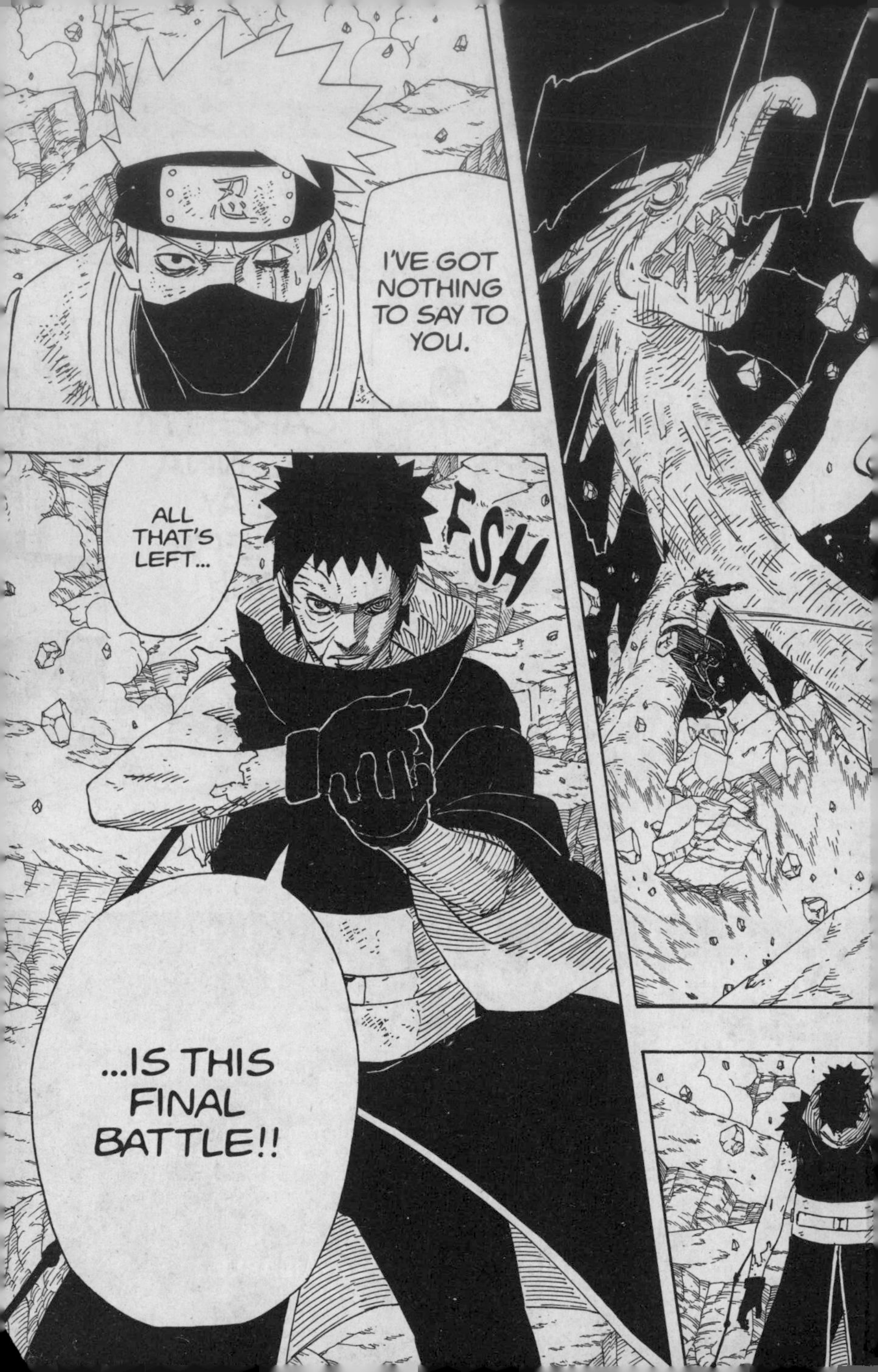
I'VE GOT NOTHING TO SAY TO YOU.
ALL THAT'S LEFT...
FSH
...IS THIS FINAL BATTLE!!

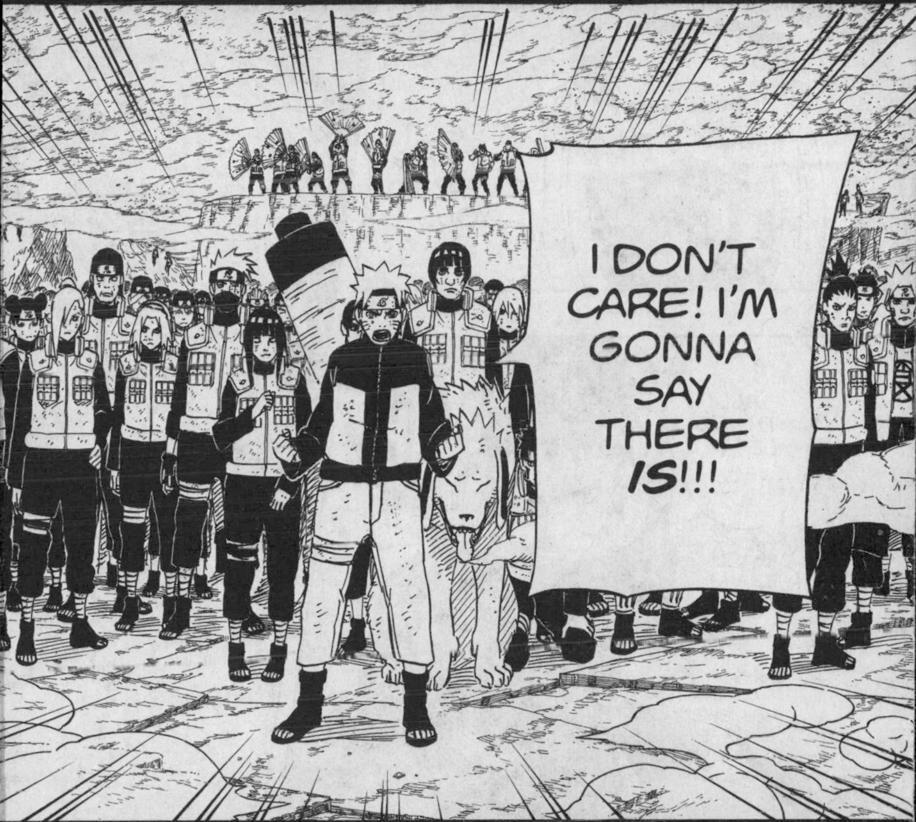
I DON'T CARE! I'M GONNA SAY THERE *IS*!!!

IN THE NEXT VOLUME...

THE ARRIVAL

When Obito is revealed to be the masked man, Kakashi's resolve is no longer unwavering, and it falls to Naruto to inspire his old master to continue the fight. As the battle rages on, Naruto must then summon all of his Nine Tails power in order to stand against the devastating team of Obito and Madara. But the Allied Shinobi Forces might be in for a much-needed and lucky break...

NARUTO 3-IN-1 EDITION VOLUME 22 AVAILABLE APRIL 2018!

NARUTO

3-in-1 Edition
Volume 21
SHONEN JUMP Manga Omnibus Edition
A compilation of the graphic novel volumes 61-63

STORY AND ART BY MASASHI KISHIMOTO

Translation/Mari Morimoto
English Adaptation/Joel Enos
Touch-up Art & Lettering/ John Hunt, Inori Fukuda Trant
Design/Sam Elzway (Original Series and Omnibus Edition)
Editor/Megan Bates (Manga Edition)
Managing Editor/Erica Yee (Omnibus Edition)

Printed in the U.S.A.

Published by VIZ Media, LLC
P.O. Box 77010
San Francisco, CA 94107

10 9 8 7 6 5 4 3 2 1
Omnibus edition first printing, January 2018

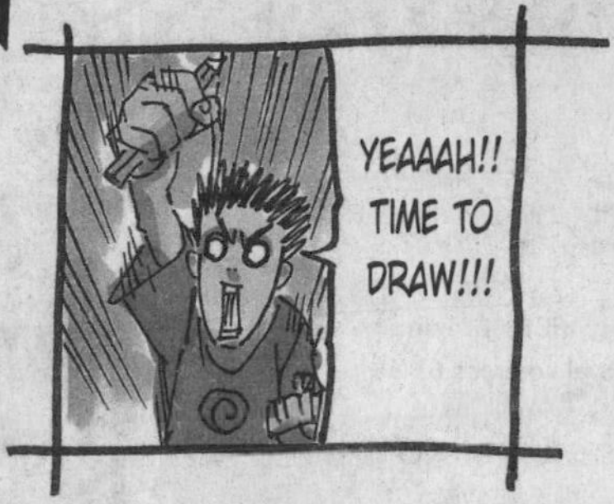
YEAAAH!! TIME TO DRAW!!!

岸本斉史

For those of you who weren't able to read the "Road to Ninja" one-shot, you can check it out on the Japanese *Shonen Jump* website!

The story is gonna get hotter and hotter! I don't want to rush anyone, but I want you to read volume 62 too!

—Masashi Kishimoto, 2012

Author/artist Masashi Kishimoto was born in 1974 in rural Okayama Prefecture, Japan. After spending time in art college, he won the Hop Step Award for new manga artists with his manga **Karakuri** (Mechanism). Kishimoto decided to base his next story on traditional Japanese culture. His first version of **Naruto**, drawn in 1997, was a one-shot story about fox spirits; his final version, which debuted in **Weekly Shonen Jump** in 1999, quickly became the most popular ninja manga in Japan.

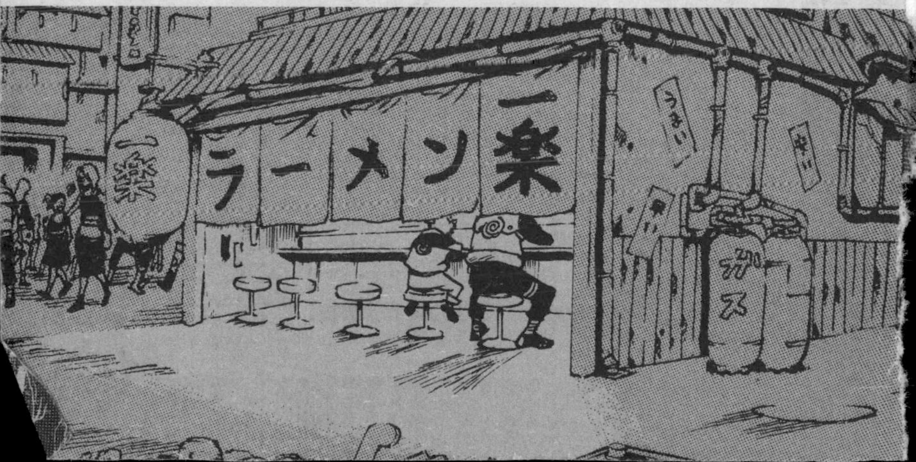
一楽
ラーメン一楽

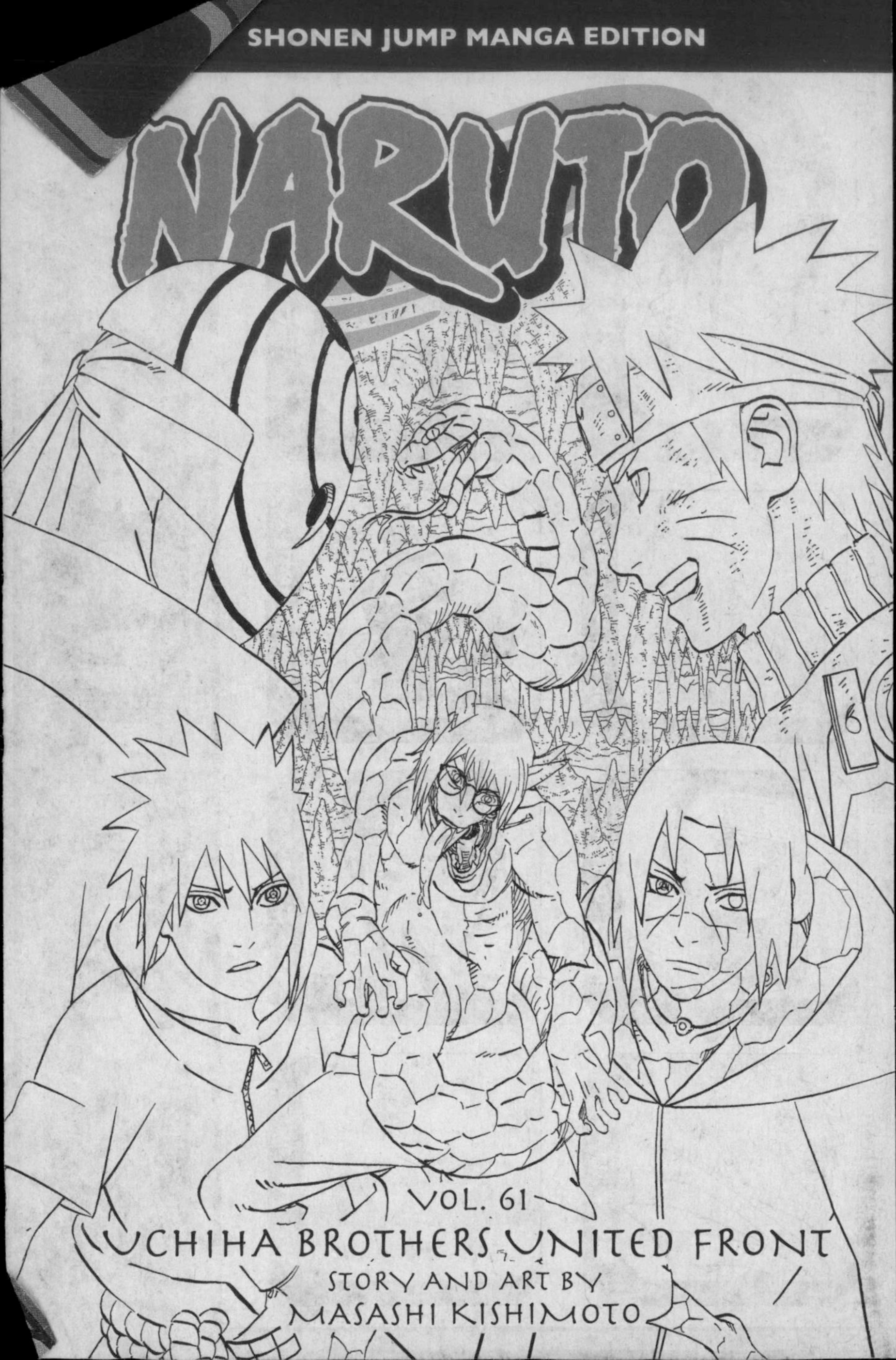
SHONEN JUMP MANGA EDITION
NARUTO
VOL. 61
UCHIHA BROTHERS UNITED FRONT
STORY AND ART BY
MASASHI KISHIMOTO

CHARACTERS

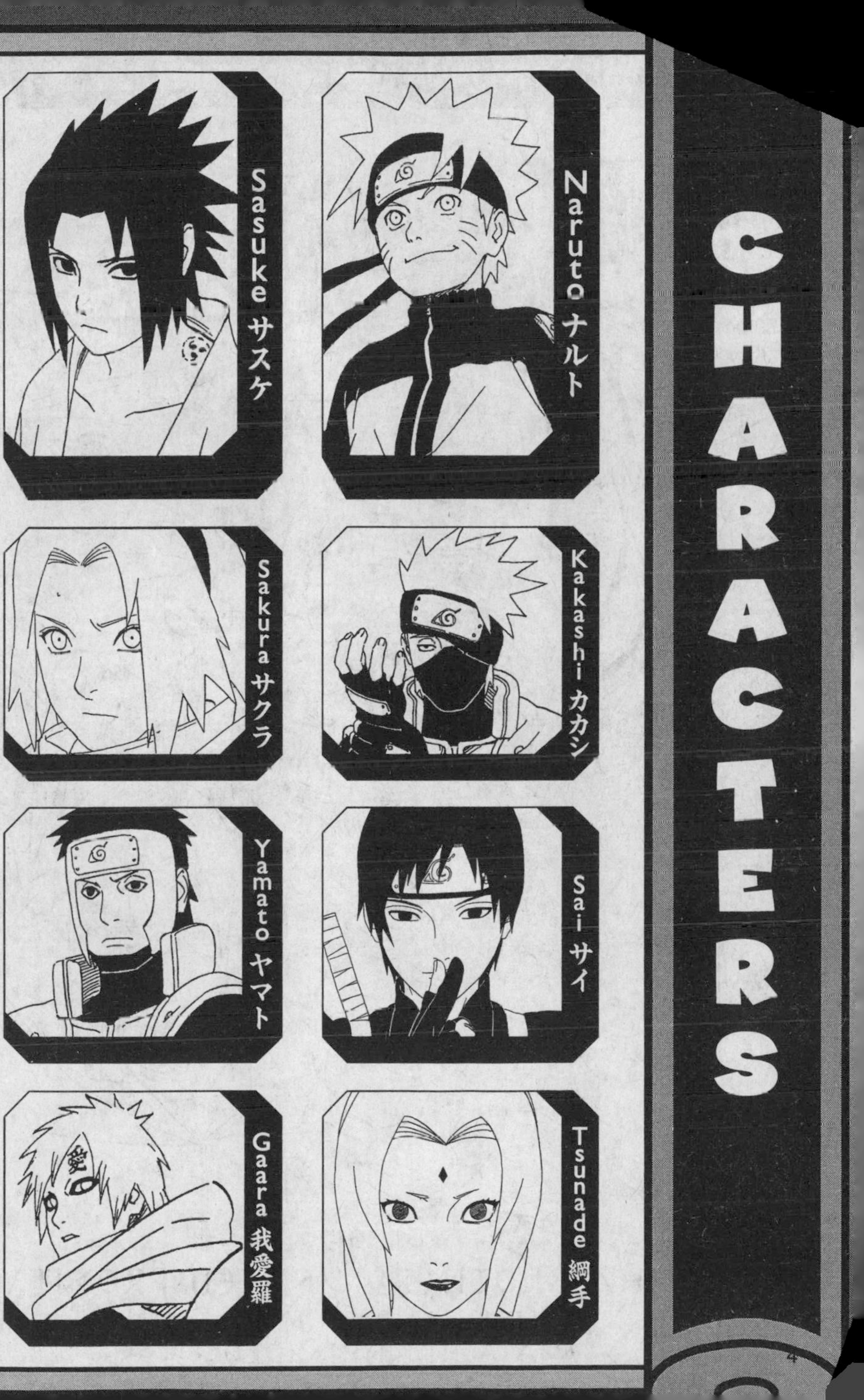
Naruto ナルト
Sasuke サスケ
Kakashi カカシ
Sakura サクラ
Sai サイ
Yamato ヤマト
Tsunade 綱手
Gaara 我愛羅

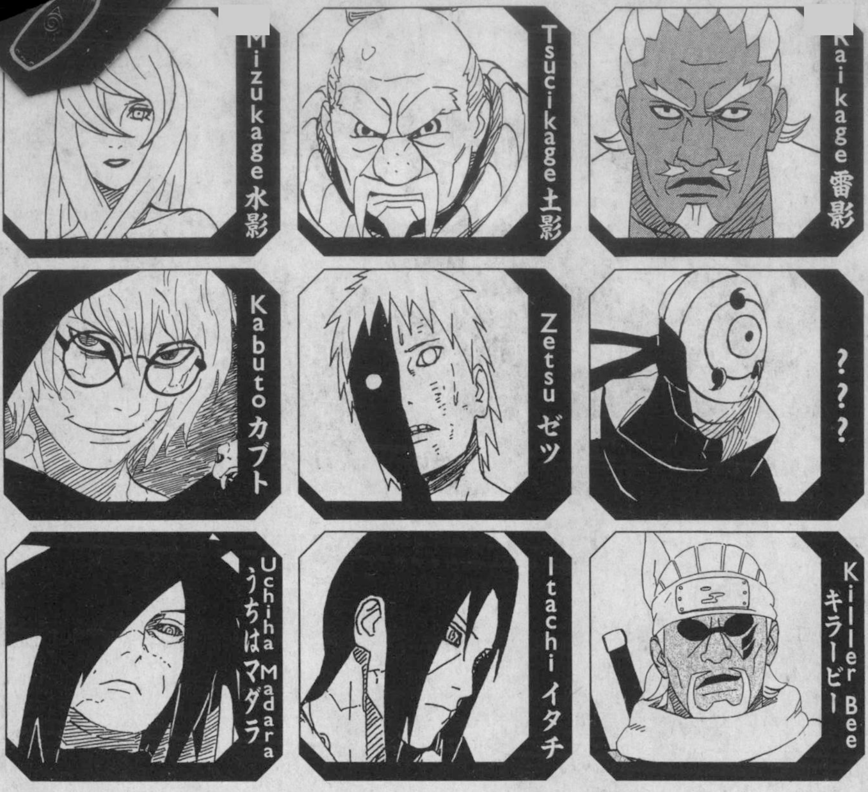
Raikage 雷影
Tsucikage 土影
Mizukage 水影
? ? ?
Zetsu ゼツ
Kabuto カブト
Killer Bee キラービー
Itachi イタチ
Uchiha Madara うちはマダラ

THE STORY SO FAR...

Naruto, the biggest troublemaker at the Ninja Academy in the Village of Konohagakure, finally becomes a ninja along with his classmates Sasuke and Sakura. They grow and mature through countless trials and battles. However, Sasuke, unable to give up his quest for vengeance, leaves Konohagakure to seek Orochimaru and his power.

Two years pass. Naruto grows up and engages in fierce battles against the Tailed Beast-targeting Akatsuki. Elsewhere, after winning the heroic battle against Itachi and learning his older brother's true intentions, Sasuke allies with the Akatsuki and sets out to destroy Konoha.

The Fourth Great Ninja War against the Akatsuki begins. The Allied Shinobi Forces begin to rally back after a series of unfavorable battles early on and have the Five Shadows assemble on the battlefield in order to stop the Edotensei-revived Madara! Naruto deepens his bond with Nine Tails and the other jinchûriki during his battle against the masked man. Meanwhile, Sasuke encounters a revived Itachi!

VOL. 61

UCHIHA BROTHERS UNITED FRONT

CONTENTS

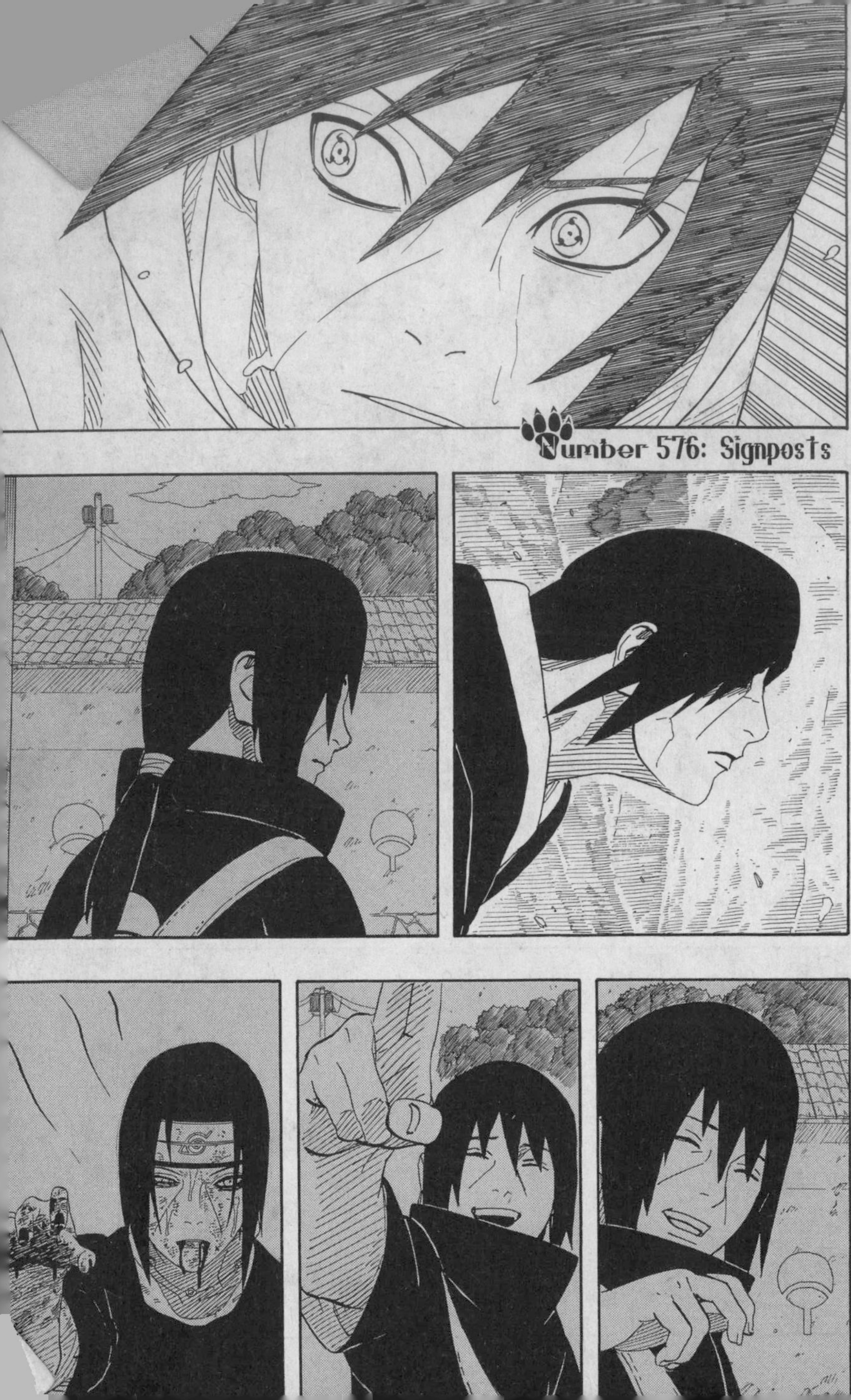
Number 576: Signposts

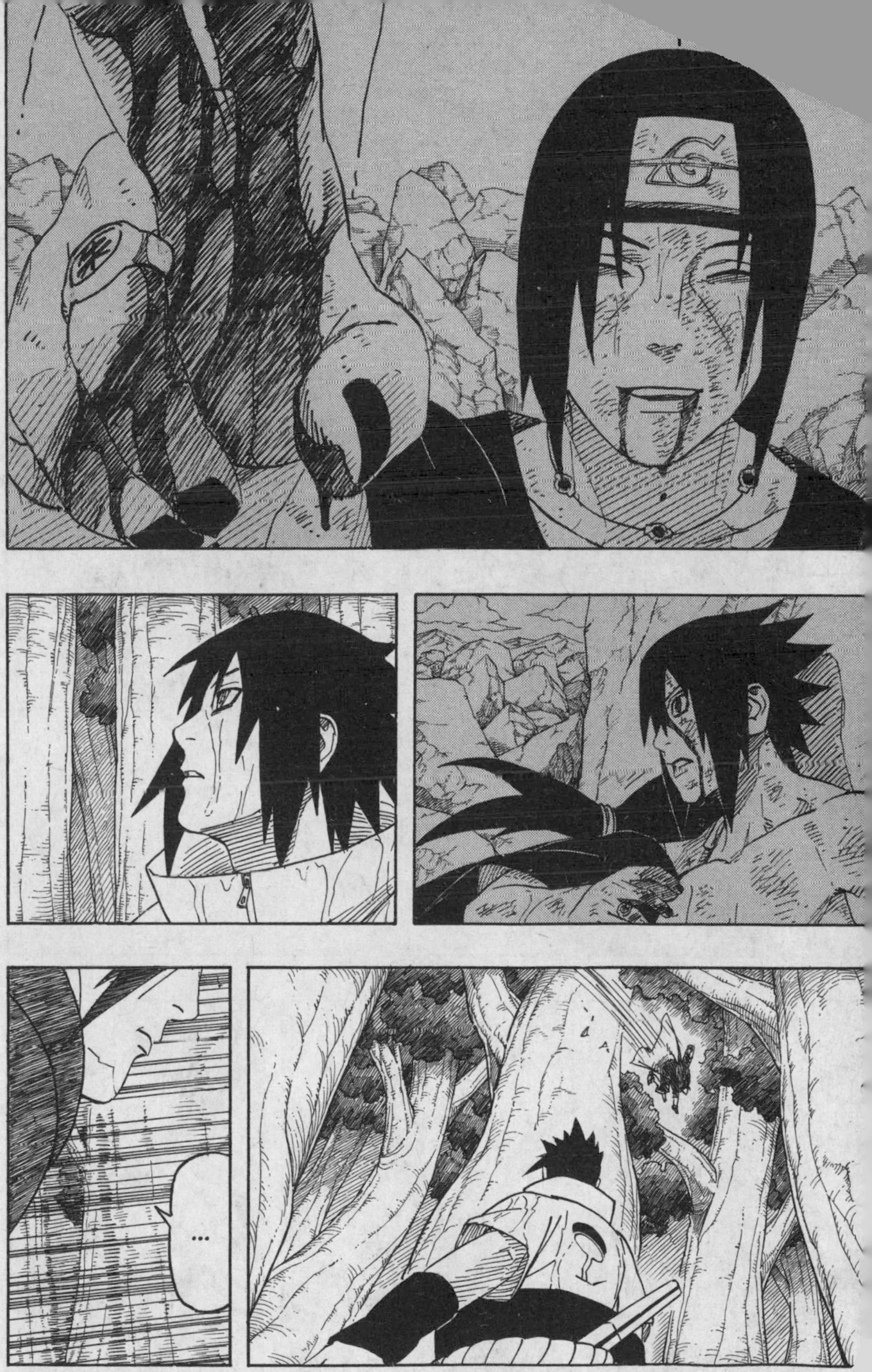
...

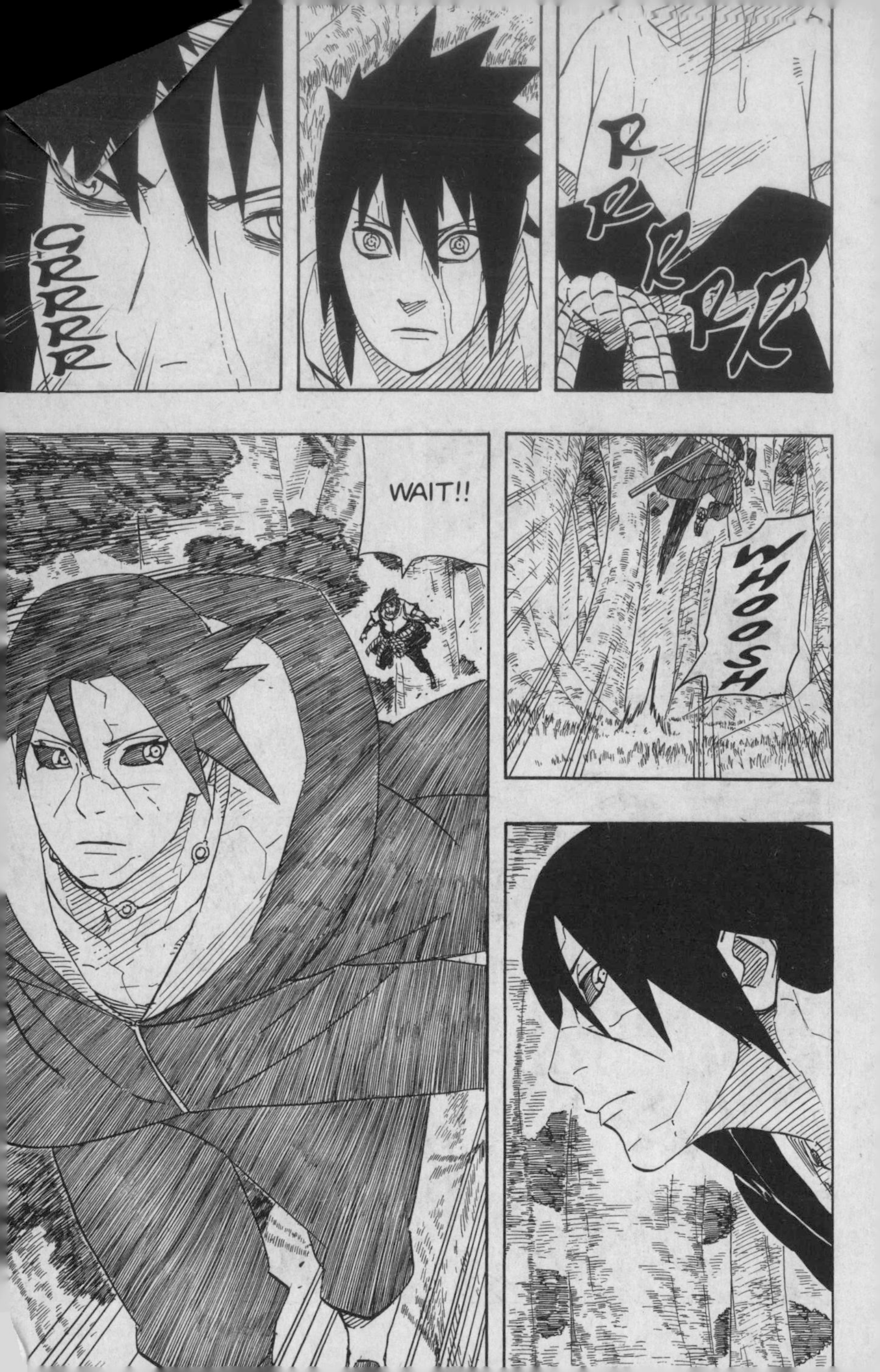
RRRRR
GRRRR
WHOOSH
WAIT!!

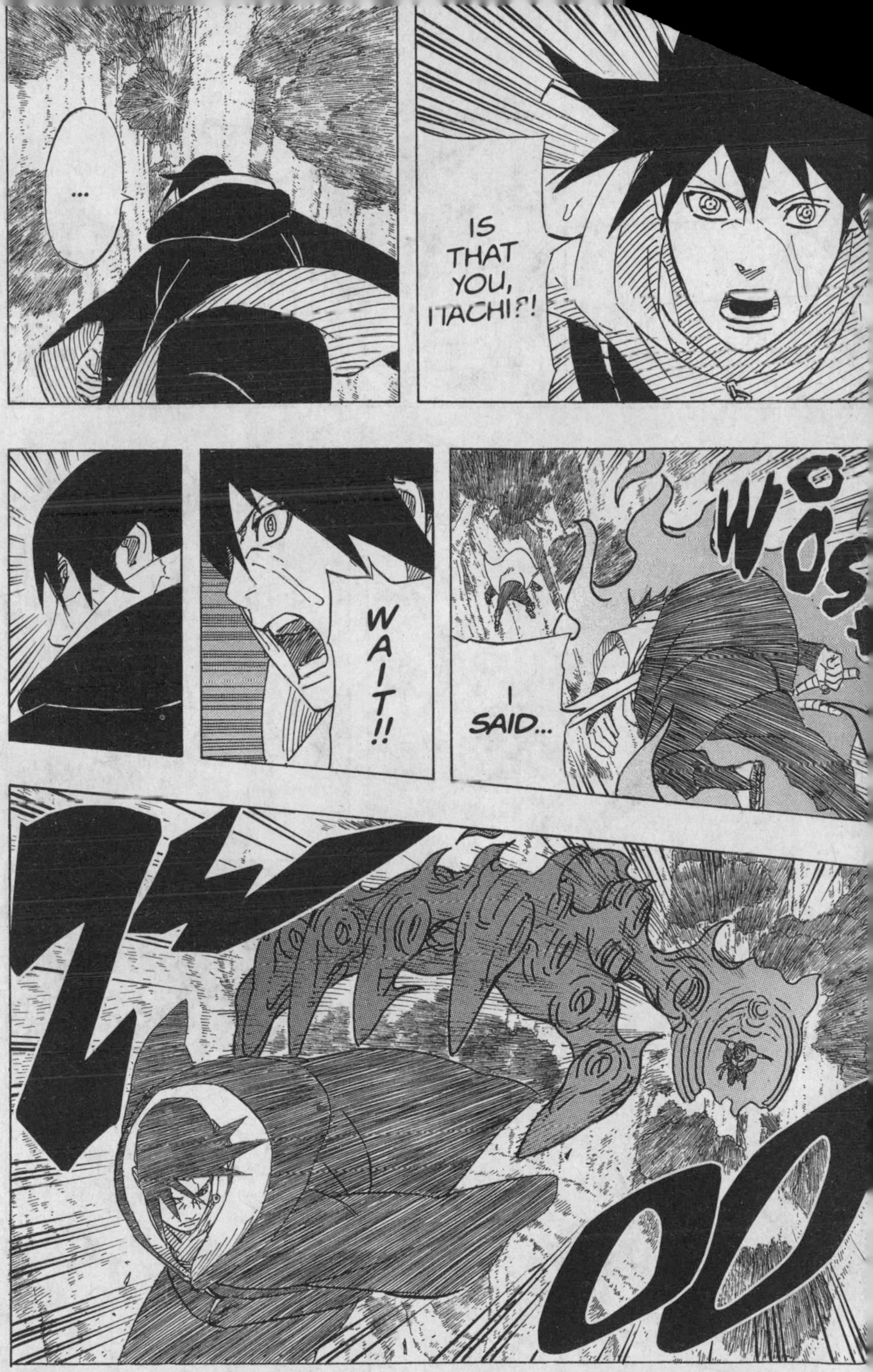
IS THAT YOU, ITACHI?!
...
I SAID...
WAIT!!

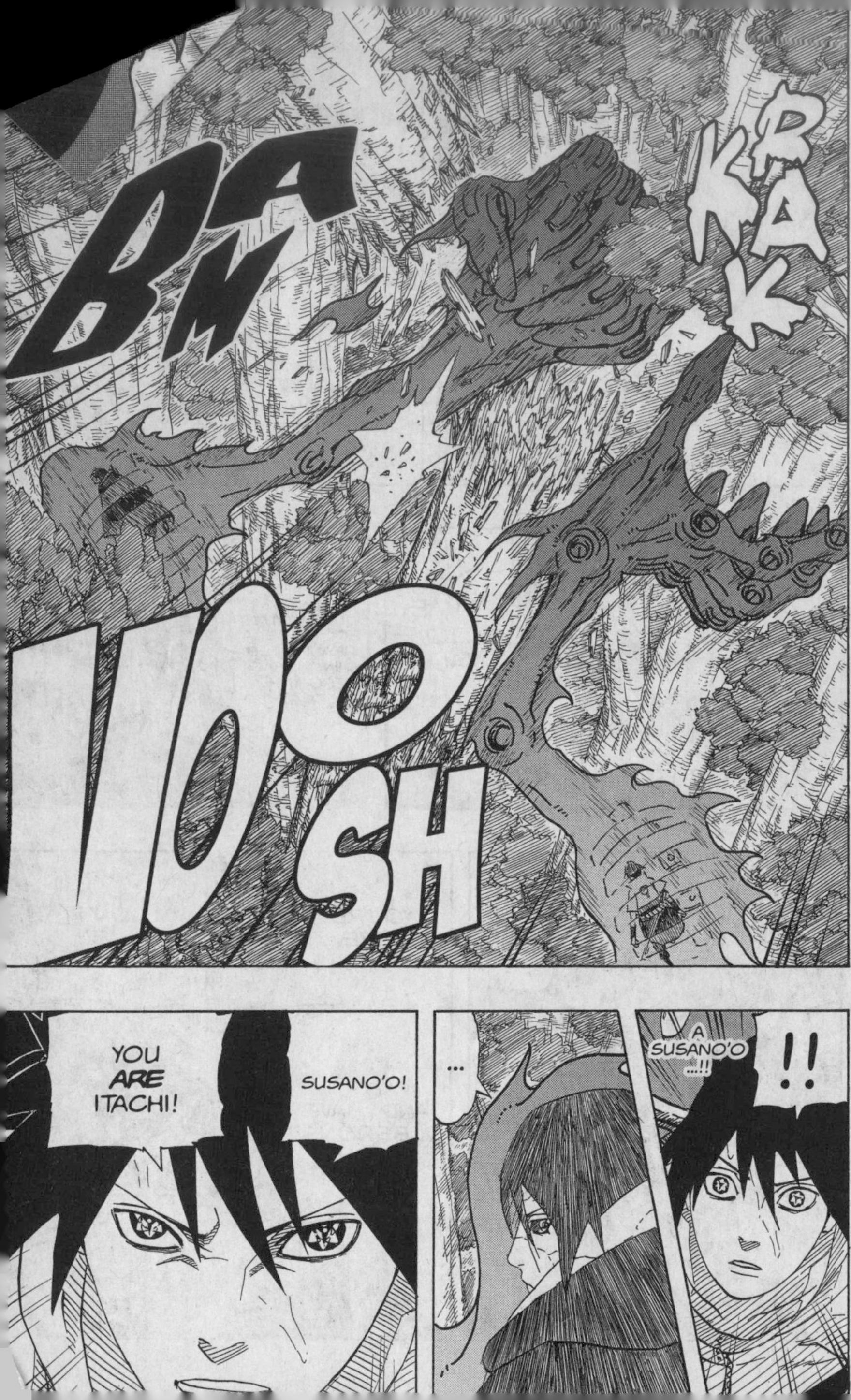
KRAK
BAM
WOOSH
A SUSANO'O ...!!
!!
...
SUSANO'O!
YOU **ARE** ITACHI!

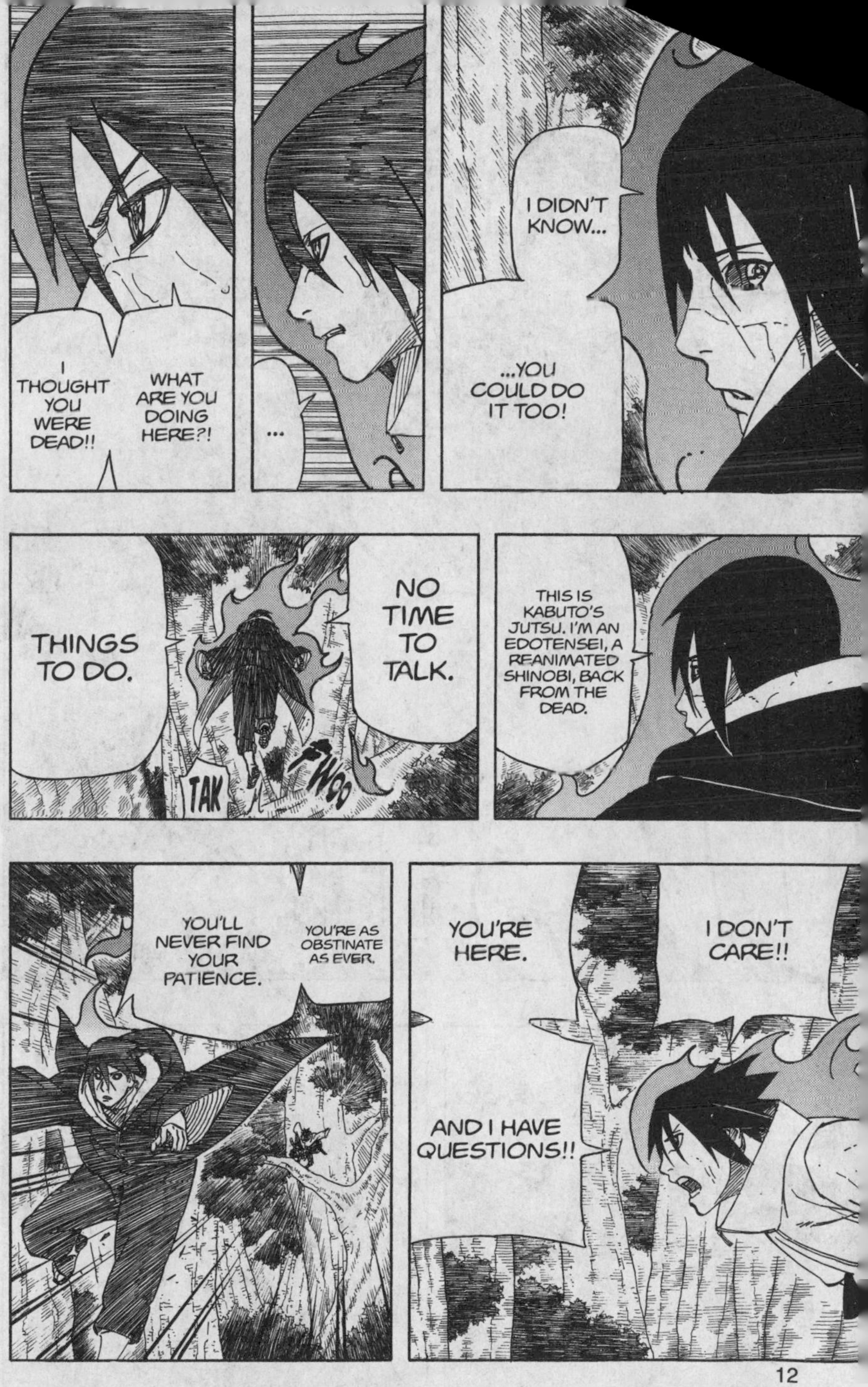
I DIDN'T KNOW...
...YOU COULD DO IT TOO!
...
WHAT ARE YOU DOING HERE?!
I THOUGHT YOU WERE DEAD!!
THIS IS KABUTO'S JUTSU. I'M AN EDOTENSEI, A REANIMATED SHINOBI, BACK FROM THE DEAD.
NO TIME TO TALK.
THINGS TO DO.
FWOO
TAK
I DON'T CARE!!
YOU'RE HERE.
AND I HAVE QUESTIONS!!
YOU'RE AS OBSTINATE AS EVER.
YOU'LL NEVER FIND YOUR PATIENCE.

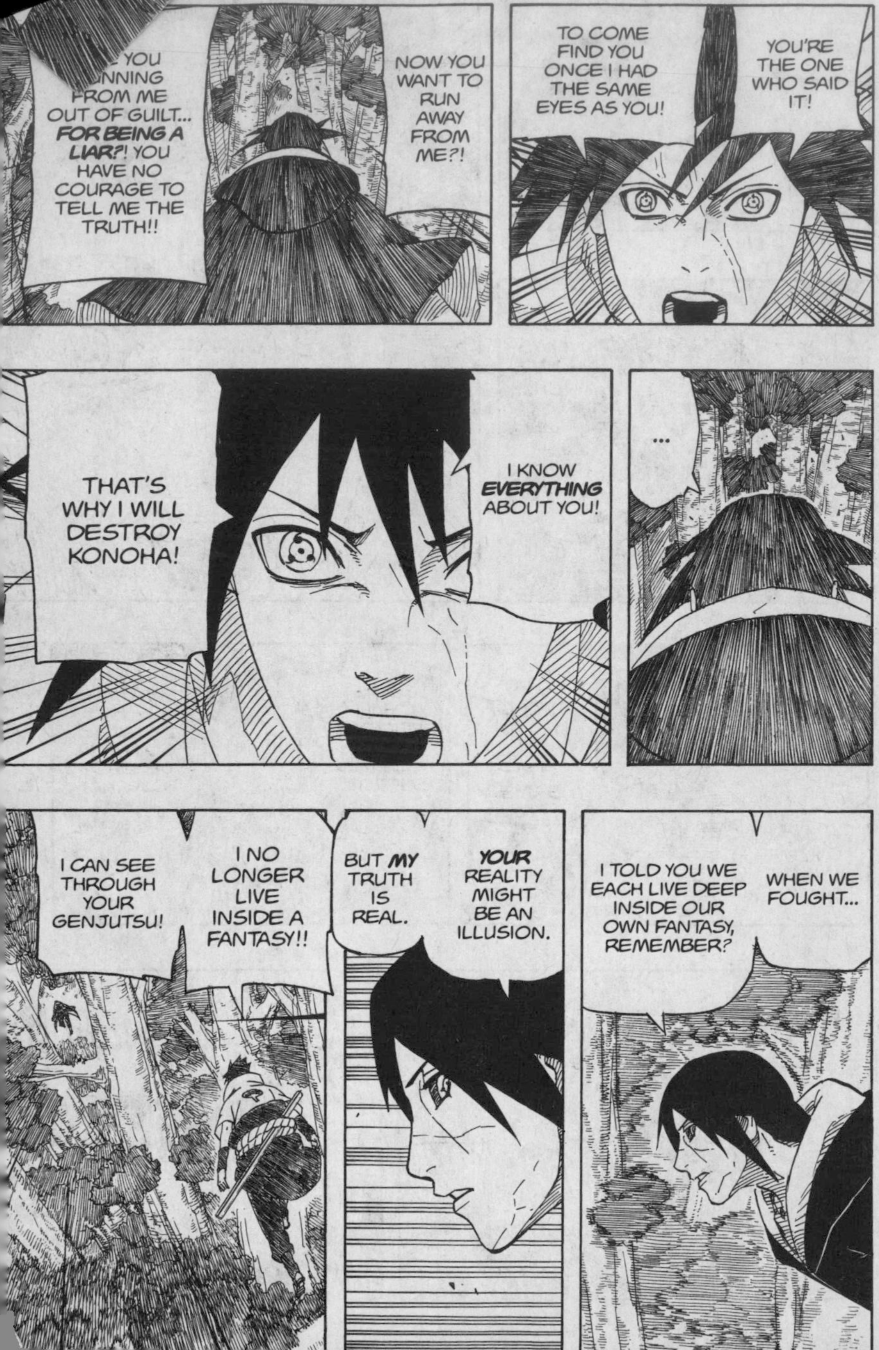
YOU'RE THE ONE WHO SAID IT!
TO COME FIND YOU ONCE I HAD THE SAME EYES AS YOU!
NOW YOU WANT TO RUN AWAY FROM ME?!
YOU ...NNING FROM ME OUT OF GUILT... ***FOR BEING A LIAR?!*** YOU HAVE NO COURAGE TO TELL ME THE TRUTH!!
...
I KNOW ***EVERYTHING*** ABOUT YOU!
THAT'S WHY I WILL DESTROY KONOHA!
WHEN WE FOUGHT...
I TOLD YOU WE EACH LIVE DEEP INSIDE OUR OWN FANTASY, REMEMBER?
YOUR REALITY MIGHT BE AN ILLUSION.
BUT ***MY*** TRUTH IS REAL.
I NO LONGER LIVE INSIDE A FANTASY!!
I CAN SEE THROUGH YOUR GENJUTSU!

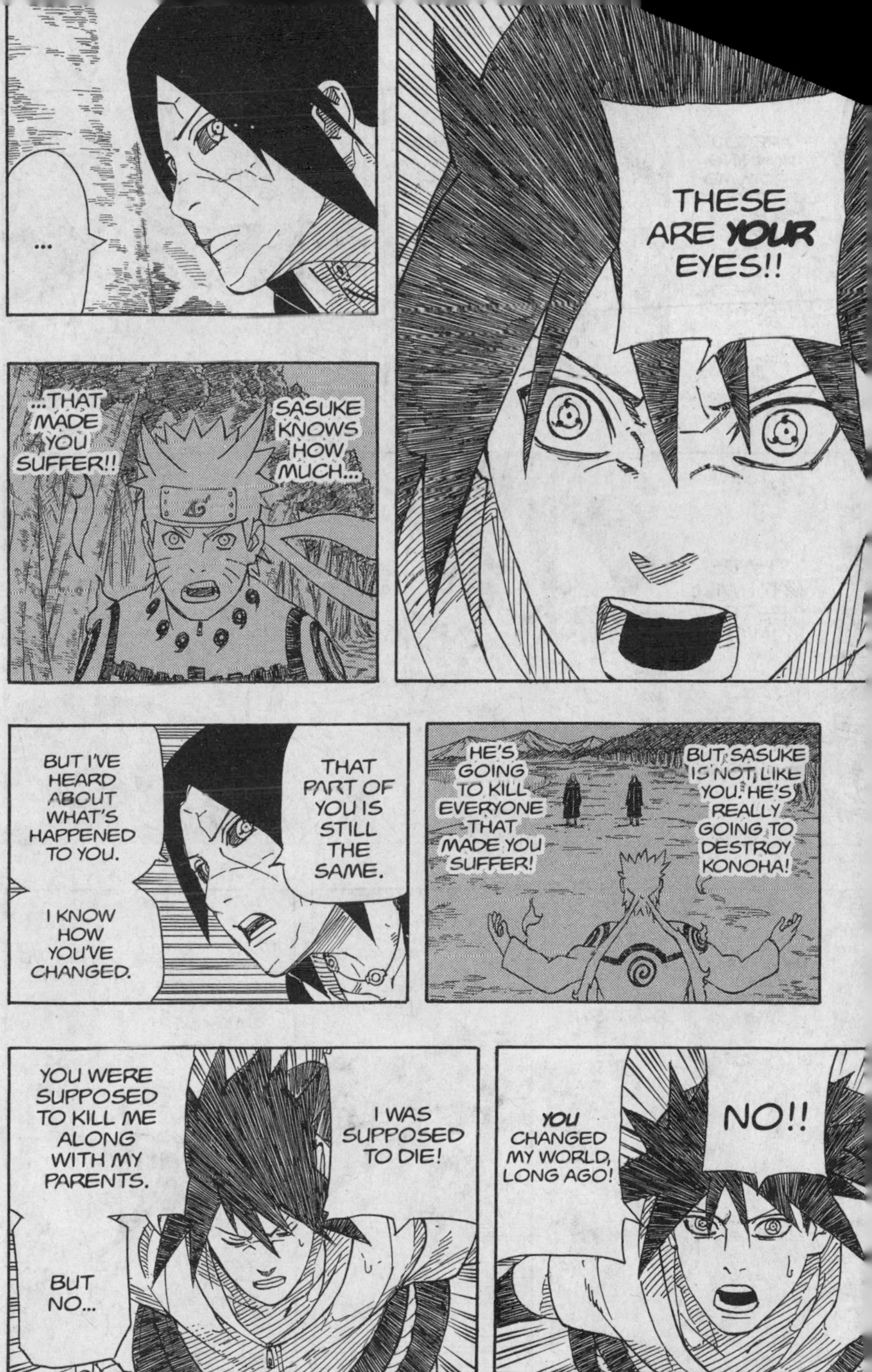
THESE ARE YOUR EYES!!
...
SASUKE KNOWS HOW MUCH...
...THAT MADE YOU SUFFER!!
BUT SASUKE IS NOT LIKE YOU. HE'S REALLY GOING TO DESTROY KONOHA!
HE'S GOING TO KILL EVERYONE THAT MADE YOU SUFFER!
THAT PART OF YOU IS STILL THE SAME.
BUT I'VE HEARD ABOUT WHAT'S HAPPENED TO YOU.
I KNOW HOW YOU'VE CHANGED.
NO!!
YOU CHANGED MY WORLD, LONG AGO!
I WAS SUPPOSED TO DIE!
YOU WERE SUPPOSED TO KILL ME ALONG WITH MY PARENTS.
BUT NO...

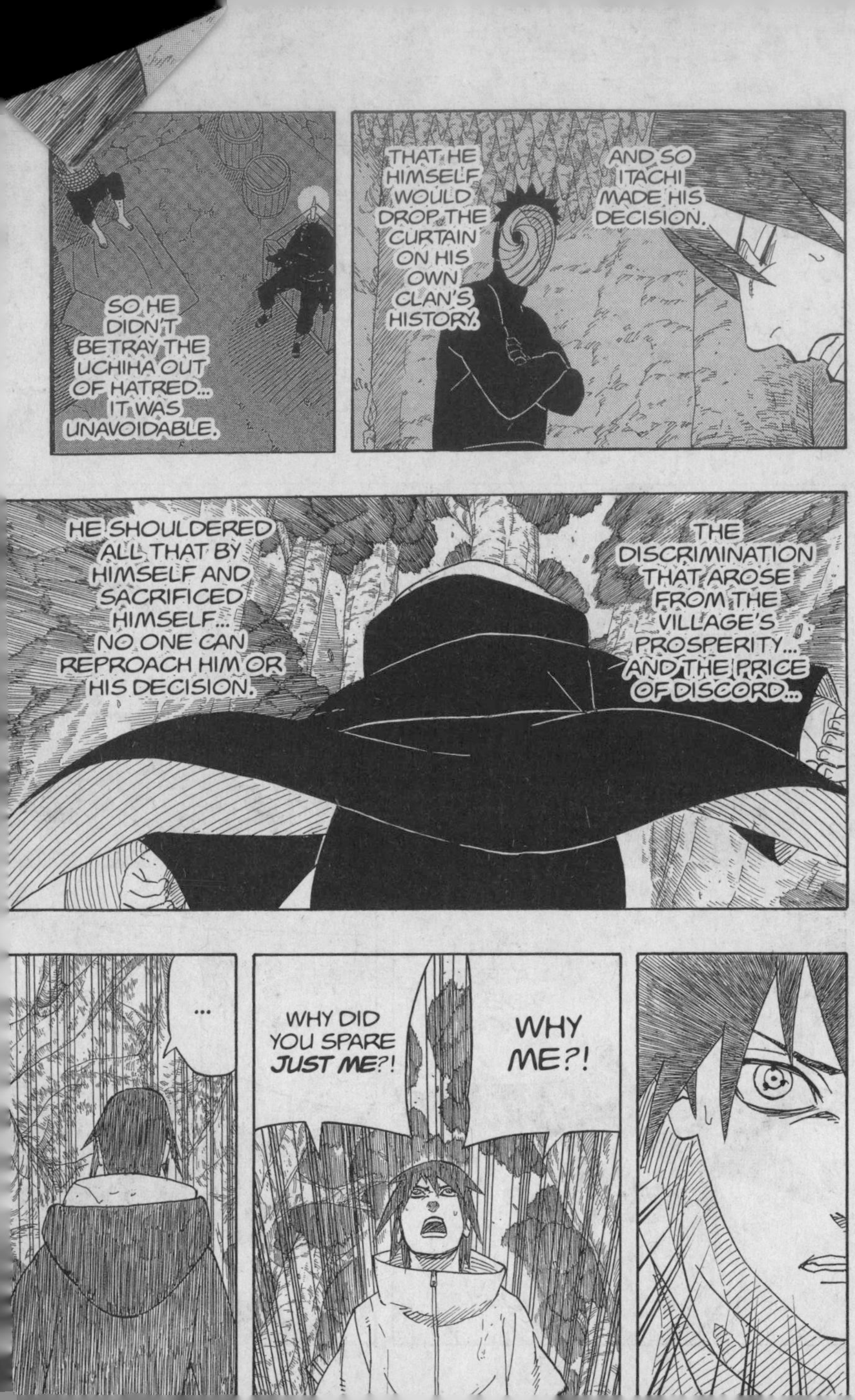
AND SO ITACHI MADE HIS DECISION.
THAT HE HIMSELF WOULD DROP THE CURTAIN ON HIS OWN CLAN'S HISTORY.
SO HE DIDN'T BETRAY THE UCHIHA OUT OF HATRED... IT WAS UNAVOIDABLE.
THE DISCRIMINATION THAT AROSE FROM THE VILLAGE'S PROSPERITY... AND THE PRICE OF DISCORD...
HE SHOULDERED ALL THAT BY HIMSELF AND SACRIFICED HIMSELF... NO ONE CAN REPROACH HIM OR HIS DECISION.
WHY ME?!
WHY DID YOU SPARE *JUST ME*?!
...

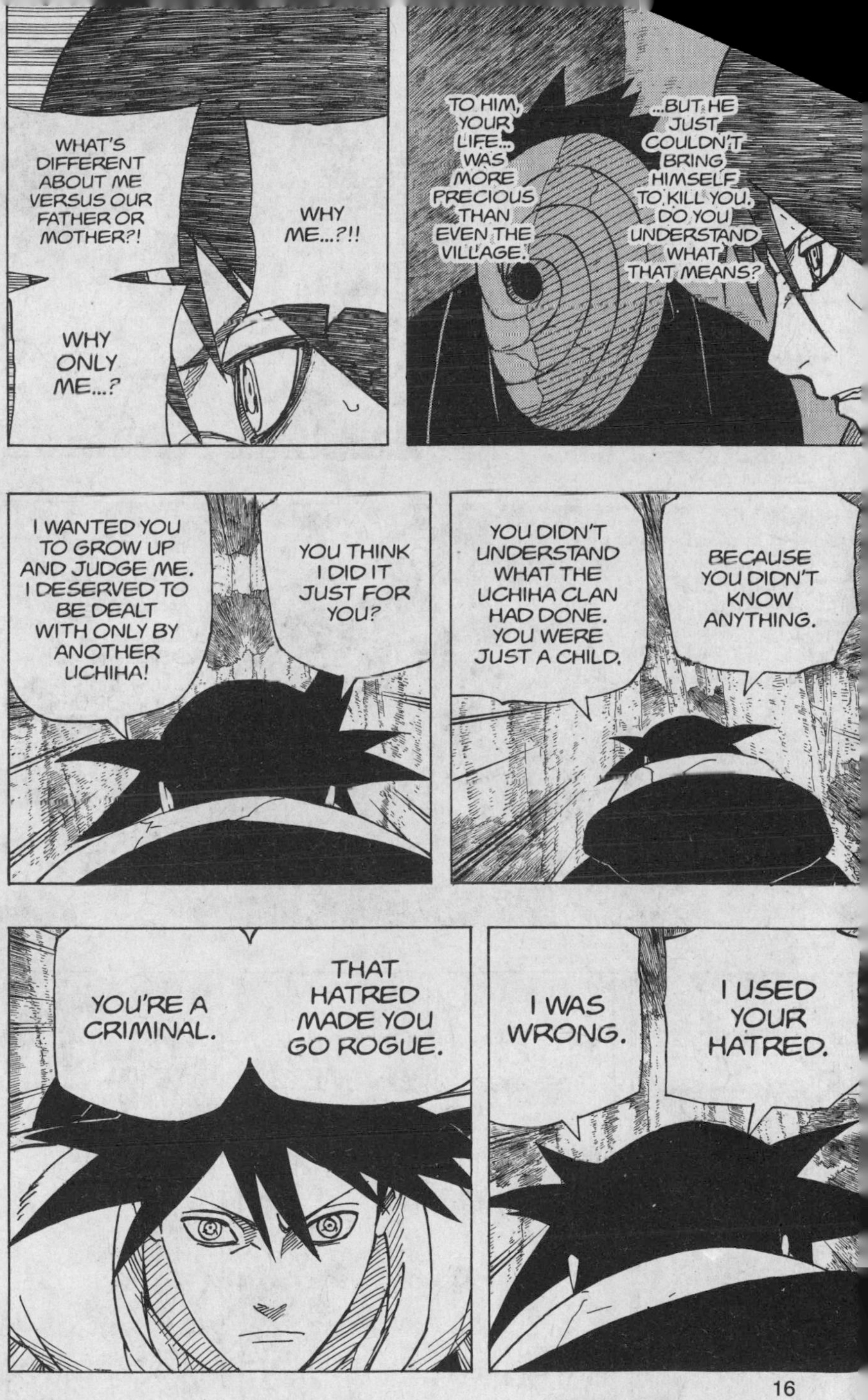
TO HIM, YOUR LIFE... WAS MORE PRECIOUS THAN EVEN THE VILLAGE.
...BUT HE JUST COULDN'T BRING HIMSELF TO KILL YOU. DO YOU UNDERSTAND WHAT THAT MEANS?
WHY ME...?!!
WHAT'S DIFFERENT ABOUT ME VERSUS OUR FATHER OR MOTHER?!
WHY ONLY ME...?
BECAUSE YOU DIDN'T KNOW ANYTHING.
YOU DIDN'T UNDERSTAND WHAT THE UCHIHA CLAN HAD DONE. YOU WERE JUST A CHILD.
YOU THINK I DID IT JUST FOR YOU?
I WANTED YOU TO GROW UP AND JUDGE ME. I DESERVED TO BE DEALT WITH ONLY BY ANOTHER UCHIHA!
I USED YOUR HATRED.
I WAS WRONG.
THAT HATRED MADE YOU GO ROGUE.
YOU'RE A CRIMINAL.

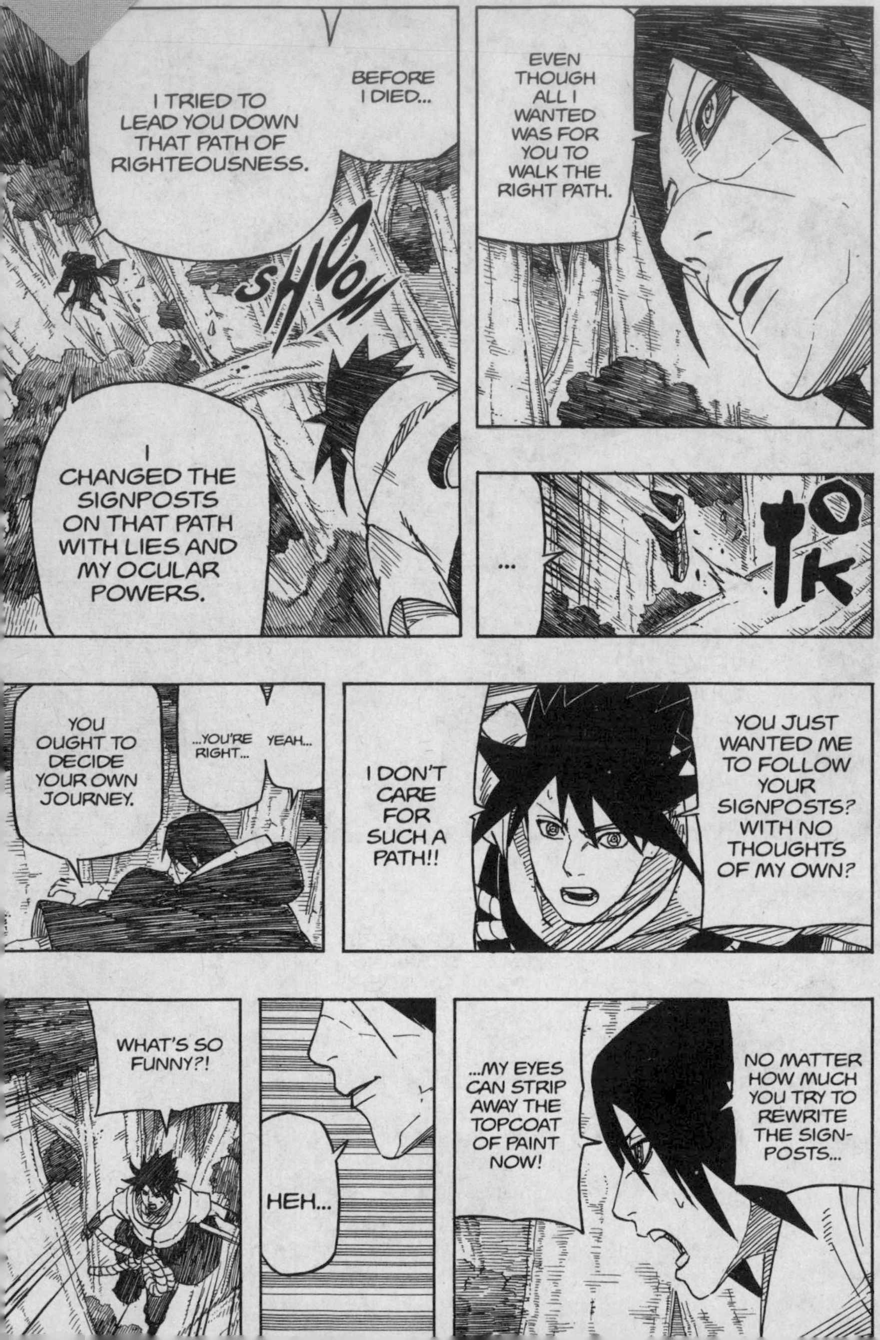
EVEN THOUGH ALL I WANTED WAS FOR YOU TO WALK THE RIGHT PATH.
...
TOK
BEFORE I DIED...
I TRIED TO LEAD YOU DOWN THAT PATH OF RIGHTEOUSNESS.
SHOOM
I CHANGED THE SIGNPOSTS ON THAT PATH WITH LIES AND MY OCULAR POWERS.
YOU JUST WANTED ME TO FOLLOW YOUR SIGNPOSTS? WITH NO THOUGHTS OF MY OWN?
I DON'T CARE FOR SUCH A PATH!!
YEAH...
...YOU'RE RIGHT...
YOU OUGHT TO DECIDE YOUR OWN JOURNEY.
NO MATTER HOW MUCH YOU TRY TO REWRITE THE SIGN-POSTS...
...MY EYES CAN STRIP AWAY THE TOPCOAT OF PAINT NOW!
HEH...
WHAT'S SO FUNNY?!

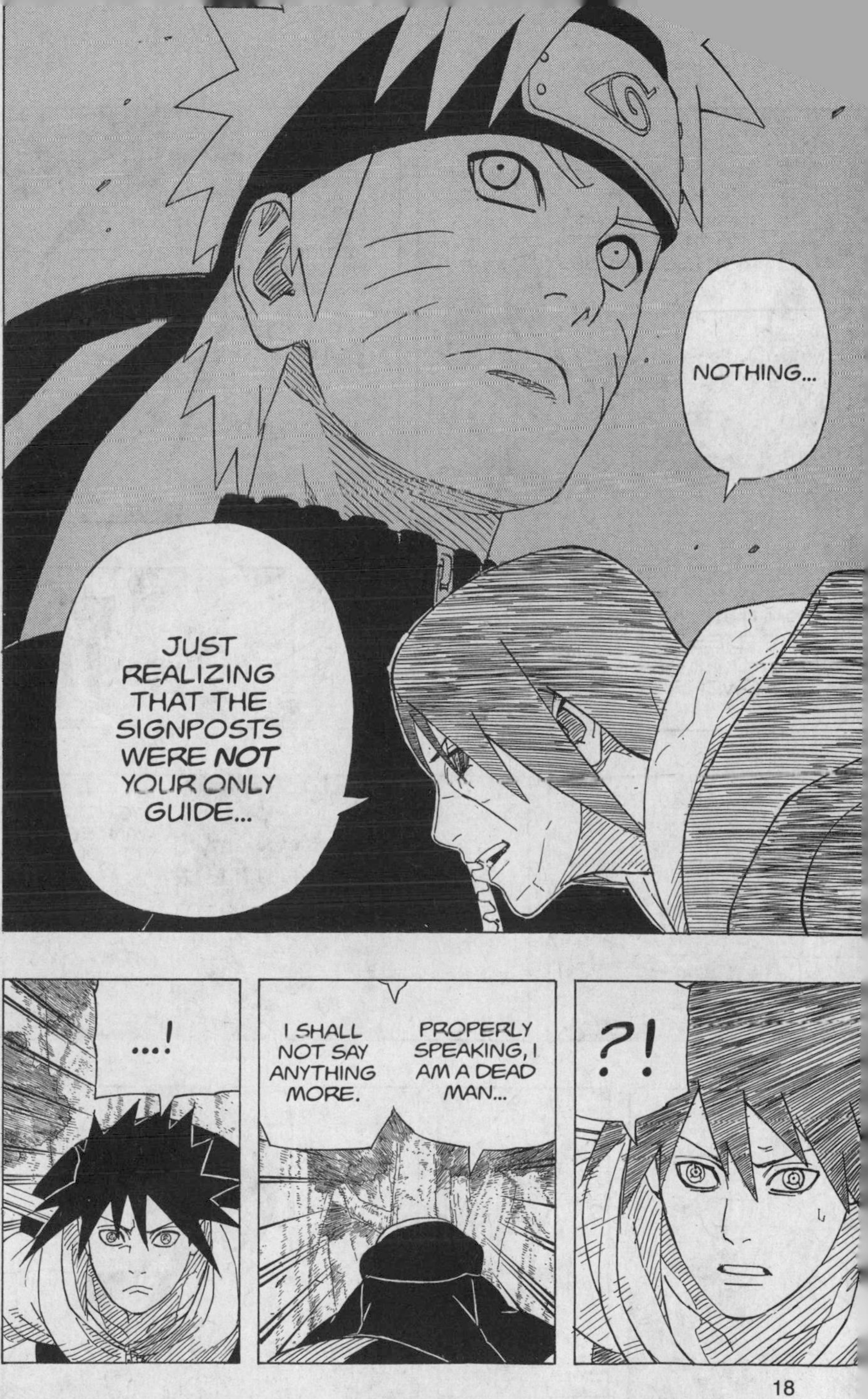
NOTHING...
JUST REALIZING THAT THE SIGNPOSTS WERE NOT YOUR ONLY GUIDE...
?!
PROPERLY SPEAKING, I AM A DEAD MAN...
I SHALL NOT SAY ANYTHING MORE.
...!

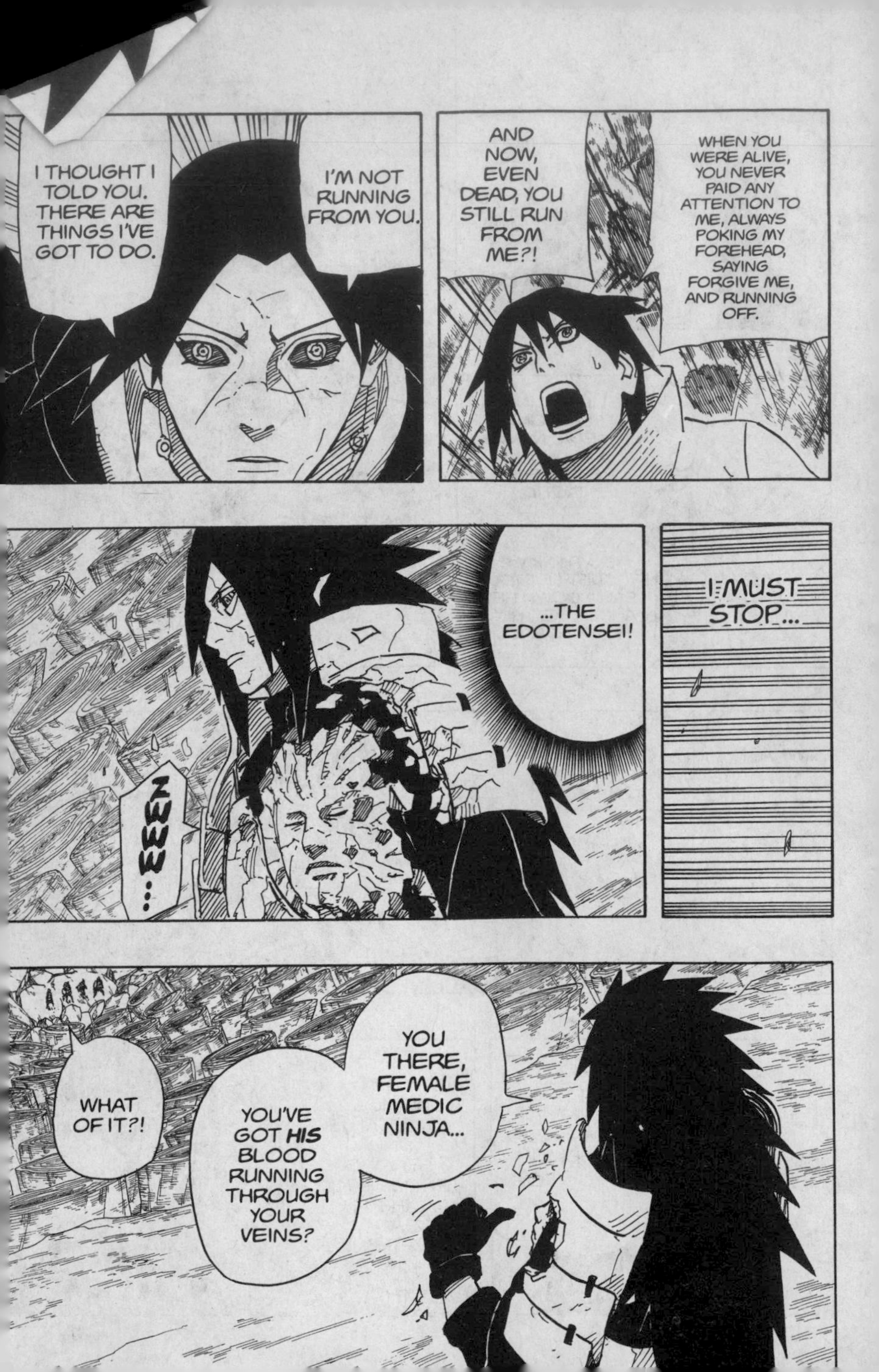
WHEN YOU WERE ALIVE, YOU NEVER PAID ANY ATTENTION TO ME, ALWAYS POKING MY FOREHEAD, SAYING FORGIVE ME, AND RUNNING OFF.
AND NOW, EVEN DEAD, YOU STILL RUN FROM ME?!
I'M NOT RUNNING FROM YOU.
I THOUGHT I TOLD YOU. THERE ARE THINGS I'VE GOT TO DO.
I MUST STOP...
...THE EDOTENSEI!
ZWWW...
YOU THERE, FEMALE MEDIC NINJA...
YOU'VE GOT **HIS** BLOOD RUNNING THROUGH YOUR VEINS?
WHAT OF IT?!

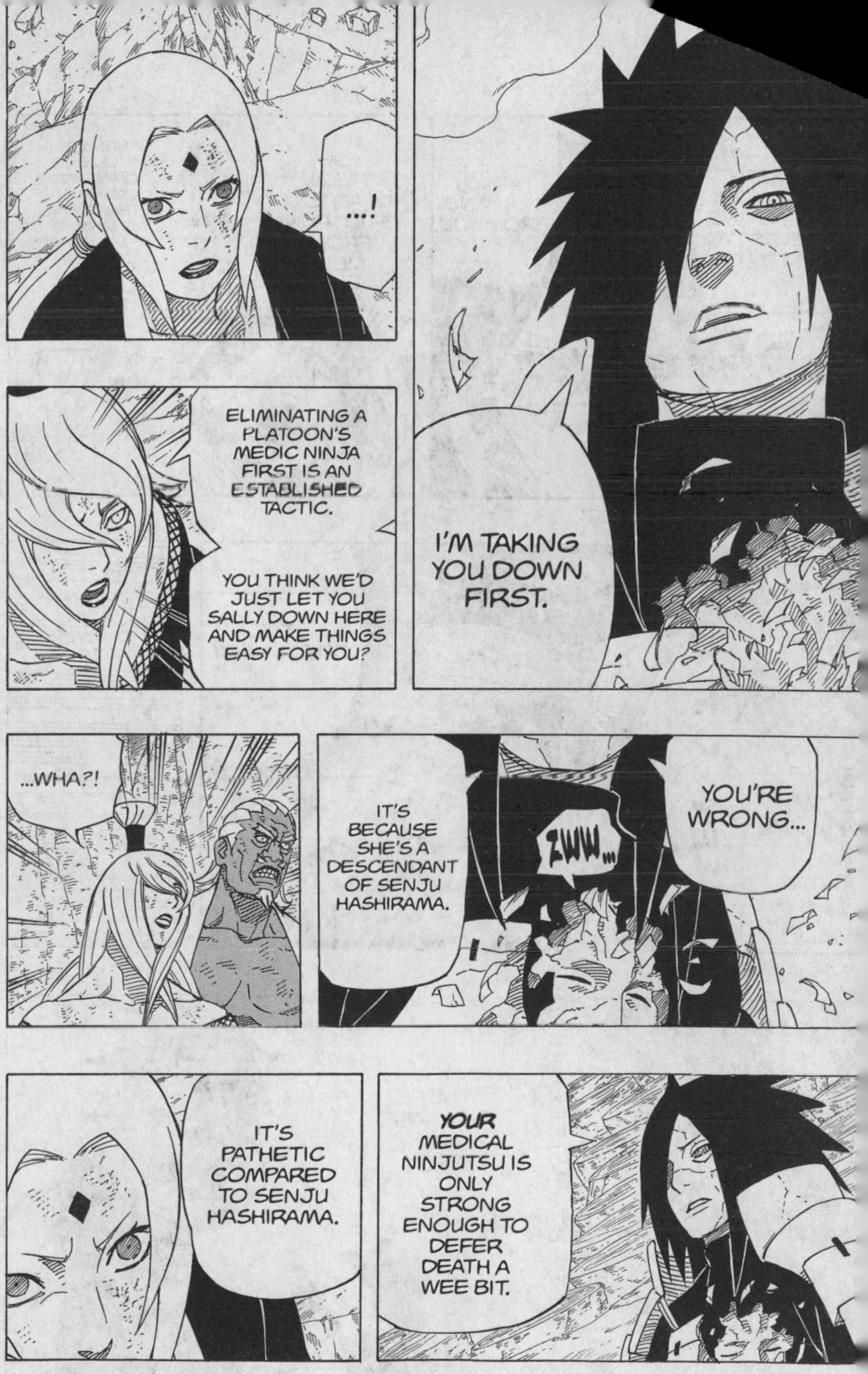
I'M TAKING YOU DOWN FIRST.
...!
ELIMINATING A PLATOON'S MEDIC NINJA FIRST IS AN ESTABLISHED TACTIC.
YOU THINK WE'D JUST LET YOU SALLY DOWN HERE AND MAKE THINGS EASY FOR YOU?
YOU'RE WRONG...
ZWW...
IT'S BECAUSE SHE'S A DESCENDANT OF SENJU HASHIRAMA.
...WHA?!
YOUR MEDICAL NINJUTSU IS ONLY STRONG ENOUGH TO DEFER DEATH A WEE BIT.
IT'S PATHETIC COMPARED TO SENJU HASHIRAMA.

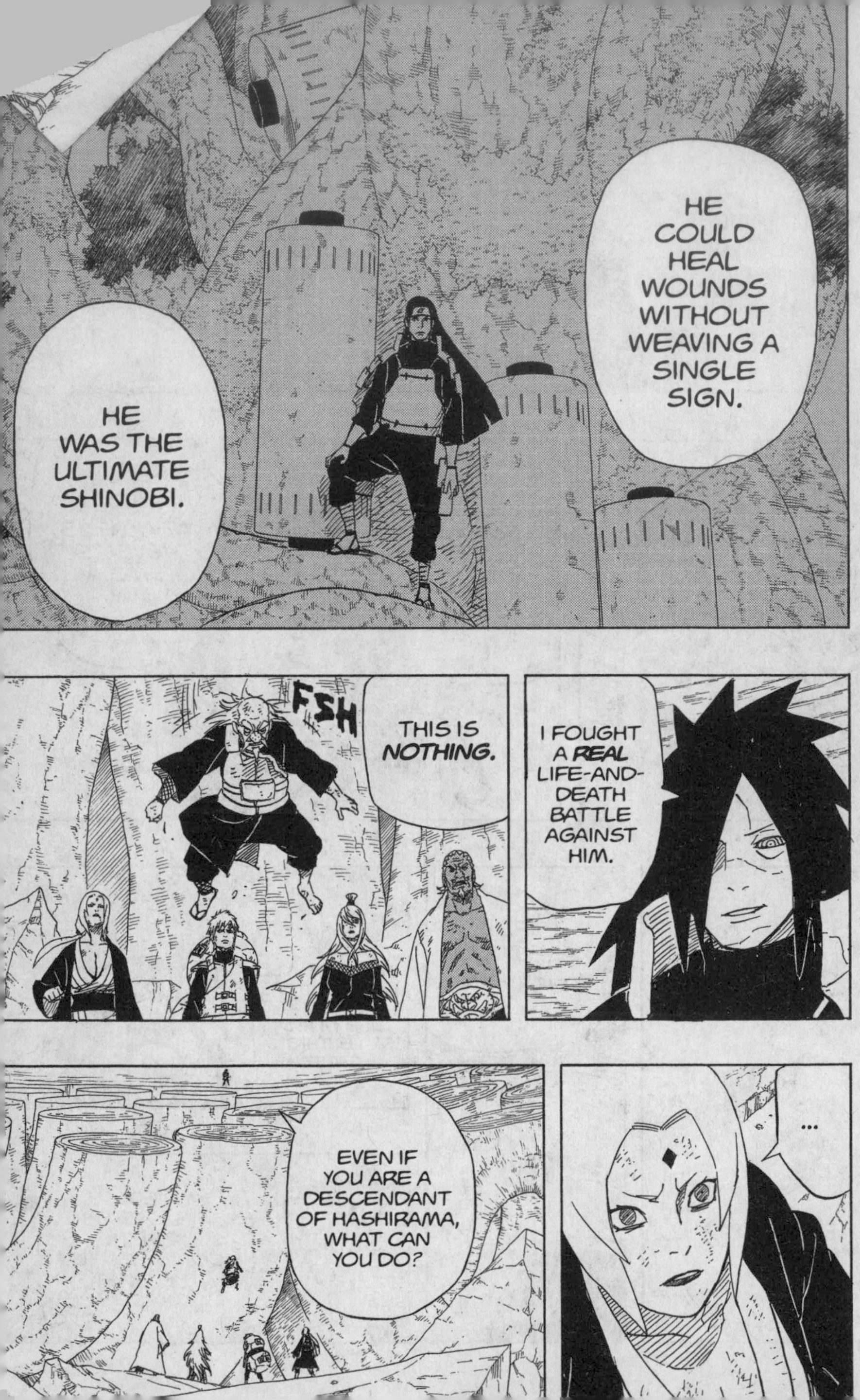
HE COULD HEAL WOUNDS WITHOUT WEAVING A SINGLE SIGN.
HE WAS THE ULTIMATE SHINOBI.
I FOUGHT A **REAL** LIFE-AND-DEATH BATTLE AGAINST HIM.
FSH
THIS IS ***NOTHING.***
...
EVEN IF YOU ARE A DESCENDANT OF HASHIRAMA, WHAT CAN YOU DO?

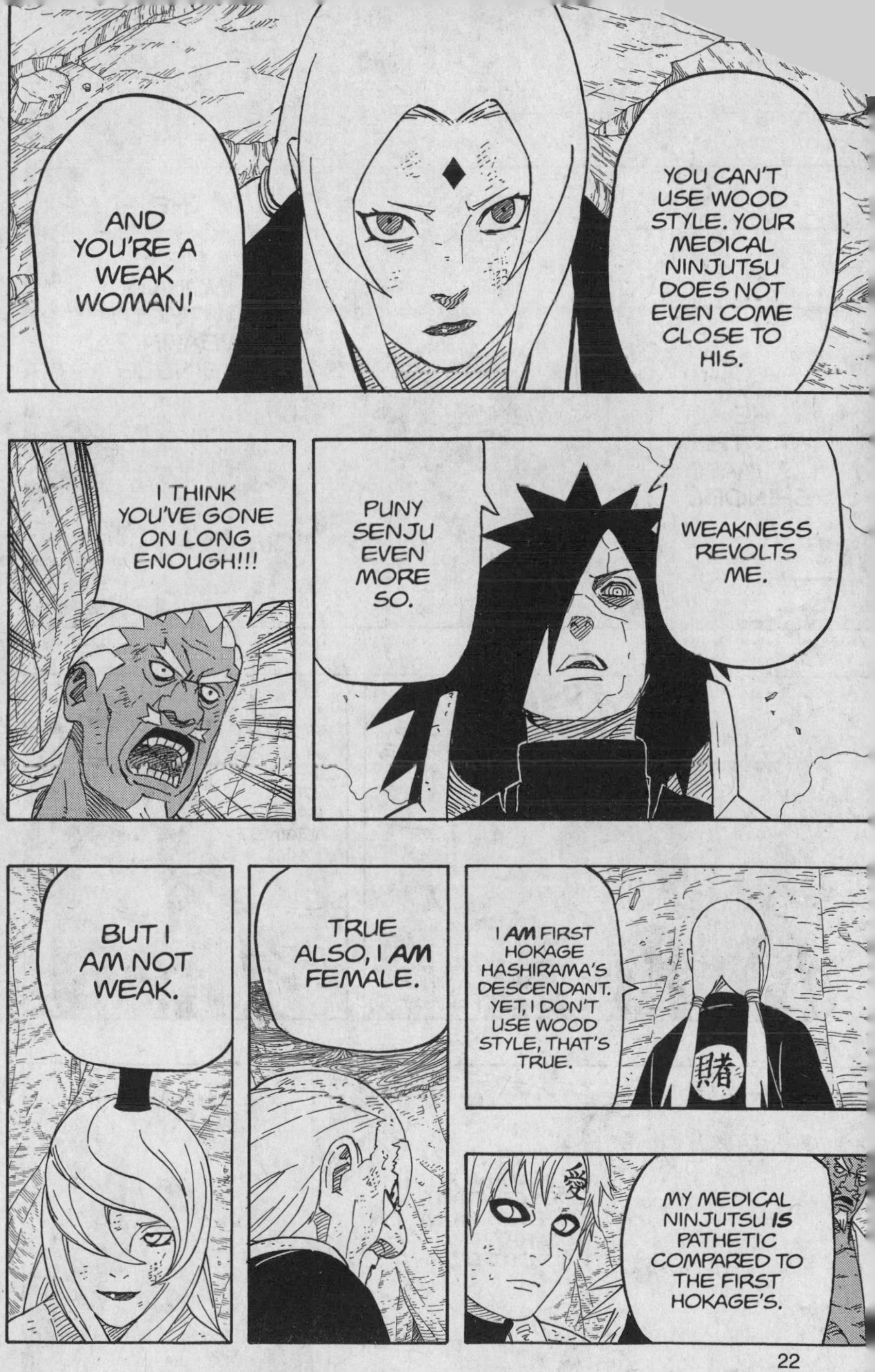
YOU CAN'T USE WOOD STYLE. YOUR MEDICAL NINJUTSU DOES NOT EVEN COME CLOSE TO HIS.
AND YOU'RE A WEAK WOMAN!
WEAKNESS REVOLTS ME.
PUNY SENJU EVEN MORE SO.
I THINK YOU'VE GONE ON LONG ENOUGH!!!
I *AM* FIRST HOKAGE HASHIRAMA'S DESCENDANT. YET, I DON'T USE WOOD STYLE, THAT'S TRUE.
MY MEDICAL NINJUTSU *IS* PATHETIC COMPARED TO THE FIRST HOKAGE'S.
TRUE ALSO, I *AM* FEMALE.
BUT I AM NOT WEAK.

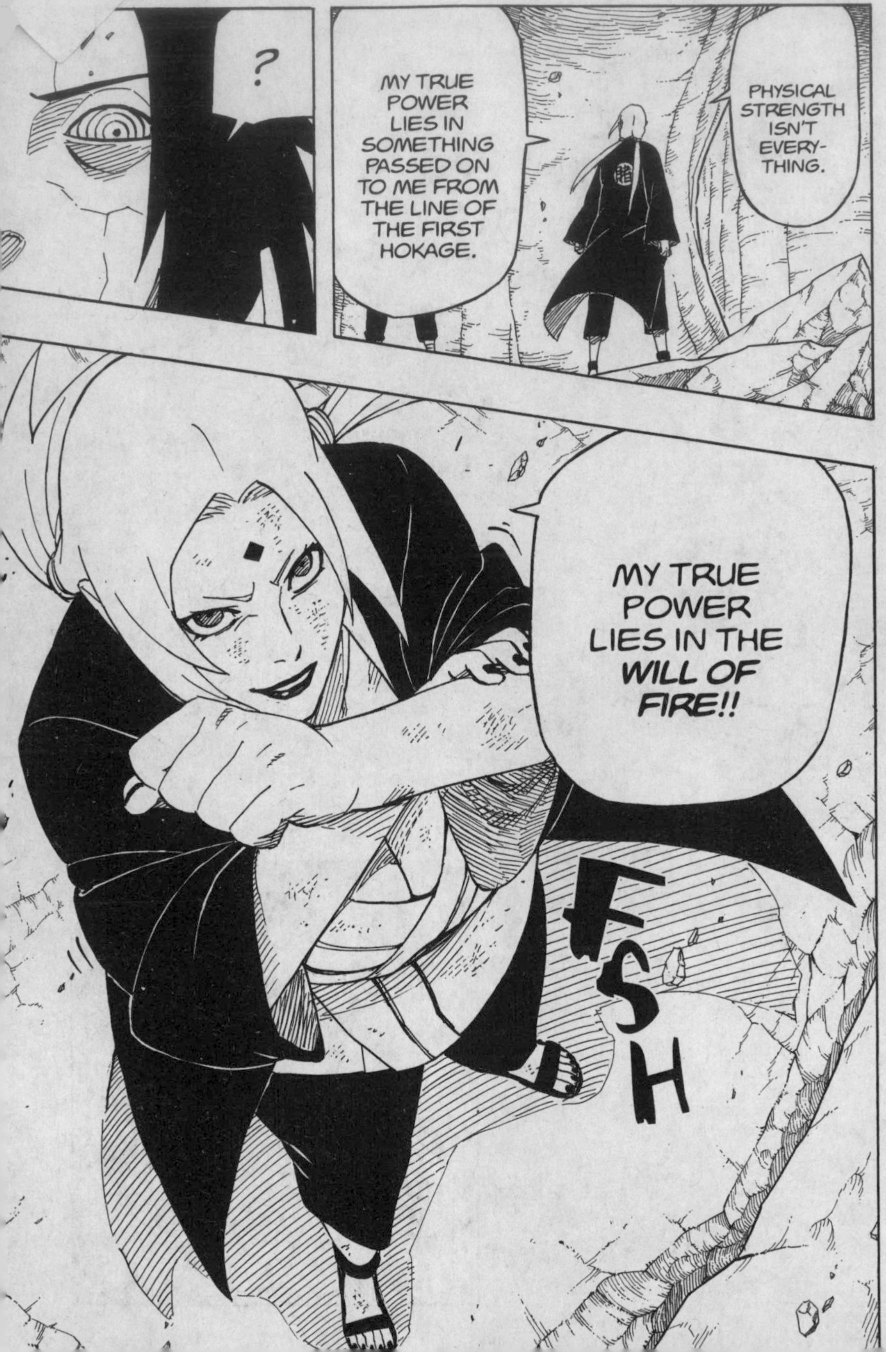
PHYSICAL STRENGTH ISN'T EVERYTHING.
MY TRUE POWER LIES IN SOMETHING PASSED ON TO ME FROM THE LINE OF THE FIRST HOKAGE.
?
MY TRUE POWER LIES IN THE *WILL OF FIRE!!*
FSH

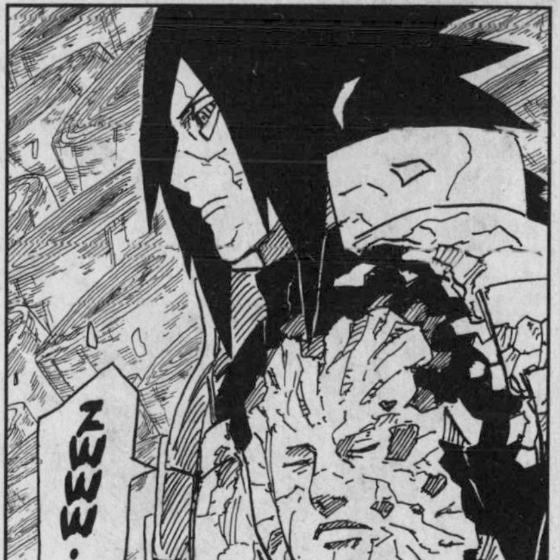

...EEEWWWN

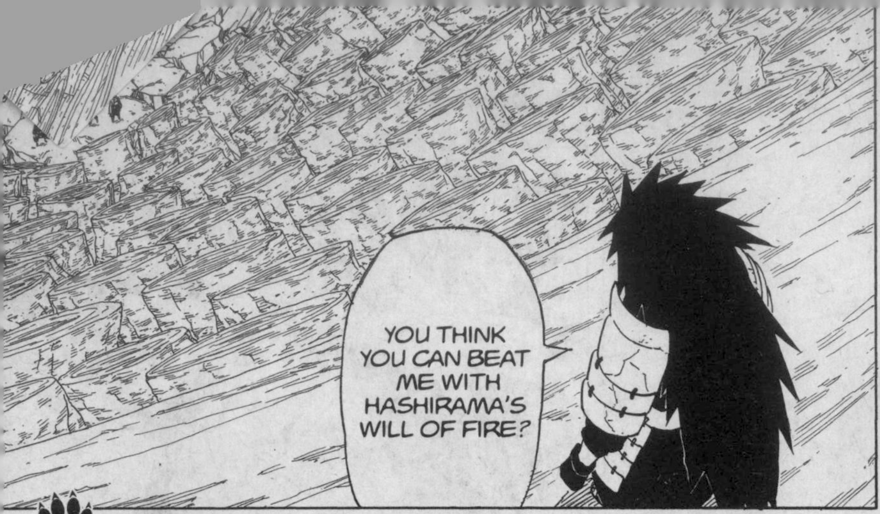
YOU THINK YOU CAN BEAT ME WITH HASHIRAMA'S WILL OF FIRE?

Number 577: Hate Blade

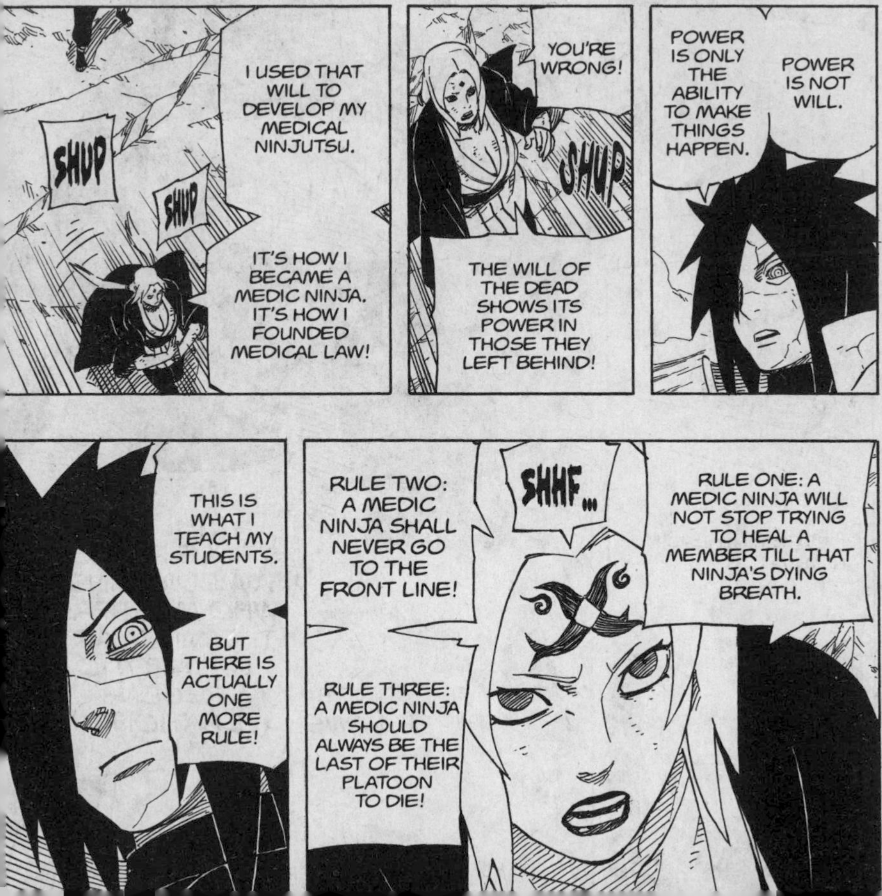
POWER IS NOT WILL.
POWER IS ONLY THE ABILITY TO MAKE THINGS HAPPEN.
YOU'RE WRONG!
SHUP
THE WILL OF THE DEAD SHOWS ITS POWER IN THOSE THEY LEFT BEHIND!
I USED THAT WILL TO DEVELOP MY MEDICAL NINJUTSU.
SHUP
SHUP
IT'S HOW I BECAME A MEDIC NINJA. IT'S HOW I FOUNDED MEDICAL LAW!
RULE ONE: A MEDIC NINJA WILL NOT STOP TRYING TO HEAL A MEMBER TILL THAT NINJA'S DYING BREATH.
SHHF...
RULE TWO: A MEDIC NINJA SHALL NEVER GO TO THE FRONT LINE!
RULE THREE: A MEDIC NINJA SHOULD ALWAYS BE THE LAST OF THEIR PLATOON TO DIE!
THIS IS WHAT I TEACH MY STUDENTS.
BUT THERE IS ACTUALLY ONE MORE RULE!

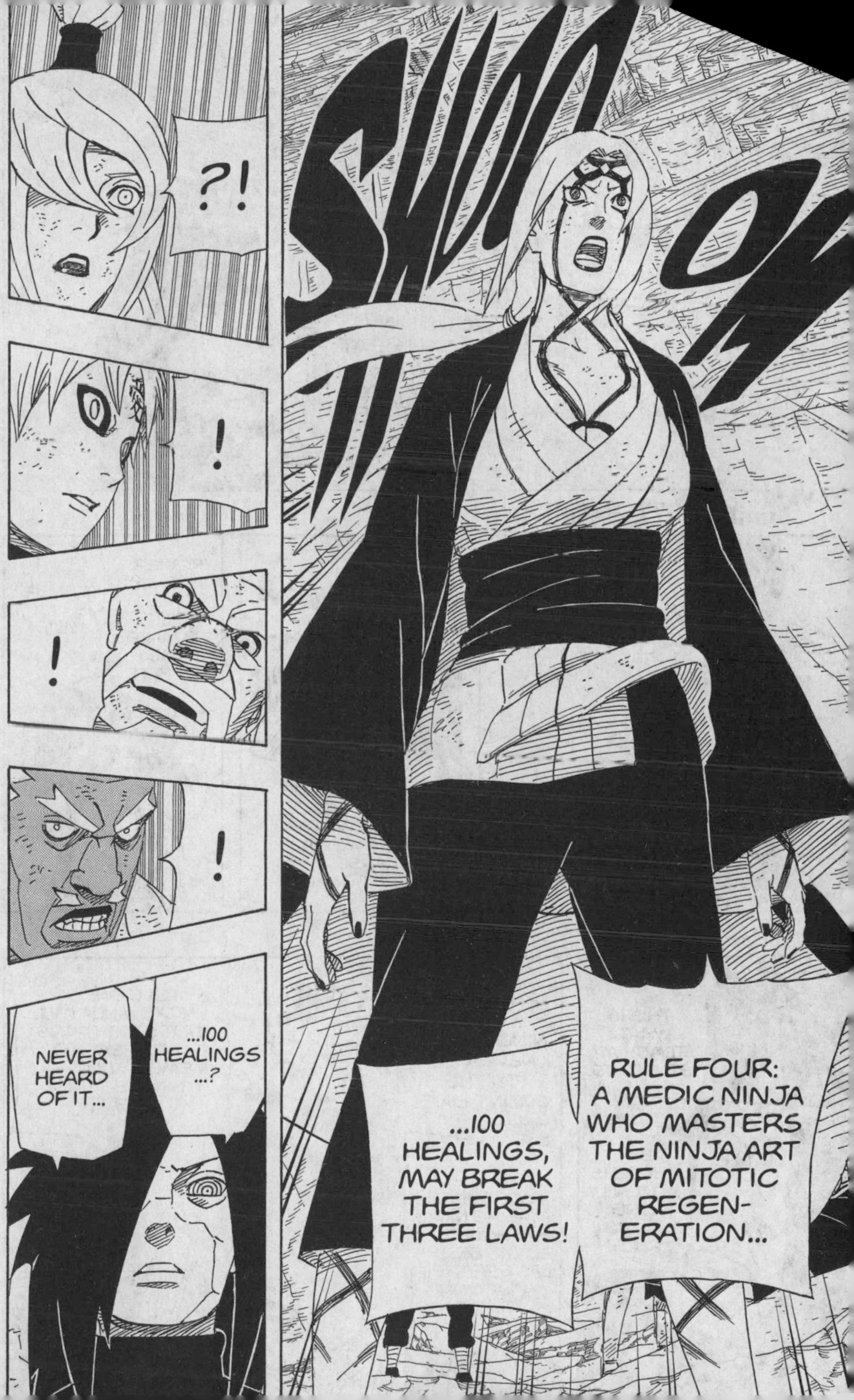
RULE FOUR: A MEDIC NINJA WHO MASTERS THE NINJA ART OF MITOTIC REGEN-ERATION...
...100 HEALINGS, MAY BREAK THE FIRST THREE LAWS!
?!
!
!
!
...100 HEALINGS ...?
NEVER HEARD OF IT...

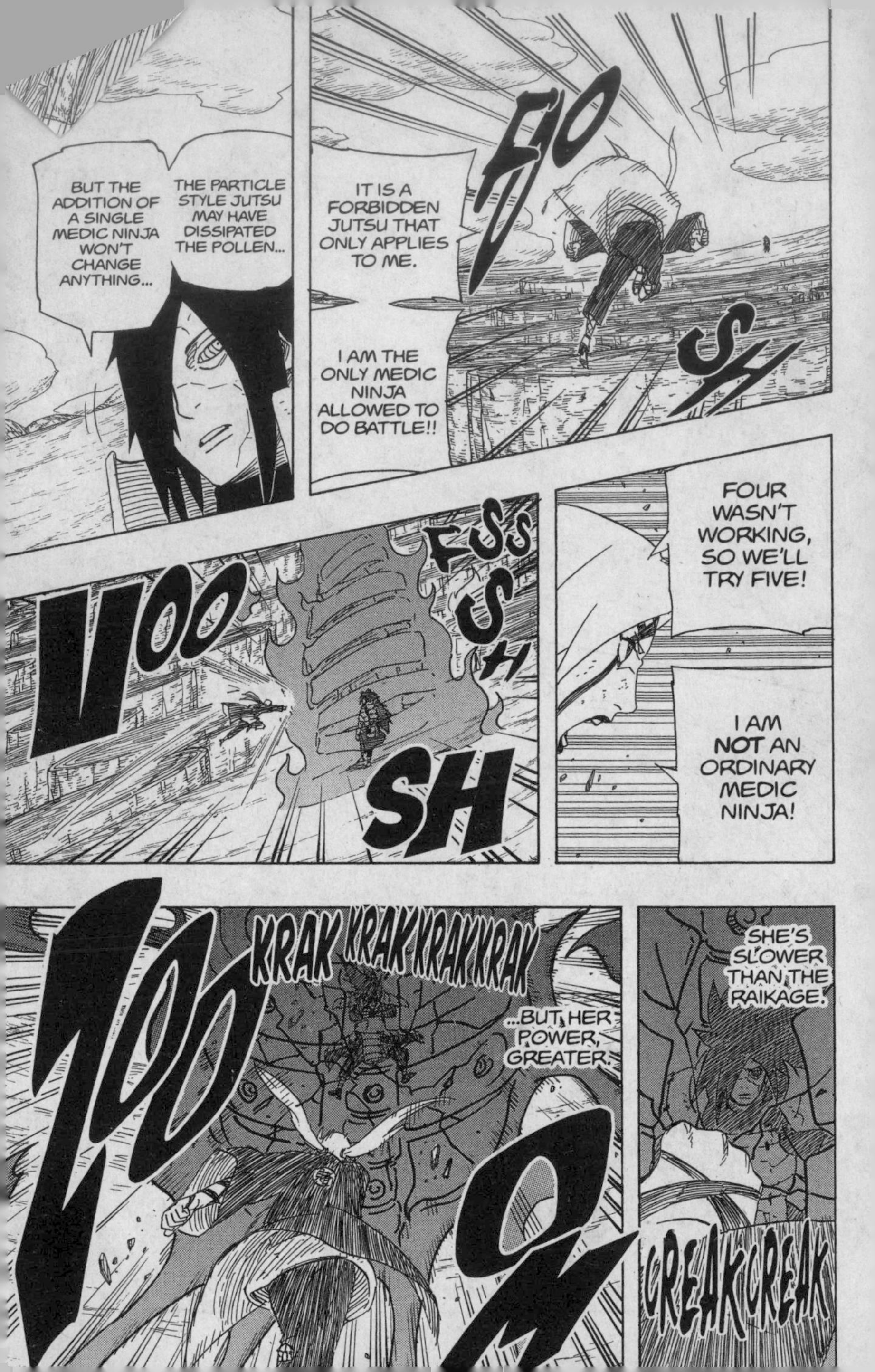
IT IS A FORBIDDEN JUTSU THAT ONLY APPLIES TO ME.
I AM THE ONLY MEDIC NINJA ALLOWED TO DO BATTLE!!
SH
THE PARTICLE STYLE JUTSU MAY HAVE DISSIPATED THE POLLEN...
BUT THE ADDITION OF A SINGLE MEDIC NINJA WON'T CHANGE ANYTHING...
FOUR WASN'T WORKING, SO WE'LL TRY FIVE!
I AM **NOT** AN ORDINARY MEDIC NINJA!
SH
SHE'S SLOWER THAN THE RAIKAGE.
CREAKCREAK
KRAK KRAK KRAK KRAK
...BUT HER POWER, GREATER.

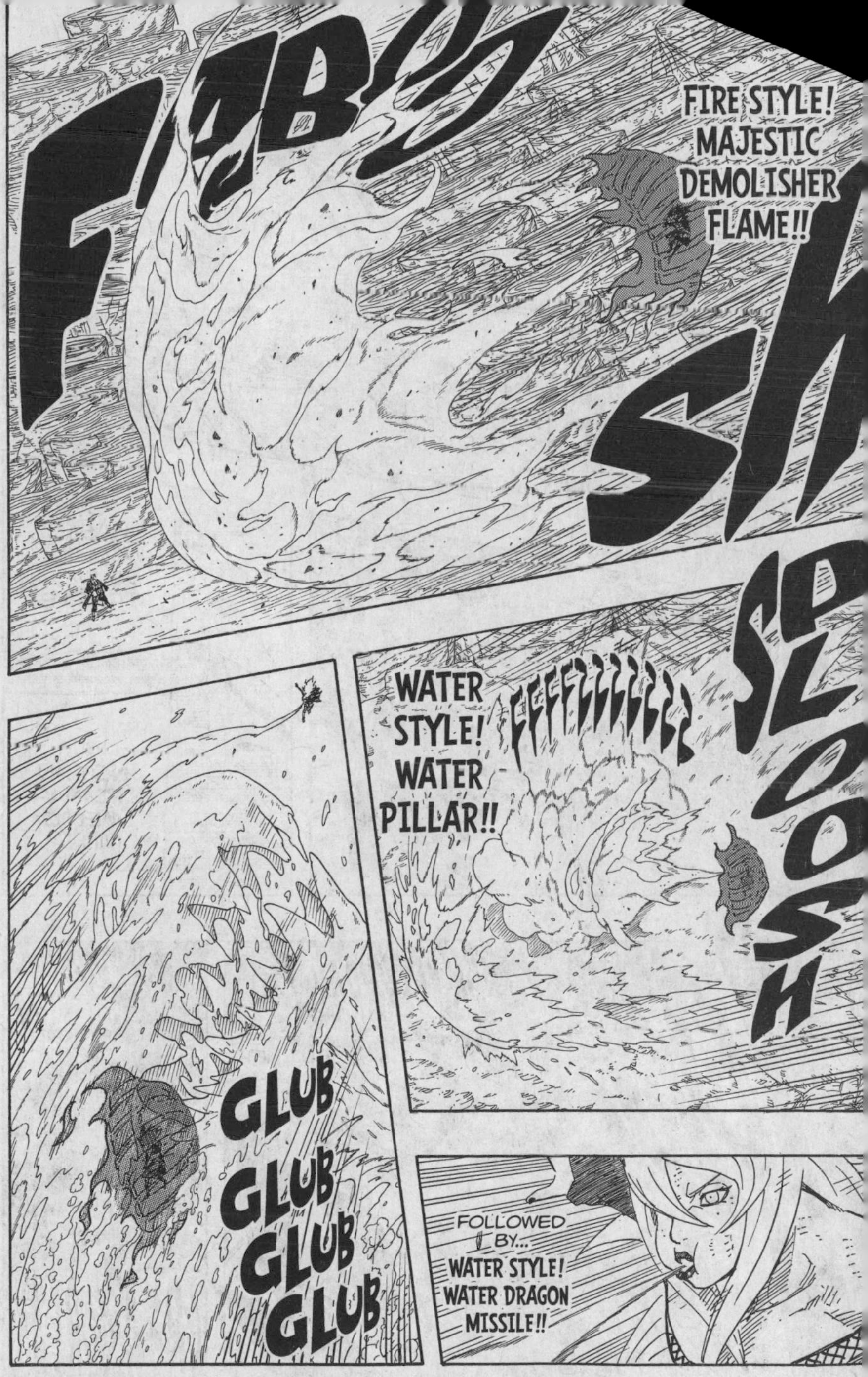
FIRE STYLE! MAJESTIC DEMOLISHER FLAME!!
SPLOOSH
WATER STYLE! WATER PILLAR!!
FOLLOWED BY...
WATER STYLE! WATER DRAGON MISSILE!!
GLUB
GLUB
GLUB
GLUB

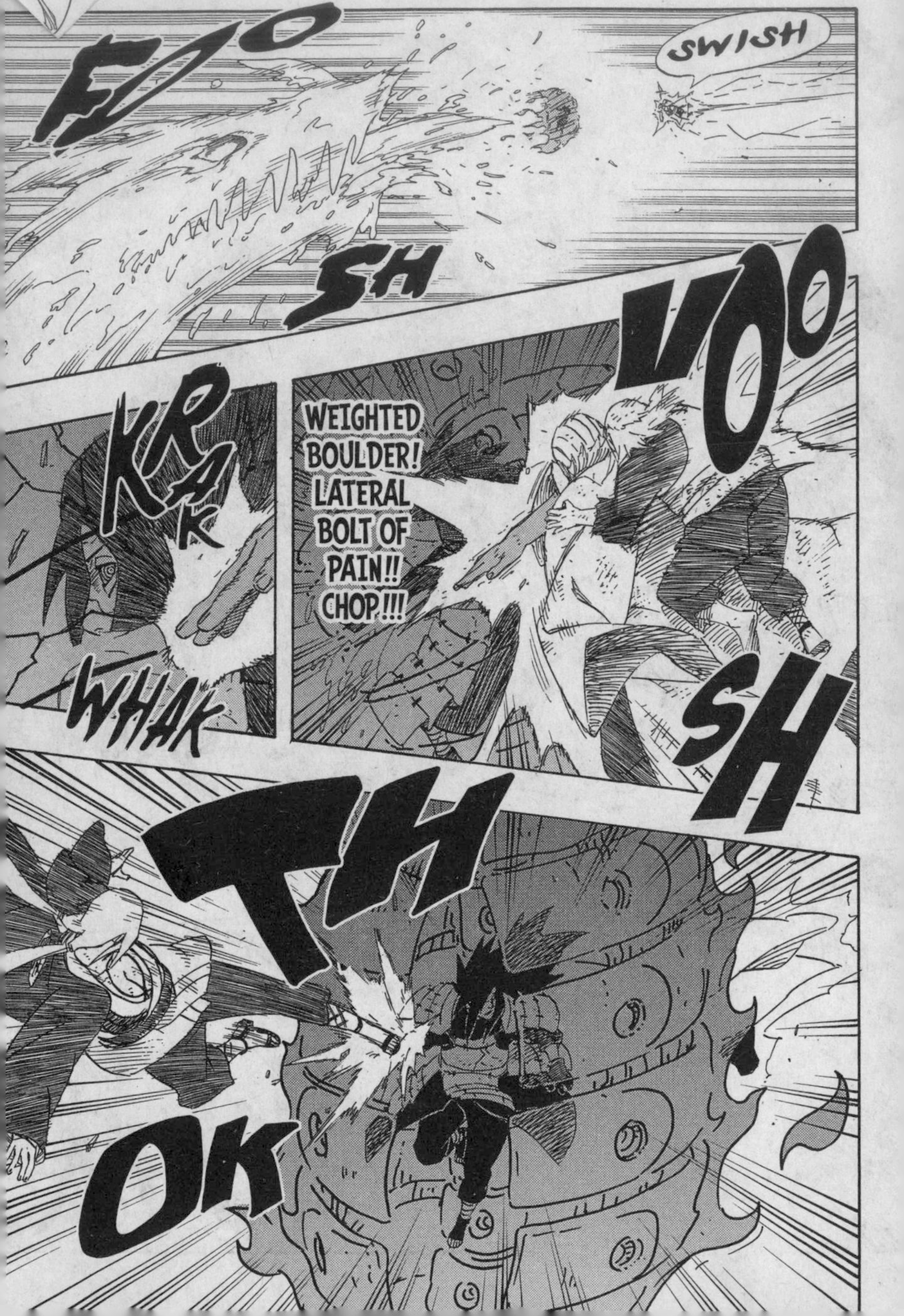
SWISH
FWOSH
VOOSH
WEIGHTED BOULDER! LATERAL BOLT OF PAIN!! CHOP!!!
KRAK
WHAK
THOK

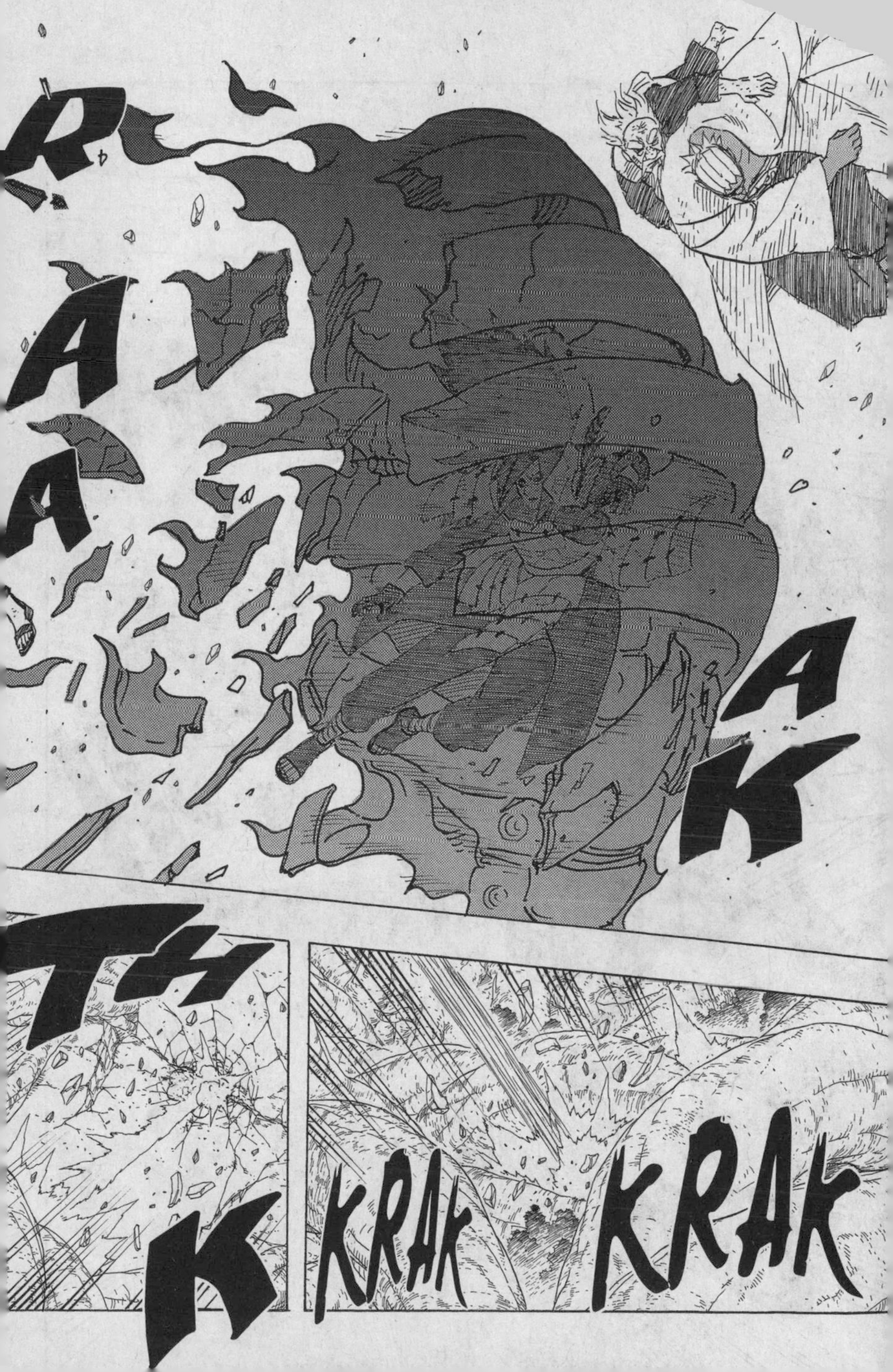
RAAAK
KRAK KRAK
THK

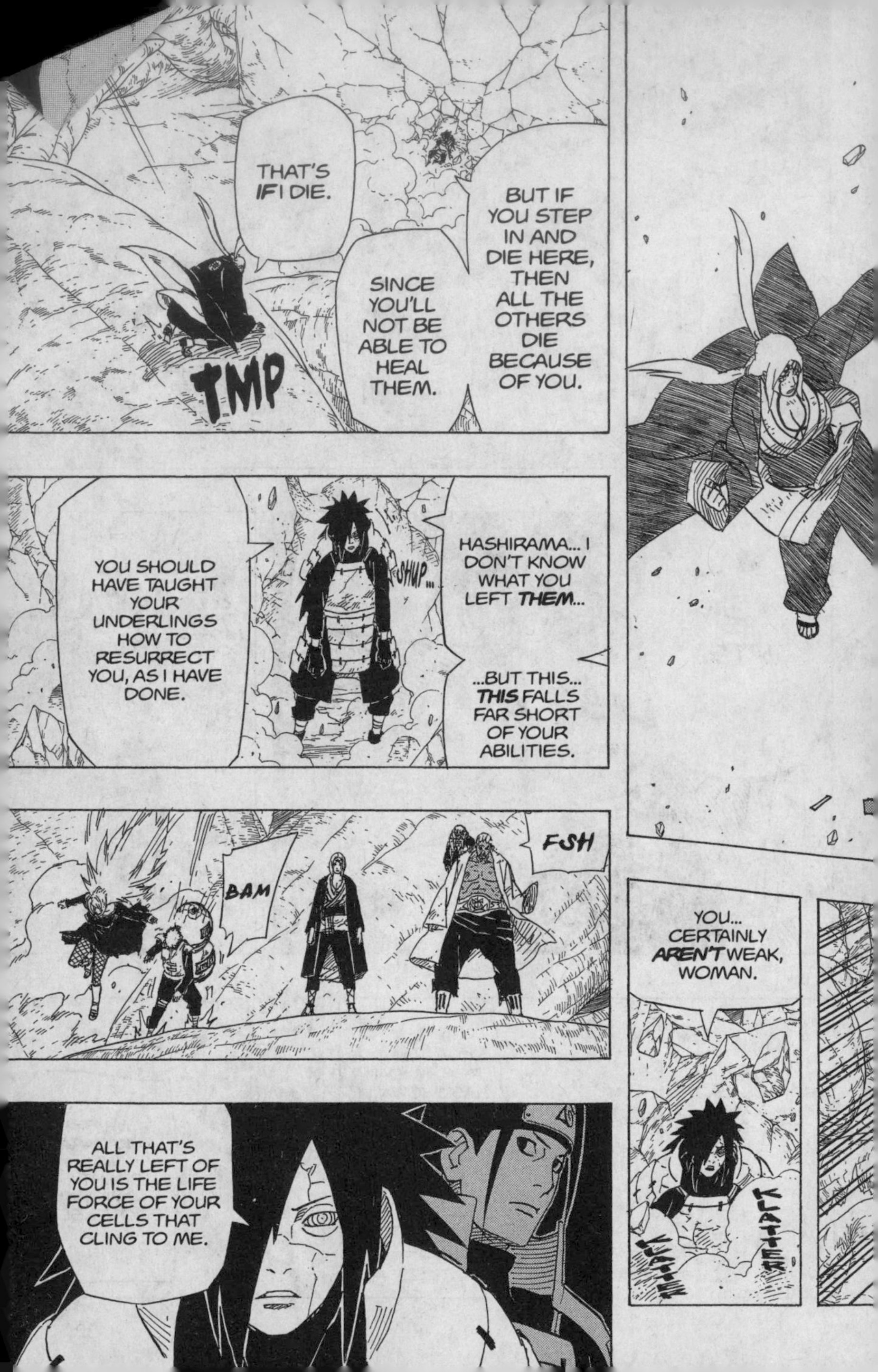
BUT IF YOU STEP IN AND DIE HERE, THEN ALL THE OTHERS DIE BECAUSE OF YOU.
SINCE YOU'LL NOT BE ABLE TO HEAL THEM.
THAT'S *IF* I DIE.
TMP
HASHIRAMA... I DON'T KNOW WHAT YOU LEFT *THEM*...
...BUT THIS... *THIS* FALLS FAR SHORT OF YOUR ABILITIES.
SHUP...
YOU SHOULD HAVE TAUGHT YOUR UNDERLINGS HOW TO RESURRECT YOU, AS I HAVE DONE.
FSH
BAM
YOU... CERTAINLY *AREN'T* WEAK, WOMAN.
KLATTER
KLATTER
ALL THAT'S REALLY LEFT OF YOU IS THE LIFE FORCE OF YOUR CELLS THAT CLING TO ME.

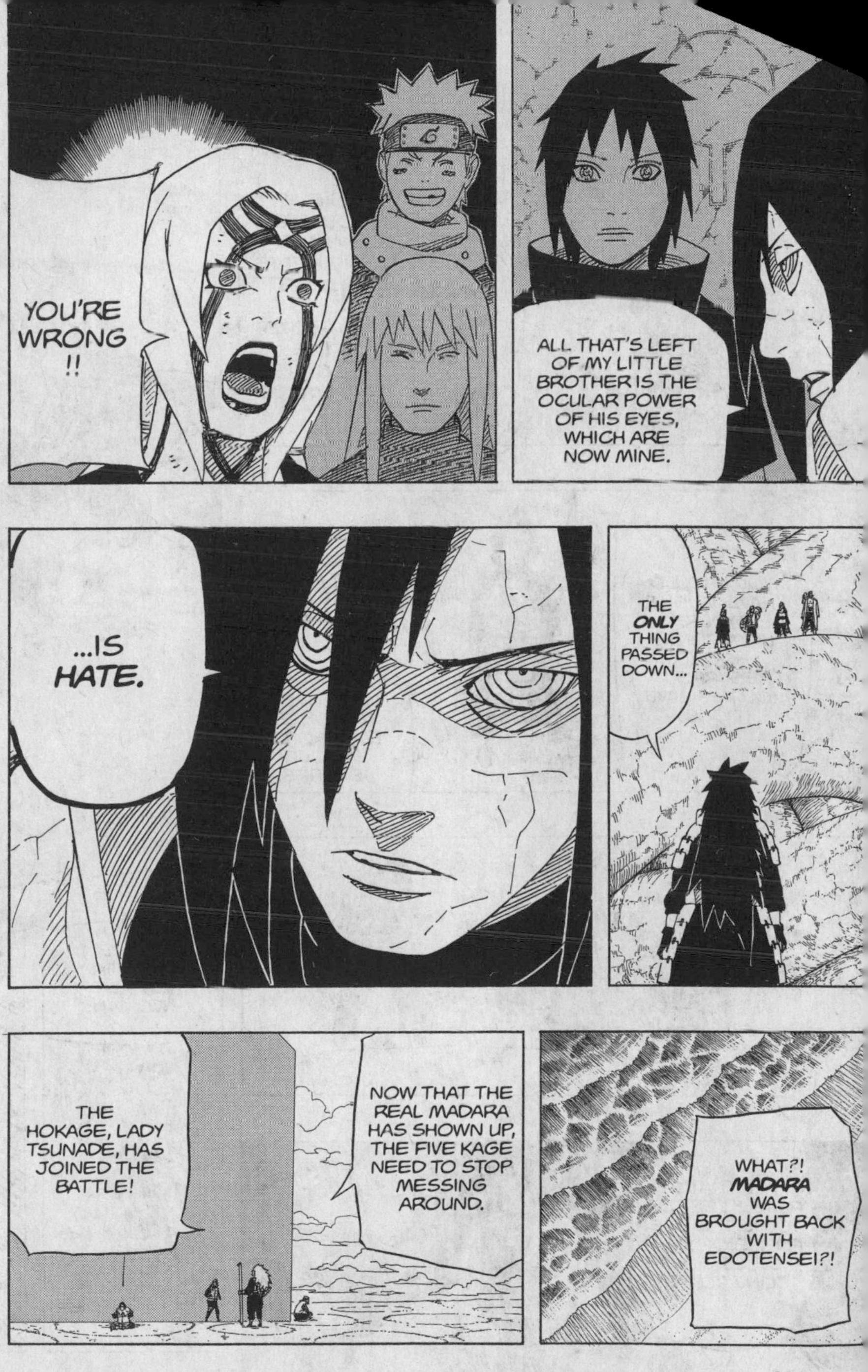
ALL THAT'S LEFT OF MY LITTLE BROTHER IS THE OCULAR POWER OF HIS EYES, WHICH ARE NOW MINE.
YOU'RE WRONG !!
THE ONLY THING PASSED DOWN...
...IS HATE.
WHAT?! MADARA WAS BROUGHT BACK WITH EDOTENSEI?!
NOW THAT THE REAL MADARA HAS SHOWN UP, THE FIVE KAGE NEED TO STOP MESSING AROUND.
THE HOKAGE, LADY TSUNADE, HAS JOINED THE BATTLE!

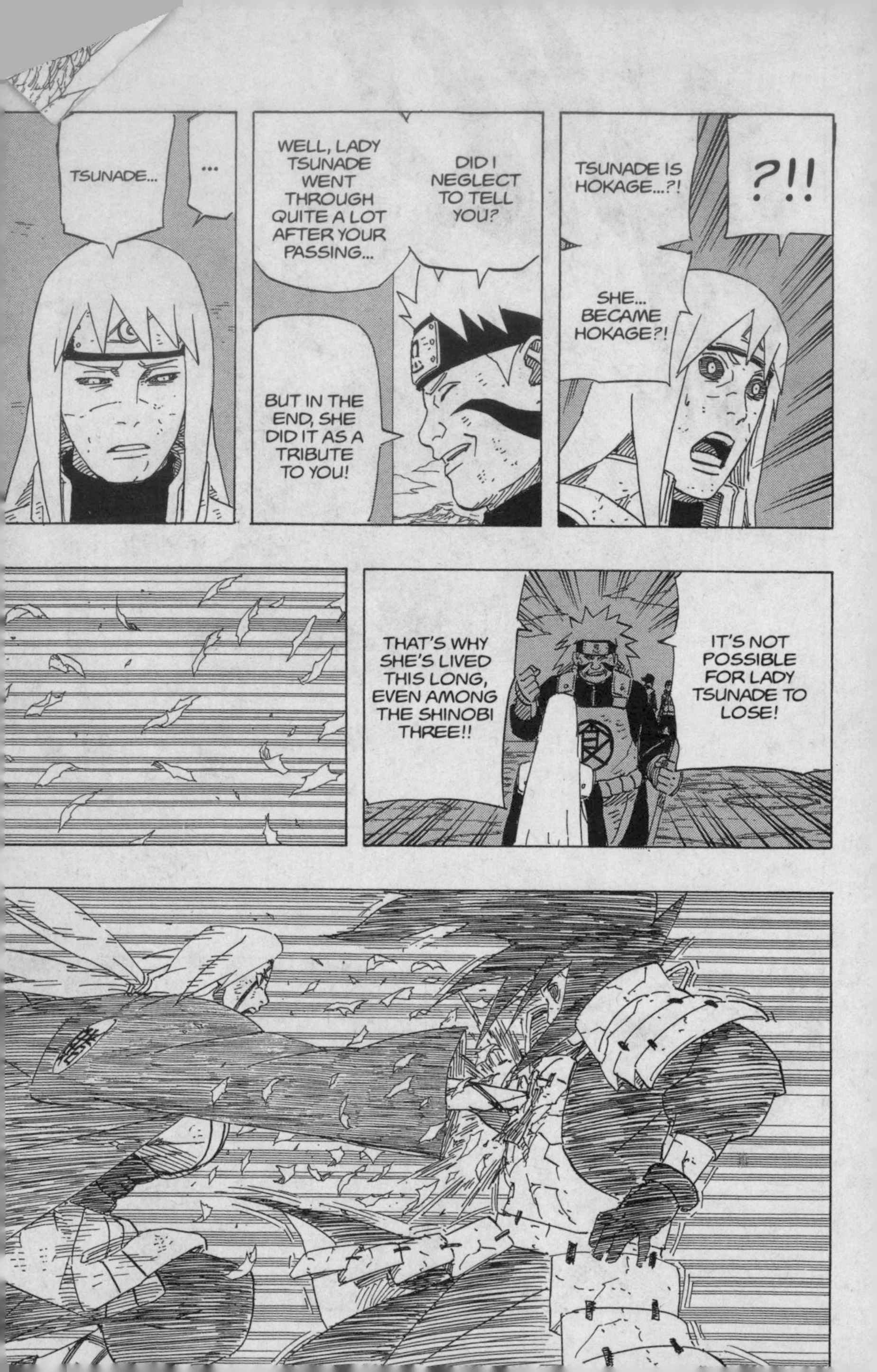
?!!
TSUNADE IS HOKAGE...?!
SHE... BECAME HOKAGE?!
DID I NEGLECT TO TELL YOU?
WELL, LADY TSUNADE WENT THROUGH QUITE A LOT AFTER YOUR PASSING...
BUT IN THE END, SHE DID IT AS A TRIBUTE TO YOU!
...
TSUNADE...
IT'S NOT POSSIBLE FOR LADY TSUNADE TO LOSE!
THAT'S WHY SHE'S LIVED THIS LONG, EVEN AMONG THE SHINOBI THREE!!

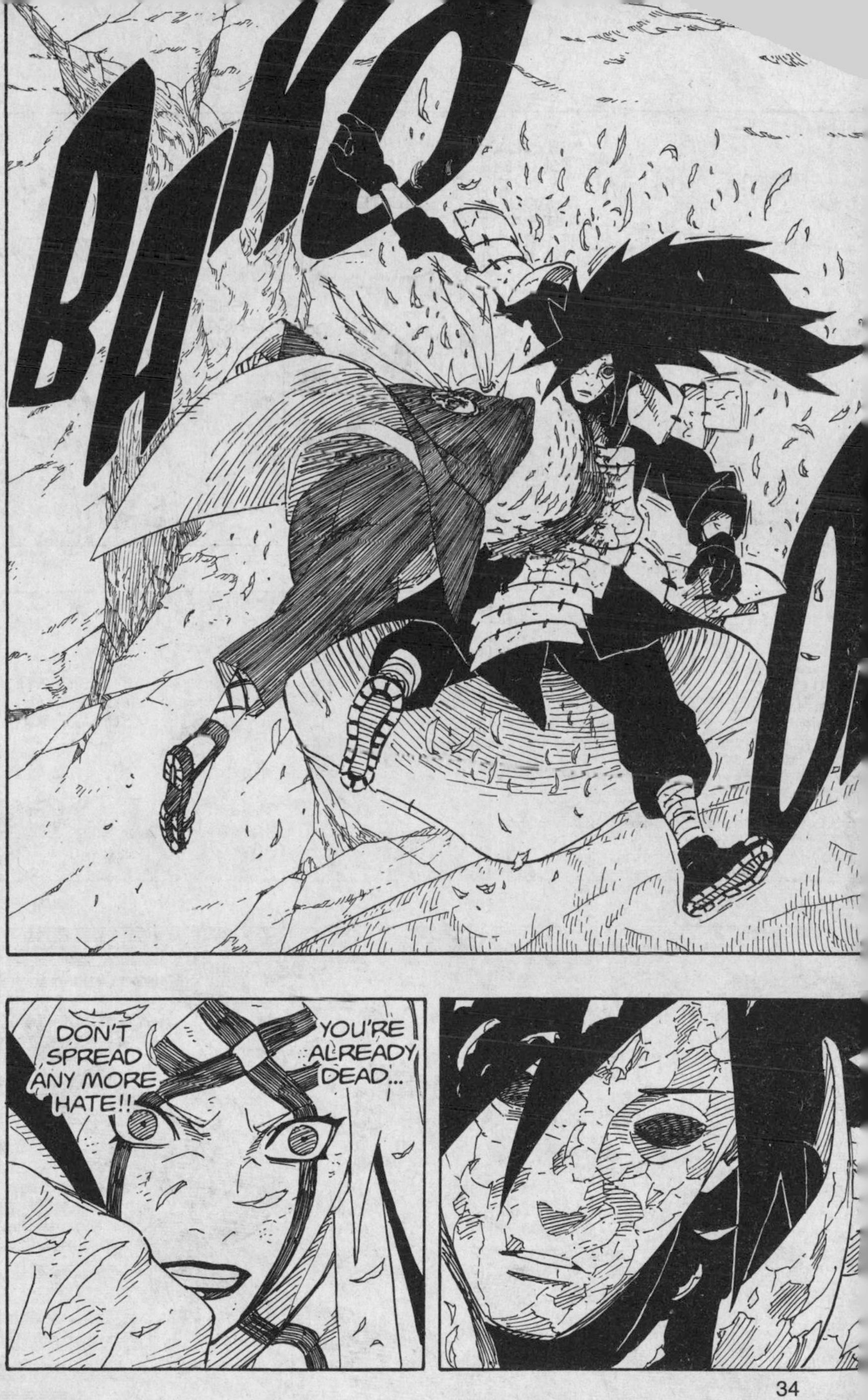
BAKO
YOU'RE ALREADY DEAD...
DON'T SPREAD ANY MORE HATE!!

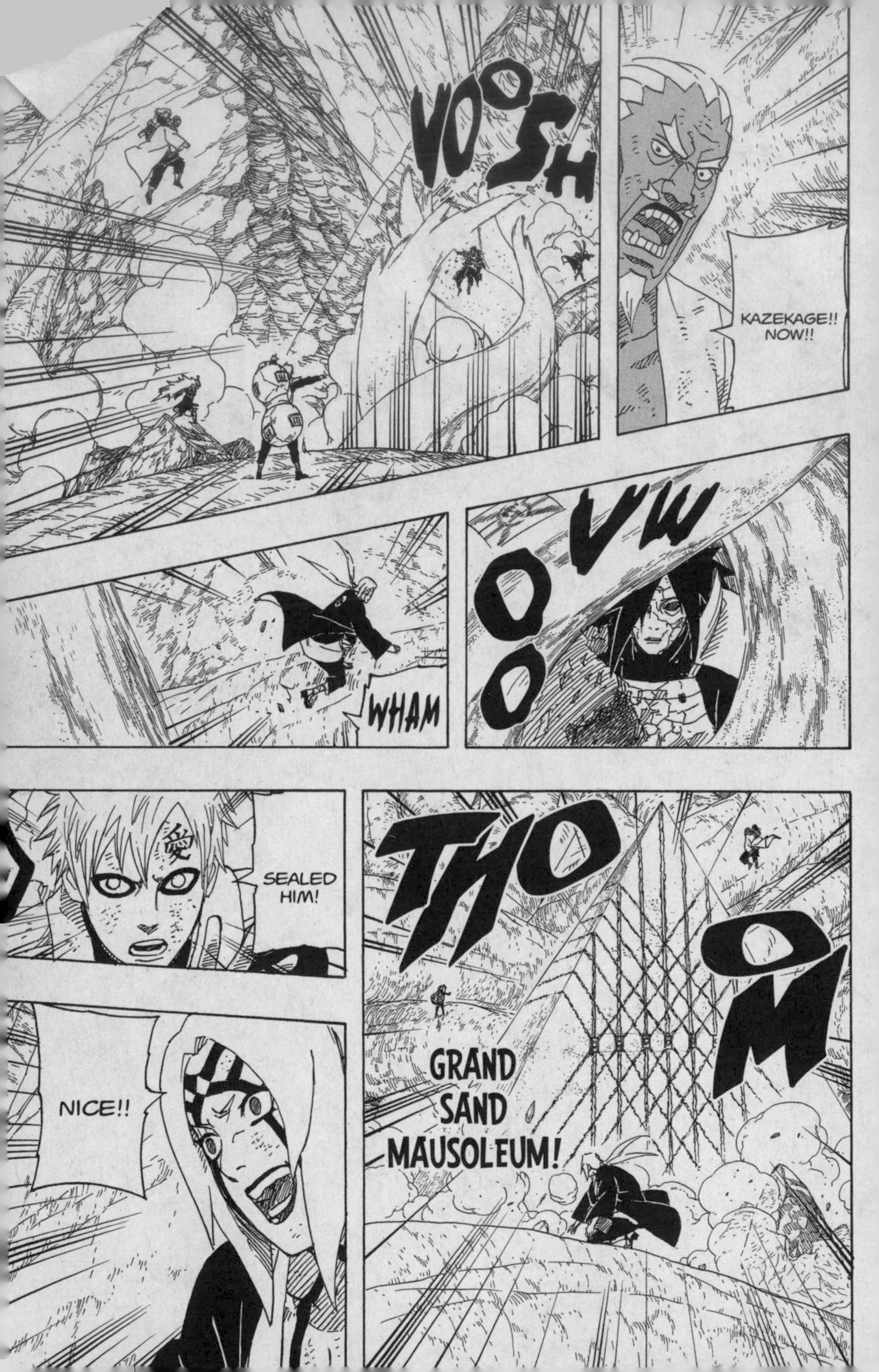
KAZEKAGE!! NOW!!
VOOSH
VWOOO
WHAM
THOOM
GRAND SAND MAUSOLEUM!
SEALED HIM!
NICE!!

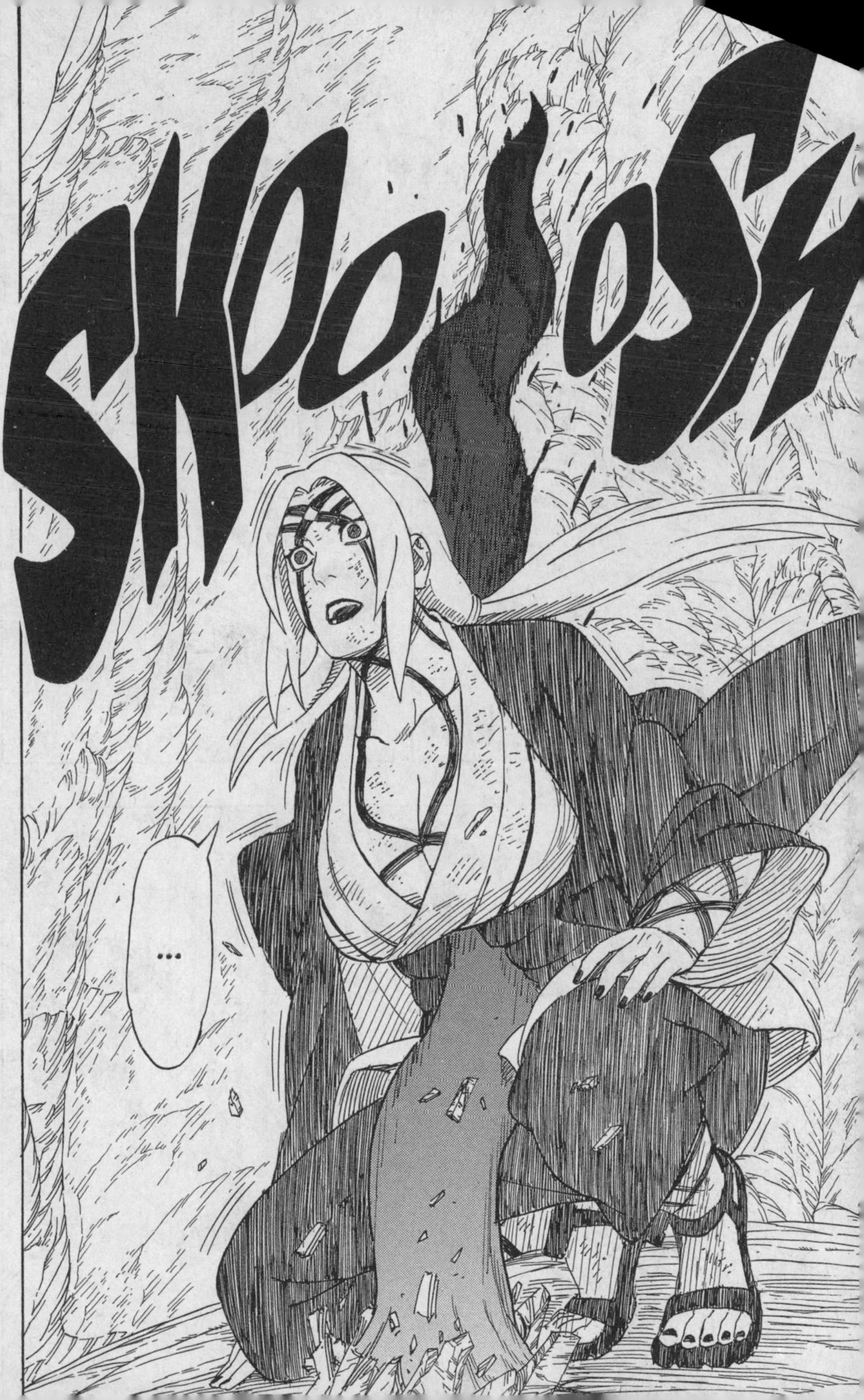
SHOOSH
...

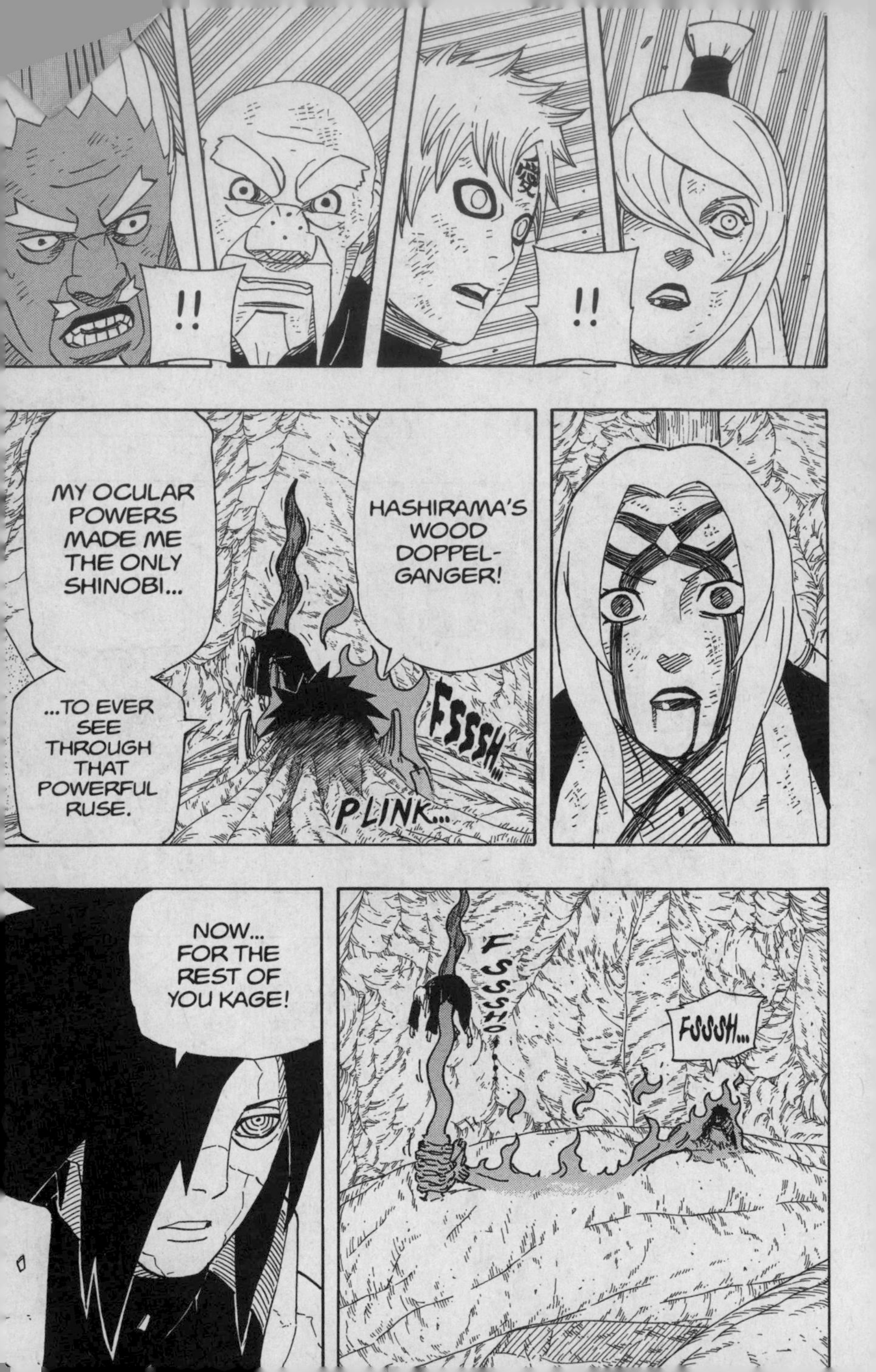
!!
!!
HASHIRAMA'S WOOD DOPPEL-GANGER!
MY OCULAR POWERS MADE ME THE ONLY SHINOBI...
...TO EVER SEE THROUGH THAT POWERFUL RUSE.
FSSSH...
PLINK...
FSSSH...
FSSSH
NOW... FOR THE REST OF YOU KAGE!

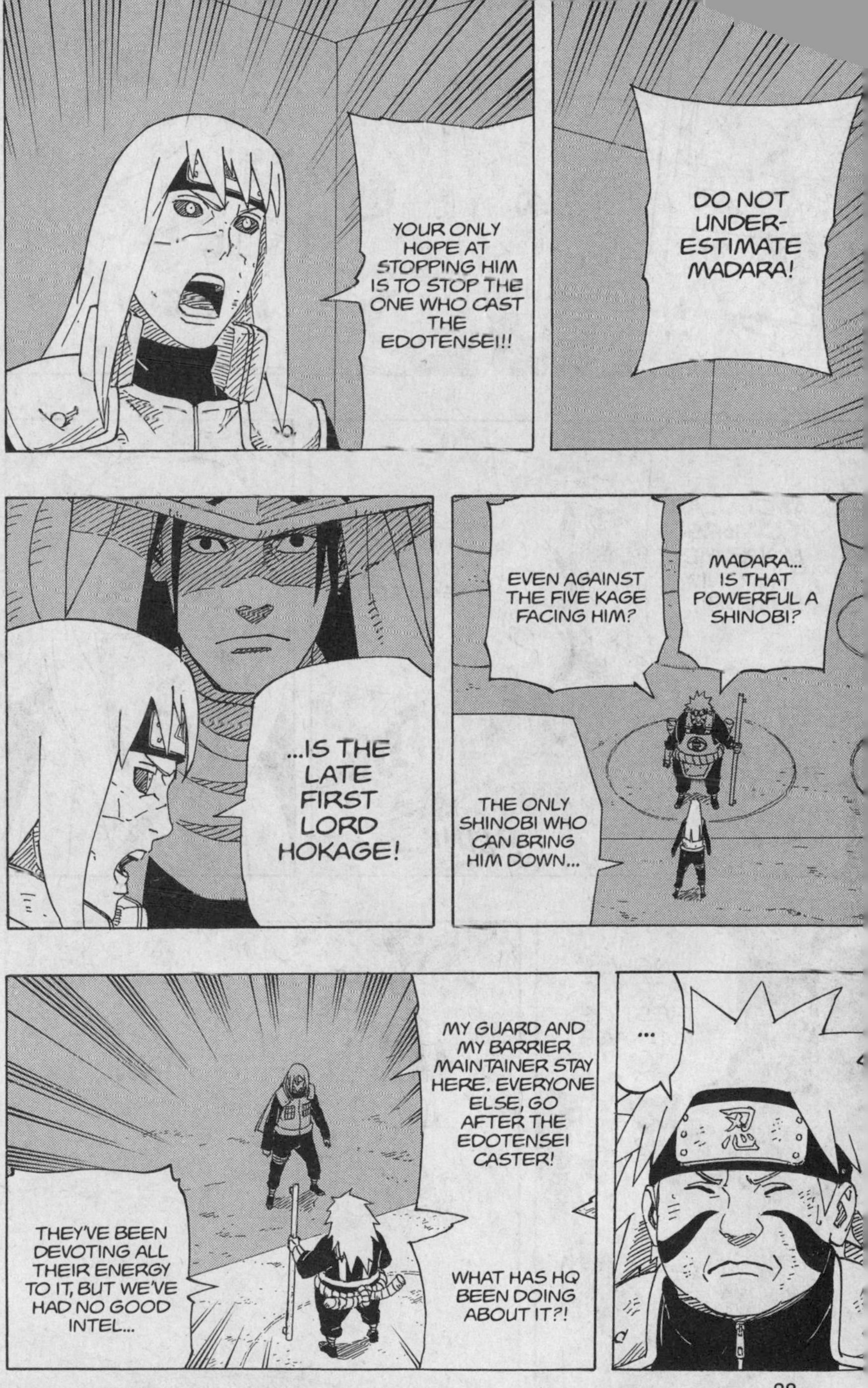
DO NOT UNDER-ESTIMATE MADARA!
YOUR ONLY HOPE AT STOPPING HIM IS TO STOP THE ONE WHO CAST THE EDOTENSEI!!
MADARA... IS THAT POWERFUL A SHINOBI?
EVEN AGAINST THE FIVE KAGE FACING HIM?
THE ONLY SHINOBI WHO CAN BRING HIM DOWN...
...IS THE LATE FIRST LORD HOKAGE!
...
MY GUARD AND MY BARRIER MAINTAINER STAY HERE. EVERYONE ELSE, GO AFTER THE EDOTENSEI CASTER!
WHAT HAS HQ BEEN DOING ABOUT IT?!
THEY'VE BEEN DEVOTING ALL THEIR ENERGY TO IT, BUT WE'VE HAD NO GOOD INTEL...

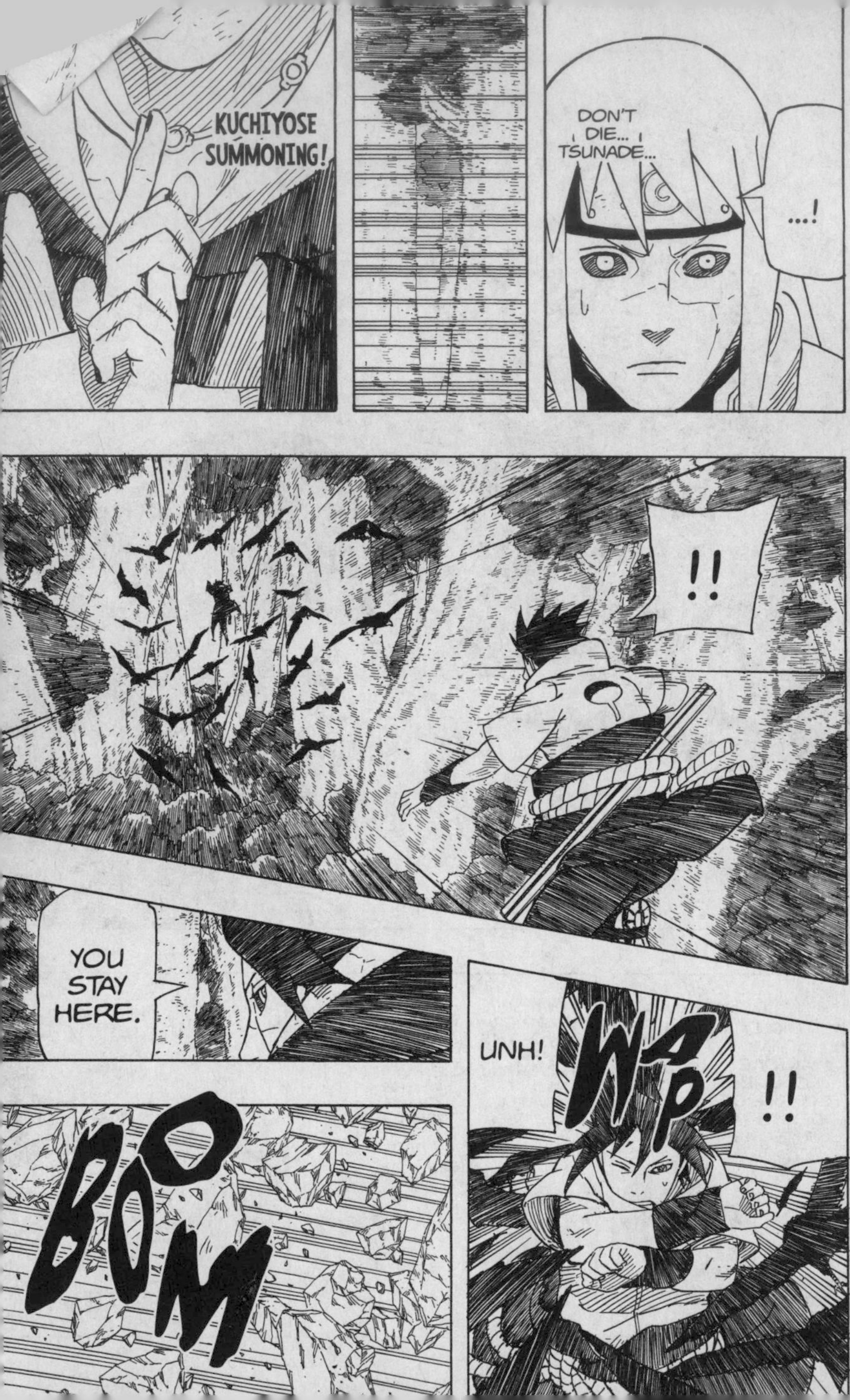
DON'T DIE... TSUNADE...
...!
KUCHIYOSE SUMMONING!
!!
UNH!
WAP
!!
YOU STAY HERE.
BOOM

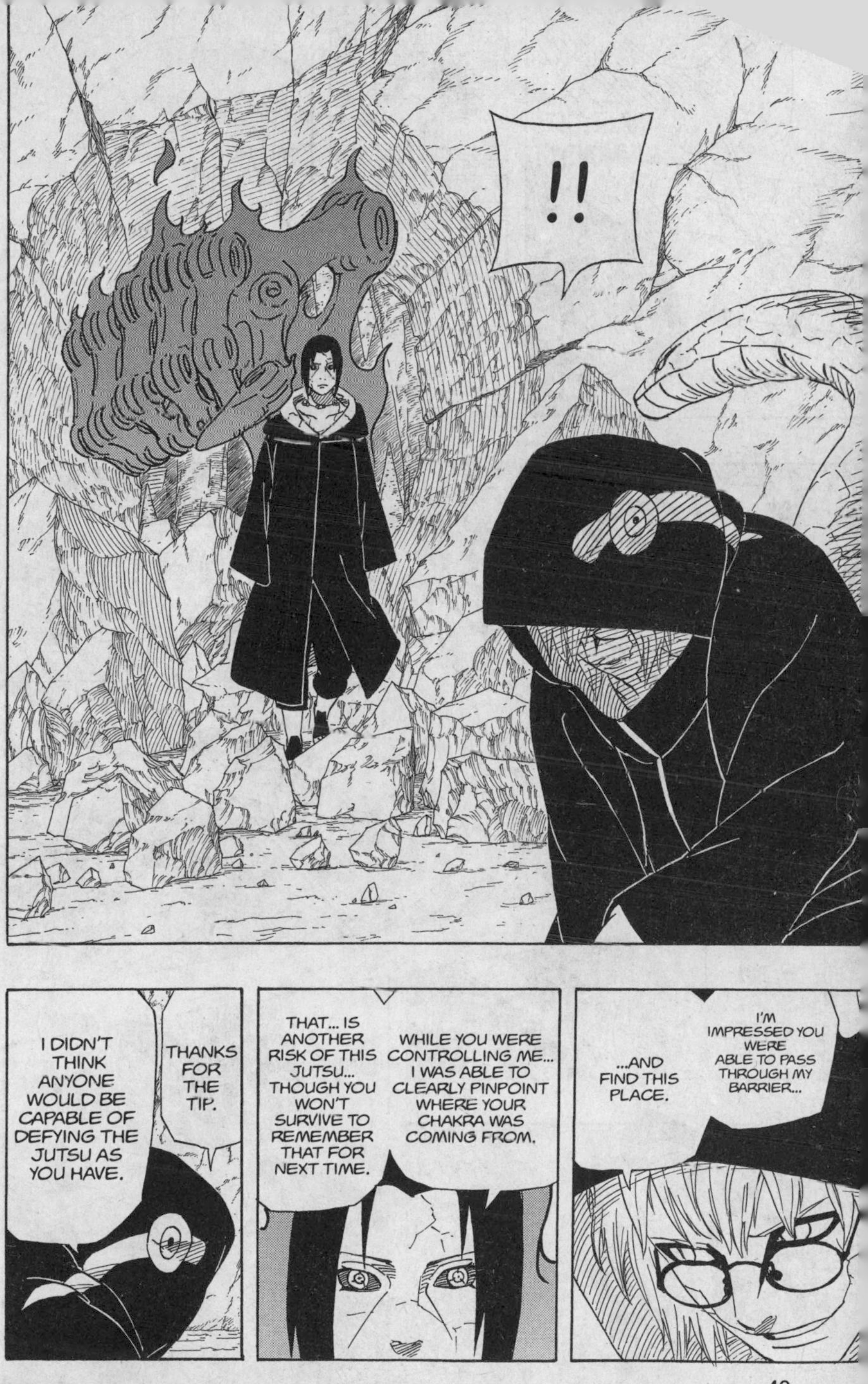
!!
I'M IMPRESSED YOU WERE ABLE TO PASS THROUGH MY BARRIER...
...AND FIND THIS PLACE.
WHILE YOU WERE CONTROLLING ME... I WAS ABLE TO CLEARLY PINPOINT WHERE YOUR CHAKRA WAS COMING FROM.
THAT... IS ANOTHER RISK OF THIS JUTSU... THOUGH YOU WON'T SURVIVE TO REMEMBER THAT FOR NEXT TIME.
THANKS FOR THE TIP.
I DIDN'T THINK ANYONE WOULD BE CAPABLE OF DEFYING THE JUTSU AS YOU HAVE.

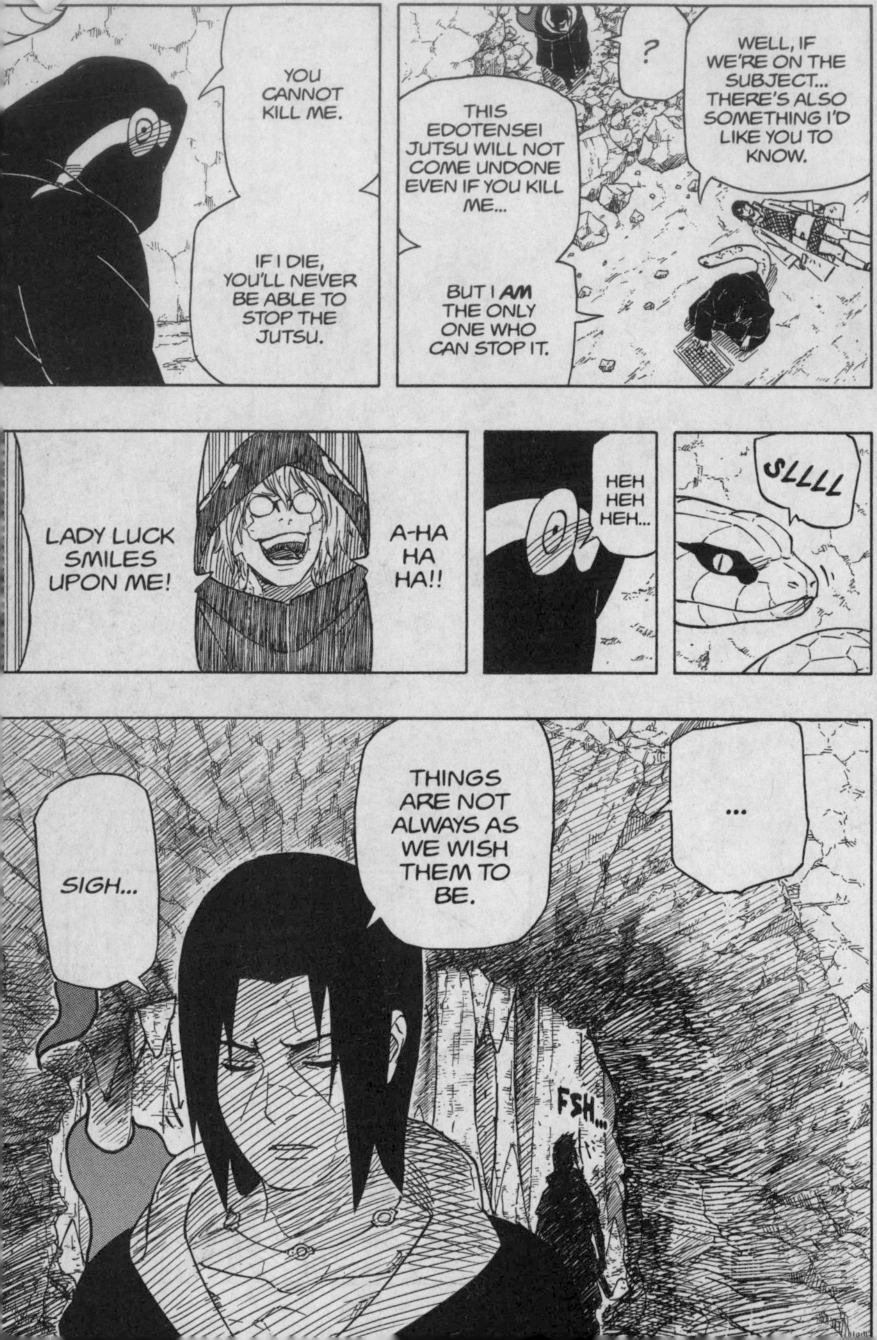
WELL, IF WE'RE ON THE SUBJECT... THERE'S ALSO SOMETHING I'D LIKE YOU TO KNOW.
?
THIS EDOTENSEI JUTSU WILL NOT COME UNDONE EVEN IF YOU KILL ME...
BUT I **AM** THE ONLY ONE WHO CAN STOP IT.
YOU CANNOT KILL ME.
IF I DIE, YOU'LL NEVER BE ABLE TO STOP THE JUTSU.
SLLLL
HEH HEH HEH...
A-HA HA HA!!
LADY LUCK SMILES UPON ME!
...
THINGS ARE NOT ALWAYS AS WE WISH THEM TO BE.
FSH...
SIGH...

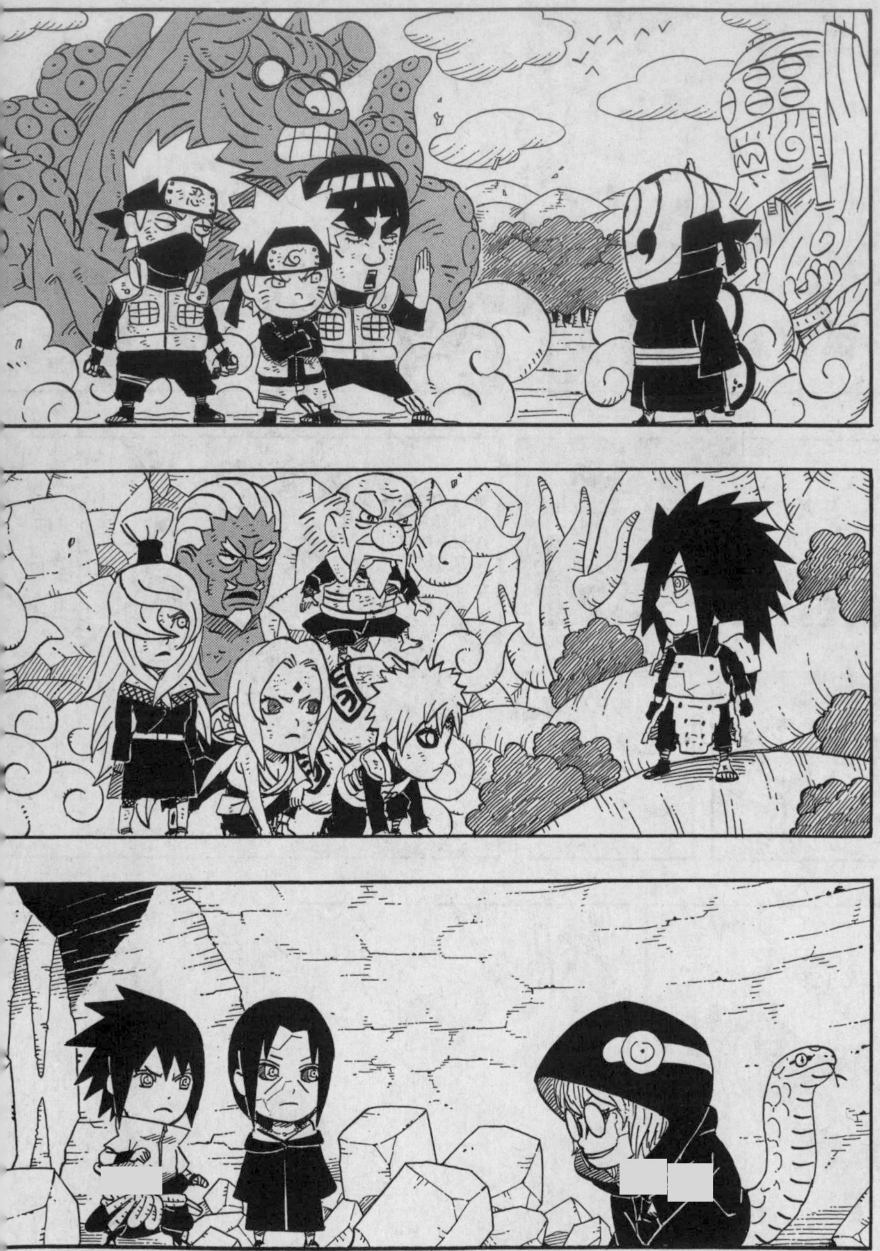

Number 578: The Weak Point of Despair!!

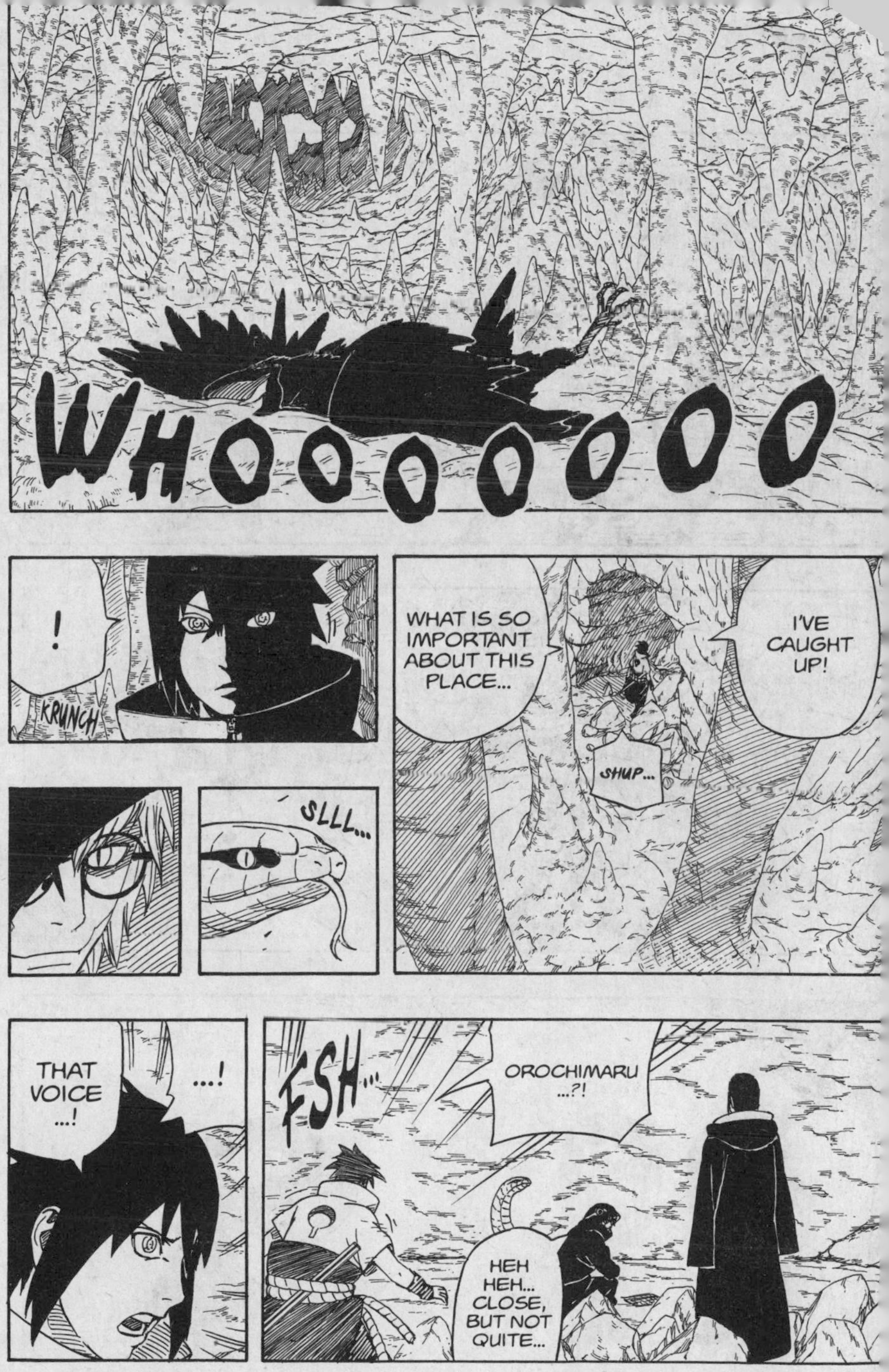
WHOOOOOOO
I'VE CAUGHT UP!
WHAT IS SO IMPORTANT ABOUT THIS PLACE...
SHUP...
!
KRUNCH
SLLL...
OROCHIMARU ...?!
FSH...
HEH HEH... CLOSE, BUT NOT QUITE...
...!
THAT VOICE ...!

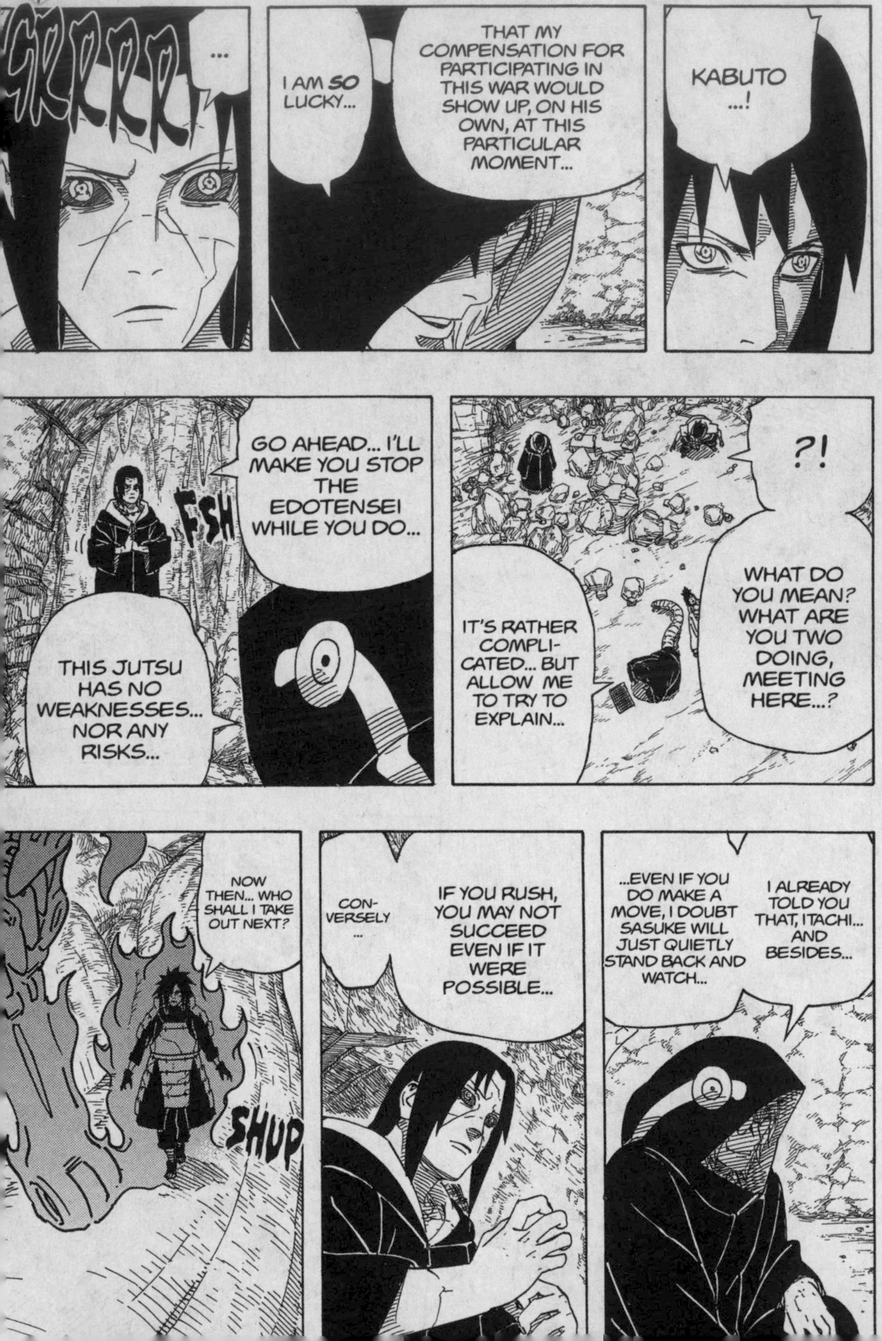
KABUTO ...!
I AM SO LUCKY...
THAT MY COMPENSATION FOR PARTICIPATING IN THIS WAR WOULD SHOW UP, ON HIS OWN, AT THIS PARTICULAR MOMENT...
...
GRRRR
?!
WHAT DO YOU MEAN? WHAT ARE YOU TWO DOING, MEETING HERE...?
IT'S RATHER COMPLICATED... BUT ALLOW ME TO TRY TO EXPLAIN...
GO AHEAD... I'LL MAKE YOU STOP THE EDOTENSEI WHILE YOU DO...
FSH
THIS JUTSU HAS NO WEAKNESSES... NOR ANY RISKS...
I ALREADY TOLD YOU THAT, ITACHI... AND BESIDES...
...EVEN IF YOU DO MAKE A MOVE, I DOUBT SASUKE WILL JUST QUIETLY STAND BACK AND WATCH...
CONVERSELY ...
IF YOU RUSH, YOU MAY NOT SUCCEED EVEN IF IT WERE POSSIBLE...
NOW THEN... WHO SHALL I TAKE OUT NEXT?
SHUP

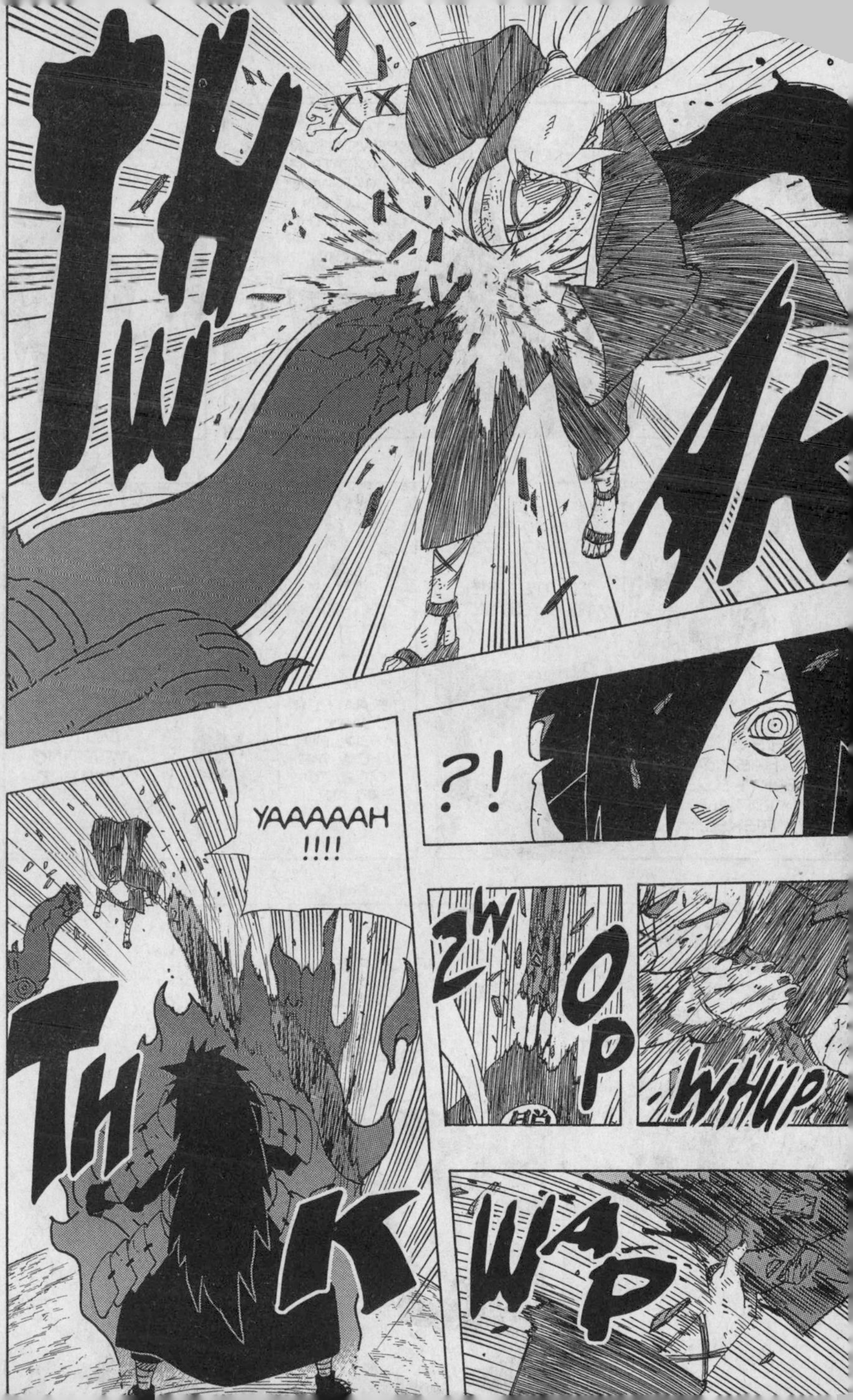
?!
WHUP
YAAAAAH
!!!!

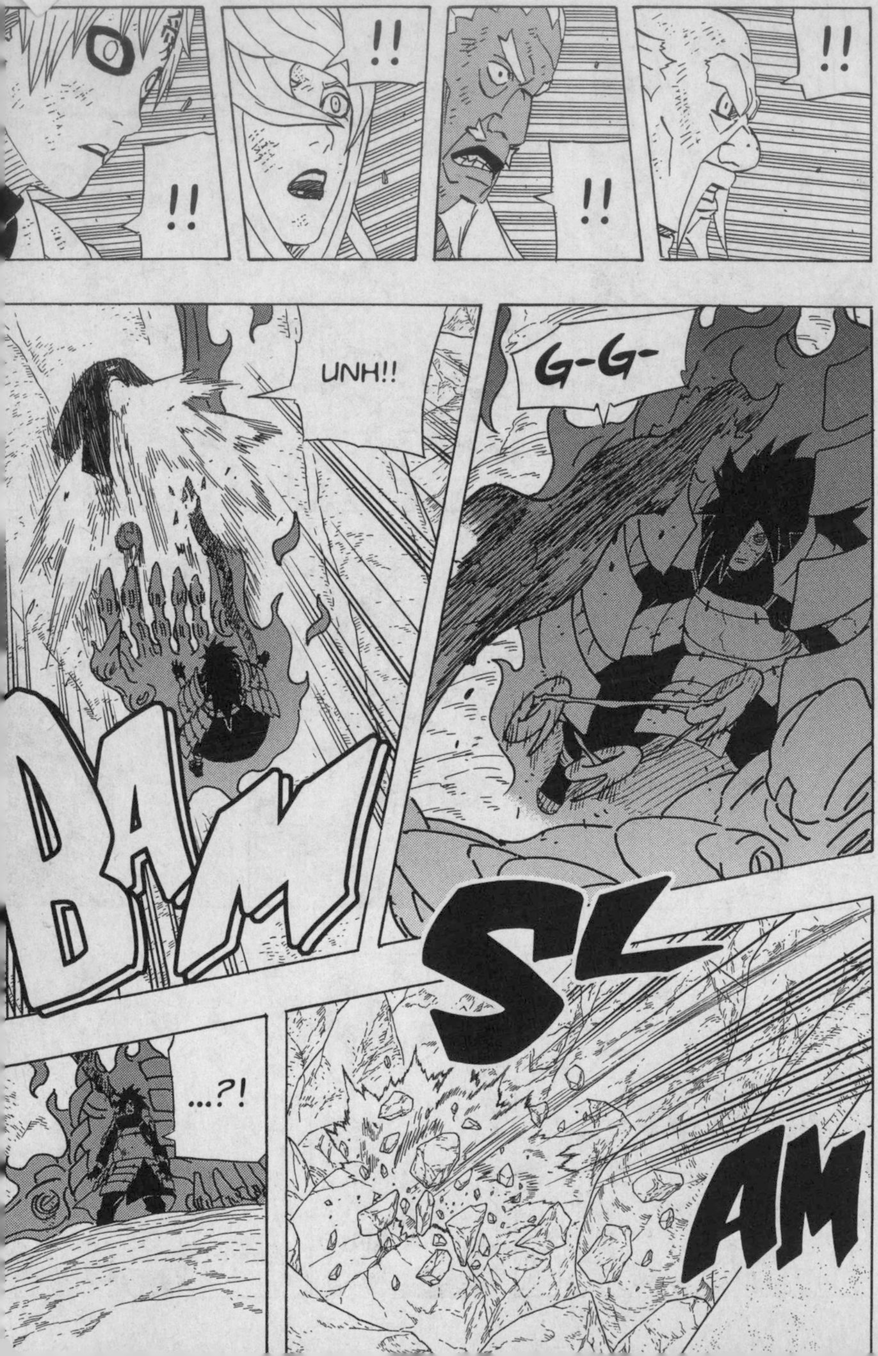
!!
!!
!!
!!
G-G-
UNH!!
BAM
SLAM
...?!

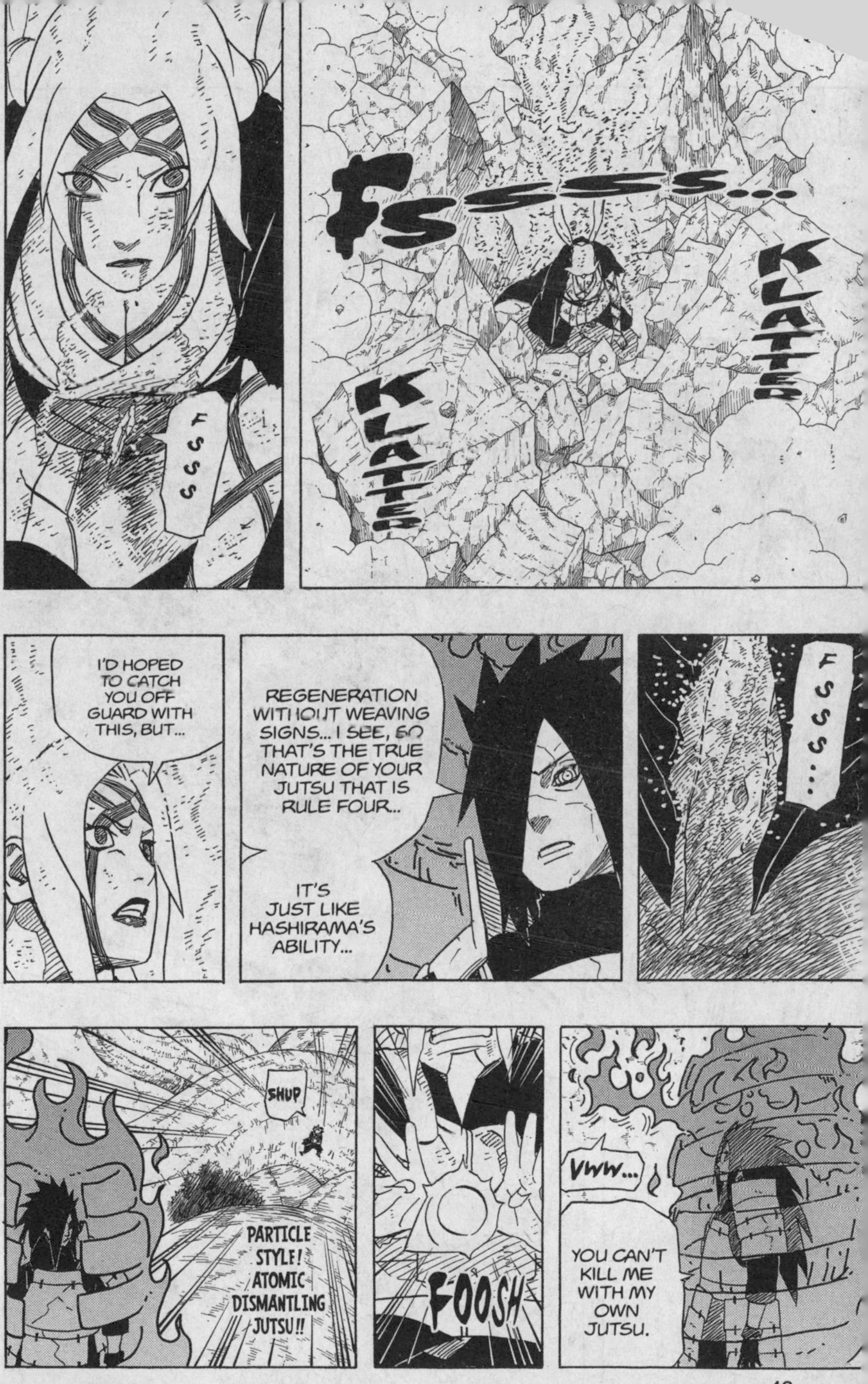
FSSSSS...
KLATTER
KLATTER
FSSS
FSSS...
REGENERATION WITHOUT WEAVING SIGNS... I SEE, SO THAT'S THE TRUE NATURE OF YOUR JUTSU THAT IS RULE FOUR...
IT'S JUST LIKE HASHIRAMA'S ABILITY...
I'D HOPED TO CATCH YOU OFF GUARD WITH THIS, BUT...
VWW...
YOU CAN'T KILL ME WITH MY OWN JUTSU.
FOOSH
SHUP
PARTICLE STYLE! ATOMIC DISMANTLING JUTSU!!

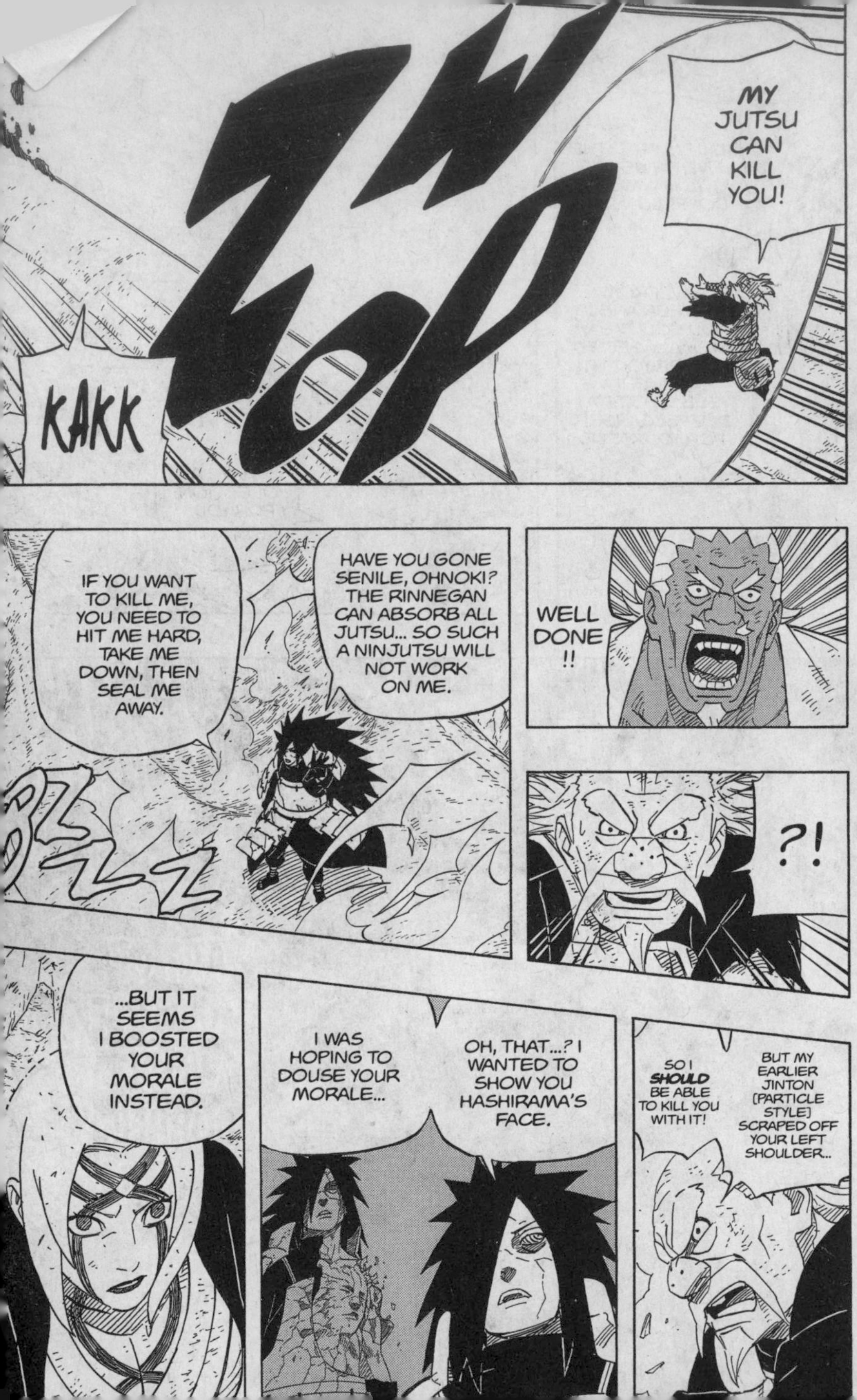
MY JUTSU CAN KILL YOU!
KAKK
WELL DONE !!
?!
HAVE YOU GONE SENILE, OHNOKI? THE RINNEGAN CAN ABSORB ALL JUTSU... SO SUCH A NINJUTSU WILL NOT WORK ON ME.
IF YOU WANT TO KILL ME, YOU NEED TO HIT ME HARD, TAKE ME DOWN, THEN SEAL ME AWAY.
BUT MY EARLIER JINTON [PARTICLE STYLE] SCRAPED OFF YOUR LEFT SHOULDER...
SO I **SHOULD** BE ABLE TO KILL YOU WITH IT!
OH, THAT...? I WANTED TO SHOW YOU HASHIRAMA'S FACE.
I WAS HOPING TO DOUSE YOUR MORALE...
...BUT IT SEEMS I BOOSTED YOUR MORALE INSTEAD.

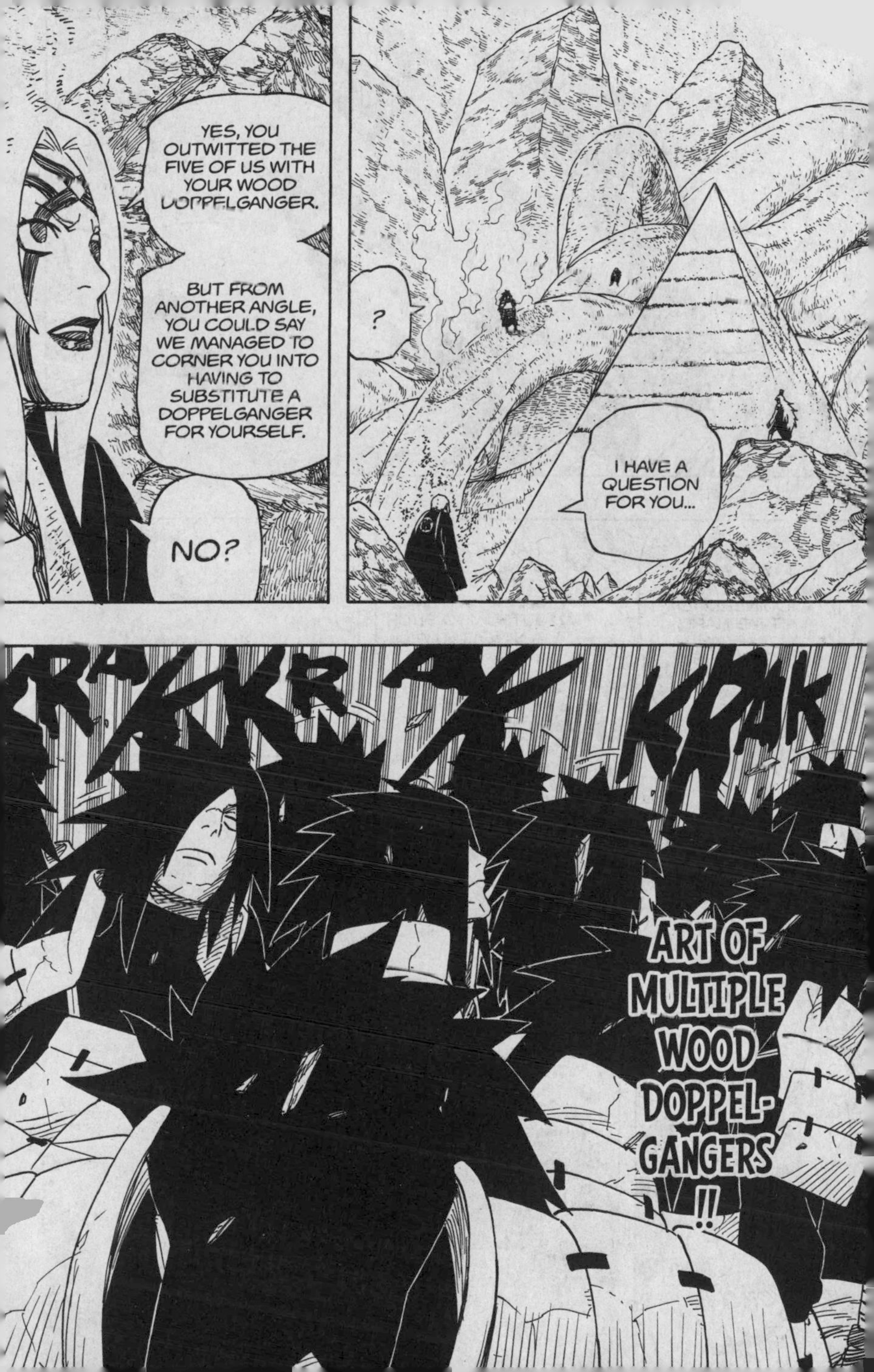
?
I HAVE A QUESTION FOR YOU...
YES, YOU OUTWITTED THE FIVE OF US WITH YOUR WOOD DOPPELGANGER.
BUT FROM ANOTHER ANGLE, YOU COULD SAY WE MANAGED TO CORNER YOU INTO HAVING TO SUBSTITUTE A DOPPELGANGER FOR YOURSELF.
NO?
KRAK
ART OF MULTIPLE WOOD DOPPEL-GANGERS!!

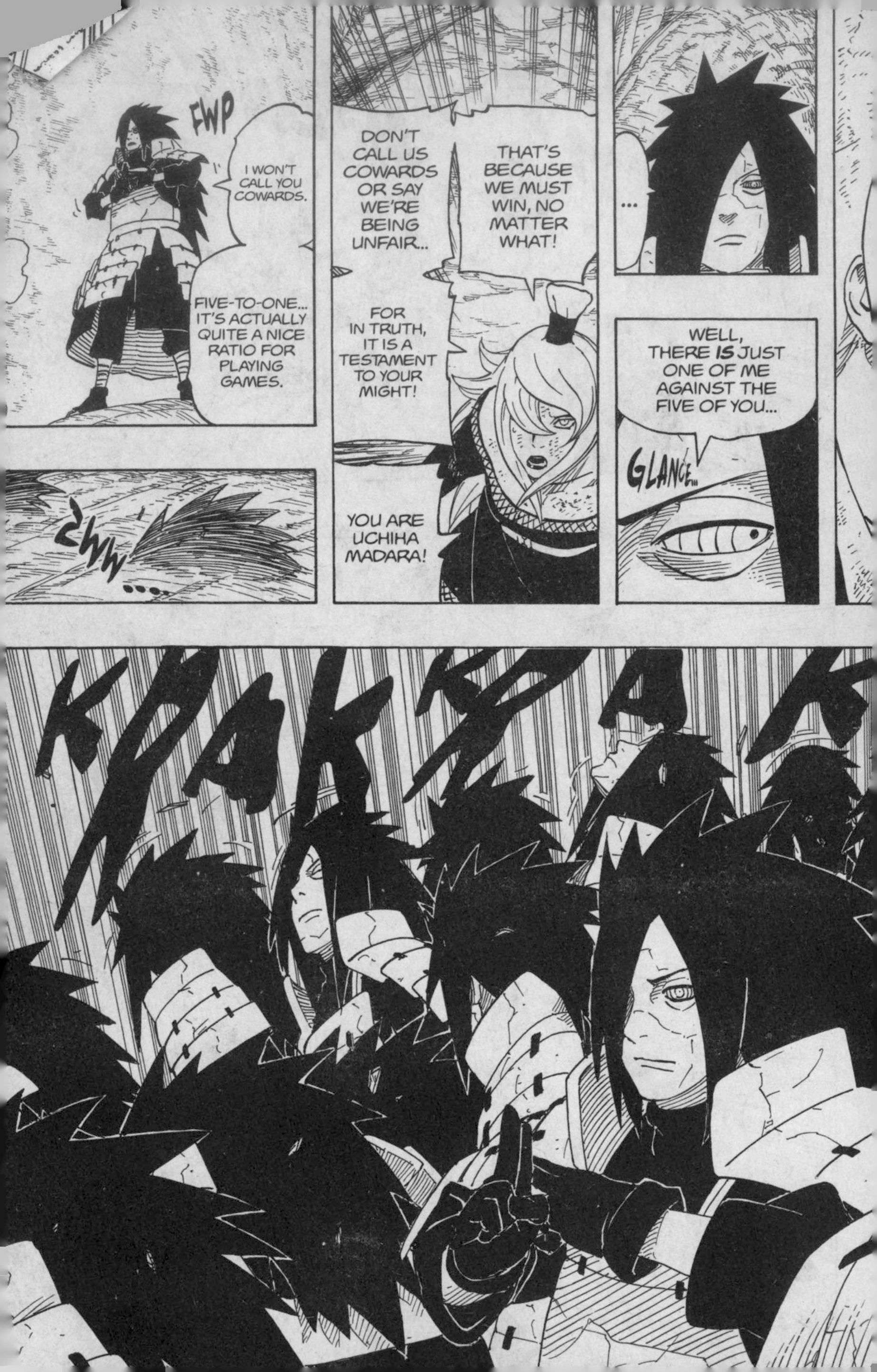
...
WELL, THERE IS JUST ONE OF ME AGAINST THE FIVE OF YOU...
GLANCE...
DON'T CALL US COWARDS OR SAY WE'RE BEING UNFAIR...
THAT'S BECAUSE WE MUST WIN, NO MATTER WHAT!
FOR IN TRUTH, IT IS A TESTAMENT TO YOUR MIGHT!
YOU ARE UCHIHA MADARA!
I WON'T CALL YOU COWARDS.
FWP
FIVE-TO-ONE... IT'S ACTUALLY QUITE A NICE RATIO FOR PLAYING GAMES.
KPAK KPAK

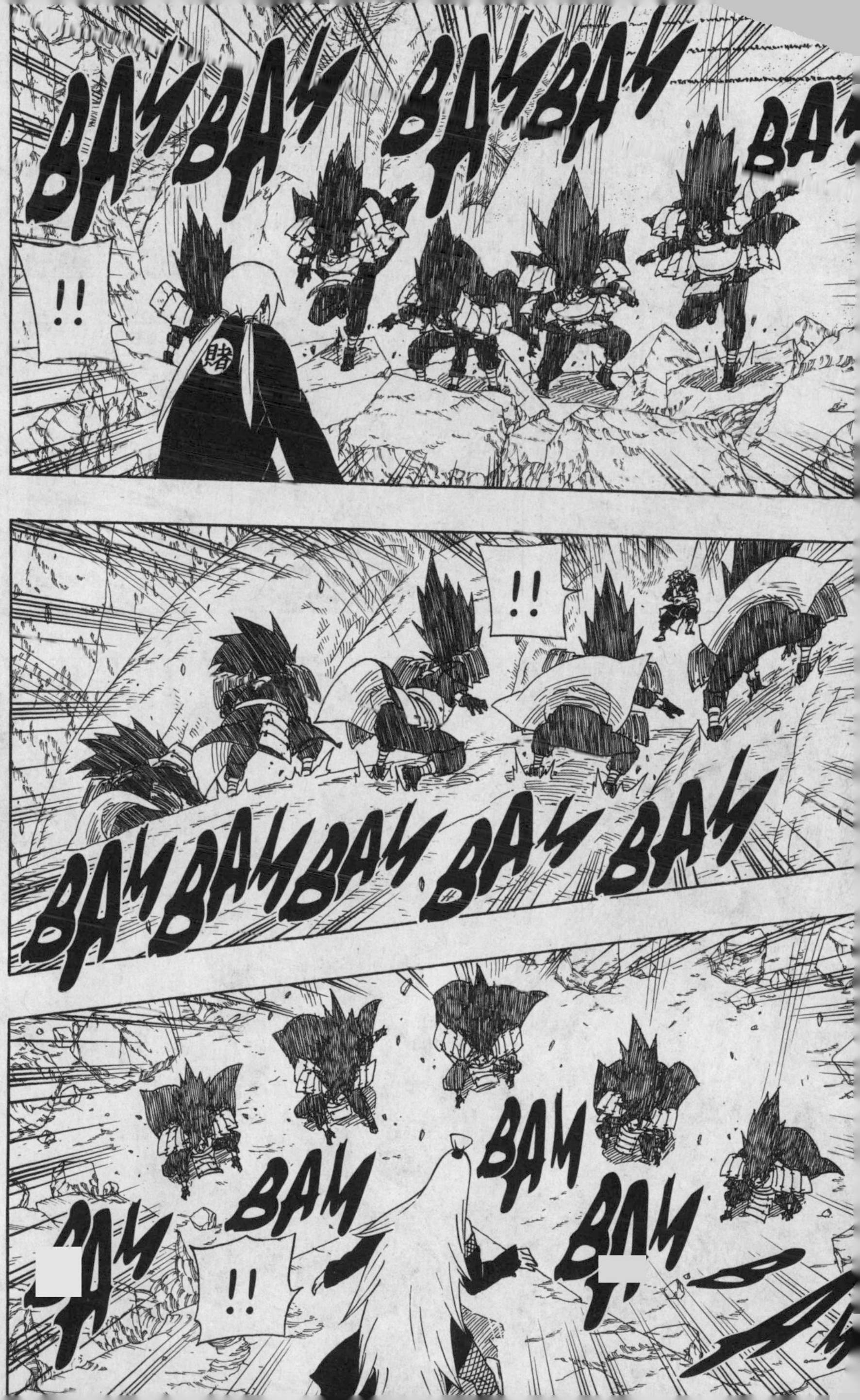

BAM BAM BAM BAM BAM
!!
!!
BAM BAM BAM BAM BAM
BAM
BAM
BAM
BAM
BAM
!!

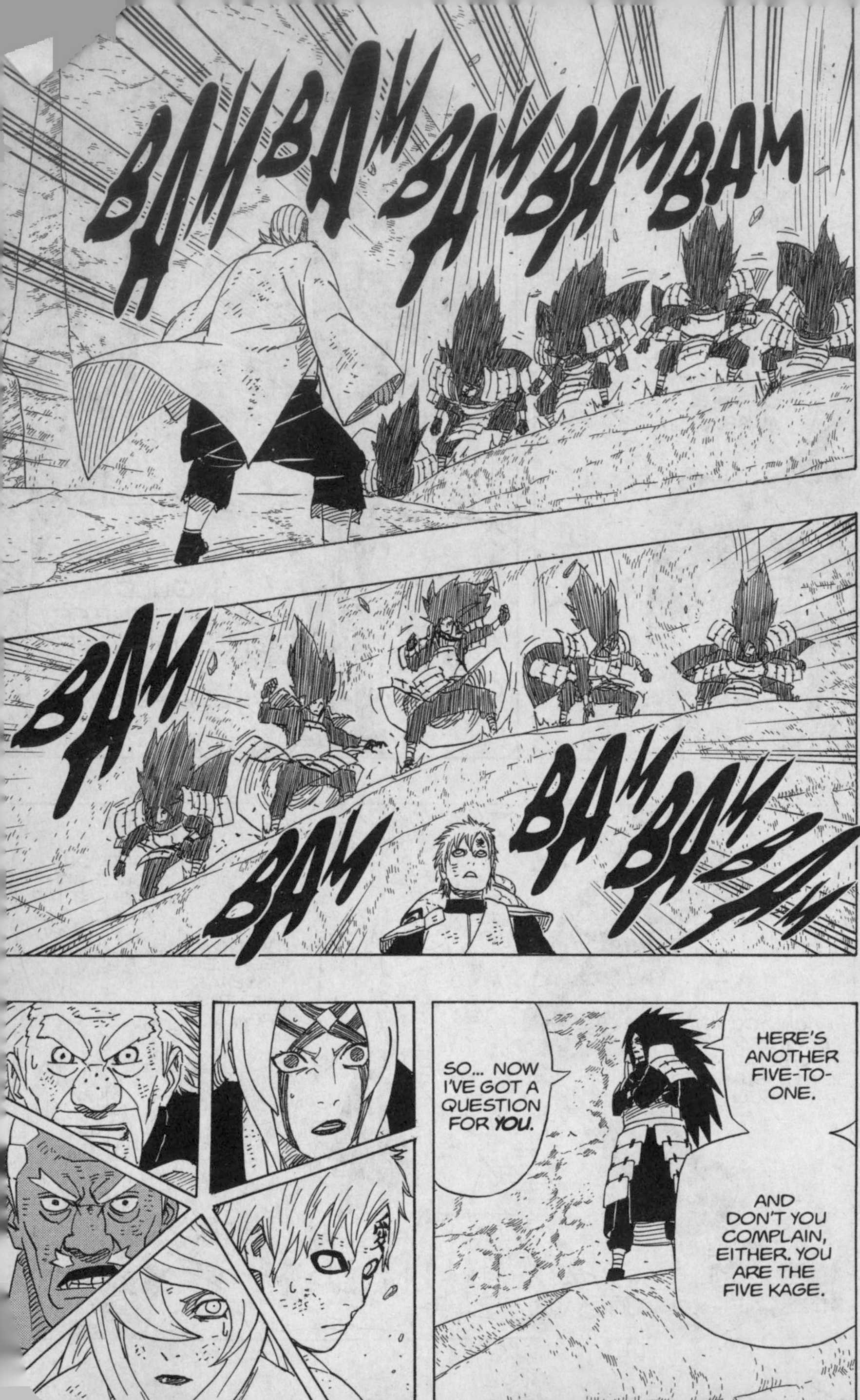
BAM BAM BAM BAM BAM
BAM BAM BAM
BAM
BAM
HERE'S ANOTHER FIVE-TO-ONE.
SO... NOW I'VE GOT A QUESTION FOR **YOU**.
AND DON'T YOU COMPLAIN, EITHER. YOU ARE THE FIVE KAGE.

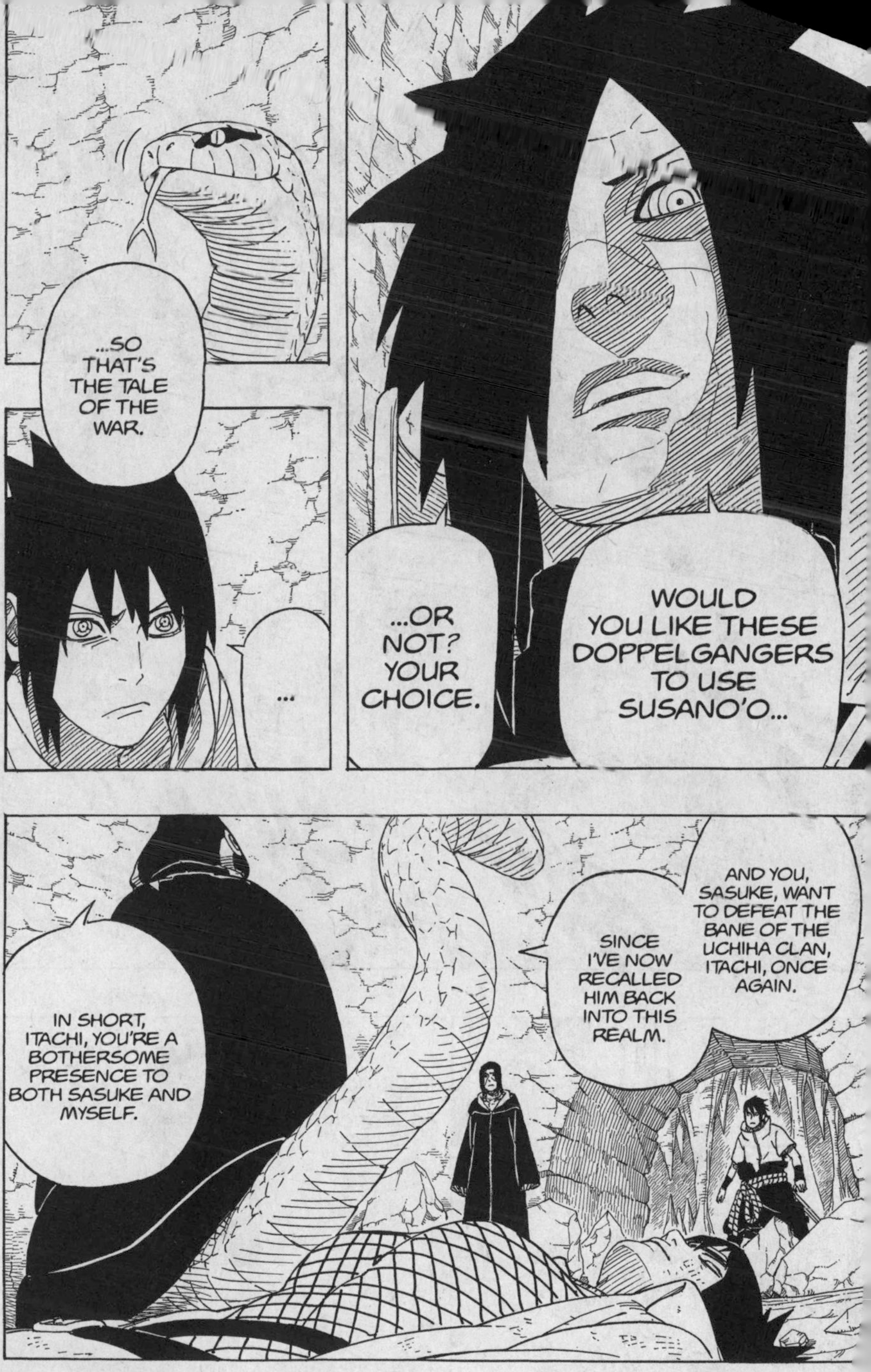
WOULD YOU LIKE THESE DOPPELGANGERS TO USE SUSANO'O...
...OR NOT? YOUR CHOICE.
...SO THAT'S THE TALE OF THE WAR.
...
AND YOU, SASUKE, WANT TO DEFEAT THE BANE OF THE UCHIHA CLAN, ITACHI, ONCE AGAIN.
SINCE I'VE NOW RECALLED HIM BACK INTO THIS REALM.
IN SHORT, ITACHI, YOU'RE A BOTHERSOME PRESENCE TO BOTH SASUKE AND MYSELF.

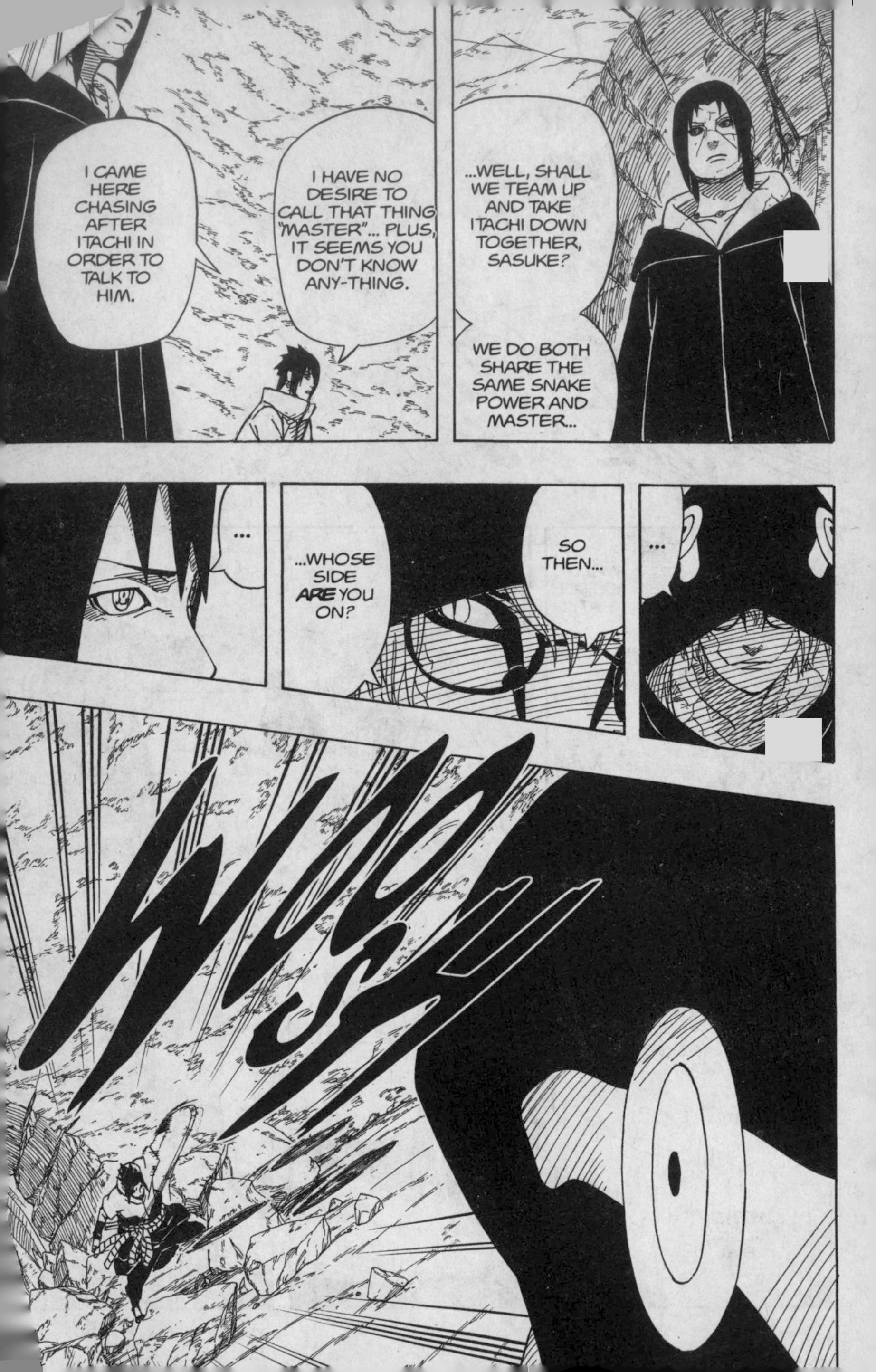
...WELL, SHALL WE TEAM UP AND TAKE ITACHI DOWN TOGETHER, SASUKE?
WE DO BOTH SHARE THE SAME SNAKE POWER AND MASTER...
I HAVE NO DESIRE TO CALL THAT THING "MASTER"... PLUS, IT SEEMS YOU DON'T KNOW ANY-THING.
I CAME HERE CHASING AFTER ITACHI IN ORDER TO TALK TO HIM.
...
SO THEN...
...WHOSE SIDE **ARE** YOU ON?
...

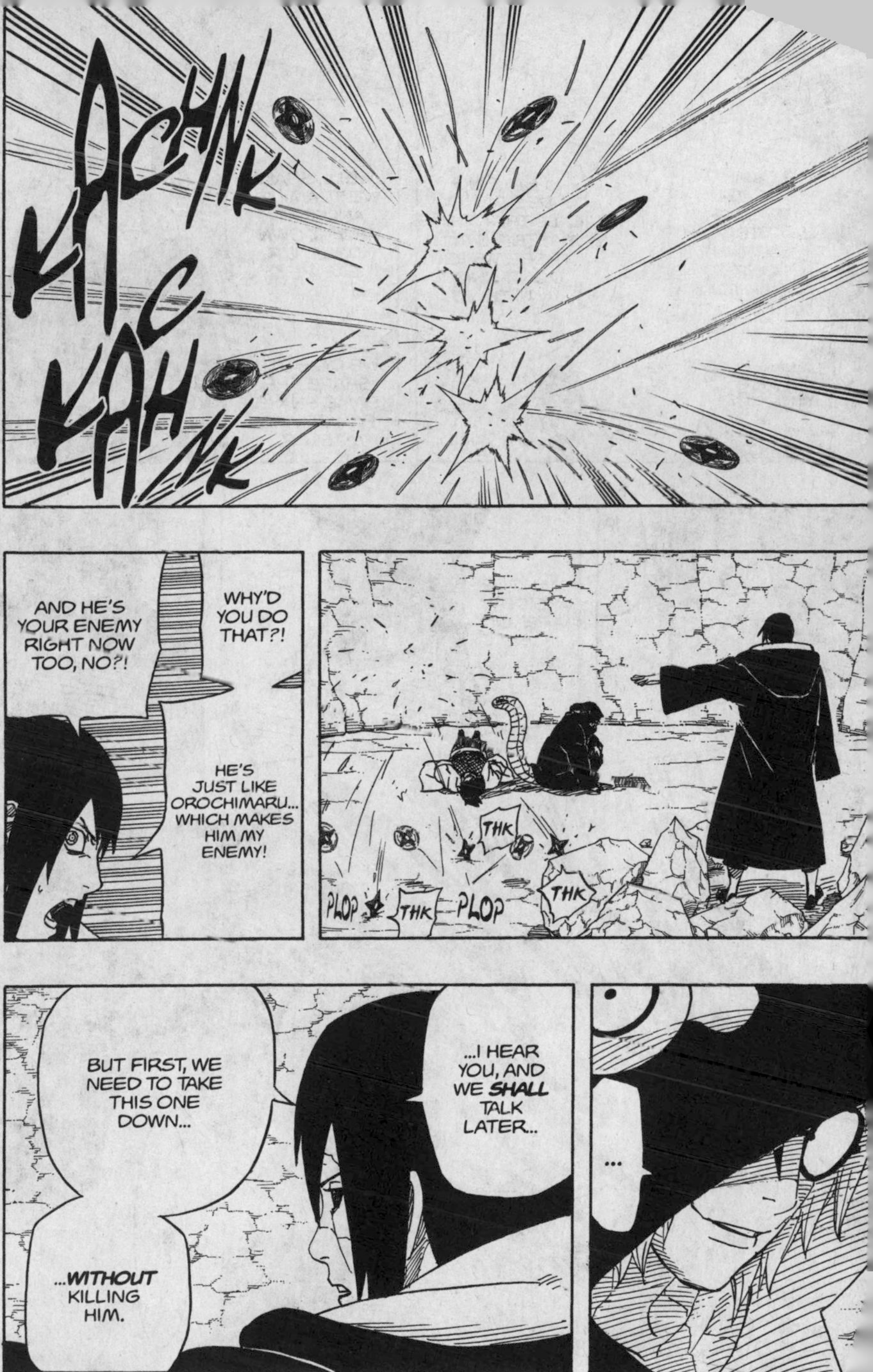

KACHINK
KCKAHNK
THK
THK
PLOP
THK
PLOP
WHY'D YOU DO THAT?!
HE'S JUST LIKE OROCHIMARU... WHICH MAKES HIM MY ENEMY!
AND HE'S YOUR ENEMY RIGHT NOW TOO, NO?!
...
...I HEAR YOU, AND WE SHALL TALK LATER..
BUT FIRST, WE NEED TO TAKE THIS ONE DOWN...
...WITHOUT KILLING HIM.

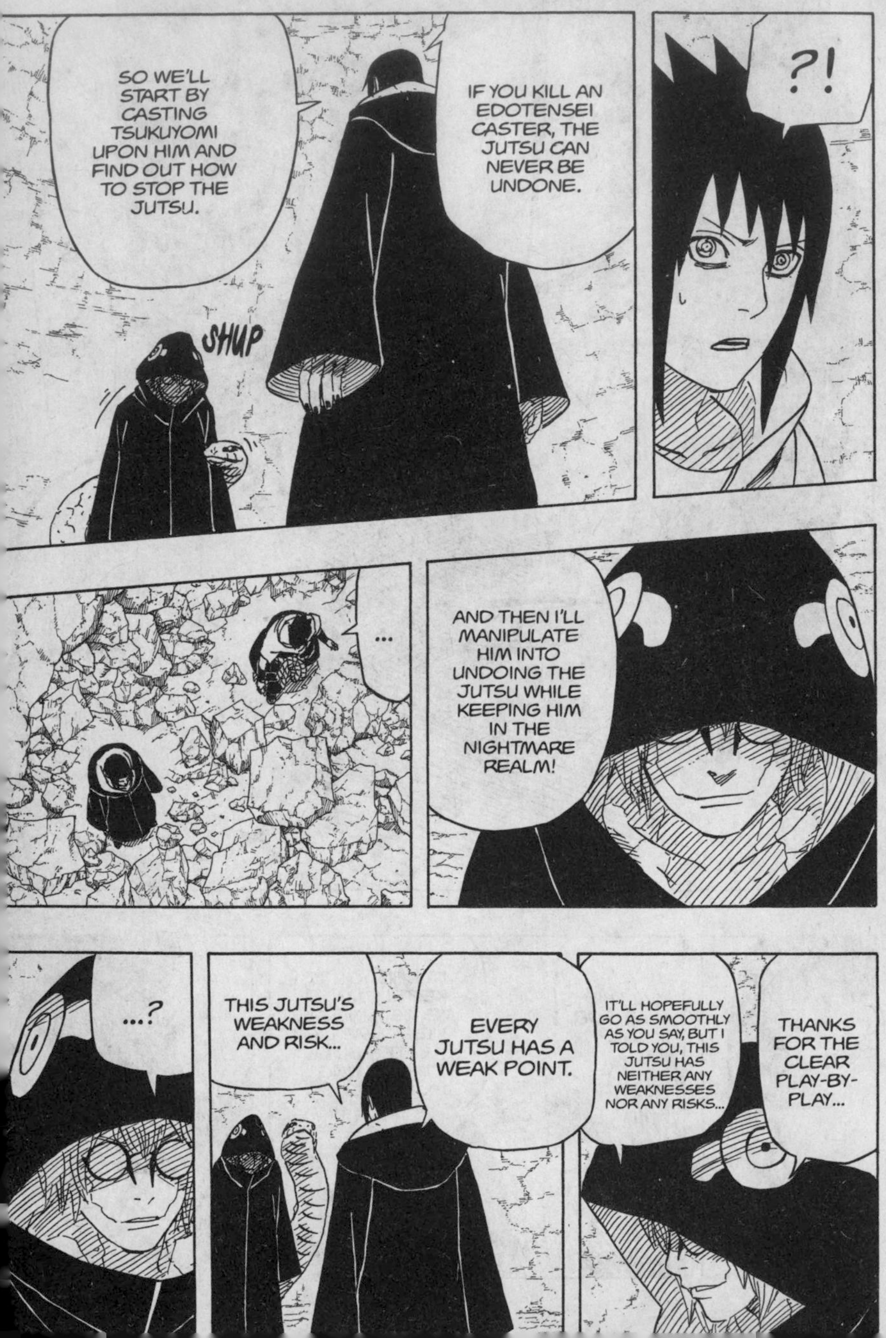
?!
IF YOU KILL AN EDOTENSEI CASTER, THE JUTSU CAN NEVER BE UNDONE.
SO WE'LL START BY CASTING TSUKUYOMI UPON HIM AND FIND OUT HOW TO STOP THE JUTSU.
SHUP
AND THEN I'LL MANIPULATE HIM INTO UNDOING THE JUTSU WHILE KEEPING HIM IN THE NIGHTMARE REALM!
...
THANKS FOR THE CLEAR PLAY-BY-PLAY...
IT'LL HOPEFULLY GO AS SMOOTHLY AS YOU SAY, BUT I TOLD YOU, THIS JUTSU HAS NEITHER ANY WEAKNESSES NOR ANY RISKS...
EVERY JUTSU HAS A WEAK POINT.
THIS JUTSU'S WEAKNESS AND RISK...
...?

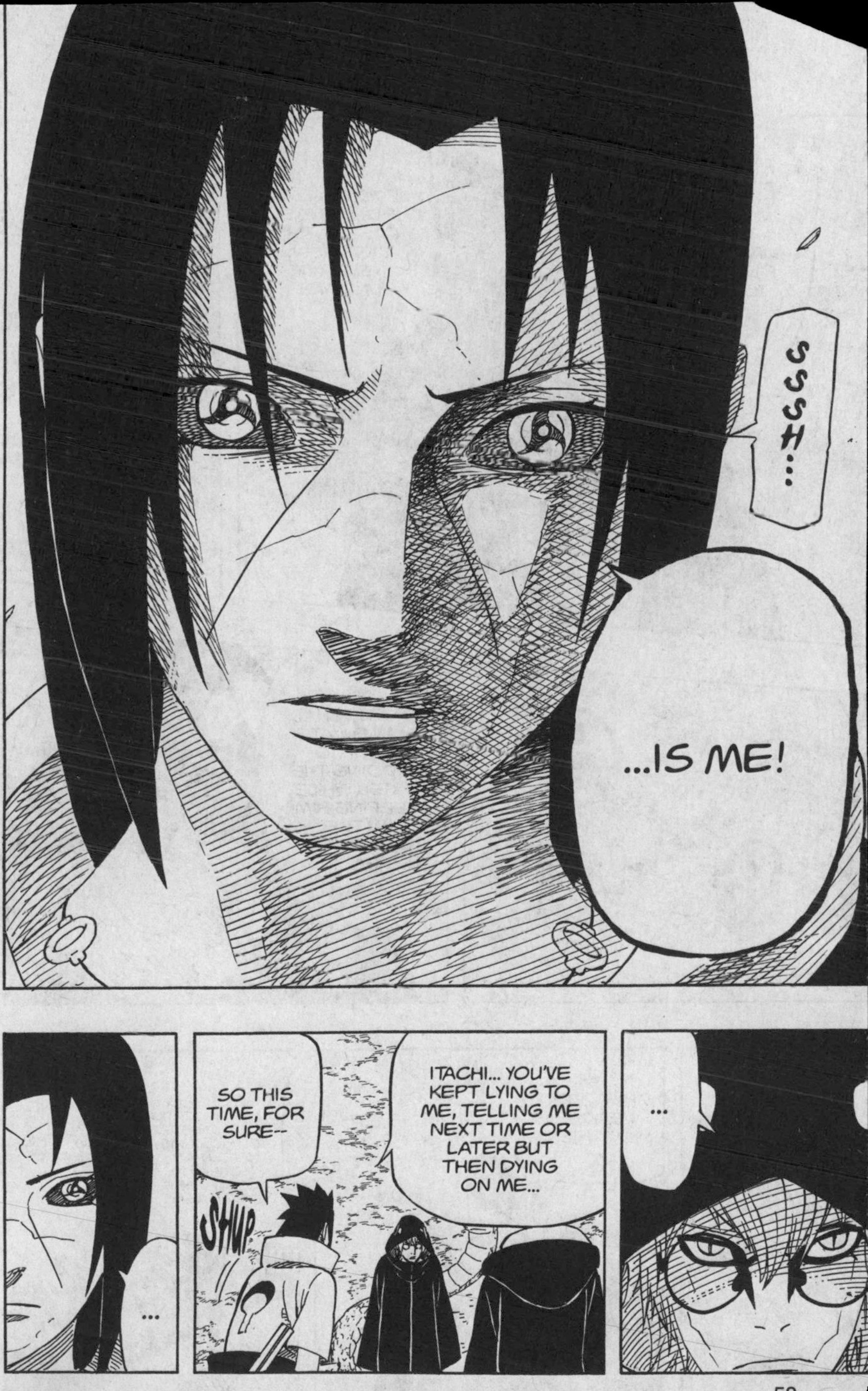
SSSH...
...IS ME!
...
ITACHI... YOU'VE KEPT LYING TO ME, TELLING ME NEXT TIME OR LATER BUT THEN DYING ON ME...
SO THIS TIME, FOR SURE--
SHUP
...

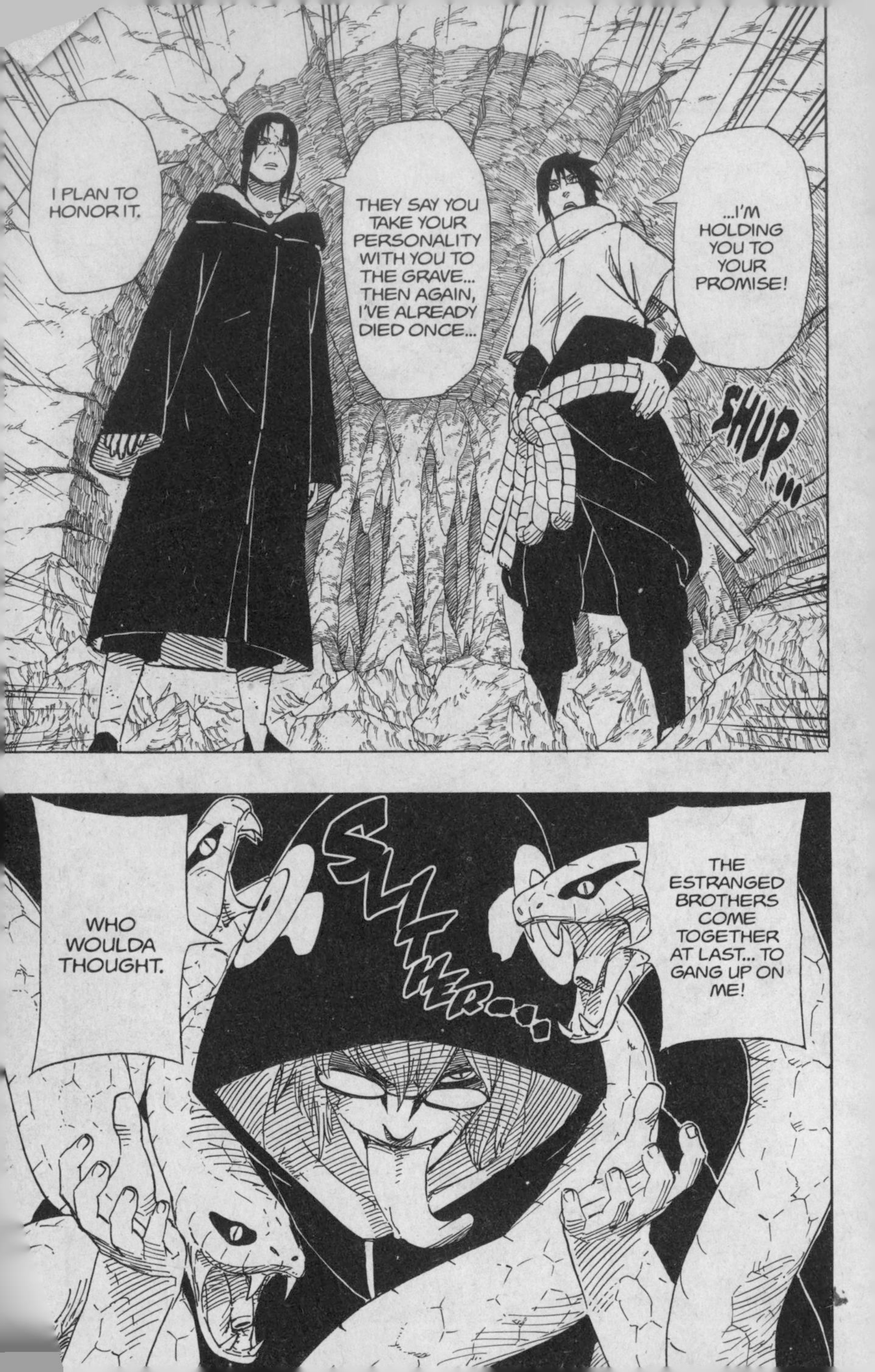
...I'M HOLDING YOU TO YOUR PROMISE!
SHUP...
THEY SAY YOU TAKE YOUR PERSONALITY WITH YOU TO THE GRAVE... THEN AGAIN, I'VE ALREADY DIED ONCE...
I PLAN TO HONOR IT.
THE ESTRANGED BROTHERS COME TOGETHER AT LAST... TO GANG UP ON ME!
SLITHER...
WHO WOULDA THOUGHT.

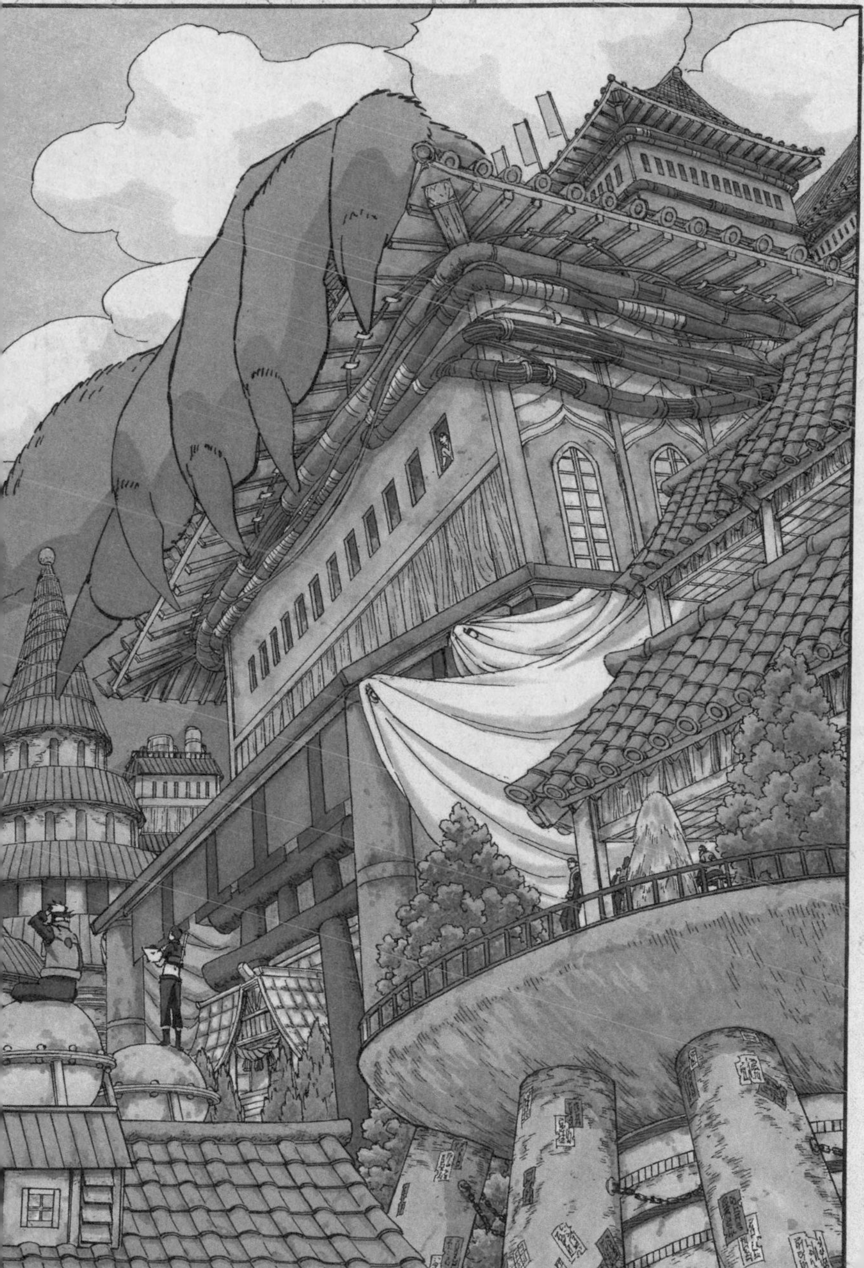

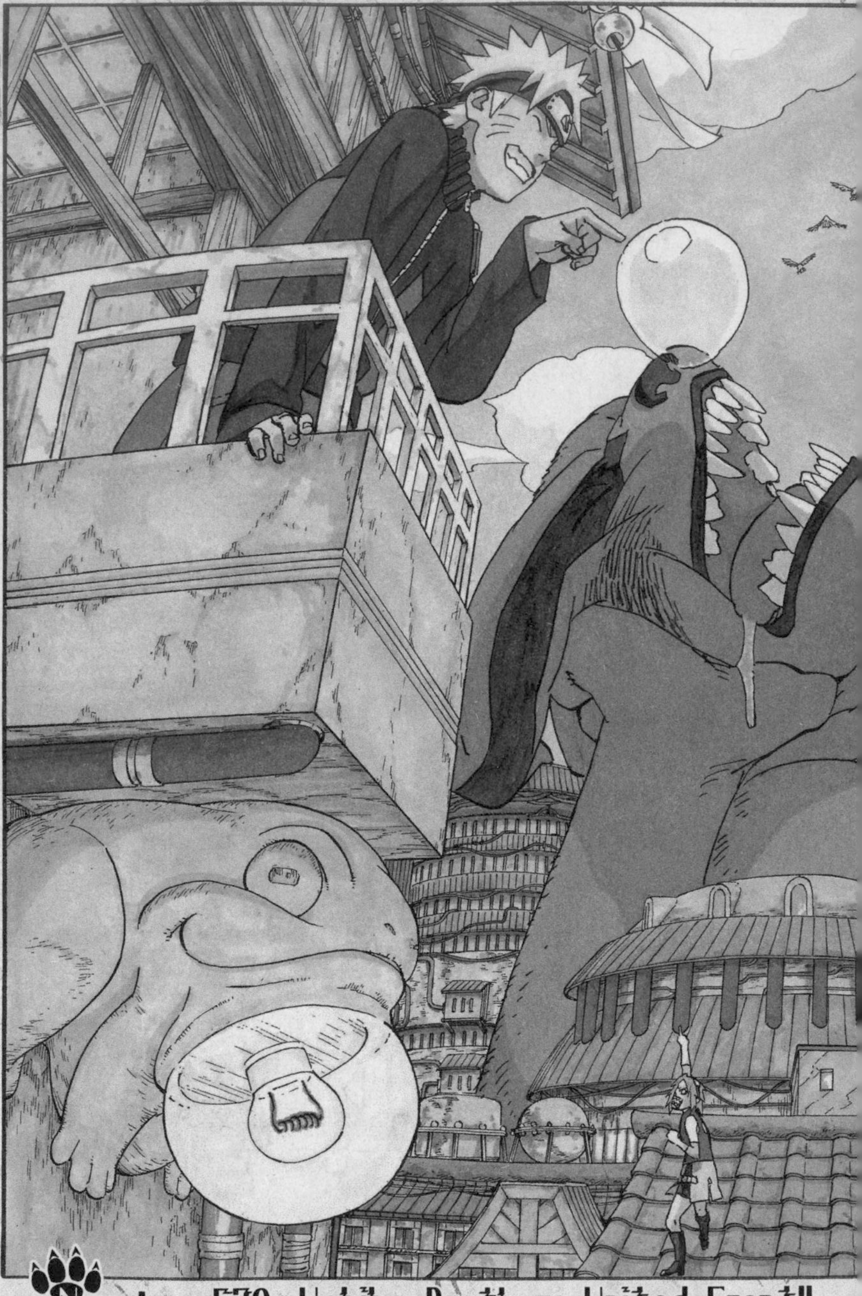

Number 579: Uchiha Brothers United Front!!

NARUTO

—ナルト—

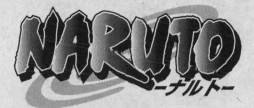

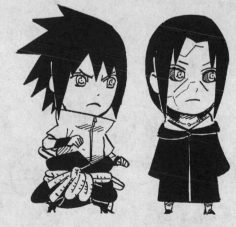

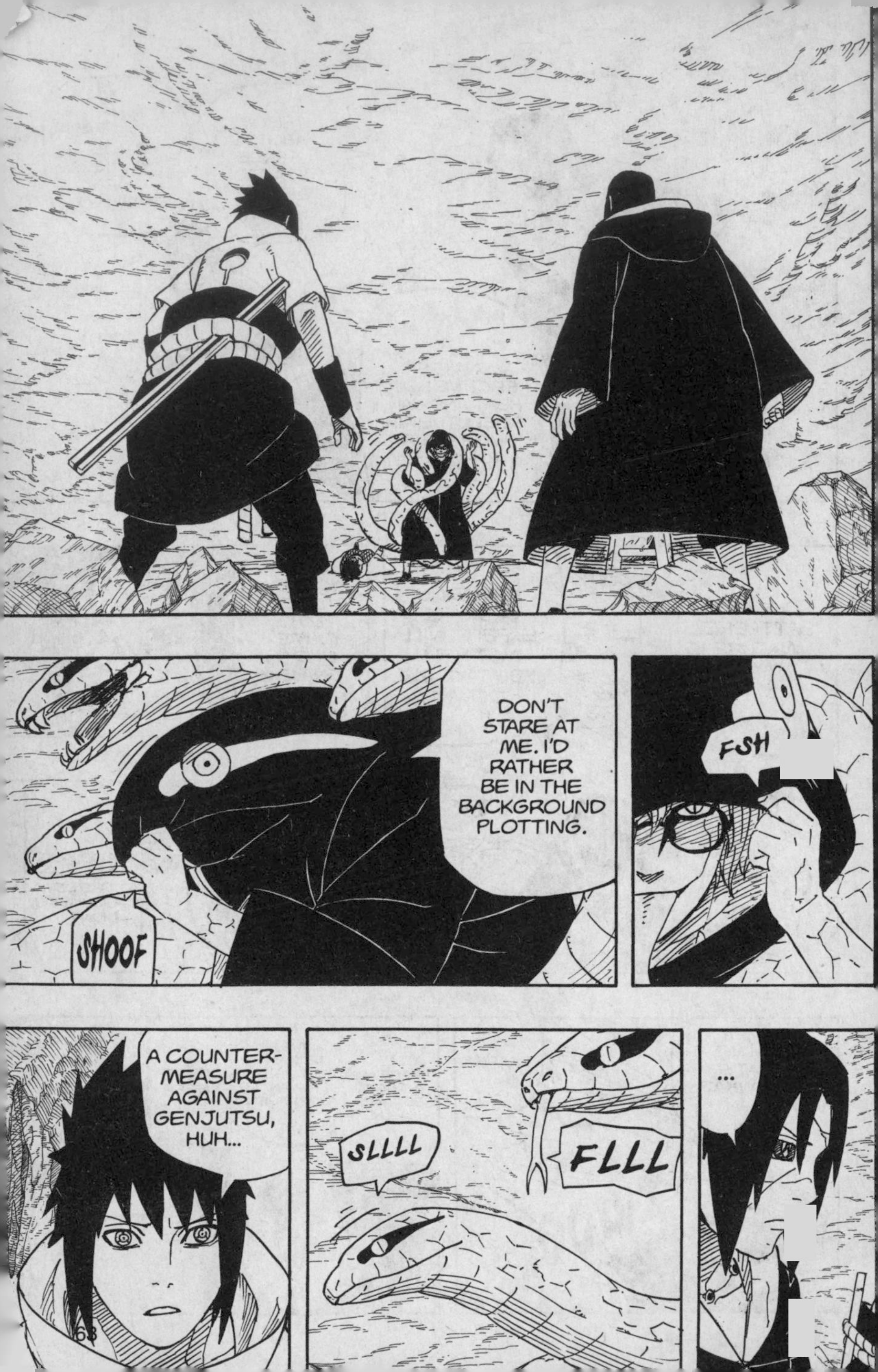
FSH
DON'T STARE AT ME. I'D RATHER BE IN THE BACKGROUND PLOTTING.
SHOOF
...
FLLL
SLLLL
A COUNTER-MEASURE AGAINST GENJUTSU, HUH...

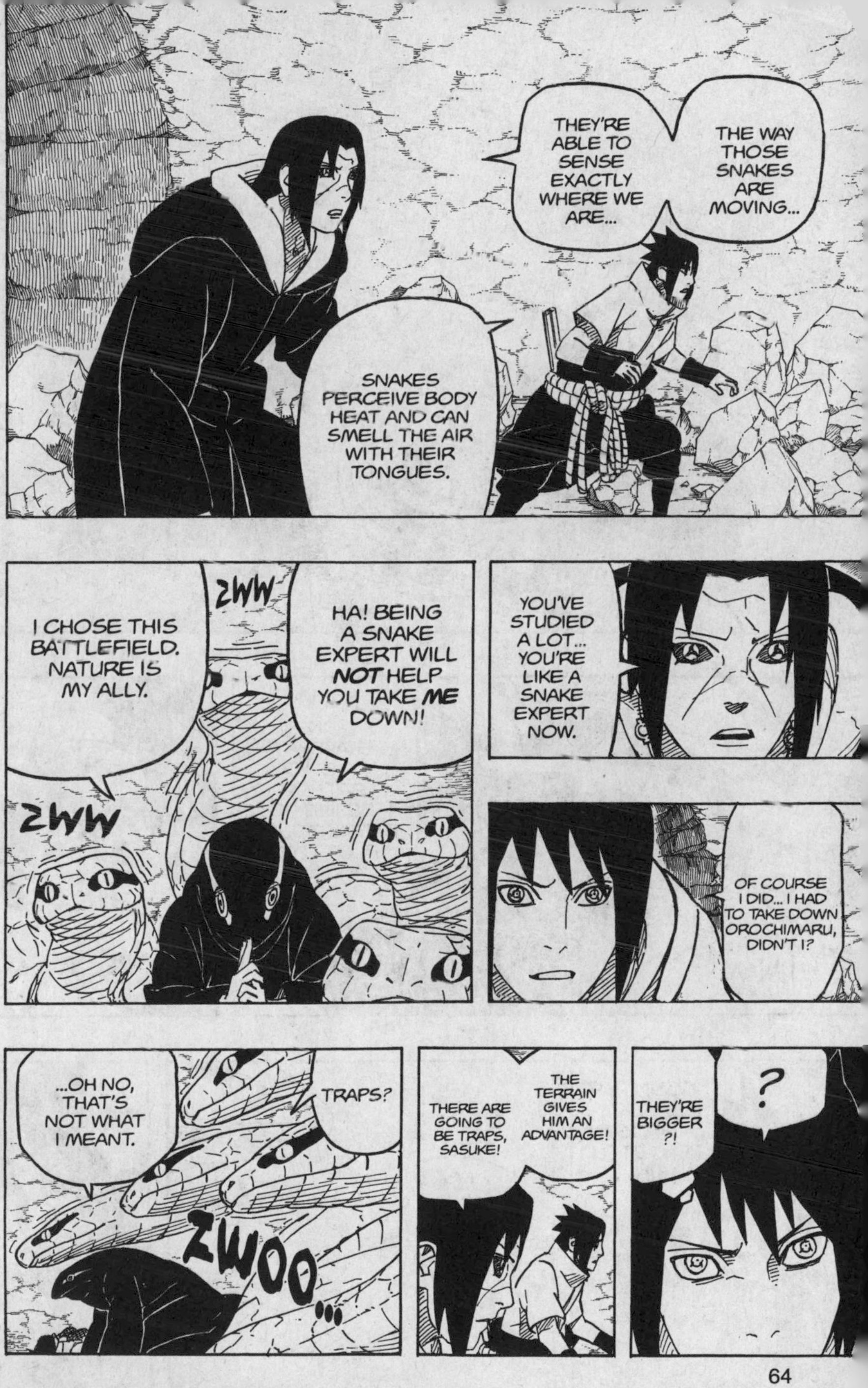
THE WAY THOSE SNAKES ARE MOVING...
THEY'RE ABLE TO SENSE EXACTLY WHERE WE ARE...
SNAKES PERCEIVE BODY HEAT AND CAN SMELL THE AIR WITH THEIR TONGUES.
YOU'VE STUDIED A LOT... YOU'RE LIKE A SNAKE EXPERT NOW.
OF COURSE I DID... I HAD TO TAKE DOWN OROCHIMARU, DIDN'T I?
HA! BEING A SNAKE EXPERT WILL **NOT** HELP YOU TAKE **ME** DOWN!
ZWW
I CHOSE THIS BATTLEFIELD. NATURE IS MY ALLY.
ZWW
?
THEY'RE BIGGER ?!
THE TERRAIN GIVES HIM AN ADVANTAGE!
THERE ARE GOING TO BE TRAPS, SASUKE!
TRAPS?
...OH NO, THAT'S NOT WHAT I MEANT.
ZWOO...

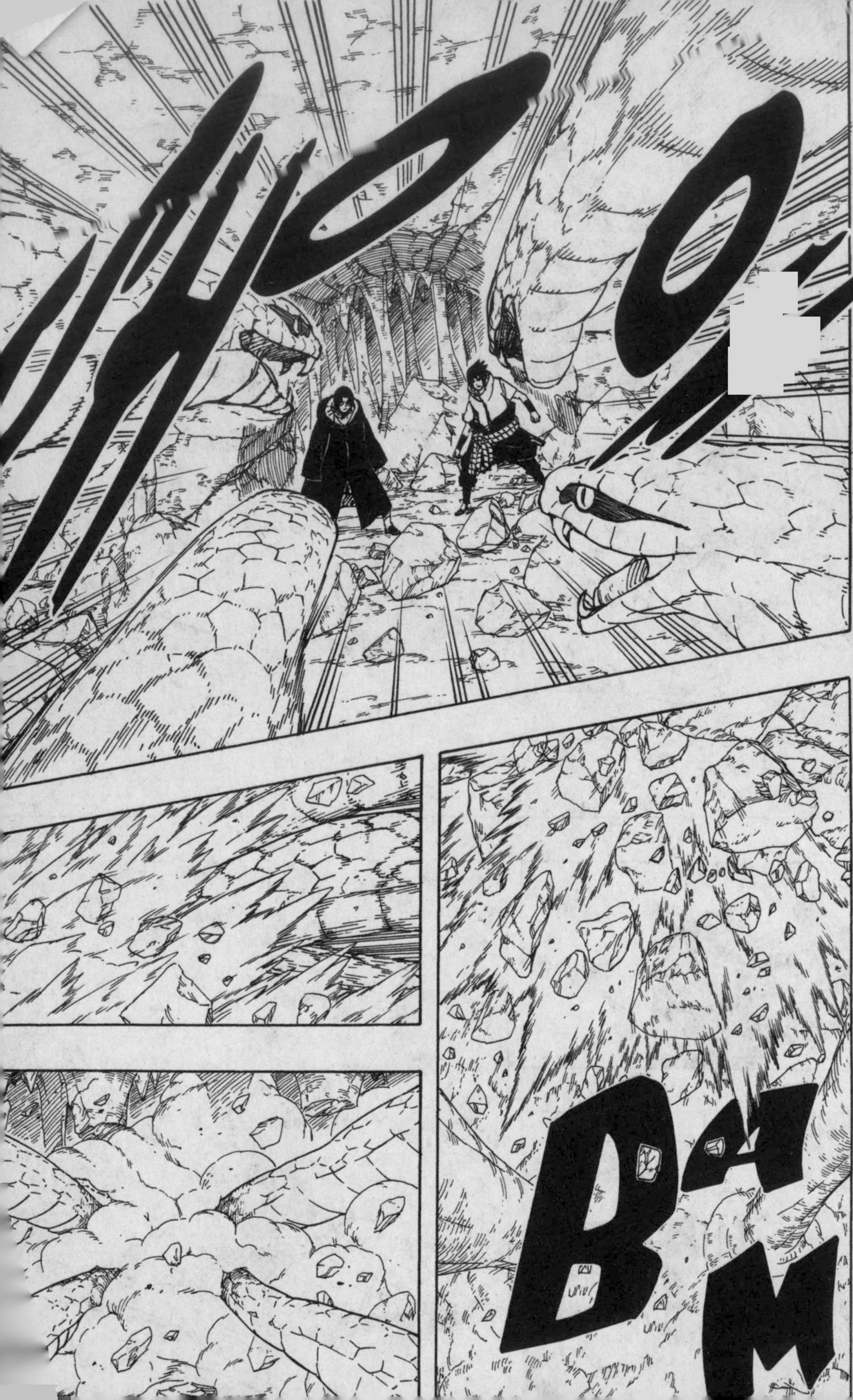
BAM

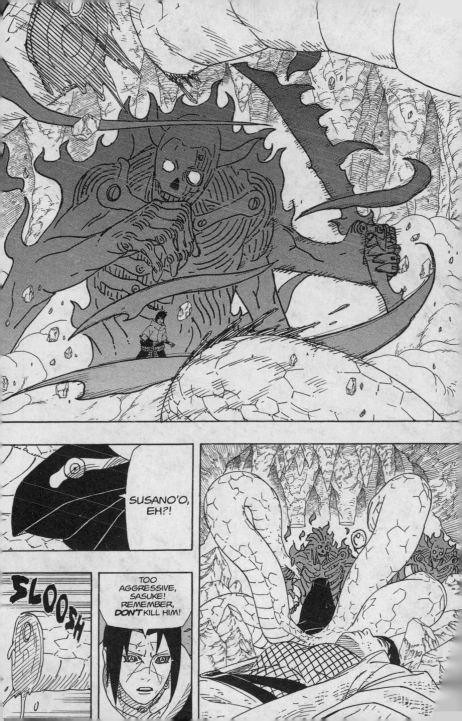

SUSANO'O, EH?!

SLOOSH

TOO AGGRESSIVE, SASUKE! REMEMBER, *DON'T* KILL HIM!

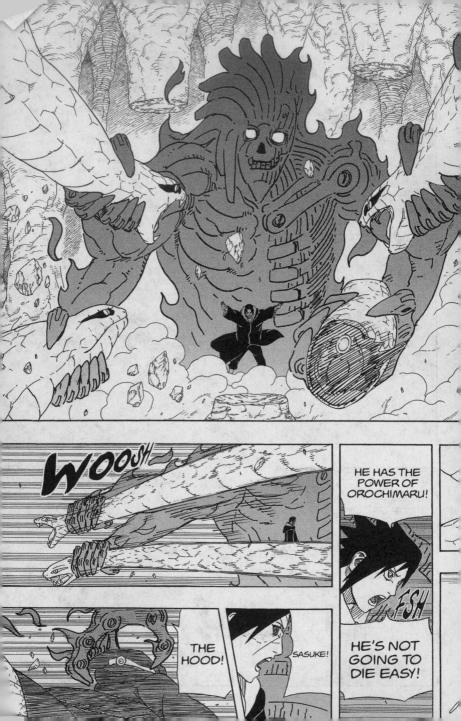

WOOSH

HE HAS THE POWER OF OROCHIMARU!

FSH

THE HOOD!

SASUKE!

HE'S NOT GOING TO DIE EASY!

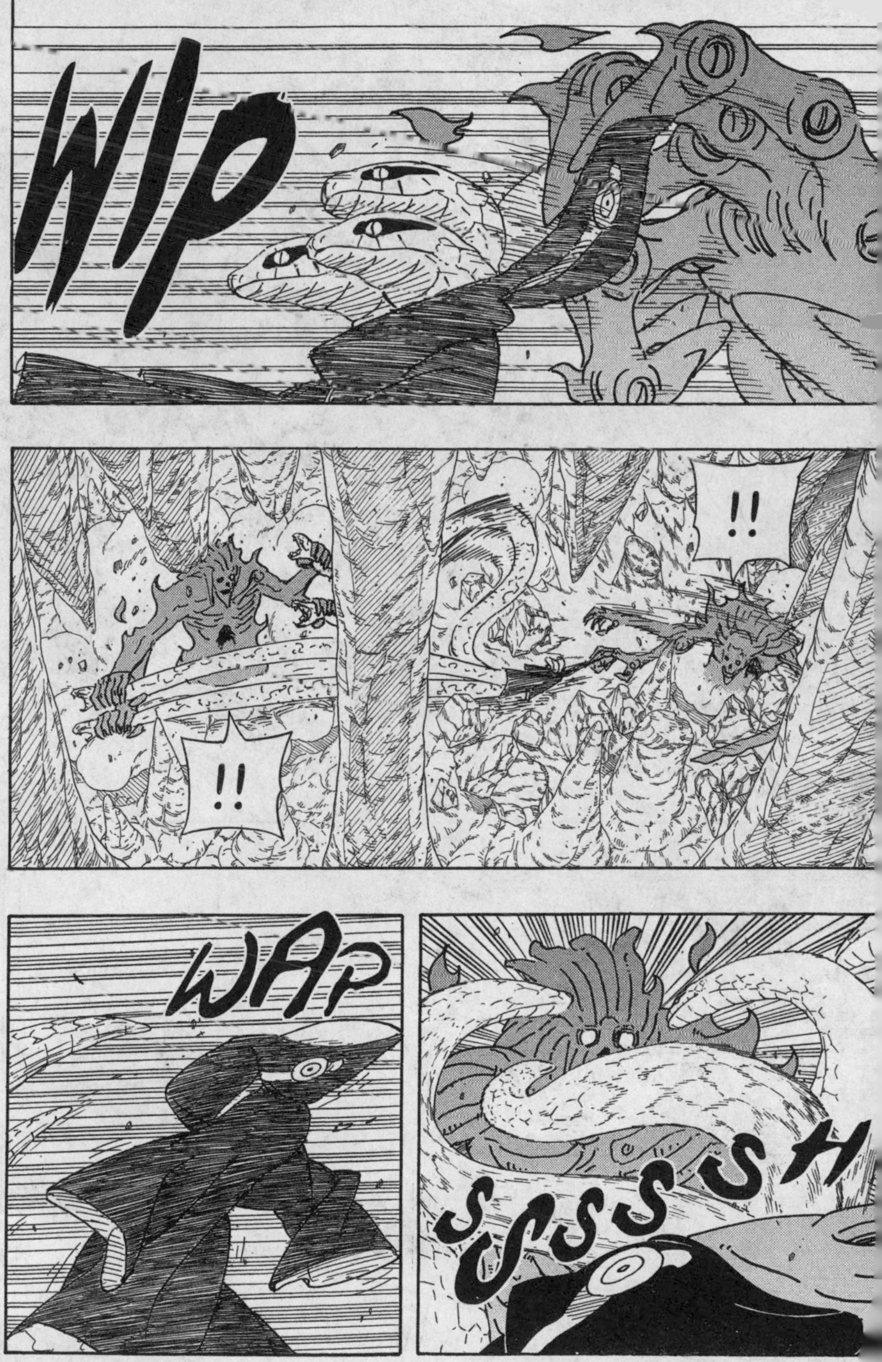
WIP
!!
!!
SSSSH
WAP

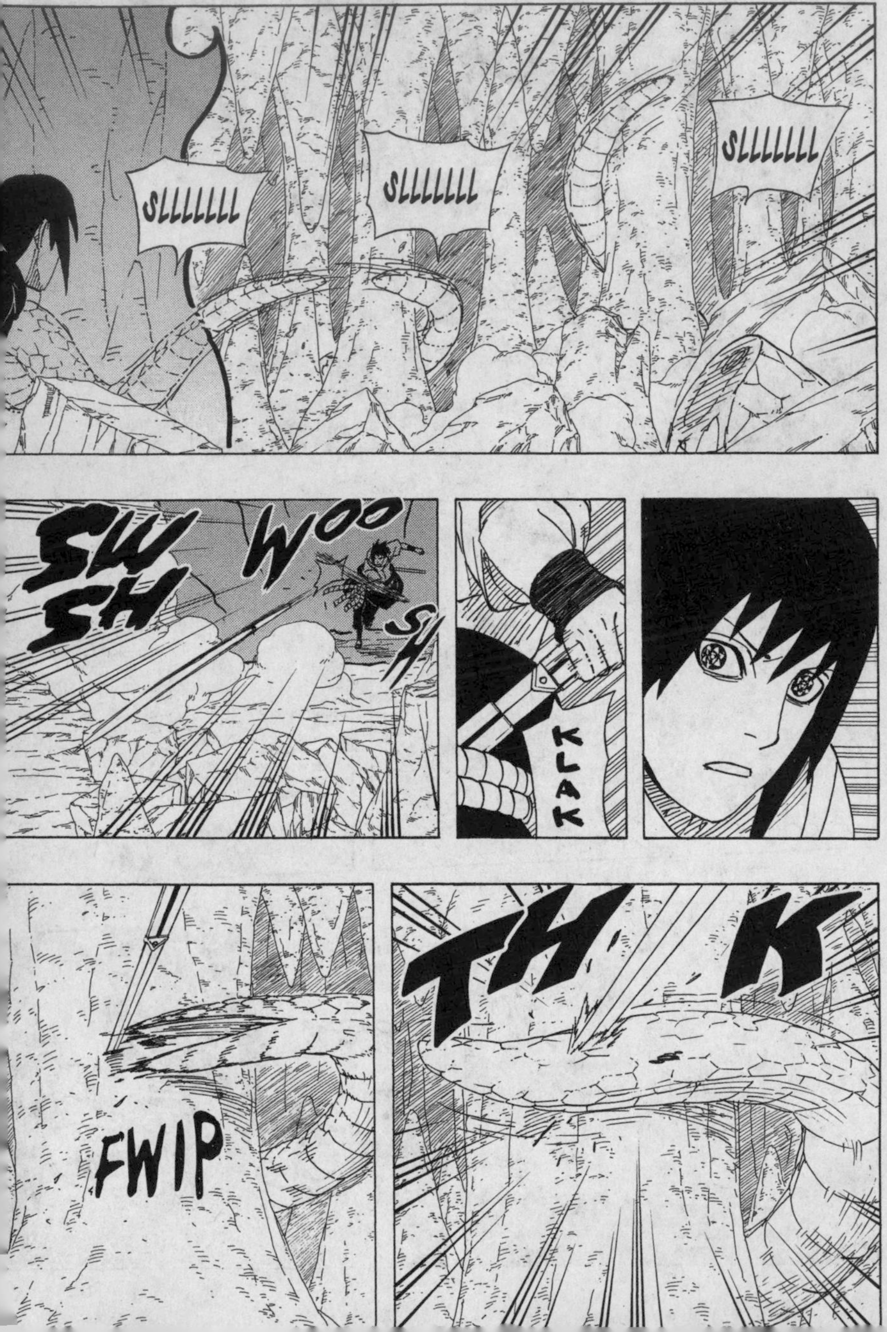
SLLLLLLL
SLLLLLLL
SLLLLLLL
KLAK
WOOSH
SWSH
THK
FWIP

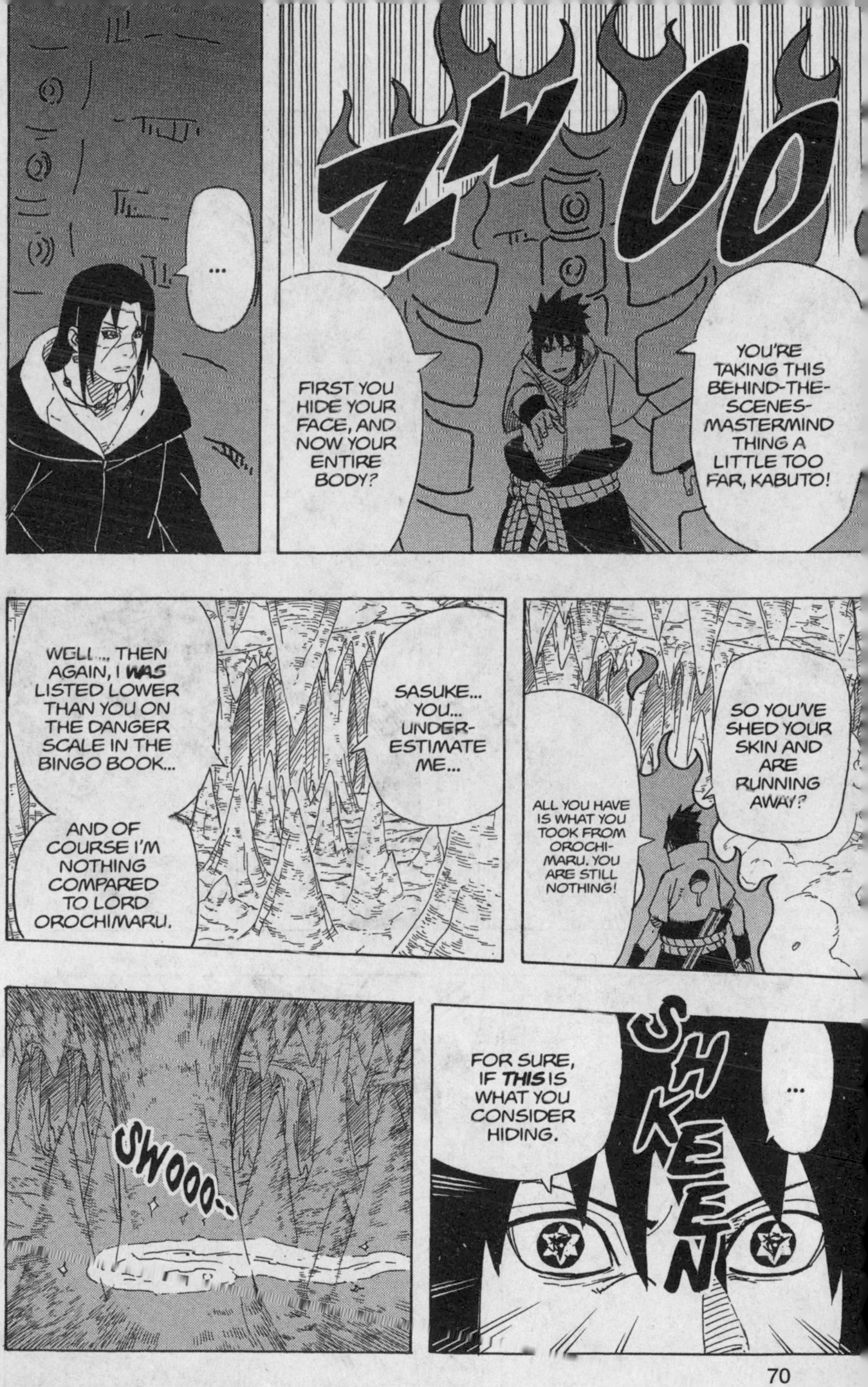
ZWOOO
YOU'RE TAKING THIS BEHIND-THE-SCENES-MASTERMIND THING A LITTLE TOO FAR, KABUTO!
FIRST YOU HIDE YOUR FACE, AND NOW YOUR ENTIRE BODY?
...
SO YOU'VE SHED YOUR SKIN AND ARE RUNNING AWAY?
ALL YOU HAVE IS WHAT YOU TOOK FROM OROCHI-MARU. YOU ARE STILL NOTHING!
SASUKE... YOU... UNDER-ESTIMATE ME...
WELL... THEN AGAIN, I WAS LISTED LOWER THAN YOU ON THE DANGER SCALE IN THE BINGO BOOK...
AND OF COURSE I'M NOTHING COMPARED TO LORD OROCHIMARU.
...
SHKEEN
FOR SURE, IF THIS IS WHAT YOU CONSIDER HIDING.
SWOOO..

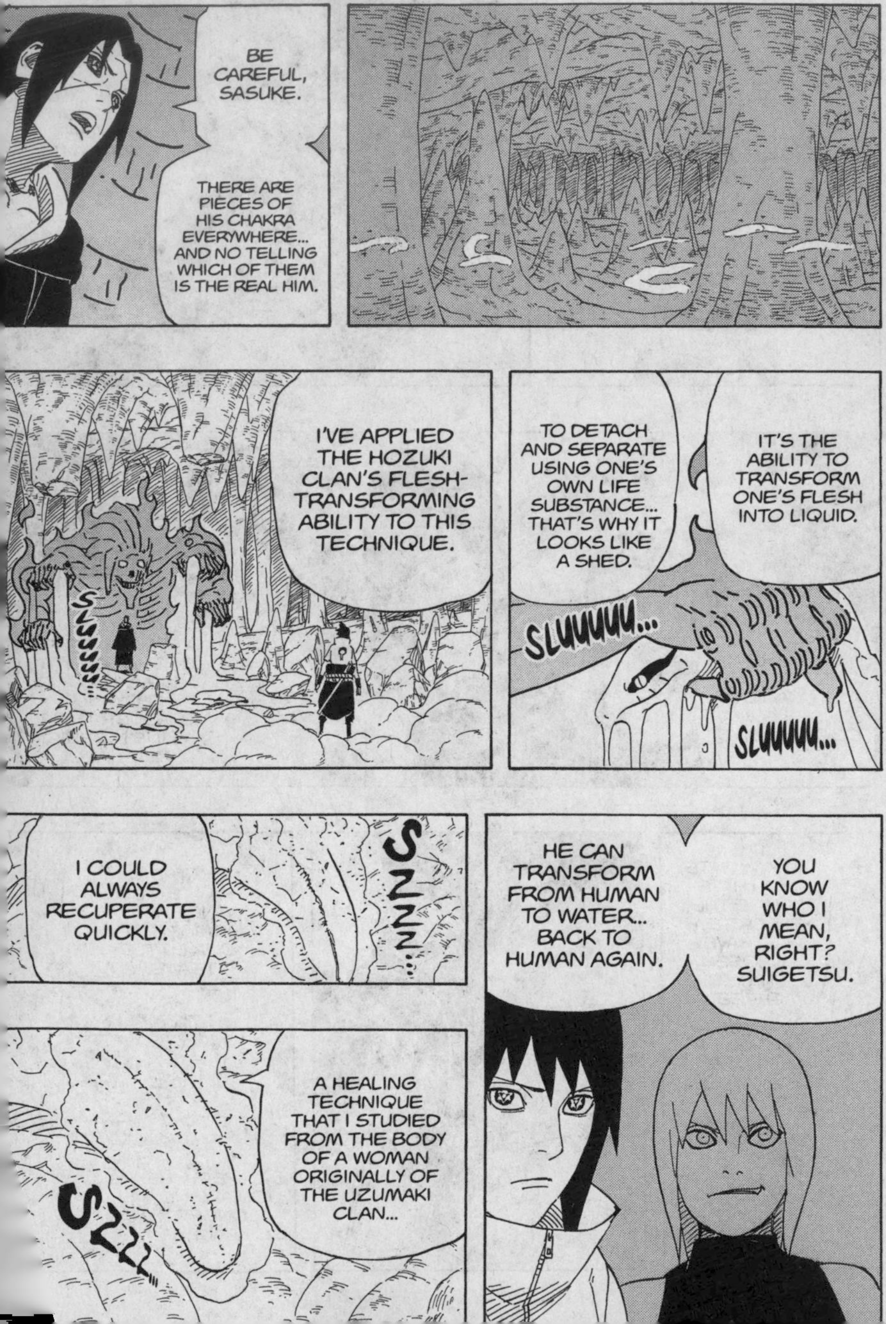
BE CAREFUL, SASUKE.
THERE ARE PIECES OF HIS CHAKRA EVERYWHERE... AND NO TELLING WHICH OF THEM IS THE REAL HIM.
IT'S THE ABILITY TO TRANSFORM ONE'S FLESH INTO LIQUID.
TO DETACH AND SEPARATE USING ONE'S OWN LIFE SUBSTANCE... THAT'S WHY IT LOOKS LIKE A SHED.
SLUUUUU...
SLUUUUU...
I'VE APPLIED THE HOZUKI CLAN'S FLESH-TRANSFORMING ABILITY TO THIS TECHNIQUE.
SLUUUUU...
YOU KNOW WHO I MEAN, RIGHT? SUIGETSU.
HE CAN TRANSFORM FROM HUMAN TO WATER... BACK TO HUMAN AGAIN.
I COULD ALWAYS RECUPERATE QUICKLY.
SZZZ...
A HEALING TECHNIQUE THAT I STUDIED FROM THE BODY OF A WOMAN ORIGINALLY OF THE UZUMAKI CLAN...
SZZZ...

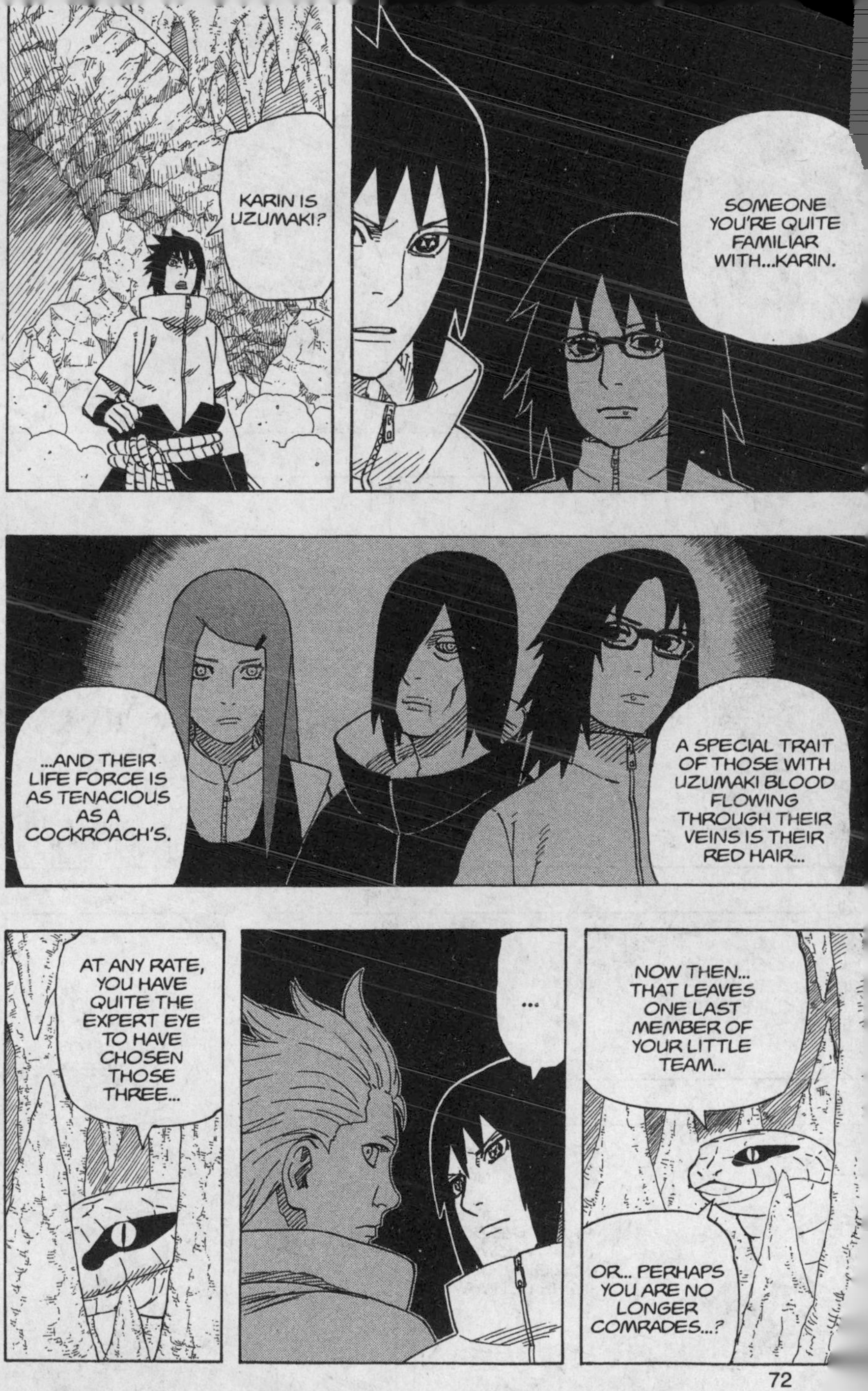
SOMEONE YOU'RE QUITE FAMILIAR WITH...KARIN.
KARIN IS UZUMAKI?
A SPECIAL TRAIT OF THOSE WITH UZUMAKI BLOOD FLOWING THROUGH THEIR VEINS IS THEIR RED HAIR...
...AND THEIR LIFE FORCE IS AS TENACIOUS AS A COCKROACH'S.
NOW THEN... THAT LEAVES ONE LAST MEMBER OF YOUR LITTLE TEAM...
OR... PERHAPS YOU ARE NO LONGER COMRADES...?
...
AT ANY RATE, YOU HAVE QUITE THE EXPERT EYE TO HAVE CHOSEN THOSE THREE...

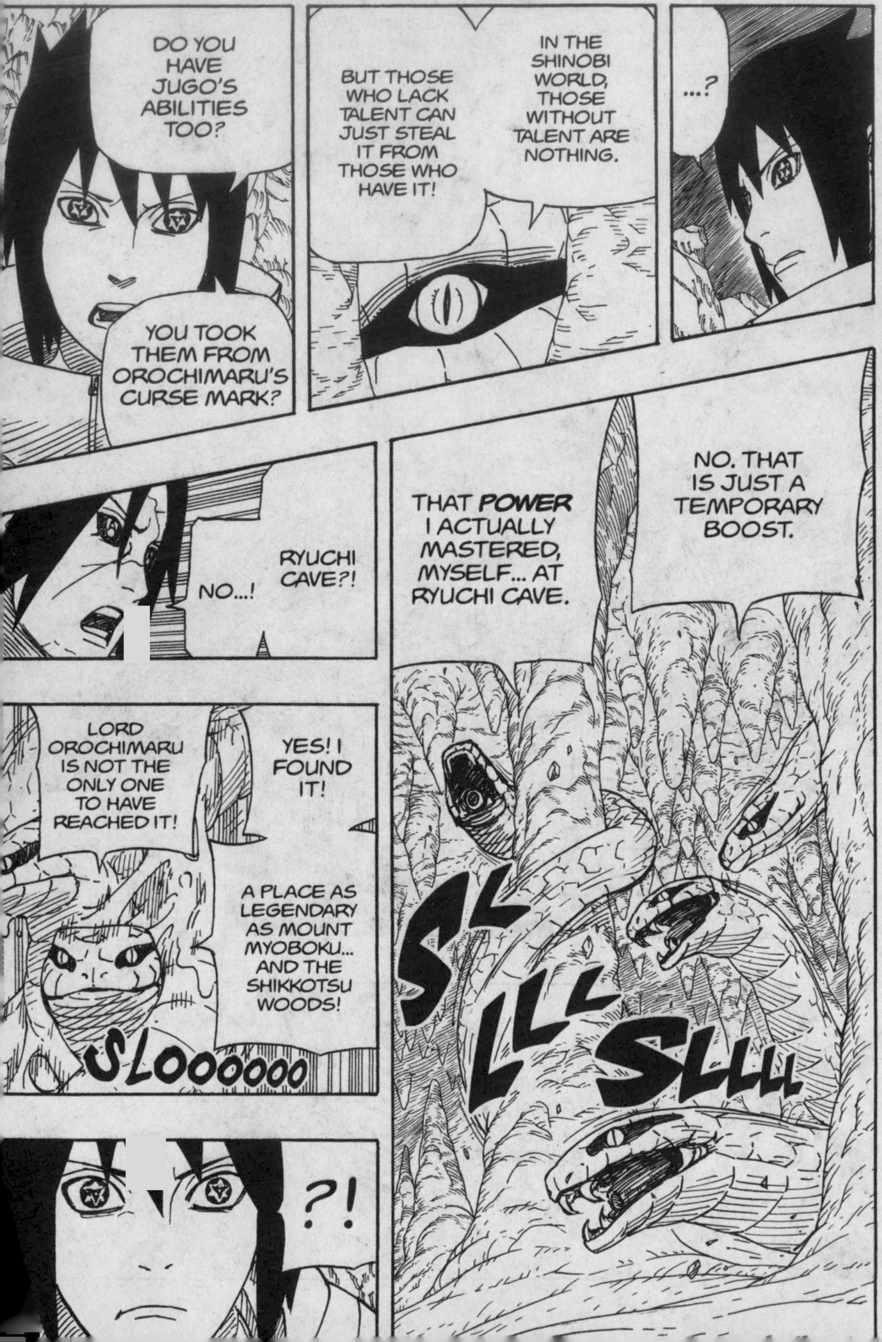
...?
IN THE SHINOBI WORLD, THOSE WITHOUT TALENT ARE NOTHING.
BUT THOSE WHO LACK TALENT CAN JUST STEAL IT FROM THOSE WHO HAVE IT!
DO YOU HAVE JUGO'S ABILITIES TOO?
YOU TOOK THEM FROM OROCHIMARU'S CURSE MARK?
NO. THAT IS JUST A TEMPORARY BOOST.
THAT POWER I ACTUALLY MASTERED, MYSELF... AT RYUCHI CAVE.
SL
LLL
SLLLL
RYUCHI CAVE?!
NO...!
YES! I FOUND IT!
LORD OROCHIMARU IS NOT THE ONLY ONE TO HAVE REACHED IT!
A PLACE AS LEGENDARY AS MOUNT MYOBOKU... AND THE SHIKKOTSU WOODS!
SLOOOOOO
?!

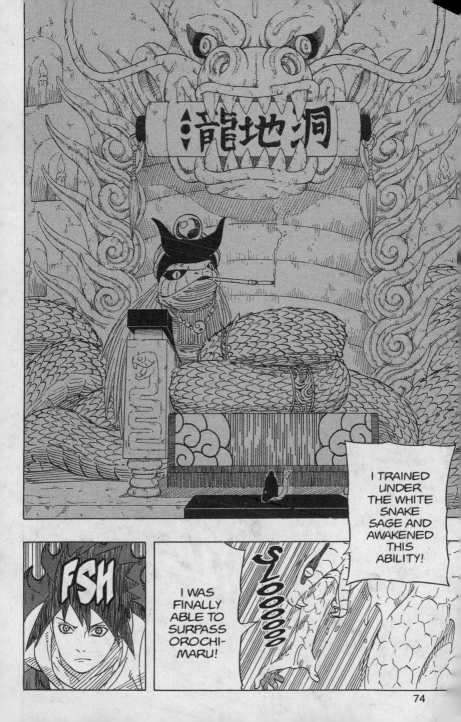

I TRAINED UNDER THE WHITE SNAKE SAGE AND AWAKENED THIS ABILITY!

I WAS FINALLY ABLE TO SURPASS OROCHI-MARU!

FSH

SLoooooo

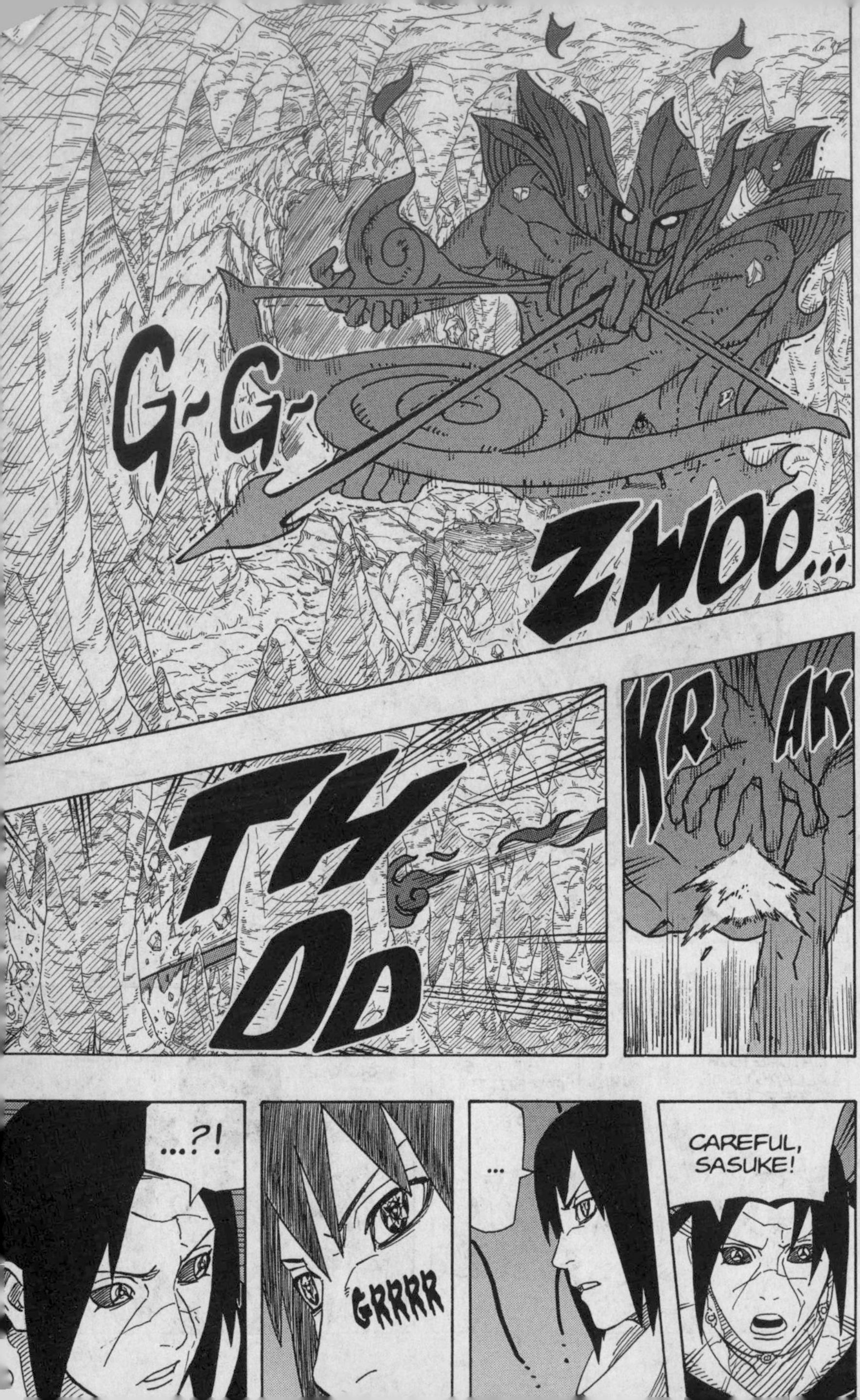
G-G-
ZWOO...
KRAK
THOD
CAREFUL, SASUKE!
...
GRRRR
...?!

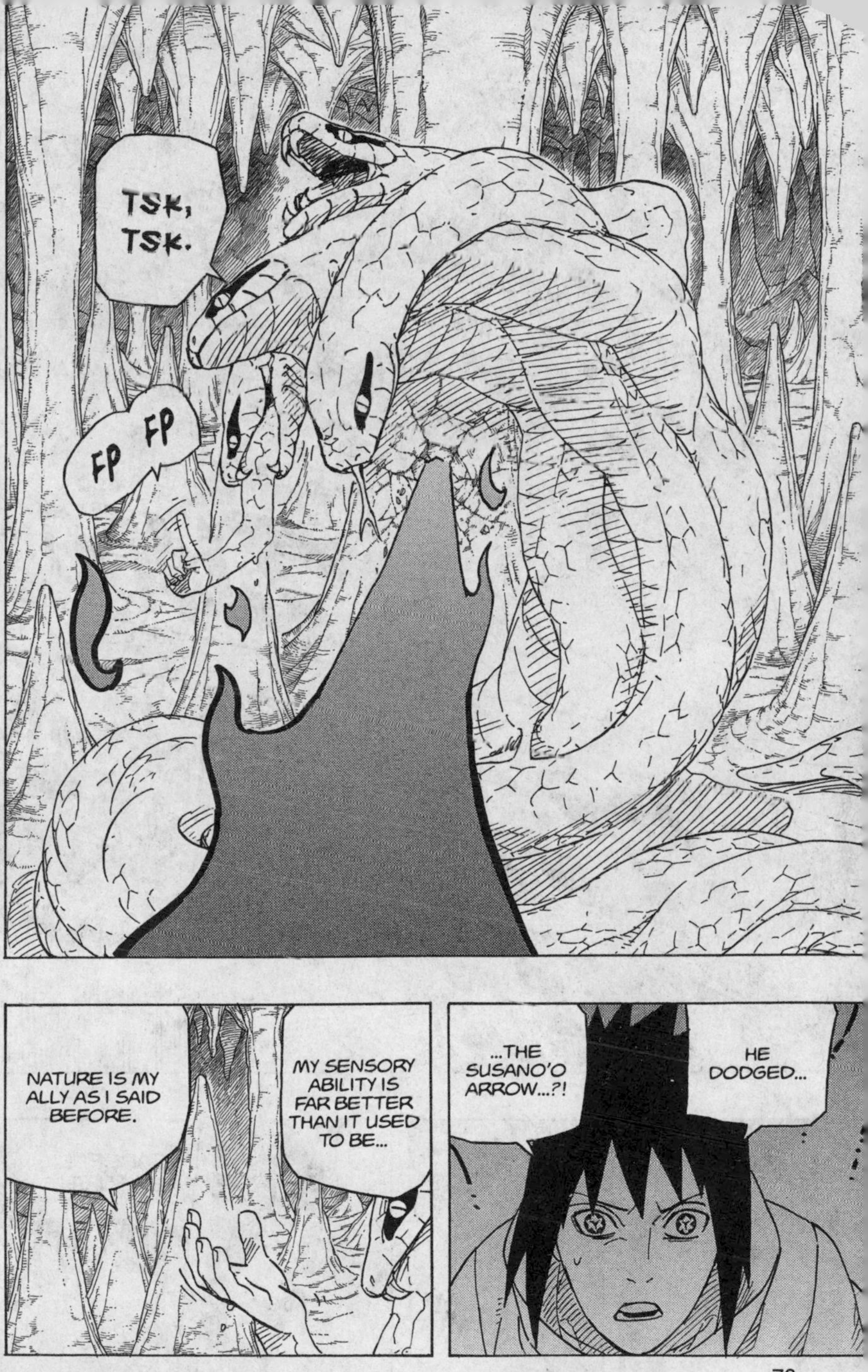
TSK, TSK.
FP FP
HE DODGED...
...THE SUSANO'O ARROW...?!
MY SENSORY ABILITY IS FAR BETTER THAN IT USED TO BE...
NATURE IS MY ALLY AS I SAID BEFORE.

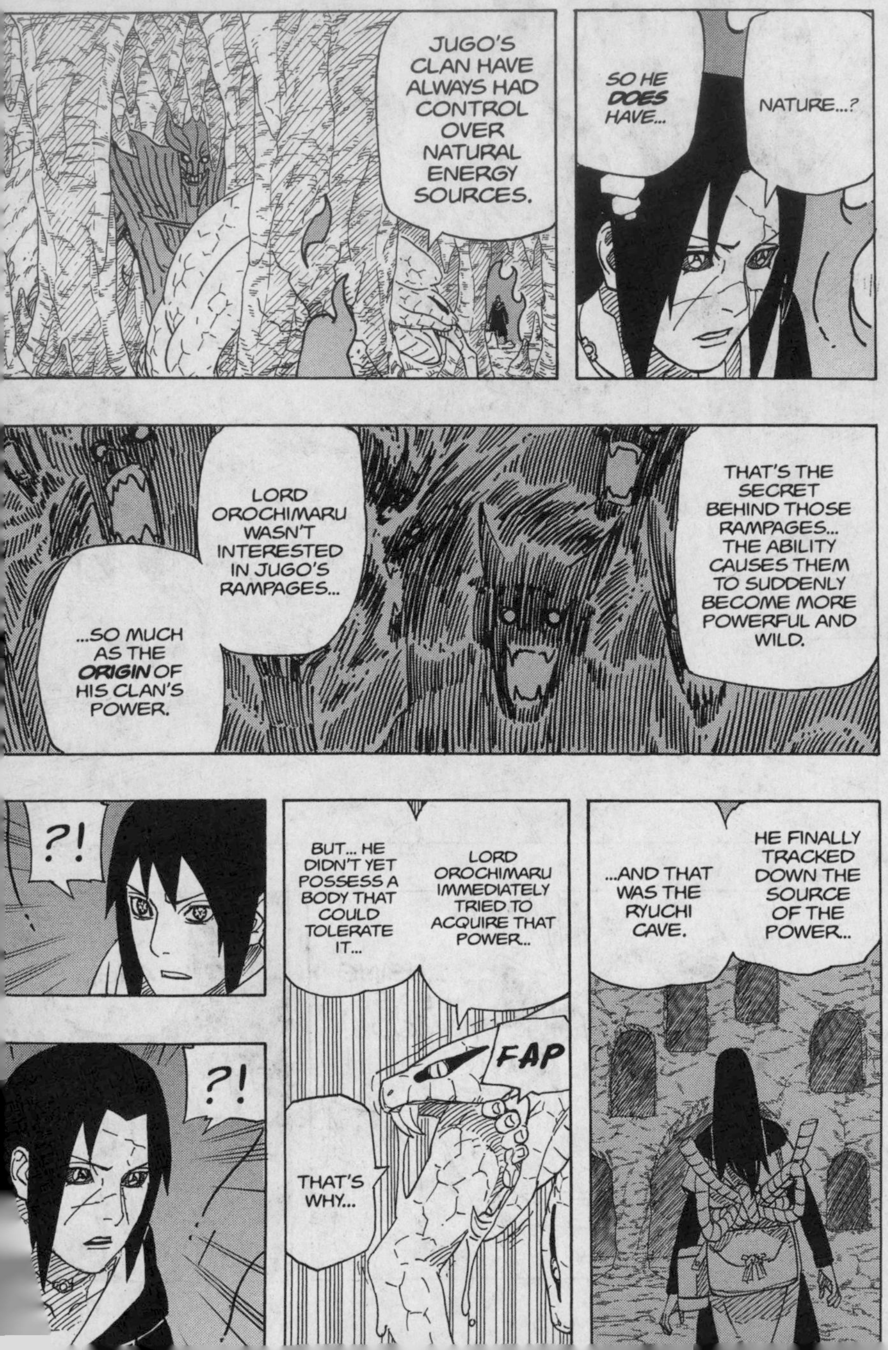
NATURE...?
SO HE **DOES** HAVE...
JUGO'S CLAN HAVE ALWAYS HAD CONTROL OVER NATURAL ENERGY SOURCES.
THAT'S THE SECRET BEHIND THOSE RAMPAGES... THE ABILITY CAUSES THEM TO SUDDENLY BECOME MORE POWERFUL AND WILD.
LORD OROCHIMARU WASN'T INTERESTED IN JUGO'S RAMPAGES...
...SO MUCH AS THE **ORIGIN** OF HIS CLAN'S POWER.
HE FINALLY TRACKED DOWN THE SOURCE OF THE POWER...
...AND THAT WAS THE RYUCHI CAVE.
LORD OROCHIMARU IMMEDIATELY TRIED TO ACQUIRE THAT POWER..
BUT... HE DIDN'T YET POSSESS A BODY THAT COULD TOLERATE IT...
FAP
THAT'S WHY...
?!
?!

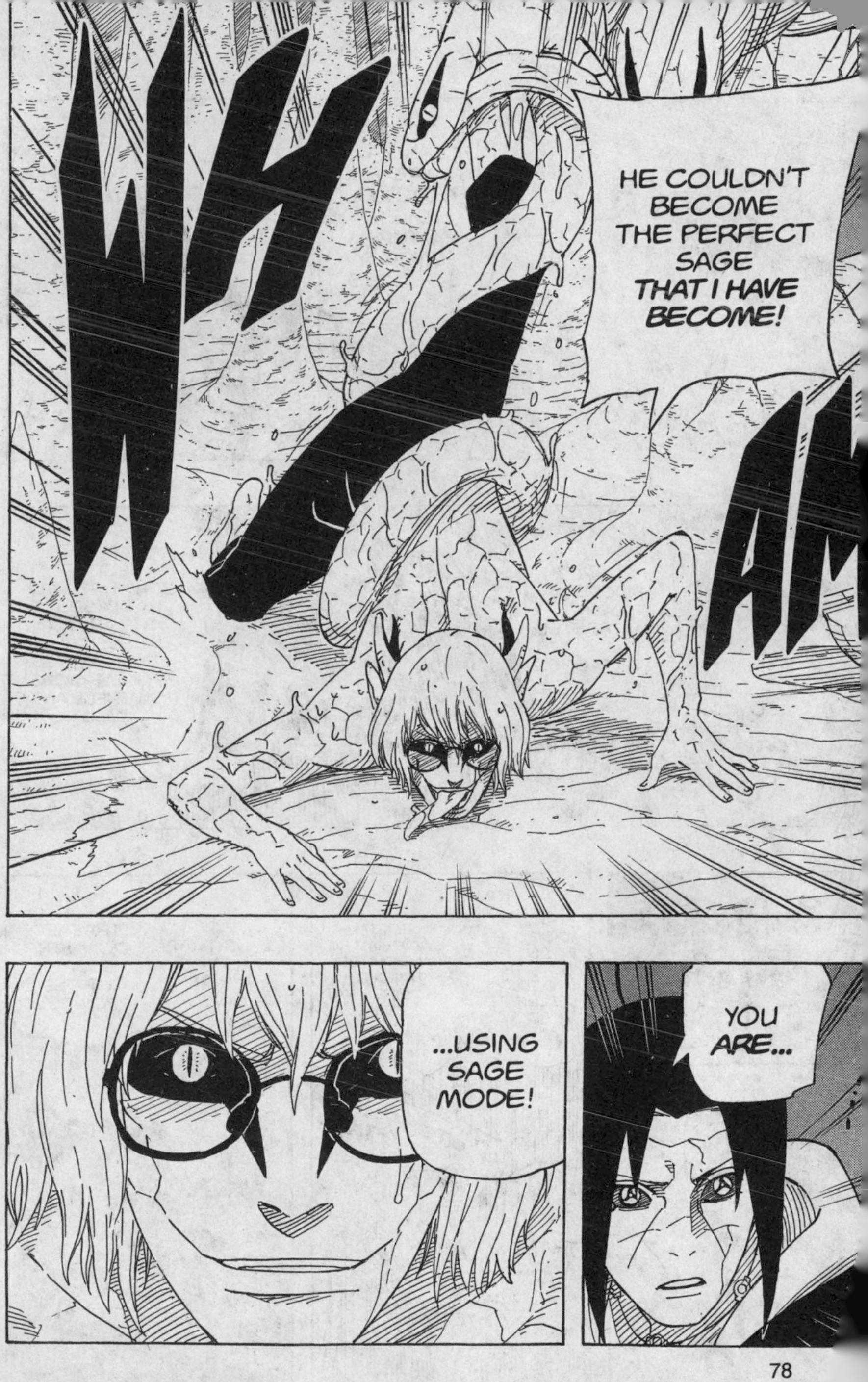
HE COULDN'T BECOME THE PERFECT SAGE THAT I HAVE BECOME!
YOU ARE...
...USING SAGE MODE!

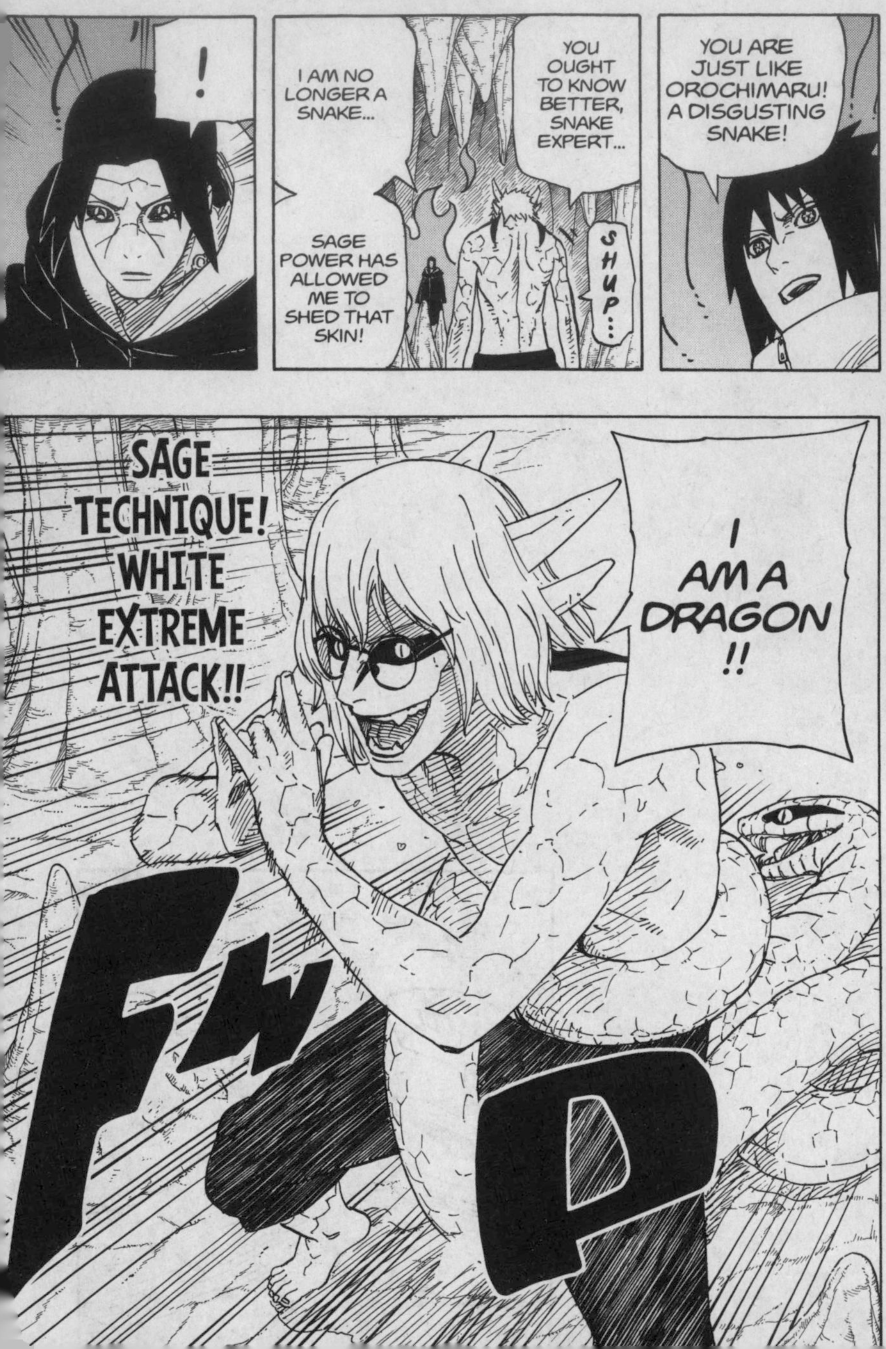
YOU ARE JUST LIKE OROCHIMARU! A DISGUSTING SNAKE!
YOU OUGHT TO KNOW BETTER, SNAKE EXPERT...
I AM NO LONGER A SNAKE...
SHUP...
SAGE POWER HAS ALLOWED ME TO SHED THAT SKIN!
!
I AM A DRAGON!!
SAGE TECHNIQUE! WHITE EXTREME ATTACK!!
FWP

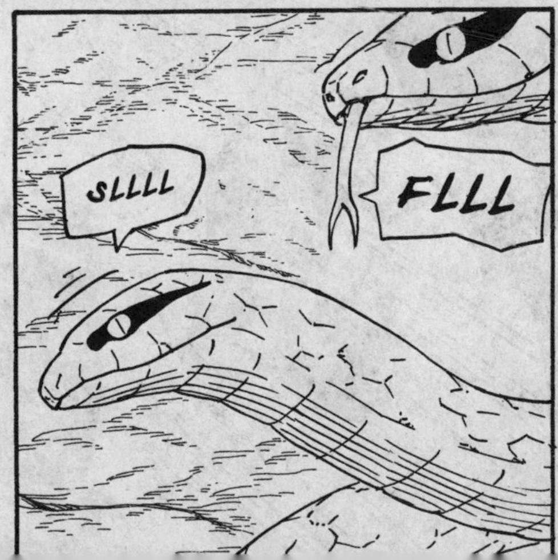
FLLL
SLLLL

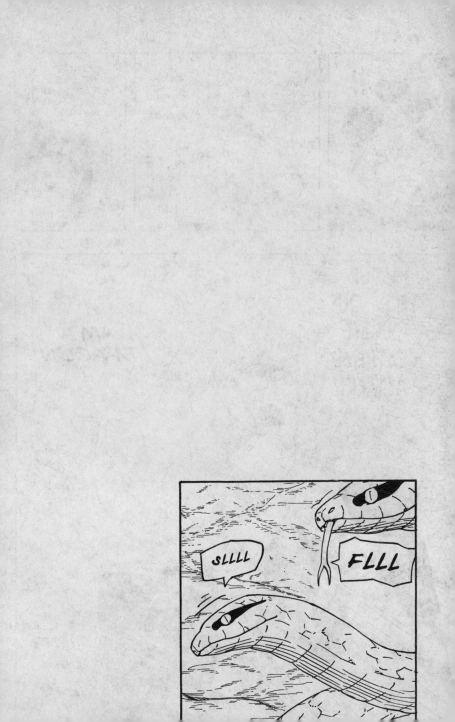

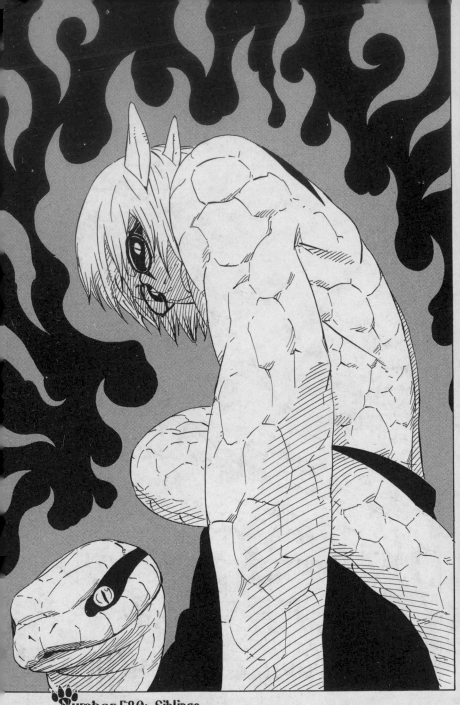

Number 580: Siblings

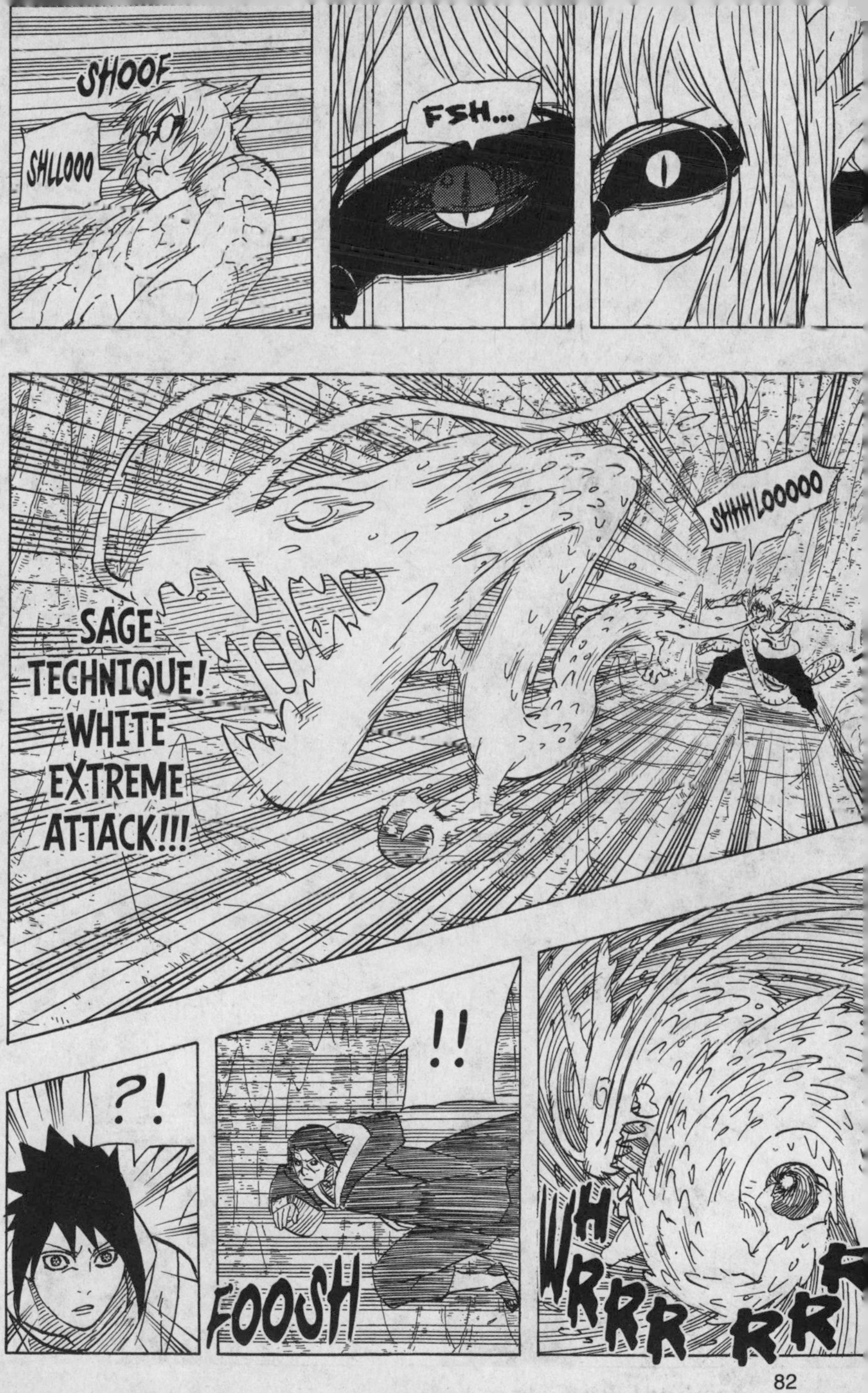
FSH...
SHOOF
SHLLOOO
SHHHLOOOOO
SAGE TECHNIQUE! WHITE EXTREME ATTACK!!!
WHRRR RRR
!!
FOOSH
?!

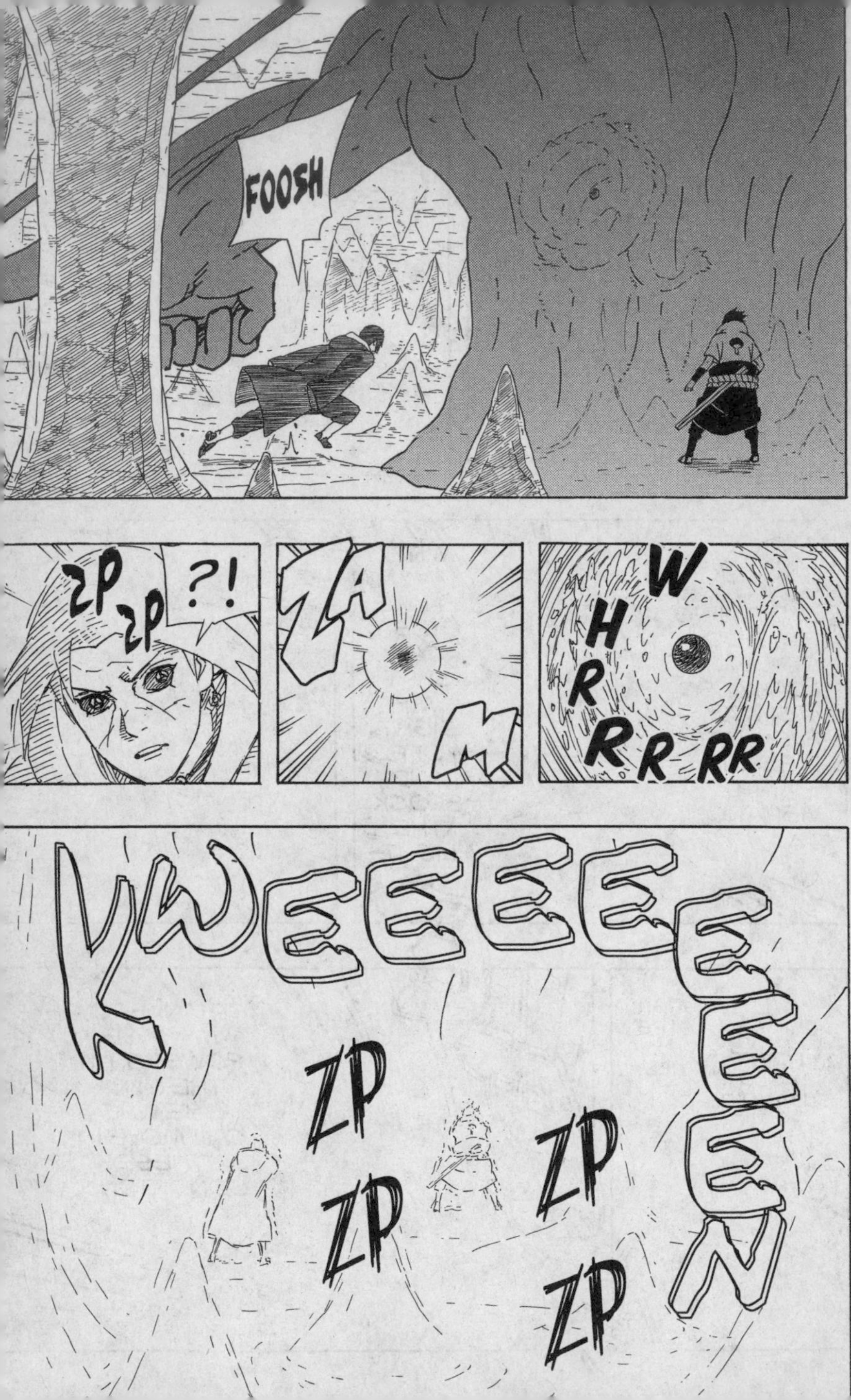
FOOSH
WHRRRRRR
ZAM
ZP ZP
?!
KWEEEEEEEEN
ZP
ZP
ZP
ZP

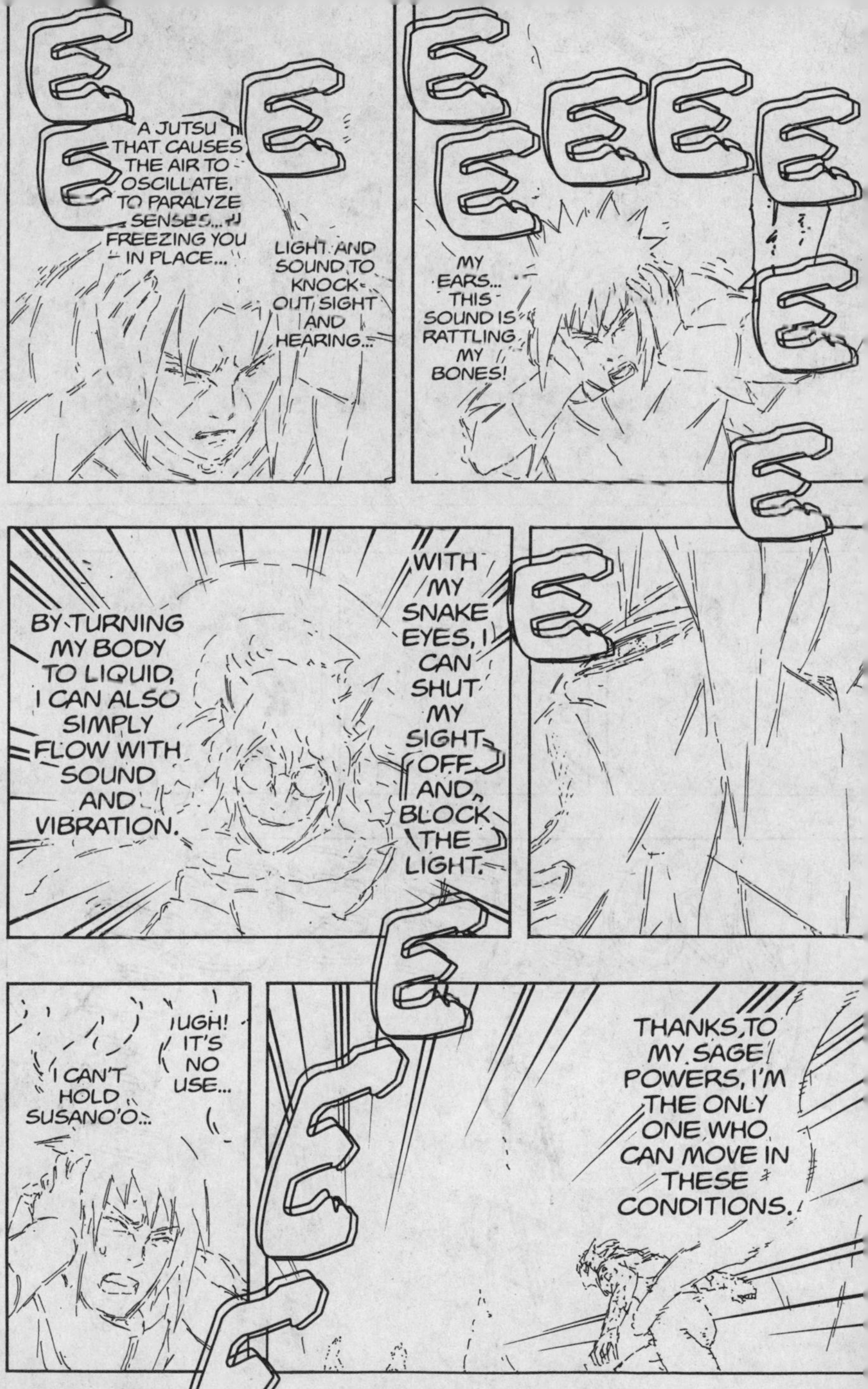
MY EARS... THIS SOUND IS RATTLING MY BONES!
A JUTSU THAT CAUSES THE AIR TO OSCILLATE, TO PARALYZE SENSES... FREEZING YOU IN PLACE...
LIGHT AND SOUND TO KNOCK OUT SIGHT AND HEARING...
WITH MY SNAKE EYES, I CAN SHUT MY SIGHT OFF AND BLOCK THE LIGHT.
BY TURNING MY BODY TO LIQUID, I CAN ALSO SIMPLY FLOW WITH SOUND AND VIBRATION.
THANKS TO MY SAGE POWERS, I'M THE ONLY ONE WHO CAN MOVE IN THESE CONDITIONS.
UGH! IT'S NO USE...
I CAN'T HOLD SUSANO'O...

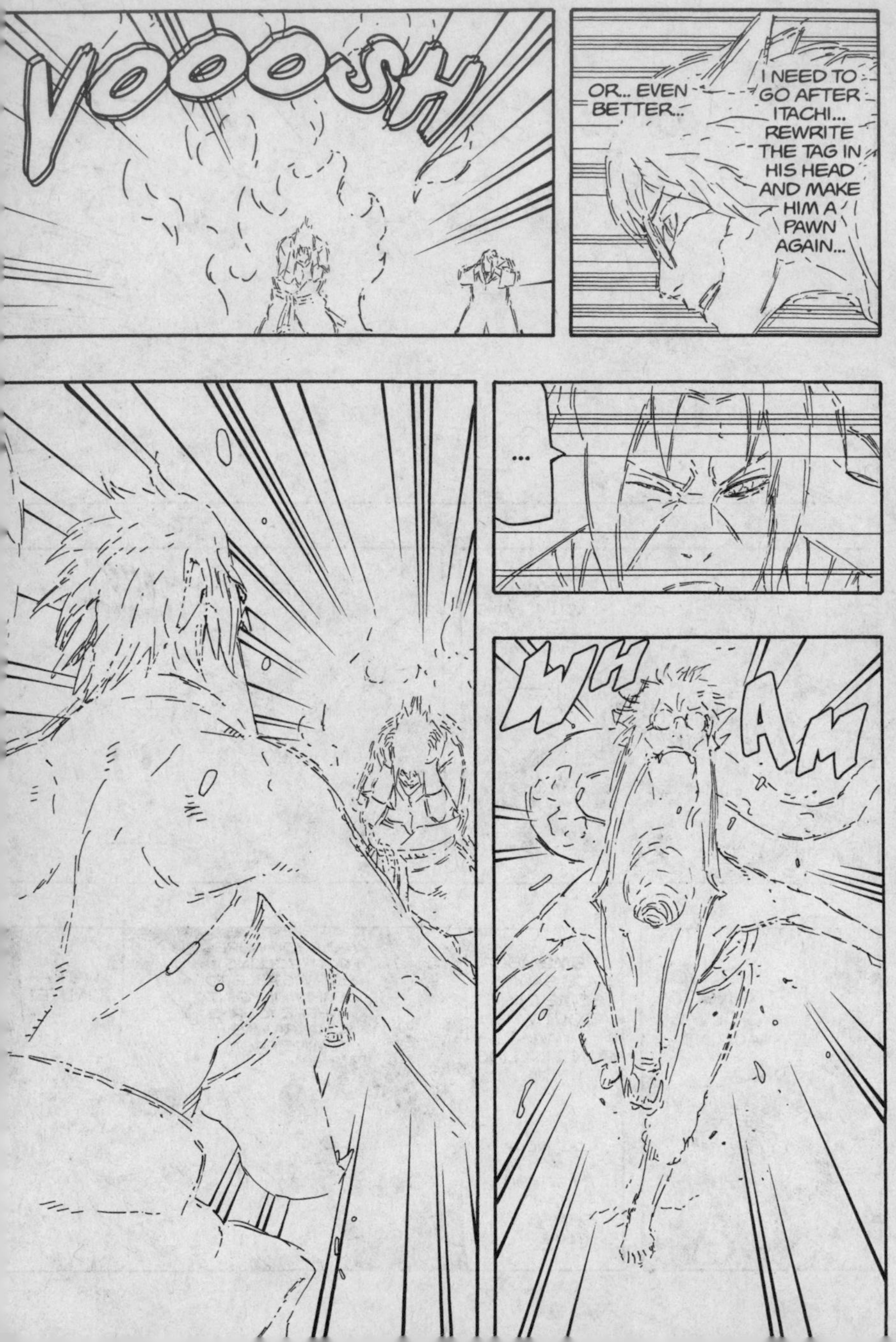
I NEED TO GO AFTER ITACHI... REWRITE THE TAG IN HIS HEAD AND MAKE HIM A PAWN AGAIN...
OR... EVEN BETTER...
VOOOSH
...
WHAM

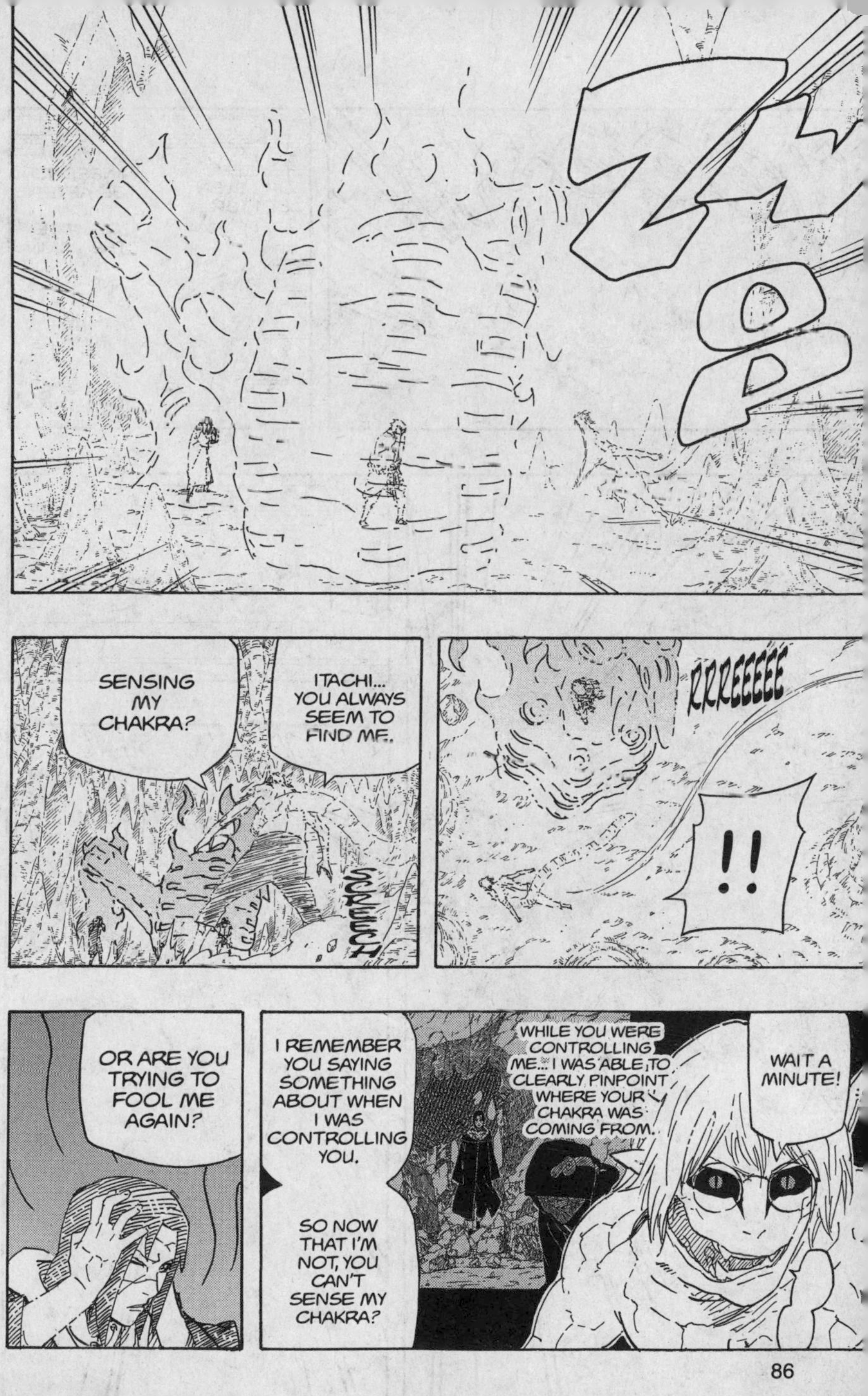
ZWOP
RRREEEEE
!!
ITACHI... YOU ALWAYS SEEM TO FIND ME.
SENSING MY CHAKRA?
SCREECH
WAIT A MINUTE!
WHILE YOU WERE CONTROLLING ME... I WAS ABLE TO CLEARLY PINPOINT WHERE YOUR CHAKRA WAS COMING FROM.
I REMEMBER YOU SAYING SOMETHING ABOUT WHEN I WAS CONTROLLING YOU.
SO NOW THAT I'M NOT, YOU CAN'T SENSE MY CHAKRA?
OR ARE YOU TRYING TO FOOL ME AGAIN?

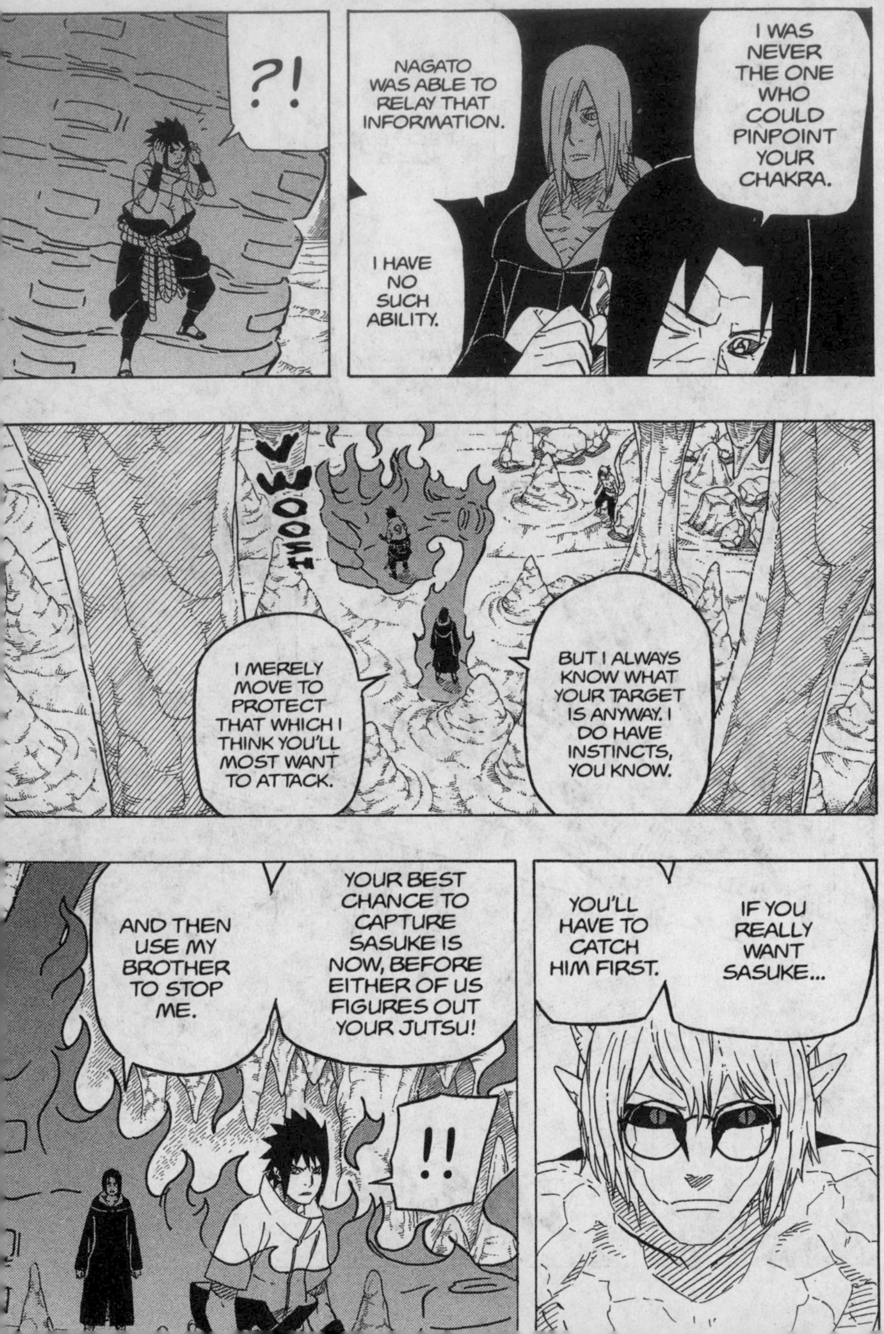
I WAS NEVER THE ONE WHO COULD PINPOINT YOUR CHAKRA.
NAGATO WAS ABLE TO RELAY THAT INFORMATION.
I HAVE NO SUCH ABILITY.
?!
VWOOSH
BUT I ALWAYS KNOW WHAT YOUR TARGET IS ANYWAY. I DO HAVE INSTINCTS, YOU KNOW.
I MERELY MOVE TO PROTECT THAT WHICH I THINK YOU'LL MOST WANT TO ATTACK.
IF YOU REALLY WANT SASUKE...
YOU'LL HAVE TO CATCH HIM FIRST.
YOUR BEST CHANCE TO CAPTURE SASUKE IS NOW, BEFORE EITHER OF US FIGURES OUT YOUR JUTSU!
AND THEN USE MY BROTHER TO STOP ME.
!!

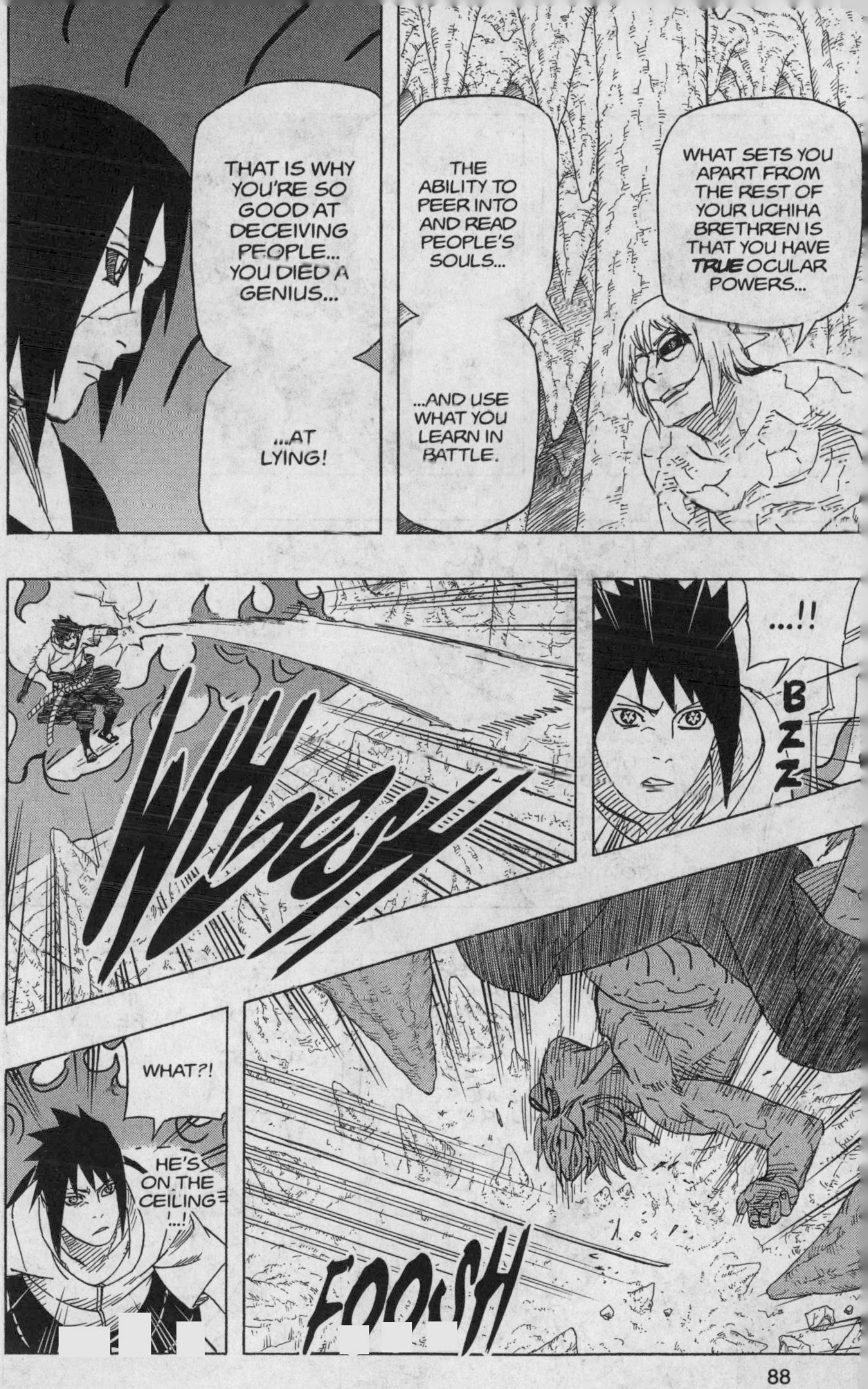
WHAT SETS YOU APART FROM THE REST OF YOUR UCHIHA BRETHREN IS THAT YOU HAVE TRUE OCULAR POWERS...
THE ABILITY TO PEER INTO AND READ PEOPLE'S SOULS...
...AND USE WHAT YOU LEARN IN BATTLE.
THAT IS WHY YOU'RE SO GOOD AT DECEIVING PEOPLE... YOU DIED A GENIUS...
...AT LYING!
...!!
BZZZ
WHOOSH
FOOSH
WHAT?!
HE'S ON THE CEILING ...!

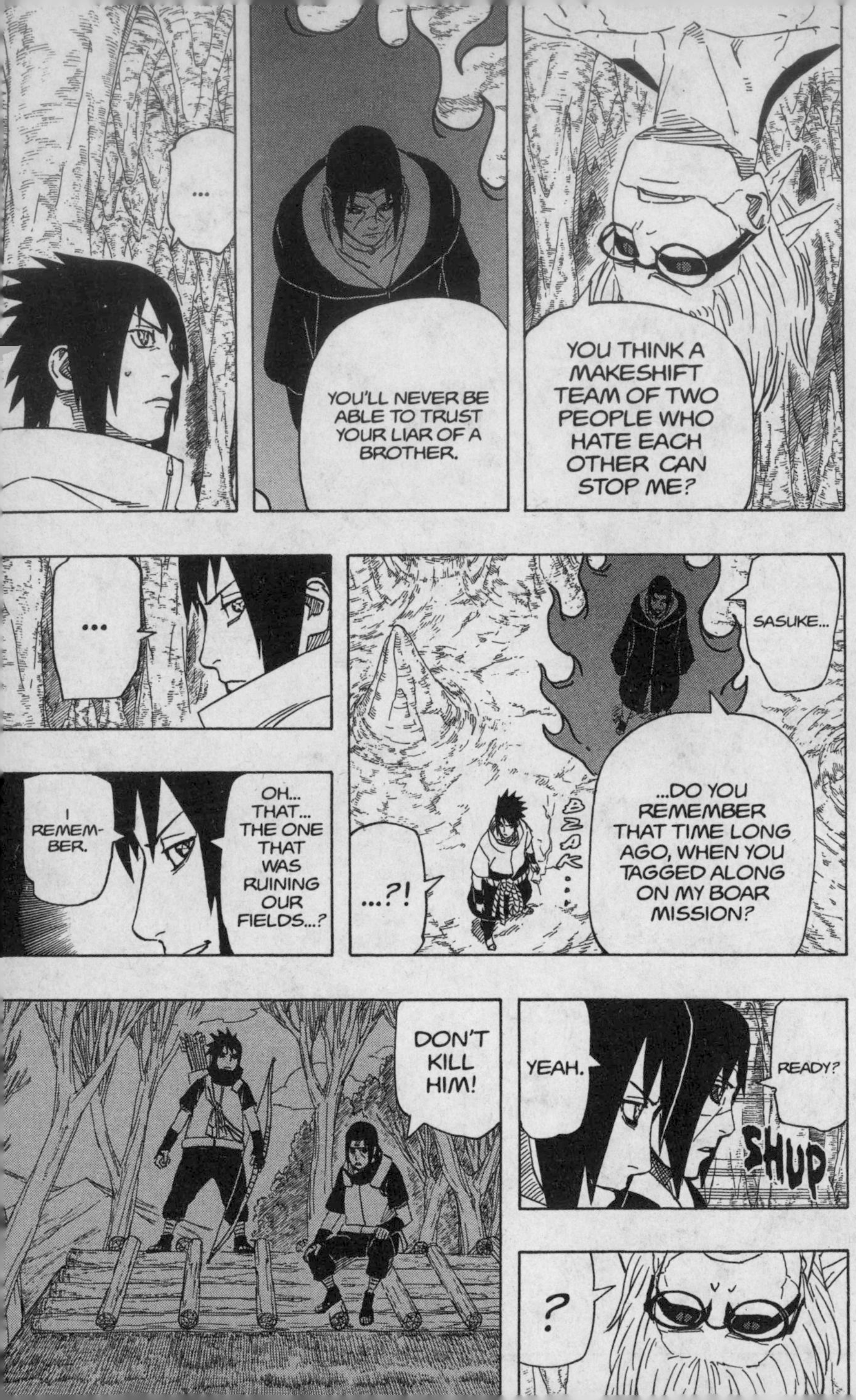
YOU THINK A MAKESHIFT TEAM OF TWO PEOPLE WHO HATE EACH OTHER CAN STOP ME?
YOU'LL NEVER BE ABLE TO TRUST YOUR LIAR OF A BROTHER.
...
SASUKE...
...DO YOU REMEMBER THAT TIME LONG AGO, WHEN YOU TAGGED ALONG ON MY BOAR MISSION?
BZAK...
...?!
...
OH... THAT... THE ONE THAT WAS RUINING OUR FIELDS...?
I REMEMBER.
READY?
YEAH.
SHUP
?
DON'T KILL HIM!

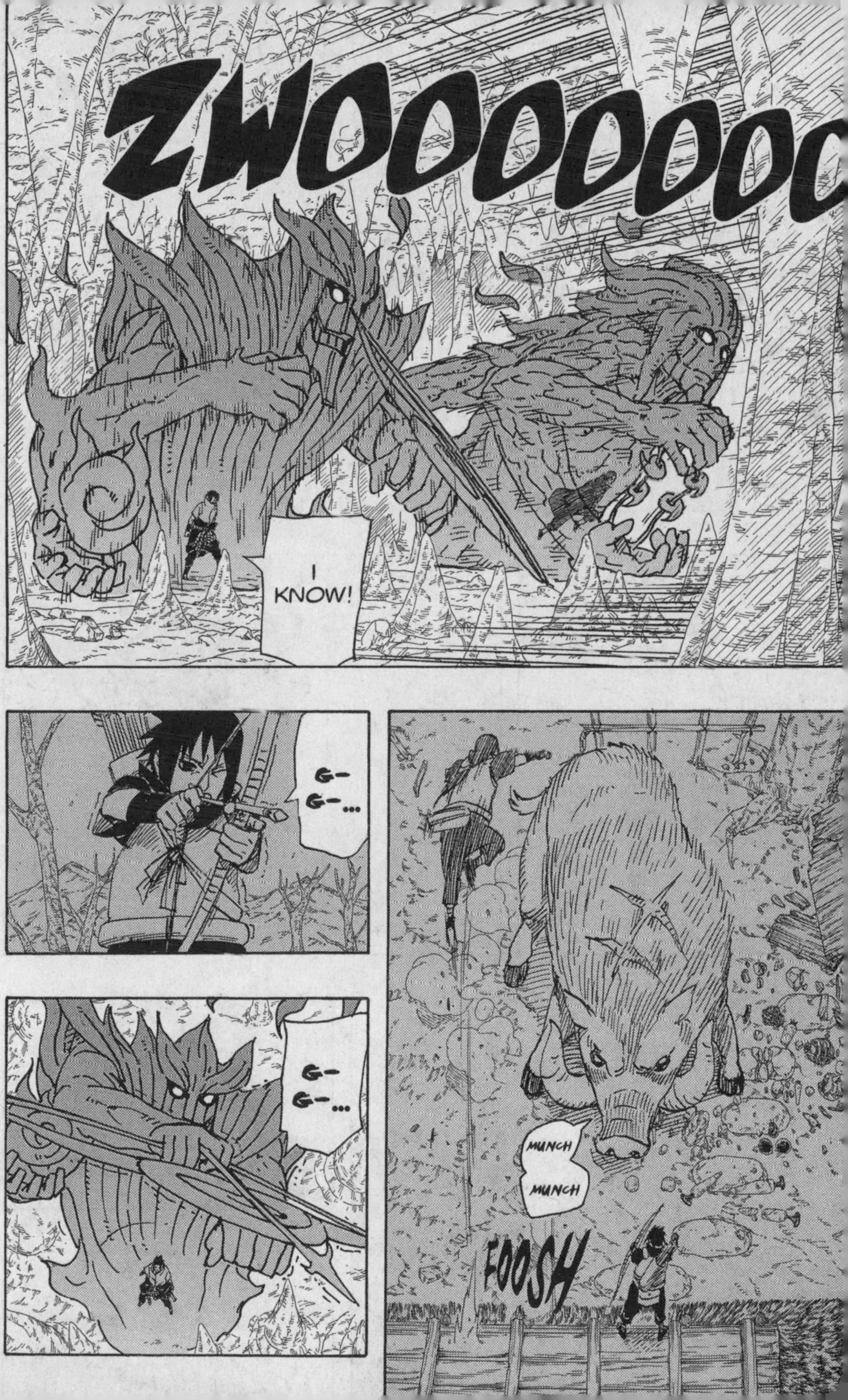
ZWOOOOOO
I KNOW!
MUNCH
MUNCH
FOOSH
G- G-...
G- G-...

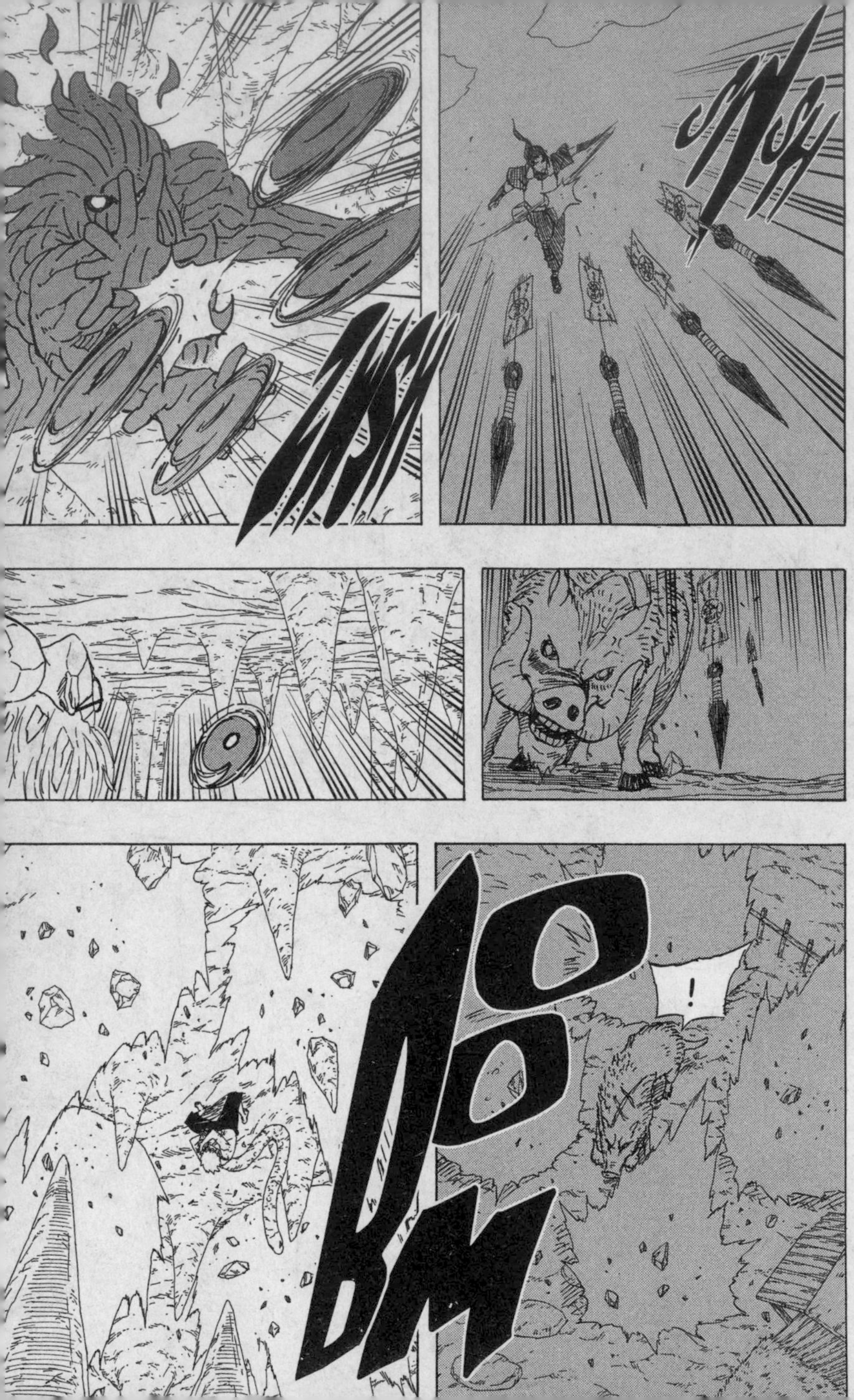
ZASH
!
BOOM

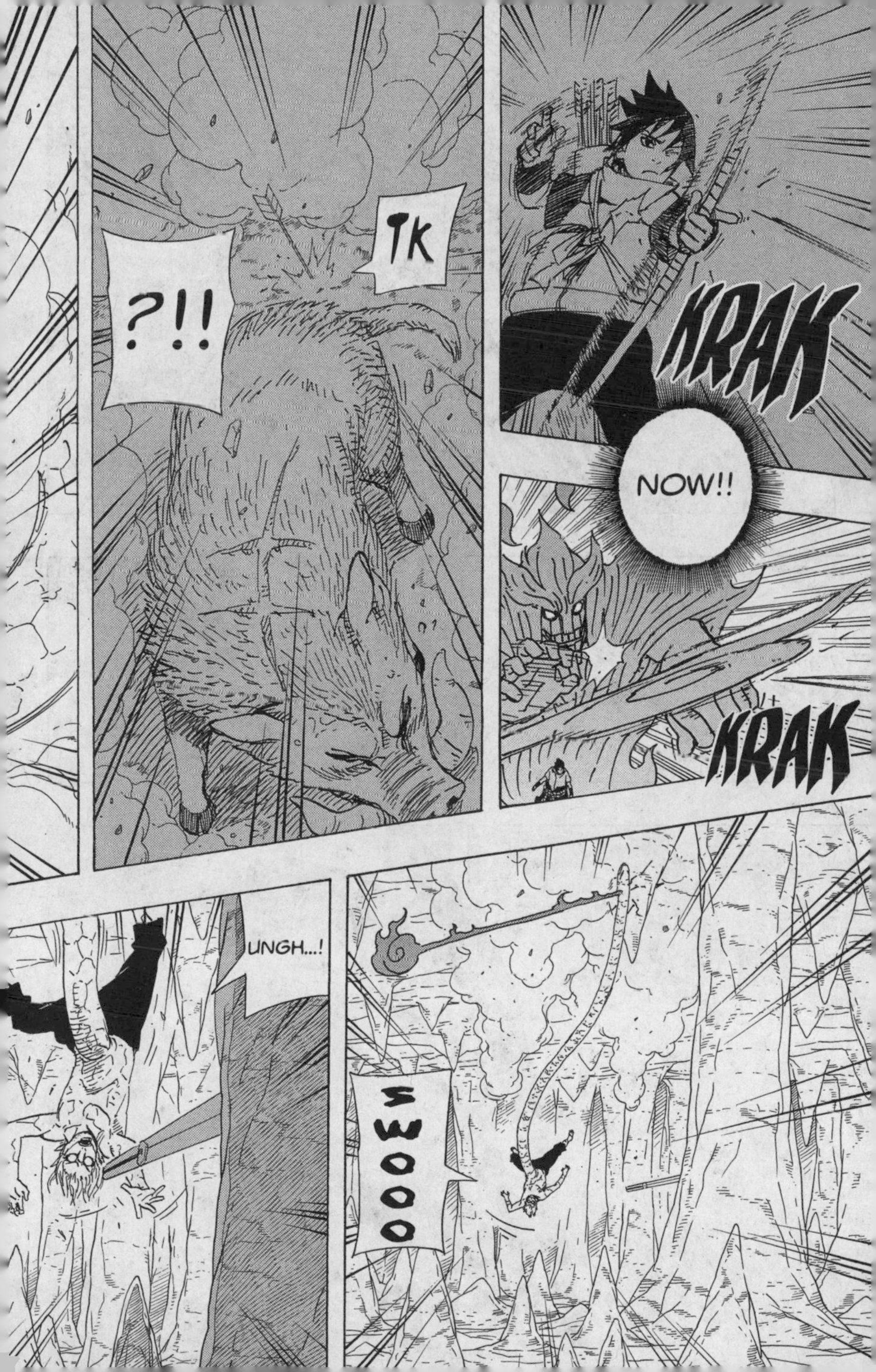
KRAK
NOW!!
KRAK
TK
?!!
SWOOO
UNGH...!

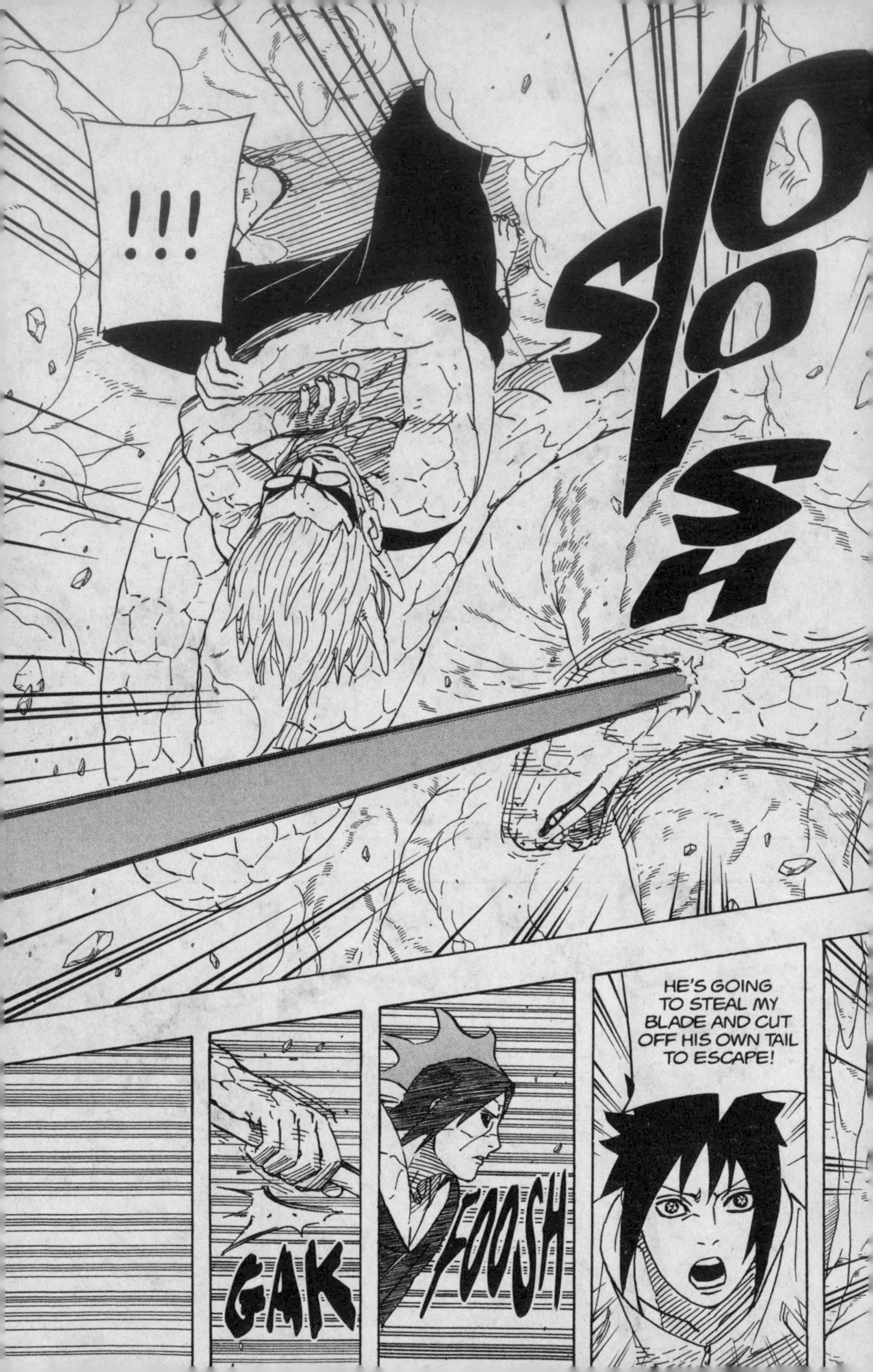
SLOOSH
!!!
HE'S GOING TO STEAL MY BLADE AND CUT OFF HIS OWN TAIL TO ESCAPE!
FOOSH
GAK

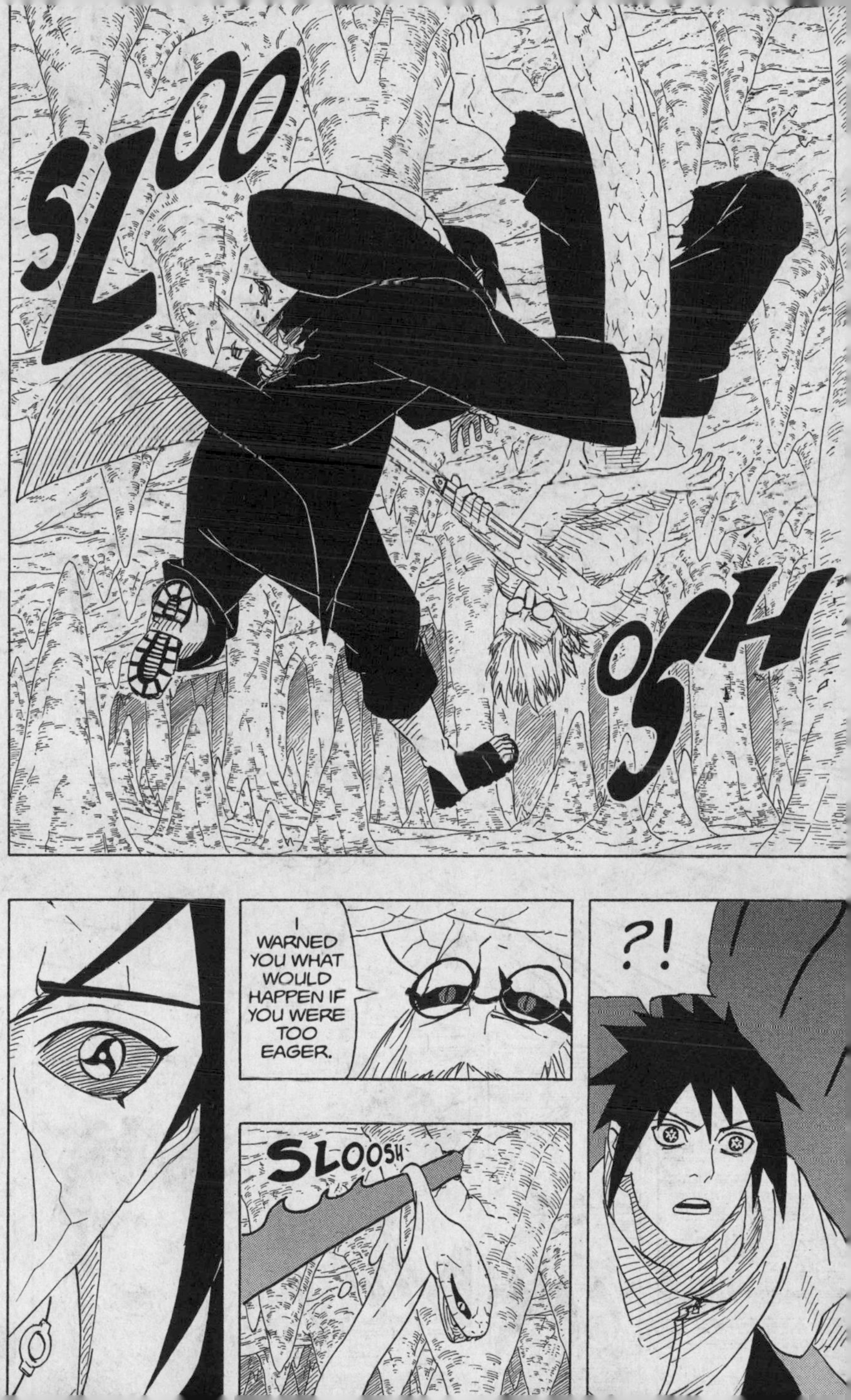
SLOO
OSH
?!
I WARNED YOU WHAT WOULD HAPPEN IF YOU WERE TOO EAGER.
SLOOSH

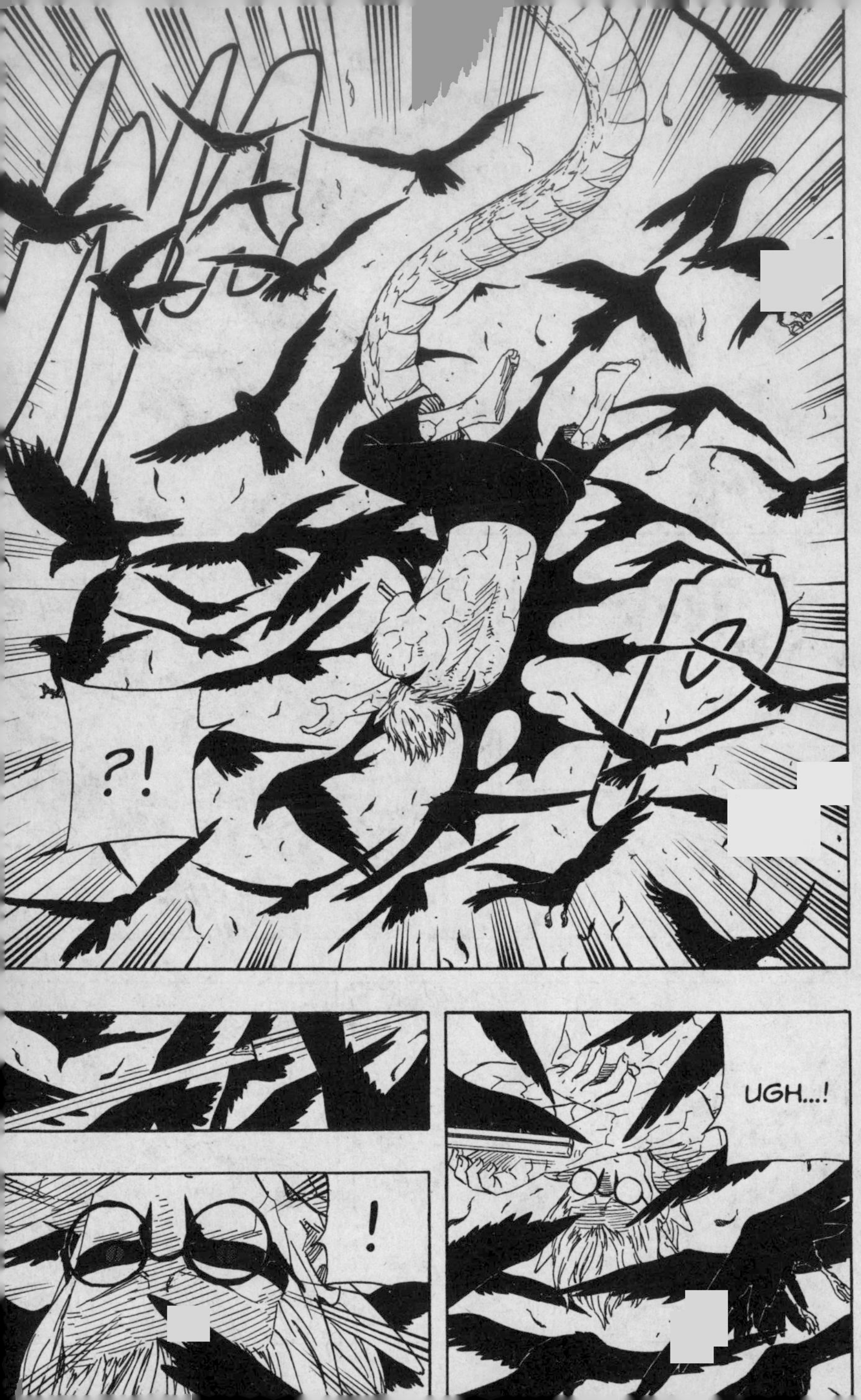
?!
UGH...!
!

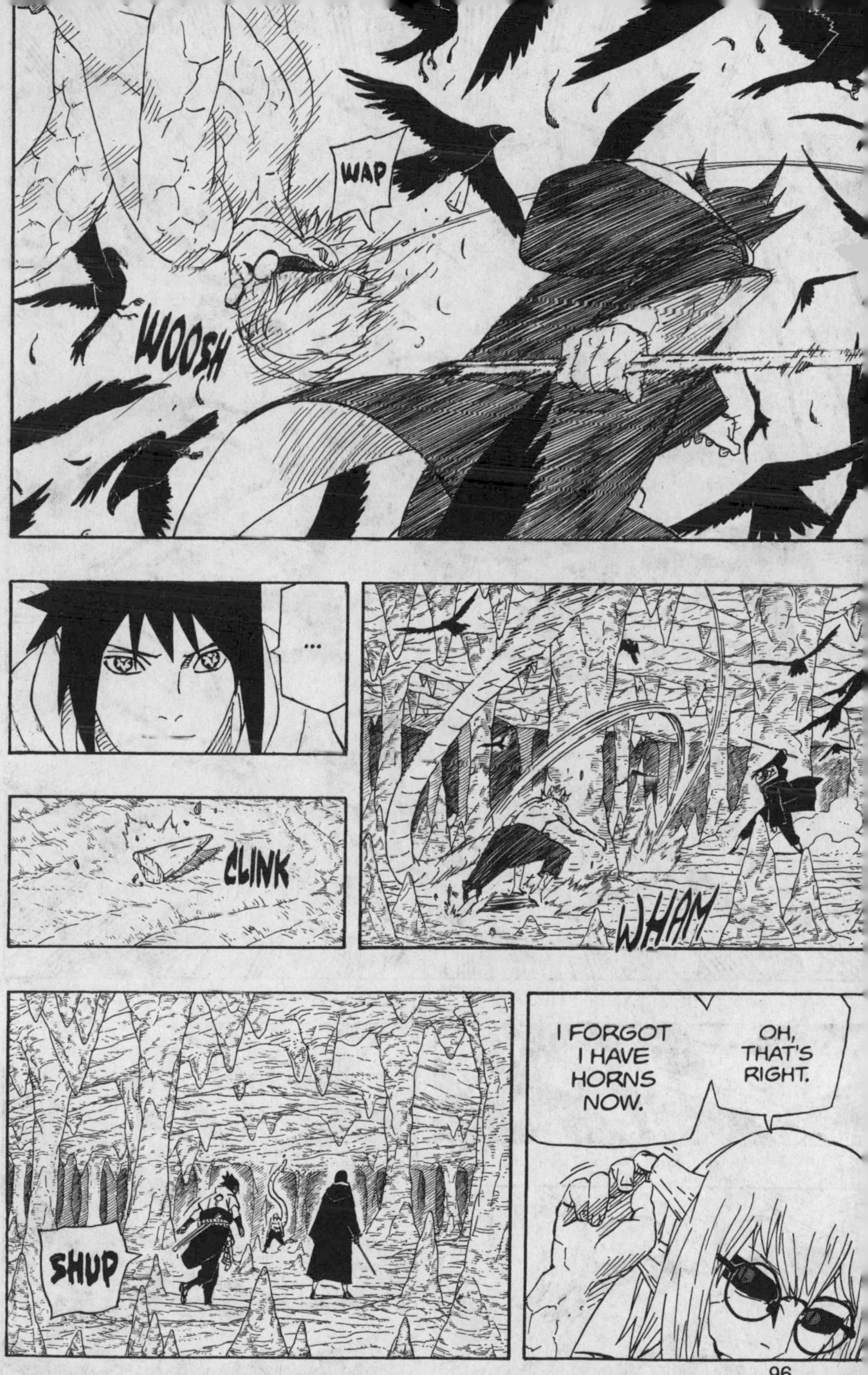
WAP
WOOSH
WHAM
...
CLINK
OH, THAT'S RIGHT.
I FORGOT I HAVE HORNS NOW.
SHUP

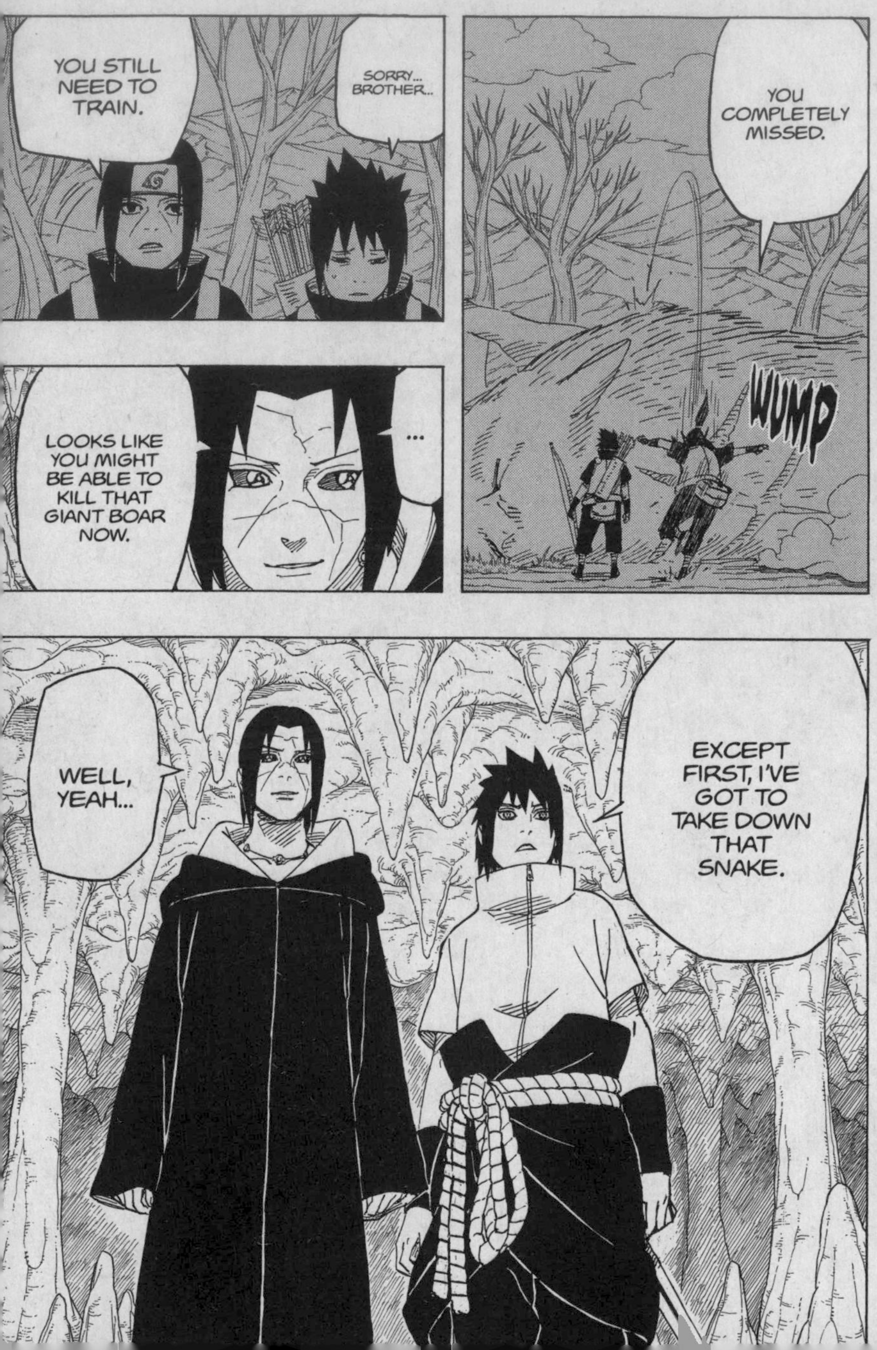
YOU COMPLETELY MISSED.
WUMP
SORRY... BROTHER..
YOU STILL NEED TO TRAIN.
...
LOOKS LIKE YOU MIGHT BE ABLE TO KILL THAT GIANT BOAR NOW.
EXCEPT FIRST, I'VE GOT TO TAKE DOWN THAT SNAKE.
WELL, YEAH...

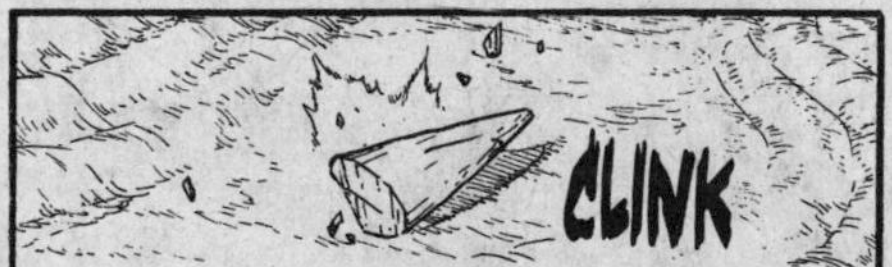
CLINK

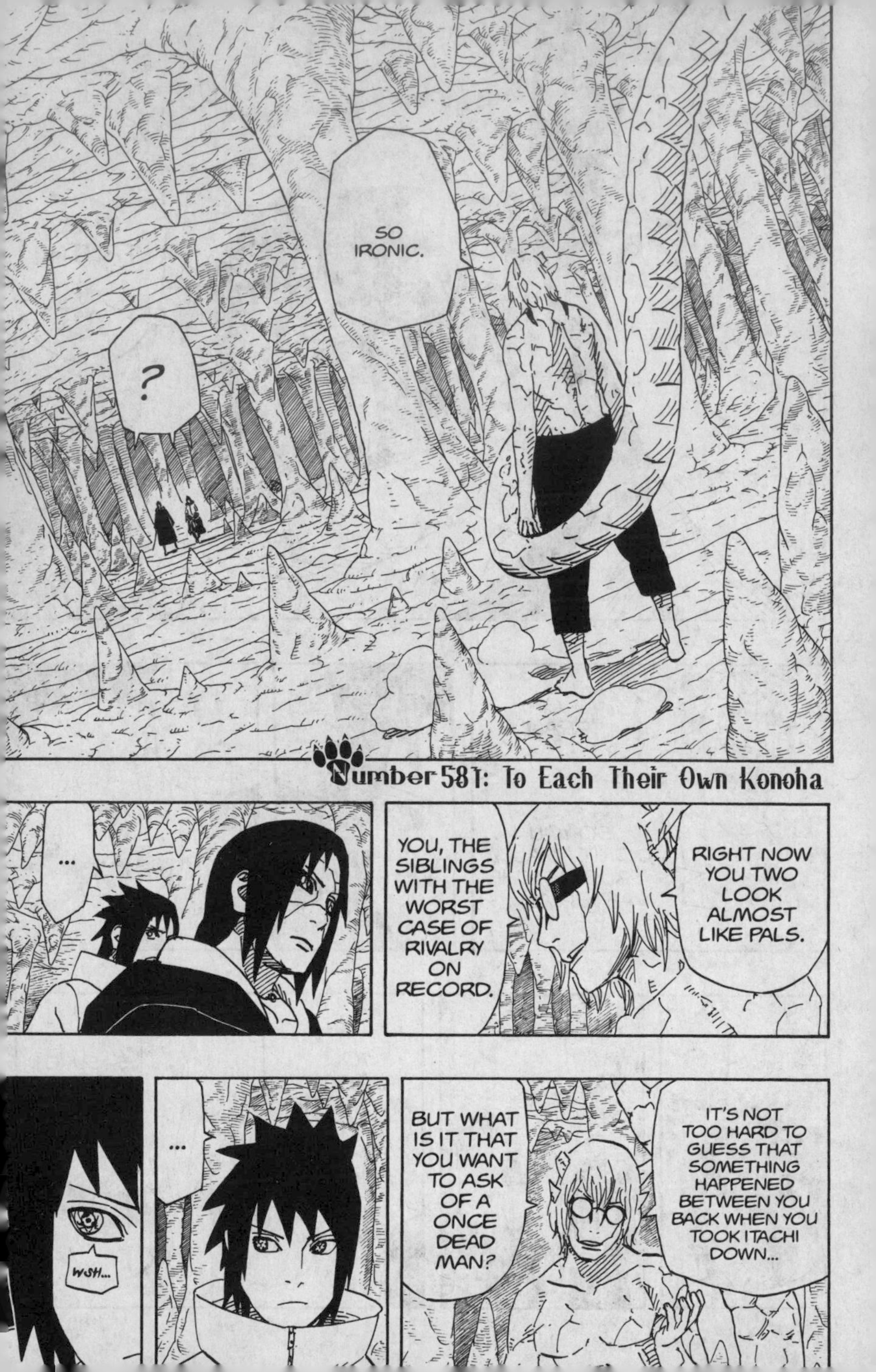
SO IRONIC.
?
Number 581: To Each Their Own Konoha
RIGHT NOW YOU TWO LOOK ALMOST LIKE PALS.
YOU, THE SIBLINGS WITH THE WORST CASE OF RIVALRY ON RECORD.
...
IT'S NOT TOO HARD TO GUESS THAT SOMETHING HAPPENED BETWEEN YOU BACK WHEN YOU TOOK ITACHI DOWN...
BUT WHAT IS IT THAT YOU WANT TO ASK OF A ONCE DEAD MAN?
...
WSH...

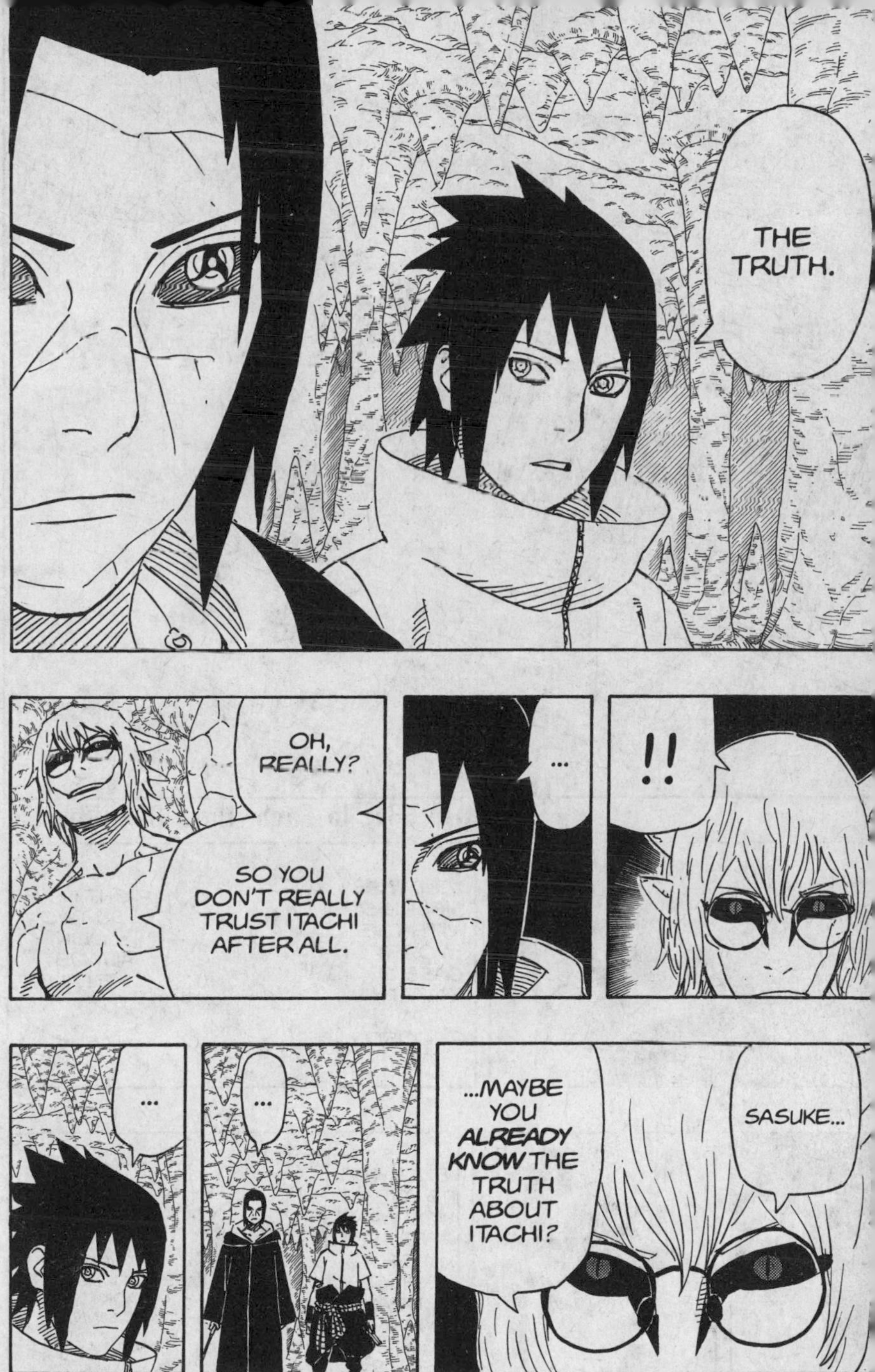
THE TRUTH.
!!
...
OH, REALLY?
SO YOU DON'T REALLY TRUST ITACHI AFTER ALL.
SASUKE...
...MAYBE YOU *ALREADY KNOW* THE TRUTH ABOUT ITACHI?
...
...

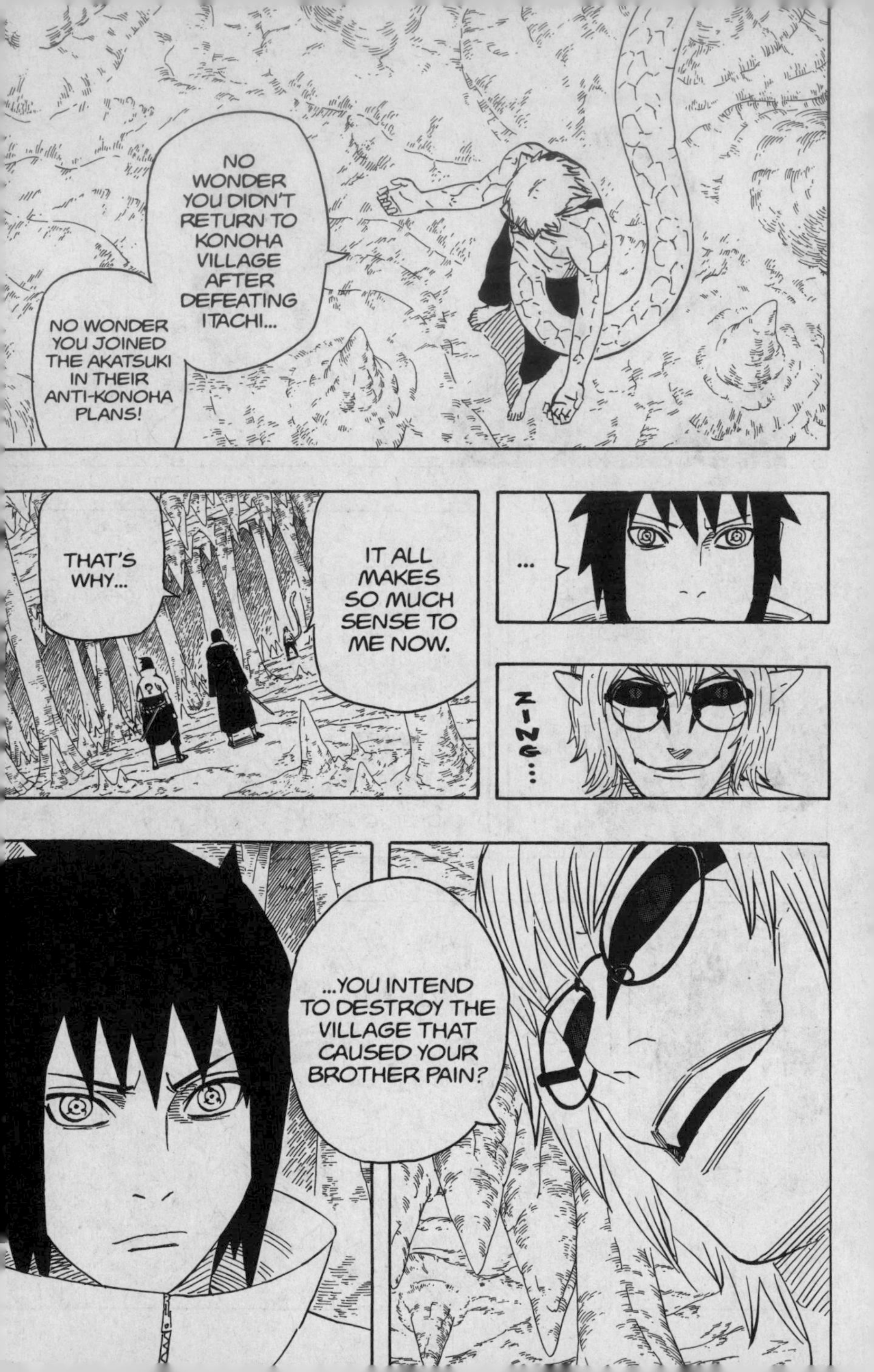
NO WONDER YOU DIDN'T RETURN TO KONOHA VILLAGE AFTER DEFEATING ITACHI...
NO WONDER YOU JOINED THE AKATSUKI IN THEIR ANTI-KONOHA PLANS!
...
ZING...
IT ALL MAKES SO MUCH SENSE TO ME NOW.
THAT'S WHY...
...YOU INTEND TO DESTROY THE VILLAGE THAT CAUSED YOUR BROTHER PAIN?

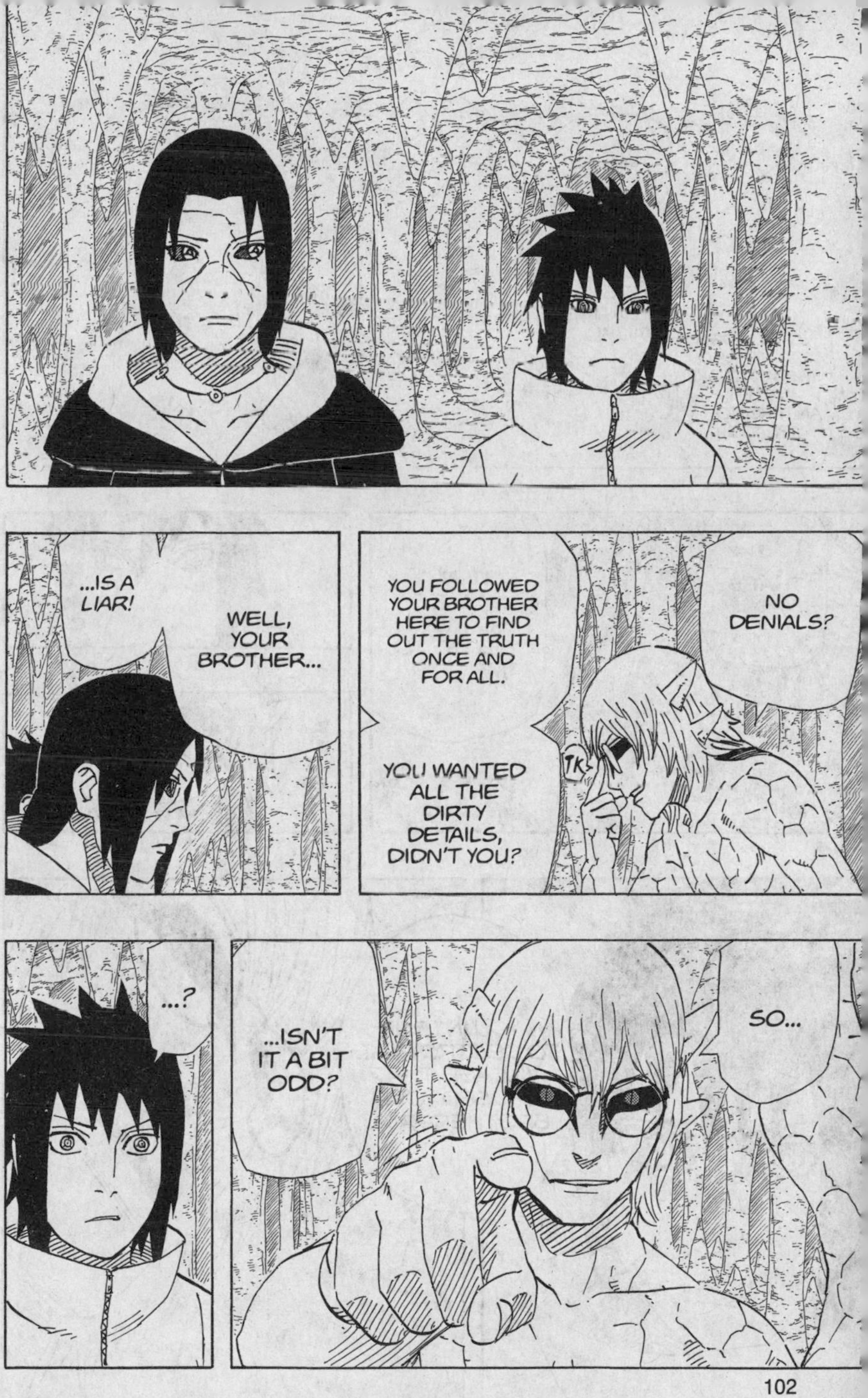
NO DENIALS?
YOU FOLLOWED YOUR BROTHER HERE TO FIND OUT THE TRUTH ONCE AND FOR ALL.
YOU WANTED ALL THE DIRTY DETAILS, DIDN'T YOU?
TK
WELL, YOUR BROTHER...
...IS A LIAR!
SO...
...ISN'T IT A BIT ODD?
...?

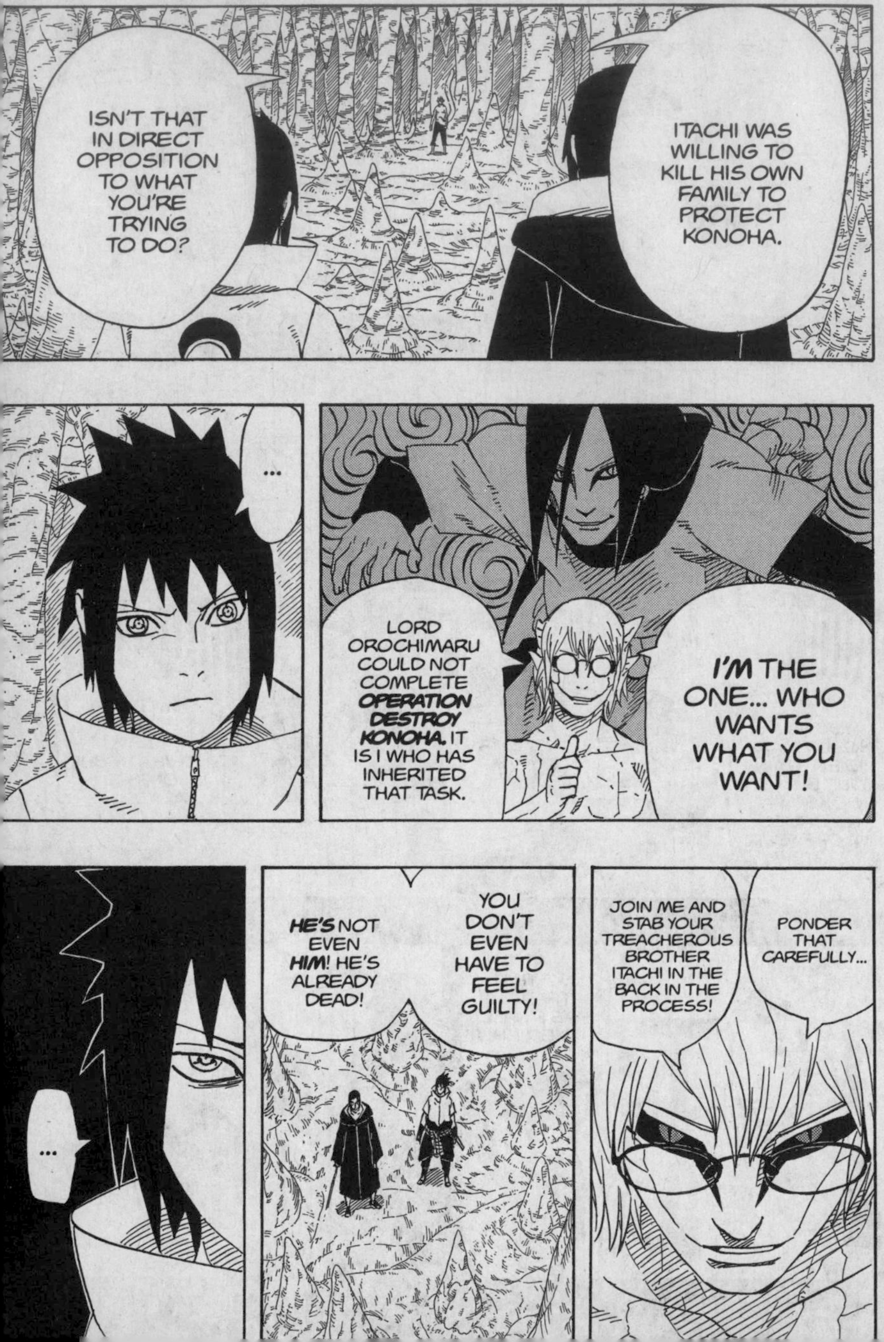
ITACHI WAS WILLING TO KILL HIS OWN FAMILY TO PROTECT KONOHA.
ISN'T THAT IN DIRECT OPPOSITION TO WHAT YOU'RE TRYING TO DO?
I'M THE ONE... WHO WANTS WHAT YOU WANT!
LORD OROCHIMARU COULD NOT COMPLETE OPERATION DESTROY KONOHA. IT IS I WHO HAS INHERITED THAT TASK.
...
PONDER THAT CAREFULLY...
JOIN ME AND STAB YOUR TREACHEROUS BROTHER ITACHI IN THE BACK IN THE PROCESS!
YOU DON'T EVEN HAVE TO FEEL GUILTY!
HE'S NOT EVEN HIM! HE'S ALREADY DEAD!
...

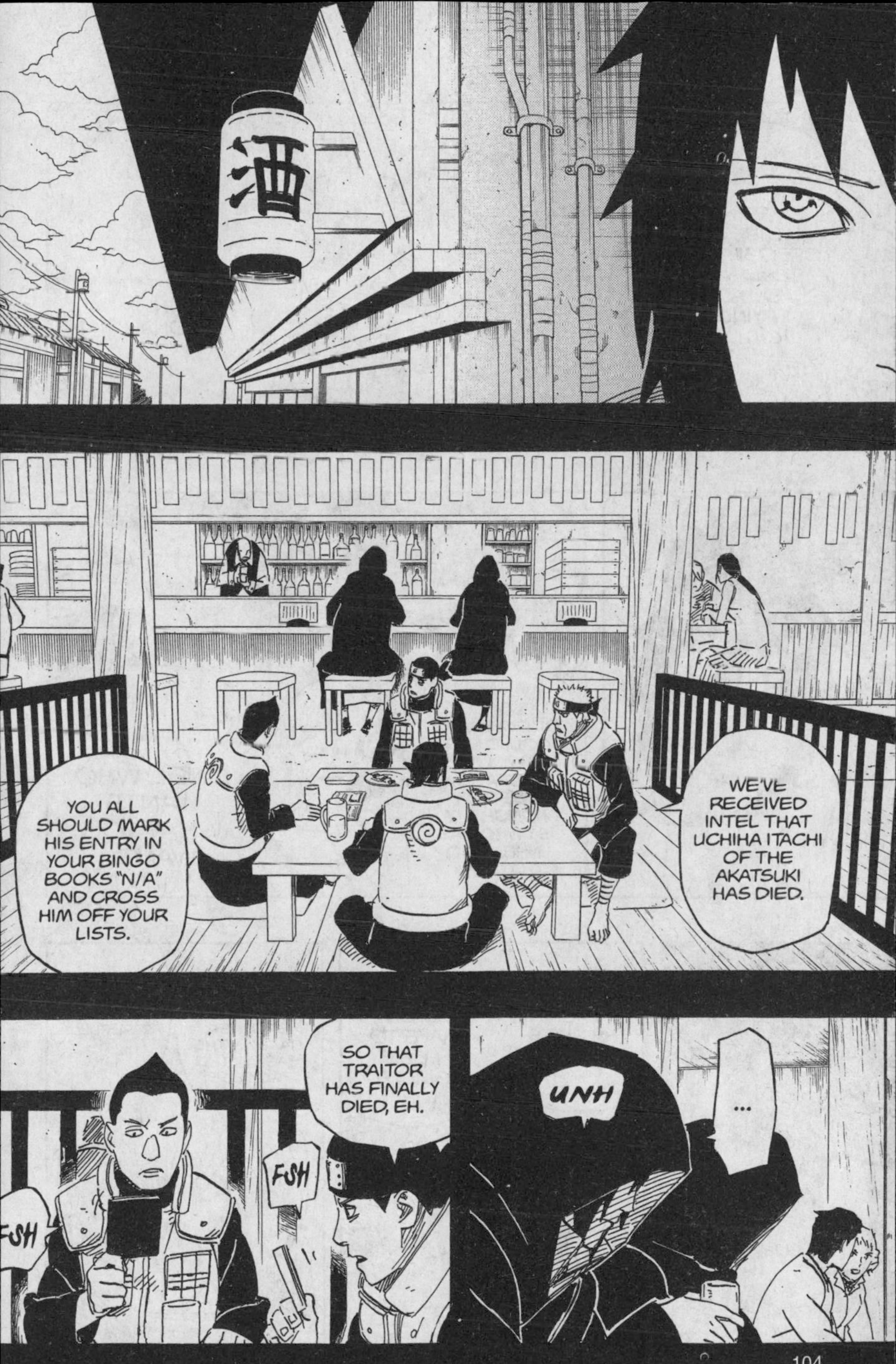

酒
WE'VE RECEIVED INTEL THAT UCHIHA ITACHI OF THE AKATSUKI HAS DIED.
YOU ALL SHOULD MARK HIS ENTRY IN YOUR BINGO BOOKS "N/A" AND CROSS HIM OFF YOUR LISTS.
...
UNH
SO THAT TRAITOR HAS FINALLY DIED, EH.
FSH
FSH

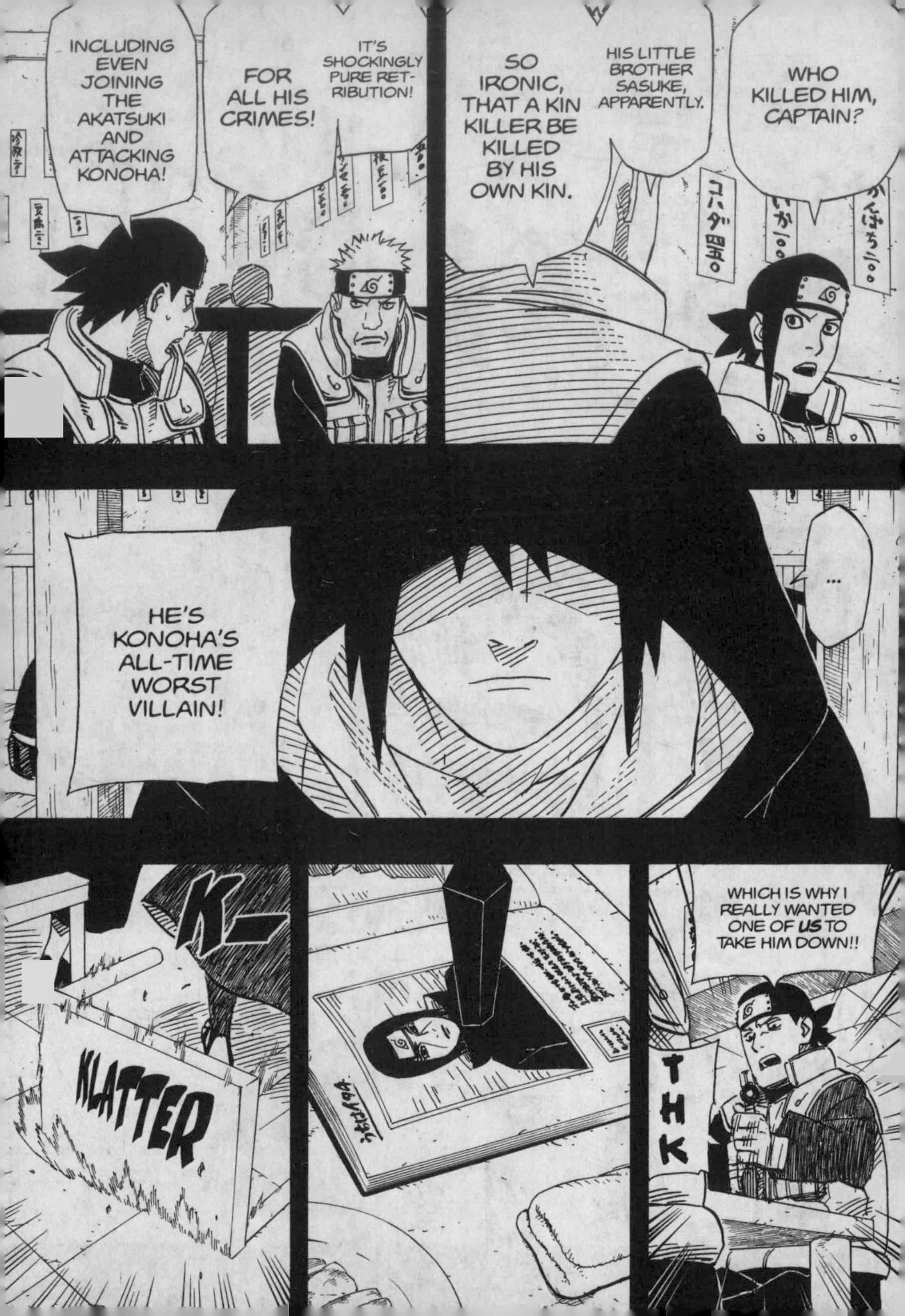
WHO KILLED HIM, CAPTAIN?
HIS LITTLE BROTHER SASUKE, APPARENTLY.
SO IRONIC, THAT A KIN KILLER BE KILLED BY HIS OWN KIN.
IT'S SHOCKINGLY PURE RETRIBUTION!
FOR ALL HIS CRIMES!
INCLUDING EVEN JOINING THE AKATSUKI AND ATTACKING KONOHA!
...
HE'S KONOHA'S ALL-TIME WORST VILLAIN!
WHICH IS WHY I REALLY WANTED ONE OF **US** TO TAKE HIM DOWN!!
THK
K-
KLATTER

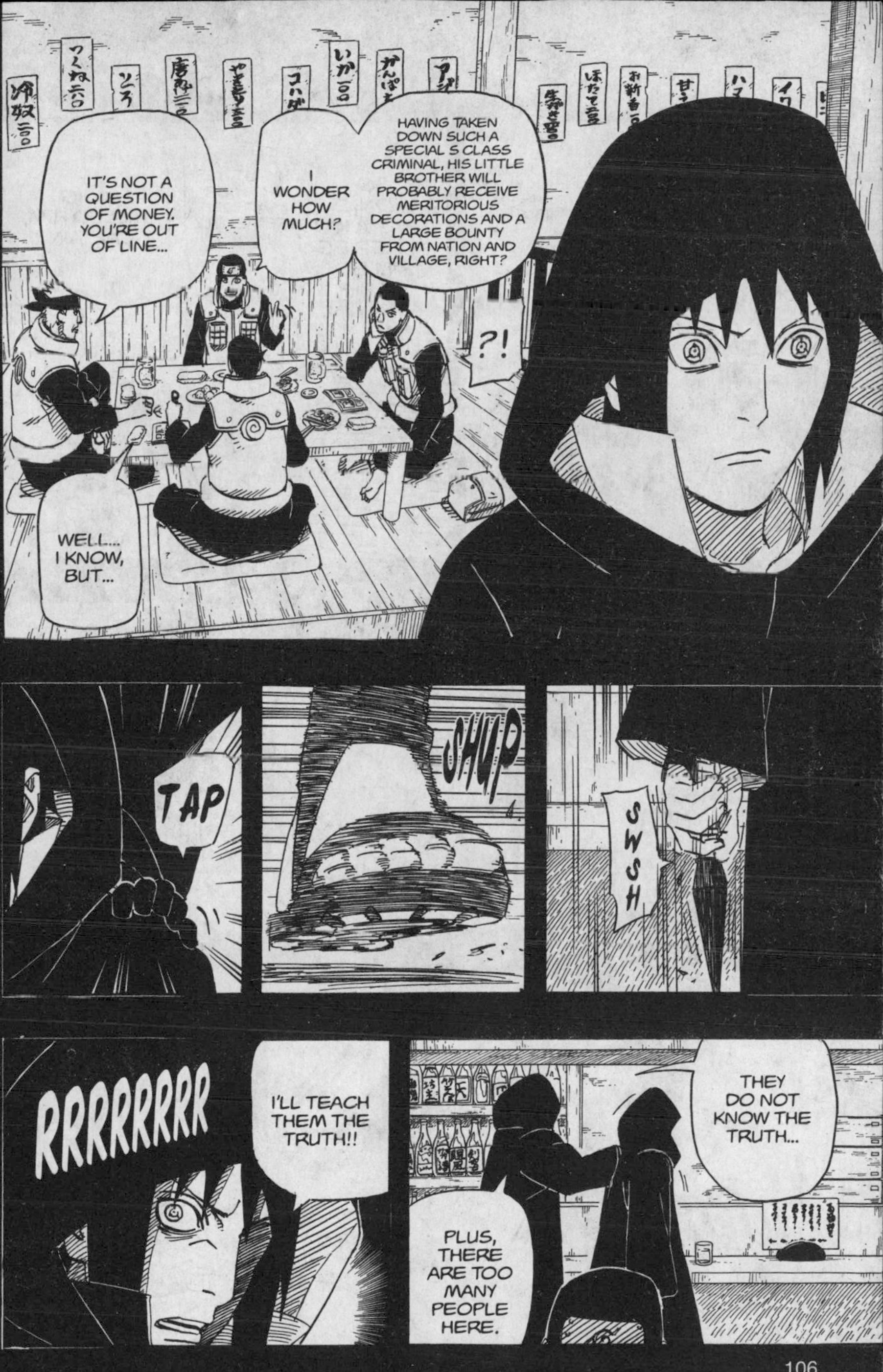
HAVING TAKEN DOWN SUCH A SPECIAL S CLASS CRIMINAL, HIS LITTLE BROTHER WILL PROBABLY RECEIVE MERITORIOUS DECORATIONS AND A LARGE BOUNTY FROM NATION AND VILLAGE, RIGHT?
I WONDER HOW MUCH?
IT'S NOT A QUESTION OF MONEY. YOU'RE OUT OF LINE...
WELL... I KNOW, BUT...
?!
SWSH
SHUP
TAP
THEY DO NOT KNOW THE TRUTH...
PLUS, THERE ARE TOO MANY PEOPLE HERE.
I'LL TEACH THEM THE TRUTH!!
RRRRRRRR

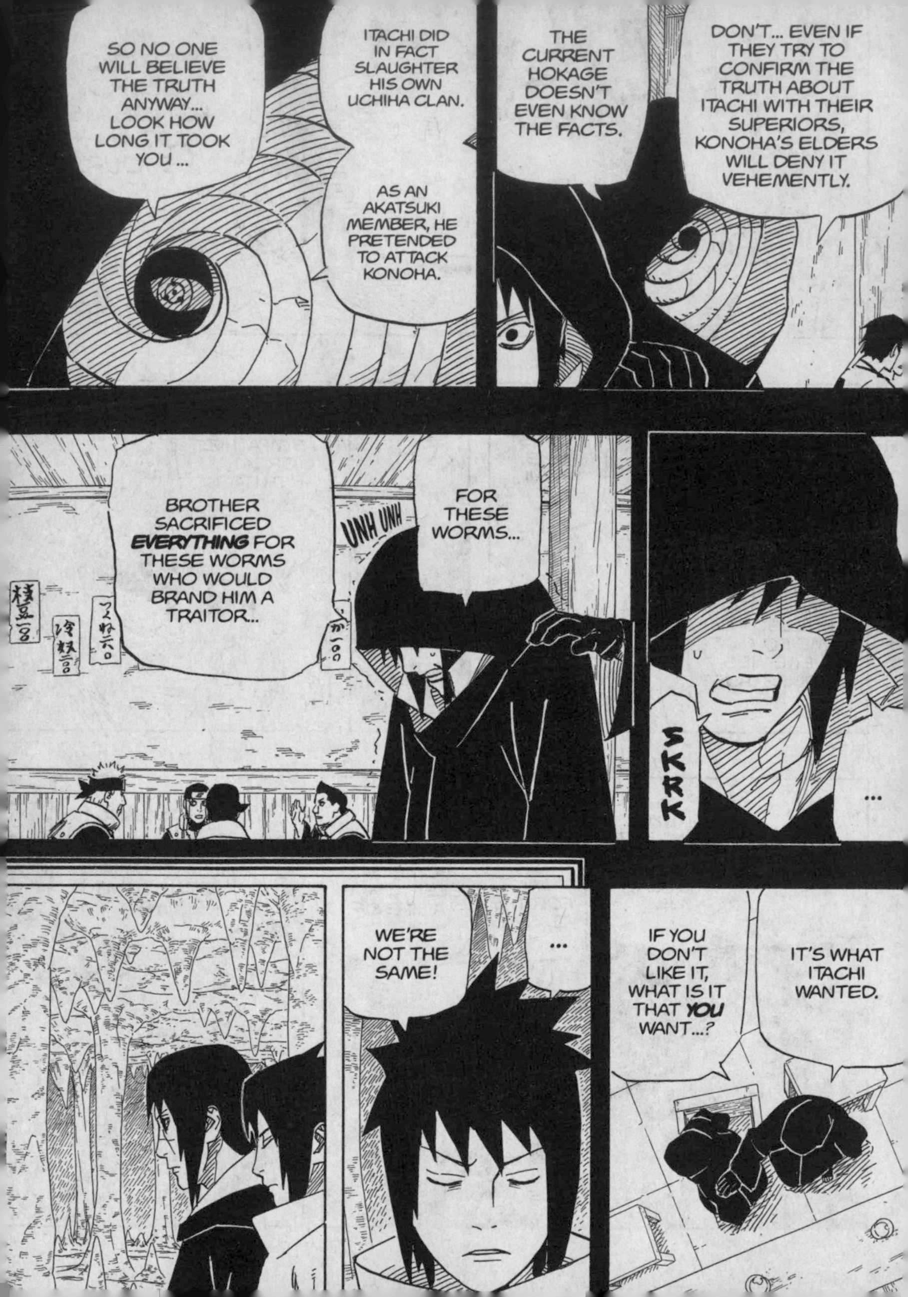
DON'T... EVEN IF THEY TRY TO CONFIRM THE TRUTH ABOUT ITACHI WITH THEIR SUPERIORS, KONOHA'S ELDERS WILL DENY IT VEHEMENTLY.
THE CURRENT HOKAGE DOESN'T EVEN KNOW THE FACTS.
ITACHI DID IN FACT SLAUGHTER HIS OWN UCHIHA CLAN.
AS AN AKATSUKI MEMBER, HE PRETENDED TO ATTACK KONOHA.
SO NO ONE WILL BELIEVE THE TRUTH ANYWAY... LOOK HOW LONG IT TOOK YOU...
...
SKRK
FOR THESE WORMS...
UNH UNH
BROTHER SACRIFICED **EVERYTHING** FOR THESE WORMS WHO WOULD BRAND HIM A TRAITOR...
IT'S WHAT ITACHI WANTED.
IF YOU DON'T LIKE IT, WHAT IS IT THAT **YOU** WANT...?
...
WE'RE NOT THE SAME!

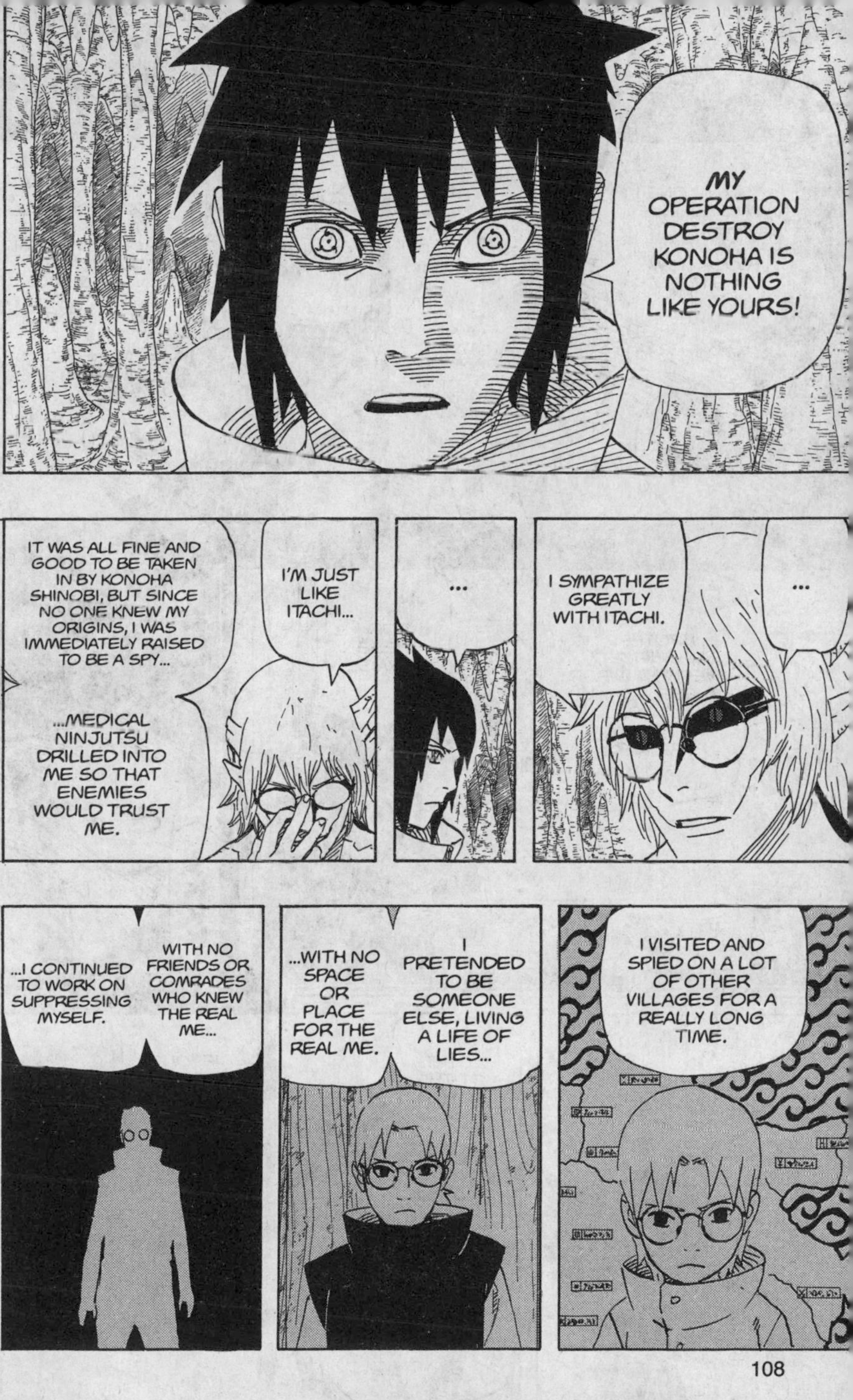
MY OPERATION DESTROY KONOHA IS NOTHING LIKE YOURS!
...
I SYMPATHIZE GREATLY WITH ITACHI.
...
I'M JUST LIKE ITACHI...
IT WAS ALL FINE AND GOOD TO BE TAKEN IN BY KONOHA SHINOBI, BUT SINCE NO ONE KNEW MY ORIGINS, I WAS IMMEDIATELY RAISED TO BE A SPY...
...MEDICAL NINJUTSU DRILLED INTO ME SO THAT ENEMIES WOULD TRUST ME.
I VISITED AND SPIED ON A LOT OF OTHER VILLAGES FOR A REALLY LONG TIME.
I PRETENDED TO BE SOMEONE ELSE, LIVING A LIFE OF LIES...
...WITH NO SPACE OR PLACE FOR THE REAL ME.
WITH NO FRIENDS OR COMRADES WHO KNEW THE REAL ME...
...I CONTINUED TO WORK ON SUPPRESSING MYSELF.

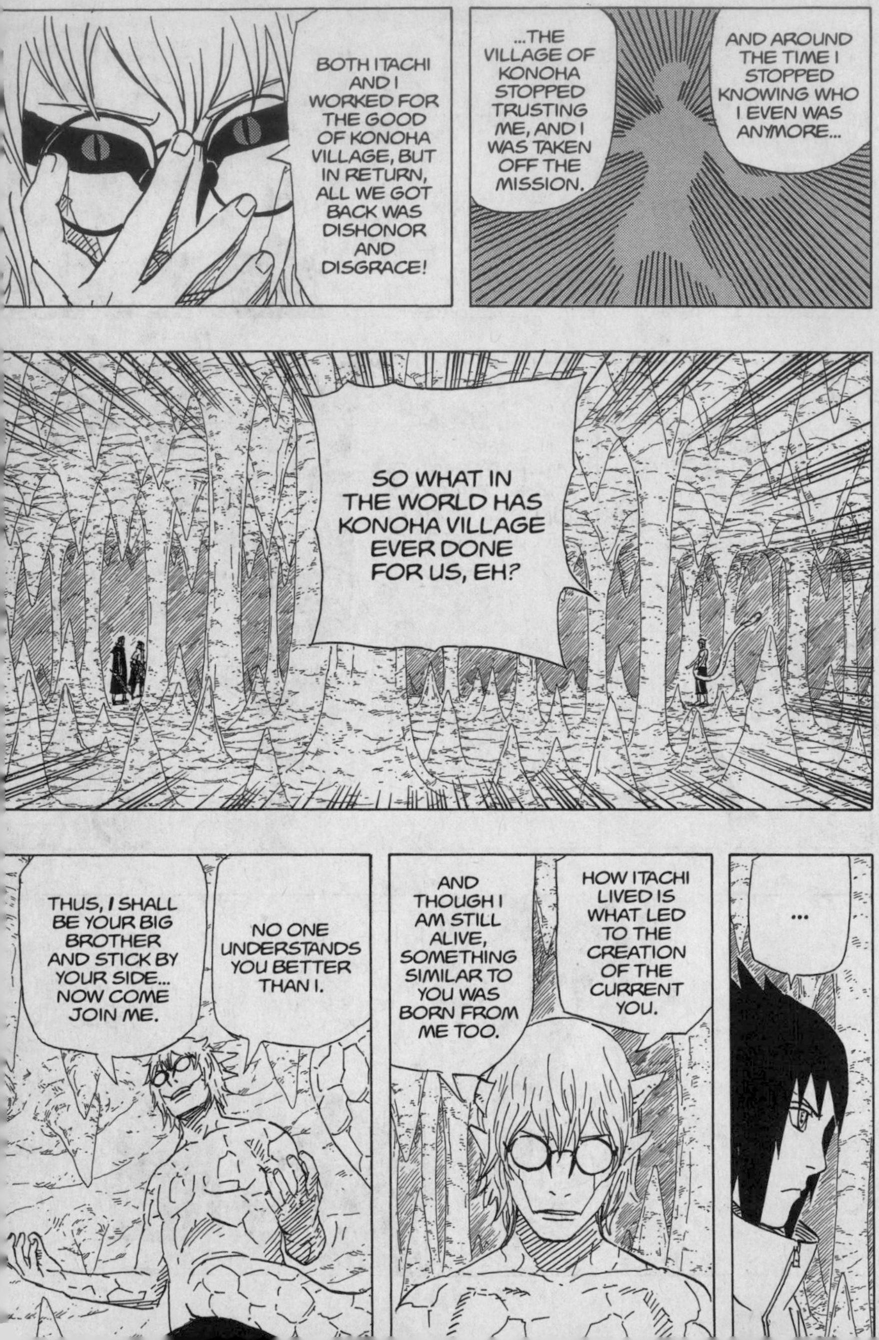
AND AROUND THE TIME I STOPPED KNOWING WHO I EVEN WAS ANYMORE...
...THE VILLAGE OF KONOHA STOPPED TRUSTING ME, AND I WAS TAKEN OFF THE MISSION.
BOTH ITACHI AND I WORKED FOR THE GOOD OF KONOHA VILLAGE, BUT IN RETURN, ALL WE GOT BACK WAS DISHONOR AND DISGRACE!
SO WHAT IN THE WORLD HAS KONOHA VILLAGE EVER DONE FOR US, EH?
...
HOW ITACHI LIVED IS WHAT LED TO THE CREATION OF THE CURRENT YOU.
AND THOUGH I AM STILL ALIVE, SOMETHING SIMILAR TO YOU WAS BORN FROM ME TOO.
NO ONE UNDERSTANDS YOU BETTER THAN I.
THUS, I SHALL BE YOUR BIG BROTHER AND STICK BY YOUR SIDE... NOW COME JOIN ME.

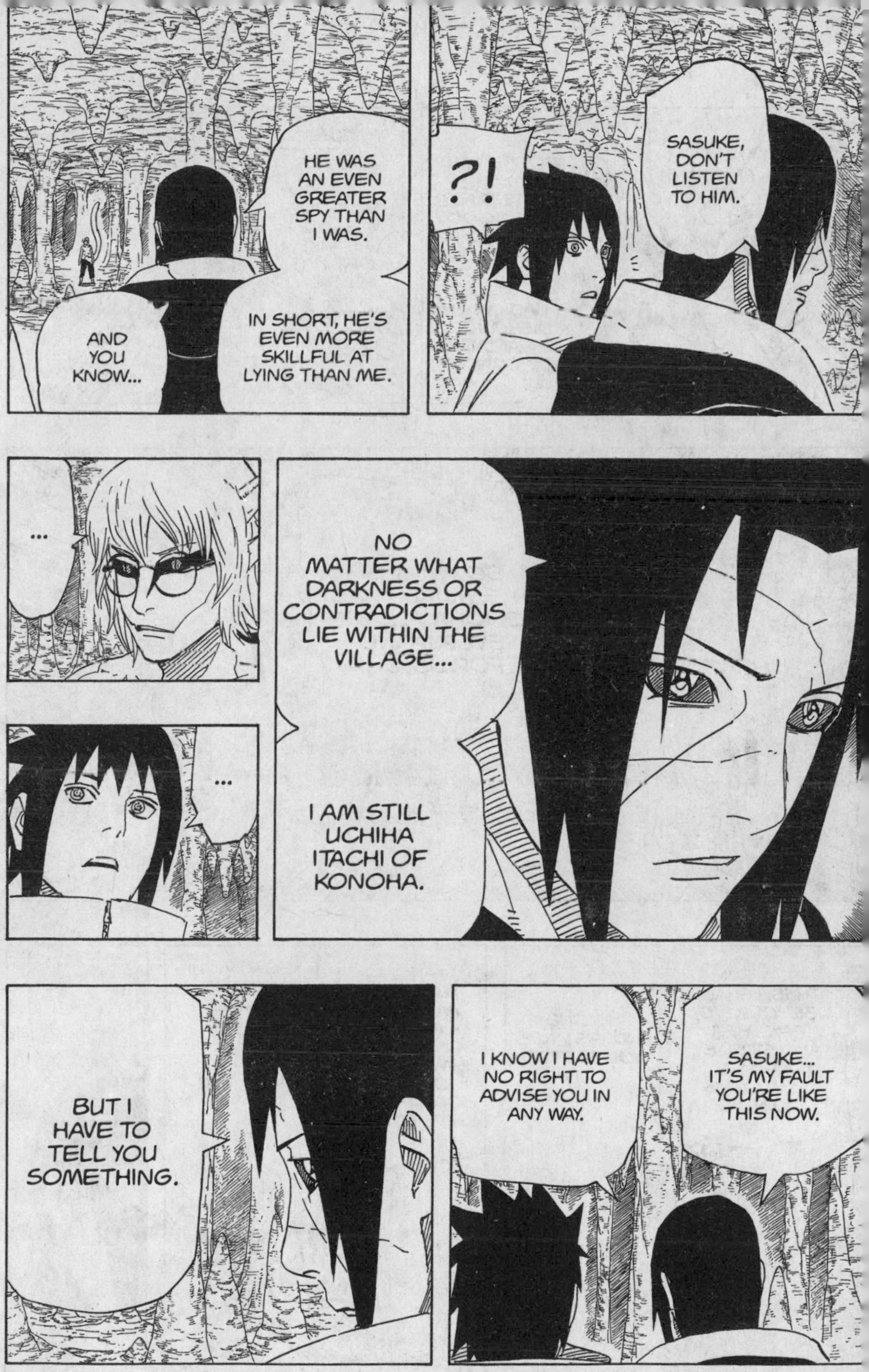
SASUKE, DON'T LISTEN TO HIM.
?!
HE WAS AN EVEN GREATER SPY THAN I WAS.
IN SHORT, HE'S EVEN MORE SKILLFUL AT LYING THAN ME.
AND YOU KNOW...
NO MATTER WHAT DARKNESS OR CONTRADICTIONS LIE WITHIN THE VILLAGE...
I AM STILL UCHIHA ITACHI OF KONOHA.
...
...
SASUKE... IT'S MY FAULT YOU'RE LIKE THIS NOW.
I KNOW I HAVE NO RIGHT TO ADVISE YOU IN ANY WAY.
BUT I HAVE TO TELL YOU SOMETHING.

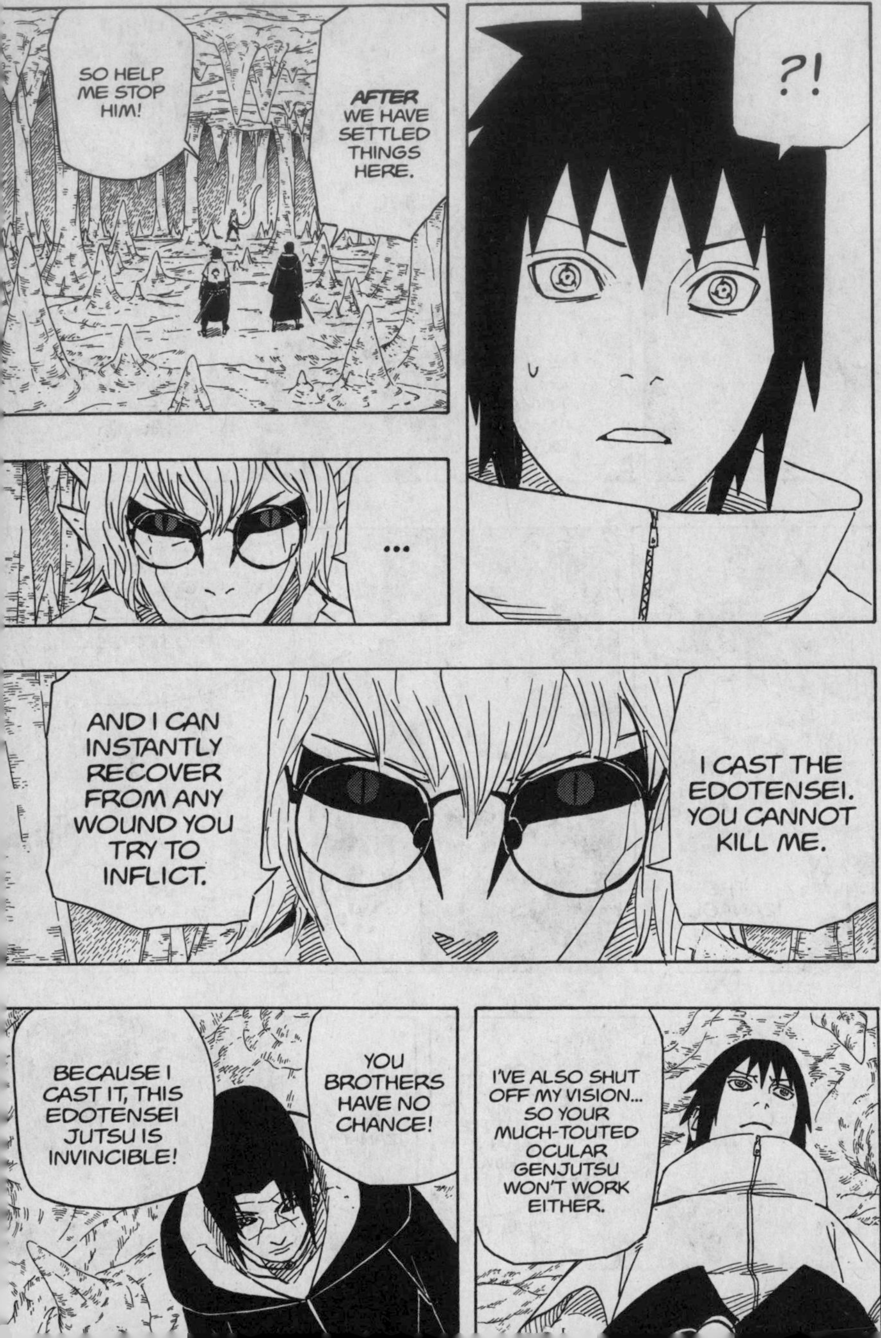
?!
AFTER WE HAVE SETTLED THINGS HERE.
SO HELP ME STOP HIM!
...
I CAST THE EDOTENSEI. YOU CANNOT KILL ME.
AND I CAN INSTANTLY RECOVER FROM ANY WOUND YOU TRY TO INFLICT.
I'VE ALSO SHUT OFF MY VISION... SO YOUR MUCH-TOUTED OCULAR GENJUTSU WON'T WORK EITHER.
YOU BROTHERS HAVE NO CHANCE!
BECAUSE I CAST IT, THIS EDOTENSEI JUTSU IS INVINCIBLE!

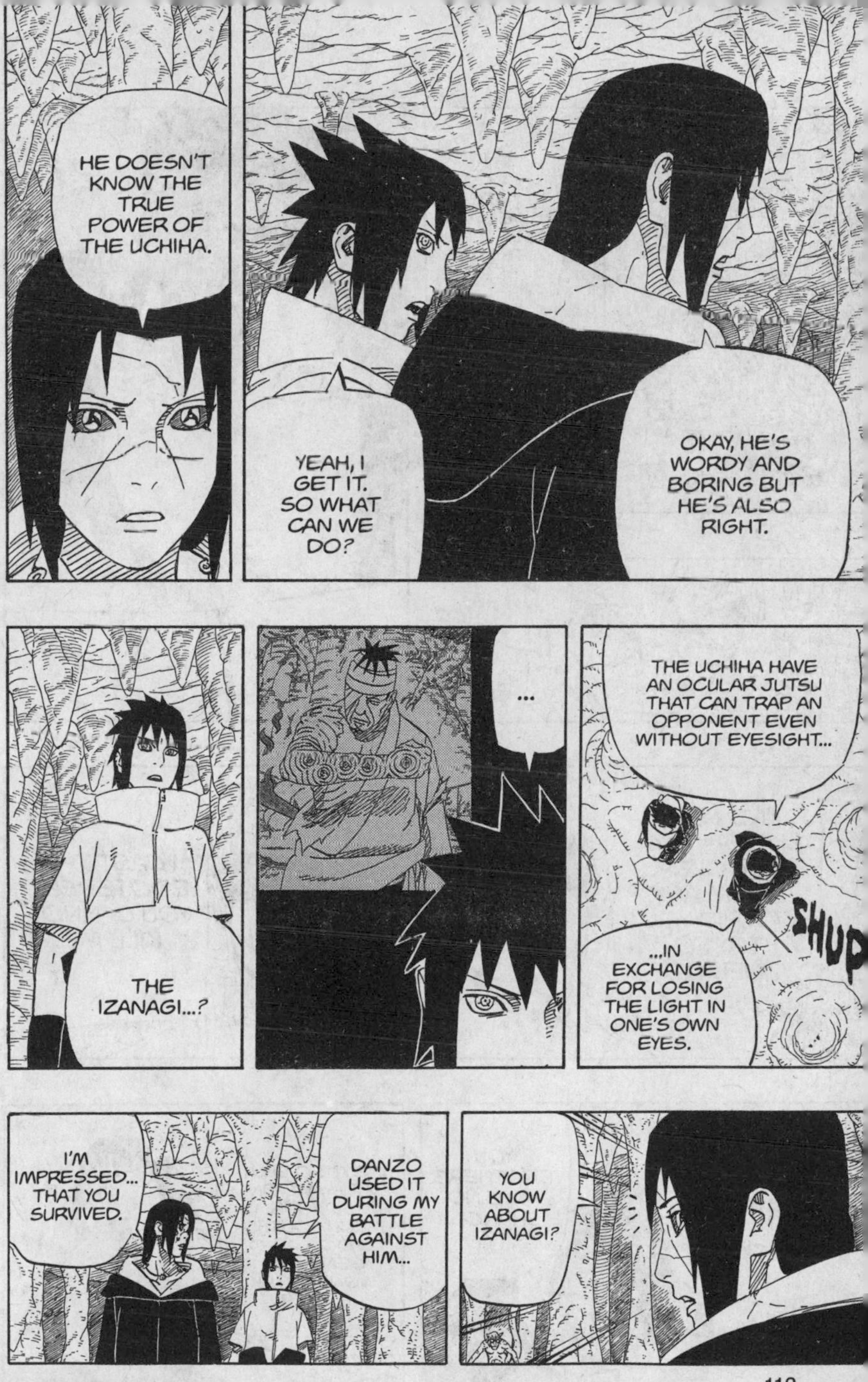
OKAY, HE'S WORDY AND BORING BUT HE'S ALSO RIGHT.
YEAH, I GET IT. SO WHAT CAN WE DO?
HE DOESN'T KNOW THE TRUE POWER OF THE UCHIHA.
THE UCHIHA HAVE AN OCULAR JUTSU THAT CAN TRAP AN OPPONENT EVEN WITHOUT EYESIGHT...
SHUP
...IN EXCHANGE FOR LOSING THE LIGHT IN ONE'S OWN EYES.
...
THE IZANAGI...?
YOU KNOW ABOUT IZANAGI?
DANZO USED IT DURING MY BATTLE AGAINST HIM...
I'M IMPRESSED... THAT YOU SURVIVED.

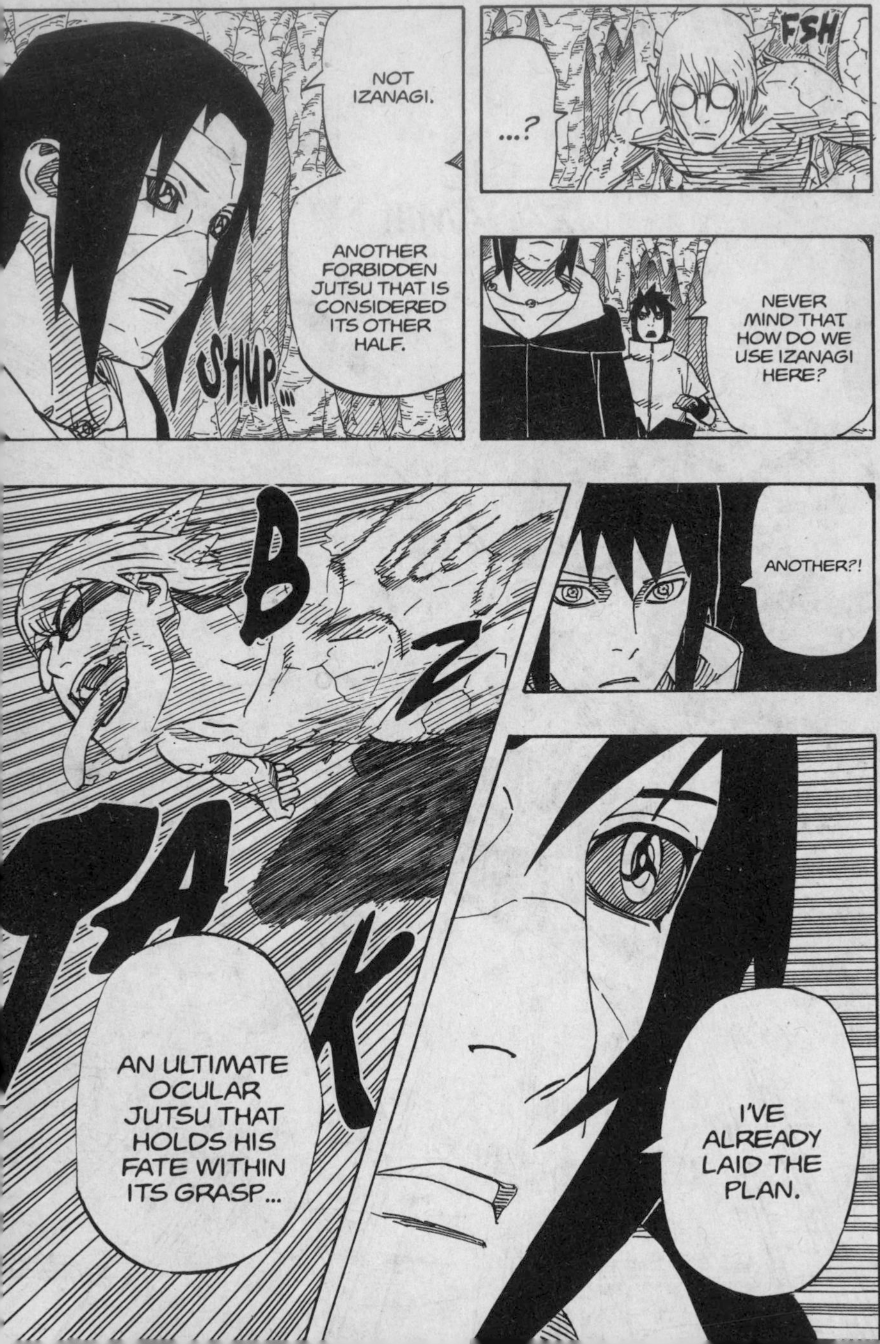

FSH
...?
NEVER MIND THAT. HOW DO WE USE IZANAGI HERE?
NOT IZANAGI.
ANOTHER FORBIDDEN JUTSU THAT IS CONSIDERED ITS OTHER HALF.
SHUP...
ANOTHER?!
I'VE ALREADY LAID THE PLAN.
BZ
TAK
AN ULTIMATE OCULAR JUTSU THAT HOLDS HIS FATE WITHIN ITS GRASP...

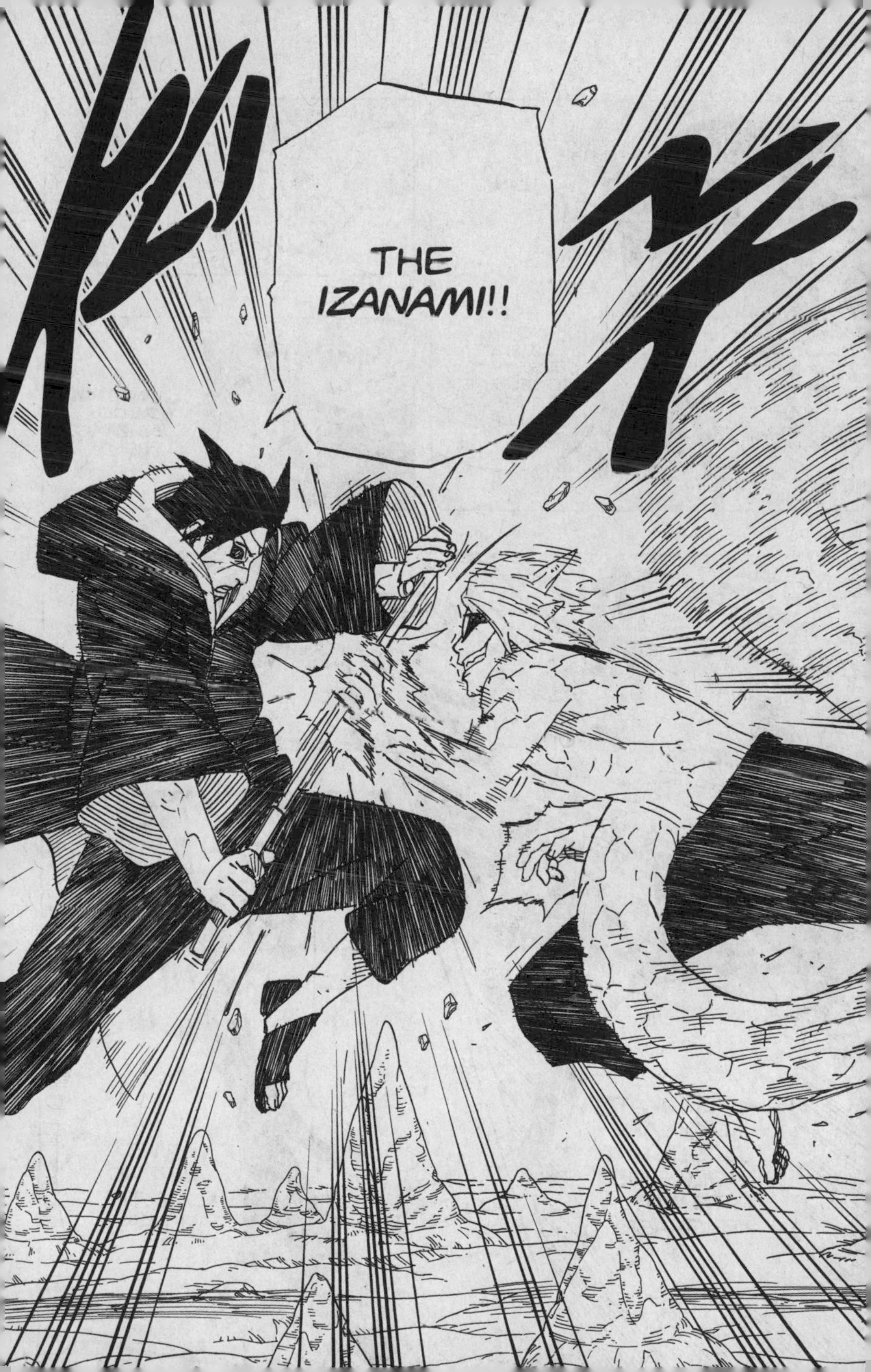
THE IZANAMI!!

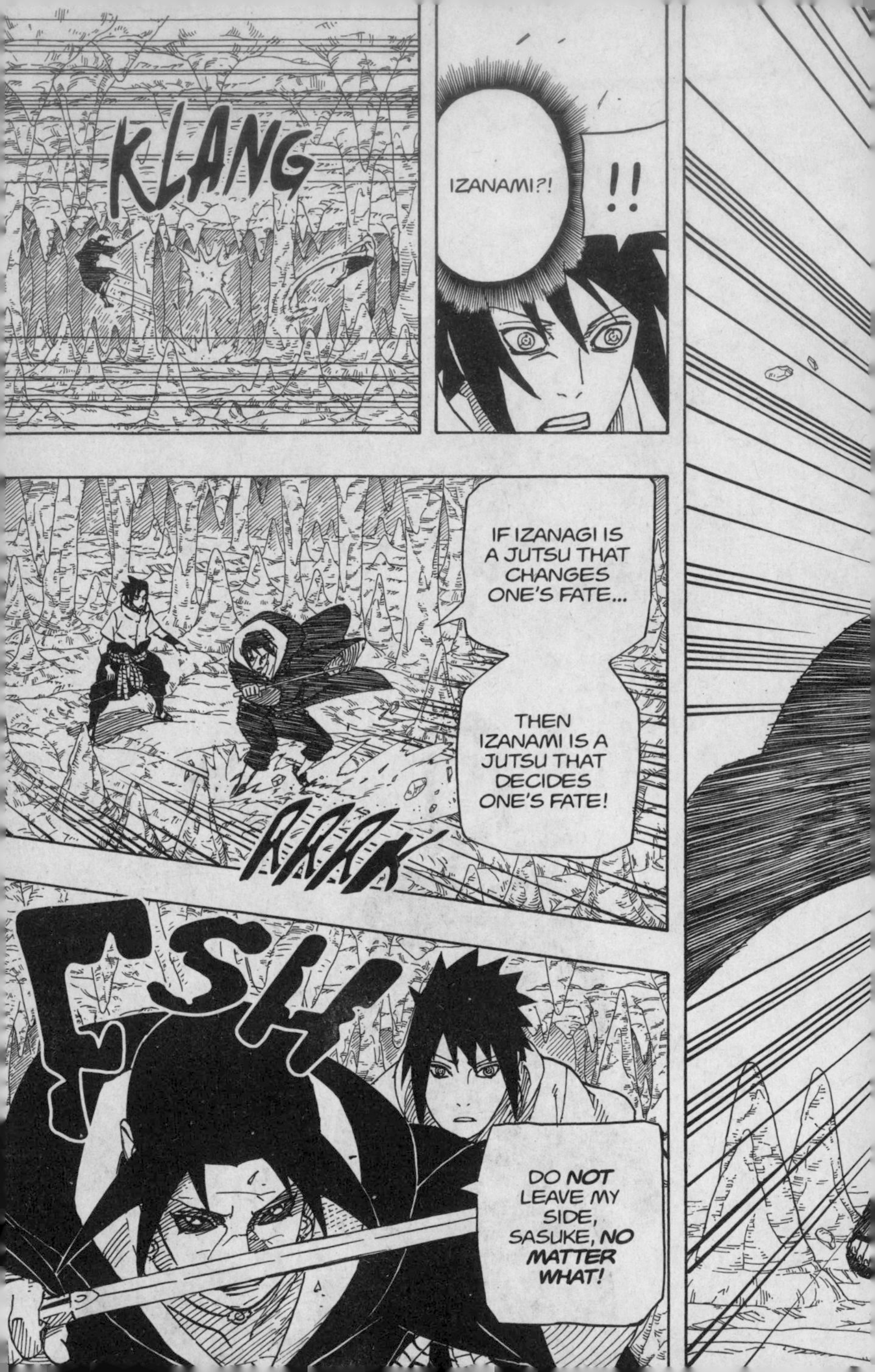
!!
IZANAMI?!
KLANG
IF IZANAGI IS A JUTSU THAT CHANGES ONE'S FATE...
THEN IZANAMI IS A JUTSU THAT DECIDES ONE'S FATE!
RRRK
FSH
DO **NOT** LEAVE MY SIDE, SASUKE, **NO** ***MATTER WHAT!***

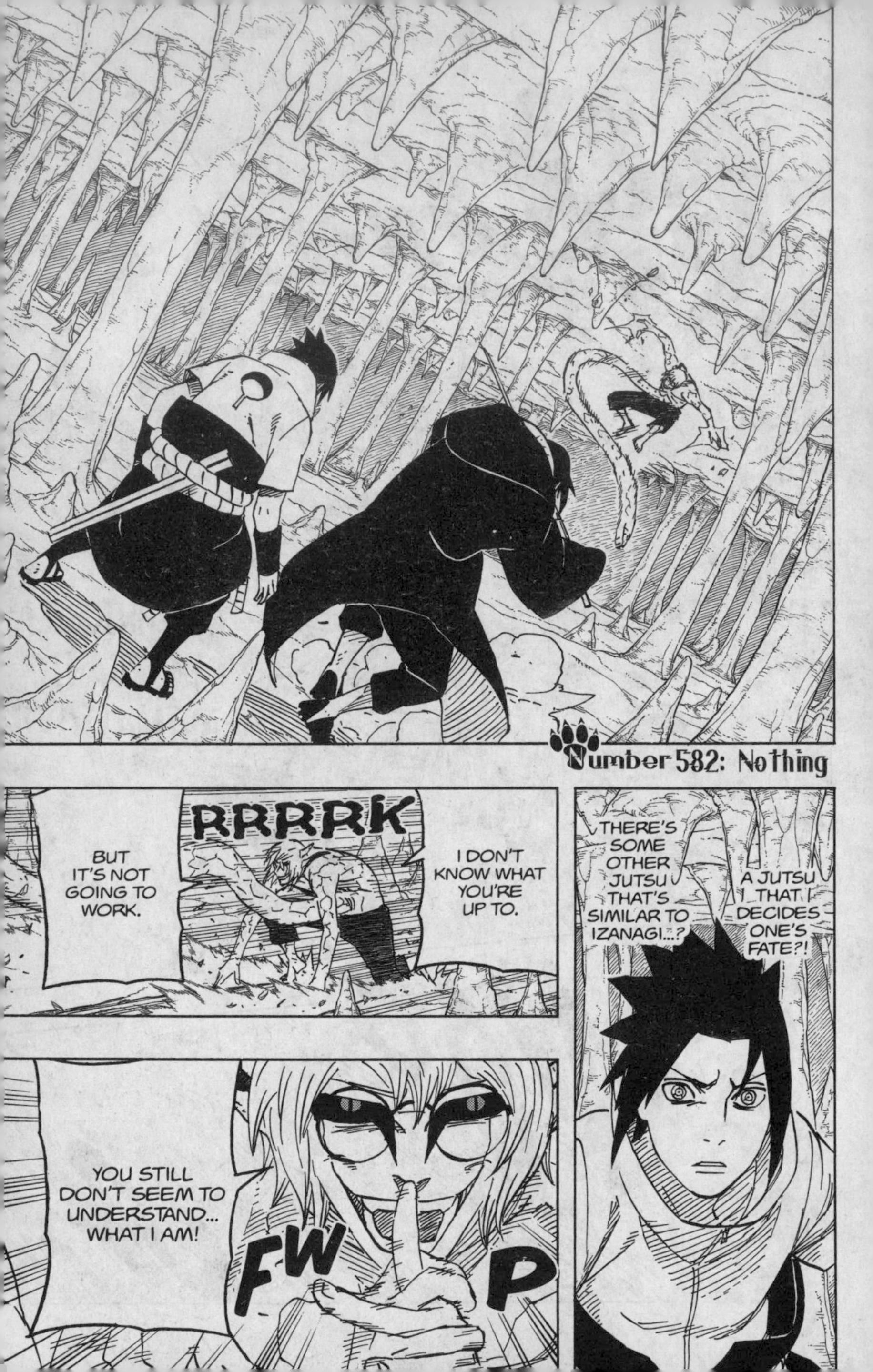
Number 582: Nothing
THERE'S SOME OTHER JUTSU THAT'S SIMILAR TO IZANAGI...?
A JUTSU THAT DECIDES ONE'S FATE?!
RRRRK
I DON'T KNOW WHAT YOU'RE UP TO.
BUT IT'S NOT GOING TO WORK.
FW P
YOU STILL DON'T SEEM TO UNDERSTAND... WHAT I AM!

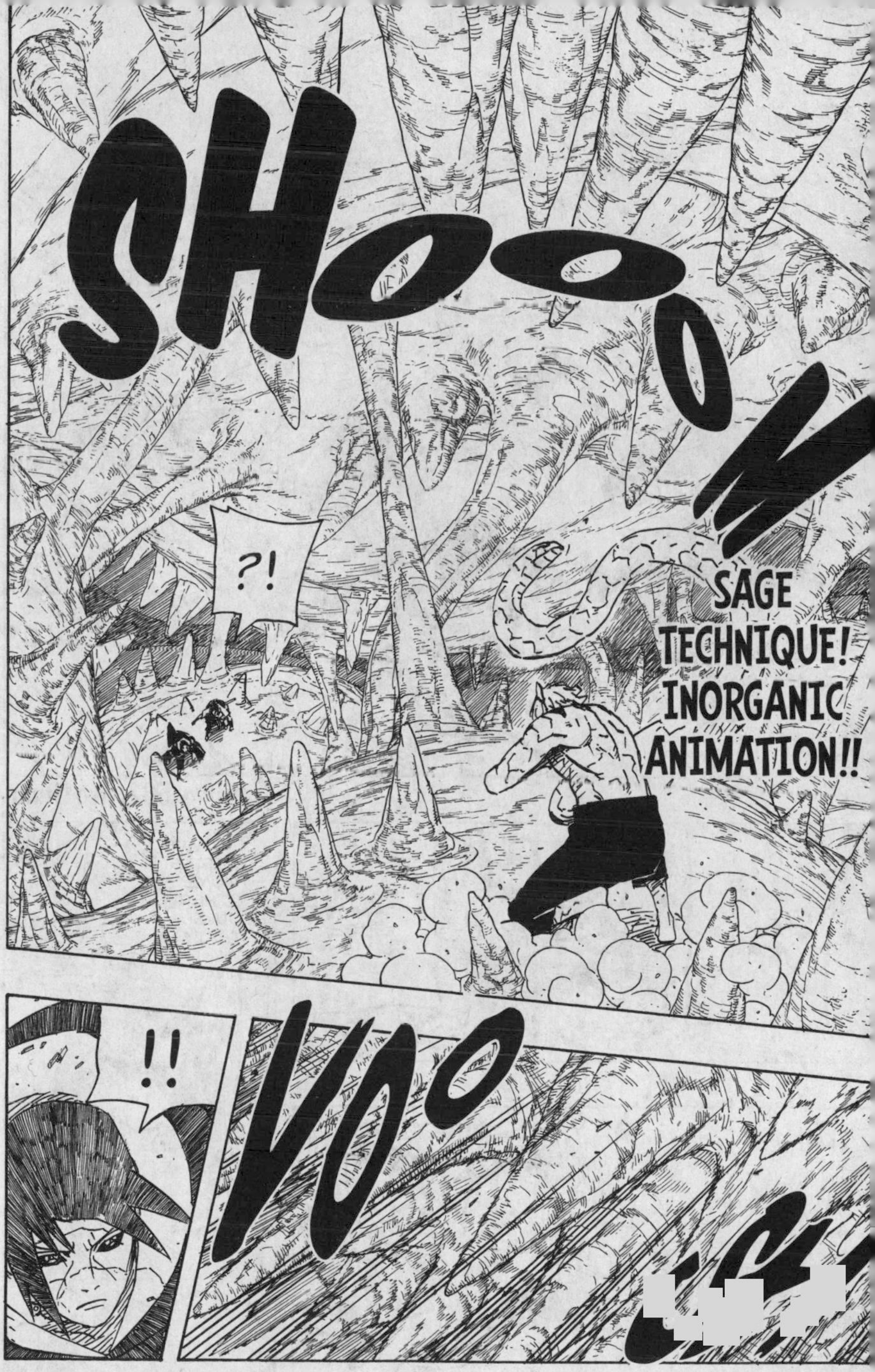
SHOOOON
SAGE TECHNIQUE! INORGANIC ANIMATION!!
?!
VOO
!!

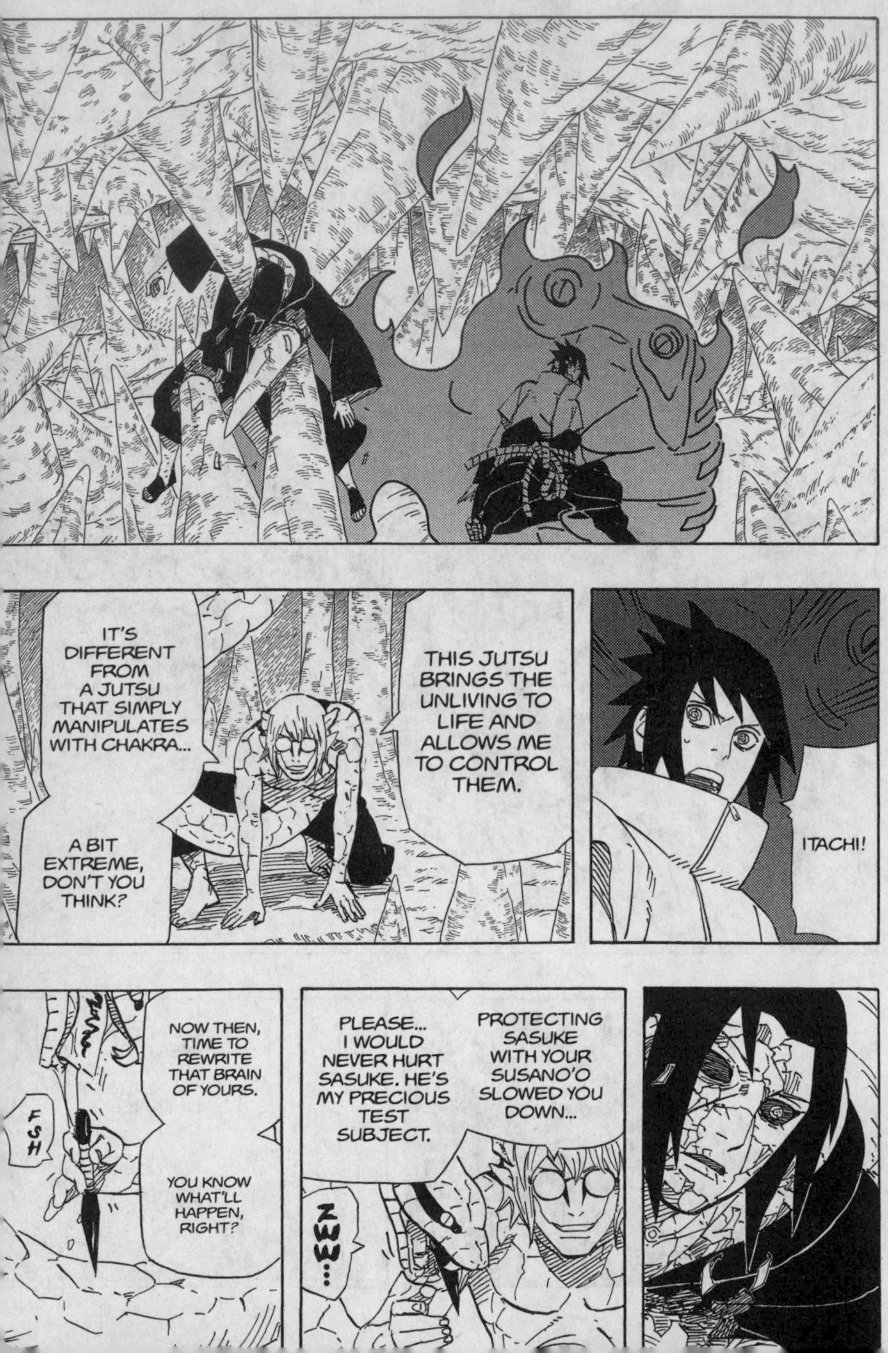
ITACHI!
THIS JUTSU BRINGS THE UNLIVING TO LIFE AND ALLOWS ME TO CONTROL THEM.
IT'S DIFFERENT FROM A JUTSU THAT SIMPLY MANIPULATES WITH CHAKRA...
A BIT EXTREME, DON'T YOU THINK?
PROTECTING SASUKE WITH YOUR SUSANO'O SLOWED YOU DOWN...
PLEASE... I WOULD NEVER HURT SASUKE. HE'S MY PRECIOUS TEST SUBJECT.
ZWW...
NOW THEN, TIME TO REWRITE THAT BRAIN OF YOURS.
YOU KNOW WHAT'LL HAPPEN, RIGHT?
FSH

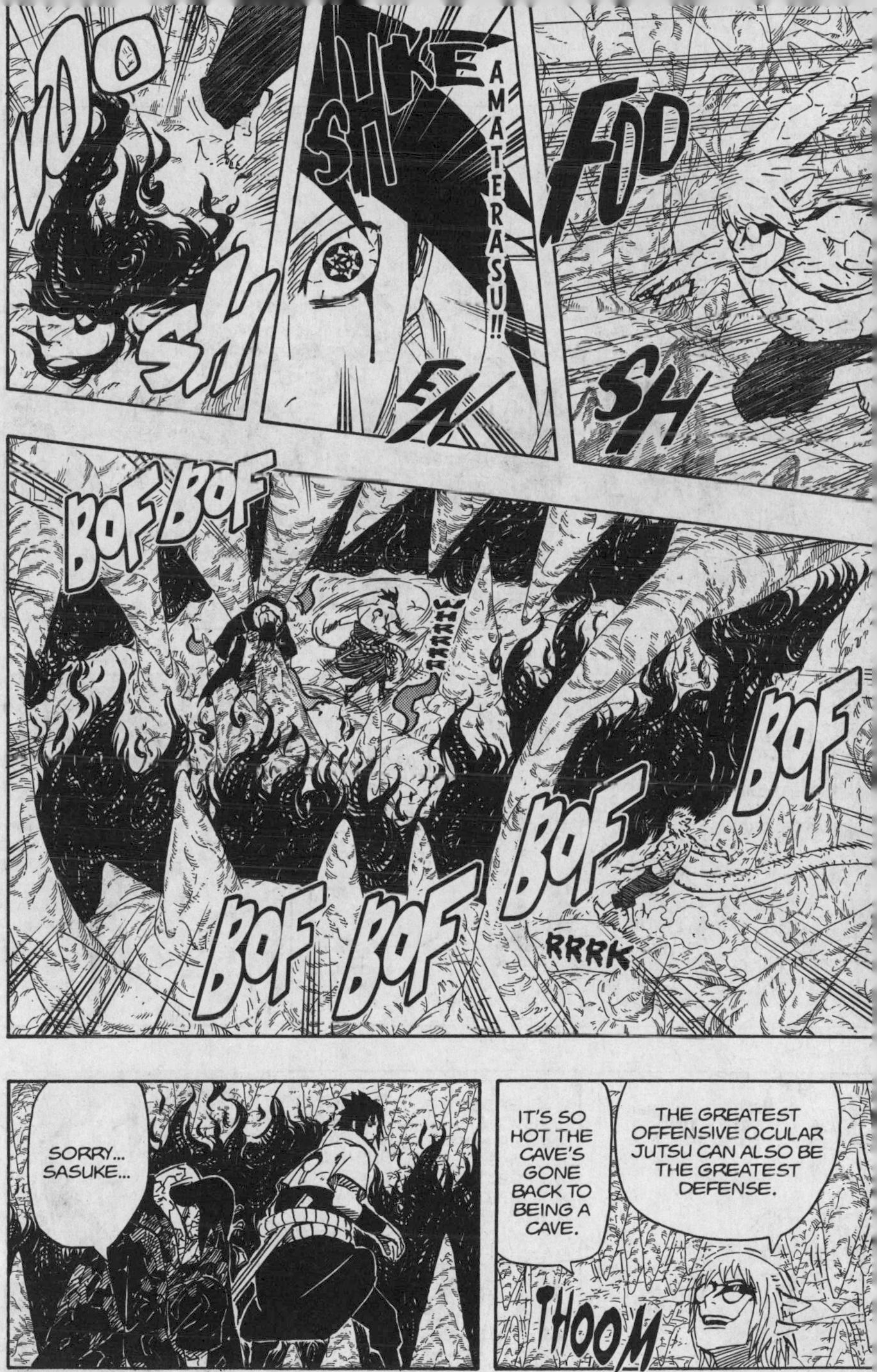
FOD
SH
AMATERASU!!
SHIKE
EN
VOO
SH
BOF
BOF
BOF
BOF
BOF BOF
BOF BOF
WHRRRR
RRRK
THE GREATEST OFFENSIVE OCULAR JUTSU CAN ALSO BE THE GREATEST DEFENSE.
IT'S SO HOT THE CAVE'S GONE BACK TO BEING A CAVE.
THOOM
SORRY... SASUKE...

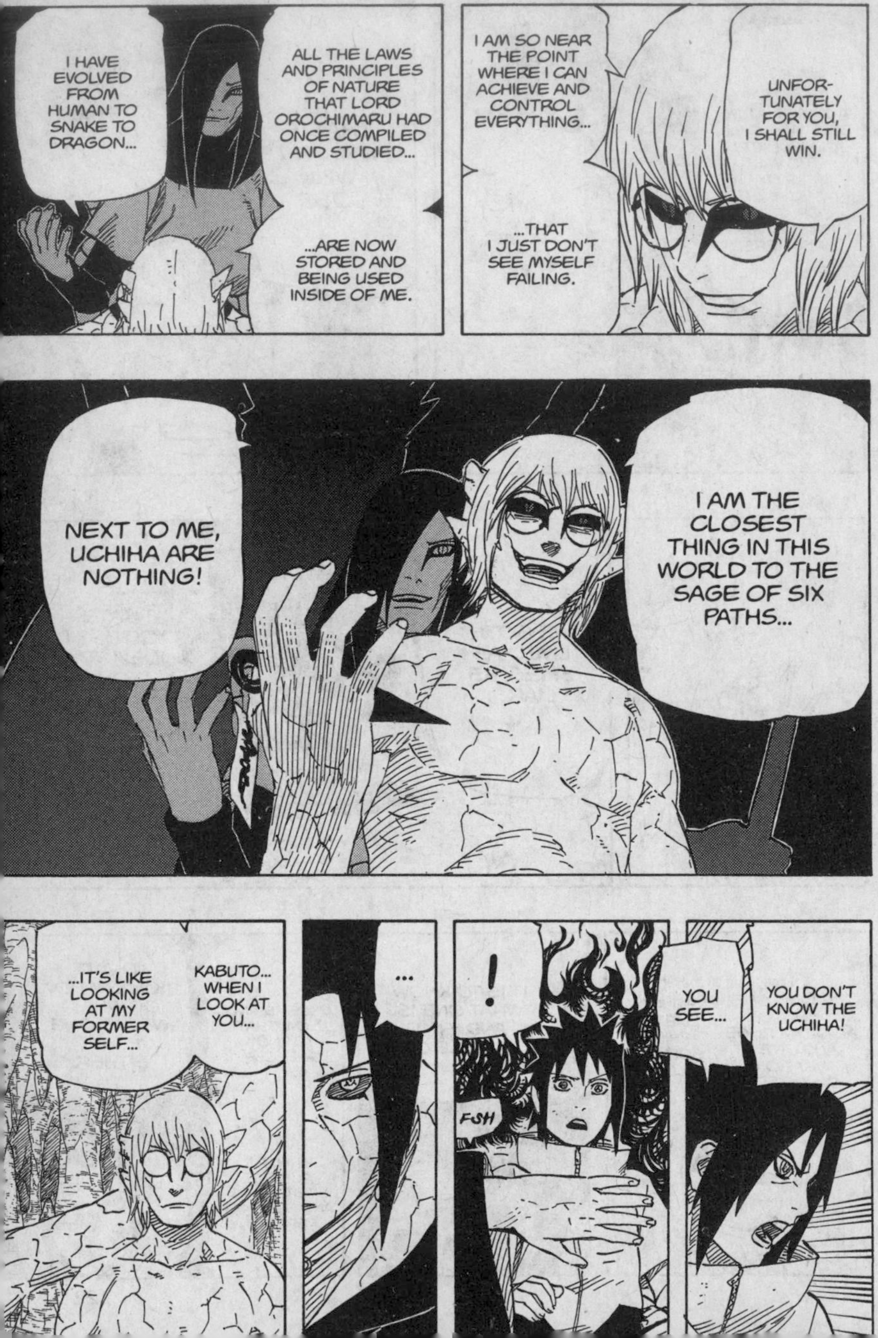
UNFORTUNATELY FOR YOU, I SHALL STILL WIN.
I AM SO NEAR THE POINT WHERE I CAN ACHIEVE AND CONTROL EVERYTHING...
...THAT I JUST DON'T SEE MYSELF FAILING.
ALL THE LAWS AND PRINCIPLES OF NATURE THAT LORD OROCHIMARU HAD ONCE COMPILED AND STUDIED...
...ARE NOW STORED AND BEING USED INSIDE OF ME.
I HAVE EVOLVED FROM HUMAN TO SNAKE TO DRAGON...
I AM THE CLOSEST THING IN THIS WORLD TO THE SAGE OF SIX PATHS...
NEXT TO ME, UCHIHA ARE NOTHING!
YOU DON'T KNOW THE UCHIHA!
YOU SEE...
!
FSH
...
KABUTO... WHEN I LOOK AT YOU...
...IT'S LIKE LOOKING AT MY FORMER SELF...

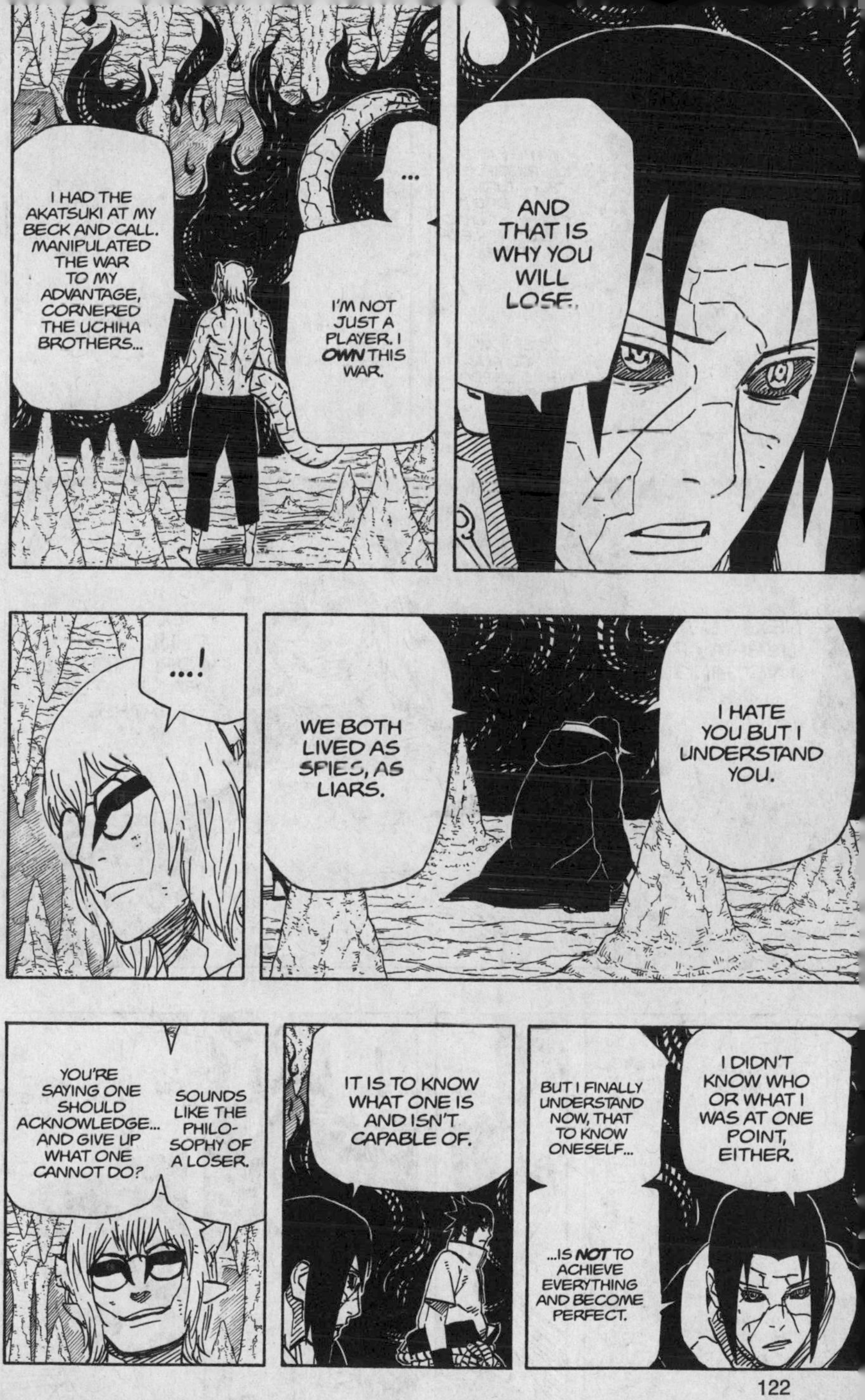
AND THAT IS WHY YOU WILL LOSE.
...
I'M NOT JUST A PLAYER. I **OWN** THIS WAR.
I HAD THE AKATSUKI AT MY BECK AND CALL. MANIPULATED THE WAR TO MY ADVANTAGE, CORNERED THE UCHIHA BROTHERS...
I HATE YOU BUT I UNDERSTAND YOU.
WE BOTH LIVED AS SPIES, AS LIARS.
...!
I DIDN'T KNOW WHO OR WHAT I WAS AT ONE POINT, EITHER.
BUT I FINALLY UNDERSTAND NOW, THAT TO KNOW ONESELF...
...IS **NOT** TO ACHIEVE EVERYTHING AND BECOME PERFECT.
IT IS TO KNOW WHAT ONE IS AND ISN'T CAPABLE OF.
SOUNDS LIKE THE PHILO-SOPHY OF A LOSER.
YOU'RE SAYING ONE SHOULD ACKNOWLEDGE... AND GIVE UP WHAT ONE CANNOT DO?

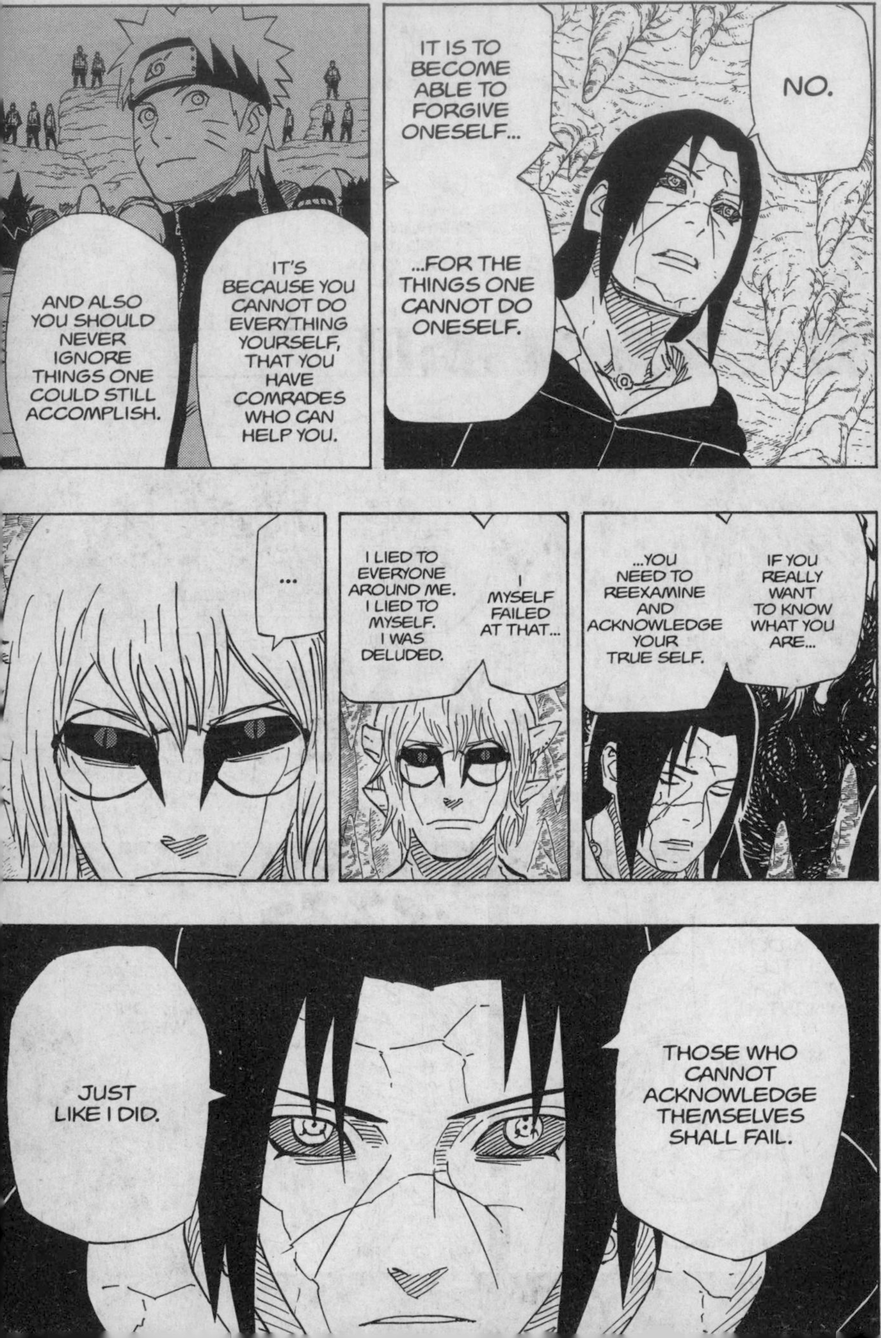
NO.
IT IS TO BECOME ABLE TO FORGIVE ONESELF...
...FOR THE THINGS ONE CANNOT DO ONESELF.
IT'S BECAUSE YOU CANNOT DO EVERYTHING YOURSELF, THAT YOU HAVE COMRADES WHO CAN HELP YOU.
AND ALSO YOU SHOULD NEVER IGNORE THINGS ONE COULD STILL ACCOMPLISH.
IF YOU REALLY WANT TO KNOW WHAT YOU ARE...
...YOU NEED TO REEXAMINE AND ACKNOWLEDGE YOUR TRUE SELF.
I MYSELF FAILED AT THAT...
I LIED TO EVERYONE AROUND ME. I LIED TO MYSELF. I WAS DELUDED.
...
THOSE WHO CANNOT ACKNOWLEDGE THEMSELVES SHALL FAIL.
JUST LIKE I DID.

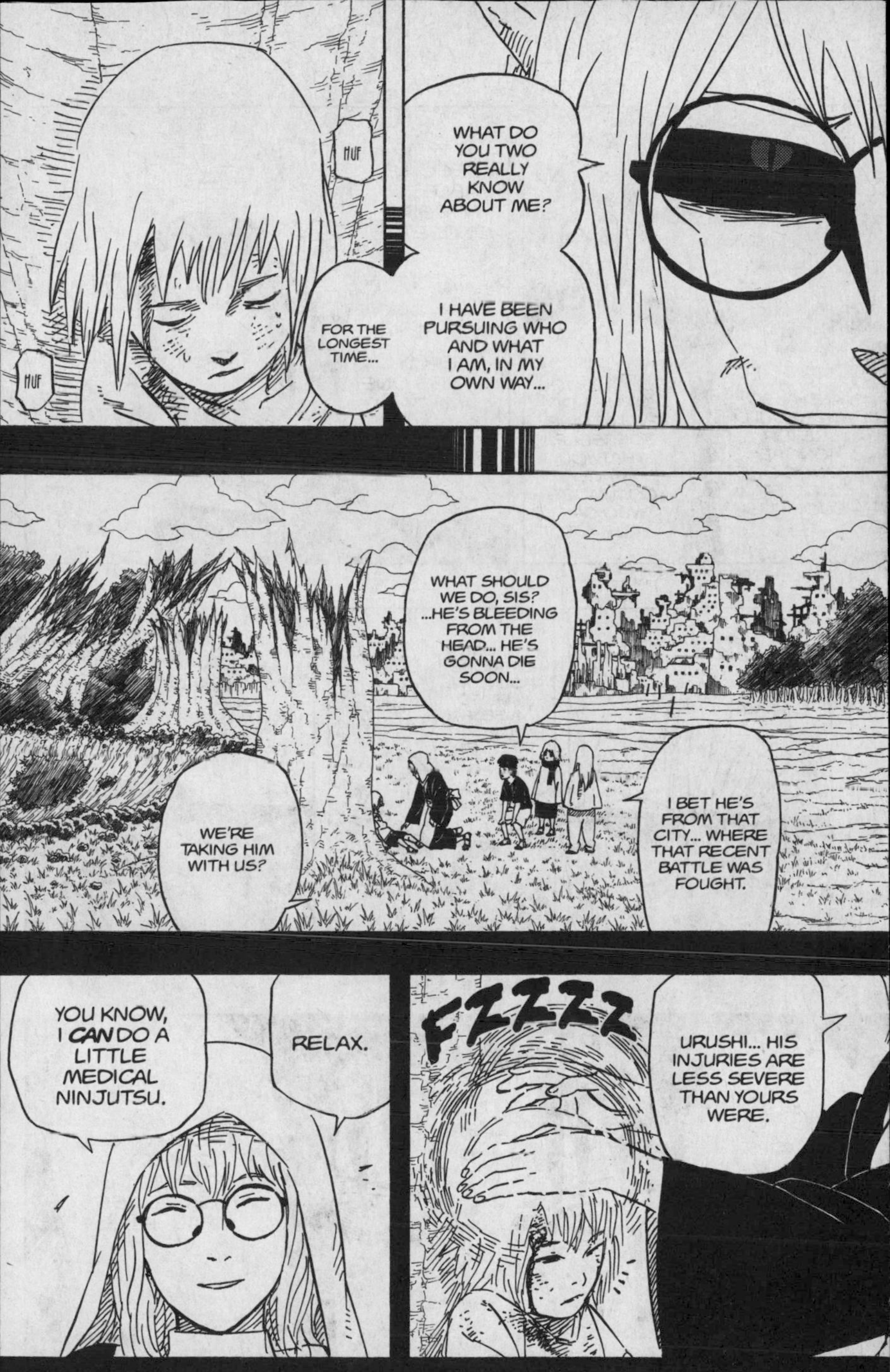
WHAT DO YOU TWO REALLY KNOW ABOUT ME?
I HAVE BEEN PURSUING WHO AND WHAT I AM, IN MY OWN WAY...
FOR THE LONGEST TIME...
HUF
HUF
WHAT SHOULD WE DO, SIS? ...HE'S BLEEDING FROM THE HEAD... HE'S GONNA DIE SOON...
I BET HE'S FROM THAT CITY... WHERE THAT RECENT BATTLE WAS FOUGHT.
WE'RE TAKING HIM WITH US?
FZZZZ
URUSHI... HIS INJURIES ARE LESS SEVERE THAN YOURS WERE.
RELAX.
YOU KNOW, I **CAN** DO A LITTLE MEDICAL NINJUTSU.

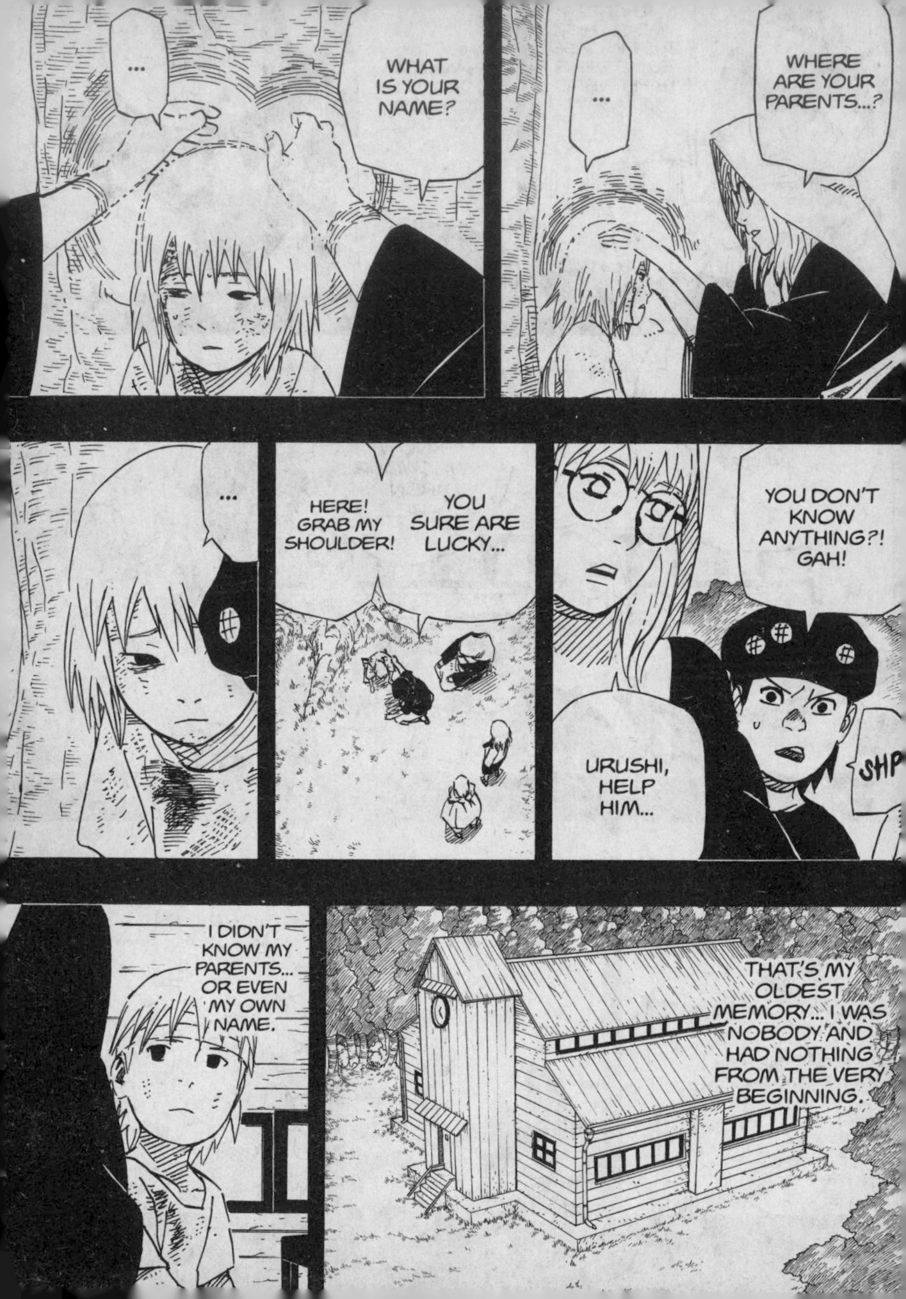
WHERE ARE YOUR PARENTS...?
...
WHAT IS YOUR NAME?
...
YOU DON'T KNOW ANYTHING?! GAH!
SHP
URUSHI, HELP HIM...
YOU SURE ARE LUCKY...
HERE! GRAB MY SHOULDER!
...
THAT'S MY OLDEST MEMORY... I WAS NOBODY AND HAD NOTHING FROM THE VERY BEGINNING.
I DIDN'T KNOW MY PARENTS... OR EVEN MY OWN NAME.

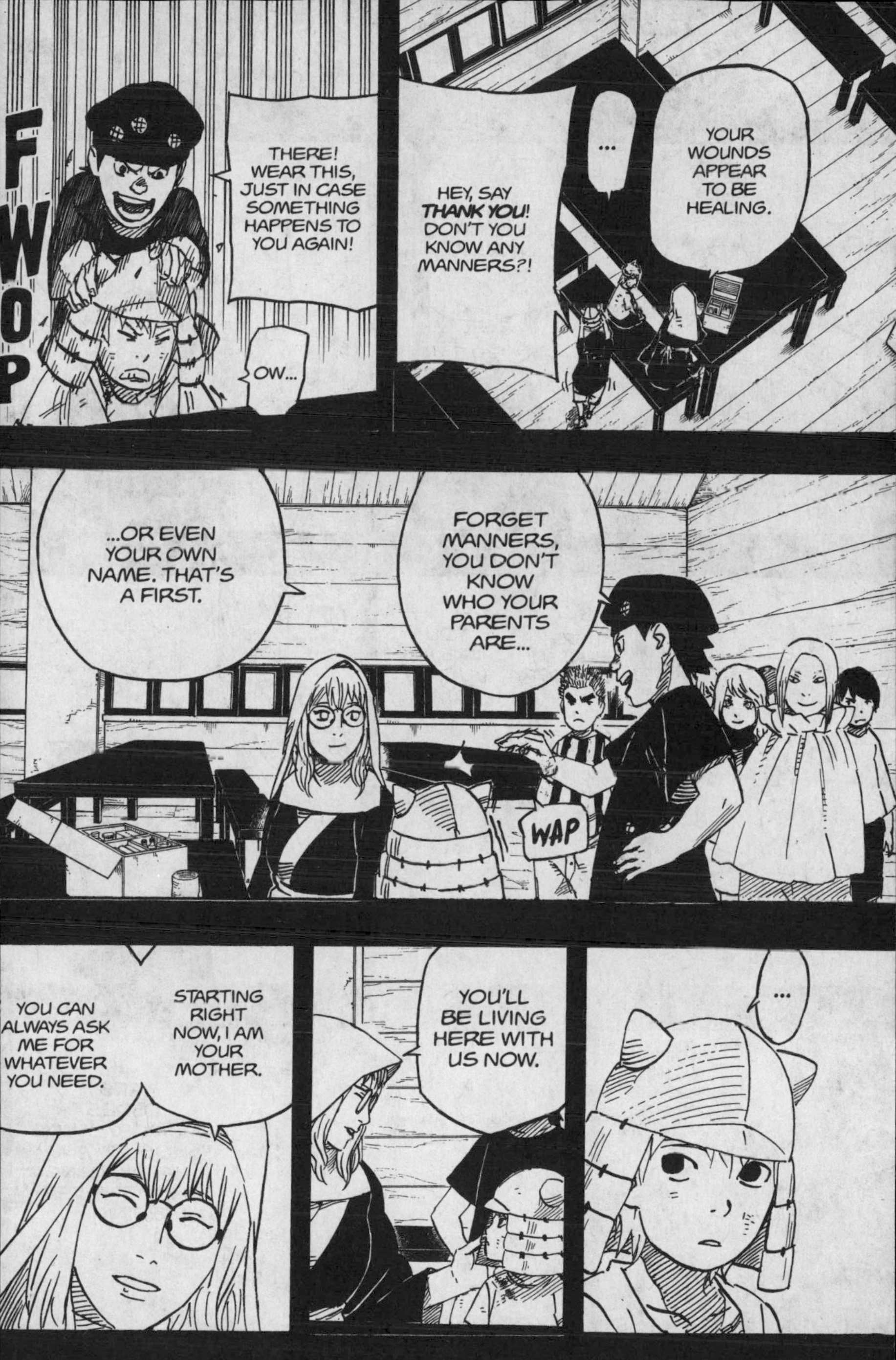
YOUR WOUNDS APPEAR TO BE HEALING.
...
HEY, SAY **THANK YOU**! DON'T YOU KNOW ANY MANNERS?!
FWOP
THERE! WEAR THIS, JUST IN CASE SOMETHING HAPPENS TO YOU AGAIN!
OW...
FORGET MANNERS, YOU DON'T KNOW WHO YOUR PARENTS ARE...
...OR EVEN YOUR OWN NAME. THAT'S A FIRST.
WAP
...
YOU'LL BE LIVING HERE WITH US NOW.
STARTING RIGHT NOW, I AM YOUR MOTHER.
YOU CAN ALWAYS ASK ME FOR WHATEVER YOU NEED.

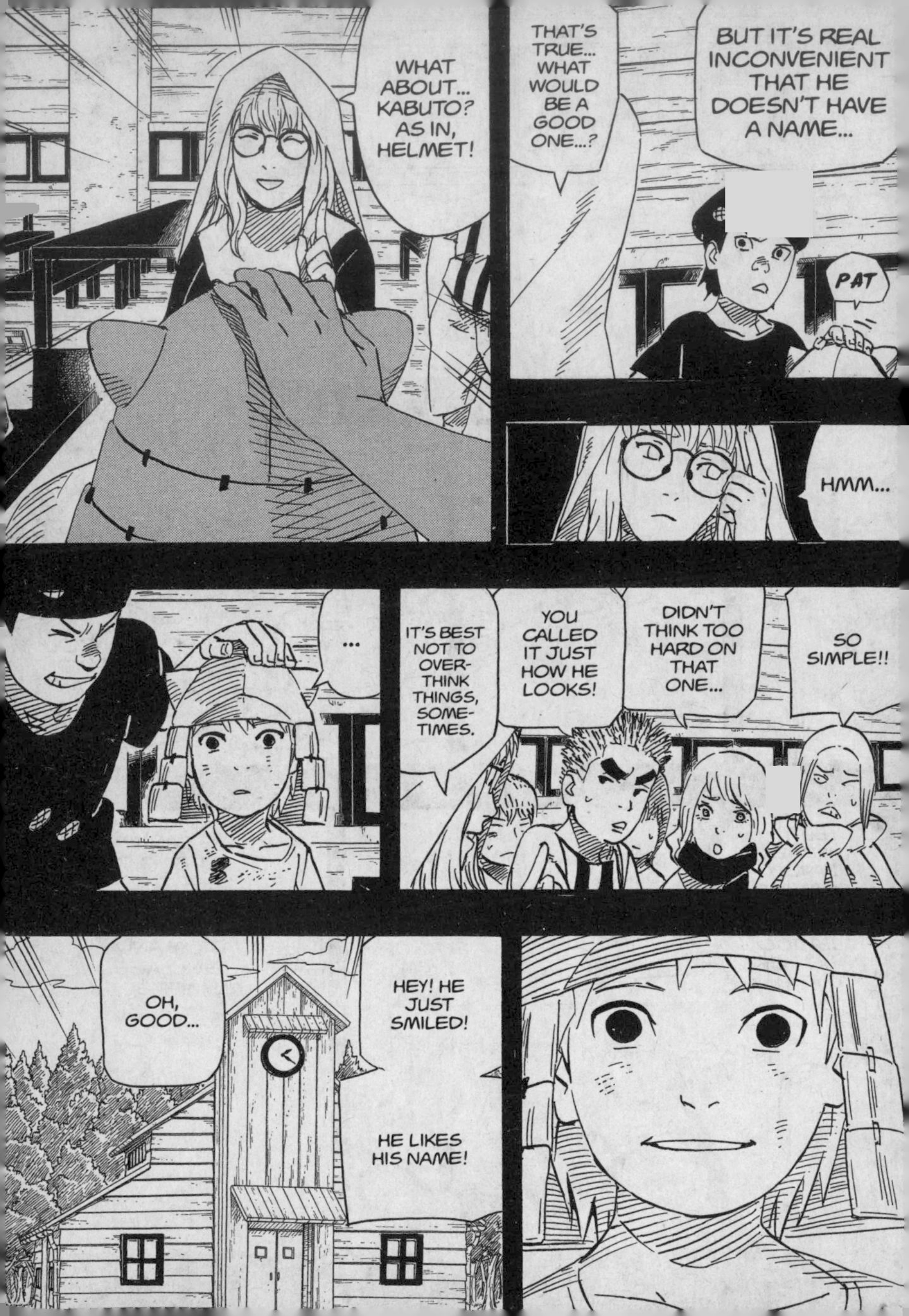
BUT IT'S REAL INCONVENIENT THAT HE DOESN'T HAVE A NAME...
THAT'S TRUE... WHAT WOULD BE A GOOD ONE...?
PAT
HMM...
WHAT ABOUT... KABUTO? AS IN, HELMET!
SO SIMPLE!!
DIDN'T THINK TOO HARD ON THAT ONE...
YOU CALLED IT JUST HOW HE LOOKS!
IT'S BEST NOT TO OVER-THINK THINGS, SOME-TIMES.
...
HEY! HE JUST SMILED!
HE LIKES HIS NAME!
OH, GOOD...

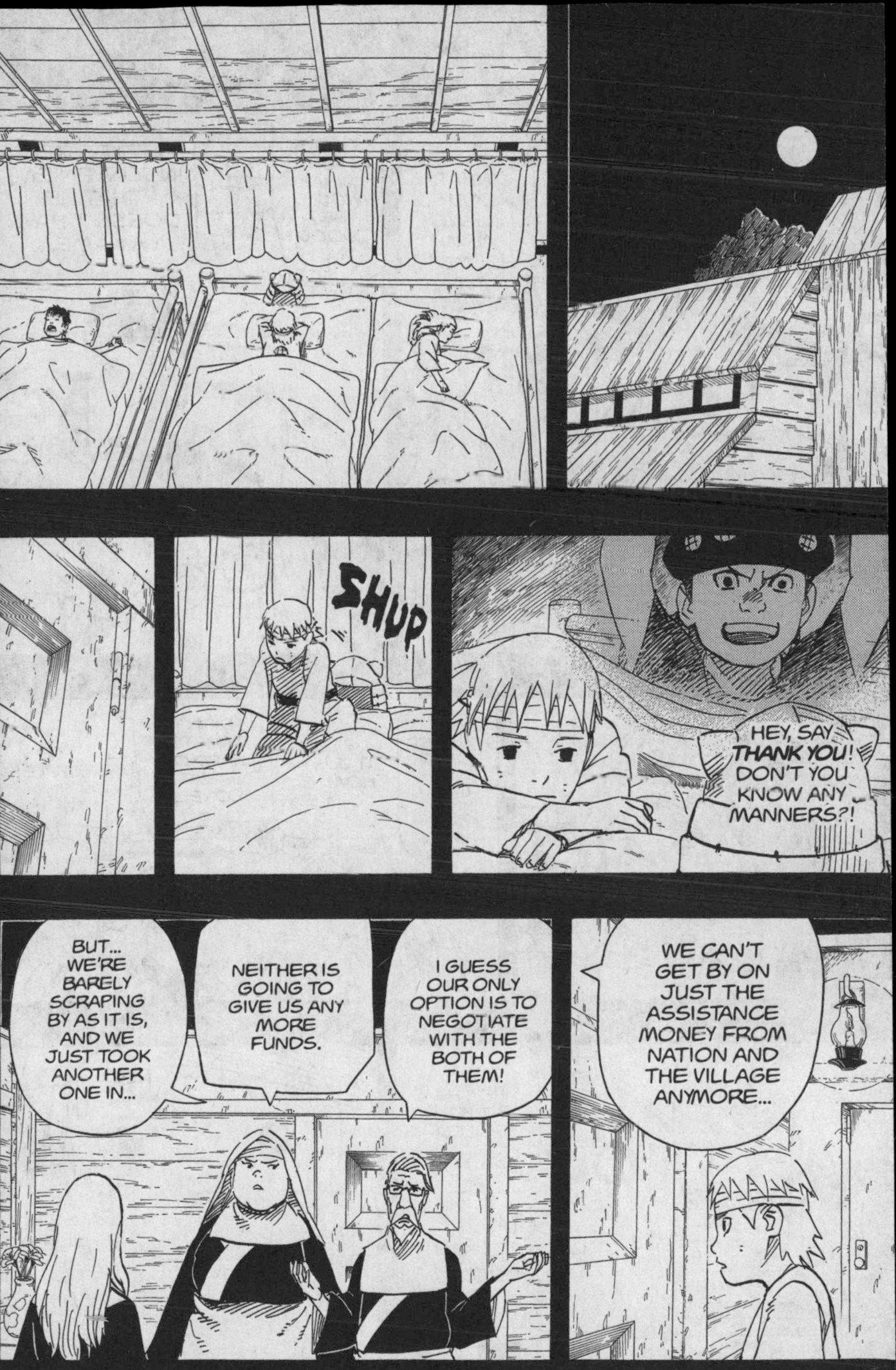
HEY, SAY THANK YOU! DON'T YOU KNOW ANY MANNERS?!
SHUP
WE CAN'T GET BY ON JUST THE ASSISTANCE MONEY FROM NATION AND THE VILLAGE ANYMORE...
I GUESS OUR ONLY OPTION IS TO NEGOTIATE WITH THE BOTH OF THEM!
NEITHER IS GOING TO GIVE US ANY MORE FUNDS.
BUT... WE'RE BARELY SCRAPING BY AS IT IS, AND WE JUST TOOK ANOTHER ONE IN...

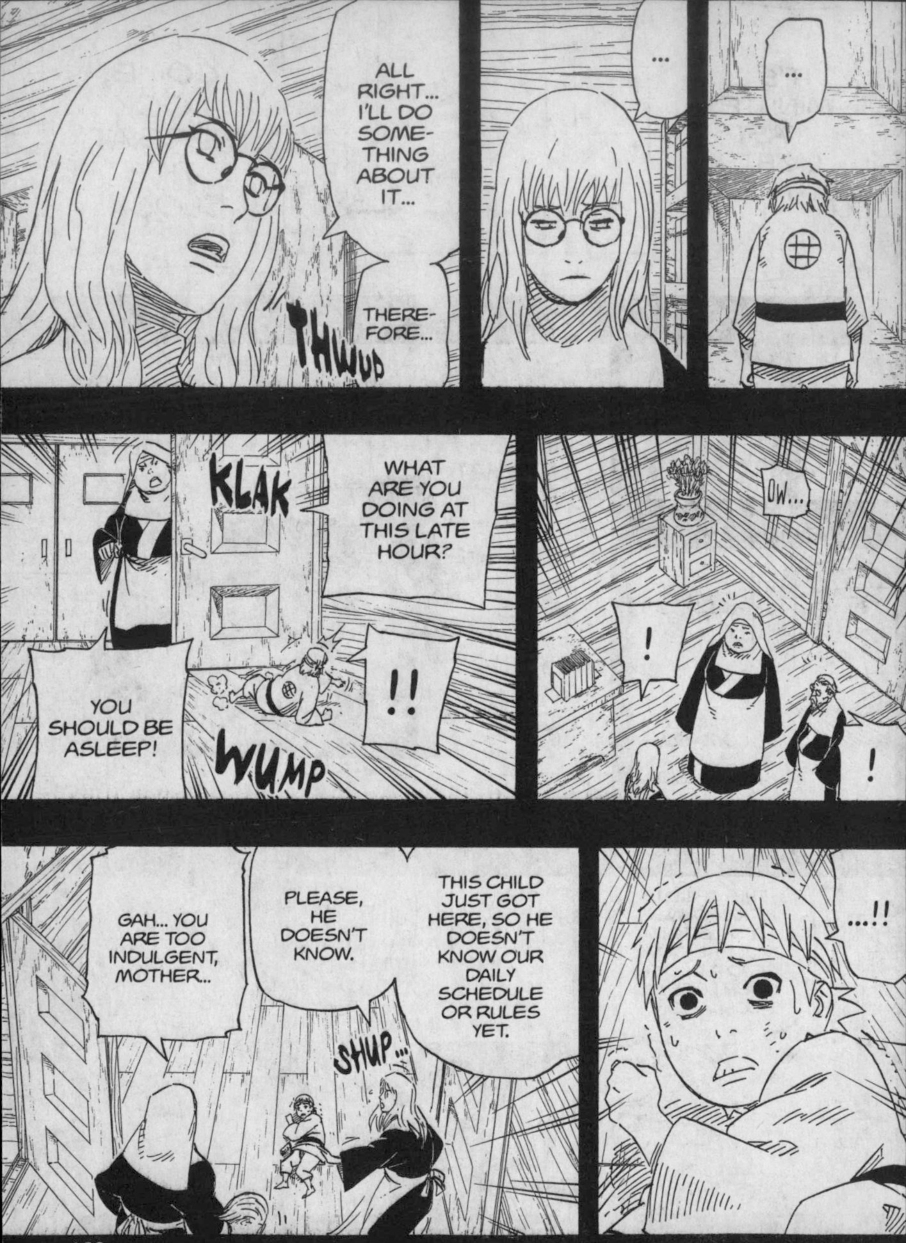
...
...
ALL RIGHT... I'LL DO SOMETHING ABOUT IT...
THEREFORE...
THWUD
OW...
!
!
WHAT ARE YOU DOING AT THIS LATE HOUR?
KLAK
!!
YOU SHOULD BE ASLEEP!
WUMP
...!!
THIS CHILD JUST GOT HERE, SO HE DOESN'T KNOW OUR DAILY SCHEDULE OR RULES YET.
PLEASE, HE DOESN'T KNOW.
GAH... YOU ARE TOO INDULGENT, MOTHER...
SHUP...

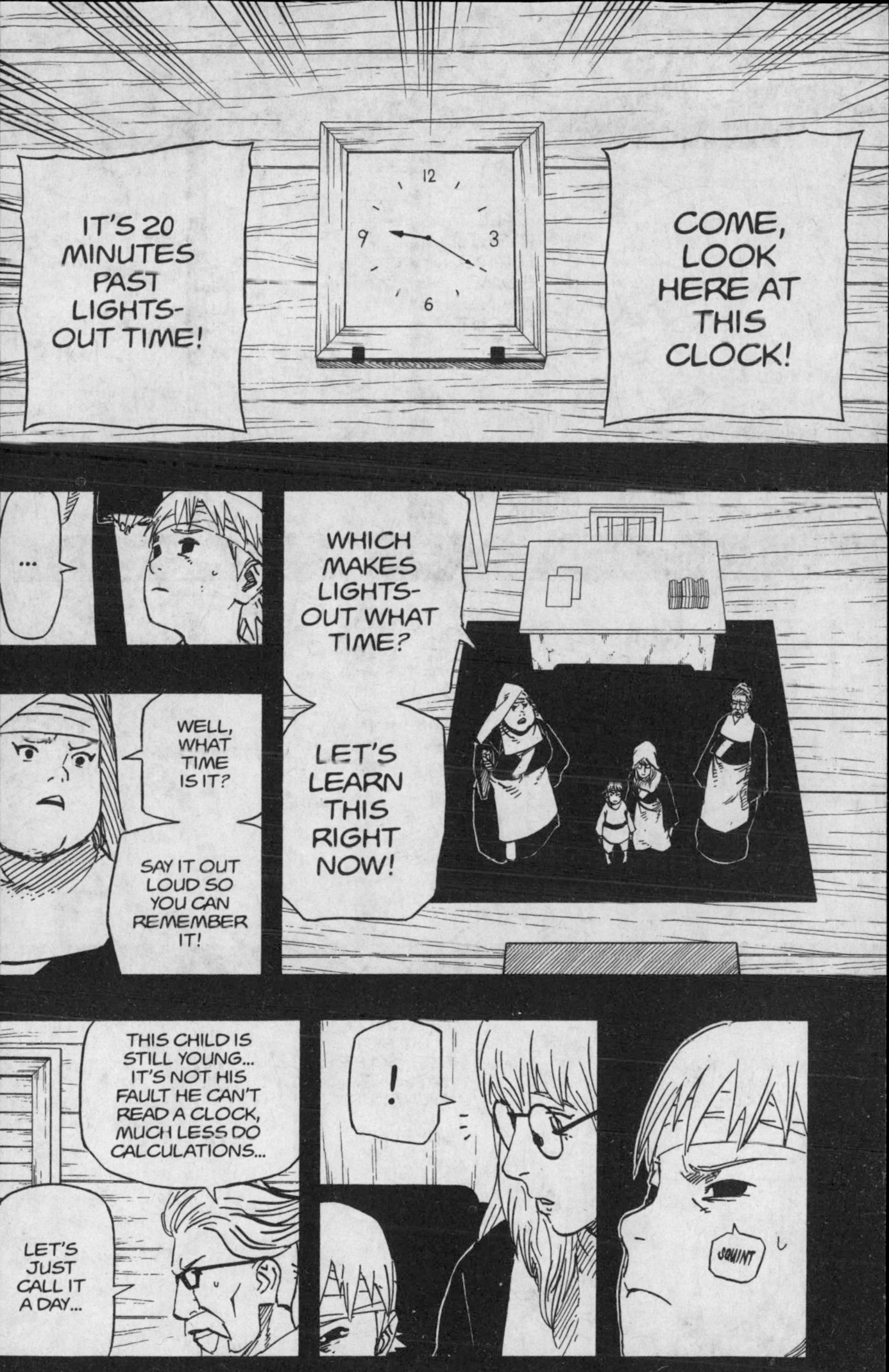
COME, LOOK HERE AT THIS CLOCK!
IT'S 20 MINUTES PAST LIGHTS-OUT TIME!
WHICH MAKES LIGHTS-OUT WHAT TIME?
LET'S LEARN THIS RIGHT NOW!
...
WELL, WHAT TIME IS IT?
SAY IT OUT LOUD SO YOU CAN REMEMBER IT!
SQUINT
!
THIS CHILD IS STILL YOUNG... IT'S NOT HIS FAULT HE CAN'T READ A CLOCK, MUCH LESS DO CALCULATIONS...
LET'S JUST CALL IT A DAY...

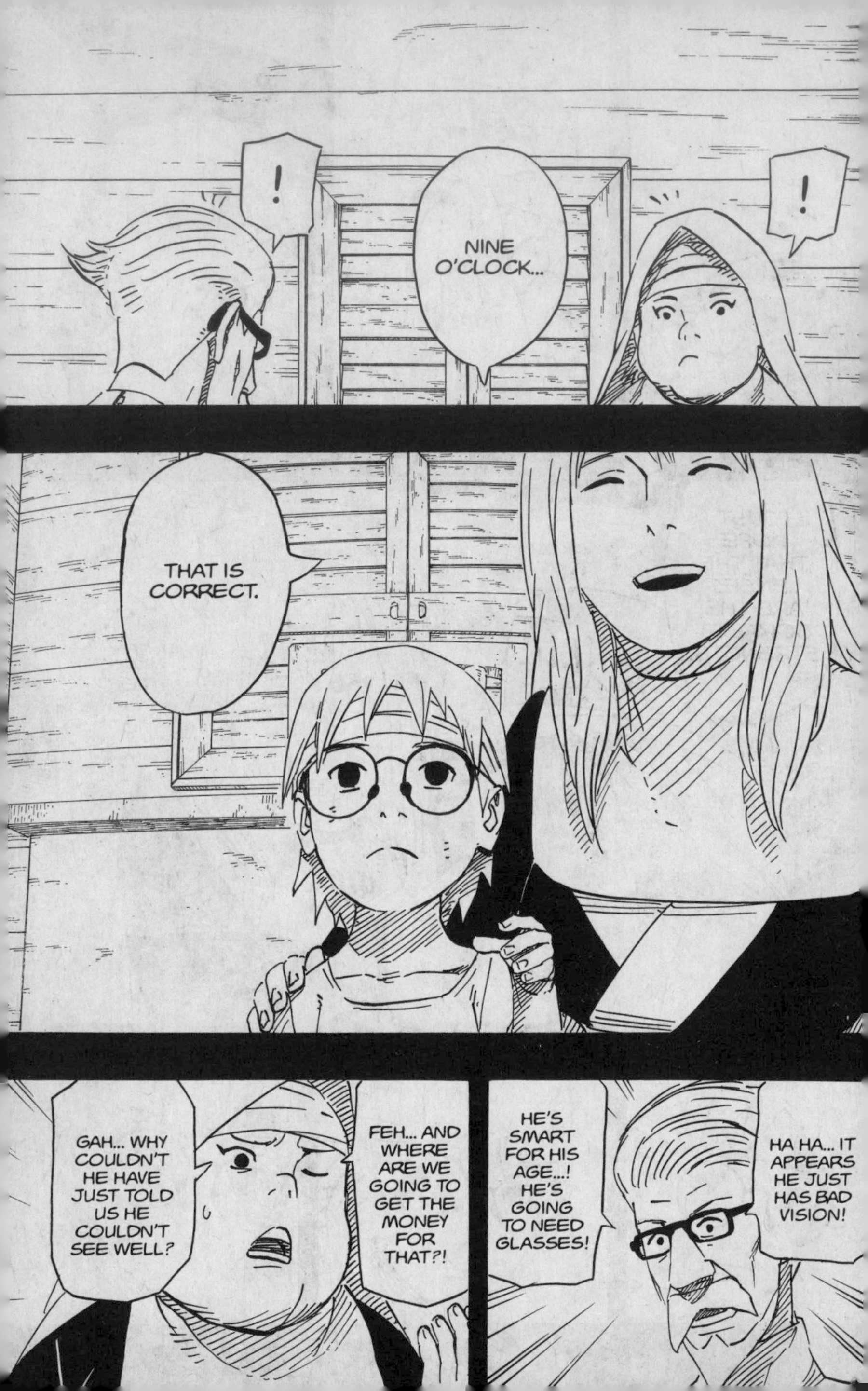
!
NINE O'CLOCK...
!
THAT IS CORRECT.
HA HA... IT APPEARS HE JUST HAS BAD VISION!
HE'S SMART FOR HIS AGE...! HE'S GOING TO NEED GLASSES!
FEH... AND WHERE ARE WE GOING TO GET THE MONEY FOR THAT?!
GAH... WHY COULDN'T HE HAVE JUST TOLD US HE COULDN'T SEE WELL?

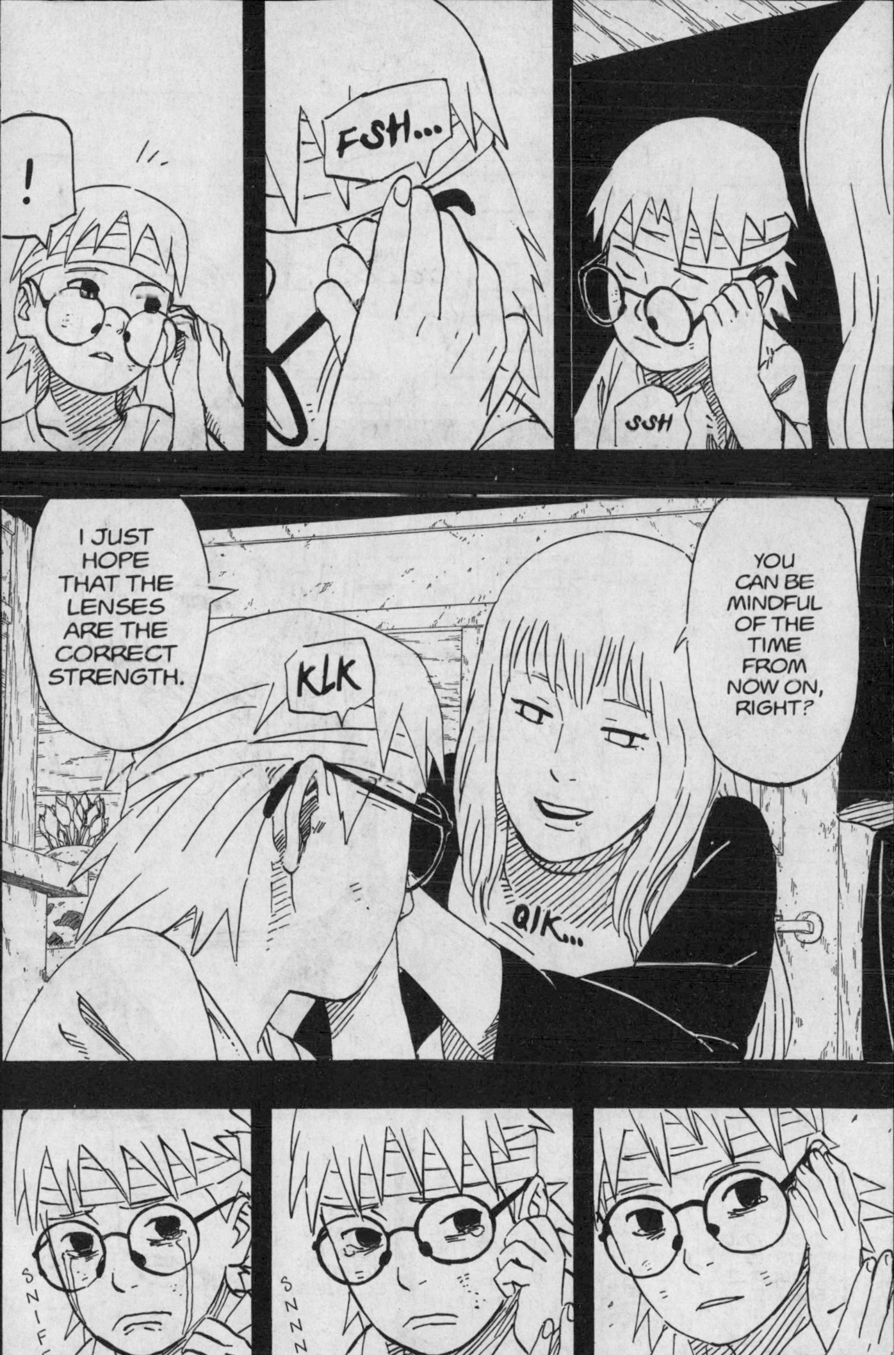
SSH
FSH...
!
YOU CAN BE MINDFUL OF THE TIME FROM NOW ON, RIGHT?
I JUST HOPE THAT THE LENSES ARE THE CORRECT STRENGTH.
KLK
QIK...
SNNN
SNIFF

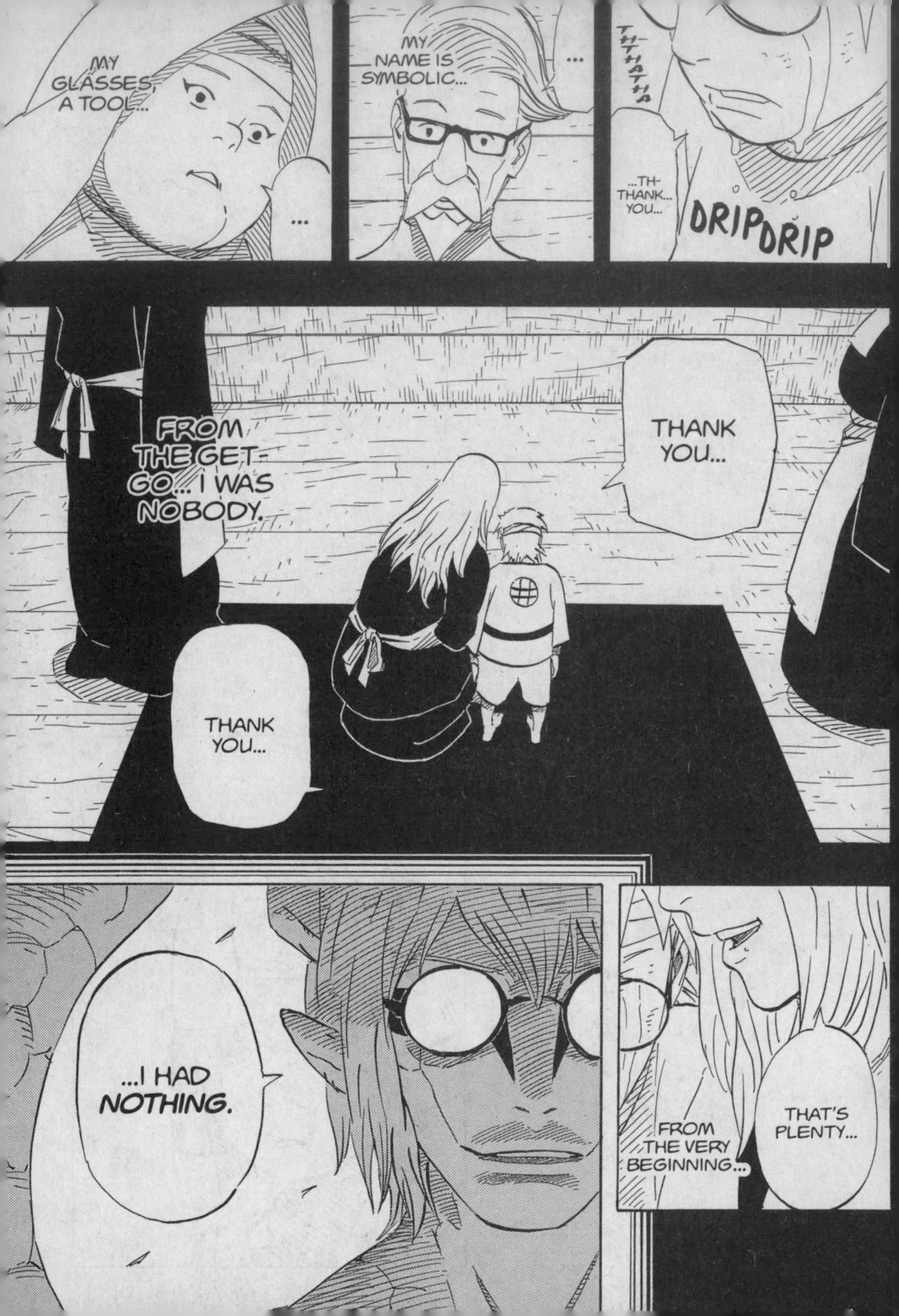
THTHATHA
...TH-THANK... YOU...
DRIPDRIP
MY NAME IS SYMBOLIC...
...
MY GLASSES, A TOOL...
...
THANK YOU...
FROM THE GET-GO... I WAS NOBODY.
THANK YOU...
THAT'S PLENTY...
FROM THE VERY BEGINNING...
...I HAD NOTHING.

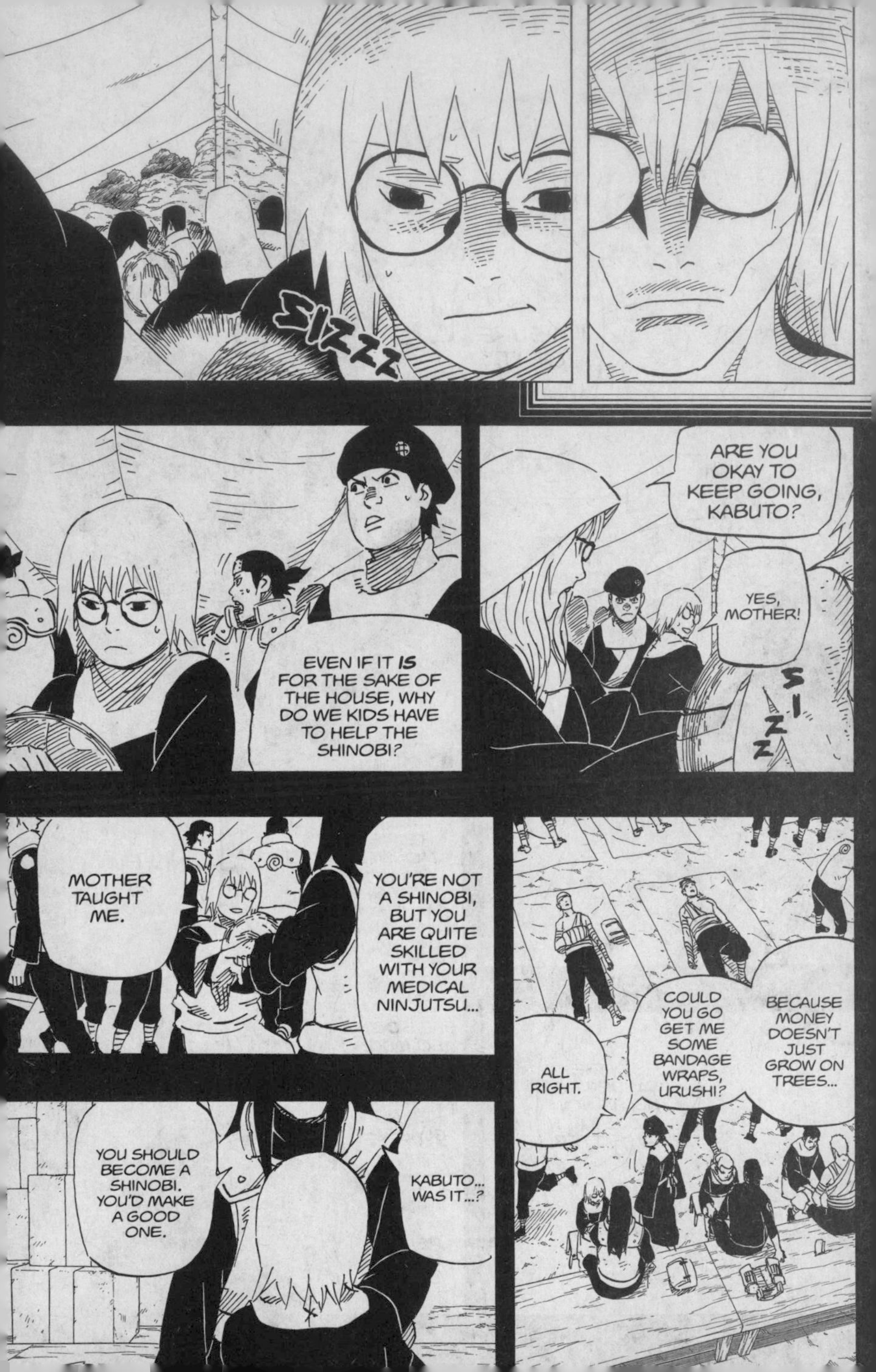
SIZZZZ
ARE YOU OKAY TO KEEP GOING, KABUTO?
YES, MOTHER!
SIZZZ
EVEN IF IT **IS** FOR THE SAKE OF THE HOUSE, WHY DO WE KIDS HAVE TO HELP THE SHINOBI?
BECAUSE MONEY DOESN'T JUST GROW ON TREES...
COULD YOU GO GET ME SOME BANDAGE WRAPS, URUSHI?
ALL RIGHT.
YOU'RE NOT A SHINOBI, BUT YOU ARE QUITE SKILLED WITH YOUR MEDICAL NINJUTSU...
MOTHER TAUGHT ME.
KABUTO... WAS IT...?
YOU SHOULD BECOME A SHINOBI. YOU'D MAKE A GOOD ONE.

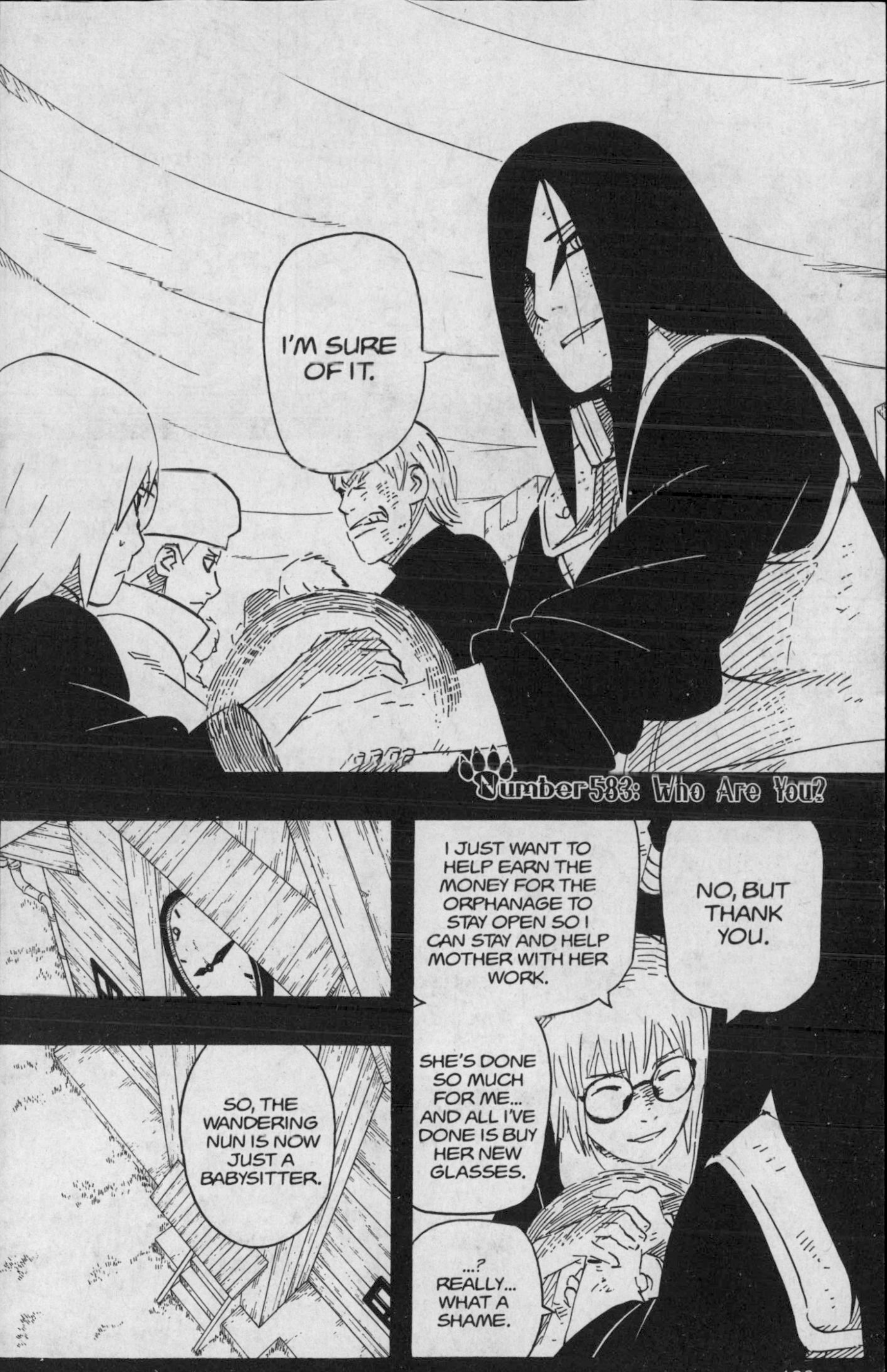
I'M SURE OF IT.
Number 583: Who Are You?
NO, BUT THANK YOU.
I JUST WANT TO HELP EARN THE MONEY FOR THE ORPHANAGE TO STAY OPEN SO I CAN STAY AND HELP MOTHER WITH HER WORK.
SHE'S DONE SO MUCH FOR ME... AND ALL I'VE DONE IS BUY HER NEW GLASSES.
...? REALLY... WHAT A SHAME.
SO, THE WANDERING NUN IS NOW JUST A BABYSITTER.

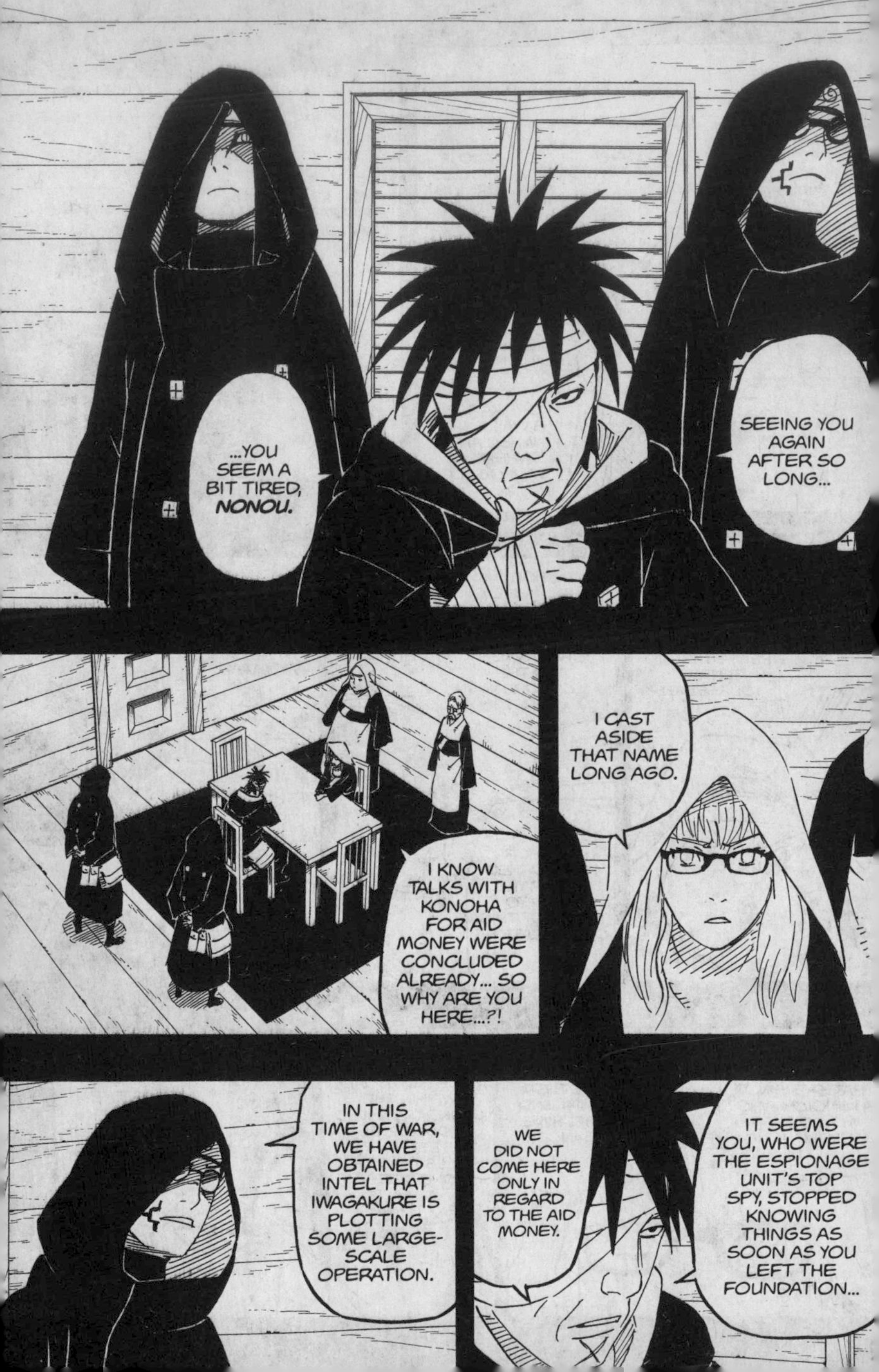
SEEING YOU AGAIN AFTER SO LONG...
...YOU SEEM A BIT TIRED, **NONOU.**
I CAST ASIDE THAT NAME LONG AGO.
I KNOW TALKS WITH KONOHA FOR AID MONEY WERE CONCLUDED ALREADY... SO WHY ARE YOU HERE...?!
IT SEEMS YOU, WHO WERE THE ESPIONAGE UNIT'S TOP SPY, STOPPED KNOWING THINGS AS SOON AS YOU LEFT THE FOUNDATION...
WE DID NOT COME HERE ONLY IN REGARD TO THE AID MONEY.
IN THIS TIME OF WAR, WE HAVE OBTAINED INTEL THAT IWAGAKURE IS PLOTTING SOME LARGE-SCALE OPERATION.

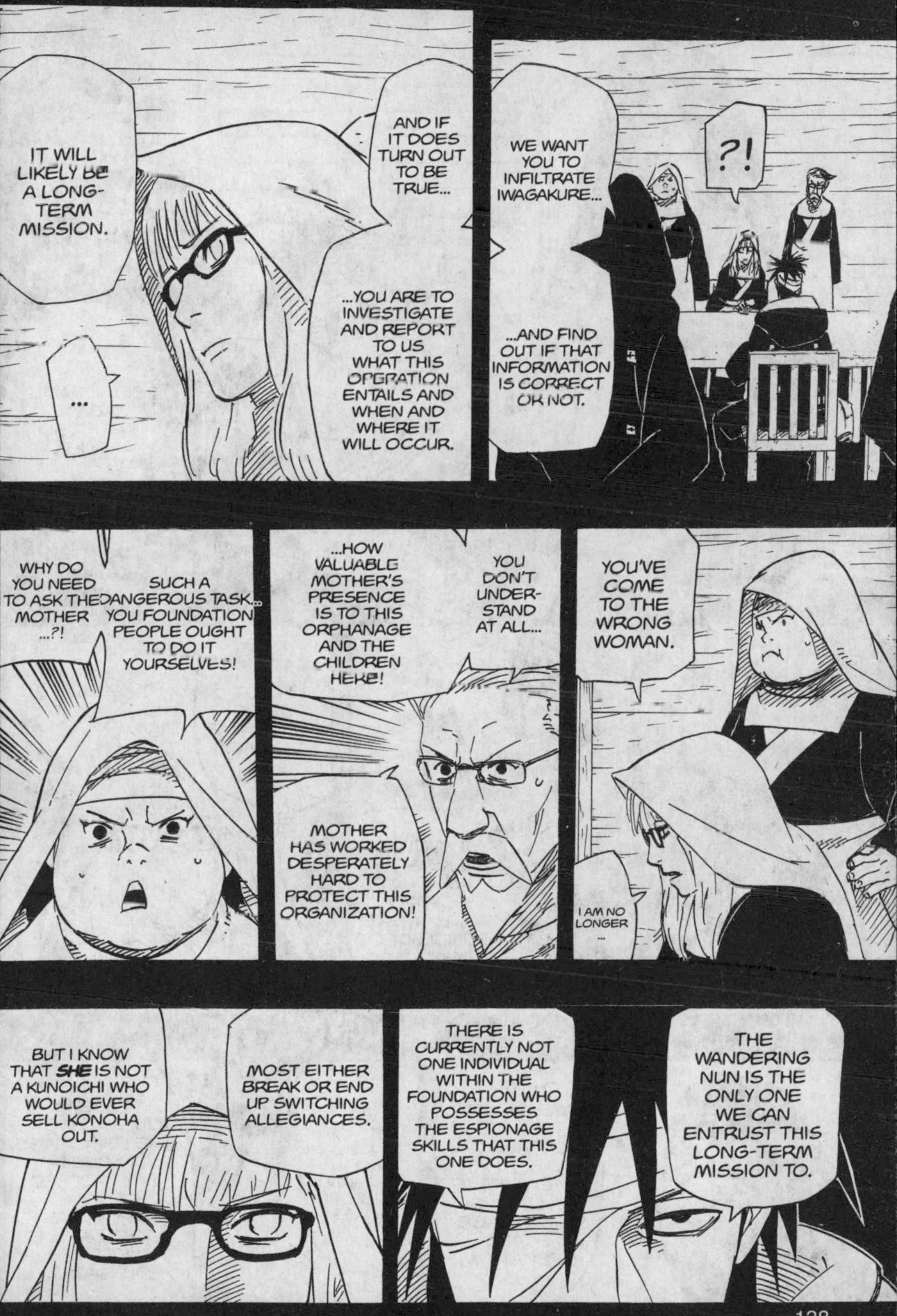
WE WANT YOU TO INFILTRATE IWAGAKURE...
...AND FIND OUT IF THAT INFORMATION IS CORRECT OR NOT.
?!
AND IF IT DOES TURN OUT TO BE TRUE...
...YOU ARE TO INVESTIGATE AND REPORT TO US WHAT THIS OPERATION ENTAILS AND WHEN AND WHERE IT WILL OCCUR.
IT WILL LIKELY BE A LONG-TERM MISSION.
...
YOU'VE COME TO THE WRONG WOMAN.
I AM NO LONGER ...
YOU DON'T UNDERSTAND AT ALL...
...HOW VALUABLE MOTHER'S PRESENCE IS TO THIS ORPHANAGE AND THE CHILDREN HERE!
MOTHER HAS WORKED DESPERATELY HARD TO PROTECT THIS ORGANIZATION!
SUCH A DANGEROUS TASK... YOU FOUNDATION PEOPLE OUGHT TO DO IT YOURSELVES!
WHY DO YOU NEED TO ASK THE MOTHER ...?!
THE WANDERING NUN IS THE ONLY ONE WE CAN ENTRUST THIS LONG-TERM MISSION TO.
THERE IS CURRENTLY NOT ONE INDIVIDUAL WITHIN THE FOUNDATION WHO POSSESSES THE ESPIONAGE SKILLS THAT THIS ONE DOES.
MOST EITHER BREAK OR END UP SWITCHING ALLEGIANCES.
BUT I KNOW THAT ***SHE*** IS NOT A KUNOICHI WHO WOULD EVER SELL KONOHA OUT.

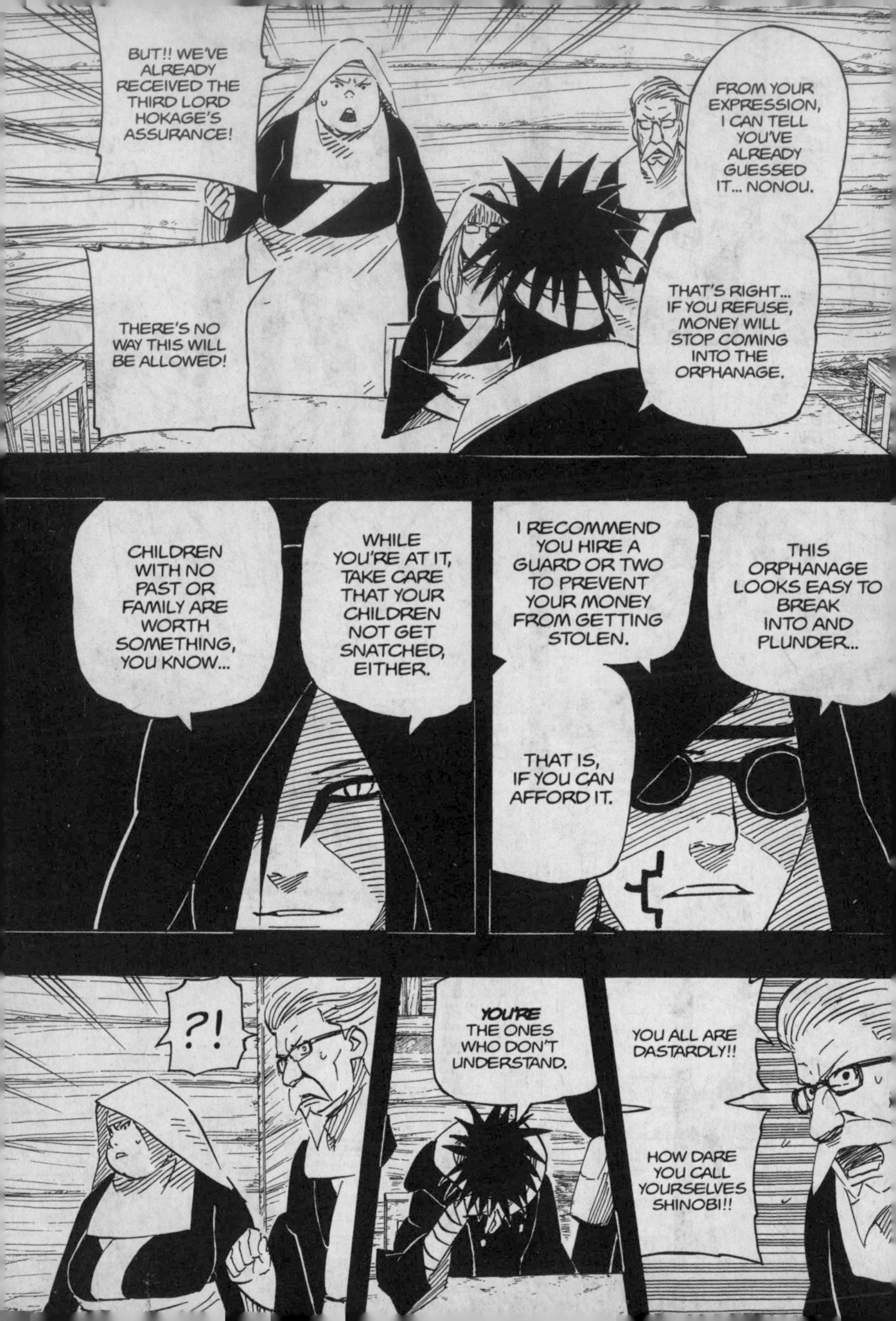
FROM YOUR EXPRESSION, I CAN TELL YOU'VE ALREADY GUESSED IT... NONOU.
THAT'S RIGHT... IF YOU REFUSE, MONEY WILL STOP COMING INTO THE ORPHANAGE.
BUT!! WE'VE ALREADY RECEIVED THE THIRD LORD HOKAGE'S ASSURANCE!
THERE'S NO WAY THIS WILL BE ALLOWED!
THIS ORPHANAGE LOOKS EASY TO BREAK INTO AND PLUNDER...
I RECOMMEND YOU HIRE A GUARD OR TWO TO PREVENT YOUR MONEY FROM GETTING STOLEN.
THAT IS, IF YOU CAN AFFORD IT.
WHILE YOU'RE AT IT, TAKE CARE THAT YOUR CHILDREN NOT GET SNATCHED, EITHER.
CHILDREN WITH NO PAST OR FAMILY ARE WORTH SOMETHING, YOU KNOW...
YOU ALL ARE DASTARDLY!!
HOW DARE YOU CALL YOURSELVES SHINOBI!!
YOU'RE THE ONES WHO DON'T UNDERSTAND.
?!

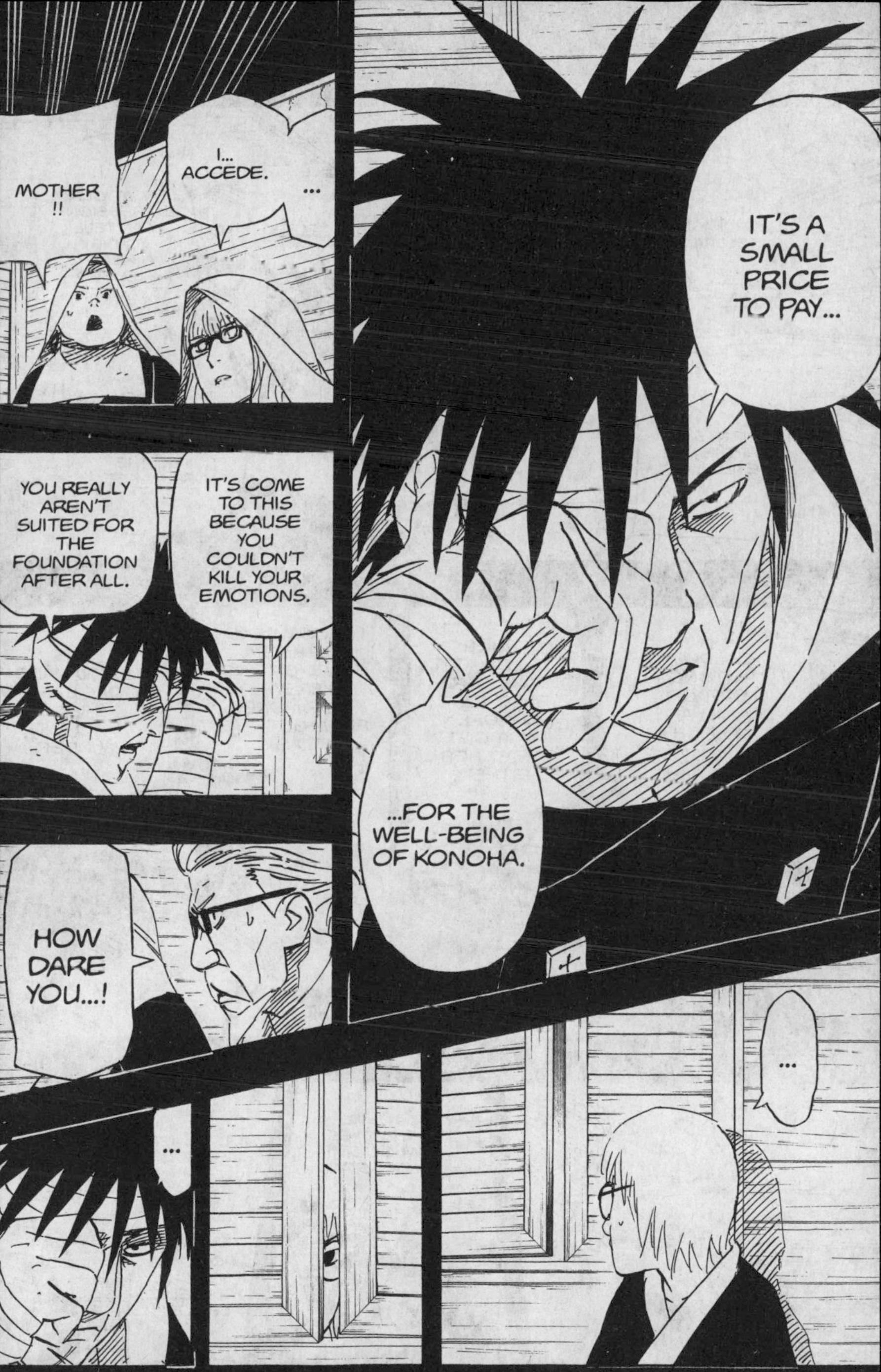
IT'S A SMALL PRICE TO PAY...
...FOR THE WELL-BEING OF KONOHA.
...
I... ACCEDE.
MOTHER !!
IT'S COME TO THIS BECAUSE YOU COULDN'T KILL YOUR EMOTIONS.
YOU REALLY AREN'T SUITED FOR THE FOUNDATION AFTER ALL.
HOW DARE YOU...!
...
...

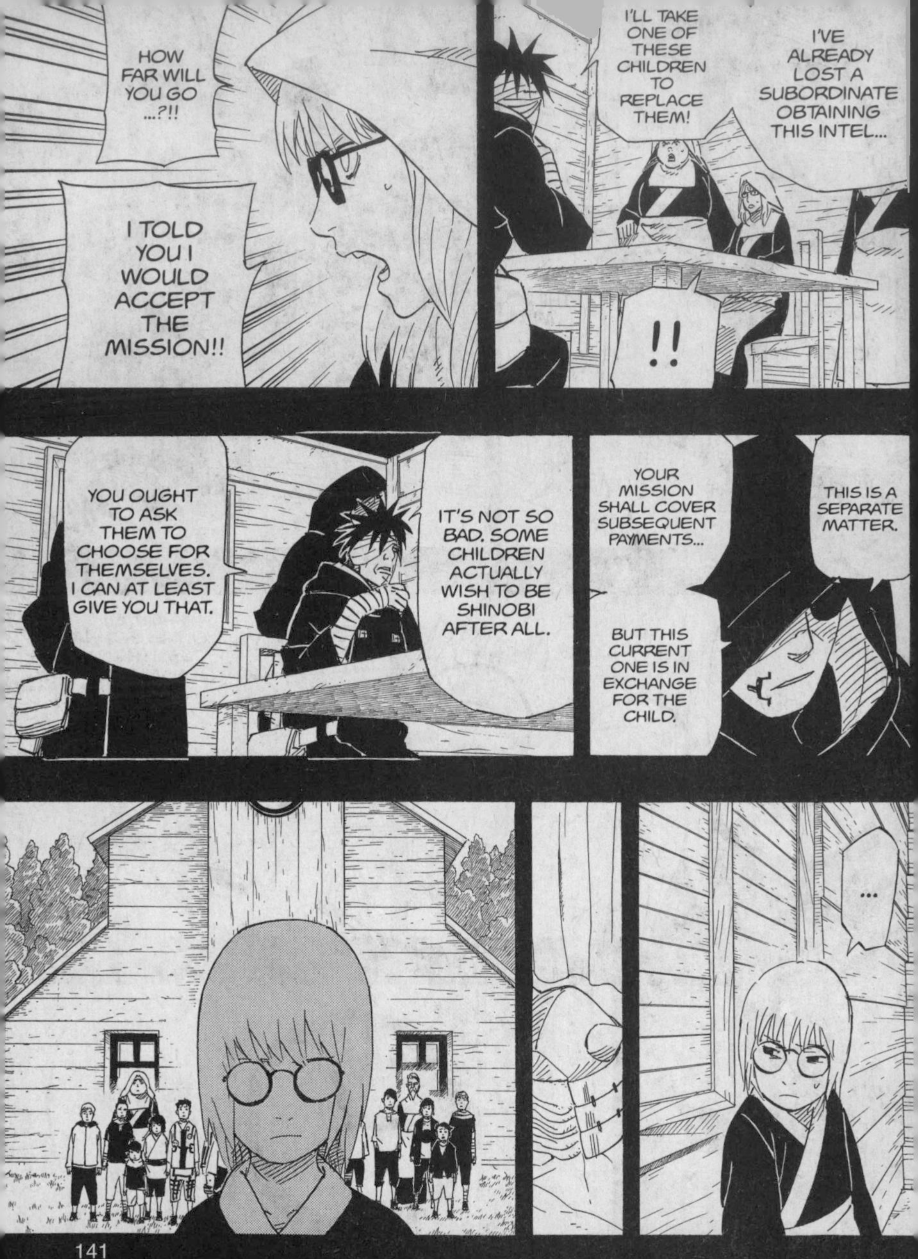
I'VE ALREADY LOST A SUBORDINATE OBTAINING THIS INTEL...
I'LL TAKE ONE OF THESE CHILDREN TO REPLACE THEM!
!!
HOW FAR WILL YOU GO ...?!!
I TOLD YOU I WOULD ACCEPT THE MISSION!!
THIS IS A SEPARATE MATTER.
YOUR MISSION SHALL COVER SUBSEQUENT PAYMENTS...
BUT THIS CURRENT ONE IS IN EXCHANGE FOR THE CHILD.
IT'S NOT SO BAD. SOME CHILDREN ACTUALLY WISH TO BE SHINOBI AFTER ALL.
YOU OUGHT TO ASK THEM TO CHOOSE FOR THEMSELVES. I CAN AT LEAST GIVE YOU THAT.
...

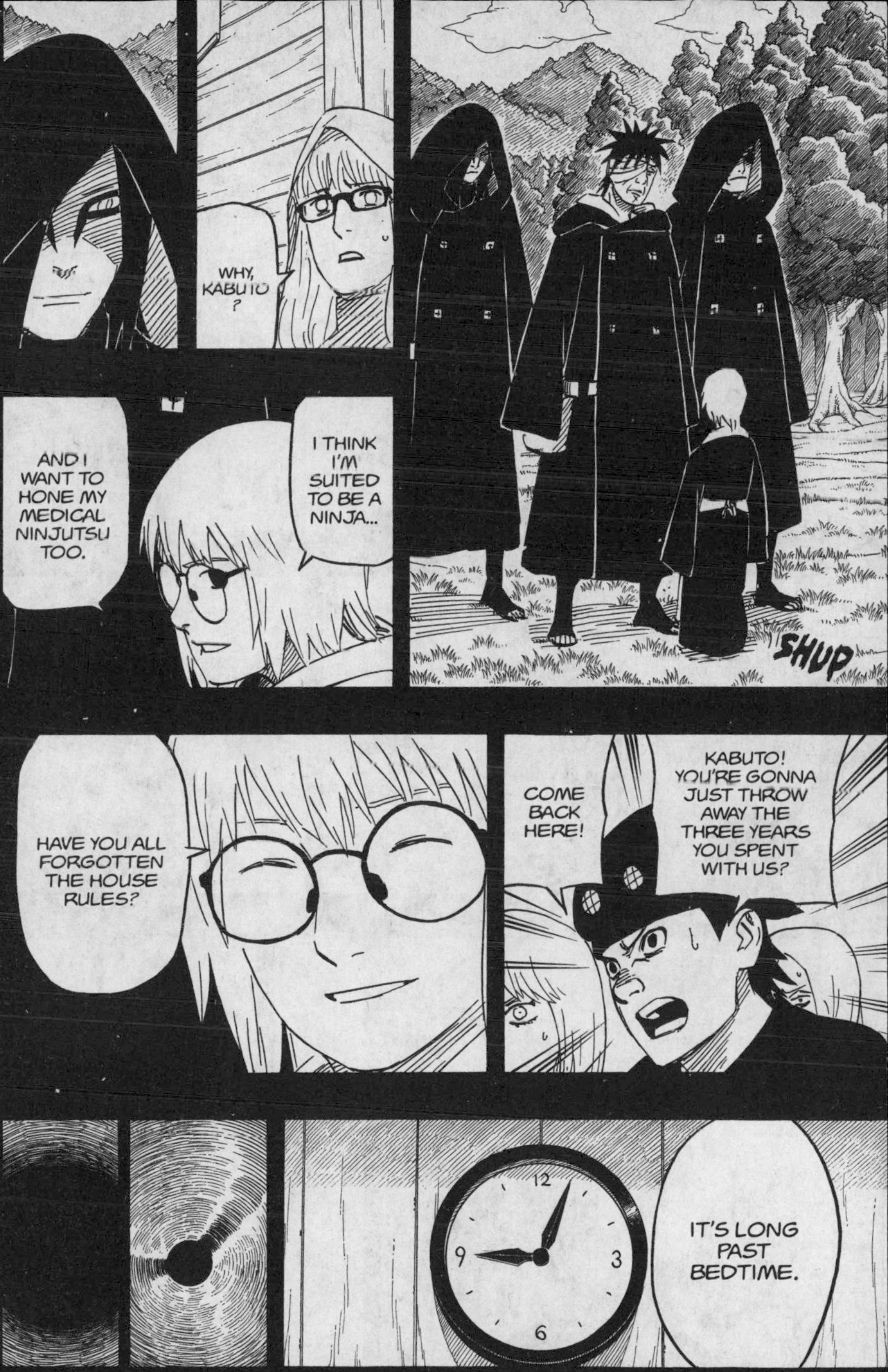
SHUP
WHY, KABUTO?
I THINK I'M SUITED TO BE A NINJA...
AND I WANT TO HONE MY MEDICAL NINJUTSU TOO.
KABUTO! YOU'RE GONNA JUST THROW AWAY THE THREE YEARS YOU SPENT WITH US?
COME BACK HERE!
HAVE YOU ALL FORGOTTEN THE HOUSE RULES?
IT'S LONG PAST BEDTIME.

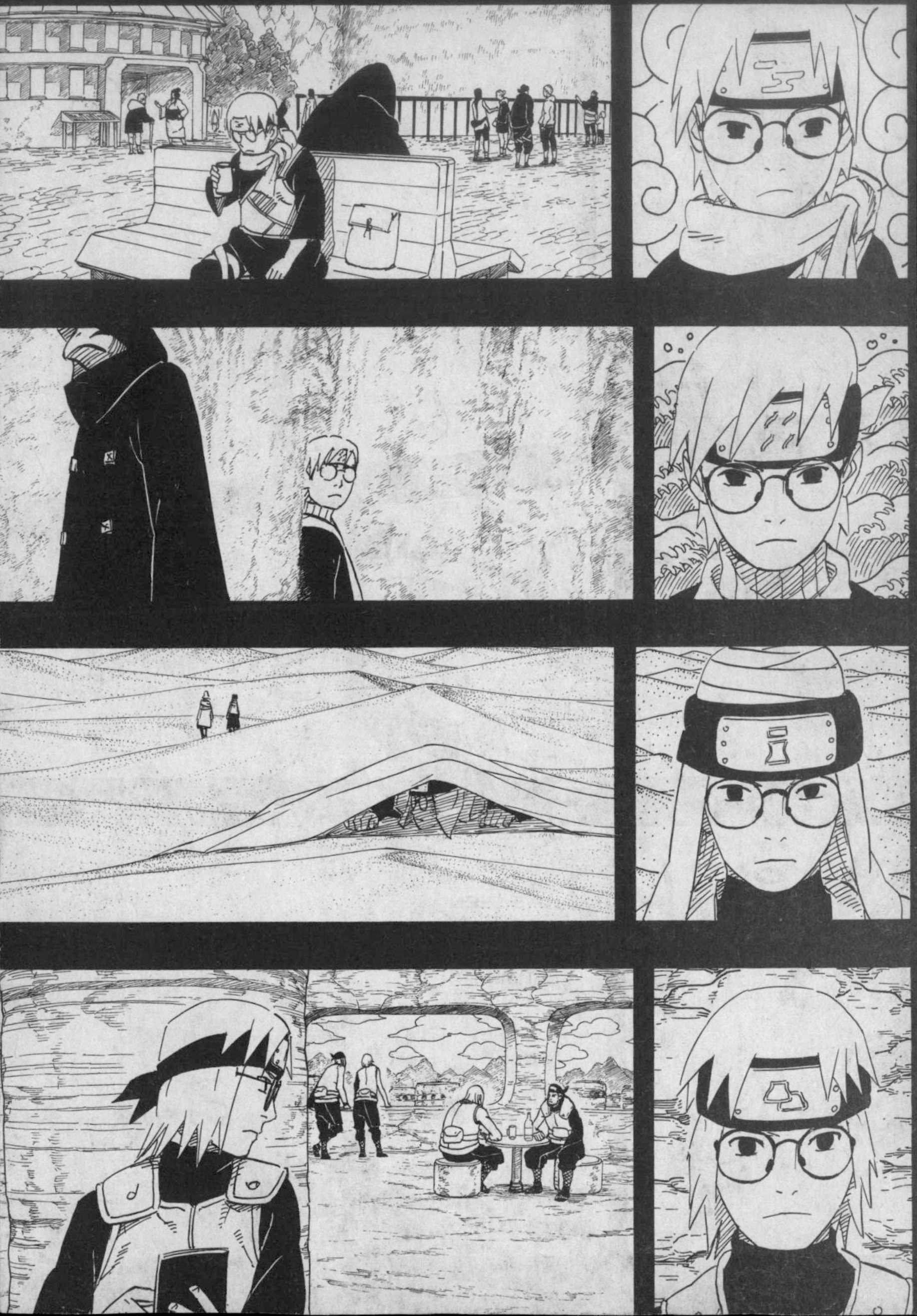

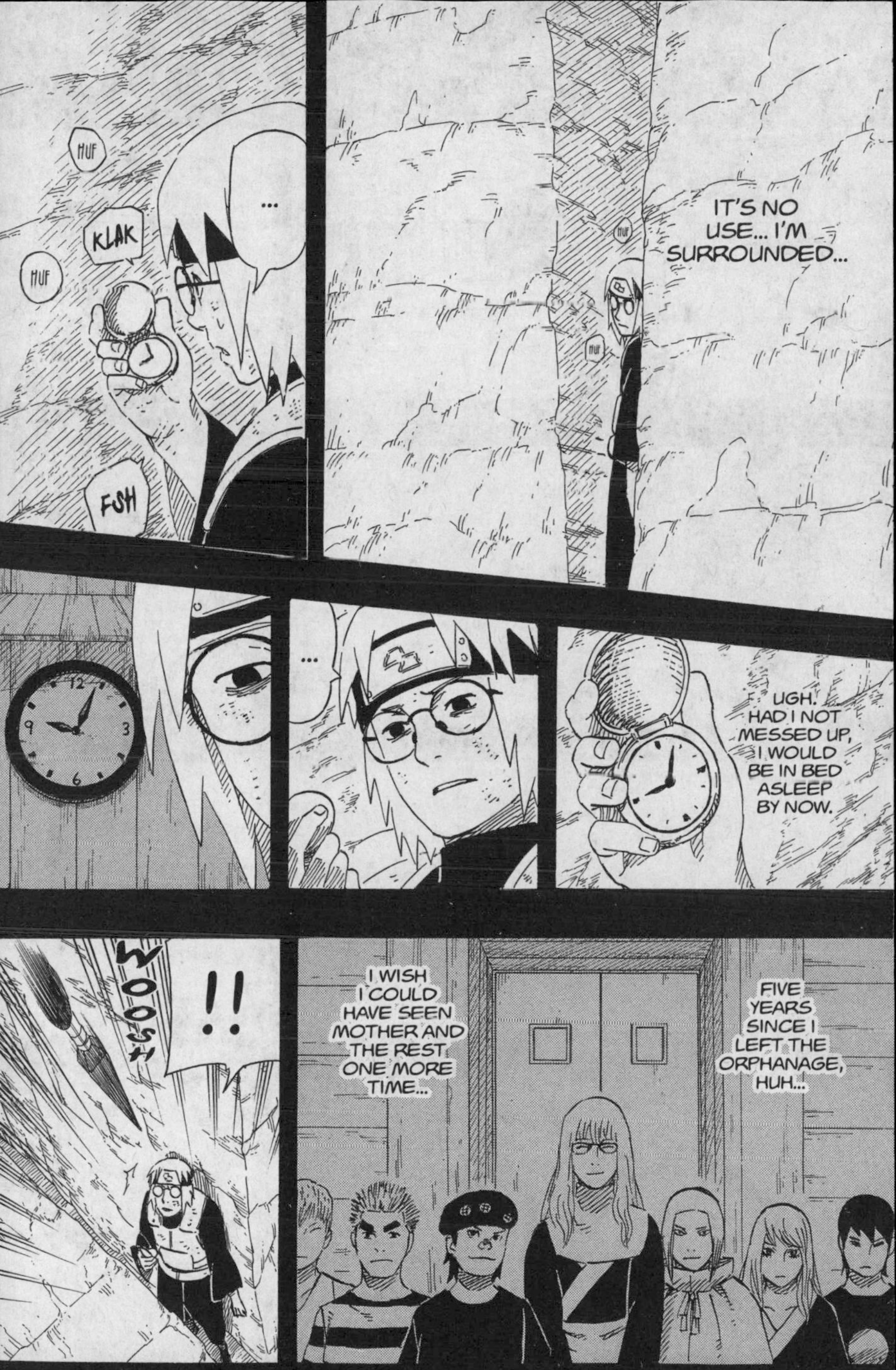
HUF
HUF
IT'S NO USE... I'M SURROUNDED...
HUF
...
KLAK
HUF
FSH
UGH. HAD I NOT MESSED UP, I WOULD BE IN BED ASLEEP BY NOW.
...
FIVE YEARS SINCE I LEFT THE ORPHANAGE, HUH...
I WISH I COULD HAVE SEEN MOTHER AND THE REST ONE MORE TIME...
!!
WOOSH

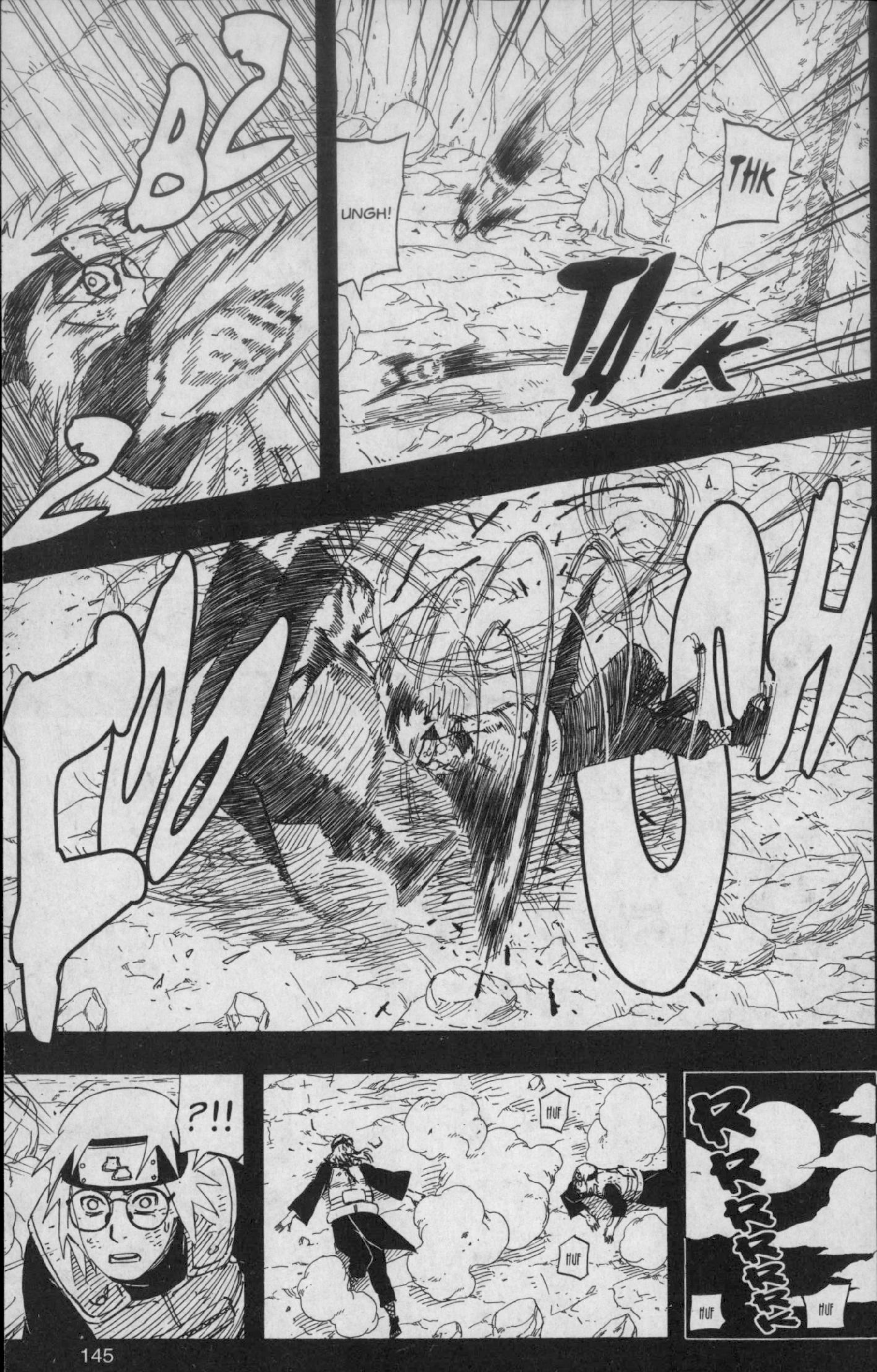
THK
UNGH!
HUF
HUF
HUF
HUF
?!!

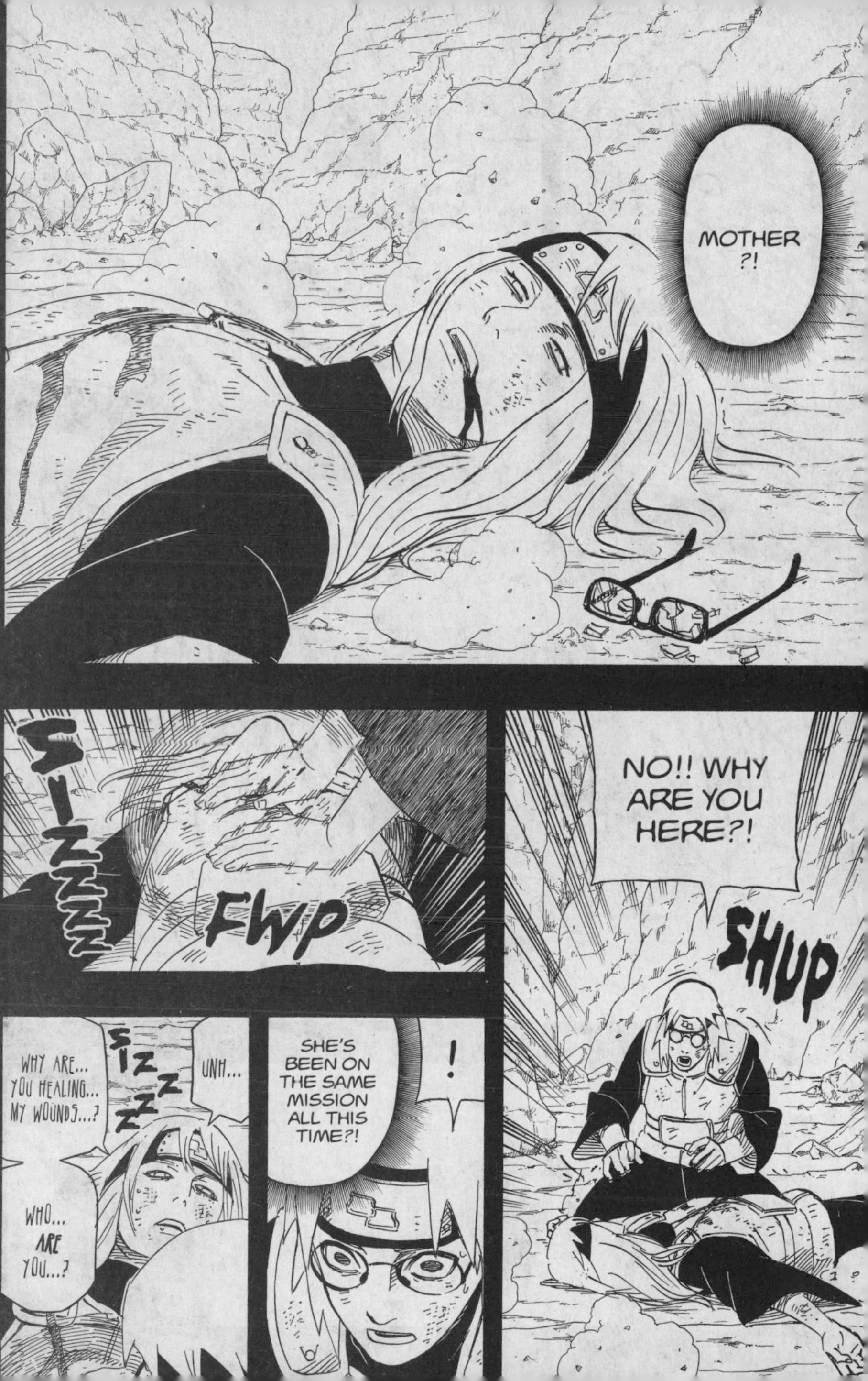
MOTHER ?!
NO!! WHY ARE YOU HERE?!
SHUP
SIZZZZ
FWP
!
SHE'S BEEN ON THE SAME MISSION ALL THIS TIME?!
UNH...
SIZZZZ
WHY ARE... YOU HEALING... MY WOUNDS...?
WHO... ARE YOU...?

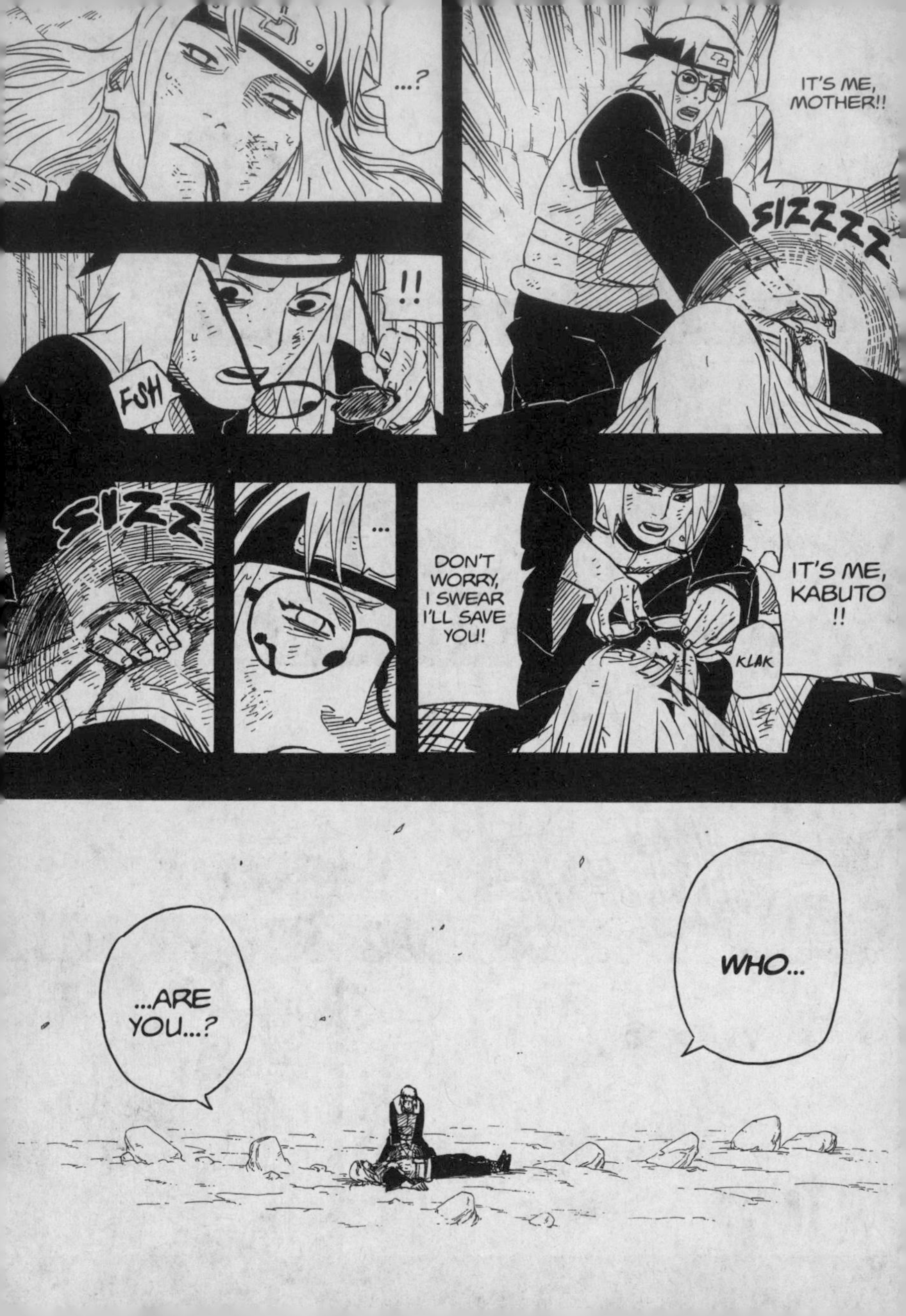
IT'S ME, MOTHER!!
SIZZZZZ
...?
!!
FSH
IT'S ME, KABUTO!!
KLAK
DON'T WORRY, I SWEAR I'LL SAVE YOU!
...
SIZZ
WHO...
...ARE YOU...?

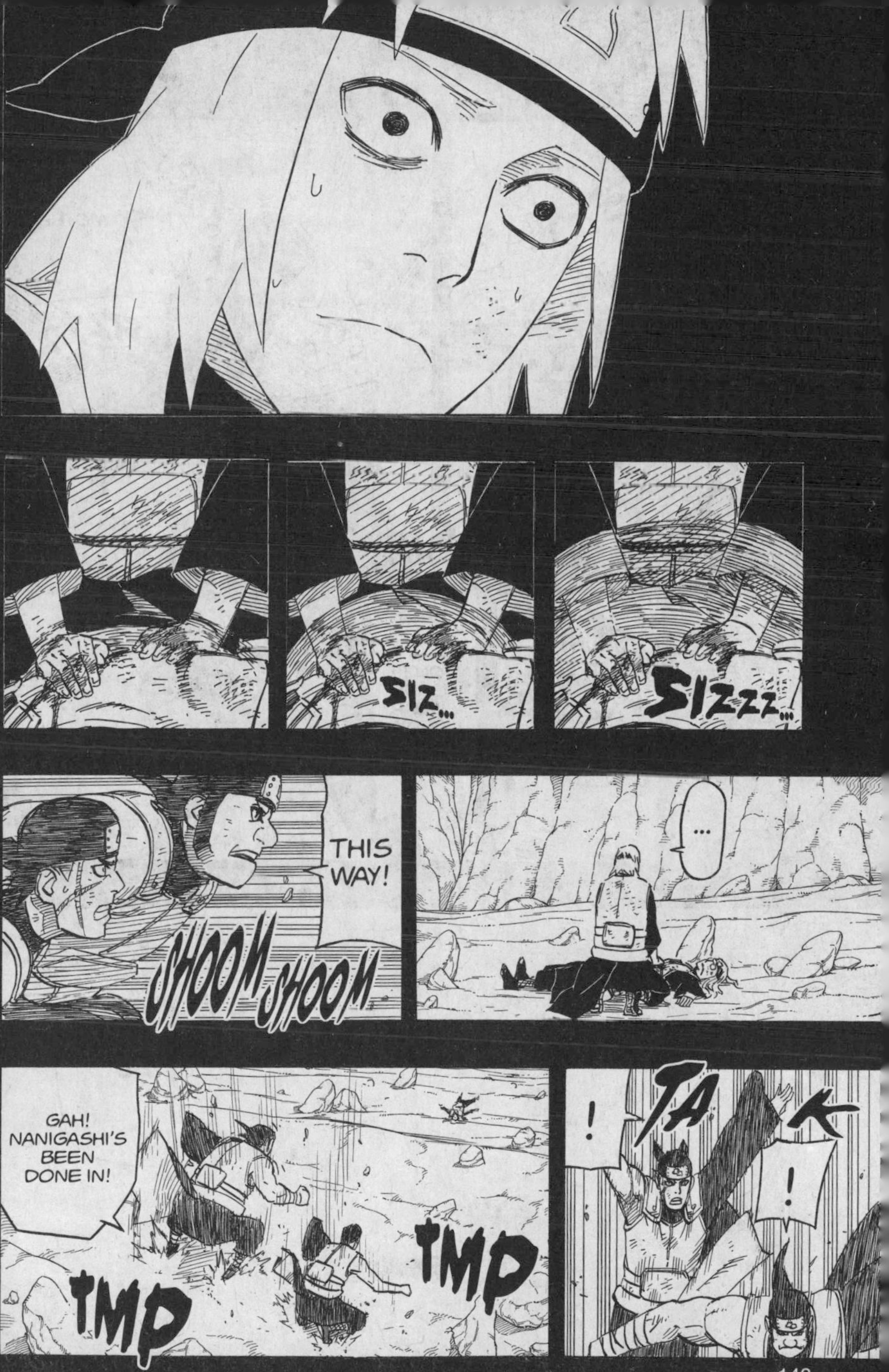
SIZZZ...
SIZ...
...
THIS WAY!
SHOOM SHOOM
TA K
!
!
GAH! NANIGASHI'S BEEN DONE IN!
TMP
TMP

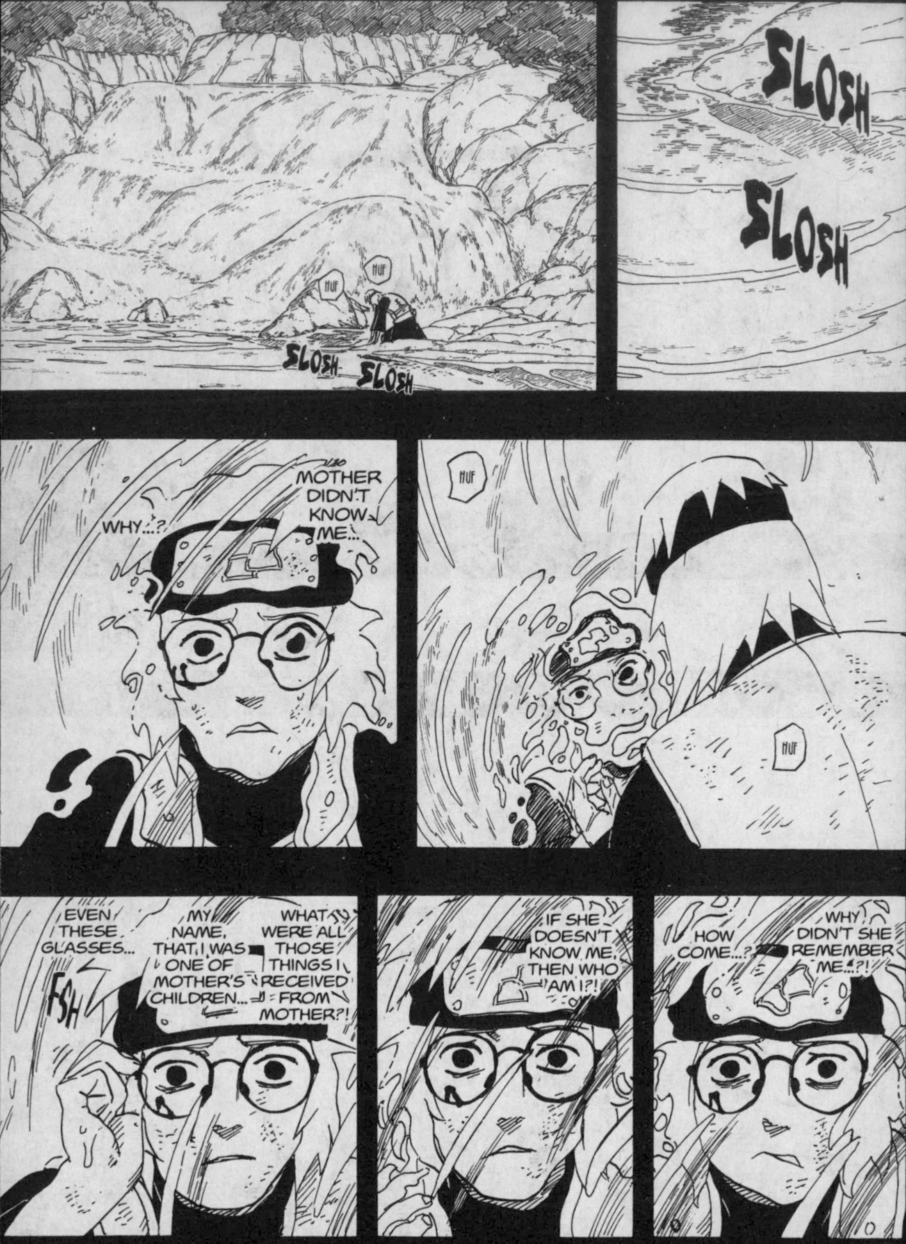
SLOSH
SLOSH
HUF
HUF
SLOSH
SLOSH
HUF
HUF
MOTHER DIDN'T KNOW ME...
WHY...?
WHY DIDN'T SHE REMEMBER ME...?!
HOW COME...?
IF SHE DOESN'T KNOW ME, THEN WHO AM I?!
WHAT WERE ALL THOSE THINGS I RECEIVED FROM MOTHER?!
MY NAME, THAT I WAS ONE OF MOTHER'S CHILDREN...
EVEN THESE GLASSES...
FSH

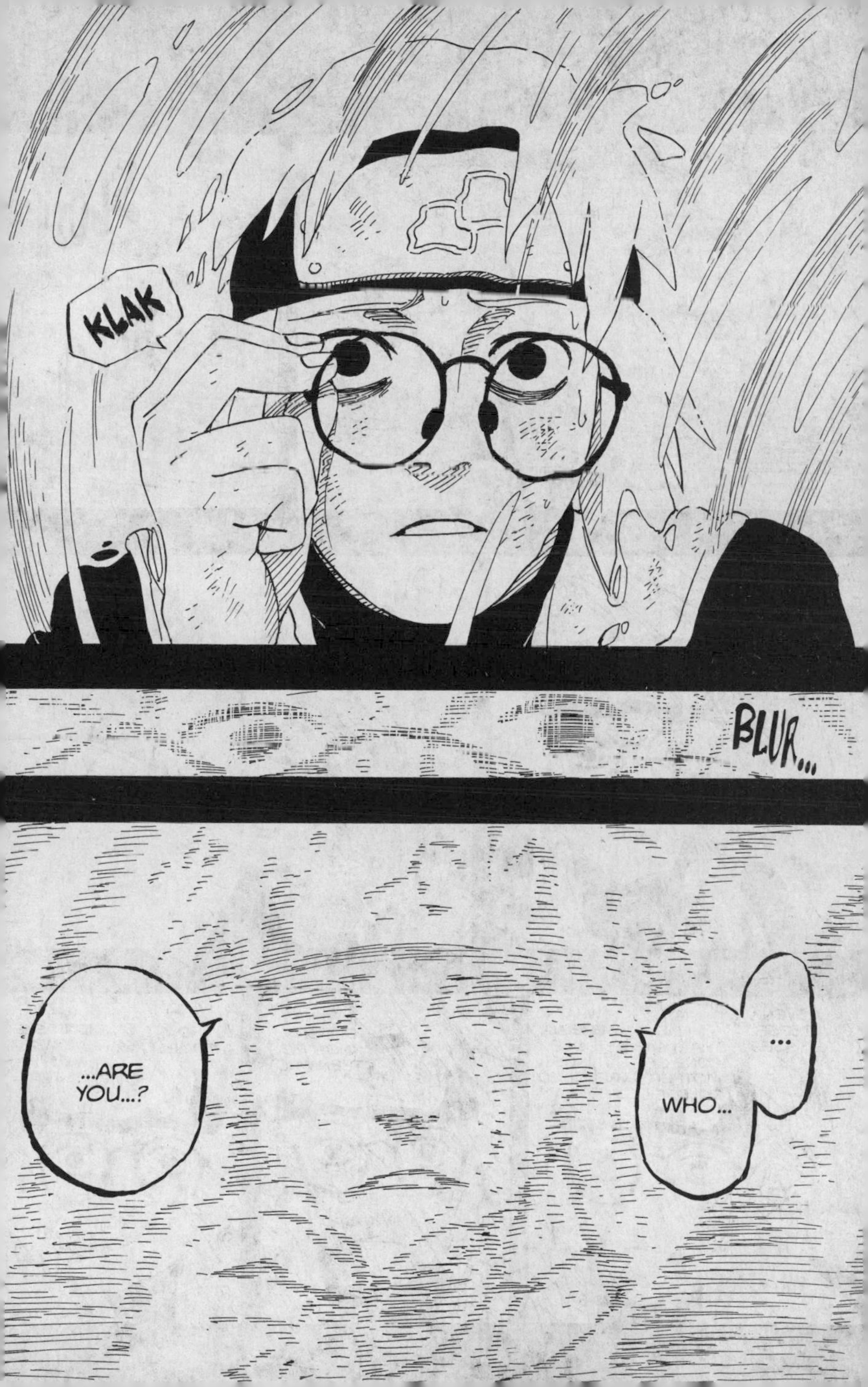
KLAK
BLUR...
...
WHO...
...ARE YOU...?

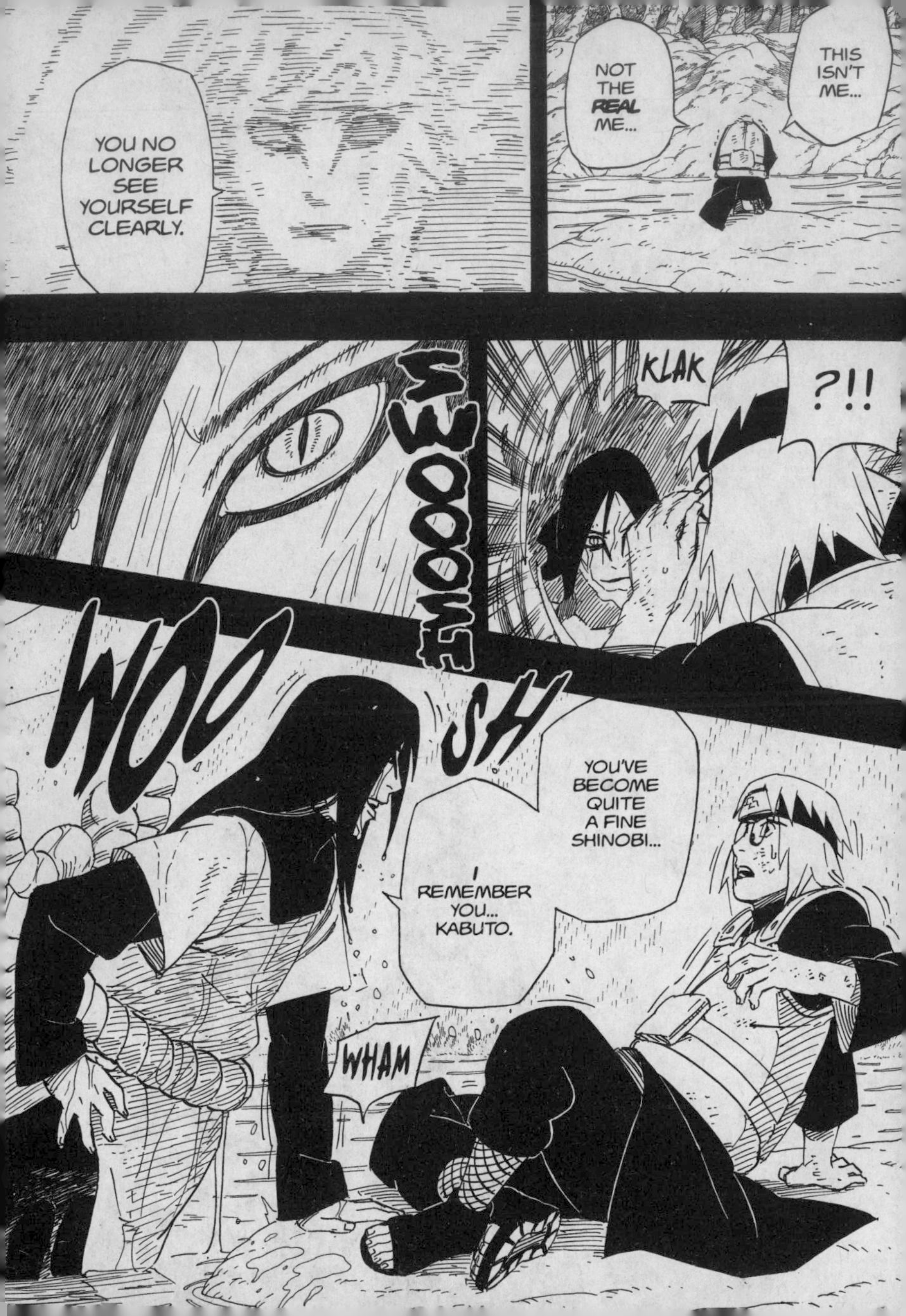
THIS ISN'T ME...
NOT THE REAL ME...
YOU NO LONGER SEE YOURSELF CLEARLY.
KLAK
?!!
WOOOMF
WOOSH
YOU'VE BECOME QUITE A FINE SHINOBI...
I REMEMBER YOU... KABUTO.
WHAM

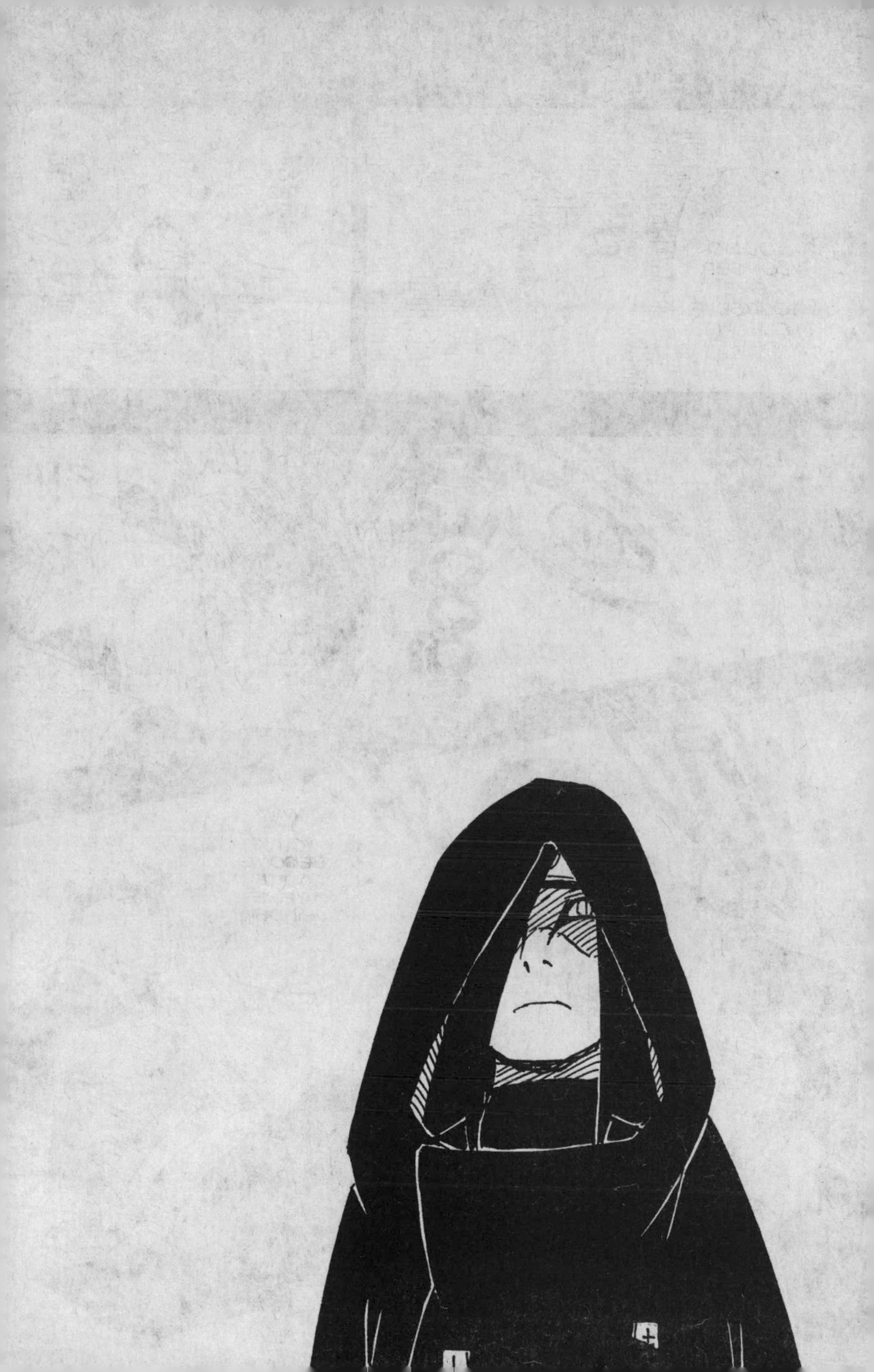

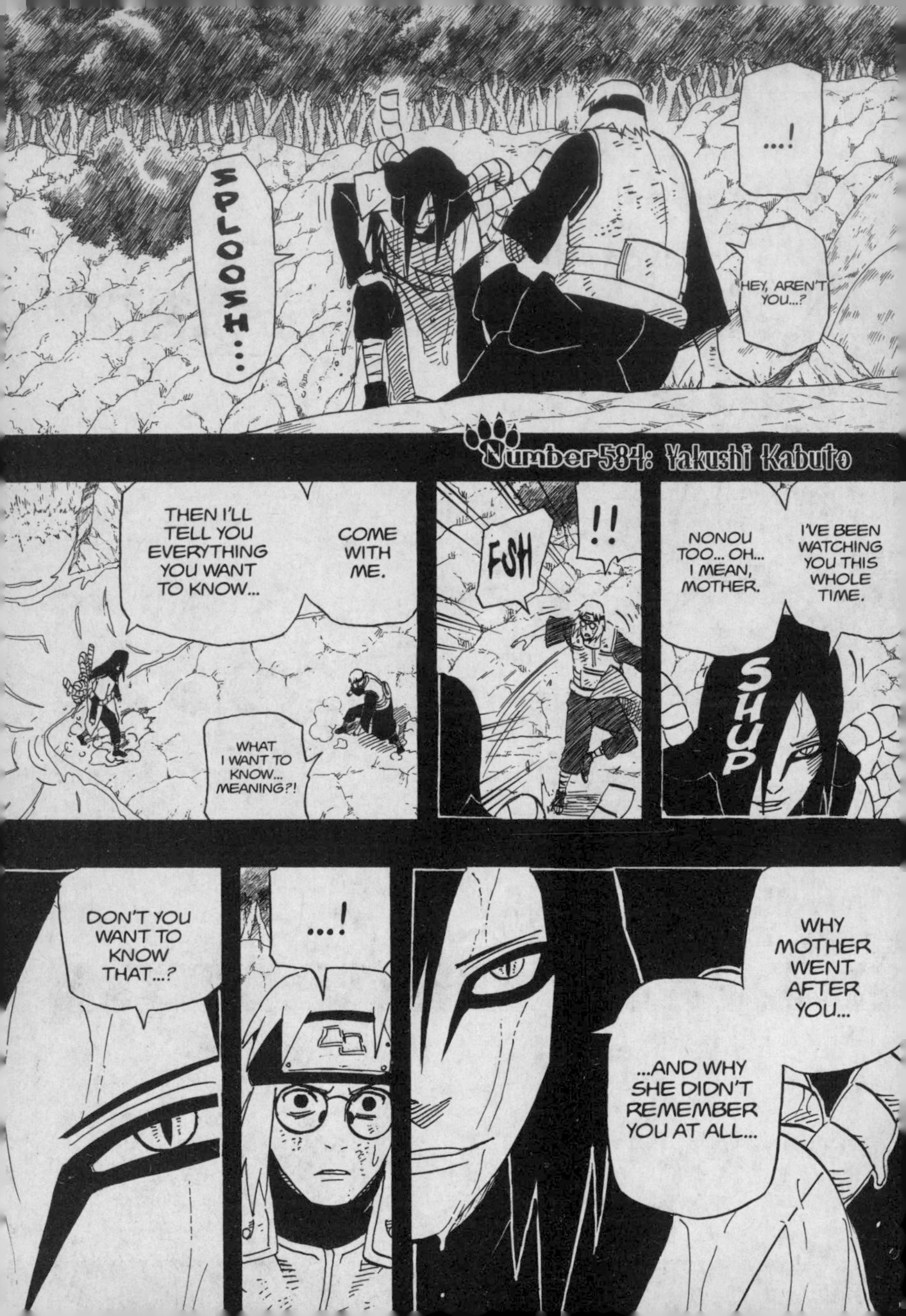
...!
HEY, AREN'T YOU...?
SPLOOSH...
Number 584: Yakushi Kabuto
I'VE BEEN WATCHING YOU THIS WHOLE TIME.
NONOU TOO... OH... I MEAN, MOTHER.
SHUP
!!
FSH
COME WITH ME.
THEN I'LL TELL YOU EVERYTHING YOU WANT TO KNOW...
WHAT I WANT TO KNOW... MEANING?!
WHY MOTHER WENT AFTER YOU...
...AND WHY SHE DIDN'T REMEMBER YOU AT ALL...
...!
DON'T YOU WANT TO KNOW THAT...?

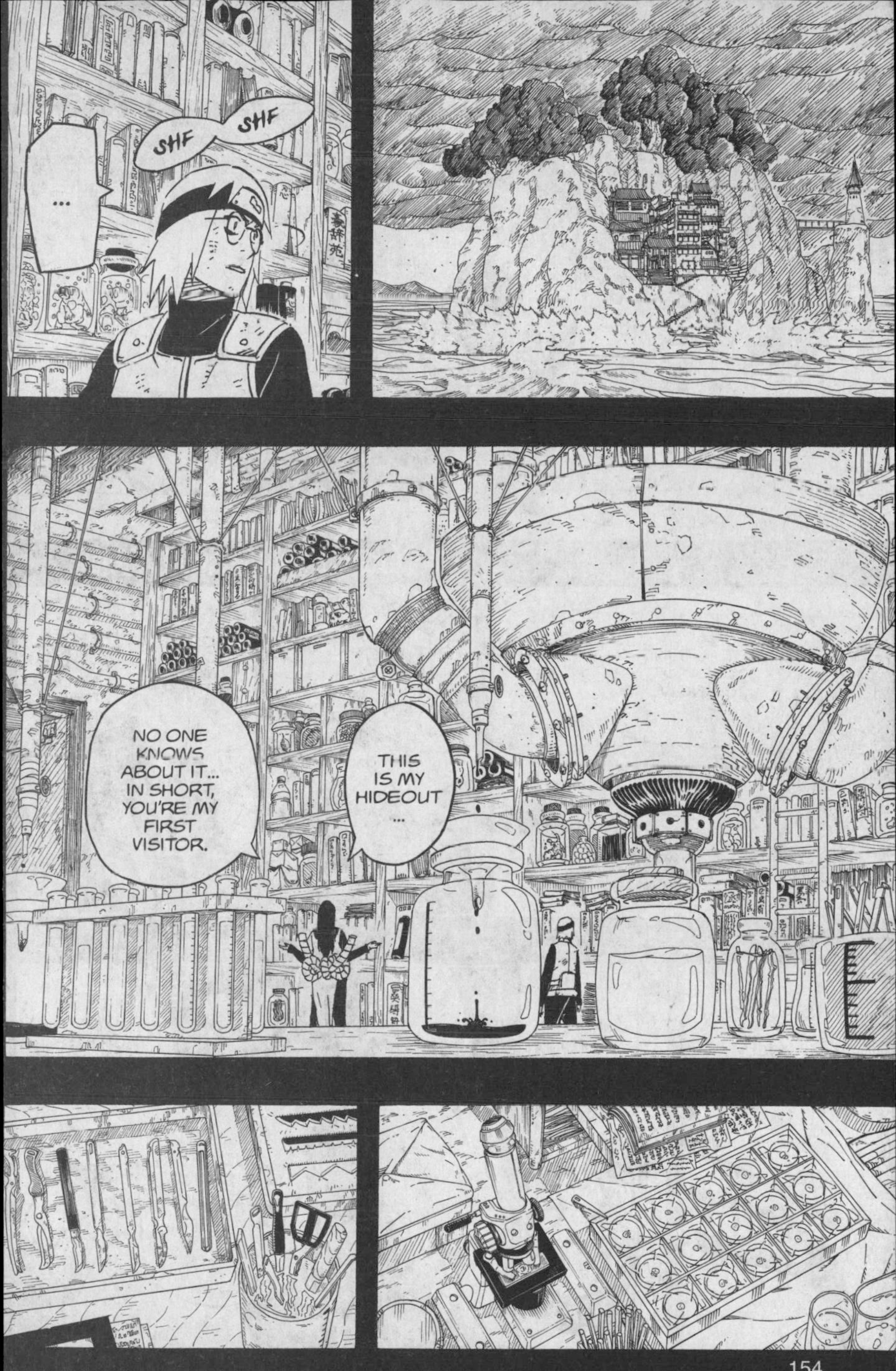
SHF
SHF
...
THIS IS MY HIDEOUT ...
NO ONE KNOWS ABOUT IT... IN SHORT, YOU'RE MY FIRST VISITOR.

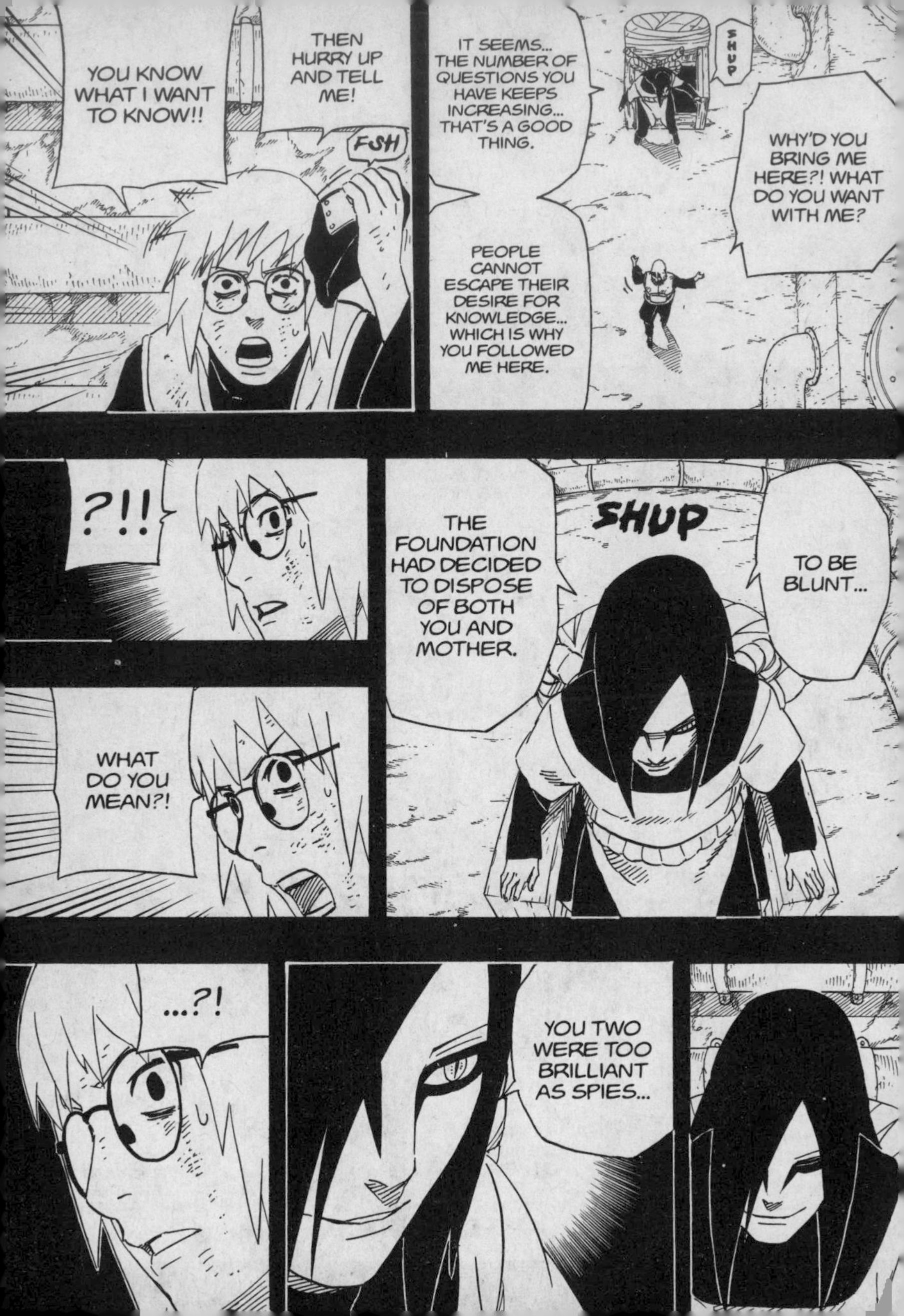
WHY'D YOU BRING ME HERE?! WHAT DO YOU WANT WITH ME?
SHUP
IT SEEMS... THE NUMBER OF QUESTIONS YOU HAVE KEEPS INCREASING... THAT'S A GOOD THING.
PEOPLE CANNOT ESCAPE THEIR DESIRE FOR KNOWLEDGE... WHICH IS WHY YOU FOLLOWED ME HERE.
THEN HURRY UP AND TELL ME!
FSH
YOU KNOW WHAT I WANT TO KNOW!!
TO BE BLUNT...
SHUP
THE FOUNDATION HAD DECIDED TO DISPOSE OF BOTH YOU AND MOTHER.
?!!
WHAT DO YOU MEAN?!
YOU TWO WERE TOO BRILLIANT AS SPIES...
...?!

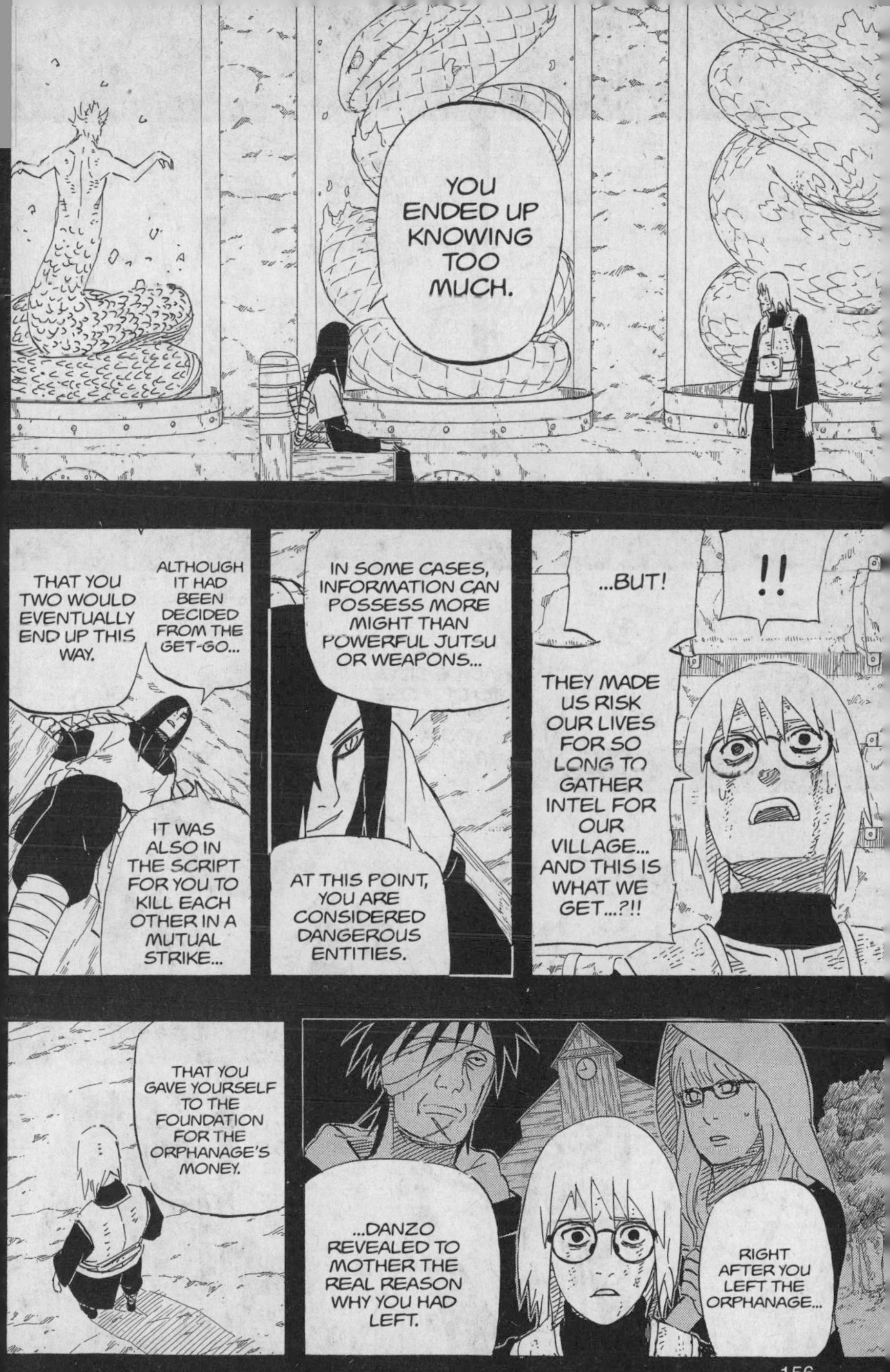
YOU ENDED UP KNOWING TOO MUCH.
!!
...BUT!
THEY MADE US RISK OUR LIVES FOR SO LONG TO GATHER INTEL FOR OUR VILLAGE... AND THIS IS WHAT WE GET...?!!
IN SOME CASES, INFORMATION CAN POSSESS MORE MIGHT THAN POWERFUL JUTSU OR WEAPONS...
AT THIS POINT, YOU ARE CONSIDERED DANGEROUS ENTITIES.
ALTHOUGH IT HAD BEEN DECIDED FROM THE GET-GO...
THAT YOU TWO WOULD EVENTUALLY END UP THIS WAY.
IT WAS ALSO IN THE SCRIPT FOR YOU TO KILL EACH OTHER IN A MUTUAL STRIKE...
RIGHT AFTER YOU LEFT THE ORPHANAGE...
...DANZO REVEALED TO MOTHER THE REAL REASON WHY YOU HAD LEFT.
THAT YOU GAVE YOURSELF TO THE FOUNDATION FOR THE ORPHANAGE'S MONEY.

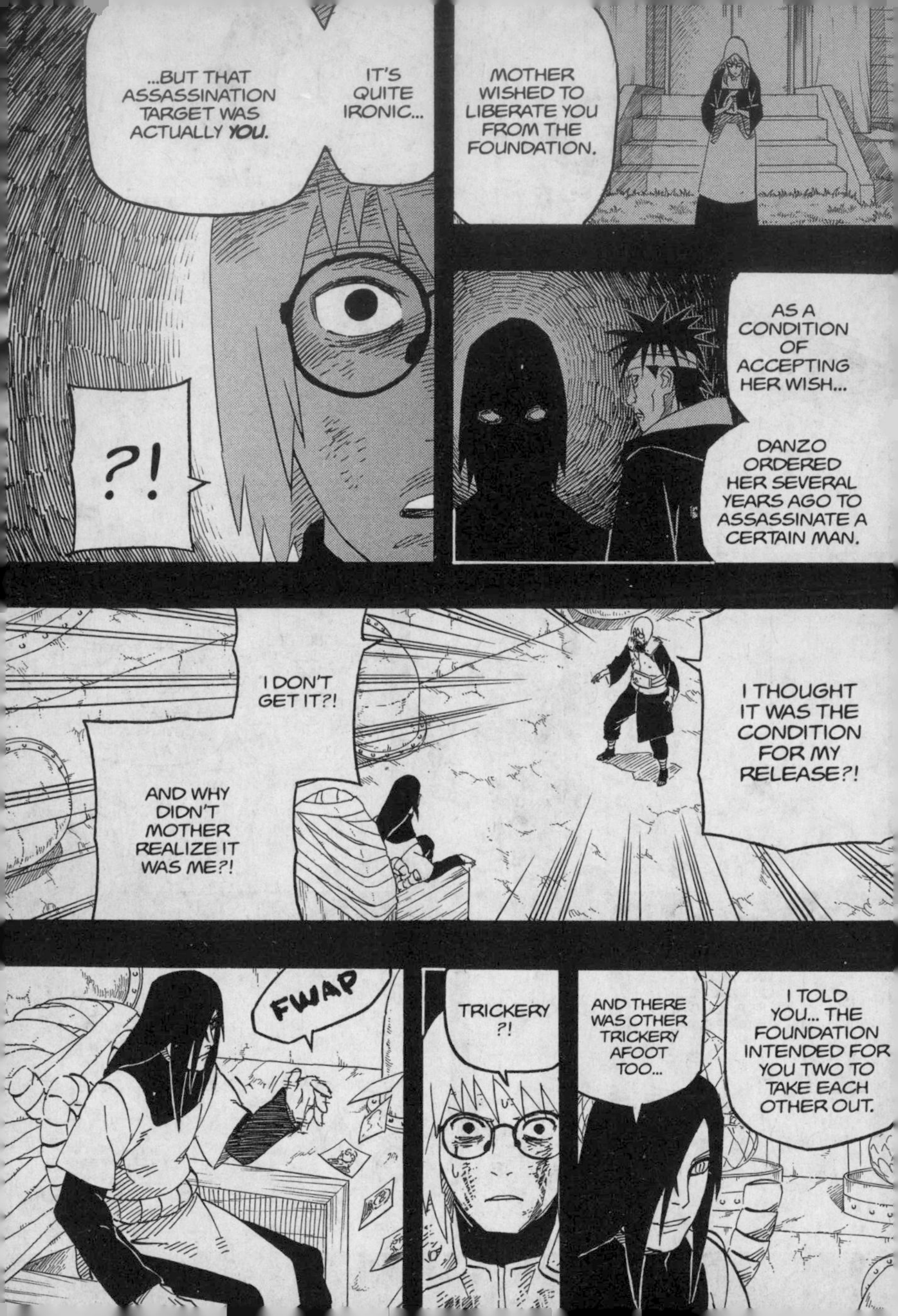
MOTHER WISHED TO LIBERATE YOU FROM THE FOUNDATION.
AS A CONDITION OF ACCEPTING HER WISH...
DANZO ORDERED HER SEVERAL YEARS AGO TO ASSASSINATE A CERTAIN MAN.
IT'S QUITE IRONIC...
...BUT THAT ASSASSINATION TARGET WAS ACTUALLY **YOU.**
?!
I THOUGHT IT WAS THE CONDITION FOR MY RELEASE?!
I DON'T GET IT?!
AND WHY DIDN'T MOTHER REALIZE IT WAS ME?!
I TOLD YOU... THE FOUNDATION INTENDED FOR YOU TWO TO TAKE EACH OTHER OUT.
AND THERE WAS OTHER TRICKERY AFOOT TOO...
TRICKERY ?!
FWAP

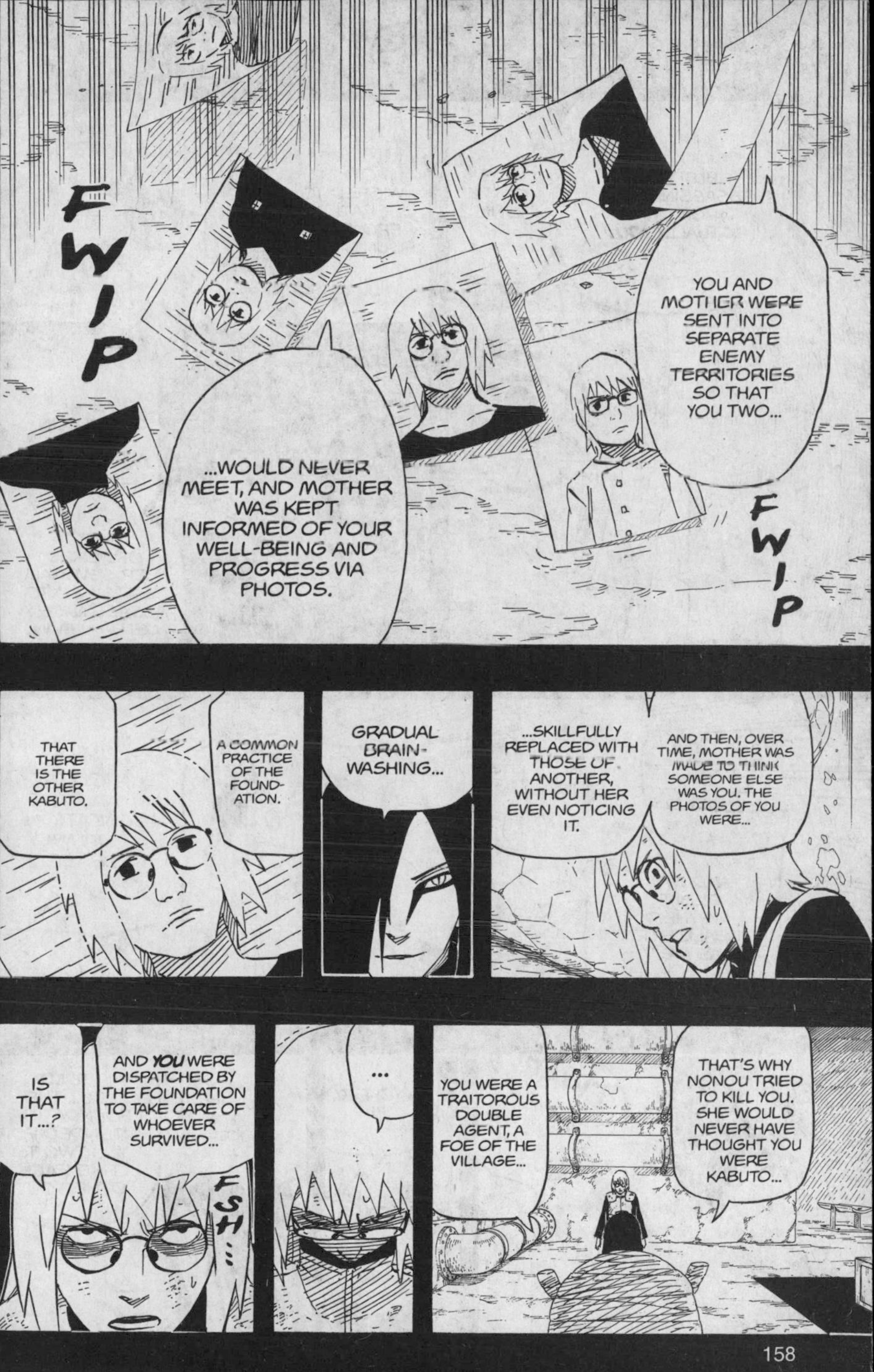
YOU AND MOTHER WERE SENT INTO SEPARATE ENEMY TERRITORIES SO THAT YOU TWO...
FWIP
...WOULD NEVER MEET, AND MOTHER WAS KEPT INFORMED OF YOUR WELL-BEING AND PROGRESS VIA PHOTOS.
FWIP
AND THEN, OVER TIME, MOTHER WAS MADE TO THINK SOMEONE ELSE WAS YOU. THE PHOTOS OF YOU WERE...
...SKILLFULLY REPLACED WITH THOSE OF ANOTHER, WITHOUT HER EVEN NOTICING IT.
GRADUAL BRAIN-WASHING...
A COMMON PRACTICE OF THE FOUNDATION.
THAT THERE IS THE OTHER KABUTO.
THAT'S WHY NONOU TRIED TO KILL YOU. SHE WOULD NEVER HAVE THOUGHT YOU WERE KABUTO...
YOU WERE A TRAITOROUS DOUBLE AGENT, A FOE OF THE VILLAGE...
...
AND *YOU* WERE DISPATCHED BY THE FOUNDATION TO TAKE CARE OF WHOEVER SURVIVED...
IS THAT IT...?
FSH...

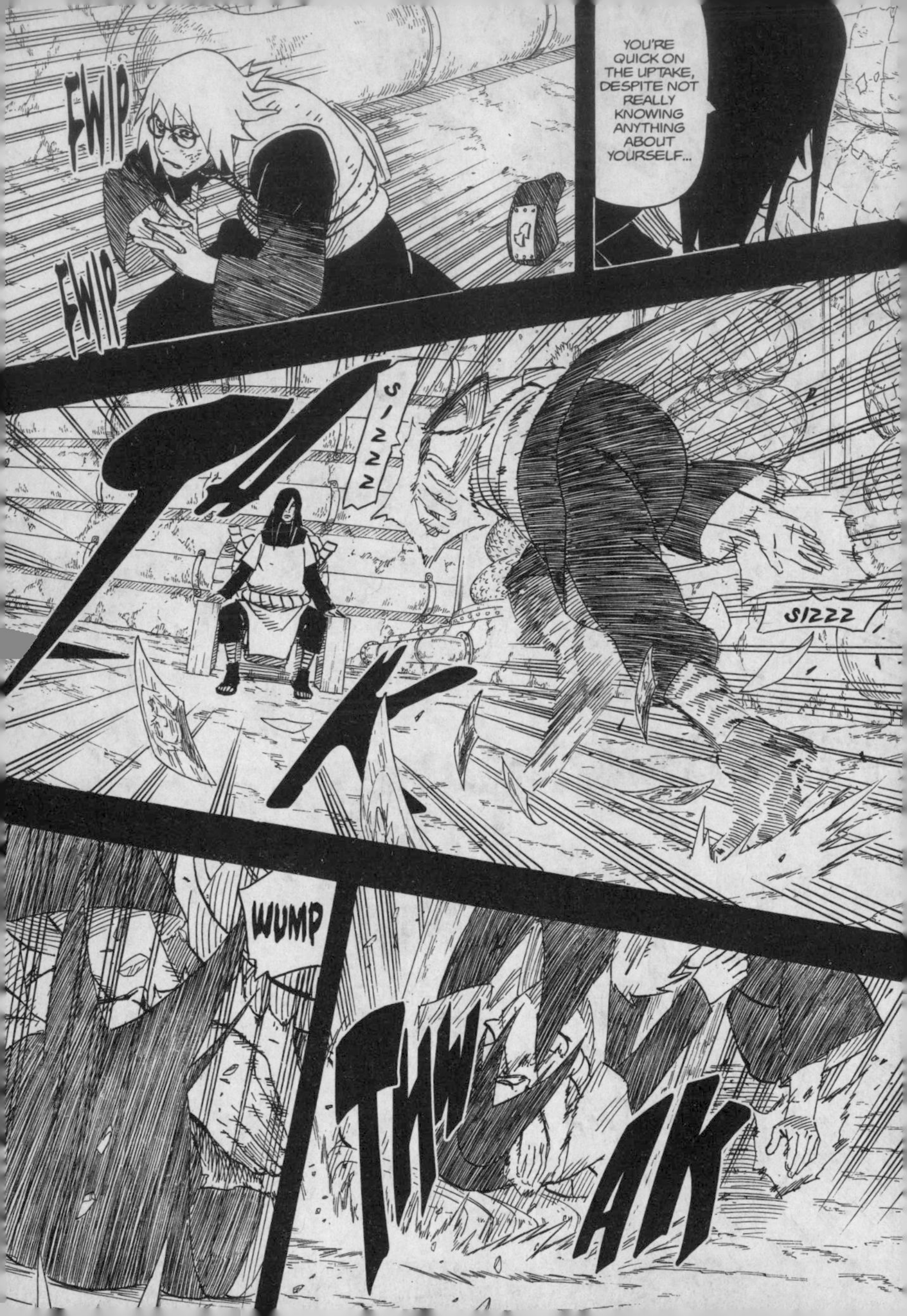
YOU'RE QUICK ON THE UPTAKE, DESPITE NOT REALLY KNOWING ANYTHING ABOUT YOURSELF...
FWIP
FWIP
SIZZZ
SIZZZ
TAK
THWAK
WUMP

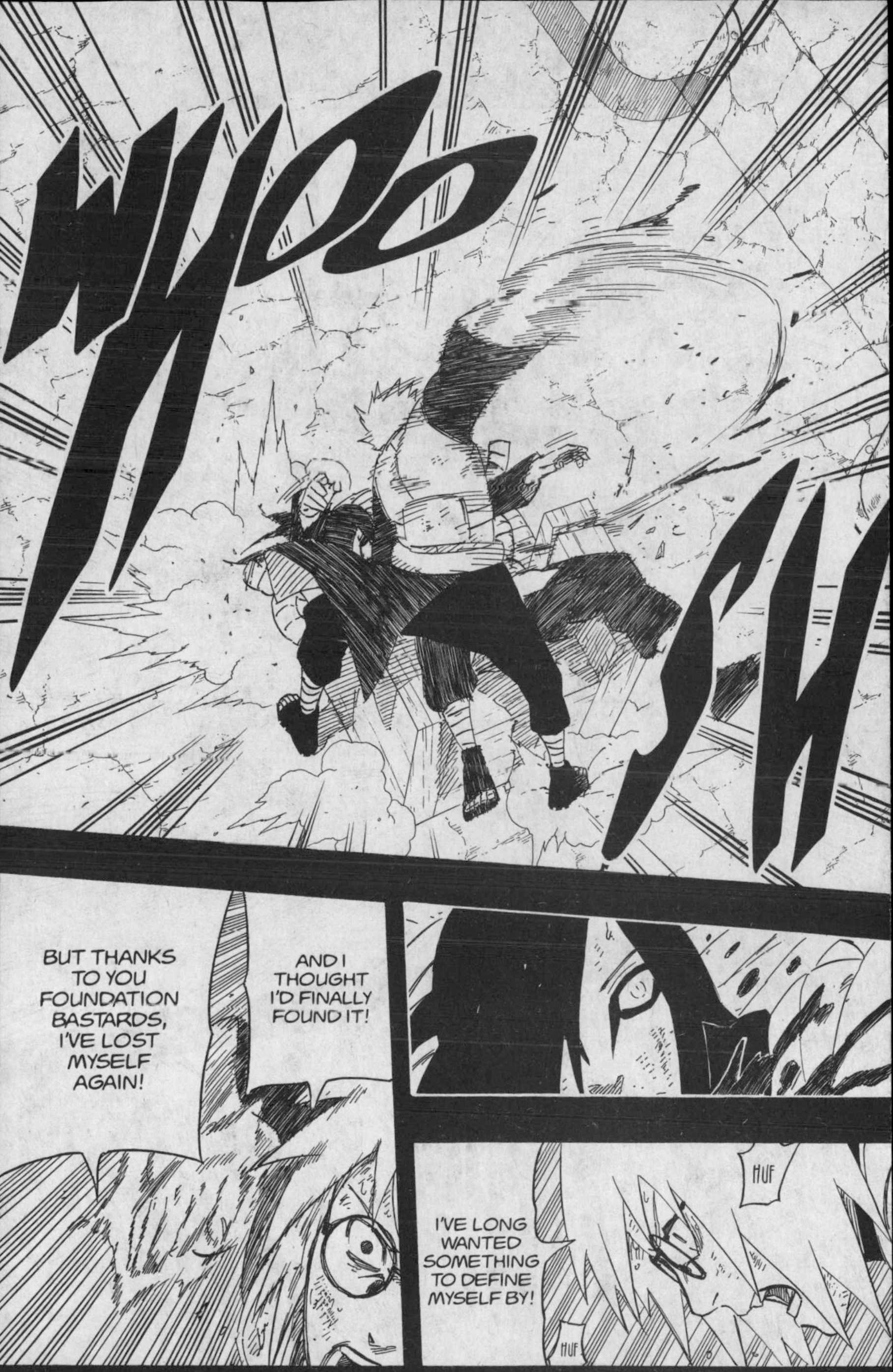
WHOOSH
HUF
I'VE LONG WANTED SOMETHING TO DEFINE MYSELF BY!
HUF
AND I THOUGHT I'D FINALLY FOUND IT!
BUT THANKS TO YOU FOUNDATION BASTARDS, I'VE LOST MYSELF AGAIN!

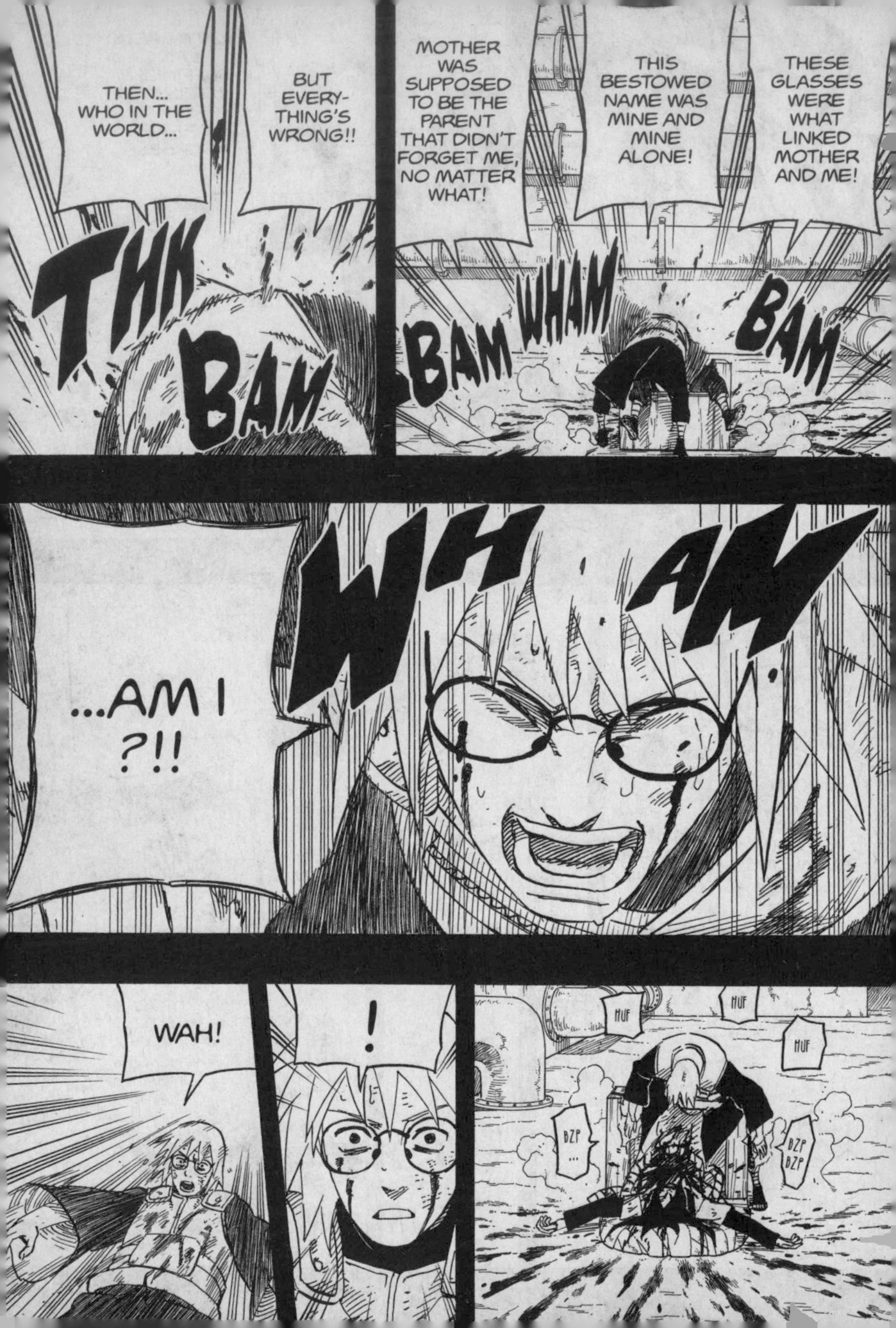
THESE GLASSES WERE WHAT LINKED MOTHER AND ME!
THIS BESTOWED NAME WAS MINE AND MINE ALONE!
MOTHER WAS SUPPOSED TO BE THE PARENT THAT DIDN'T FORGET ME, NO MATTER WHAT!
BAM
WHAM
BAM
BUT EVERY-THING'S WRONG!!
THEN... WHO IN THE WORLD...
THK
BAM
WHAM
...AM I ?!!
HUF
HUF
HUF
BZP BZP
BZP ...
!
WAH!

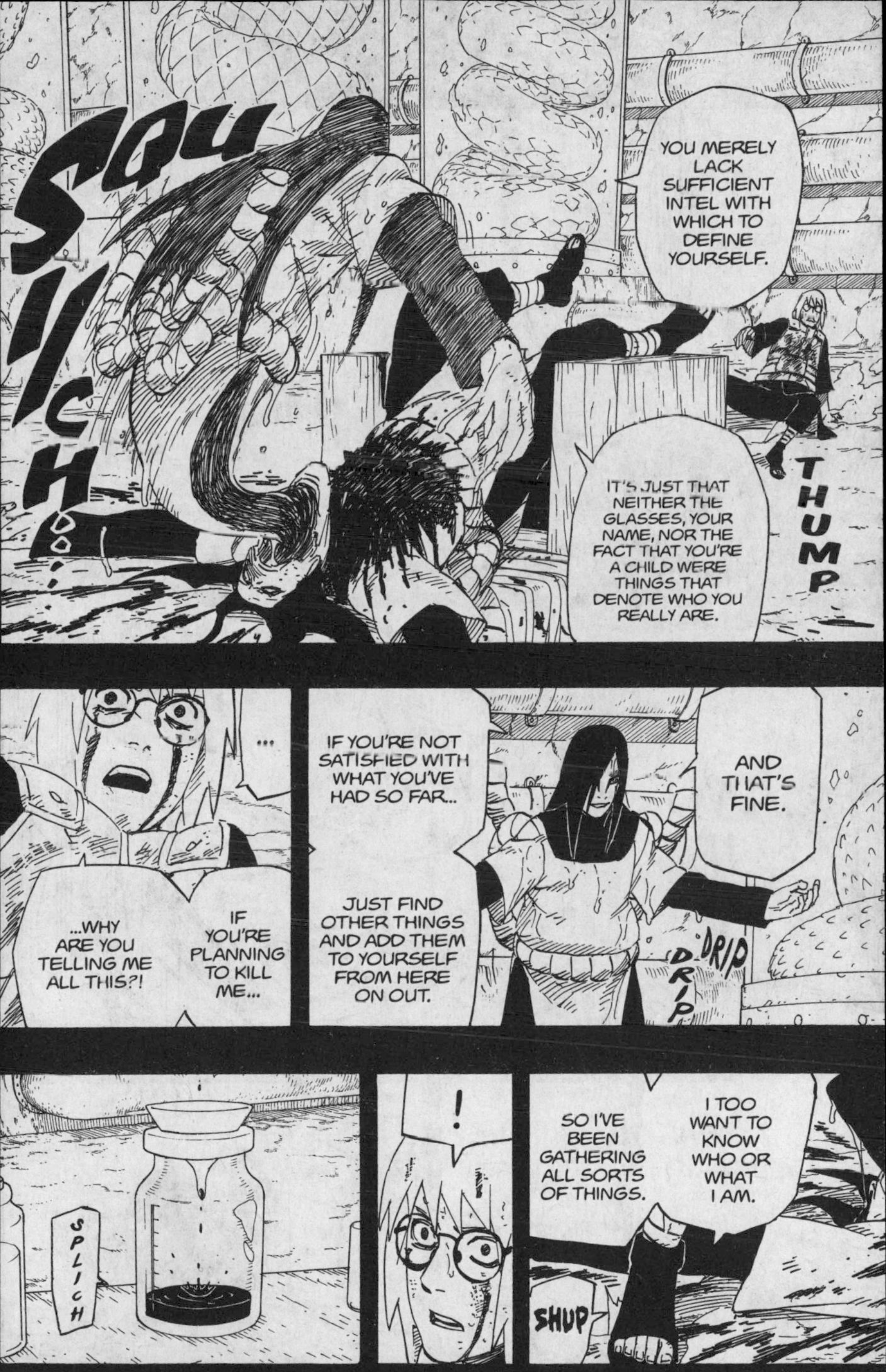
YOU MERELY LACK SUFFICIENT INTEL WITH WHICH TO DEFINE YOURSELF.
IT'S JUST THAT NEITHER THE GLASSES, YOUR NAME, NOR THE FACT THAT YOU'RE A CHILD WERE THINGS THAT DENOTE WHO YOU REALLY ARE.
THUMP
AND THAT'S FINE.
IF YOU'RE NOT SATISFIED WITH WHAT YOU'VE HAD SO FAR...
JUST FIND OTHER THINGS AND ADD THEM TO YOURSELF FROM HERE ON OUT.
DRIP
DRIP
DRIP
...
IF YOU'RE PLANNING TO KILL ME...
...WHY ARE YOU TELLING ME ALL THIS?!
I TOO WANT TO KNOW WHO OR WHAT I AM.
SO I'VE BEEN GATHERING ALL SORTS OF THINGS.
SHUP
!
SPLICH

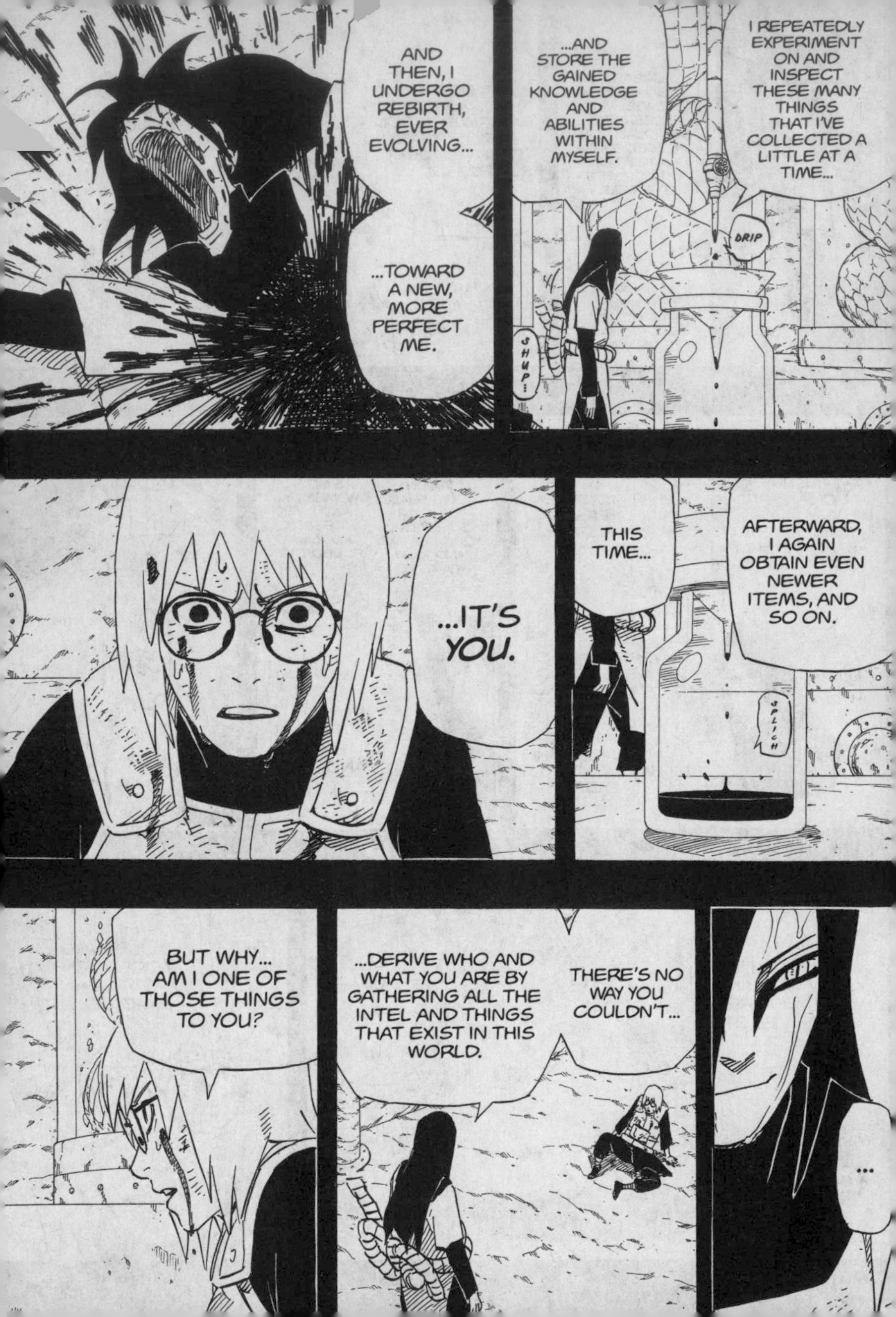

I REPEATEDLY EXPERIMENT ON AND INSPECT THESE MANY THINGS THAT I'VE COLLECTED A LITTLE AT A TIME...
...AND STORE THE GAINED KNOWLEDGE AND ABILITIES WITHIN MYSELF.
DRIP
SHUP
AND THEN, I UNDERGO REBIRTH, EVER EVOLVING...
...TOWARD A NEW, MORE PERFECT ME.
AFTERWARD, I AGAIN OBTAIN EVEN NEWER ITEMS, AND SO ON.
THIS TIME...
SPLICH
...IT'S YOU.
...
THERE'S NO WAY YOU COULDN'T...
...DERIVE WHO AND WHAT YOU ARE BY GATHERING ALL THE INTEL AND THINGS THAT EXIST IN THIS WORLD.
BUT WHY... AM I ONE OF THOSE THINGS TO YOU?

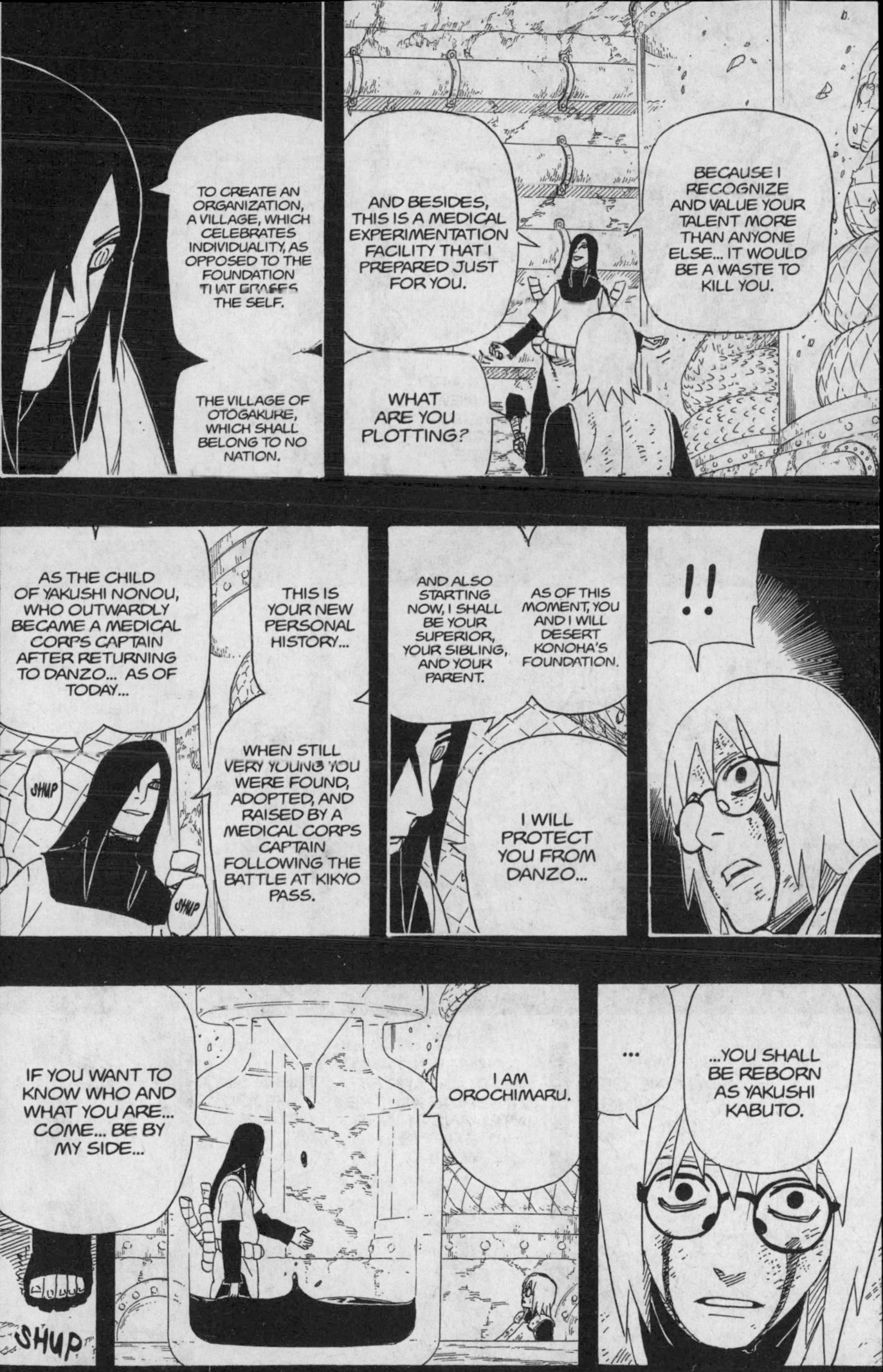
BECAUSE I RECOGNIZE AND VALUE YOUR TALENT MORE THAN ANYONE ELSE... IT WOULD BE A WASTE TO KILL YOU.
AND BESIDES, THIS IS A MEDICAL EXPERIMENTATION FACILITY THAT I PREPARED JUST FOR YOU.
WHAT ARE YOU PLOTTING?
TO CREATE AN ORGANIZATION, A VILLAGE, WHICH CELEBRATES INDIVIDUALITY, AS OPPOSED TO THE FOUNDATION THAT ERASES THE SELF.
THE VILLAGE OF OTOGAKURE, WHICH SHALL BELONG TO NO NATION.
!!
AS OF THIS MOMENT, YOU AND I WILL DESERT KONOHA'S FOUNDATION.
AND ALSO STARTING NOW, I SHALL BE YOUR SUPERIOR, YOUR SIBLING, AND YOUR PARENT.
I WILL PROTECT YOU FROM DANZO...
THIS IS YOUR NEW PERSONAL HISTORY...
AS THE CHILD OF YAKUSHI NONOU, WHO OUTWARDLY BECAME A MEDICAL CORPS CAPTAIN AFTER RETURNING TO DANZO... AS OF TODAY...
WHEN STILL VERY YOUNG YOU WERE FOUND, ADOPTED, AND RAISED BY A MEDICAL CORPS CAPTAIN FOLLOWING THE BATTLE AT KIKYO PASS.
SHUP
SHUP
...
...YOU SHALL BE REBORN AS YAKUSHI KABUTO.
I AM OROCHIMARU.
IF YOU WANT TO KNOW WHO AND WHAT YOU ARE... COME... BE BY MY SIDE...
SHUP

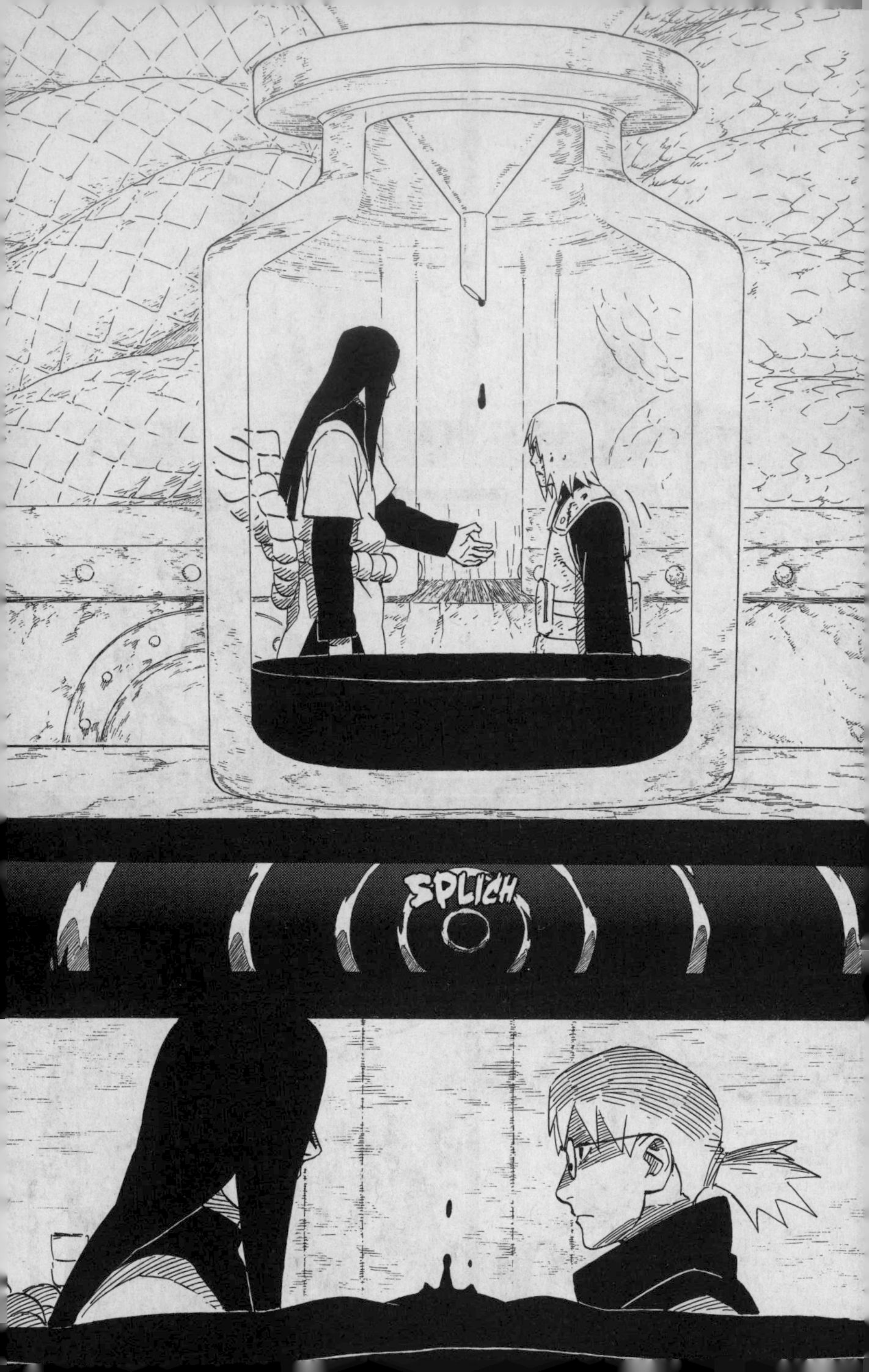
SPLICH

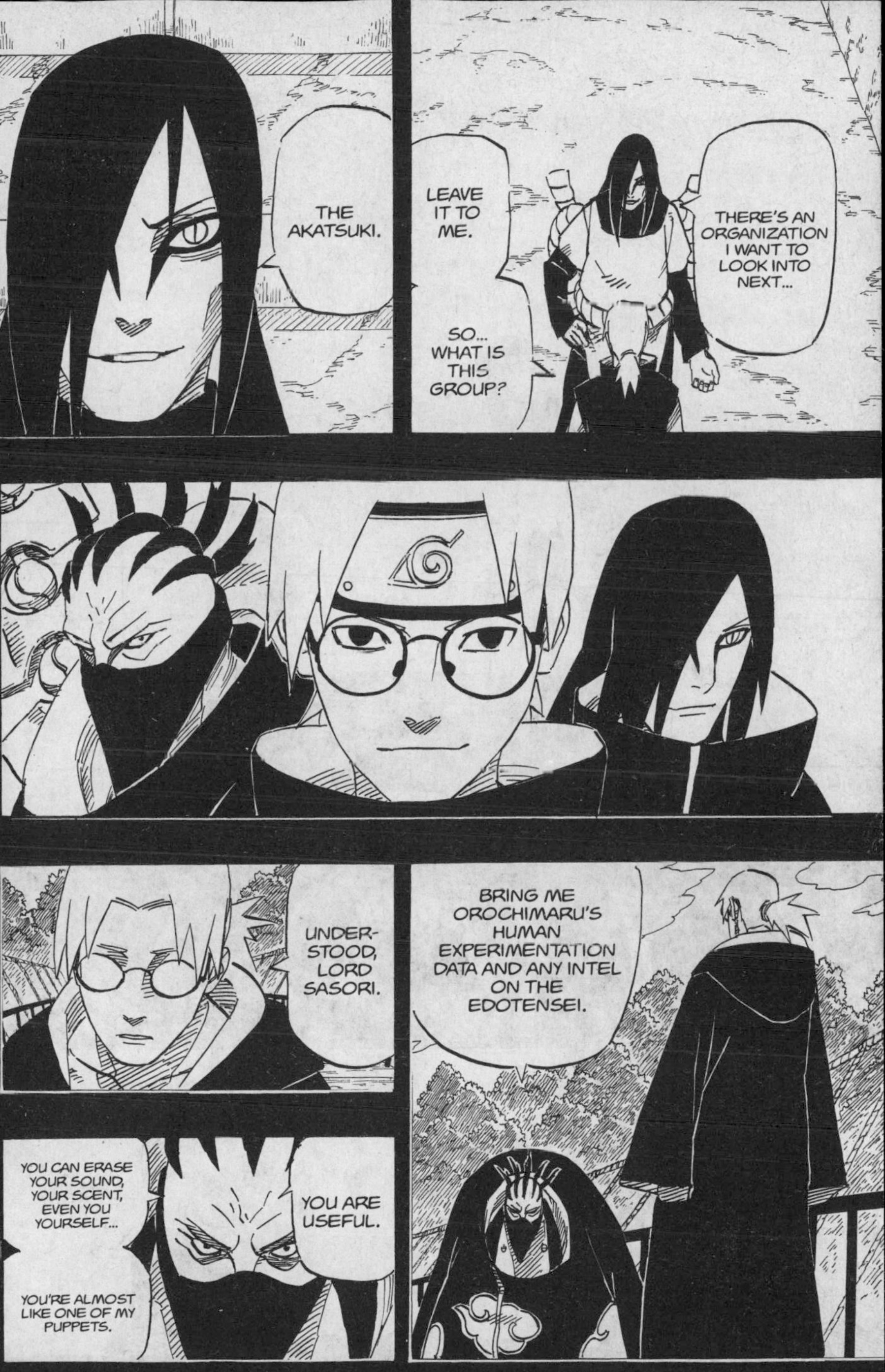
THERE'S AN ORGANIZATION I WANT TO LOOK INTO NEXT...
LEAVE IT TO ME.
SO... WHAT IS THIS GROUP?
THE AKATSUKI.
BRING ME OROCHIMARU'S HUMAN EXPERIMENTATION DATA AND ANY INTEL ON THE EDOTENSEI.
UNDER-STOOD, LORD SASORI.
YOU ARE USEFUL.
YOU CAN ERASE YOUR SOUND, YOUR SCENT, EVEN YOU YOURSELF...
YOU'RE ALMOST LIKE ONE OF MY PUPPETS.

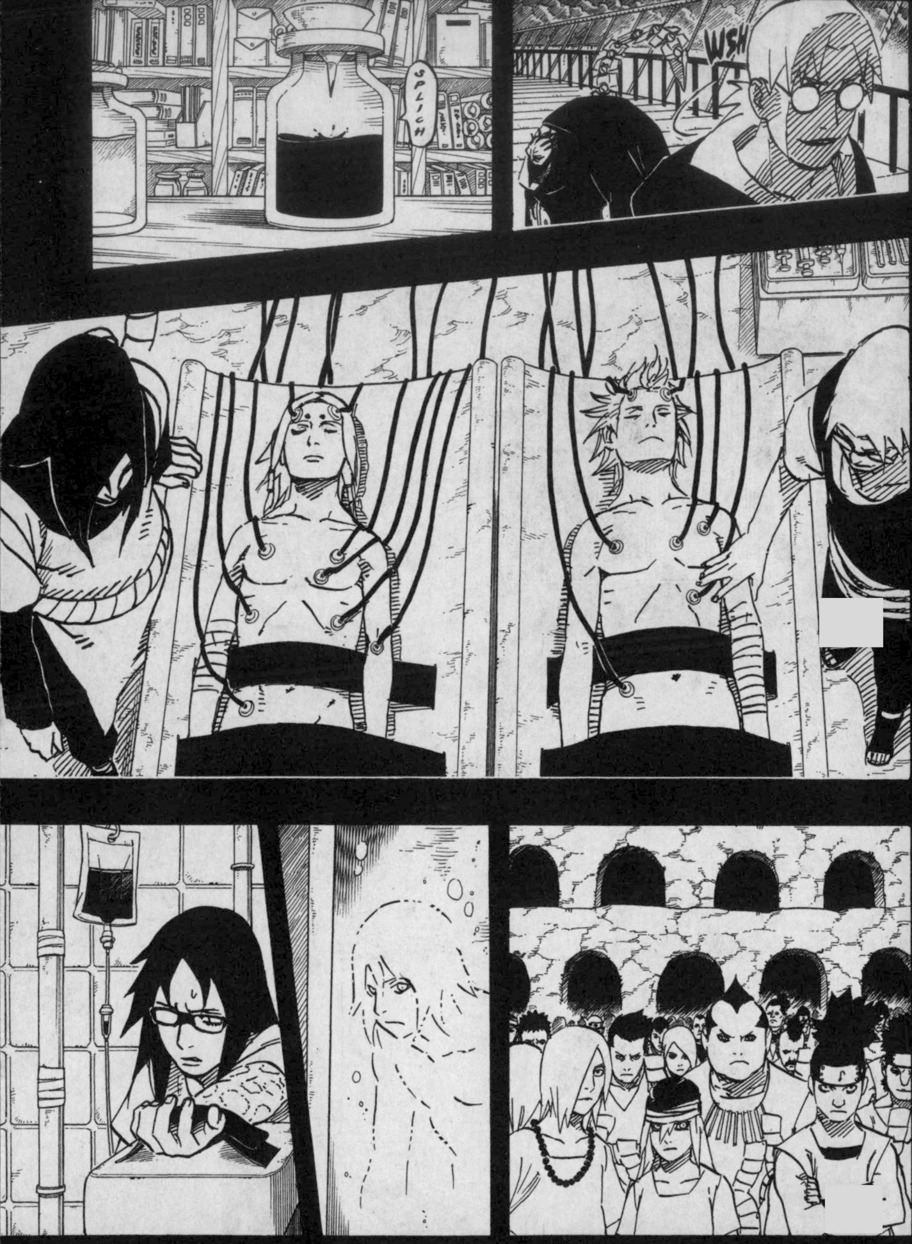
WSH
SPLICH

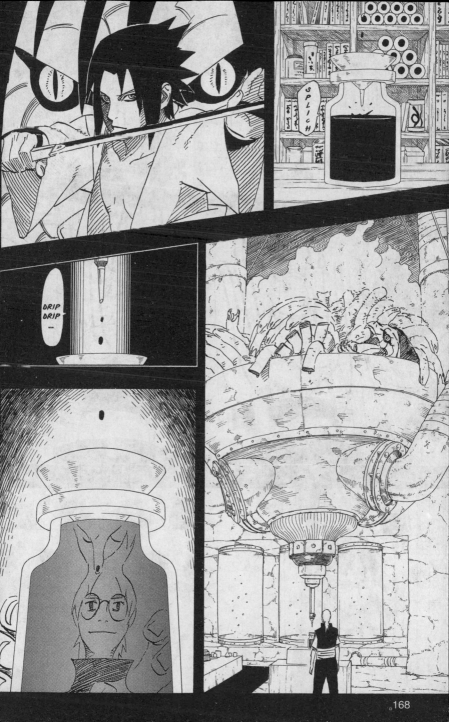

SPLICH

DRIP
DRIP
...

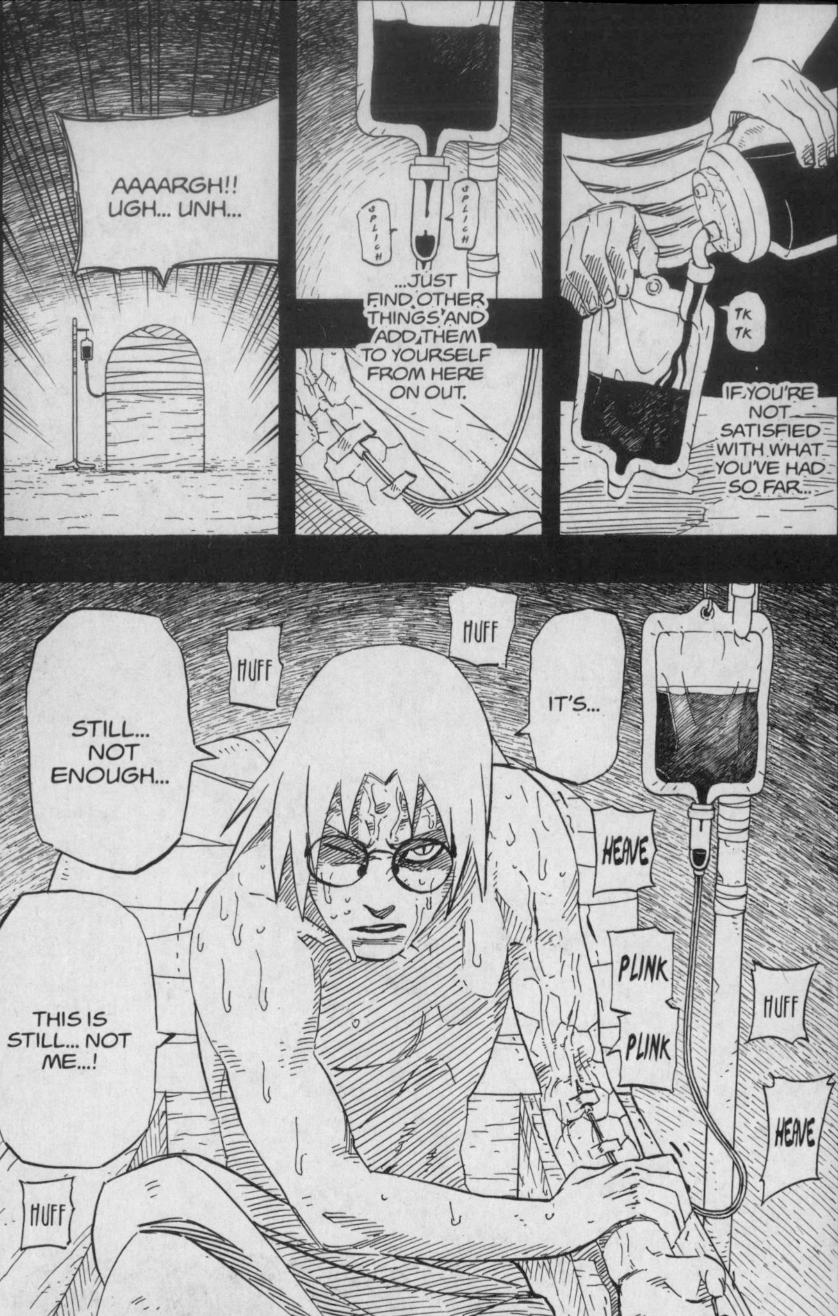
TK TK
IF YOU'RE NOT SATISFIED WITH WHAT YOU'VE HAD SO FAR...
SPLICH
SPLICH
...JUST FIND OTHER THINGS AND ADD THEM TO YOURSELF FROM HERE ON OUT.
AAAARGH!! UGH... UNH...
HUFF
HEAVE
PLINK
PLINK
HEAVE
IT'S...
HUFF
HUFF
STILL... NOT ENOUGH...
THIS IS STILL... NOT ME...!
HUFF

NARUTO

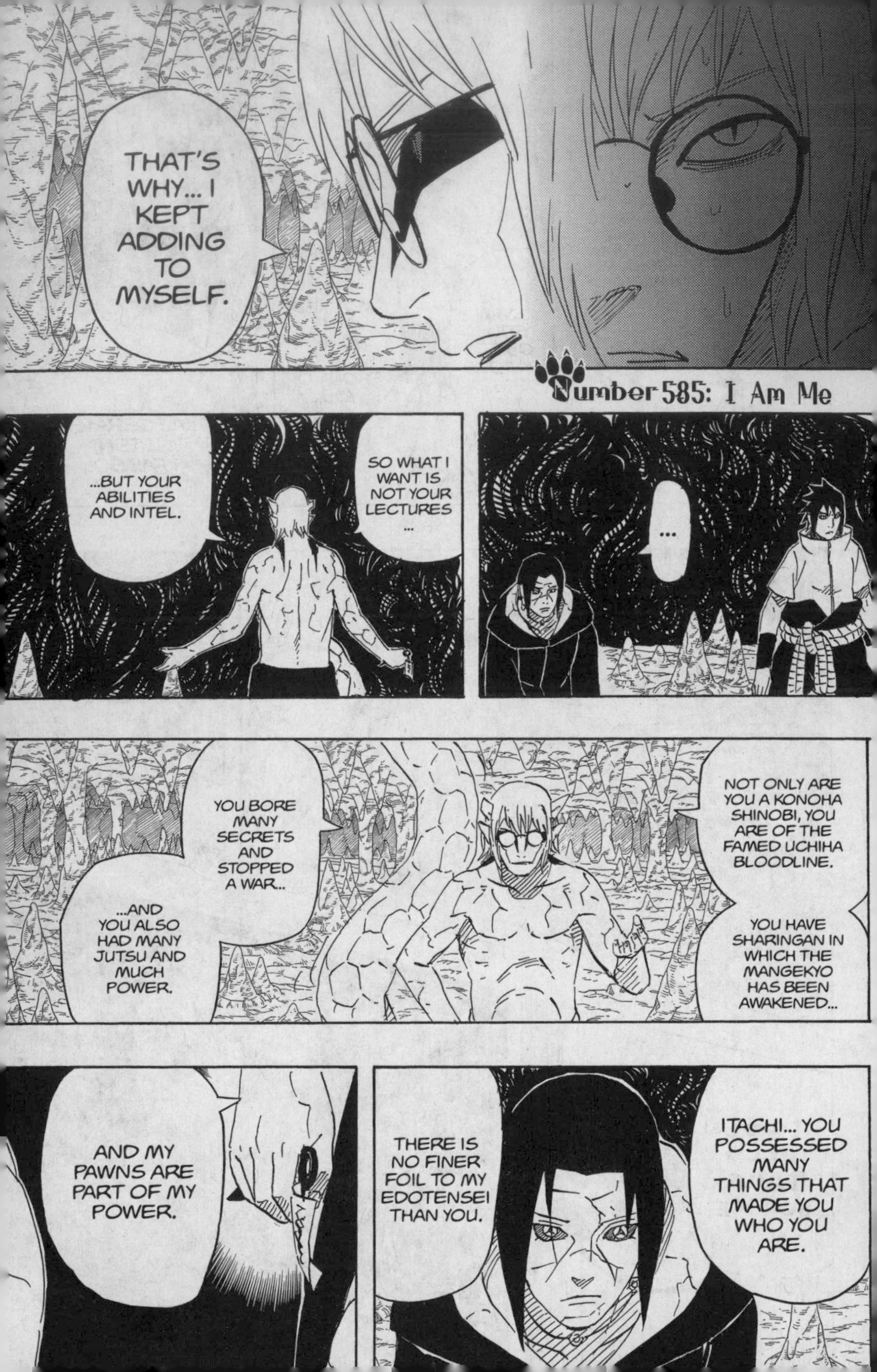
THAT'S WHY... I KEPT ADDING TO MYSELF.
Number 585: I Am Me
...
SO WHAT I WANT IS NOT YOUR LECTURES ...
...BUT YOUR ABILITIES AND INTEL.
NOT ONLY ARE YOU A KONOHA SHINOBI, YOU ARE OF THE FAMED UCHIHA BLOODLINE.
YOU HAVE SHARINGAN IN WHICH THE MANGEKYO HAS BEEN AWAKENED...
YOU BORE MANY SECRETS AND STOPPED A WAR...
...AND YOU ALSO HAD MANY JUTSU AND MUCH POWER.
ITACHI... YOU POSSESSED MANY THINGS THAT MADE YOU WHO YOU ARE.
THERE IS NO FINER FOIL TO MY EDOTENSEI THAN YOU.
AND MY PAWNS ARE PART OF MY POWER.

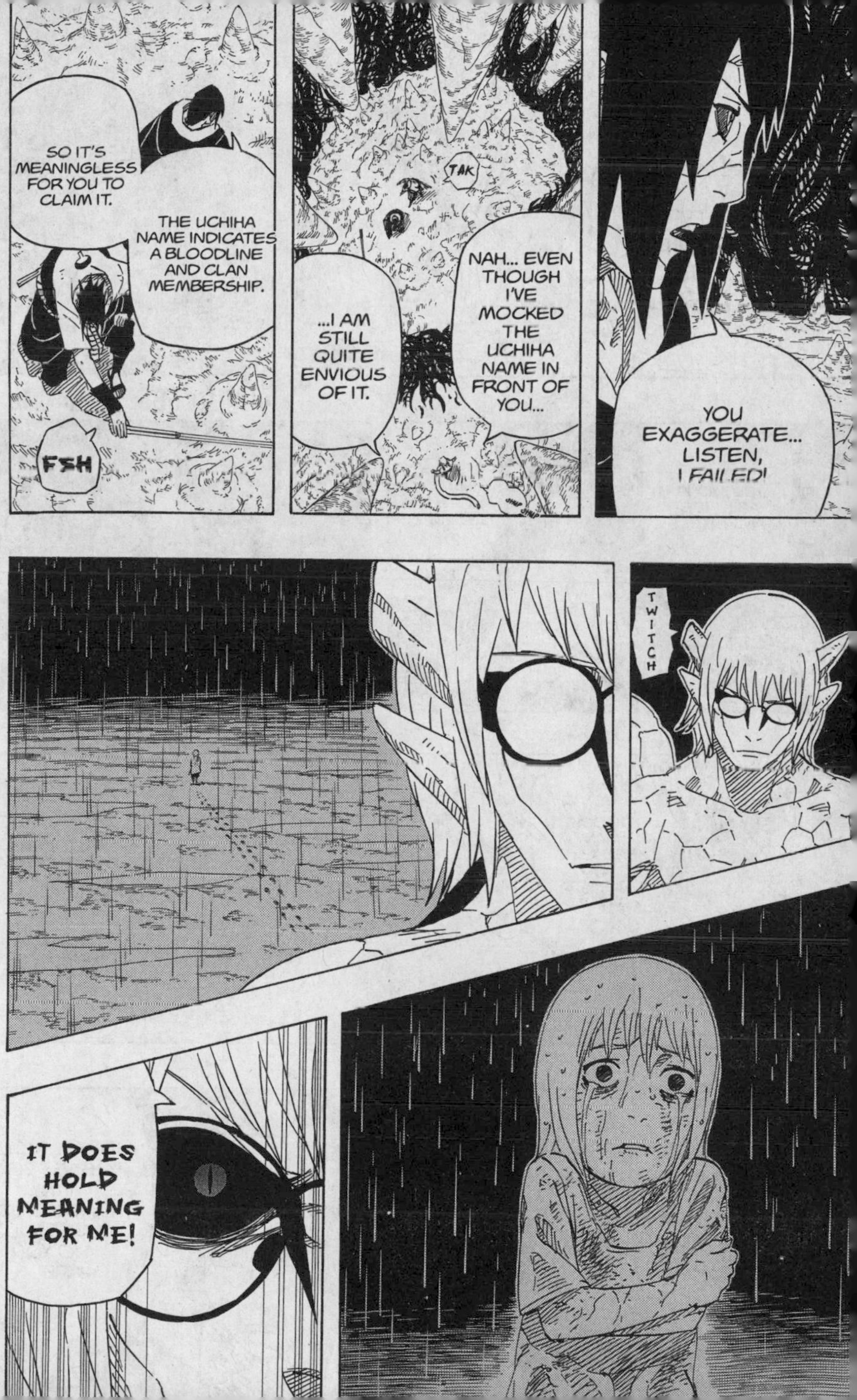
YOU EXAGGERATE... LISTEN, I FAILED!
TAK
NAH... EVEN THOUGH I'VE MOCKED THE UCHIHA NAME IN FRONT OF YOU...
...I AM STILL QUITE ENVIOUS OF IT.
THE UCHIHA NAME INDICATES A BLOODLINE AND CLAN MEMBERSHIP.
SO IT'S MEANINGLESS FOR YOU TO CLAIM IT.
FSH
TWITCH
IT DOES HOLD MEANING FOR ME!

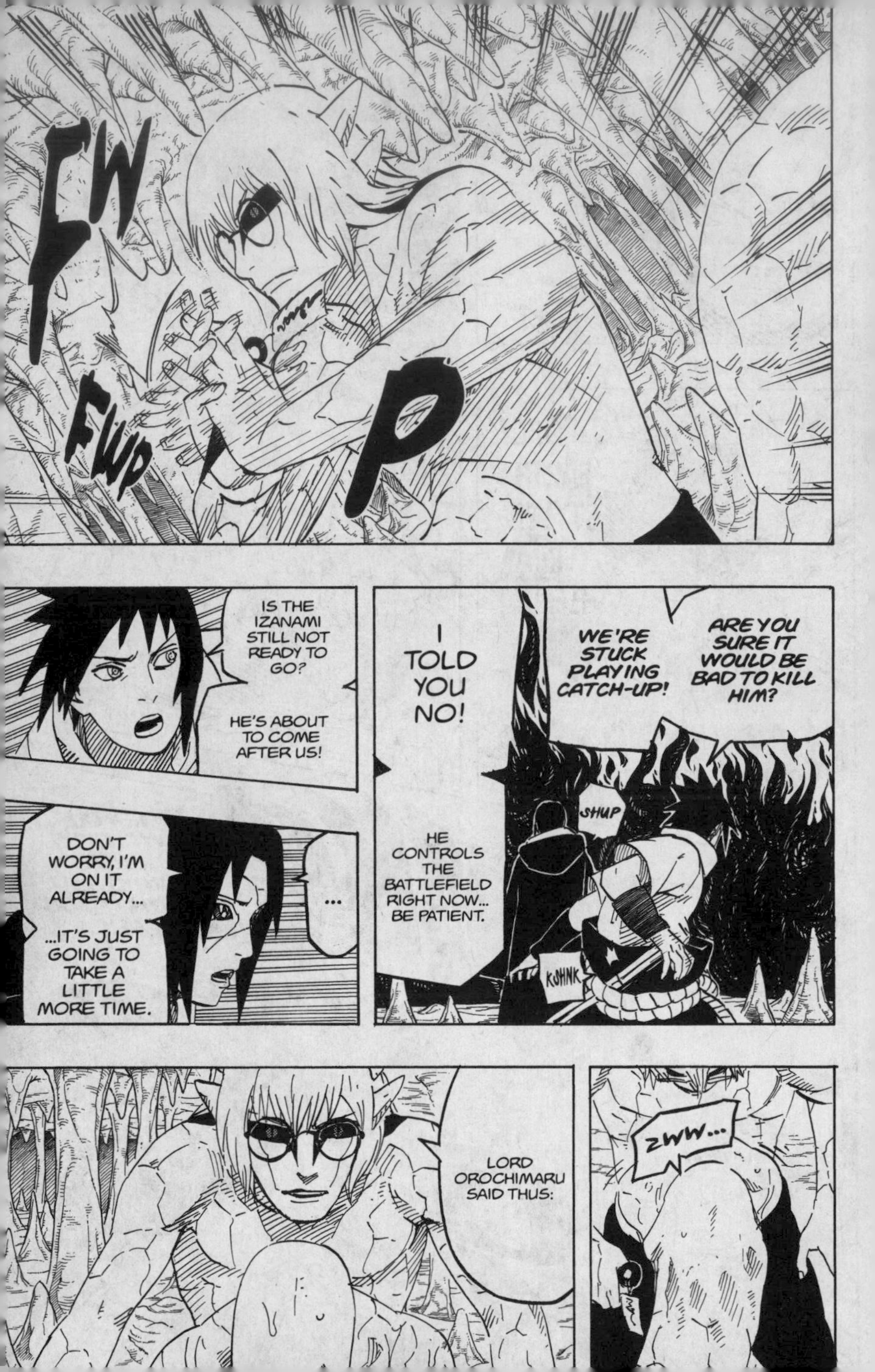
FW
FWP
ARE YOU SURE IT WOULD BE BAD TO KILL HIM?
WE'RE STUCK PLAYING CATCH-UP!
I TOLD YOU NO!
HE CONTROLS THE BATTLEFIELD RIGHT NOW... BE PATIENT.
SHUP
KCHNK
IS THE IZANAMI STILL NOT READY TO GO?
HE'S ABOUT TO COME AFTER US!
...
DON'T WORRY, I'M ON IT ALREADY...
...IT'S JUST GOING TO TAKE A LITTLE MORE TIME.
ZWW...
LORD OROCHIMARU SAID THUS:

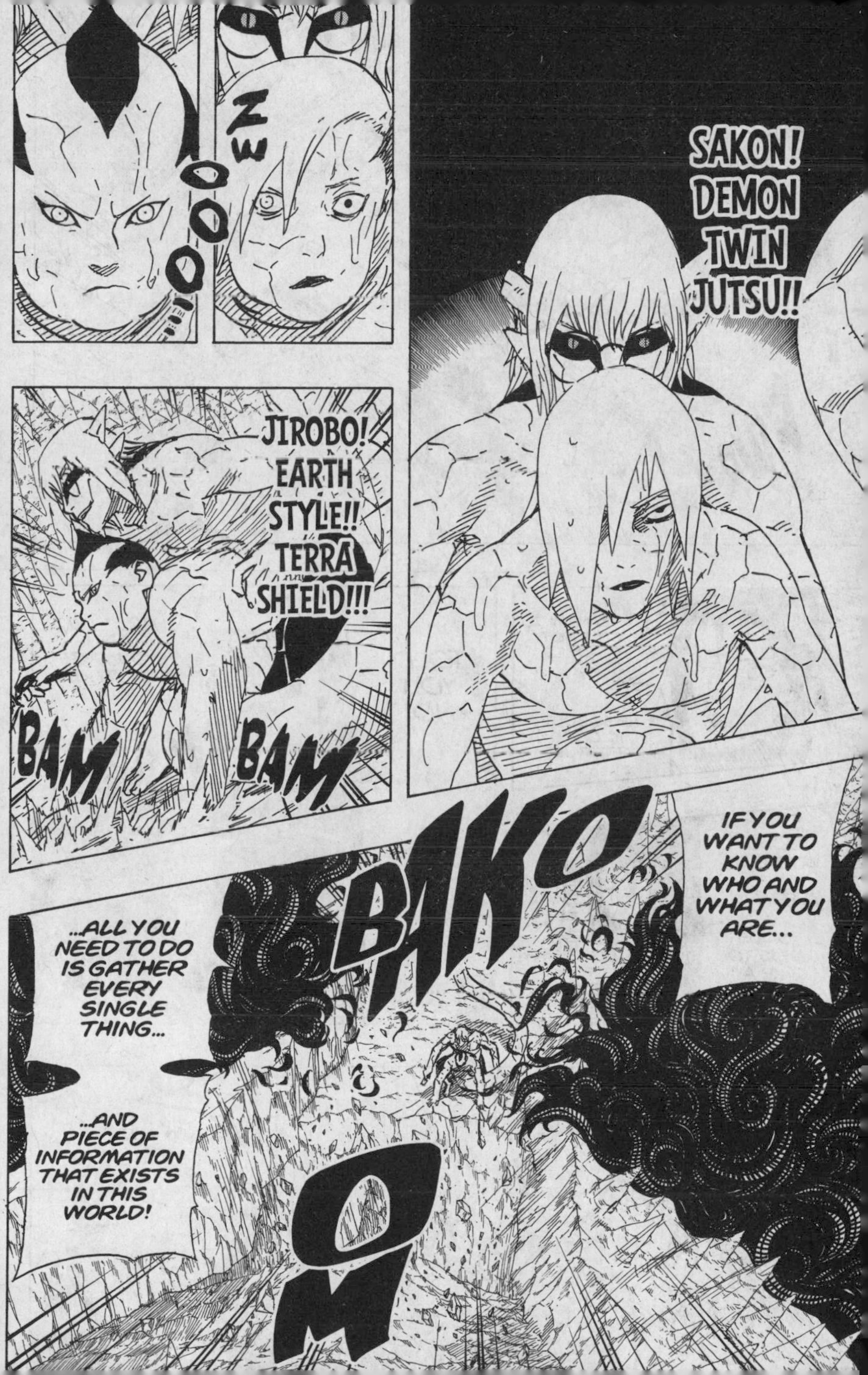

SAKON! DEMON TWIN JUTSU!!
ZWOOO...!!
JIROBO! EARTH STYLE!! TERRA SHIELD!!!
BAM
BAM
IF YOU WANT TO KNOW WHO AND WHAT YOU ARE...
BAKOOM
...ALL YOU NEED TO DO IS GATHER EVERY SINGLE THING...
...AND PIECE OF INFORMATION THAT EXISTS IN THIS WORLD!

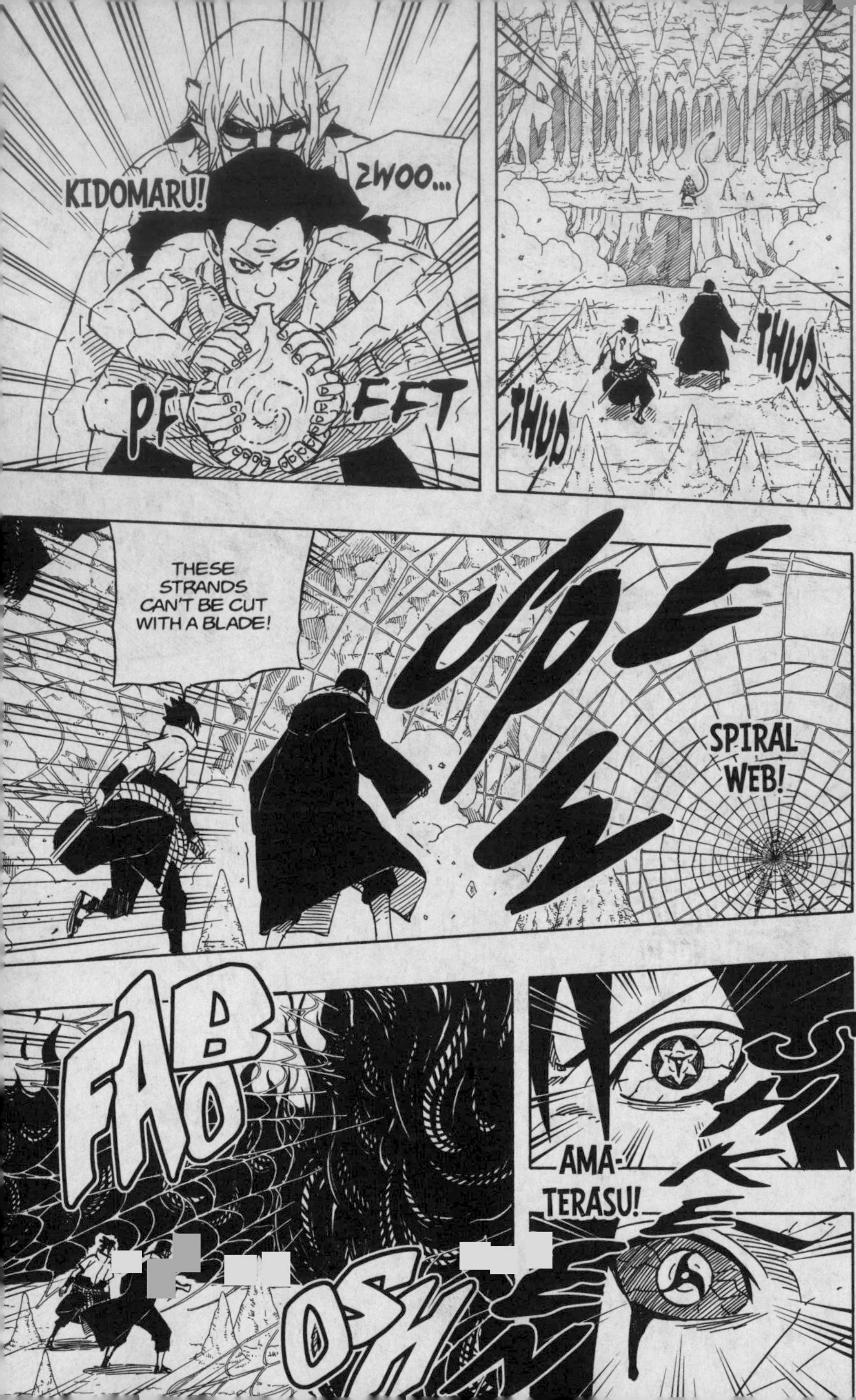
THUD
THUD
ZWOO...
KIDOMARU!
PF
FFT
THESE STRANDS CAN'T BE CUT WITH A BLADE!
SPIRAL WEB!
AMA-TERASU!
FAB

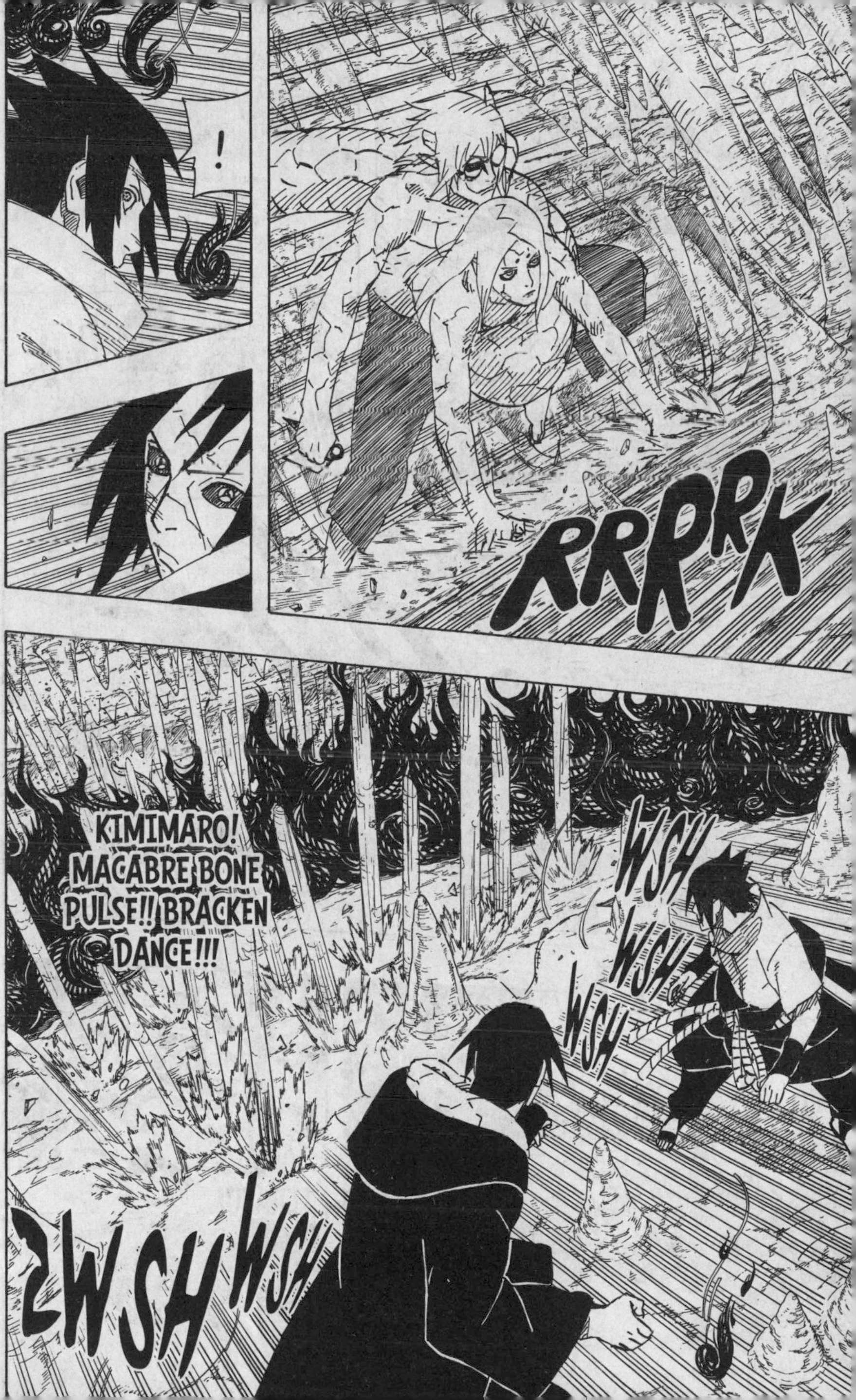
RRRRK
!
WSH
WSH
WSH
KIMIMARO! MACABRE BONE PULSE!! BRACKEN DANCE!!!
WSH
WSH
WSH

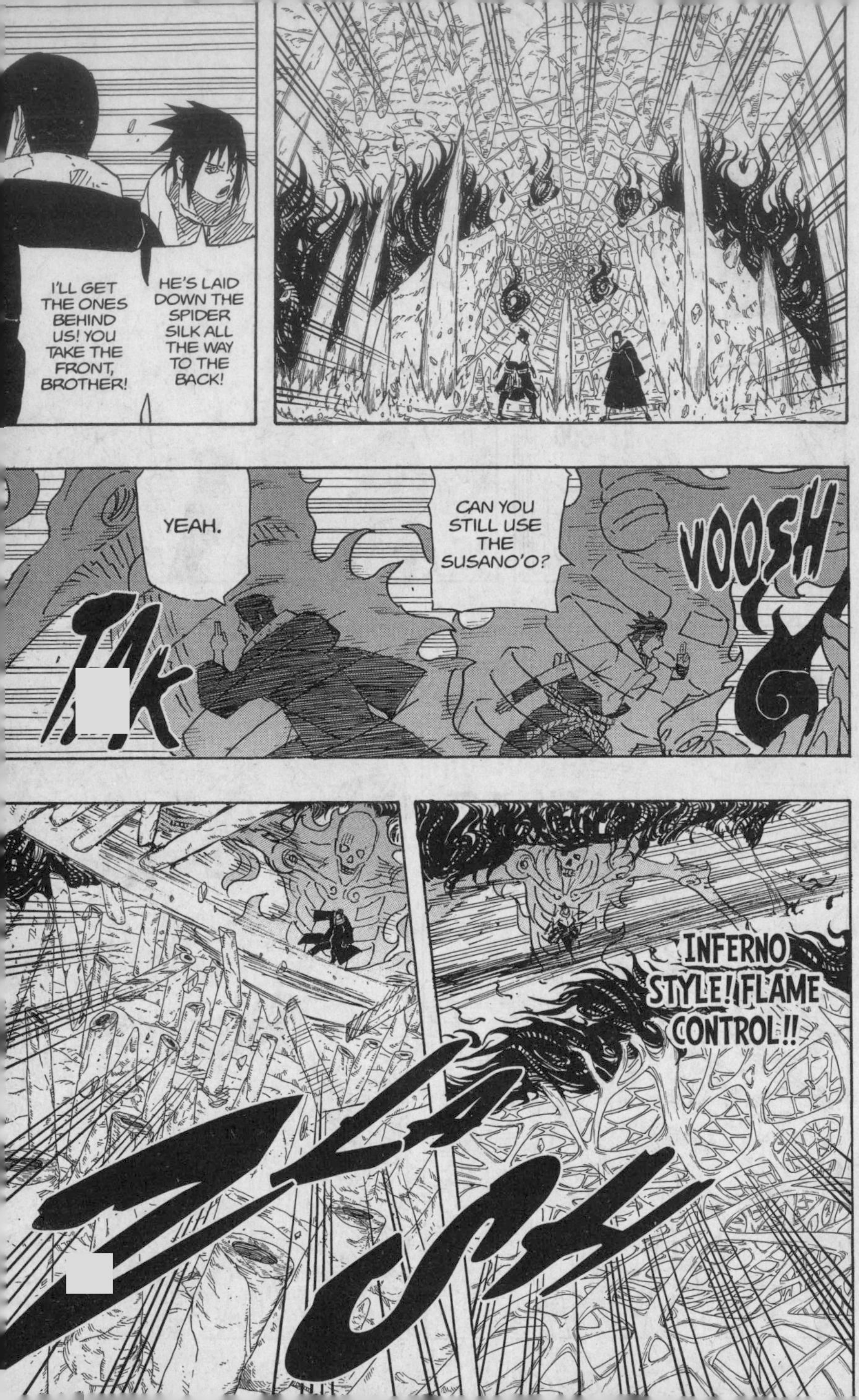
HE'S LAID DOWN THE SPIDER SILK ALL THE WAY TO THE BACK!
I'LL GET THE ONES BEHIND US! YOU TAKE THE FRONT, BROTHER!
VOOSH
CAN YOU STILL USE THE SUSANO'O?
YEAH.
TAK
INFERNO STYLE! FLAME CONTROL!!

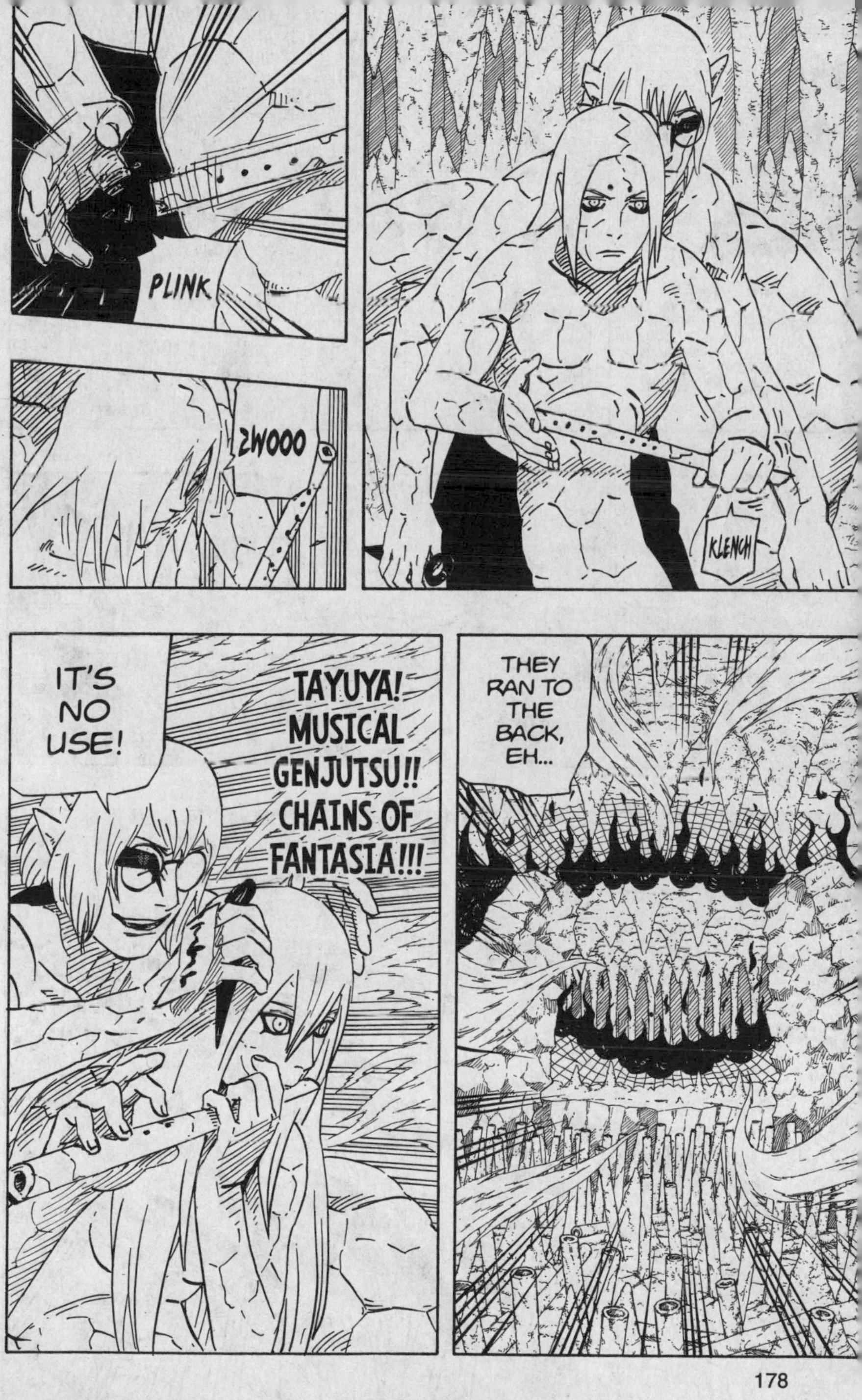
KLENCH
PLINK
ZWOOO
THEY RAN TO THE BACK, EH...
IT'S NO USE!
TAYUYA! MUSICAL GENJUTSU!! CHAINS OF FANTASIA!!!

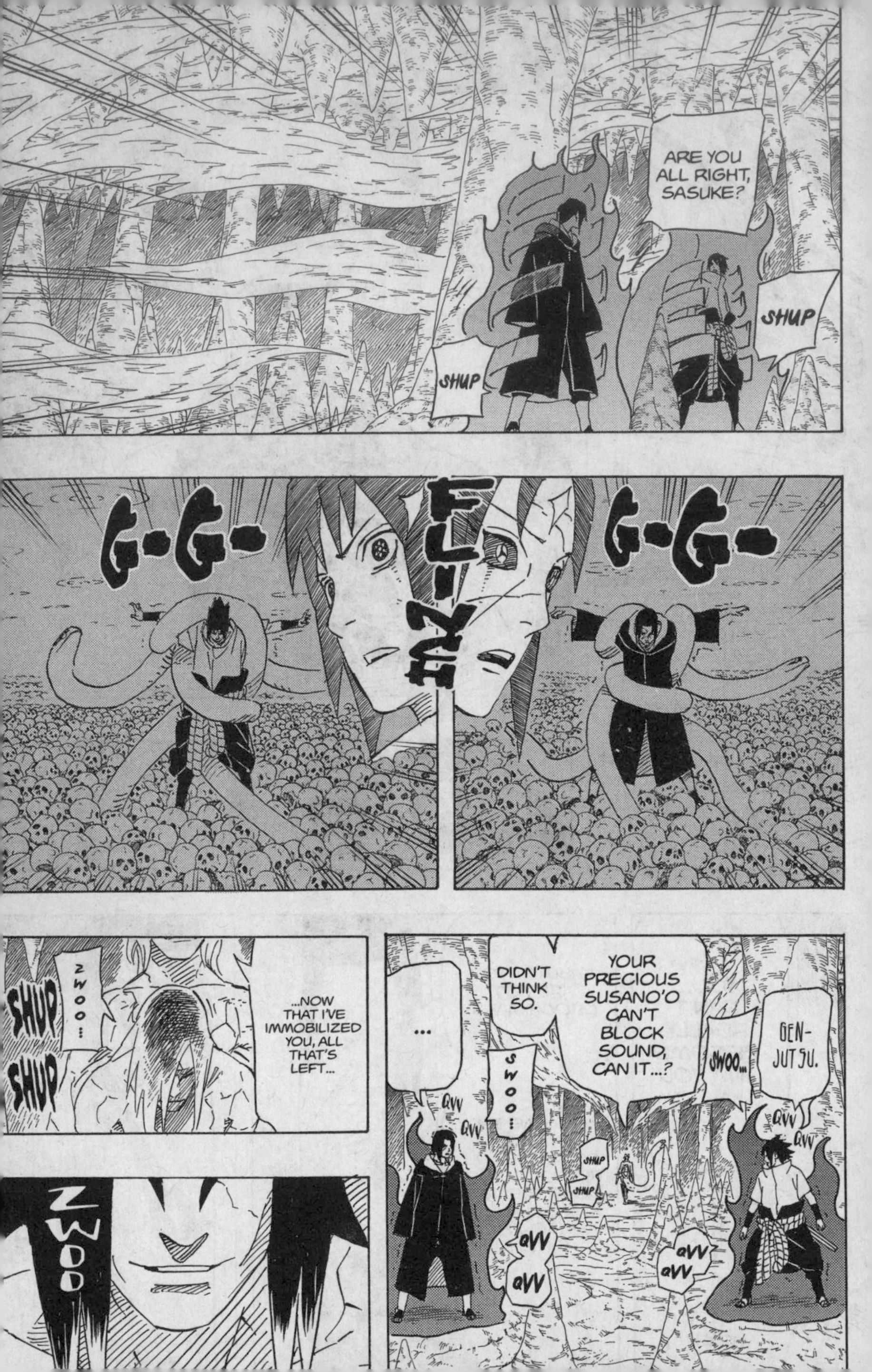
ARE YOU ALL RIGHT, SASUKE?
SHUP
SHUP
G-G-
FLING
G-G-
GEN-JUTSU.
QVV QVV
SWOO...
YOUR PRECIOUS SUSANO'O CAN'T BLOCK SOUND, CAN IT...?
DIDN'T THINK SO.
SWOO...
...
QVV QVV
SHUP
SHUP
QVV QVV
QVV QVV
ZWOO...
SHUP SHUP
...NOW THAT I'VE IMMOBILIZED YOU, ALL THAT'S LEFT...
ZWOO

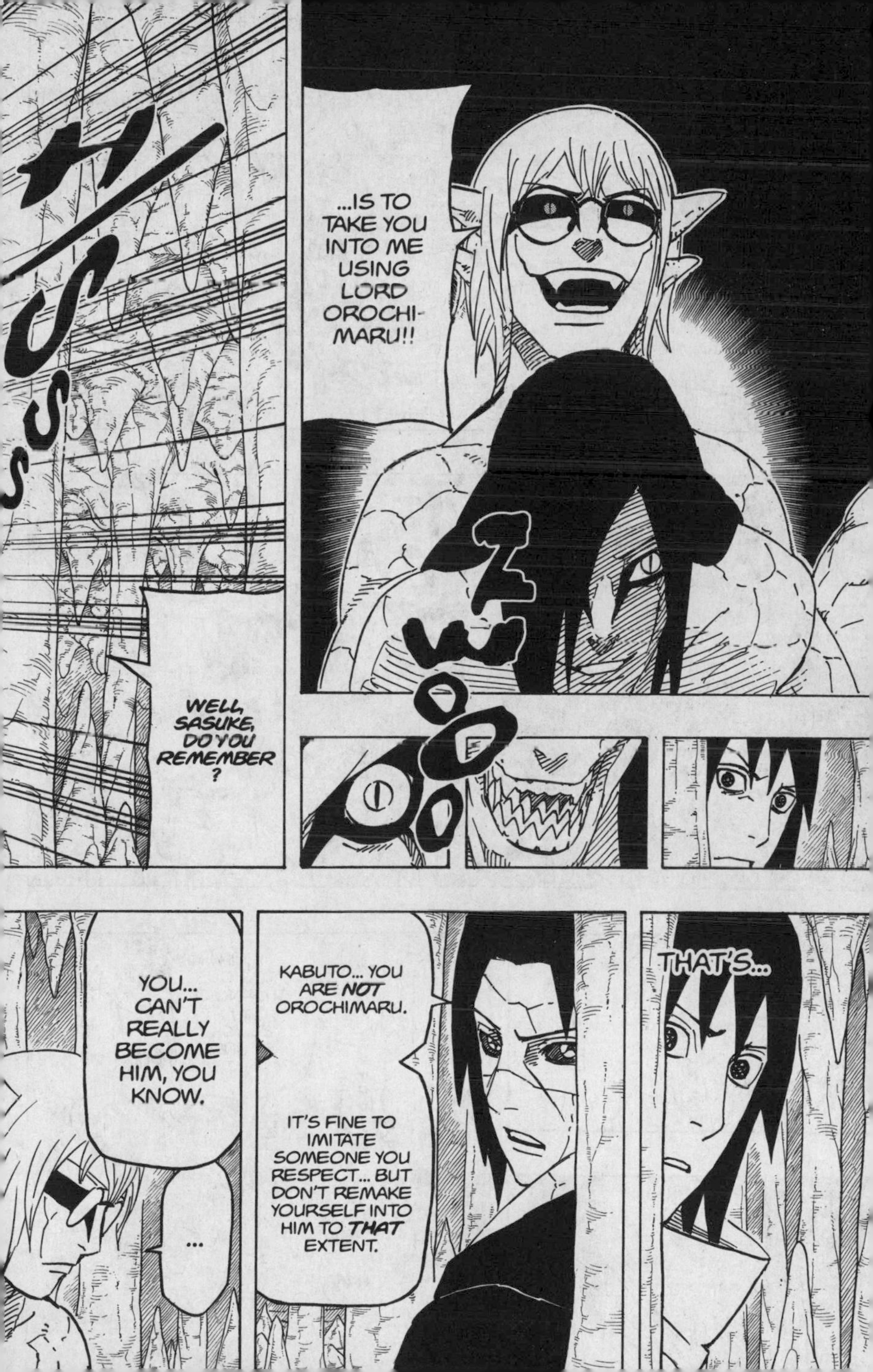
...IS TO TAKE YOU INTO ME USING LORD OROCHIMARU!!
WELL, SASUKE, DO YOU REMEMBER?
THAT'S...
KABUTO... YOU ARE *NOT* OROCHIMARU.
IT'S FINE TO IMITATE SOMEONE YOU RESPECT... BUT DON'T REMAKE YOURSELF INTO HIM TO *THAT* EXTENT.
YOU... CAN'T REALLY BECOME HIM, YOU KNOW.
...

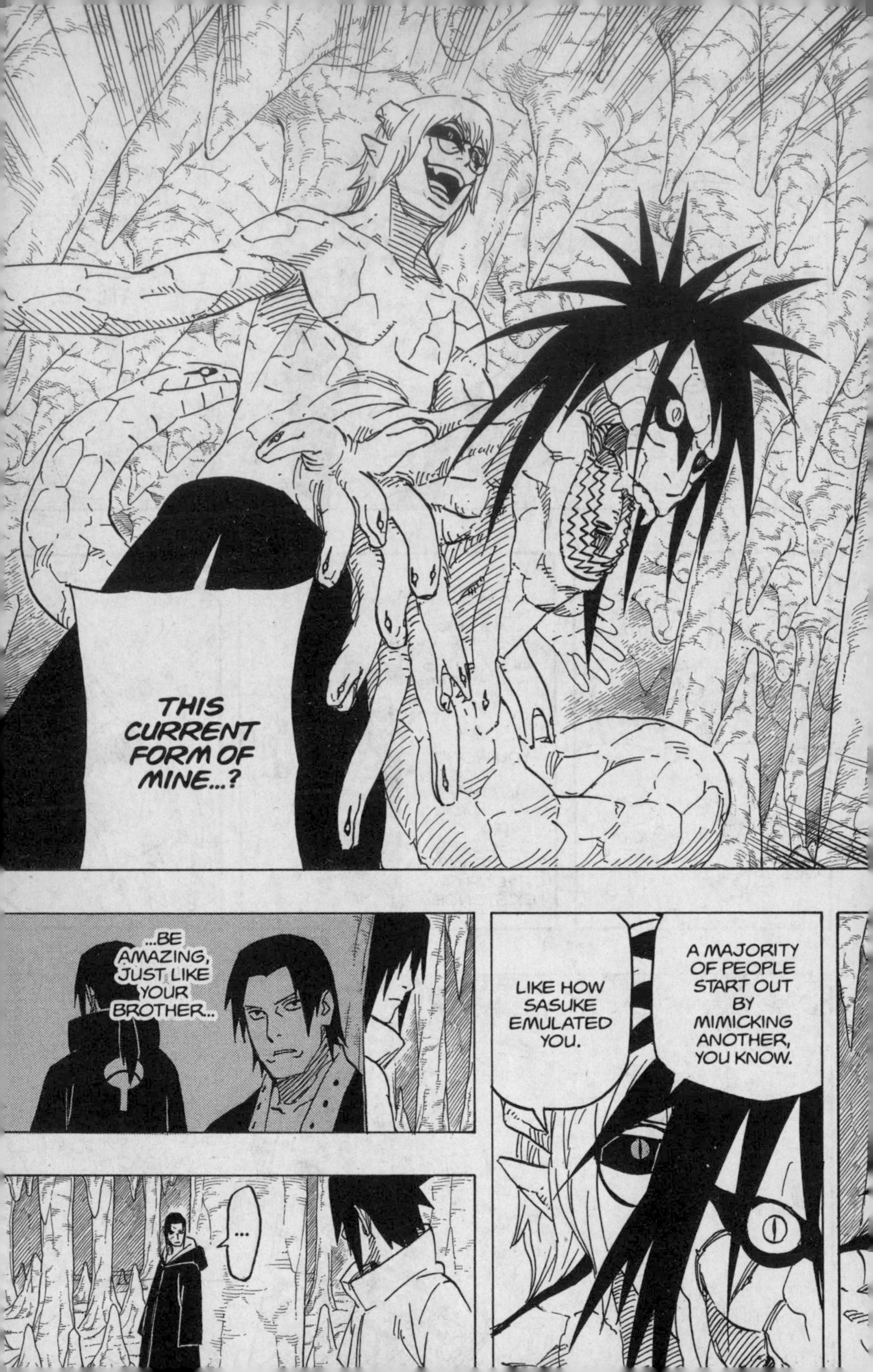
THIS CURRENT FORM OF MINE...?
A MAJORITY OF PEOPLE START OUT BY MIMICKING ANOTHER, YOU KNOW.
LIKE HOW SASUKE EMULATED YOU.
...BE AMAZING, JUST LIKE YOUR BROTHER...
...

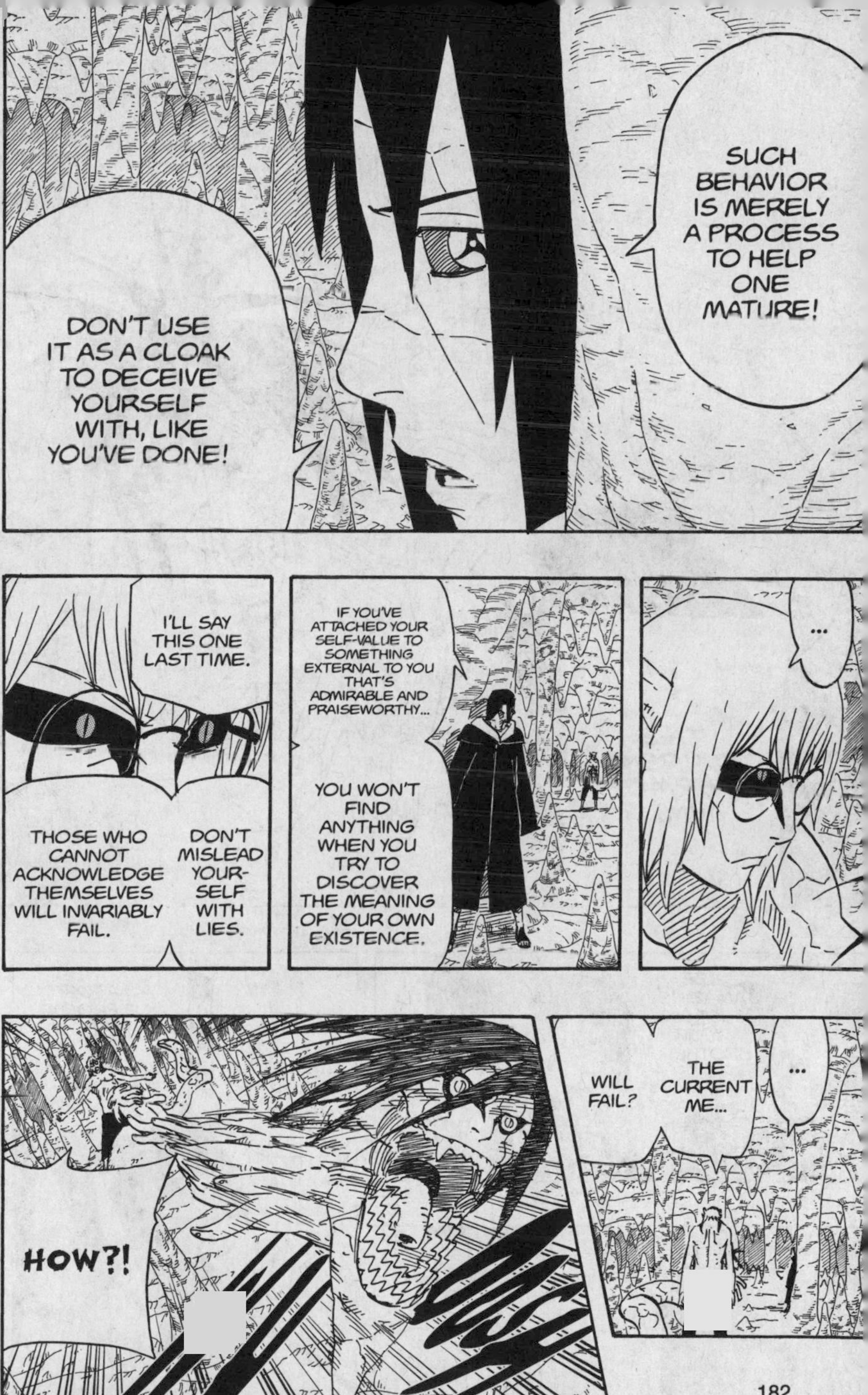
SUCH BEHAVIOR IS MERELY A PROCESS TO HELP ONE MATURE!
DON'T USE IT AS A CLOAK TO DECEIVE YOURSELF WITH, LIKE YOU'VE DONE!
...
IF YOU'VE ATTACHED YOUR SELF-VALUE TO SOMETHING EXTERNAL TO YOU THAT'S ADMIRABLE AND PRAISEWORTHY...
YOU WON'T FIND ANYTHING WHEN YOU TRY TO DISCOVER THE MEANING OF YOUR OWN EXISTENCE.
I'LL SAY THIS ONE LAST TIME.
DON'T MISLEAD YOURSELF WITH LIES.
THOSE WHO CANNOT ACKNOWLEDGE THEMSELVES WILL INVARIABLY FAIL.
...
THE CURRENT ME...
WILL FAIL?
HOW?!

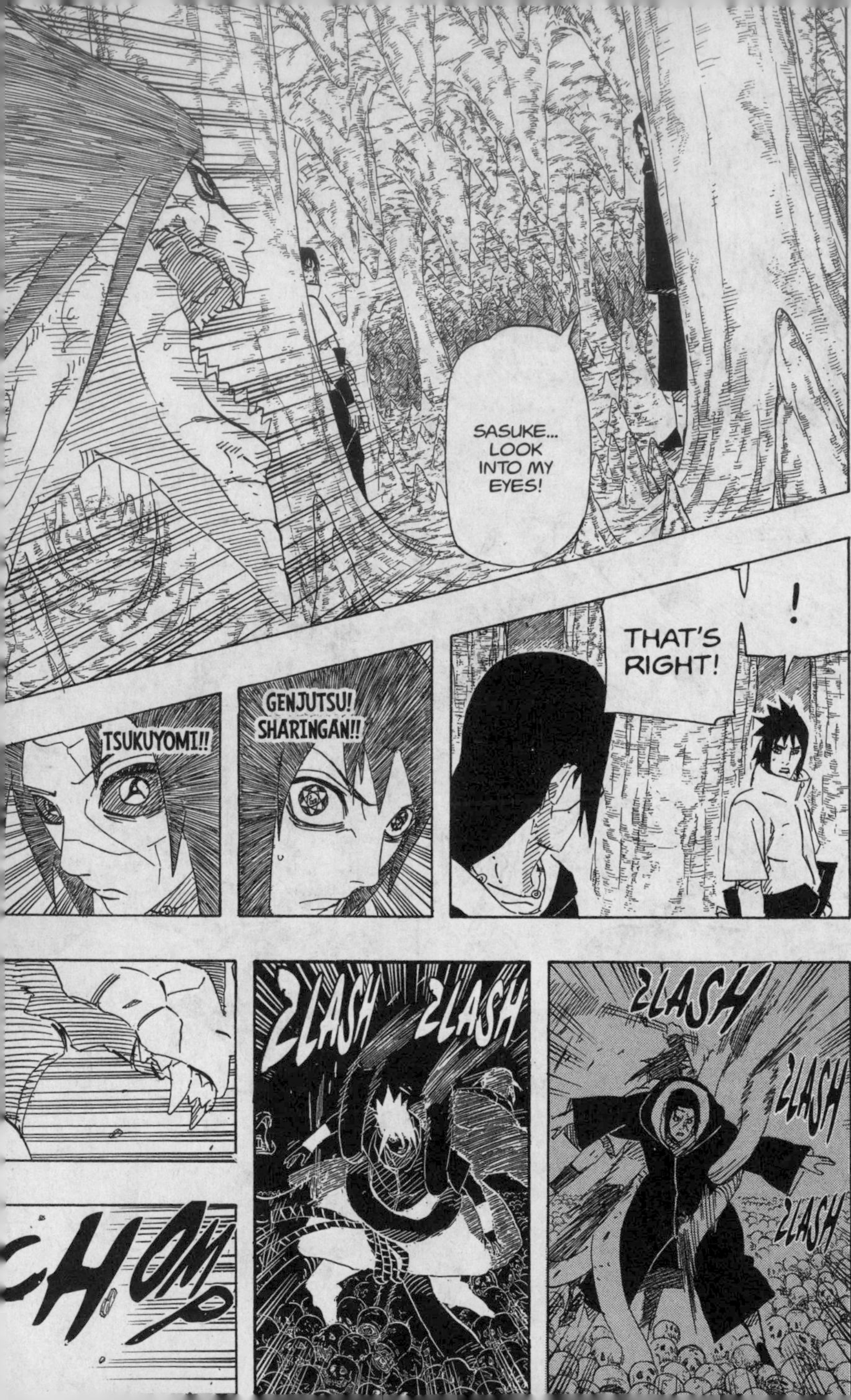
SASUKE... LOOK INTO MY EYES!
!
THAT'S RIGHT!
GENJUTSU! SHARINGAN!!
TSUKUYOMI!!
SLASH
SLASH
SLASH
SLASH
SLASH
CHOMP

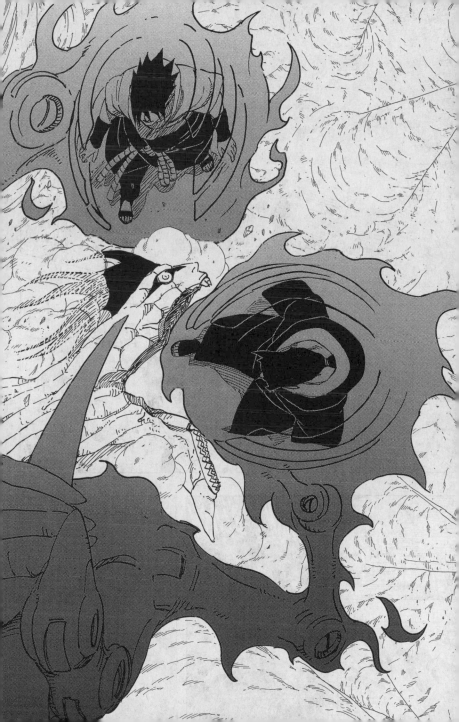

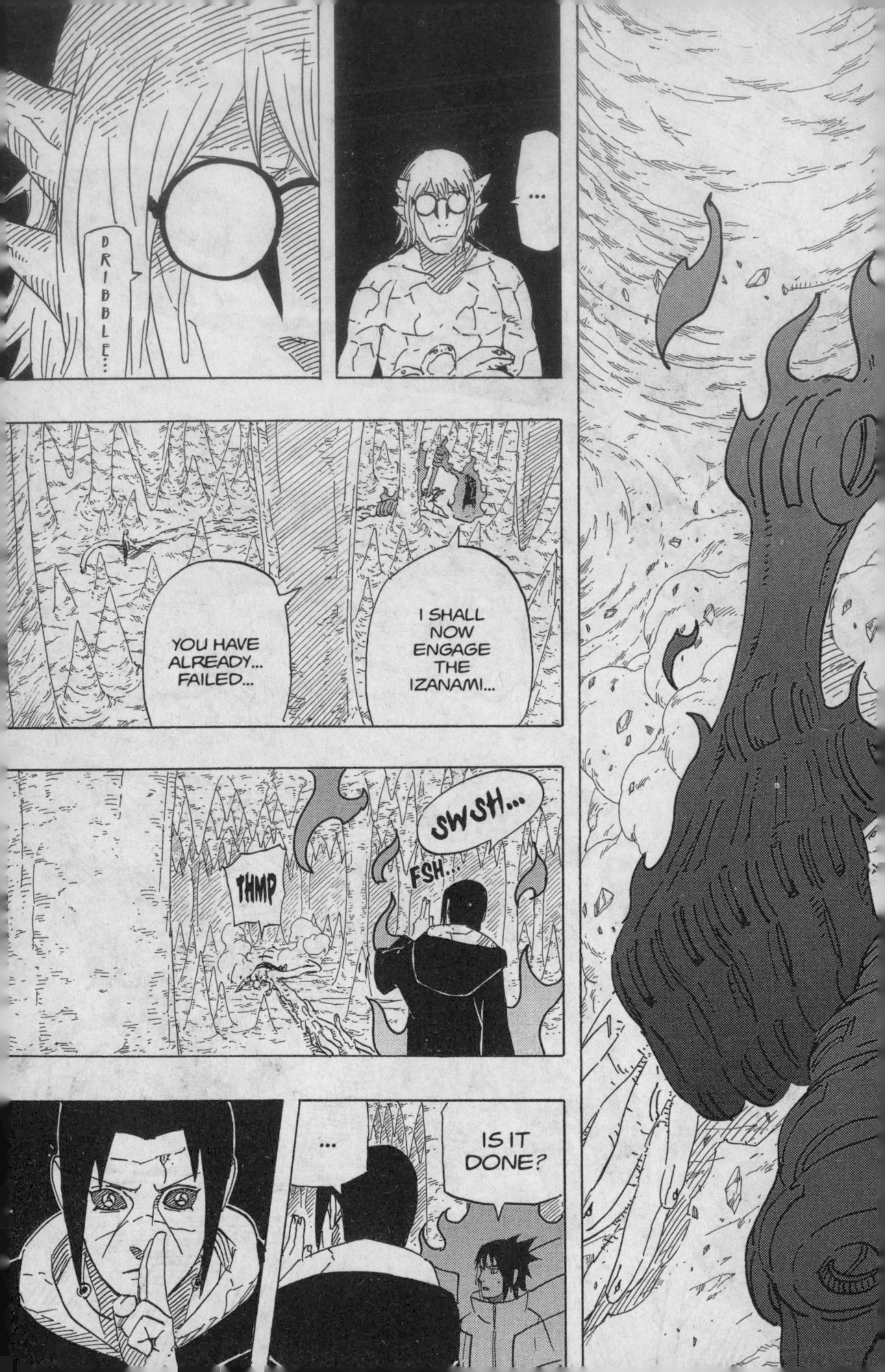
...
DRIBBLE...
I SHALL NOW ENGAGE THE IZANAMI...
YOU HAVE ALREADY... FAILED...
SWSH...
FSH...
THMP
IS IT DONE?
...

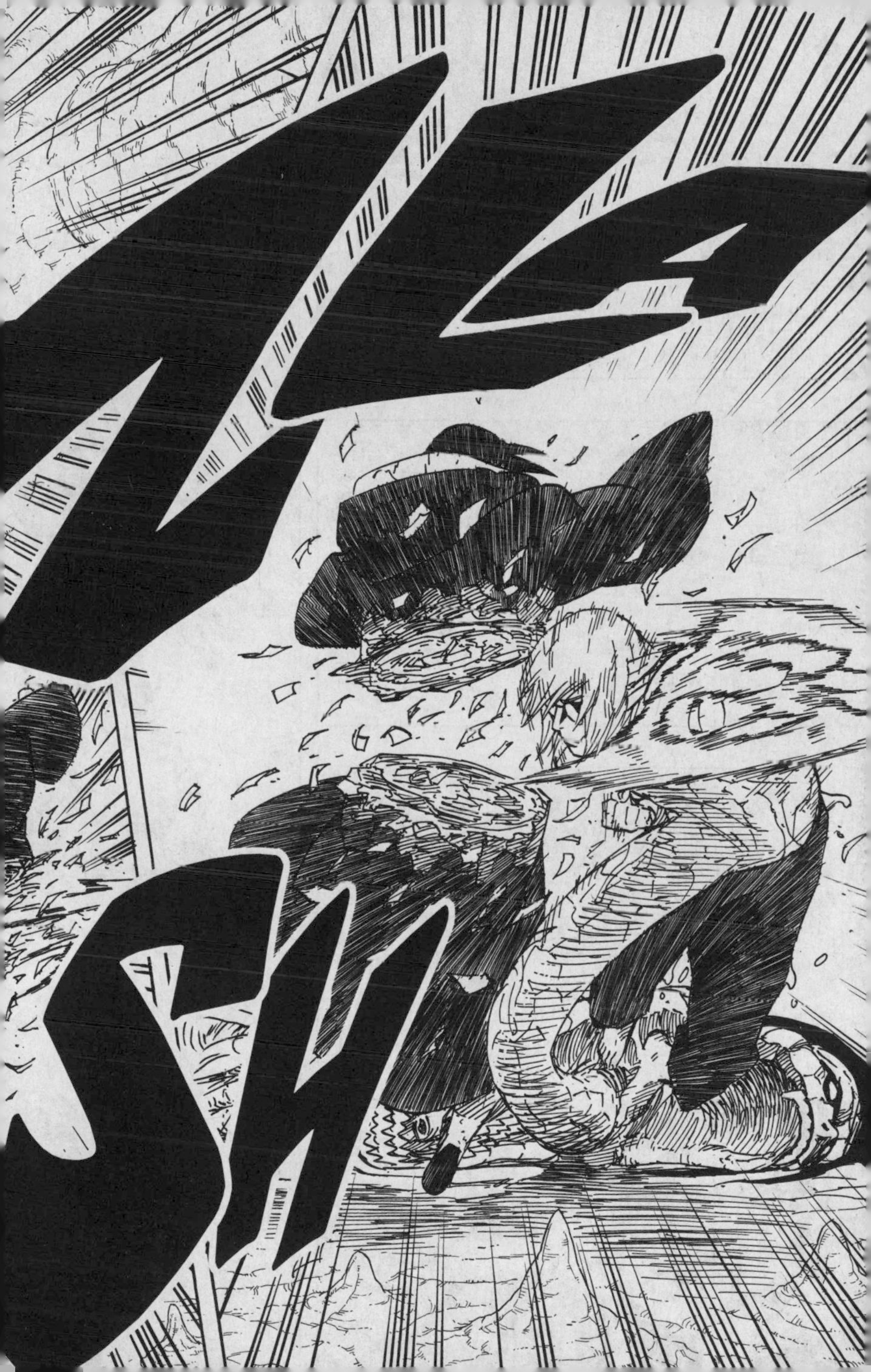

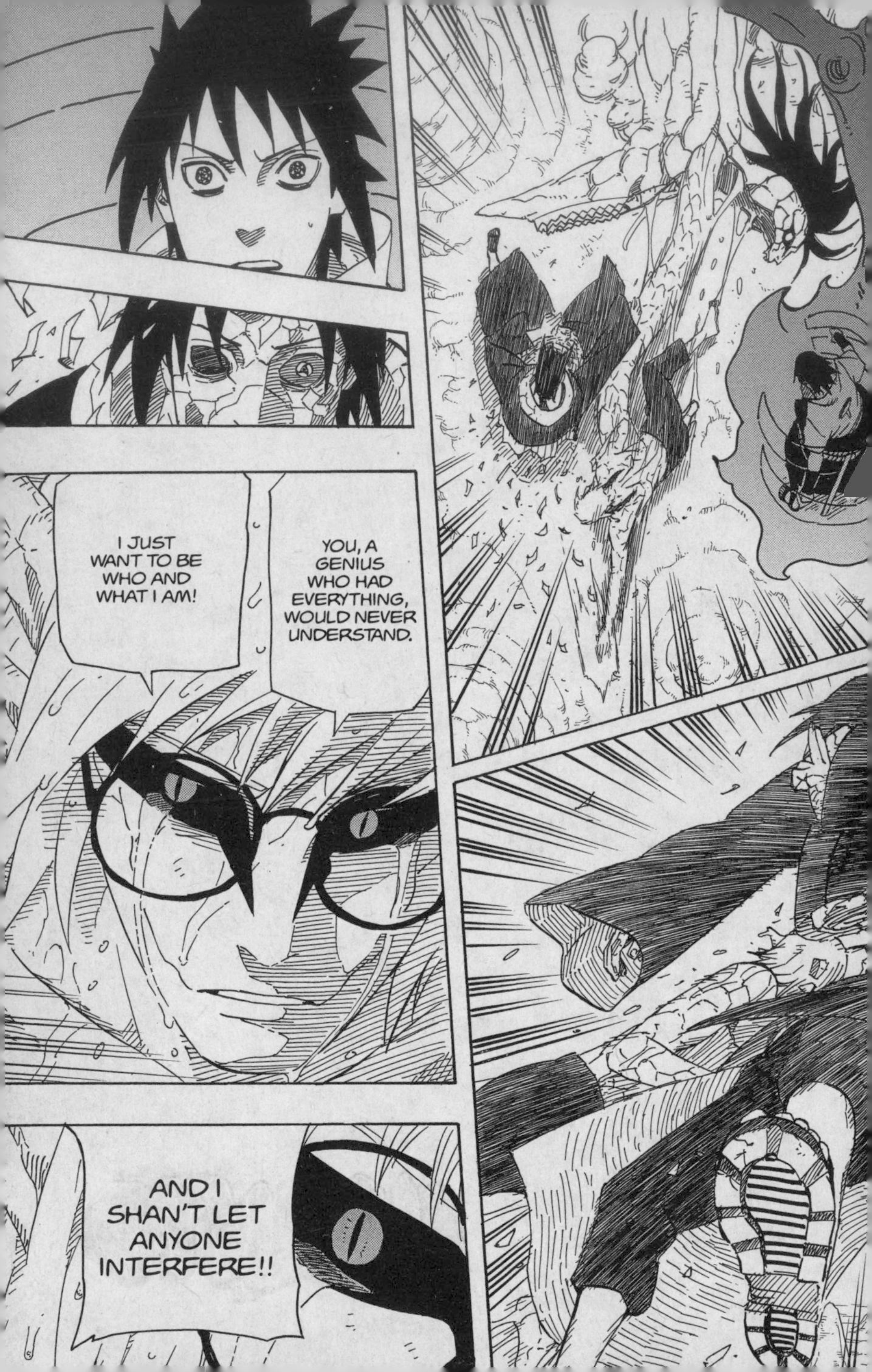
YOU, A GENIUS WHO HAD EVERYTHING, WOULD NEVER UNDERSTAND.
I JUST WANT TO BE WHO AND WHAT I AM!
AND I SHAN'T LET ANYONE INTERFERE!!

NARUTO

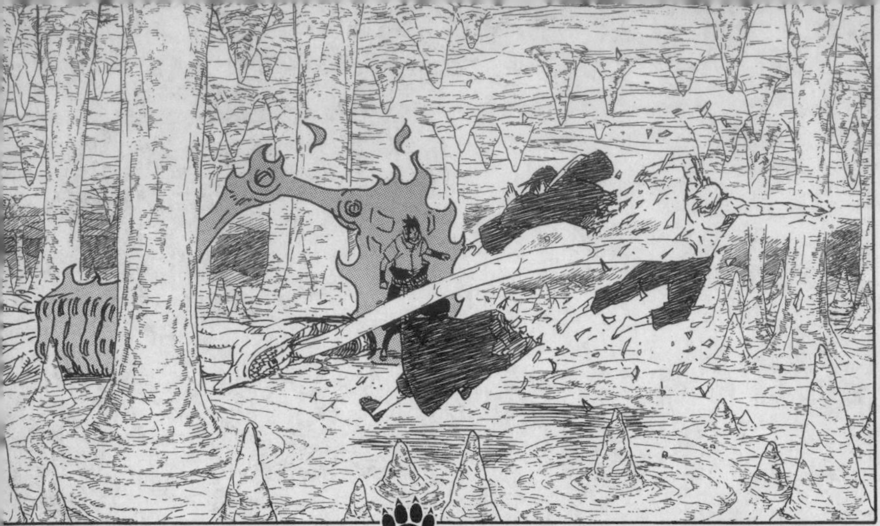

Number 586: The Izanami Activated

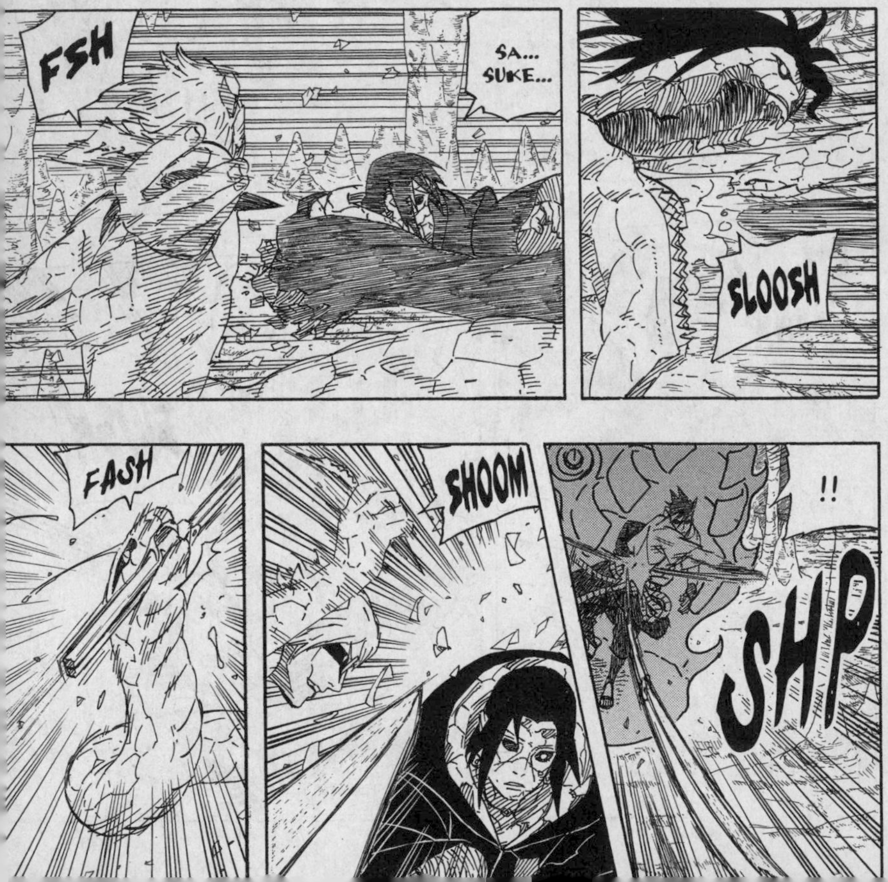
SLOOSH
FSH
SA... SUKE...
!!
SHP
SHOOM
FASH

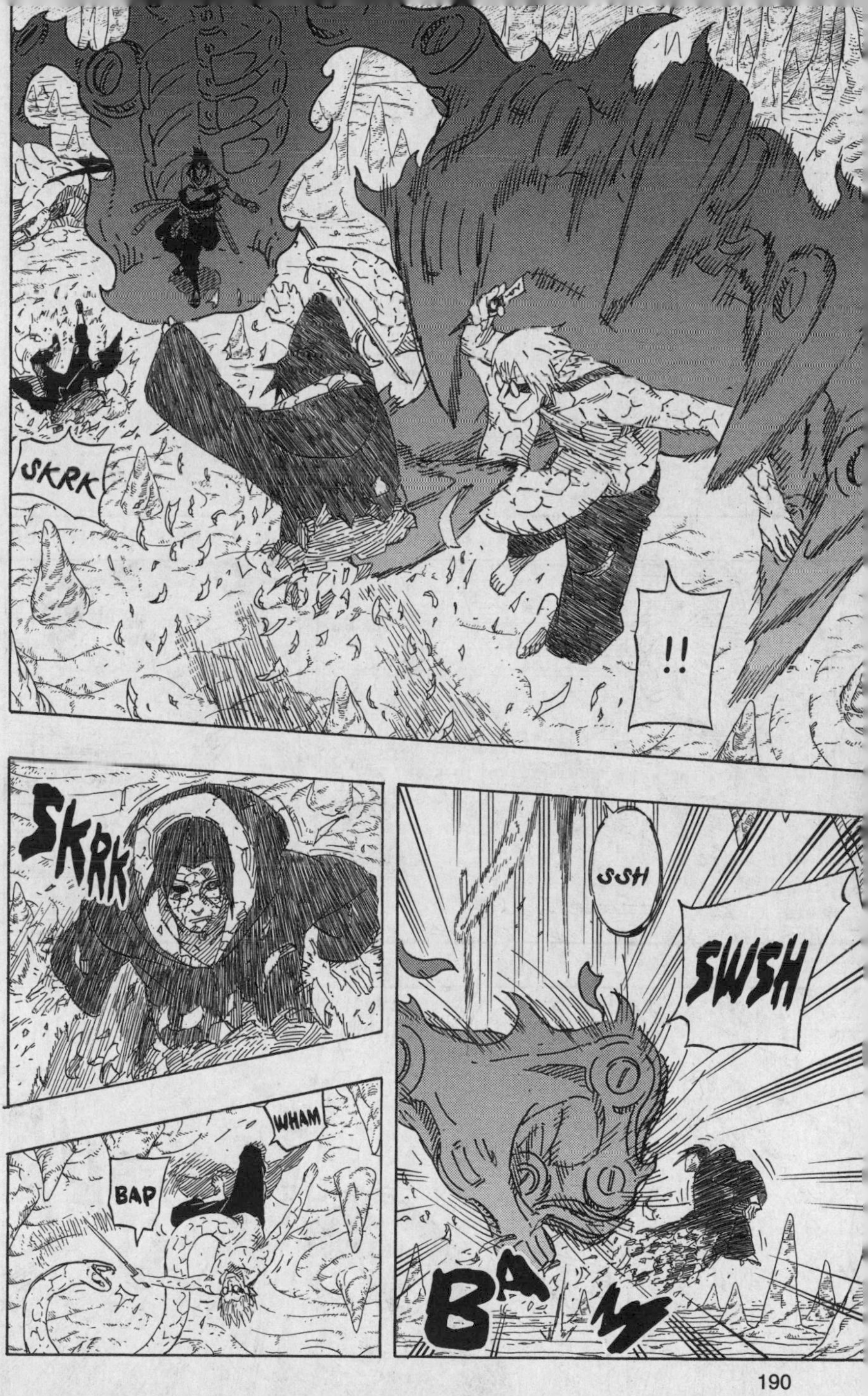
!!
SKRK
SSH
SWSH
BAM
SKRK
WHAM
BAP

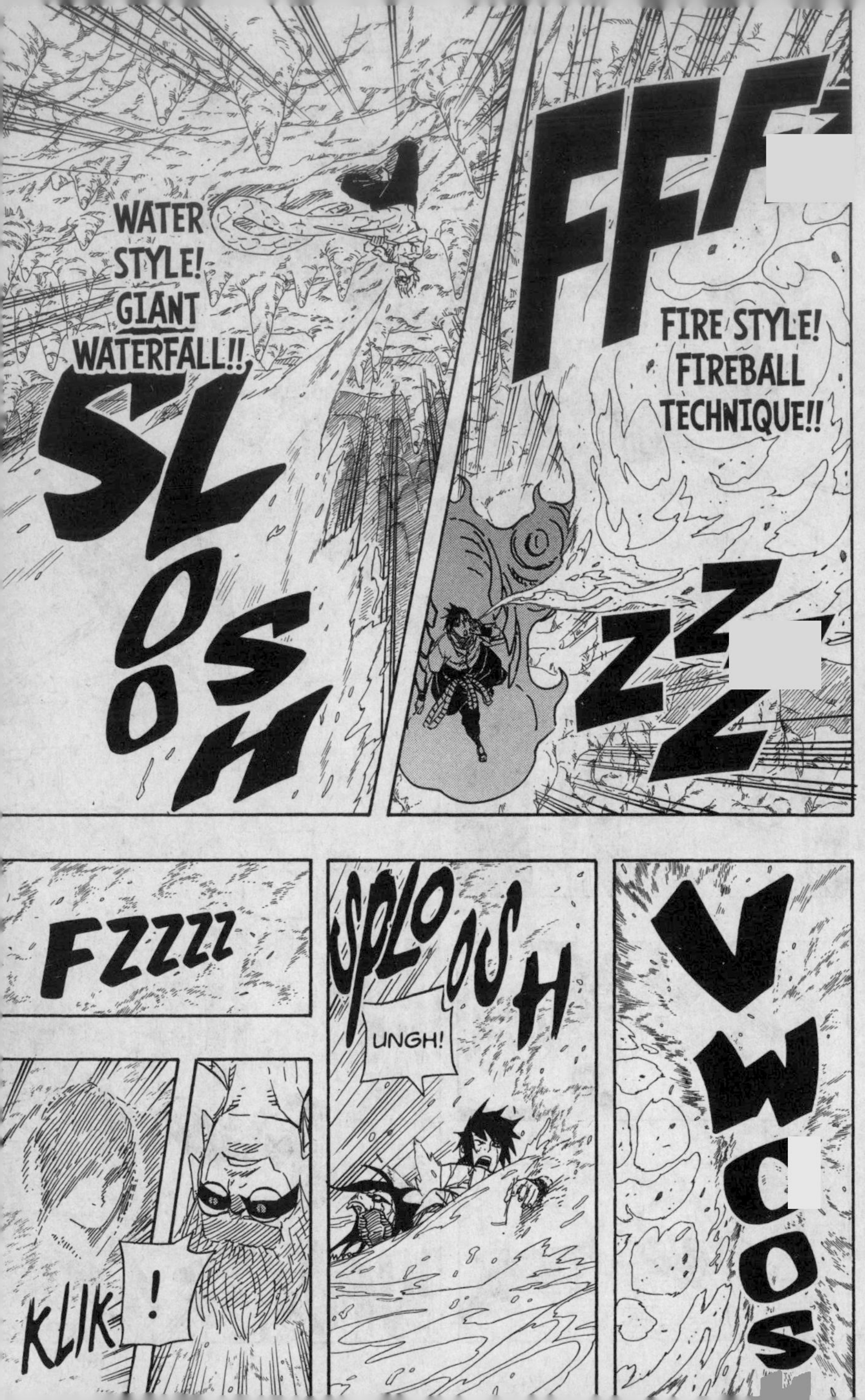
FFF
FIRE STYLE! FIREBALL TECHNIQUE!!
ZZZ
WATER STYLE! GIANT WATERFALL!!
SLOOSH
VWOOS
SPLOOSH
UNGH!
FZZZZ
!
KLIK

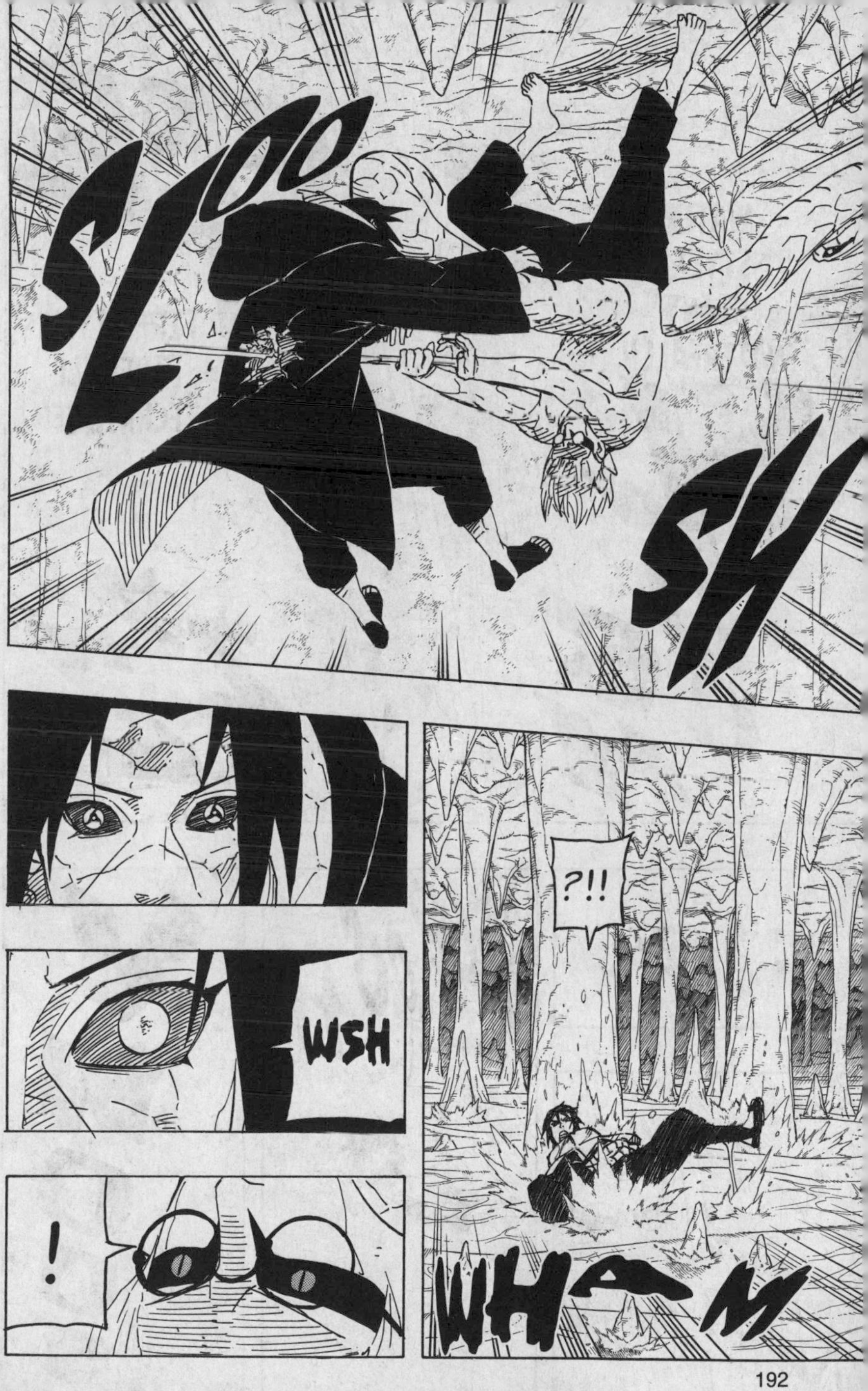
SLOO
SH
?!!
WHAM
WSH
!

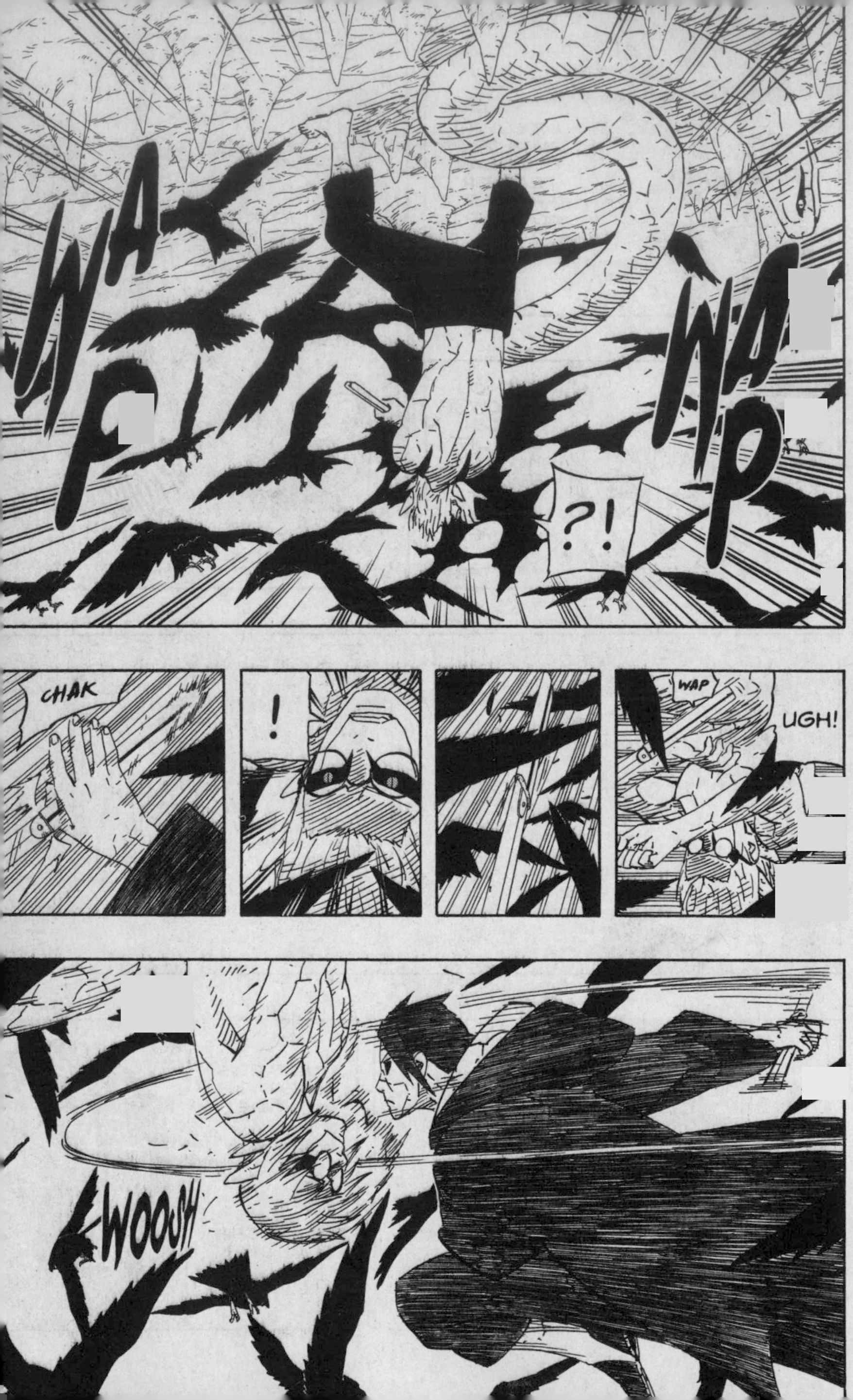
WAP
?!
WAP
WAP
UGH!
!
CHAK
WOOSH

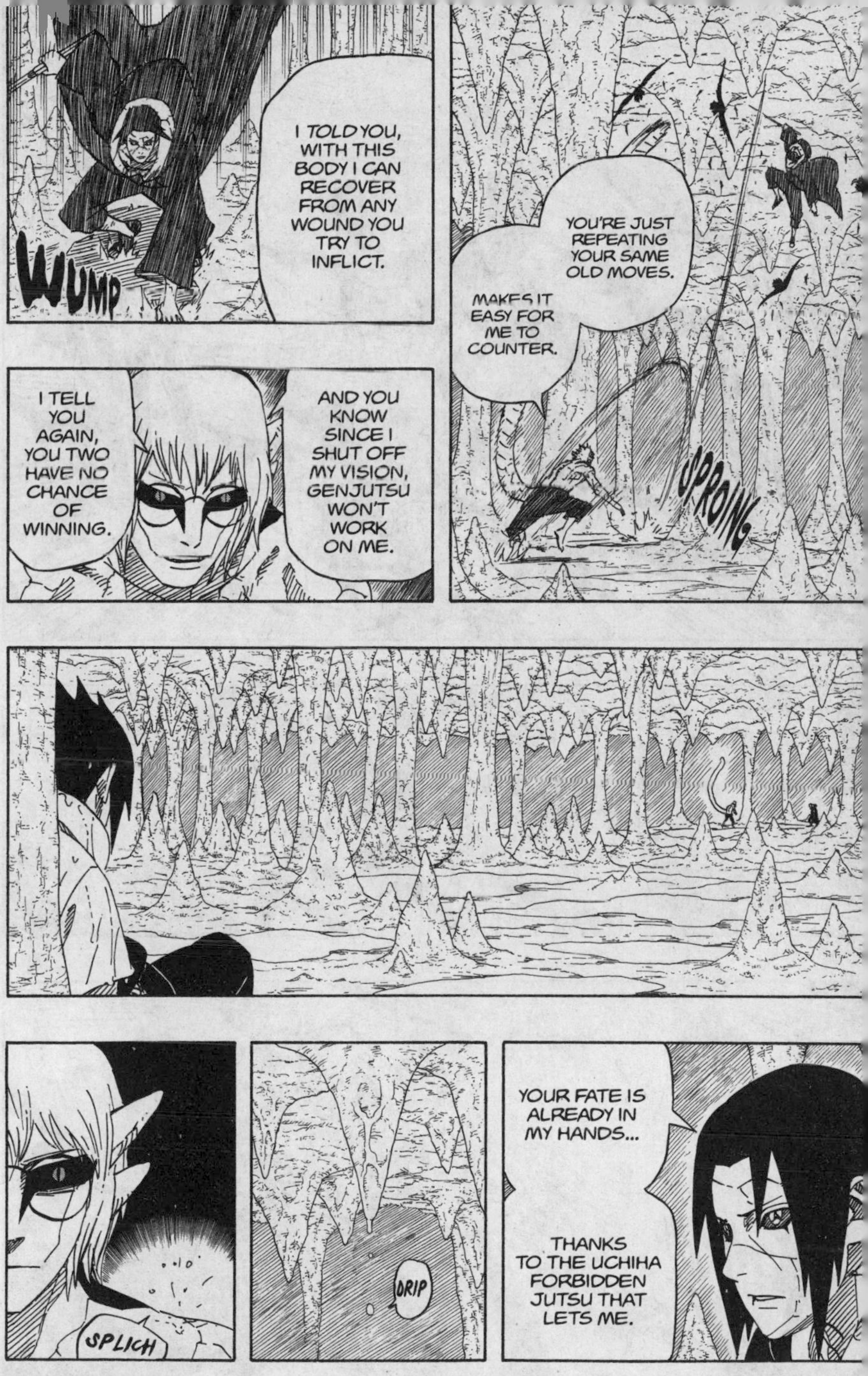

YOU'RE JUST REPEATING YOUR SAME OLD MOVES.
MAKES IT EASY FOR ME TO COUNTER.
SPROING
I *TOLD* YOU, WITH THIS BODY I CAN RECOVER FROM ANY WOUND YOU TRY TO INFLICT.
WUMP
AND YOU KNOW SINCE I SHUT OFF MY VISION, GENJUTSU WON'T WORK ON ME.
I TELL YOU AGAIN, YOU TWO HAVE NO CHANCE OF WINNING.
YOUR FATE IS ALREADY IN MY HANDS...
THANKS TO THE UCHIHA FORBIDDEN JUTSU THAT LETS ME.
DRIP
SPLICH

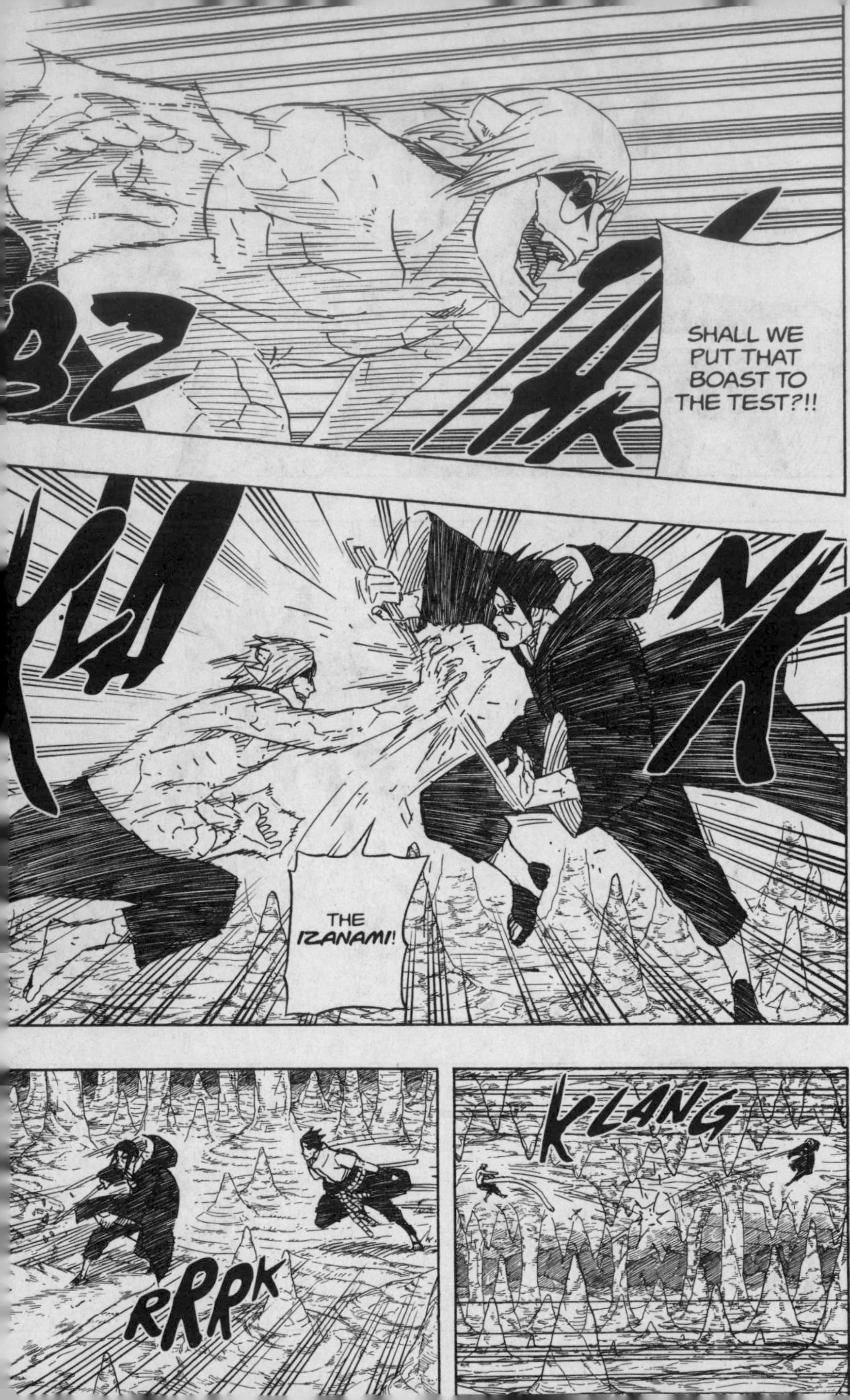
SHALL WE PUT THAT BOAST TO THE TEST?!!
THE IZANAMI!
KLANG

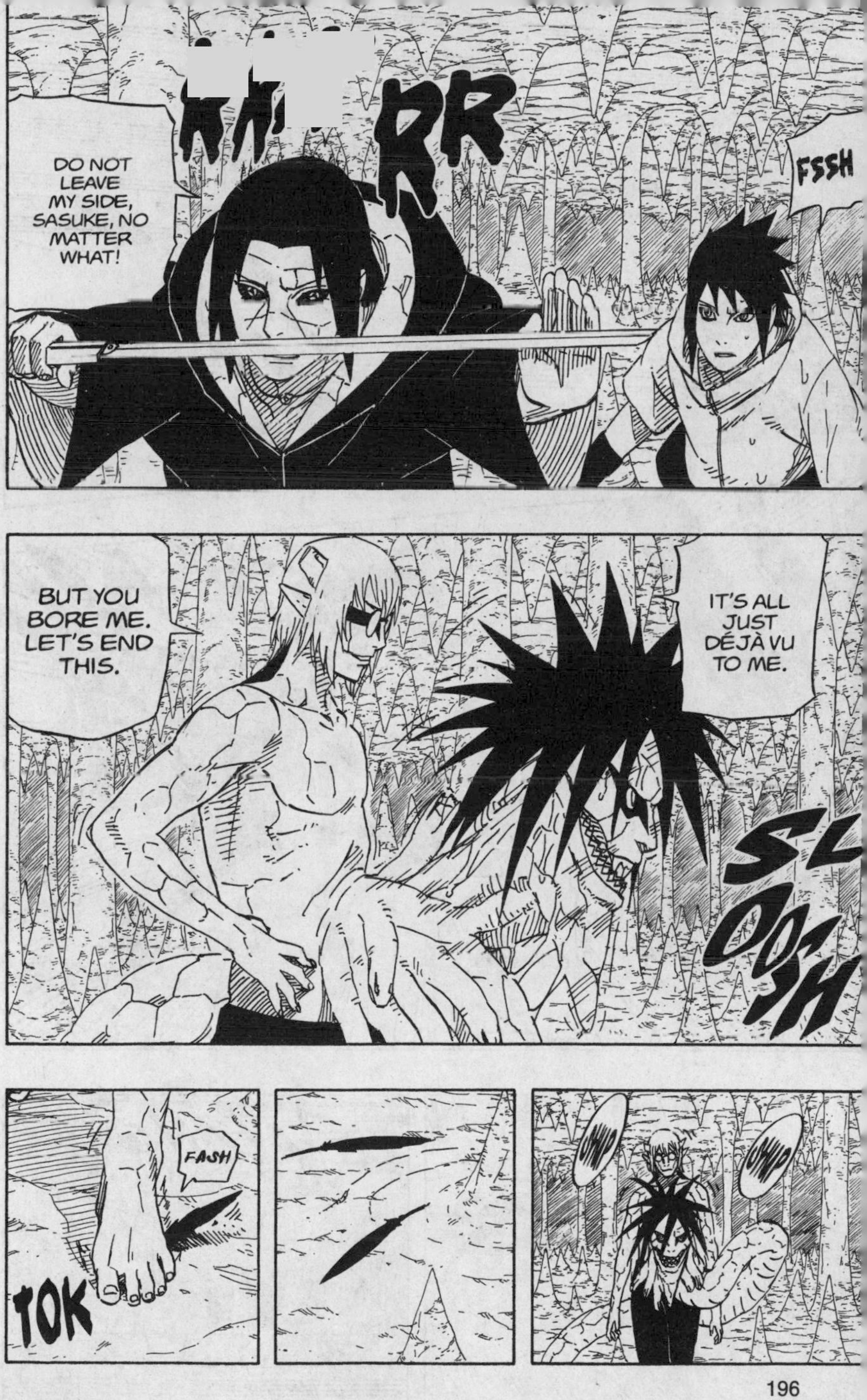
FSSH
DO NOT LEAVE MY SIDE, SASUKE, NO MATTER WHAT!
IT'S ALL JUST DÉJÀ VU TO ME.
SLOOSH
BUT YOU BORE ME. LET'S END THIS.
FASH
TOK

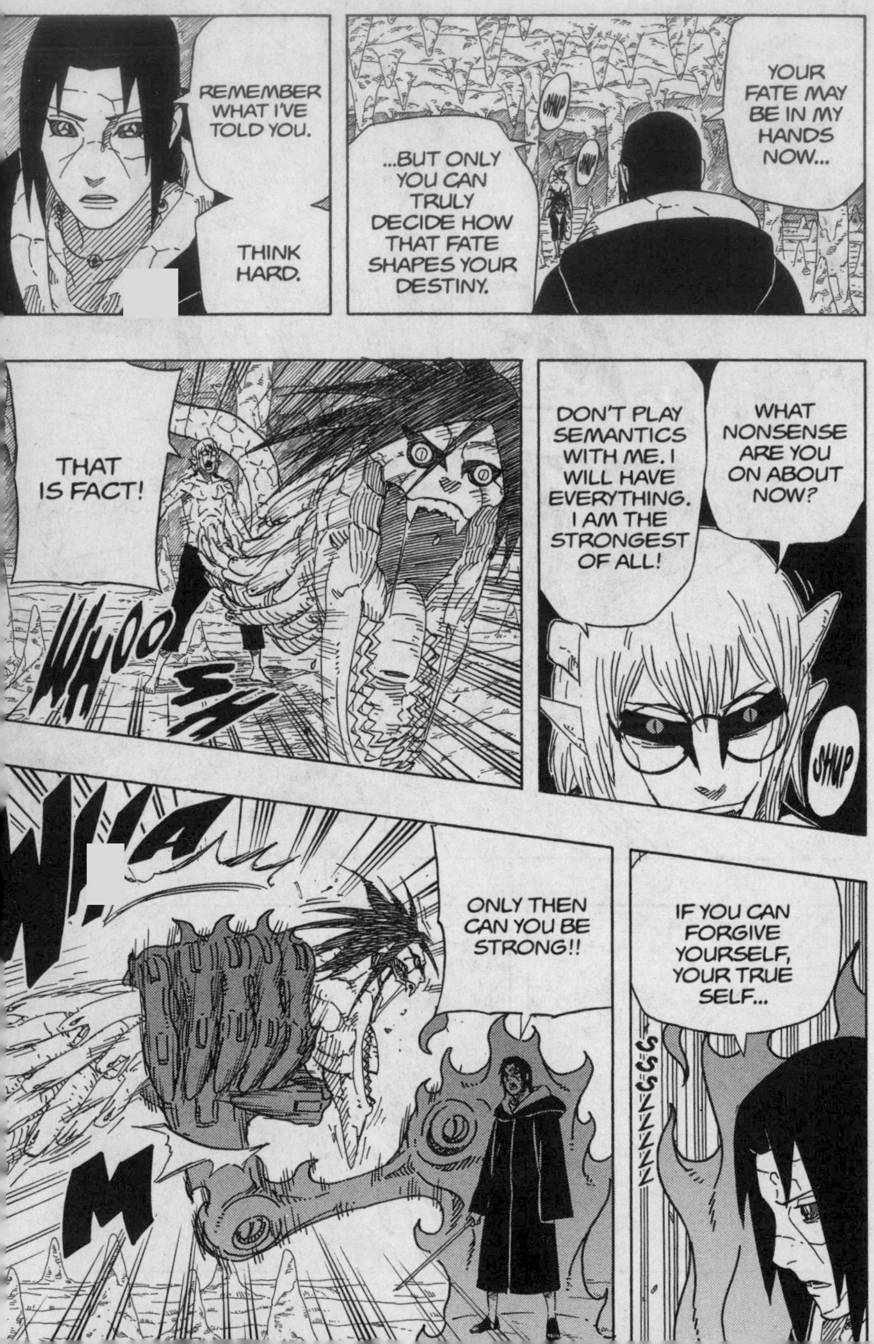
YOUR FATE MAY BE IN MY HANDS NOW...
...BUT ONLY YOU CAN TRULY DECIDE HOW THAT FATE SHAPES YOUR DESTINY.
REMEMBER WHAT I'VE TOLD YOU.
THINK HARD.
WHAT NONSENSE ARE YOU ON ABOUT NOW?
DON'T PLAY SEMANTICS WITH ME. I WILL HAVE EVERYTHING. I AM THE STRONGEST OF ALL!
THAT IS FACT!
WHOOSH
IF YOU CAN FORGIVE YOURSELF, YOUR TRUE SELF...
ONLY THEN CAN YOU BE STRONG!!

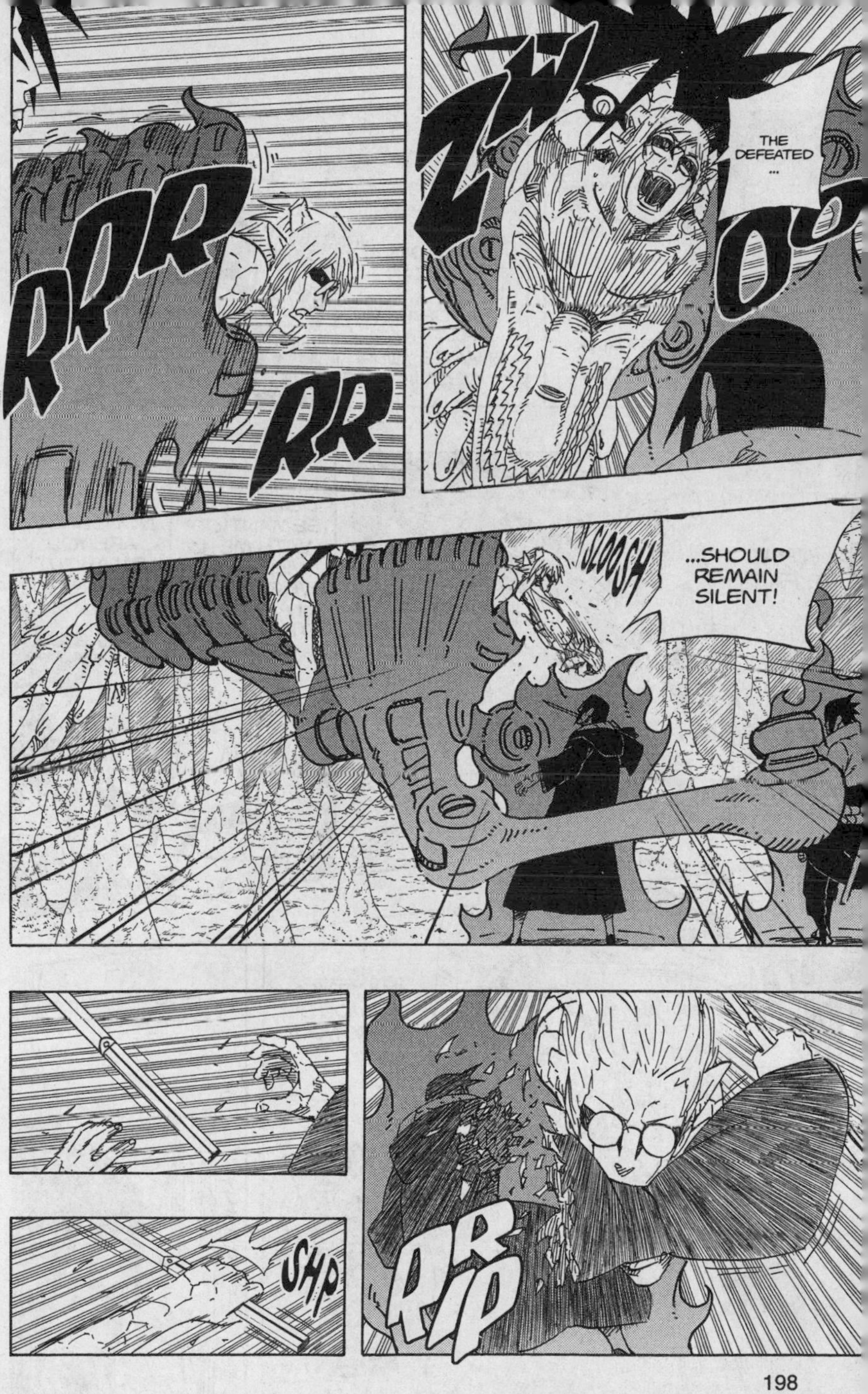
ZWOO
THE DEFEATED ...
RRRR
RR
SLOOSH
...SHOULD REMAIN SILENT!
RRIP
SHP

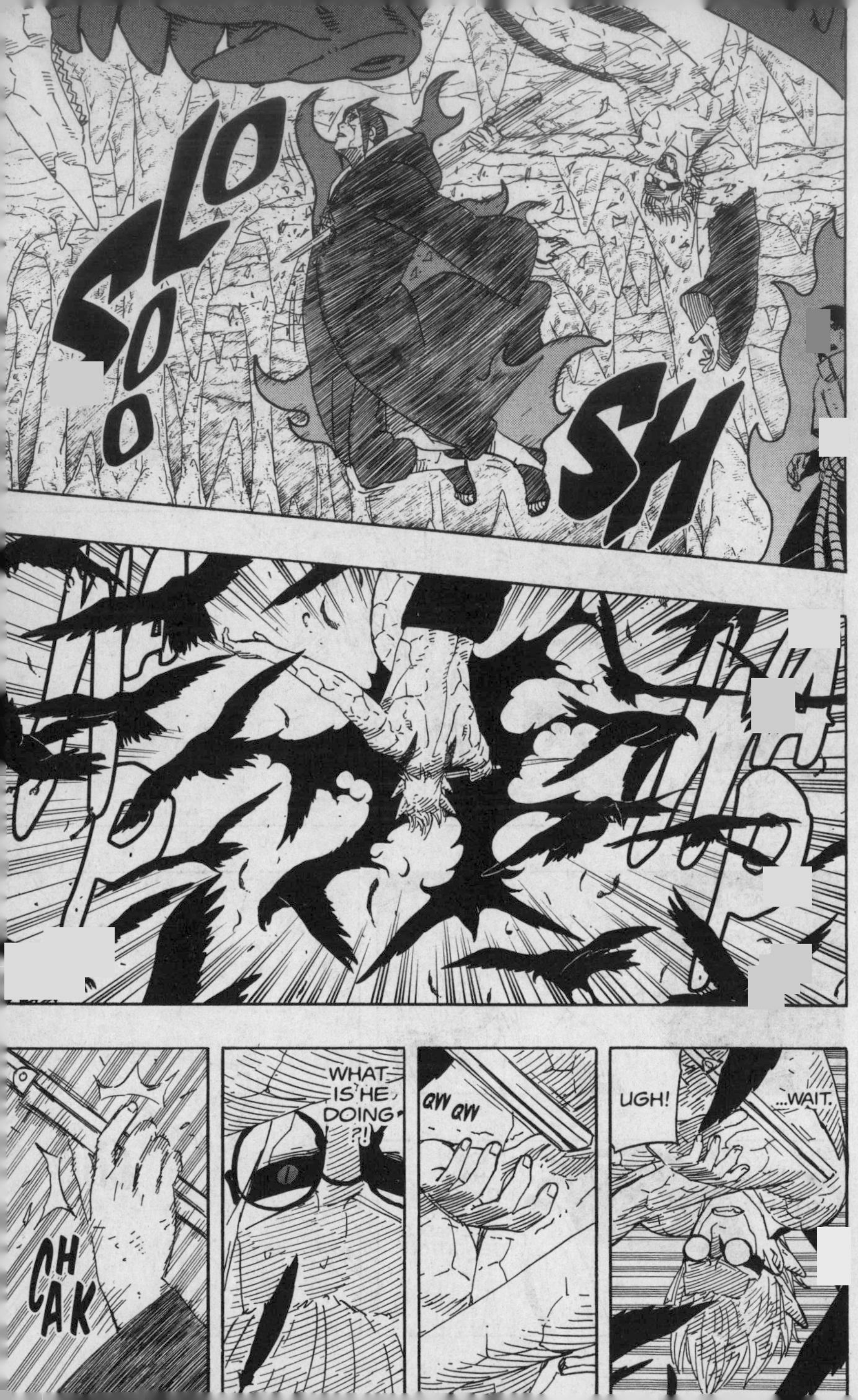
SLOOOO
SH
...WAIT.
UGH!
QW QW
WHAT IS HE DOING?!
CHAK

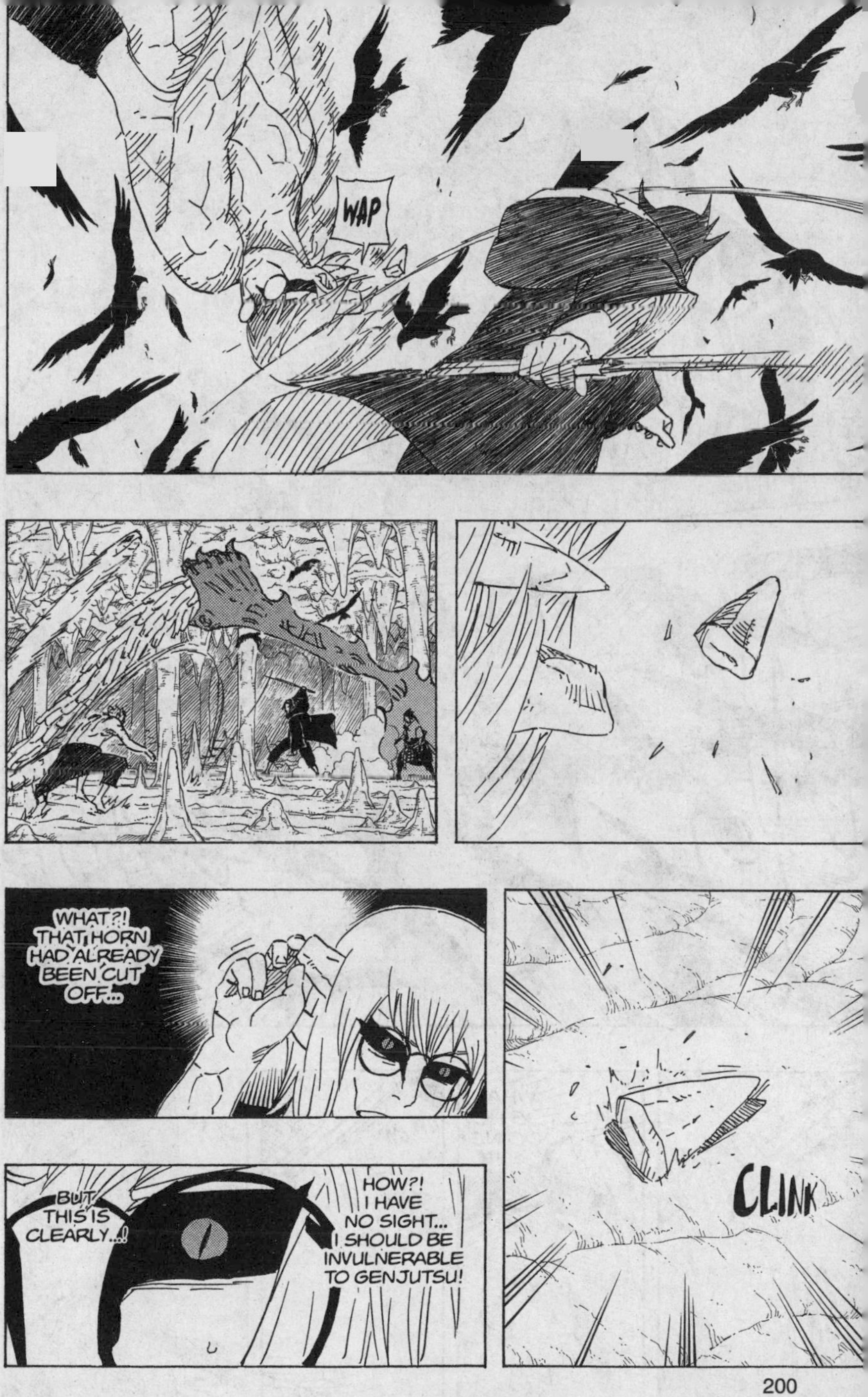
WAP
CLINK
WHAT?! THAT HORN HAD ALREADY BEEN CUT OFF...
HOW?! I HAVE NO SIGHT... I SHOULD BE INVULNERABLE TO GENJUTSU!
BUT THIS IS CLEARLY...!

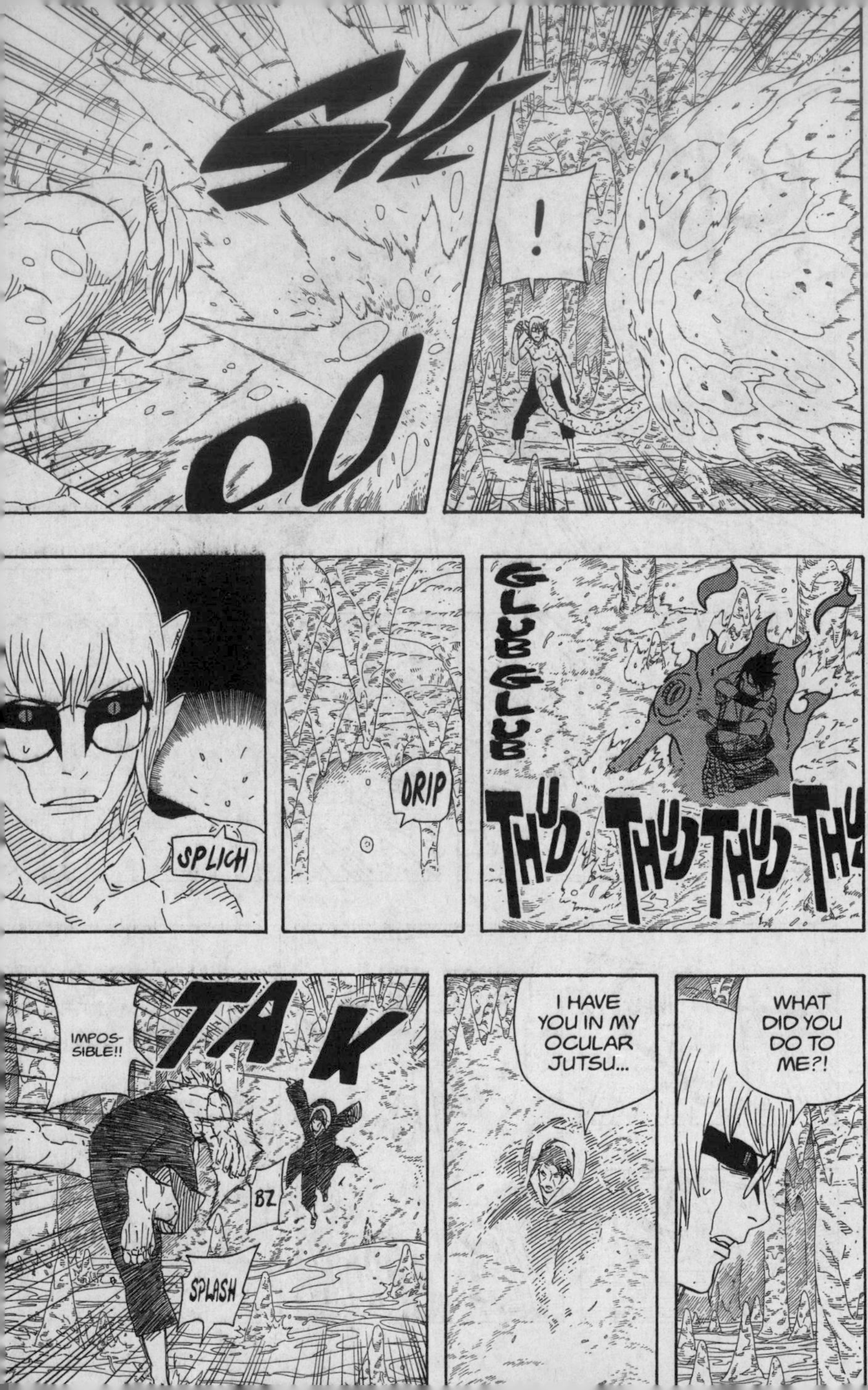
!
SPLOO
GLUB GLUB
THUD THUD THUD THU
DRIP
SPLICH
WHAT DID YOU DO TO ME?!
I HAVE YOU IN MY OCULAR JUTSU...
IMPOSSIBLE!!
TAK
BZ
SPLASH

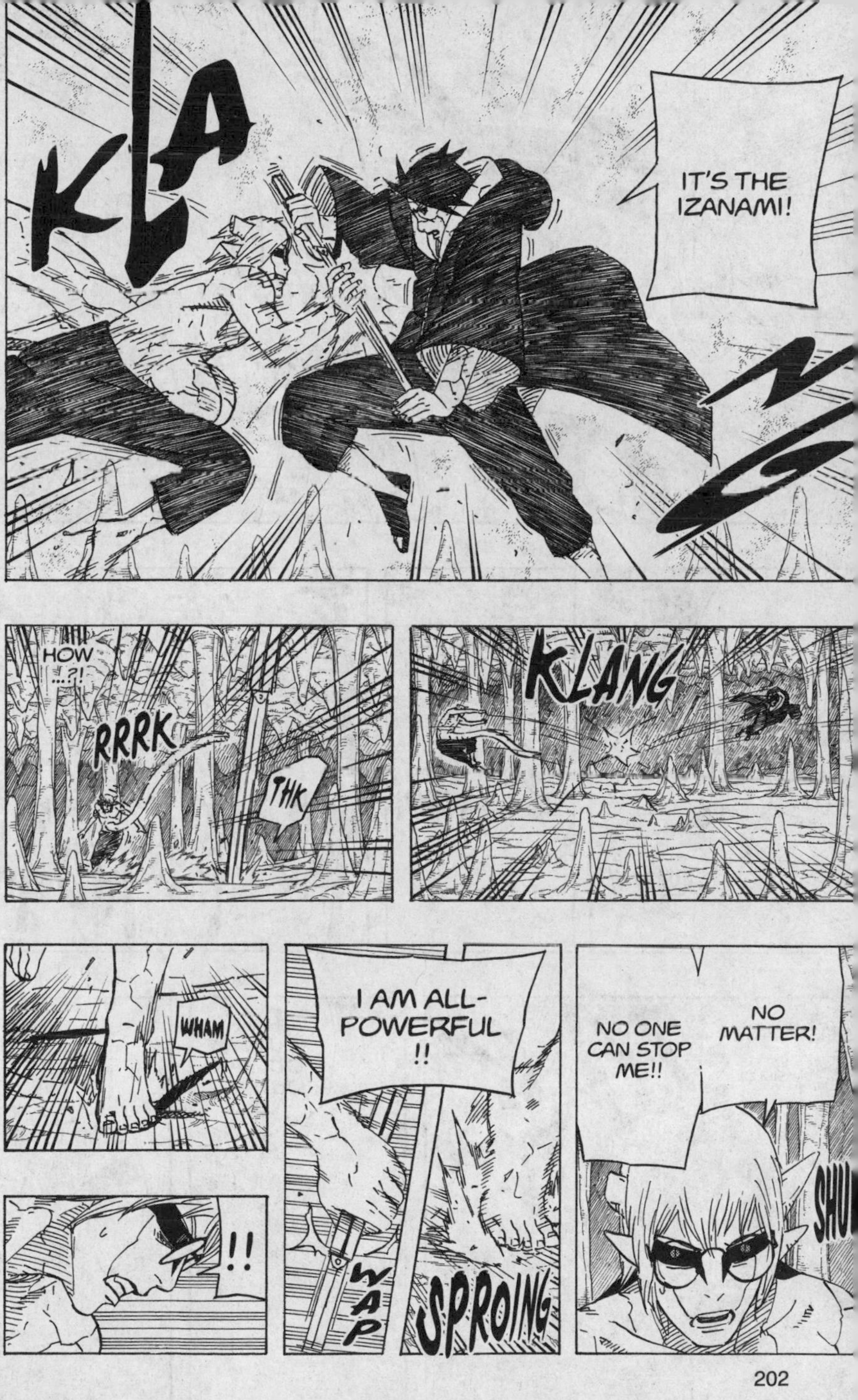
IT'S THE IZANAMI!
KLA
KLANG
HOW ...?!
RRRK
THK
NO MATTER!
NO ONE CAN STOP ME!!
I AM ALL-POWERFUL !!
WAP
SPROING
WHAM
!!

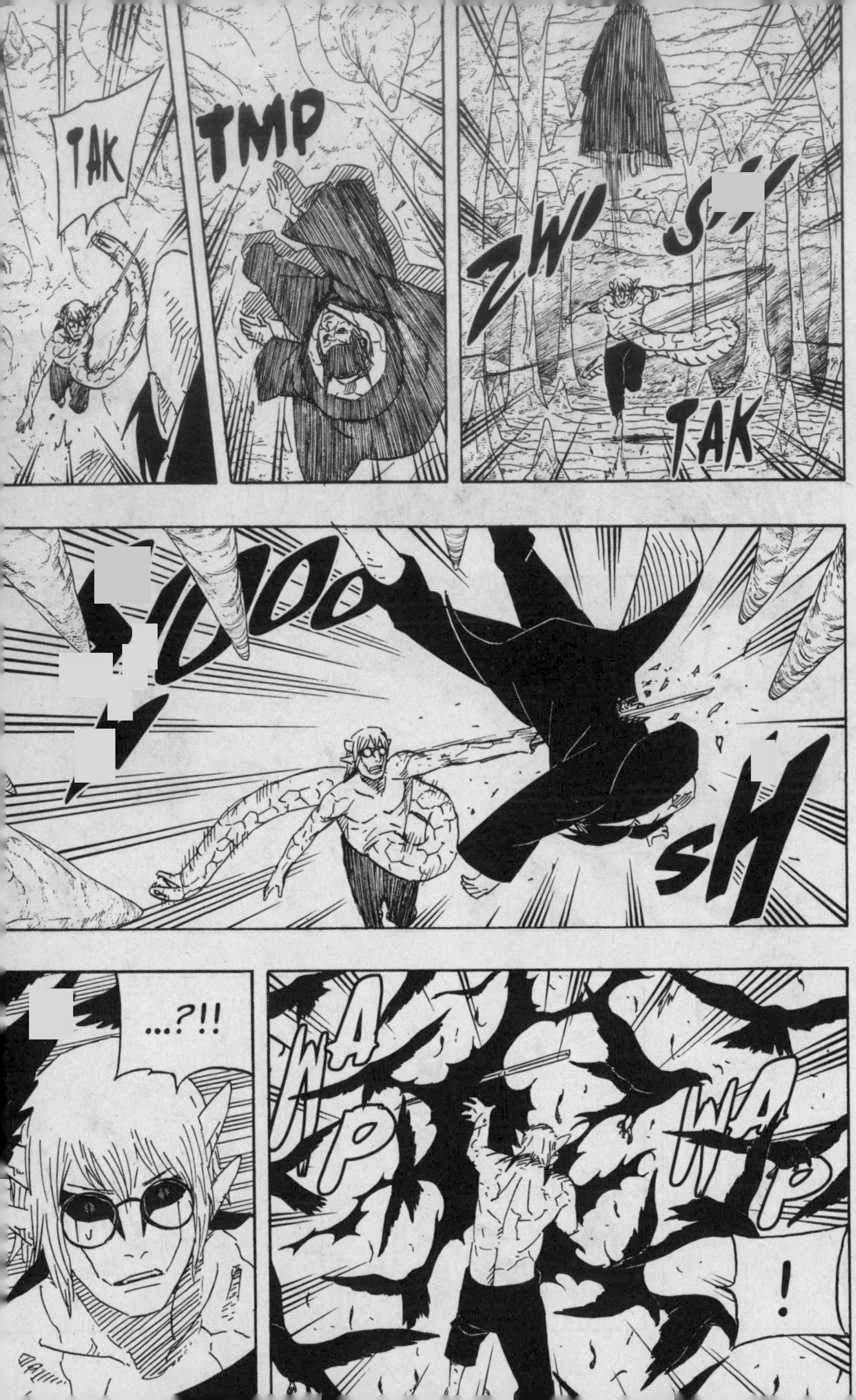
ZWI
S
TAK
TMP
TAK
OOO
SH
WAP
WAP
!
...?!!

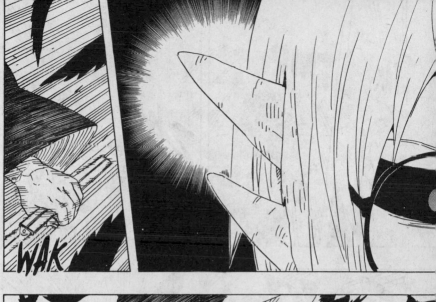

WAK

WAP

?!

RRRK

CLINK

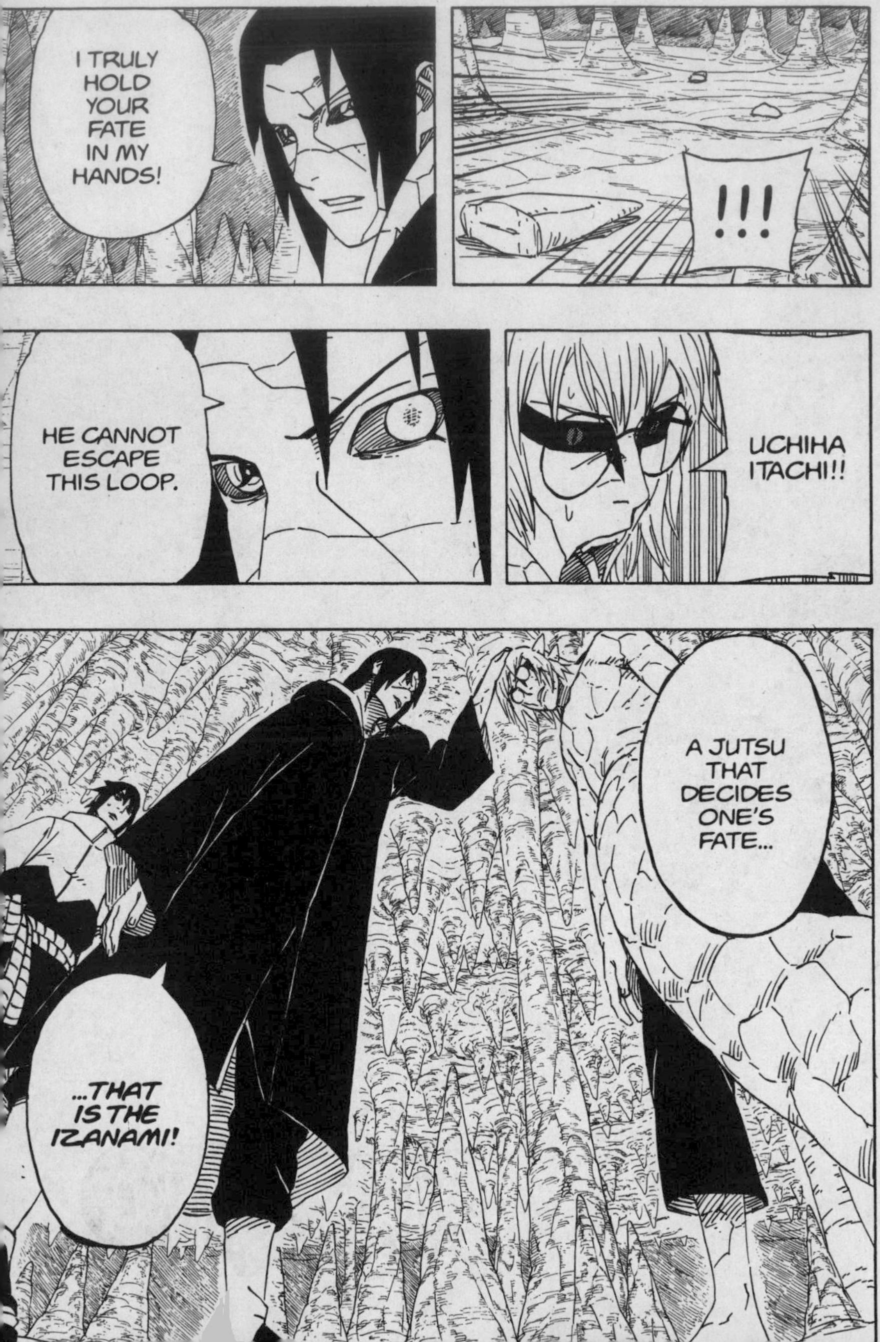
!!!
I TRULY HOLD YOUR FATE IN MY HANDS!
UCHIHA ITACHI!!
HE CANNOT ESCAPE THIS LOOP.
A JUTSU THAT DECIDES ONE'S FATE...
...THAT IS THE IZANAMI!

NARUTO

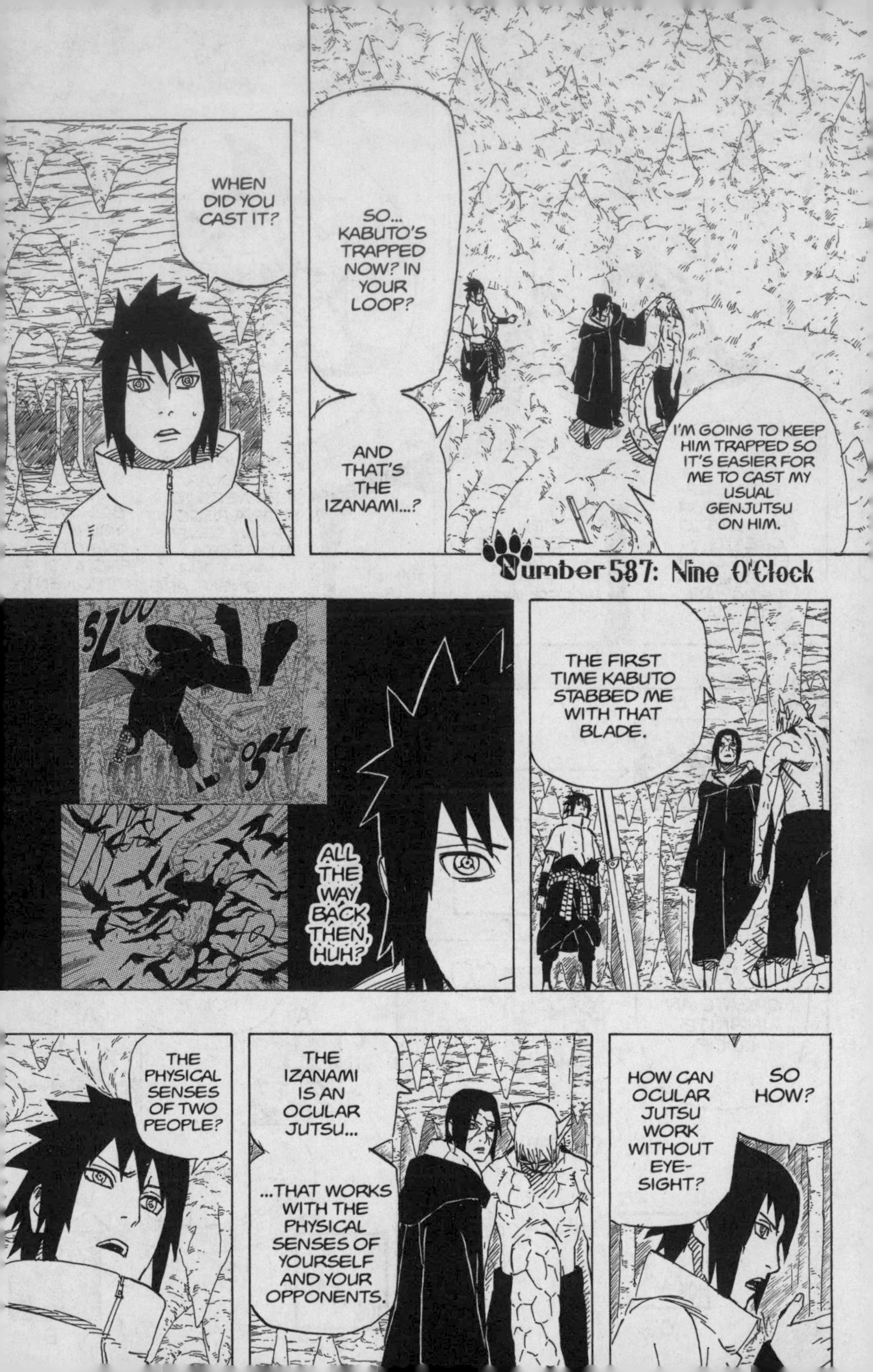
SO... KABUTO'S TRAPPED NOW? IN YOUR LOOP?
I'M GOING TO KEEP HIM TRAPPED SO IT'S EASIER FOR ME TO CAST MY USUAL GENJUTSU ON HIM.
AND THAT'S THE IZANAMI...?
WHEN DID YOU CAST IT?
Number 587: Nine O'Clock
THE FIRST TIME KABUTO STABBED ME WITH THAT BLADE.
ALL THE WAY BACK THEN, HUH?
SO HOW?
HOW CAN OCULAR JUTSU WORK WITHOUT EYE-SIGHT?
THE IZANAMI IS AN OCULAR JUTSU...
...THAT WORKS WITH THE PHYSICAL SENSES OF YOURSELF AND YOUR OPPONENTS.
THE PHYSICAL SENSES OF TWO PEOPLE?

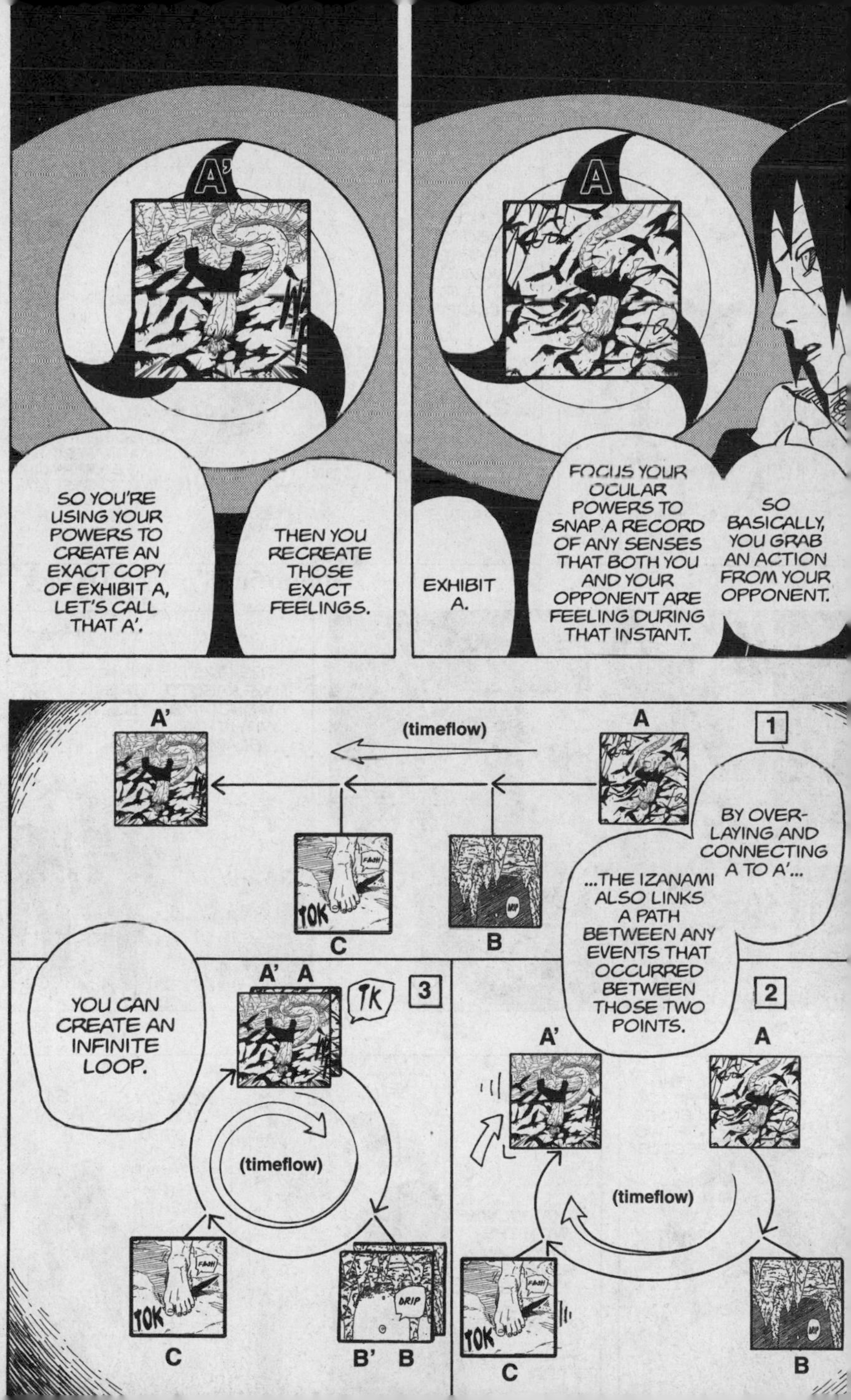
A
SO BASICALLY, YOU GRAB AN ACTION FROM YOUR OPPONENT.
FOCUS YOUR OCULAR POWERS TO SNAP A RECORD OF ANY SENSES THAT BOTH YOU AND YOUR OPPONENT ARE FEELING DURING THAT INSTANT.
EXHIBIT A.
A'
SO YOU'RE USING YOUR POWERS TO CREATE AN EXACT COPY OF EXHIBIT A, LET'S CALL THAT A'.
THEN YOU RECREATE THOSE EXACT FEELINGS.
1
A
(timeflow)
A'
BY OVER-LAYING AND CONNECTING A TO A'...
B
C
FASH
TOK
...THE IZANAMI ALSO LINKS A PATH BETWEEN ANY EVENTS THAT OCCURRED BETWEEN THOSE TWO POINTS.
2
A
A'
(timeflow)
B
C
FASH
TOK
3
A' A
TK
YOU CAN CREATE AN INFINITE LOOP.
(timeflow)
B' B
DRIP
C
FASH
TOK

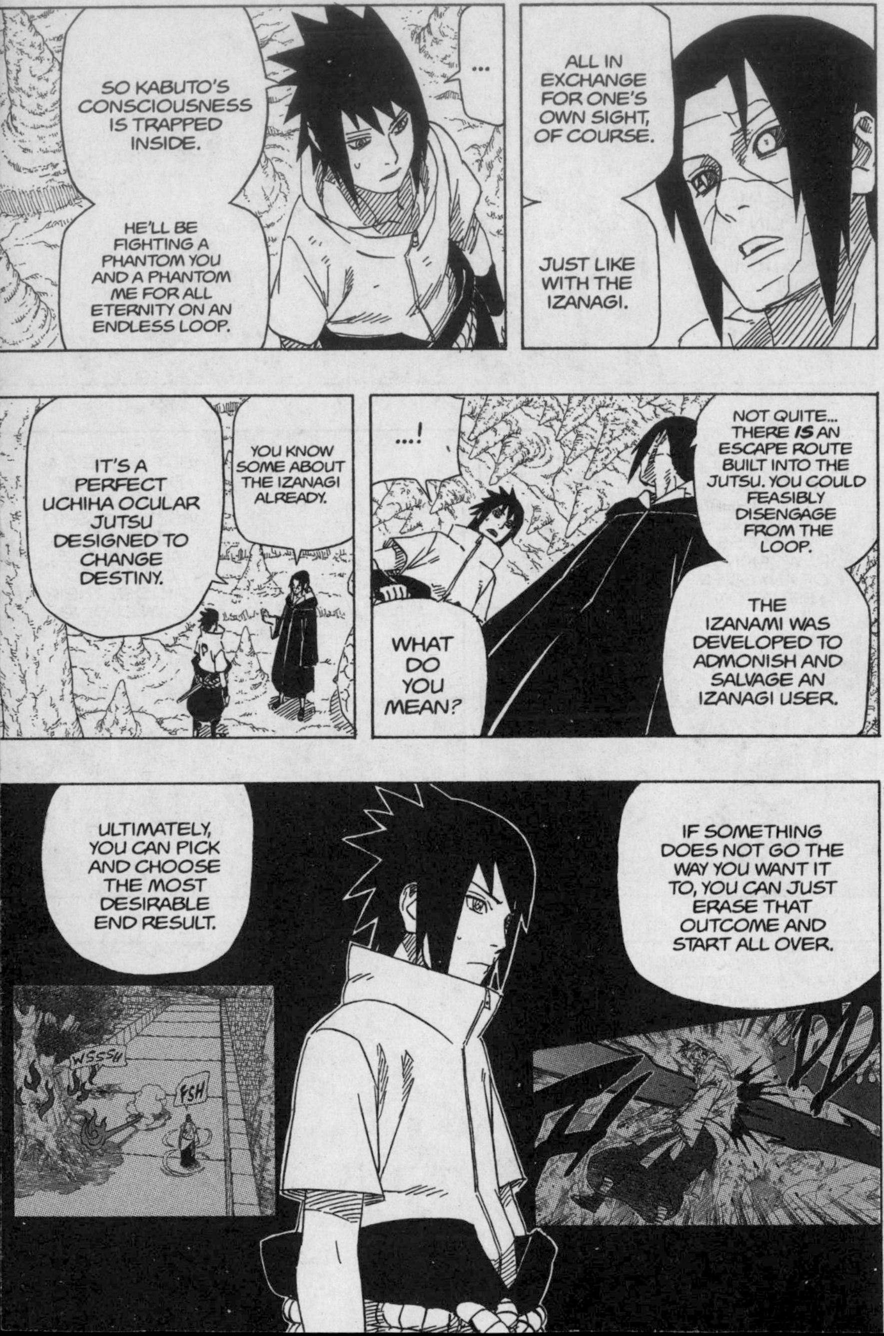
ALL IN EXCHANGE FOR ONE'S OWN SIGHT, OF COURSE.
JUST LIKE WITH THE IZANAGI.
...
SO KABUTO'S CONSCIOUSNESS IS TRAPPED INSIDE.
HE'LL BE FIGHTING A PHANTOM YOU AND A PHANTOM ME FOR ALL ETERNITY ON AN ENDLESS LOOP.
NOT QUITE... THERE ***IS*** AN ESCAPE ROUTE BUILT INTO THE JUTSU. YOU COULD FEASIBLY DISENGAGE FROM THE LOOP.
...!
THE IZANAMI WAS DEVELOPED TO ADMONISH AND SALVAGE AN IZANAGI USER.
WHAT DO YOU MEAN?
YOU KNOW SOME ABOUT THE IZANAGI ALREADY.
IT'S A PERFECT UCHIHA OCULAR JUTSU DESIGNED TO CHANGE DESTINY.
IF SOMETHING DOES NOT GO THE WAY YOU WANT IT TO, YOU CAN JUST ERASE THAT OUTCOME AND START ALL OVER.
ULTIMATELY, YOU CAN PICK AND CHOOSE THE MOST DESIRABLE END RESULT.
WSSSH
FSH

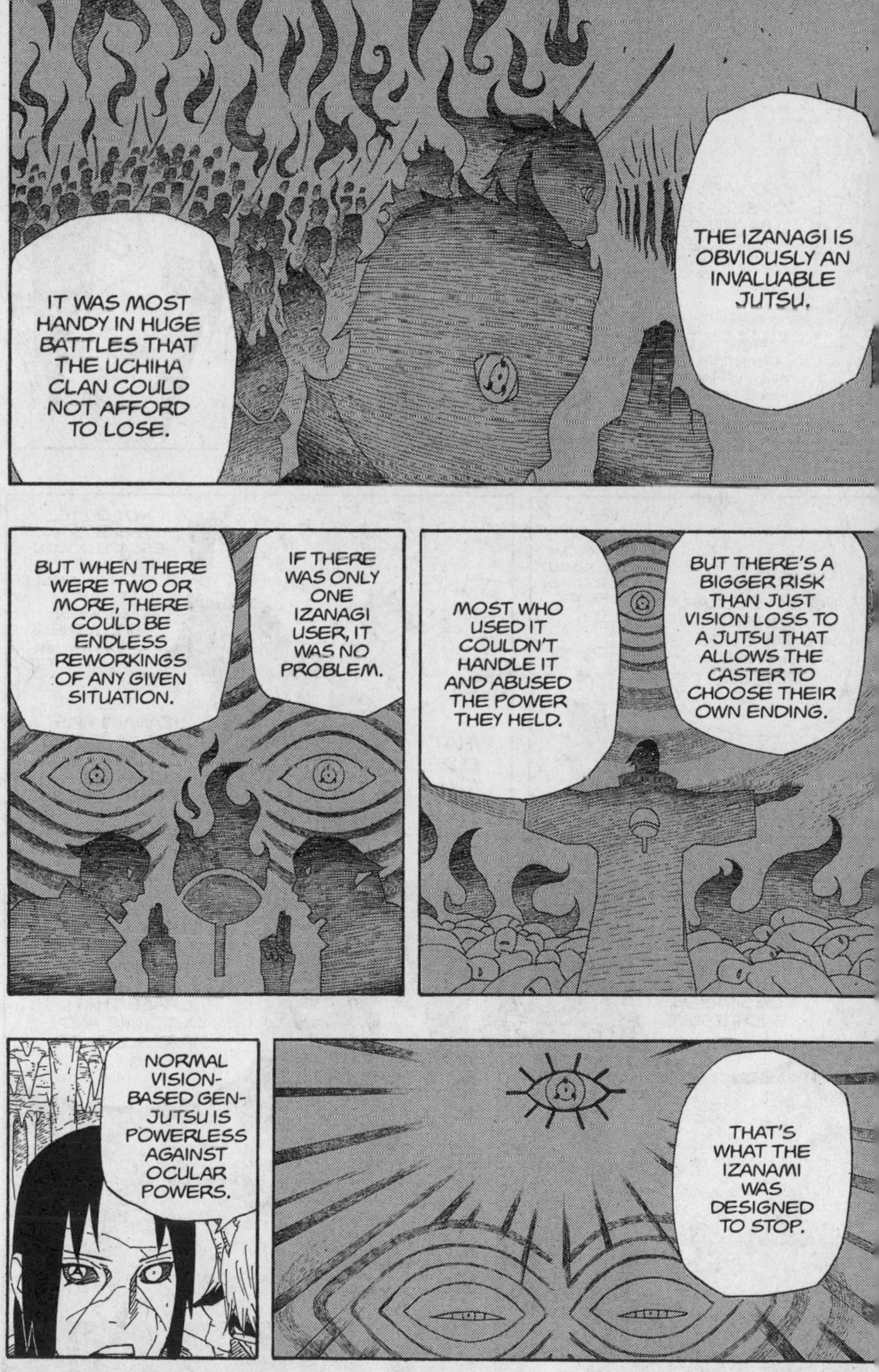
THE IZANAGI IS OBVIOUSLY AN INVALUABLE JUTSU.
IT WAS MOST HANDY IN HUGE BATTLES THAT THE UCHIHA CLAN COULD NOT AFFORD TO LOSE.
BUT THERE'S A BIGGER RISK THAN JUST VISION LOSS TO A JUTSU THAT ALLOWS THE CASTER TO CHOOSE THEIR OWN ENDING.
MOST WHO USED IT COULDN'T HANDLE IT AND ABUSED THE POWER THEY HELD.
IF THERE WAS ONLY ONE IZANAGI USER, IT WAS NO PROBLEM.
BUT WHEN THERE WERE TWO OR MORE, THERE COULD BE ENDLESS REWORKINGS OF ANY GIVEN SITUATION.
THAT'S WHAT THE IZANAMI WAS DESIGNED TO STOP.
NORMAL VISION-BASED GEN-JUTSU IS POWERLESS AGAINST OCULAR POWERS.

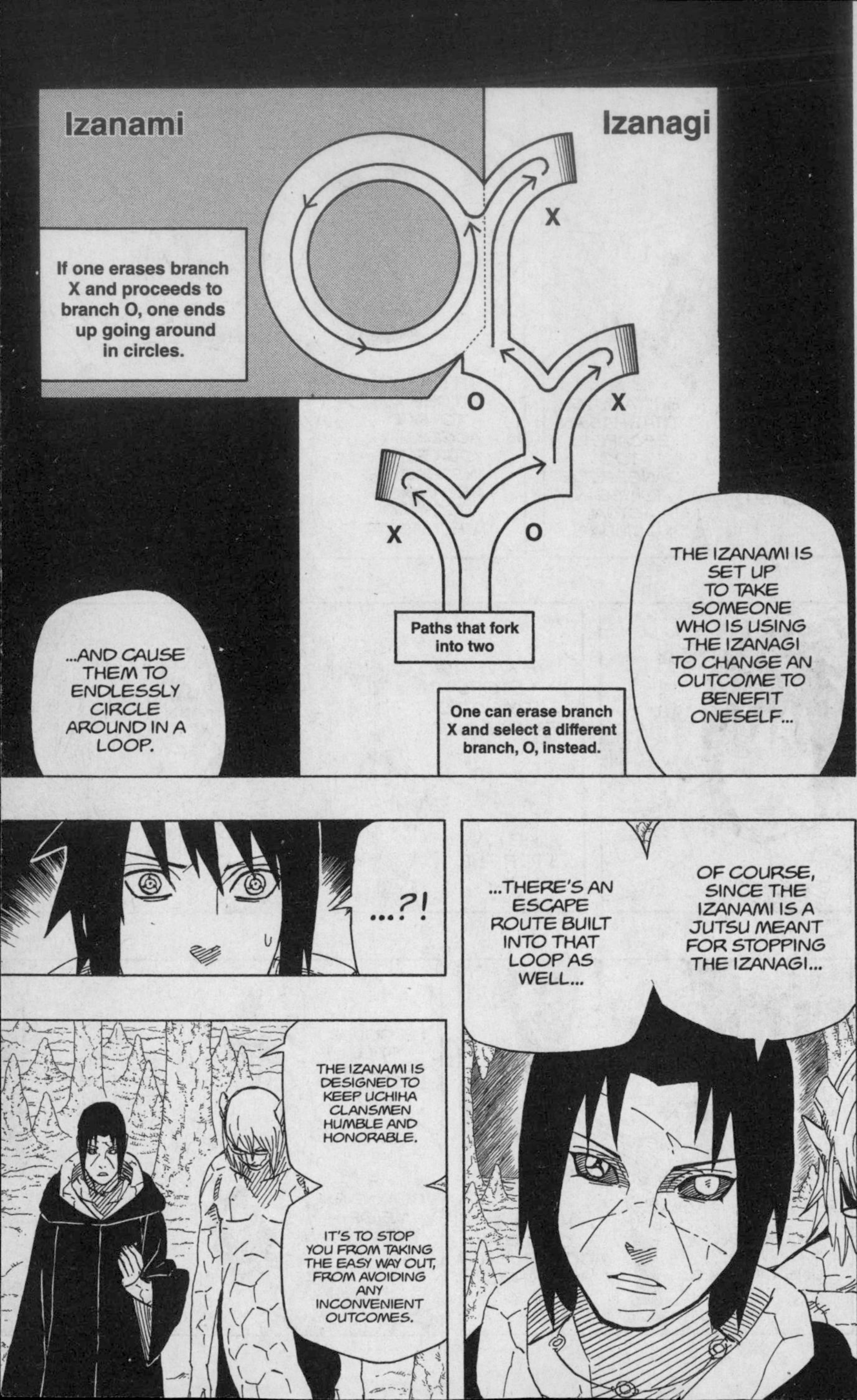
THE IZANAMI IS SET UP TO TAKE SOMEONE WHO IS USING THE IZANAGI TO CHANGE AN OUTCOME TO BENEFIT ONESELF...
Izanagi
X
X
O
X
O
Paths that fork into two
One can erase branch X and select a different branch, O, instead.
Izanami
If one erases branch X and proceeds to branch O, one ends up going around in circles.
...AND CAUSE THEM TO ENDLESSLY CIRCLE AROUND IN A LOOP.
OF COURSE, SINCE THE IZANAMI IS A JUTSU MEANT FOR STOPPING THE IZANAGI...
...THERE'S AN ESCAPE ROUTE BUILT INTO THAT LOOP AS WELL...
...?!
THE IZANAMI IS DESIGNED TO KEEP UCHIHA CLANSMEN HUMBLE AND HONORABLE.
IT'S TO STOP YOU FROM TAKING THE EASY WAY OUT, FROM AVOIDING ANY INCONVENIENT OUTCOMES.

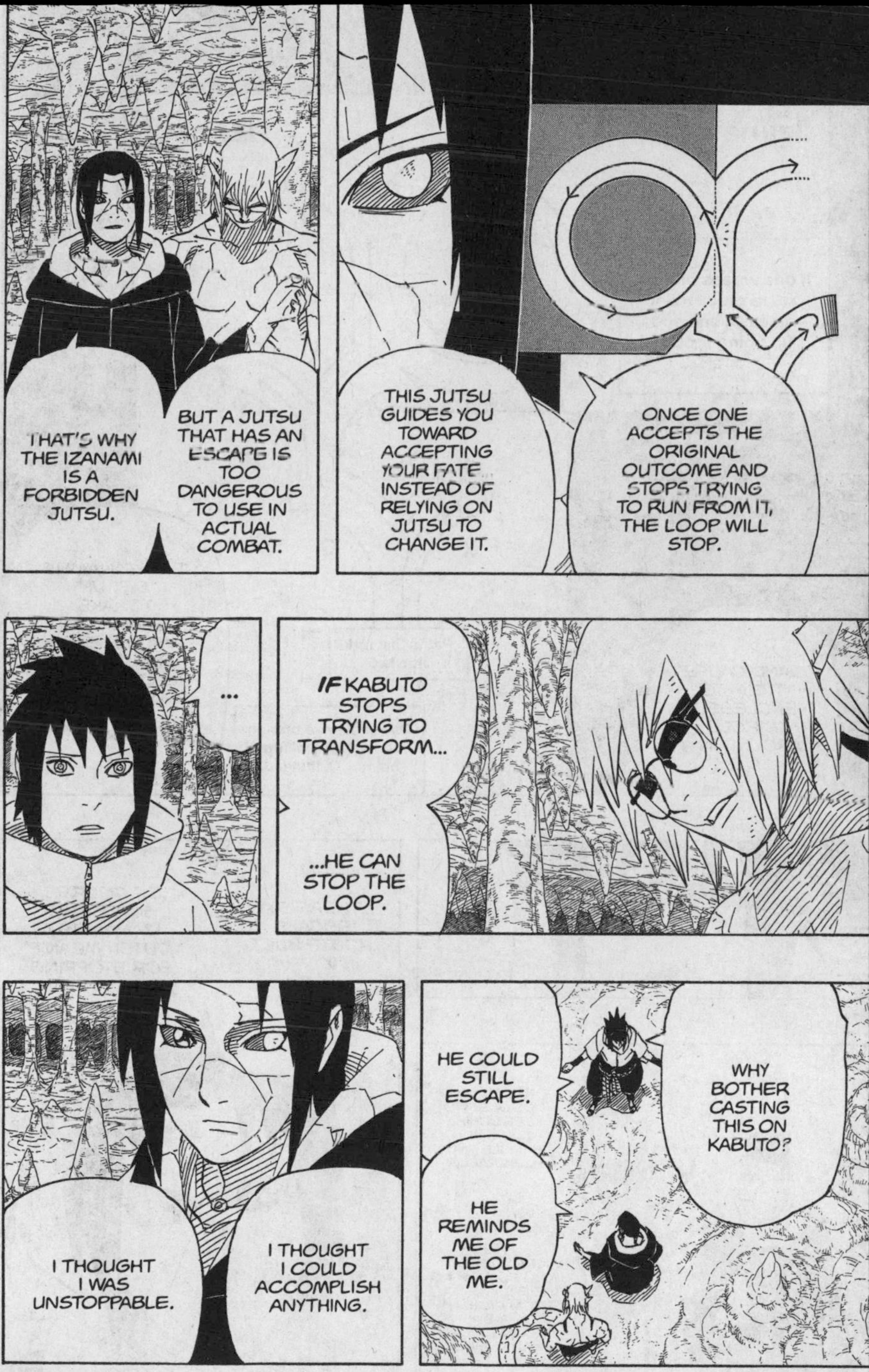
ONCE ONE ACCEPTS THE ORIGINAL OUTCOME AND STOPS TRYING TO RUN FROM IT, THE LOOP WILL STOP.
THIS JUTSU GUIDES YOU TOWARD ACCEPTING YOUR FATE... INSTEAD OF RELYING ON JUTSU TO CHANGE IT.
BUT A JUTSU THAT HAS AN ESCAPE IS TOO DANGEROUS TO USE IN ACTUAL COMBAT.
THAT'S WHY THE IZANAMI IS A FORBIDDEN JUTSU.
IF KABUTO STOPS TRYING TO TRANSFORM...
...HE CAN STOP THE LOOP.
...
WHY BOTHER CASTING THIS ON KABUTO?
HE COULD STILL ESCAPE.
HE REMINDS ME OF THE OLD ME.
I THOUGHT I COULD ACCOMPLISH ANYTHING.
I THOUGHT I WAS UNSTOPPABLE.

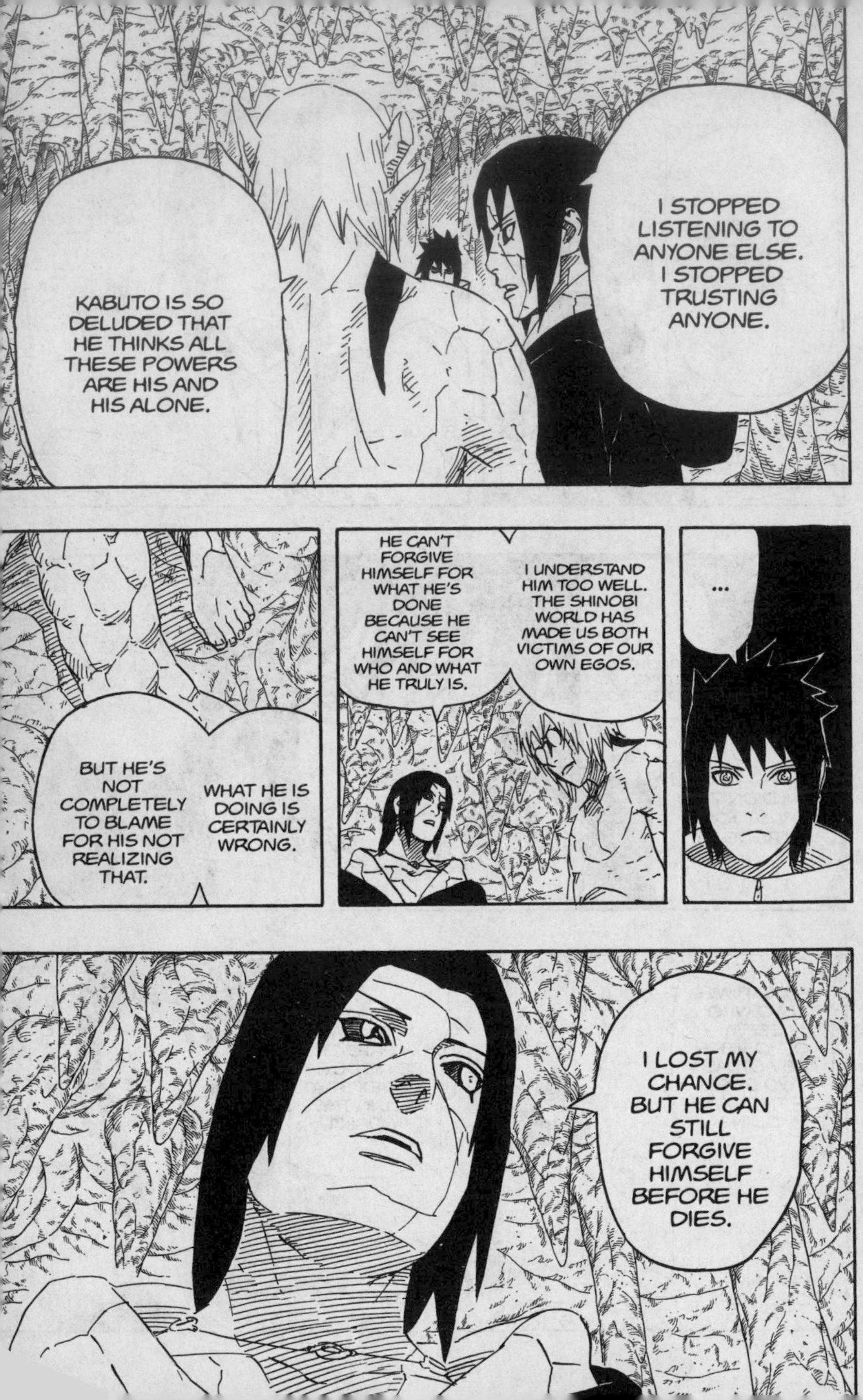
I STOPPED LISTENING TO ANYONE ELSE. I STOPPED TRUSTING ANYONE.
KABUTO IS SO DELUDED THAT HE THINKS ALL THESE POWERS ARE HIS AND HIS ALONE.
...
I UNDERSTAND HIM TOO WELL. THE SHINOBI WORLD HAS MADE US BOTH VICTIMS OF OUR OWN EGOS.
HE CAN'T FORGIVE HIMSELF FOR WHAT HE'S DONE BECAUSE HE CAN'T SEE HIMSELF FOR WHO AND WHAT HE TRULY IS.
WHAT HE IS DOING IS CERTAINLY WRONG.
BUT HE'S NOT COMPLETELY TO BLAME FOR HIS NOT REALIZING THAT.
I LOST MY CHANCE. BUT HE CAN STILL FORGIVE HIMSELF BEFORE HE DIES.

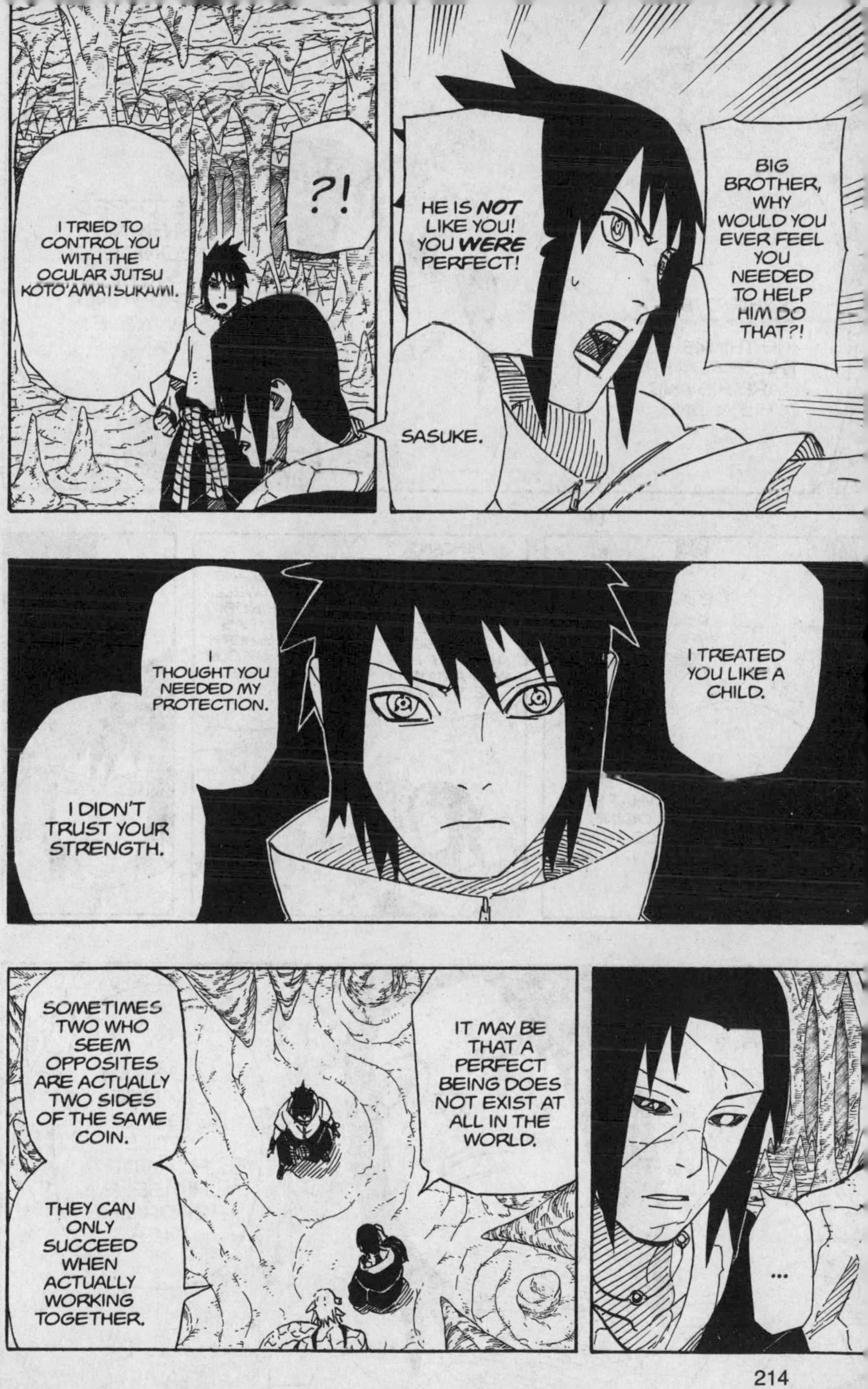
BIG BROTHER, WHY WOULD YOU EVER FEEL YOU NEEDED TO HELP HIM DO THAT?!
HE IS **NOT** LIKE YOU! YOU **WERE** PERFECT!
SASUKE.
?!
I TRIED TO CONTROL YOU WITH THE OCULAR JUTSU KOTO'AMATSUKAMI.
I TREATED YOU LIKE A CHILD.
I THOUGHT YOU NEEDED MY PROTECTION.
I DIDN'T TRUST YOUR STRENGTH.
...
IT MAY BE THAT A PERFECT BEING DOES NOT EXIST AT ALL IN THE WORLD.
SOMETIMES TWO WHO SEEM OPPOSITES ARE ACTUALLY TWO SIDES OF THE SAME COIN.
THEY CAN ONLY SUCCEED WHEN ACTUALLY WORKING TOGETHER.

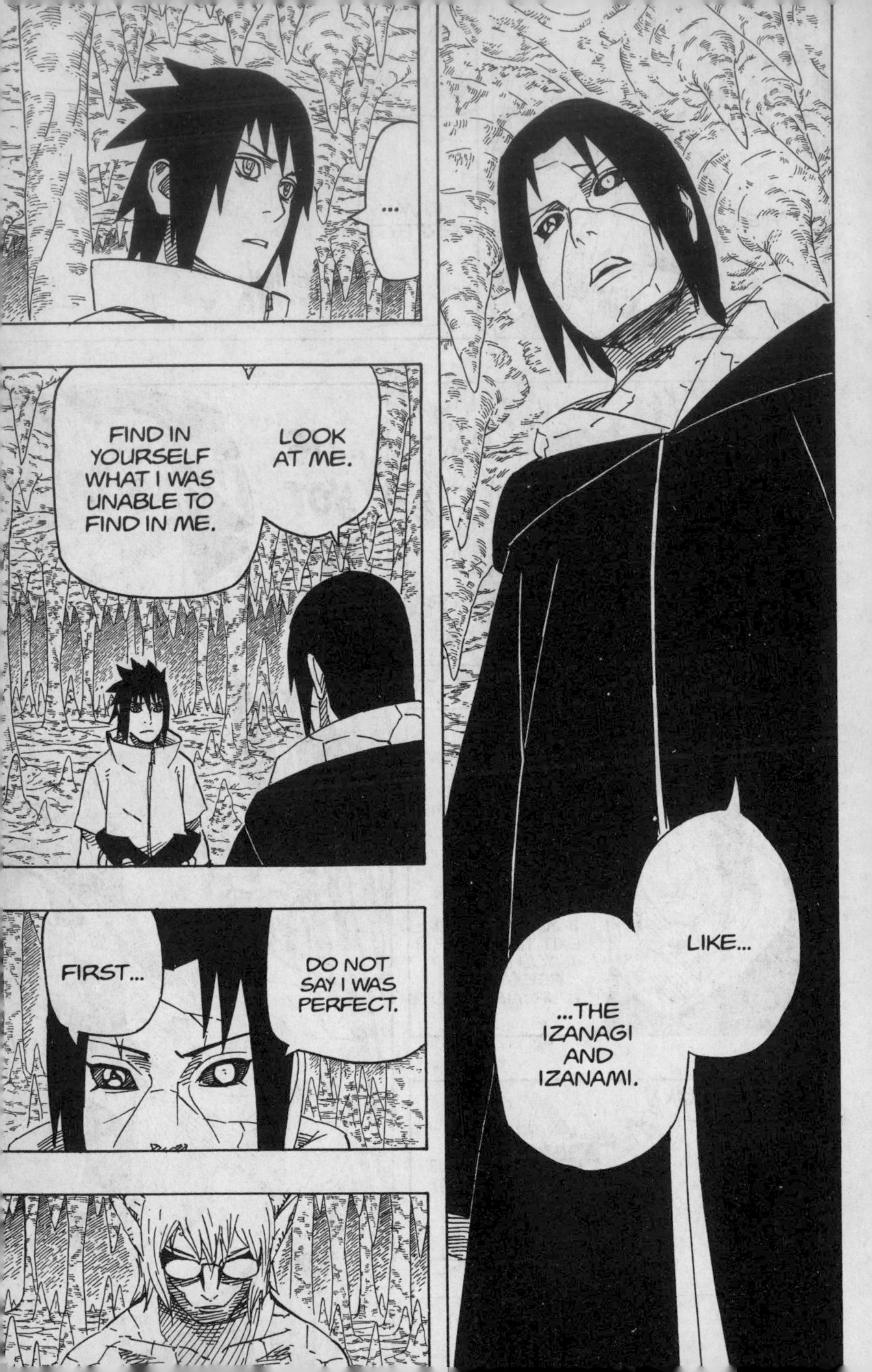
LIKE...
...THE IZANAGI AND IZANAMI.
...
LOOK AT ME.
FIND IN YOURSELF WHAT I WAS UNABLE TO FIND IN ME.
DO NOT SAY I WAS PERFECT.
FIRST...

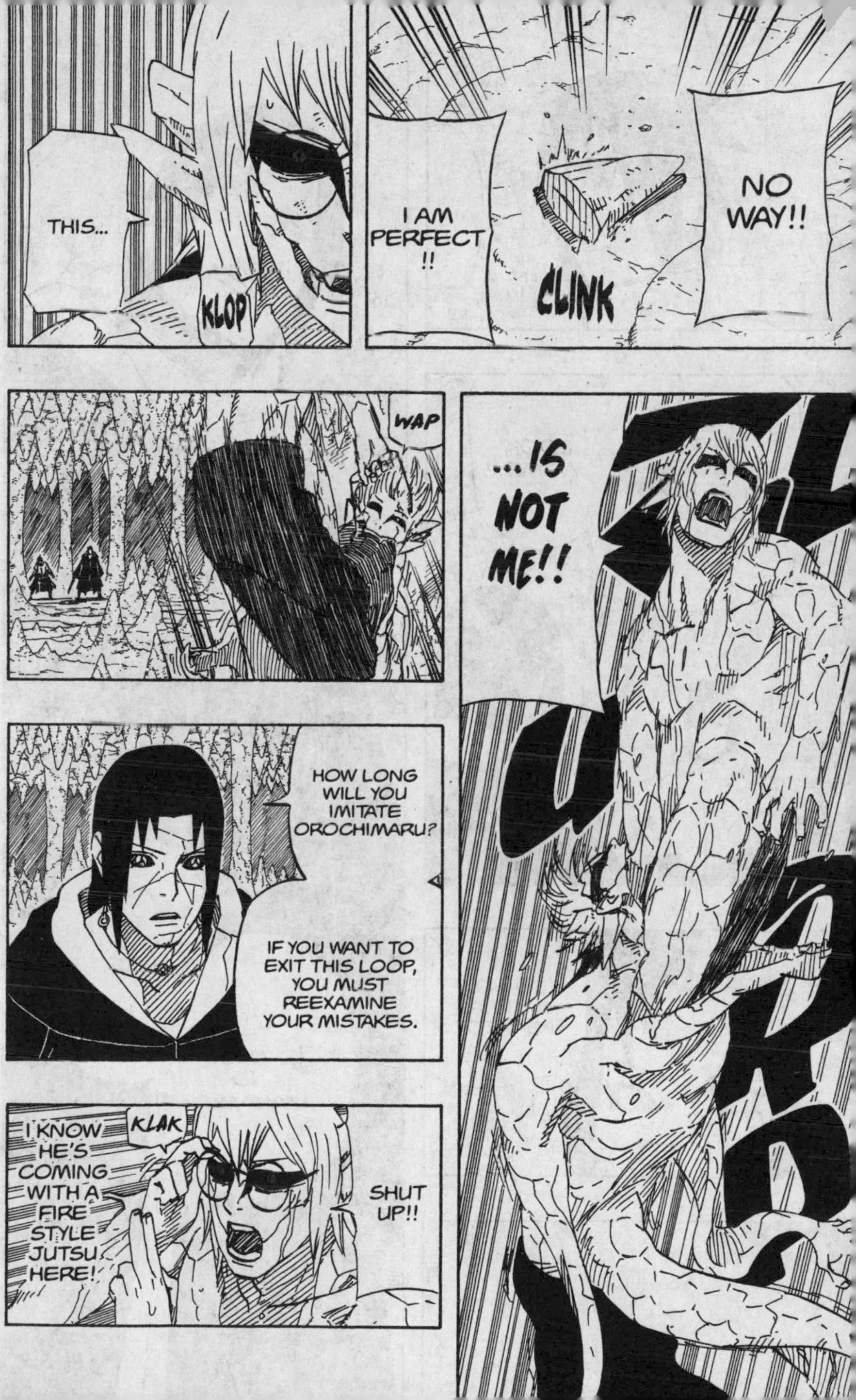
NO WAY!!
I AM PERFECT !!
CLINK
THIS...
KLOP
...IS NOT ME!!
WAP
HOW LONG WILL YOU IMITATE OROCHIMARU?
IF YOU WANT TO EXIT THIS LOOP, YOU MUST REEXAMINE YOUR MISTAKES.
SHUT UP!!
KLAK
I KNOW HE'S COMING WITH A FIRE STYLE JUTSU HERE!

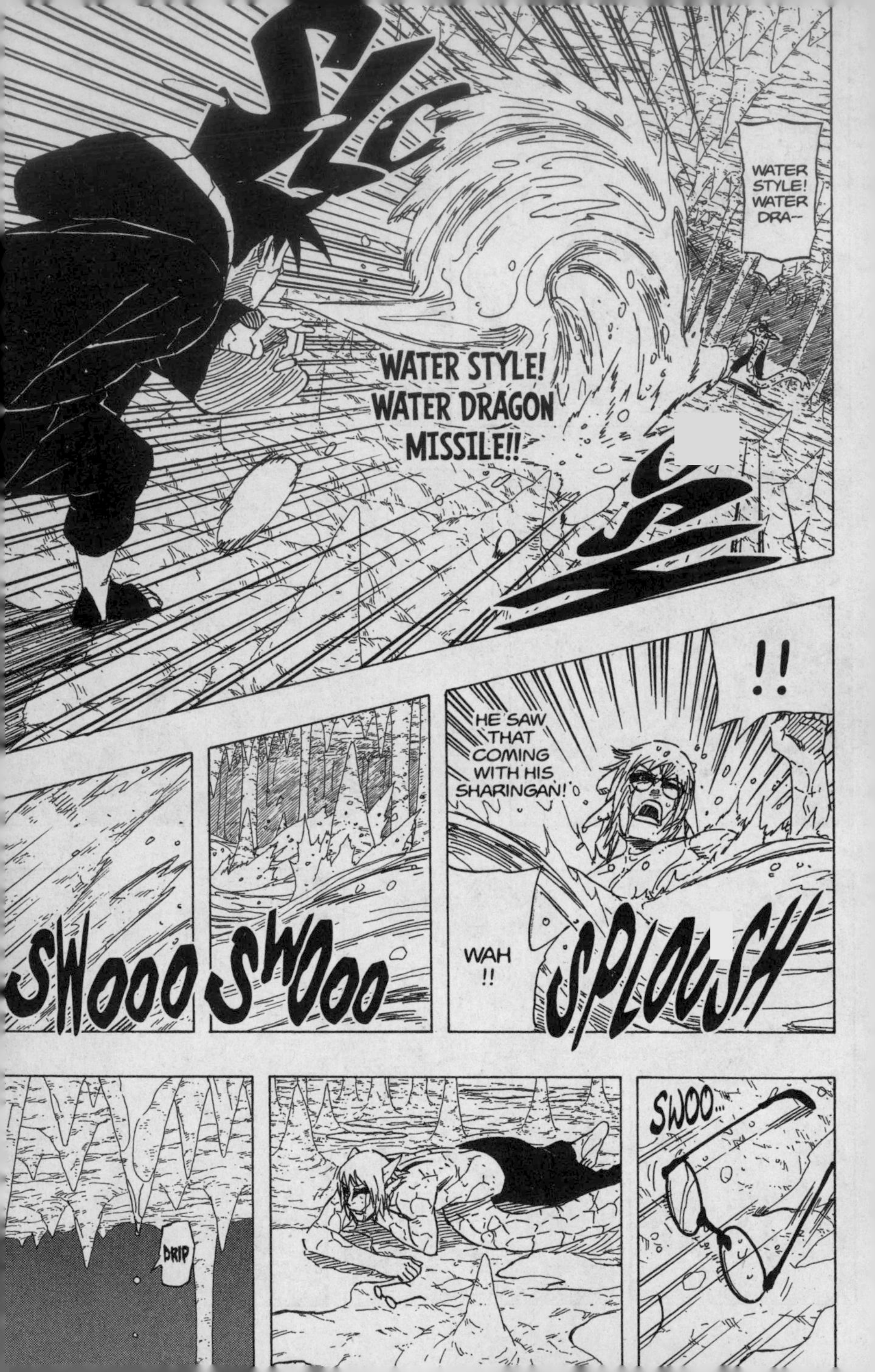
WATER STYLE! WATER DRA--
WATER STYLE! WATER DRAGON MISSILE!!
!!
HE SAW THAT COMING WITH HIS SHARINGAN!
WAH !!
SPLOUSH
SWOOO
SWOOO
SWOO...
DRIP

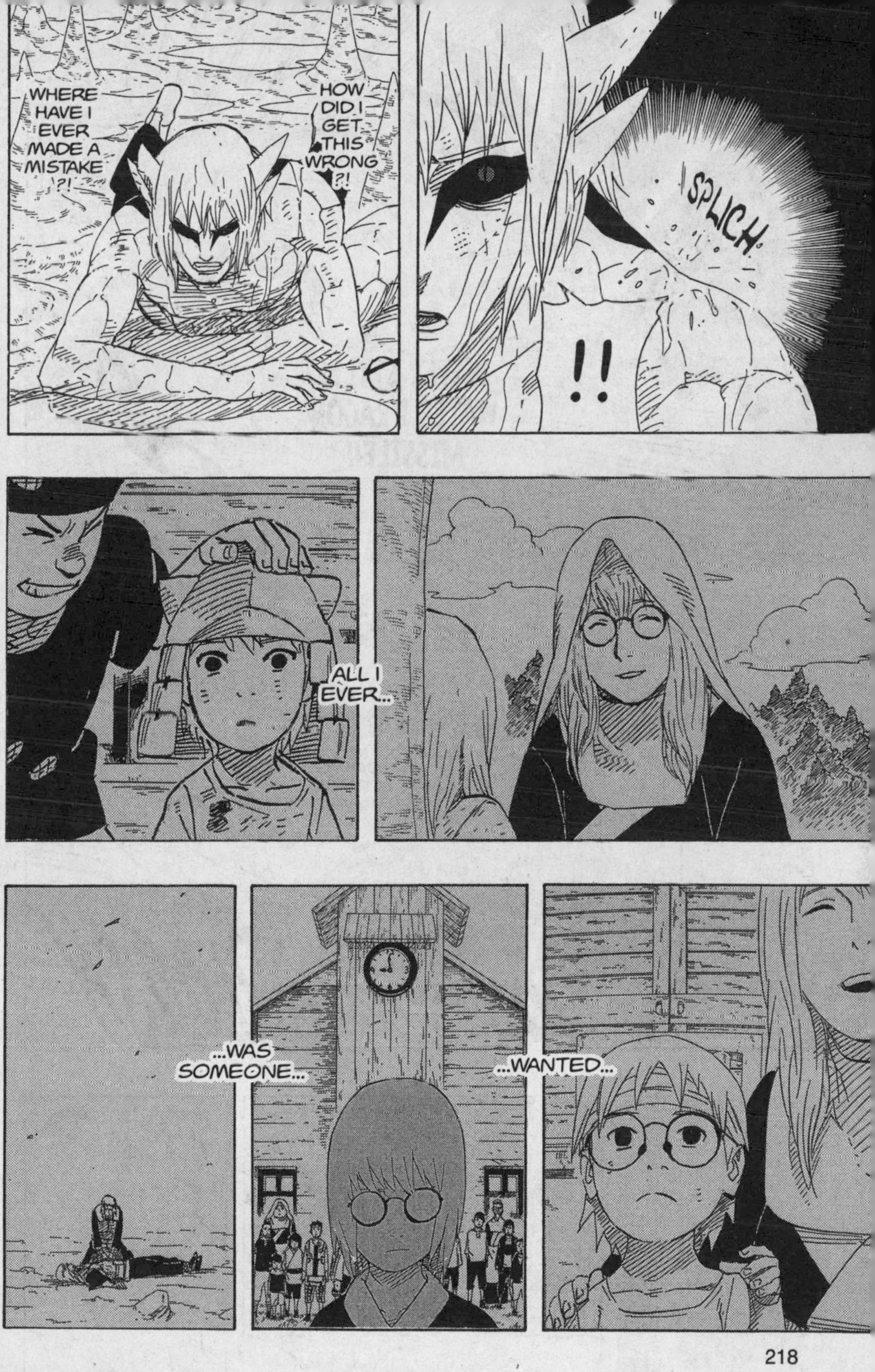
SPLICH
!!
HOW DID I GET THIS WRONG ?!
WHERE HAVE I EVER MADE A MISTAKE ?!
ALL I EVER...
...WANTED...
...WAS SOMEONE...

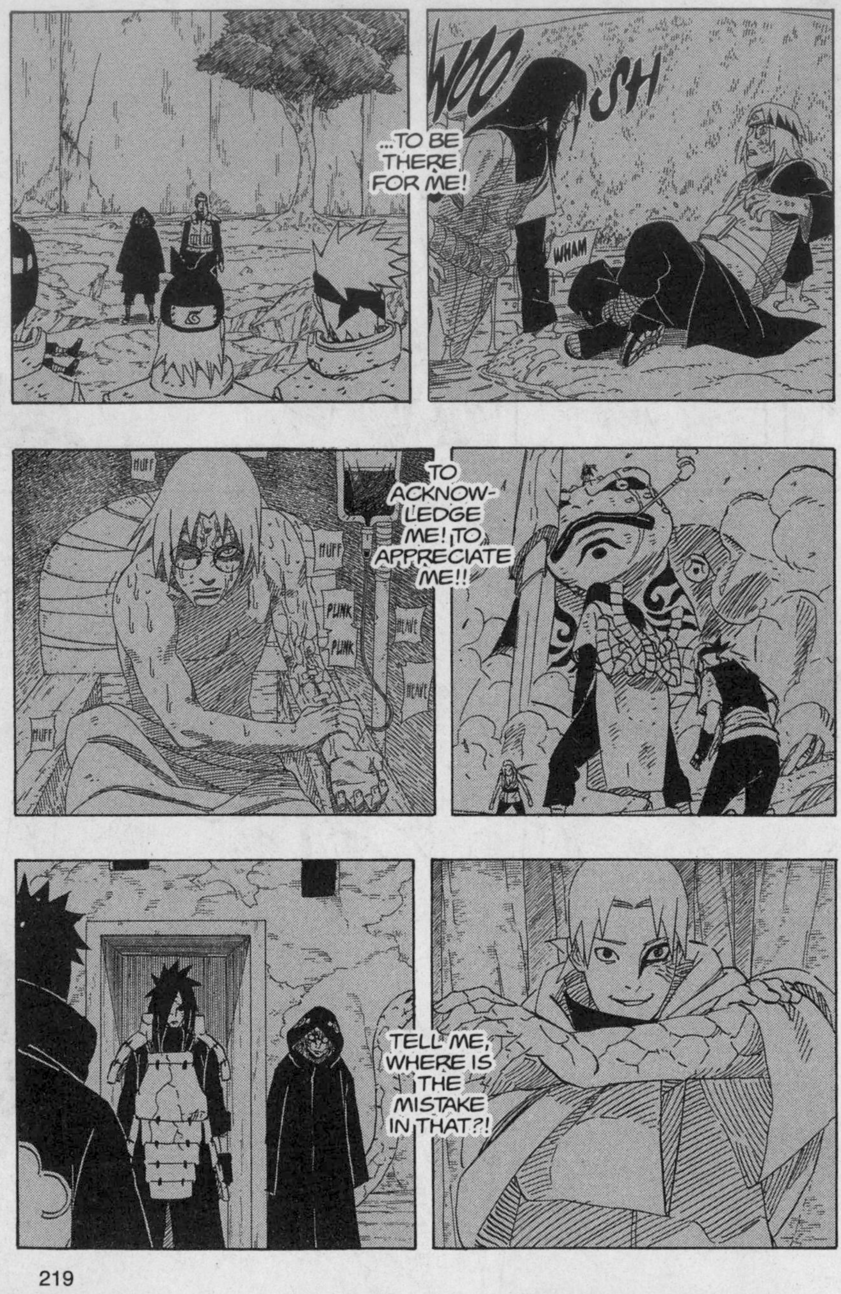
WHOOSH
WHAM
...TO BE THERE FOR ME!
TO ACKNOWLEDGE ME! TO APPRECIATE ME!!
HUFF
HUFF
PLINK
PLINK
HEAVE
HEAVE
HUFF
TELL ME, WHERE IS THE MISTAKE IN THAT?!

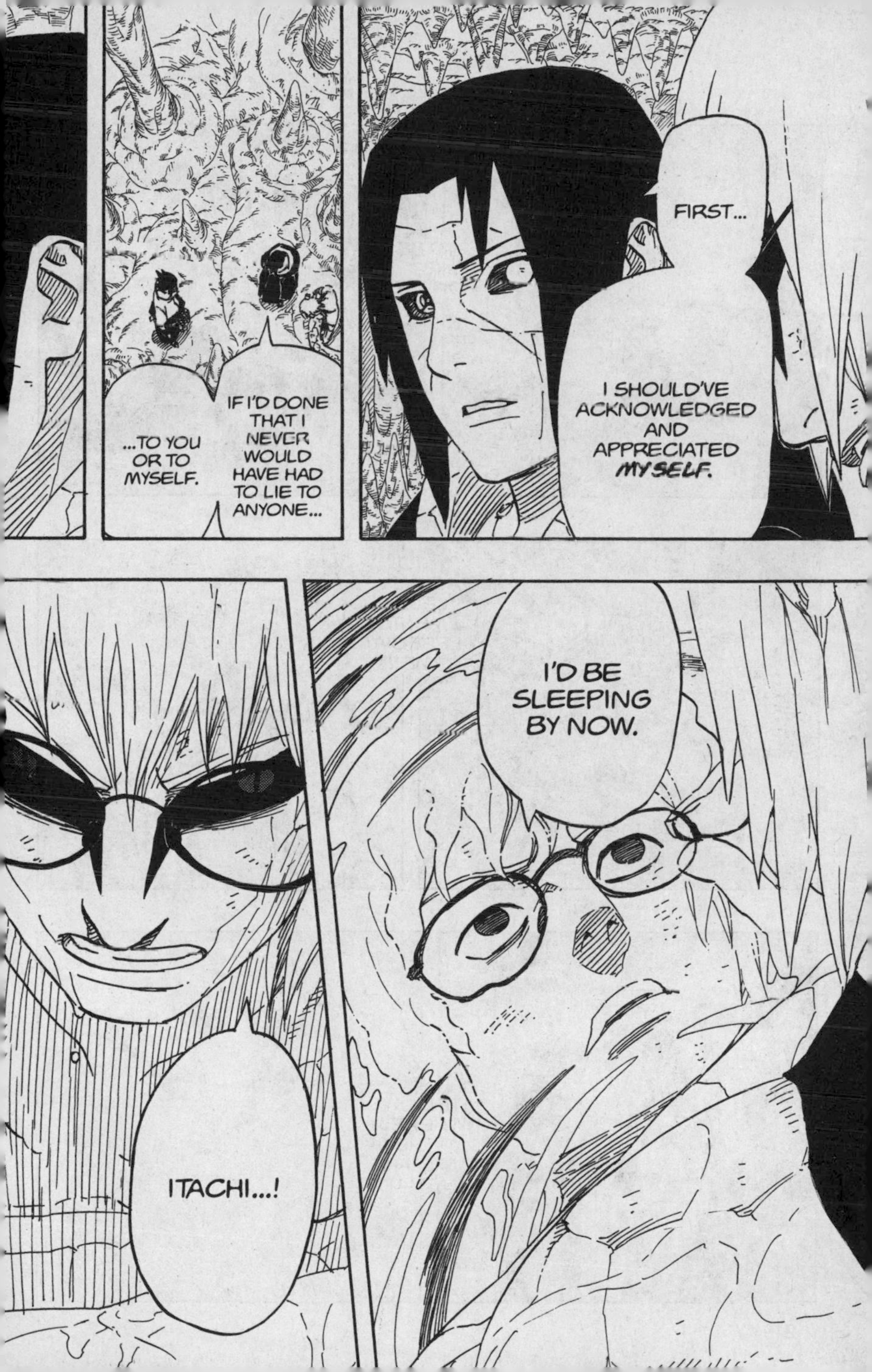
FIRST...
I SHOULD'VE ACKNOWLEDGED AND APPRECIATED *MYSELF*.
IF I'D DONE THAT I NEVER WOULD HAVE HAD TO LIE TO ANYONE...
...TO YOU OR TO MYSELF.
I'D BE SLEEPING BY NOW.
ITACHI...!

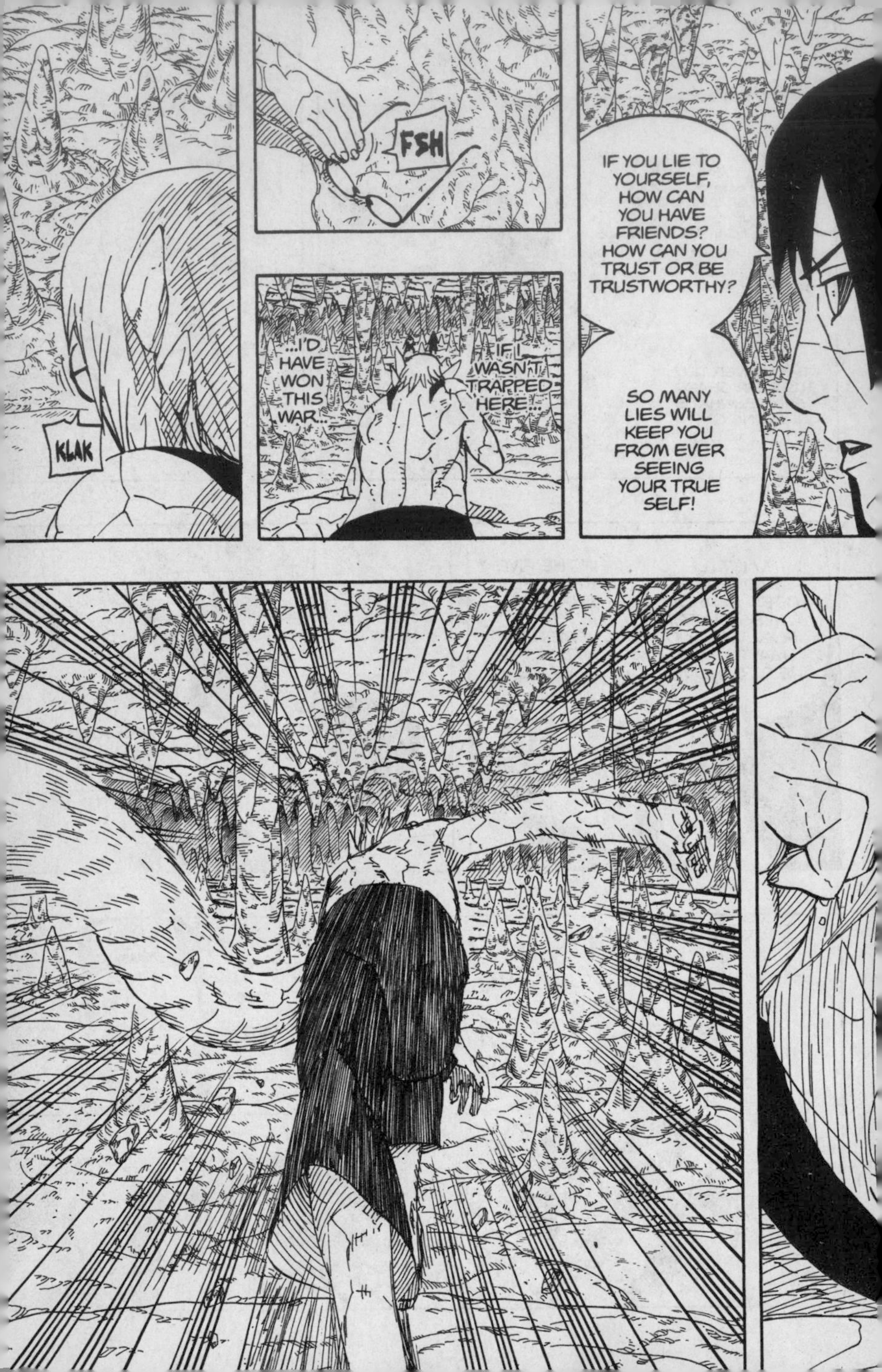
IF YOU LIE TO YOURSELF, HOW CAN YOU HAVE FRIENDS? HOW CAN YOU TRUST OR BE TRUSTWORTHY?
SO MANY LIES WILL KEEP YOU FROM EVER SEEING YOUR TRUE SELF!
FSH
IF I WASN'T TRAPPED HERE...
...I'D HAVE WON THIS WAR..
KLAK

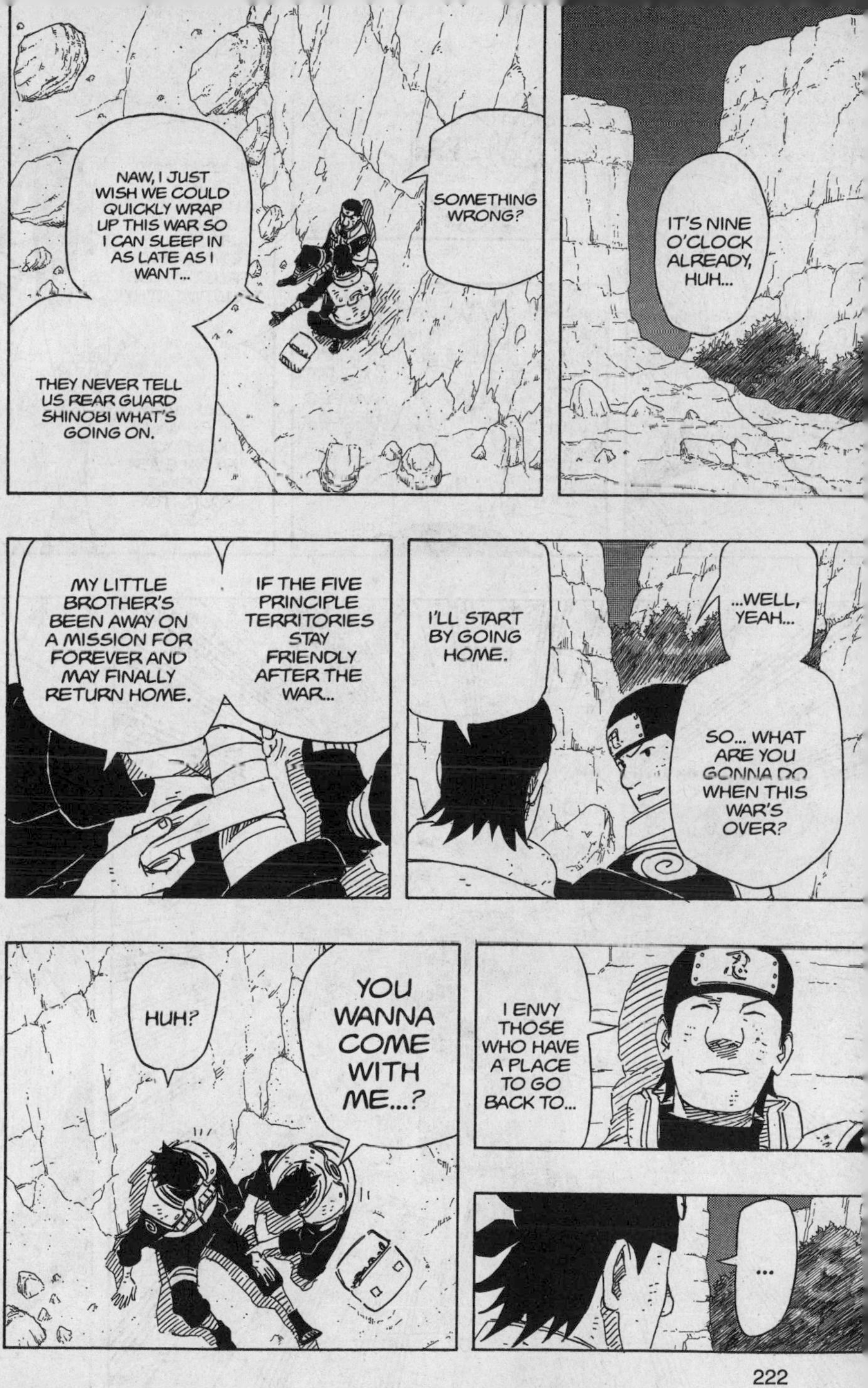
IT'S NINE O'CLOCK ALREADY, HUH...
SOMETHING WRONG?
NAW, I JUST WISH WE COULD QUICKLY WRAP UP THIS WAR SO I CAN SLEEP IN AS LATE AS I WANT...
THEY NEVER TELL US REAR GUARD SHINOBI WHAT'S GOING ON.
...WELL, YEAH...
SO... WHAT ARE YOU GONNA DO WHEN THIS WAR'S OVER?
I'LL START BY GOING HOME.
IF THE FIVE PRINCIPLE TERRITORIES STAY FRIENDLY AFTER THE WAR...
MY LITTLE BROTHER'S BEEN AWAY ON A MISSION FOR FOREVER AND MAY FINALLY RETURN HOME.
I ENVY THOSE WHO HAVE A PLACE TO GO BACK TO...
...
YOU WANNA COME WITH ME...?
HUH?

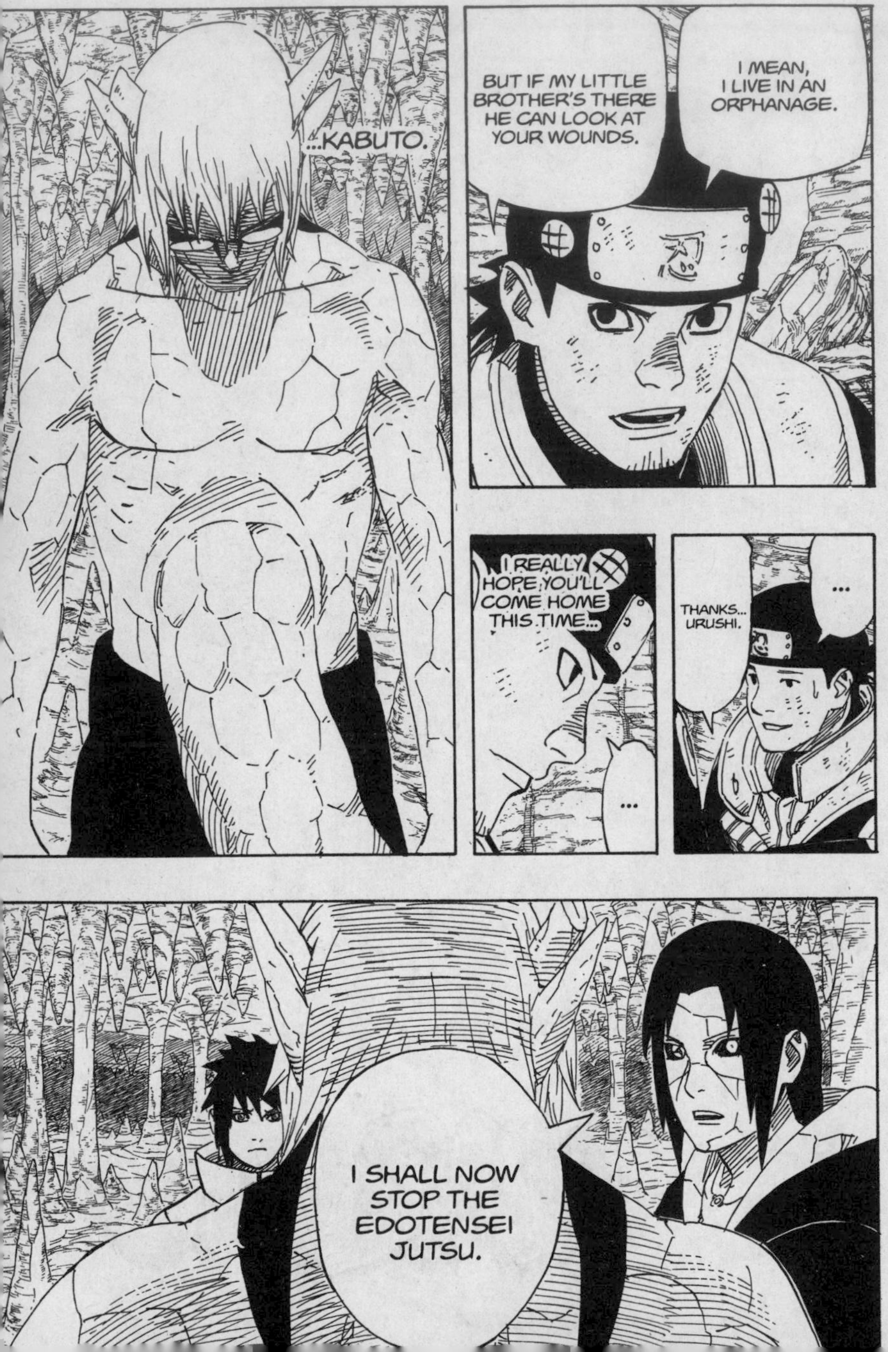
I MEAN, I LIVE IN AN ORPHANAGE.
BUT IF MY LITTLE BROTHER'S THERE HE CAN LOOK AT YOUR WOUNDS.
...
THANKS... URUSHI.
I REALLY HOPE YOU'LL COME HOME THIS TIME...
...
...KABUTO.
I SHALL NOW STOP THE EDOTENSEI JUTSU.

NARUTO

62
NARUTO
61
NARUTO

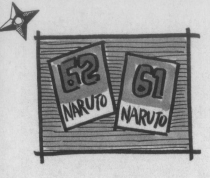

Sasuke and Itachi's tale concludes in this volume. I actually wanted to put it all in volume 61 so that you could read it all at once, but it just wasn't possible. (D'oh!) Please read volume 61 before 62! Please!

岸本斉史

—Masashi Kishimoto, 2012

一楽
ラーメン一楽
うまい

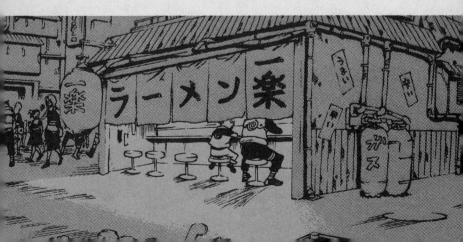

NARUTO

SHONEN JUMP MANGA EDITION

NARUTO

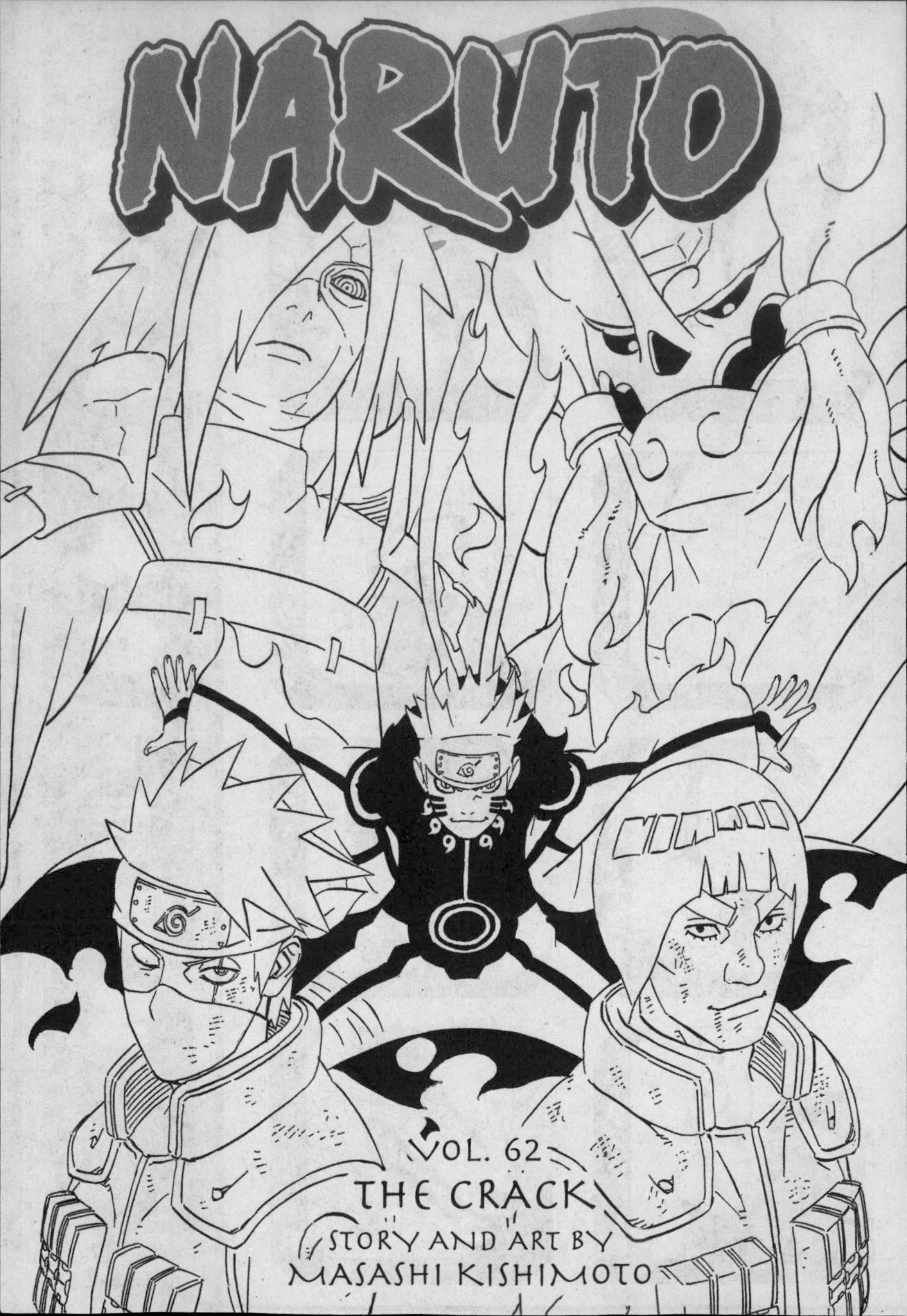

VOL. 62

THE CRACK

STORY AND ART BY

MASASHI KISHIMOTO

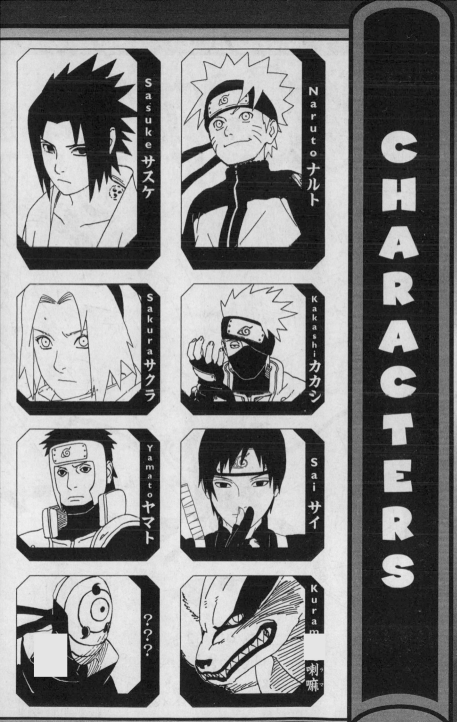

Sasuke サスケ

Naruto ナルト

Sakura サクラ

Kakashi カカシ

Yamato ヤマト

Sai サイ

？？？

Kuram

喇嘛

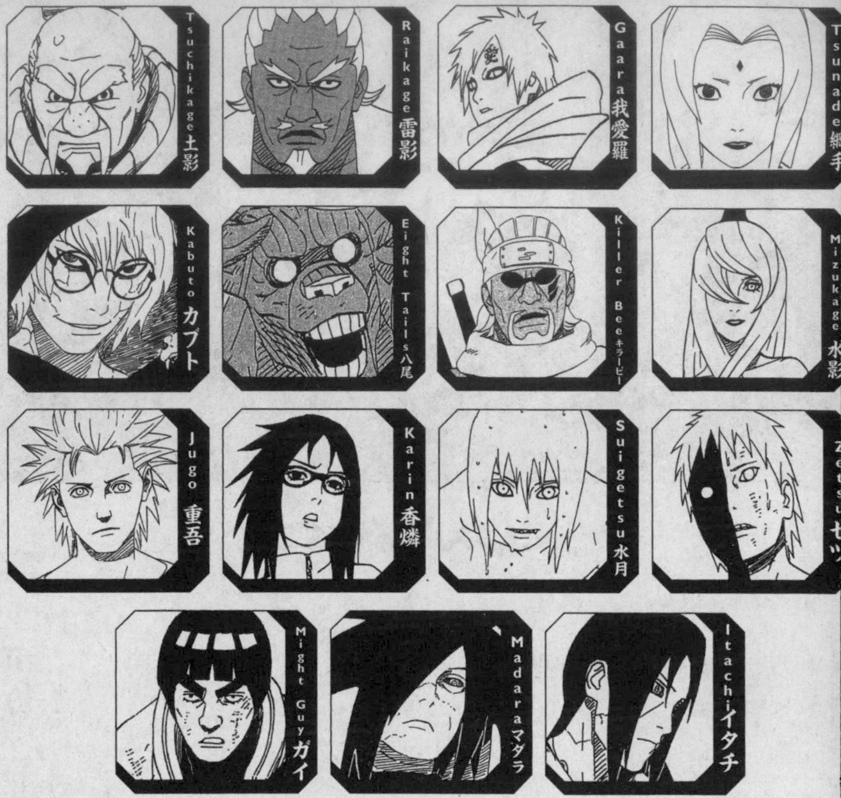
Tsunade 綱手
Gaara 我愛羅
Raikage 雷影
Tsuchikage 土影
Mizukage 水影
Killer Bee キラービー
Eight Tails 八尾
Kabuto カブト
Zetsu
Suigetsu 水月
Karin 香燐
Jugo 重吾
Itachi イタチ
Madara マダラ
Might Guy ガイ

THE STORY SO FAR...

Naruto, the biggest troublemaker at the Ninja Academy in the Village of Konohagakure, finally becomes a ninja along with his classmates Sasuke and Sakura. They grow and mature through countless trials and battles. However, Sasuke, unable to give up his quest for vengeance, leaves Konohagakure to seek Orochimaru and his power...

Two years pass. Naruto grows up and engages in fierce battles against the Tailed Beast-targeting Akatsuki. Elsewhere, after winning the heroic battle against Itachi and learning his older brother's true intentions, Sasuke allies with Akatsuki and sets out to destroy Konoha.

The Fourth Great Ninja War against the Akatsuki begins. The Five Shadows seem powerless against the revived Madara's power. Meanwhile, Sasuke and Itachi confront Kabuto, who is dragging the battlefield into a vortex of chaos. Having surmounted their past differences, will the brothers' united front finally succeed in stopping Kabuto?!

NARUTO

VOL. 62
THE CRACK

CONTENTS

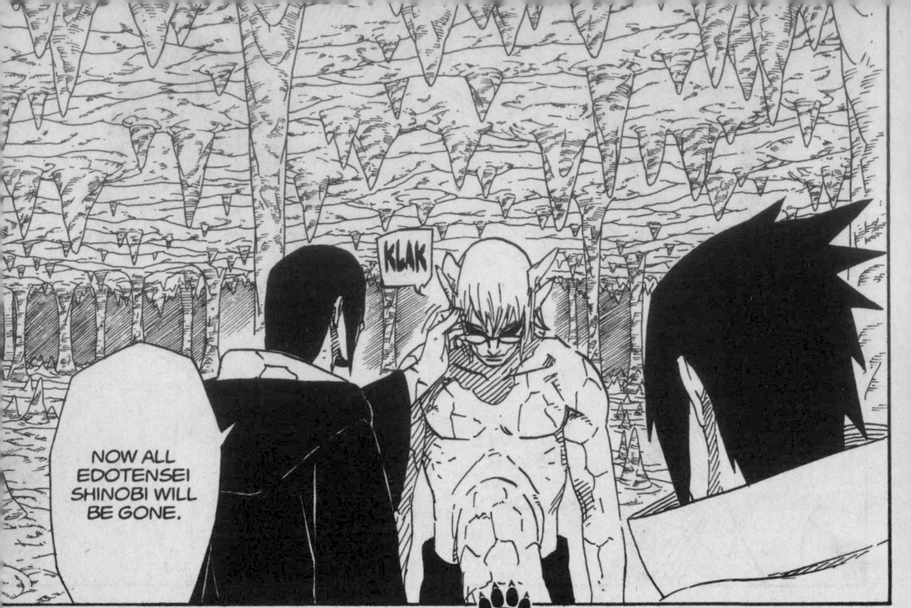
KLAK
NOW ALL EDOTENSEI SHINOBI WILL BE GONE.

Number 588: Burden of a Kage

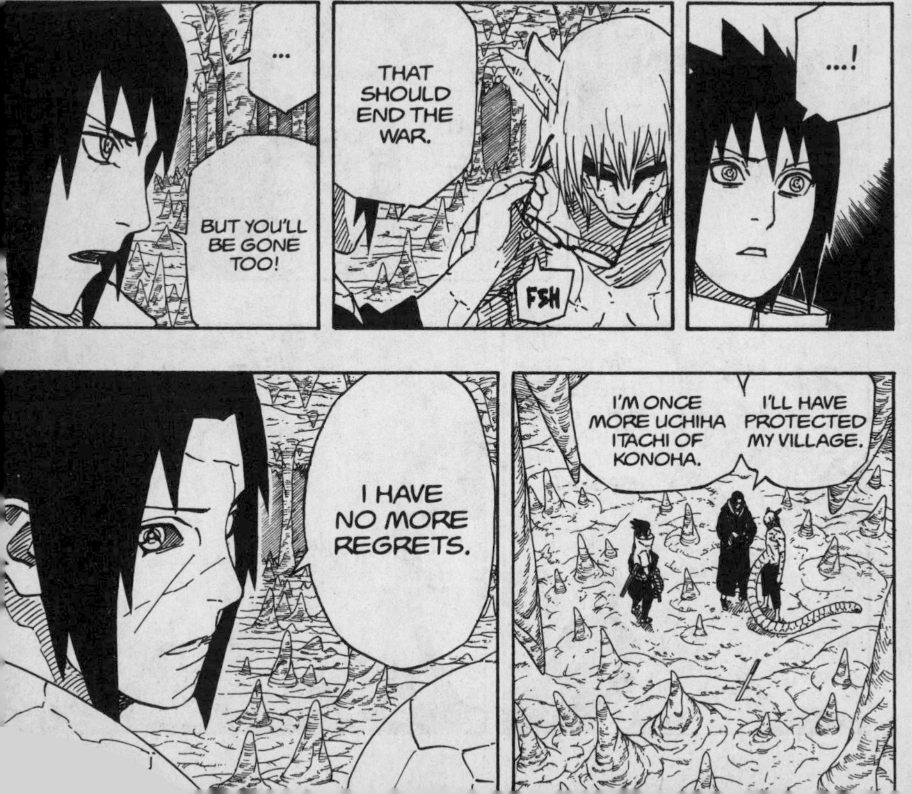
...!
THAT SHOULD END THE WAR.
FSH
...
BUT YOU'LL BE GONE TOO!
I'LL HAVE PROTECTED MY VILLAGE.
I'M ONCE MORE UCHIHA ITACHI OF KONOHA.
I HAVE NO MORE REGRETS.

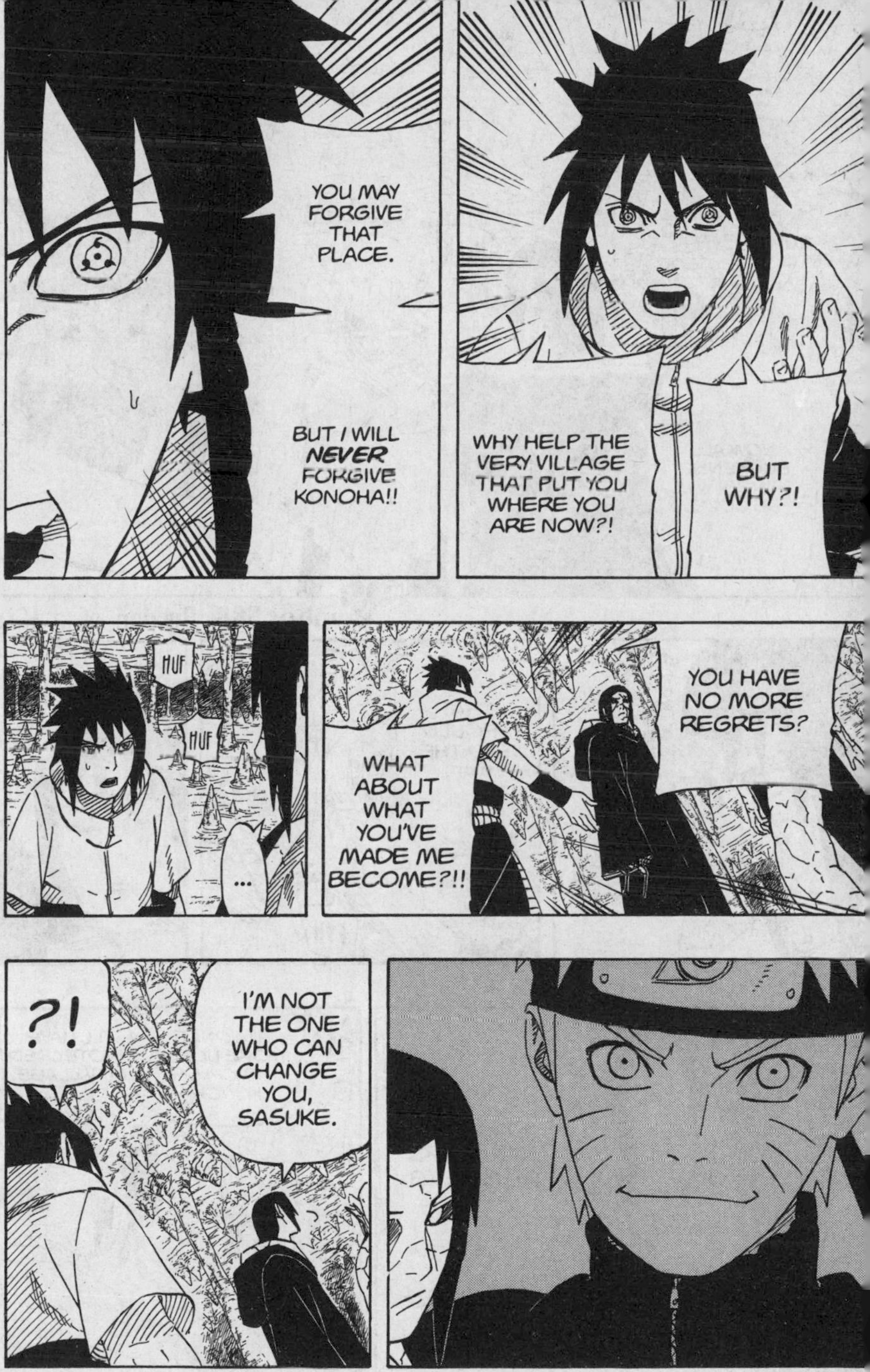
BUT WHY?!
WHY HELP THE VERY VILLAGE THAT PUT YOU WHERE YOU ARE NOW?!
YOU MAY FORGIVE THAT PLACE.
BUT I WILL ***NEVER*** FORGIVE KONOHA!!
YOU HAVE NO MORE REGRETS?
WHAT ABOUT WHAT YOU'VE MADE ME BECOME?!!
HUF
HUF
...
?!
I'M NOT THE ONE WHO CAN CHANGE YOU, SASUKE.

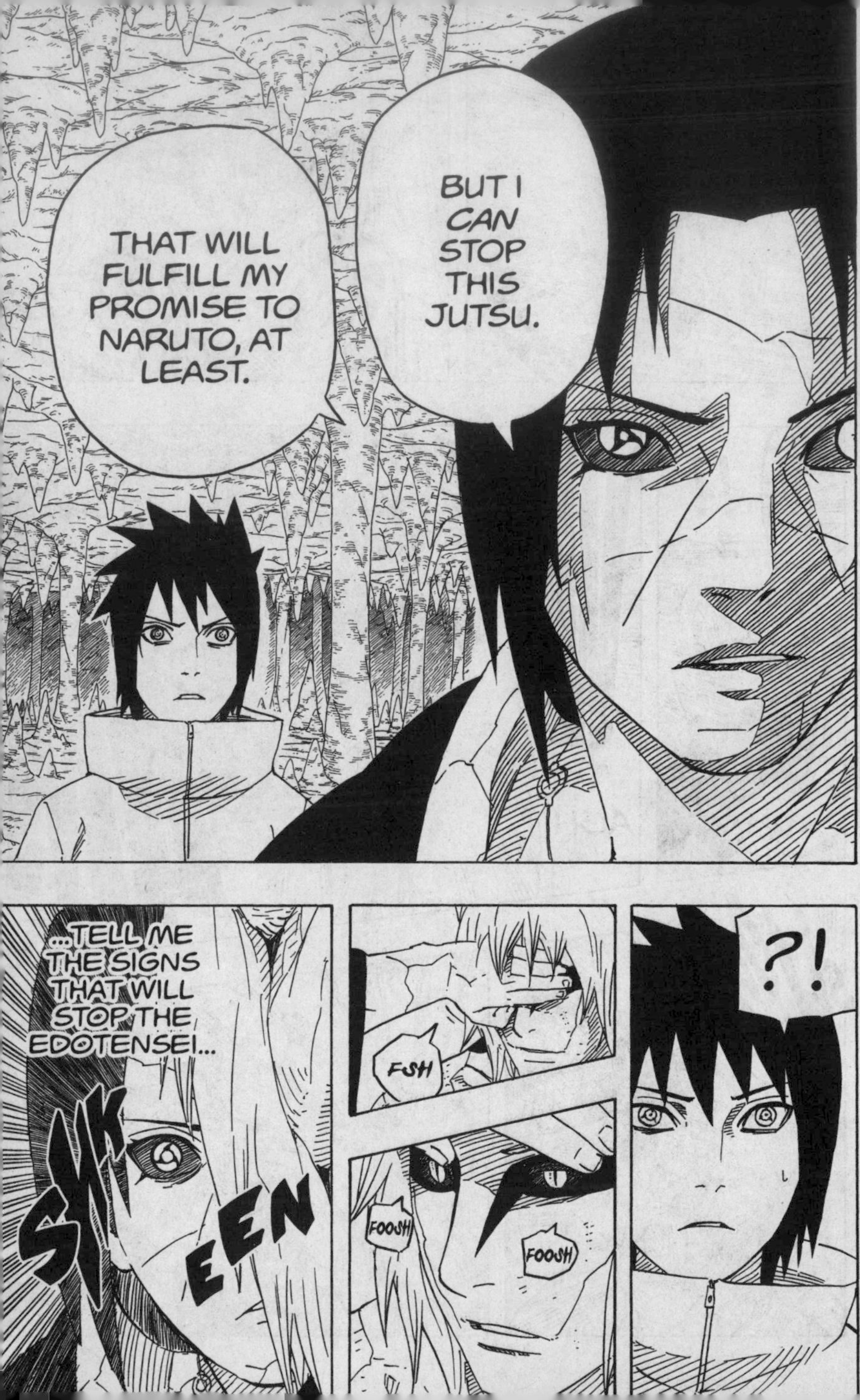
BUT I CAN STOP THIS JUTSU.
THAT WILL FULFILL MY PROMISE TO NARUTO, AT LEAST.
?!
FSH
FOOSH
FOOSH
...TELL ME THE SIGNS THAT WILL STOP THE EDOTENSEI...
SHKEEN

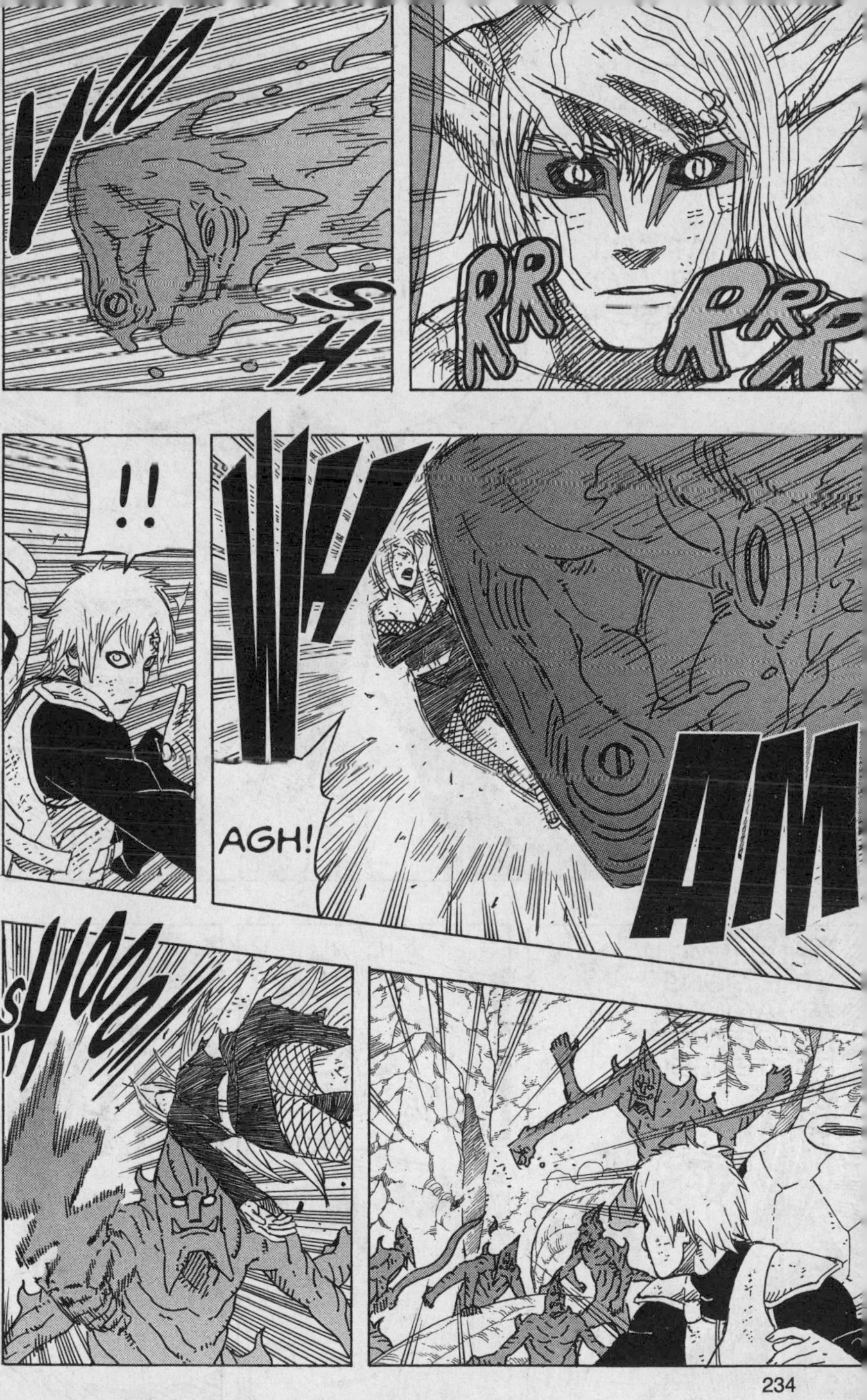
AGH!
!!

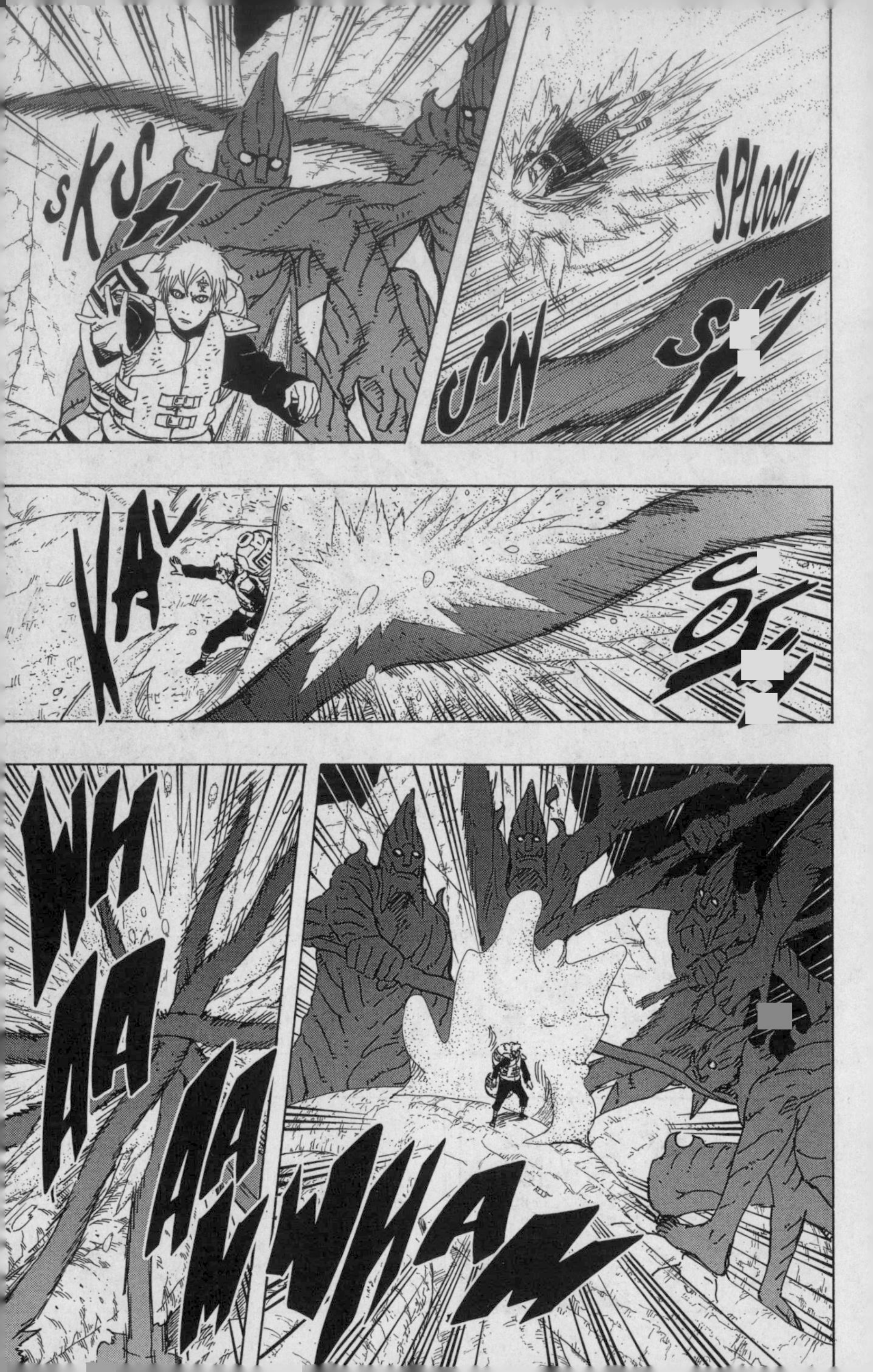
SPLOOSH
SKSH

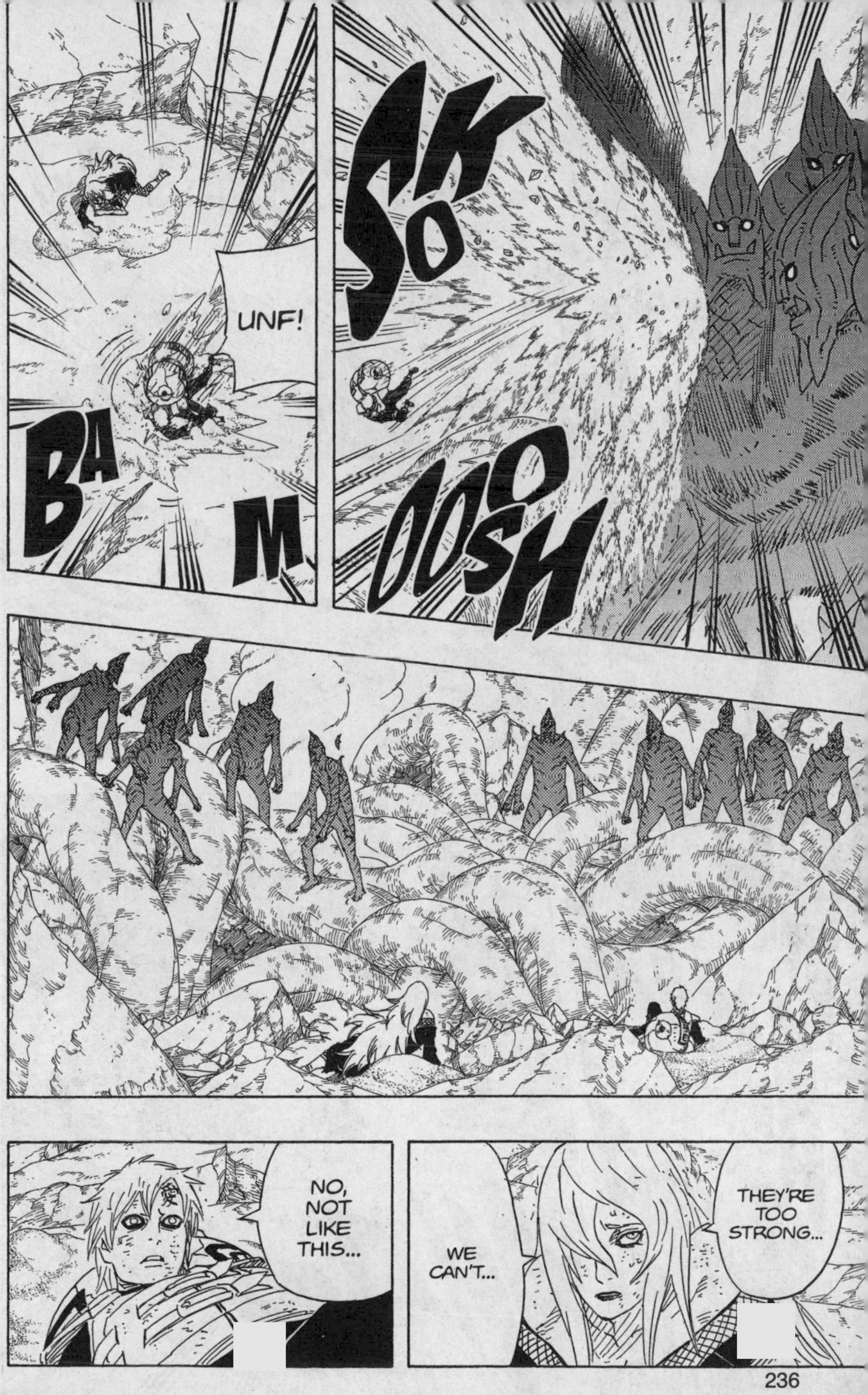
UNF!
BAM
THEY'RE TOO STRONG...
WE CAN'T...
NO, NOT LIKE THIS...

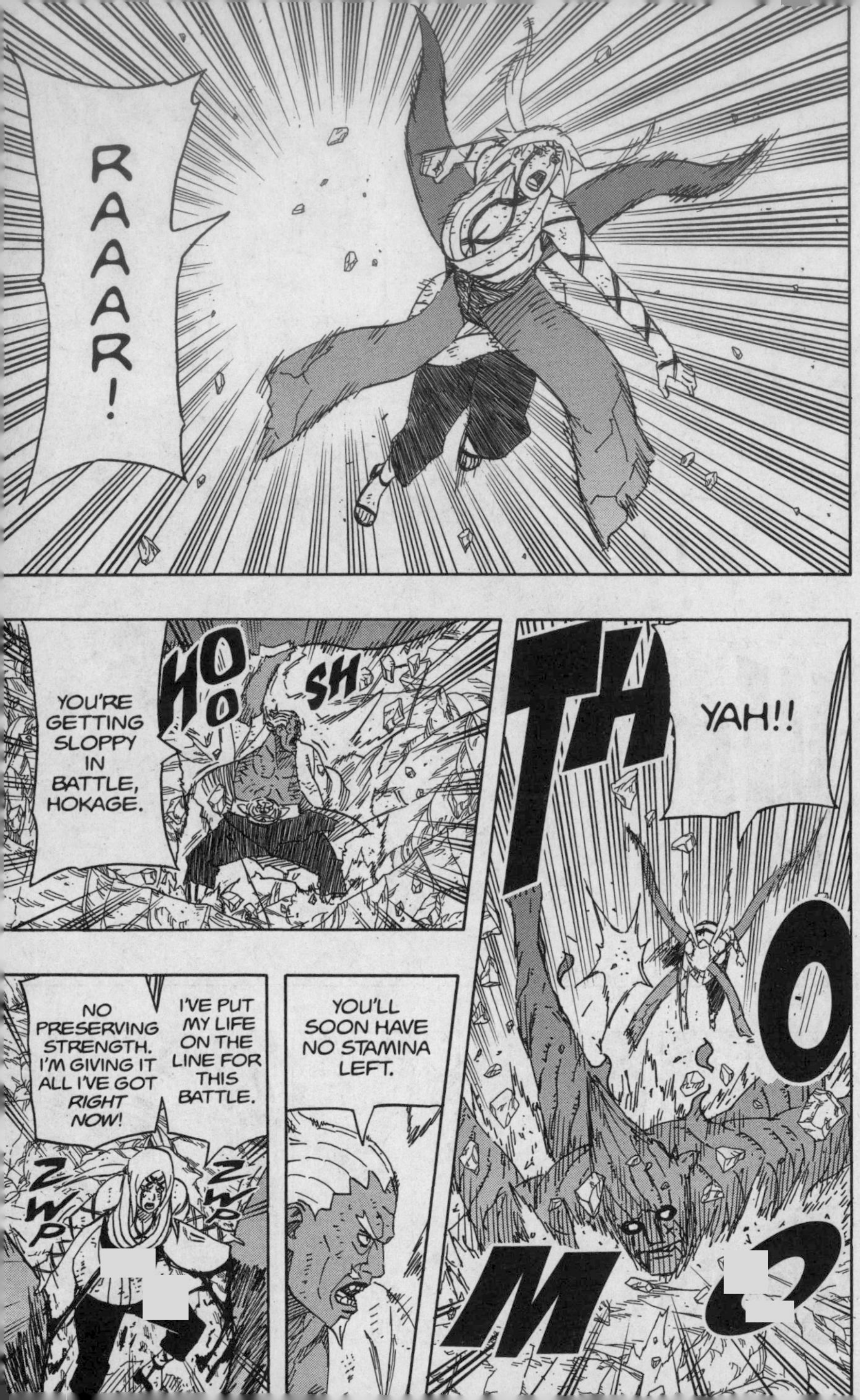
RAAAR!
TH
YAH!!
O
M
HOOSH
YOU'RE GETTING SLOPPY IN BATTLE, HOKAGE.
YOU'LL SOON HAVE NO STAMINA LEFT.
NO PRESERVING STRENGTH. I'M GIVING IT ALL I'VE GOT RIGHT NOW!
I'VE PUT MY LIFE ON THE LINE FOR THIS BATTLE.
ZWP
ZWP

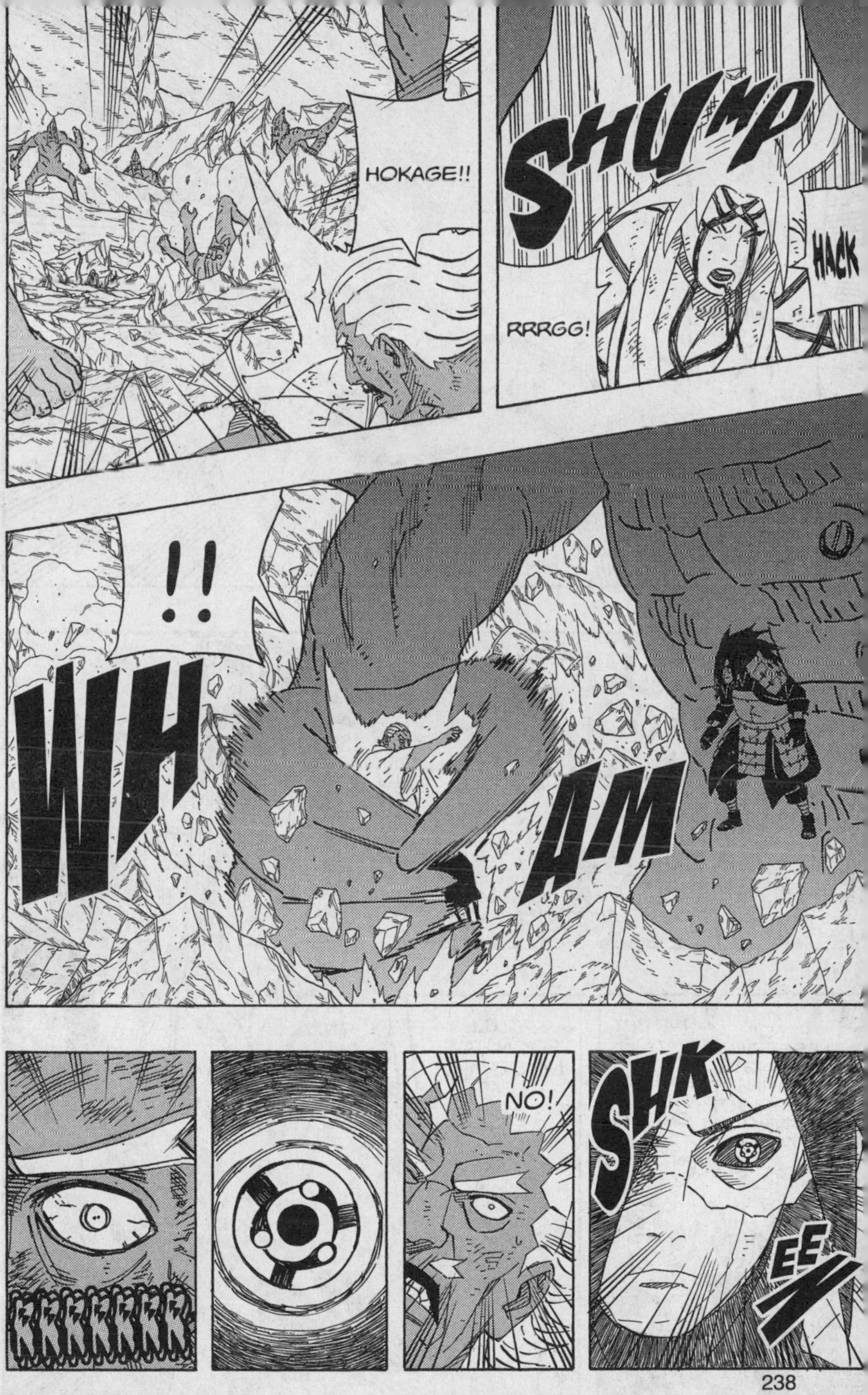
SHUMP
HACK
RRRGG!
HOKAGE!!
!!
WHAM
SHK
EEN
NO!

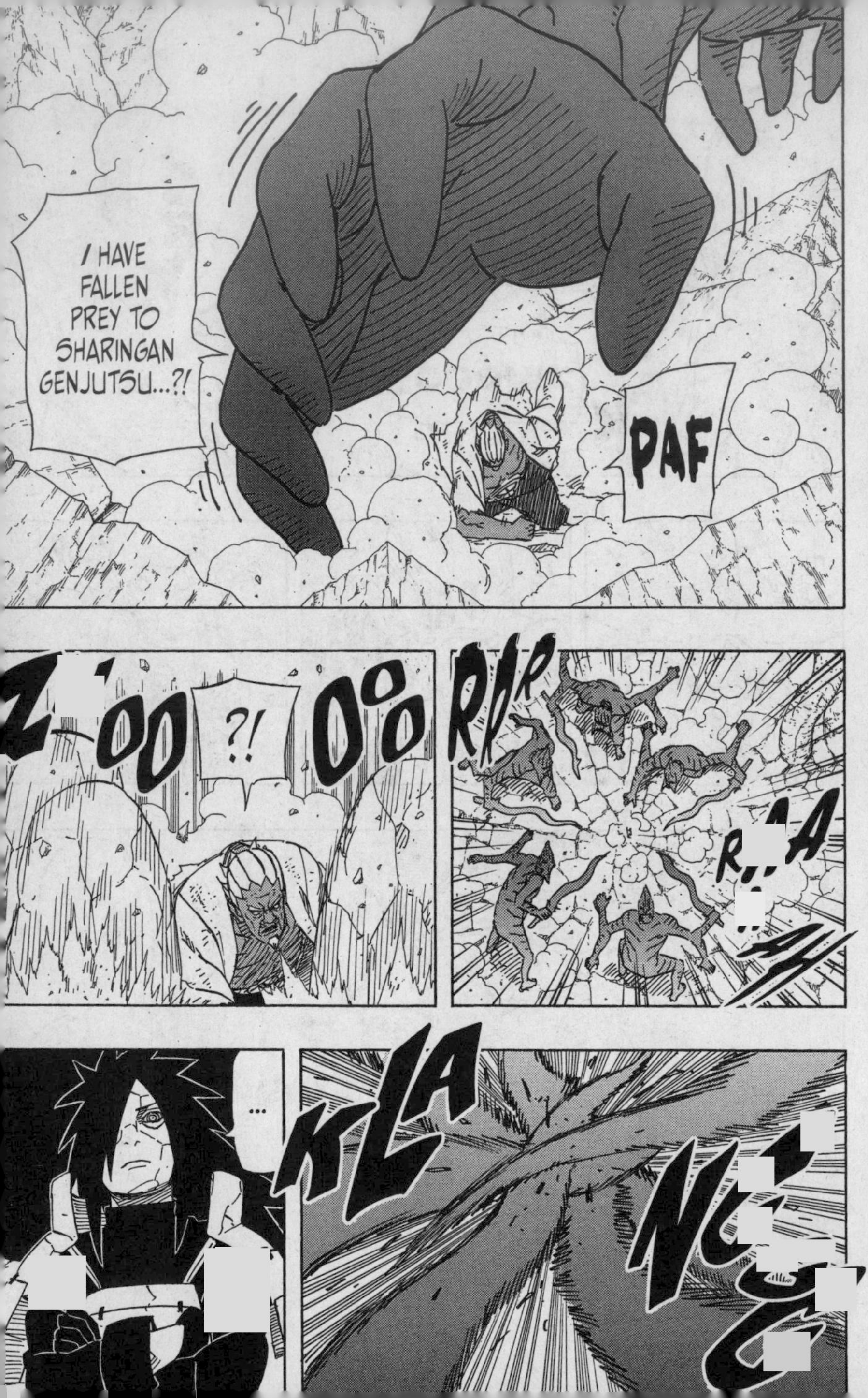
I HAVE FALLEN PREY TO SHARINGAN GENJUTSU...?!
PAF
?!
...

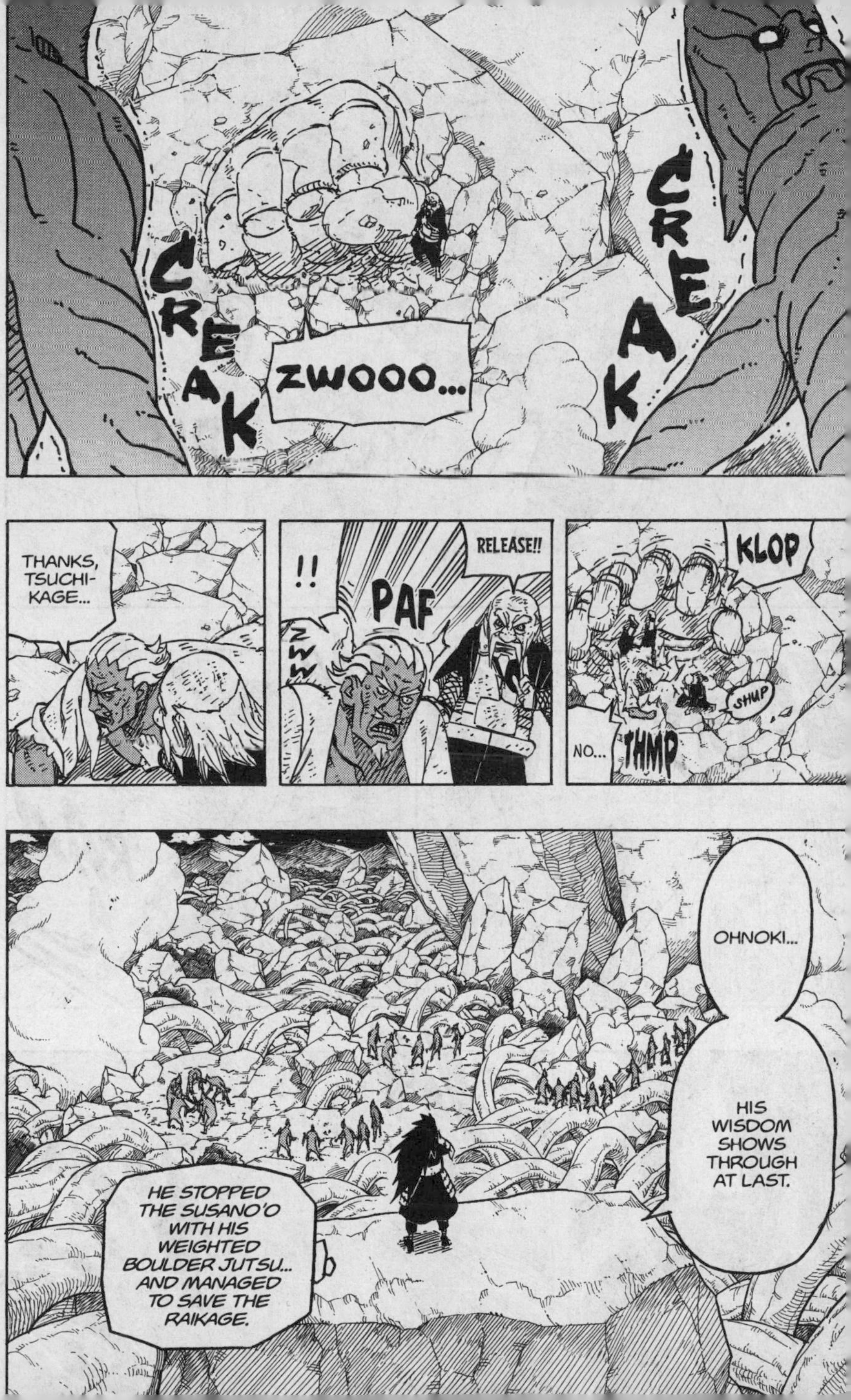
CREAK
CREAK
ZWOOO...
KLOP
SHUP
THMP
NO...
RELEASE!!
PAF
!!
ZWW
THANKS, TSUCHI-KAGE...
OHNOKI...
HIS WISDOM SHOWS THROUGH AT LAST.
HE STOPPED THE SUSANO'O WITH HIS WEIGHTED BOULDER JUTSU... AND MANAGED TO SAVE THE RAIKAGE.

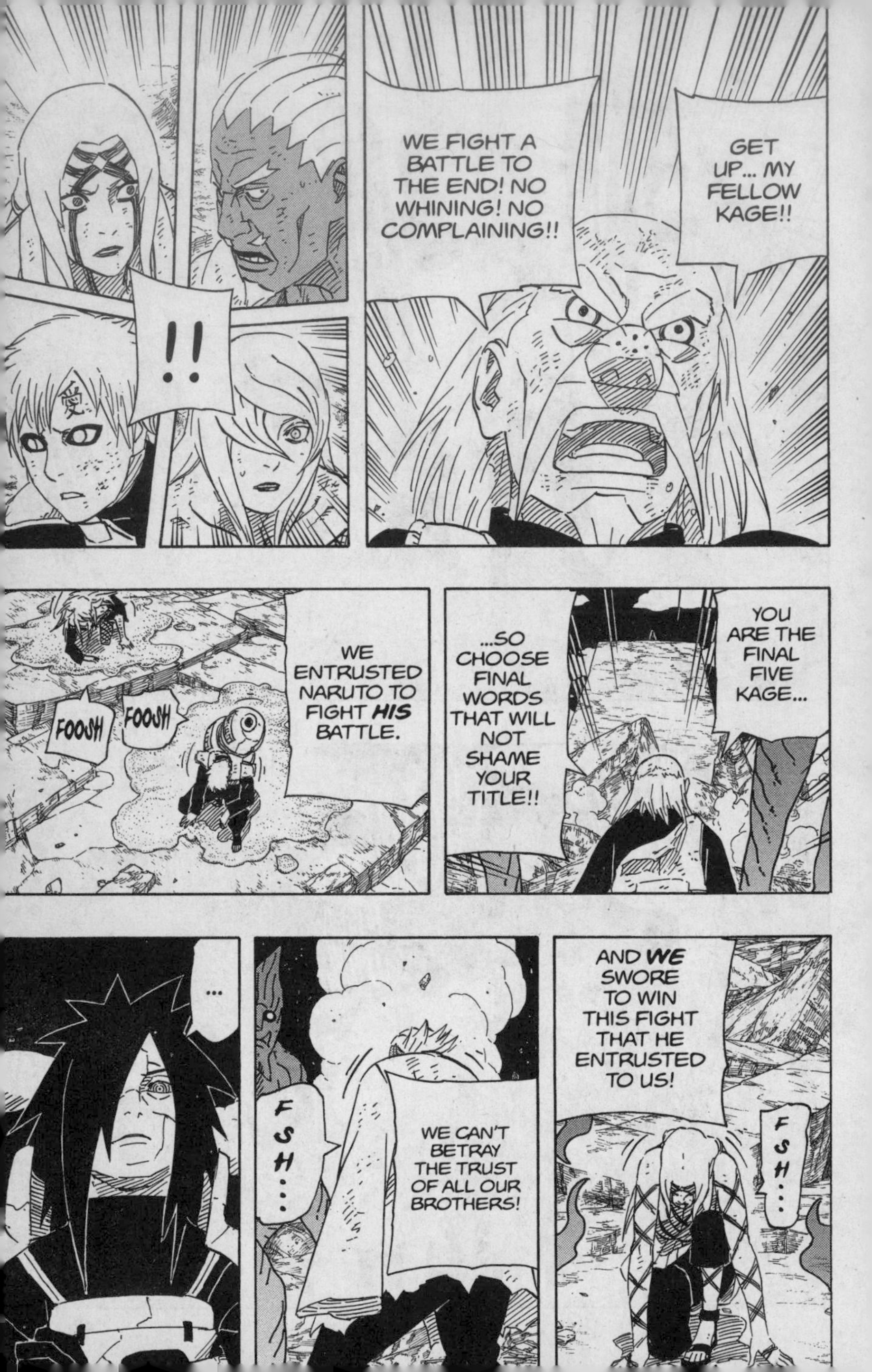
GET UP... MY FELLOW KAGE!!
WE FIGHT A BATTLE TO THE END! NO WHINING! NO COMPLAINING!!
!!
YOU ARE THE FINAL FIVE KAGE...
...SO CHOOSE FINAL WORDS THAT WILL NOT SHAME YOUR TITLE!!
WE ENTRUSTED NARUTO TO FIGHT *HIS* BATTLE.
FOOSH
FOOSH
AND *WE* SWORE TO WIN THIS FIGHT THAT HE ENTRUSTED TO US!
FSH...
FSH...
WE CAN'T BETRAY THE TRUST OF ALL OUR BROTHERS!
...

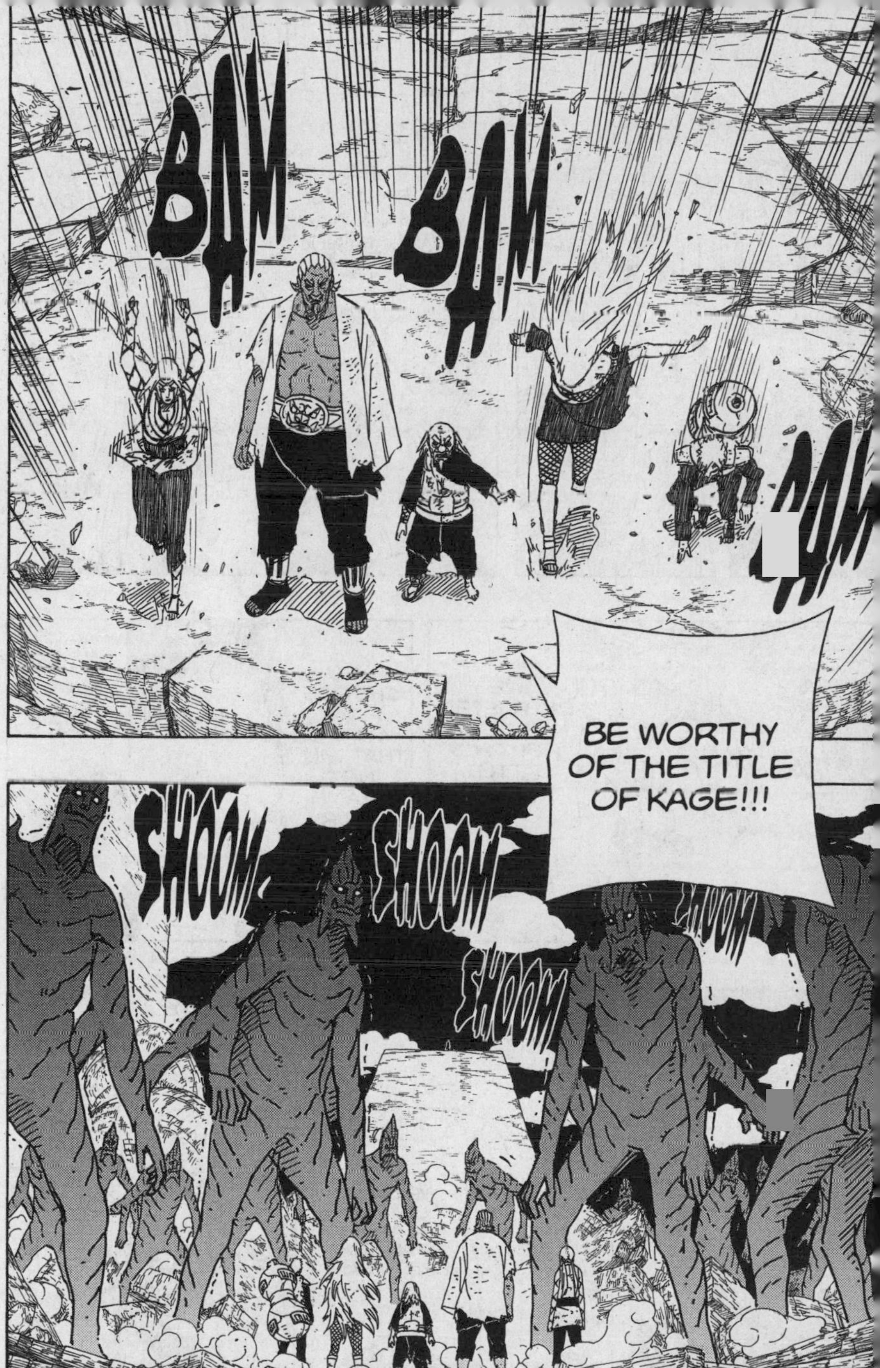
BAM
BAM
BAM
BE WORTHY OF THE TITLE OF KAGE!!!
SHOOM
SHOOM
SHOOM
SHOOM

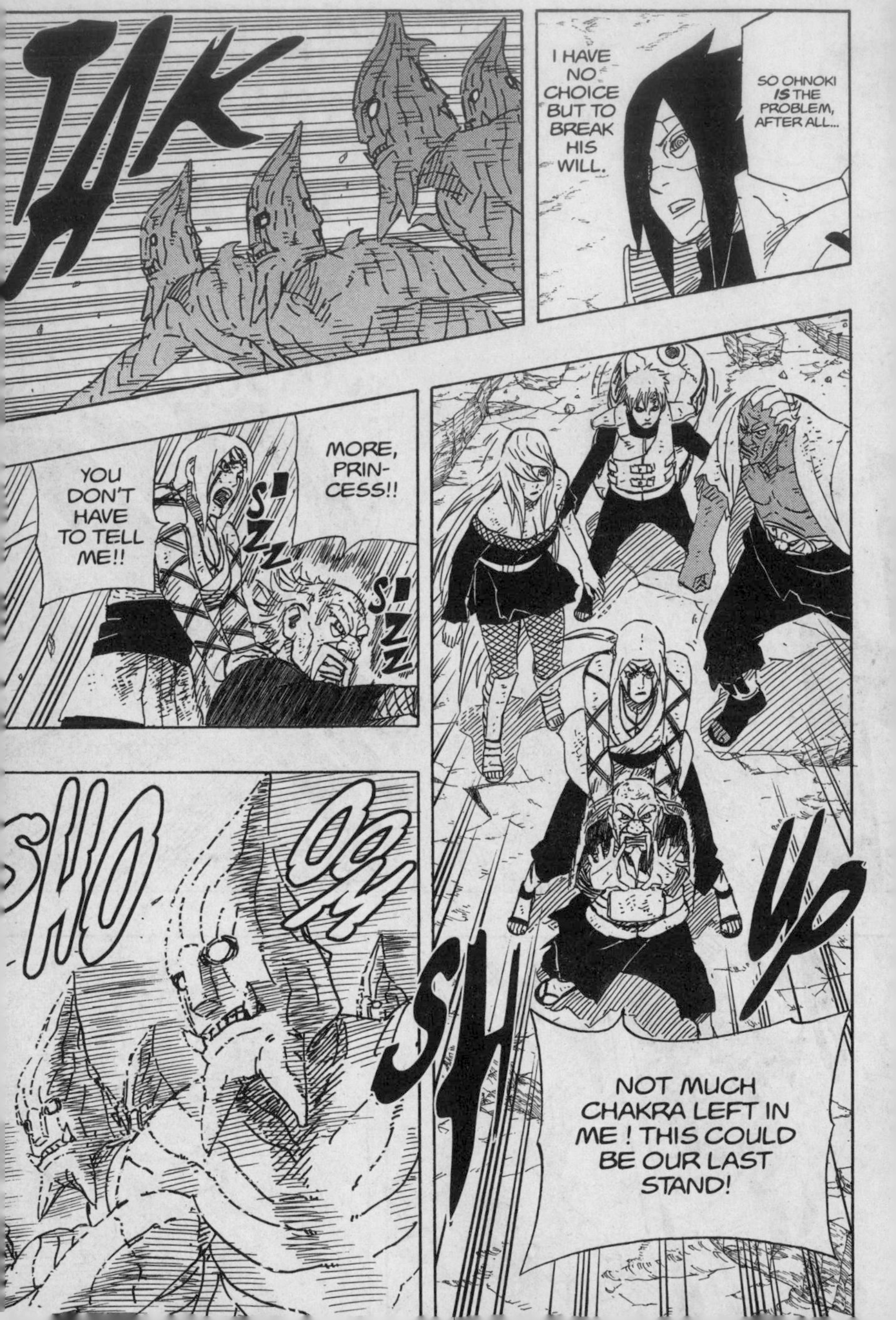
SO OHNOKI IS THE PROBLEM, AFTER ALL...
I HAVE NO CHOICE BUT TO BREAK HIS WILL.
TAK
SH
UP
NOT MUCH CHAKRA LEFT IN ME ! THIS COULD BE OUR LAST STAND!
MORE, PRIN-CESS!!
YOU DON'T HAVE TO TELL ME!!
SZZZ
SZZZ
SHO
OOM

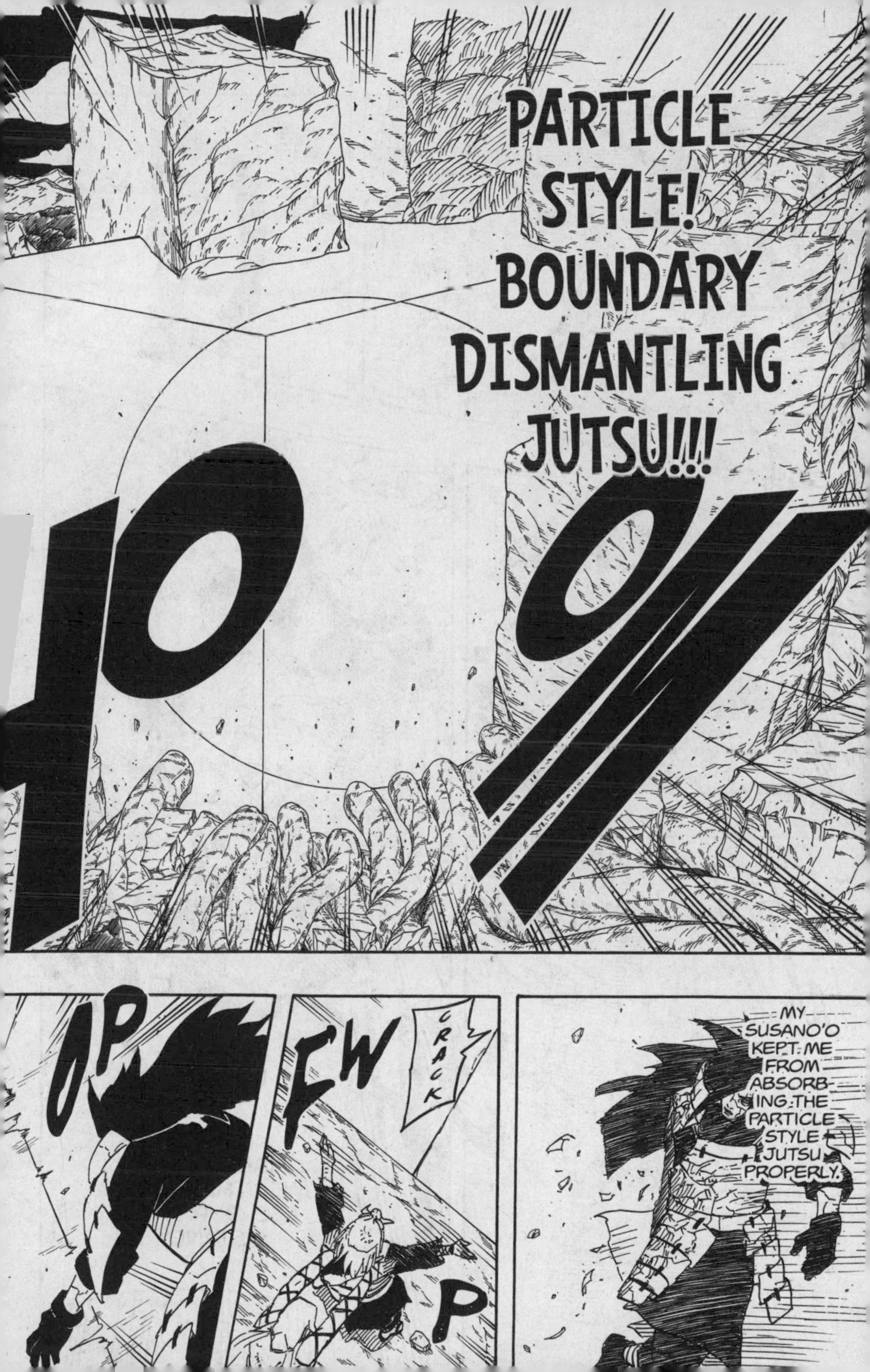
PARTICLE STYLE! BOUNDARY DISMANTLING JUTSU!!!
MY SUSANO'O KEPT ME FROM ABSORBING THE PARTICLE STYLE JUTSU PROPERLY.
CRACK

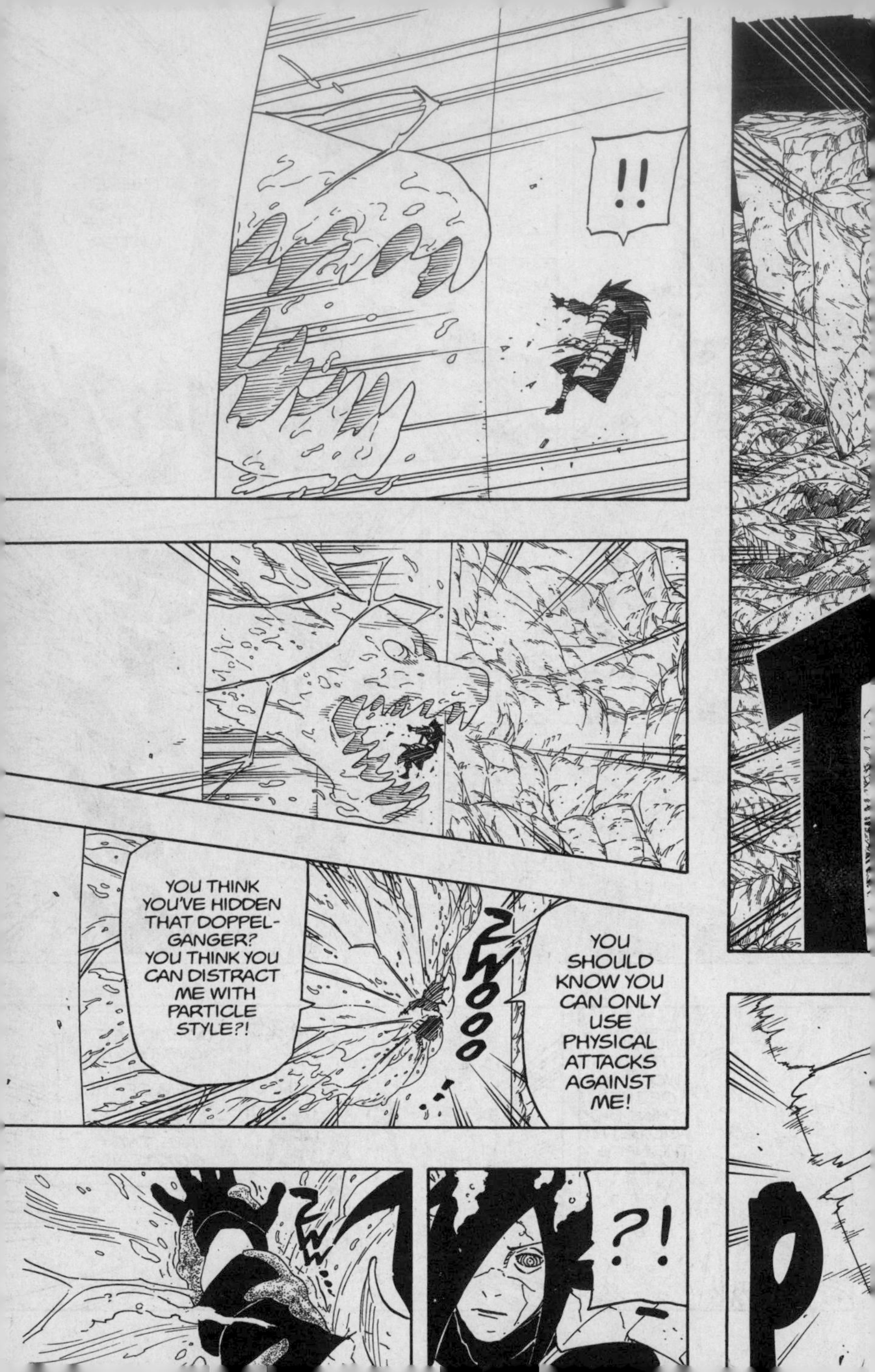
!!
YOU SHOULD KNOW YOU CAN ONLY USE PHYSICAL ATTACKS AGAINST ME!
ZWOOOO
YOU THINK YOU'VE HIDDEN THAT DOPPEL-GANGER? YOU THINK YOU CAN DISTRACT ME WITH PARTICLE STYLE?!
?!
ZWW

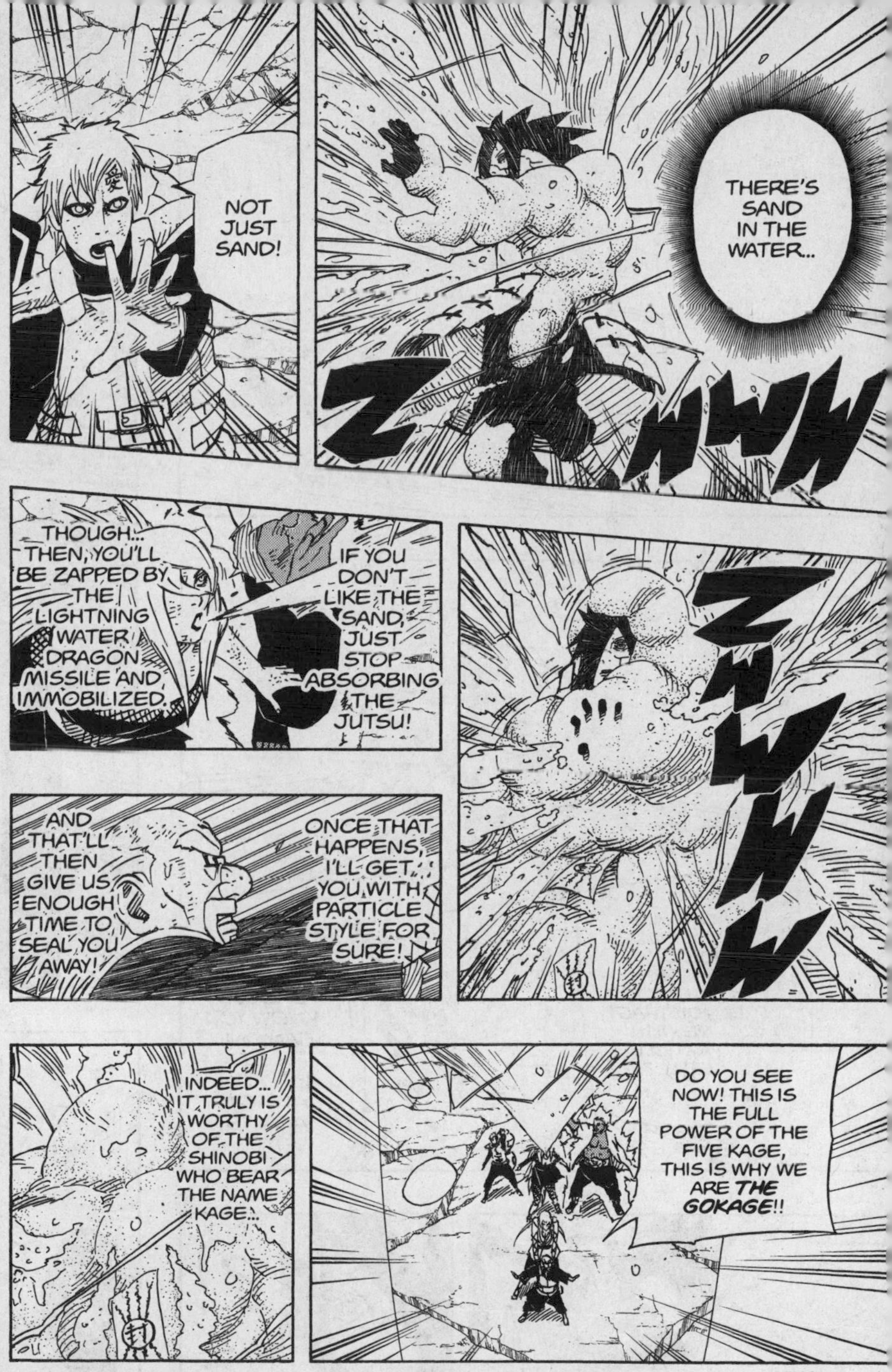
THERE'S SAND IN THE WATER...
NOT JUST SAND!
IF YOU DON'T LIKE THE SAND, JUST STOP ABSORBING THE JUTSU!
THOUGH... THEN, YOU'LL BE ZAPPED BY THE LIGHTNING WATER DRAGON MISSILE AND IMMOBILIZED.
ONCE THAT HAPPENS, I'LL GET YOU WITH PARTICLE STYLE FOR SURE!
AND THAT'LL THEN GIVE US ENOUGH TIME TO SEAL YOU AWAY!
DO YOU SEE NOW! THIS IS THE FULL POWER OF THE FIVE KAGE, THIS IS WHY WE ARE ***THE GOKAGE***!!
INDEED... IT TRULY IS WORTHY OF THE SHINOBI WHO BEAR THE NAME KAGE...

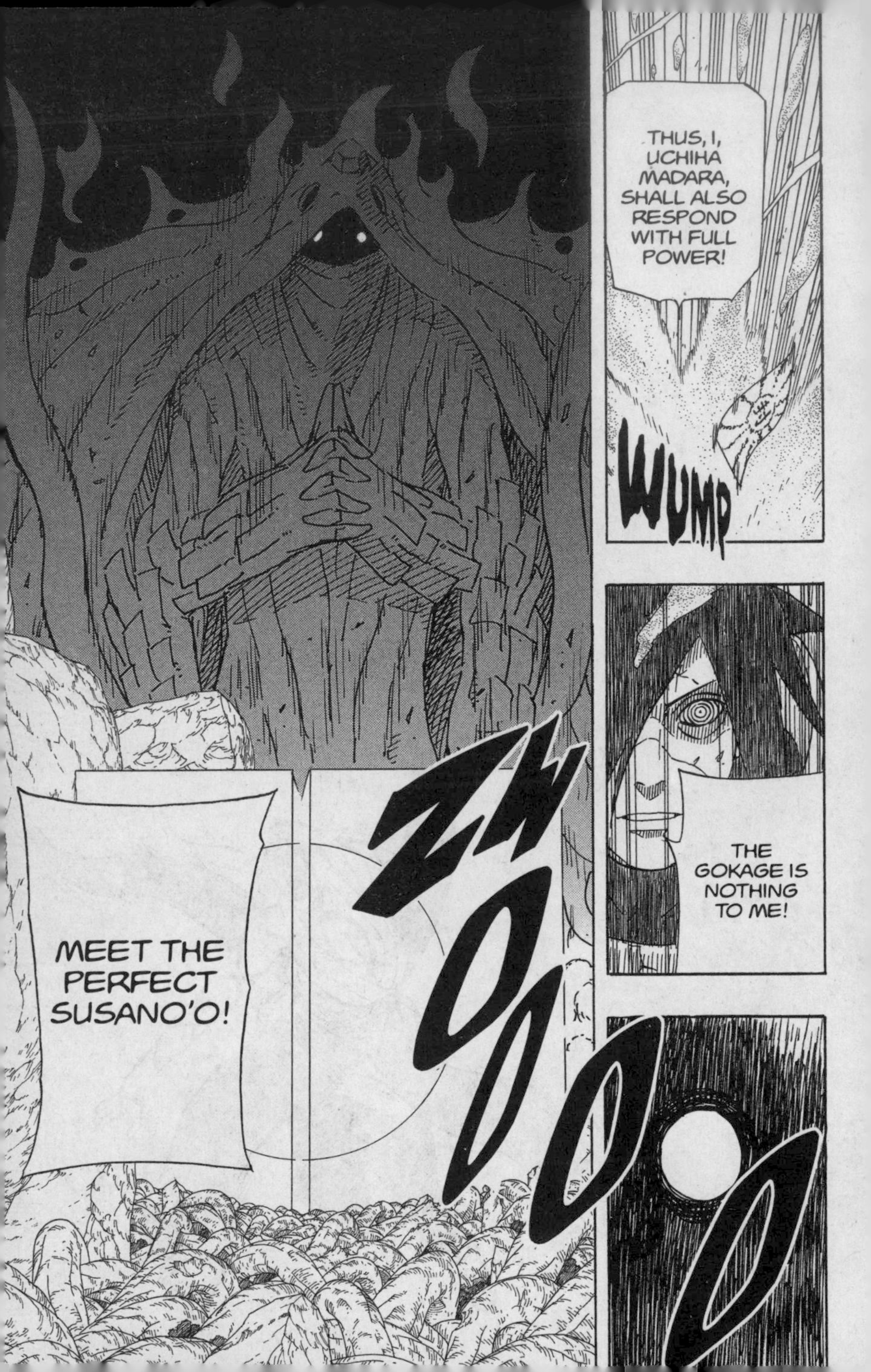
THUS, I, UCHIHA MADARA, SHALL ALSO RESPOND WITH FULL POWER!
WUMP
THE GOKAGE IS NOTHING TO ME!
MEET THE PERFECT SUSANO'O!

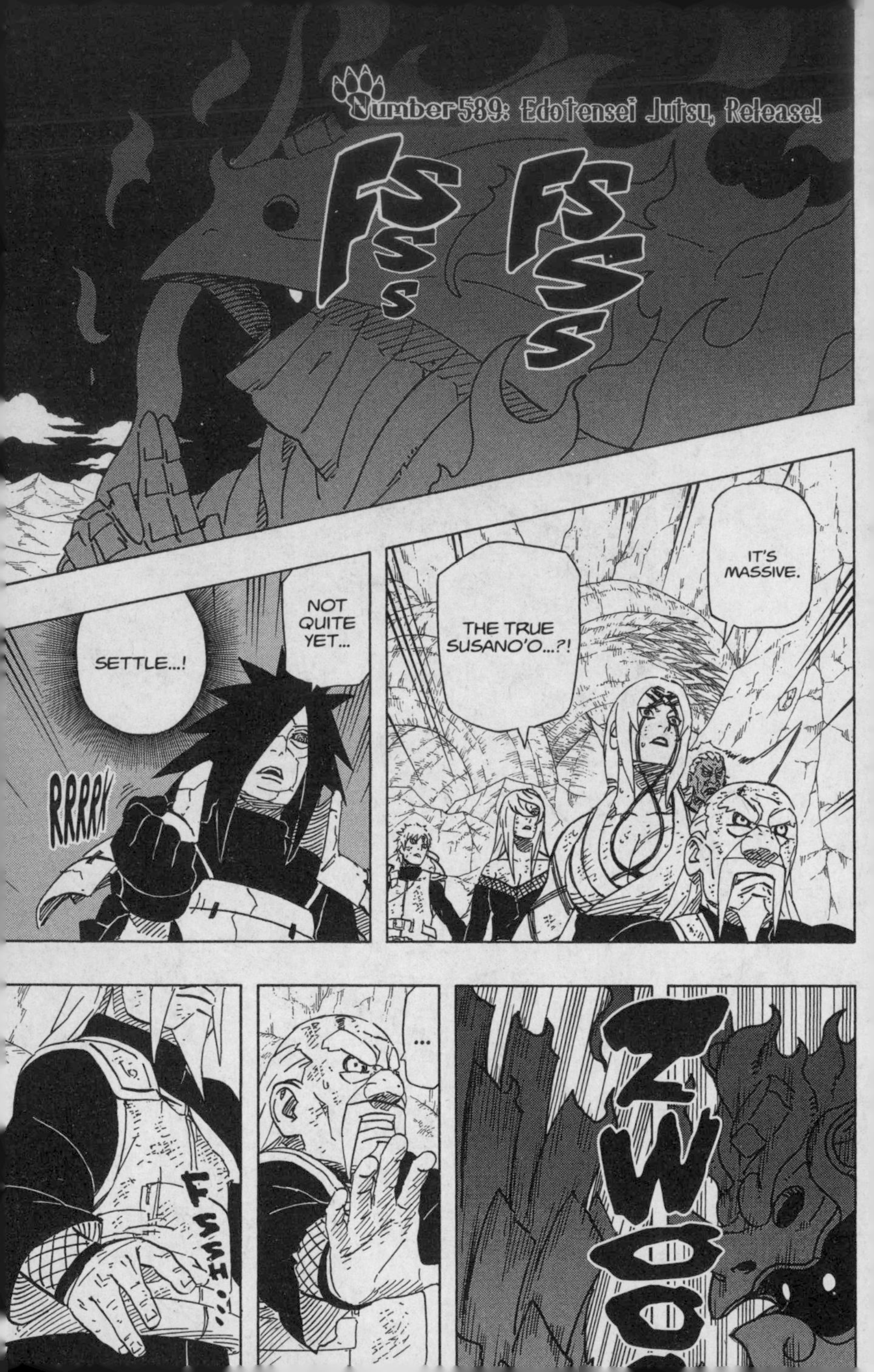
Number 589: Edotensei Jutsu, Release!
FSS FSS
IT'S MASSIVE.
THE TRUE SUSANO'O...?!
NOT QUITE YET...
SETTLE...!
RRRRK
ZWOO
...
FSSH...!

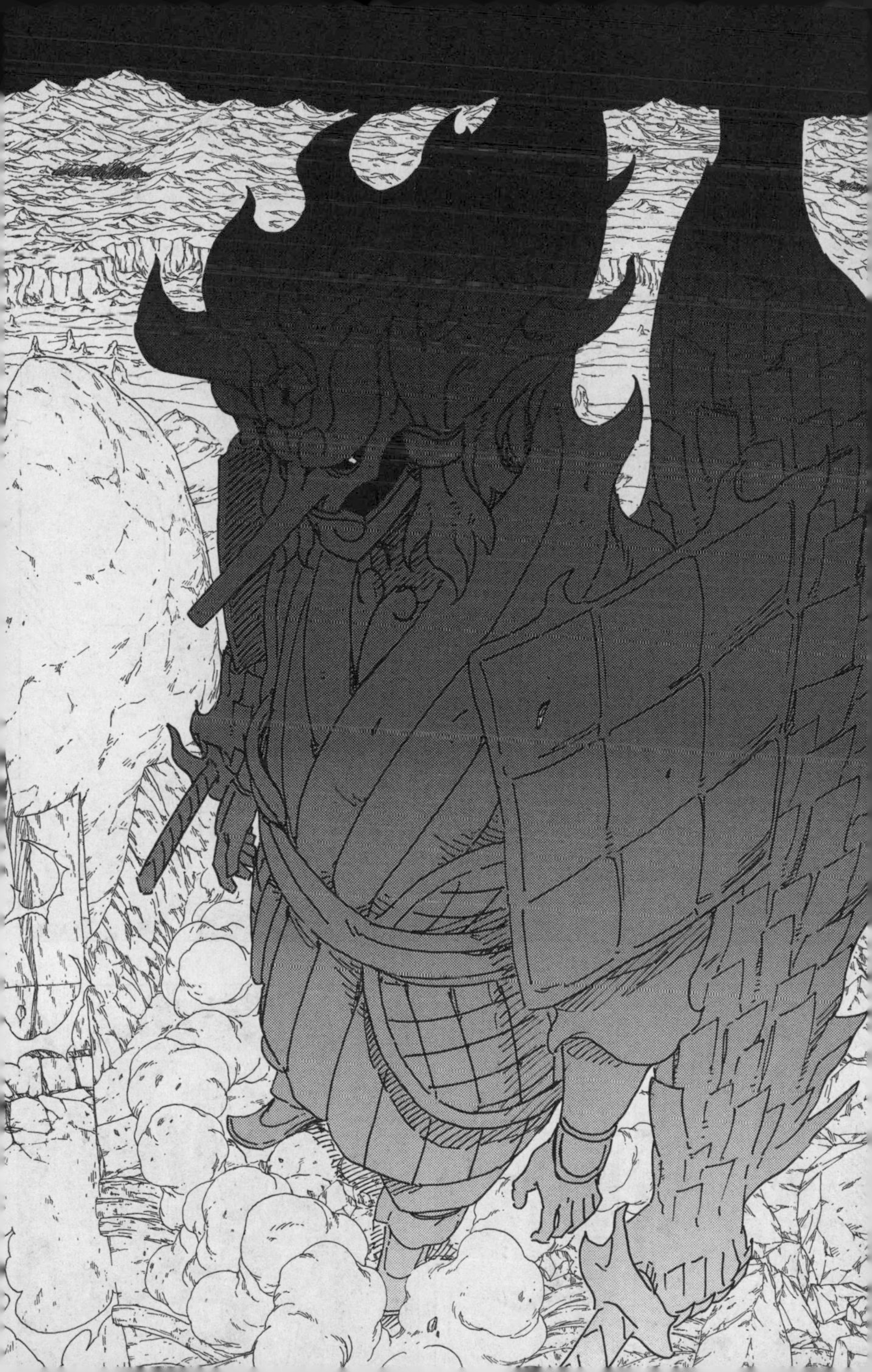

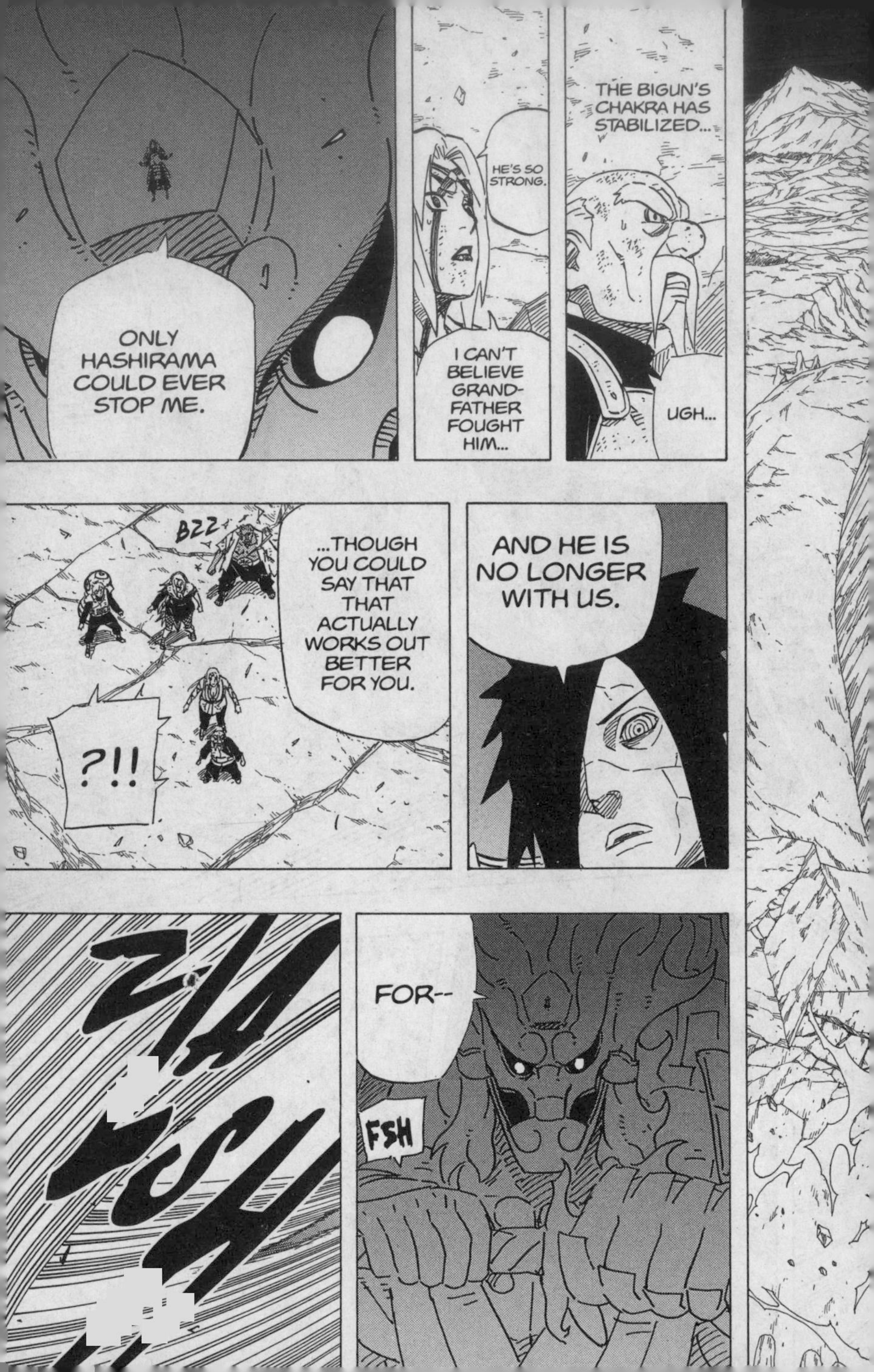
THE BIGUN'S CHAKRA HAS STABILIZED...
UGH...
HE'S SO STRONG.
I CAN'T BELIEVE GRANDFATHER FOUGHT HIM...
ONLY HASHIRAMA COULD EVER STOP ME.
AND HE IS NO LONGER WITH US.
...THOUGH YOU COULD SAY THAT THAT ACTUALLY WORKS OUT BETTER FOR YOU.
BZZ
?!!
FOR--
FSH

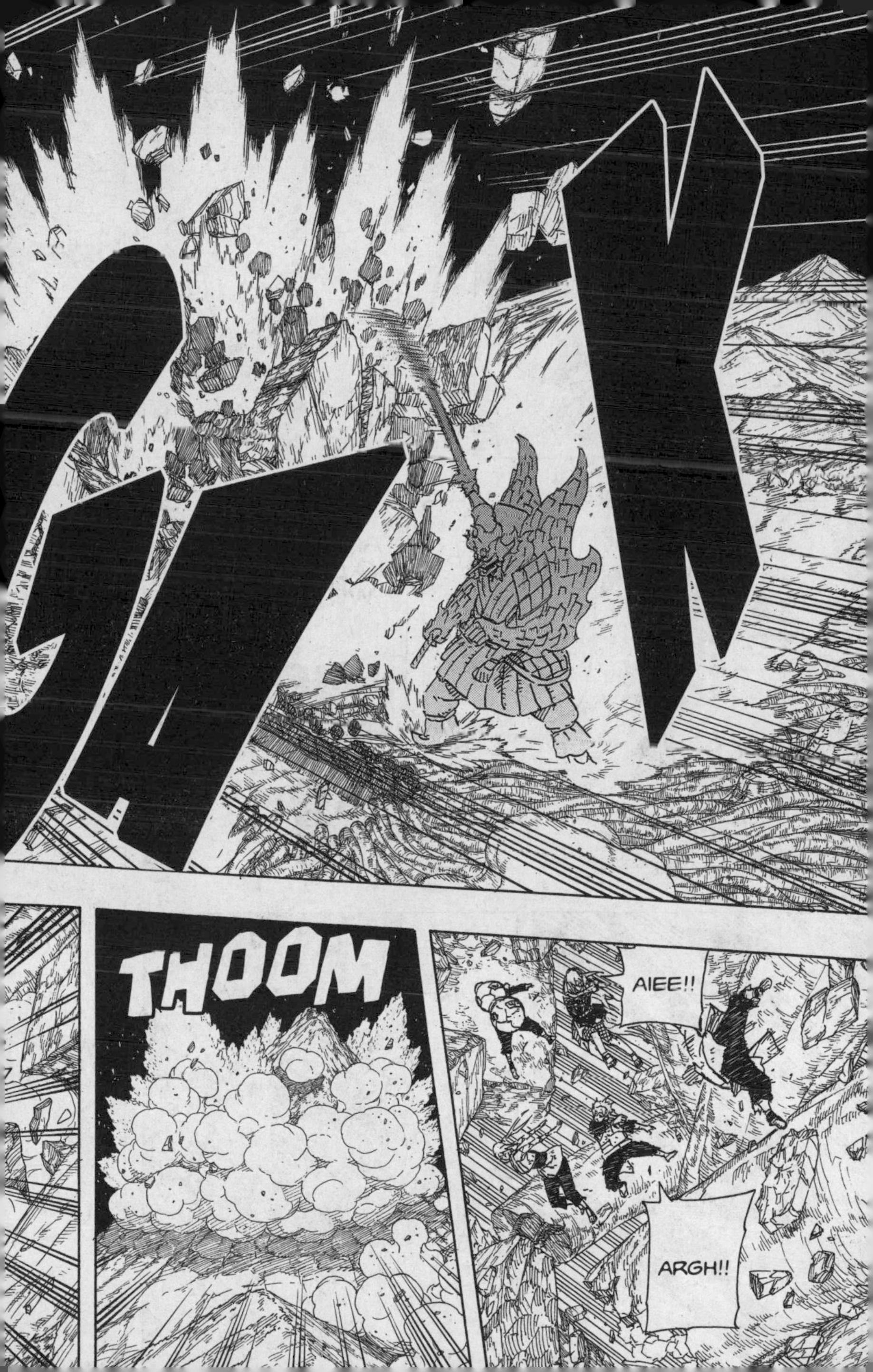
AIEE!!
ARGH!!
THOOM

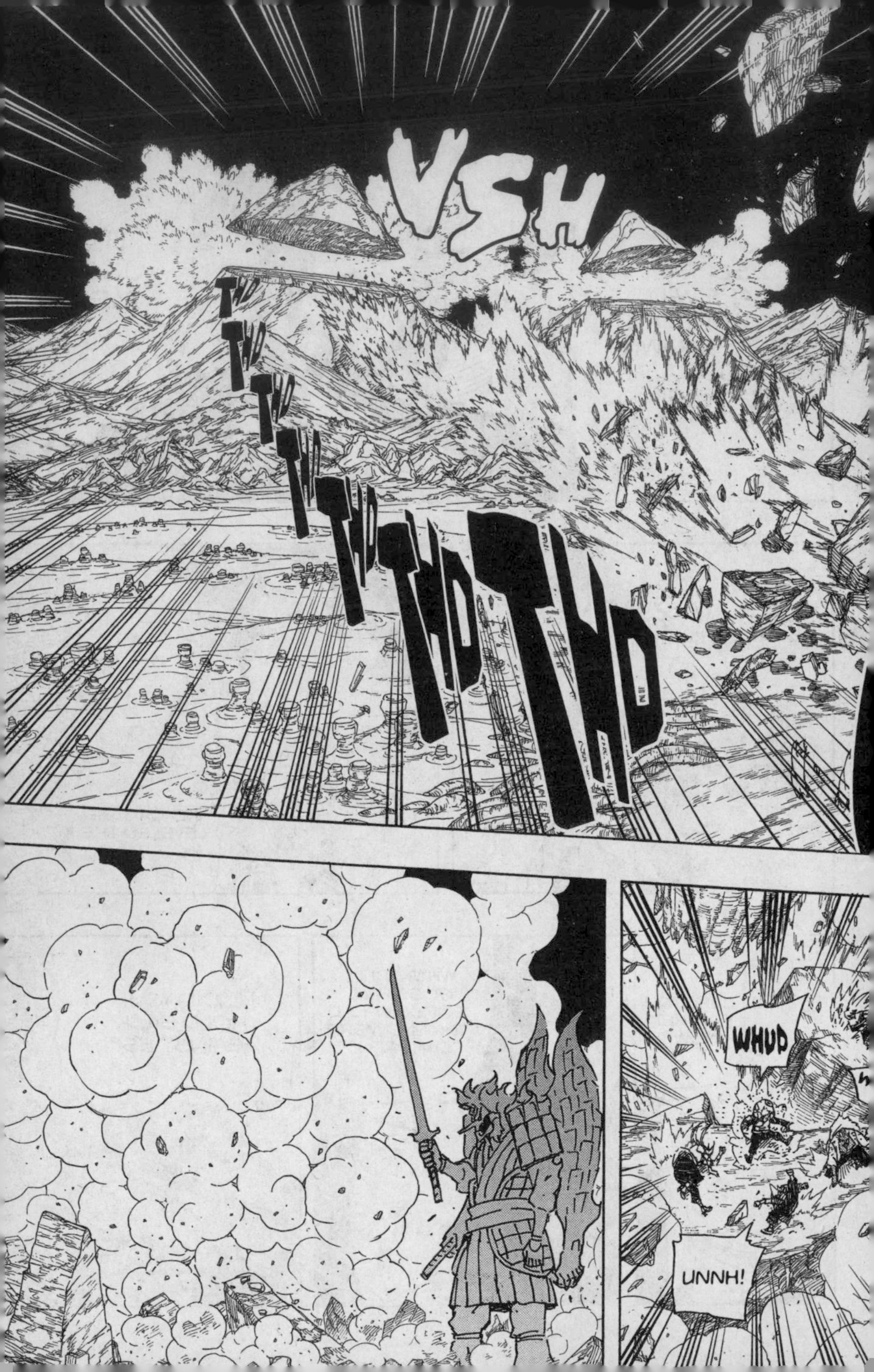
VSH
THD
THD
THD
THD
THD
THD
THD
THD
WHUD
UNNH!

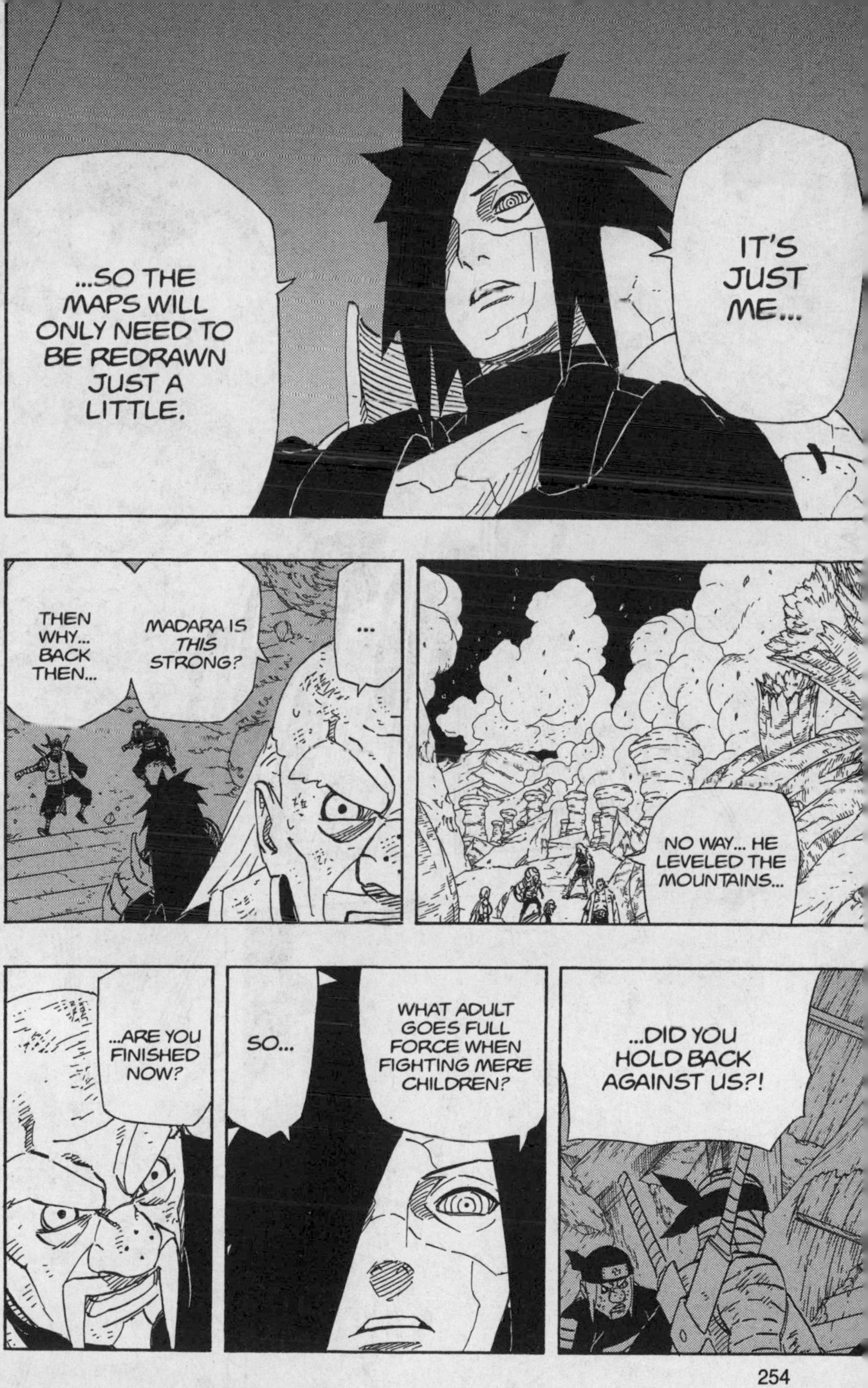
IT'S JUST ME...
...SO THE MAPS WILL ONLY NEED TO BE REDRAWN JUST A LITTLE.
NO WAY... HE LEVELED THE MOUNTAINS...
...
MADARA IS THIS STRONG?
THEN WHY... BACK THEN...
...DID YOU HOLD BACK AGAINST US?!
WHAT ADULT GOES FULL FORCE WHEN FIGHTING MERE CHILDREN?
SO...
...ARE YOU FINISHED NOW?

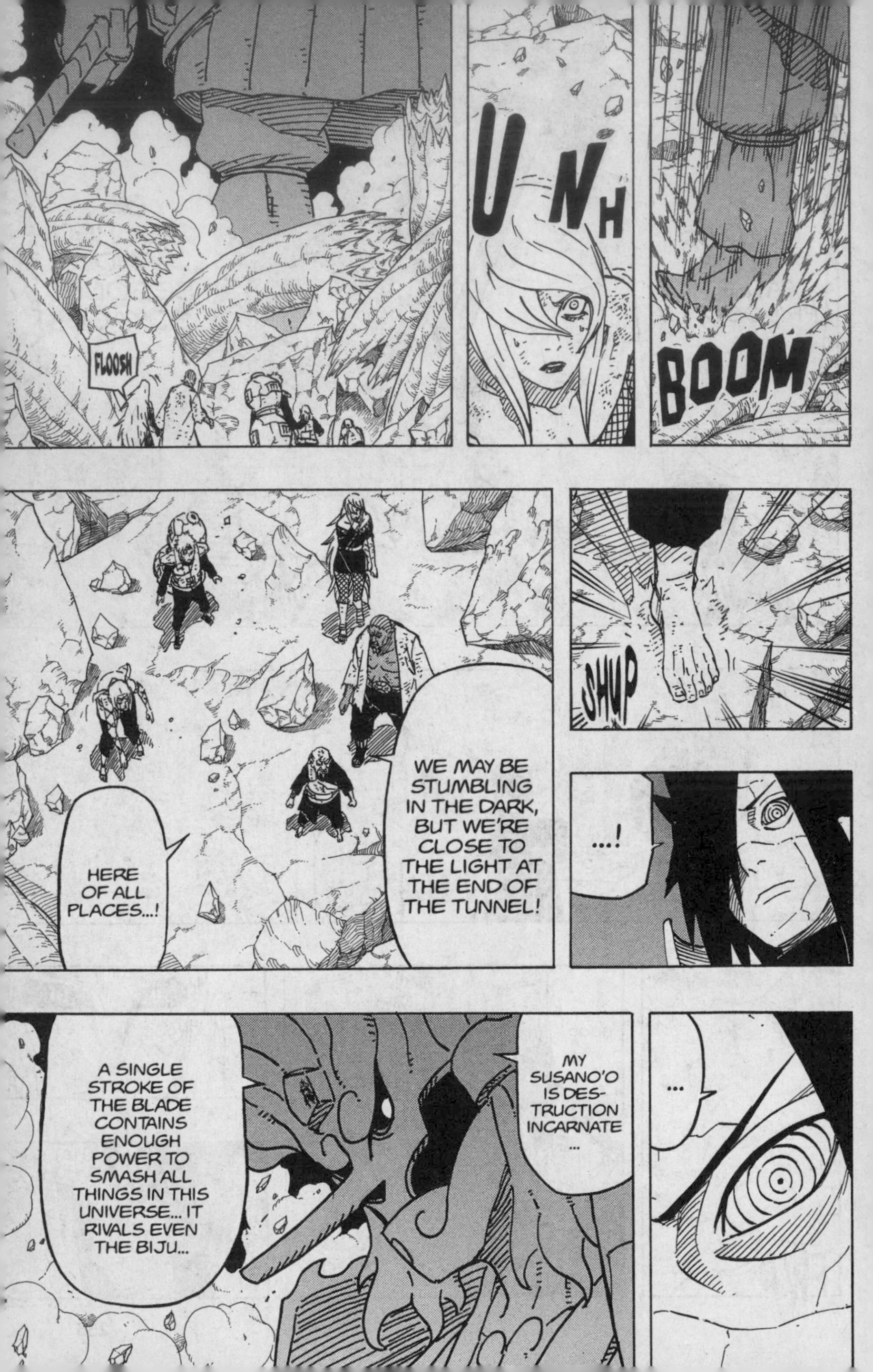
BOOM
UNH
FLOOSH
SHUP
...!
WE MAY BE STUMBLING IN THE DARK, BUT WE'RE CLOSE TO THE LIGHT AT THE END OF THE TUNNEL!
HERE OF ALL PLACES...!
...
MY SUSANO'O IS DES-TRUCTION INCARNATE ...
A SINGLE STROKE OF THE BLADE CONTAINS ENOUGH POWER TO SMASH ALL THINGS IN THIS UNIVERSE... IT RIVALS EVEN THE BIJU...

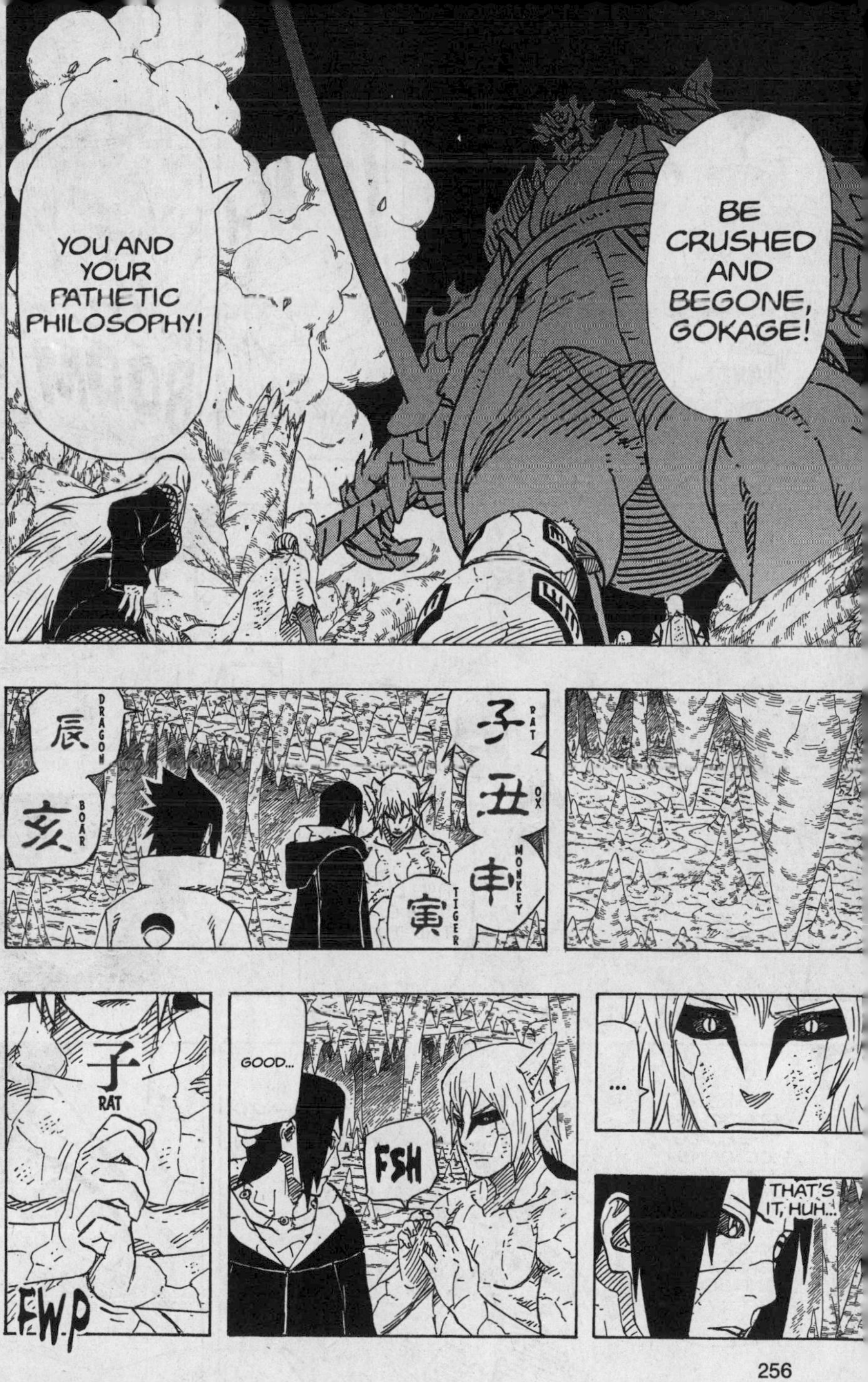
BE CRUSHED AND BEGONE, GOKAGE!
YOU AND YOUR PATHETIC PHILOSOPHY!
子 RAT
丑 OX
申 MONKEY
寅 TIGER
辰 DRAGON
亥 BOAR
...
THAT'S IT, HUH...
GOOD...
FSH
子 RAT
F.W.P

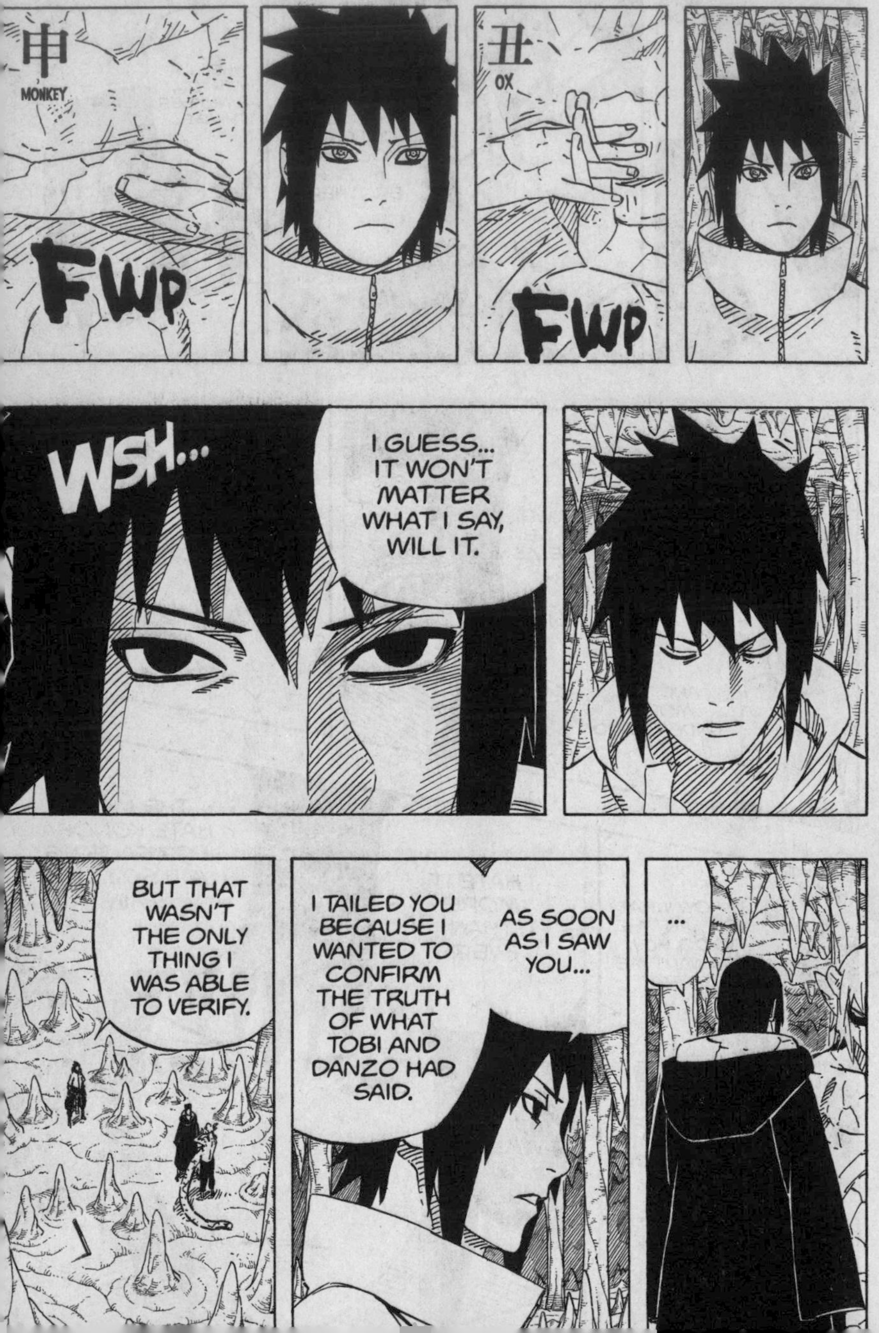
丑
OX
FWP
申
MONKEY
FWP
I GUESS... IT WON'T MATTER WHAT I SAY, WILL IT.
WSH...
...
AS SOON AS I SAW YOU...
I TAILED YOU BECAUSE I WANTED TO CONFIRM THE TRUTH OF WHAT TOBI AND DANZO HAD SAID.
BUT THAT WASN'T THE ONLY THING I WAS ABLE TO VERIFY.

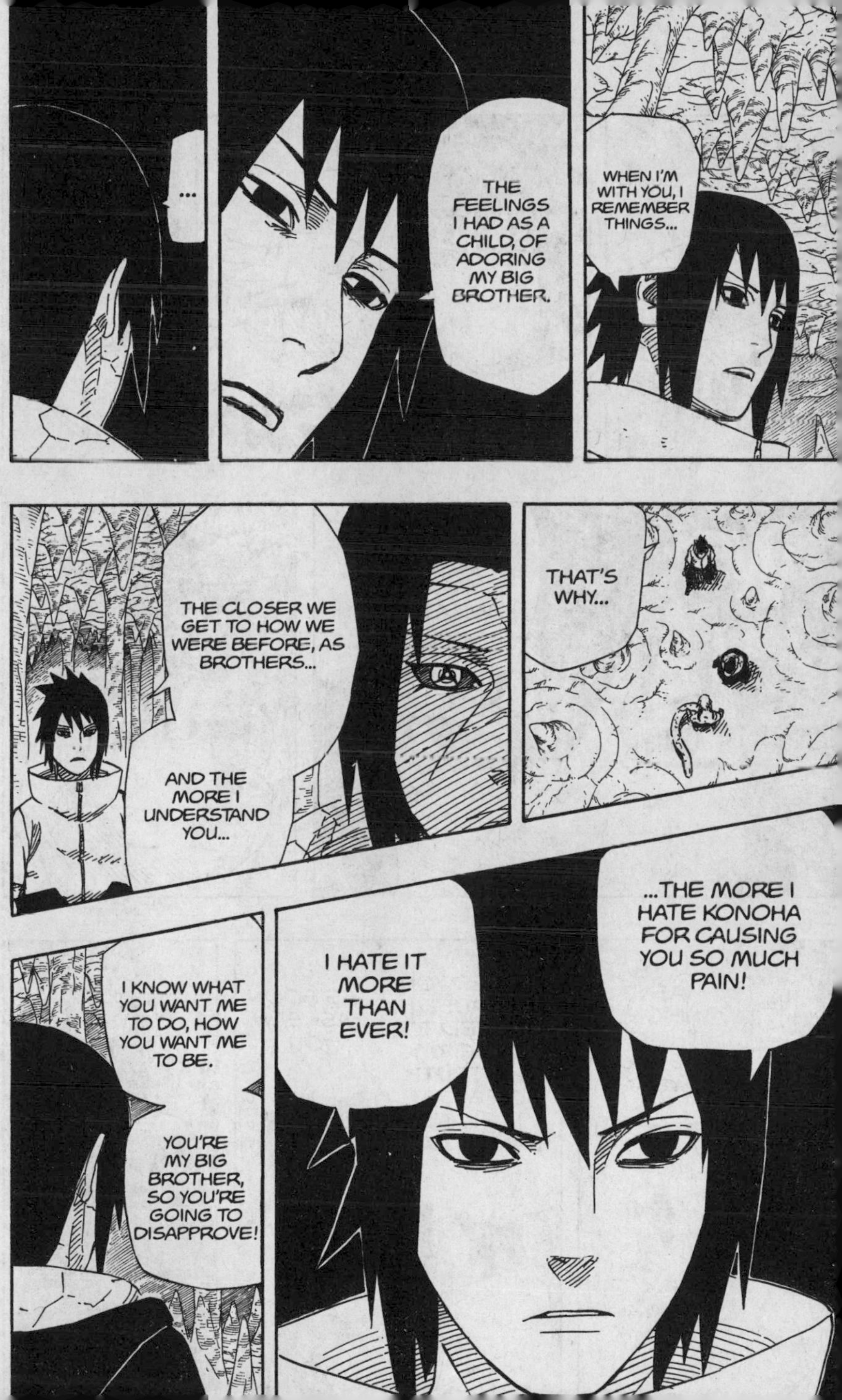
WHEN I'M WITH YOU, I REMEMBER THINGS...
THE FEELINGS I HAD AS A CHILD, OF ADORING MY BIG BROTHER.
...
THAT'S WHY...
THE CLOSER WE GET TO HOW WE WERE BEFORE, AS BROTHERS...
AND THE MORE I UNDERSTAND YOU...
...THE MORE I HATE KONOHA FOR CAUSING YOU SO MUCH PAIN!
I HATE IT MORE THAN EVER!
I KNOW WHAT YOU WANT ME TO DO, HOW YOU WANT ME TO BE.
YOU'RE MY BIG BROTHER, SO YOU'RE GOING TO DISAPPROVE!

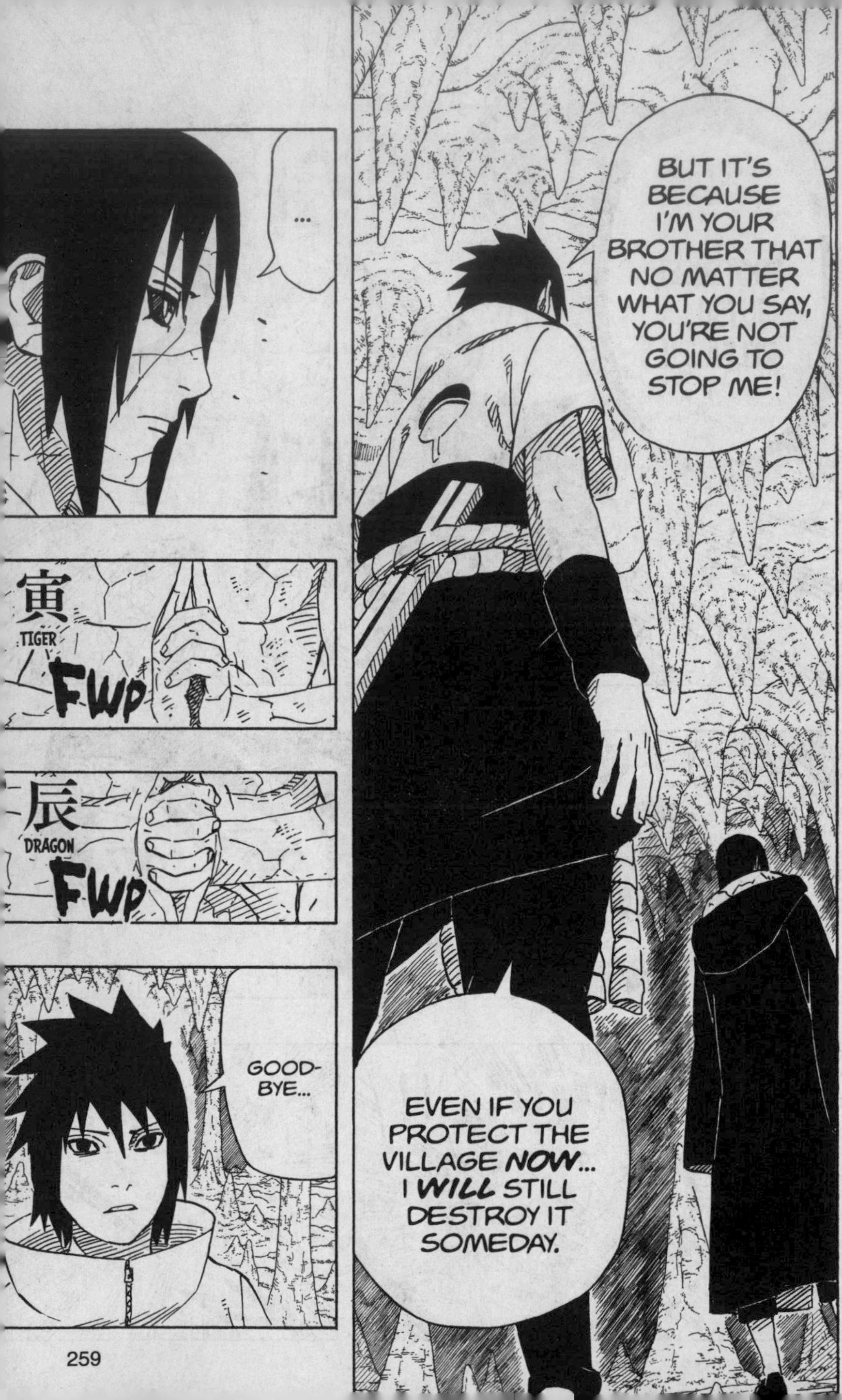
BUT IT'S BECAUSE I'M YOUR BROTHER THAT NO MATTER WHAT YOU SAY, YOU'RE NOT GOING TO STOP ME!
EVEN IF YOU PROTECT THE VILLAGE NOW... I WILL STILL DESTROY IT SOMEDAY.
...
寅
TIGER
FWP
辰
DRAGON
FWP
GOOD-BYE...

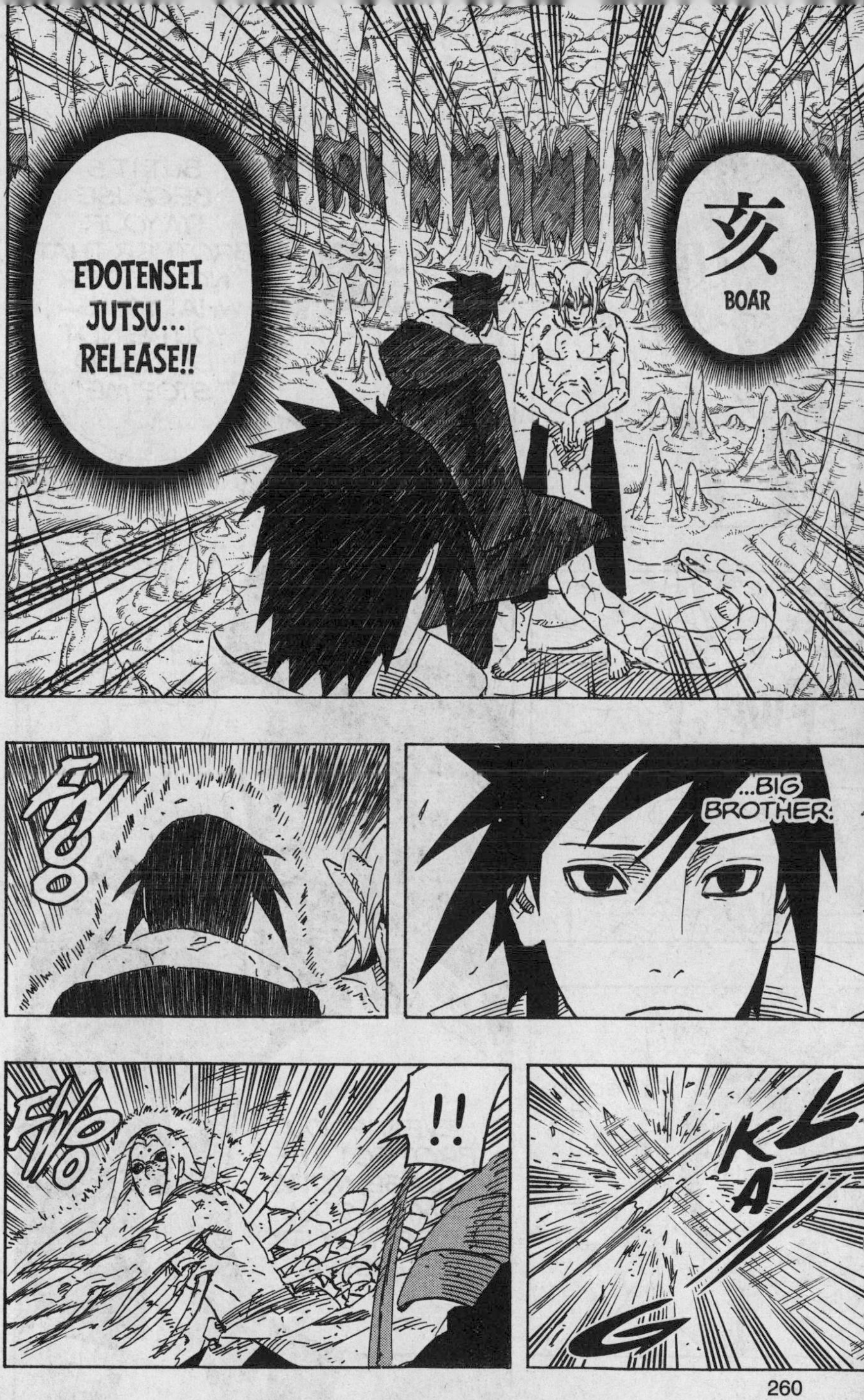
亥
BOAR
EDOTENSEI JUTSU... RELEASE!!
...BIG BROTHER.
FWOO
KLANG
!!
FWOO

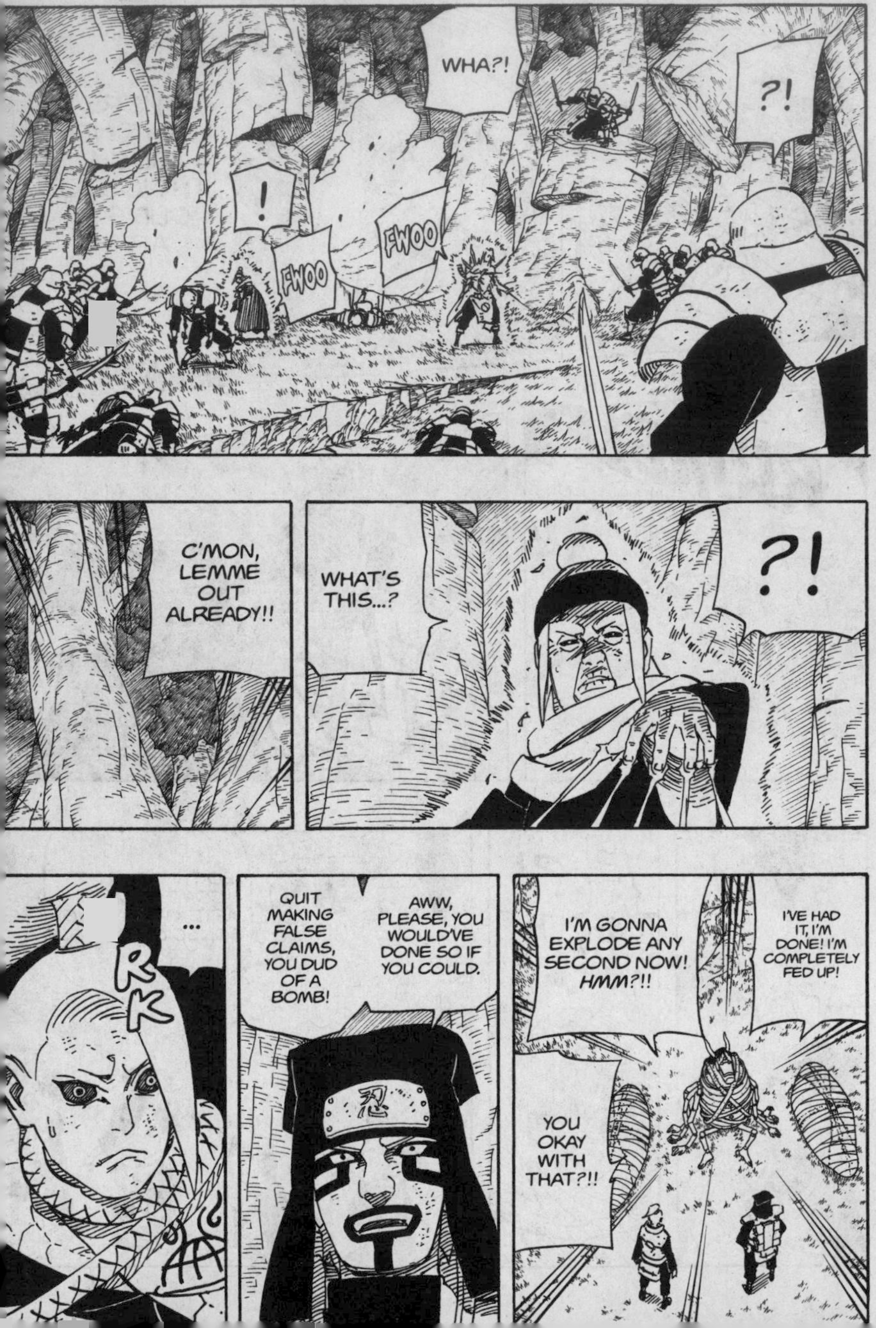
?!
WHA?!
FWOO
!
FWOO
?!
WHAT'S THIS...?
C'MON, LEMME OUT ALREADY!!
I'VE HAD IT, I'M DONE! I'M COMPLETELY FED UP!
I'M GONNA EXPLODE ANY SECOND NOW! HMM?!!
YOU OKAY WITH THAT?!!
AWW, PLEASE, YOU WOULD'VE DONE SO IF YOU COULD.
QUIT MAKING FALSE CLAIMS, YOU DUD OF A BOMB!
...
RK

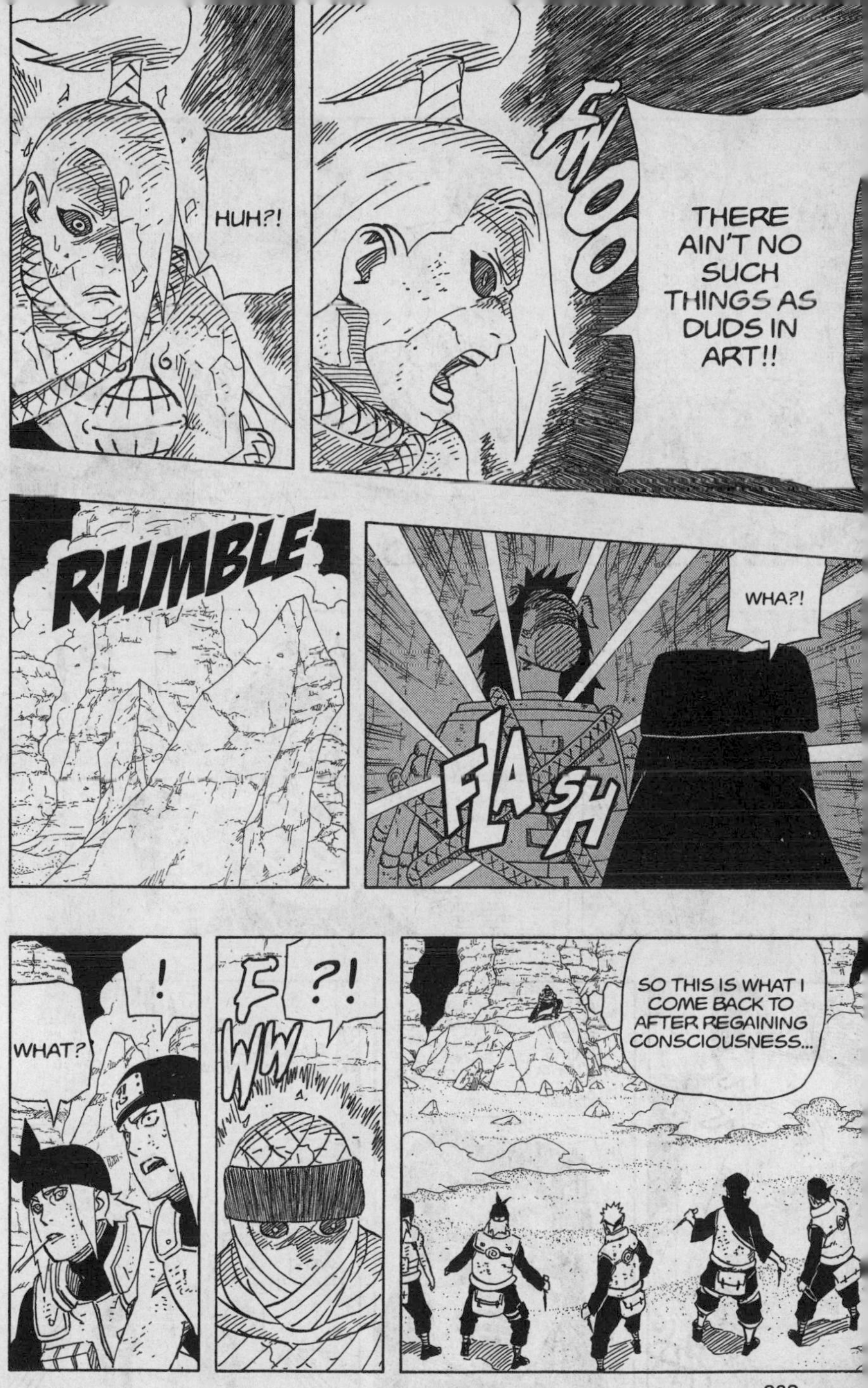
FWOO
THERE AIN'T NO SUCH THINGS AS DUDS IN ART!!
HUH?!
WHA?!
FLASH
RUMBLE
SO THIS IS WHAT I COME BACK TO AFTER REGAINING CONSCIOUSNESS...
?!
FWW
!
WHAT?

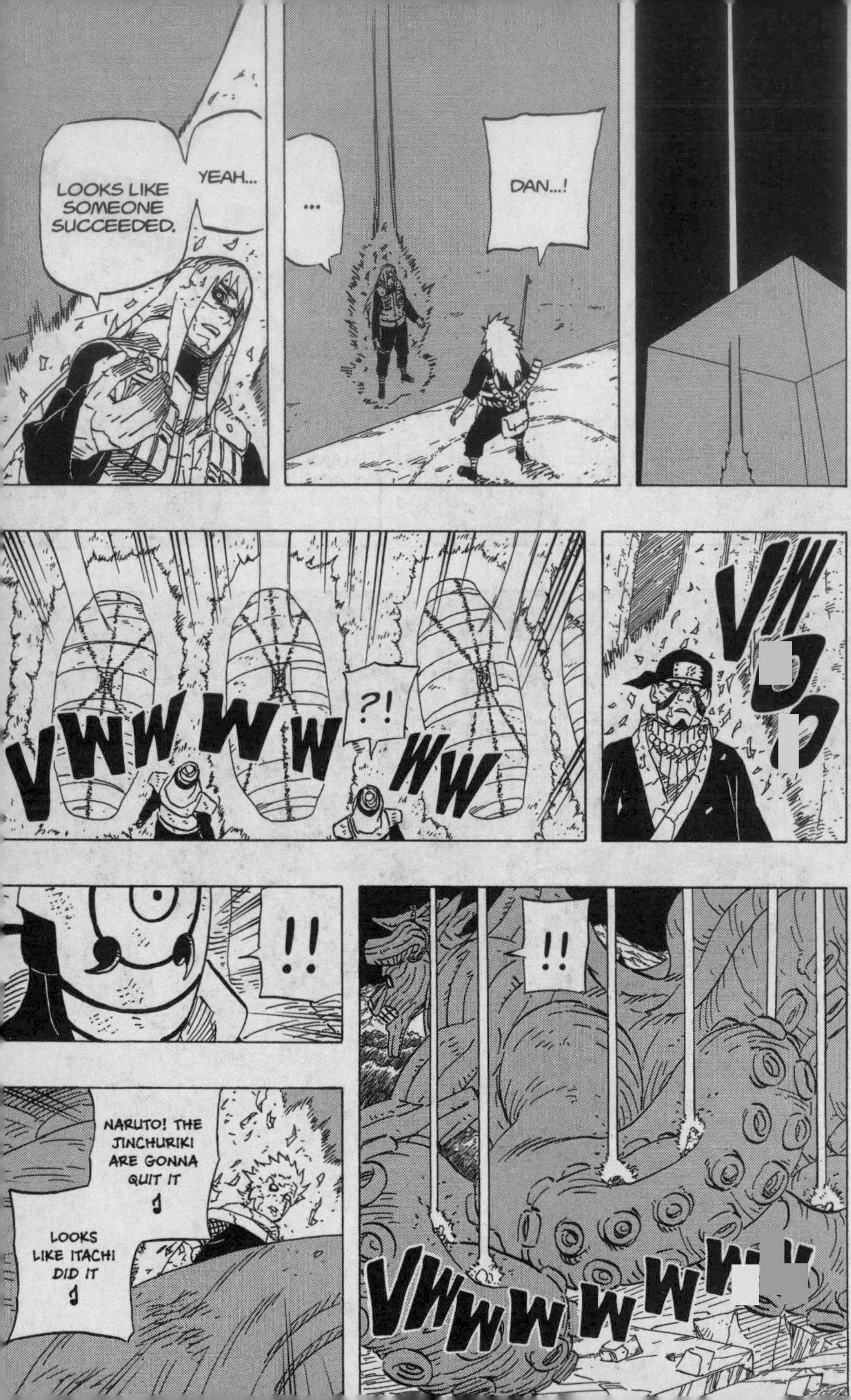
DAN...!
...
YEAH...
LOOKS LIKE SOMEONE SUCCEEDED.
?!
VWWWWW
WW
!!
VWWWWWW
!!
NARUTO! THE JINCHURIKI ARE GONNA QUIT IT ♪
LOOKS LIKE ITACHI DID IT ♪

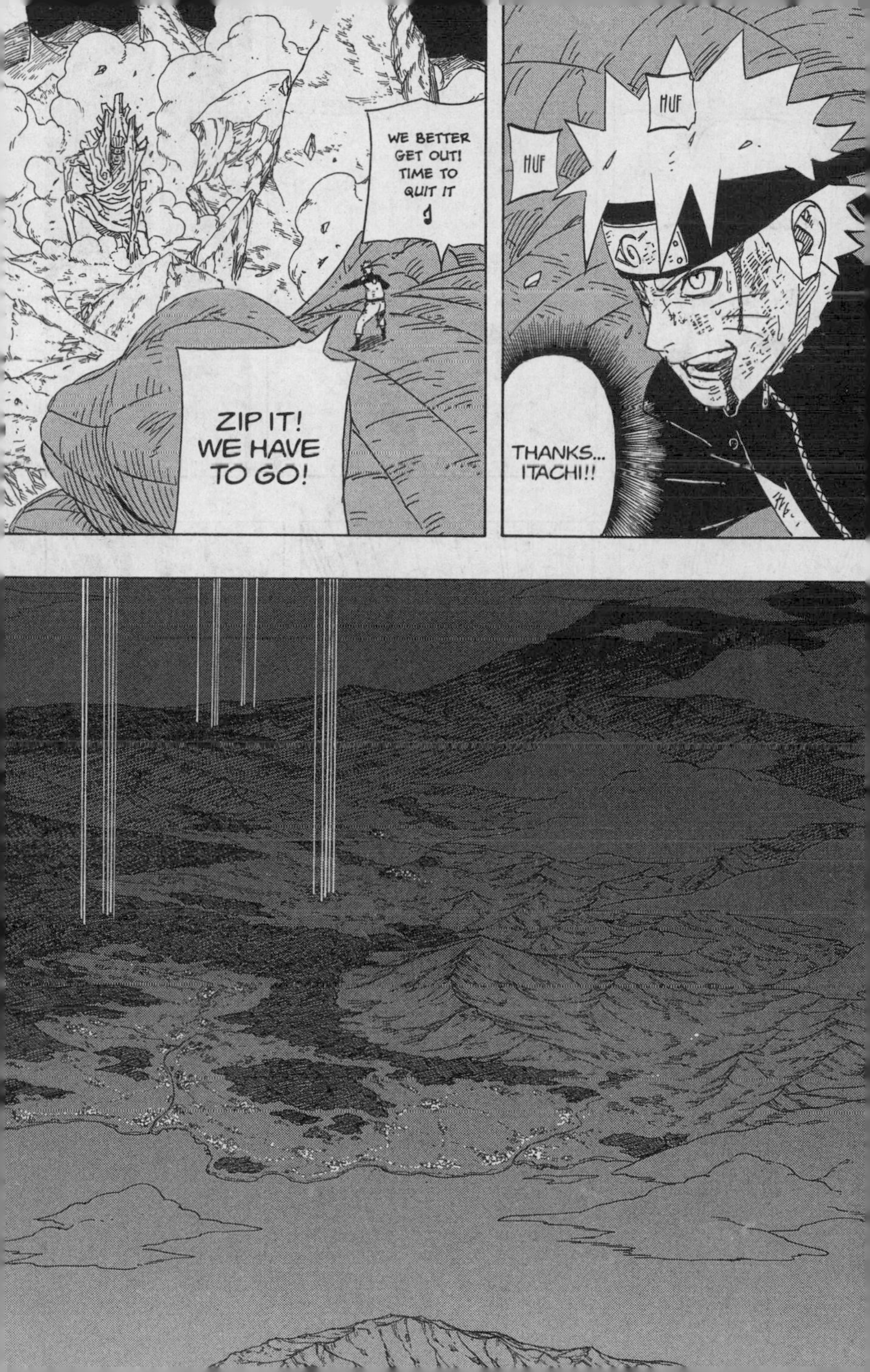
HUF
HUF
THANKS... ITACHI!!
WE BETTER GET OUT! TIME TO QUIT IT ♪
ZIP IT! WE HAVE TO GO!

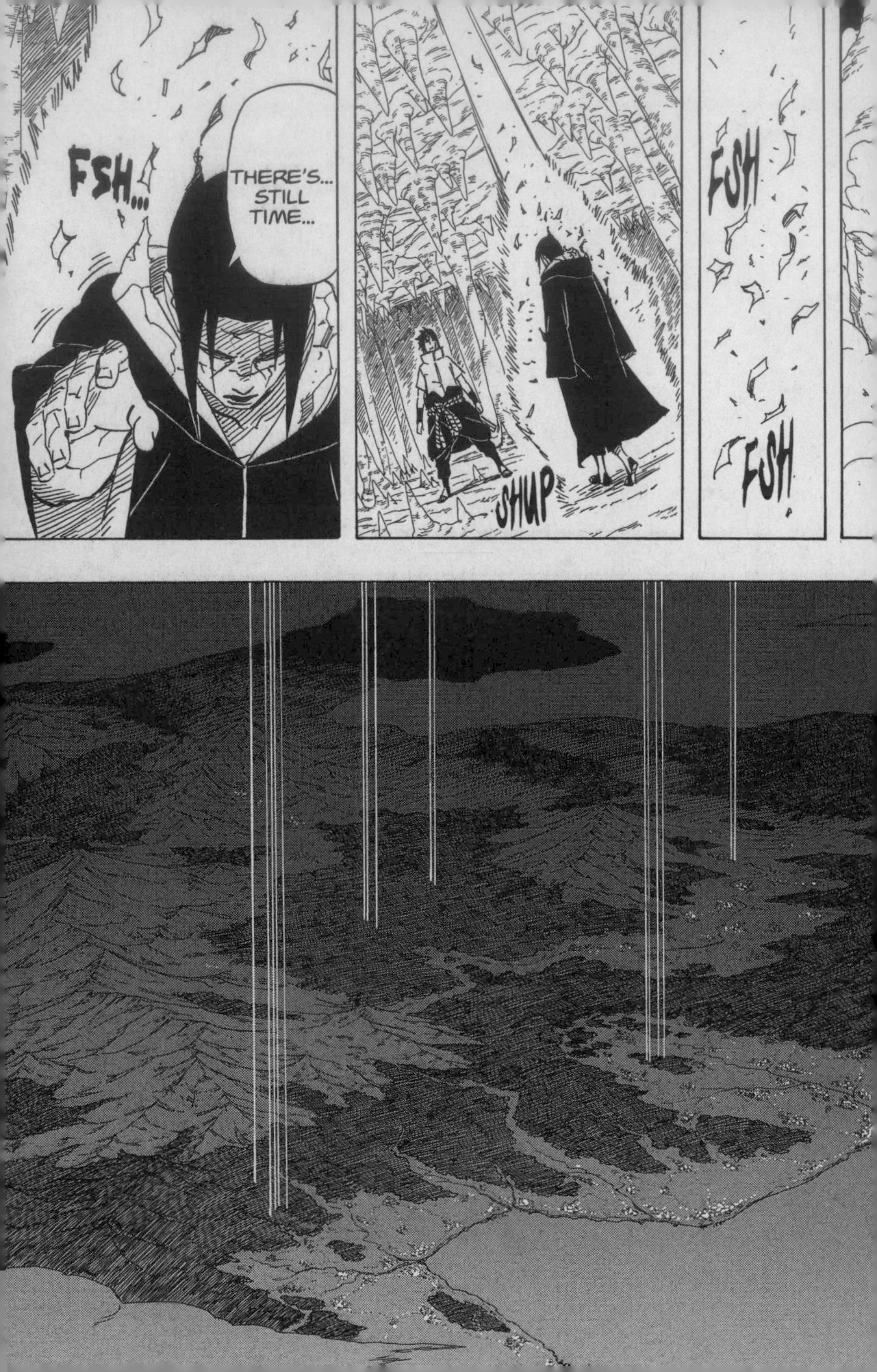
FSH
FSH
SHUP
FSH...
THERE'S... STILL TIME...

NARUTO

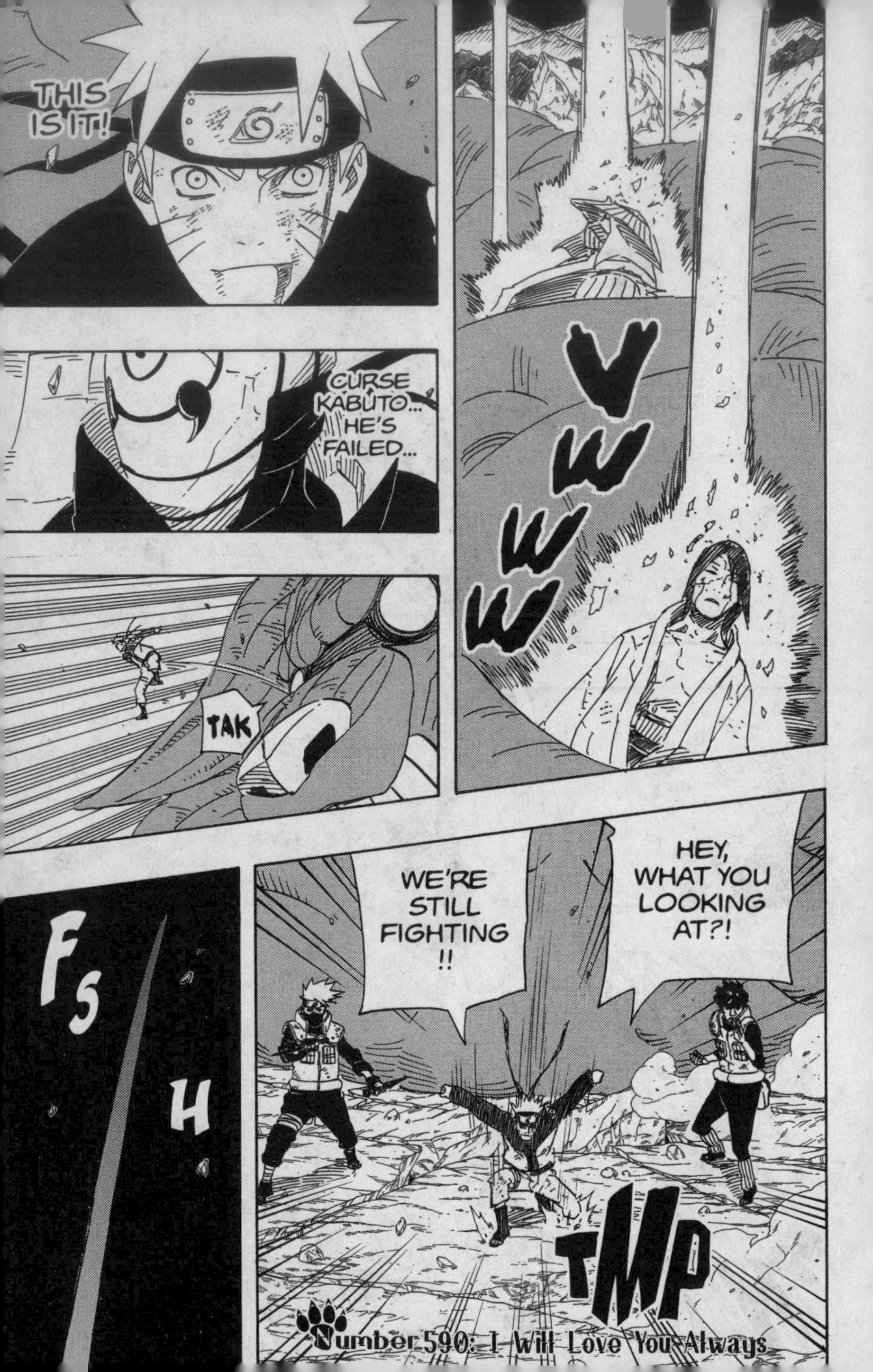

VWWWW
THIS IS IT!
CURSE KABUTO... HE'S FAILED...
TAK
HEY, WHAT YOU LOOKING AT?!
WE'RE STILL FIGHTING!!
TMP
FSH
Number 590: I Will Love You Always

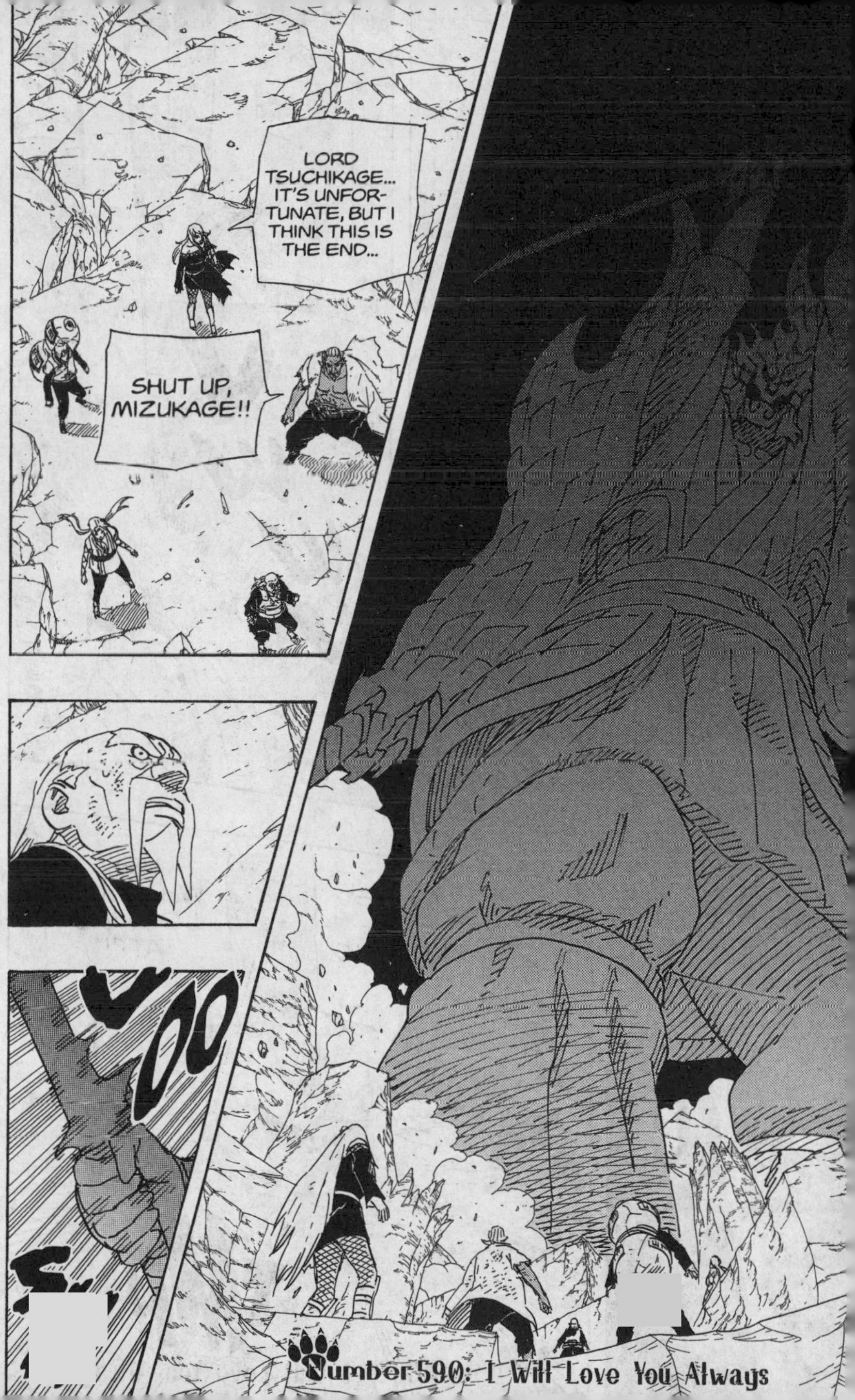
Number 590: I Will Love You Always
LORD TSUCHIKAGE... IT'S UNFOR-TUNATE, BUT I THINK THIS IS THE END...
SHUT UP, MIZUKAGE!!

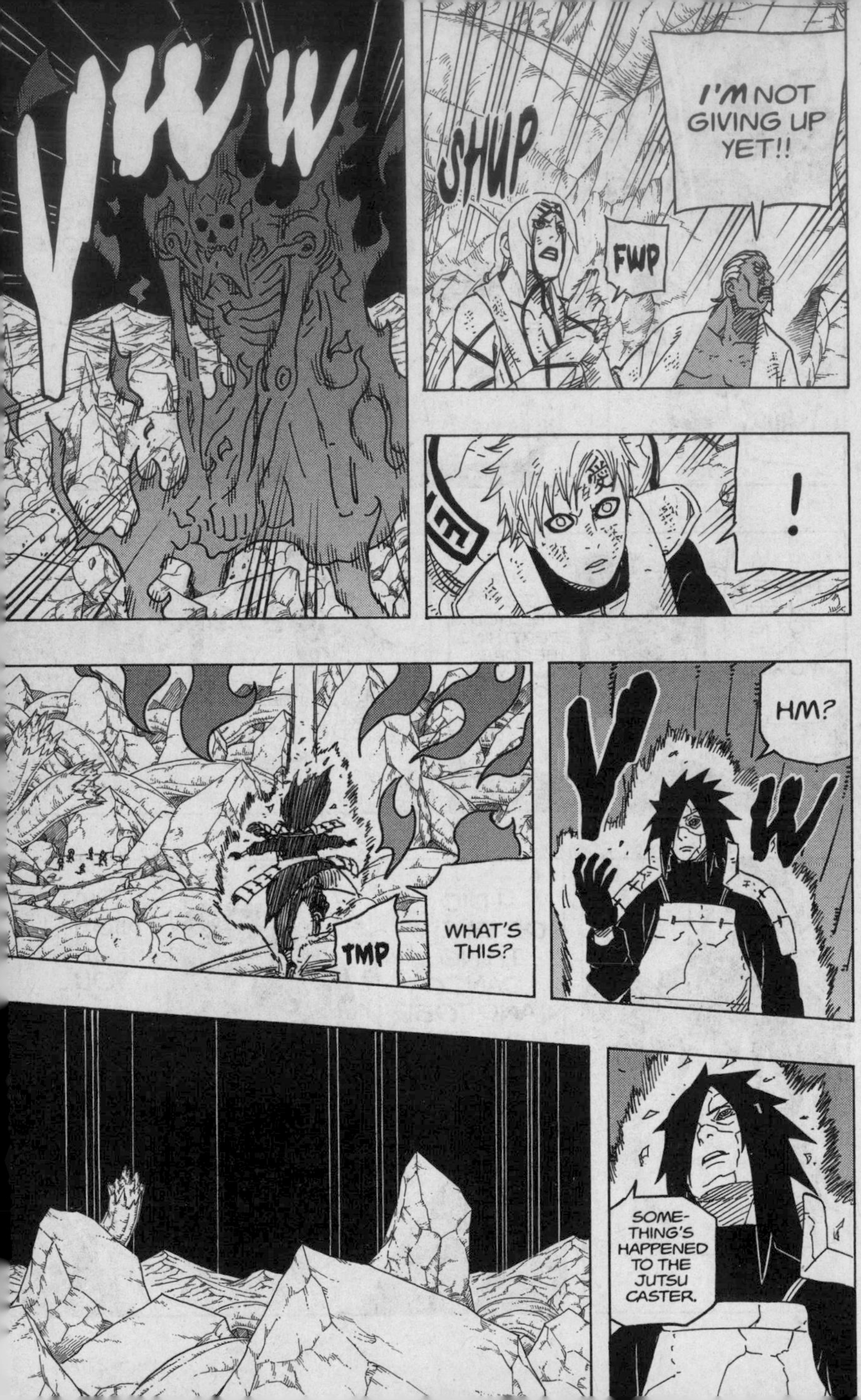
I'M NOT GIVING UP YET!!
SHUP
FWP
!
VWW
HM?
VW
WHAT'S THIS?
TMP
SOME-THING'S HAPPENED TO THE JUTSU CASTER.

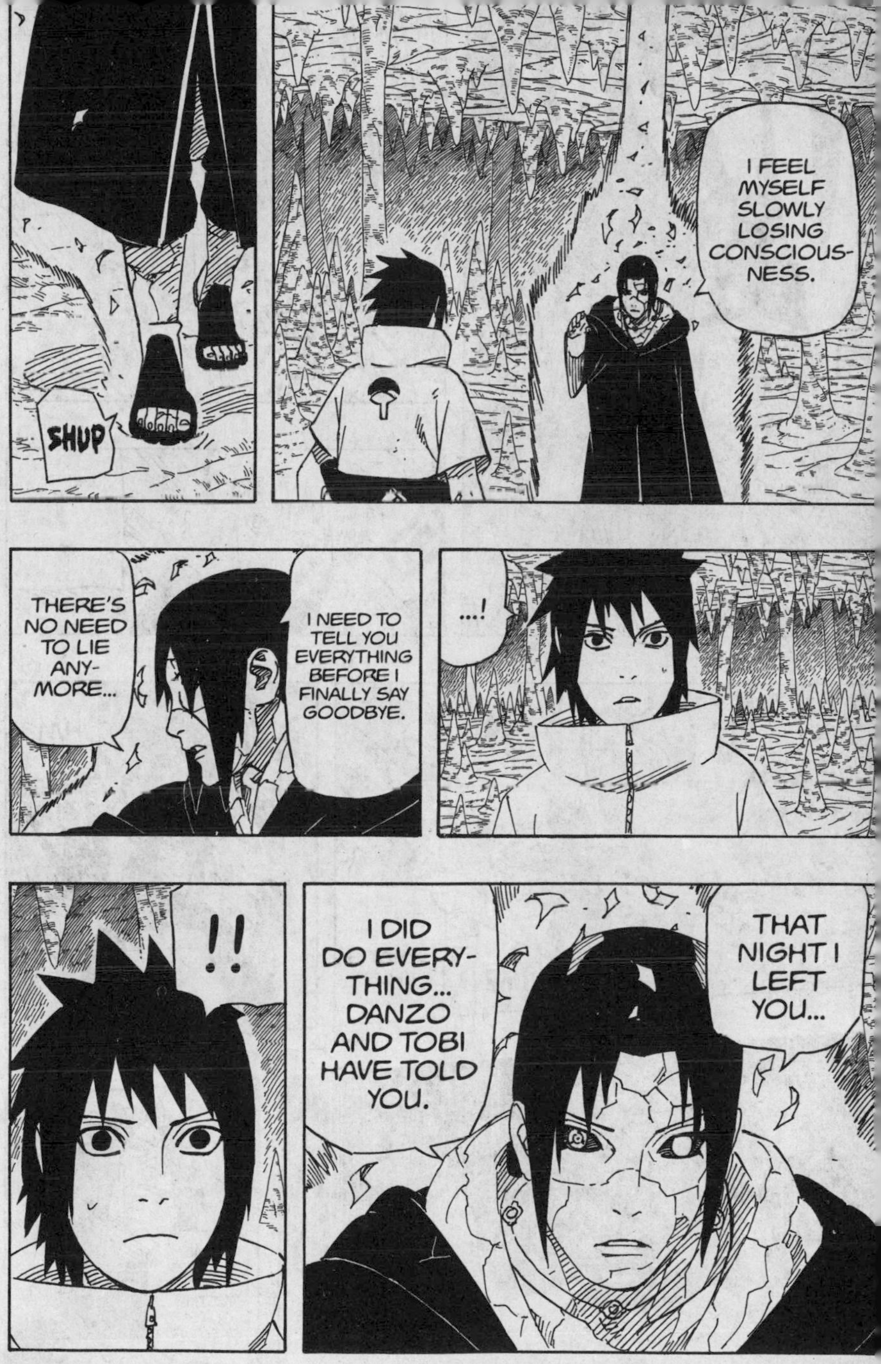
I FEEL MYSELF SLOWLY LOSING CONSCIOUS-NESS.
SHUP
...!
I NEED TO TELL YOU EVERYTHING BEFORE I FINALLY SAY GOODBYE.
THERE'S NO NEED TO LIE ANYMORE...
THAT NIGHT I LEFT YOU...
I DID DO EVERYTHING... DANZO AND TOBI HAVE TOLD YOU.
!!

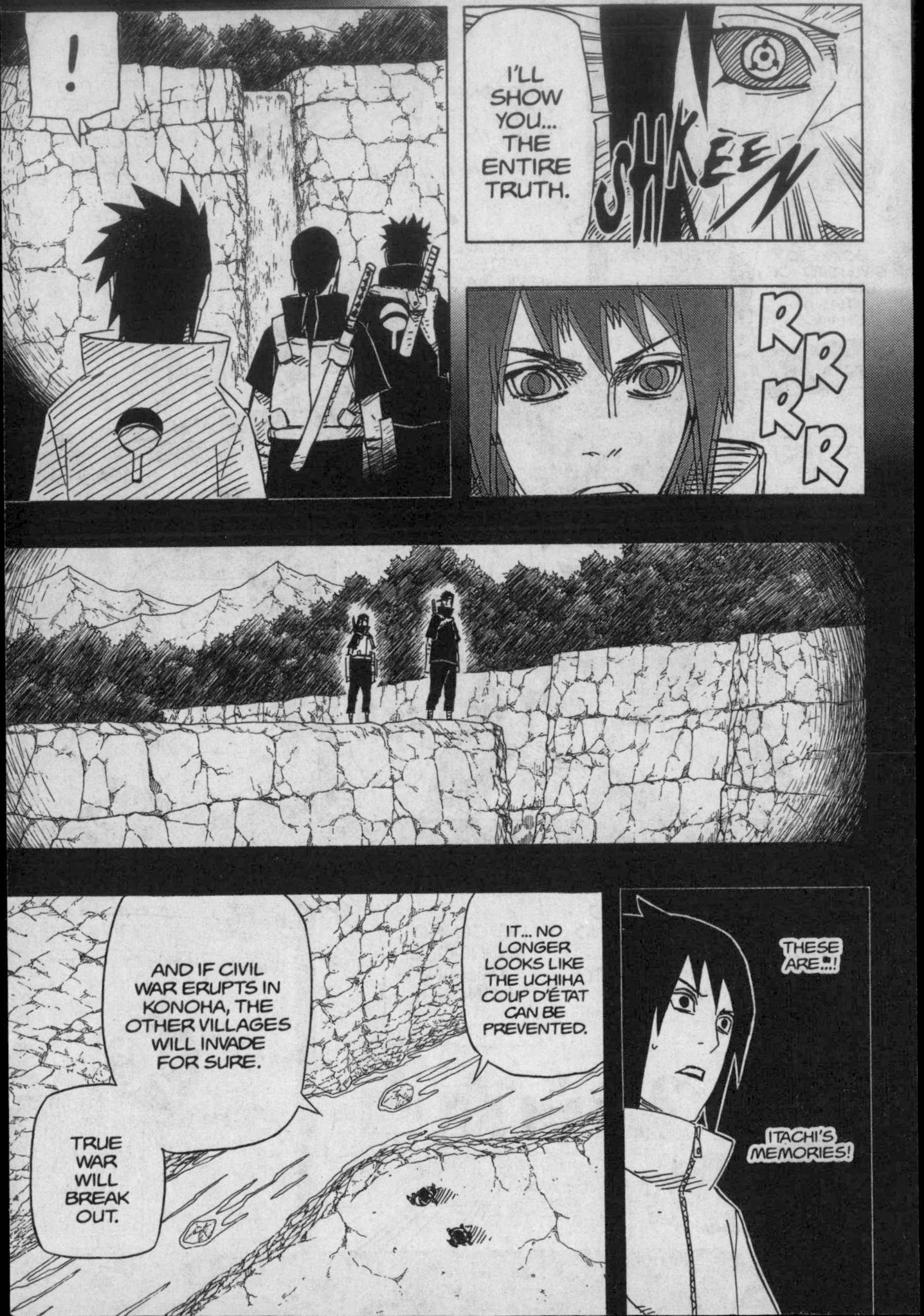
I'LL SHOW YOU... THE ENTIRE TRUTH.
SHKEEN
RRRR
!
THESE ARE...!
ITACHI'S MEMORIES!
IT... NO LONGER LOOKS LIKE THE UCHIHA COUP D'ÉTAT CAN BE PREVENTED.
AND IF CIVIL WAR ERUPTS IN KONOHA, THE OTHER VILLAGES WILL INVADE FOR SURE.
TRUE WAR WILL BREAK OUT.

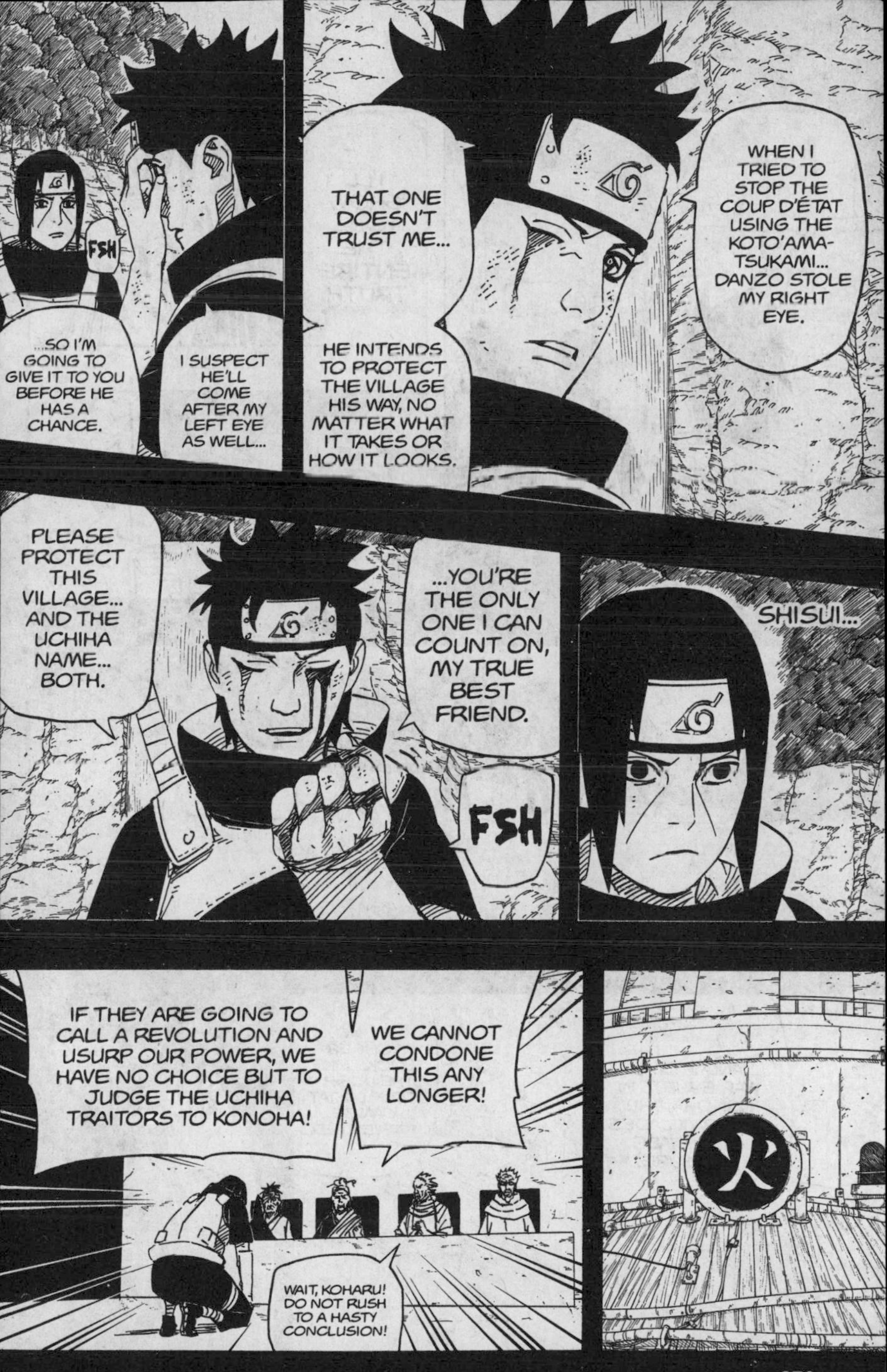
WHEN I TRIED TO STOP THE COUP D'ÉTAT USING THE KOTO'AMATSUKAMI... DANZO STOLE MY RIGHT EYE.
THAT ONE DOESN'T TRUST ME...
HE INTENDS TO PROTECT THE VILLAGE HIS WAY, NO MATTER WHAT IT TAKES OR HOW IT LOOKS.
FSH
I SUSPECT HE'LL COME AFTER MY LEFT EYE AS WELL...
...SO I'M GOING TO GIVE IT TO YOU BEFORE HE HAS A CHANCE.
SHISUI...
...YOU'RE THE ONLY ONE I CAN COUNT ON, MY TRUE BEST FRIEND.
FSH
PLEASE PROTECT THIS VILLAGE... AND THE UCHIHA NAME... BOTH.
WE CANNOT CONDONE THIS ANY LONGER!
IF THEY ARE GOING TO CALL A REVOLUTION AND USURP OUR POWER, WE HAVE NO CHOICE BUT TO JUDGE THE UCHIHA TRAITORS TO KONOHA!
WAIT, KOHARU! DO NOT RUSH TO A HASTY CONCLUSION!

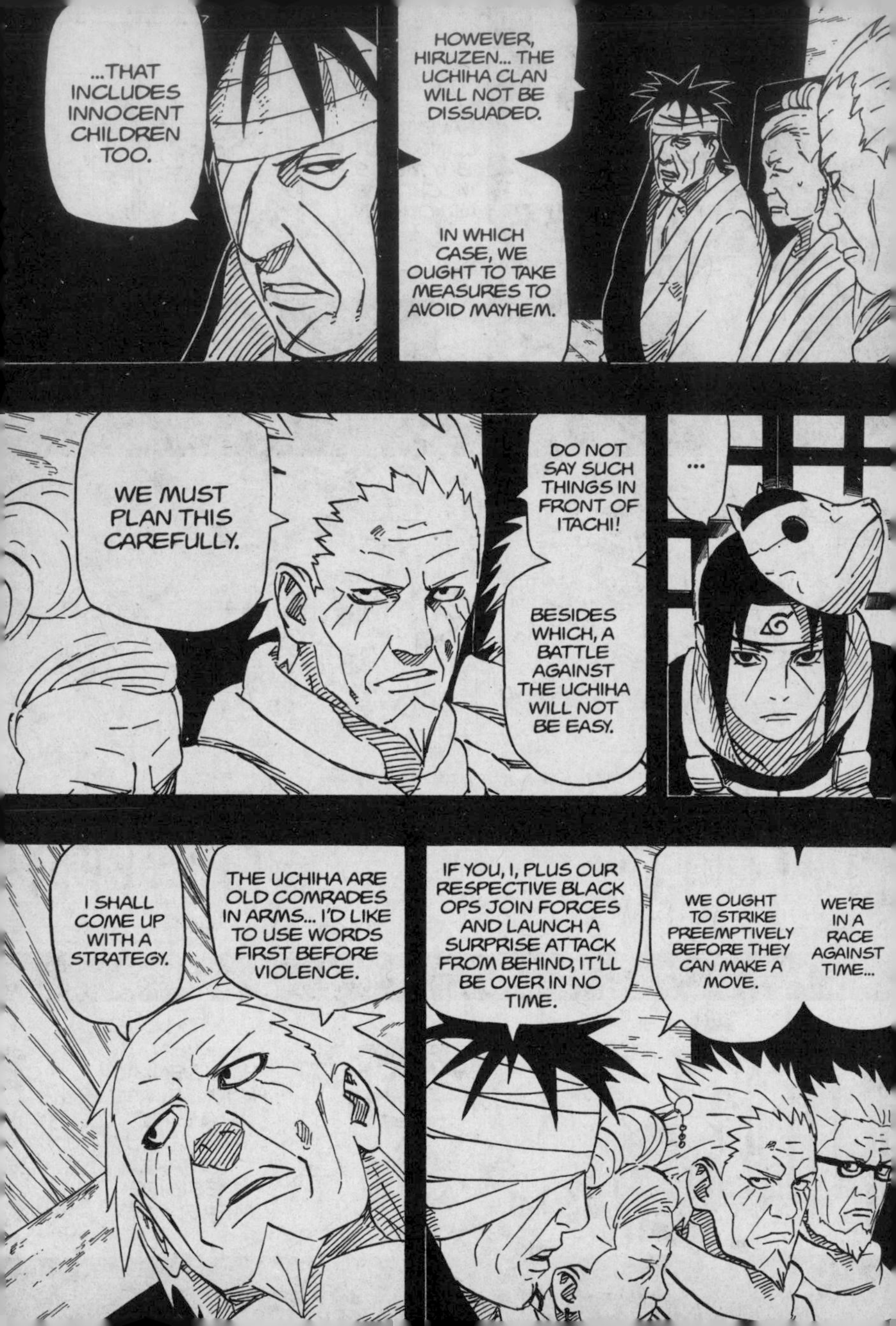
HOWEVER, HIRUZEN... THE UCHIHA CLAN WILL NOT BE DISSUADED.
IN WHICH CASE, WE OUGHT TO TAKE MEASURES TO AVOID MAYHEM.
...THAT INCLUDES INNOCENT CHILDREN TOO.
...
DO NOT SAY SUCH THINGS IN FRONT OF ITACHI!
BESIDES WHICH, A BATTLE AGAINST THE UCHIHA WILL NOT BE EASY.
WE MUST PLAN THIS CAREFULLY.
WE'RE IN A RACE AGAINST TIME...
WE OUGHT TO STRIKE PREEMPTIVELY BEFORE THEY CAN MAKE A MOVE.
IF YOU, I, PLUS OUR RESPECTIVE BLACK OPS JOIN FORCES AND LAUNCH A SURPRISE ATTACK FROM BEHIND, IT'LL BE OVER IN NO TIME.
THE UCHIHA ARE OLD COMRADES IN ARMS... I'D LIKE TO USE WORDS FIRST BEFORE VIOLENCE.
I SHALL COME UP WITH A STRATEGY.

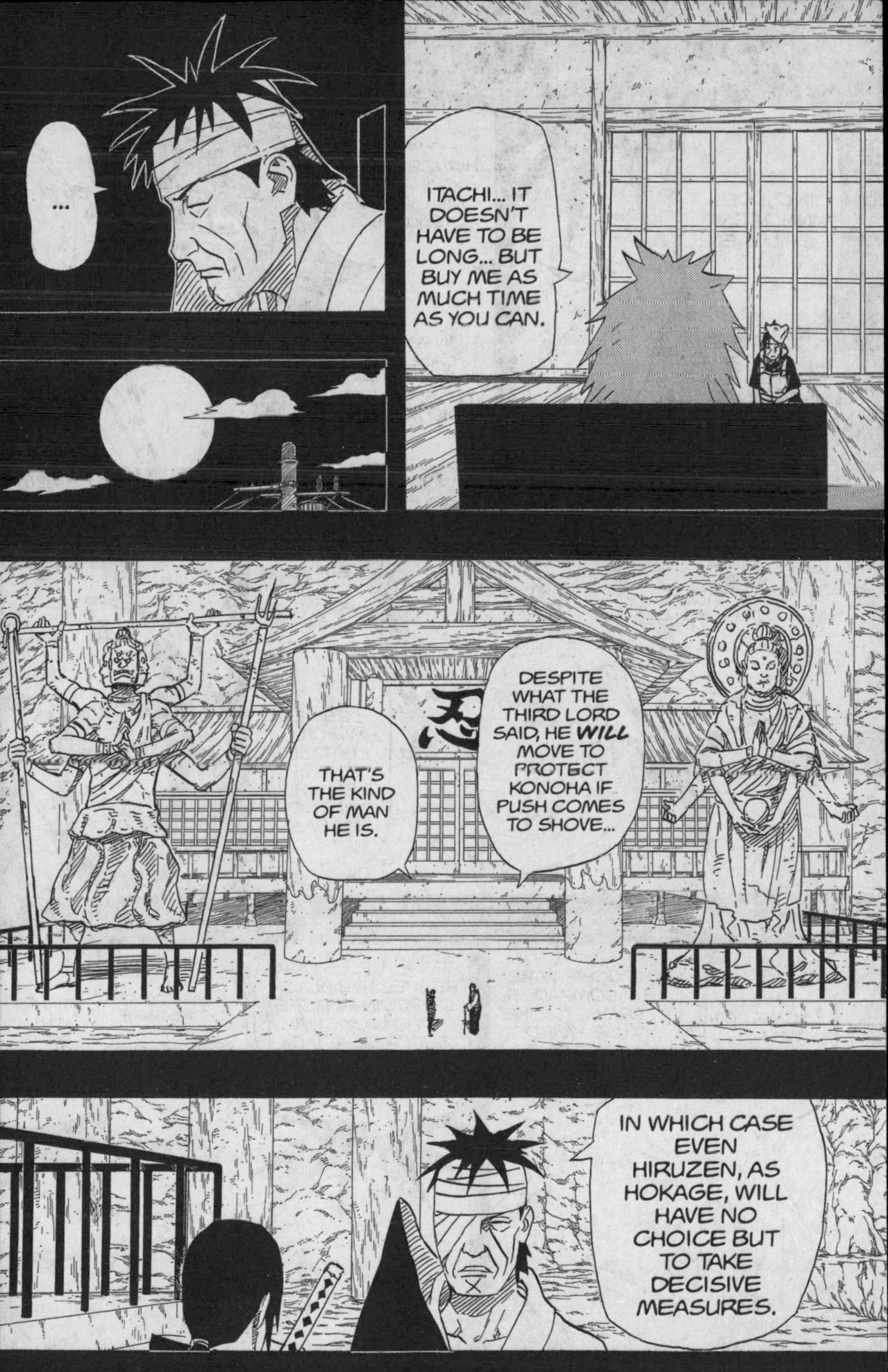
ITACHI... IT DOESN'T HAVE TO BE LONG... BUT BUY ME AS MUCH TIME AS YOU CAN.
...
DESPITE WHAT THE THIRD LORD SAID, HE *WILL* MOVE TO PROTECT KONOHA IF PUSH COMES TO SHOVE...
THAT'S THE KIND OF MAN HE IS.
IN WHICH CASE EVEN HIRUZEN, AS HOKAGE, WILL HAVE NO CHOICE BUT TO TAKE DECISIVE MEASURES.

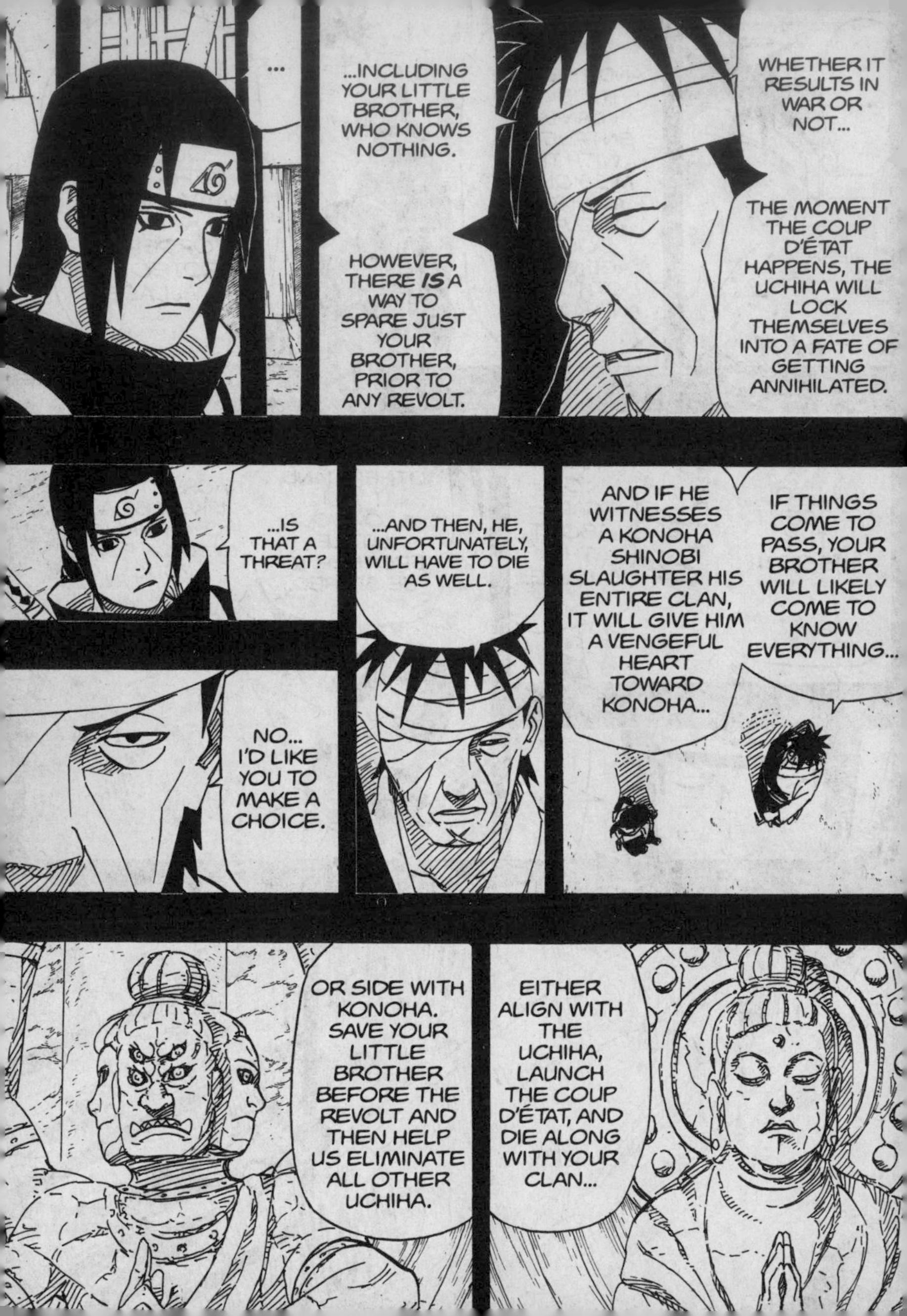
WHETHER IT RESULTS IN WAR OR NOT...
THE MOMENT THE COUP D'ÉTAT HAPPENS, THE UCHIHA WILL LOCK THEMSELVES INTO A FATE OF GETTING ANNIHILATED.
...INCLUDING YOUR LITTLE BROTHER, WHO KNOWS NOTHING.
HOWEVER, THERE *IS* A WAY TO SPARE JUST YOUR BROTHER, PRIOR TO ANY REVOLT.
...
IF THINGS COME TO PASS, YOUR BROTHER WILL LIKELY COME TO KNOW EVERYTHING...
AND IF HE WITNESSES A KONOHA SHINOBI SLAUGHTER HIS ENTIRE CLAN, IT WILL GIVE HIM A VENGEFUL HEART TOWARD KONOHA...
...AND THEN, HE, UNFORTUNATELY, WILL HAVE TO DIE AS WELL.
...IS THAT A THREAT?
NO... I'D LIKE YOU TO MAKE A CHOICE.
EITHER ALIGN WITH THE UCHIHA, LAUNCH THE COUP D'ÉTAT, AND DIE ALONG WITH YOUR CLAN...
OR SIDE WITH KONOHA. SAVE YOUR LITTLE BROTHER BEFORE THE REVOLT AND THEN HELP US ELIMINATE ALL OTHER UCHIHA.

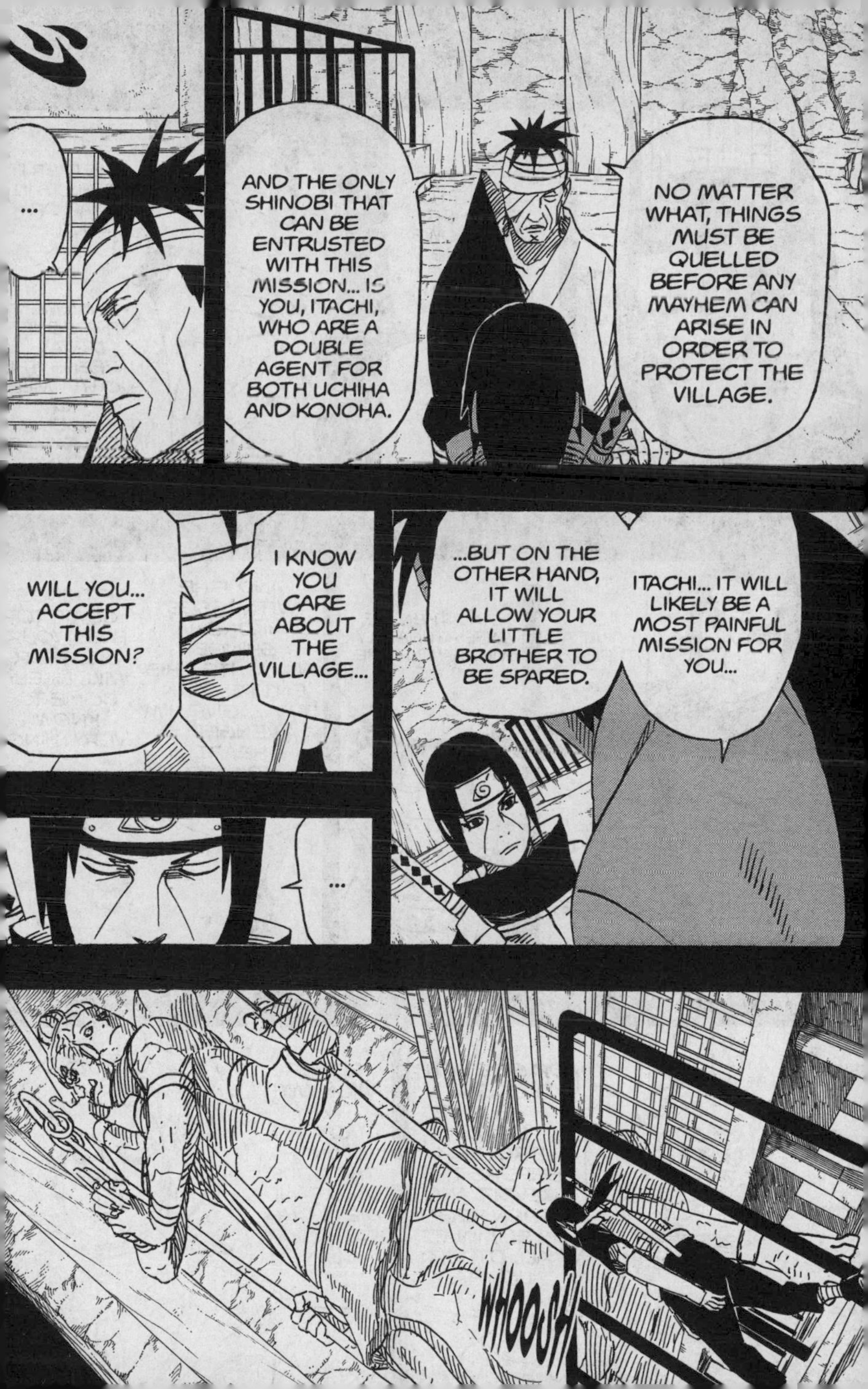
NO MATTER WHAT, THINGS MUST BE QUELLED BEFORE ANY MAYHEM CAN ARISE IN ORDER TO PROTECT THE VILLAGE.
AND THE ONLY SHINOBI THAT CAN BE ENTRUSTED WITH THIS MISSION... IS YOU, ITACHI, WHO ARE A DOUBLE AGENT FOR BOTH UCHIHA AND KONOHA.
...
ITACHI... IT WILL LIKELY BE A MOST PAINFUL MISSION FOR YOU...
...BUT ON THE OTHER HAND, IT WILL ALLOW YOUR LITTLE BROTHER TO BE SPARED.
I KNOW YOU CARE ABOUT THE VILLAGE...
WILL YOU... ACCEPT THIS MISSION?
...
WHOOSH

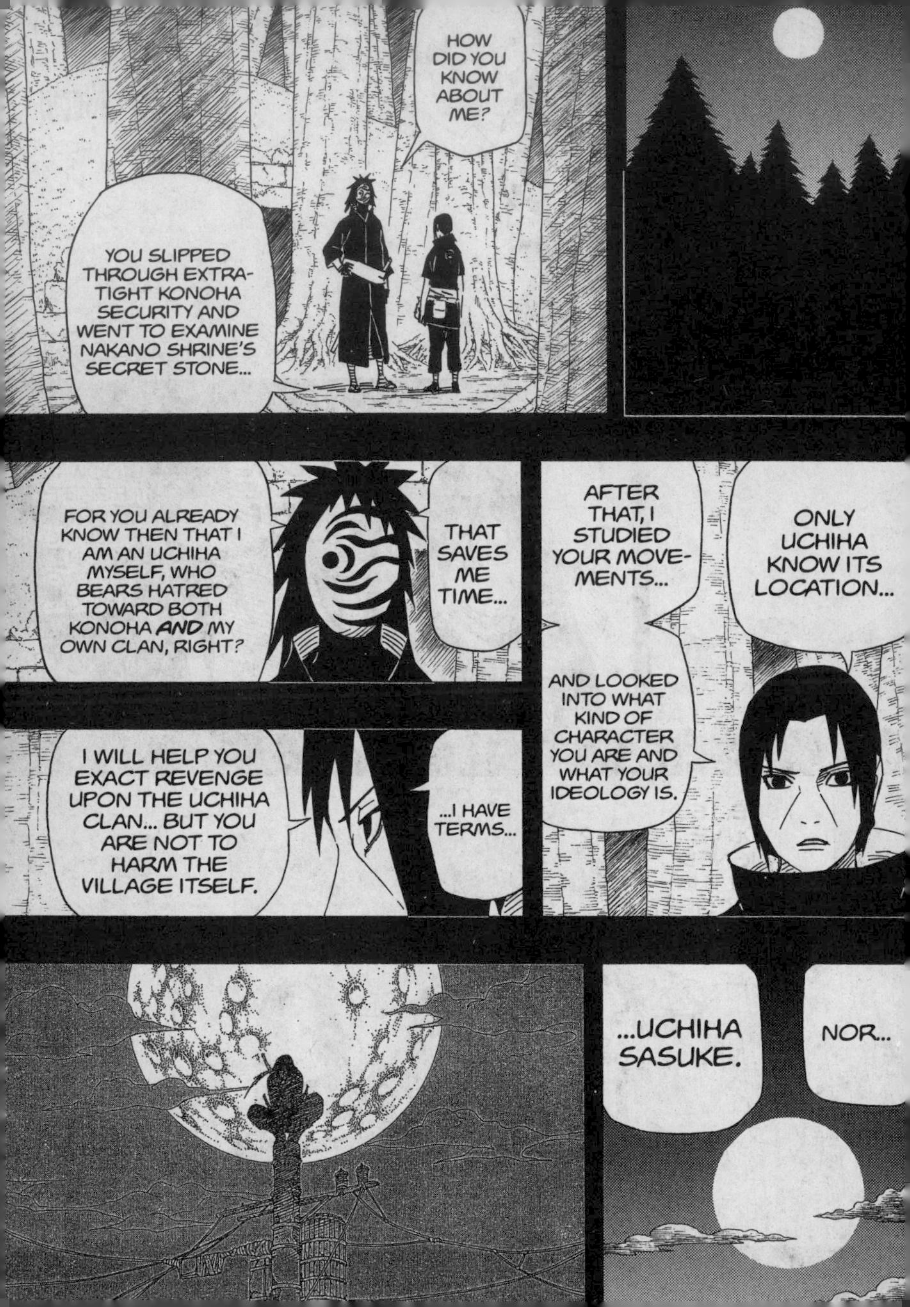
HOW DID YOU KNOW ABOUT ME?
YOU SLIPPED THROUGH EXTRA-TIGHT KONOHA SECURITY AND WENT TO EXAMINE NAKANO SHRINE'S SECRET STONE...
ONLY UCHIHA KNOW ITS LOCATION...
AFTER THAT, I STUDIED YOUR MOVEMENTS...
AND LOOKED INTO WHAT KIND OF CHARACTER YOU ARE AND WHAT YOUR IDEOLOGY IS.
THAT SAVES ME TIME...
FOR YOU ALREADY KNOW THEN THAT I AM AN UCHIHA MYSELF, WHO BEARS HATRED TOWARD BOTH KONOHA *AND* MY OWN CLAN, RIGHT?
...I HAVE TERMS...
I WILL HELP YOU EXACT REVENGE UPON THE UCHIHA CLAN... BUT YOU ARE NOT TO HARM THE VILLAGE ITSELF.
NOR...
...UCHIHA SASUKE.

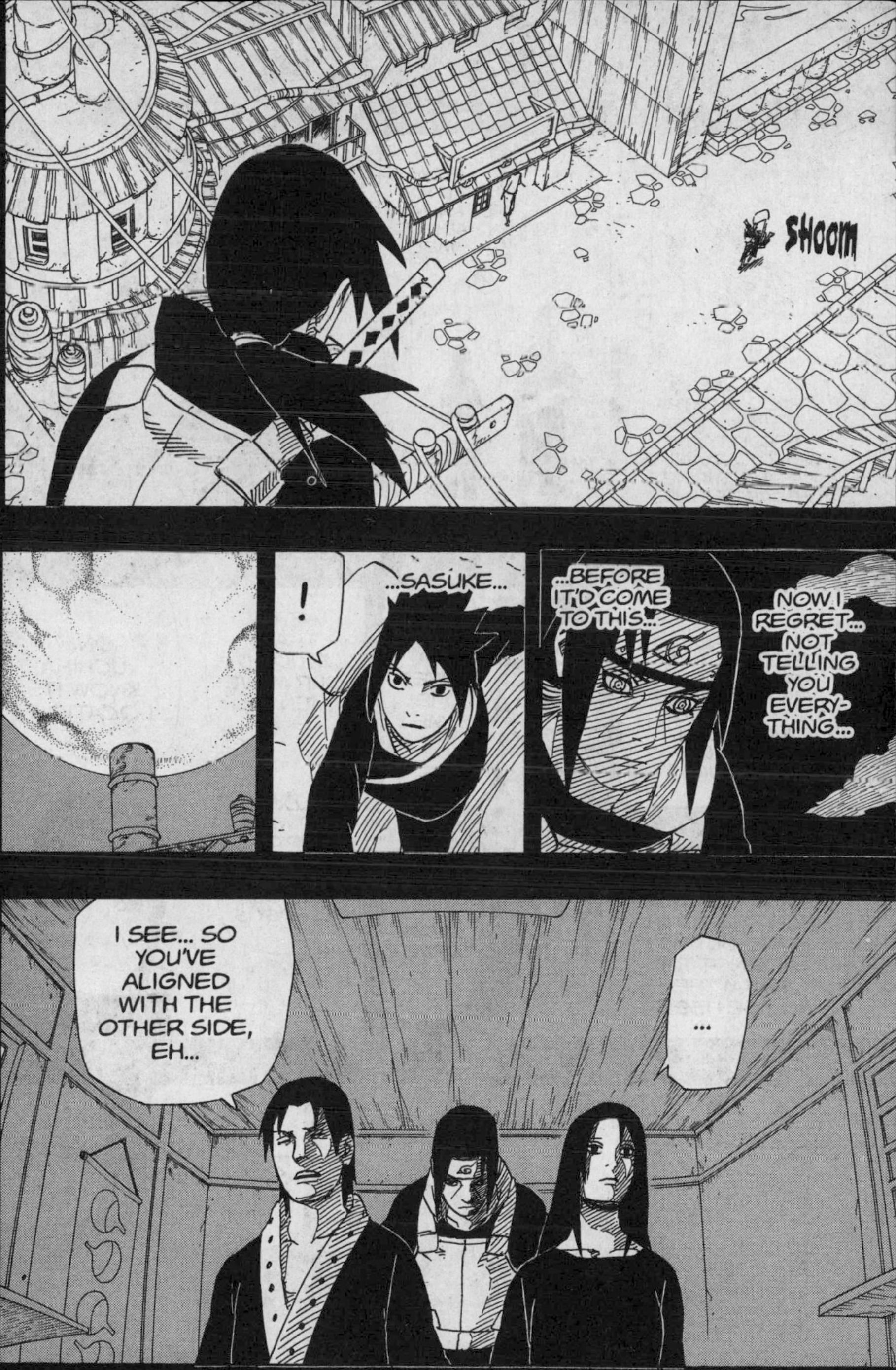
SHOOM
NOW I REGRET... NOT TELLING YOU EVERYTHING...
...BEFORE IT'D COME TO THIS...
...SASUKE...
!
...
I SEE... SO YOU'VE ALIGNED WITH THE OTHER SIDE, EH...

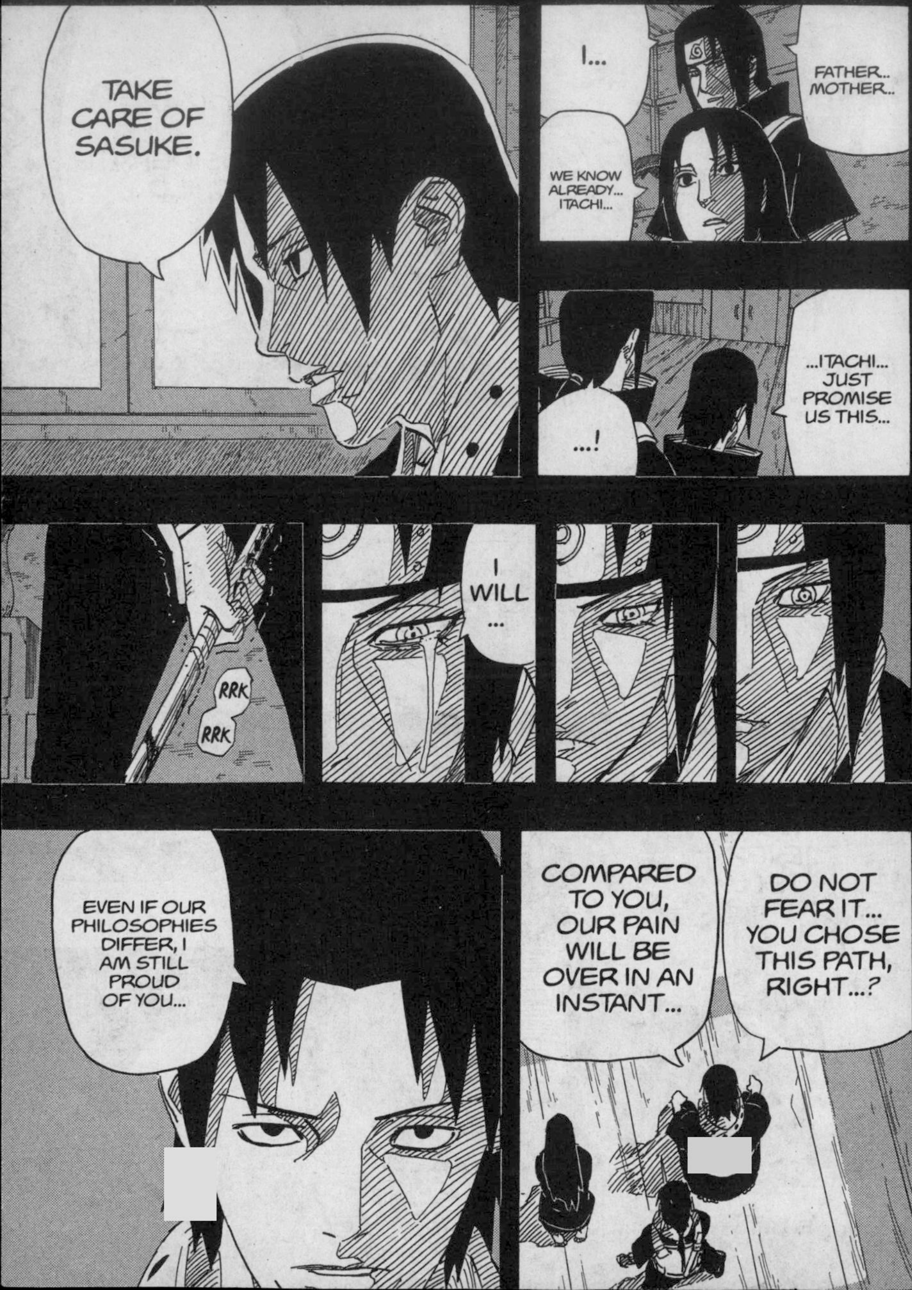
FATHER.. MOTHER..
I...
WE KNOW ALREADY... ITACHI...
...ITACHI... JUST PROMISE US THIS...
...!
TAKE CARE OF SASUKE.
I WILL ...
RRK
RRK
DO NOT FEAR IT... YOU CHOSE THIS PATH, RIGHT...?
COMPARED TO YOU, OUR PAIN WILL BE OVER IN AN INSTANT...
EVEN IF OUR PHILOSOPHIES DIFFER, I AM STILL PROUD OF YOU...

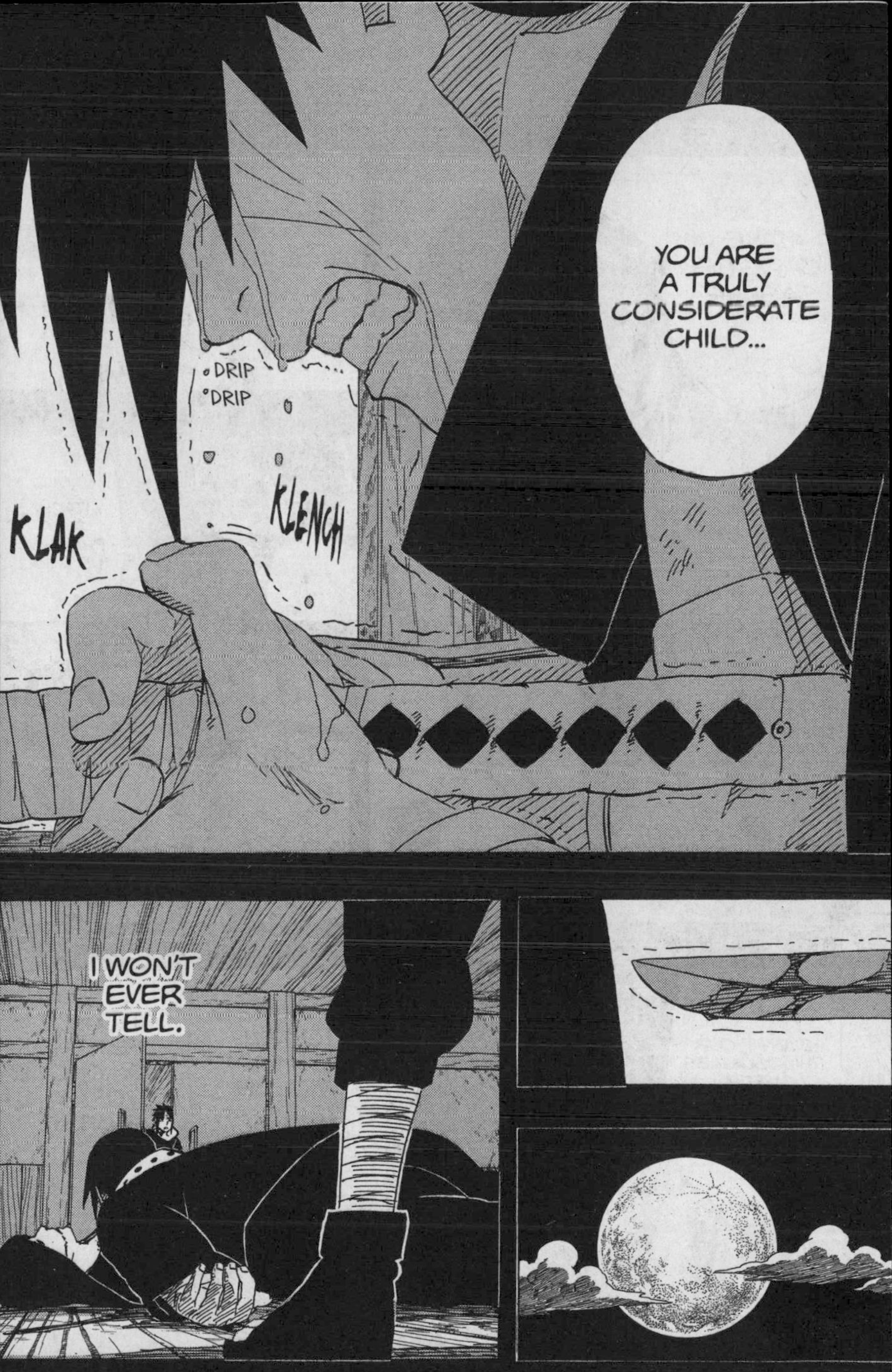
YOU ARE A TRULY CONSIDERATE CHILD...
DRIP
DRIP
KLENCH
KLAK
I WON'T EVER TELL.

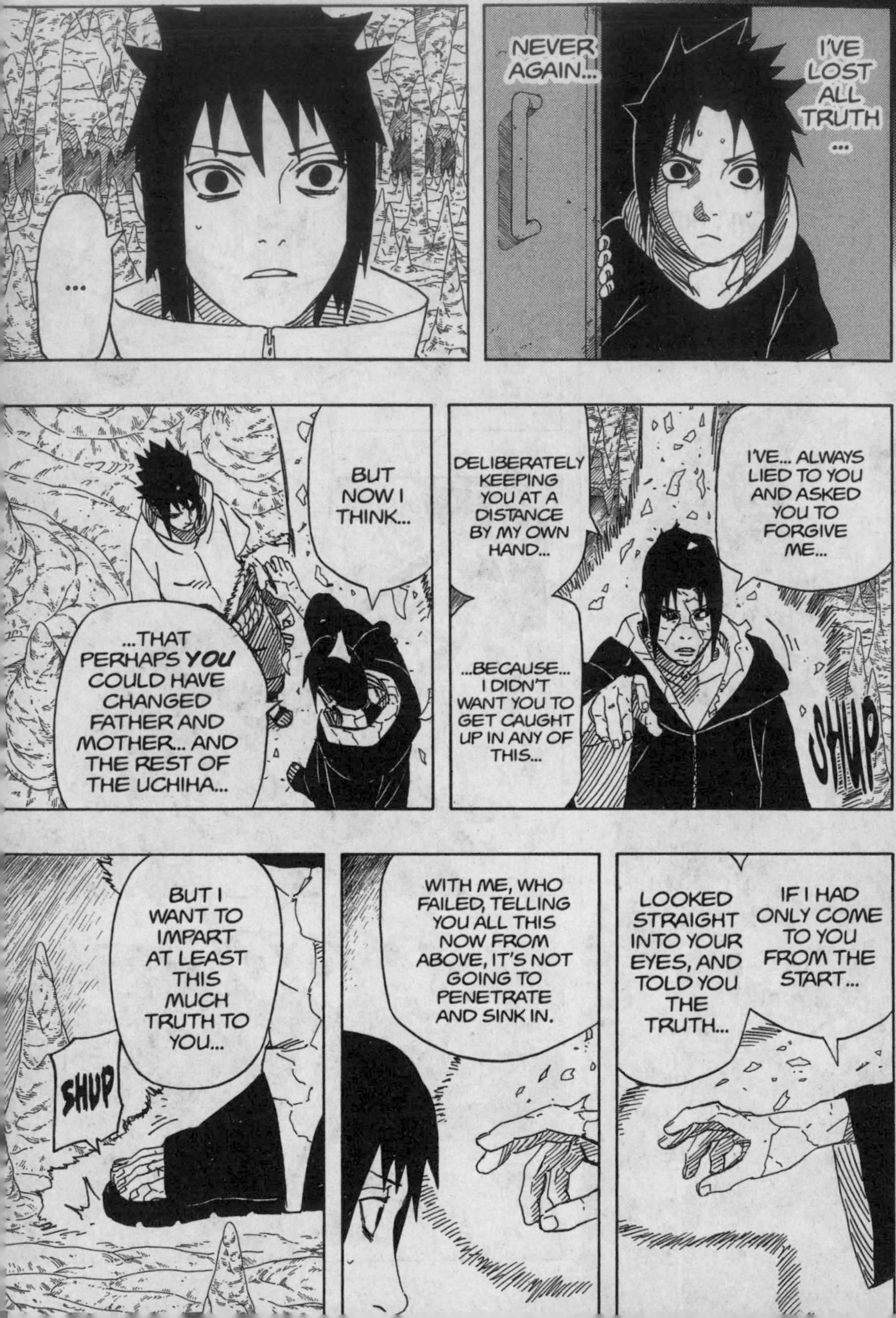
I'VE LOST ALL TRUTH...
NEVER AGAIN...
...
I'VE... ALWAYS LIED TO YOU AND ASKED YOU TO FORGIVE ME...
DELIBERATELY KEEPING YOU AT A DISTANCE BY MY OWN HAND...
...BECAUSE... I DIDN'T WANT YOU TO GET CAUGHT UP IN ANY OF THIS...
SHUP
BUT NOW I THINK...
...THAT PERHAPS *YOU* COULD HAVE CHANGED FATHER AND MOTHER... AND THE REST OF THE UCHIHA...
IF I HAD ONLY COME TO YOU FROM THE START...
LOOKED STRAIGHT INTO YOUR EYES, AND TOLD YOU THE TRUTH...
WITH ME, WHO FAILED, TELLING YOU ALL THIS NOW FROM ABOVE, IT'S NOT GOING TO PENETRATE AND SINK IN.
BUT I WANT TO IMPART AT LEAST THIS MUCH TRUTH TO YOU...
SHUP

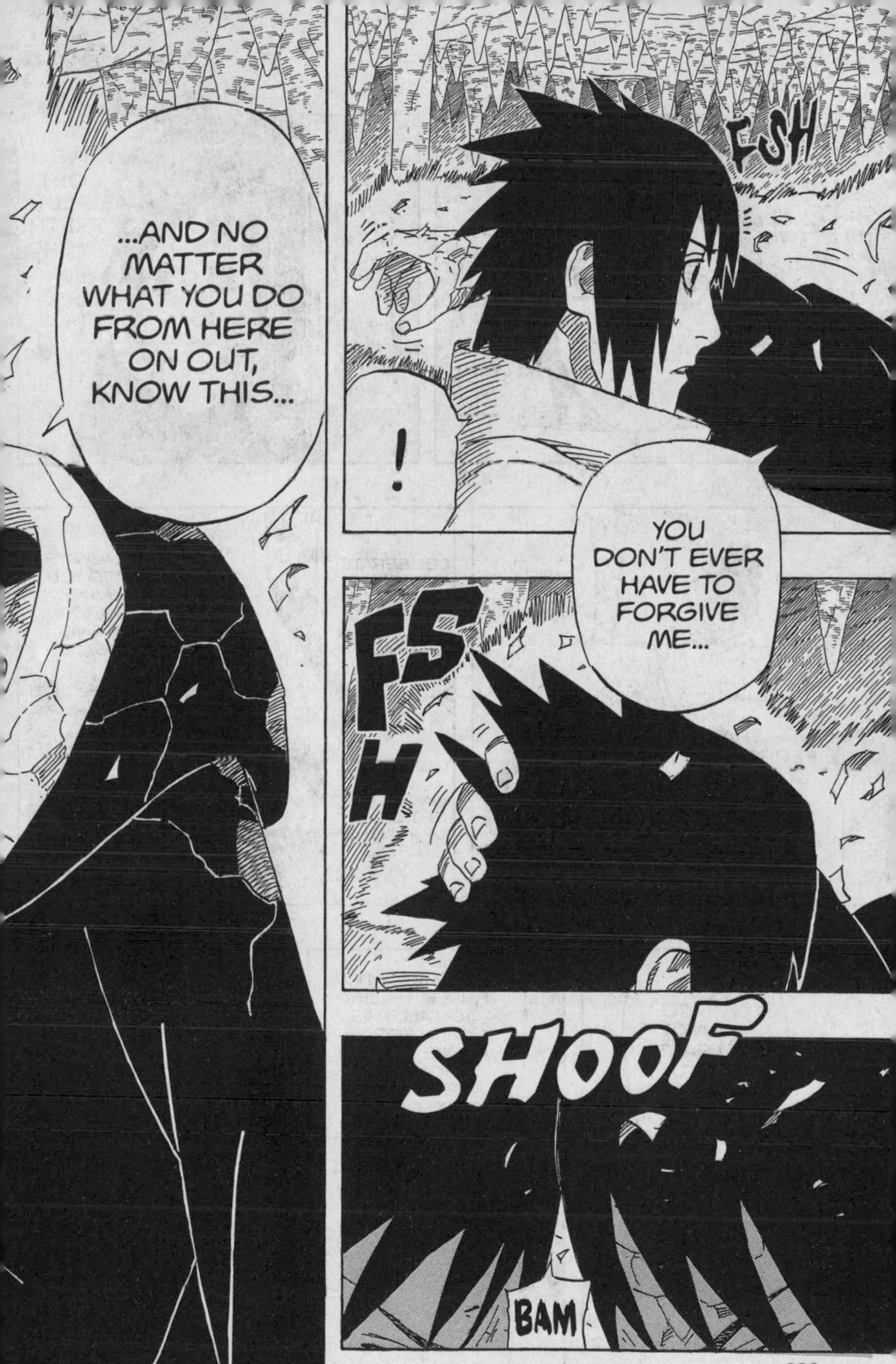
FSH
!
YOU DON'T EVER HAVE TO FORGIVE ME...
FSH
SHOOF
BAM
...AND NO MATTER WHAT YOU DO FROM HERE ON OUT, KNOW THIS...

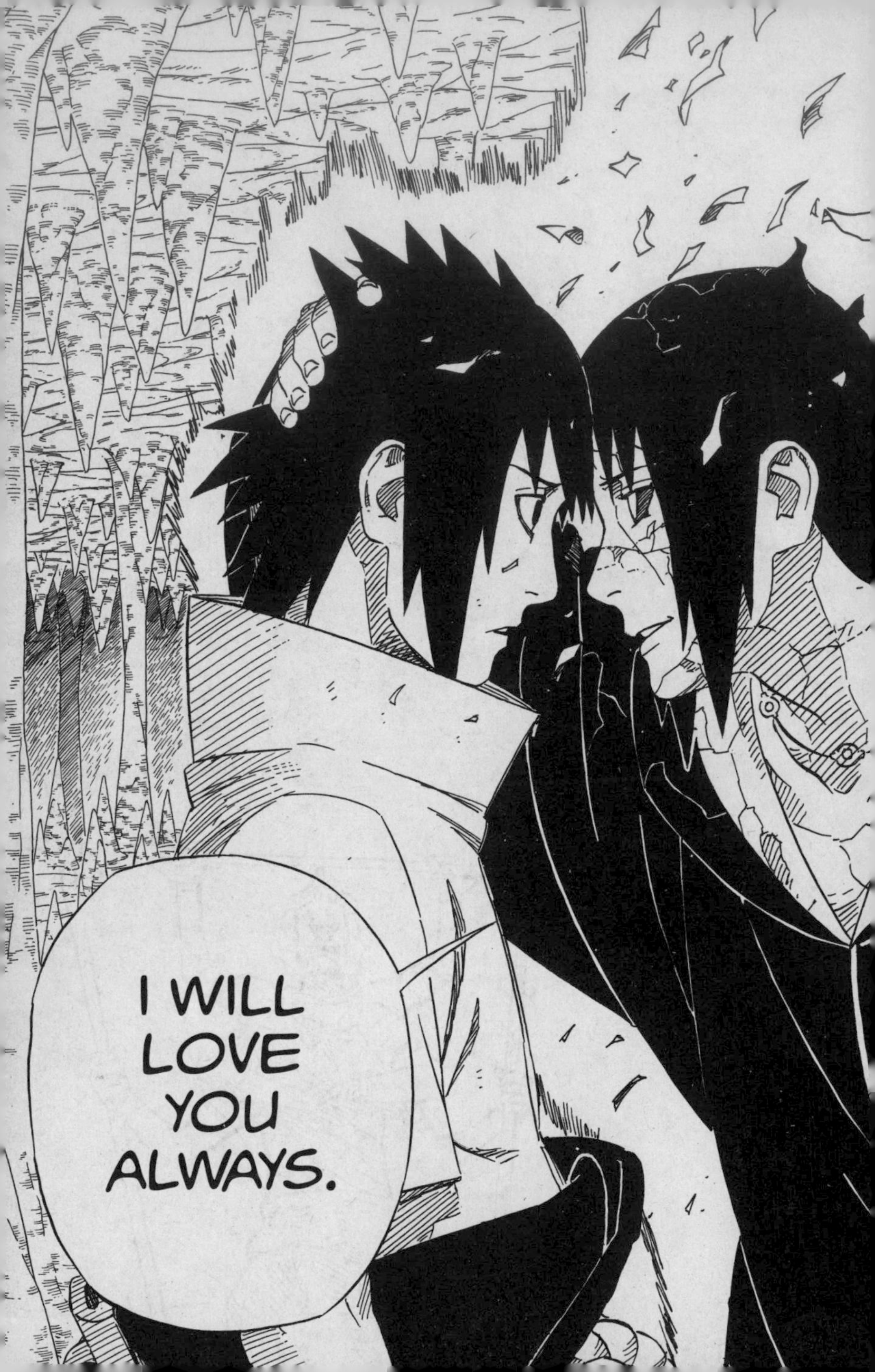
I WILL LOVE YOU ALWAYS.

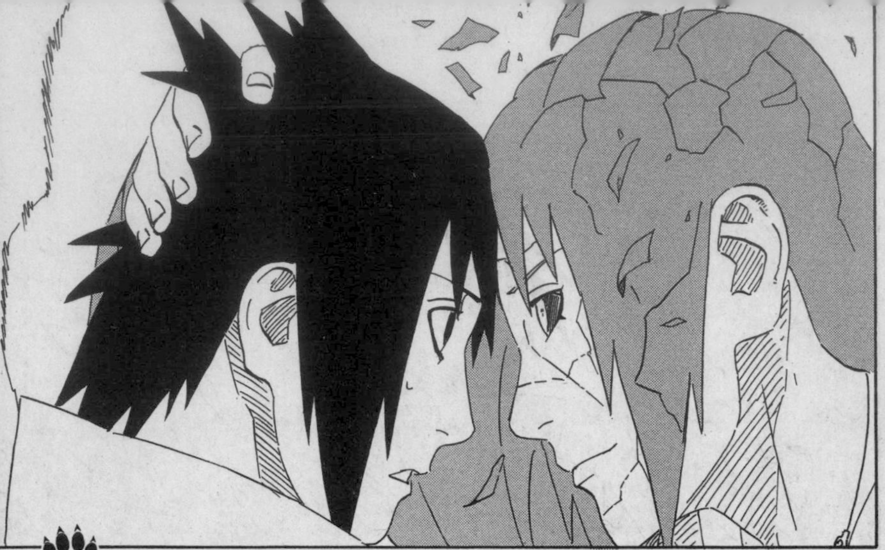

Number 591: Risk

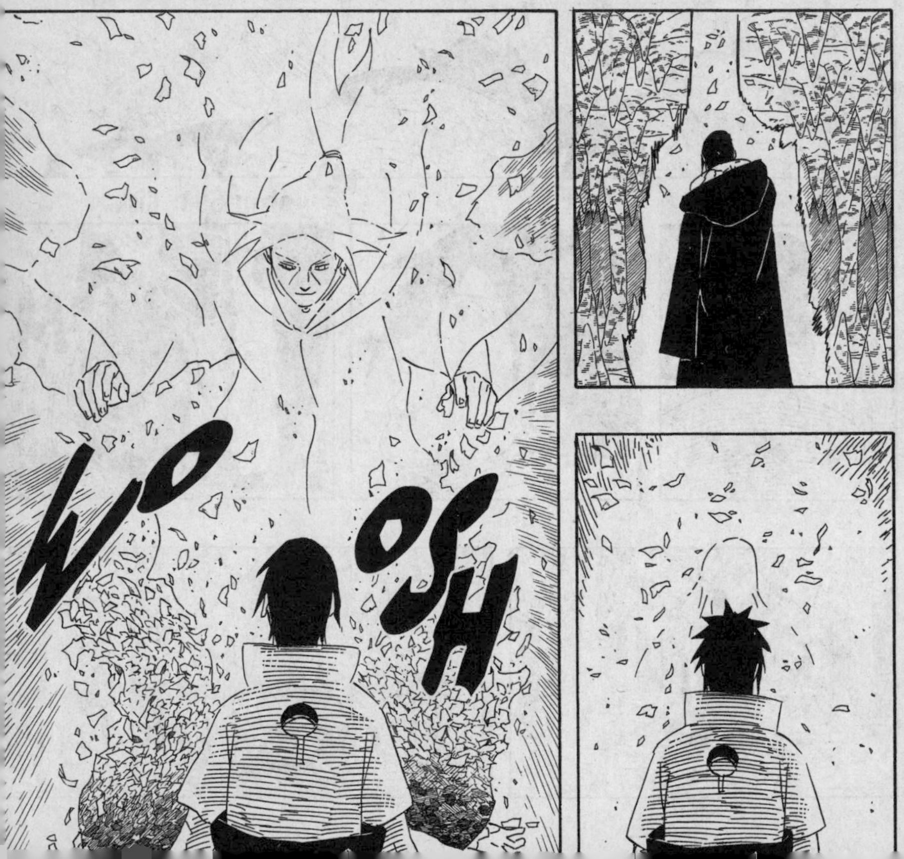
WOOSH

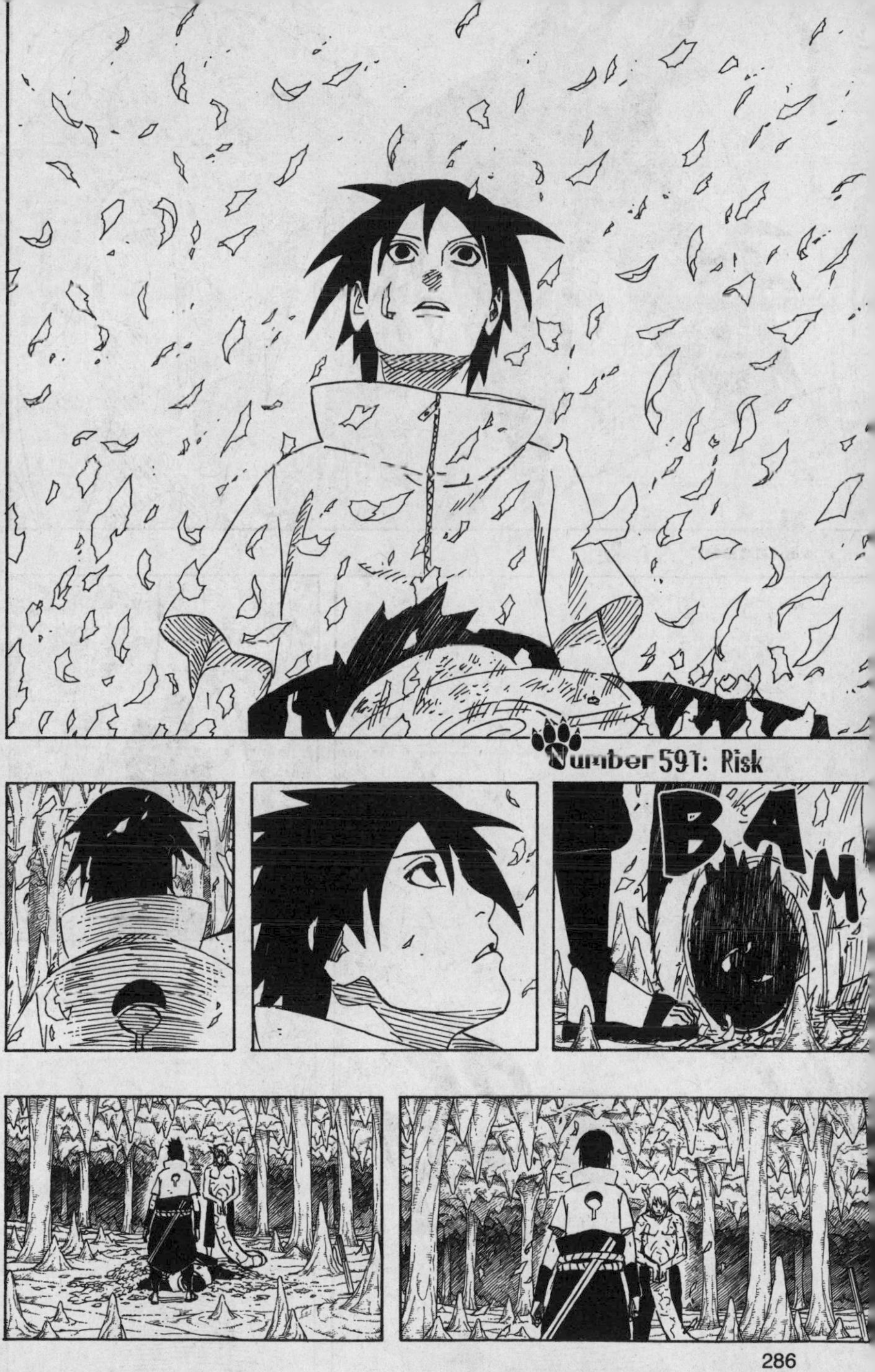
Number 591: Risk
BAM

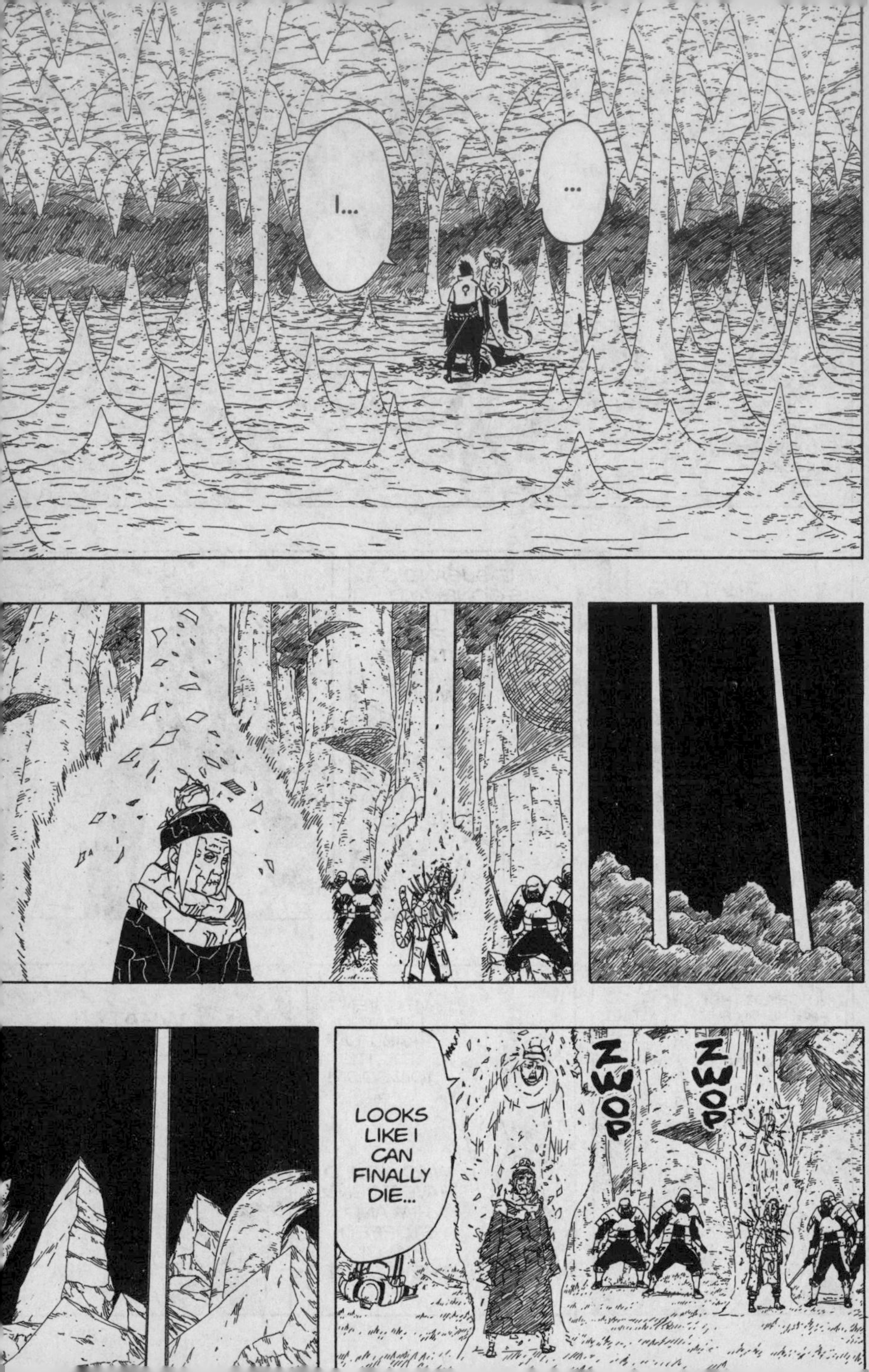
...
I...
ZWOP
ZWOP
LOOKS LIKE I CAN FINALLY DIE...

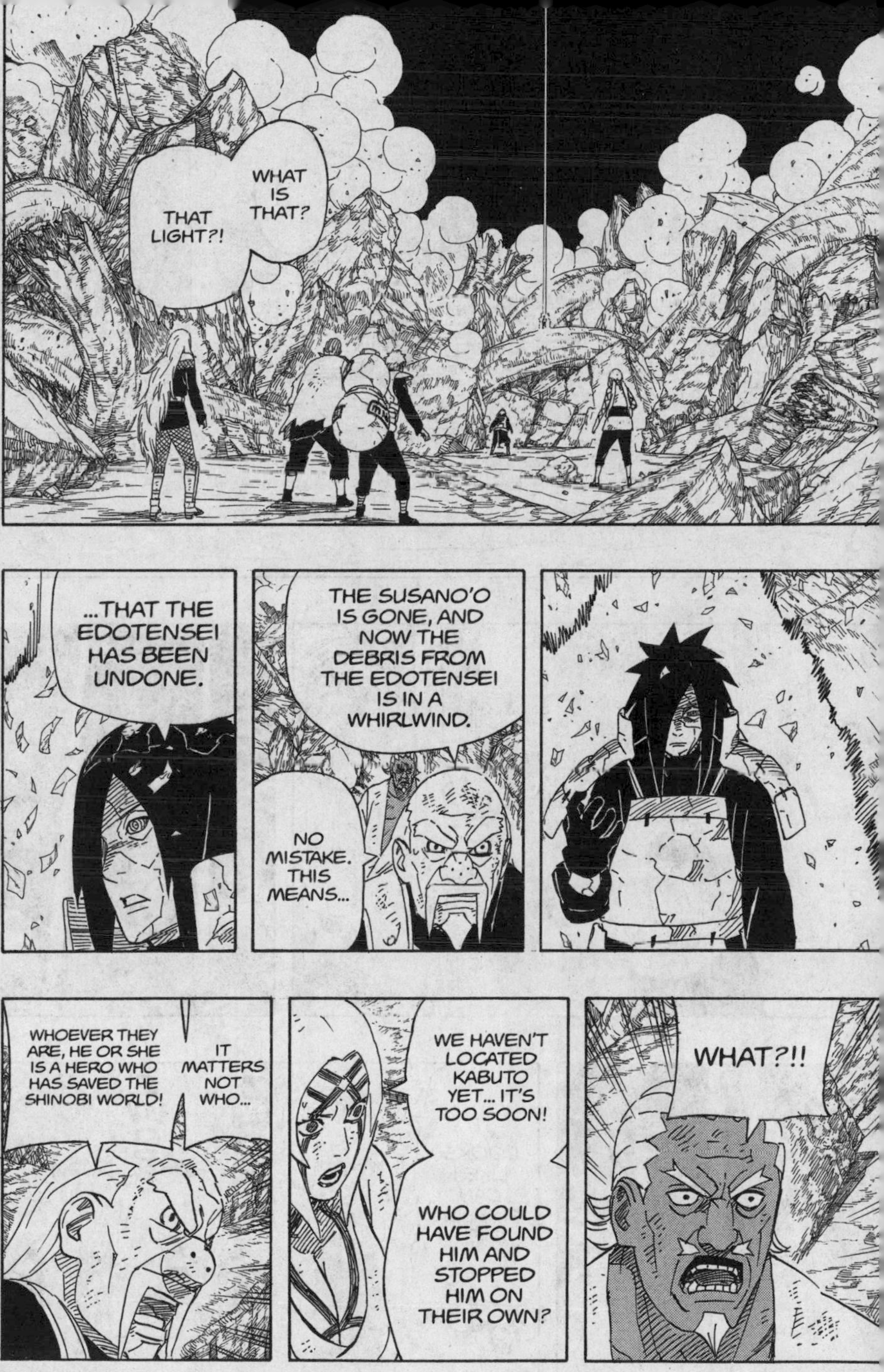
WHAT IS THAT?
THAT LIGHT?!
THE SUSANO'O IS GONE, AND NOW THE DEBRIS FROM THE EDOTENSEI IS IN A WHIRLWIND.
NO MISTAKE. THIS MEANS...
...THAT THE EDOTENSEI HAS BEEN UNDONE.
WHAT?!!
WE HAVEN'T LOCATED KABUTO YET... IT'S TOO SOON!
WHO COULD HAVE FOUND HIM AND STOPPED HIM ON THEIR OWN?
IT MATTERS NOT WHO...
WHOEVER THEY ARE, HE OR SHE IS A HERO WHO HAS SAVED THE SHINOBI WORLD!

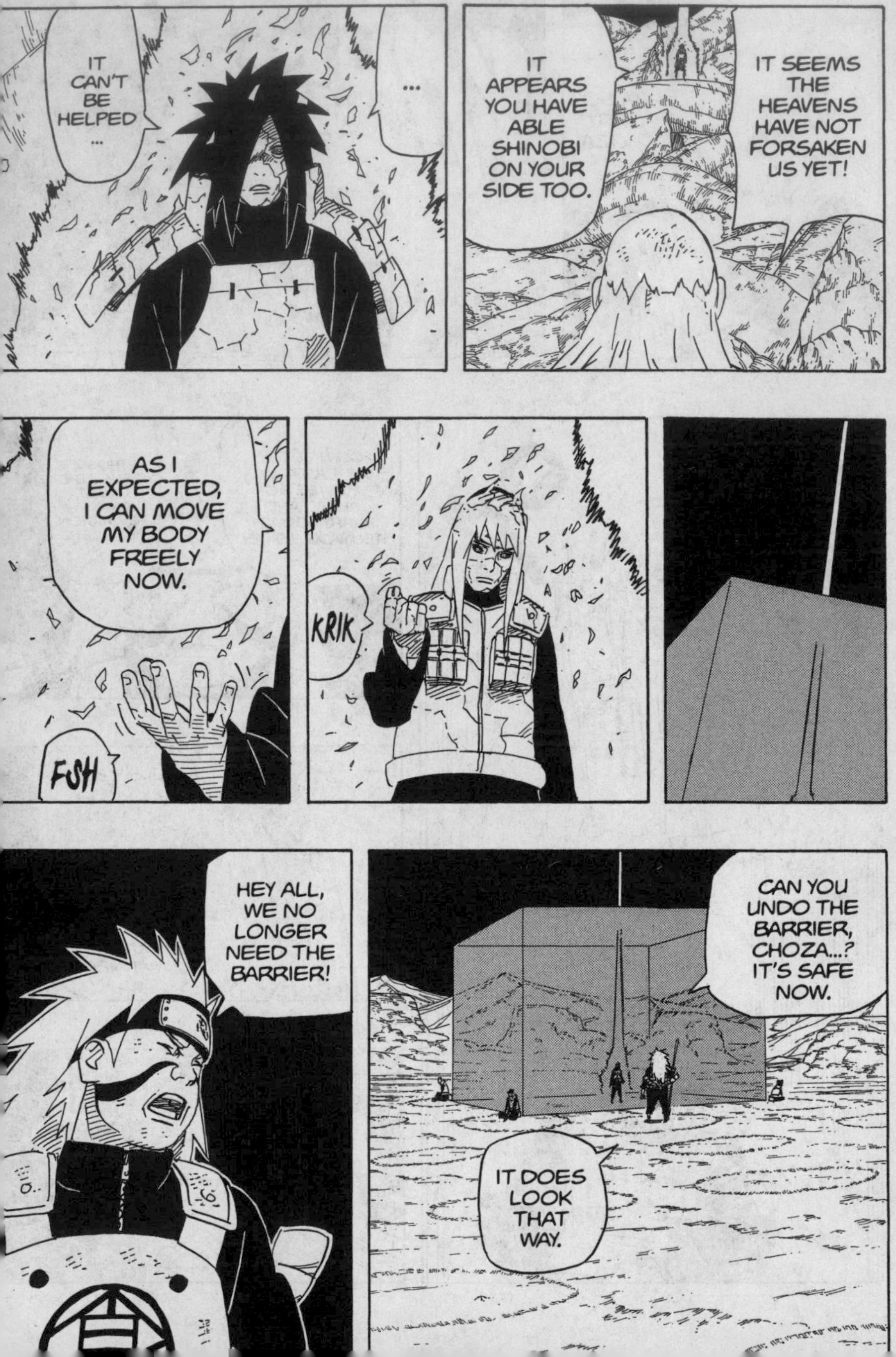
IT SEEMS THE HEAVENS HAVE NOT FORSAKEN US YET!
IT APPEARS YOU HAVE ABLE SHINOBI ON YOUR SIDE TOO.
...
IT CAN'T BE HELPED ...
KRIK
AS I EXPECTED, I CAN MOVE MY BODY FREELY NOW.
FSH
CAN YOU UNDO THE BARRIER, CHOZA...? IT'S SAFE NOW.
IT DOES LOOK THAT WAY.
HEY ALL, WE NO LONGER NEED THE BARRIER!

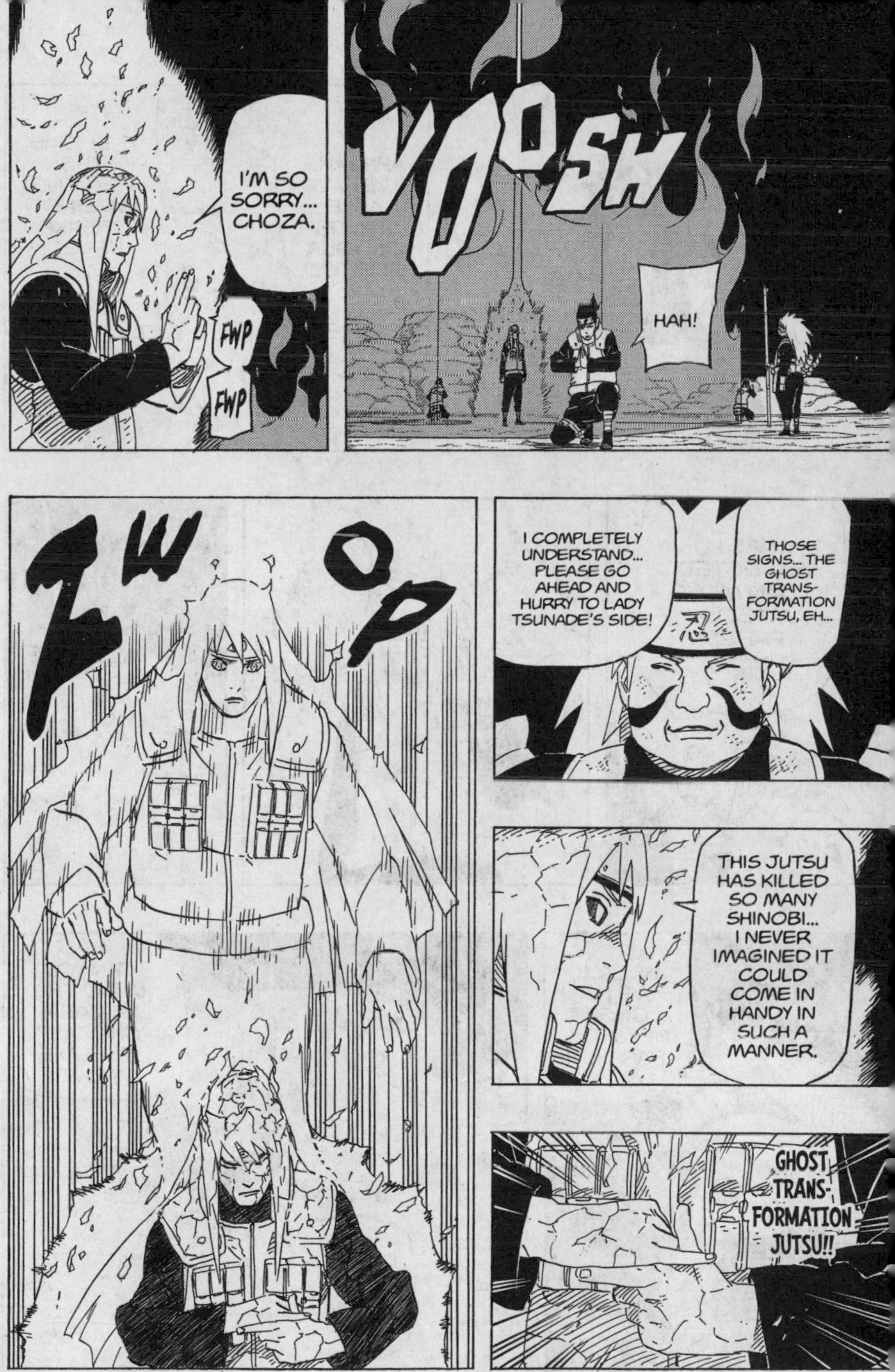
VOOSH
HAH!
I'M SO SORRY... CHOZA.
FWP
FWP
THOSE SIGNS... THE GHOST TRANSFORMATION JUTSU, EH...
I COMPLETELY UNDERSTAND... PLEASE GO AHEAD AND HURRY TO LADY TSUNADE'S SIDE!
THIS JUTSU HAS KILLED SO MANY SHINOBI... I NEVER IMAGINED IT COULD COME IN HANDY IN SUCH A MANNER.
GHOST TRANSFORMATION JUTSU!!
ZWOP

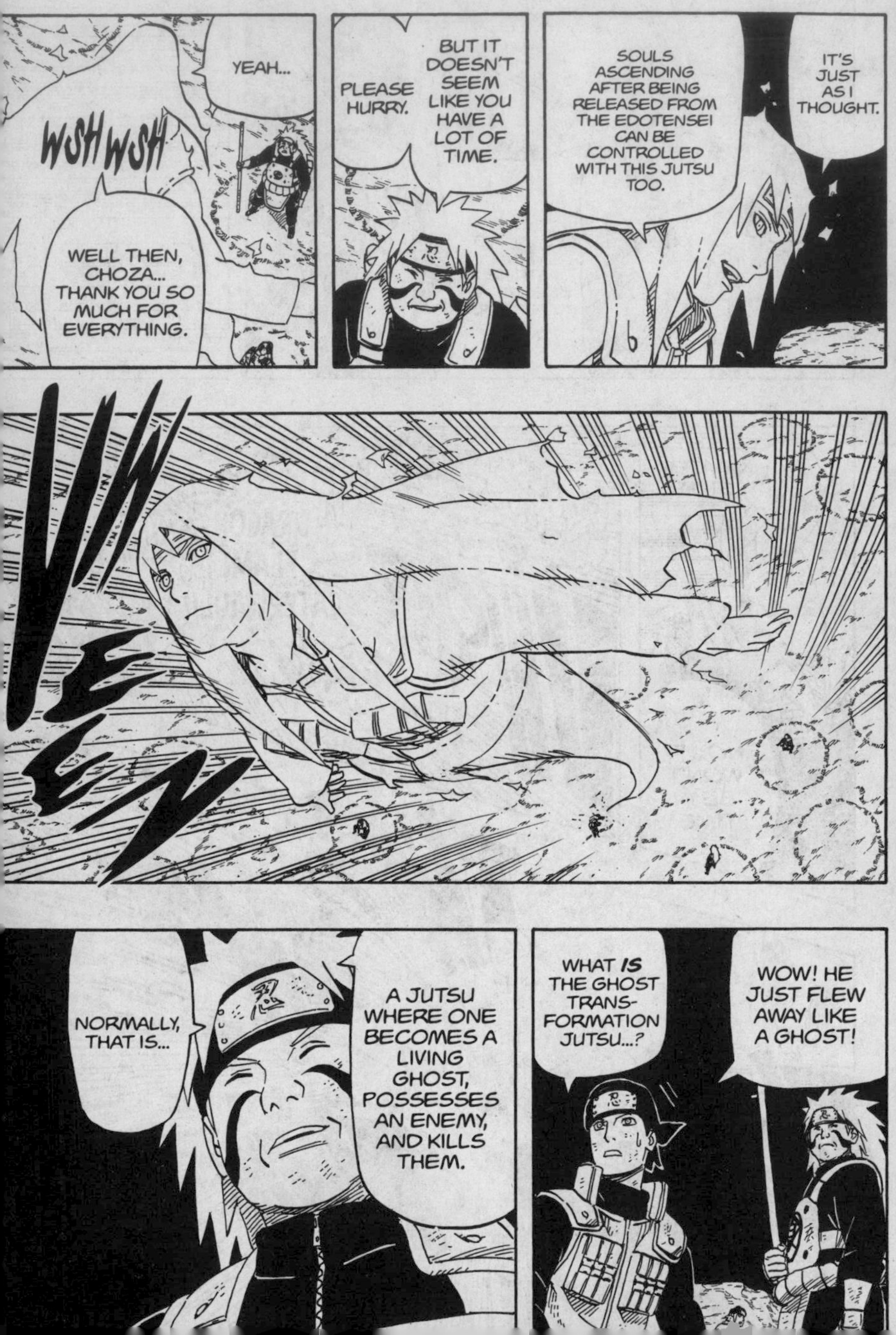
IT'S JUST AS I THOUGHT.
SOULS ASCENDING AFTER BEING RELEASED FROM THE EDOTENSEI CAN BE CONTROLLED WITH THIS JUTSU TOO.
BUT IT DOESN'T SEEM LIKE YOU HAVE A LOT OF TIME.
PLEASE HURRY.
YEAH...
WSH WSH
WELL THEN, CHOZA... THANK YOU SO MUCH FOR EVERYTHING.
VWEEN
WOW! HE JUST FLEW AWAY LIKE A GHOST!
WHAT *IS* THE GHOST TRANS-FORMATION JUTSU...?
A JUTSU WHERE ONE BECOMES A LIVING GHOST, POSSESSES AN ENEMY, AND KILLS THEM.
NORMALLY, THAT IS...

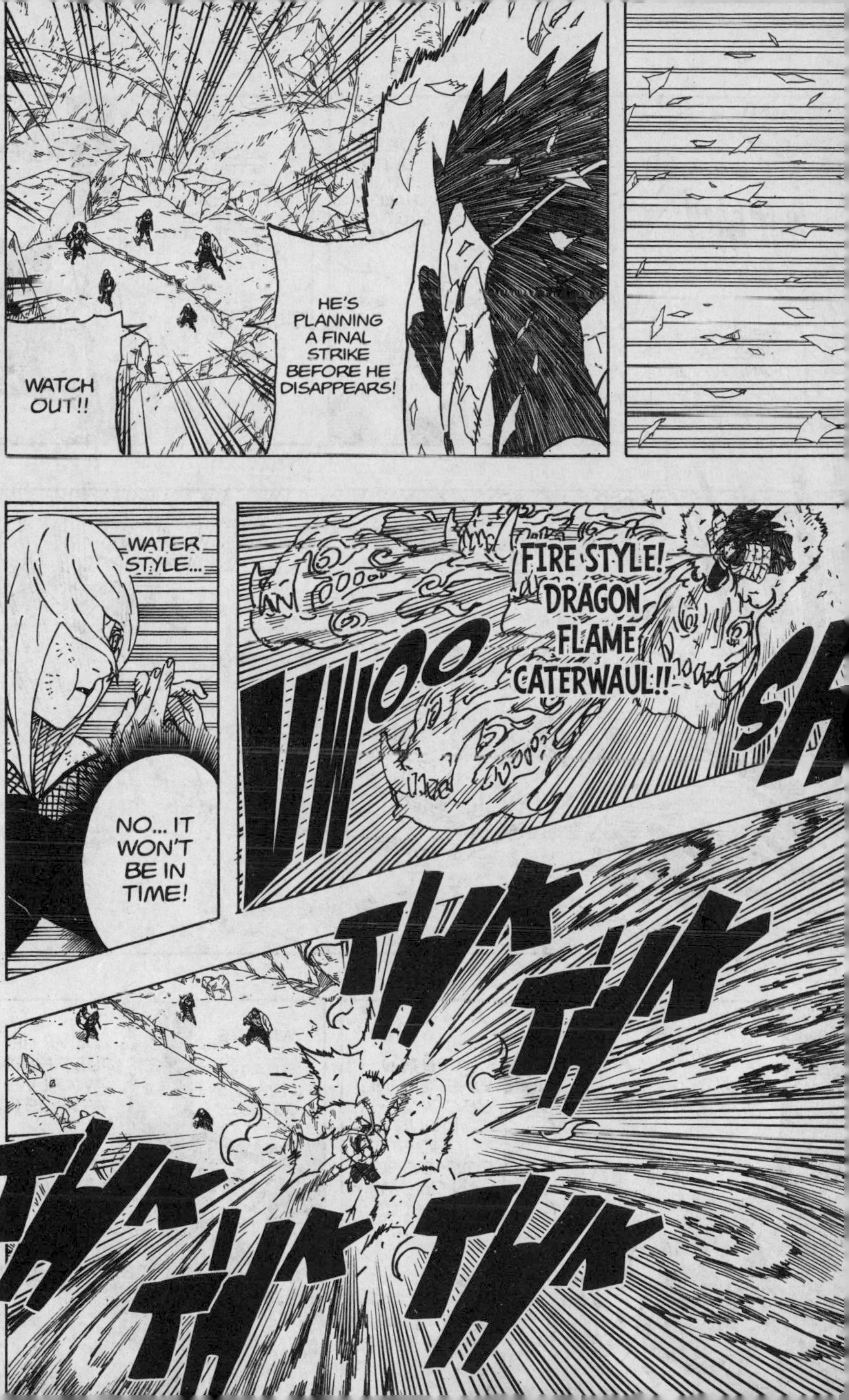
HE'S PLANNING A FINAL STRIKE BEFORE HE DISAPPEARS!
WATCH OUT!!
FIRE STYLE! DRAGON FLAME CATERWAUL!!
VWOO
SH
WATER STYLE...
NO... IT WON'T BE IN TIME!
THA THA THA
THA THA THA THA

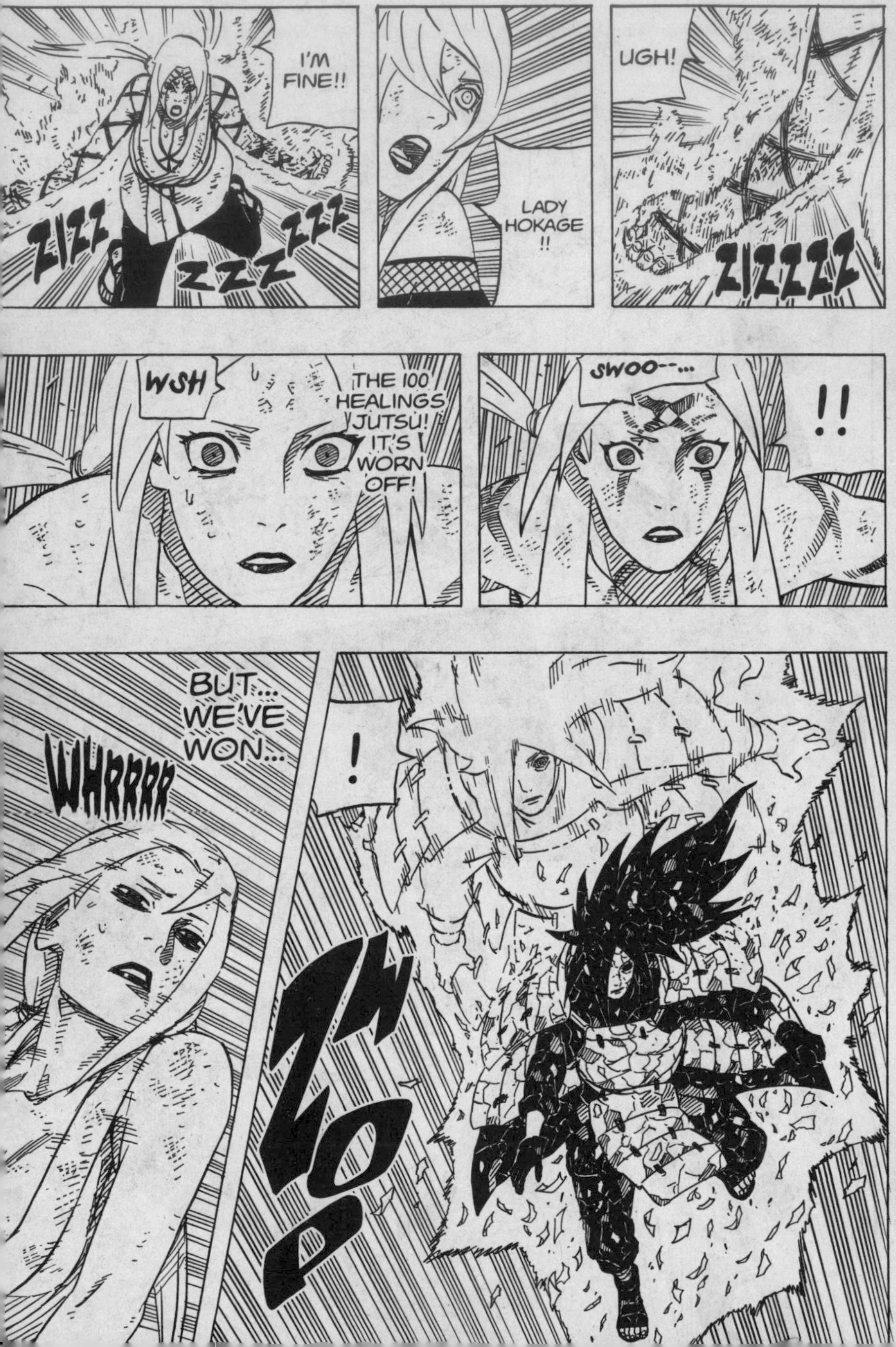
UGH!
ZIZZZZ
LADY HOKAGE !!
I'M FINE!!
ZIZZ
ZZZ
ZZZ
SWOO--...
!!
WSH
THE 100 HEALINGS JUTSU! IT'S WORN OFF!
!
BUT... WE'VE WON...
WHRRRR

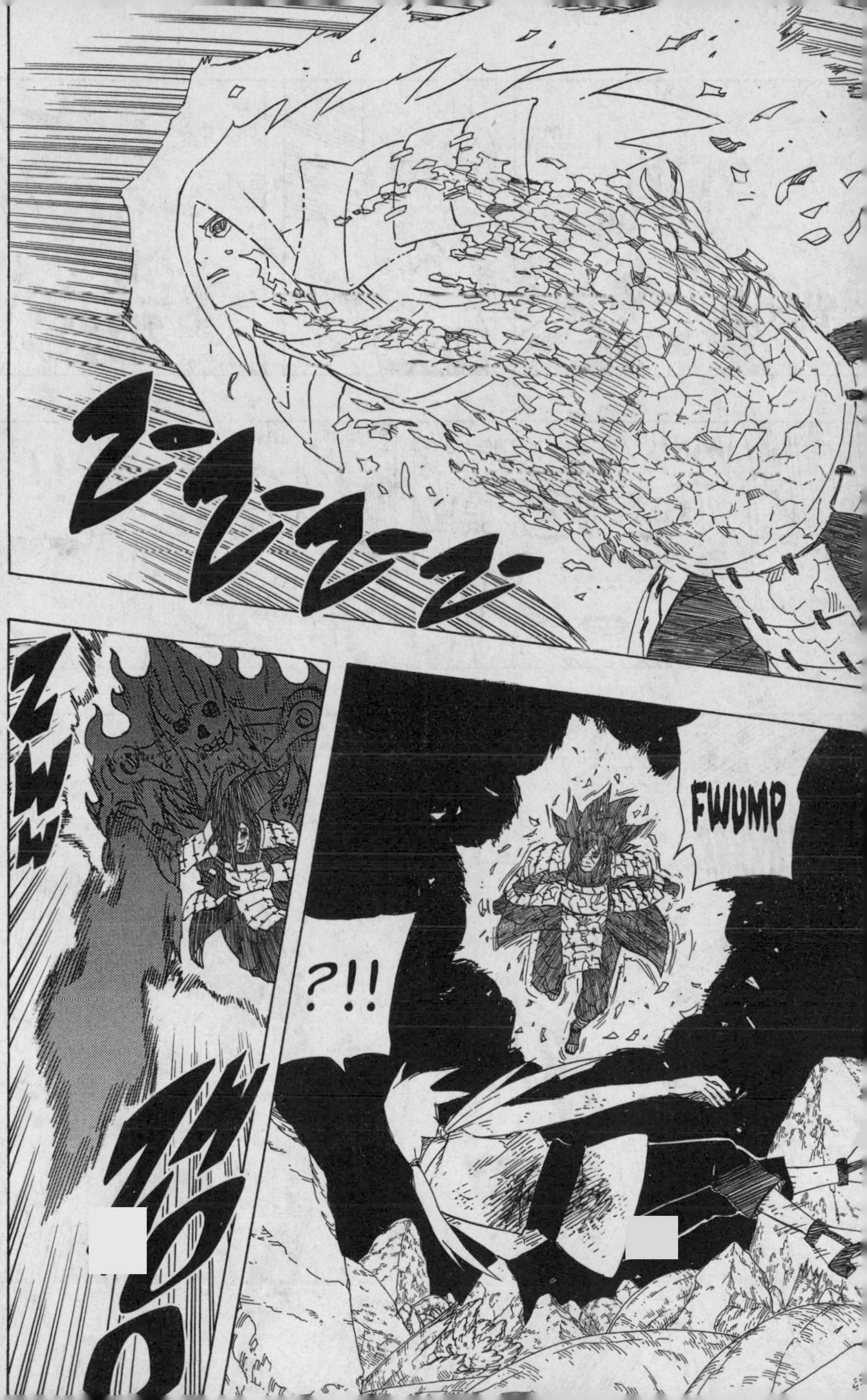
FWUMP
?!!

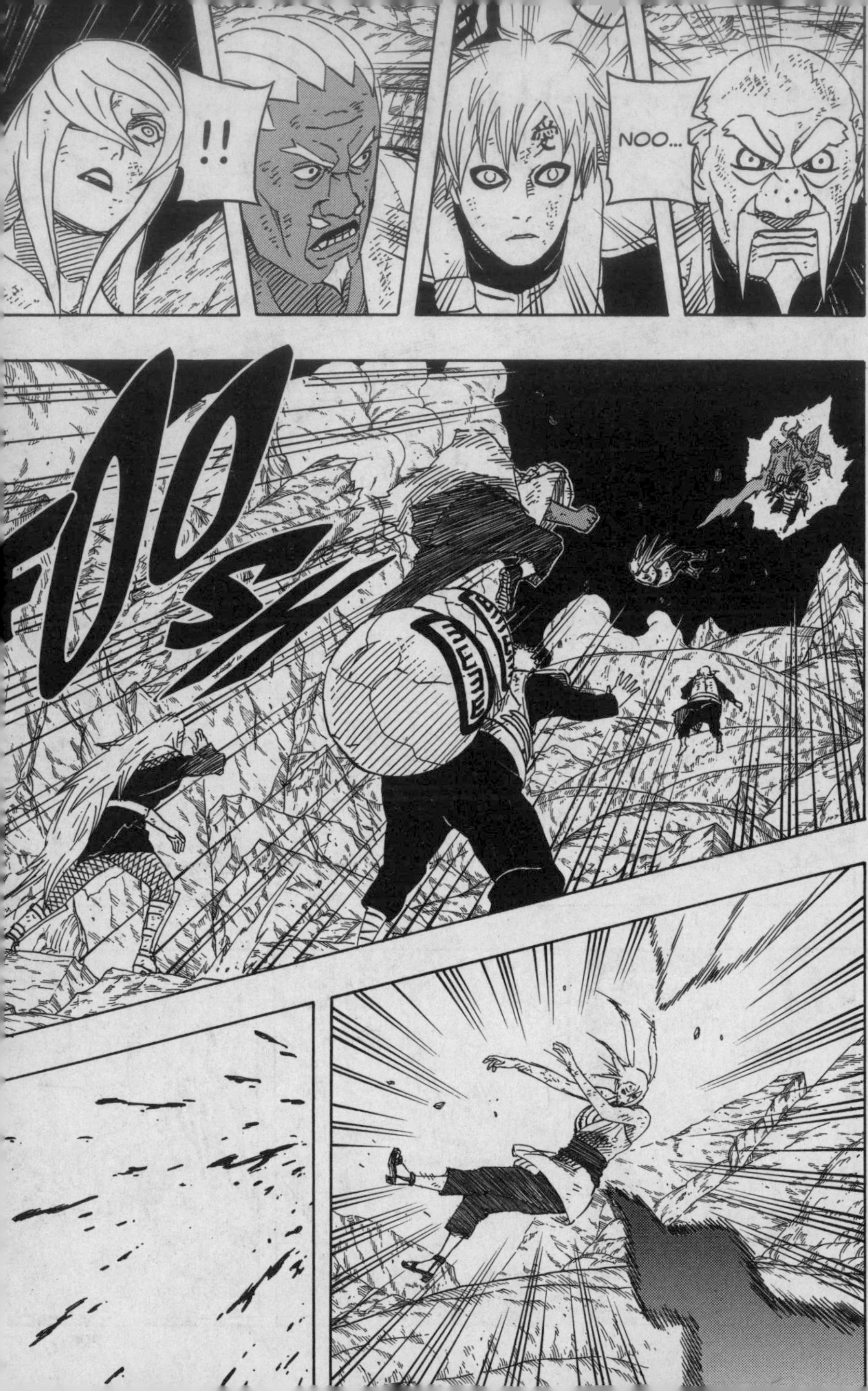
NOO...
!!
FOOSH

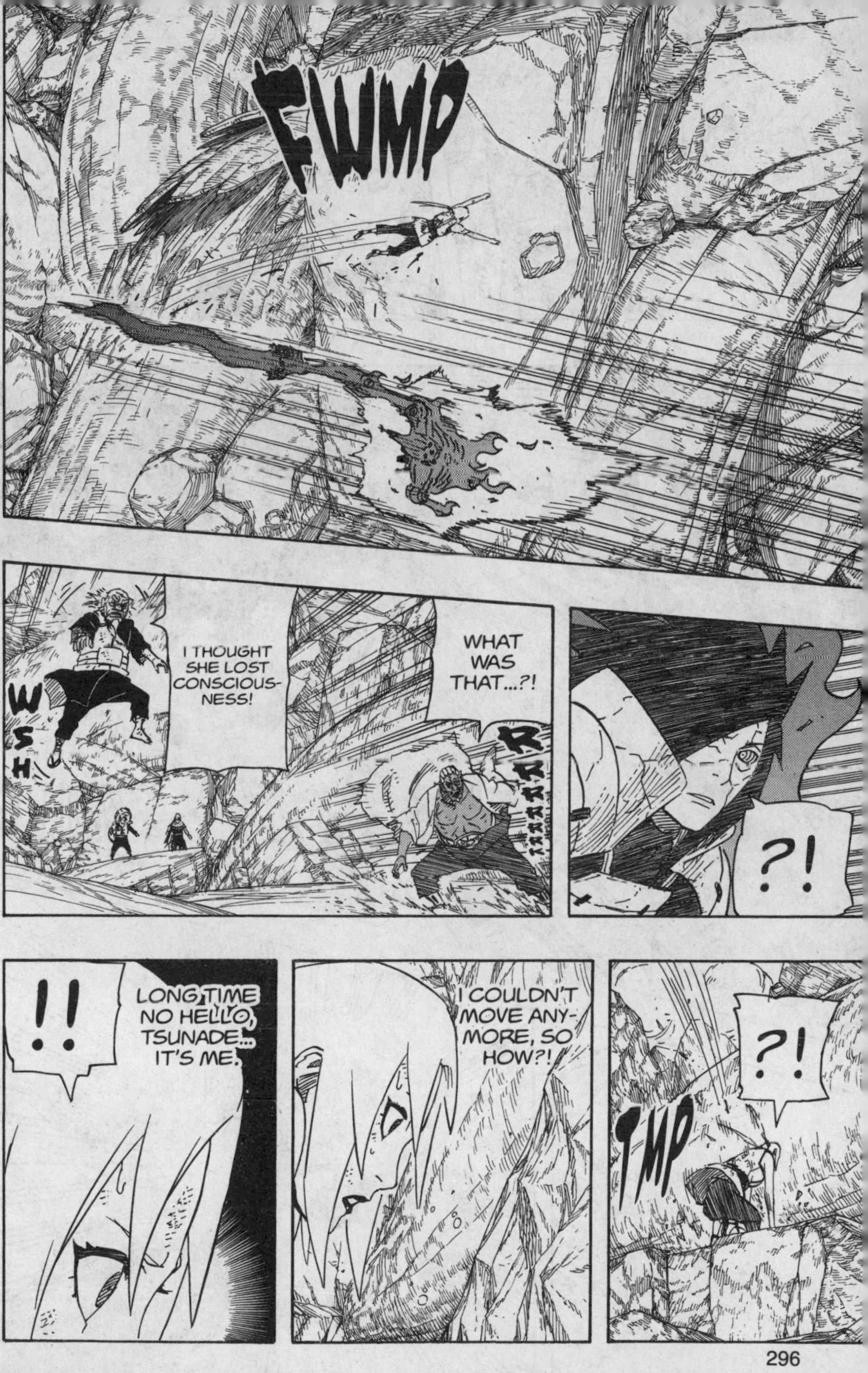
FWUMP
?!
WHAT WAS THAT...?!
RRRRRRRR
I THOUGHT SHE LOST CONSCIOUS-NESS!
WSH
?!
TMP
I COULDN'T MOVE ANY-MORE, SO HOW?!
LONG TIME NO HELLO, TSUNADE... IT'S ME.
!!

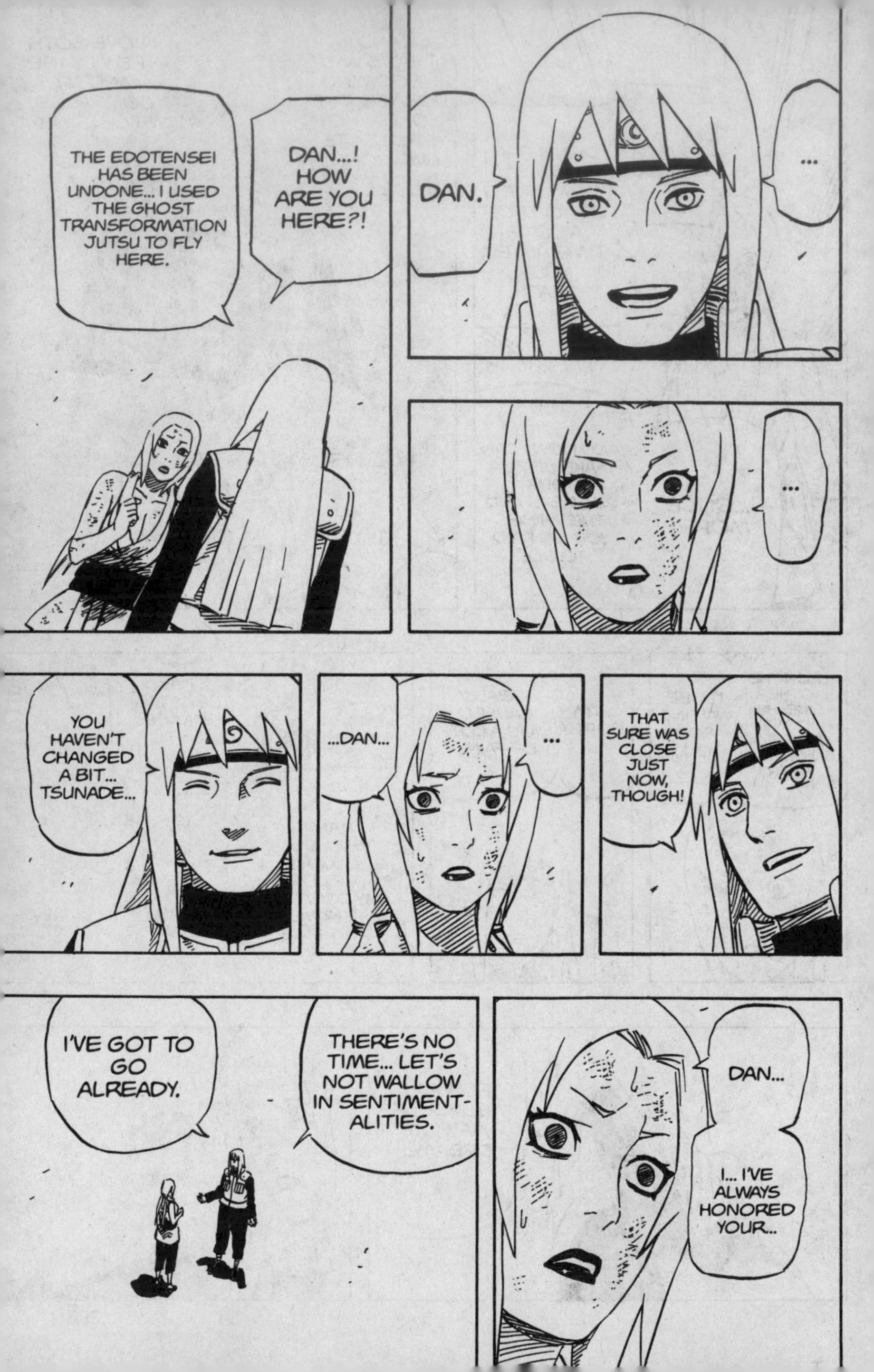
...
DAN.
...
DAN...! HOW ARE YOU HERE?!
THE EDOTENSEI HAS BEEN UNDONE... I USED THE GHOST TRANSFORMATION JUTSU TO FLY HERE.
THAT SURE WAS CLOSE JUST NOW, THOUGH!
...
...DAN...
YOU HAVEN'T CHANGED A BIT... TSUNADE...
DAN...
I... I'VE ALWAYS HONORED YOUR...
THERE'S NO TIME... LET'S NOT WALLOW IN SENTIMENT-ALITIES.
I'VE GOT TO GO ALREADY.

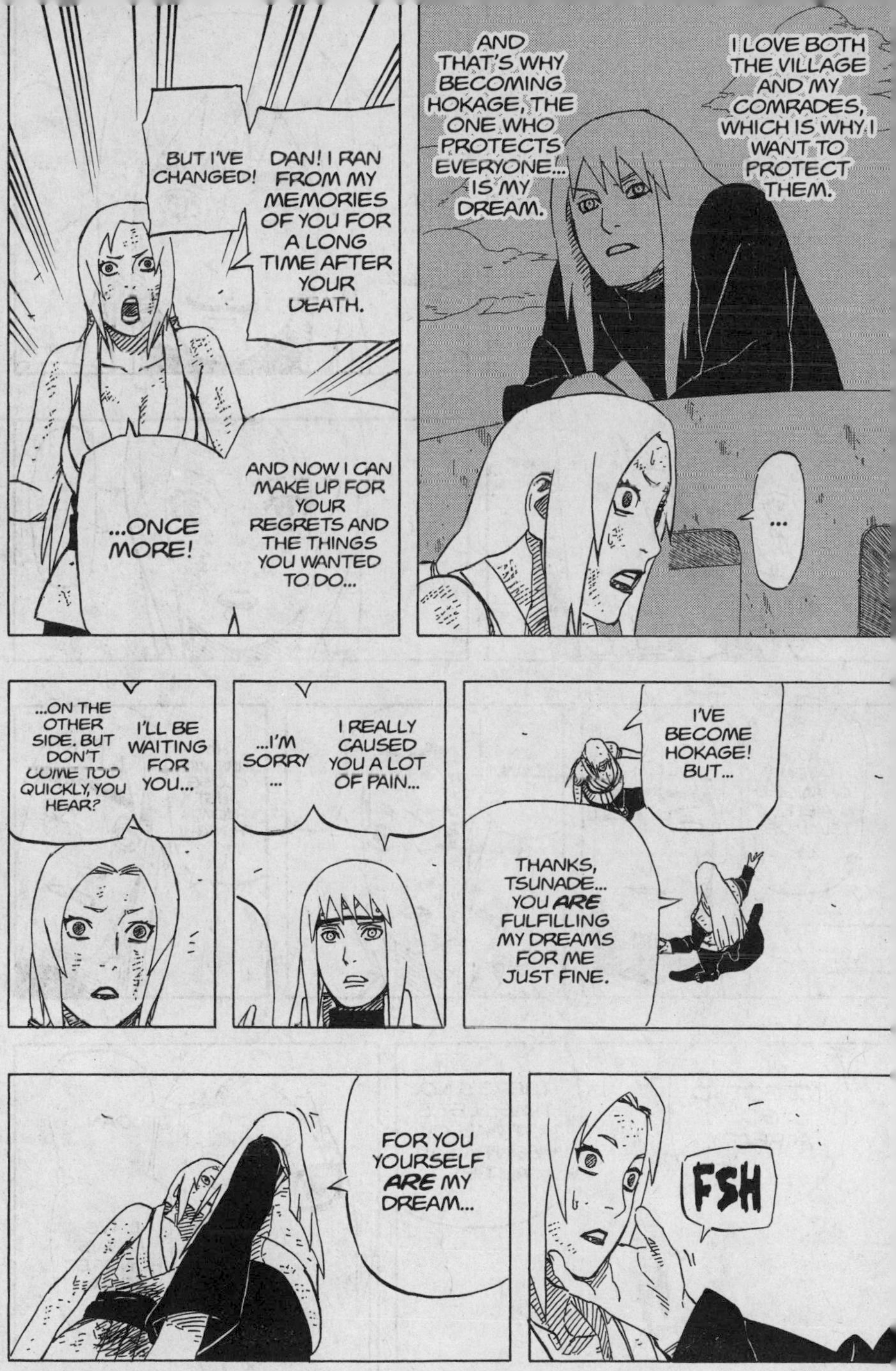
I LOVE BOTH THE VILLAGE AND MY COMRADES, WHICH IS WHY I WANT TO PROTECT THEM.
AND THAT'S WHY BECOMING HOKAGE, THE ONE WHO PROTECTS EVERYONE... IS MY DREAM.
...
DAN! I RAN FROM MY MEMORIES OF YOU FOR A LONG TIME AFTER YOUR DEATH.
BUT I'VE CHANGED!
AND NOW I CAN MAKE UP FOR YOUR REGRETS AND THE THINGS YOU WANTED TO DO...
...ONCE MORE!
I'VE BECOME HOKAGE! BUT...
THANKS, TSUNADE... YOU *ARE* FULFILLING MY DREAMS FOR ME JUST FINE.
I REALLY CAUSED YOU A LOT OF PAIN...
...I'M SORRY ...
I'LL BE WAITING FOR YOU...
...ON THE OTHER SIDE. BUT DON'T COME TOO QUICKLY, YOU HEAR?
FSH
FOR YOU YOURSELF *ARE* MY DREAM...

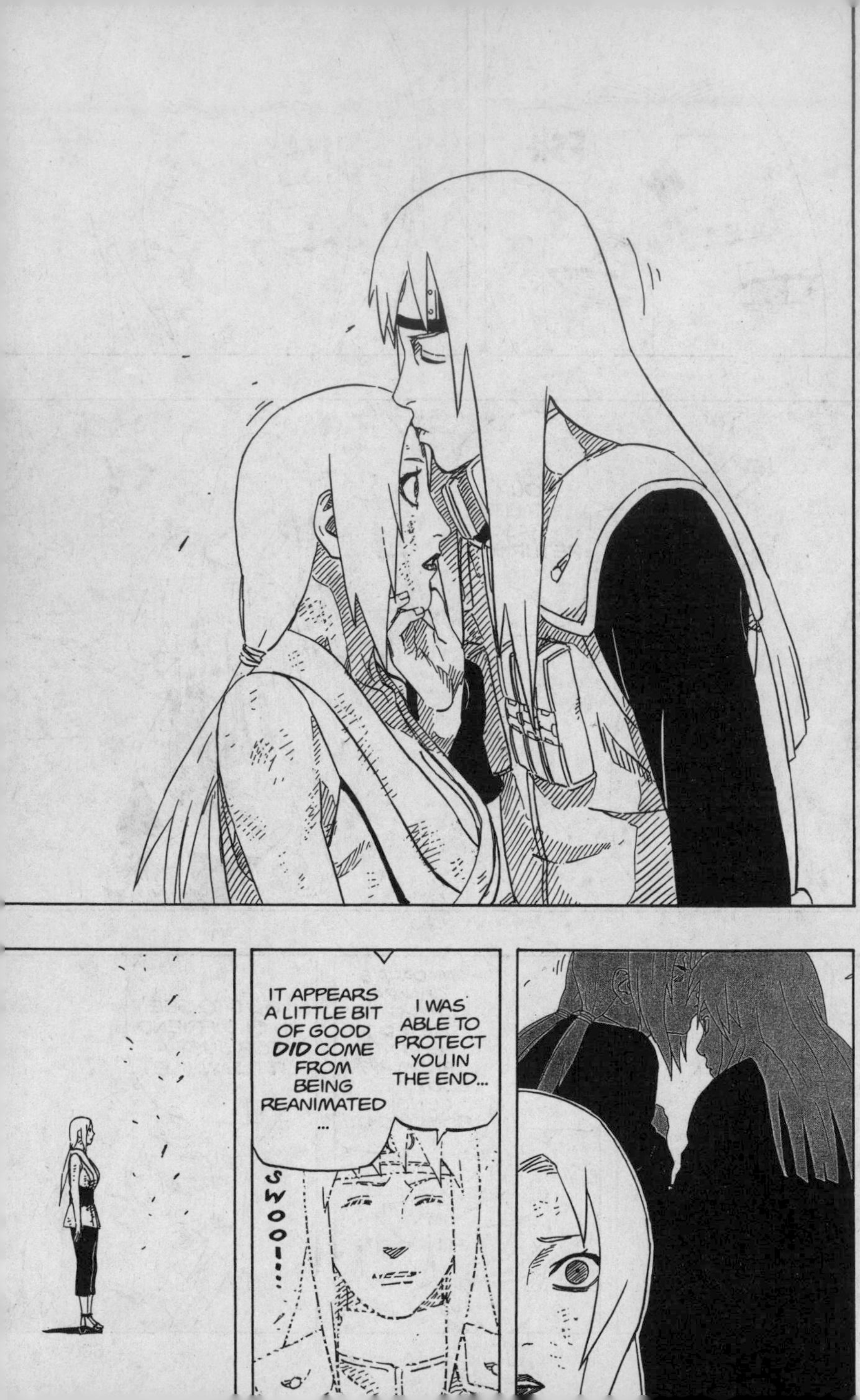
I WAS ABLE TO PROTECT YOU IN THE END...
IT APPEARS A LITTLE BIT OF GOOD DID COME FROM BEING REANIMATED ...
SWOO!!

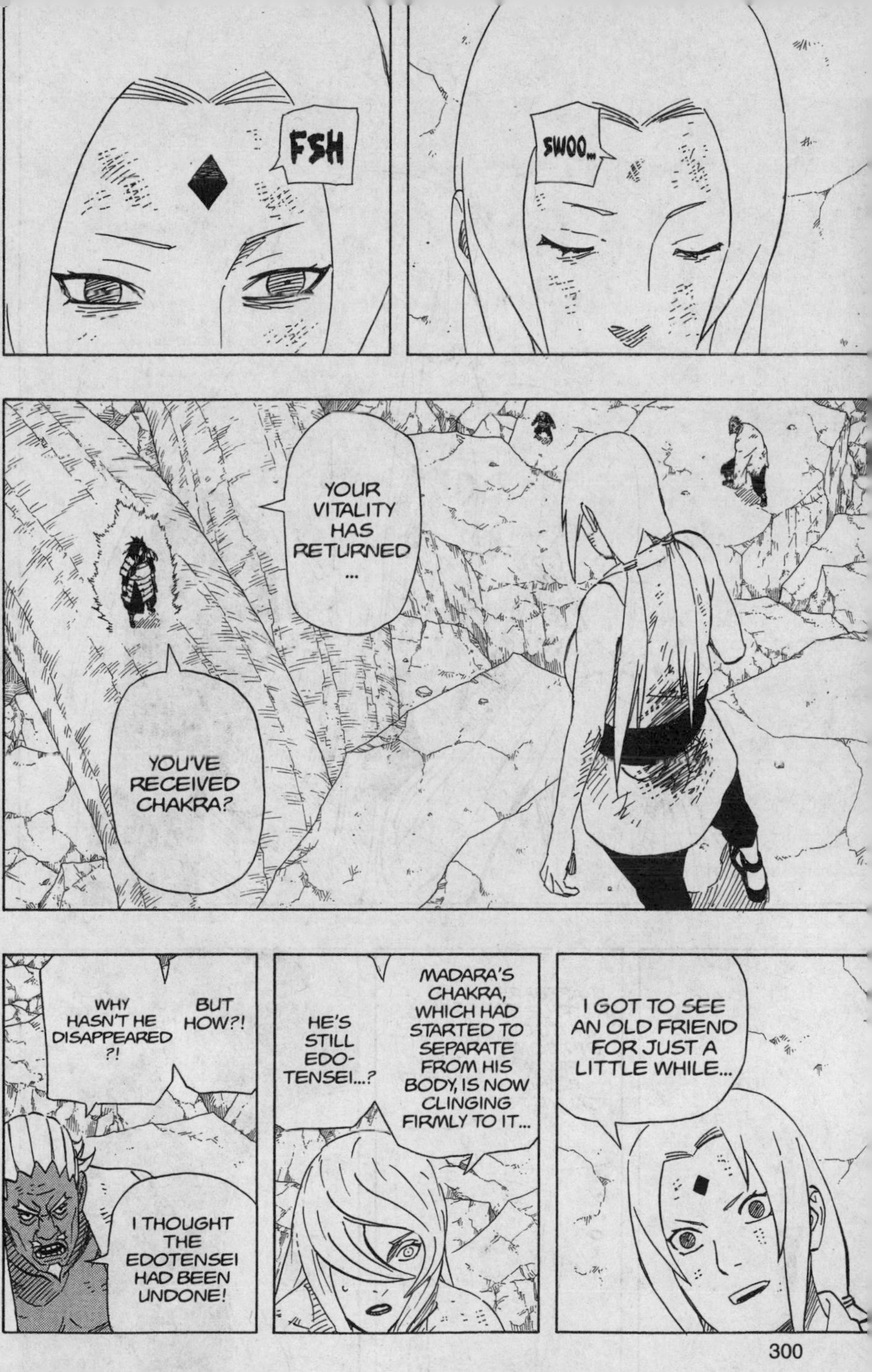
SWOO...
FSH
YOUR VITALITY HAS RETURNED ...
YOU'VE RECEIVED CHAKRA?
I GOT TO SEE AN OLD FRIEND FOR JUST A LITTLE WHILE...
MADARA'S CHAKRA, WHICH HAD STARTED TO SEPARATE FROM HIS BODY, IS NOW CLINGING FIRMLY TO IT...
HE'S STILL EDO-TENSEI...?
BUT HOW?!
WHY HASN'T HE DISAPPEARED?!
I THOUGHT THE EDOTENSEI HAD BEEN UNDONE!

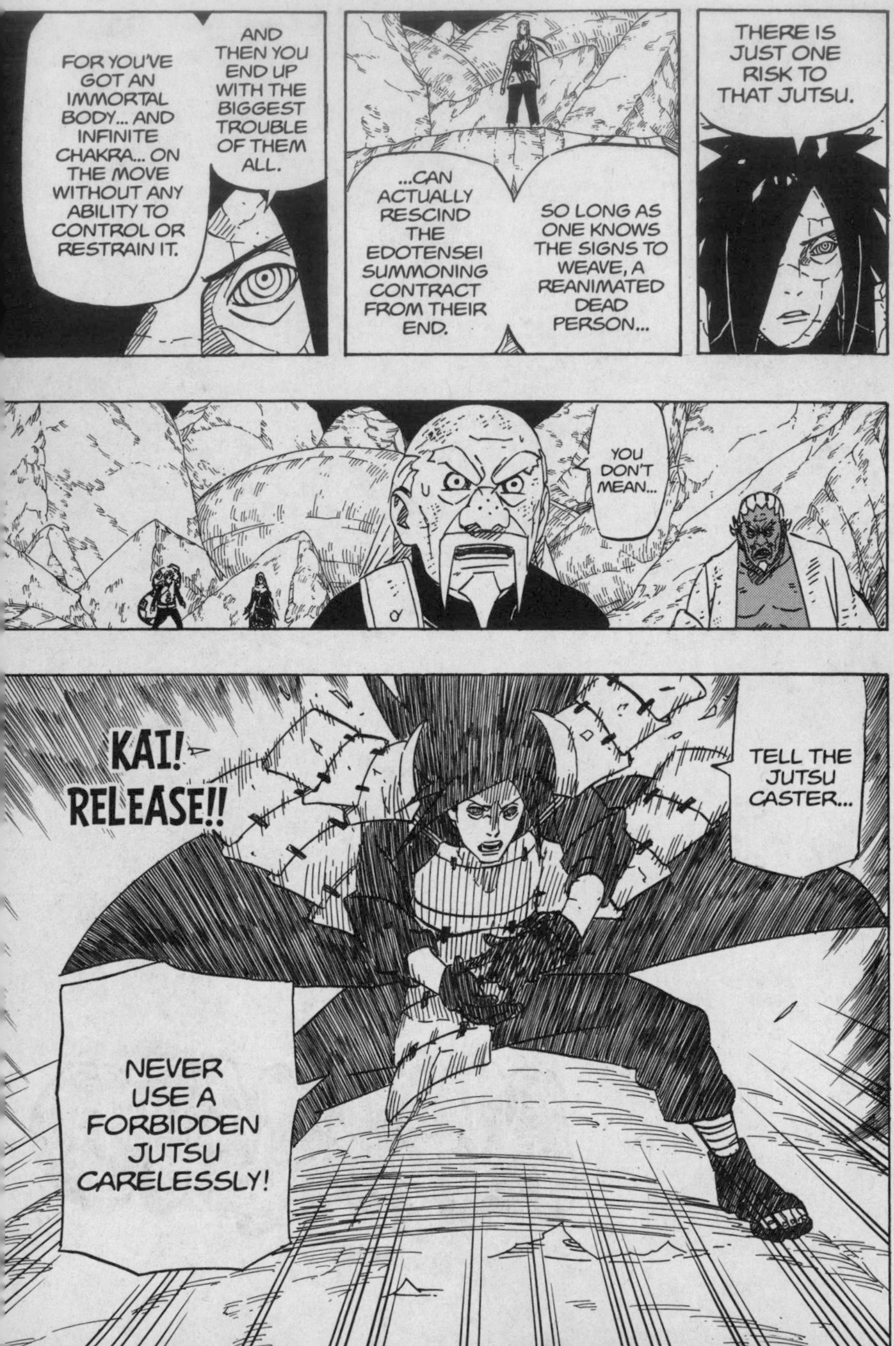
THERE IS JUST ONE RISK TO THAT JUTSU.
SO LONG AS ONE KNOWS THE SIGNS TO WEAVE, A REANIMATED DEAD PERSON...
...CAN ACTUALLY RESCIND THE EDOTENSEI SUMMONING CONTRACT FROM THEIR END.
FOR YOU'VE GOT AN IMMORTAL BODY... AND INFINITE CHAKRA... ON THE MOVE WITHOUT ANY ABILITY TO CONTROL OR RESTRAIN IT.
AND THEN YOU END UP WITH THE BIGGEST TROUBLE OF THEM ALL.
YOU DON'T MEAN...
TELL THE JUTSU CASTER...
KAI! RELEASE!!
NEVER USE A FORBIDDEN JUTSU CARELESSLY!

NARUTO

Number 592: A Third Force

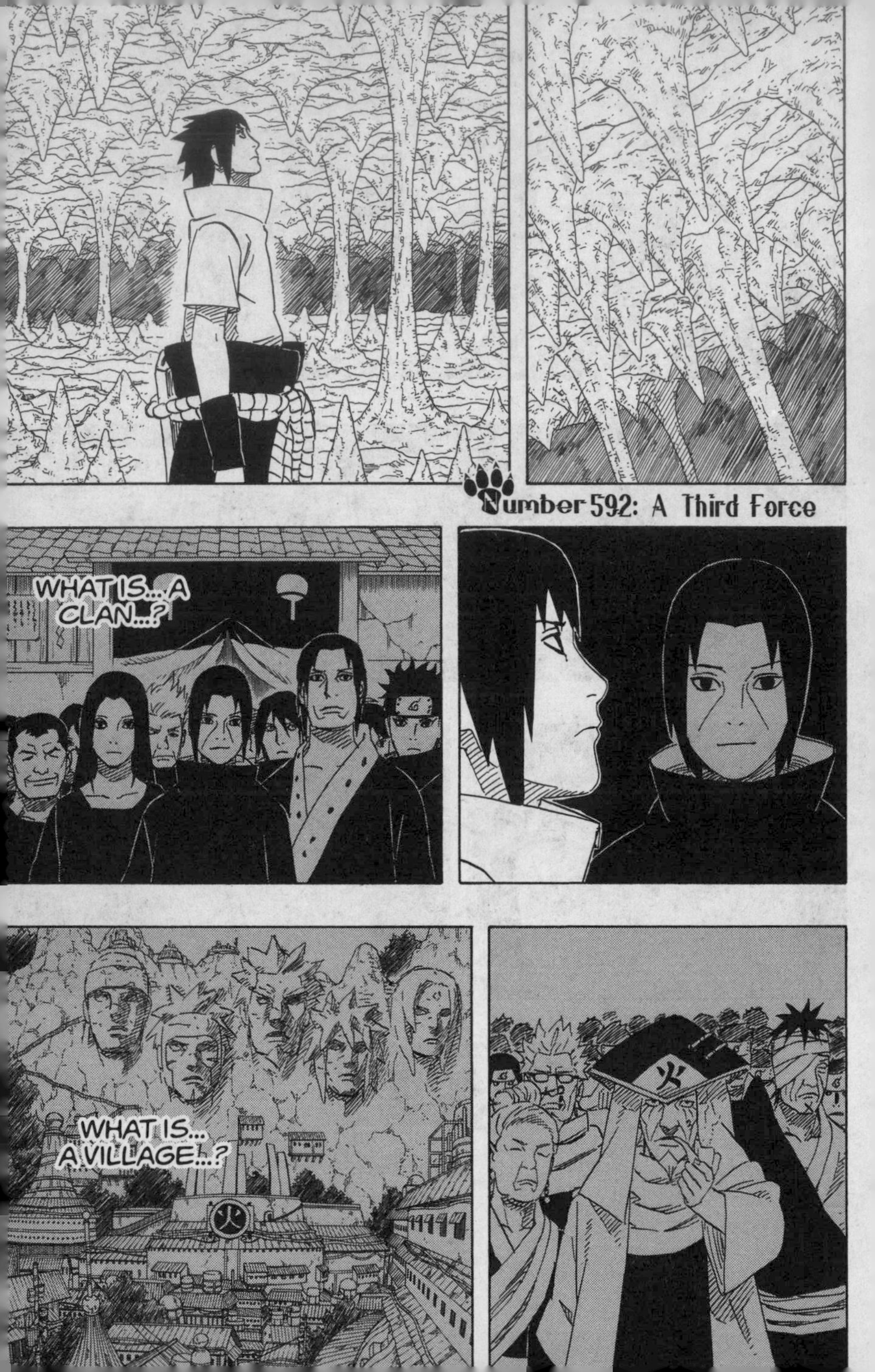
WHAT IS... A CLAN...?
WHAT IS... A VILLAGE...?

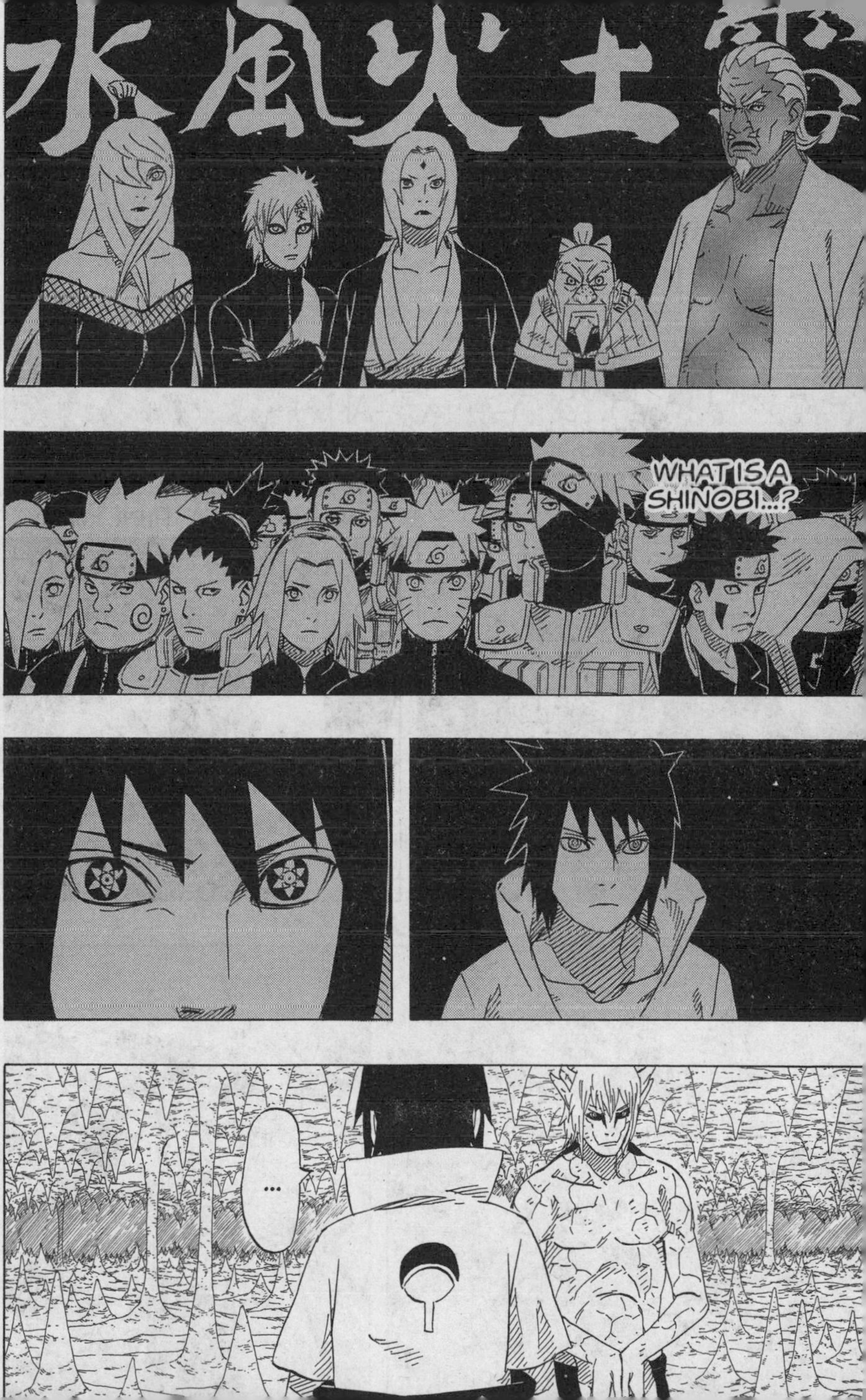
水風火土雷
WHAT IS A SHINOBI...?
...

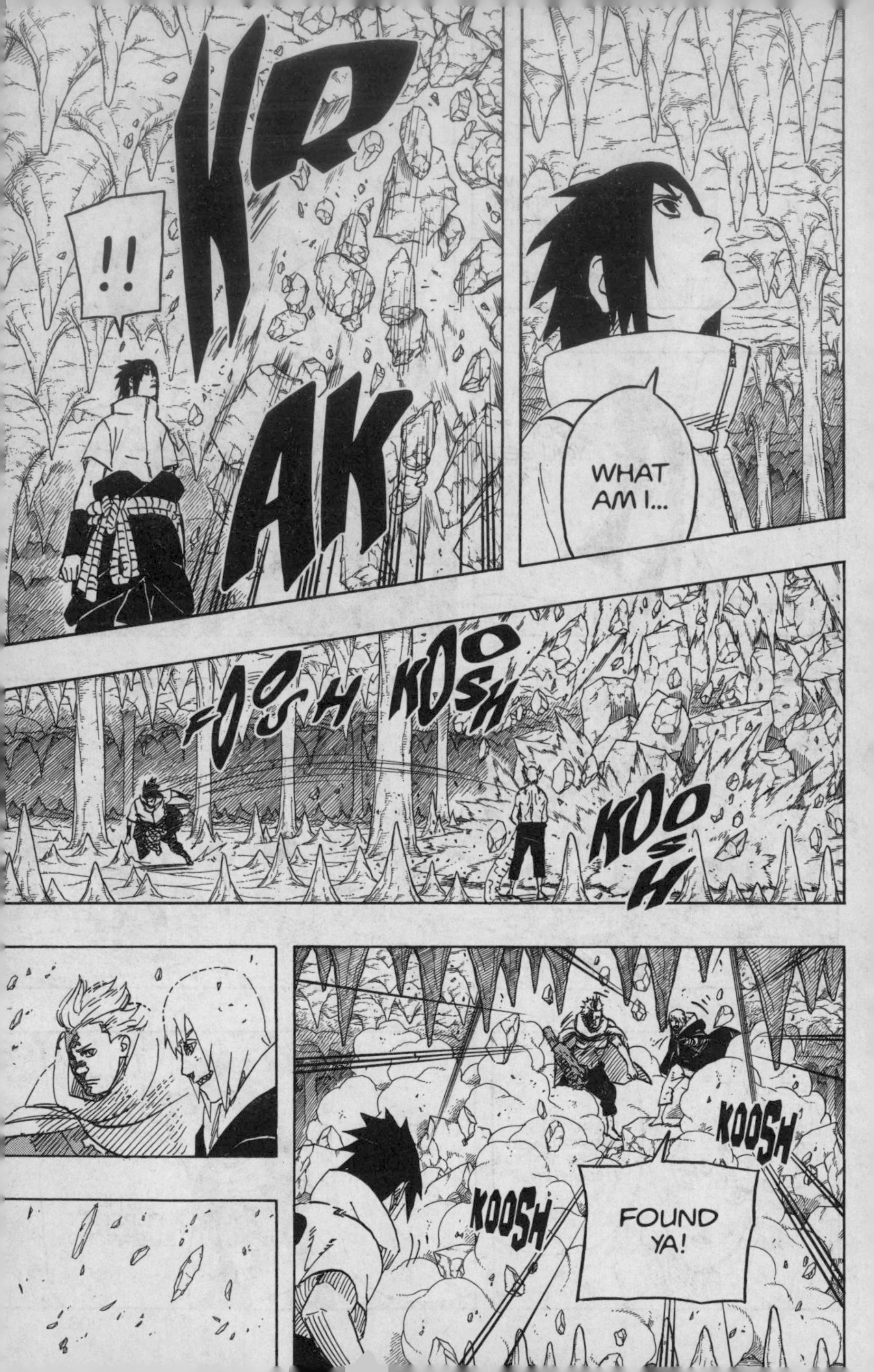
WHAT AM I...
!!
KRAK
KOOSH
FOOSH
KOOSH
KOOSH
FOUND YA!
KOOSH

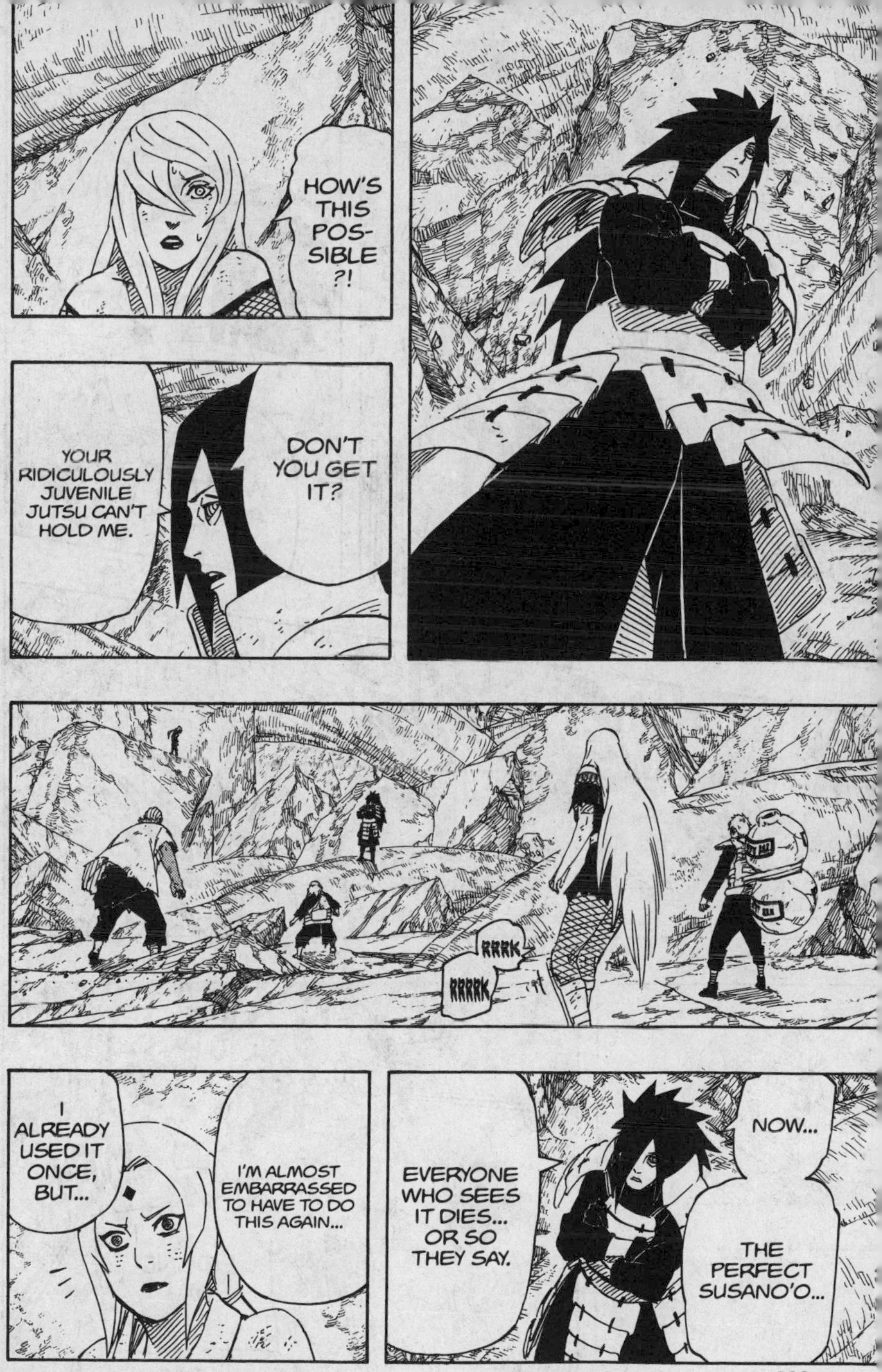
HOW'S THIS POSSIBLE?!
DON'T YOU GET IT?
YOUR RIDICULOUSLY JUVENILE JUTSU CAN'T HOLD ME.
RRRK
RRRRK
NOW...
THE PERFECT SUSANO'O...
EVERYONE WHO SEES IT DIES... OR SO THEY SAY.
I'M ALMOST EMBARRASSED TO HAVE TO DO THIS AGAIN...
I ALREADY USED IT ONCE, BUT...

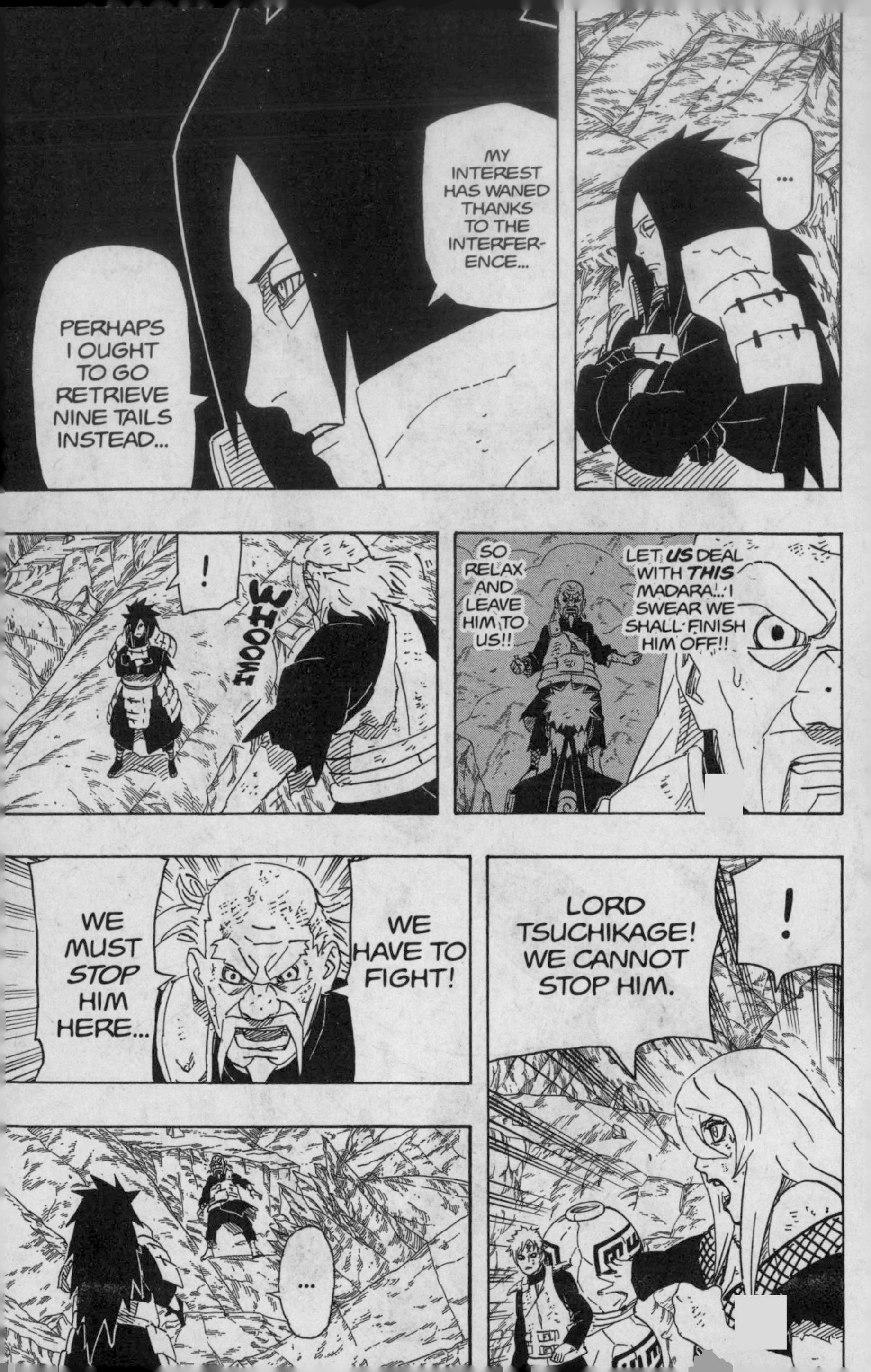
...
MY INTEREST HAS WANED THANKS TO THE INTERFERENCE...
PERHAPS I OUGHT TO GO RETRIEVE NINE TAILS INSTEAD...
LET US DEAL WITH THIS MADARA...! I SWEAR WE SHALL FINISH HIM OFF!!
SO RELAX AND LEAVE HIM TO US!!
!
WHOOSH
!
LORD TSUCHIKAGE! WE CANNOT STOP HIM.
WE HAVE TO FIGHT!
WE MUST STOP HIM HERE...
...

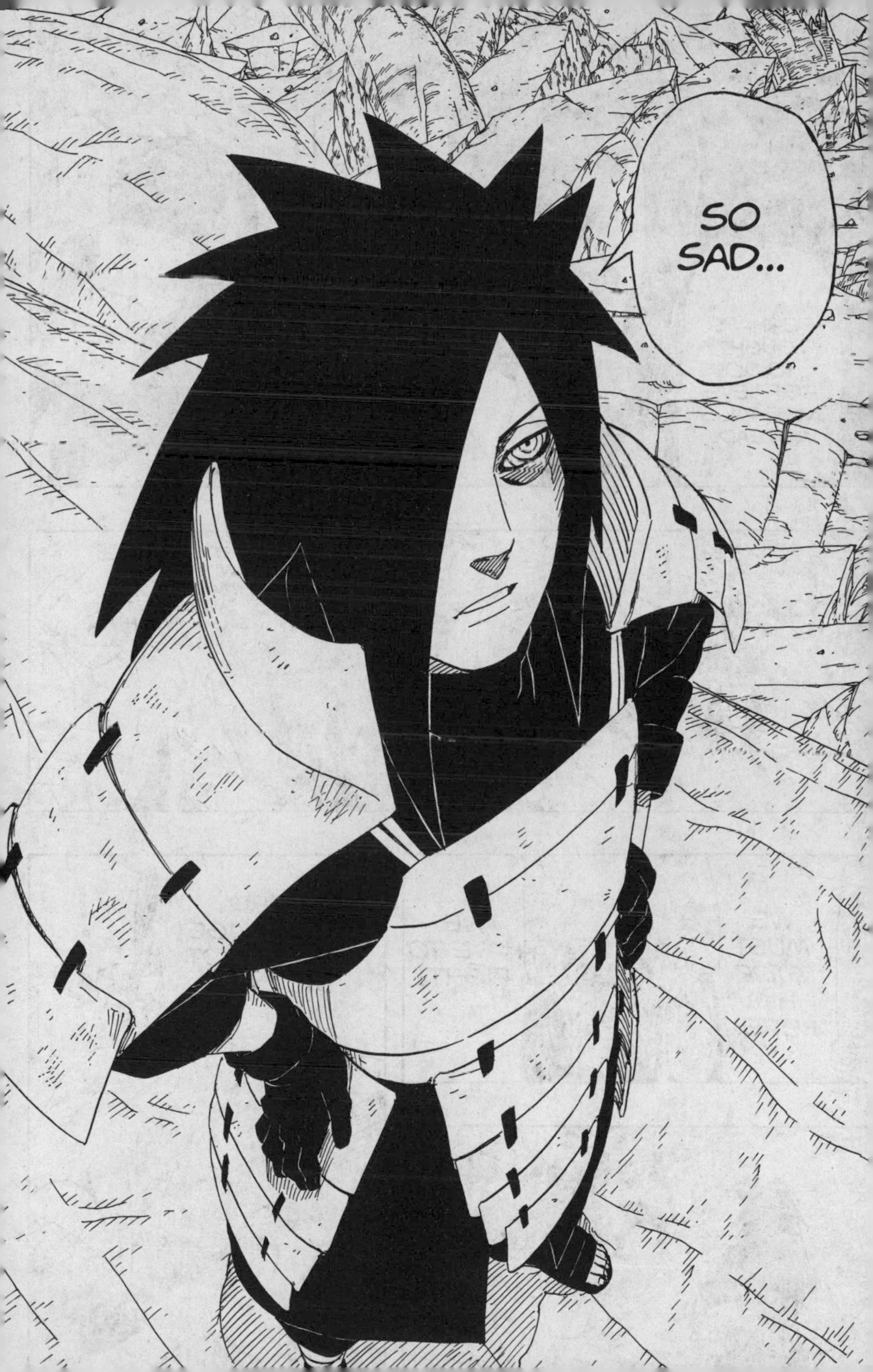
SO SAD...

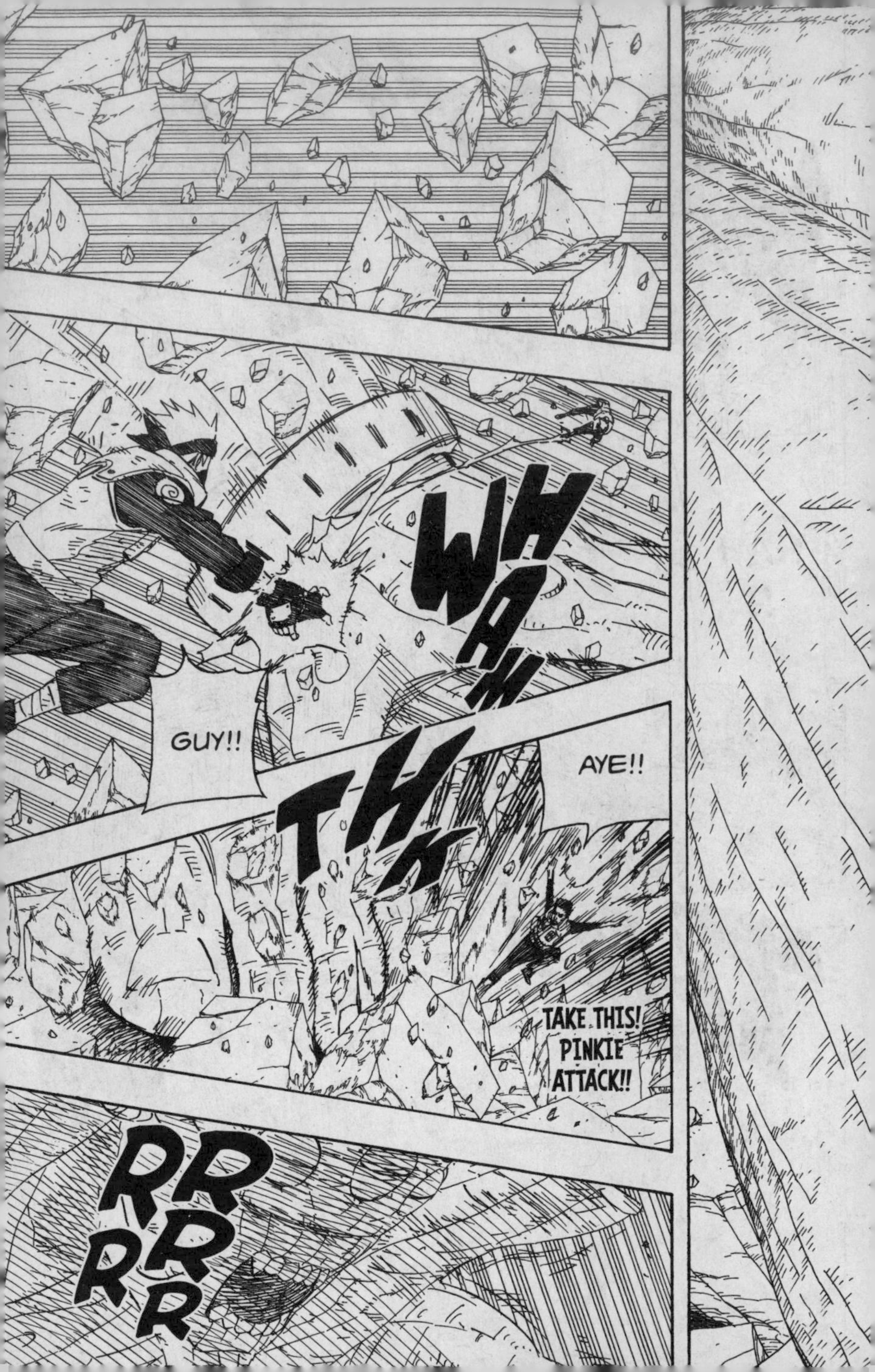
WHAM
GUY!!
AYE!!
THK
TAKE THIS! PINKIE ATTACK!!
RRRRRR

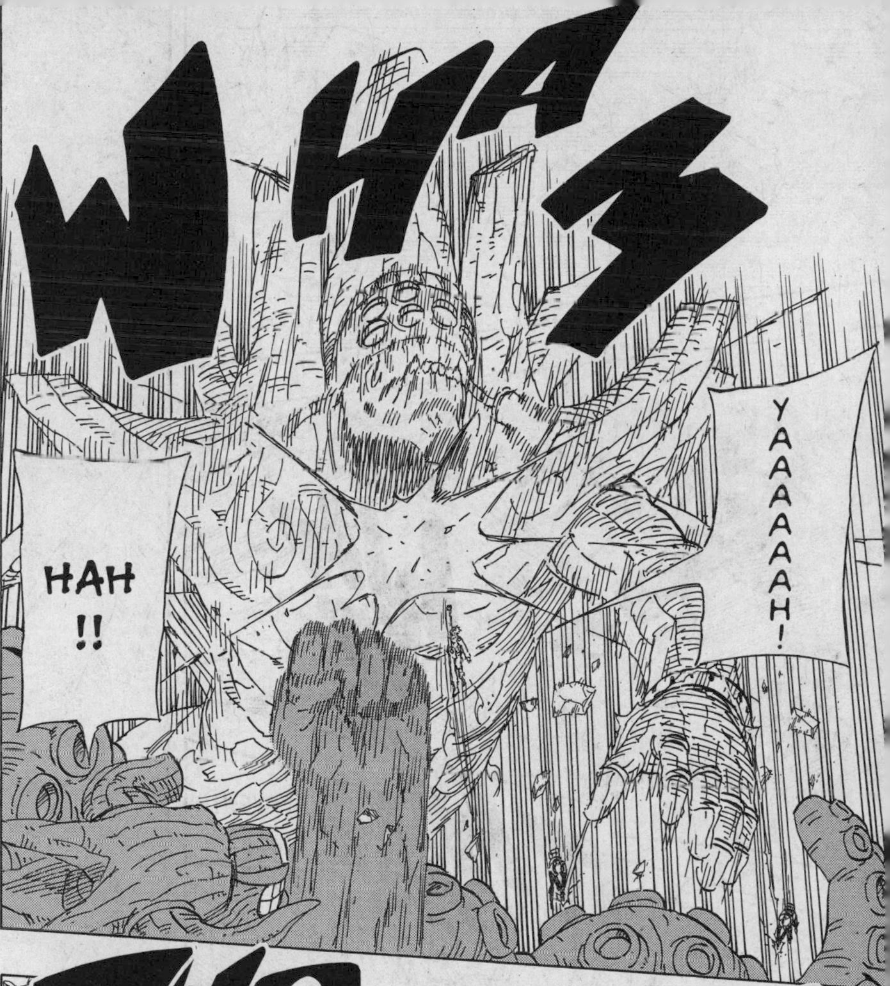
WHAM
YAAAAAAH!
HAH!!
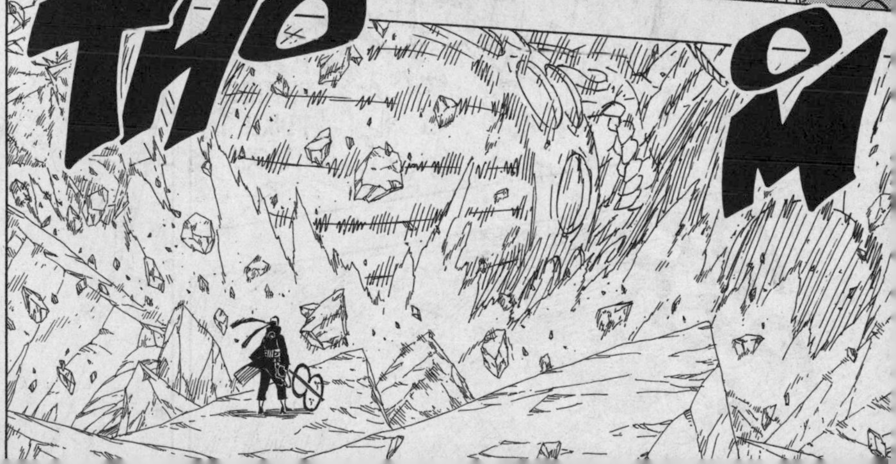
THOOM

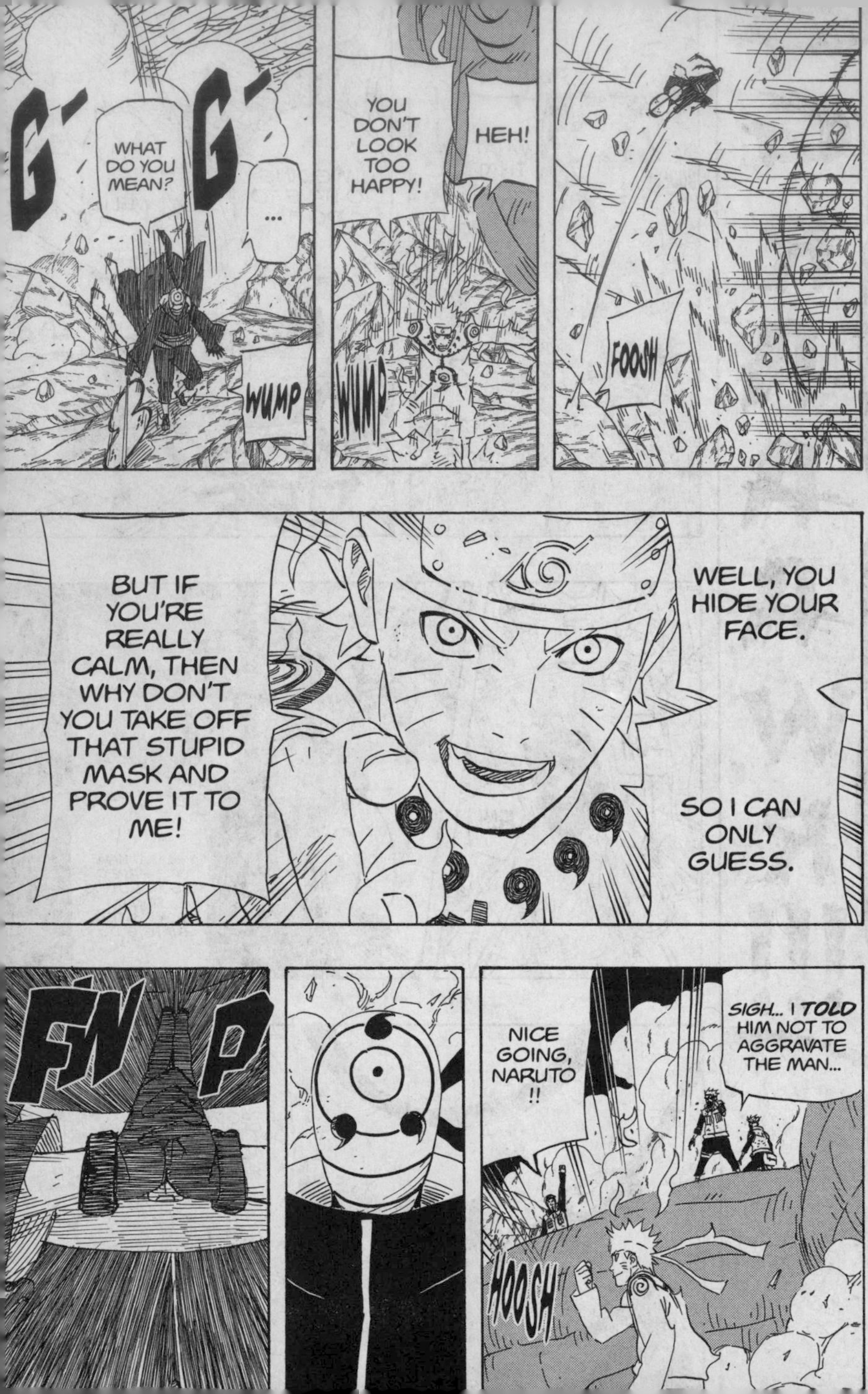
FOOSH
HEH!
YOU DON'T LOOK TOO HAPPY!
WUMP
...
WHAT DO YOU MEAN?
G- G-
WUMP
WELL, YOU HIDE YOUR FACE.
SO I CAN ONLY GUESS.
BUT IF YOU'RE REALLY CALM, THEN WHY DON'T YOU TAKE OFF THAT STUPID MASK AND PROVE IT TO ME!
SIGH... I TOLD HIM NOT TO AGGRAVATE THE MAN...
NICE GOING, NARUTO!!
HOOSH
FWP

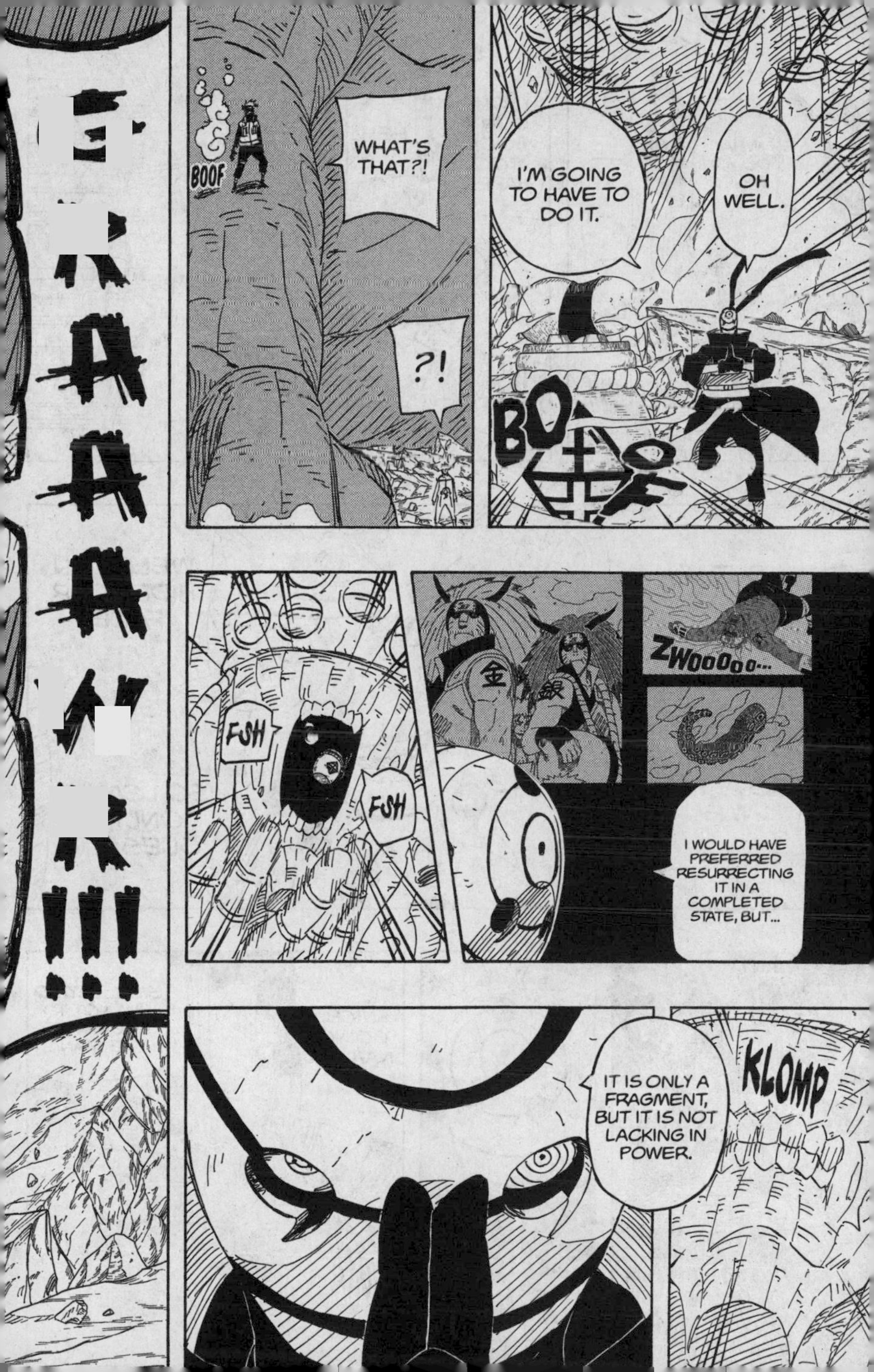
OH WELL.
I'M GOING TO HAVE TO DO IT.
WHAT'S THAT?!
BOOF
?!
ZWOOOOO...
I WOULD HAVE PREFERRED RESURRECTING IT IN A COMPLETED STATE, BUT...
FSH
FSH
KLOMP
IT IS ONLY A FRAGMENT, BUT IT IS NOT LACKING IN POWER.

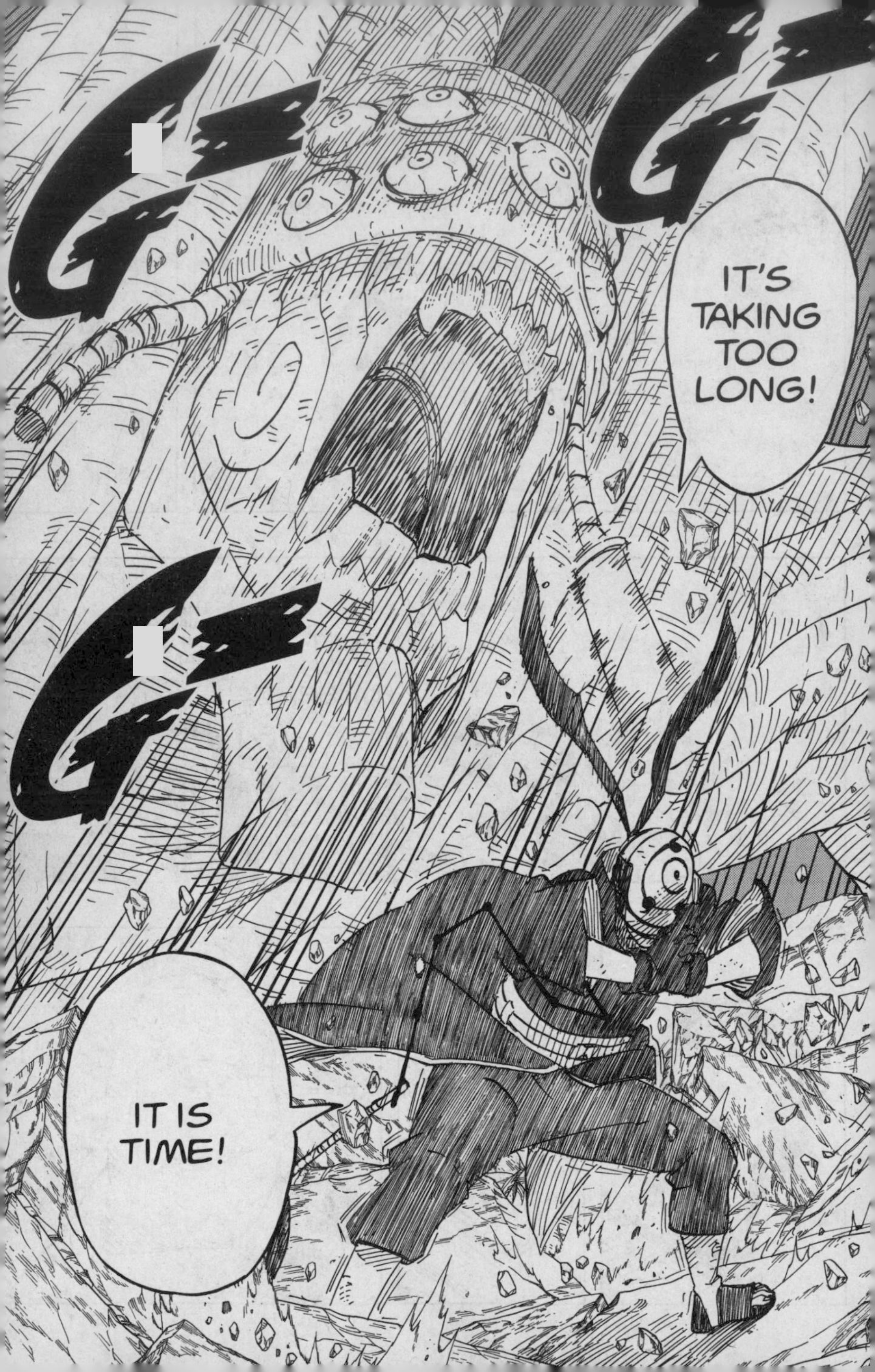
IT'S TAKING TOO LONG!
IT IS TIME!

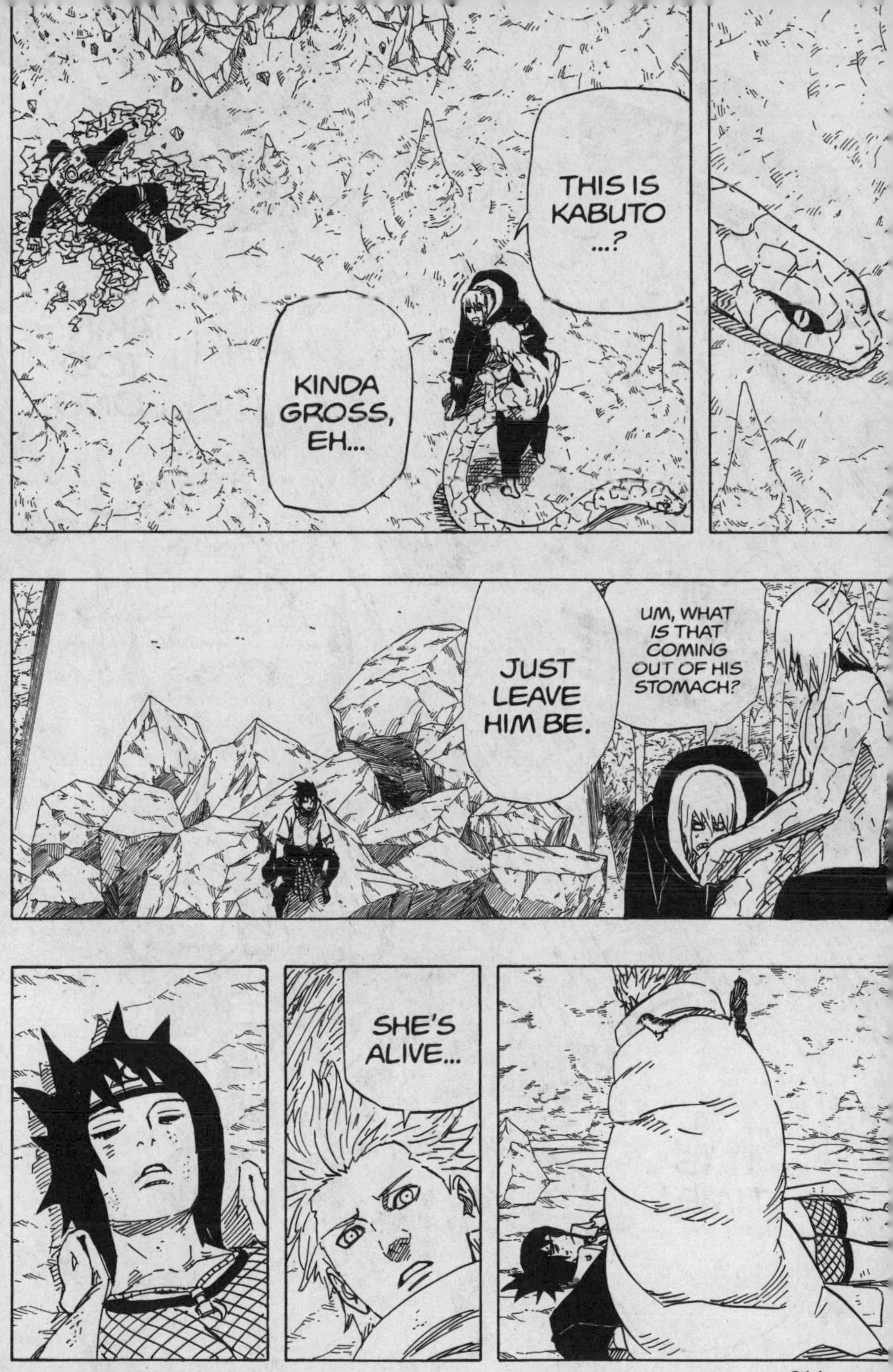
THIS IS KABUTO ...?
KINDA GROSS, EH...
UM, WHAT IS THAT COMING OUT OF HIS STOMACH?
JUST LEAVE HIM BE.
SHE'S ALIVE...

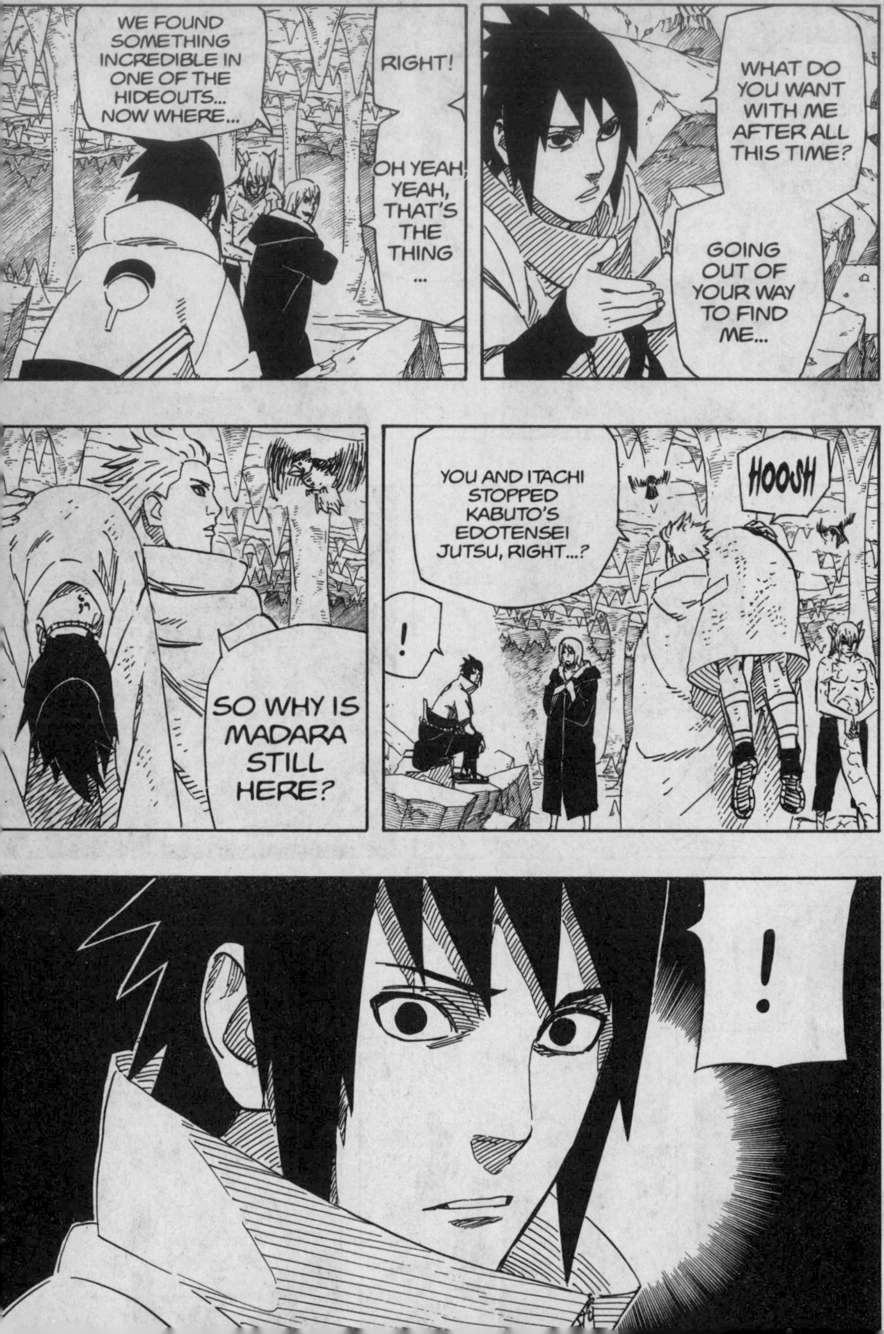
WHAT DO YOU WANT WITH ME AFTER ALL THIS TIME?
GOING OUT OF YOUR WAY TO FIND ME...
WE FOUND SOMETHING INCREDIBLE IN ONE OF THE HIDEOUTS... NOW WHERE...
RIGHT!
OH YEAH, YEAH, THAT'S THE THING ...
HOOSH
YOU AND ITACHI STOPPED KABUTO'S EDOTENSEI JUTSU, RIGHT...?
!
SO WHY IS MADARA STILL HERE?
!

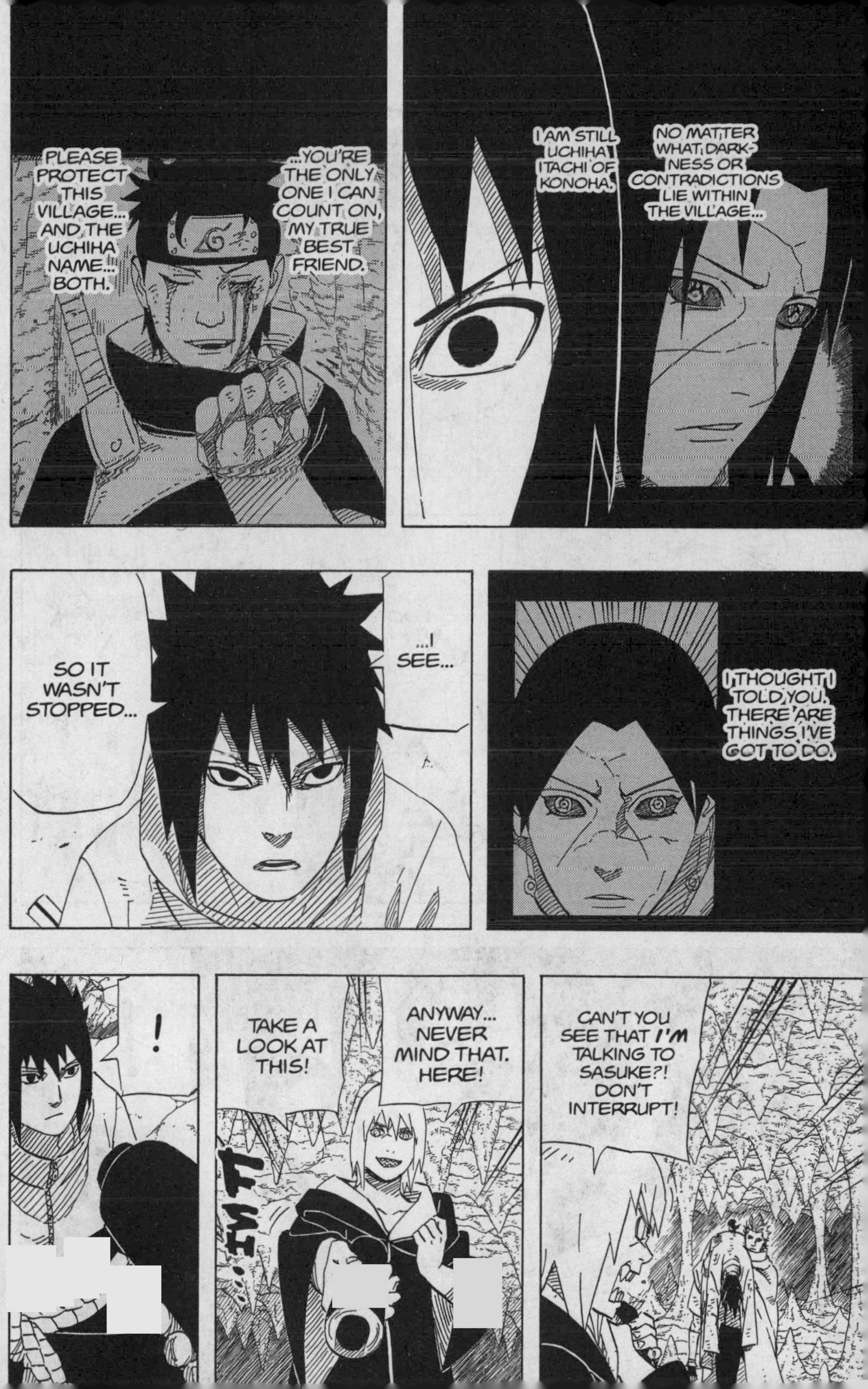
NO MATTER WHAT DARK-NESS OR CONTRADICTIONS LIE WITHIN THE VILLAGE...
I AM STILL UCHIHA ITACHI OF KONOHA.
...YOU'RE THE ONLY ONE I CAN COUNT ON, MY TRUE BEST FRIEND.
PLEASE PROTECT THIS VILLAGE... AND THE UCHIHA NAME... BOTH.
I THOUGHT I TOLD YOU. THERE ARE THINGS I'VE GOT TO DO.
...I SEE...
SO IT WASN'T STOPPED...
CAN'T YOU SEE THAT I'M TALKING TO SASUKE?! DON'T INTERRUPT!
ANYWAY... NEVER MIND THAT. HERE!
TAKE A LOOK AT THIS!
!

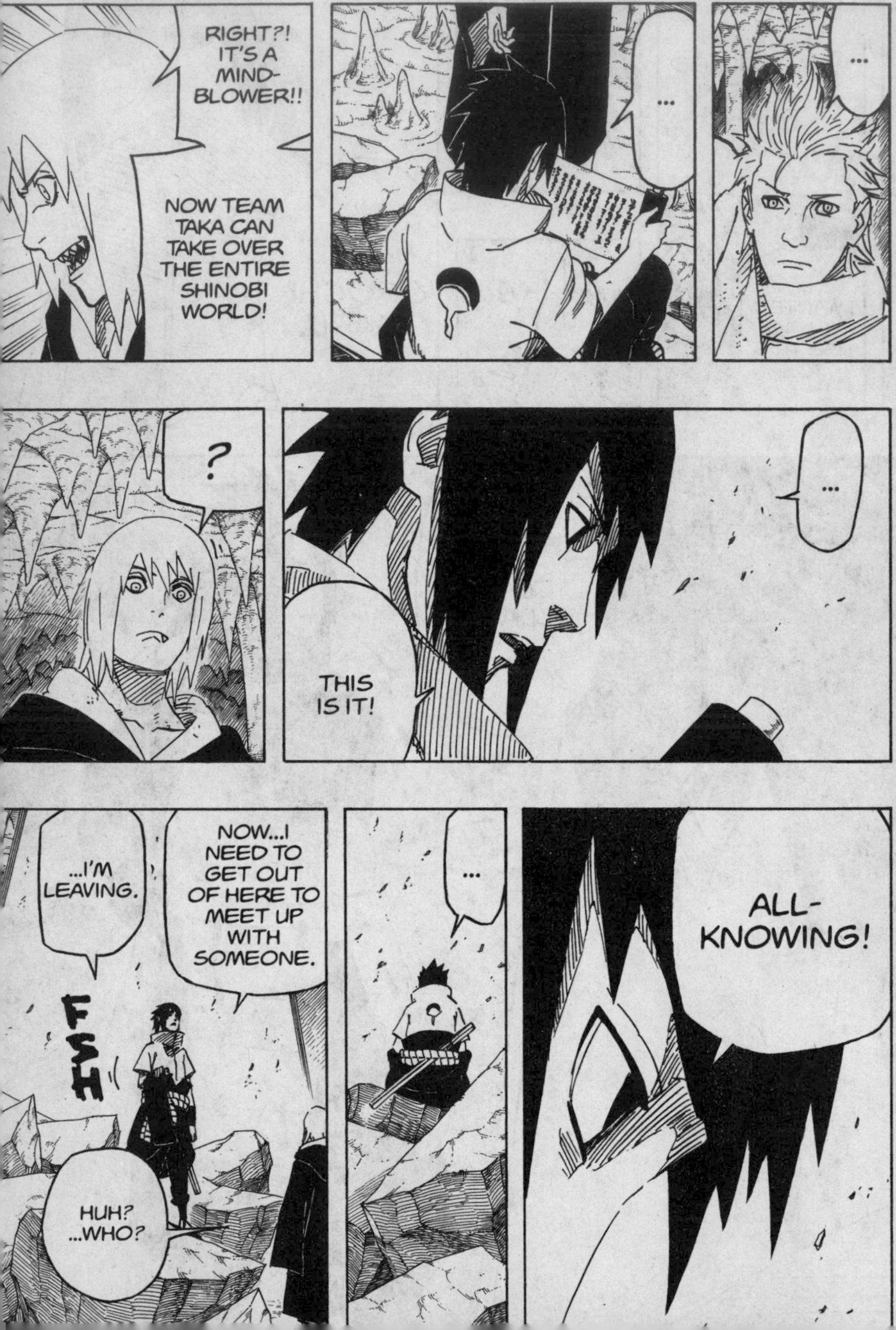
...
...
RIGHT?! IT'S A MIND-BLOWER!!
NOW TEAM TAKA CAN TAKE OVER THE ENTIRE SHINOBI WORLD!
...
THIS IS IT!
?
ALL-KNOWING!
...
NOW...I NEED TO GET OUT OF HERE TO MEET UP WITH SOMEONE.
...I'M LEAVING.
FSH
HUH? ...WHO?

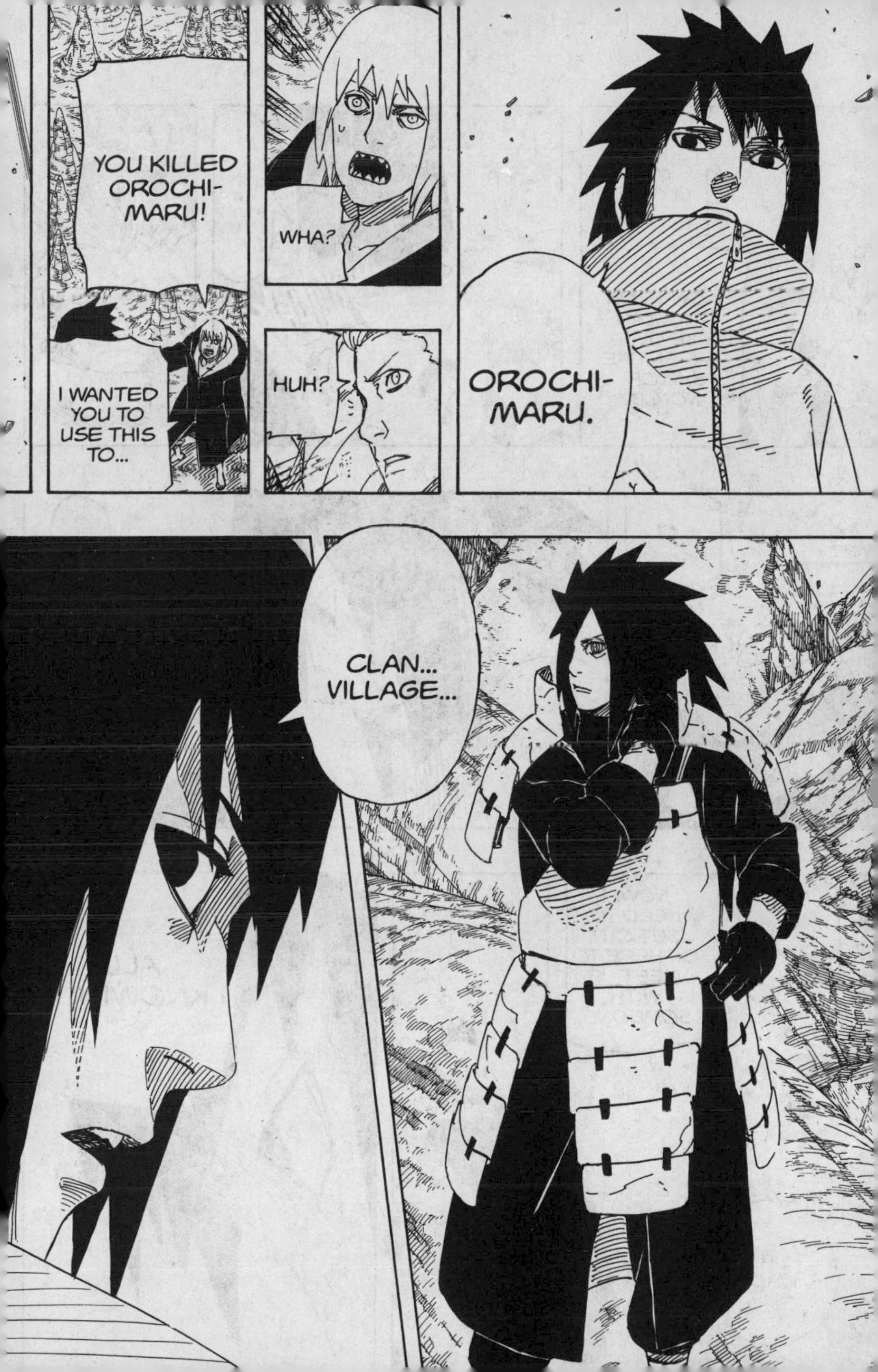
OROCHI-MARU.
WHA?
HUH?
YOU KILLED OROCHI-MARU!
I WANTED YOU TO USE THIS TO...
CLAN... VILLAGE...

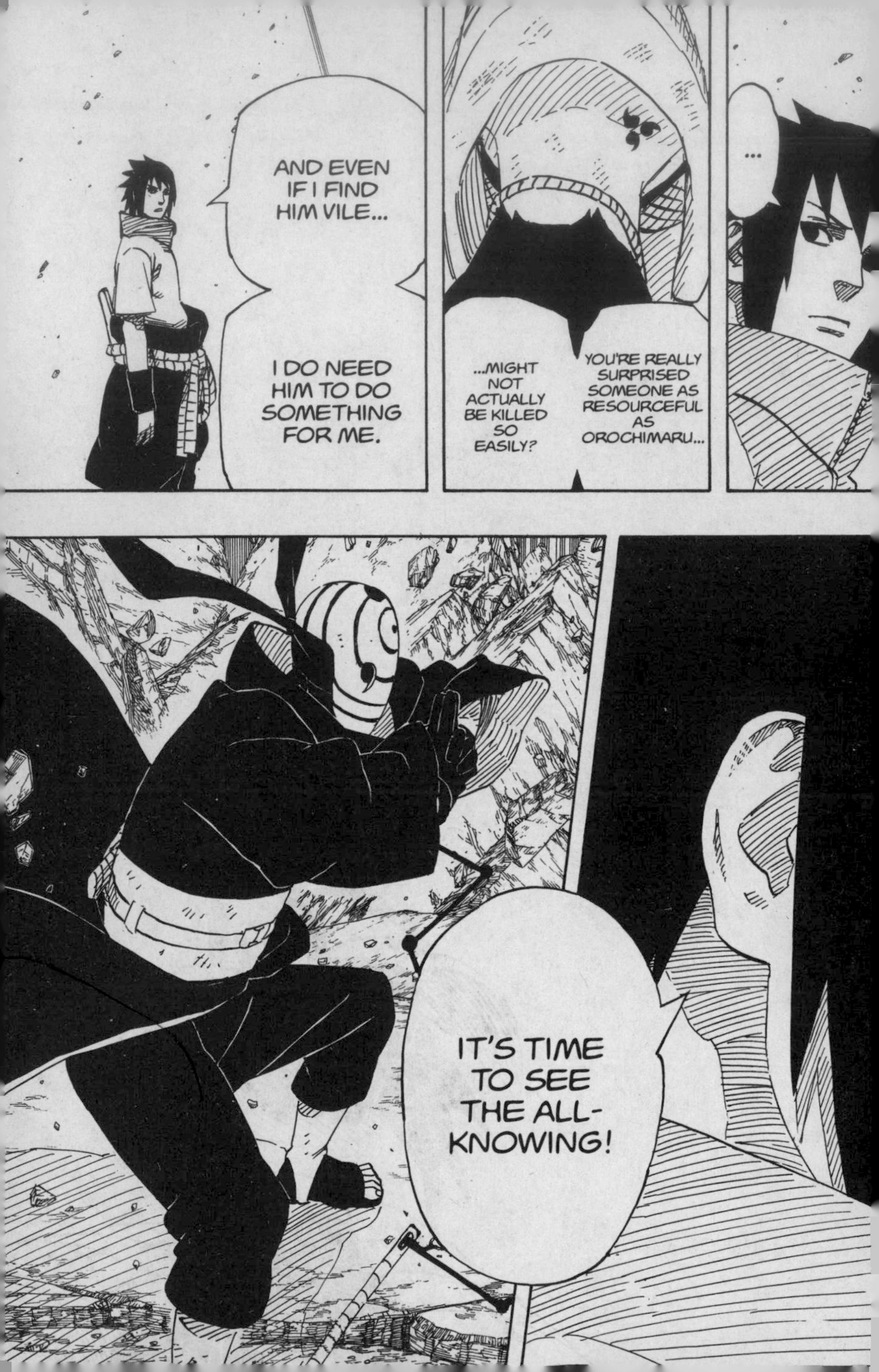
...
YOU'RE REALLY SURPRISED SOMEONE AS RESOURCEFUL AS OROCHIMARU...
...MIGHT NOT ACTUALLY BE KILLED SO EASILY?
AND EVEN IF I FIND HIM VILE...
I DO NEED HIM TO DO SOMETHING FOR ME.
IT'S TIME TO SEE THE ALL-KNOWING!

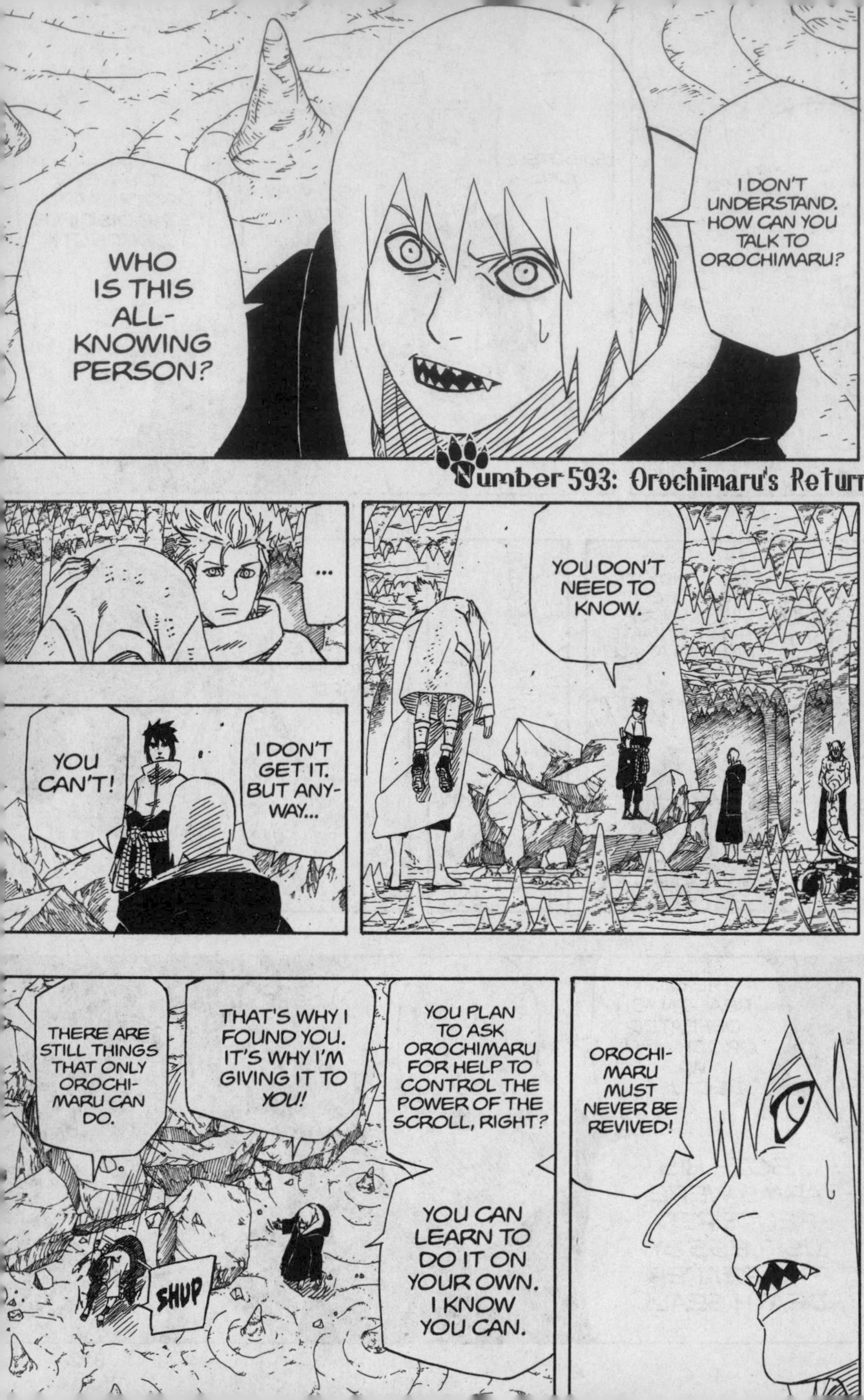
I DON'T UNDERSTAND. HOW CAN YOU TALK TO OROCHIMARU?
WHO IS THIS ALL-KNOWING PERSON?
Number 593: Orochimaru's Return
YOU DON'T NEED TO KNOW.
...
I DON'T GET IT. BUT ANYWAY...
YOU CAN'T!
OROCHIMARU MUST NEVER BE REVIVED!
YOU PLAN TO ASK OROCHIMARU FOR HELP TO CONTROL THE POWER OF THE SCROLL, RIGHT?
THAT'S WHY I FOUND YOU. IT'S WHY I'M GIVING IT TO YOU!
THERE ARE STILL THINGS THAT ONLY OROCHIMARU CAN DO.
YOU CAN LEARN TO DO IT ON YOUR OWN. I KNOW YOU CAN.
SHUP

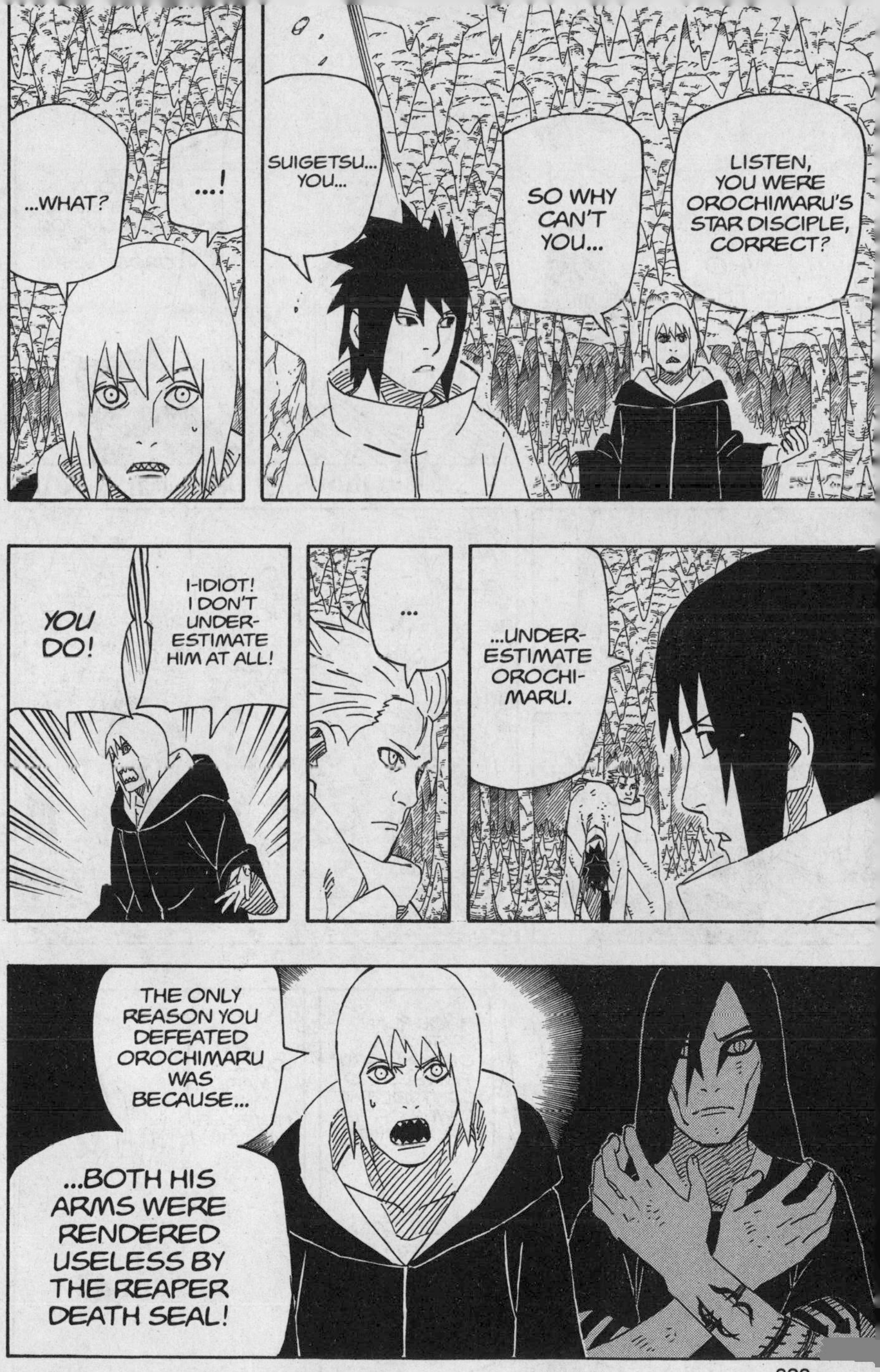

LISTEN, YOU WERE OROCHIMARU'S STAR DISCIPLE, CORRECT?
SO WHY CAN'T YOU...
SUIGETSU... YOU...
...!
...WHAT?
...UNDER-ESTIMATE OROCHI-MARU.
...
I-IDIOT! I DON'T UNDER-ESTIMATE HIM AT ALL!
YOU DO!
THE ONLY REASON YOU DEFEATED OROCHIMARU WAS BECAUSE...
...BOTH HIS ARMS WERE RENDERED USELESS BY THE REAPER DEATH SEAL!

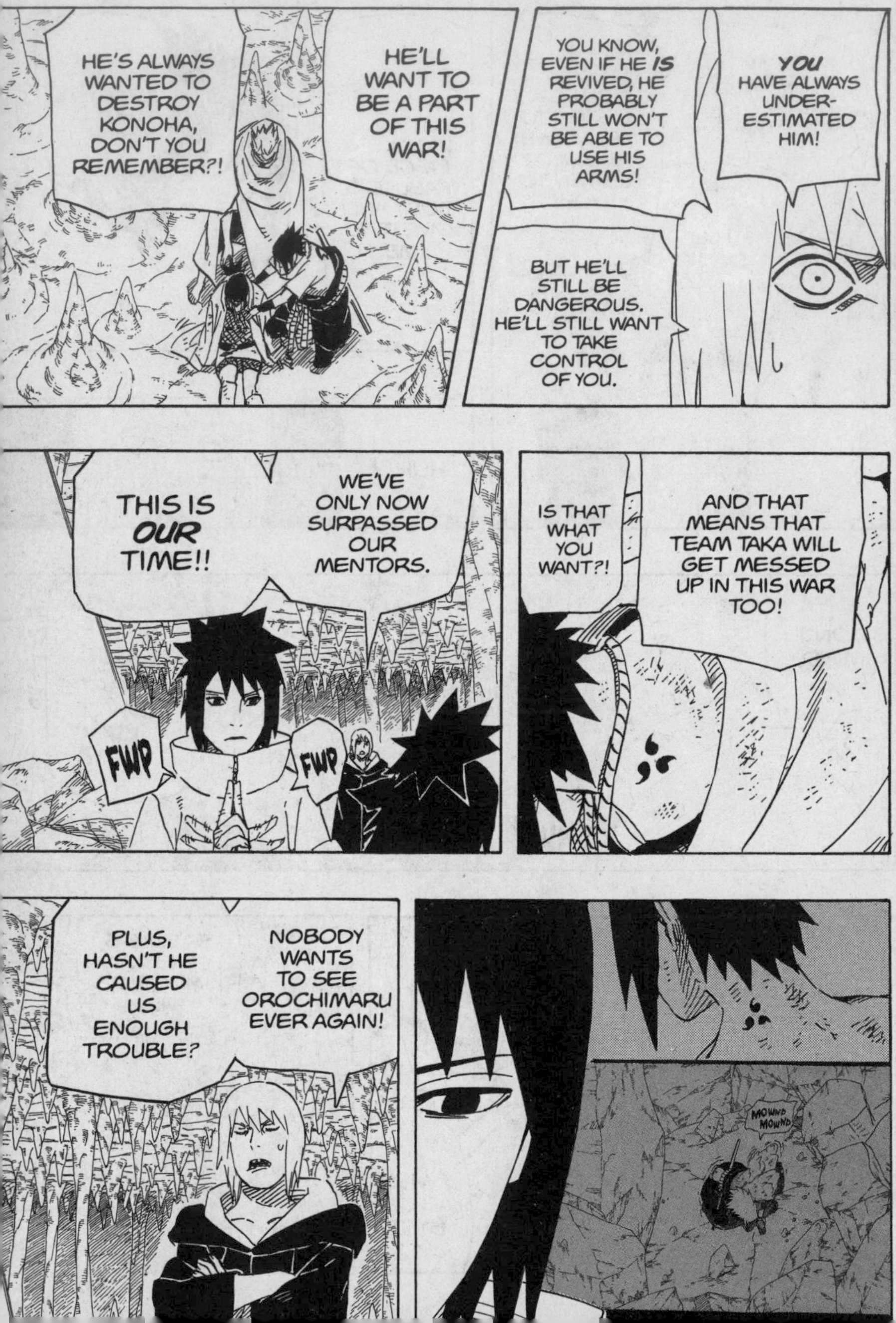
YOU HAVE ALWAYS UNDER-ESTIMATED HIM!
YOU KNOW, EVEN IF HE IS REVIVED, HE PROBABLY STILL WON'T BE ABLE TO USE HIS ARMS!
BUT HE'LL STILL BE DANGEROUS. HE'LL STILL WANT TO TAKE CONTROL OF YOU.
HE'LL WANT TO BE A PART OF THIS WAR!
HE'S ALWAYS WANTED TO DESTROY KONOHA, DON'T YOU REMEMBER?!
AND THAT MEANS THAT TEAM TAKA WILL GET MESSED UP IN THIS WAR TOO!
IS THAT WHAT YOU WANT?!
WE'VE ONLY NOW SURPASSED OUR MENTORS.
THIS IS OUR TIME!!
FWP
FWP
MOWND MOWND
NOBODY WANTS TO SEE OROCHIMARU EVER AGAIN!
PLUS, HASN'T HE CAUSED US ENOUGH TROUBLE?

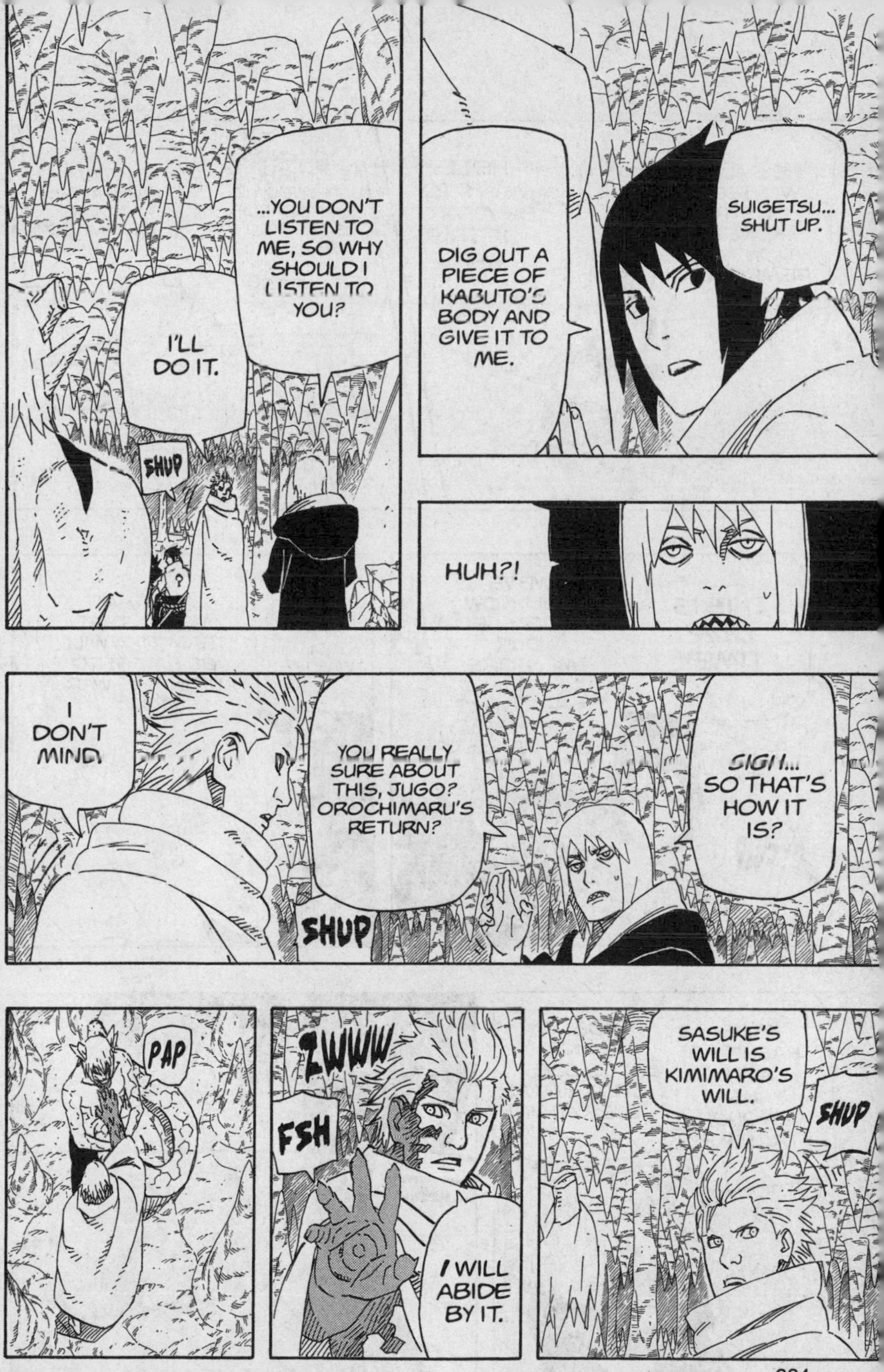
SUIGETSU... SHUT UP.
DIG OUT A PIECE OF KABUTO'S BODY AND GIVE IT TO ME.
HUH?!
...YOU DON'T LISTEN TO ME, SO WHY SHOULD I LISTEN TO YOU?
I'LL DO IT.
SHUP
SIGH... SO THAT'S HOW IT IS?
YOU REALLY SURE ABOUT THIS, JUGO? OROCHIMARU'S RETURN?
SHUP
I DON'T MIND.
SASUKE'S WILL IS KIMIMARO'S WILL.
SHUP
ZWWW
FSH
I WILL ABIDE BY IT.
PAP

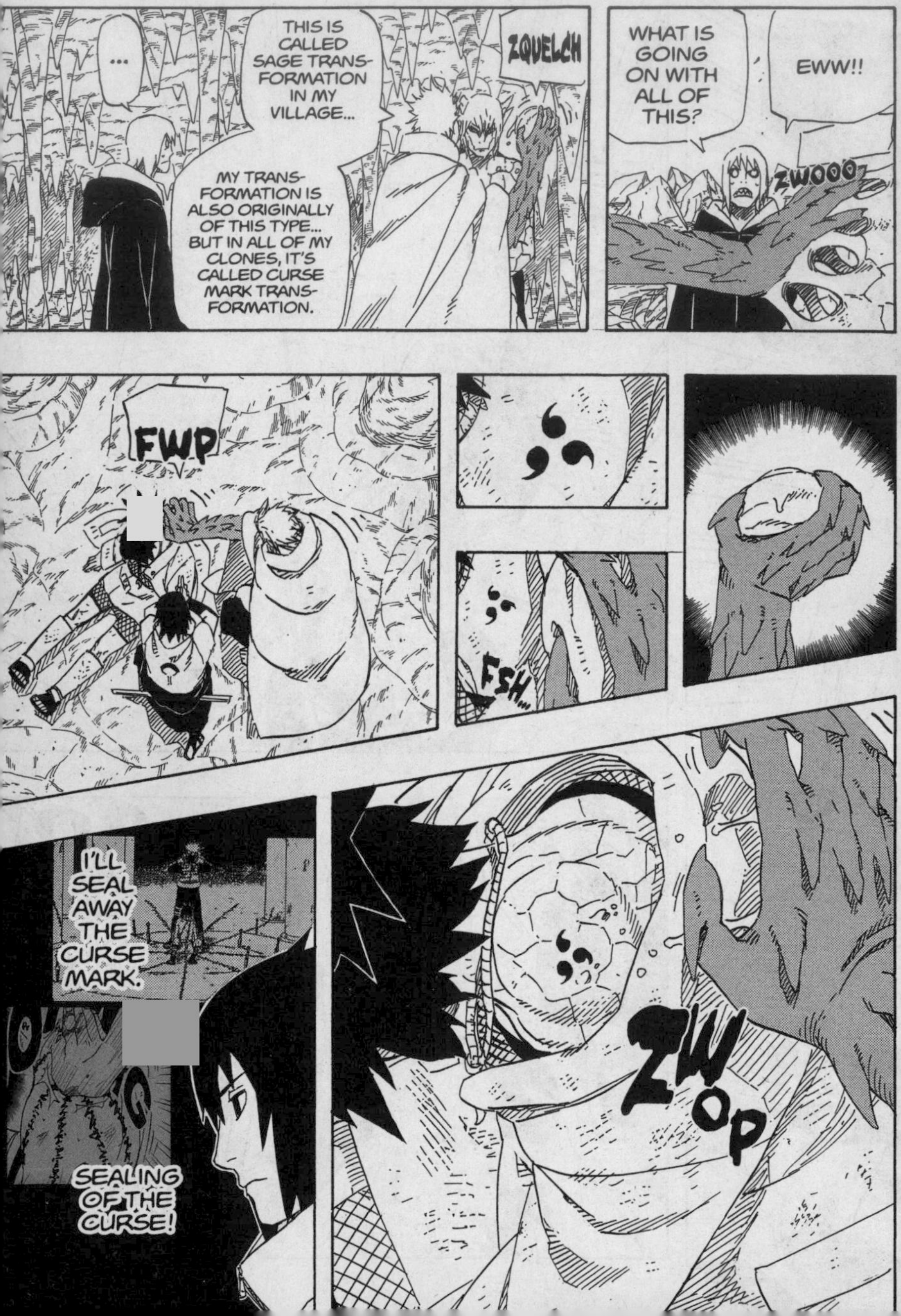
EWW!!
WHAT IS GOING ON WITH ALL OF THIS?
ZWOOO
ZQUELCH
THIS IS CALLED SAGE TRANS-FORMATION IN MY VILLAGE...
MY TRANS-FORMATION IS ALSO ORIGINALLY OF THIS TYPE... BUT IN ALL OF MY CLONES, IT'S CALLED CURSE MARK TRANS-FORMATION.
...
FSH...
FWP
ZWOOP
I'LL SEAL AWAY THE CURSE MARK.
SEALING OF THE CURSE!

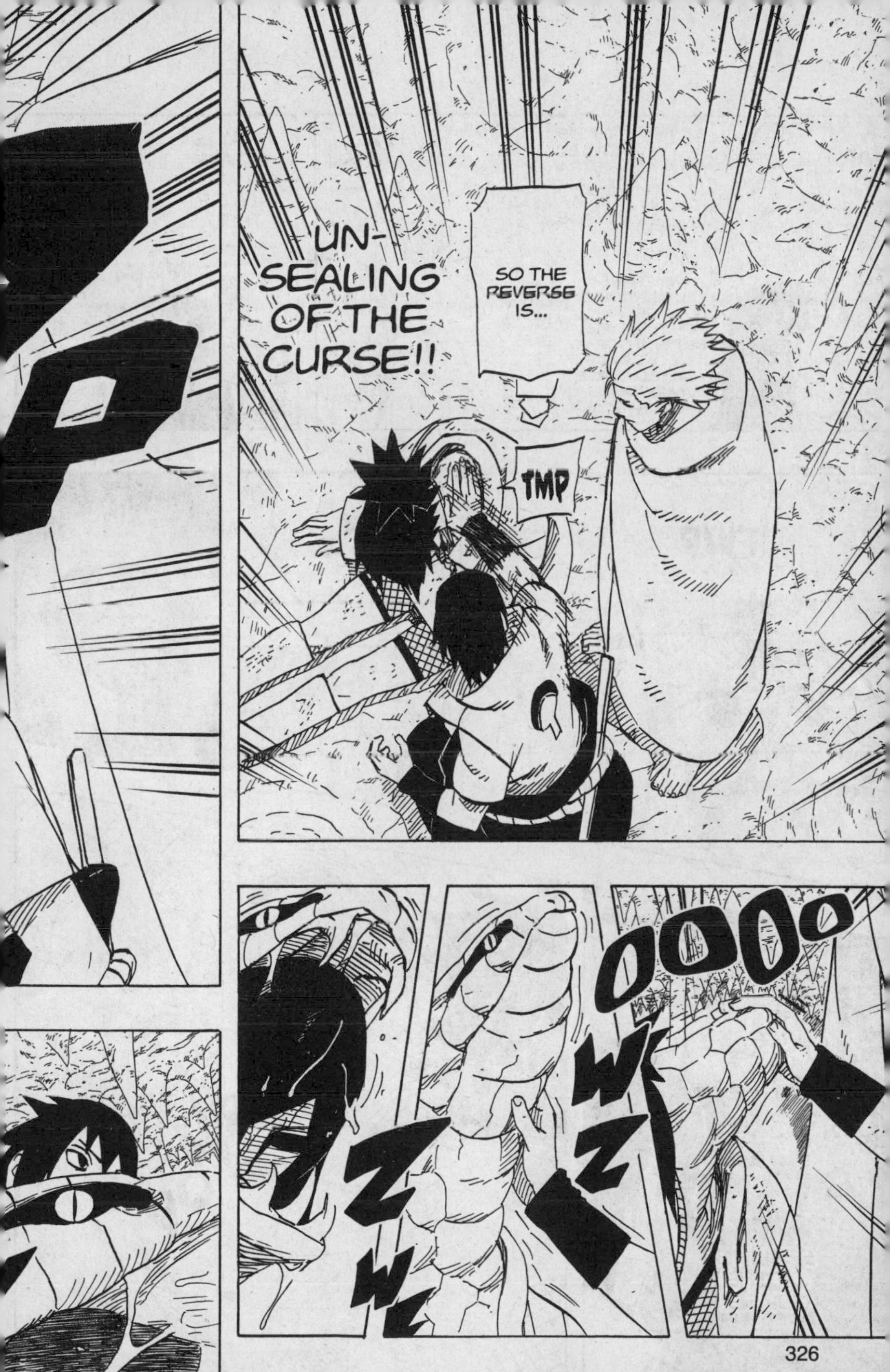
SO THE REVERSE IS...
UN-SEALING OF THE CURSE!!
TMP
OOOO

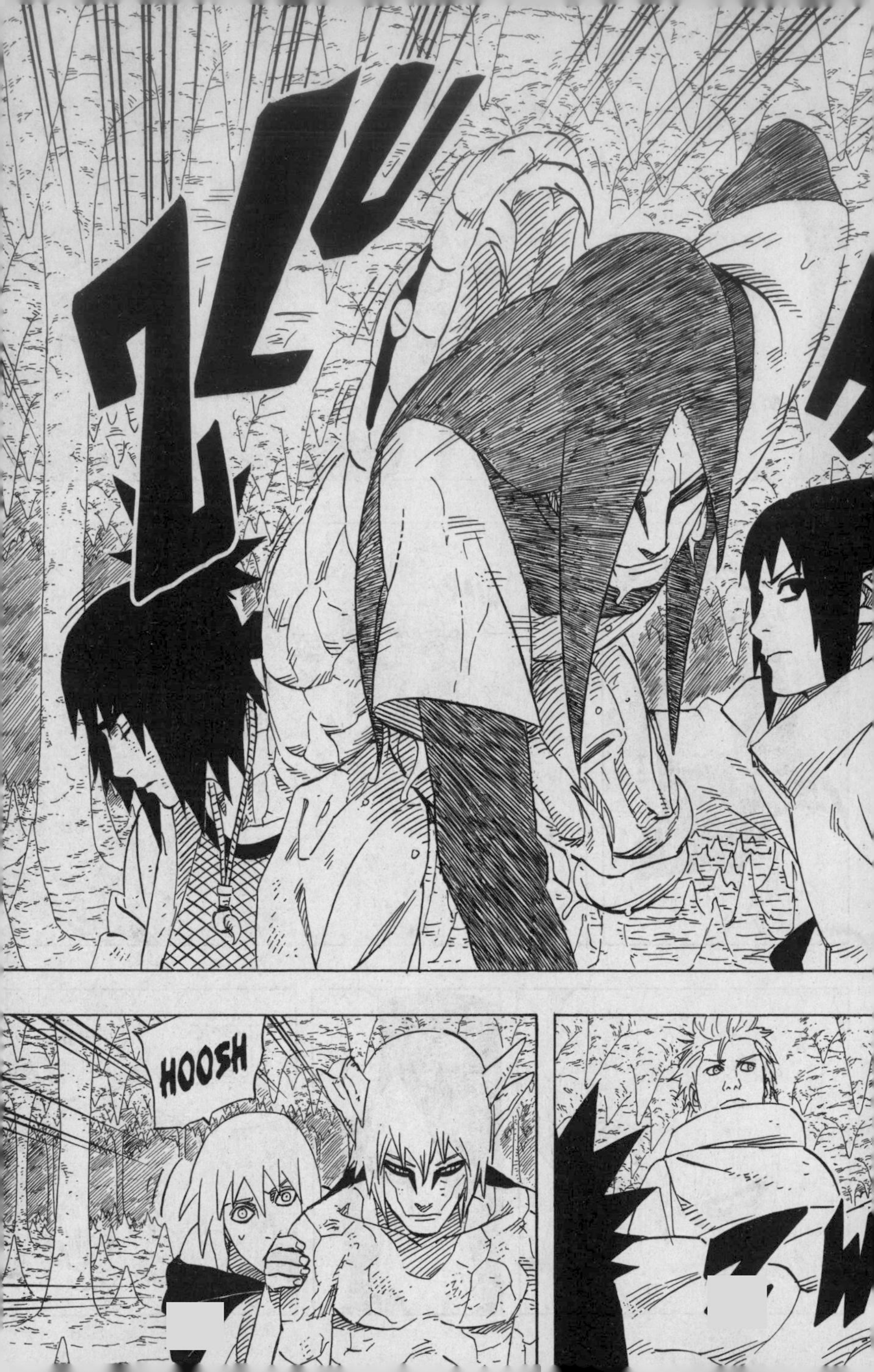
HOOSH

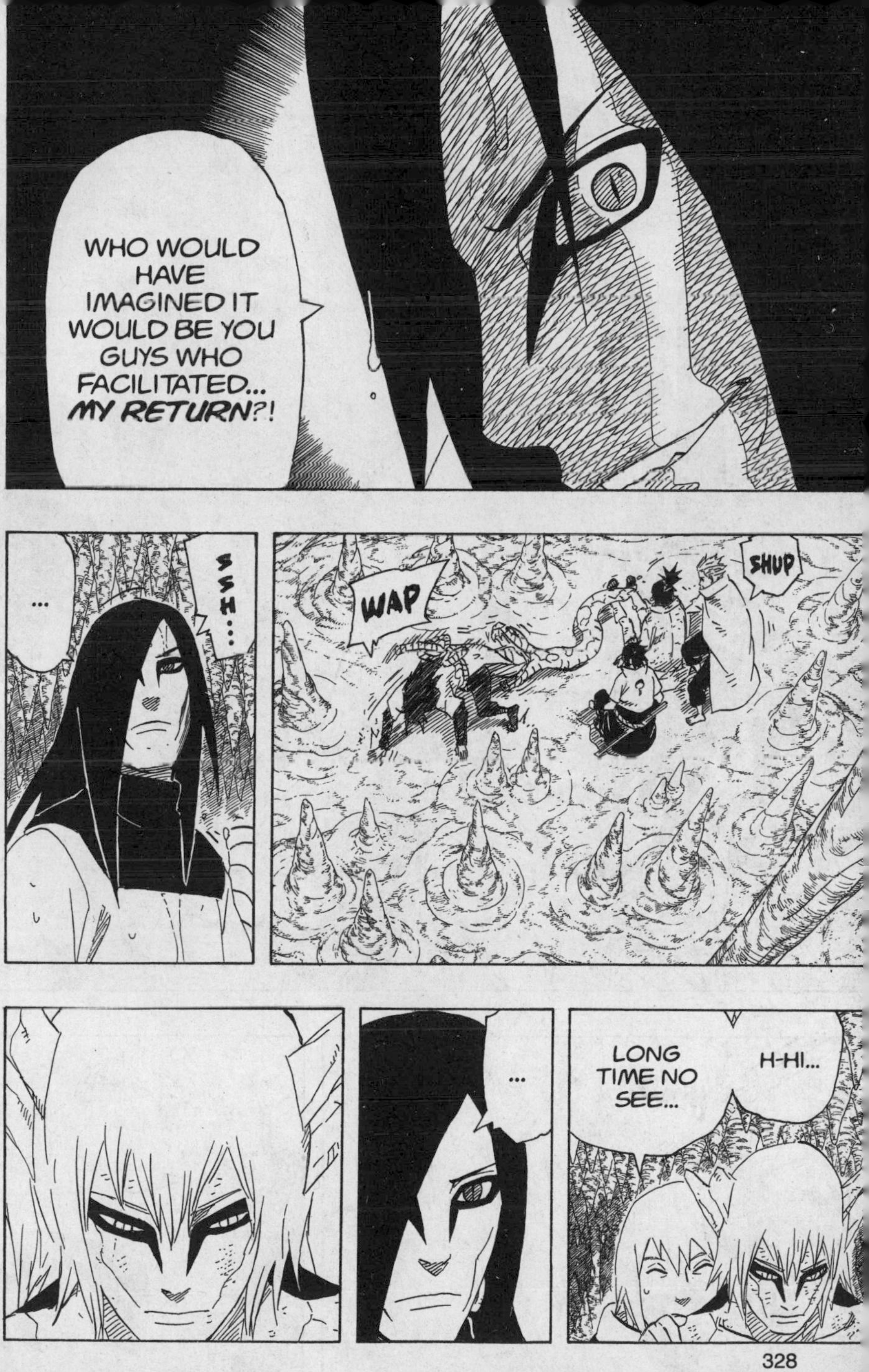
WHO WOULD HAVE IMAGINED IT WOULD BE YOU GUYS WHO FACILITATED... MY RETURN?!
SHUP
WAP
SSH...
...
H-HI...
LONG TIME NO SEE...
...

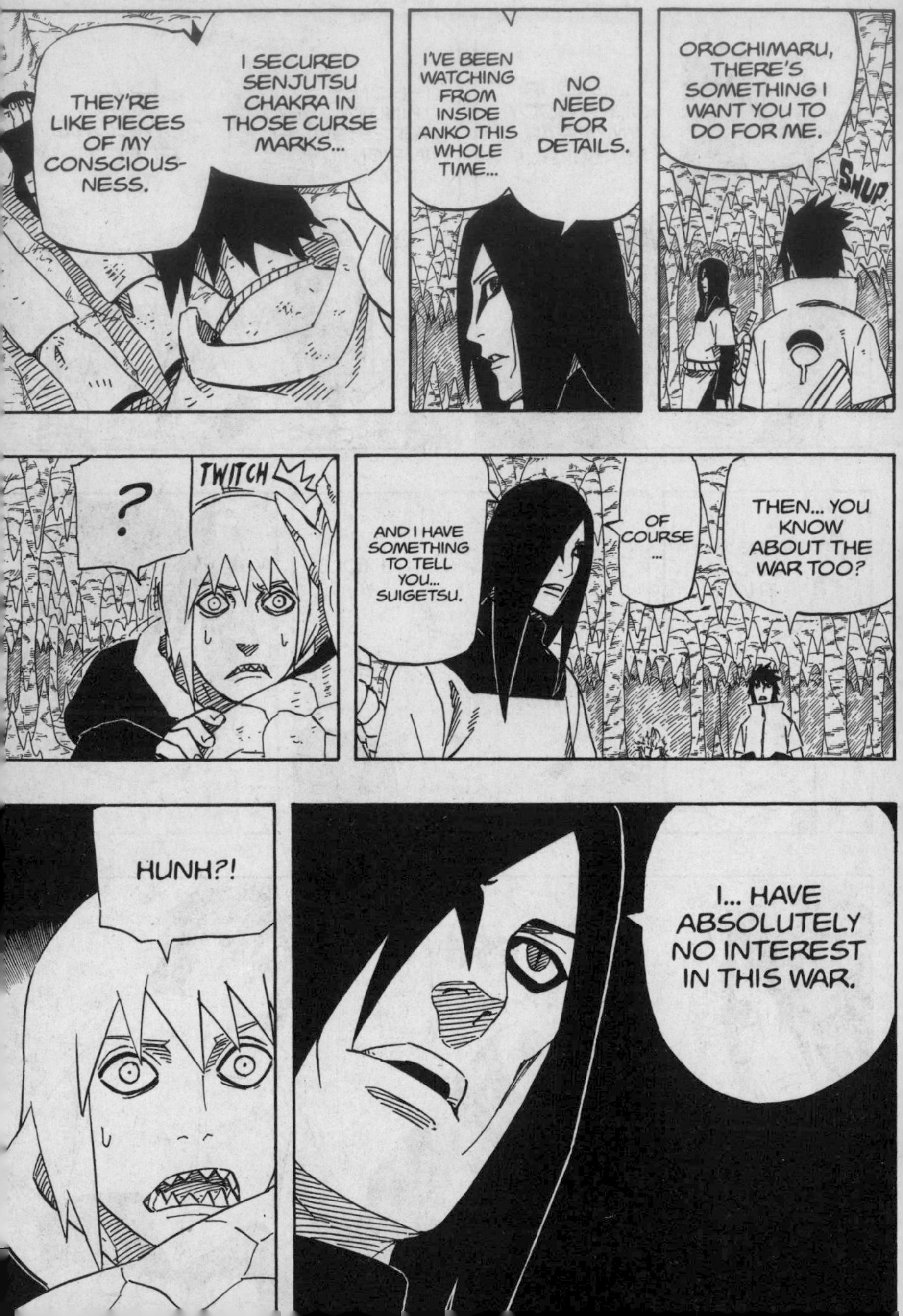
OROCHIMARU, THERE'S SOMETHING I WANT YOU TO DO FOR ME.
SHUP
NO NEED FOR DETAILS.
I'VE BEEN WATCHING FROM INSIDE ANKO THIS WHOLE TIME...
I SECURED SENJUTSU CHAKRA IN THOSE CURSE MARKS...
THEY'RE LIKE PIECES OF MY CONSCIOUSNESS.
THEN... YOU KNOW ABOUT THE WAR TOO?
OF COURSE...
AND I HAVE SOMETHING TO TELL YOU... SUIGETSU.
TWITCH
?
I... HAVE ABSOLUTELY NO INTEREST IN THIS WAR.
HUNH?!

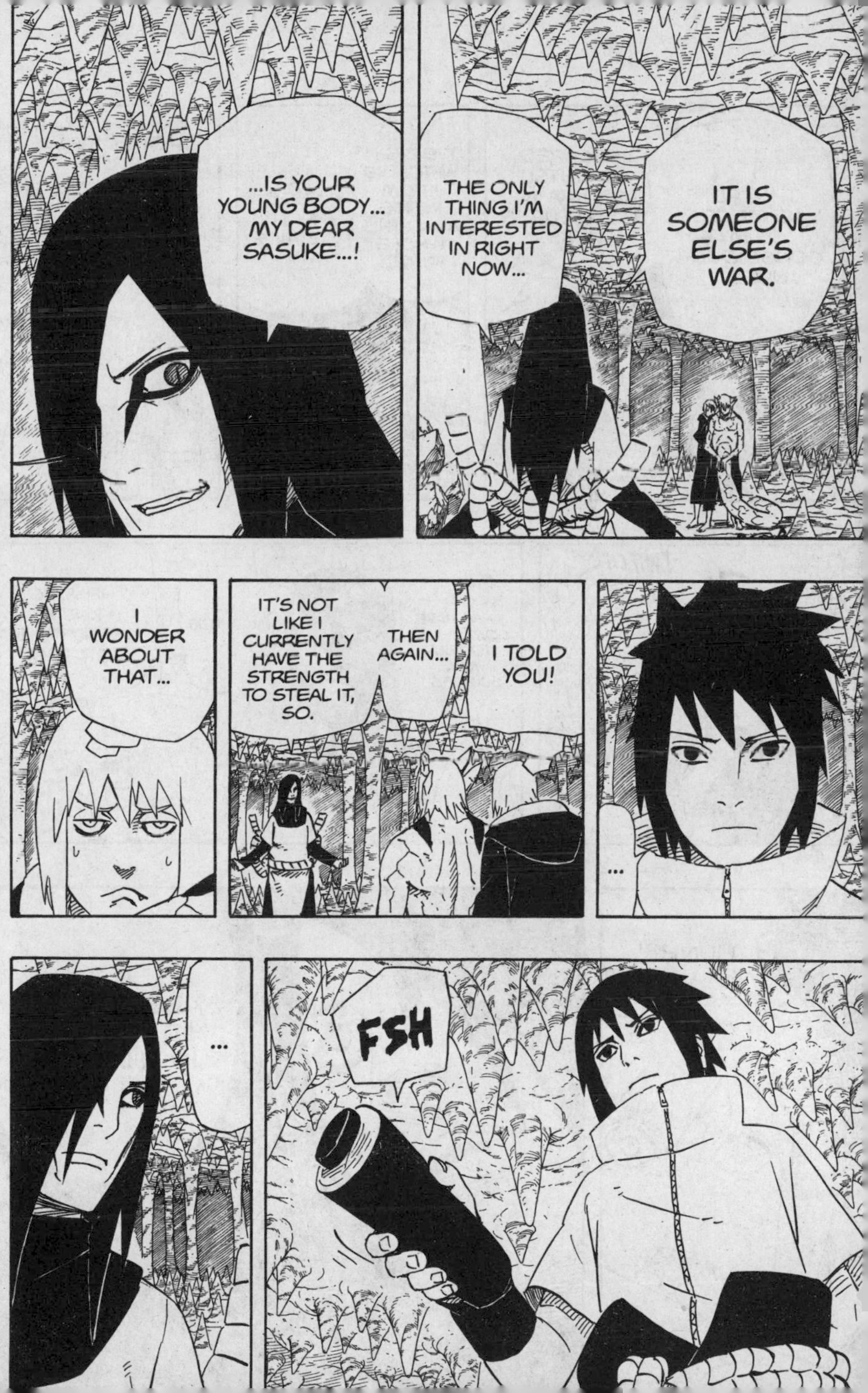
IT IS SOMEONE ELSE'S WAR.
THE ONLY THING I'M INTERESTED IN RIGHT NOW...
...IS YOUR YOUNG BODY... MY DEAR SASUKE...!
...
I TOLD YOU!
THEN AGAIN...
IT'S NOT LIKE I CURRENTLY HAVE THE STRENGTH TO STEAL IT, SO.
I WONDER ABOUT THAT...
FSH
...

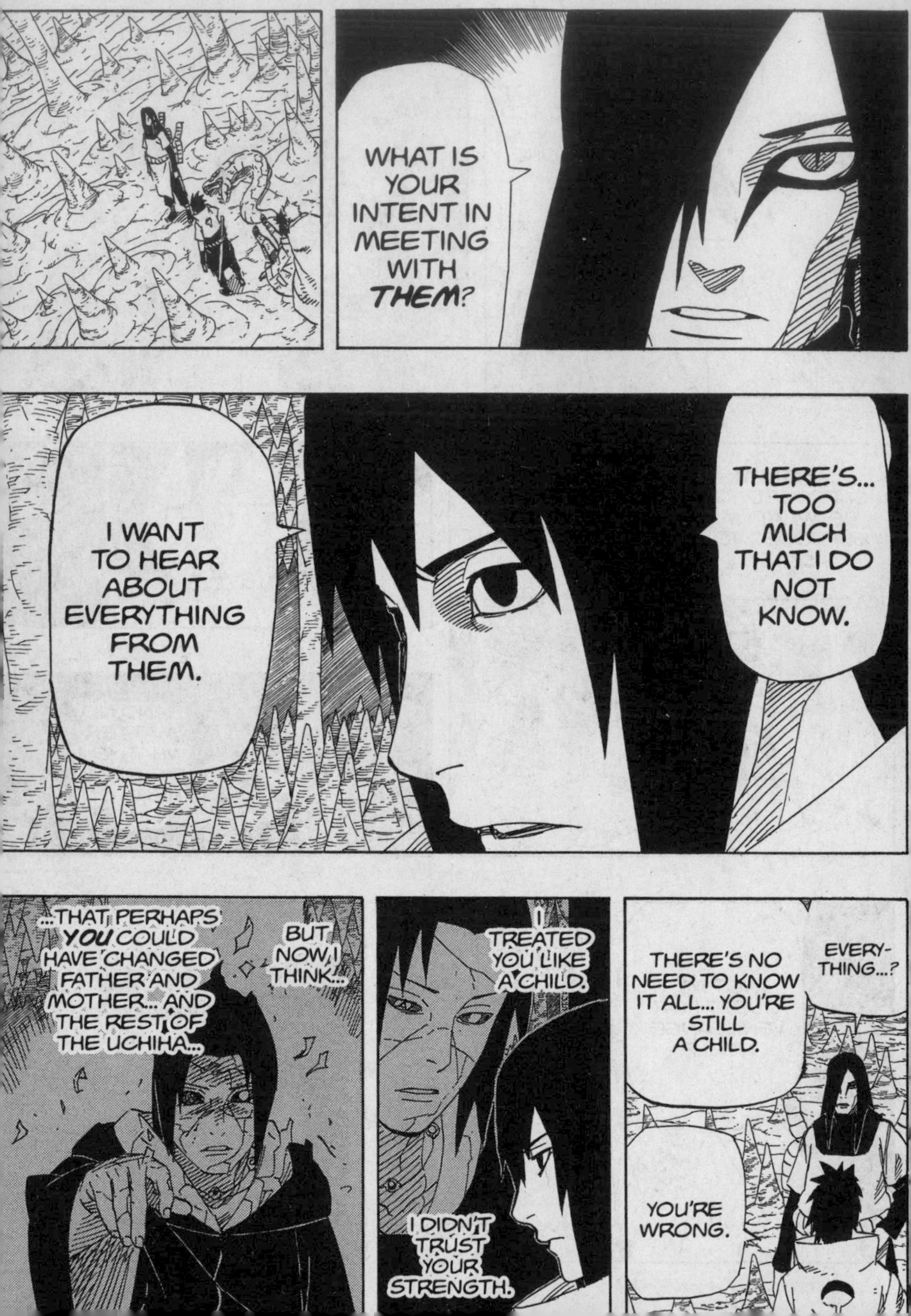
WHAT IS YOUR INTENT IN MEETING WITH *THEM*?
THERE'S... TOO MUCH THAT I DO NOT KNOW.
I WANT TO HEAR ABOUT EVERYTHING FROM THEM.
EVERY-THING...?
THERE'S NO NEED TO KNOW IT ALL... YOU'RE STILL A CHILD.
YOU'RE WRONG.
I TREATED YOU LIKE A CHILD.
I DIDN'T TRUST YOUR STRENGTH.
BUT NOW, I THINK...
...THAT PERHAPS *YOU* COULD HAVE CHANGED FATHER AND MOTHER... AND THE REST OF THE UCHIHA...

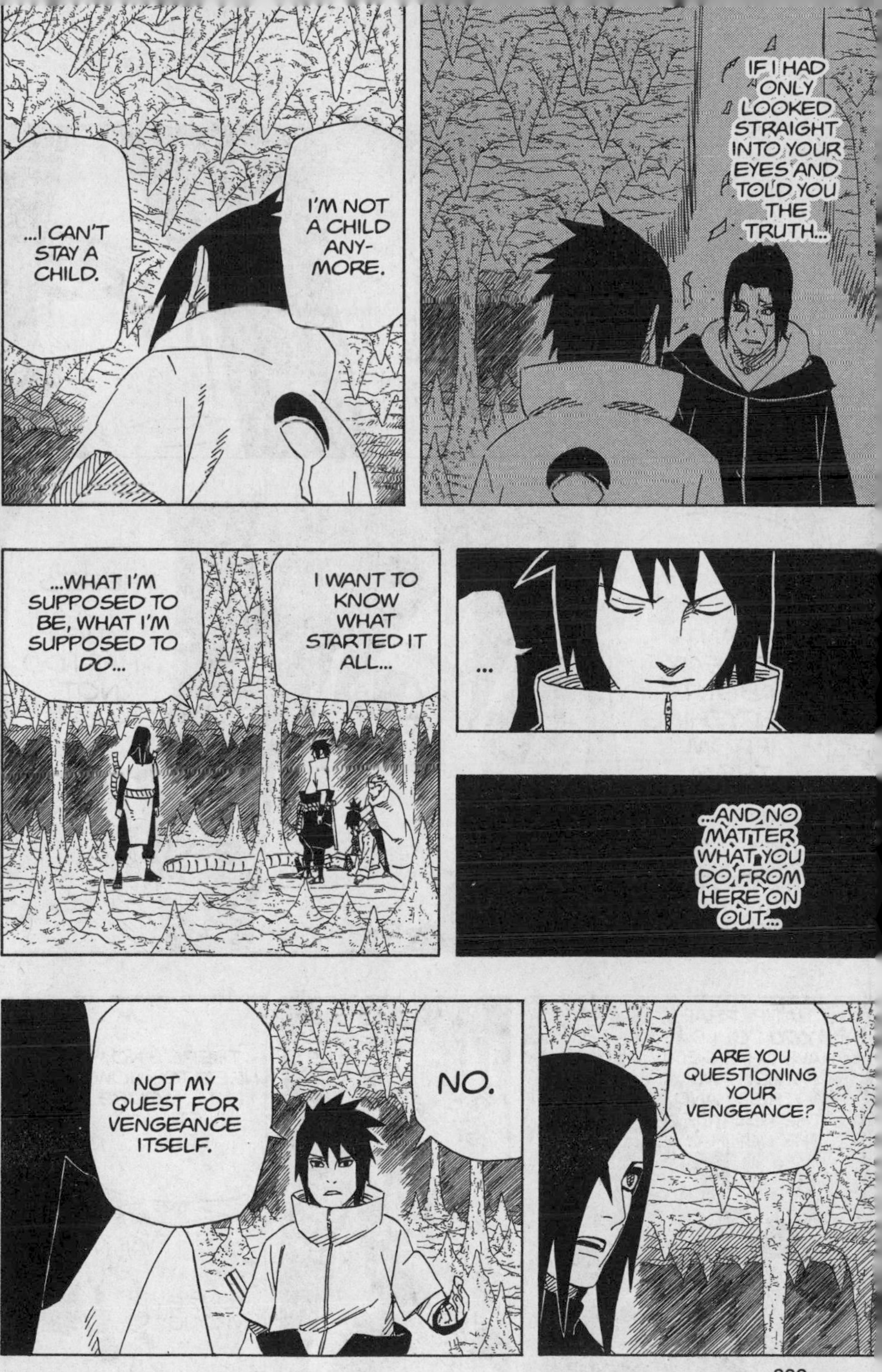
IF I HAD ONLY LOOKED STRAIGHT INTO YOUR EYES AND TOLD YOU THE TRUTH...
I'M NOT A CHILD ANYMORE.
...I CAN'T STAY A CHILD.
...
...AND NO MATTER WHAT YOU DO FROM HERE ON OUT...
I WANT TO KNOW WHAT STARTED IT ALL...
...WHAT I'M SUPPOSED TO BE, WHAT I'M SUPPOSED TO DO...
ARE YOU QUESTIONING YOUR VENGEANCE?
NO.
NOT MY QUEST FOR VENGEANCE ITSELF.

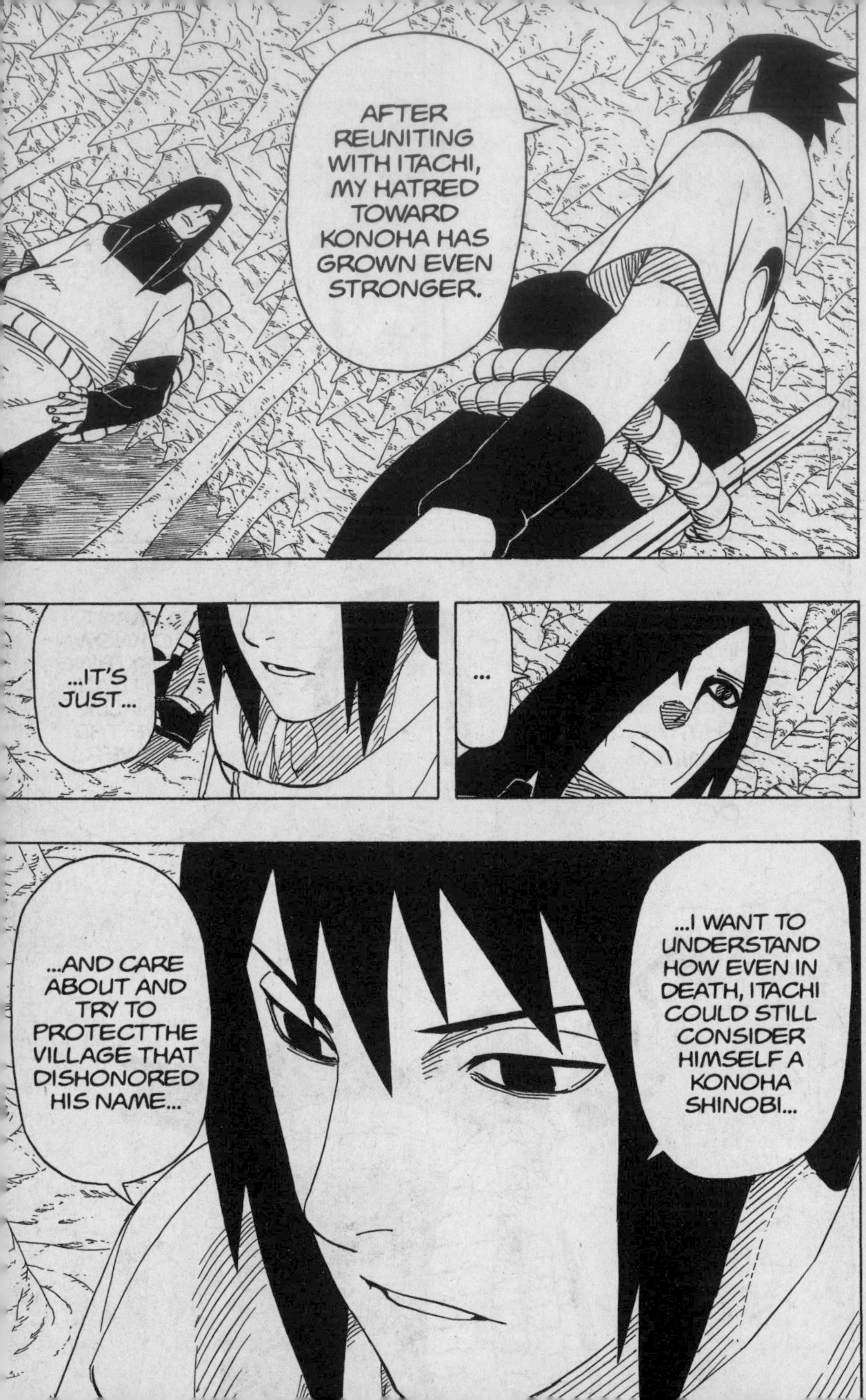
AFTER REUNITING WITH ITACHI, MY HATRED TOWARD KONOHA HAS GROWN EVEN STRONGER.
...
...IT'S JUST...
...I WANT TO UNDERSTAND HOW EVEN IN DEATH, ITACHI COULD STILL CONSIDER HIMSELF A KONOHA SHINOBI...
...AND CARE ABOUT AND TRY TO PROTECTTHE VILLAGE THAT DISHONORED HIS NAME...

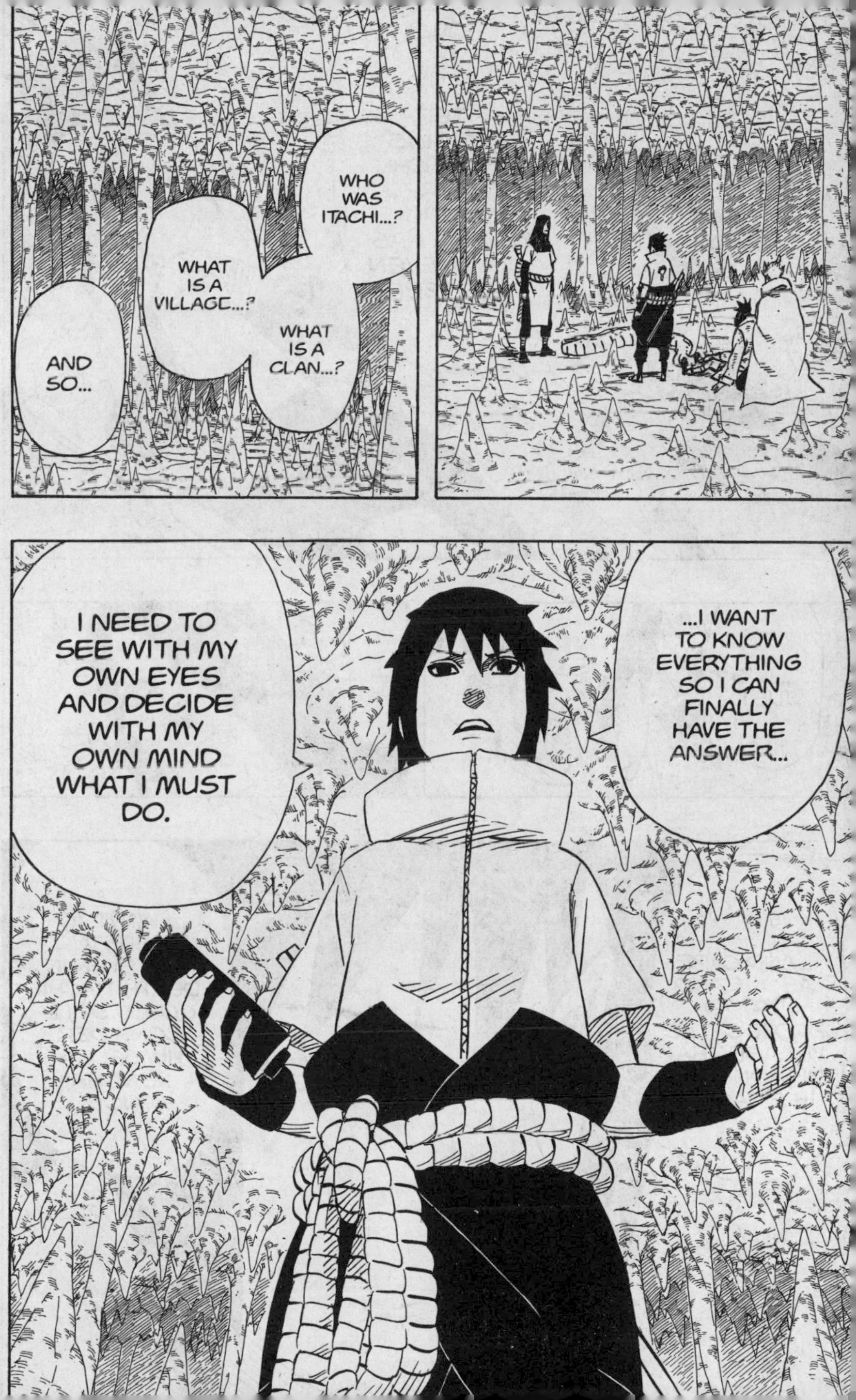
WHO WAS ITACHI...?
WHAT IS A VILLAGE...?
WHAT IS A CLAN...?
AND SO...
...I WANT TO KNOW EVERYTHING SO I CAN FINALLY HAVE THE ANSWER...
I NEED TO SEE WITH MY OWN EYES AND DECIDE WITH MY OWN MIND WHAT I MUST DO.

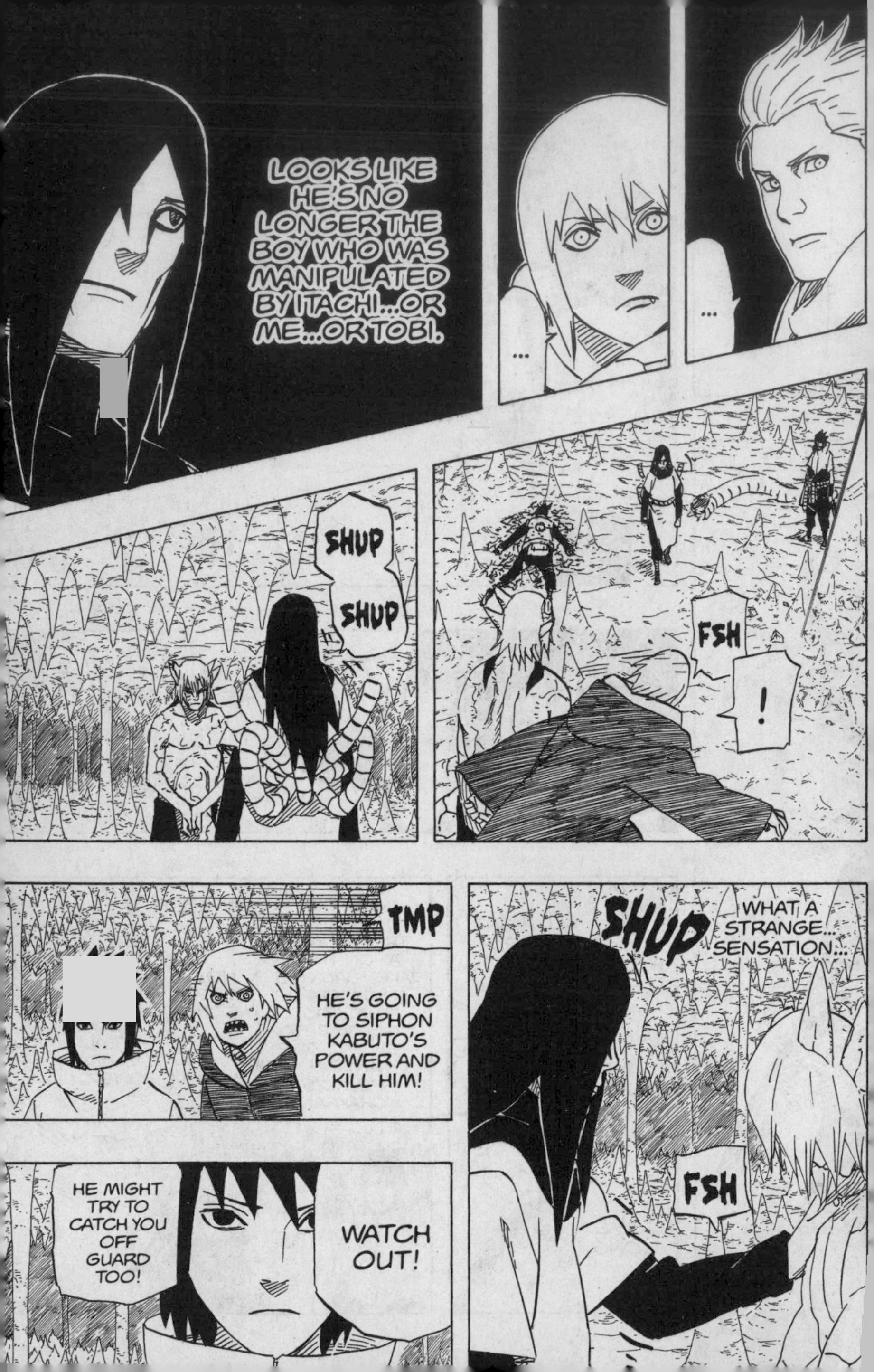
...
...
LOOKS LIKE HE'S NO LONGER THE BOY WHO WAS MANIPULATED BY ITACHI...OR ME...OR TOBI.
FSH
!
SHUP
SHUP
SHUP
WHAT A STRANGE... SENSATION...
FSH
TMP
HE'S GOING TO SIPHON KABUTO'S POWER AND KILL HIM!
WATCH OUT!
HE MIGHT TRY TO CATCH YOU OFF GUARD TOO!

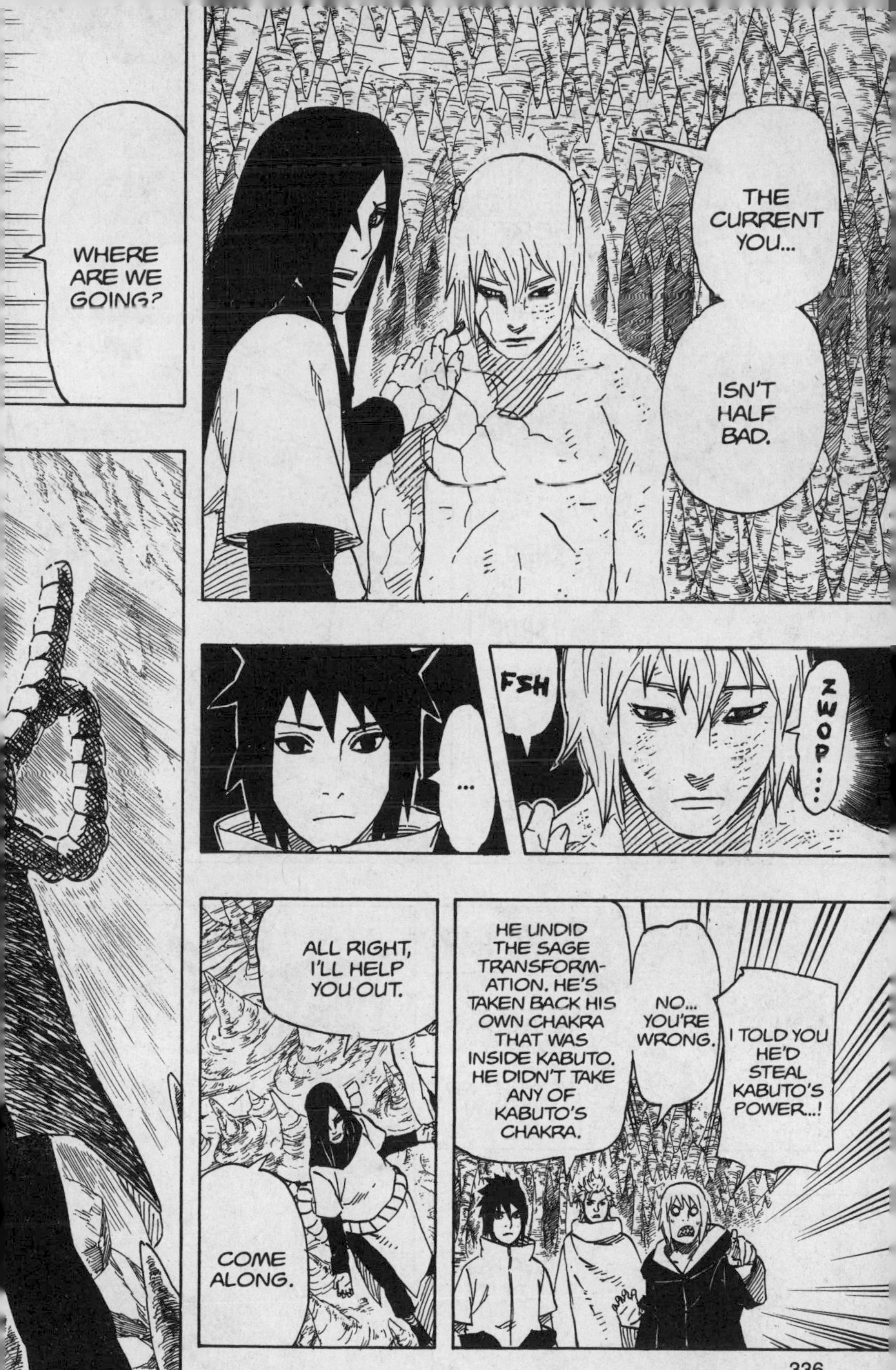
THE CURRENT YOU...
ISN'T HALF BAD.
ZWOP....
FSH
...
I TOLD YOU HE'D STEAL KABUTO'S POWER...!
NO... YOU'RE WRONG.
HE UNDID THE SAGE TRANSFORM-ATION. HE'S TAKEN BACK HIS OWN CHAKRA THAT WAS INSIDE KABUTO. HE DIDN'T TAKE ANY OF KABUTO'S CHAKRA.
ALL RIGHT, I'LL HELP YOU OUT.
COME ALONG.
WHERE ARE WE GOING?

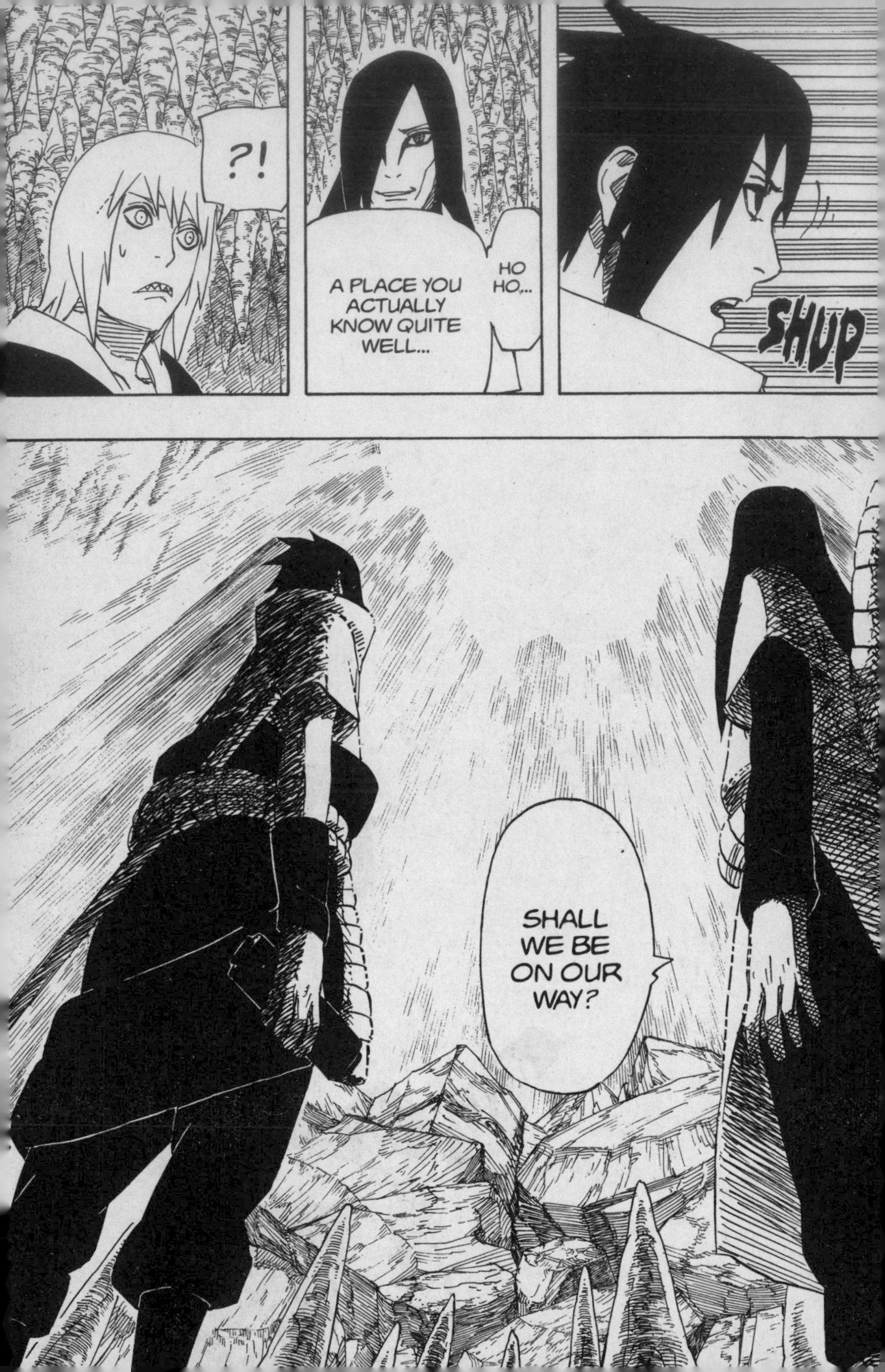
SHUP
HO HO...
A PLACE YOU ACTUALLY KNOW QUITE WELL...
?!
SHALL WE BE ON OUR WAY?

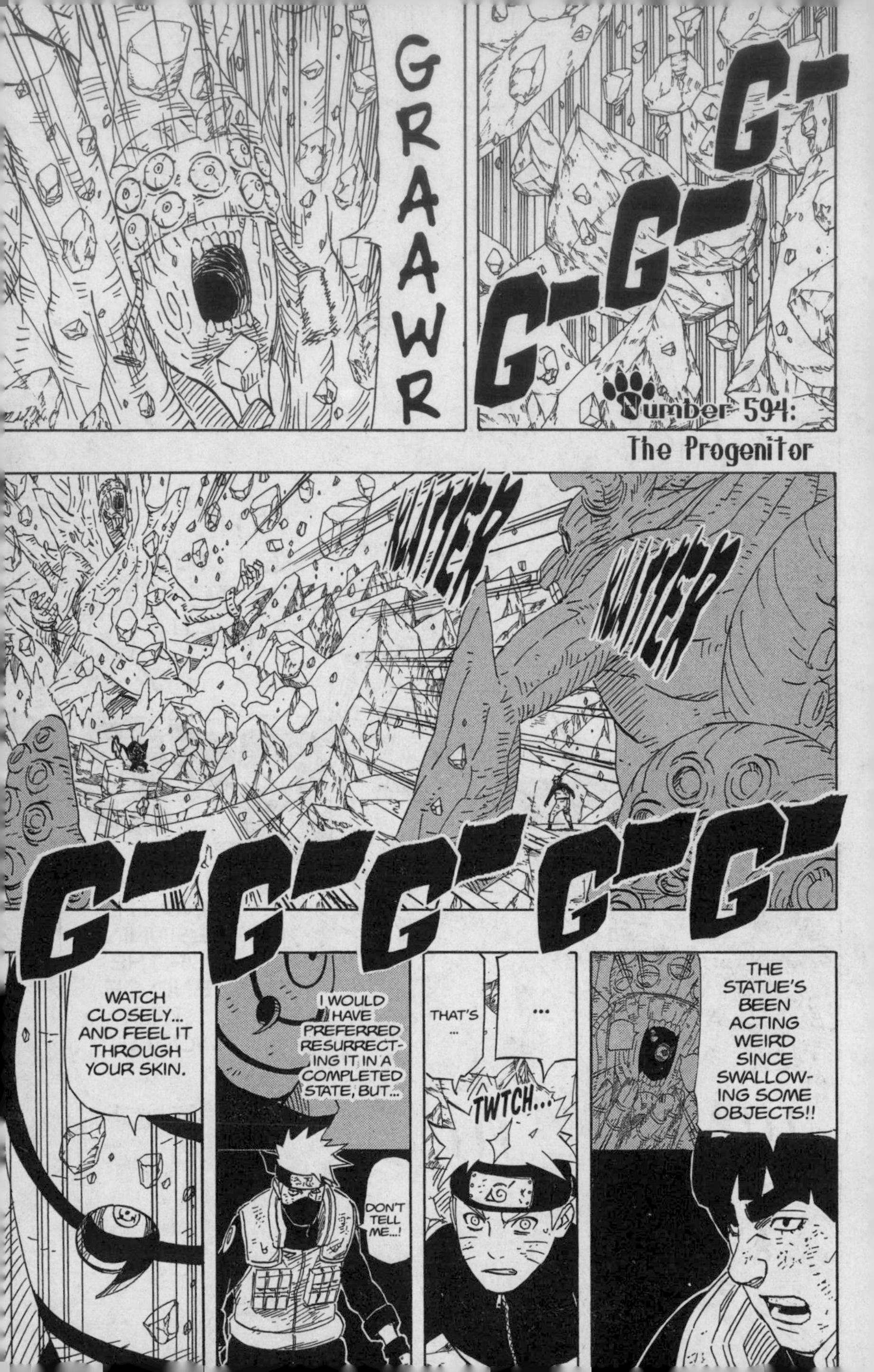
G-G-G-
Number 594:
The Progenitor
GRAWR
KLATTER
KLATTER
G-G-G-G-G-G
THE STATUE'S BEEN ACTING WEIRD SINCE SWALLOWING SOME OBJECTS!!
...
THAT'S ...
TWTCH...
I WOULD HAVE PREFERRED RESURRECTING IT IN A COMPLETED STATE, BUT...
DON'T TELL ME...!
WATCH CLOSELY... AND FEEL IT THROUGH YOUR SKIN.

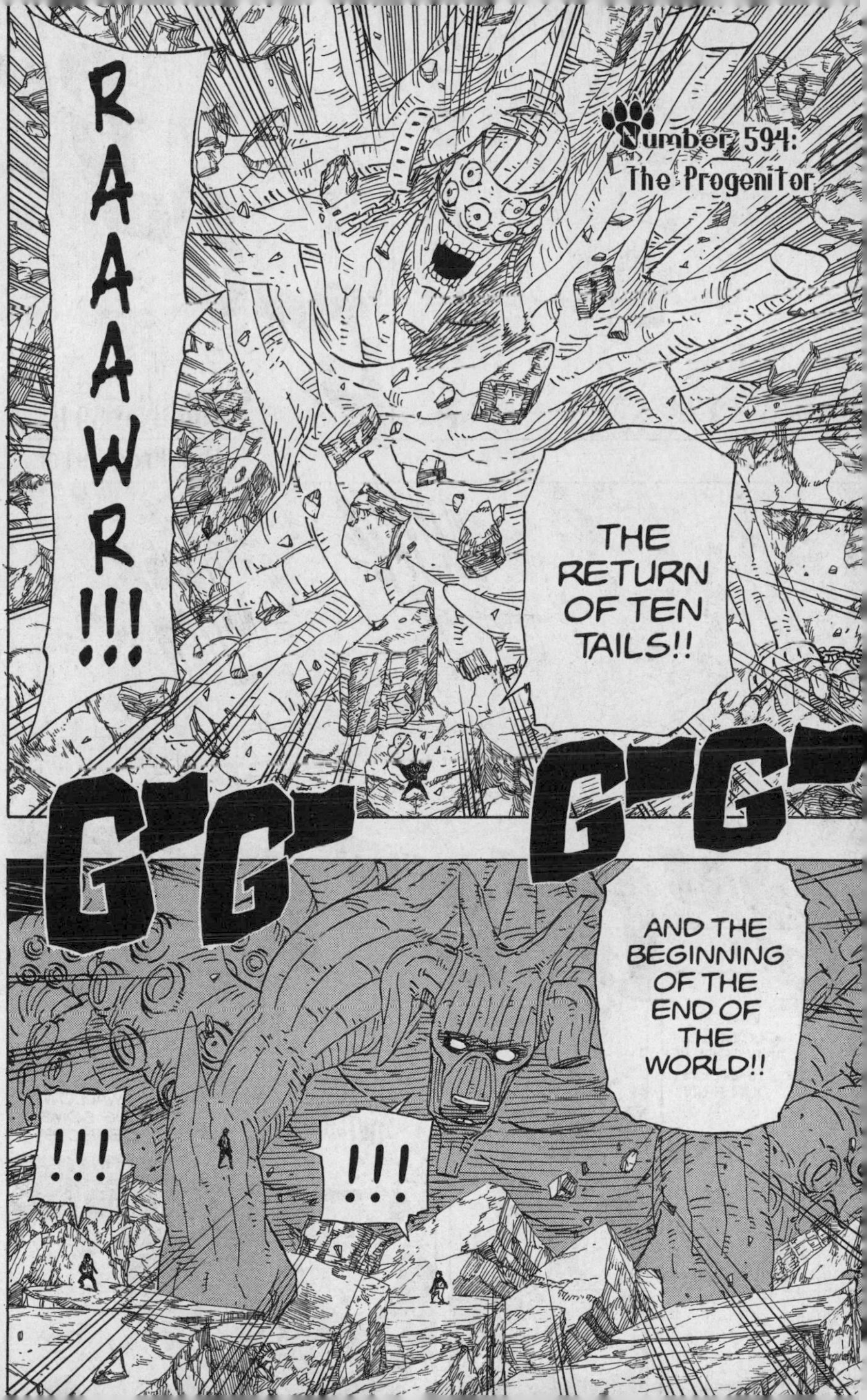
Number 594:
The Progenitor
THE RETURN OF TEN TAILS!!
RAAAWR!!!
GG GG
AND THE BEGINNING OF THE END OF THE WORLD!!
!!!
!!!

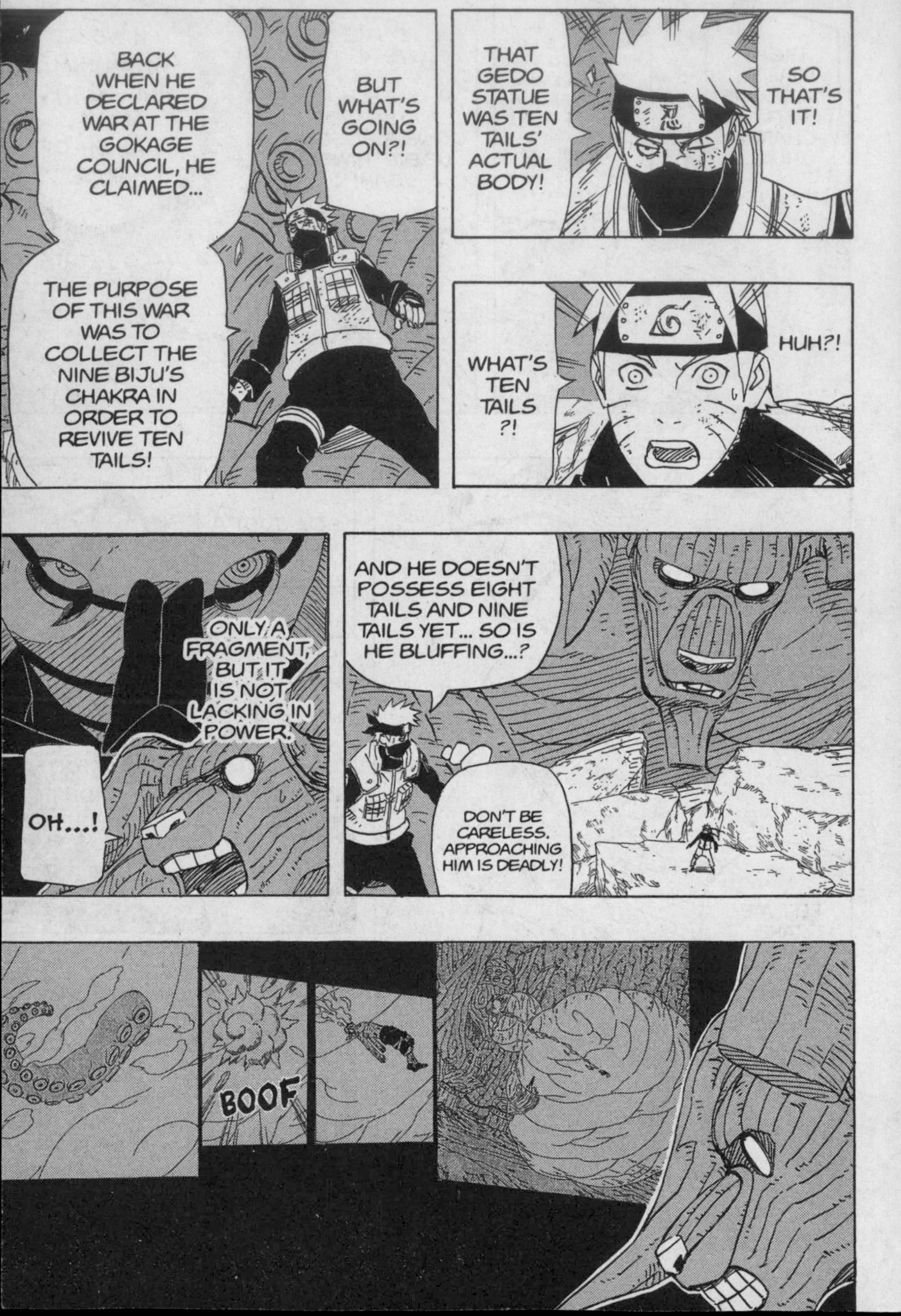
SO THAT'S IT!
THAT GEDO STATUE WAS TEN TAILS' ACTUAL BODY!
HUH?!
WHAT'S TEN TAILS ?!
BUT WHAT'S GOING ON?!
BACK WHEN HE DECLARED WAR AT THE GOKAGE COUNCIL, HE CLAIMED...
THE PURPOSE OF THIS WAR WAS TO COLLECT THE NINE BIJU'S CHAKRA IN ORDER TO REVIVE TEN TAILS!
AND HE DOESN'T POSSESS EIGHT TAILS AND NINE TAILS YET... SO IS HE BLUFFING...?
DON'T BE CARELESS. APPROACHING HIM IS DEADLY!
ONLY A FRAGMENT, BUT IT IS NOT LACKING IN POWER.
OH...!
BOOF

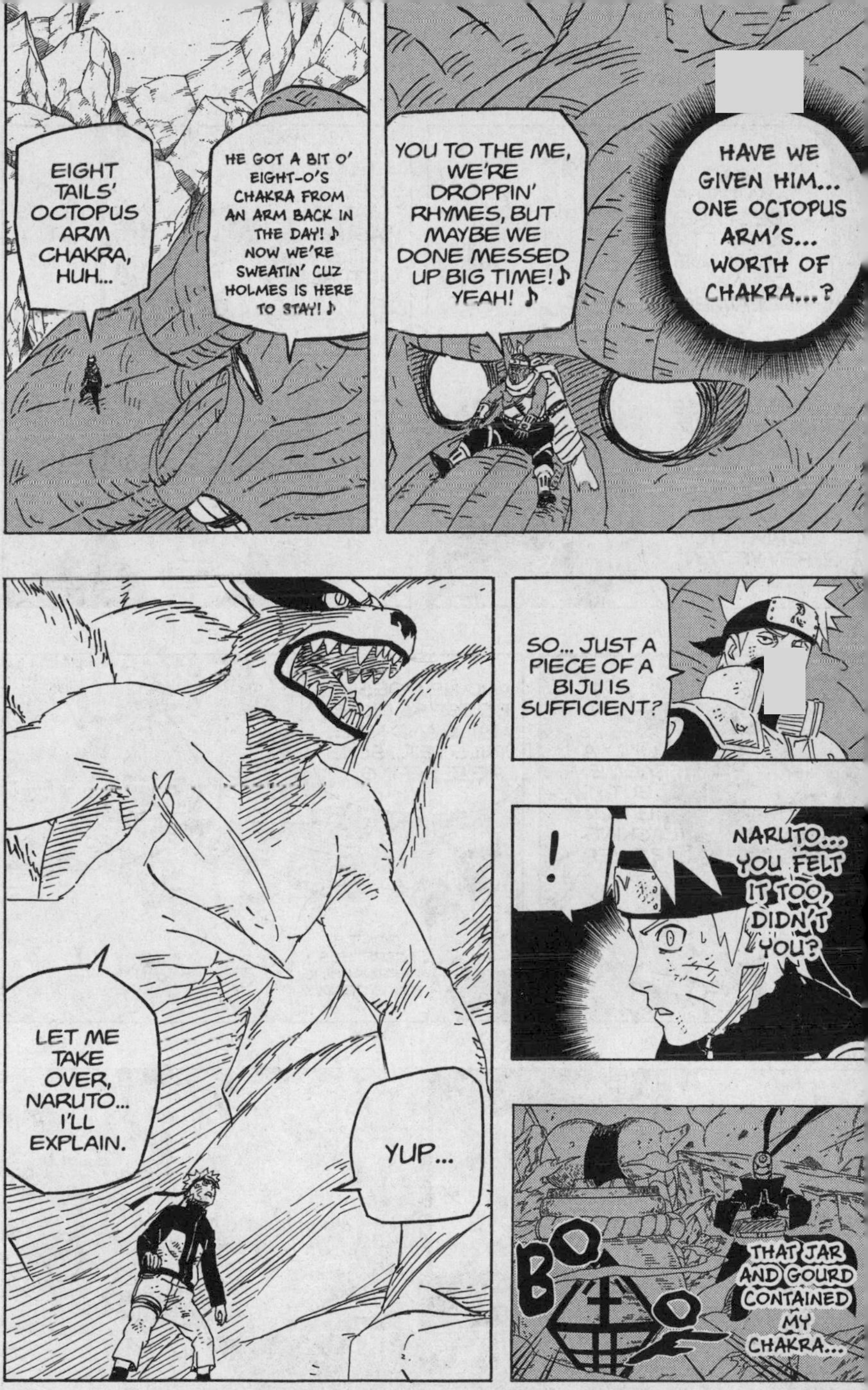
HAVE WE GIVEN HIM... ONE OCTOPUS ARM'S... WORTH OF CHAKRA...?
YOU TO THE ME, WE'RE DROPPIN' RHYMES, BUT MAYBE WE DONE MESSED UP BIG TIME! ♪ YEAH! ♪
HE GOT A BIT O' EIGHT-O'S CHAKRA FROM AN ARM BACK IN THE DAY! ♪ NOW WE'RE SWEATIN' CUZ HOLMES IS HERE TO STAY! ♪
EIGHT TAILS' OCTOPUS ARM CHAKRA, HUH...
SO... JUST A PIECE OF A BIJU IS SUFFICIENT?
NARUTO... YOU FELT IT TOO, DIDN'T YOU?
!
THAT JAR AND GOURD CONTAINED MY CHAKRA...
BO-O
YUP...
LET ME TAKE OVER, NARUTO... I'LL EXPLAIN.

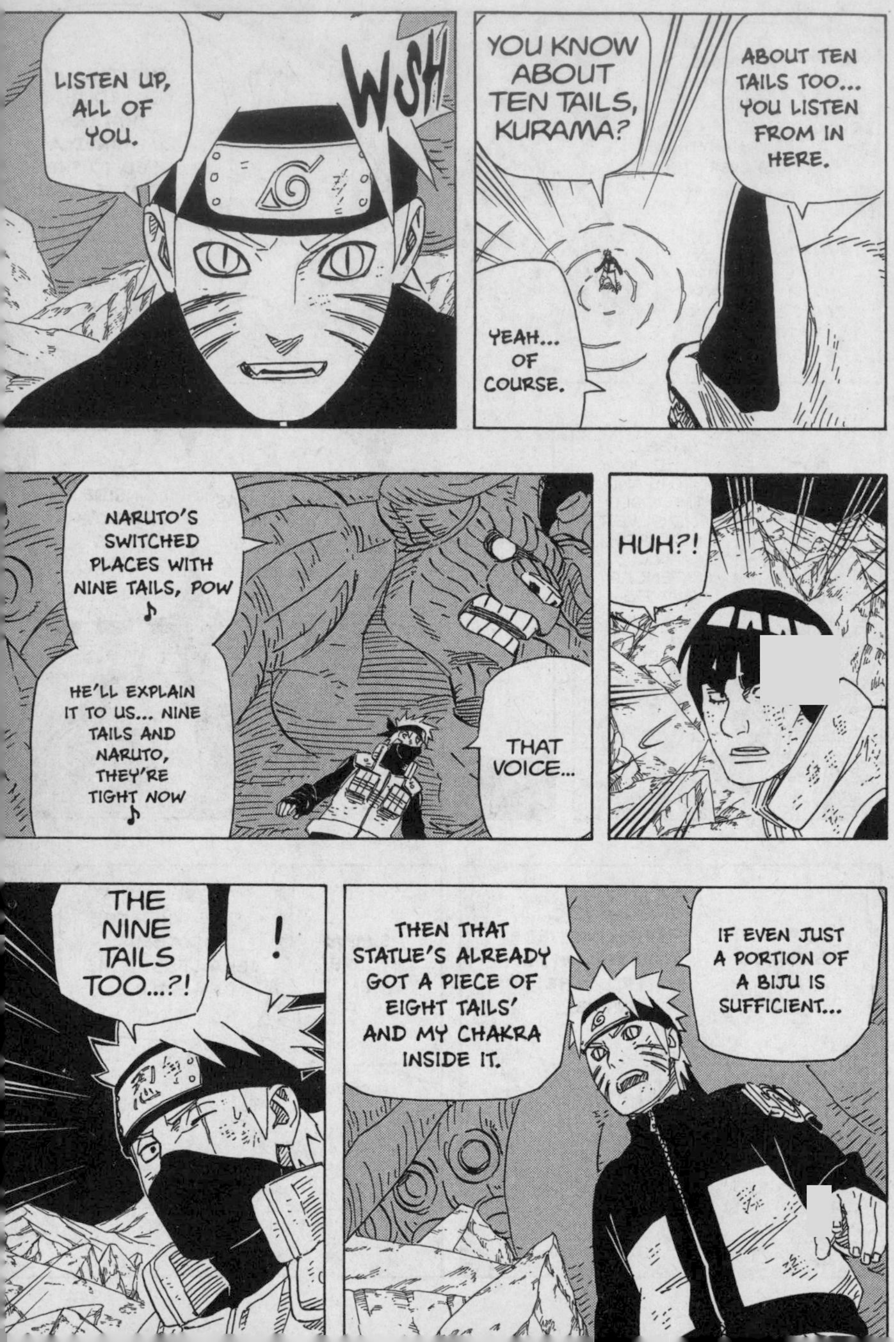
ABOUT TEN TAILS TOO... YOU LISTEN FROM IN HERE.
YOU KNOW ABOUT TEN TAILS, KURAMA?
YEAH... OF COURSE.
WSH
LISTEN UP, ALL OF YOU.
HUH?!
THAT VOICE...
NARUTO'S SWITCHED PLACES WITH NINE TAILS, POW ♪
HE'LL EXPLAIN IT TO US... NINE TAILS AND NARUTO, THEY'RE TIGHT NOW ♪
IF EVEN JUST A PORTION OF A BIJU IS SUFFICIENT...
THEN THAT STATUE'S ALREADY GOT A PIECE OF EIGHT TAILS' AND MY CHAKRA INSIDE IT.
!
THE NINE TAILS TOO...?!

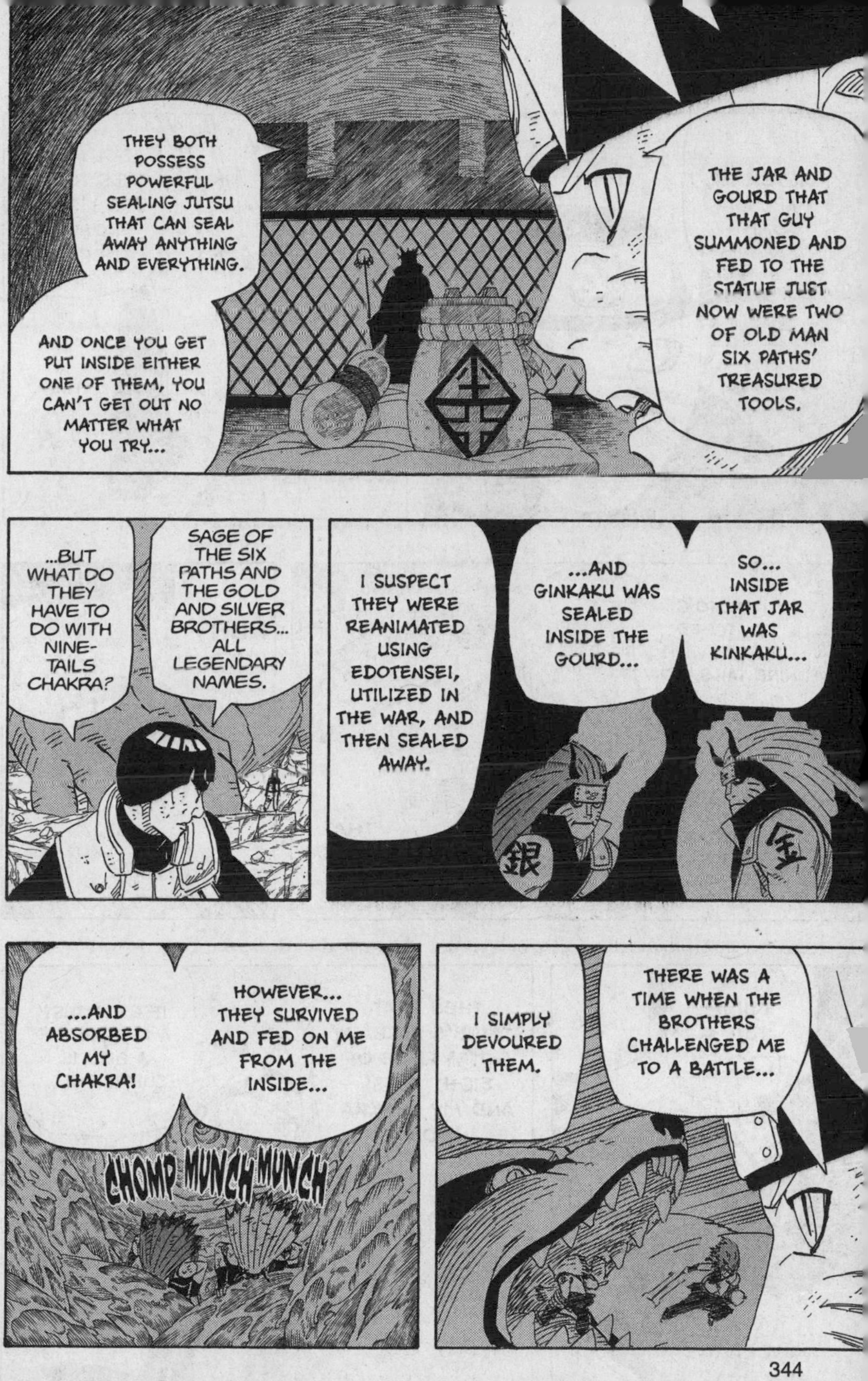
THE JAR AND GOURD THAT THAT GUY SUMMONED AND FED TO THE STATUE JUST NOW WERE TWO OF OLD MAN SIX PATHS' TREASURED TOOLS.
THEY BOTH POSSESS POWERFUL SEALING JUTSU THAT CAN SEAL AWAY ANYTHING AND EVERYTHING.
AND ONCE YOU GET PUT INSIDE EITHER ONE OF THEM, YOU CAN'T GET OUT NO MATTER WHAT YOU TRY...
SO... INSIDE THAT JAR WAS KINKAKU...
...AND GINKAKU WAS SEALED INSIDE THE GOURD...
I SUSPECT THEY WERE REANIMATED USING EDOTENSEI, UTILIZED IN THE WAR, AND THEN SEALED AWAY.
SAGE OF THE SIX PATHS AND THE GOLD AND SILVER BROTHERS... ALL LEGENDARY NAMES.
...BUT WHAT DO THEY HAVE TO DO WITH NINE-TAILS CHAKRA?
THERE WAS A TIME WHEN THE BROTHERS CHALLENGED ME TO A BATTLE...
I SIMPLY DEVOURED THEM.
HOWEVER... THEY SURVIVED AND FED ON ME FROM THE INSIDE...
...AND ABSORBED MY CHAKRA!
CHOMP MUNCH MUNCH

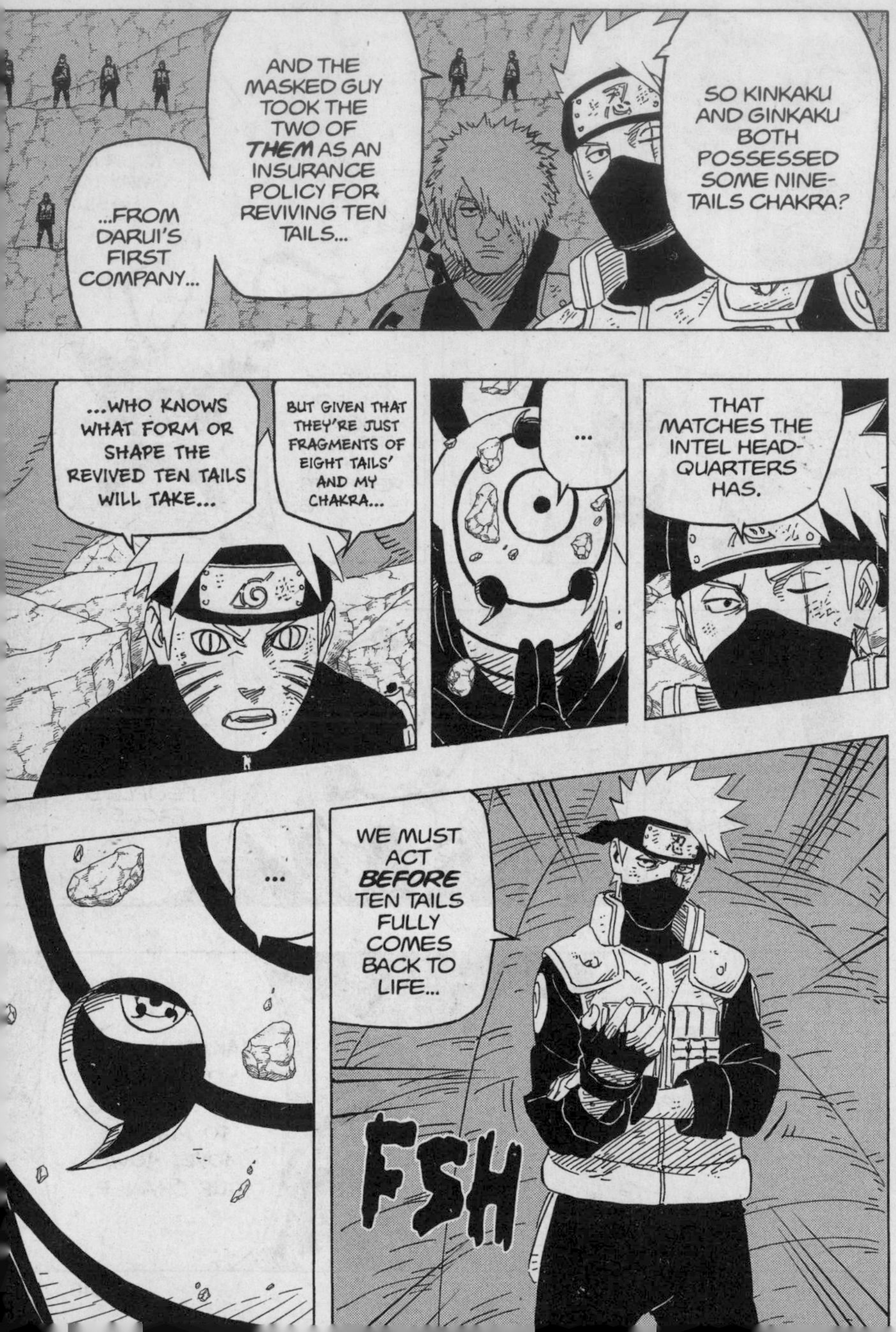
SO KINKAKU AND GINKAKU BOTH POSSESSED SOME NINE-TAILS CHAKRA?
AND THE MASKED GUY TOOK THE TWO OF THEM AS AN INSURANCE POLICY FOR REVIVING TEN TAILS...
...FROM DARUI'S FIRST COMPANY...
THAT MATCHES THE INTEL HEAD-QUARTERS HAS.
...
BUT GIVEN THAT THEY'RE JUST FRAGMENTS OF EIGHT TAILS' AND MY CHAKRA...
...WHO KNOWS WHAT FORM OR SHAPE THE REVIVED TEN TAILS WILL TAKE...
WE MUST ACT BEFORE TEN TAILS FULLY COMES BACK TO LIFE...
FSH
...

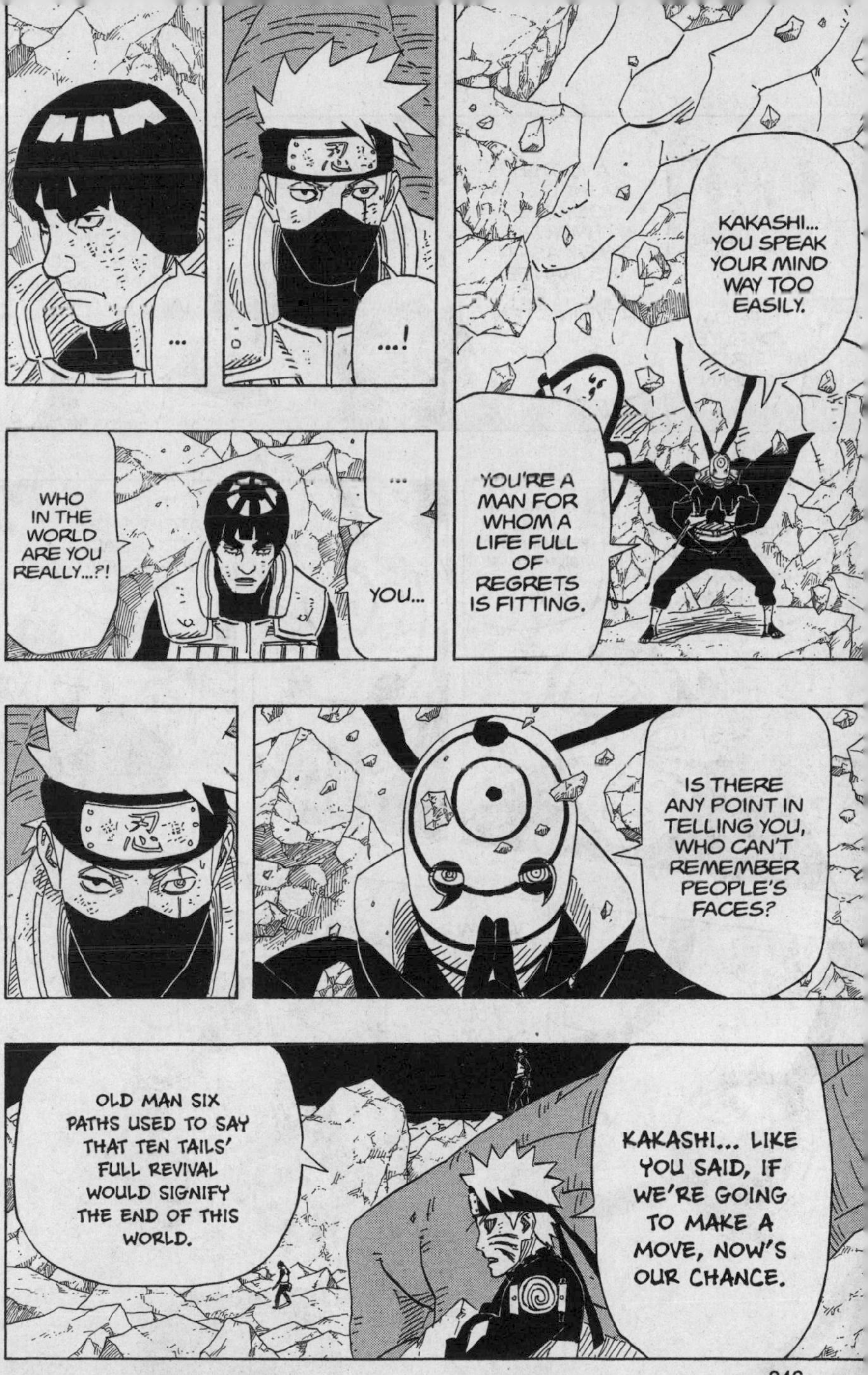
KAKASHI... YOU SPEAK YOUR MIND WAY TOO EASILY.
YOU'RE A MAN FOR WHOM A LIFE FULL OF REGRETS IS FITTING.
...!
...
... YOU...
WHO IN THE WORLD ARE YOU REALLY...?!
IS THERE ANY POINT IN TELLING YOU, WHO CAN'T REMEMBER PEOPLE'S FACES?
KAKASHI... LIKE YOU SAID, IF WE'RE GOING TO MAKE A MOVE, NOW'S OUR CHANCE.
OLD MAN SIX PATHS USED TO SAY THAT TEN TAILS' FULL REVIVAL WOULD SIGNIFY THE END OF THIS WORLD.

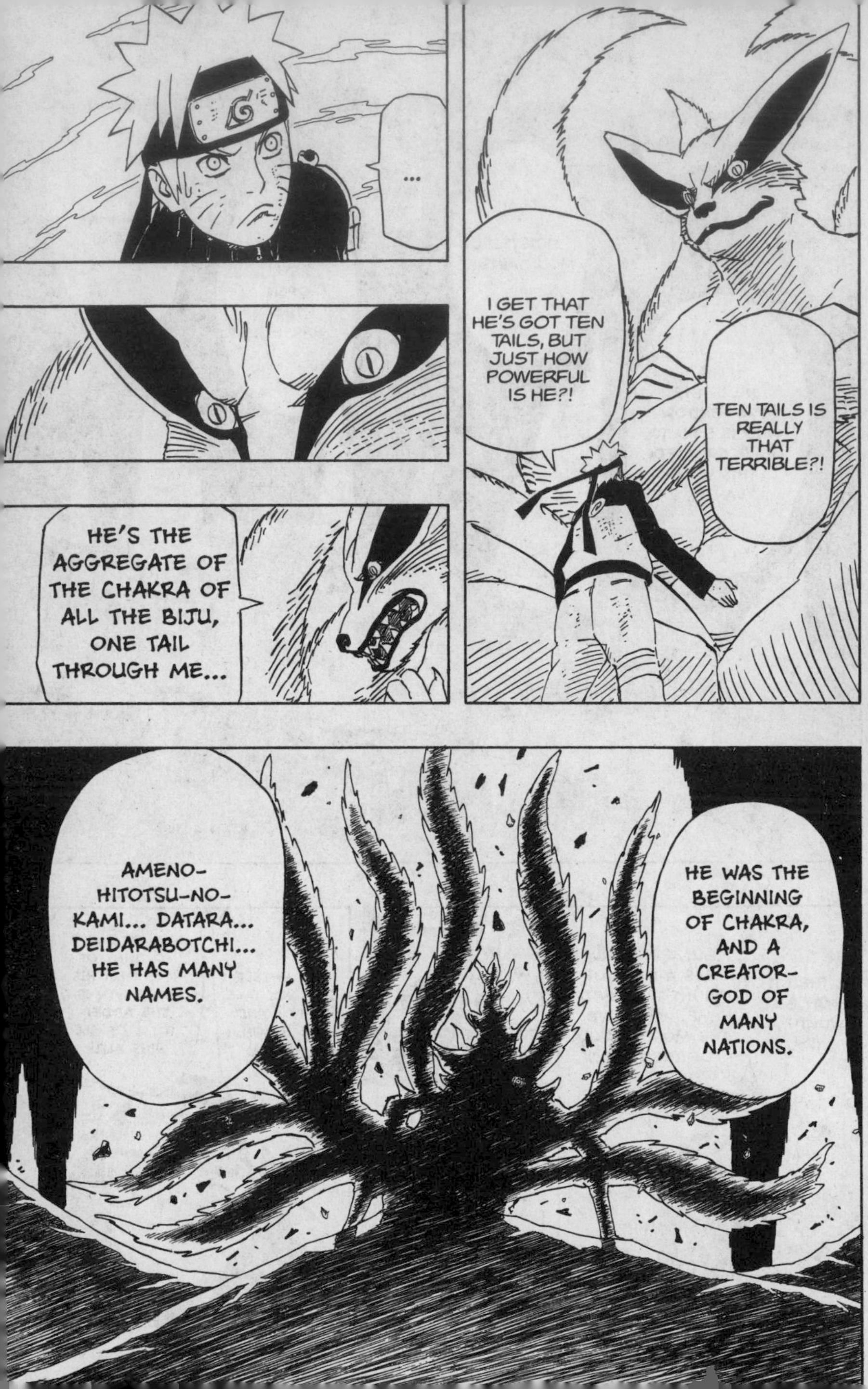
TEN TAILS IS REALLY THAT TERRIBLE?!
I GET THAT HE'S GOT TEN TAILS, BUT JUST HOW POWERFUL IS HE?!
...
HE'S THE AGGREGATE OF THE CHAKRA OF ALL THE BIJU, ONE TAIL THROUGH ME...
HE WAS THE BEGINNING OF CHAKRA, AND A CREATOR-GOD OF MANY NATIONS.
AMENO-HITOTSU-NO-KAMI... DATARA... DEIDARABOTCHI... HE HAS MANY NAMES.

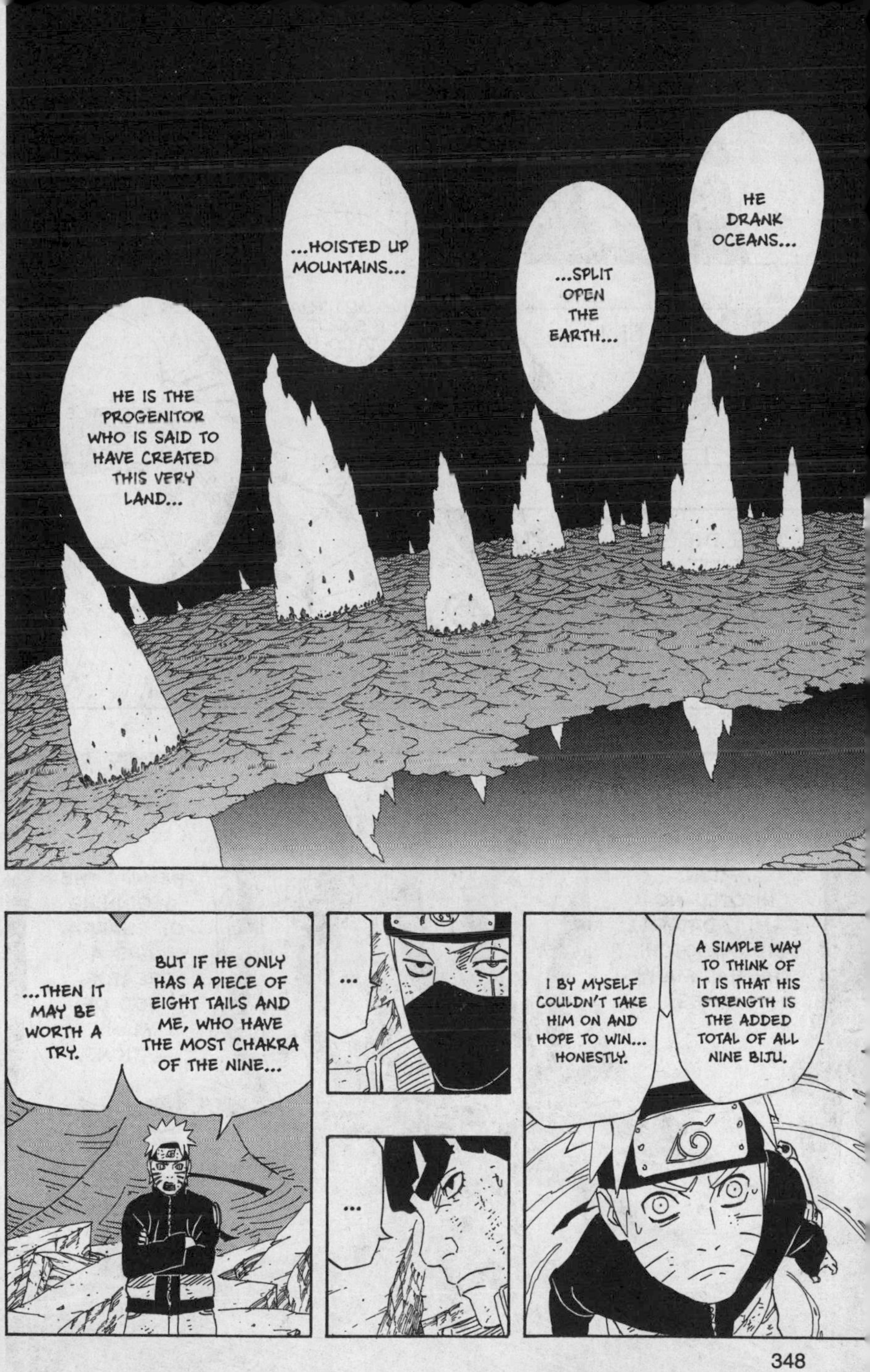
HE DRANK OCEANS...
...SPLIT OPEN THE EARTH...
...HOISTED UP MOUNTAINS...
HE IS THE PROGENITOR WHO IS SAID TO HAVE CREATED THIS VERY LAND...
A SIMPLE WAY TO THINK OF IT IS THAT HIS STRENGTH IS THE ADDED TOTAL OF ALL NINE BIJU.
I BY MYSELF COULDN'T TAKE HIM ON AND HOPE TO WIN... HONESTLY.
...
...
BUT IF HE ONLY HAS A PIECE OF EIGHT TAILS AND ME, WHO HAVE THE MOST CHAKRA OF THE NINE...
...THEN IT MAY BE WORTH A TRY.

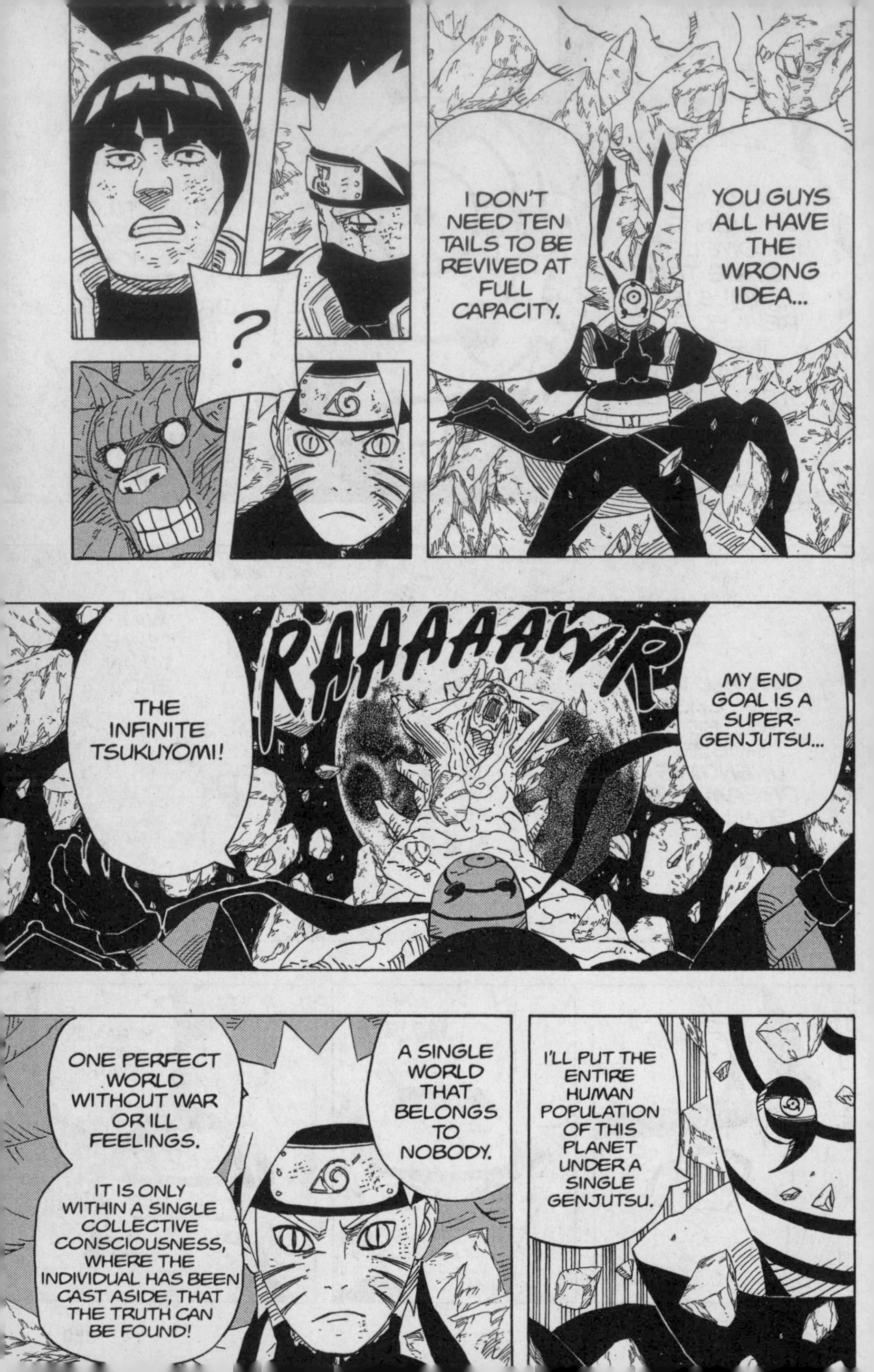
YOU GUYS ALL HAVE THE WRONG IDEA...
I DON'T NEED TEN TAILS TO BE REVIVED AT FULL CAPACITY.
?
MY END GOAL IS A SUPER-GENJUTSU...
RAAAAAWR
THE INFINITE TSUKUYOMI!
I'LL PUT THE ENTIRE HUMAN POPULATION OF THIS PLANET UNDER A SINGLE GENJUTSU.
A SINGLE WORLD THAT BELONGS TO NOBODY.
ONE PERFECT WORLD WITHOUT WAR OR ILL FEELINGS.
IT IS ONLY WITHIN A SINGLE COLLECTIVE CONSCIOUSNESS, WHERE THE INDIVIDUAL HAS BEEN CAST ASIDE, THAT THE TRUTH CAN BE FOUND!

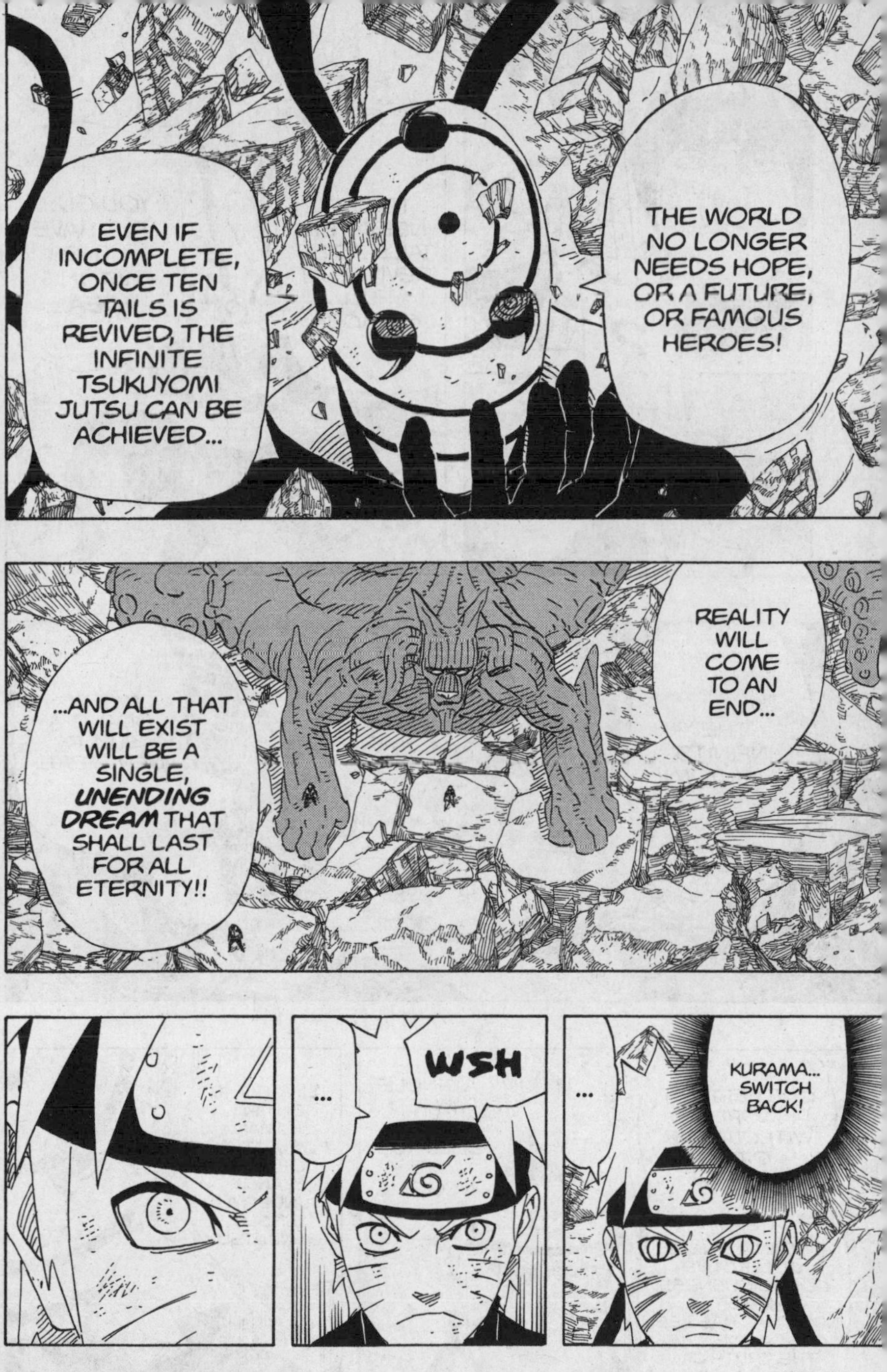
THE WORLD NO LONGER NEEDS HOPE, OR A FUTURE, OR FAMOUS HEROES!
EVEN IF INCOMPLETE, ONCE TEN TAILS IS REVIVED, THE INFINITE TSUKUYOMI JUTSU CAN BE ACHIEVED...
REALITY WILL COME TO AN END...
...AND ALL THAT WILL EXIST WILL BE A SINGLE, ***UNENDING DREAM*** THAT SHALL LAST FOR ALL ETERNITY!!
KURAMA... SWITCH BACK!
...
WSH
...

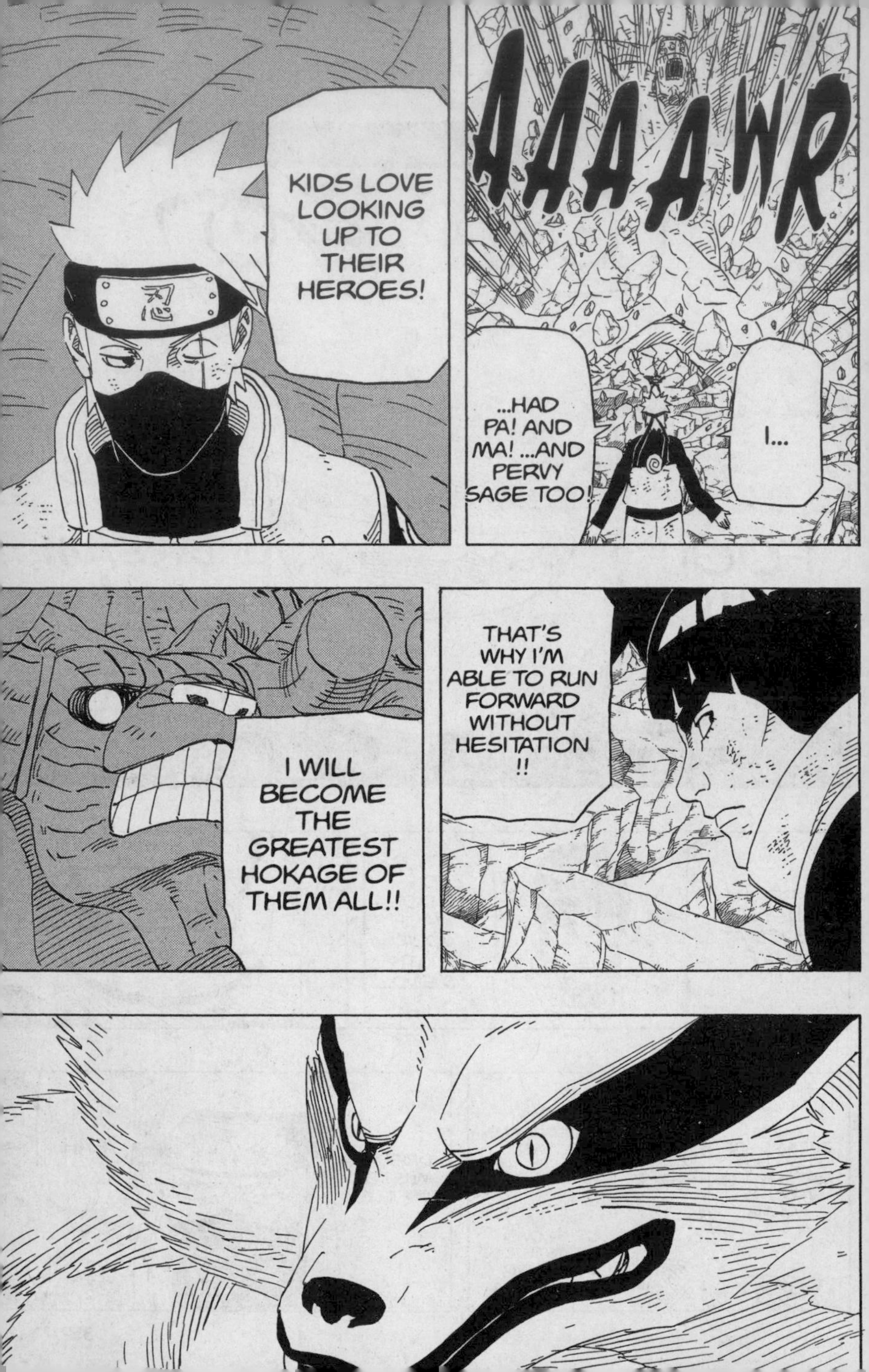
AAAAWR
I...
...HAD PA! AND MA! ...AND PERVY SAGE TOO!
KIDS LOVE LOOKING UP TO THEIR HEROES!
THAT'S WHY I'M ABLE TO RUN FORWARD WITHOUT HESITATION !!
I WILL BECOME THE GREATEST HOKAGE OF THEM ALL!!

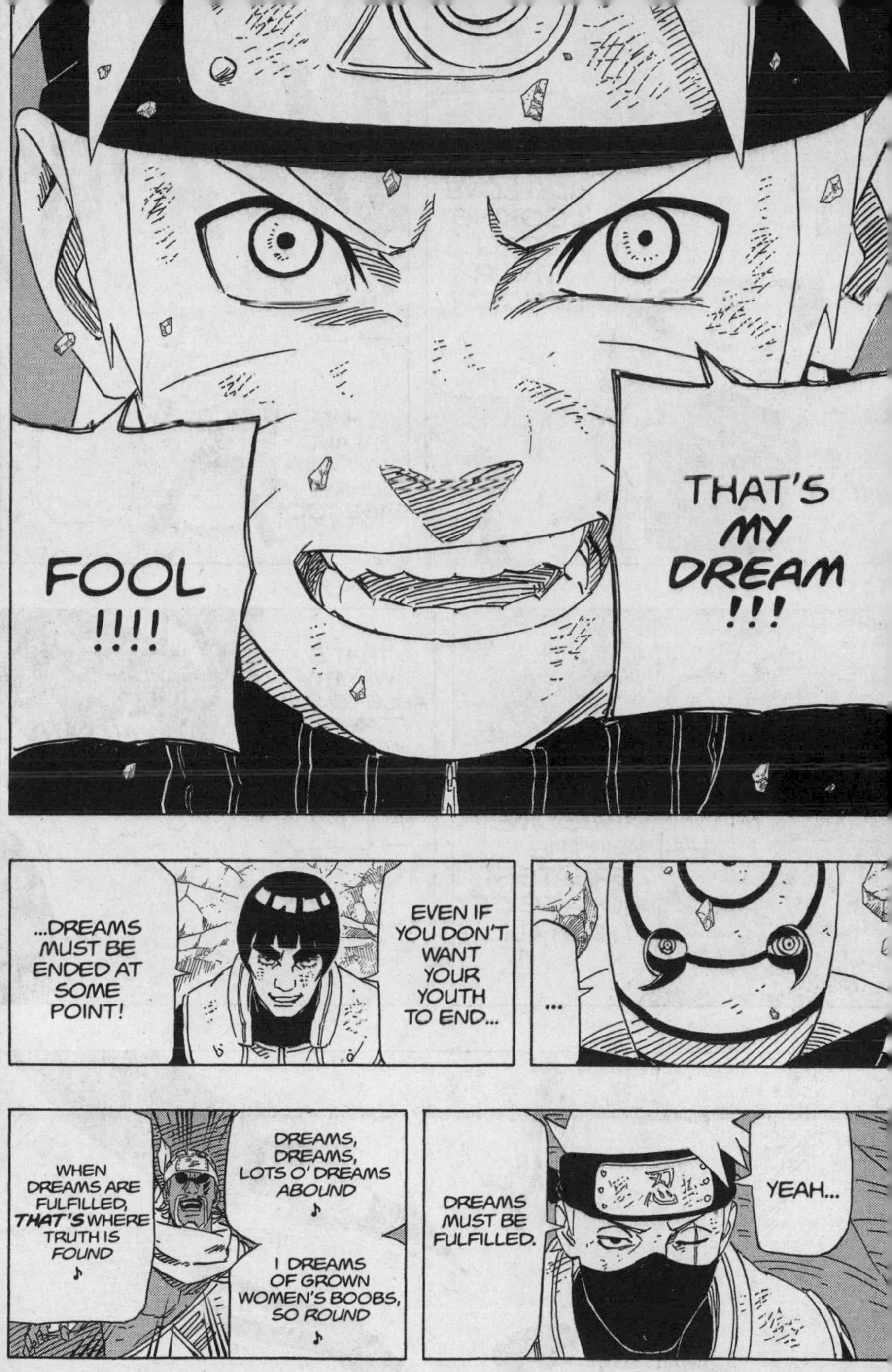
THAT'S MY DREAM!!!
FOOL!!!!
...
EVEN IF YOU DON'T WANT YOUR YOUTH TO END...
...DREAMS MUST BE ENDED AT SOME POINT!
YEAH...
DREAMS MUST BE FULFILLED.
DREAMS, DREAMS, LOTS O' DREAMS ABOUND ♪
WHEN DREAMS ARE FULFILLED, THAT'S WHERE TRUTH IS FOUND ♪
I DREAMS OF GROWN WOMEN'S BOOBS, SO ROUND ♪

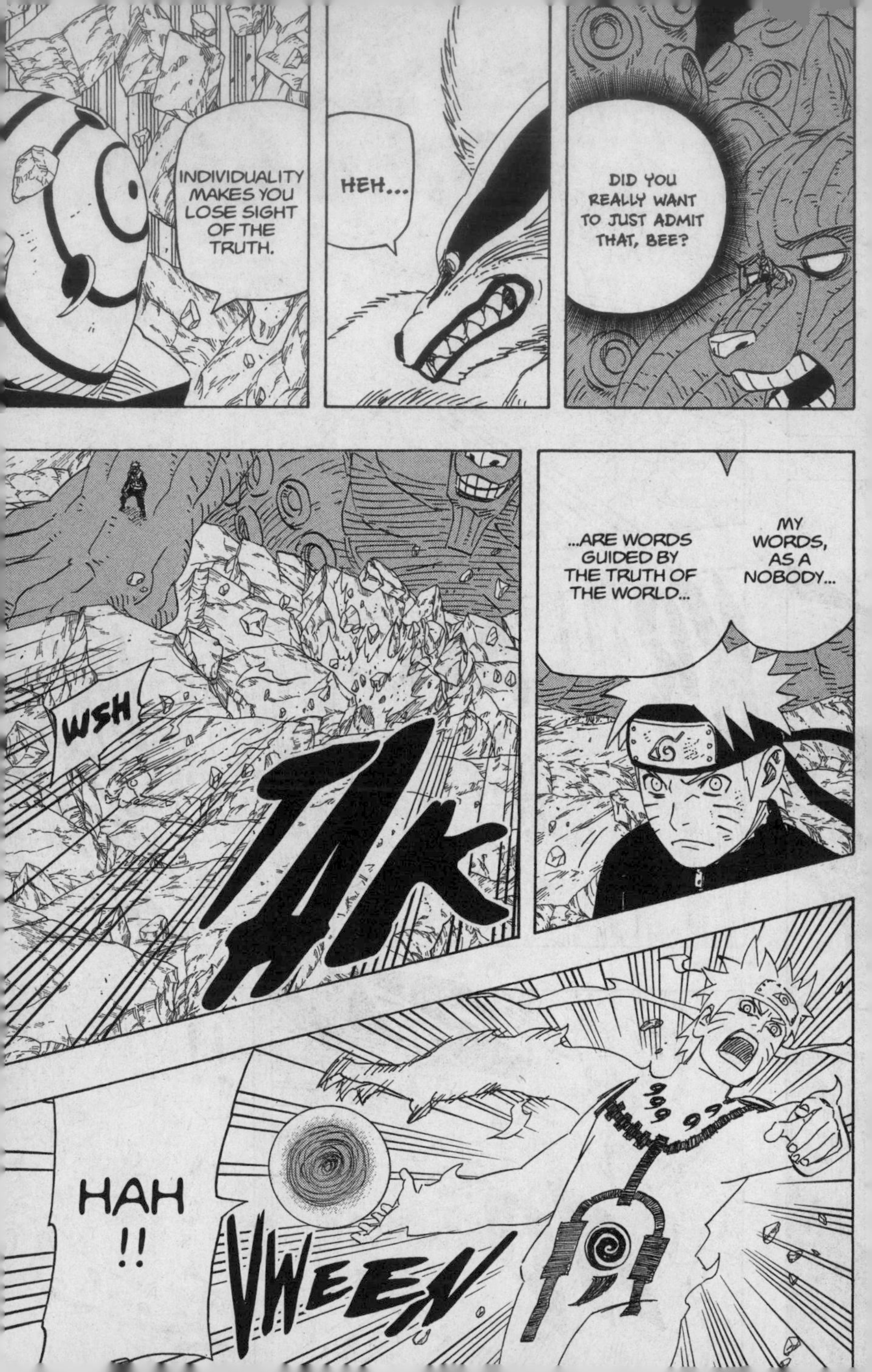
DID YOU REALLY WANT TO JUST ADMIT THAT, BEE?
HEH...
INDIVIDUALITY MAKES YOU LOSE SIGHT OF THE TRUTH.
MY WORDS, AS A NOBODY...
...ARE WORDS GUIDED BY THE TRUTH OF THE WORLD...
WSH
TAK
HAH !!
VWEEN

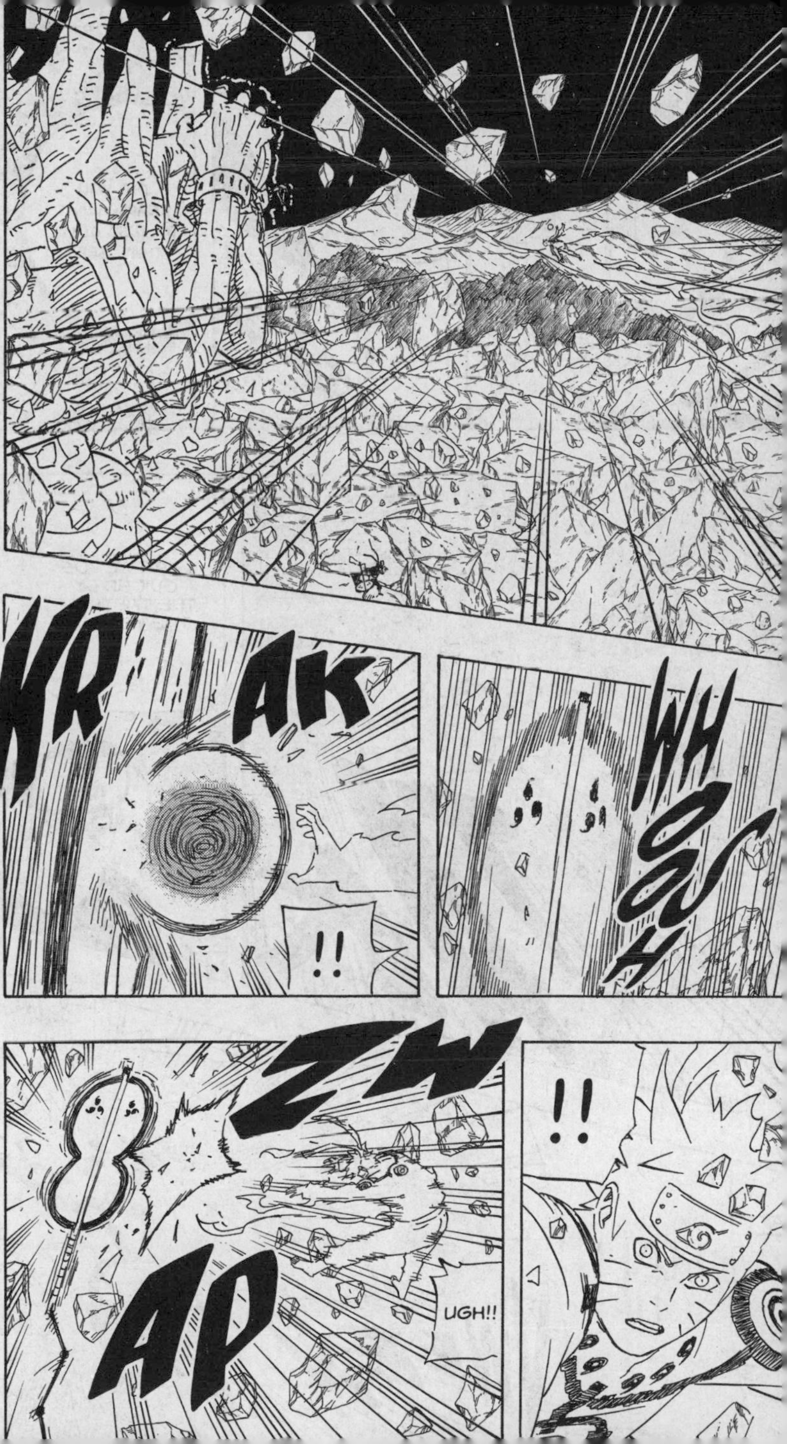
WHOSH
KRAK
!!
!!
ZWAP
UGH!!

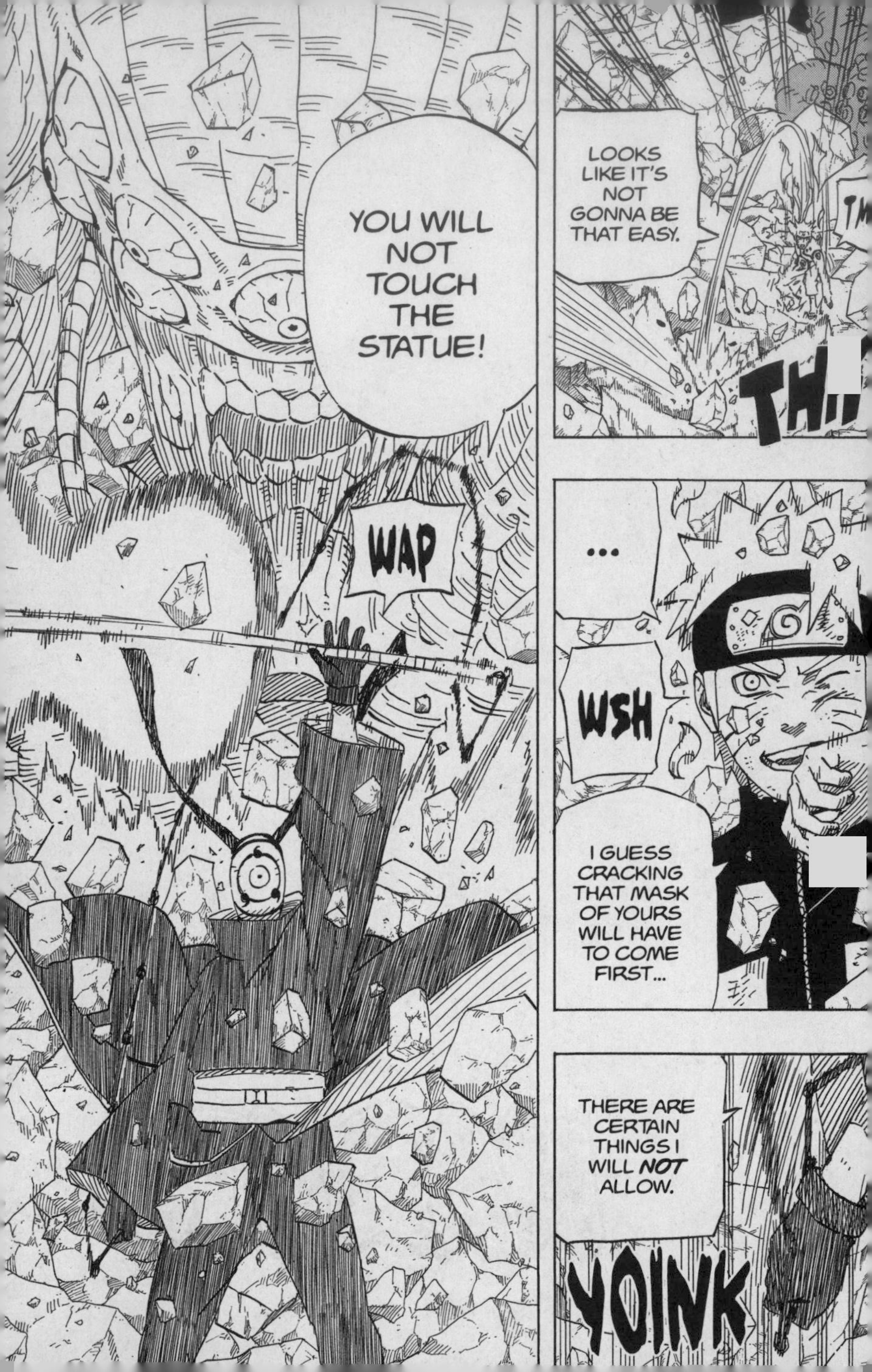
LOOKS LIKE IT'S NOT GONNA BE THAT EASY.
...
WSH
I GUESS CRACKING THAT MASK OF YOURS WILL HAVE TO COME FIRST...
THERE ARE CERTAIN THINGS I WILL *NOT* ALLOW.
YOINK
YOU WILL NOT TOUCH THE STATUE!
WAP

NARUTO

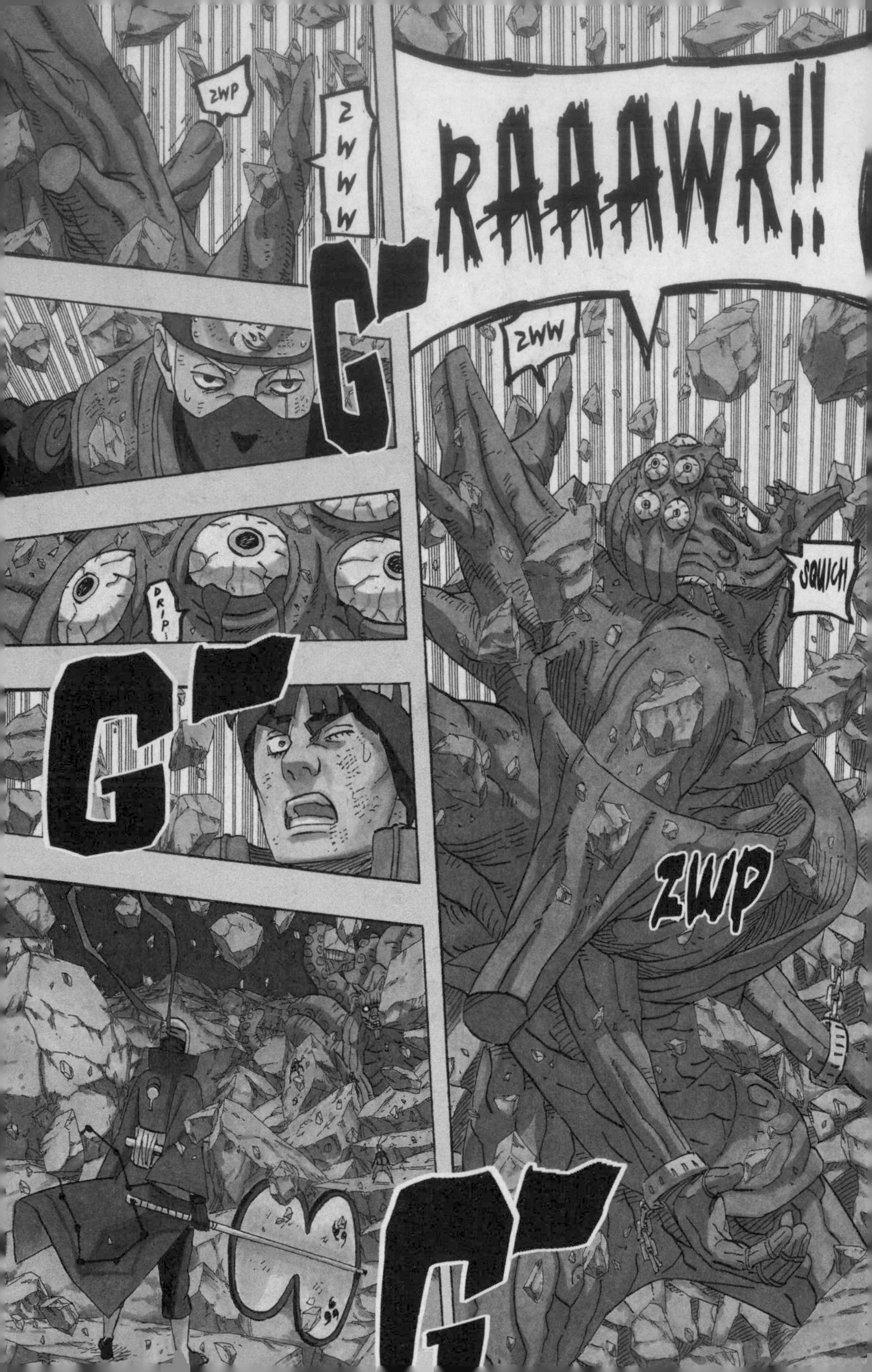

RAAAWR!!
ZWW
SQUICH
ZWP
G'
ZWP
ZWWW
G'
DRIP
G'

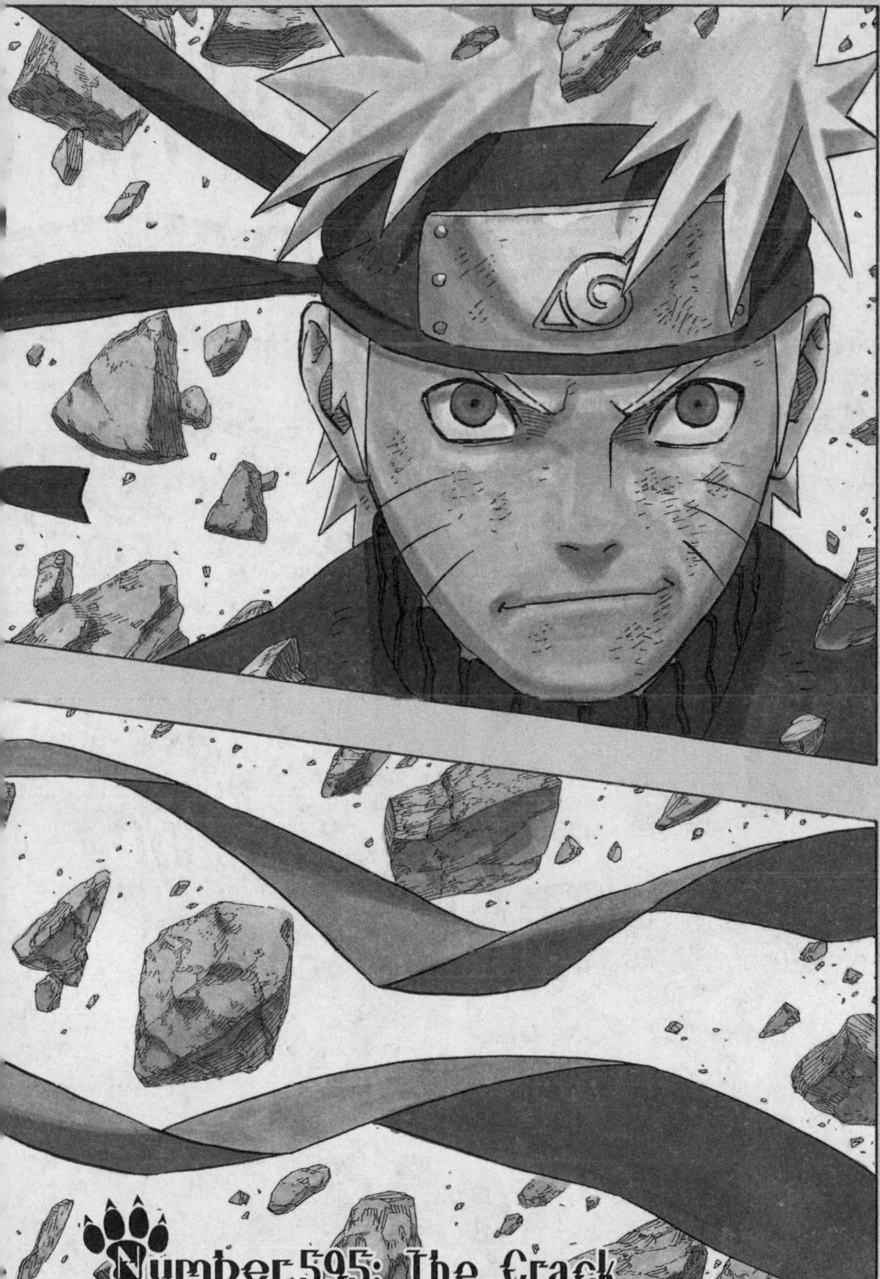
Number 595: The Crack

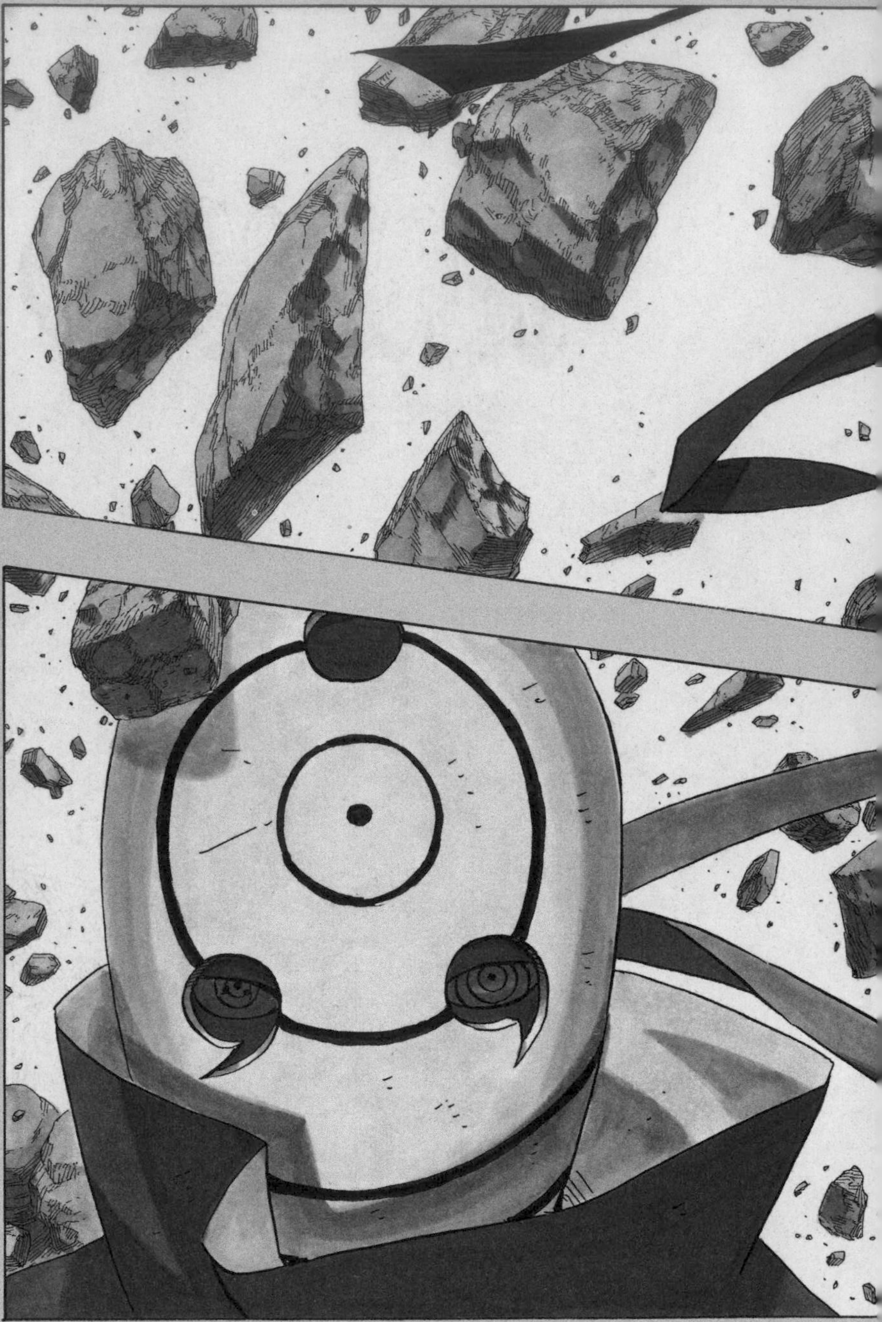

NARUTO

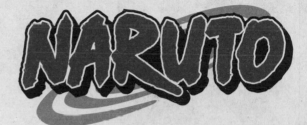

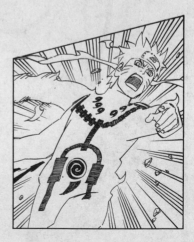

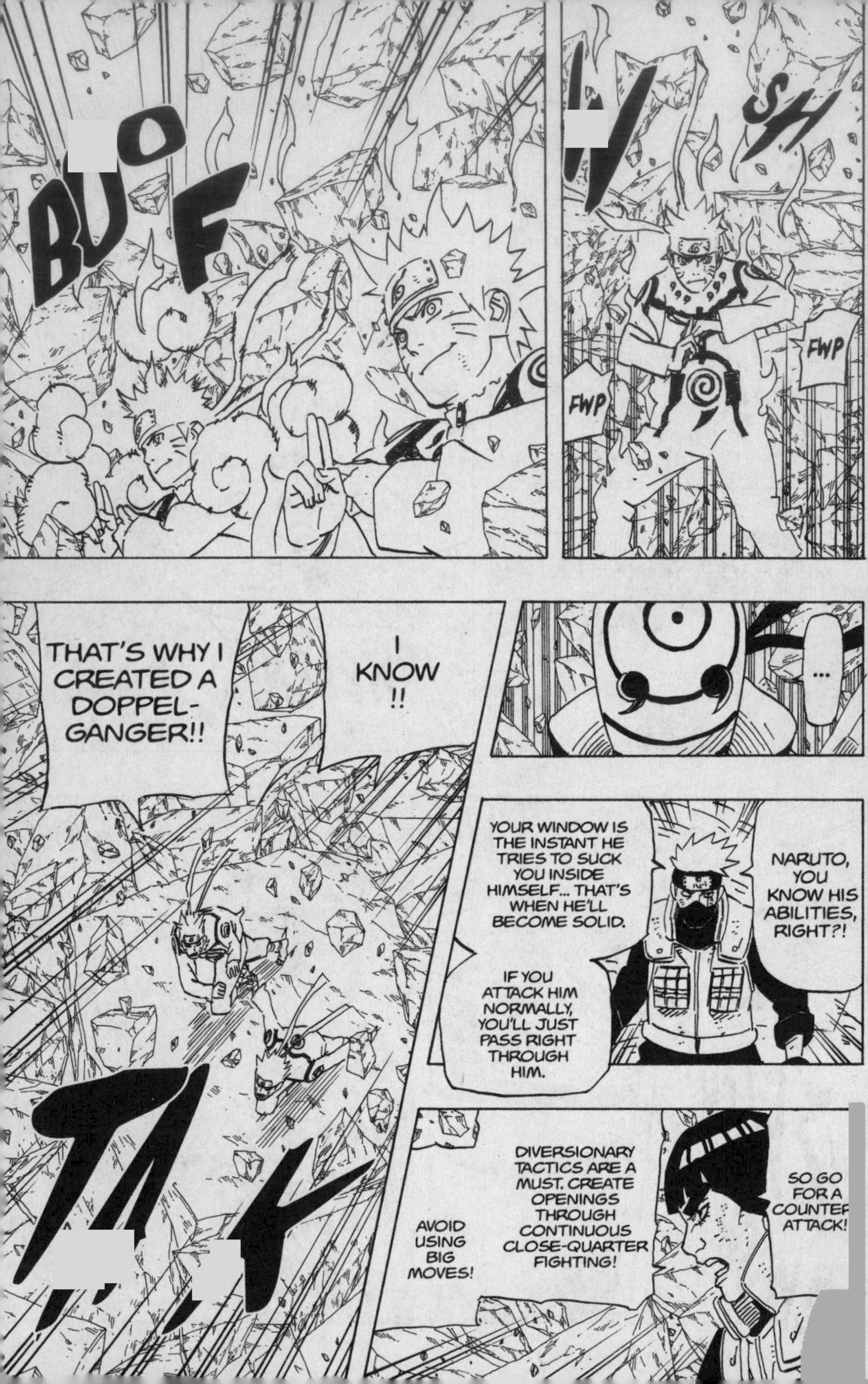
SH
FWP
FWP
...
NARUTO, YOU KNOW HIS ABILITIES, RIGHT?!
YOUR WINDOW IS THE INSTANT HE TRIES TO SUCK YOU INSIDE HIMSELF... THAT'S WHEN HE'LL BECOME SOLID.
IF YOU ATTACK HIM NORMALLY, YOU'LL JUST PASS RIGHT THROUGH HIM.
SO GO FOR A COUNTER ATTACK!
DIVERSIONARY TACTICS ARE A MUST. CREATE OPENINGS THROUGH CONTINUOUS CLOSE-QUARTER FIGHTING!
AVOID USING BIG MOVES!
I KNOW !!
THAT'S WHY I CREATED A DOPPEL-GANGER!!

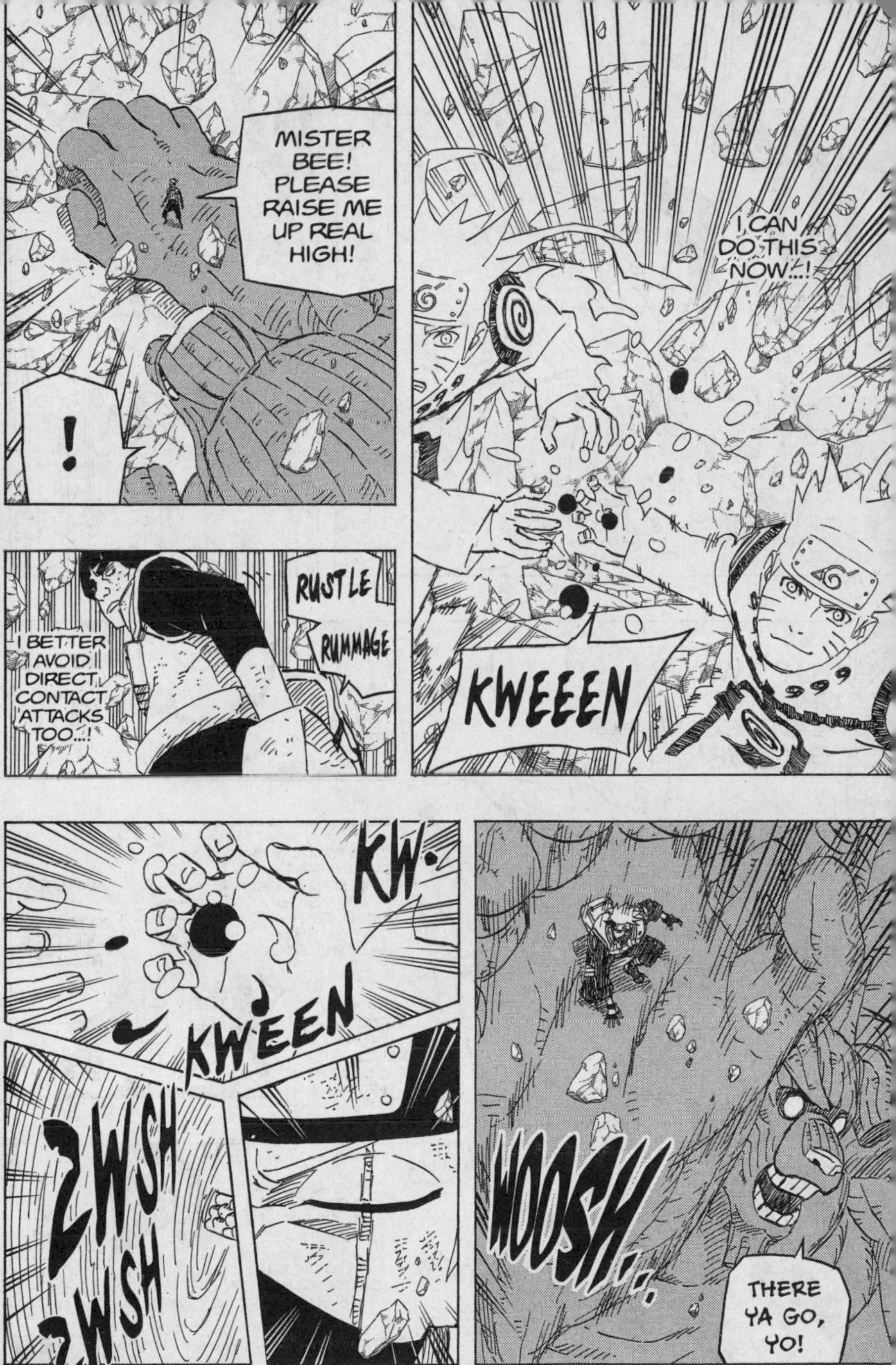
I CAN DO THIS NOW...!
KWEEEN
MISTER BEE! PLEASE RAISE ME UP REAL HIGH!
!
RUSTLE
RUMMAGE
I BETTER AVOID DIRECT CONTACT ATTACKS TOO...!
WOOSH..
THERE YA GO, YO!
KW
KWEEN
ZWSH
ZWSH

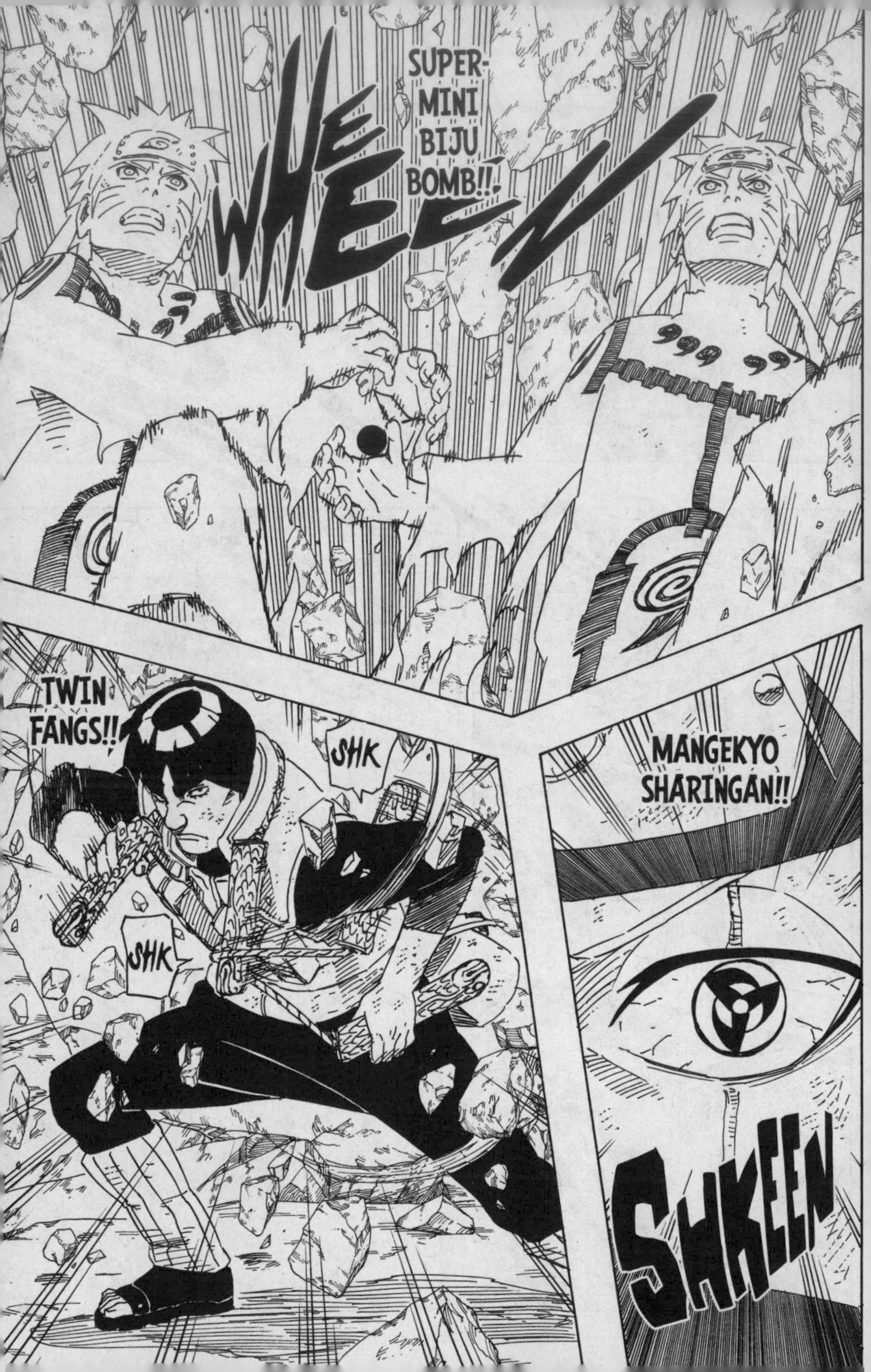
SUPER-MINI BIJU BOMB!!
WHEEN
MANGEKYO SHARINGAN!!
SHKEEN
TWIN FANGS!!
SHK
SHK

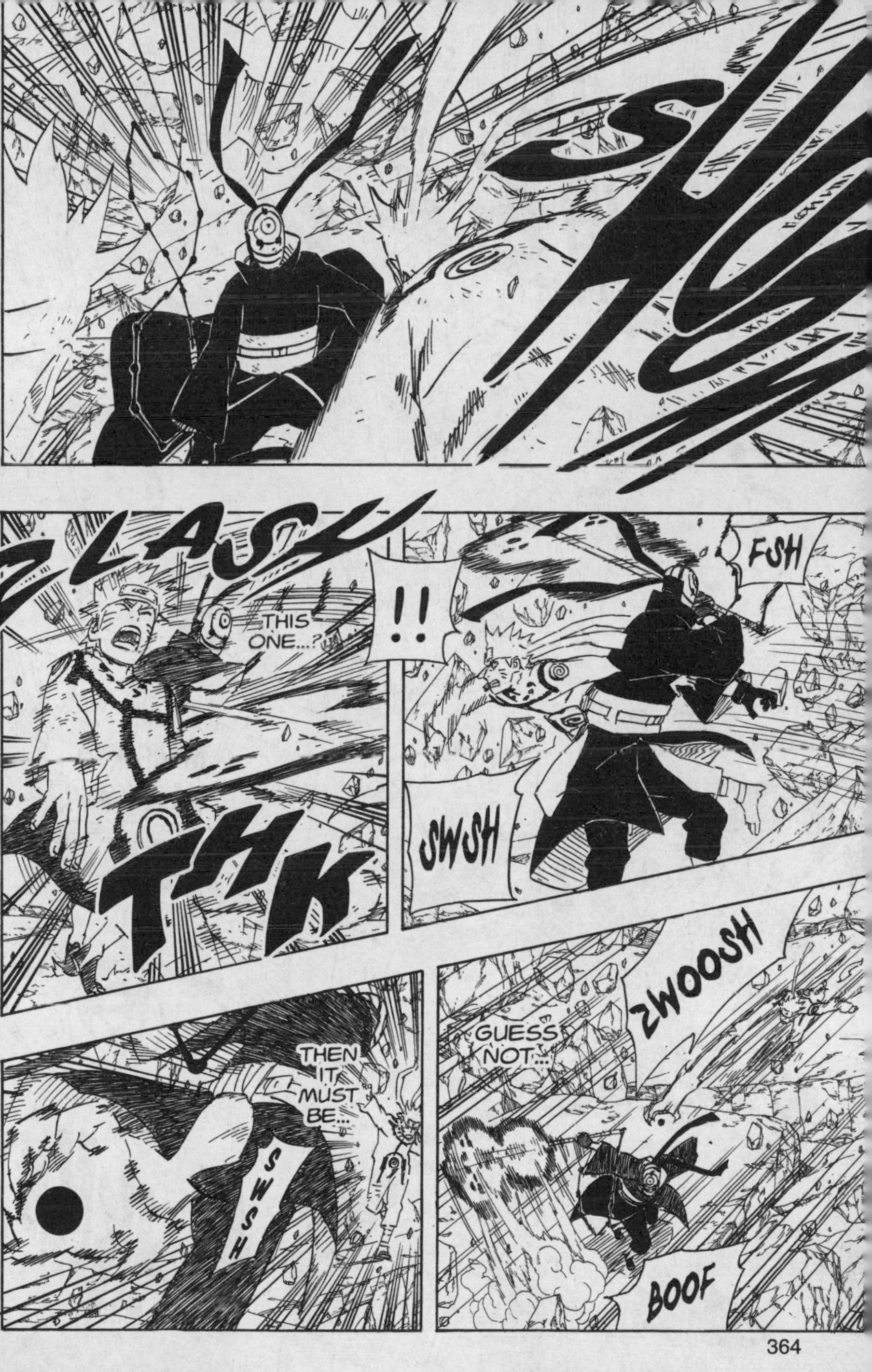

FSH
!!
SWSH
ZLASH
THIS ONE...?
THK
ZWOOSH
GUESS NOT...
BOOF
THEN IT MUST BE...
SWSH

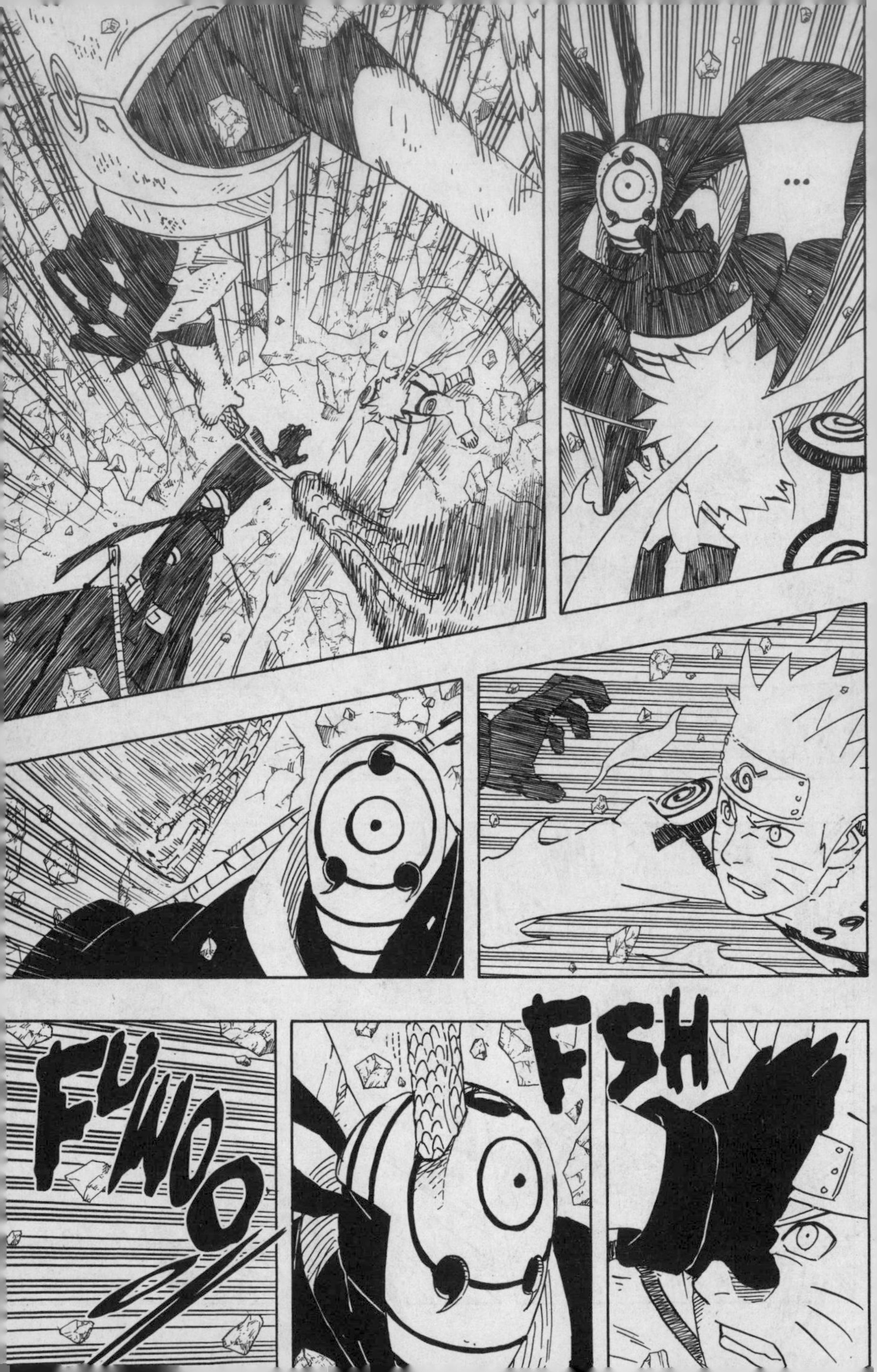
...
FSH
FWOOSH

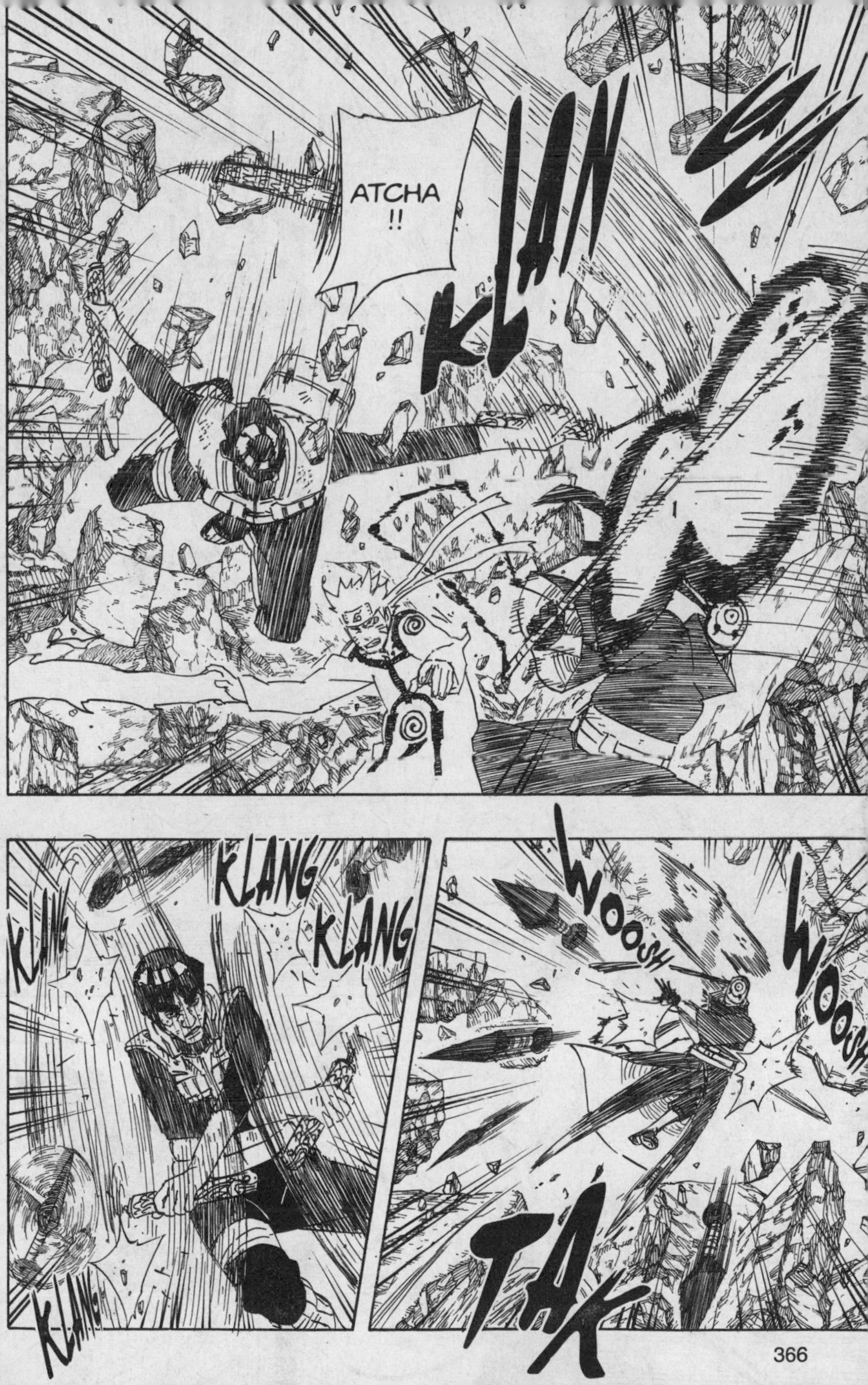

ATCHA !!
KLAN
WOOOSH
WOOOSH
TAK
KLANG
KLANG
KLANG
KLANG

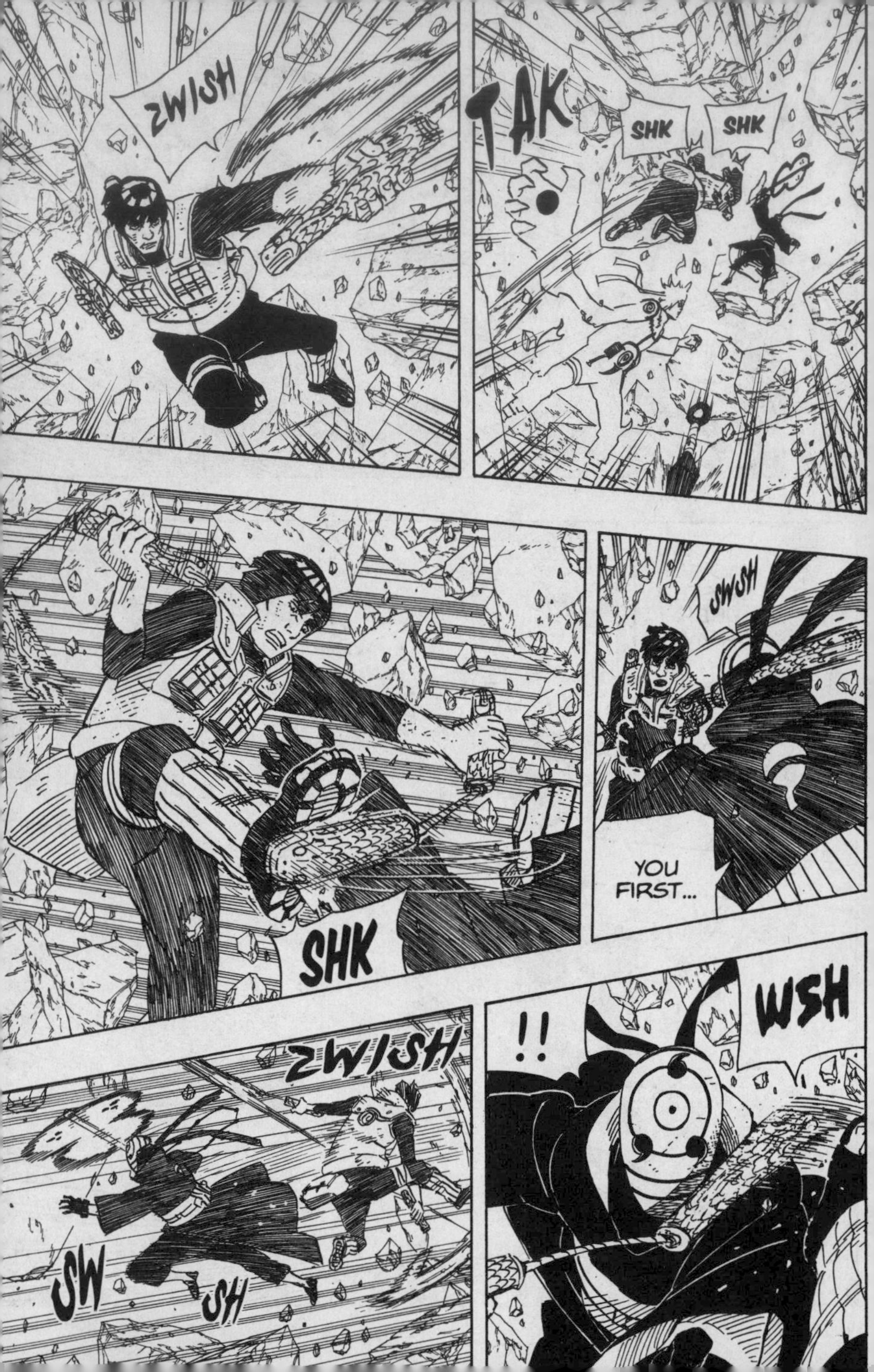
TAK
SHK
SHK
ZWISH
SWSH
YOU FIRST...
SHK
WSH
!!
ZWISH
SW
SH

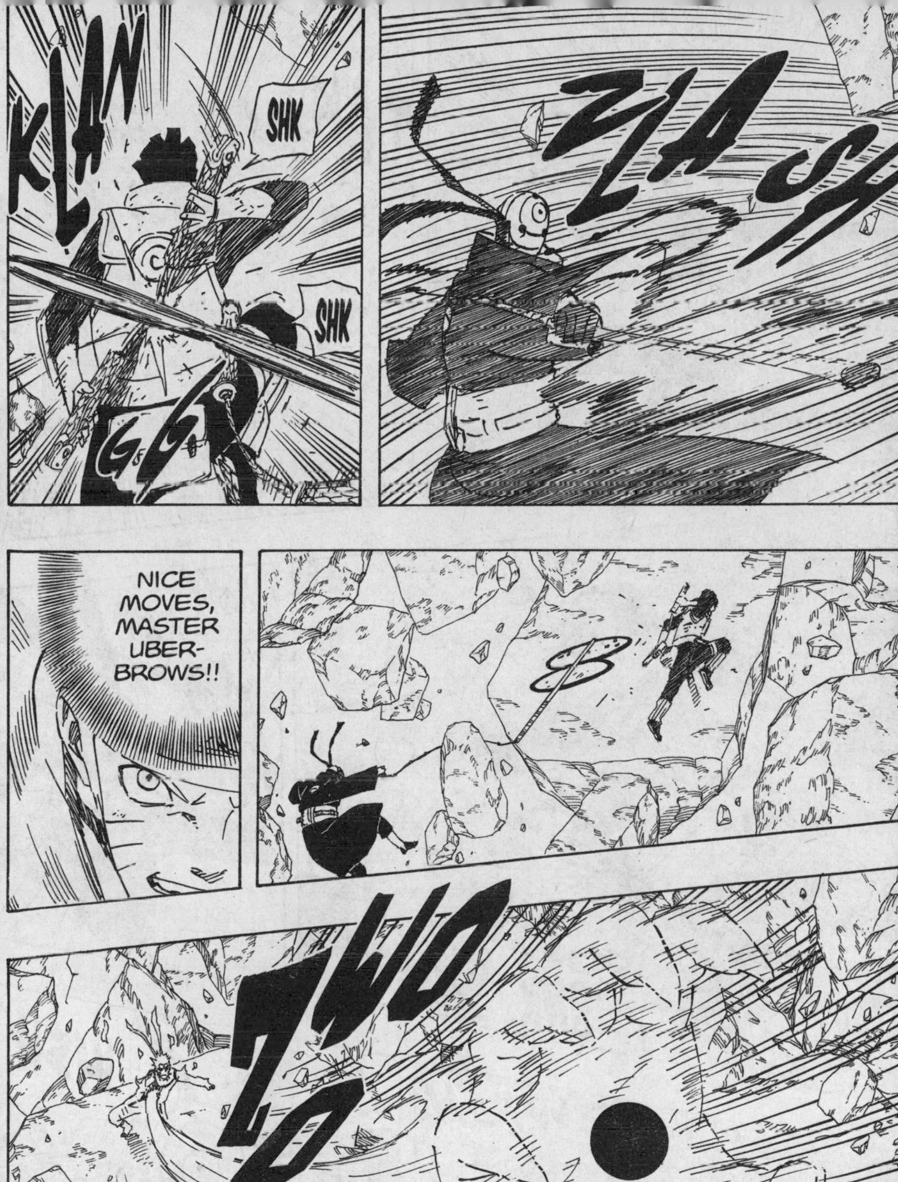
KLAN
SHK
SHK
NICE MOVES, MASTER UBER-BROWS!!

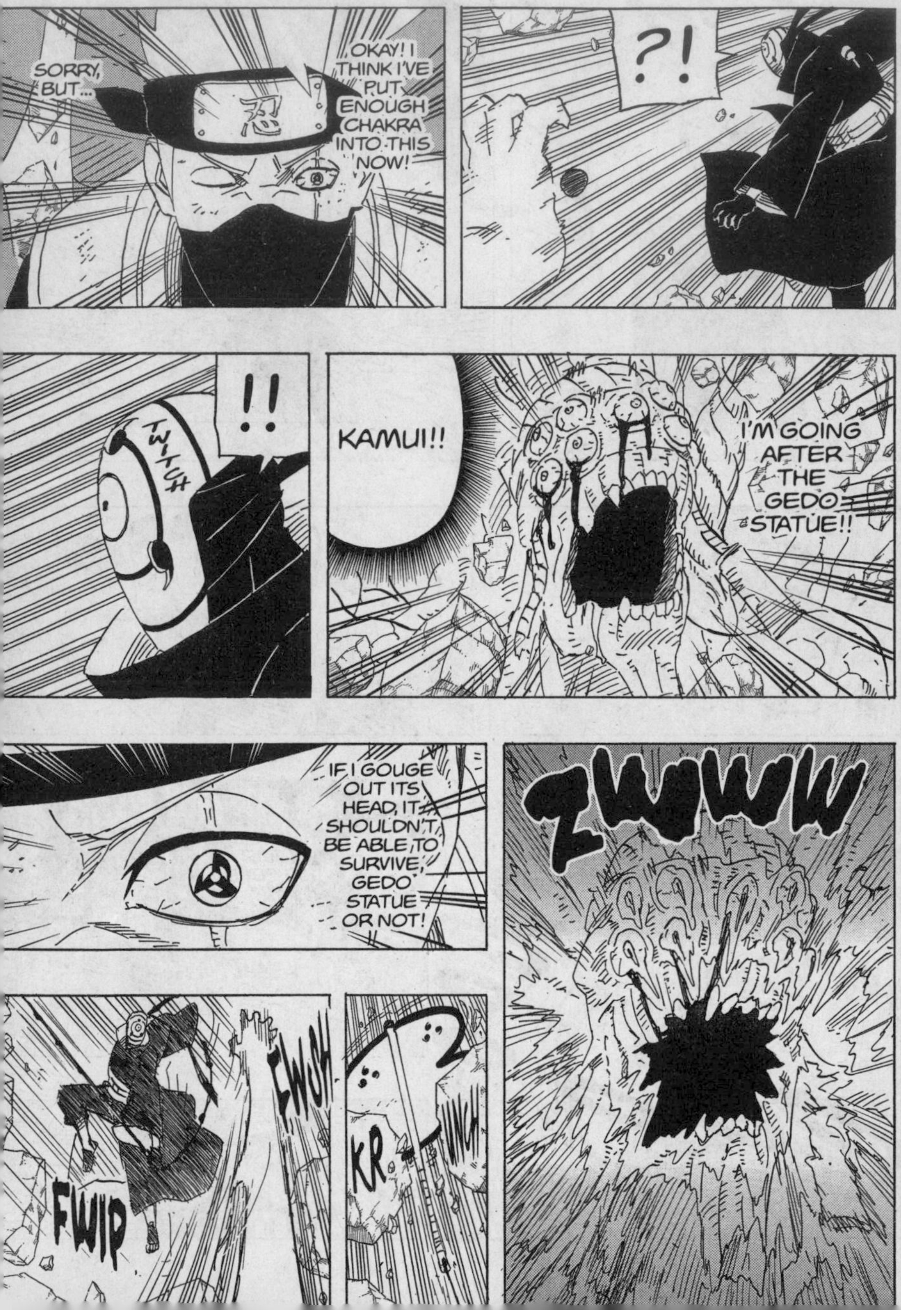
?!
OKAY! I THINK I'VE PUT ENOUGH CHAKRA INTO THIS NOW!
SORRY, BUT...
I'M GOING AFTER THE GEDO STATUE!!
KAMUI!!
!!
TWITCH
ZWWW
IF I GOUGE OUT ITS HEAD, IT SHOULDN'T BE ABLE TO SURVIVE, GEDO STATUE OR NOT!
KRUNCH
FWSH
FWIP

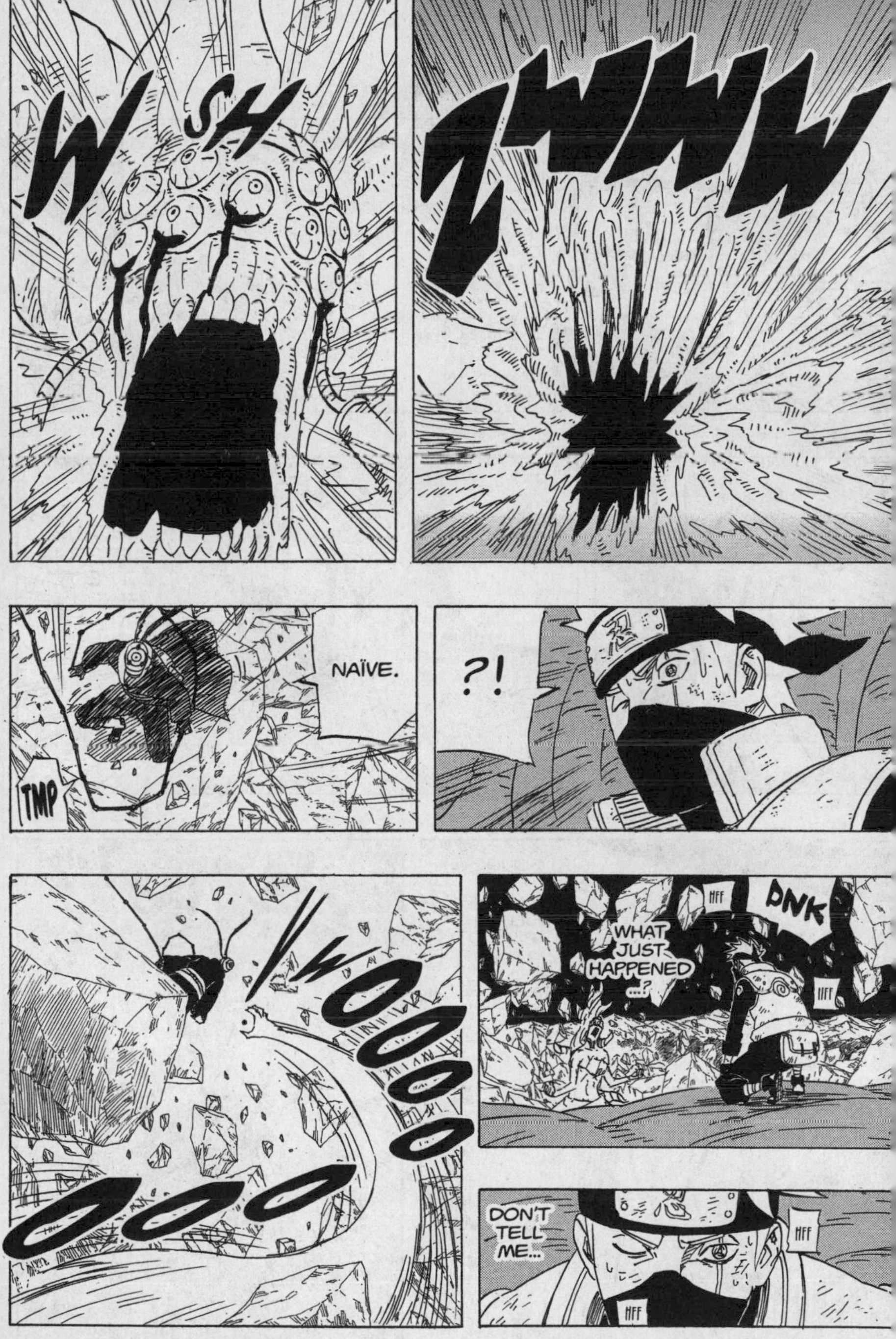
WSH
?!
NAÏVE.
TMP
DNK
HFF
WHAT JUST HAPPENED ...?
HFF
DON'T TELL ME...
HFF
HFF
WOOOOOOOOO

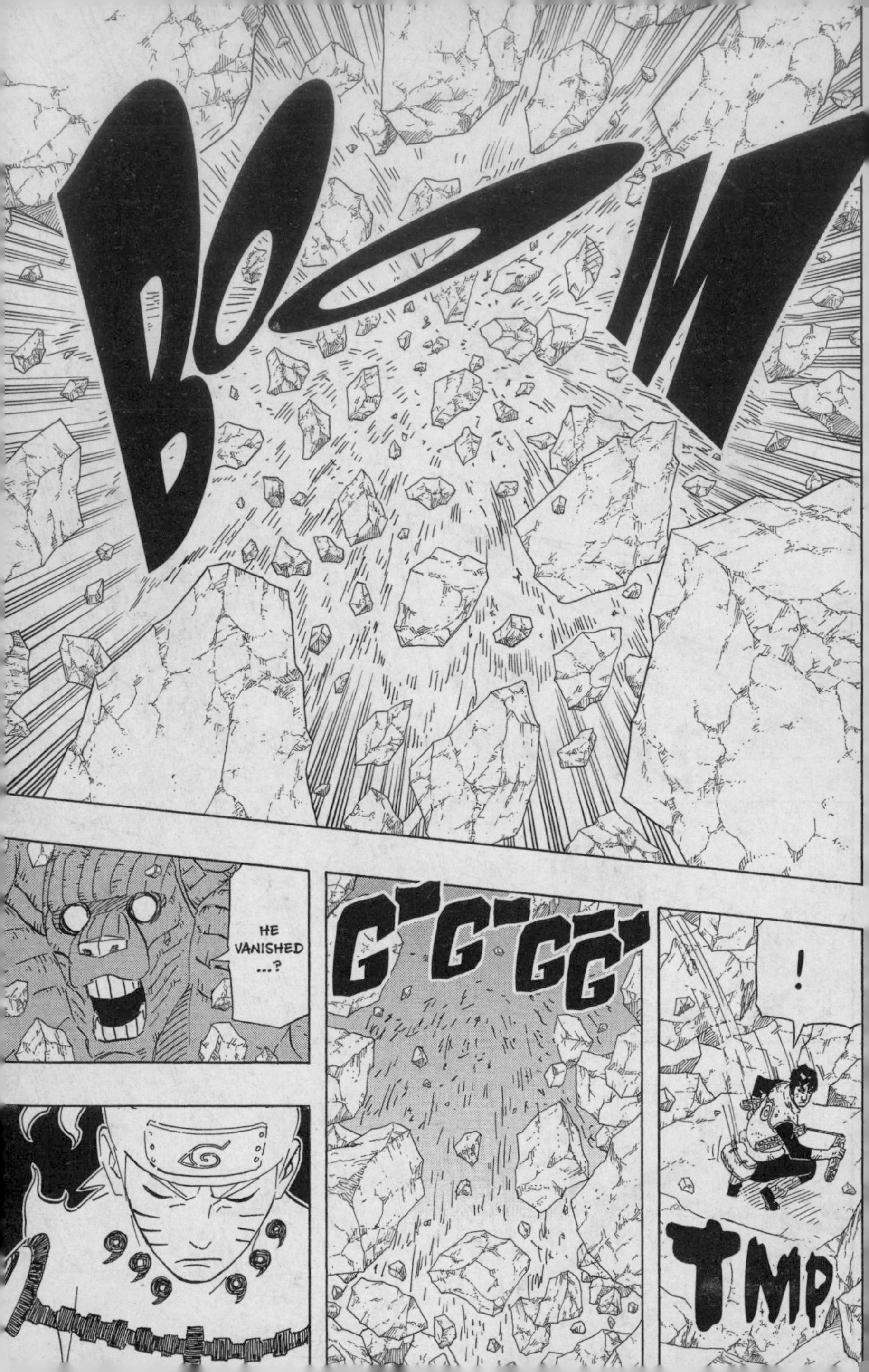
BOOM
!
TMP
G G GG
HE VANISHED ...?

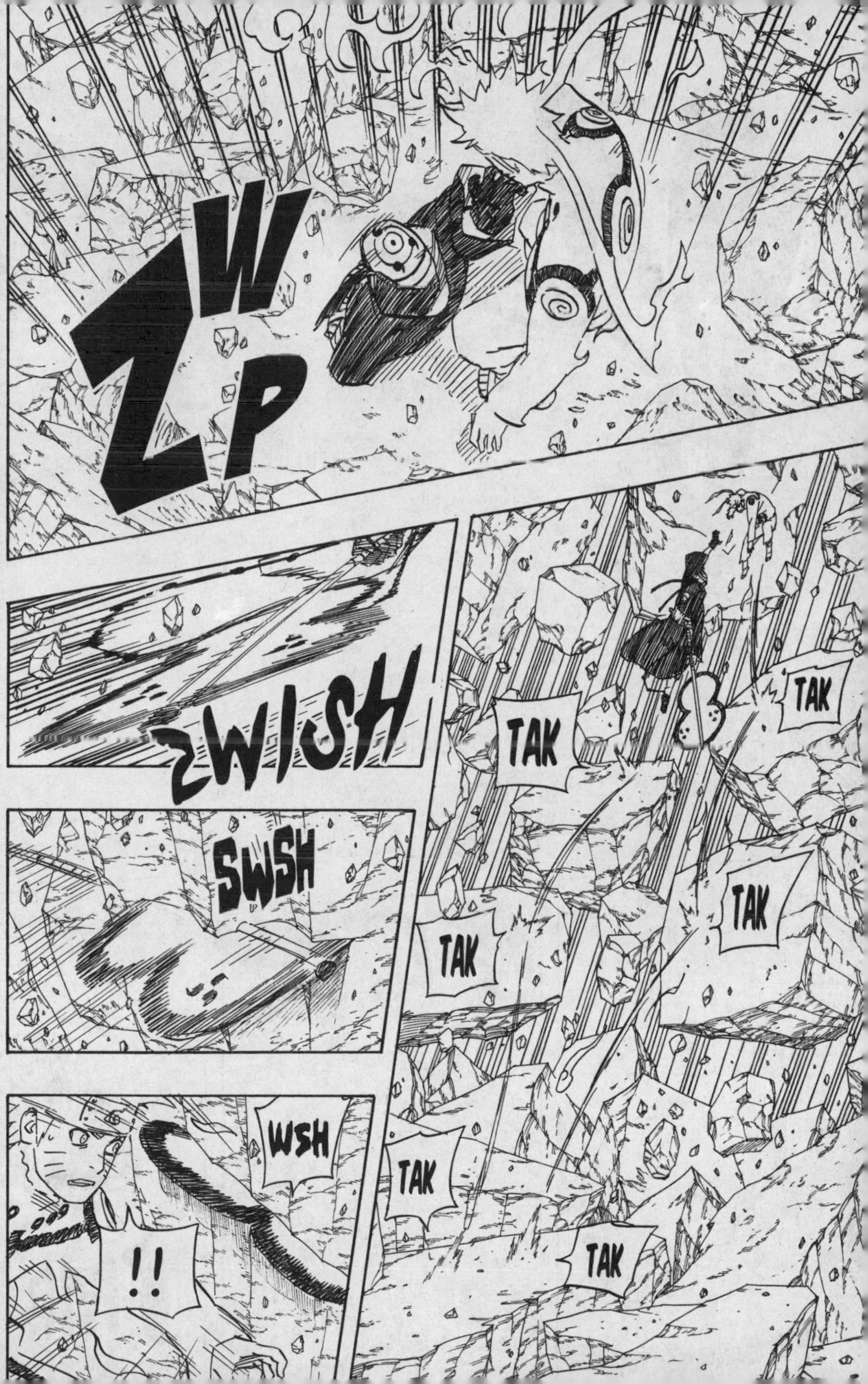
ZWIP
TAK
TAK
TAK
TAK
TAK
TAK
ZWISH
SWSH
WSH
!!

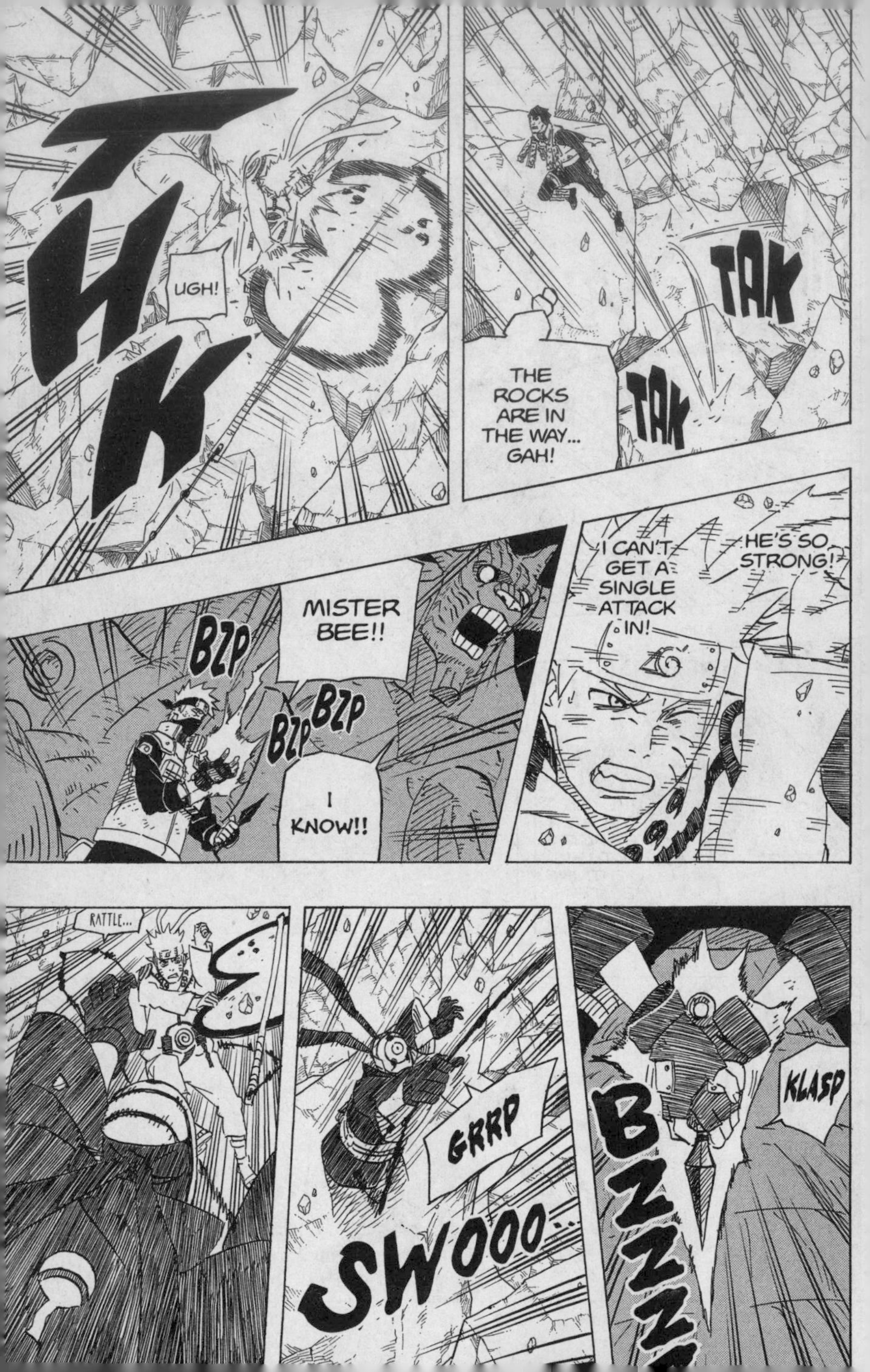
TAK
TAK
THE ROCKS ARE IN THE WAY... GAH!
UGH!
HE'S SO STRONG!
I CAN'T GET A SINGLE ATTACK IN!
MISTER BEE!!
BZP
BZP
BZP
I KNOW!!
KLASP
GRRP
SWOOO...
RATTLE...

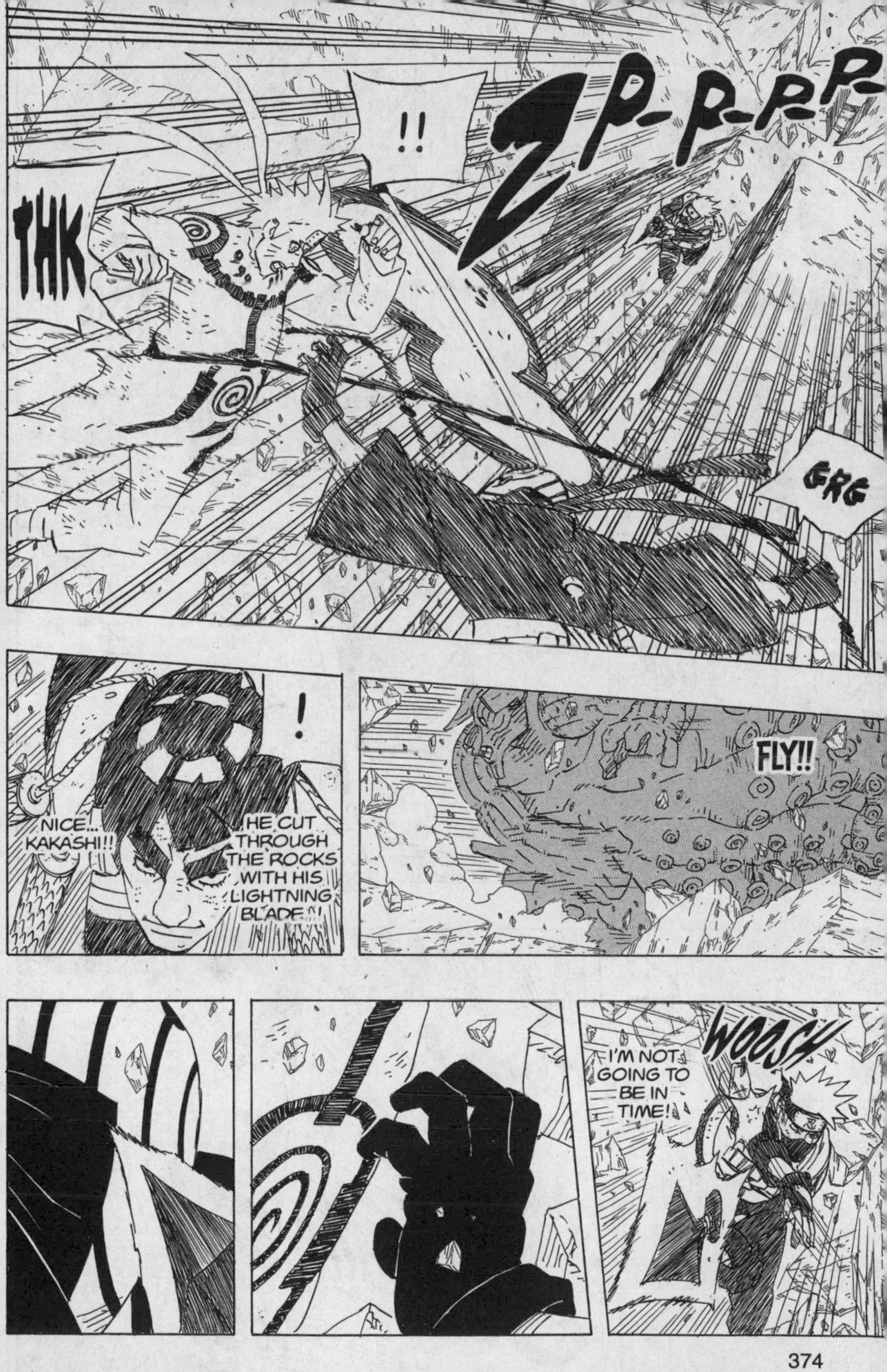
ZP-P-P-P
!!
GRG
THK
FLY!!
!
HE CUT THROUGH THE ROCKS WITH HIS LIGHTNING BLADE...!!
NICE... KAKASHI!!
WOOSH
I'M NOT GOING TO BE IN TIME!

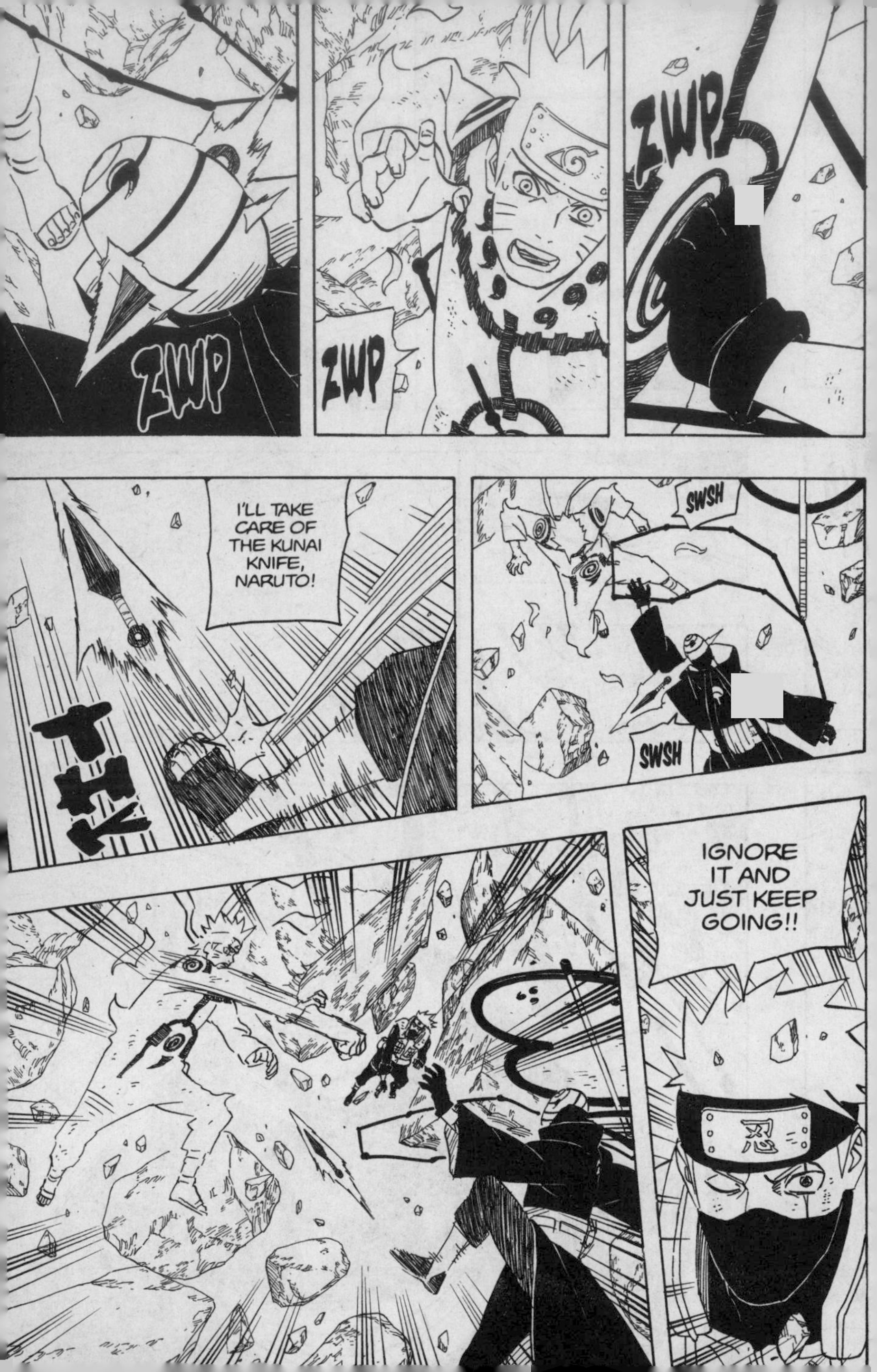
ZWP
ZWP
ZWP
SWSH
SWSH
I'LL TAKE CARE OF THE KUNAI KNIFE, NARUTO!
IGNORE IT AND JUST KEEP GOING!!

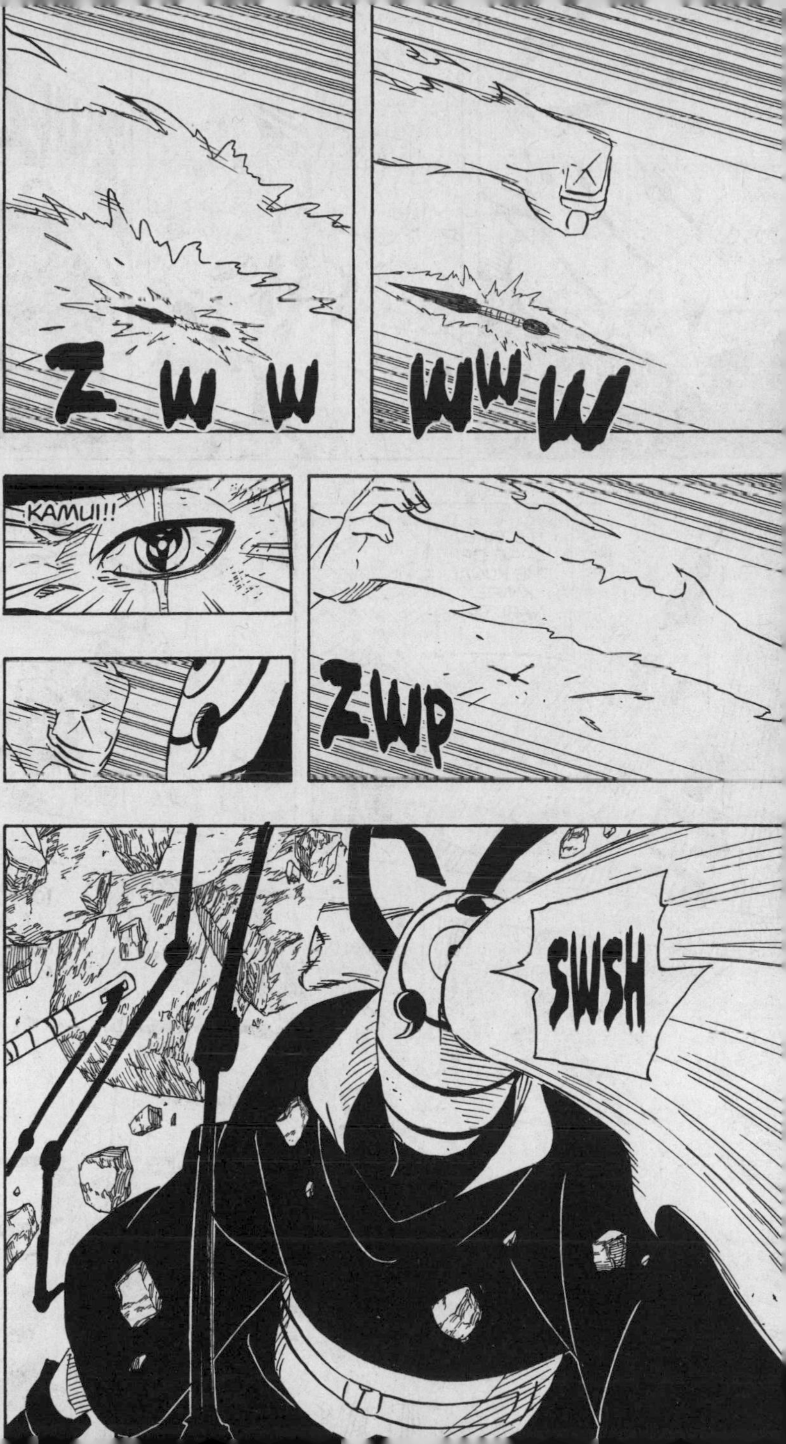
ZWWWWWW
ZWP
KAMUI!!
SWSH

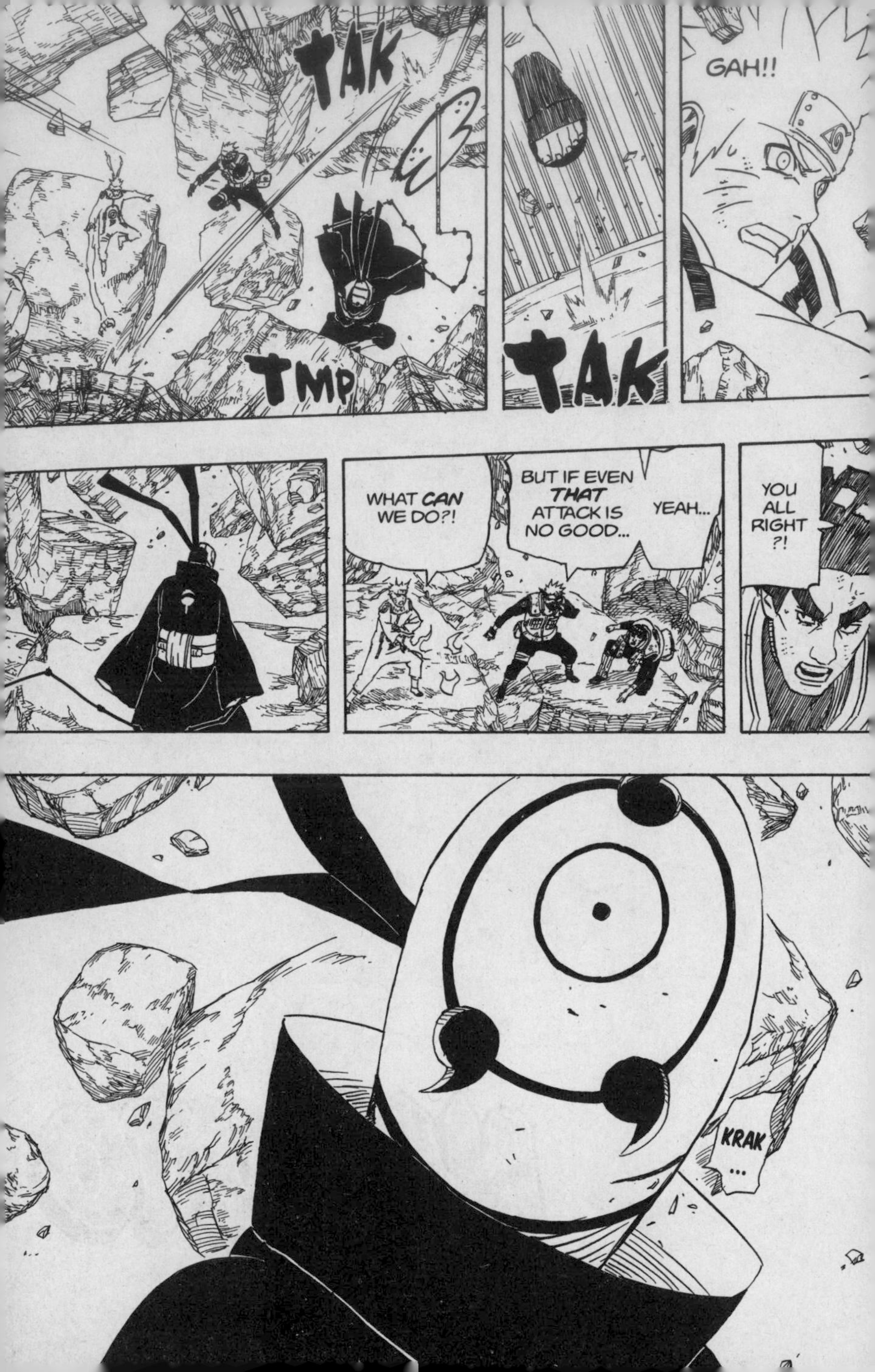
GAH!!
TAK
TAK
TMP
YOU ALL RIGHT?!
YEAH...
BUT IF EVEN THAT ATTACK IS NO GOOD...
WHAT CAN WE DO?!
KRAK
...

NARUTO

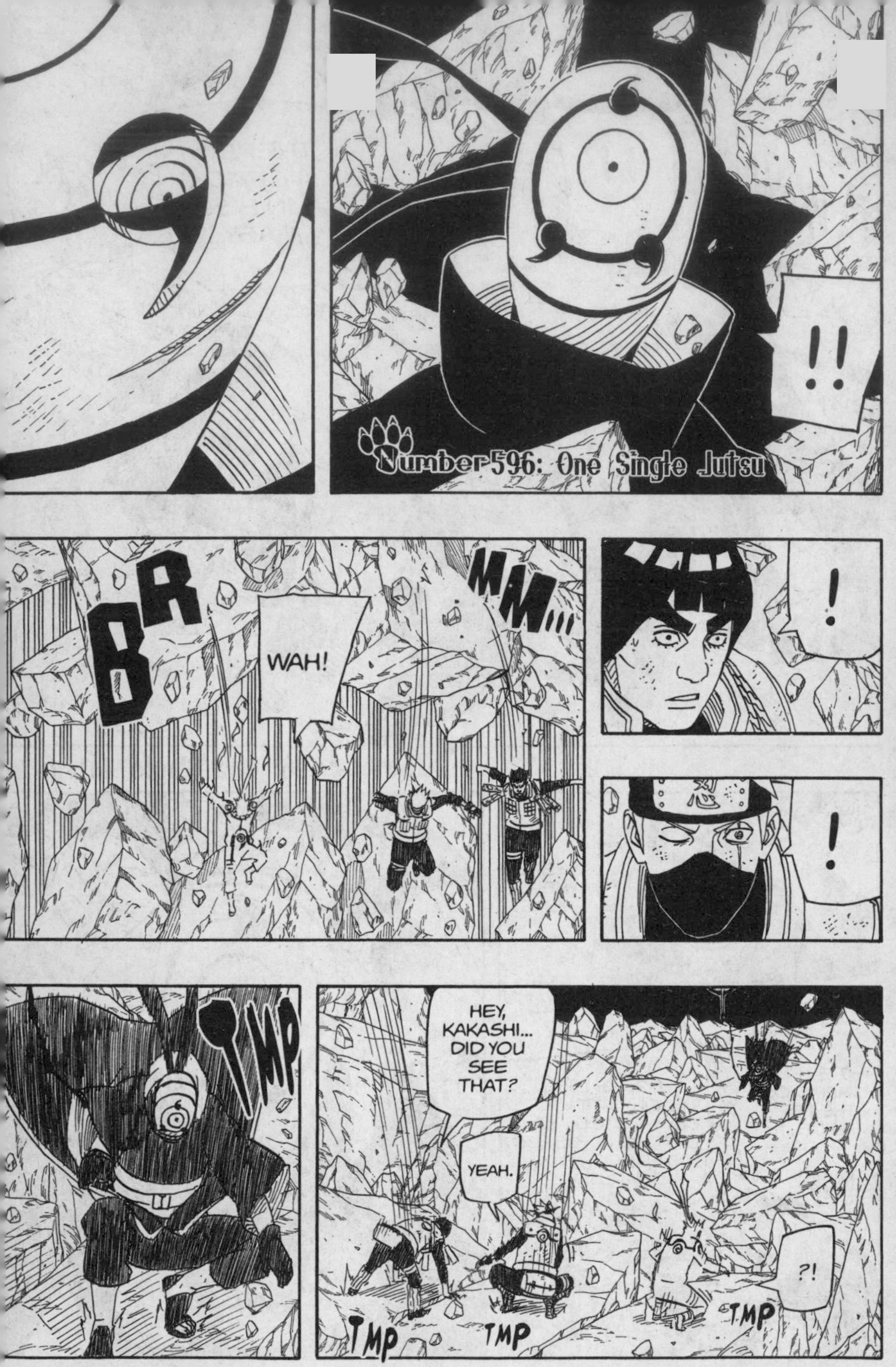
!!
Number 596: One Single Jutsu
!
!
BRMM...
WAH!
HEY, KAKASHI... DID YOU SEE THAT?
YEAH.
?!
TMP
TMP
TMP
TMP

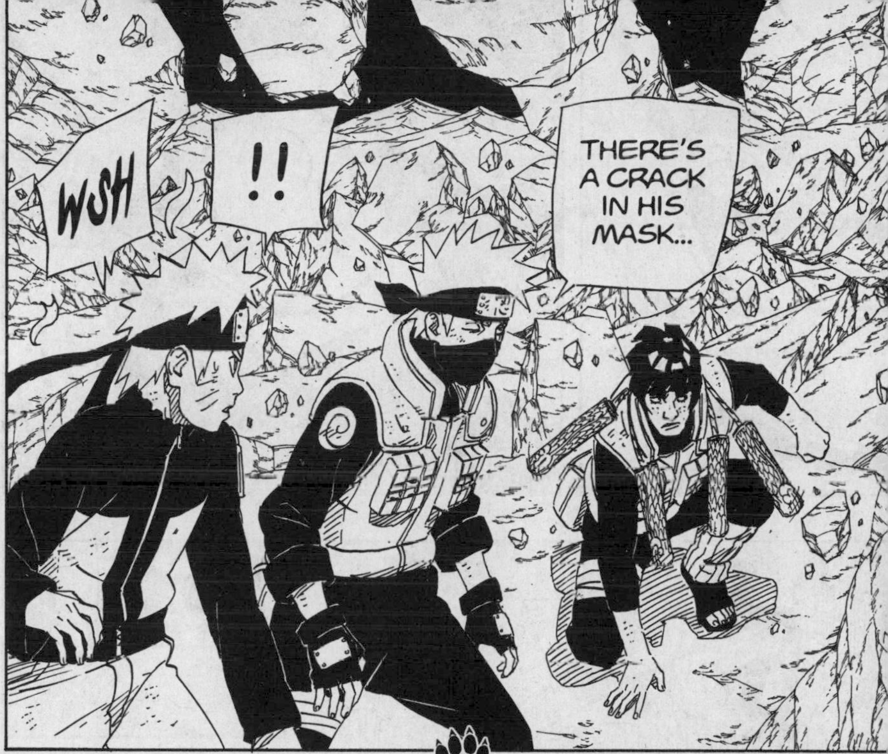
THERE'S A CRACK IN HIS MASK...
!!
WSH

Number 596: One Single Jutsu

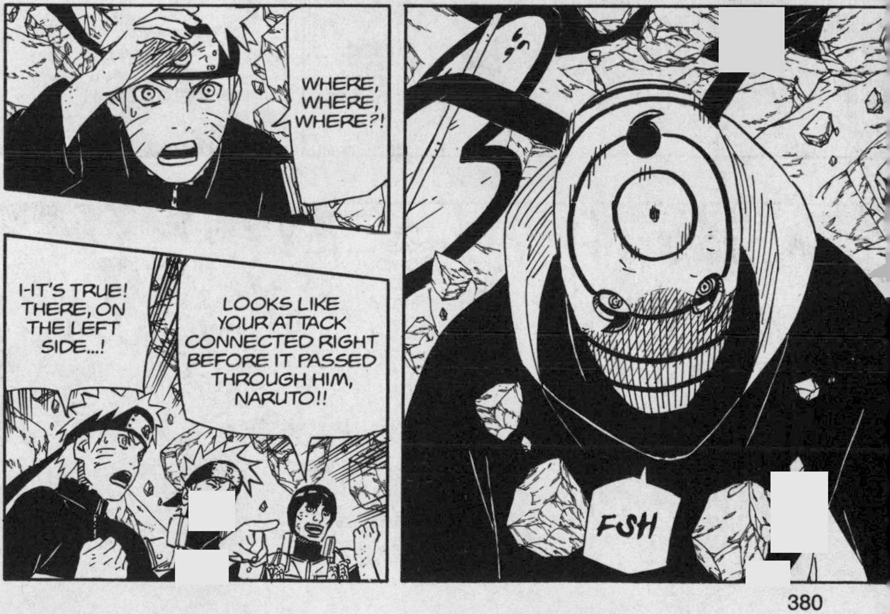
FSH
WHERE, WHERE, WHERE?!
LOOKS LIKE YOUR ATTACK CONNECTED RIGHT BEFORE IT PASSED THROUGH HIM, NARUTO!!
I-IT'S TRUE! THERE, ON THE LEFT SIDE...!

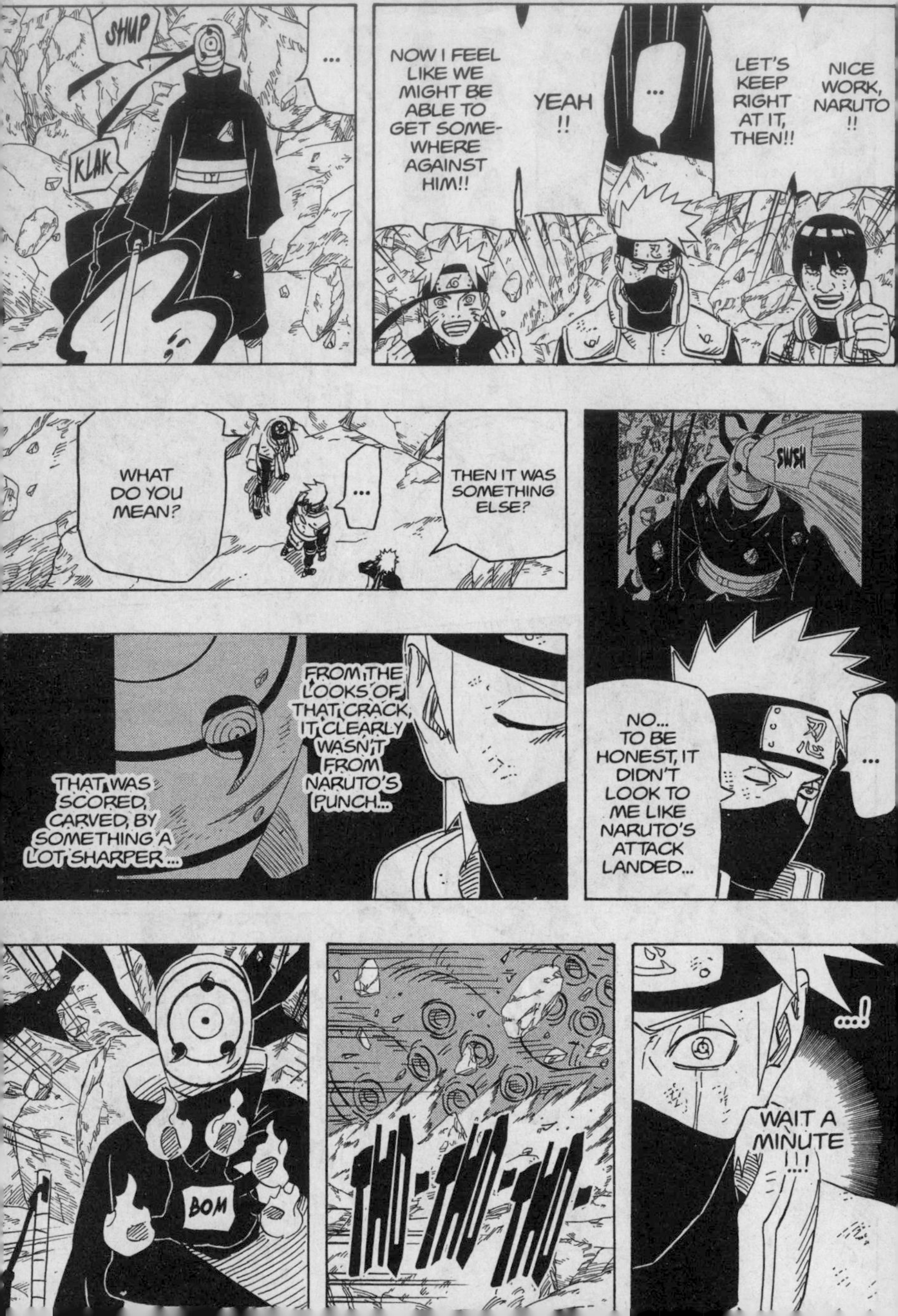
NICE WORK, NARUTO !!
LET'S KEEP RIGHT AT IT, THEN!!
...
YEAH !!
NOW I FEEL LIKE WE MIGHT BE ABLE TO GET SOME-WHERE AGAINST HIM!!
...
SHUP
KLAK
SWISH
THEN IT WAS SOMETHING ELSE?
...
WHAT DO YOU MEAN?
...
NO... TO BE HONEST, IT DIDN'T LOOK TO ME LIKE NARUTO'S ATTACK LANDED...
FROM THE LOOKS OF THAT CRACK, IT CLEARLY WASN'T FROM NARUTO'S PUNCH...
THAT WAS SCORED, CARVED, BY SOMETHING A LOT SHARPER...
...!
WAIT A MINUTE !!!
THD-THD-THD-
BOM

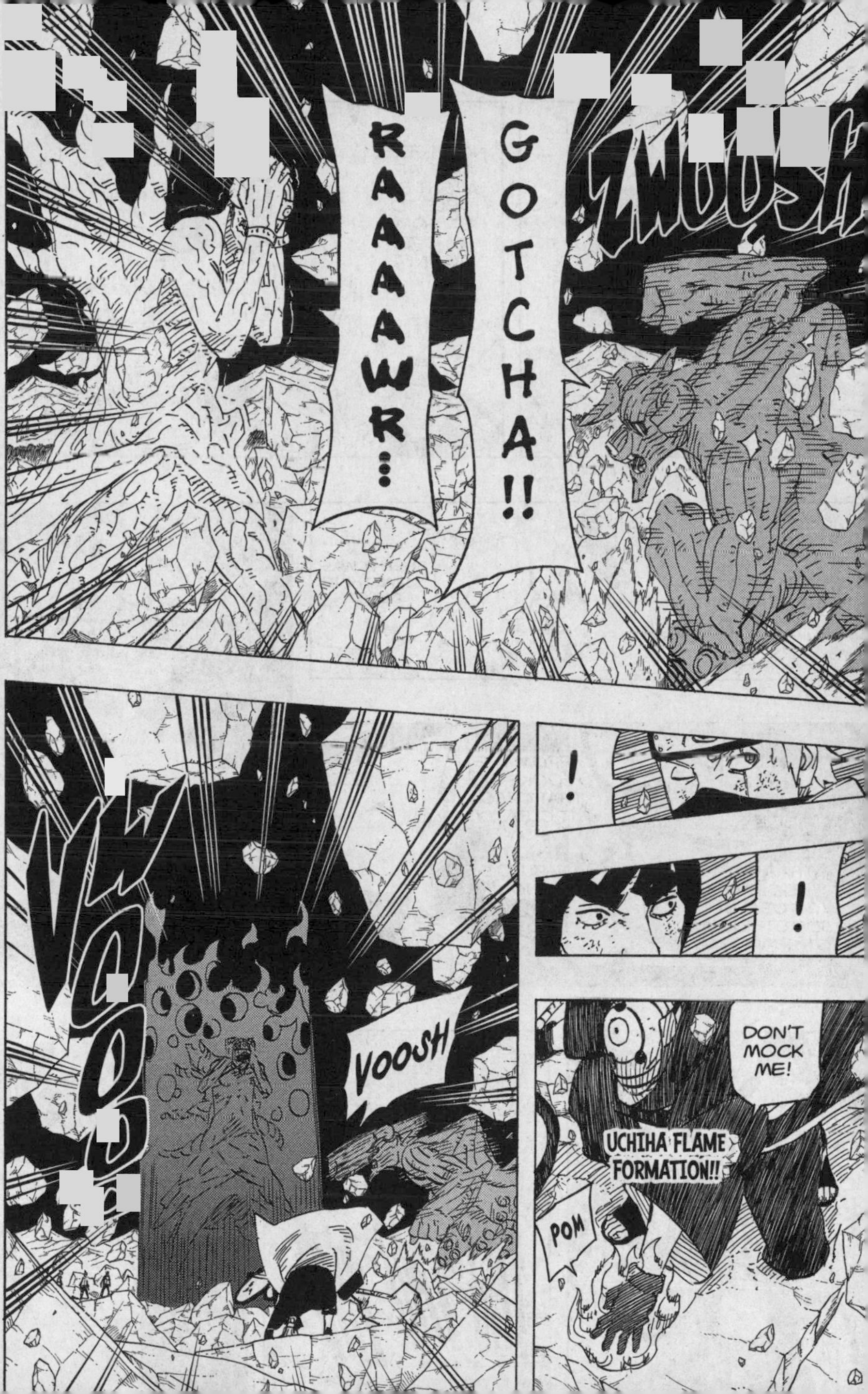
ZWOOSH
GOTCHA!!
RAAAAWR...
!
!
DON'T MOCK ME!
UCHIHA FLAME FORMATION!!
POM
VOOSH

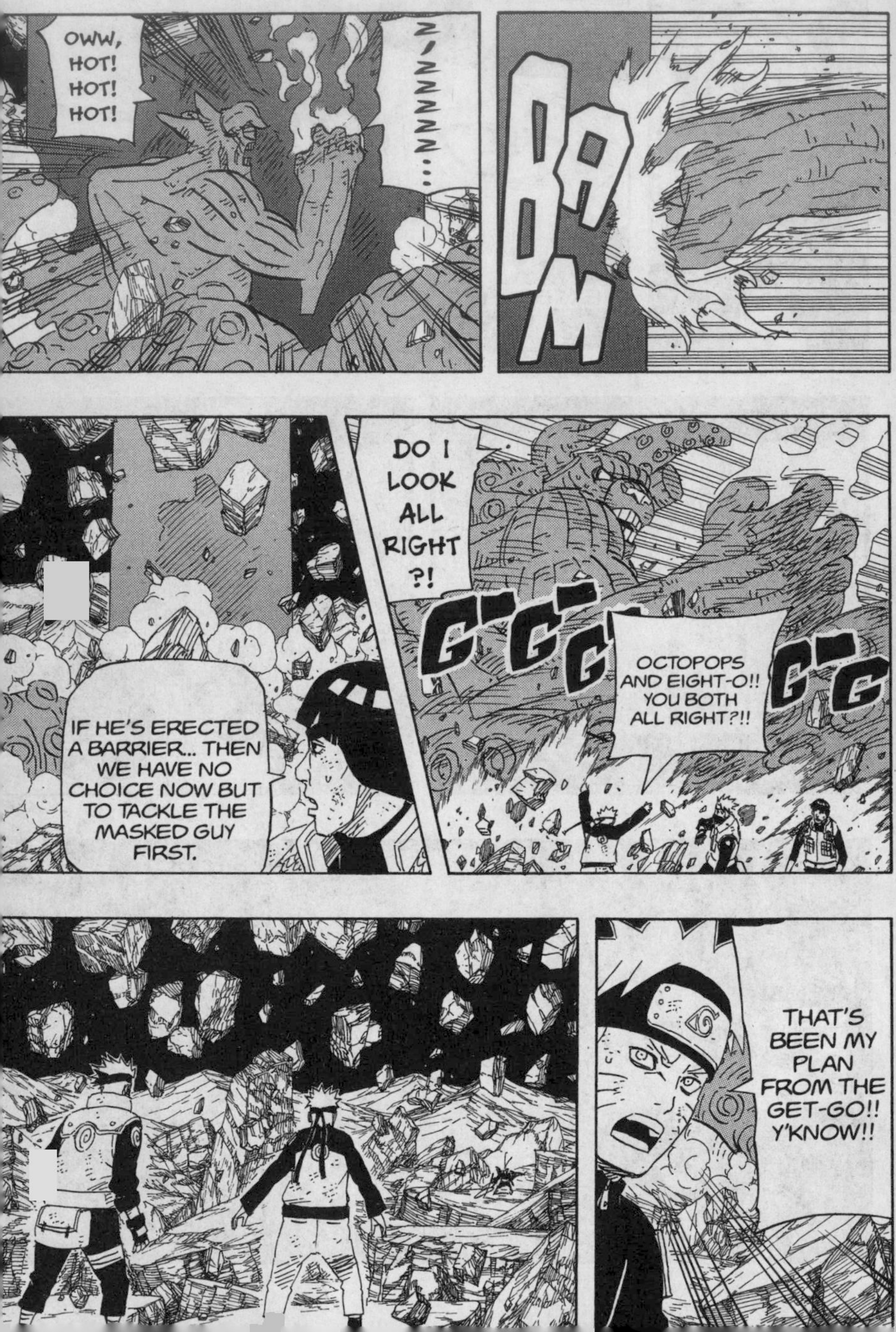
BAM
OWW, HOT! HOT! HOT!
ZZZZZZZ...
DO I LOOK ALL RIGHT?!
G-G-G
OCTOPOPS AND EIGHT-O!! YOU BOTH ALL RIGHT?!!
G-G
IF HE'S ERECTED A BARRIER... THEN WE HAVE NO CHOICE NOW BUT TO TACKLE THE MASKED GUY FIRST.
THAT'S BEEN MY PLAN FROM THE GET-GO!! Y'KNOW!!

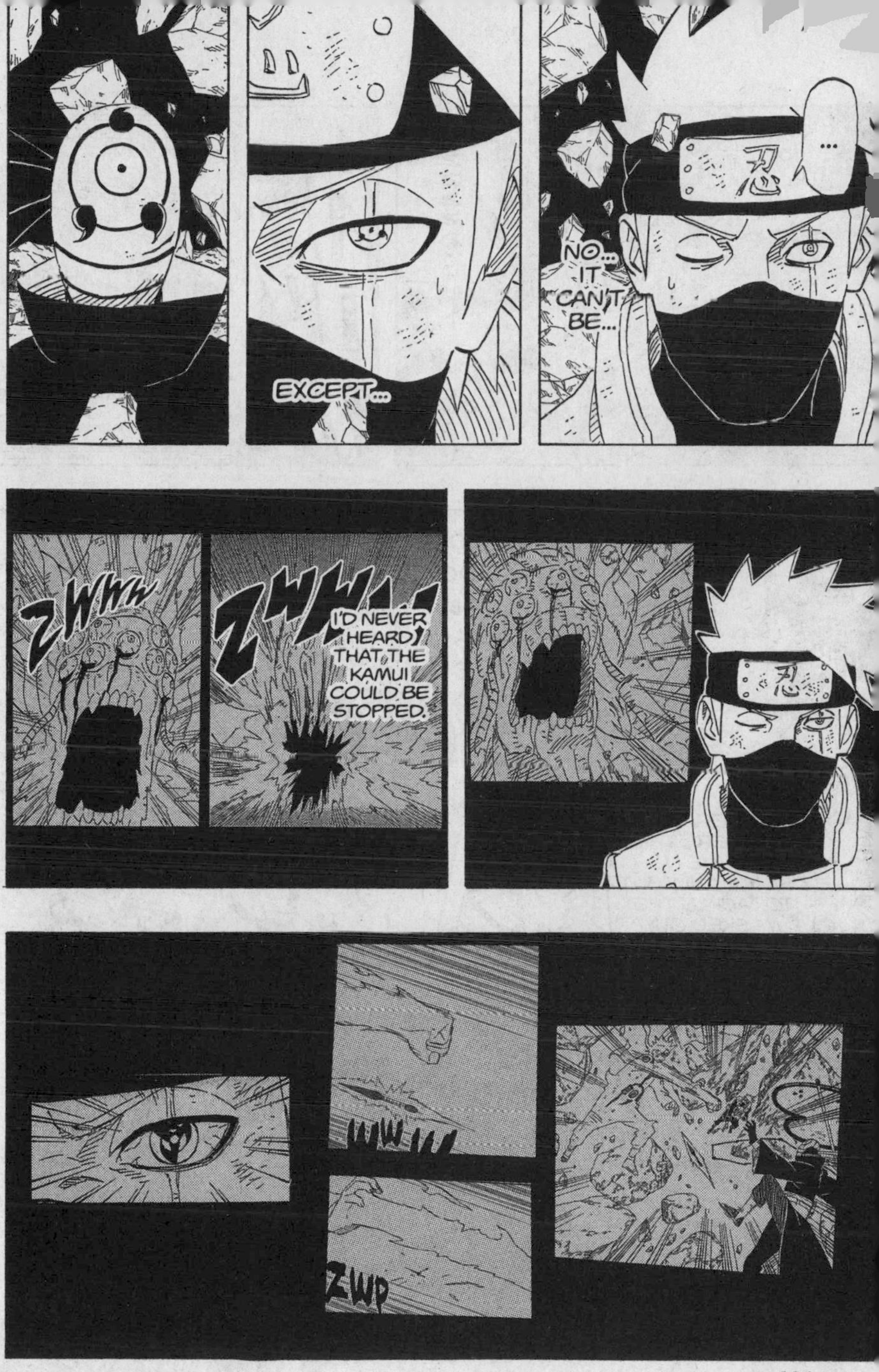
...
NO... IT CAN'T BE...
EXCEPT...
I'D NEVER HEARD THAT THE KAMUI COULD BE STOPPED.
ZWWW
ZWP

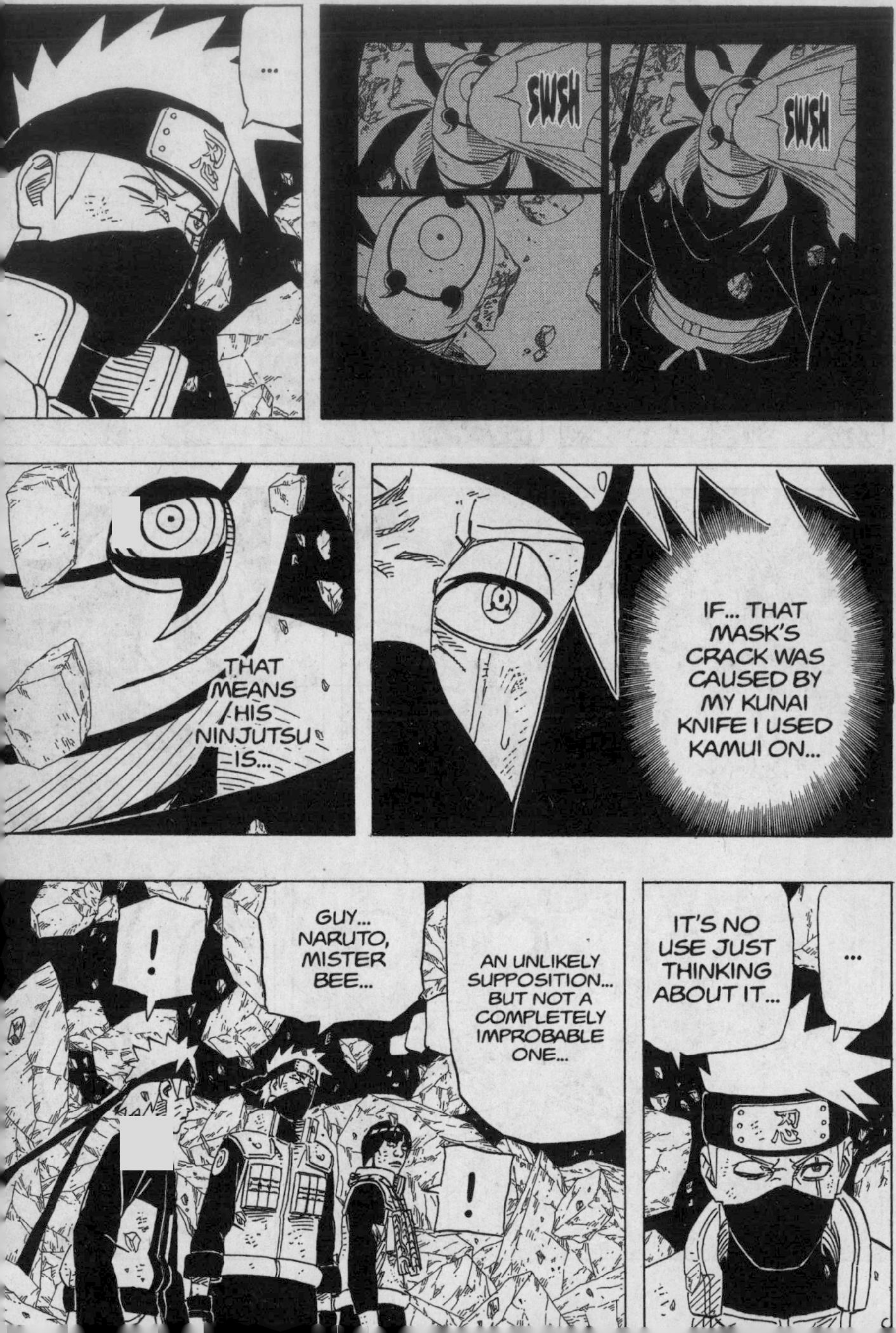
SWSH
SWSH
...
IF... THAT MASK'S CRACK WAS CAUSED BY MY KUNAI KNIFE I USED KAMUI ON...
THAT MEANS HIS NINJUTSU IS...
...
IT'S NO USE JUST THINKING ABOUT IT...
AN UNLIKELY SUPPOSITION... BUT NOT A COMPLETELY IMPROBABLE ONE...
GUY... NARUTO, MISTER BEE...
!
!

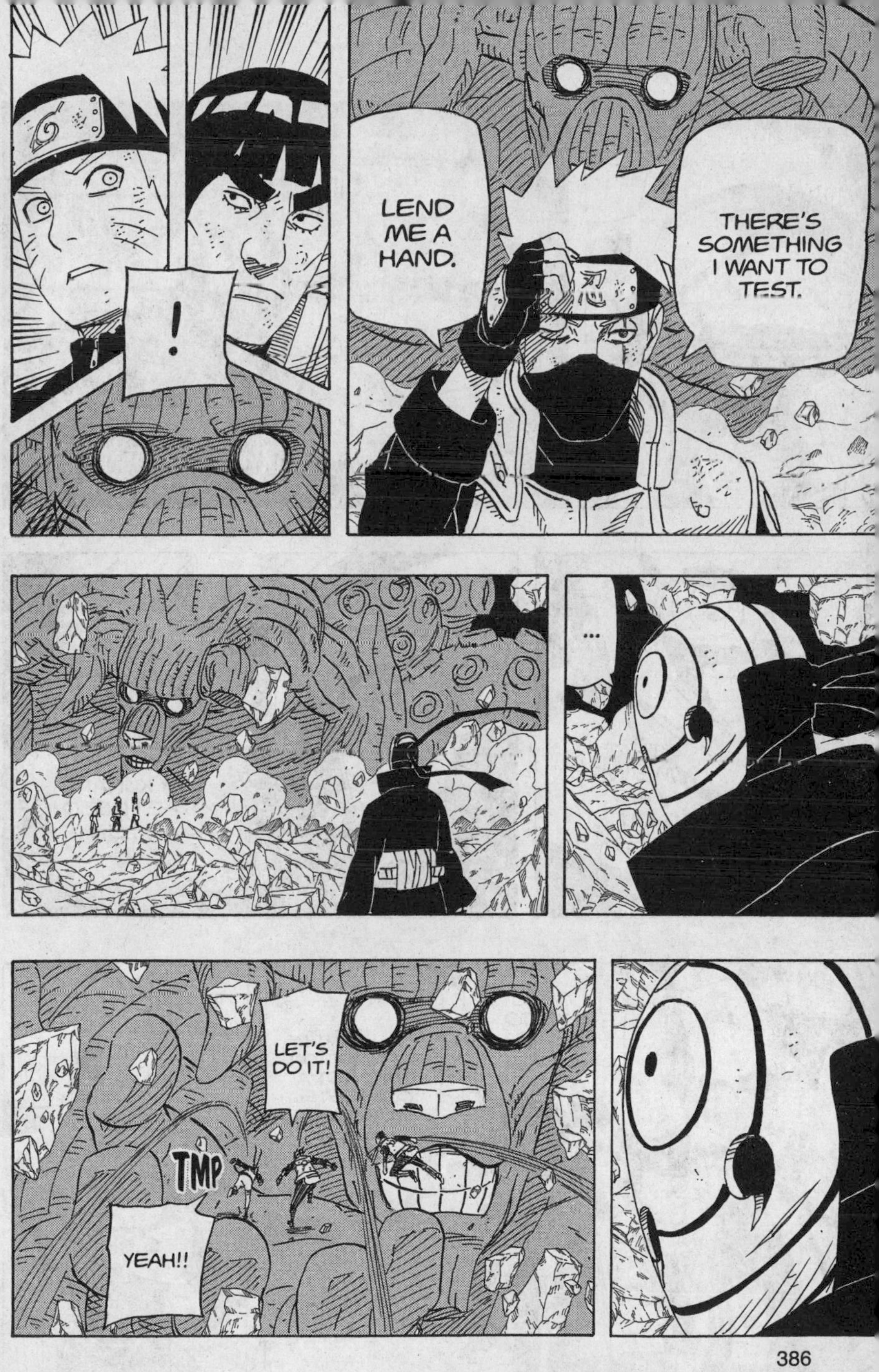
THERE'S SOMETHING I WANT TO TEST.
LEND ME A HAND.
!
...
LET'S DO IT!
TMP
YEAH!!

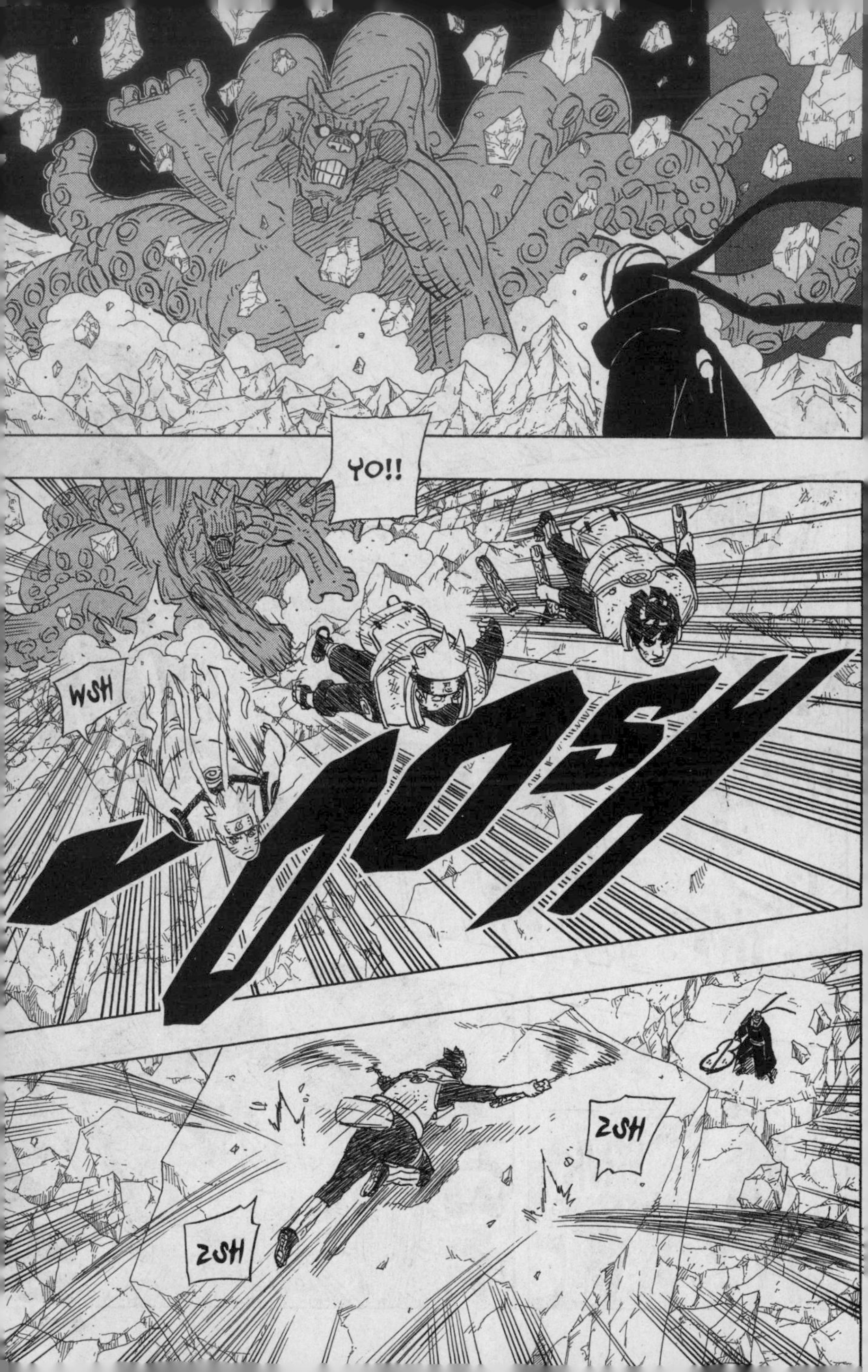
YO!!
WSH
ZSH
ZSH

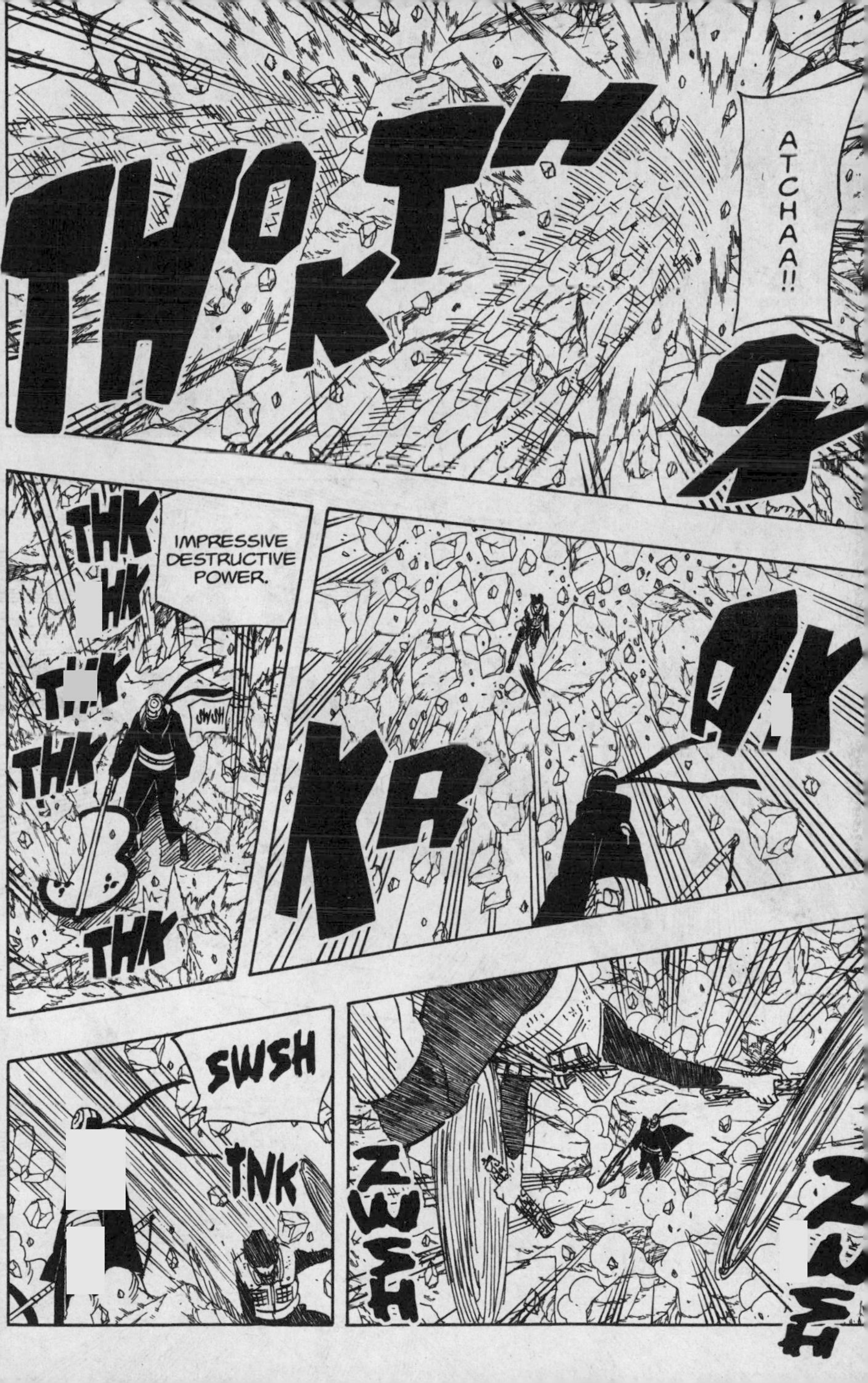
ATCHAA!!
THK
IMPRESSIVE DESTRUCTIVE POWER.
SWSH
THK
ZWSH
SWSH
TNK

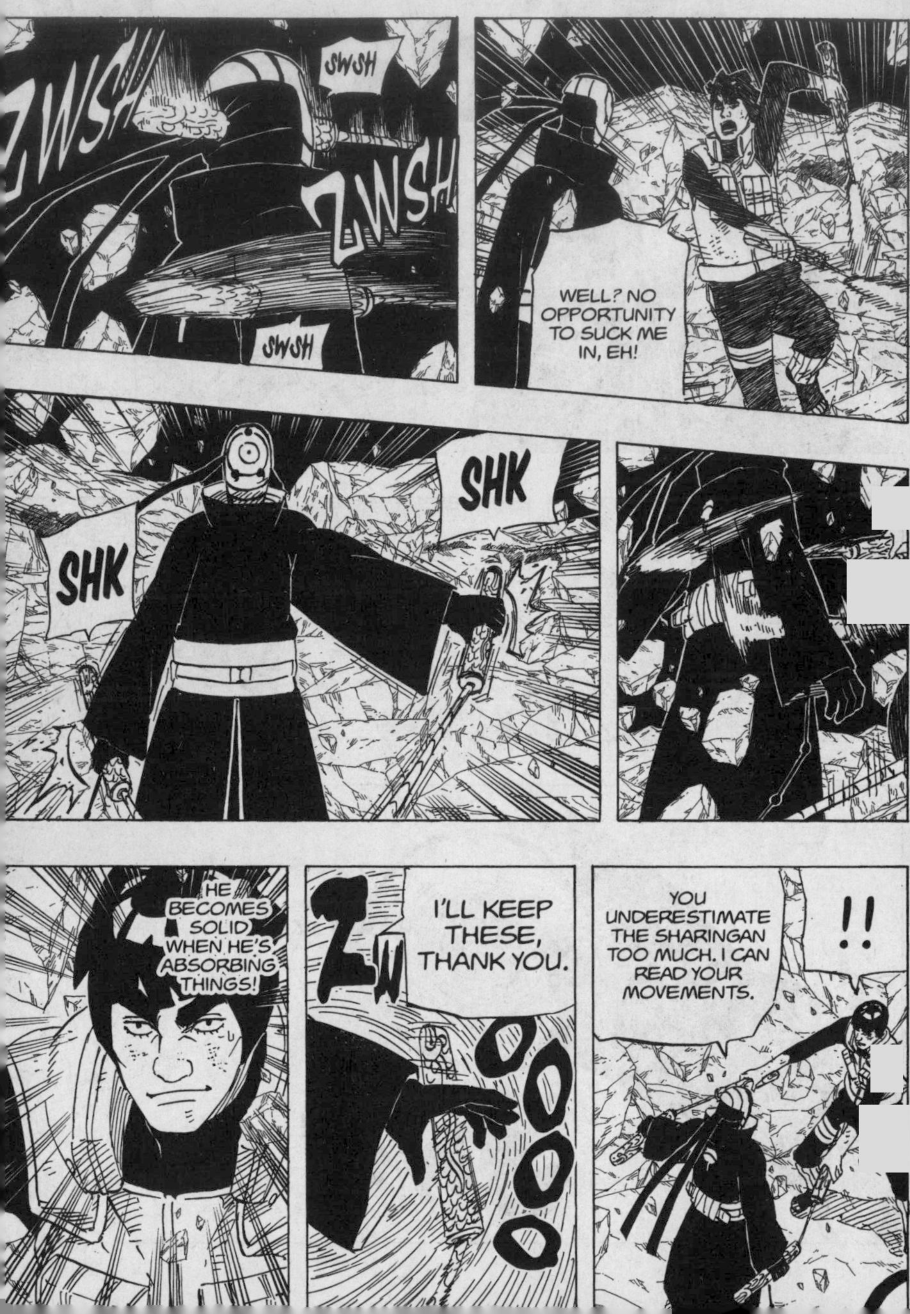
WELL? NO OPPORTUNITY TO SUCK ME IN, EH!
SWSH
ZWSH
ZWSH
SWSH
SHK
SHK
!!
YOU UNDERESTIMATE THE SHARINGAN TOO MUCH. I CAN READ YOUR MOVEMENTS.
I'LL KEEP THESE, THANK YOU.
ZW
HE BECOMES SOLID WHEN HE'S ABSORBING THINGS!

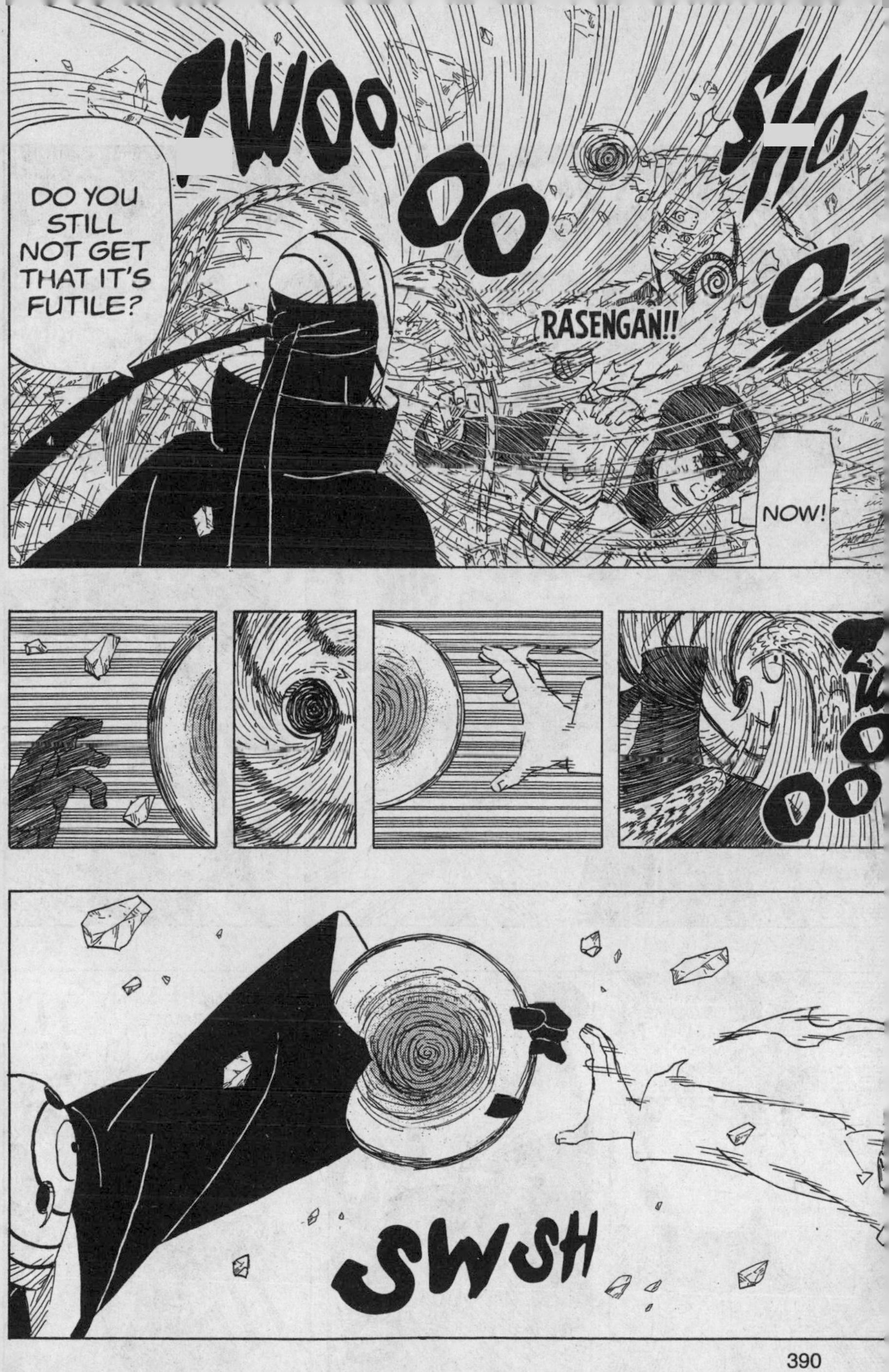
SHOOM
NOW!
RASENGAN!!
TWOOOO
DO YOU STILL NOT GET THAT IT'S FUTILE?
ZWOOOO
SWSH

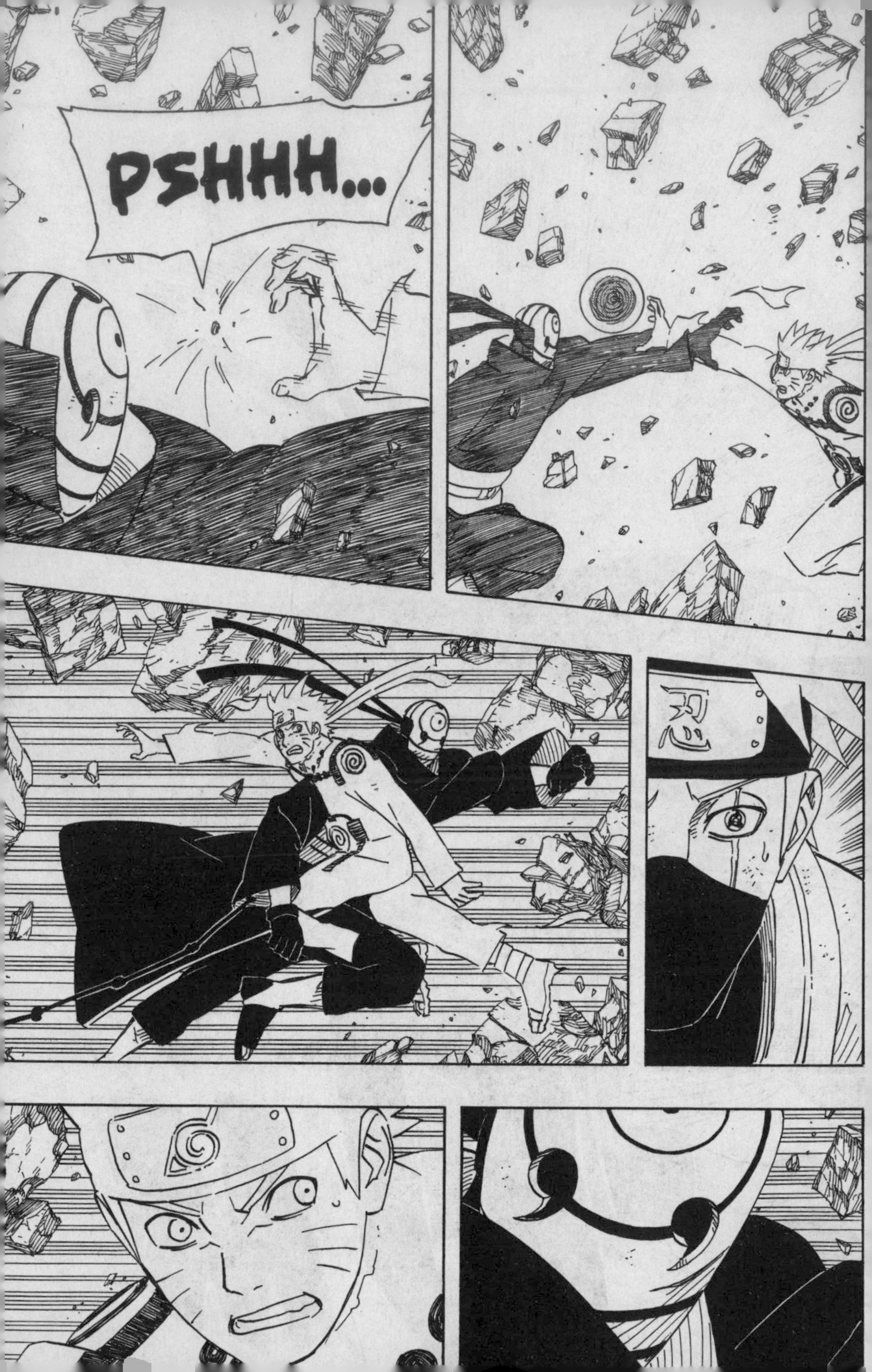
PSHHH...
忍

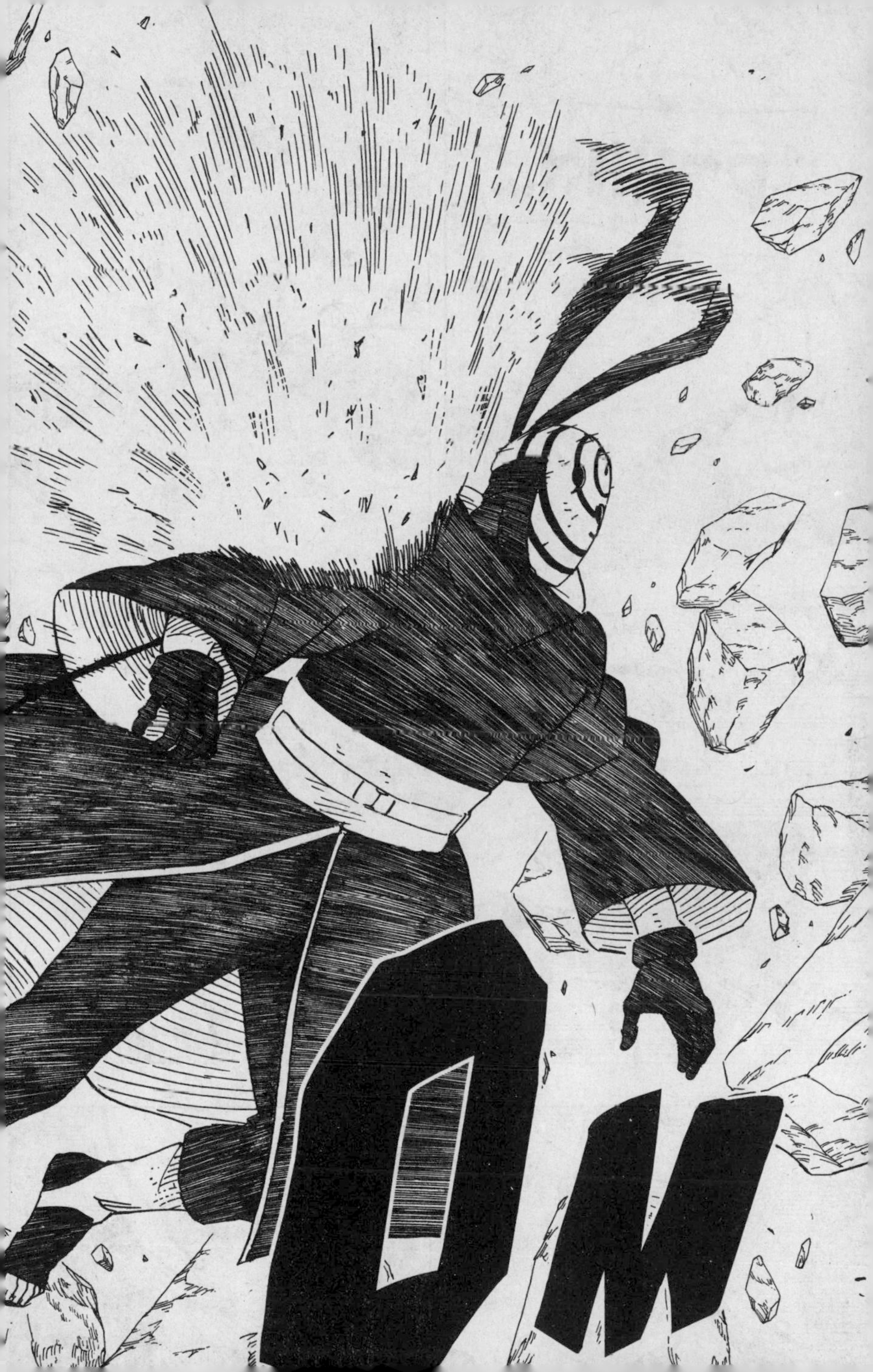
OM

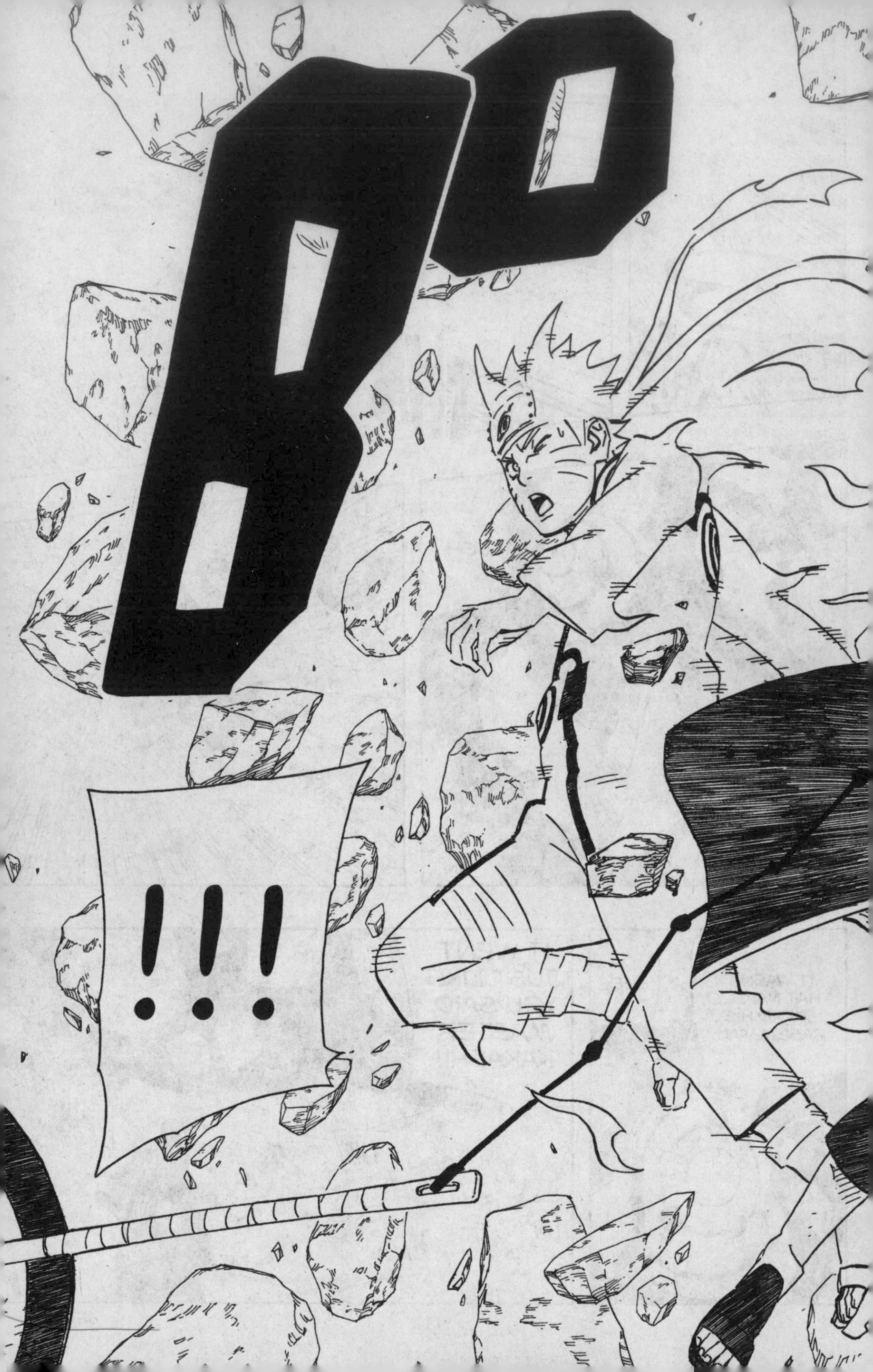
BA
!!!

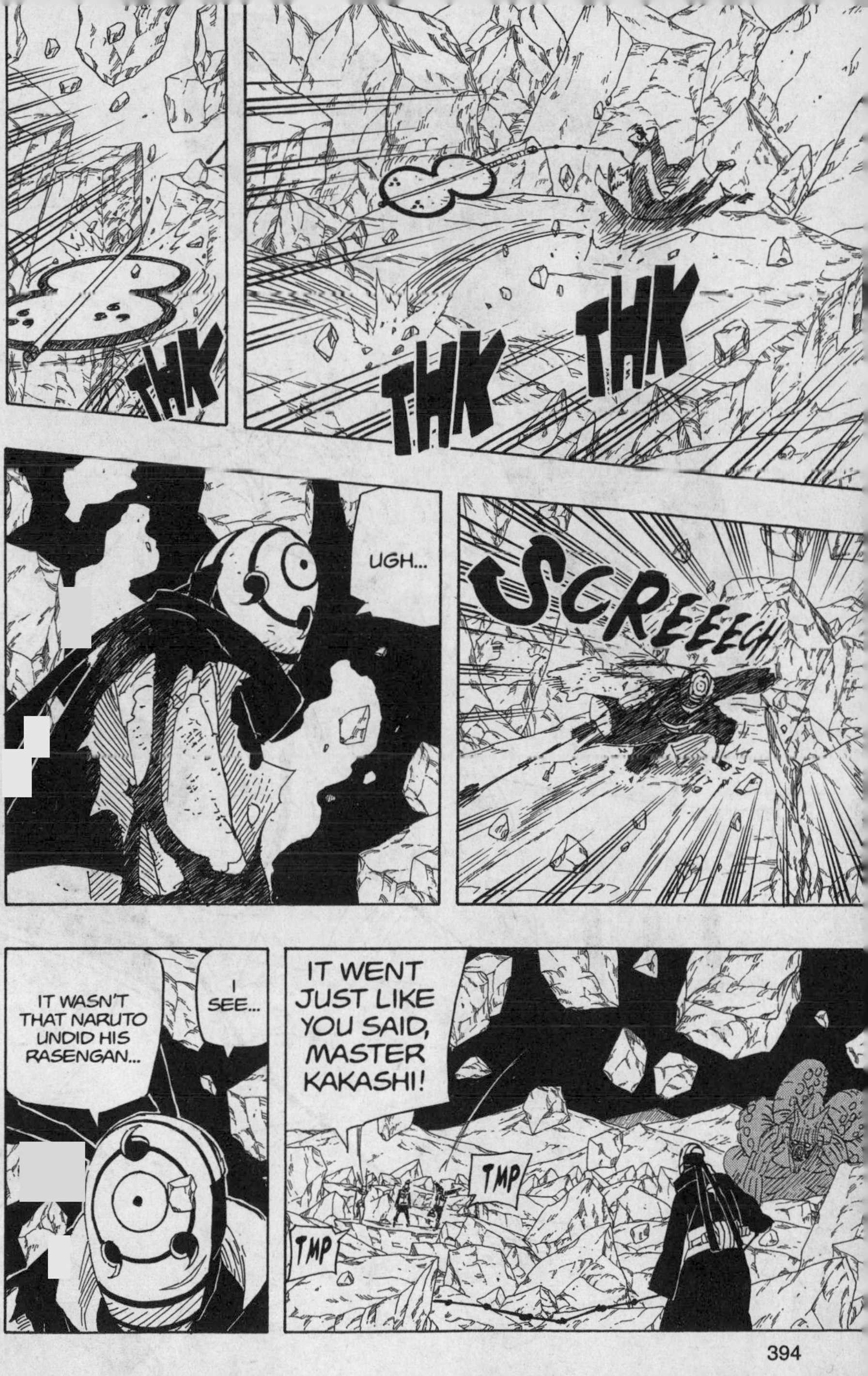
THK
THK
THK
SCREEECH
UGH...
IT WENT JUST LIKE YOU SAID, MASTER KAKASHI!
TMP
TMP
I SEE...
IT WASN'T THAT NARUTO UNDID HIS RASENGAN...

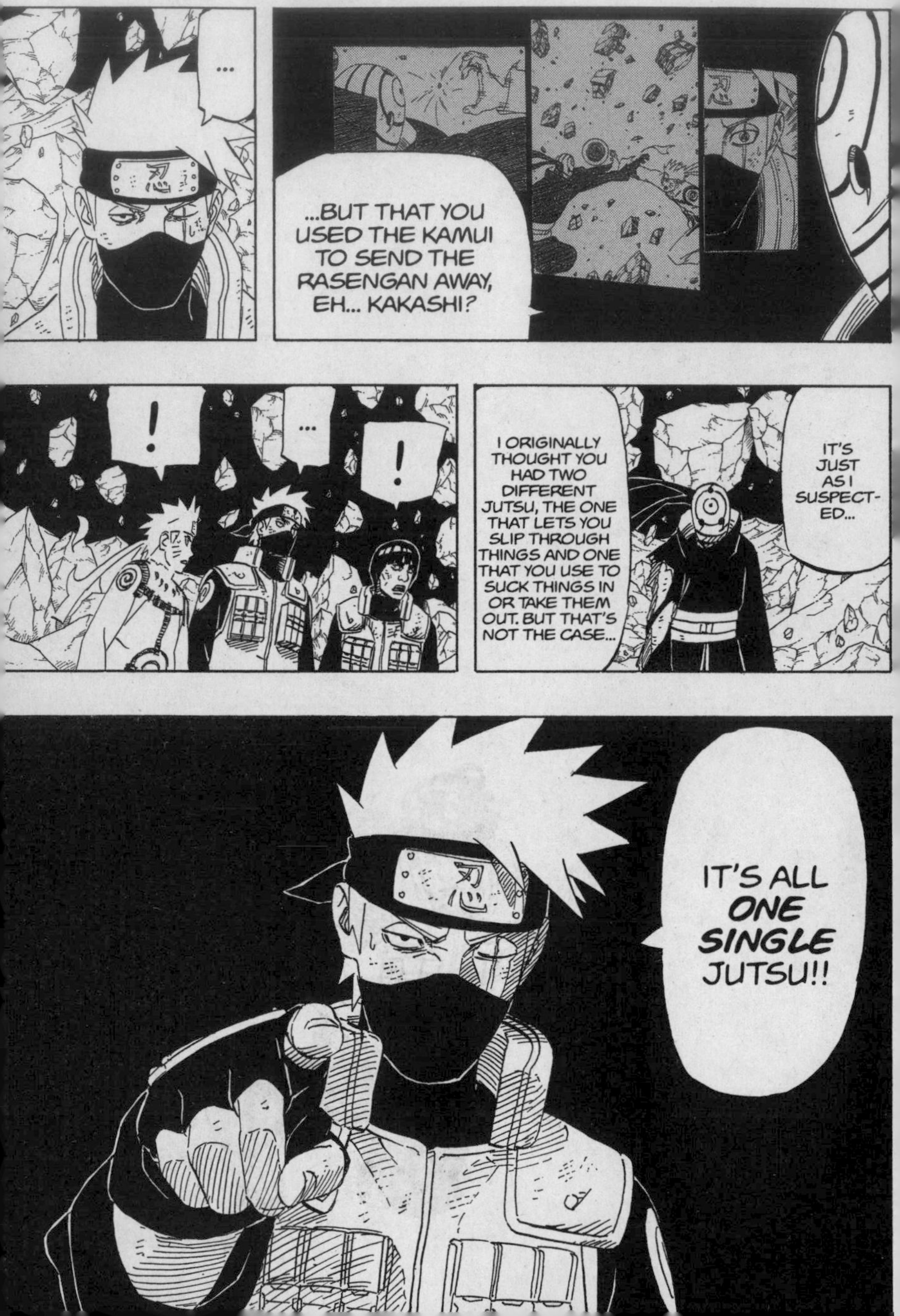
...BUT THAT YOU USED THE KAMUI TO SEND THE RASENGAN AWAY, EH... KAKASHI?
...
IT'S JUST AS I SUSPECTED...
I ORIGINALLY THOUGHT YOU HAD TWO DIFFERENT JUTSU, THE ONE THAT LETS YOU SLIP THROUGH THINGS AND ONE THAT YOU USE TO SUCK THINGS IN OR TAKE THEM OUT. BUT THAT'S NOT THE CASE...
!
...
!
IT'S ALL *ONE SINGLE* JUTSU!!

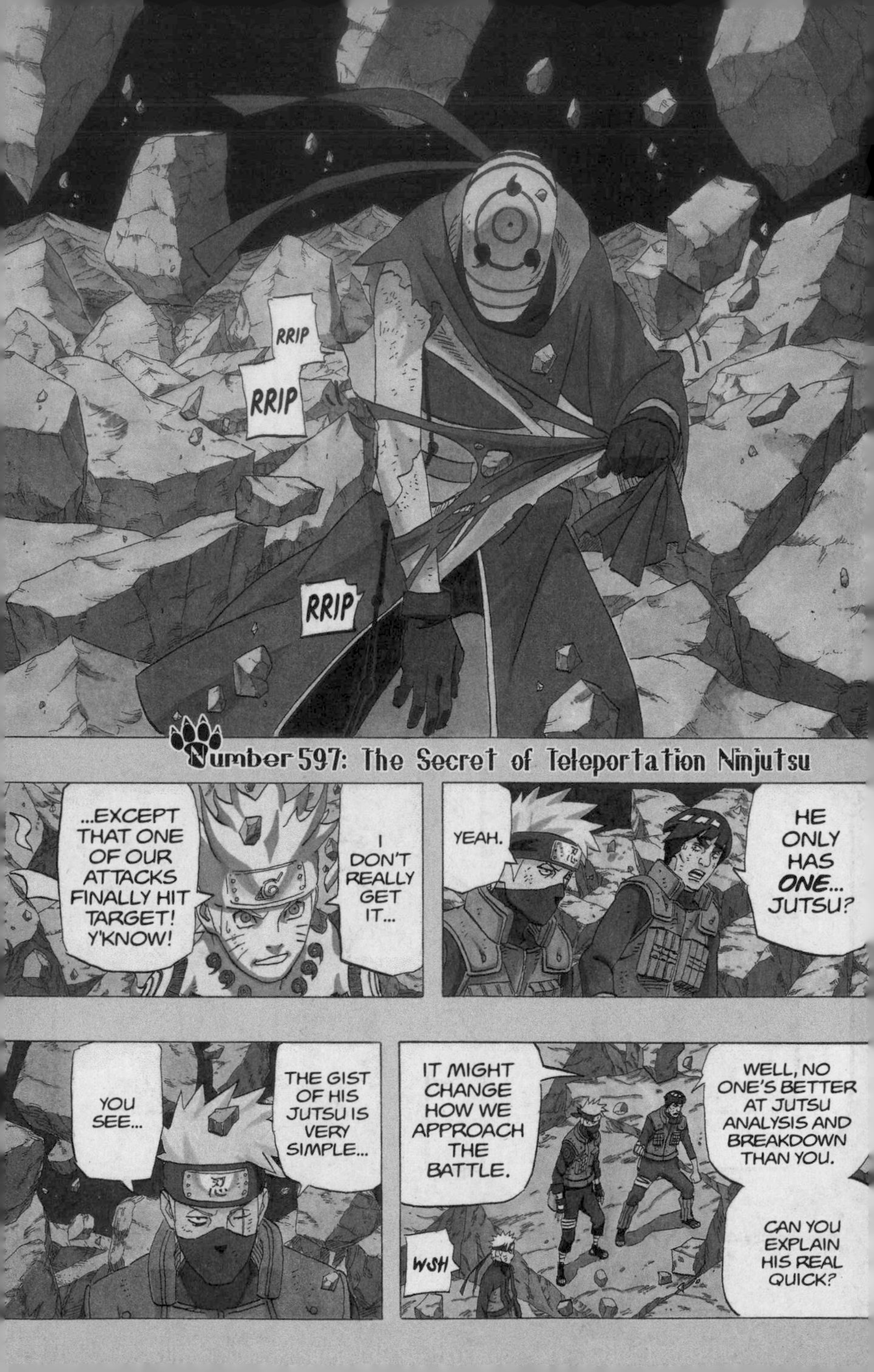
RRIP
RRIP
RRIP
Number 597: The Secret of Teleportation Ninjutsu
HE ONLY HAS ONE... JUTSU?
YEAH.
I DON'T REALLY GET IT...
...EXCEPT THAT ONE OF OUR ATTACKS FINALLY HIT TARGET! Y'KNOW!
WELL, NO ONE'S BETTER AT JUTSU ANALYSIS AND BREAKDOWN THAN YOU.
CAN YOU EXPLAIN HIS REAL QUICK?
IT MIGHT CHANGE HOW WE APPROACH THE BATTLE.
WSH
THE GIST OF HIS JUTSU IS VERY SIMPLE...
YOU SEE...

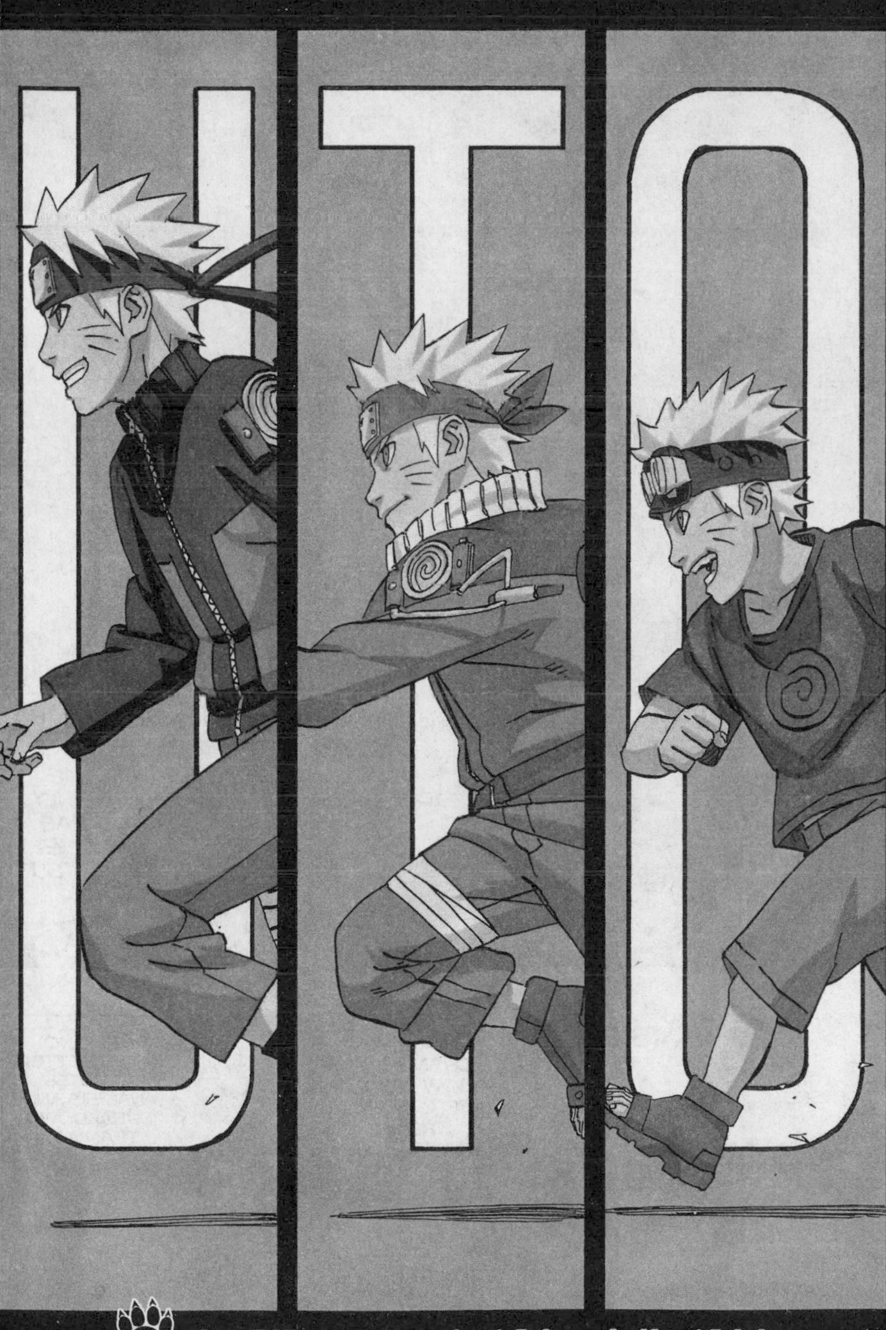

Number 597: The Secret of Teleportation Ninjutsu

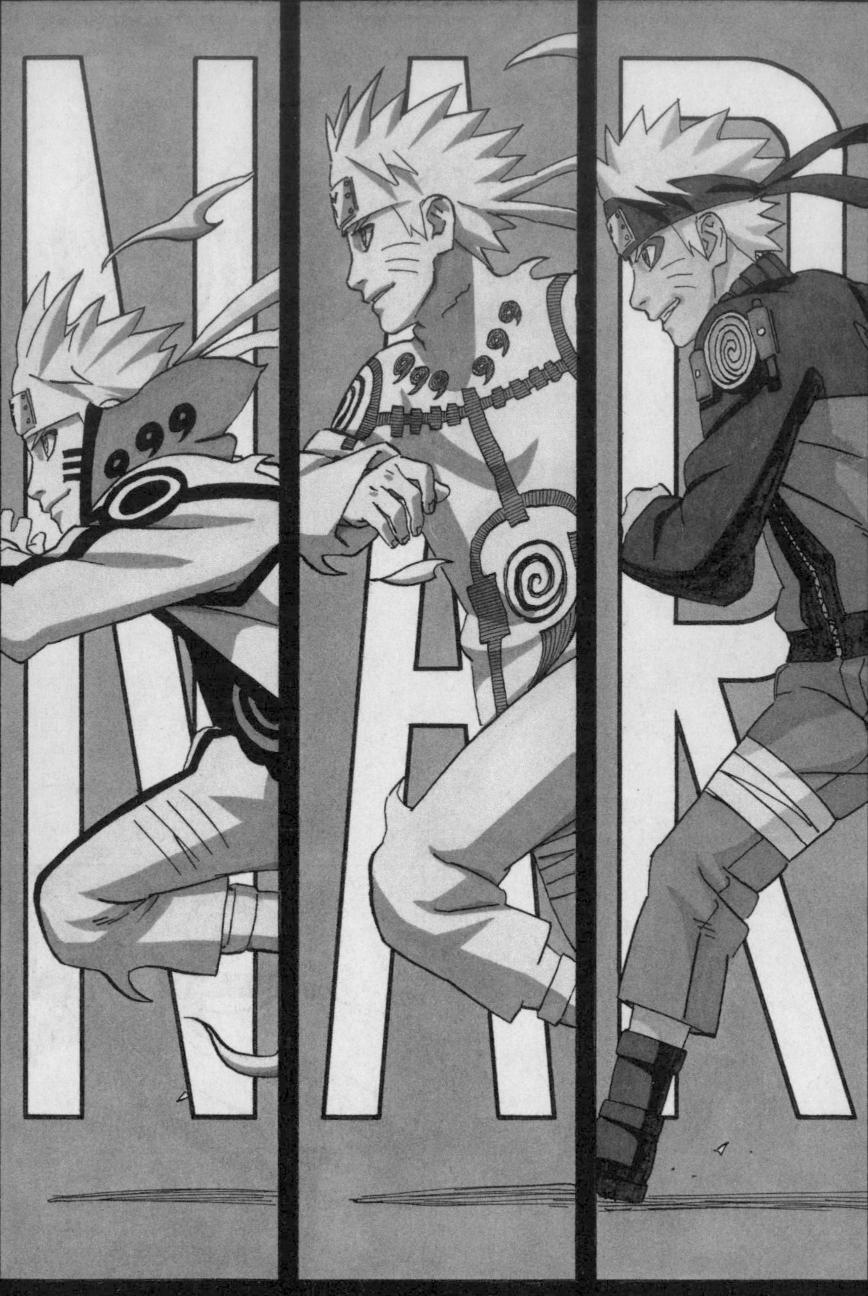

NARUTO

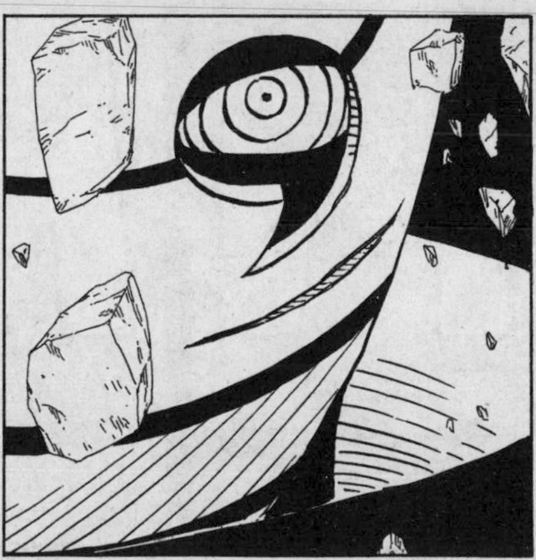

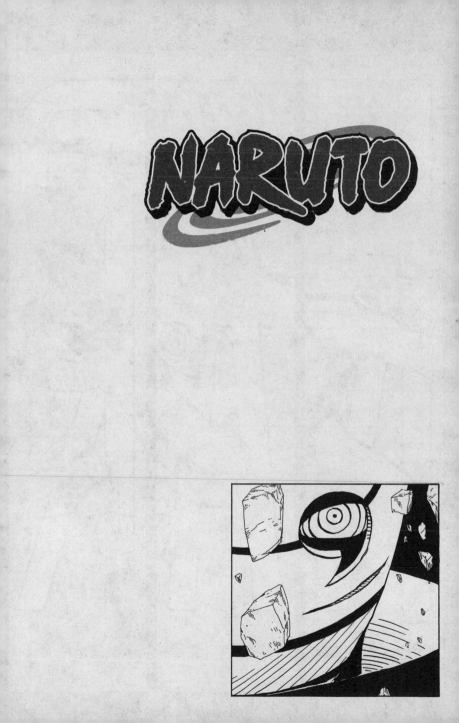

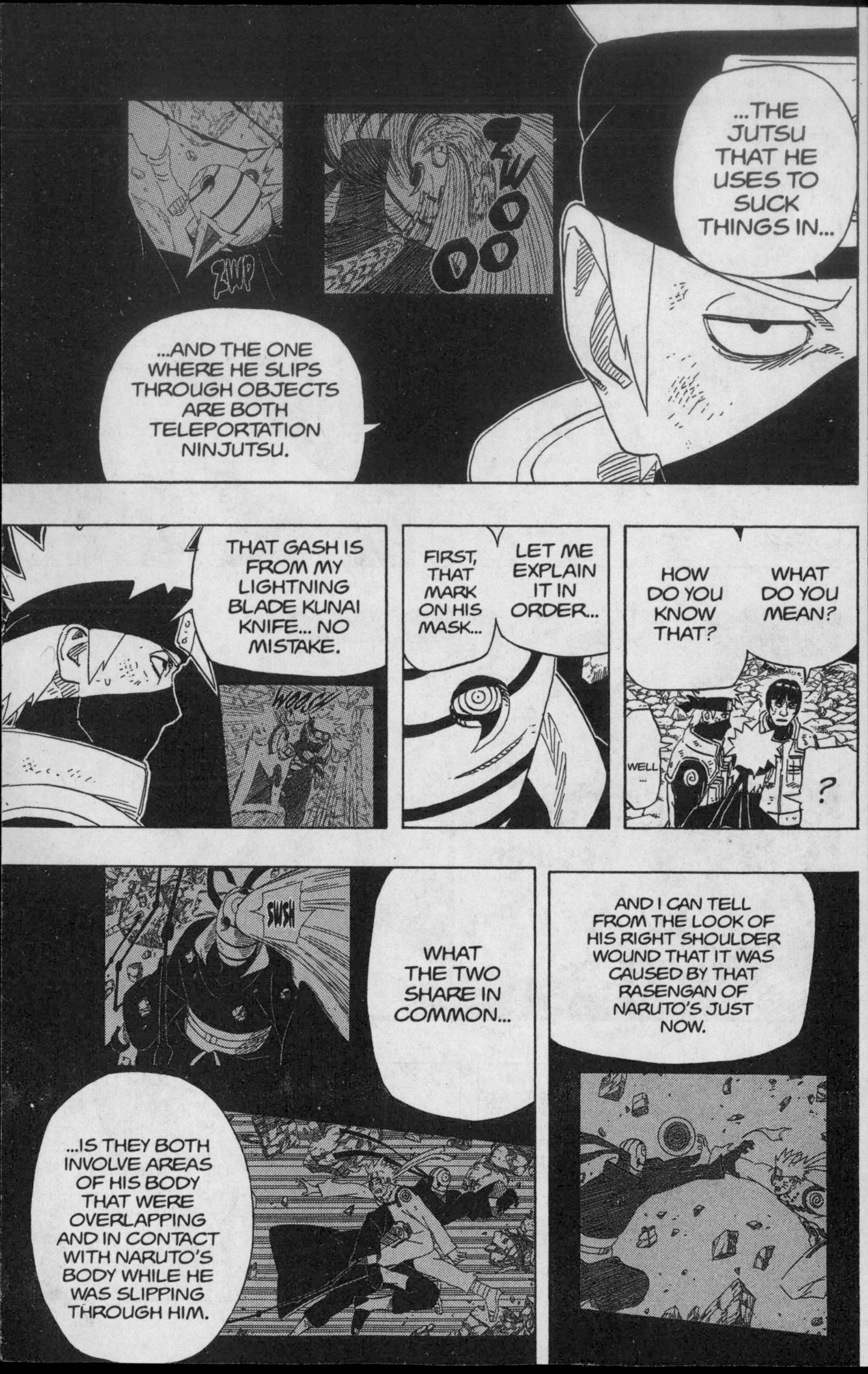
...THE JUTSU THAT HE USES TO SUCK THINGS IN...
ZWOOOO
ZWIP
...AND THE ONE WHERE HE SLIPS THROUGH OBJECTS ARE BOTH TELEPORTATION NINJUTSU.
WHAT DO YOU MEAN?
HOW DO YOU KNOW THAT?
WELL...
?
LET ME EXPLAIN IT IN ORDER...
FIRST, THAT MARK ON HIS MASK...
THAT GASH IS FROM MY LIGHTNING BLADE KUNAI KNIFE... NO MISTAKE.
AND I CAN TELL FROM THE LOOK OF HIS RIGHT SHOULDER WOUND THAT IT WAS CAUSED BY THAT RASENGAN OF NARUTO'S JUST NOW.
WHAT THE TWO SHARE IN COMMON...
SWSH
...IS THEY BOTH INVOLVE AREAS OF HIS BODY THAT WERE OVERLAPPING AND IN CONTACT WITH NARUTO'S BODY WHILE HE WAS SLIPPING THROUGH HIM.

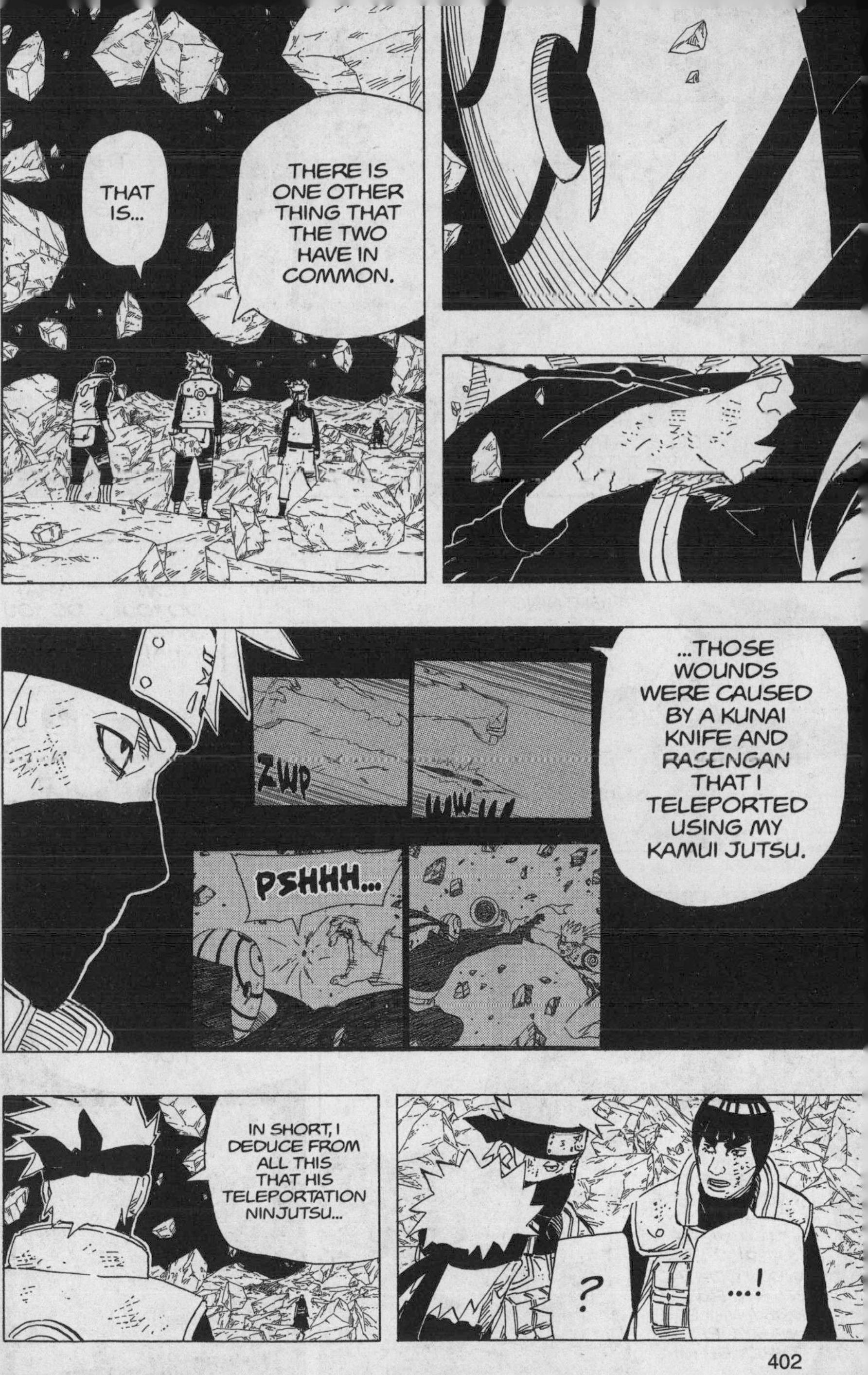
THERE IS ONE OTHER THING THAT THE TWO HAVE IN COMMON.
THAT IS...
...THOSE WOUNDS WERE CAUSED BY A KUNAI KNIFE AND RASENGAN THAT I TELEPORTED USING MY KAMUI JUTSU.
ZWP
PSHHH...
...!
?
IN SHORT, I DEDUCE FROM ALL THIS THAT HIS TELEPORTATION NINJUTSU...

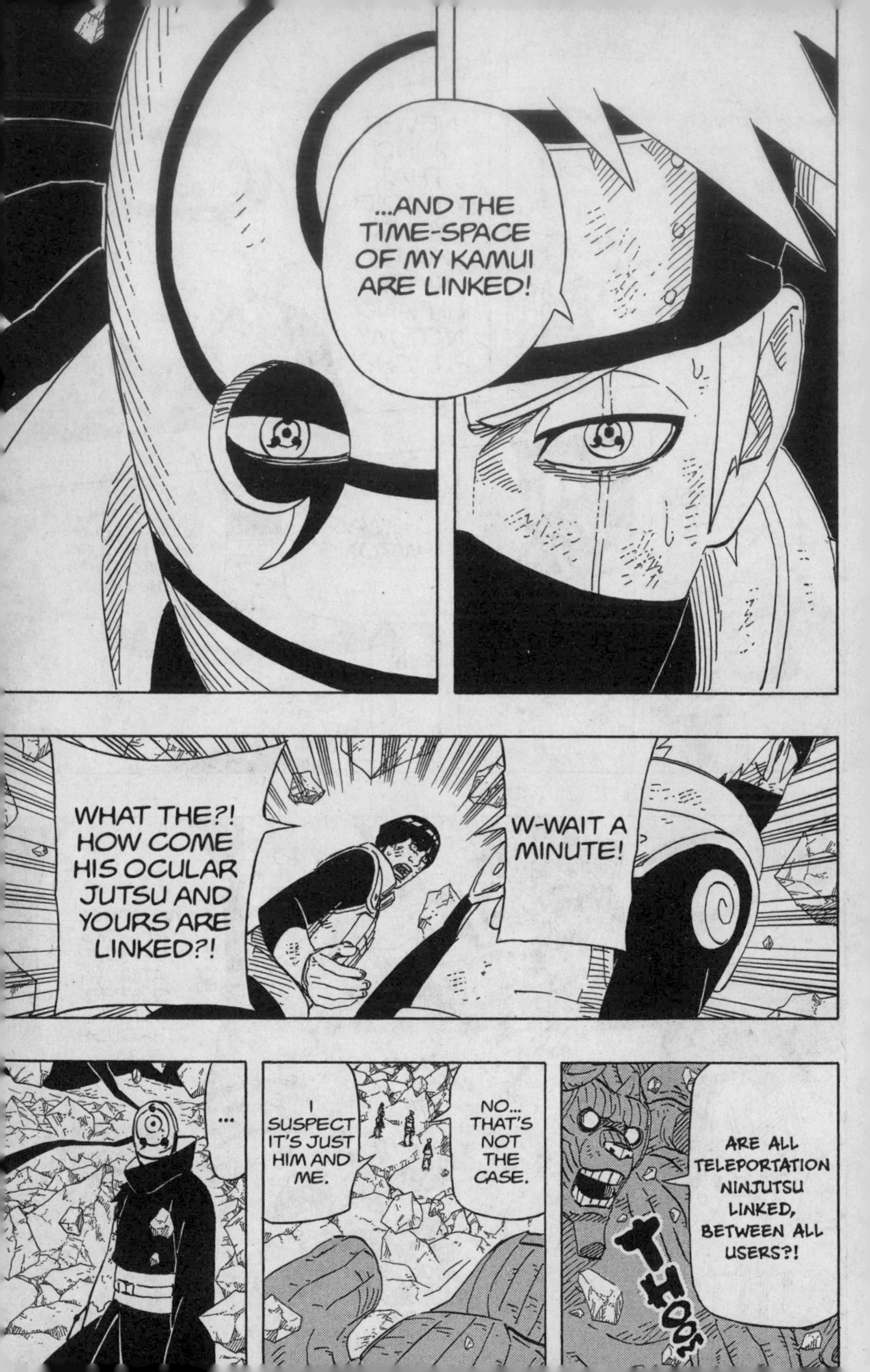

...AND THE TIME-SPACE OF MY KAMUI ARE LINKED!
W-WAIT A MINUTE!
WHAT THE?! HOW COME HIS OCULAR JUTSU AND YOURS ARE LINKED?!
ARE ALL TELEPORTATION NINJUTSU LINKED, BETWEEN ALL USERS?!
THOOM
NO... THAT'S NOT THE CASE.
I SUSPECT IT'S JUST HIM AND ME.
...

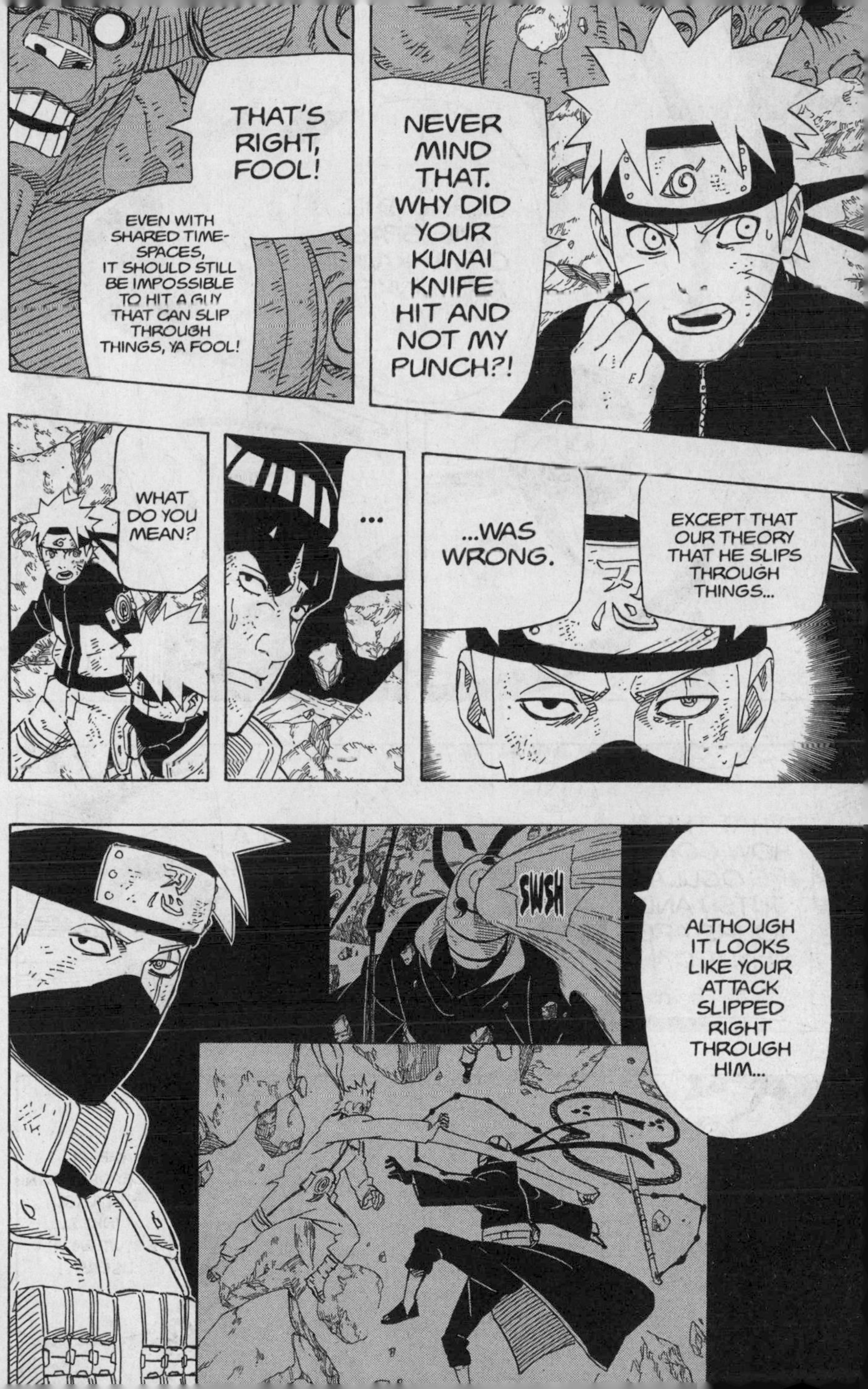
NEVER MIND THAT. WHY DID YOUR KUNAI KNIFE HIT AND NOT MY PUNCH?!
THAT'S RIGHT, FOOL!
EVEN WITH SHARED TIME-SPACES, IT SHOULD STILL BE IMPOSSIBLE TO HIT A GUY THAT CAN SLIP THROUGH THINGS, YA FOOL!
EXCEPT THAT OUR THEORY THAT HE SLIPS THROUGH THINGS...
...WAS WRONG.
...
WHAT DO YOU MEAN?
ALTHOUGH IT LOOKS LIKE YOUR ATTACK SLIPPED RIGHT THROUGH HIM...
SWSH

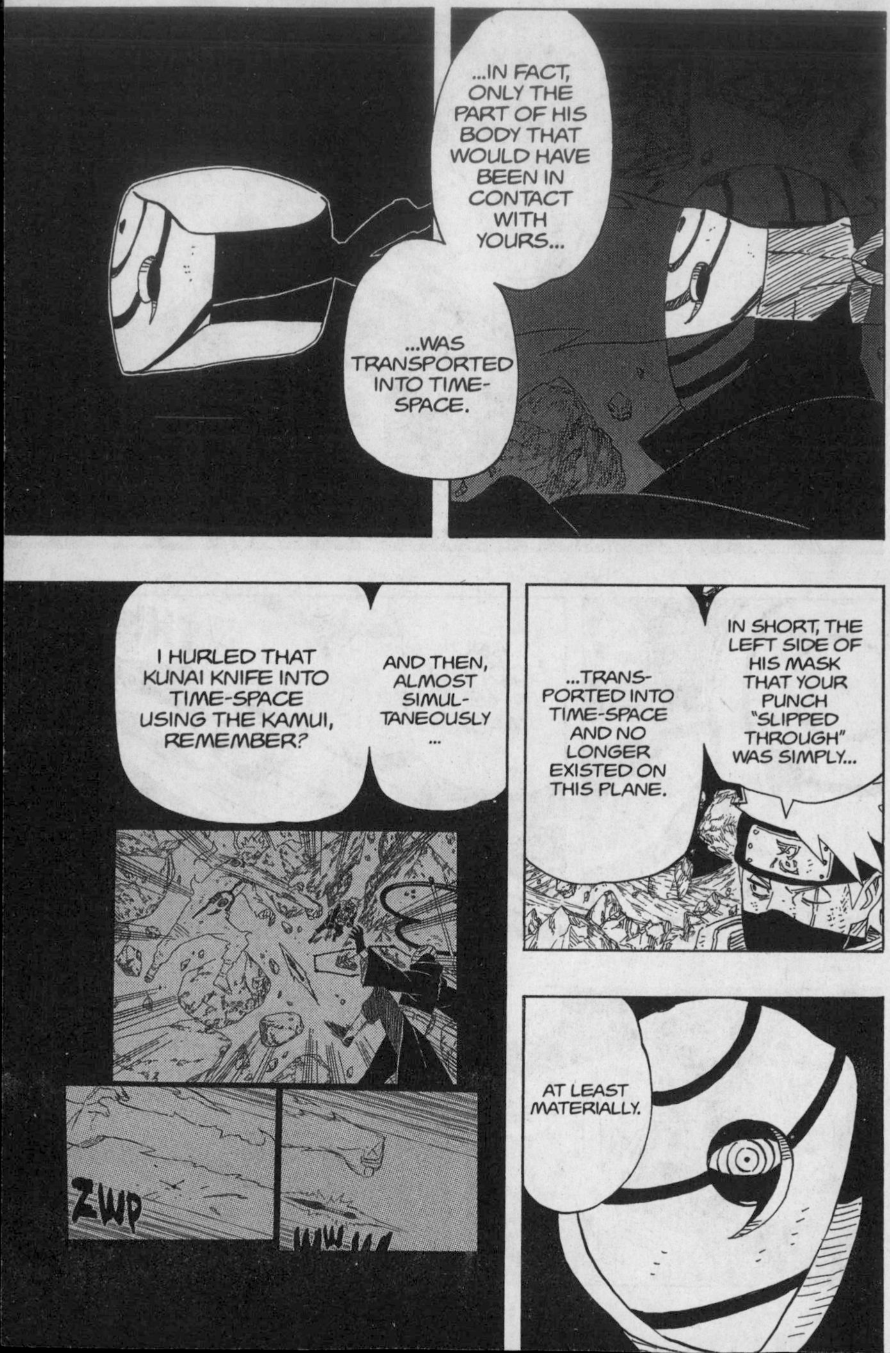
...IN FACT, ONLY THE PART OF HIS BODY THAT WOULD HAVE BEEN IN CONTACT WITH YOURS...
...WAS TRANSPORTED INTO TIME-SPACE.
IN SHORT, THE LEFT SIDE OF HIS MASK THAT YOUR PUNCH "SLIPPED THROUGH" WAS SIMPLY...
...TRANS-PORTED INTO TIME-SPACE AND NO LONGER EXISTED ON THIS PLANE.
AT LEAST MATERIALLY.
I HURLED THAT KUNAI KNIFE INTO TIME-SPACE USING THE KAMUI, REMEMBER?
AND THEN, ALMOST SIMUL-TANEOUSLY ...
ZWP

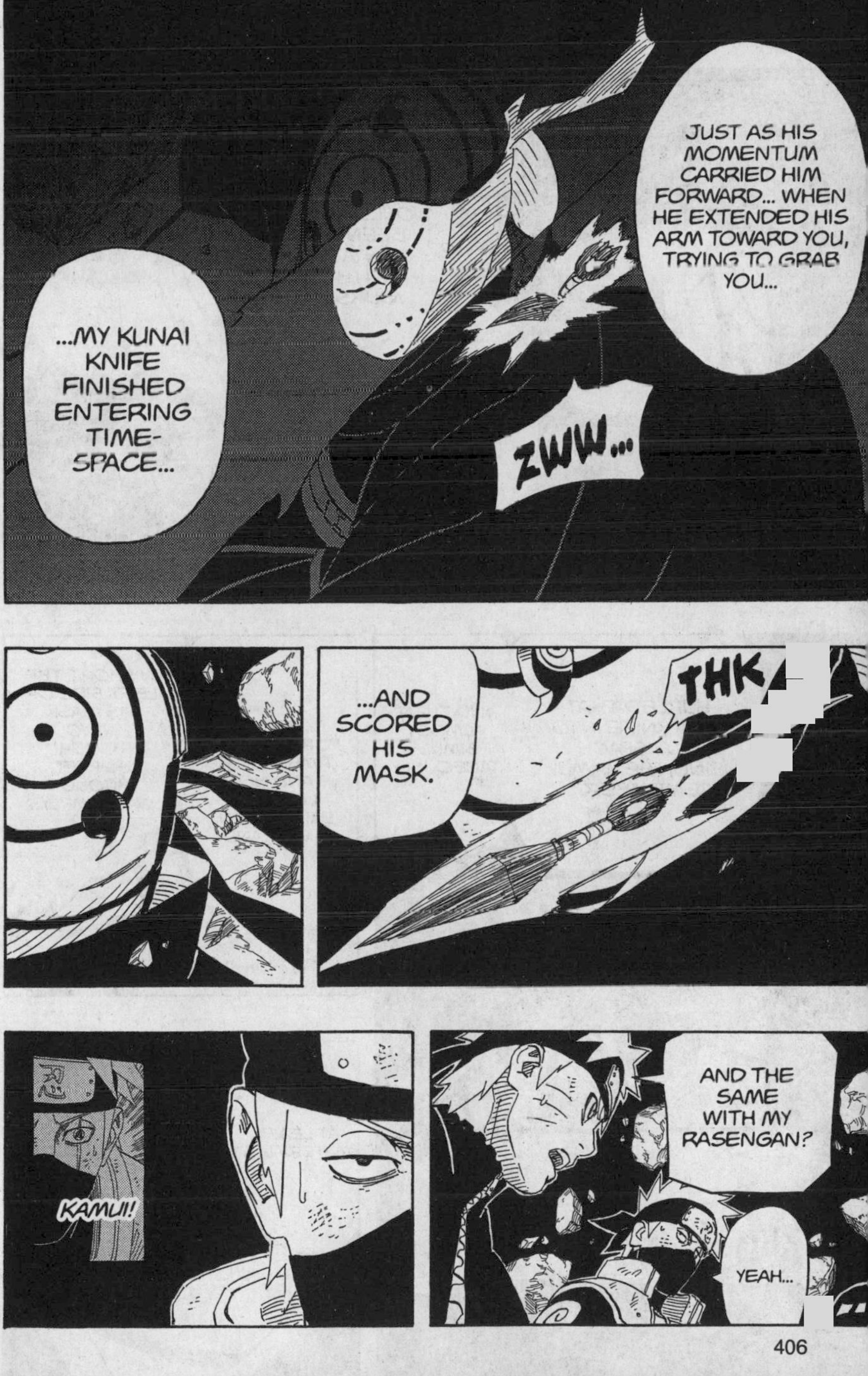

JUST AS HIS MOMENTUM CARRIED HIM FORWARD... WHEN HE EXTENDED HIS ARM TOWARD YOU, TRYING TO GRAB YOU...
...MY KUNAI KNIFE FINISHED ENTERING TIME-SPACE...
ZWW...
THK
...AND SCORED HIS MASK.
AND THE SAME WITH MY RASENGAN?
YEAH...
KAMUI!

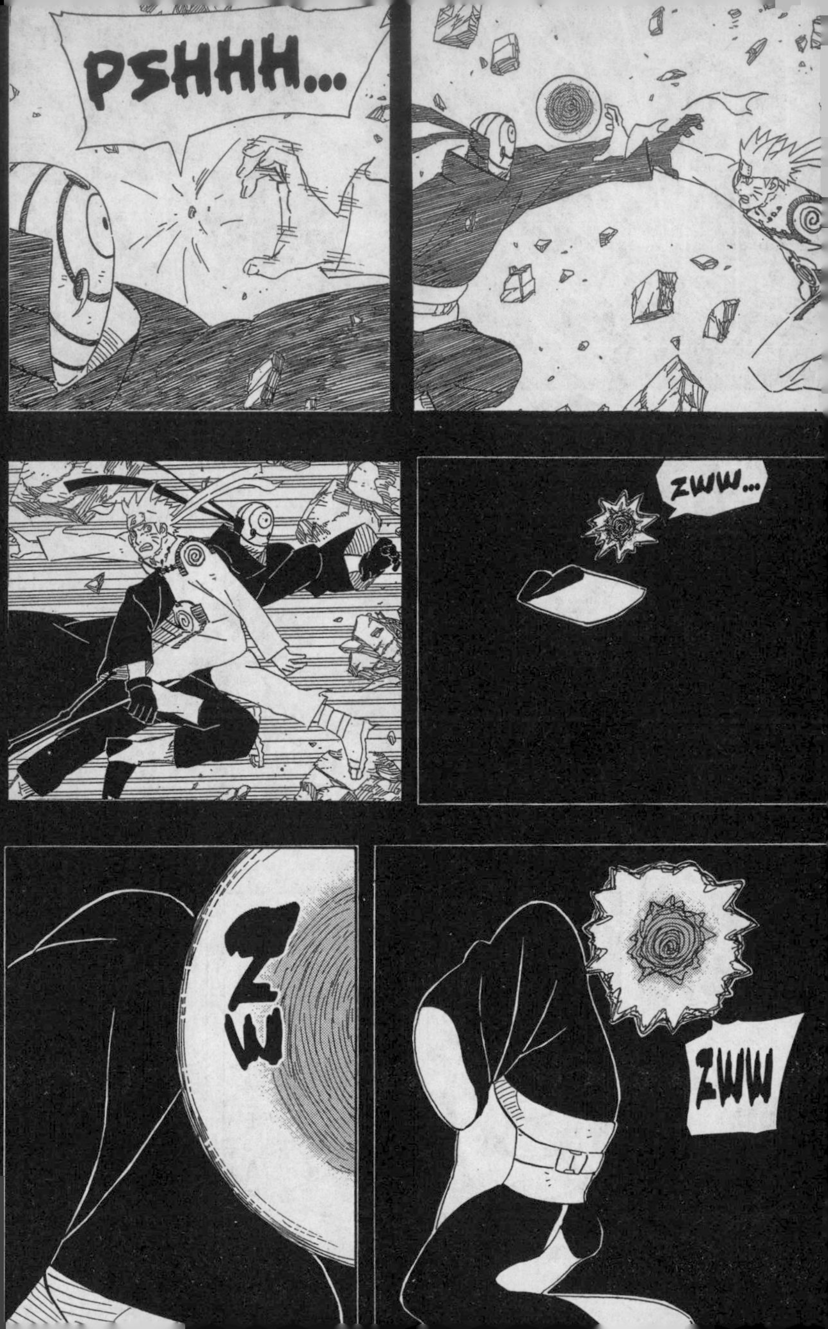
PSHHH...
ZWW...
ZWW
ZW

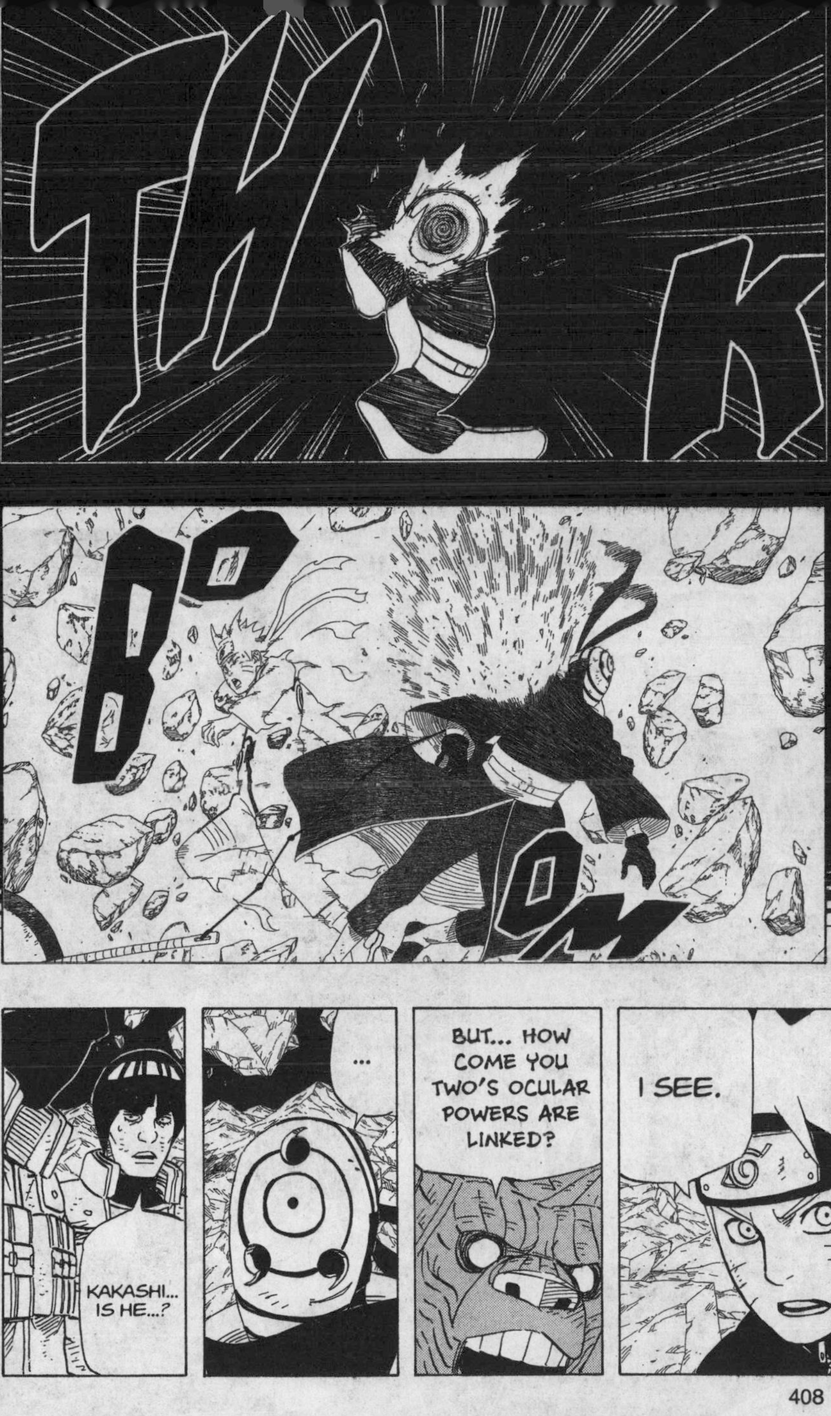
TH
K
BOOM
I SEE.
BUT... HOW COME YOU TWO'S OCULAR POWERS ARE LINKED?
...
KAKASHI... IS HE...?

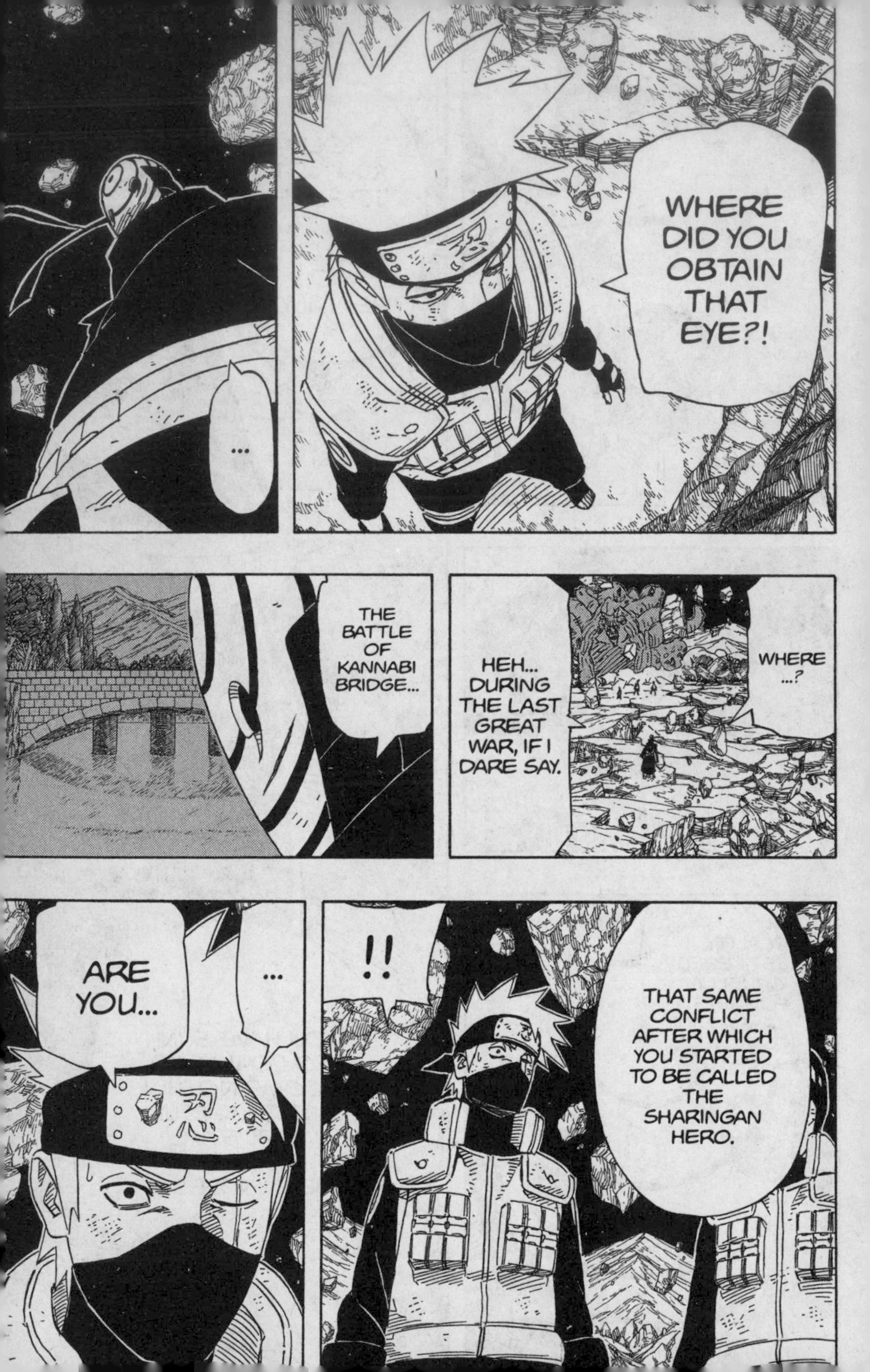
WHERE DID YOU OBTAIN THAT EYE?!
...
WHERE ...?
HEH... DURING THE LAST GREAT WAR, IF I DARE SAY.
THE BATTLE OF KANNABI BRIDGE...
THAT SAME CONFLICT AFTER WHICH YOU STARTED TO BE CALLED THE SHARINGAN HERO.
!!
...
ARE YOU...

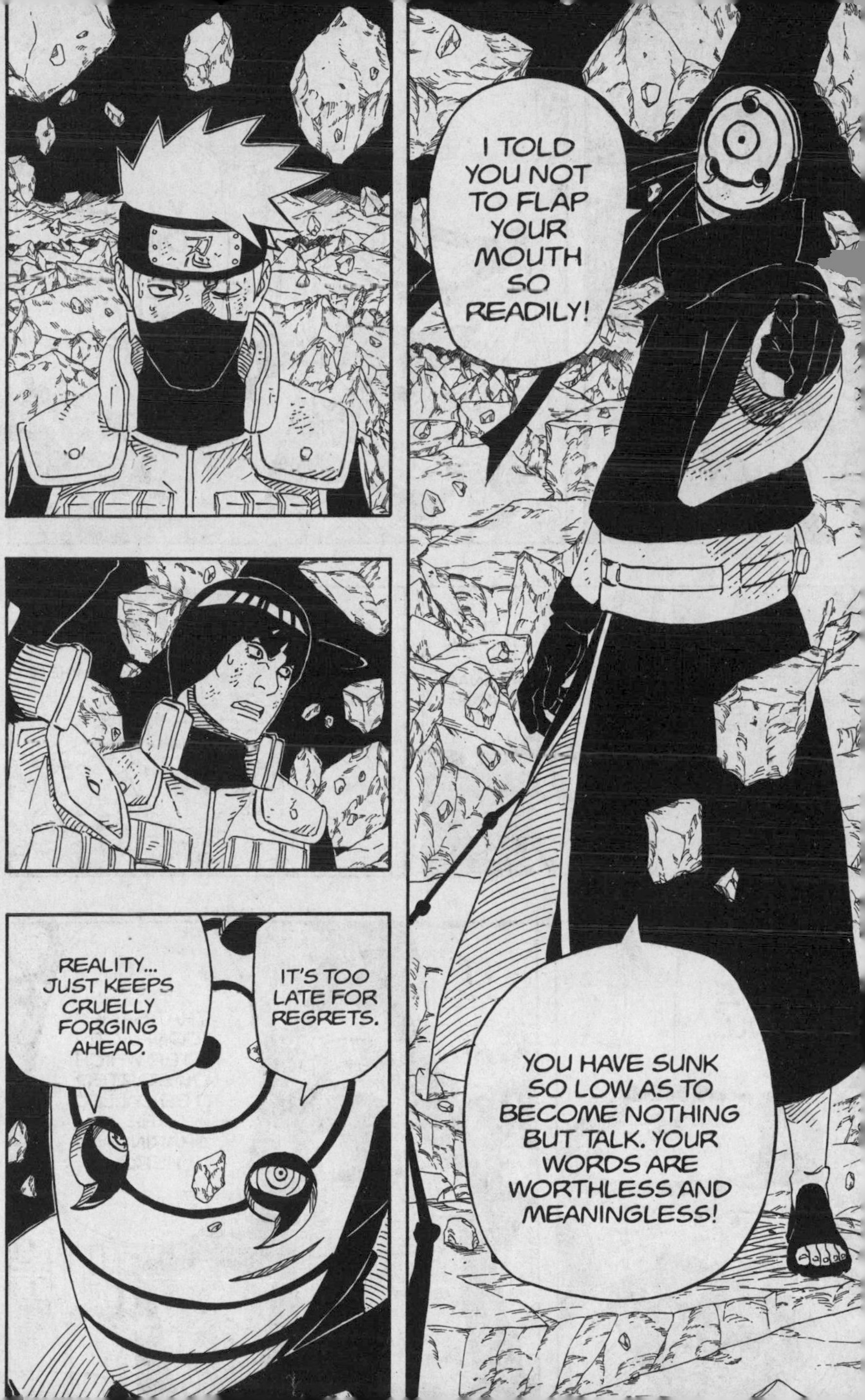
I TOLD YOU NOT TO FLAP YOUR MOUTH SO READILY!
YOU HAVE SUNK SO LOW AS TO BECOME NOTHING BUT TALK. YOUR WORDS ARE WORTHLESS AND MEANINGLESS!
IT'S TOO LATE FOR REGRETS.
REALITY... JUST KEEPS CRUELLY FORGING AHEAD.

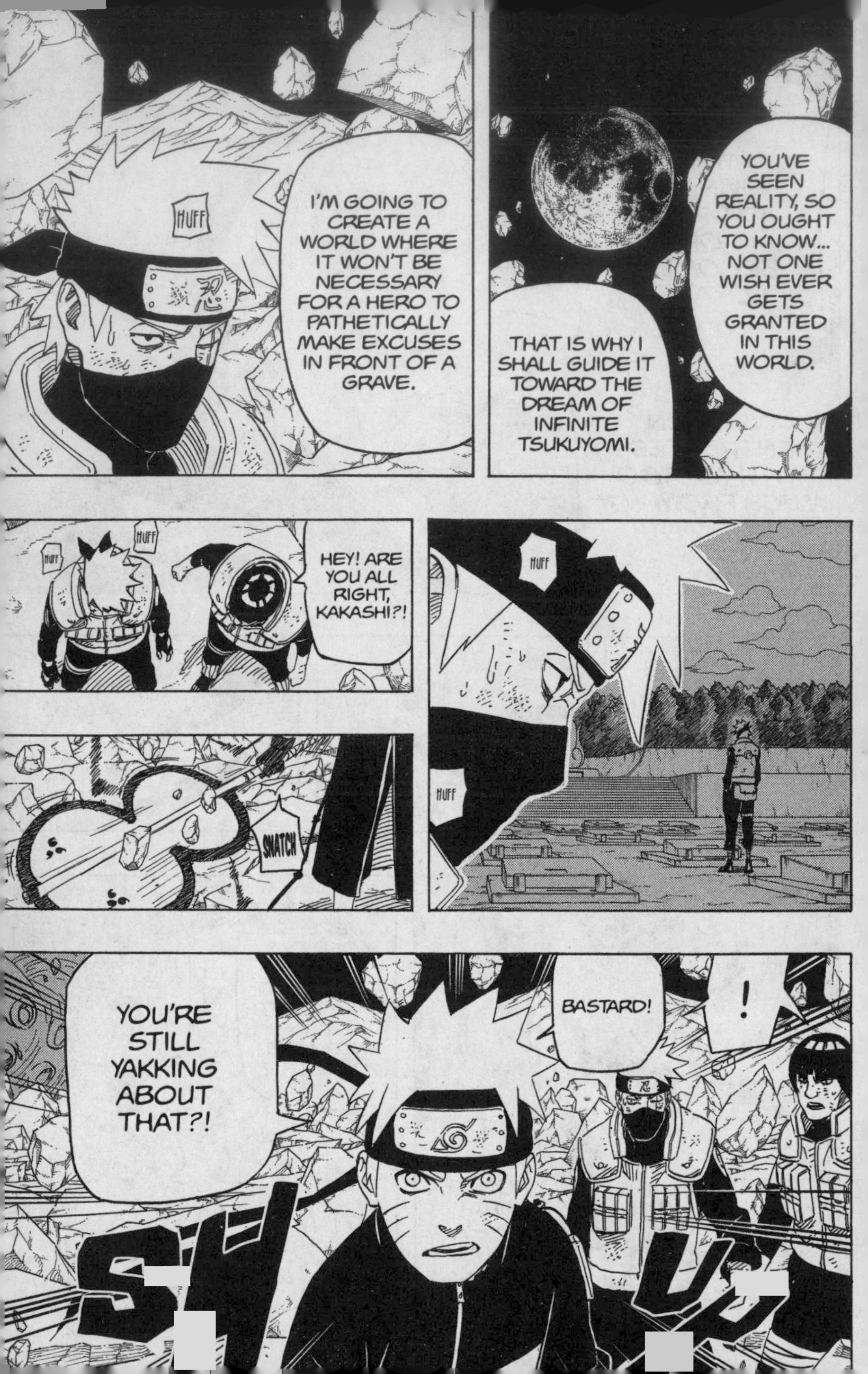
YOU'VE SEEN REALITY, SO YOU OUGHT TO KNOW... NOT ONE WISH EVER GETS GRANTED IN THIS WORLD.
THAT IS WHY I SHALL GUIDE IT TOWARD THE DREAM OF INFINITE TSUKUYOMI.
HUFF
I'M GOING TO CREATE A WORLD WHERE IT WON'T BE NECESSARY FOR A HERO TO PATHETICALLY MAKE EXCUSES IN FRONT OF A GRAVE.
HUFF
HUFF
HUFF
HUFF
HEY! ARE YOU ALL RIGHT, KAKASHI?!
SNATCH
!
BASTARD!
YOU'RE STILL YAKKING ABOUT THAT?!

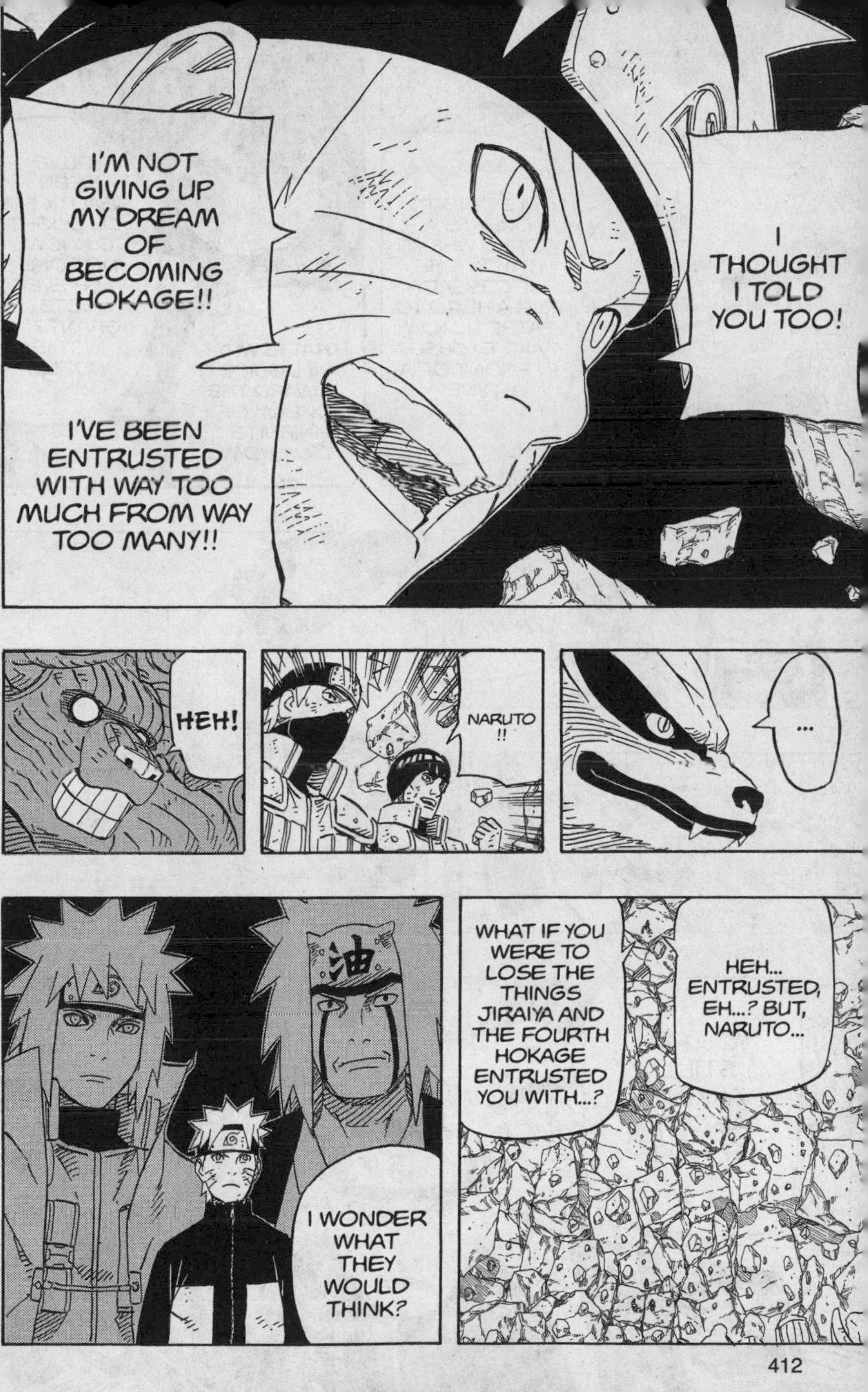
I THOUGHT I TOLD YOU TOO!
I'M NOT GIVING UP MY DREAM OF BECOMING HOKAGE!!
I'VE BEEN ENTRUSTED WITH WAY TOO MUCH FROM WAY TOO MANY!!
...
NARUTO !!
HEH!
HEH... ENTRUSTED, EH...? BUT, NARUTO...
WHAT IF YOU WERE TO LOSE THE THINGS JIRAIYA AND THE FOURTH HOKAGE ENTRUSTED YOU WITH...?
油
I WONDER WHAT THEY WOULD THINK?

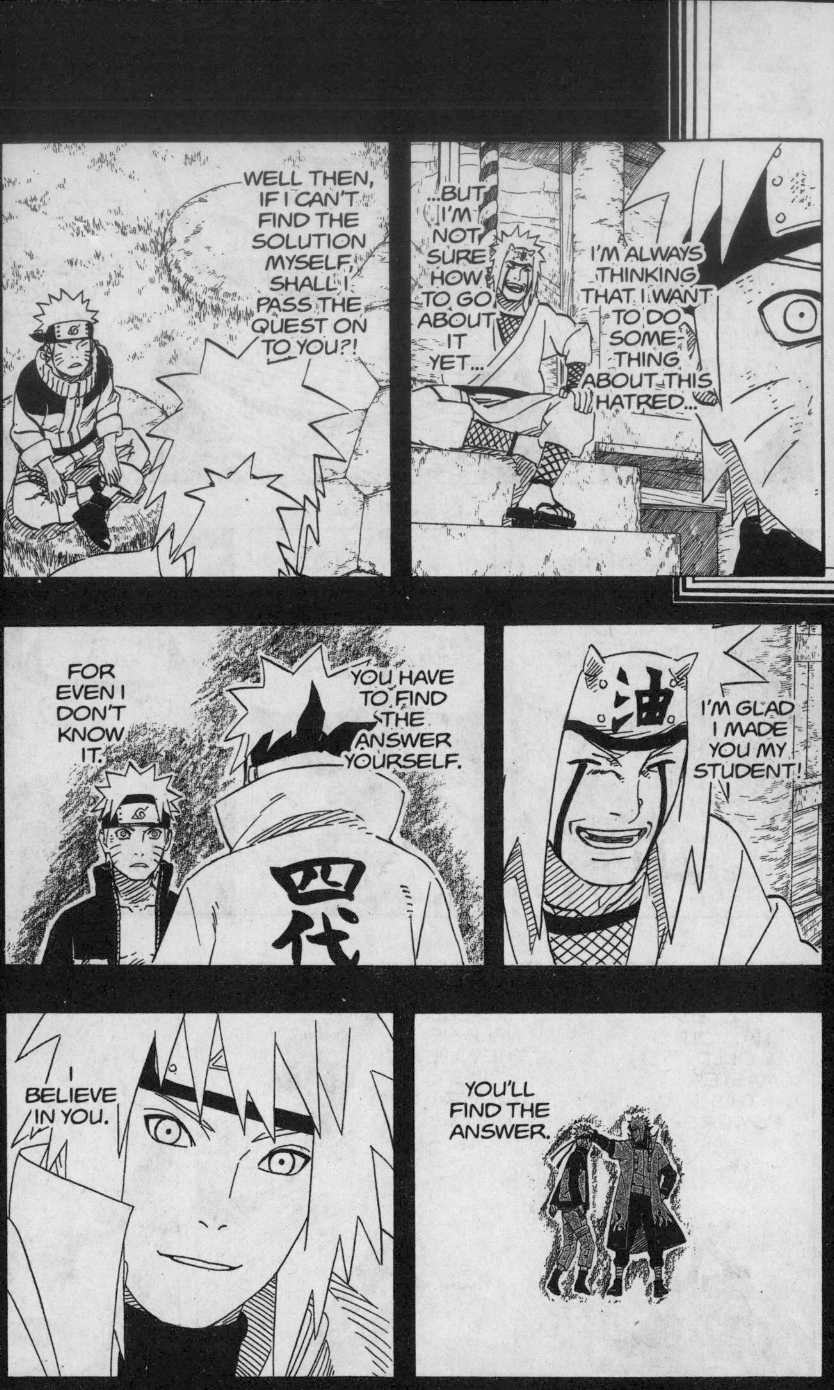
I'M ALWAYS THINKING THAT I WANT TO DO SOMETHING ABOUT THIS HATRED...
...BUT I'M NOT SURE HOW TO GO ABOUT IT YET...
WELL THEN, IF I CAN'T FIND THE SOLUTION MYSELF, SHALL I PASS THE QUEST ON TO YOU?!
I'M GLAD I MADE YOU MY STUDENT!
油
YOU HAVE TO FIND THE ANSWER YOURSELF.
FOR EVEN I DON'T KNOW IT.
四代
YOU'LL FIND THE ANSWER.
I BELIEVE IN YOU.

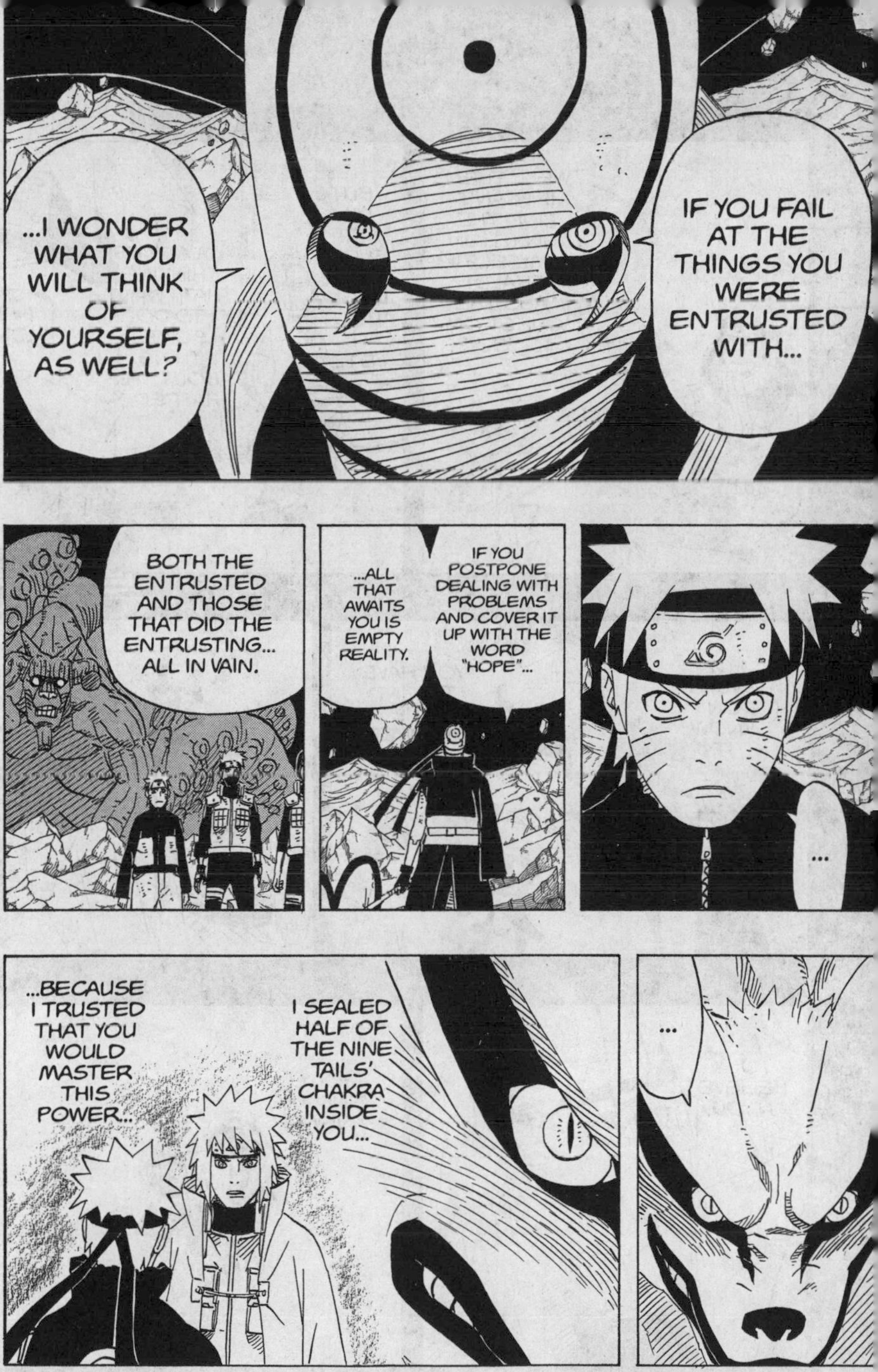
IF YOU FAIL AT THE THINGS YOU WERE ENTRUSTED WITH...
...I WONDER WHAT YOU WILL THINK OF YOURSELF, AS WELL?
...
IF YOU POSTPONE DEALING WITH PROBLEMS AND COVER IT UP WITH THE WORD "HOPE"...
...ALL THAT AWAITS YOU IS EMPTY REALITY.
BOTH THE ENTRUSTED AND THOSE THAT DID THE ENTRUSTING... ALL IN VAIN.
...
I SEALED HALF OF THE NINE TAILS' CHAKRA INSIDE YOU...
...BECAUSE I TRUSTED THAT YOU WOULD MASTER THIS POWER...

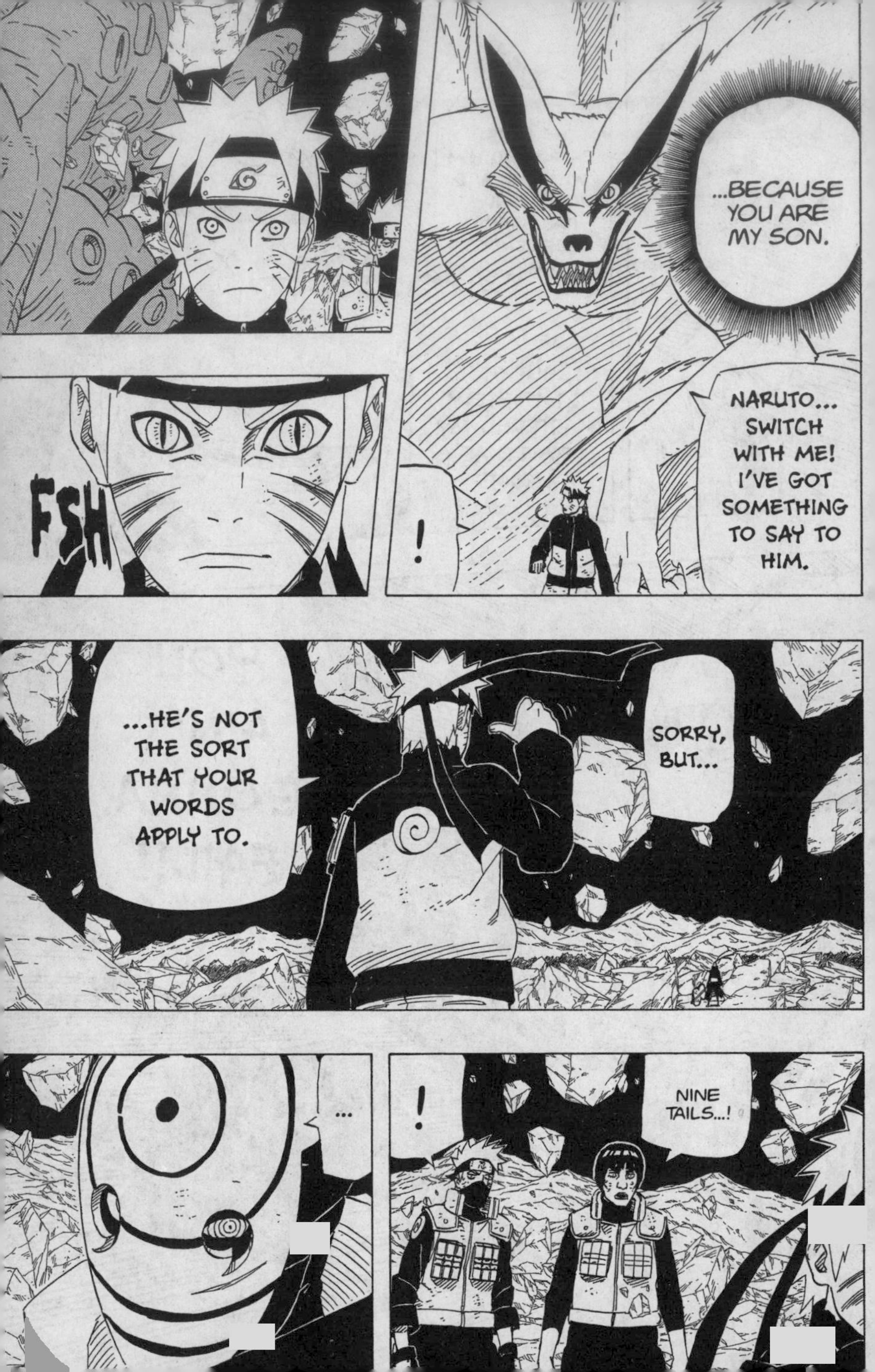
...BECAUSE YOU ARE MY SON.
NARUTO... SWITCH WITH ME! I'VE GOT SOMETHING TO SAY TO HIM.
!
FSH
SORRY, BUT...
...HE'S NOT THE SORT THAT YOUR WORDS APPLY TO.
NINE TAILS...!
!
...

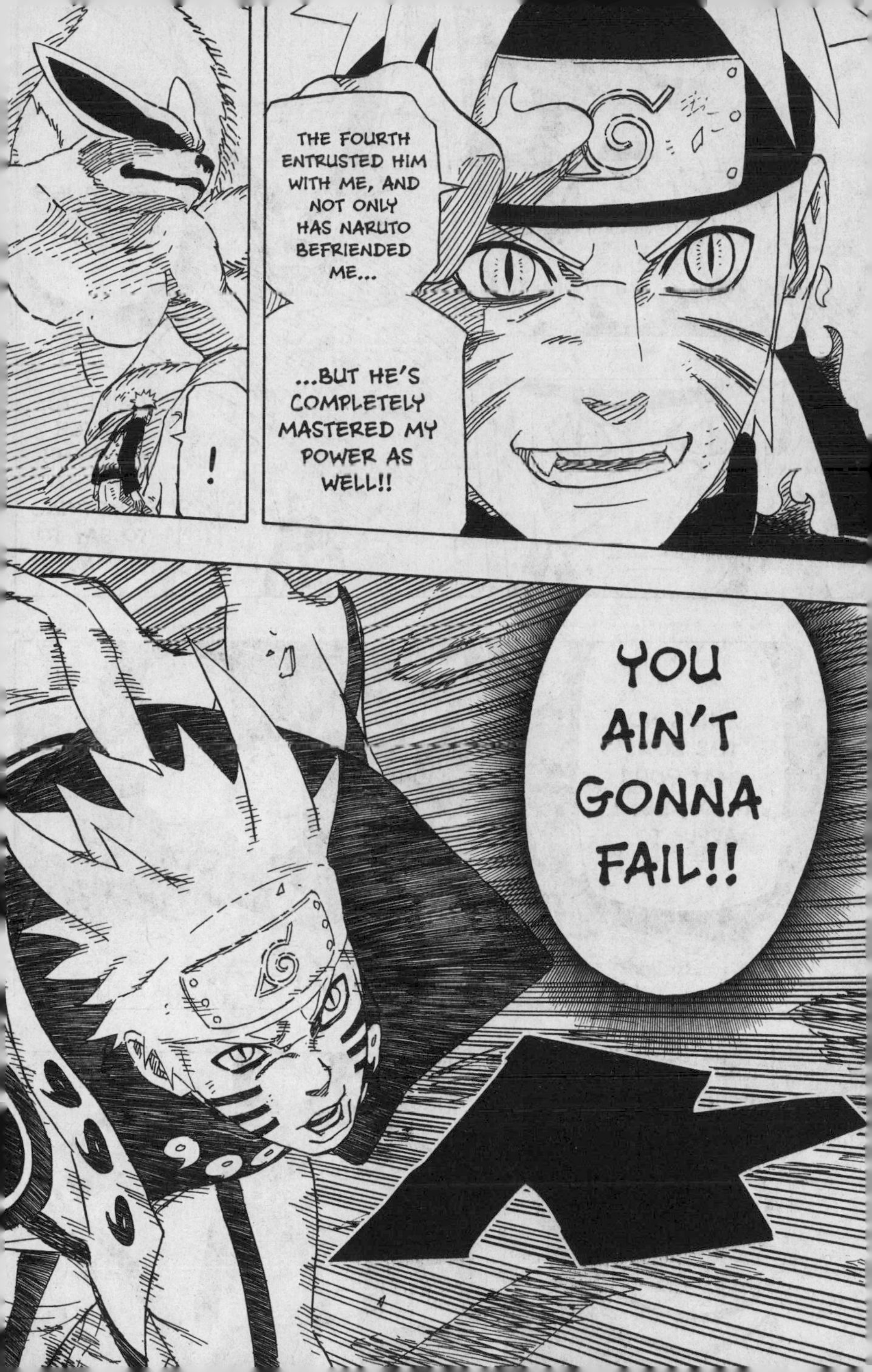
THE FOURTH ENTRUSTED HIM WITH ME, AND NOT ONLY HAS NARUTO BEFRIENDED ME...
...BUT HE'S COMPLETELY MASTERED MY POWER AS WELL!!
!
YOU AIN'T GONNA FAIL!!

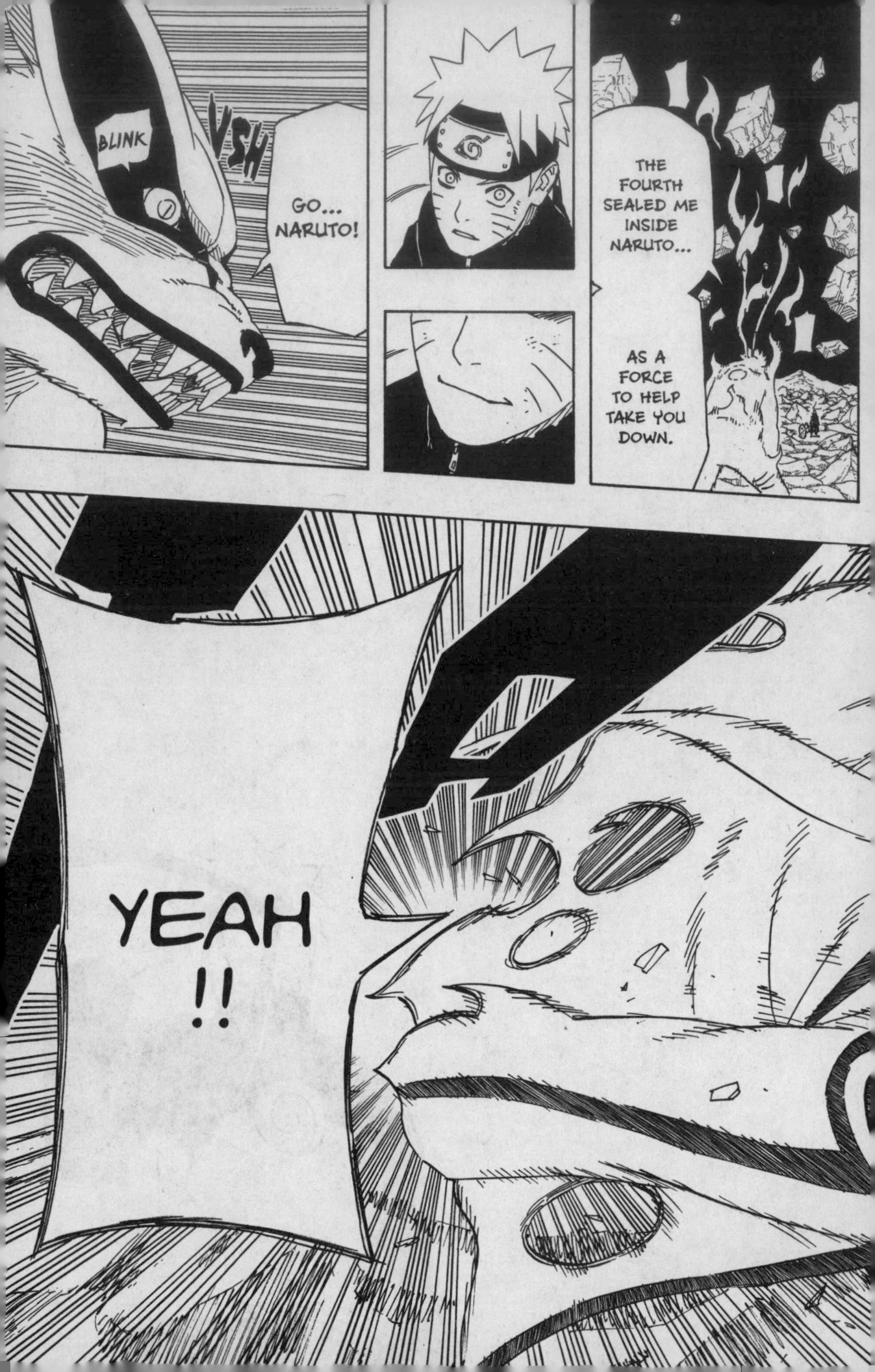
THE FOURTH SEALED ME INSIDE NARUTO...
AS A FORCE TO HELP TAKE YOU DOWN.
VSH
GO... NARUTO!
BLINK
YEAH !!

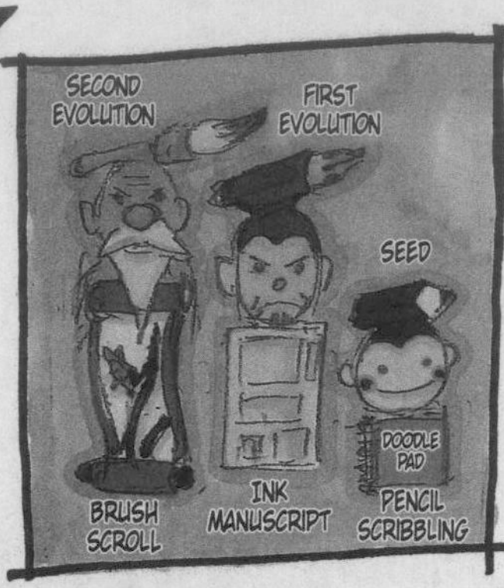
SECOND EVOLUTION
FIRST EVOLUTION
SEED
DOODLE PAD
PENCIL SCRIBBLING
INK MANUSCRIPT
BRUSH SCROLL

岸本斉史

It's really hitting me these days, that I've aged... No matter how much I sleep, I'm still tired and my eyes are blurry. Yet I can't sleep for very long. I recall writing here before that I was starting to become an old man, but I've already completed my first evolution and am now in the middle of my second evolution from old man to geezer! Pokémon evolve and get stronger, but humans just get weaker! But I'm gonna keep drawing manga!

—Masashi Kishimoto, 2012

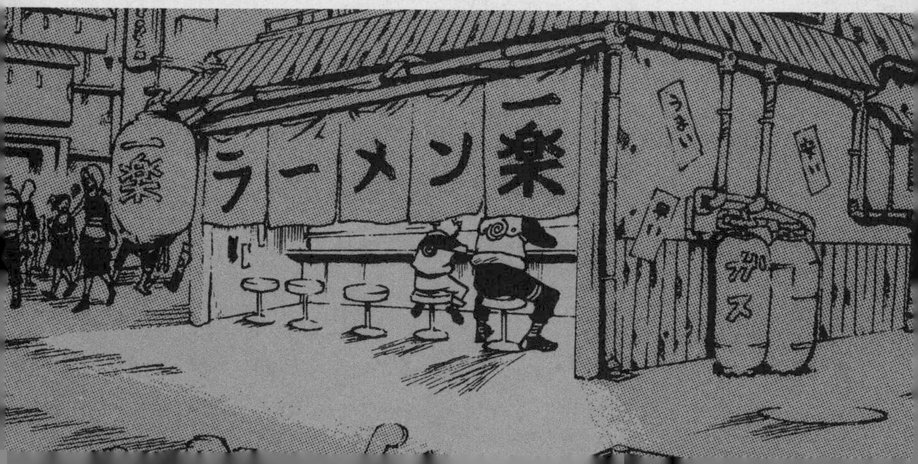
ラーメン一楽
一楽
うまい

NARUTO

SHONEN JUMP MANGA EDITION

NARUTO

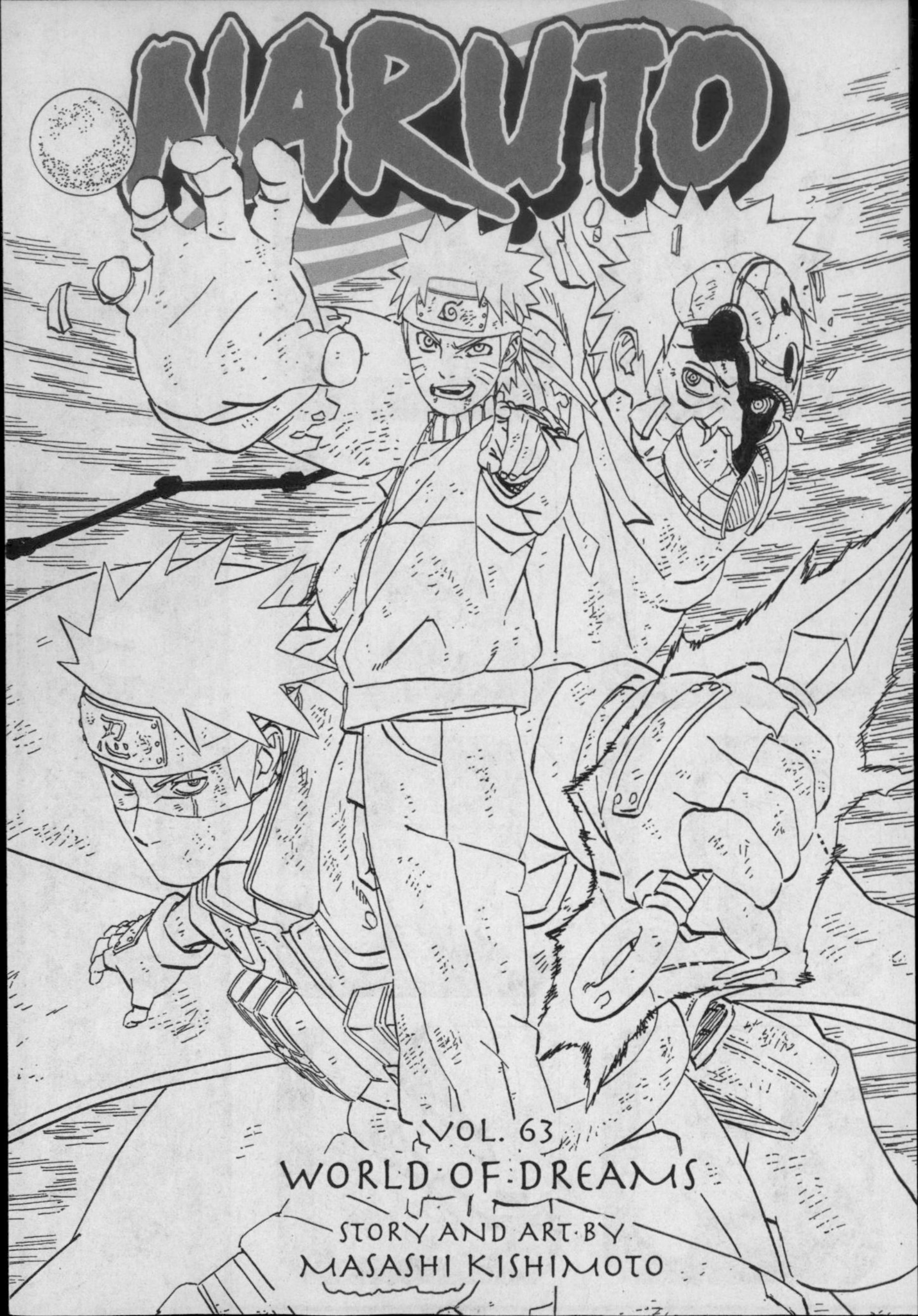

VOL. 63

WORLD OF DREAMS

STORY AND ART BY
MASASHI KISHIMOTO

CHARACTERS

Naruto ナルト

Sasuke サスケ

Kakashi カカシ

Sakura サクラ

Sai サイ

Yamato ヤマト

Kurama 九喇嘛

???

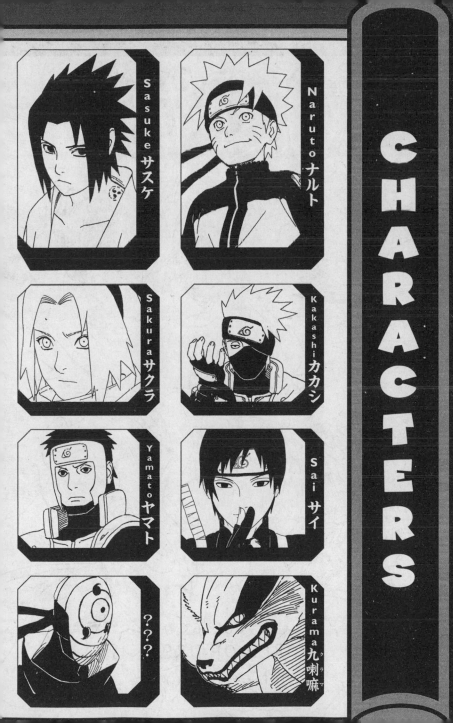

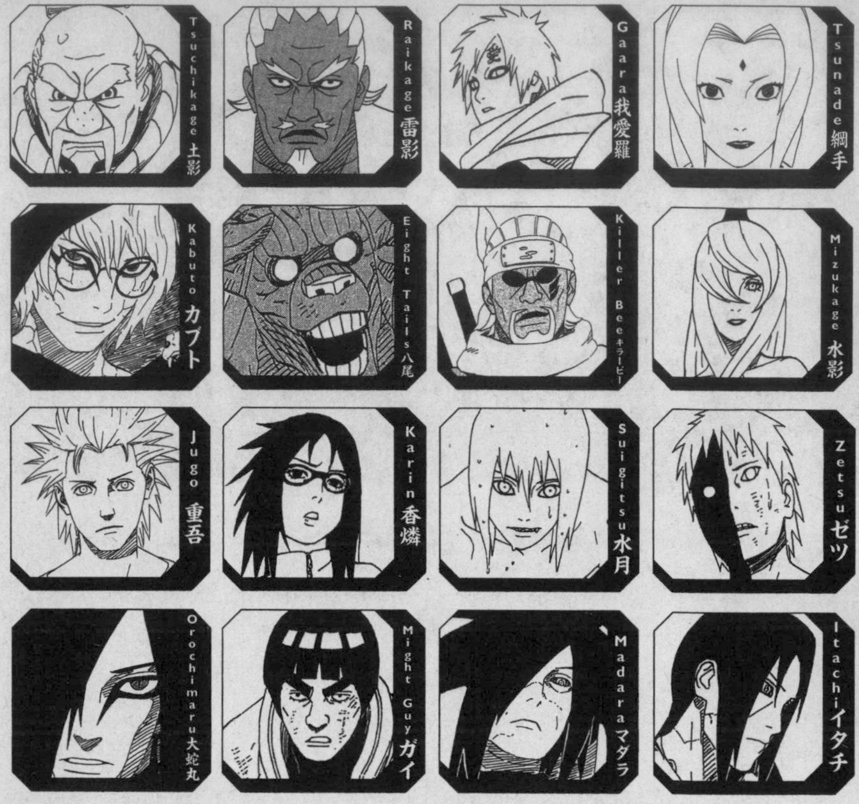

Tsunade 綱手
Gaara 我愛羅
Raikage 雷影
Tsuchikage 土影
Mizukage 水影
Killer Bee キラービー
Eight Tails 八尾
Kabuto カブト
Zetsu ゼツ
Suigetsu 水月
Karin 香燐
Jugo 重吾
Itachi イタチ
Madara マダラ
Might Guy ガイ
Orochimaru 大蛇丸

THE STORY SO FAR...

Naruto, the biggest troublemaker at the Ninja Academy in the Village of Konohagakure, finally becomes a ninja along with his classmates Sasuke and Sakura. They grow and mature through countless trials and battles. However, Sasuke, unable to give up his quest for vengeance, leaves Konohagakure to seek Orochimaru and his power.

Two years pass. Naruto grows up and engages in fierce battles against the Tailed Beast-targeting Akatsuki. Elsewhere, after winning the heroic battle against Itachi and learning his older brother's true intentions, Sasuke allies with the Akatsuki and sets out to destroy Konoha.

The Fourth Great Ninja War against the Akatsuki begins. The Five Shadows seem powerless against the revived Madara's power. Sasuke and Itachi are able to stop Kabuto and undo his jutsu, but even that's not enough to stop Madara. Meanwhile, Naruto and Kakashi team up to fight the mysterious Tobi. Can they unmask this foe once and for all?!

NARUTO

VOL. 63
WORLD OF DREAMS

CONTENTS

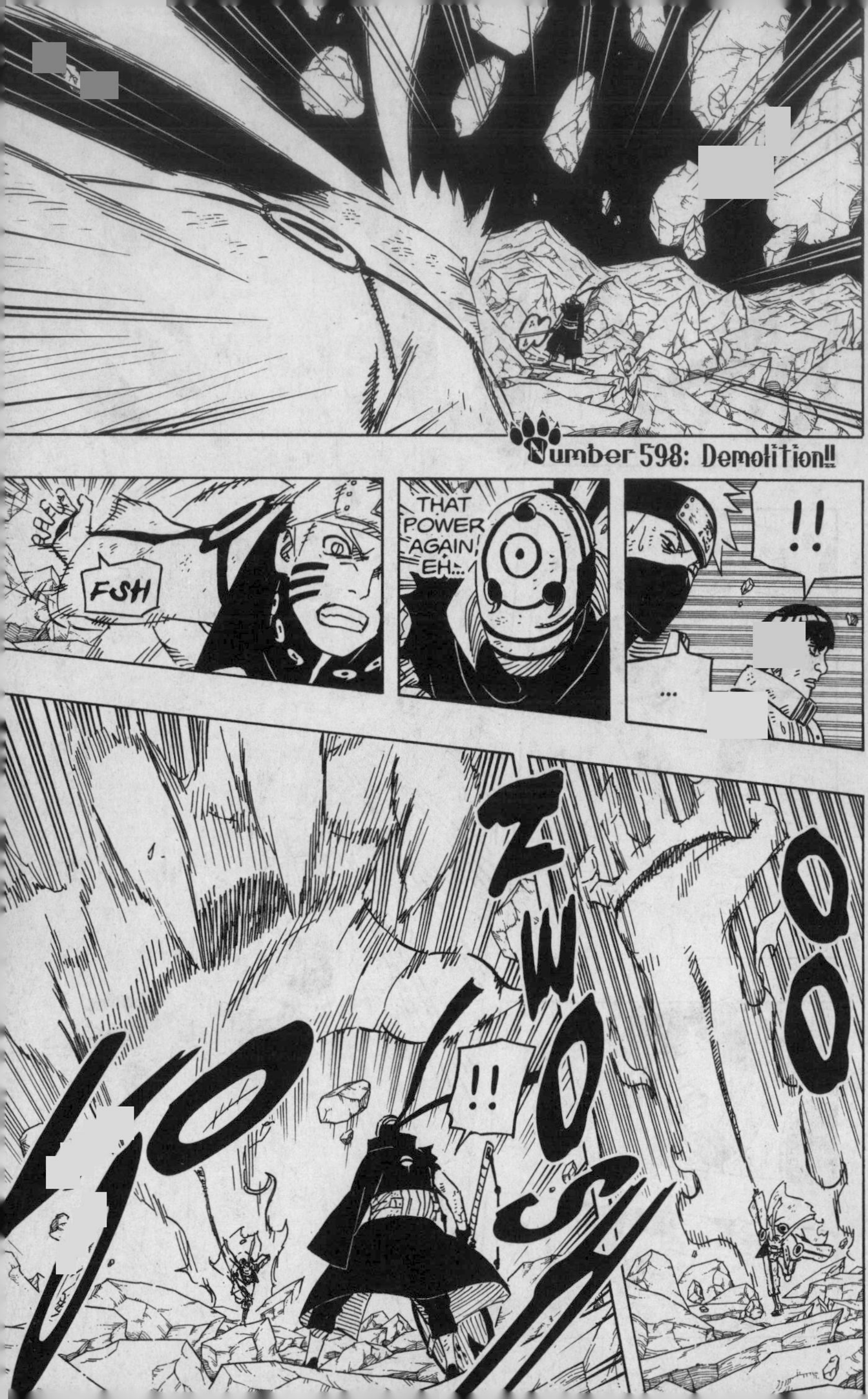
Number 598: Demolition!!
!!
...
THAT POWER AGAIN, EH...
FSH
!!
ZWOOSH

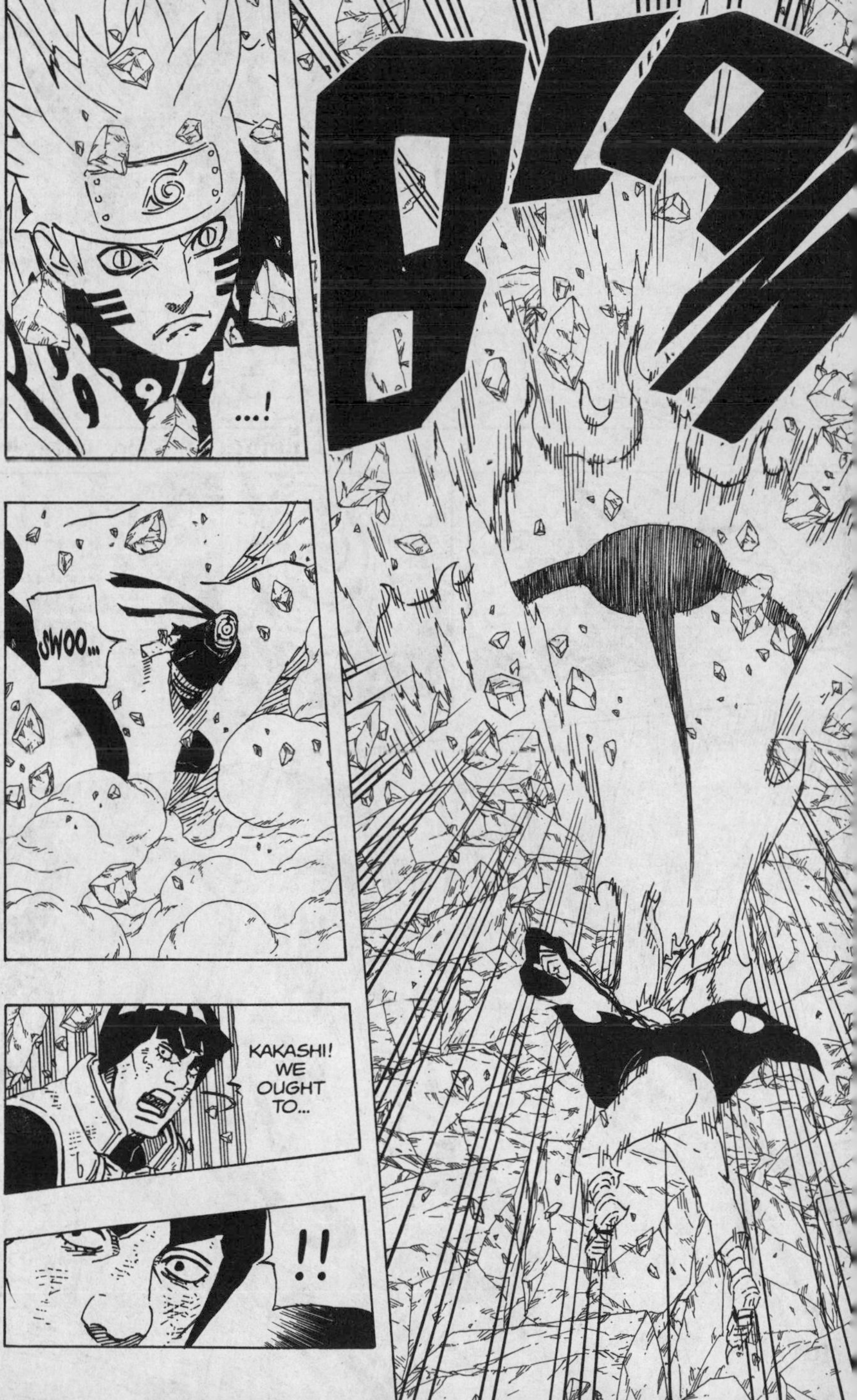
...!
SWOO...
KAKASHI! WE OUGHT TO...
!!

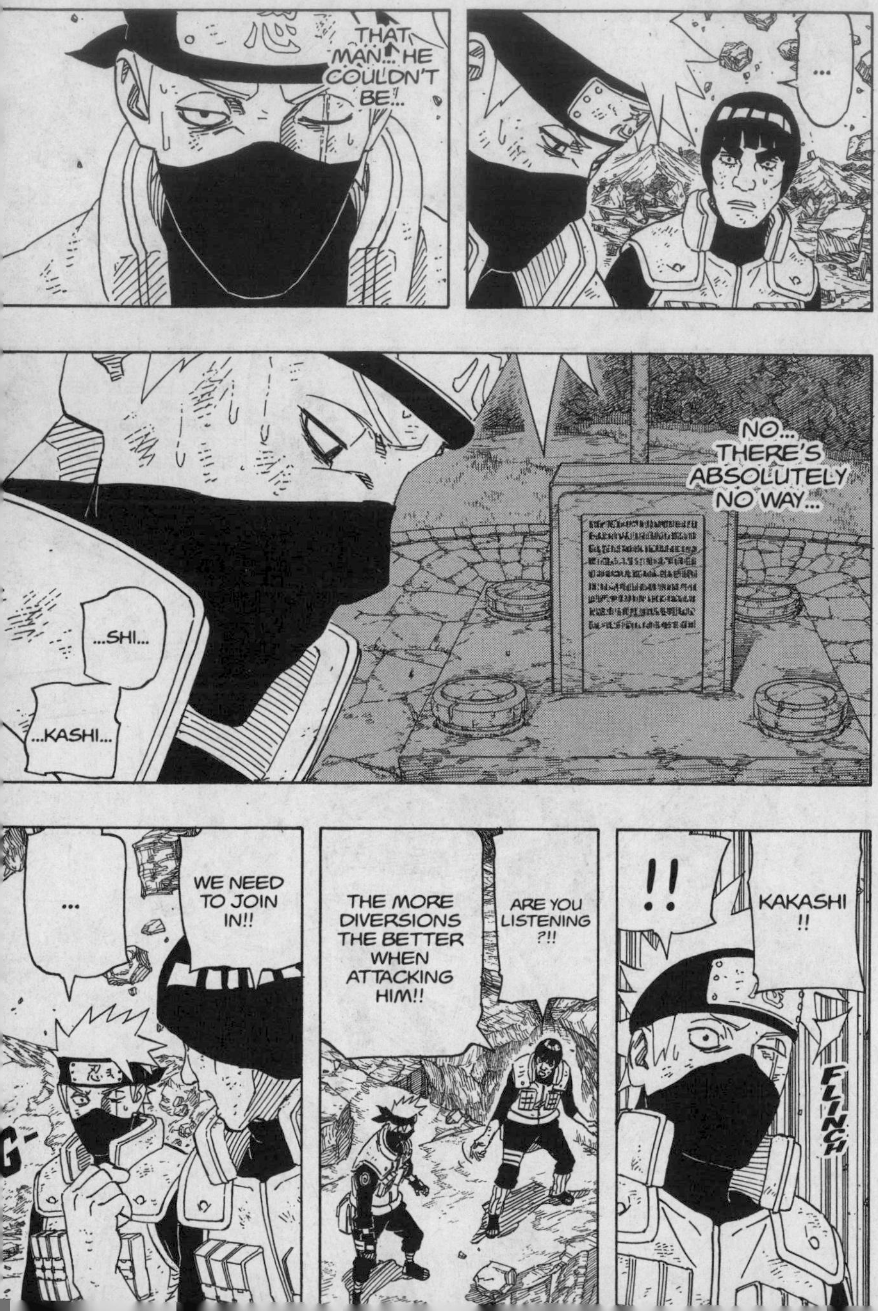
...
THAT MAN... HE COULDN'T BE...
NO... THERE'S ABSOLUTELY NO WAY...
...SHI...
...KASHI...
KAKASHI !!
!!
FLINCH
ARE YOU LISTENING ?!!
THE MORE DIVERSIONS THE BETTER WHEN ATTACKING HIM!!
WE NEED TO JOIN IN!!
...

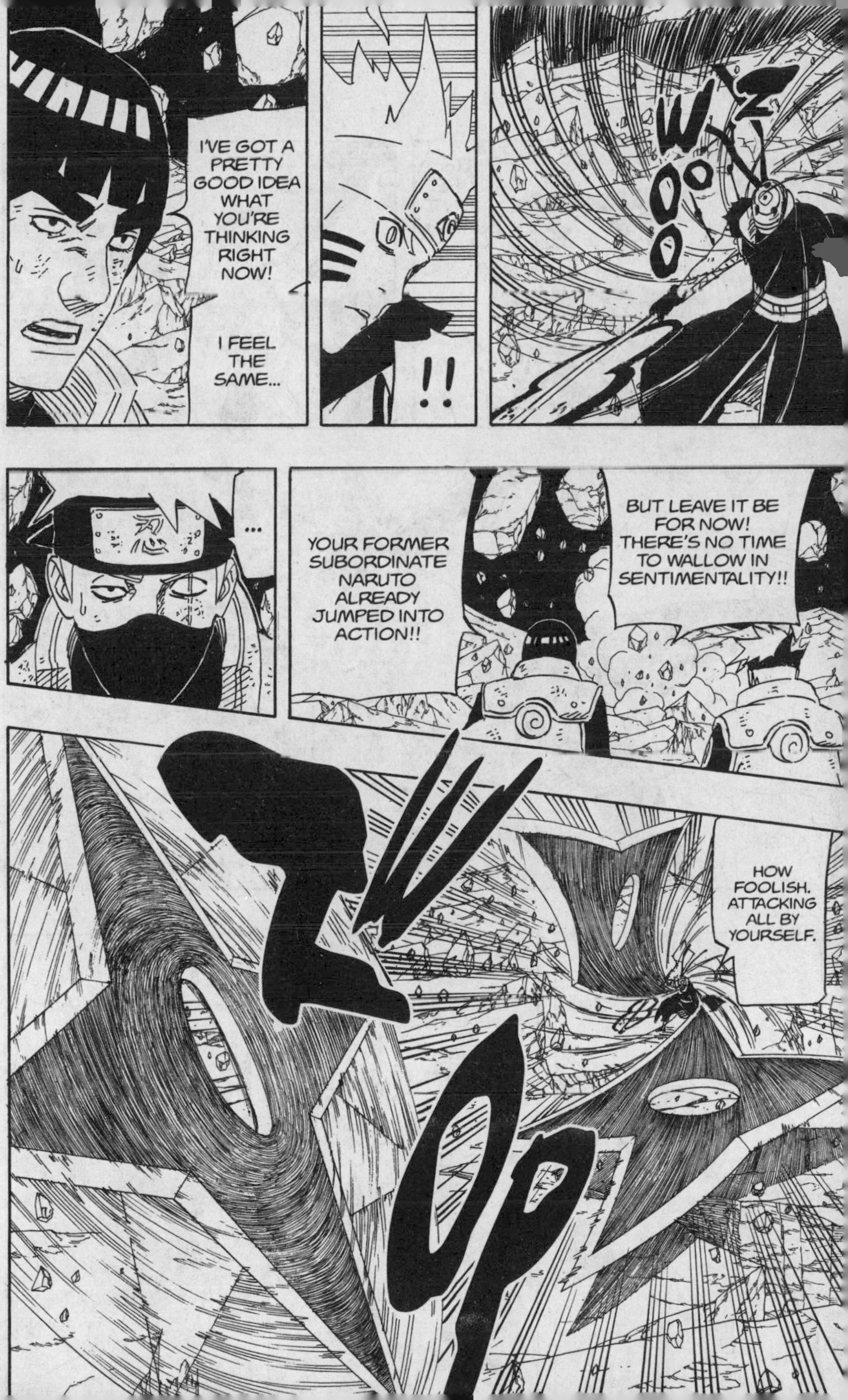
!!
I'VE GOT A PRETTY GOOD IDEA WHAT YOU'RE THINKING RIGHT NOW!
I FEEL THE SAME...
BUT LEAVE IT BE FOR NOW! THERE'S NO TIME TO WALLOW IN SENTIMENTALITY!!
YOUR FORMER SUBORDINATE NARUTO ALREADY JUMPED INTO ACTION!!
...
HOW FOOLISH. ATTACKING ALL BY YOURSELF.

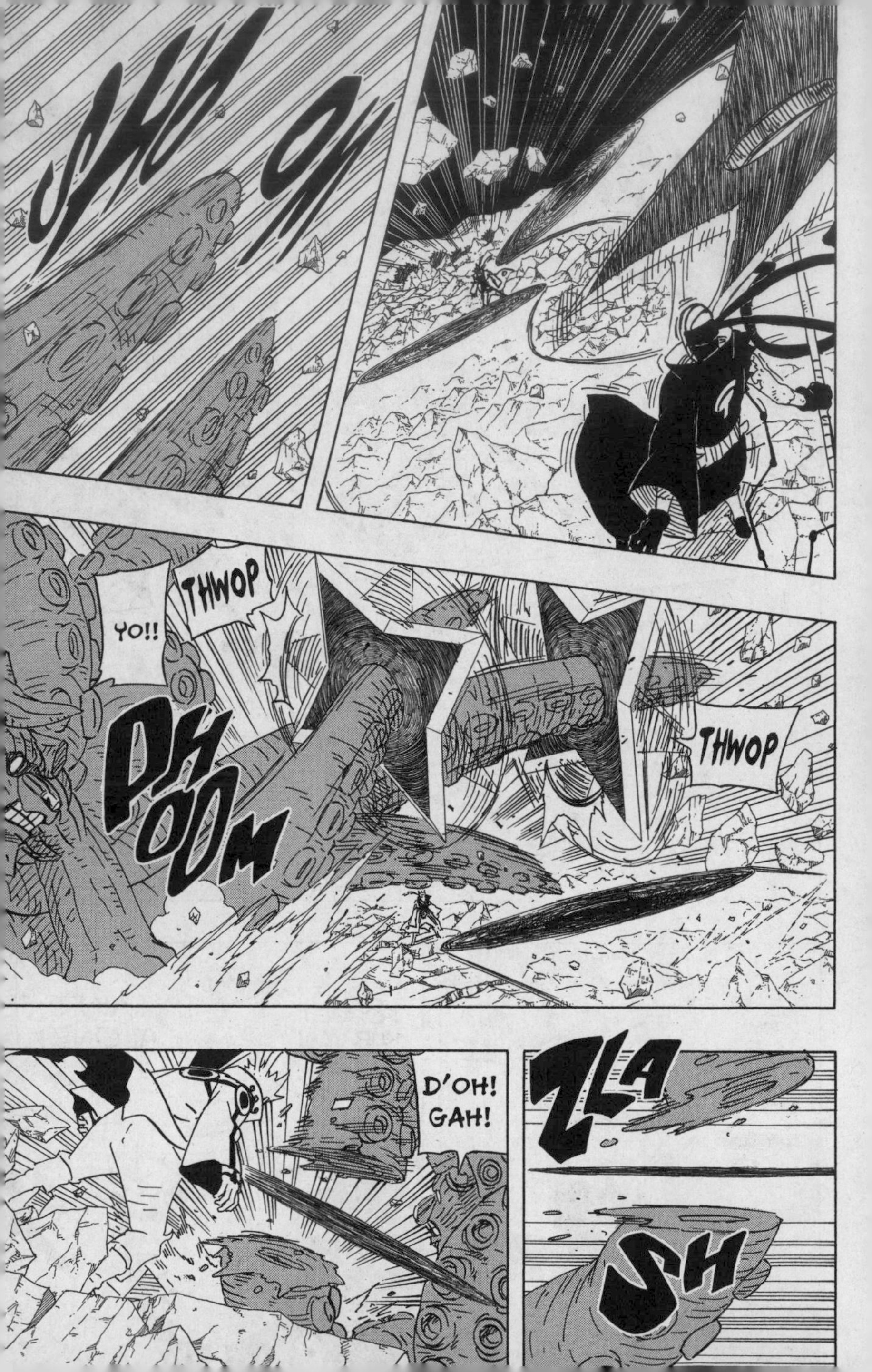
THWOP
THWOP
YO!!
D'OH! GAH!

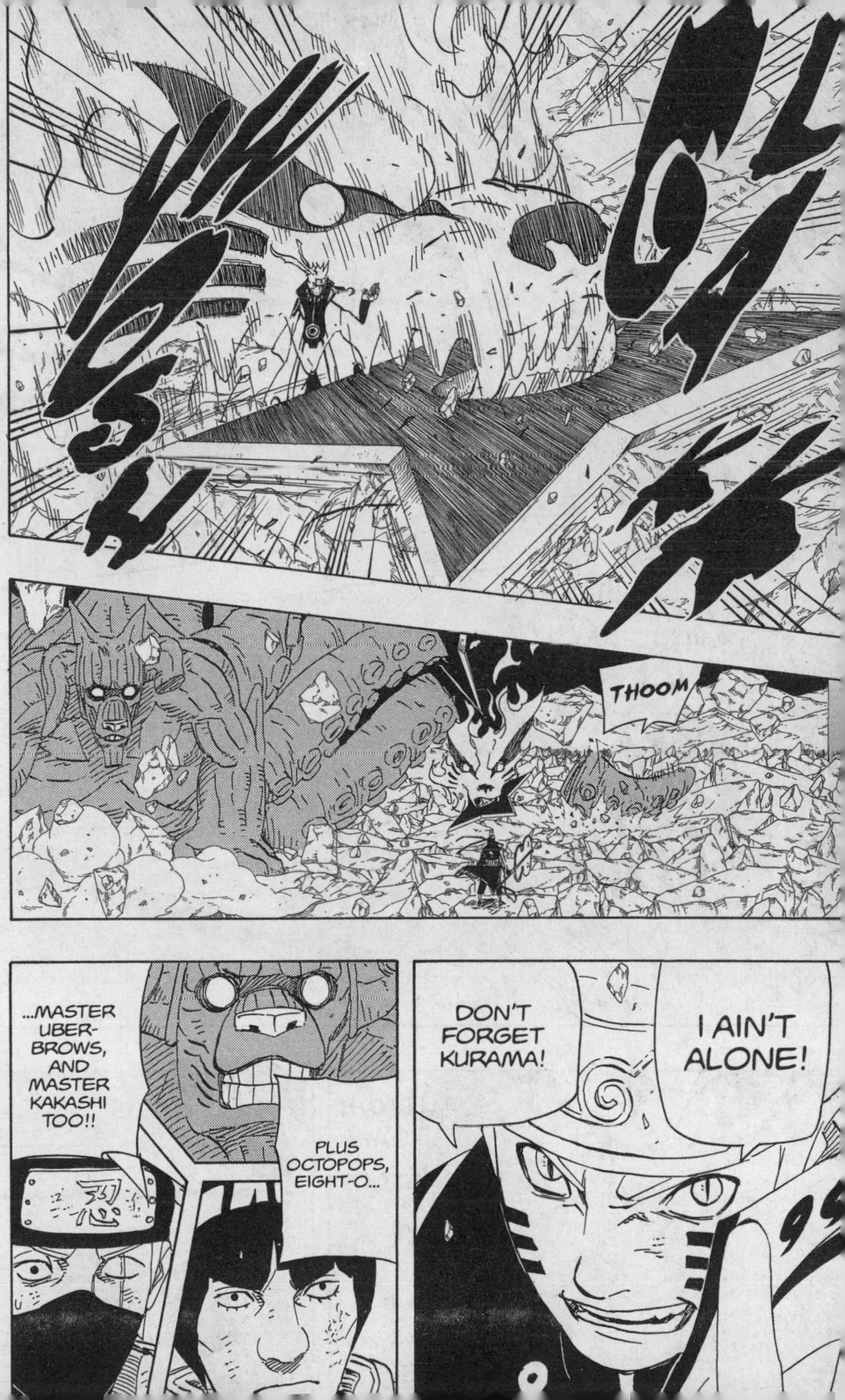
THOOM
I AIN'T ALONE!
DON'T FORGET KURAMA!
PLUS OCTOPOPS, EIGHT-O...
...MASTER UBER-BROWS, AND MASTER KAKASHI TOO!!

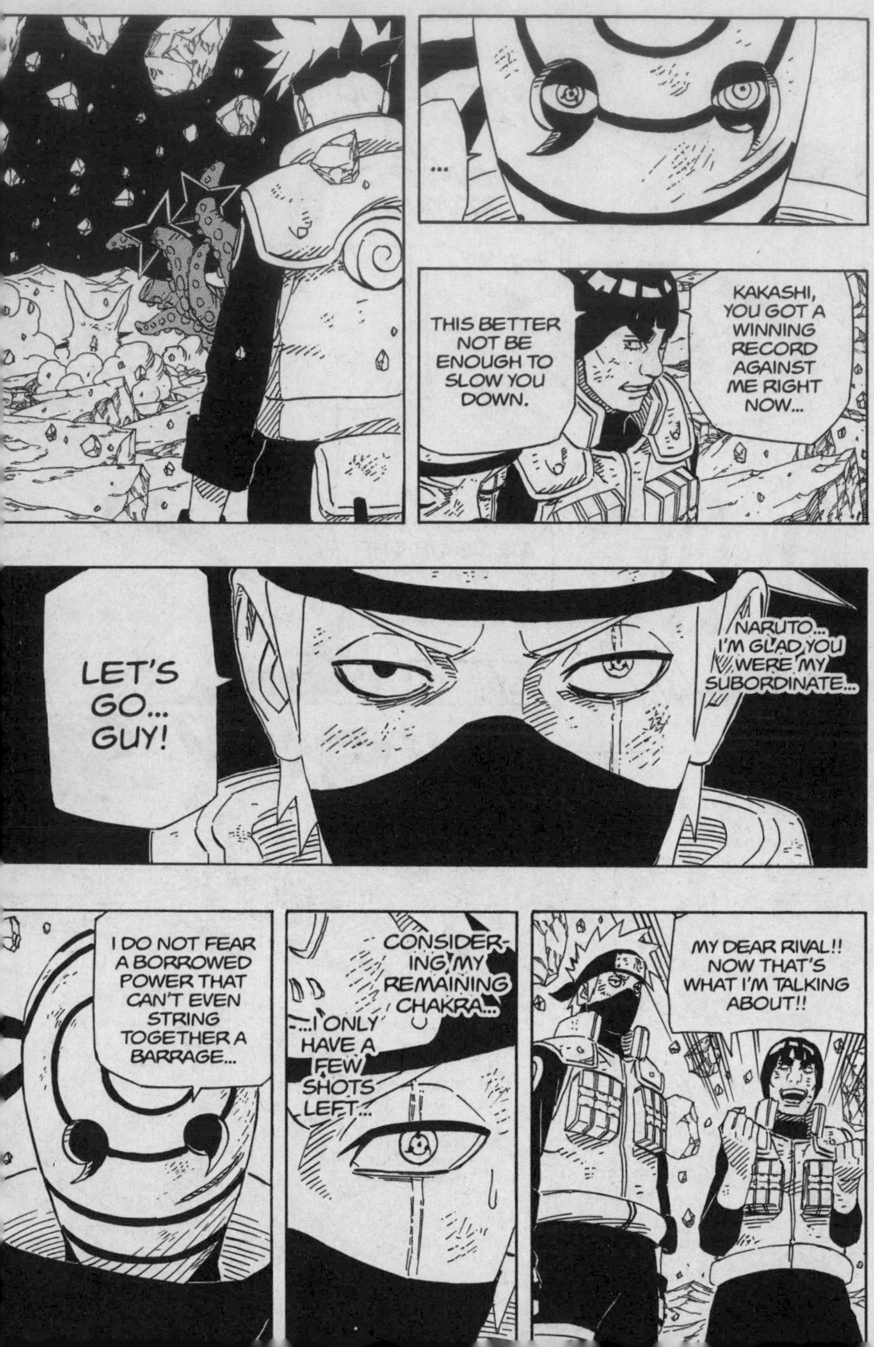
...
KAKASHI, YOU GOT A WINNING RECORD AGAINST ME RIGHT NOW...
THIS BETTER NOT BE ENOUGH TO SLOW YOU DOWN.
NARUTO... I'M GLAD YOU WERE MY SUBORDINATE...
LET'S GO... GUY!
MY DEAR RIVAL!! NOW THAT'S WHAT I'M TALKING ABOUT!!
CONSIDER-ING MY REMAINING CHAKRA...
...I ONLY HAVE A FEW SHOTS LEFT...
I DO NOT FEAR A BORROWED POWER THAT CAN'T EVEN STRING TOGETHER A BARRAGE...

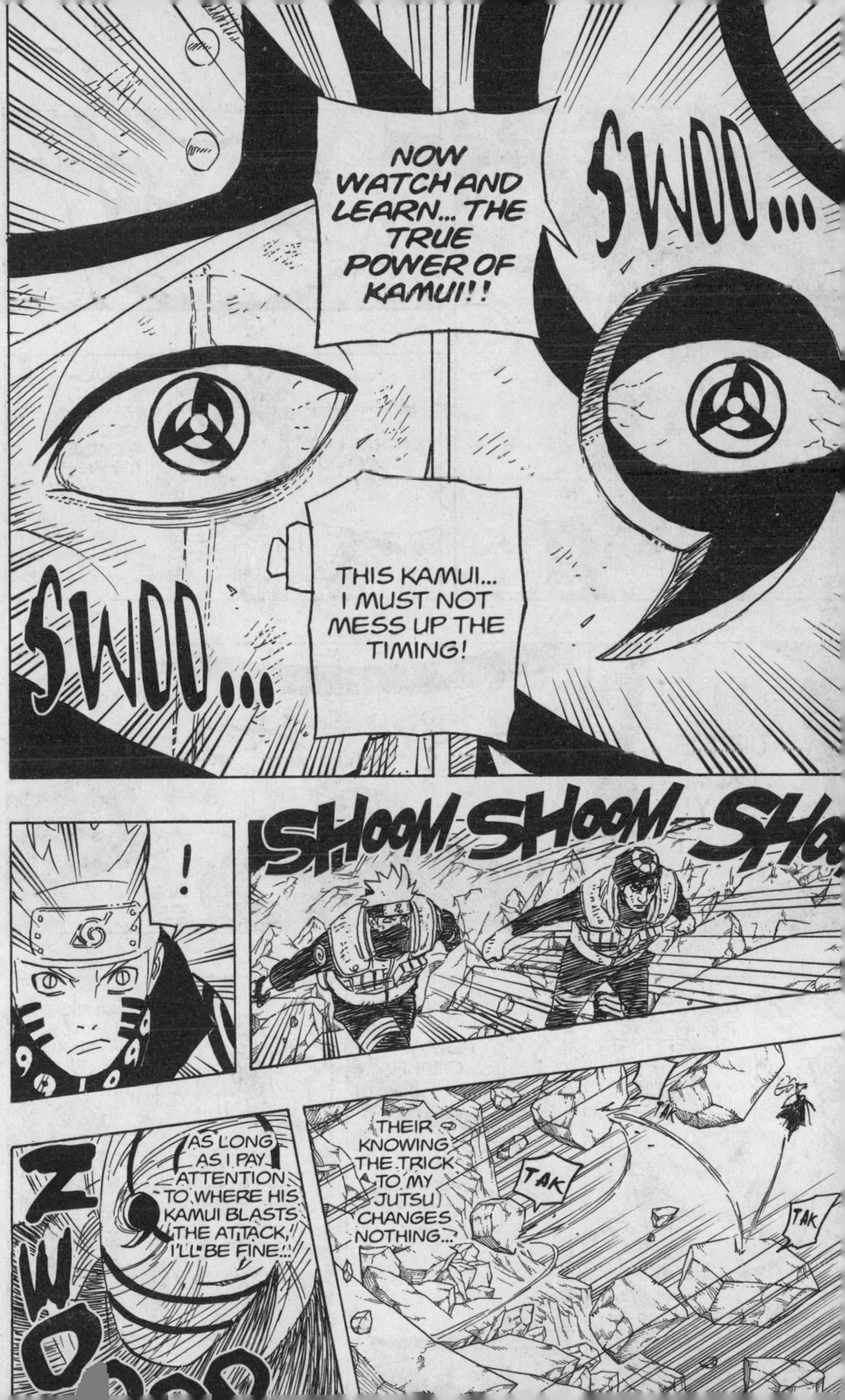
SWOO...
NOW WATCH AND LEARN... THE TRUE POWER OF KAMUI!!
THIS KAMUI... I MUST NOT MESS UP THE TIMING!
SWOO...
SHOOM SHOOM SHA
!
TAK
TAK
TAK
THEIR KNOWING THE TRICK TO MY JUTSU CHANGES NOTHING...
AS LONG AS I PAY ATTENTION TO WHERE HIS KAMUI BLASTS THE ATTACK, I'LL BE FINE...!
ZWOO

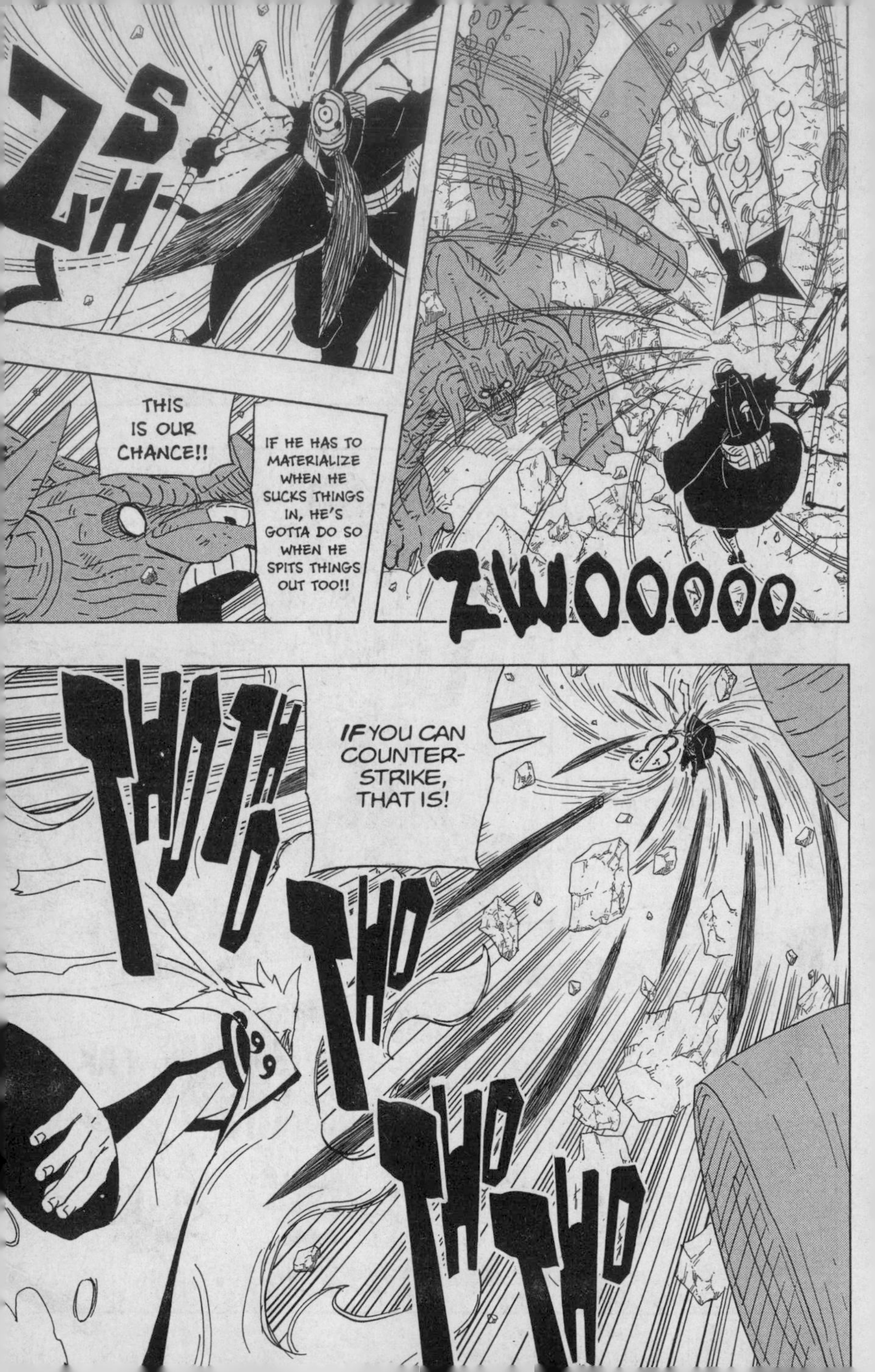
ZWOOOOO
ZSH-H
THIS IS OUR CHANCE!!
IF HE HAS TO MATERIALIZE WHEN HE SUCKS THINGS IN, HE'S GOTTA DO SO WHEN HE SPITS THINGS OUT TOO!!
IF YOU CAN COUNTER-STRIKE, THAT IS!
THO
THO
THO
THO

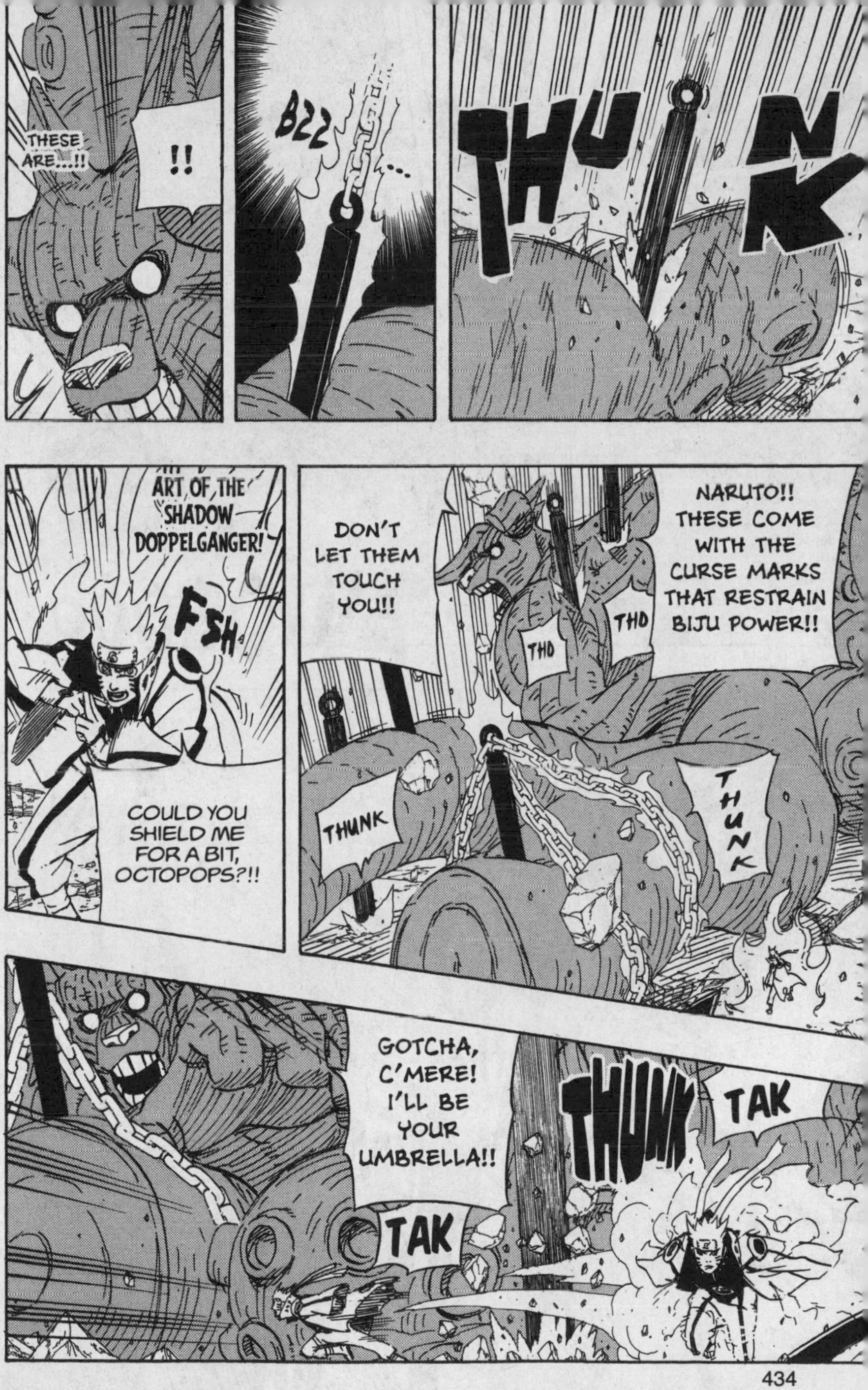
THUNK
BZZ...
!!
THESE ARE...!!
NARUTO!! THESE COME WITH THE CURSE MARKS THAT RESTRAIN BIJU POWER!!
DON'T LET THEM TOUCH YOU!!
THD
THD
THUNK
THUNK
ART OF THE SHADOW DOPPELGANGER!
FSH
COULD YOU SHIELD ME FOR A BIT, OCTOPOPS?!!
TAK
THUNK
GOTCHA, C'MERE! I'LL BE YOUR UMBRELLA!!
TAK

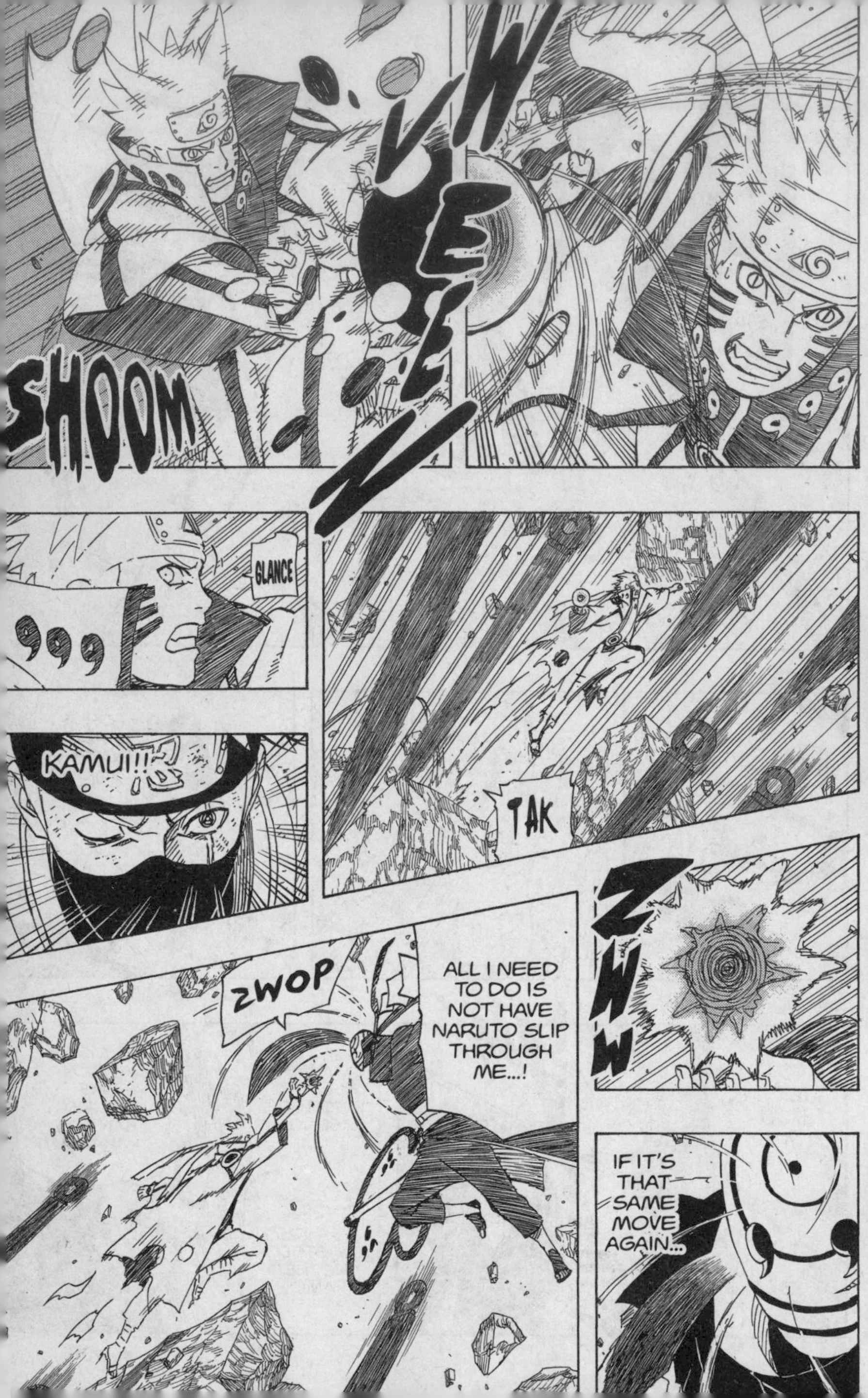
VWEEEN
SHOOM
TAK
GLANCE
KAMUI!!
ZWW
IF IT'S THAT SAME MOVE AGAIN...
ZWOP
ALL I NEED TO DO IS NOT HAVE NARUTO SLIP THROUGH ME...!

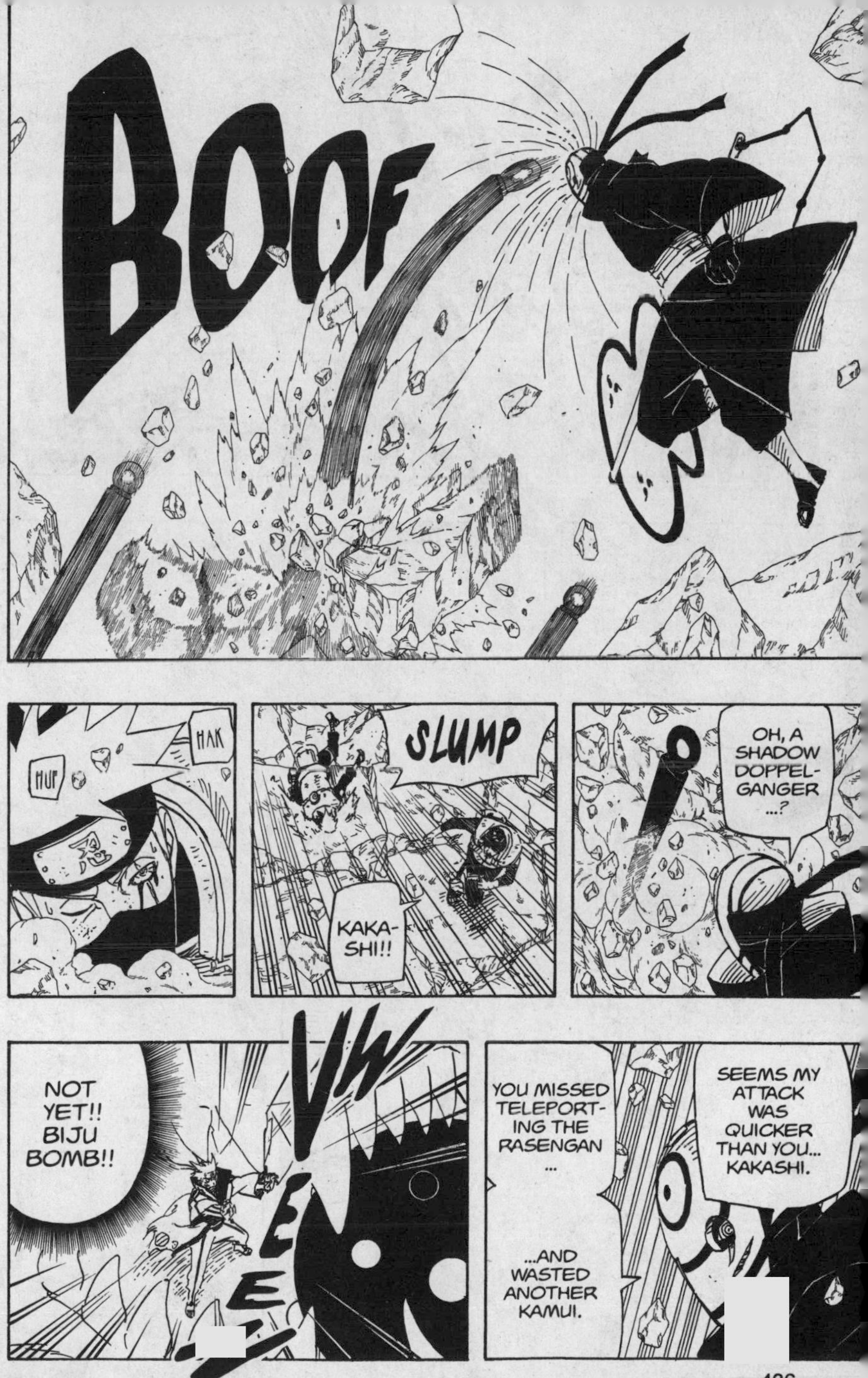
BOOF
OH, A SHADOW DOPPEL-GANGER ...?
SLUMP
KAKA-SHI!!
HAK
HUF
SEEMS MY ATTACK WAS QUICKER THAN YOU... KAKASHI.
YOU MISSED TELEPORT-ING THE RASENGAN ...
...AND WASTED ANOTHER KAMUI.
VWEE
NOT YET!! BIJU BOMB!!

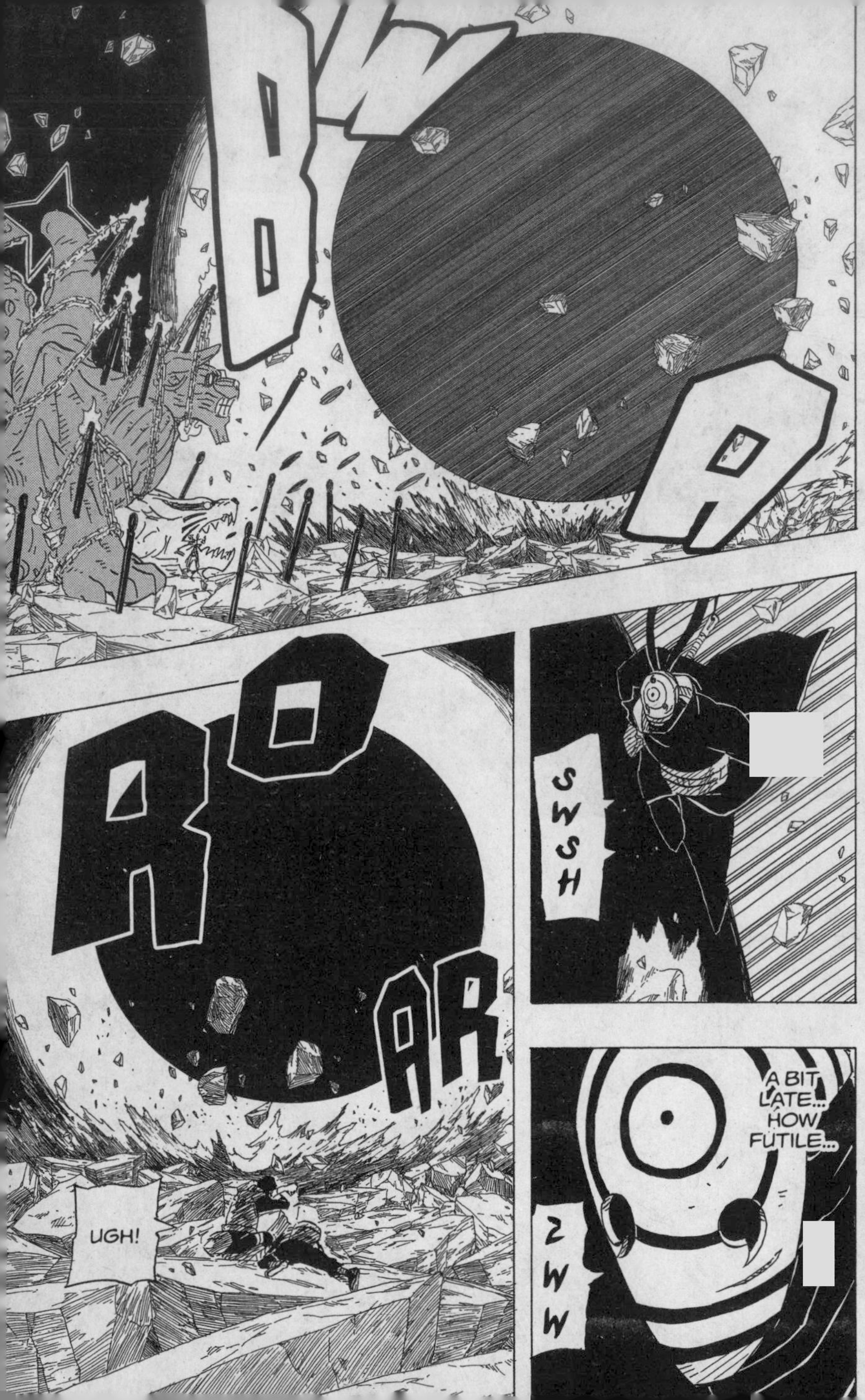
SWSH
A BIT LATE... HOW FUTILE...
ZWW
ROAR
UGH!

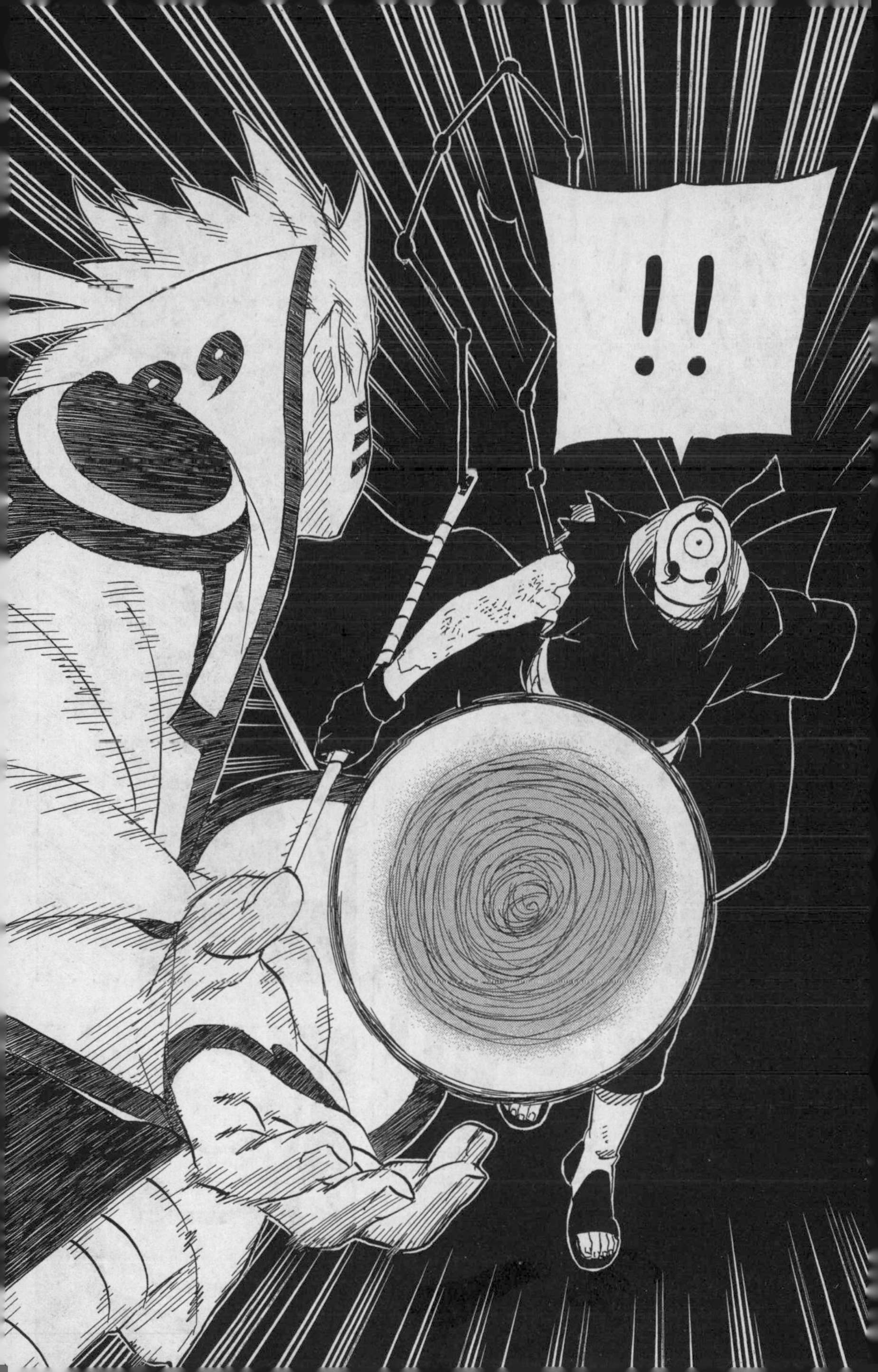
!!

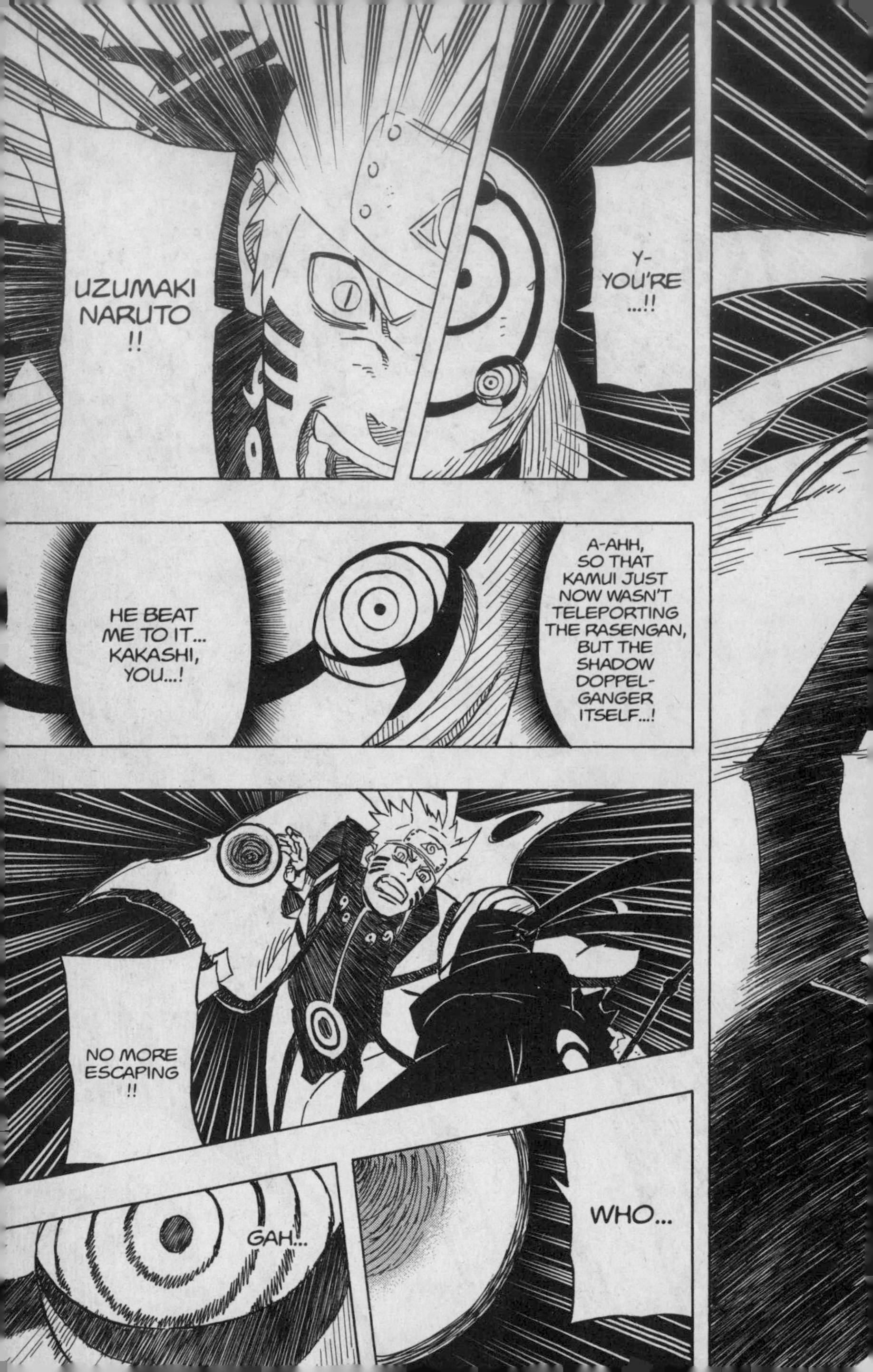
Y- YOU'RE ...!!
UZUMAKI NARUTO !!
A-AHH, SO THAT KAMUI JUST NOW WASN'T TELEPORTING THE RASENGAN, BUT THE SHADOW DOPPEL-GANGER ITSELF...!
HE BEAT ME TO IT... KAKASHI, YOU...!
NO MORE ESCAPING !!
WHO...
GAH...

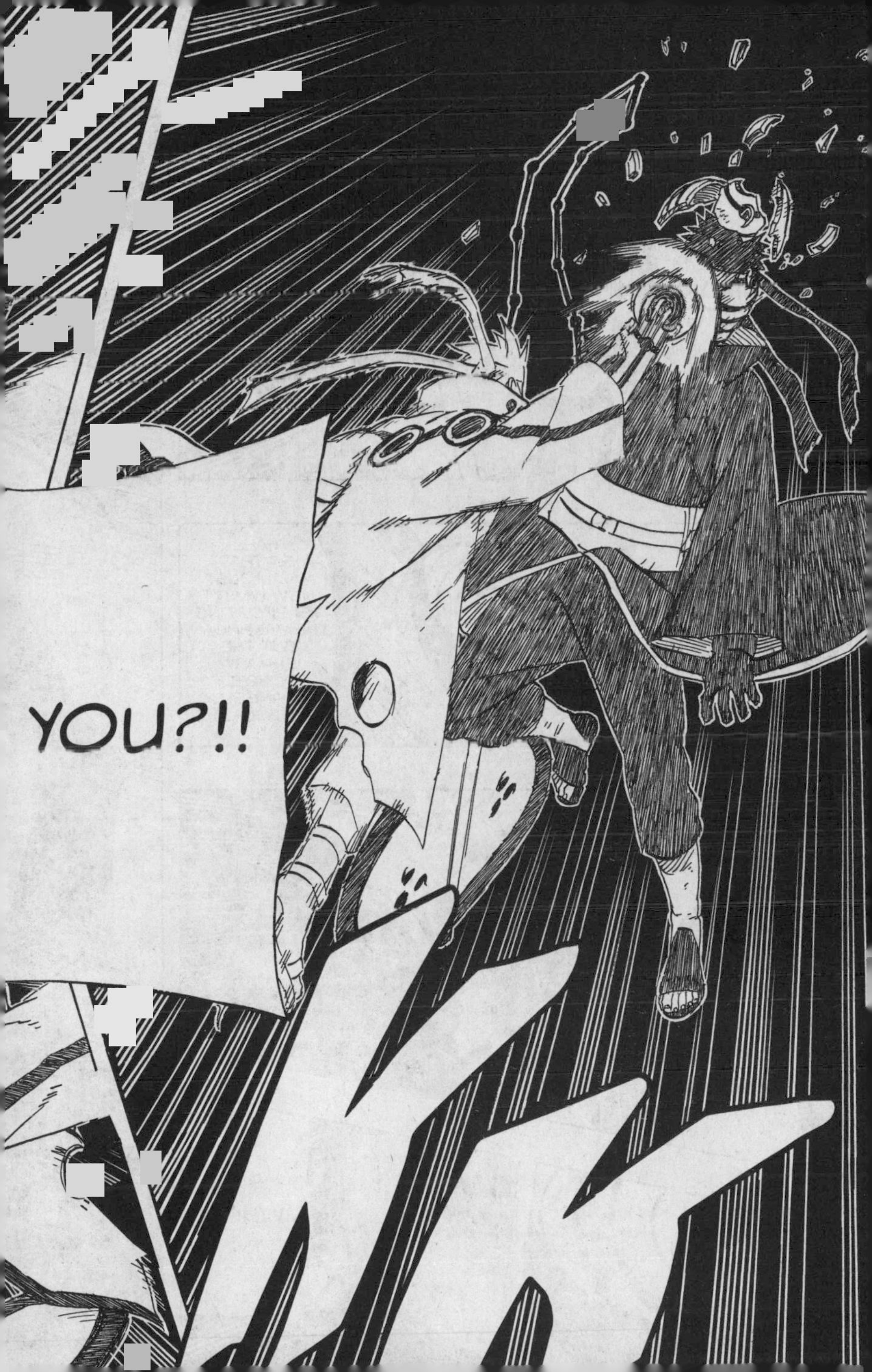
YOU?!!

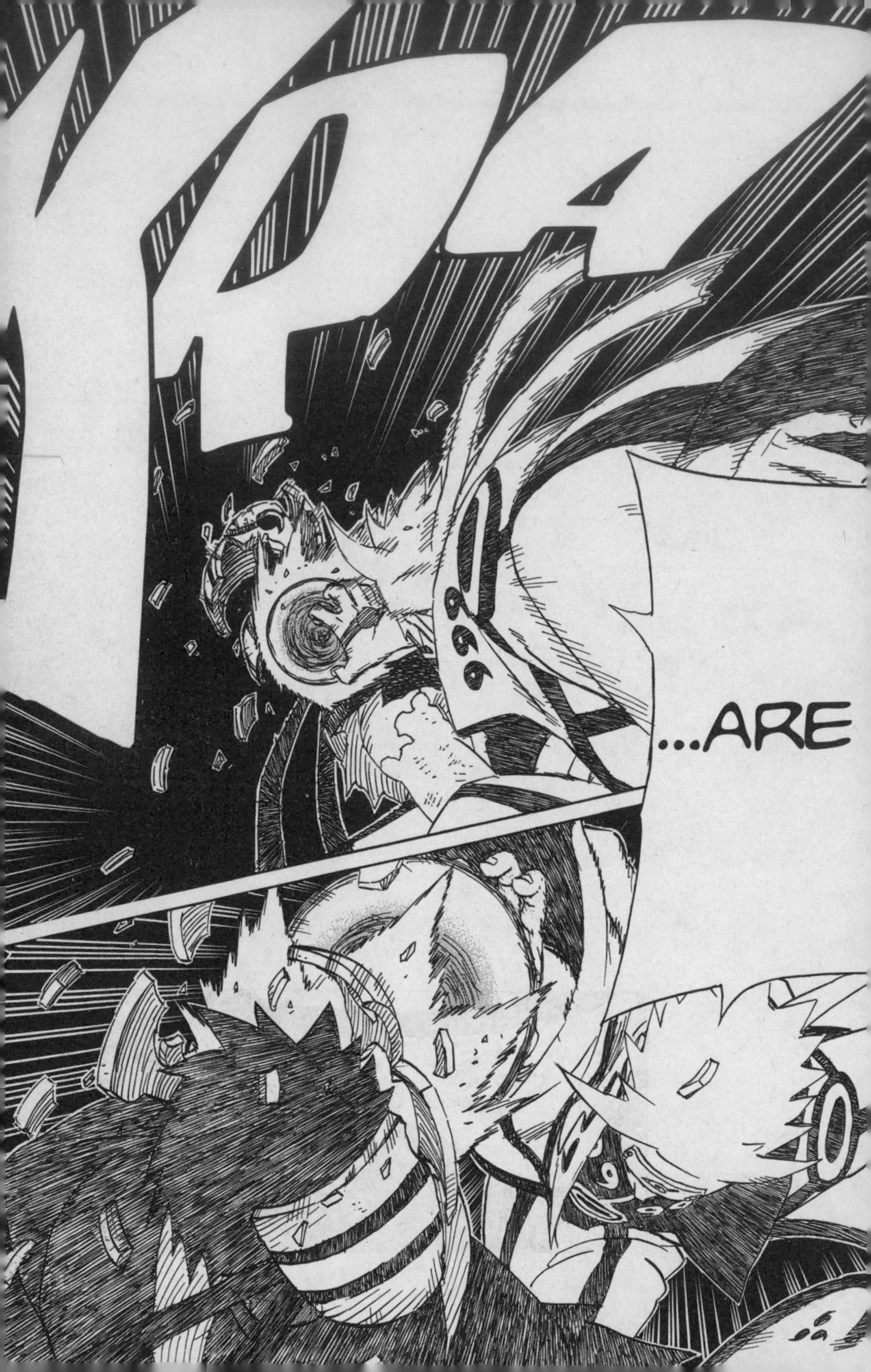
...ARE

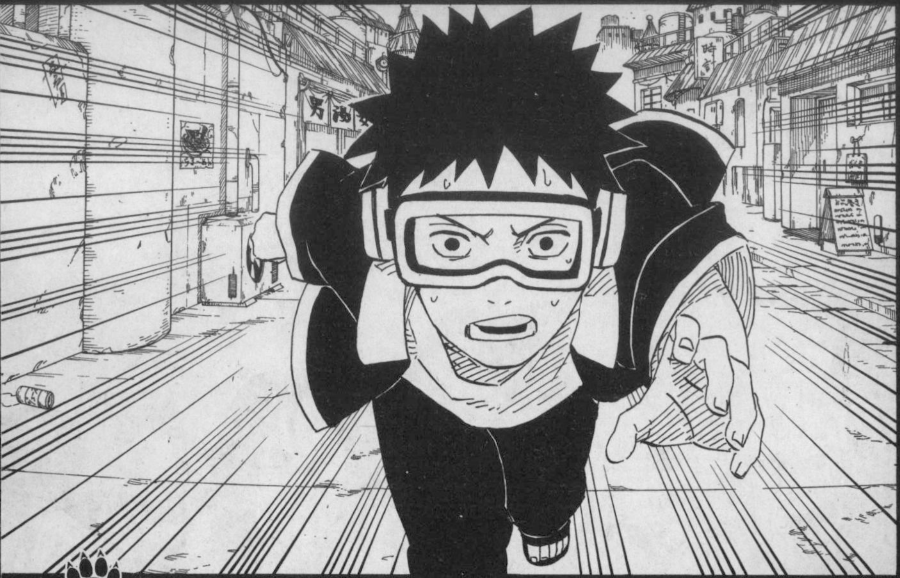

Number 599: Uchiha Obito

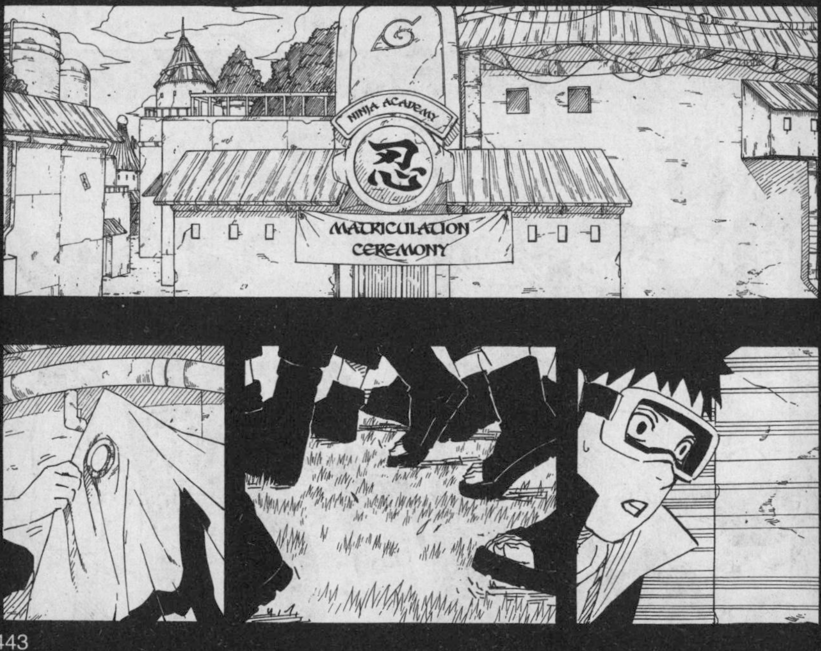
NINJA ACADEMY
忍
MATRICULATION CEREMONY

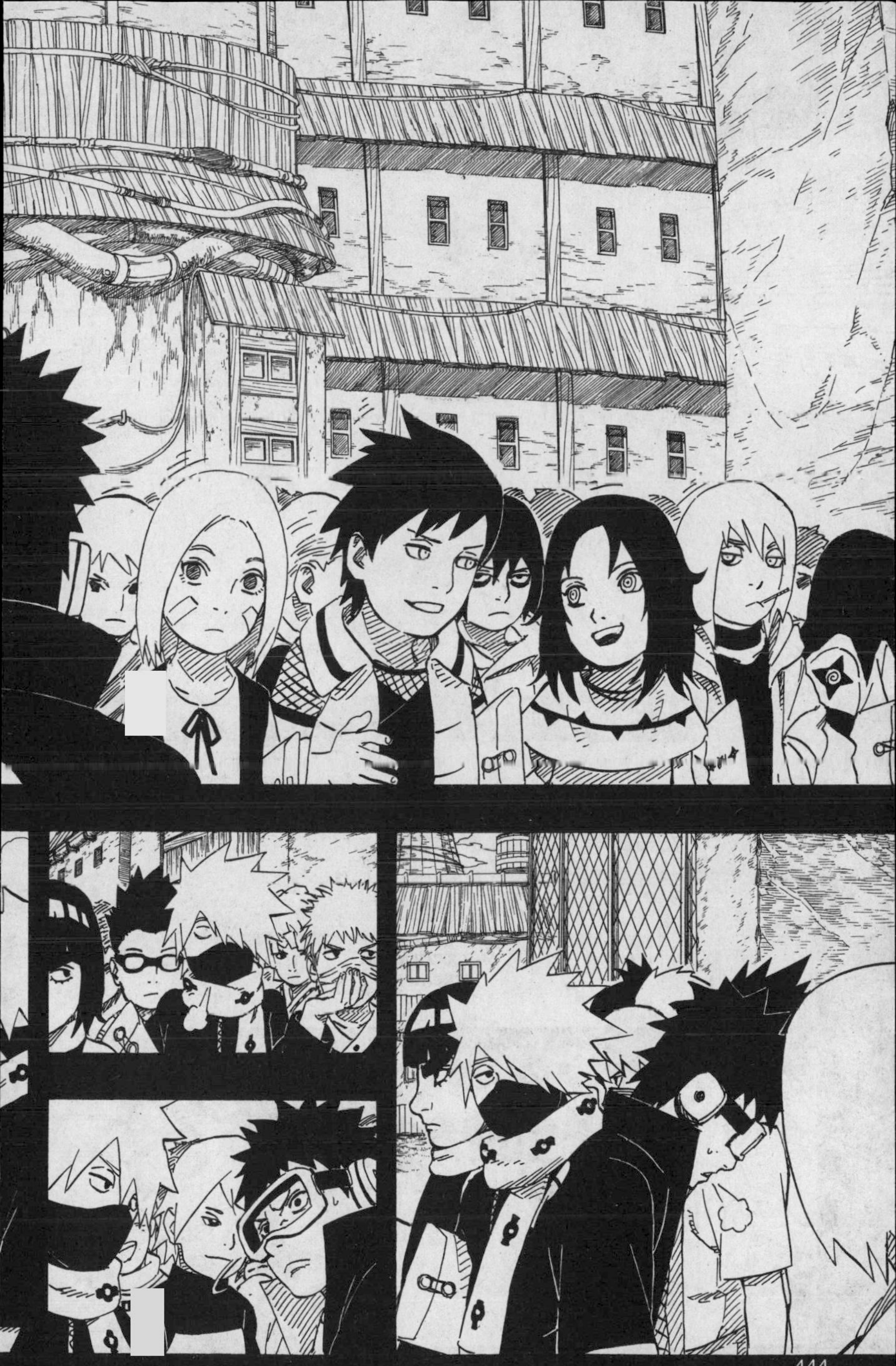

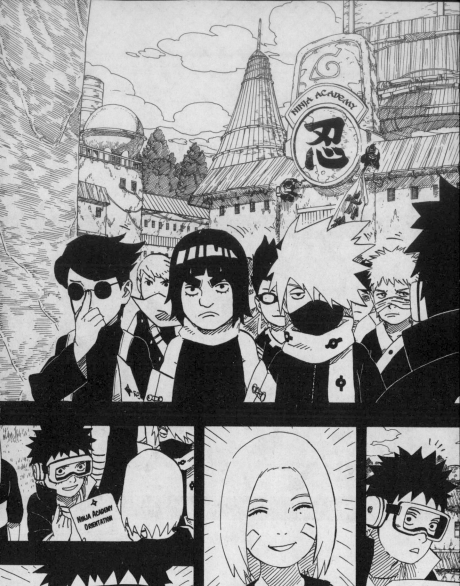

NINJA ACADEMY
忍

NINJA ACADEMY
ORIENTATION

NINJA ACADEMY
ORIENTATION

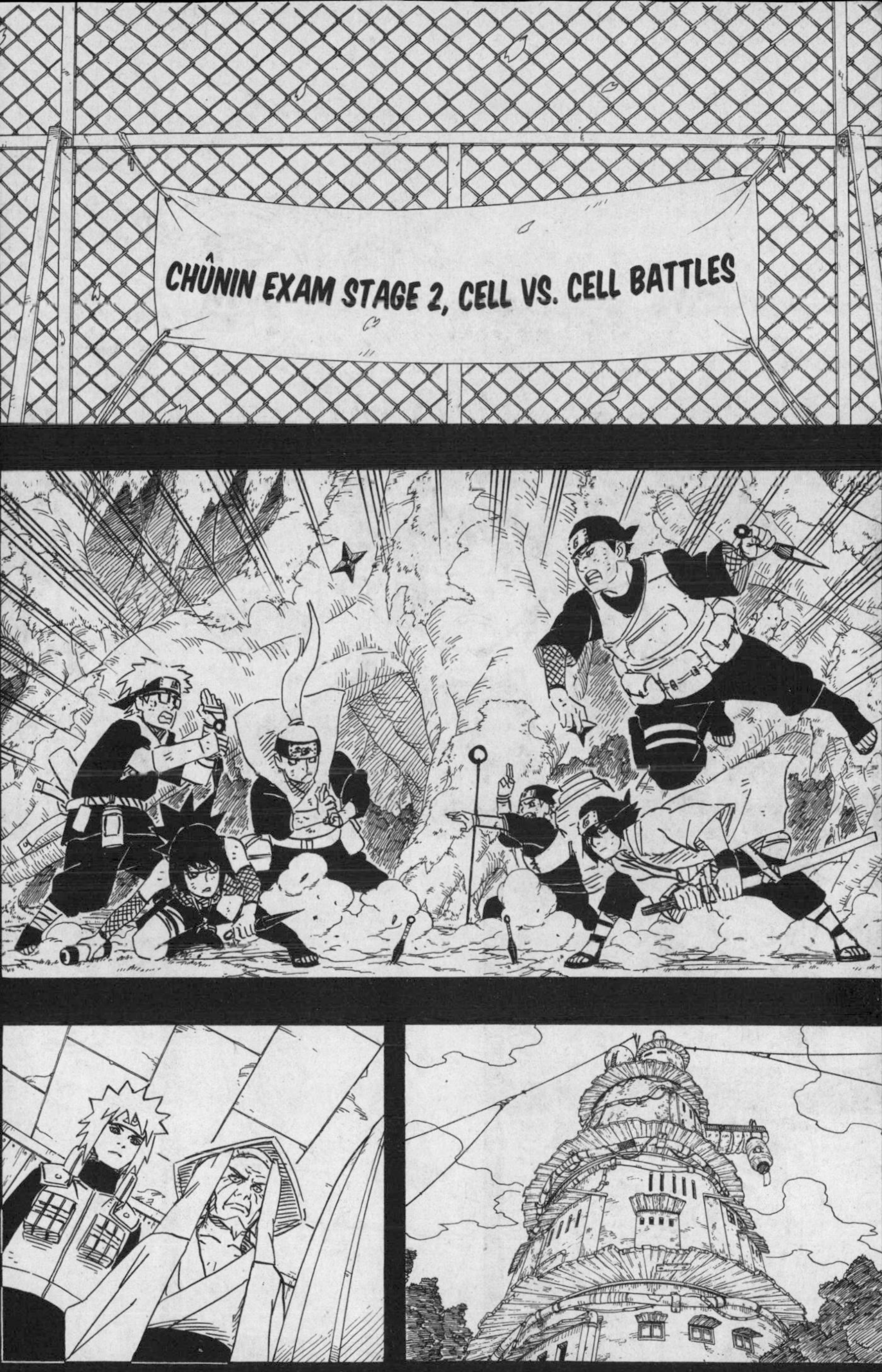
CHÛNIN EXAM STAGE 2, CELL VS. CELL BATTLES

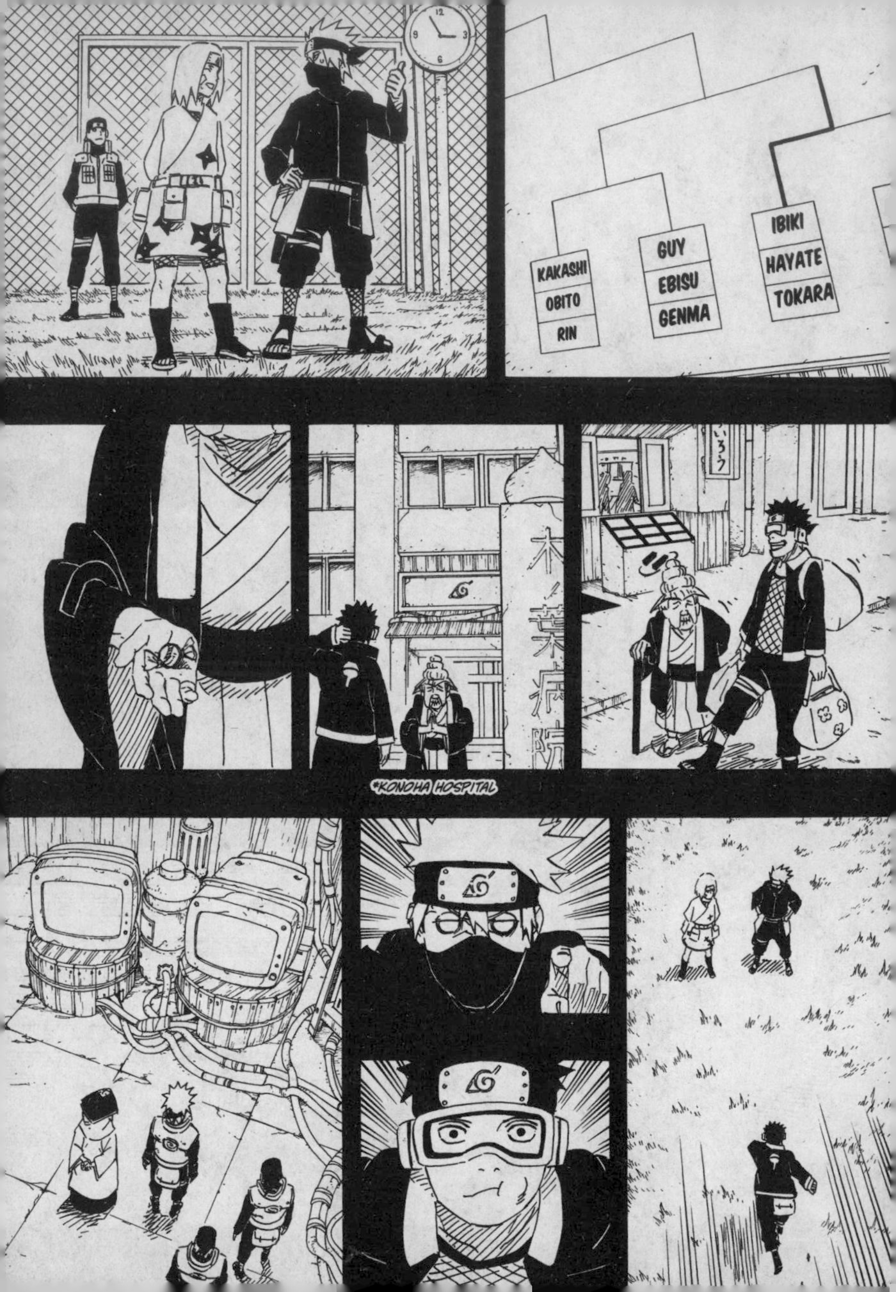
IBIKI
HAYATE
TOKARA
GUY
EBISU
GENMA
KAKASHI
OBITO
RIN
木ノ葉病院
*KONOHA HOSPITAL

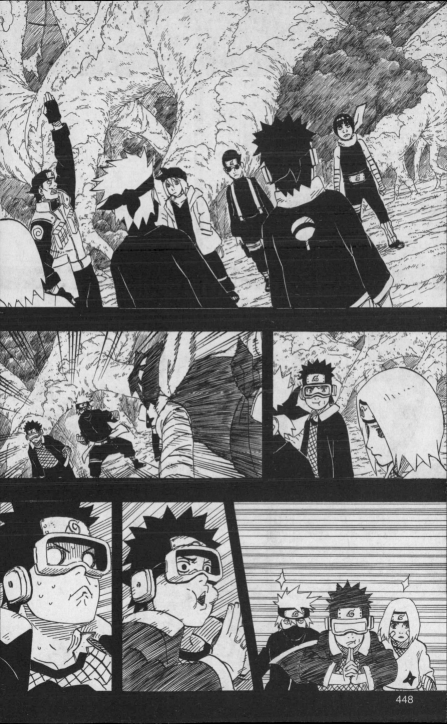

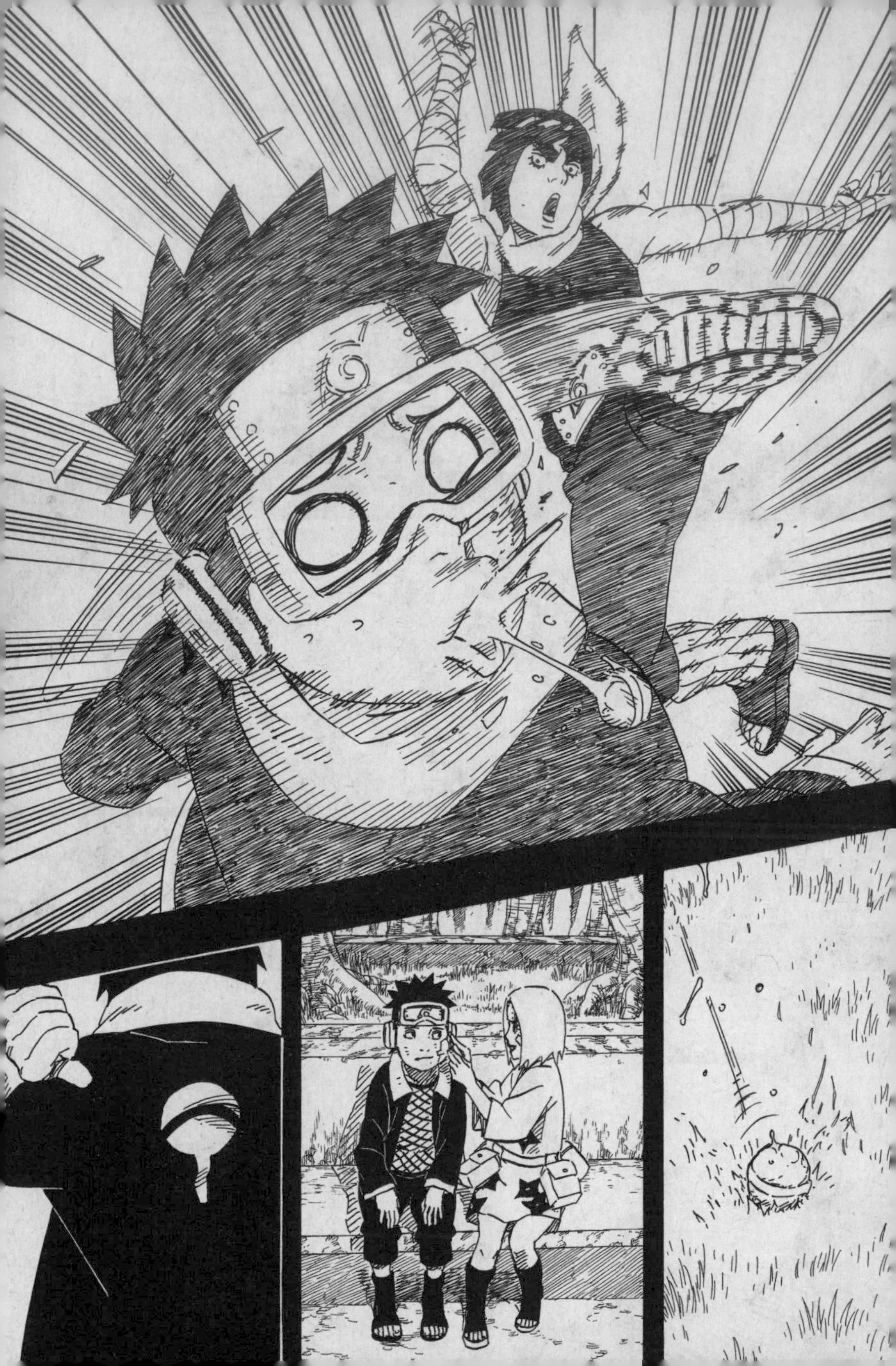

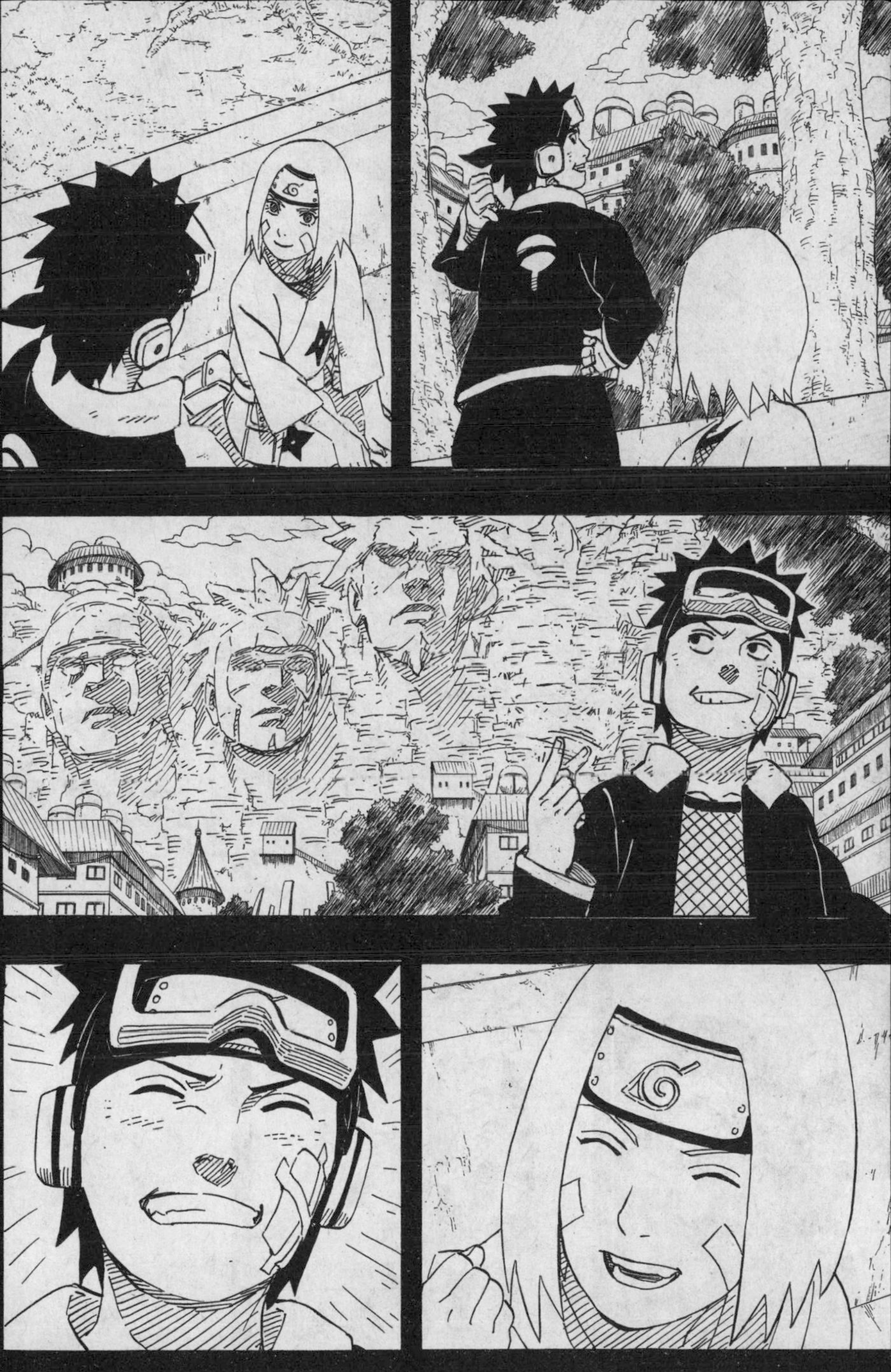

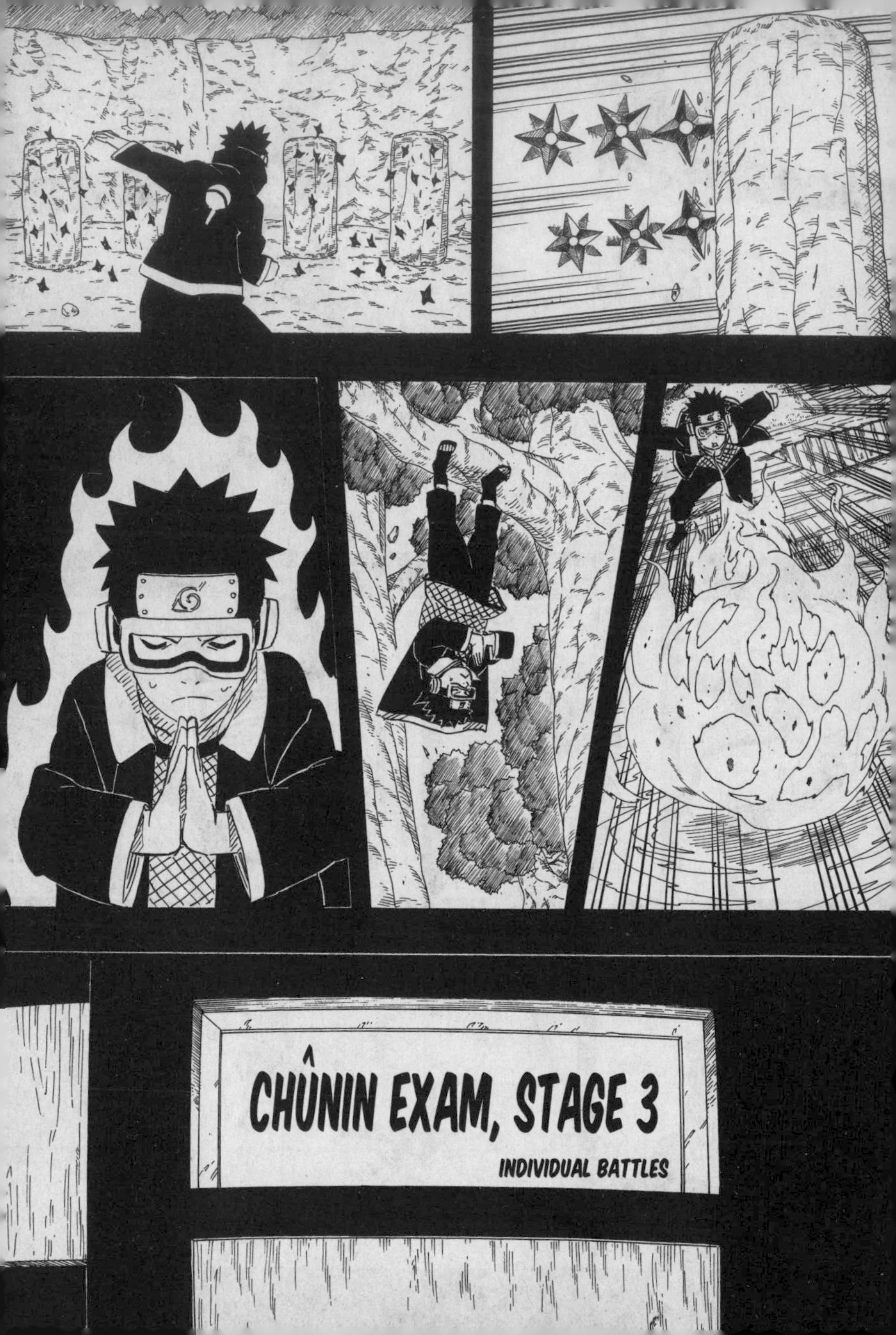
CHÛNIN EXAM, STAGE 3
INDIVIDUAL BATTLES

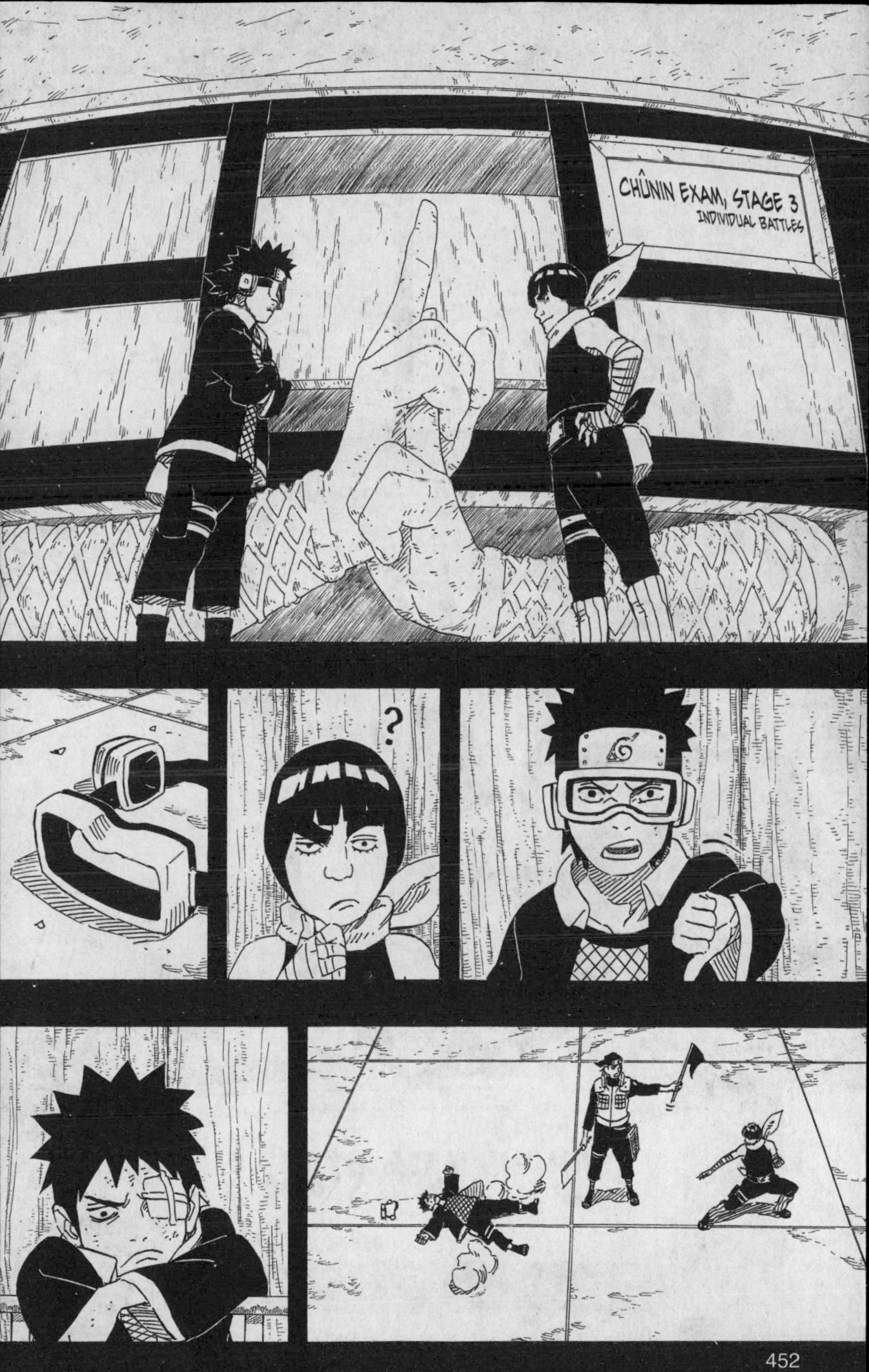
CHŪNIN EXAM, STAGE 3
INDIVIDUAL BATTLES
?

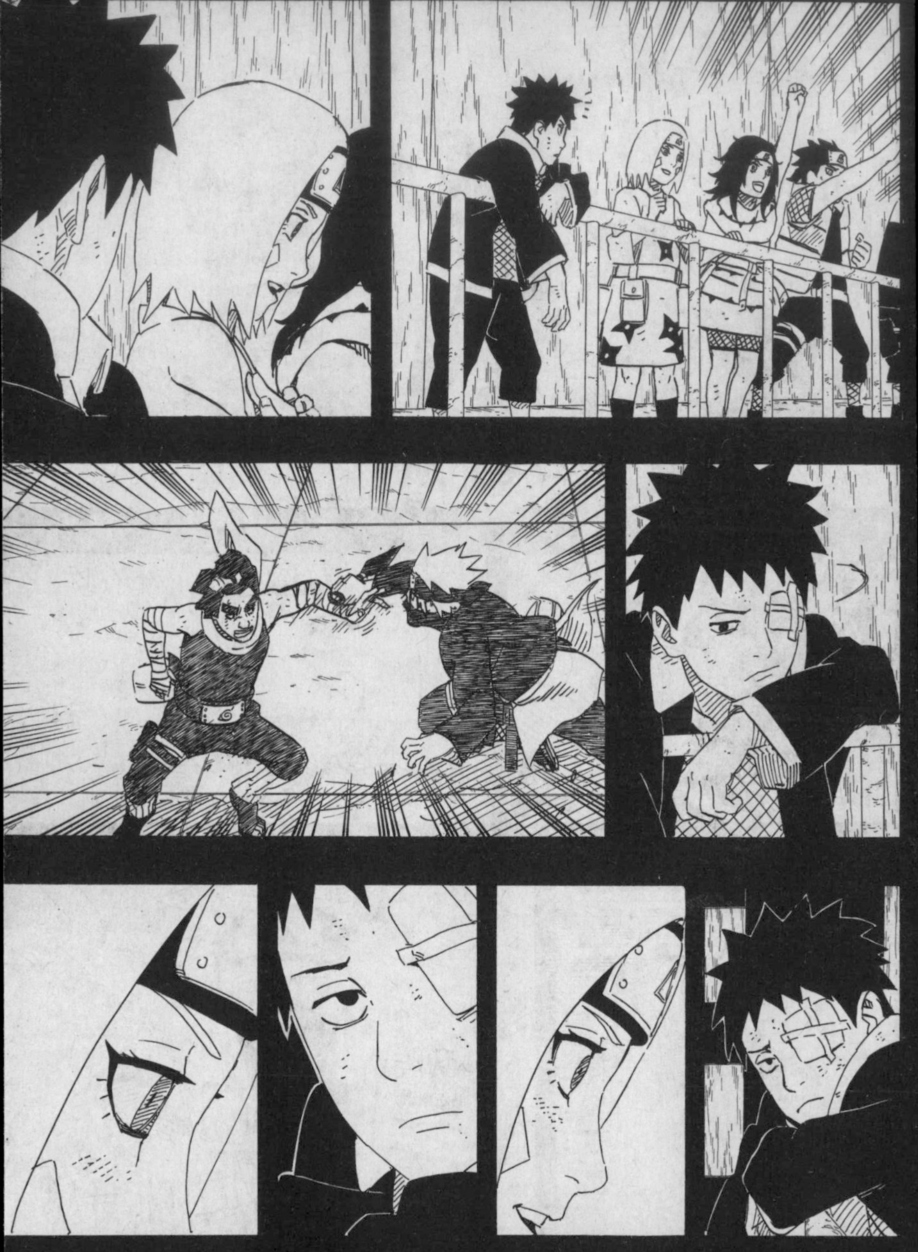

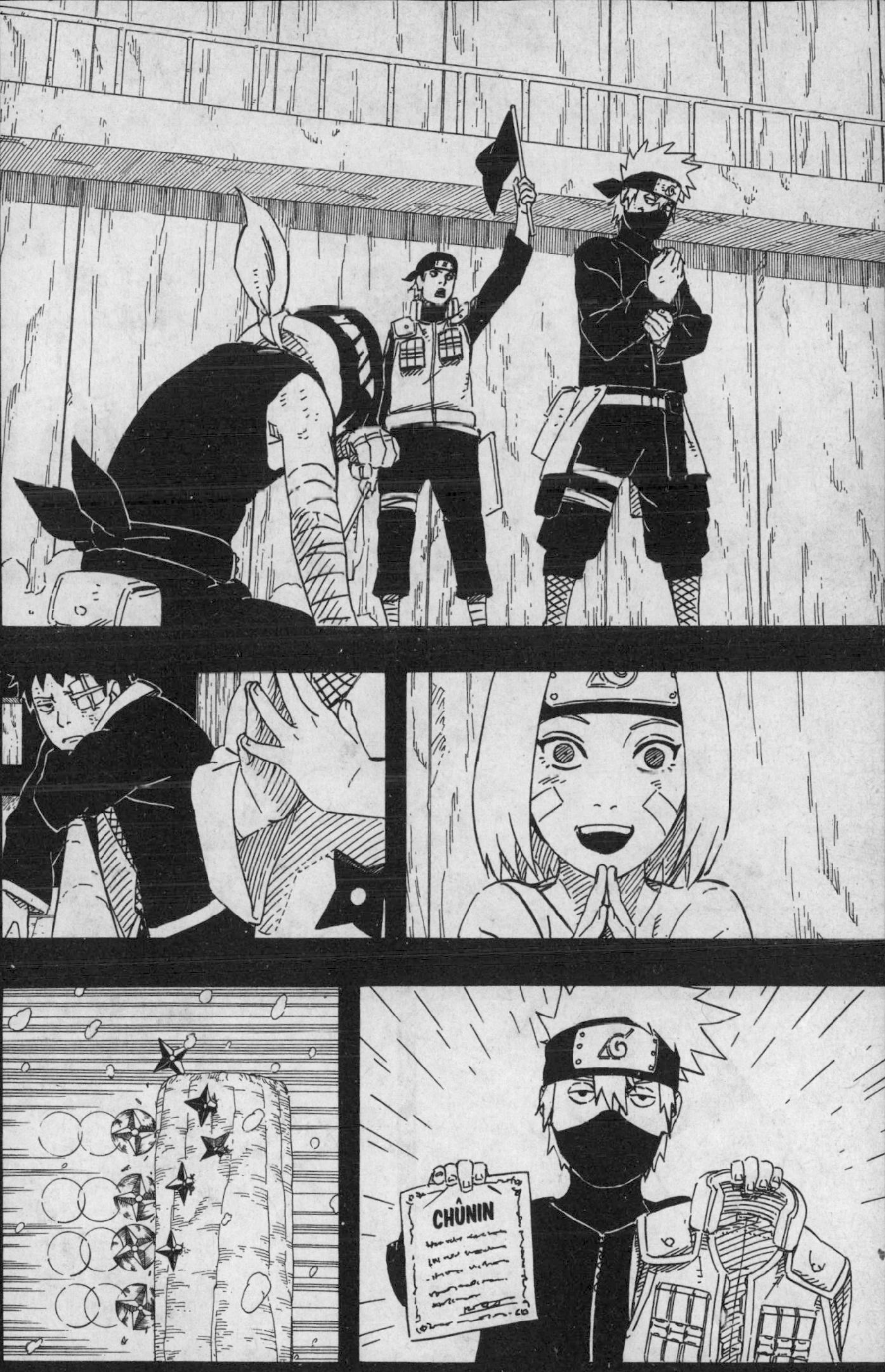
CHÛNIN

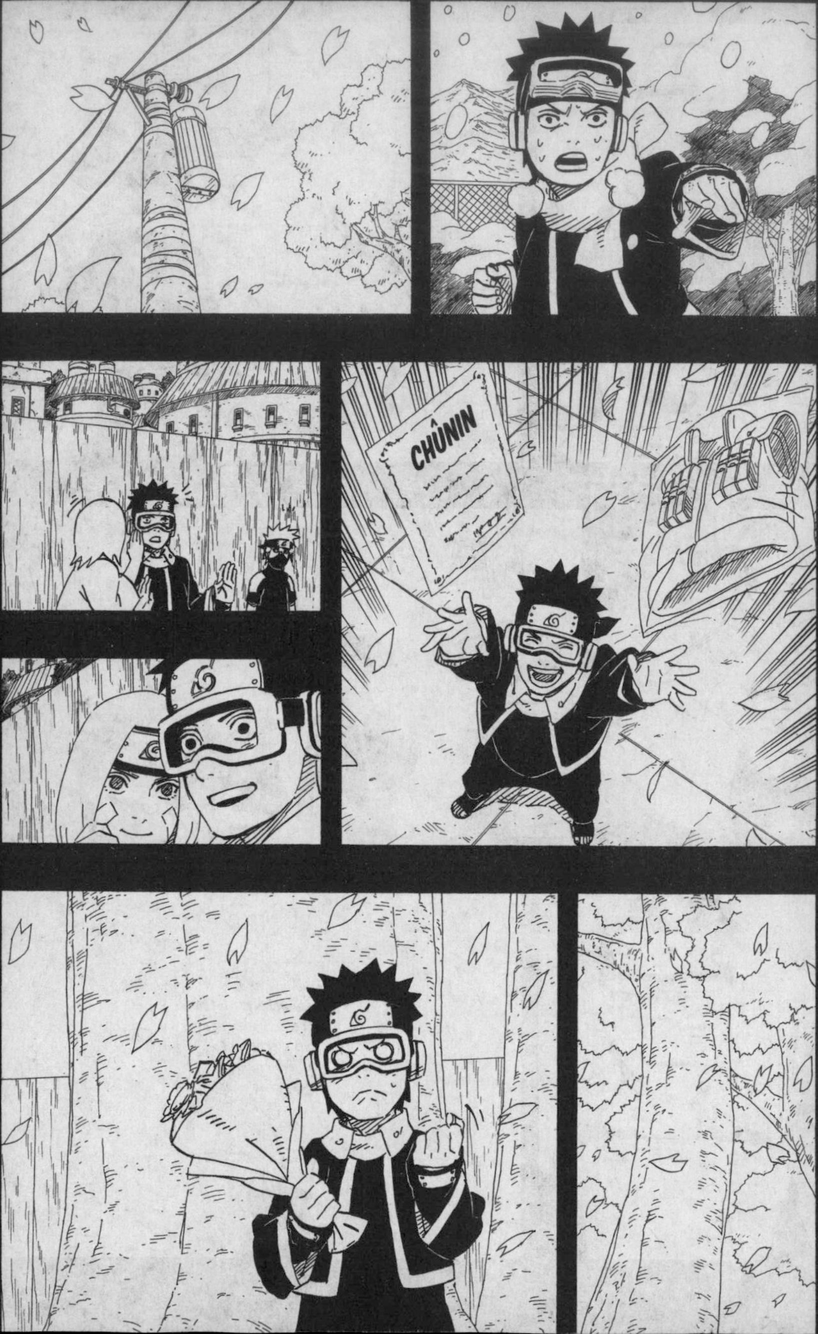
CHÛNIN

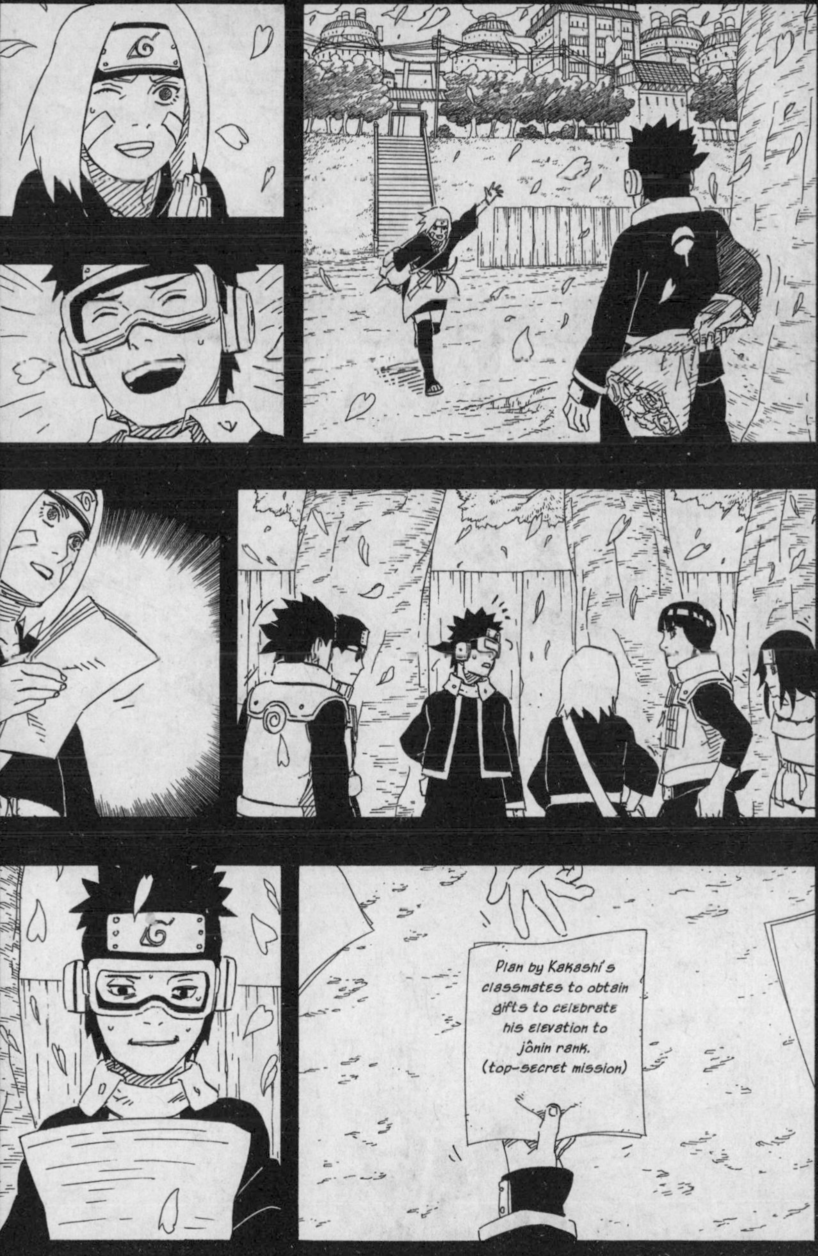
Plan by Kakashi's
classmates to obtain
gifts to celebrate
his elevation to
jônin rank.
(top-secret mission)

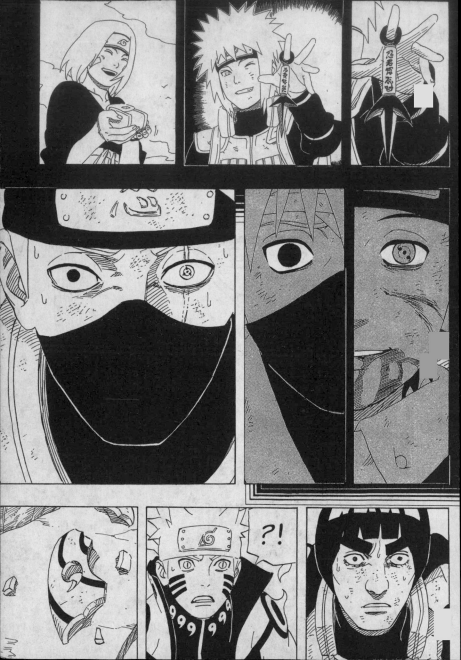

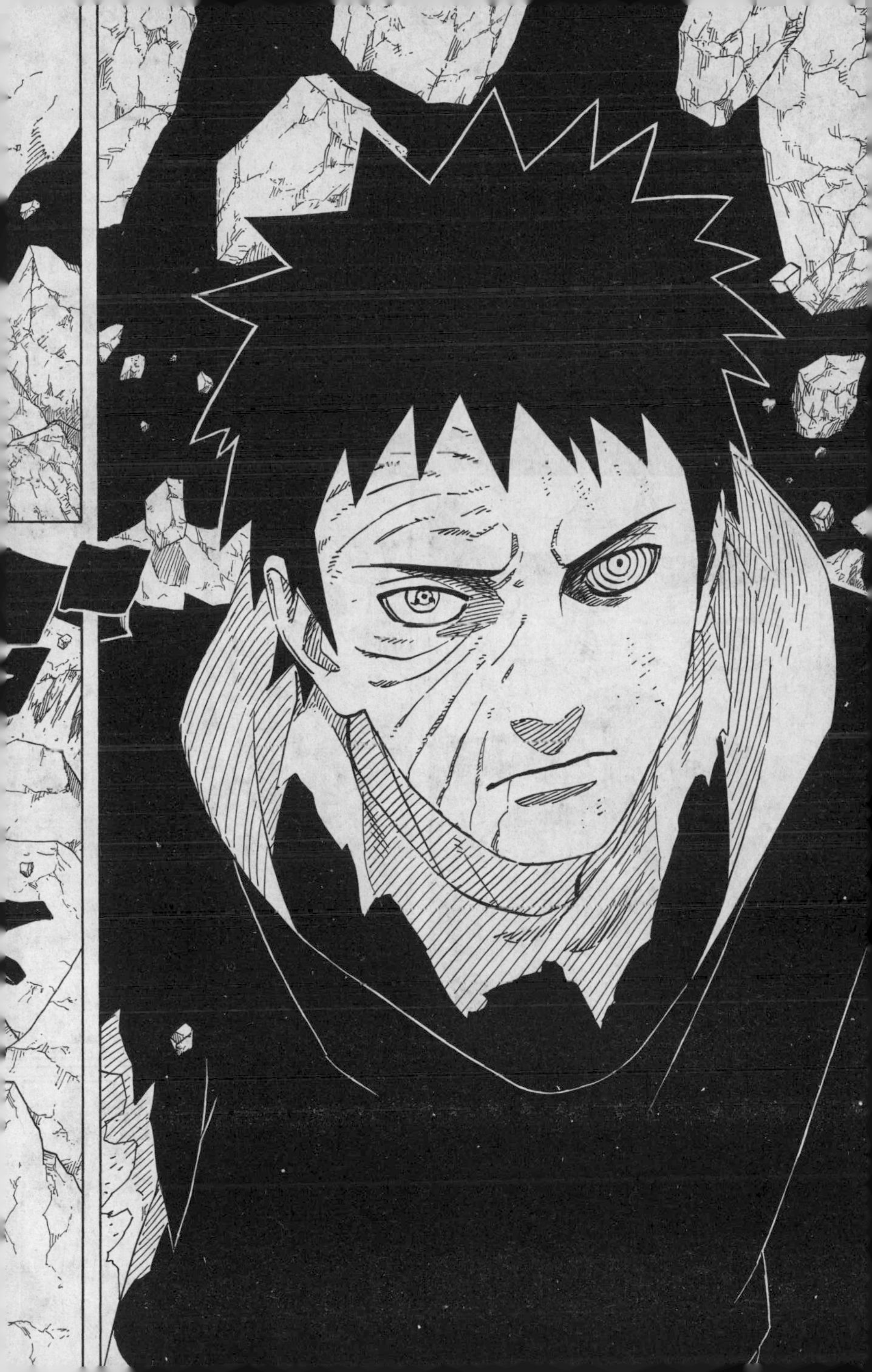

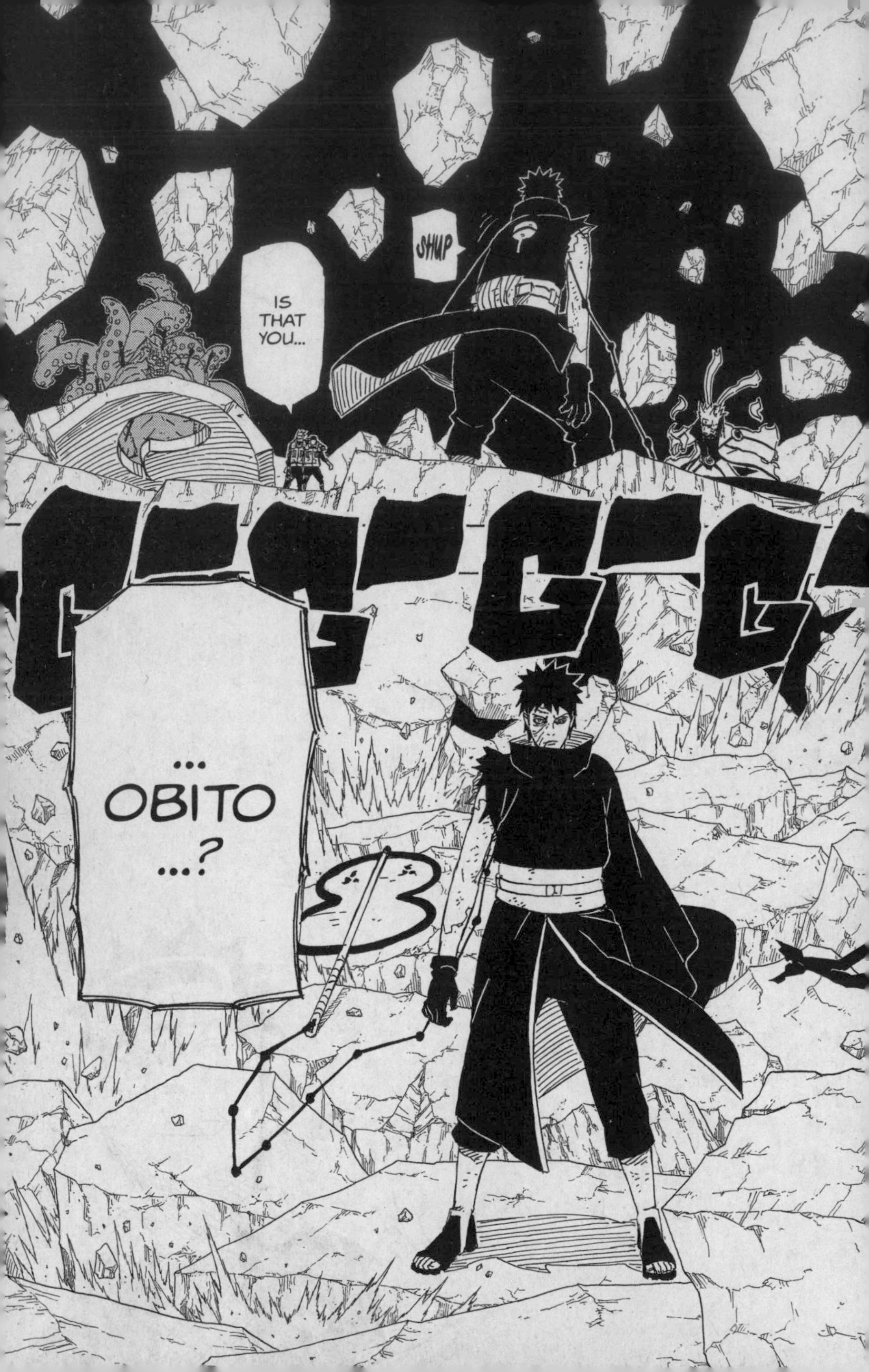
SHUP
IS THAT YOU...
... OBITO ...?

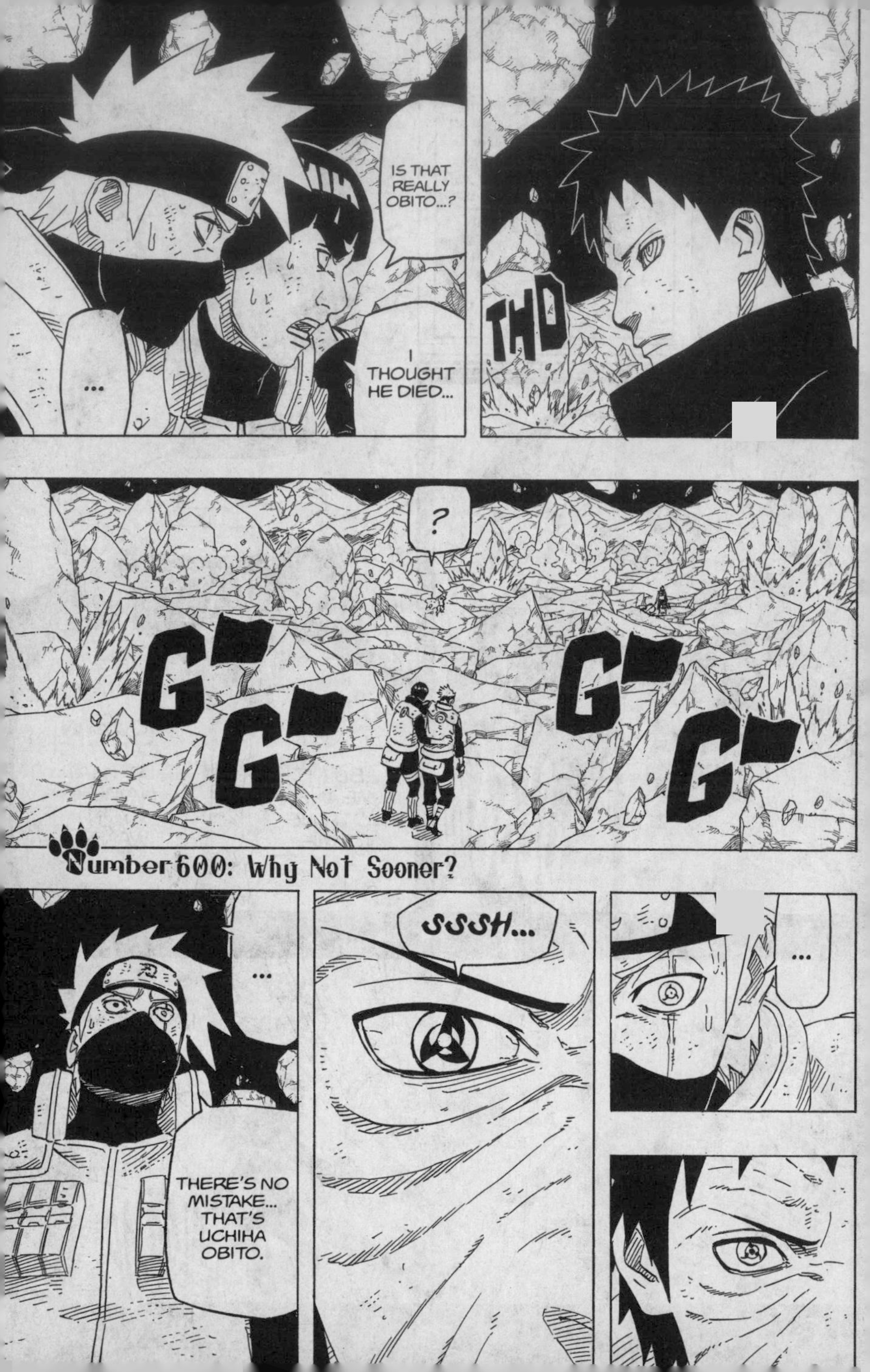
THD
IS THAT REALLY OBITO...?
I THOUGHT HE DIED...
...
?
G G
G G
Number 600: Why Not Sooner?
...
SSSH...
...
THERE'S NO MISTAKE... THAT'S UCHIHA OBITO.

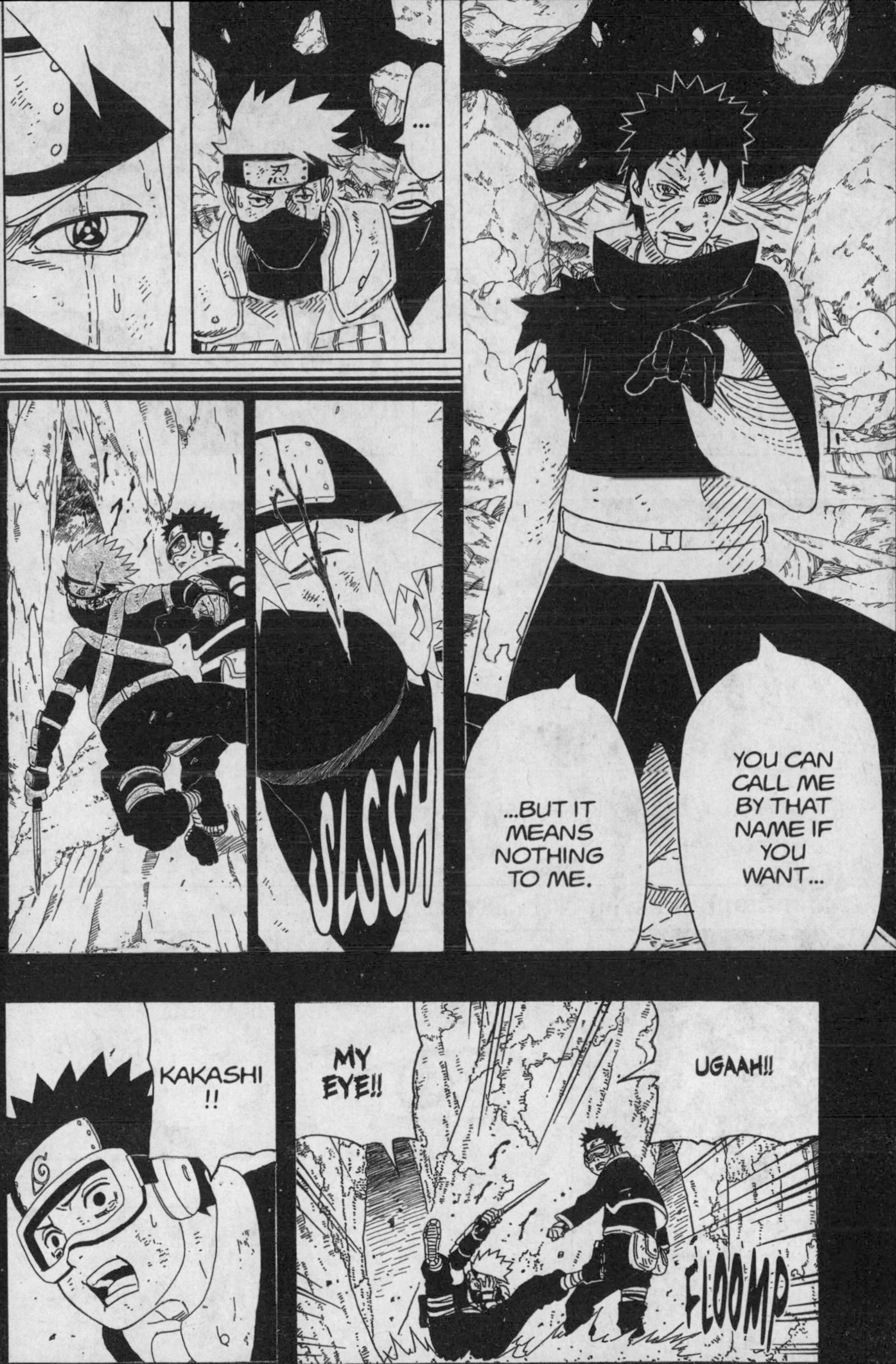

YOU CAN CALL ME BY THAT NAME IF YOU WANT...
...BUT IT MEANS NOTHING TO ME.
...
SLSSH
UGAAH!!
MY EYE!!
FLOOMP
KAKASHI !!

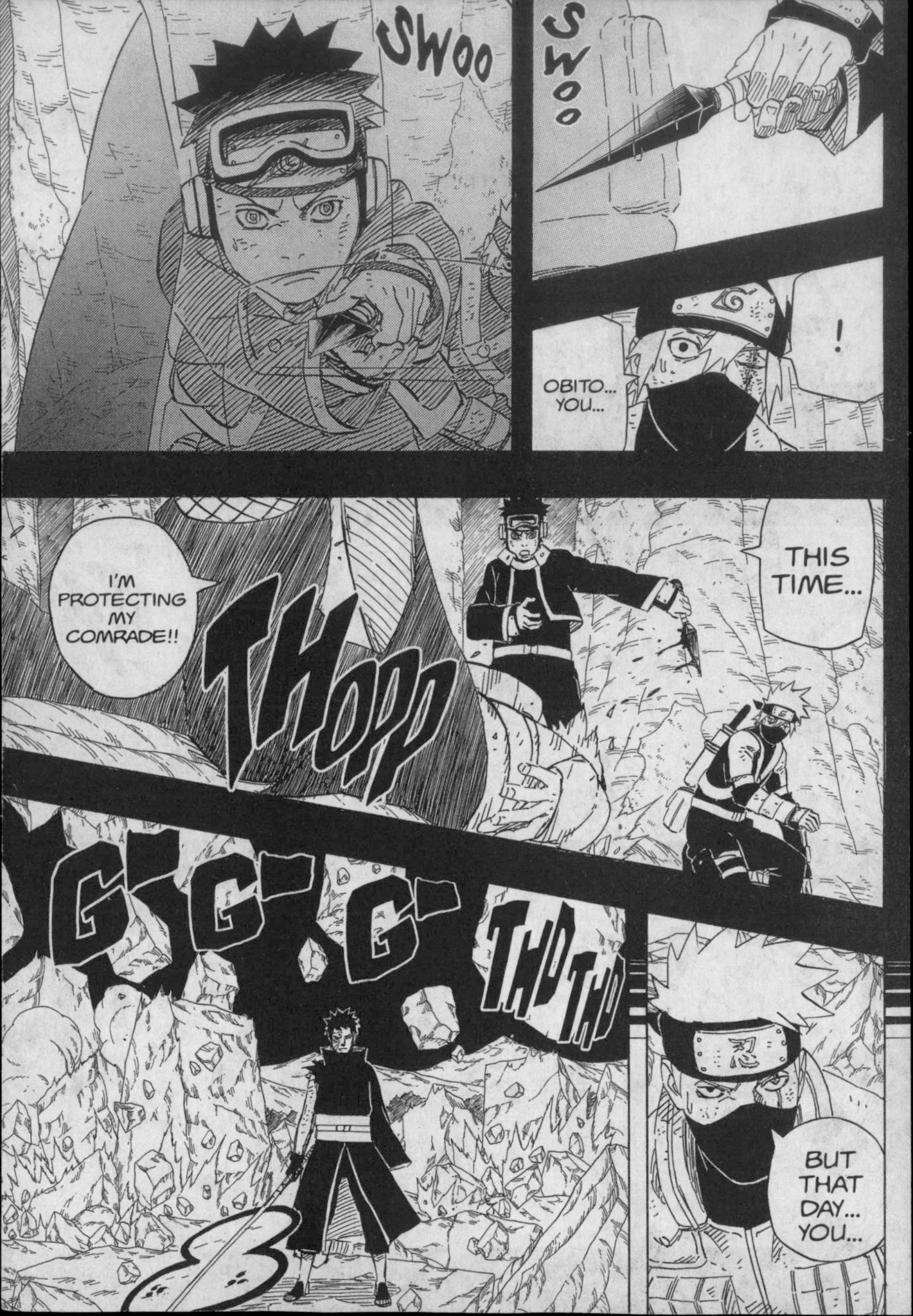
SWOO
!
OBITO... YOU...
SWOO
THIS TIME...
I'M PROTECTING MY COMRADE!!
THOPP
BUT THAT DAY... YOU...
G' G' G'
THD THD

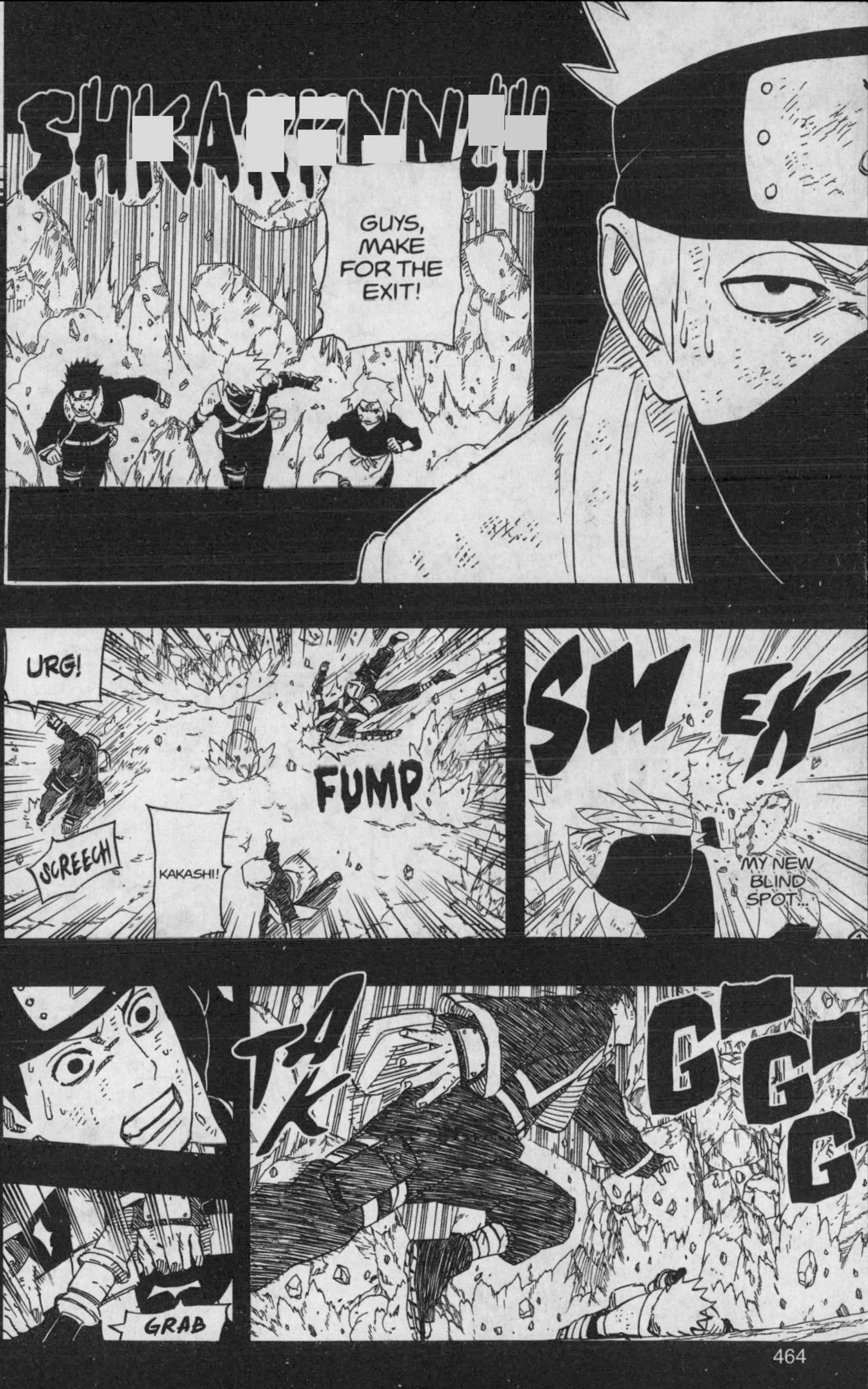
GUYS, MAKE FOR THE EXIT!
SMEK
MY NEW BLIND SPOT...
URG!
FUMP
SCREECH
KAKASHI!
TAK
GRAB

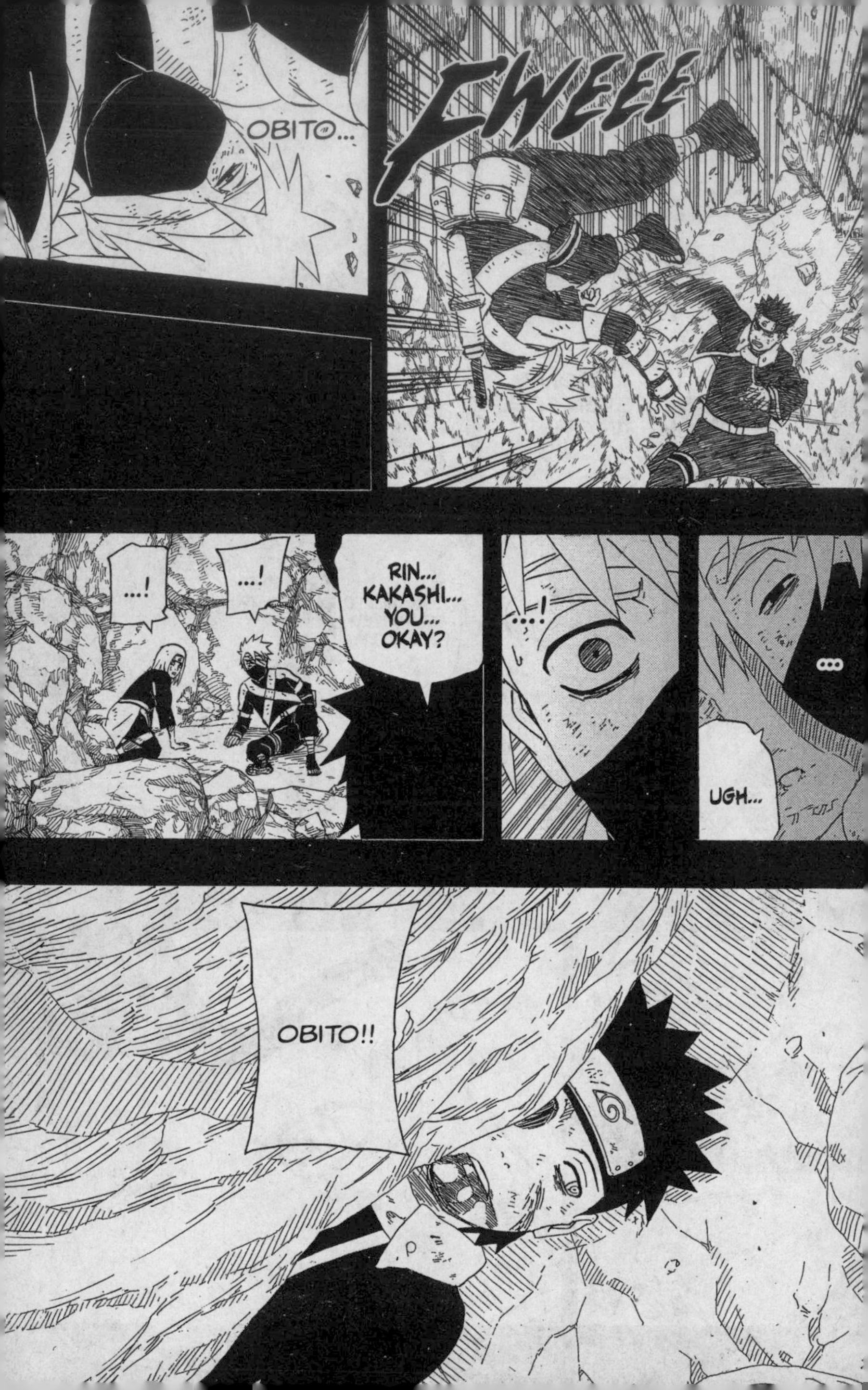
EWEEE
OBITO...
...
UGH...
...!
RIN... KAKASHI... YOU... OKAY?
...!
...!
OBITO!!

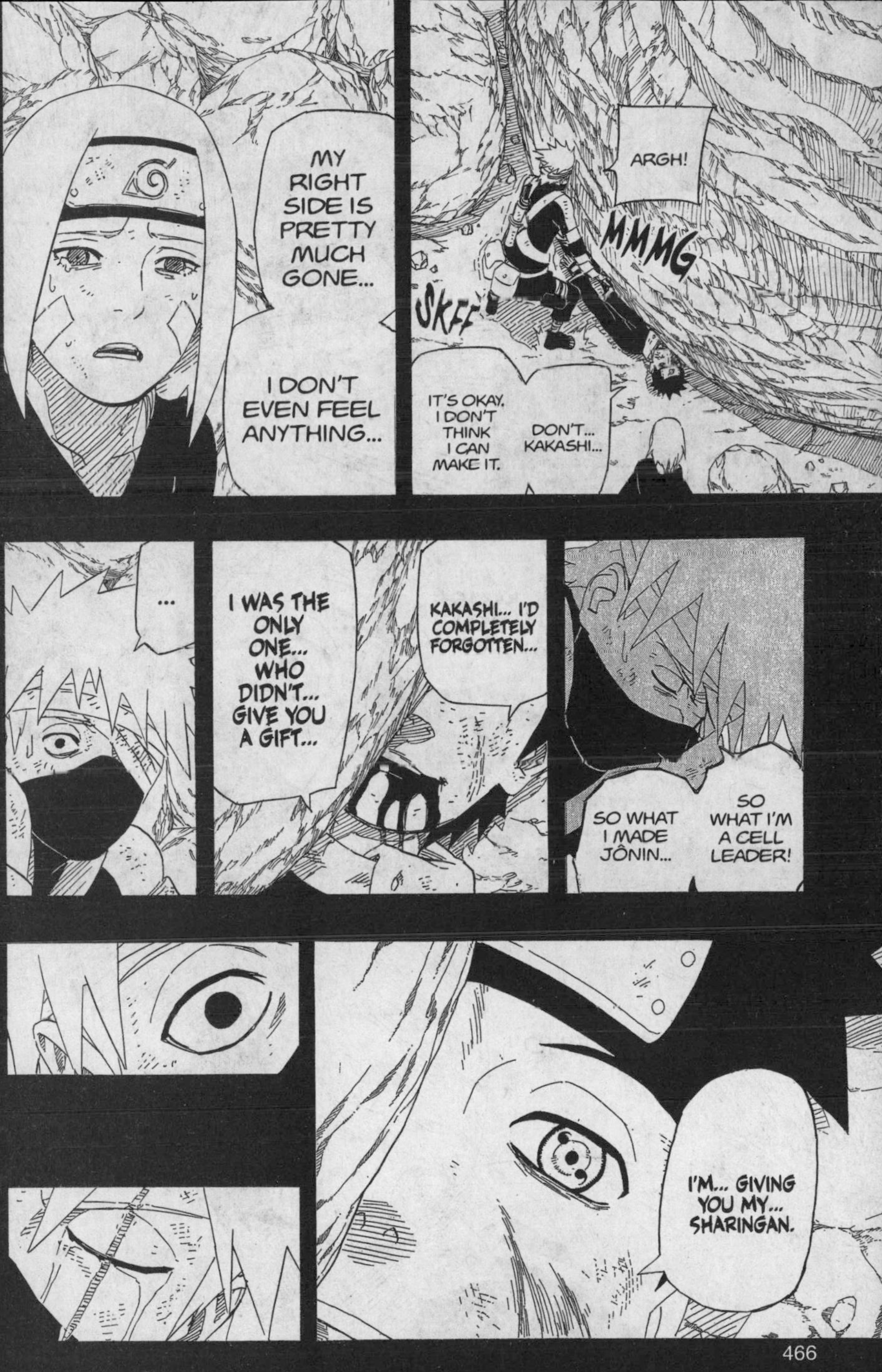
ARGH!
MMMG
SKFF
DON'T... KAKASHI...
IT'S OKAY. I DON'T THINK I CAN MAKE IT.
MY RIGHT SIDE IS PRETTY MUCH GONE...
I DON'T EVEN FEEL ANYTHING...
SO WHAT I'M A CELL LEADER!
SO WHAT I MADE JÔNIN...
KAKASHI... I'D COMPLETELY FORGOTTEN...
I WAS THE ONLY ONE... WHO DIDN'T... GIVE YOU A GIFT...
...
I'M... GIVING YOU MY... SHARINGAN.

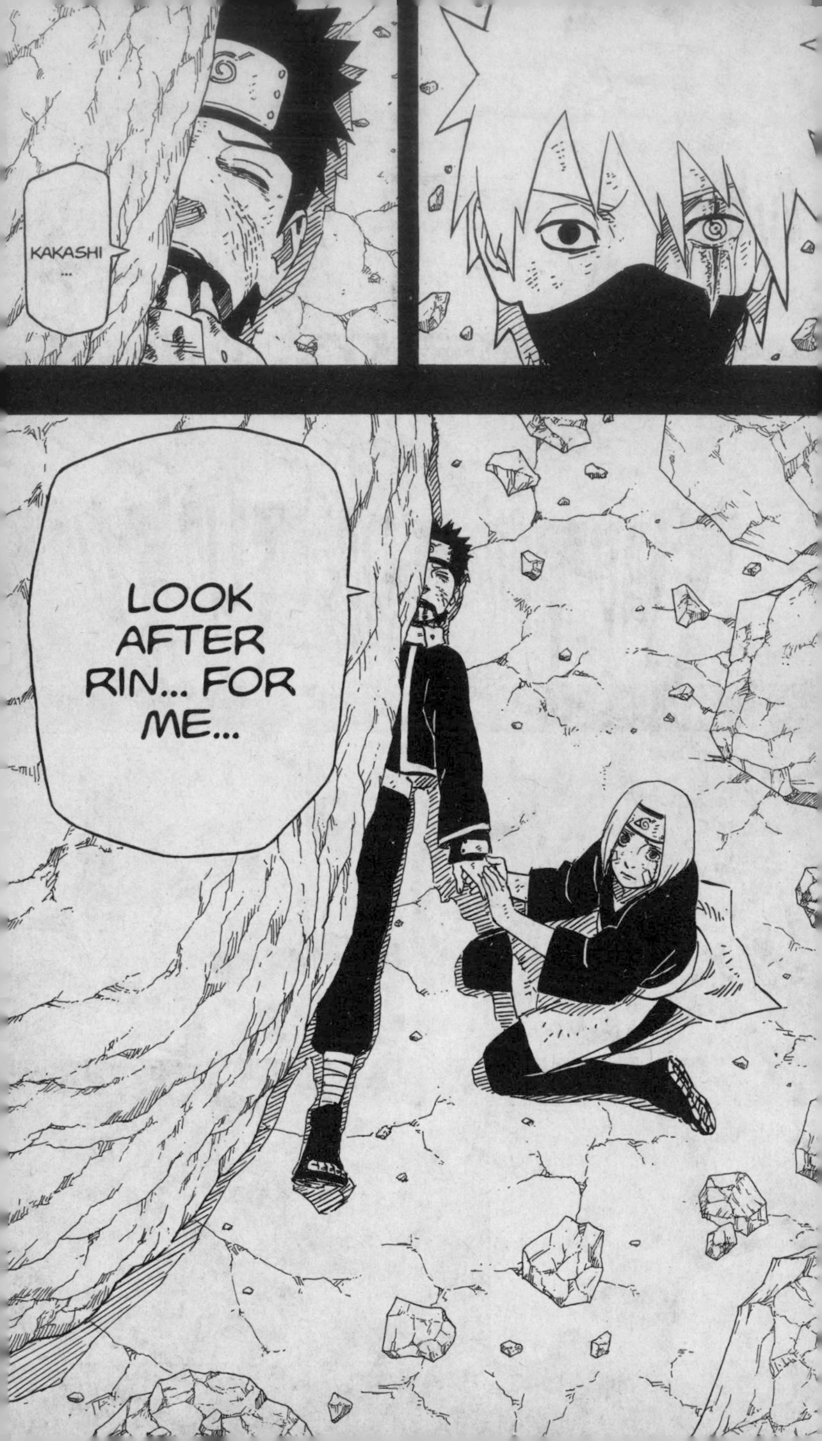
KAKASHI ...
LOOK AFTER RIN... FOR ME...

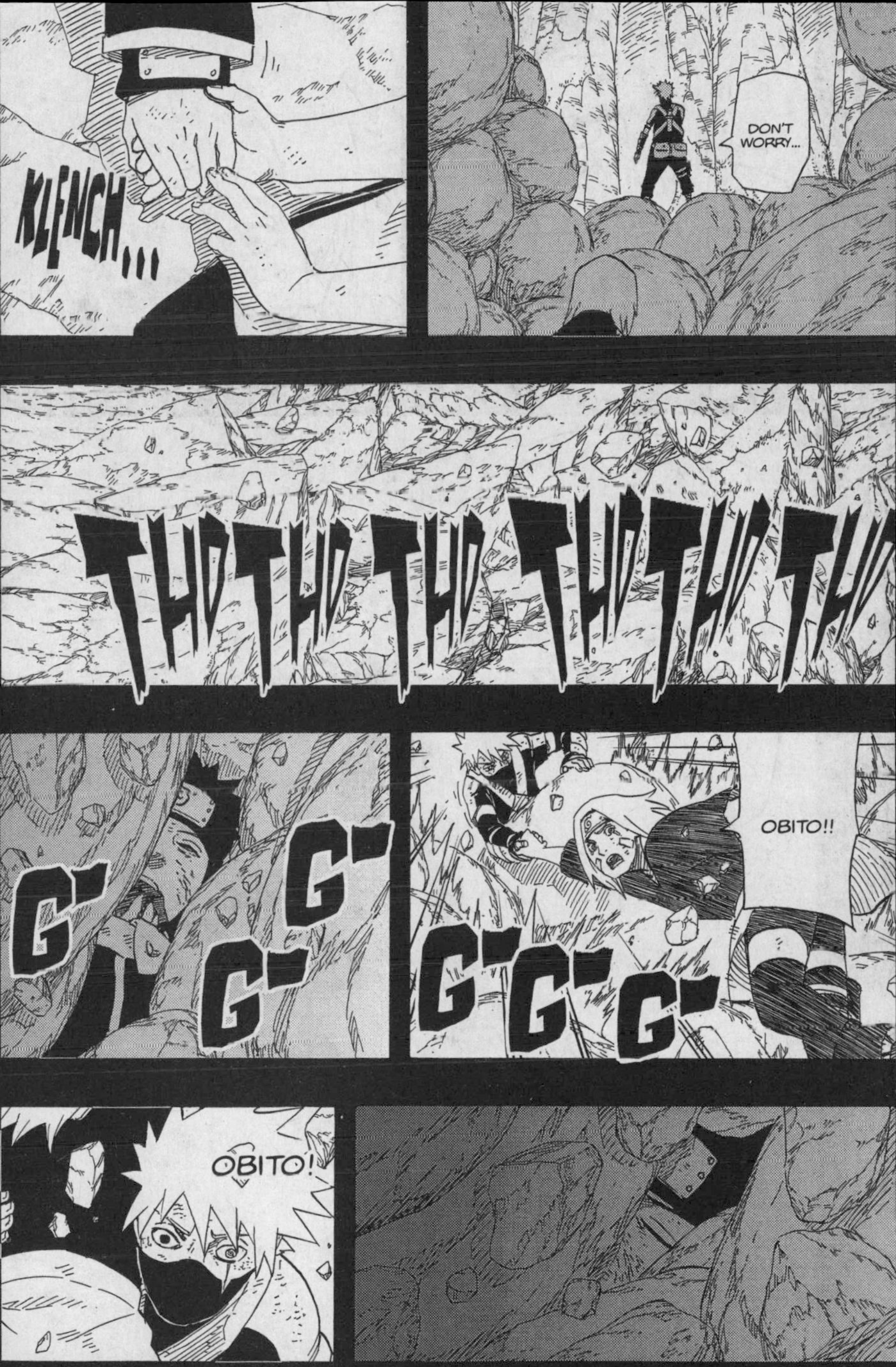
DON'T WORRY...
KLENCH...
THD THD THD THD THD THD
OBITO!!
G-G-G-
G- G G-
OBITO!

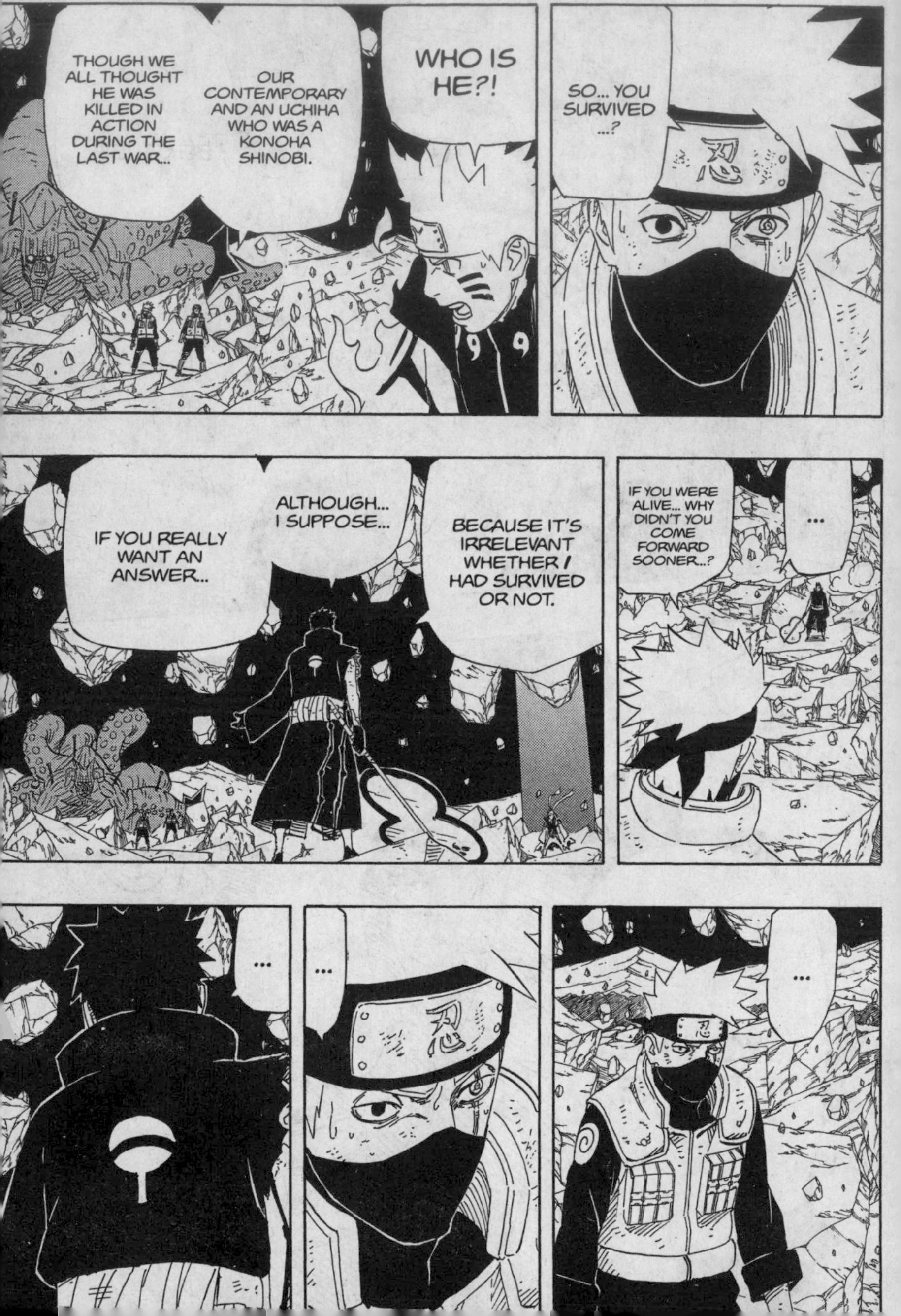
SO... YOU SURVIVED ...?
WHO IS HE?!
OUR CONTEMPORARY AND AN UCHIHA WHO WAS A KONOHA SHINOBI.
THOUGH WE ALL THOUGHT HE WAS KILLED IN ACTION DURING THE LAST WAR...
...
IF YOU WERE ALIVE... WHY DIDN'T YOU COME FORWARD SOONER...?
BECAUSE IT'S IRRELEVANT WHETHER I HAD SURVIVED OR NOT.
ALTHOUGH... I SUPPOSE...
IF YOU REALLY WANT AN ANSWER...
...
...
...

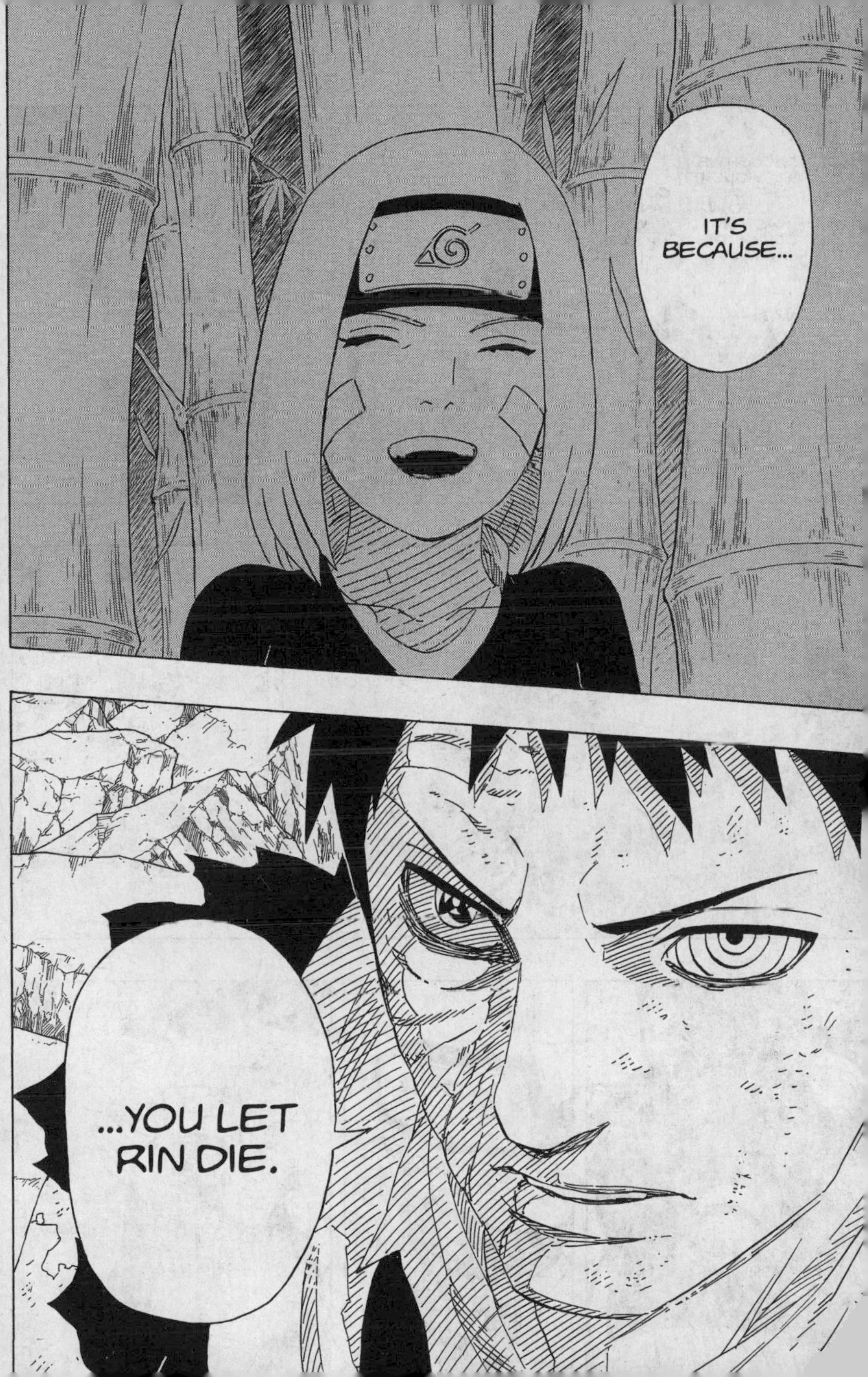
IT'S BECAUSE...
...YOU LET RIN DIE.

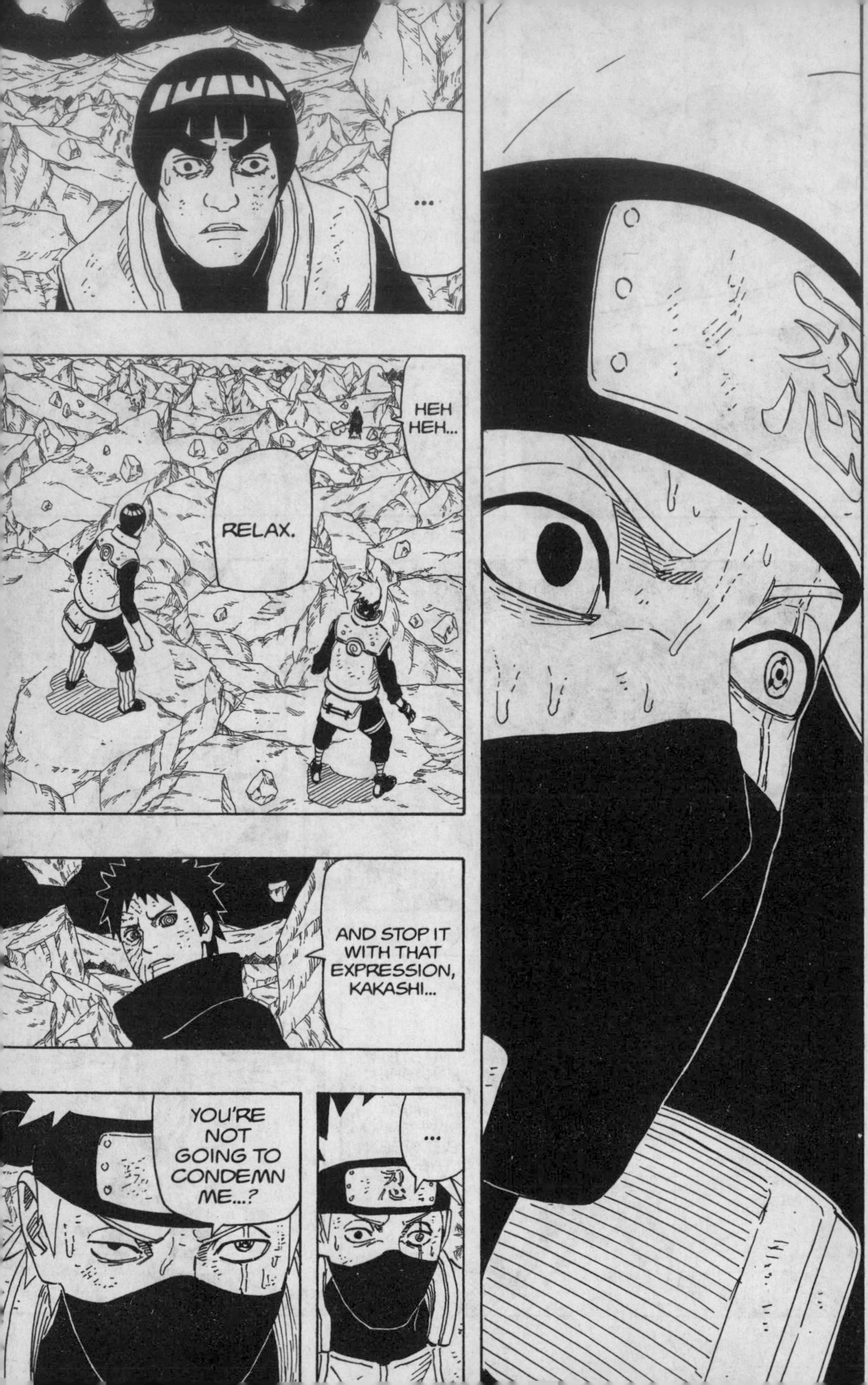
...
HEH HEH...
RELAX.
AND STOP IT WITH THAT EXPRESSION, KAKASHI...
...
YOU'RE NOT GOING TO CONDEMN ME...?

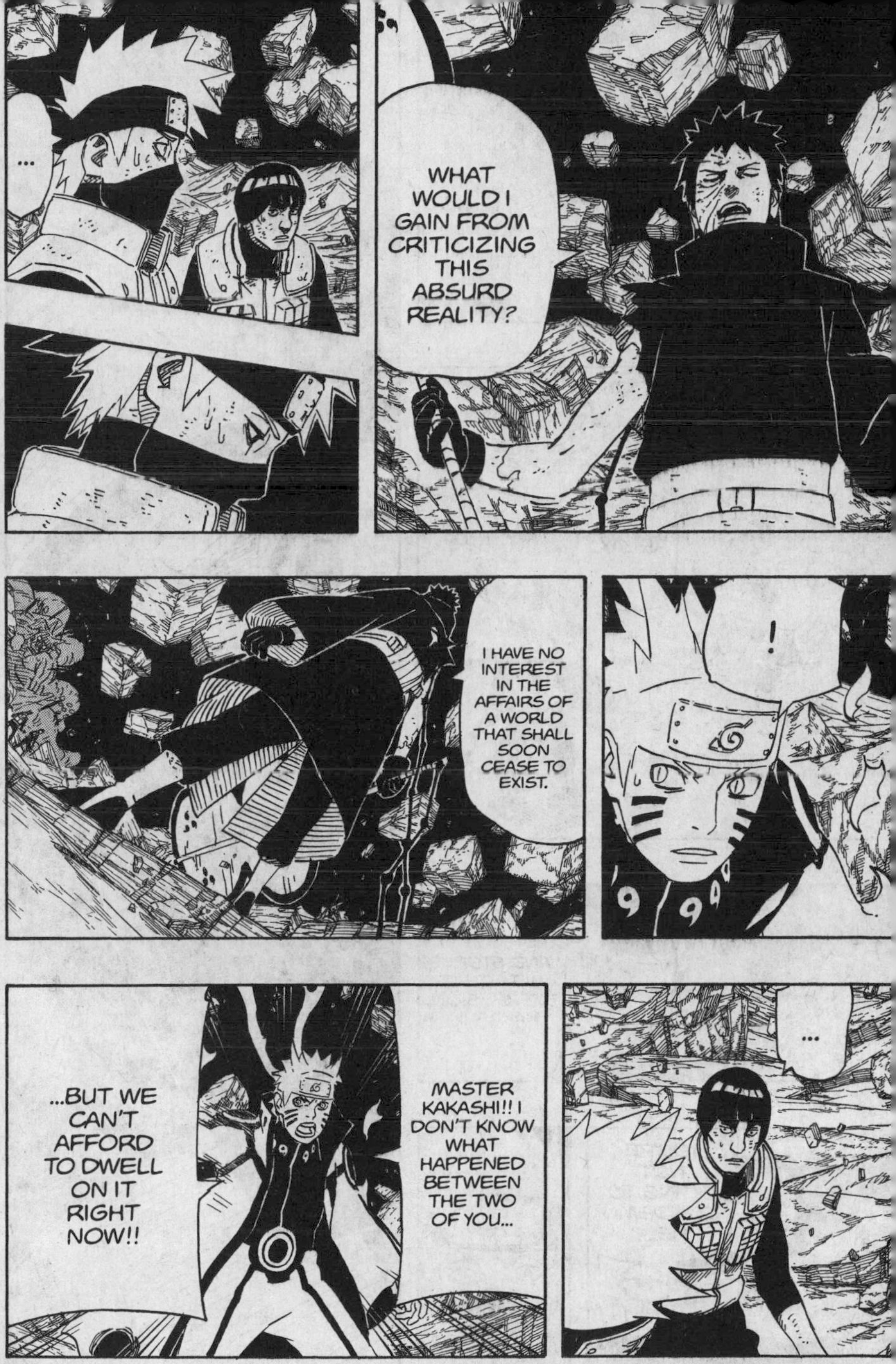
WHAT WOULD I GAIN FROM CRITICIZING THIS ABSURD REALITY?
...
!
I HAVE NO INTEREST IN THE AFFAIRS OF A WORLD THAT SHALL SOON CEASE TO EXIST.
...
MASTER KAKASHI!! I DON'T KNOW WHAT HAPPENED BETWEEN THE TWO OF YOU...
...BUT WE CAN'T AFFORD TO DWELL ON IT RIGHT NOW!!

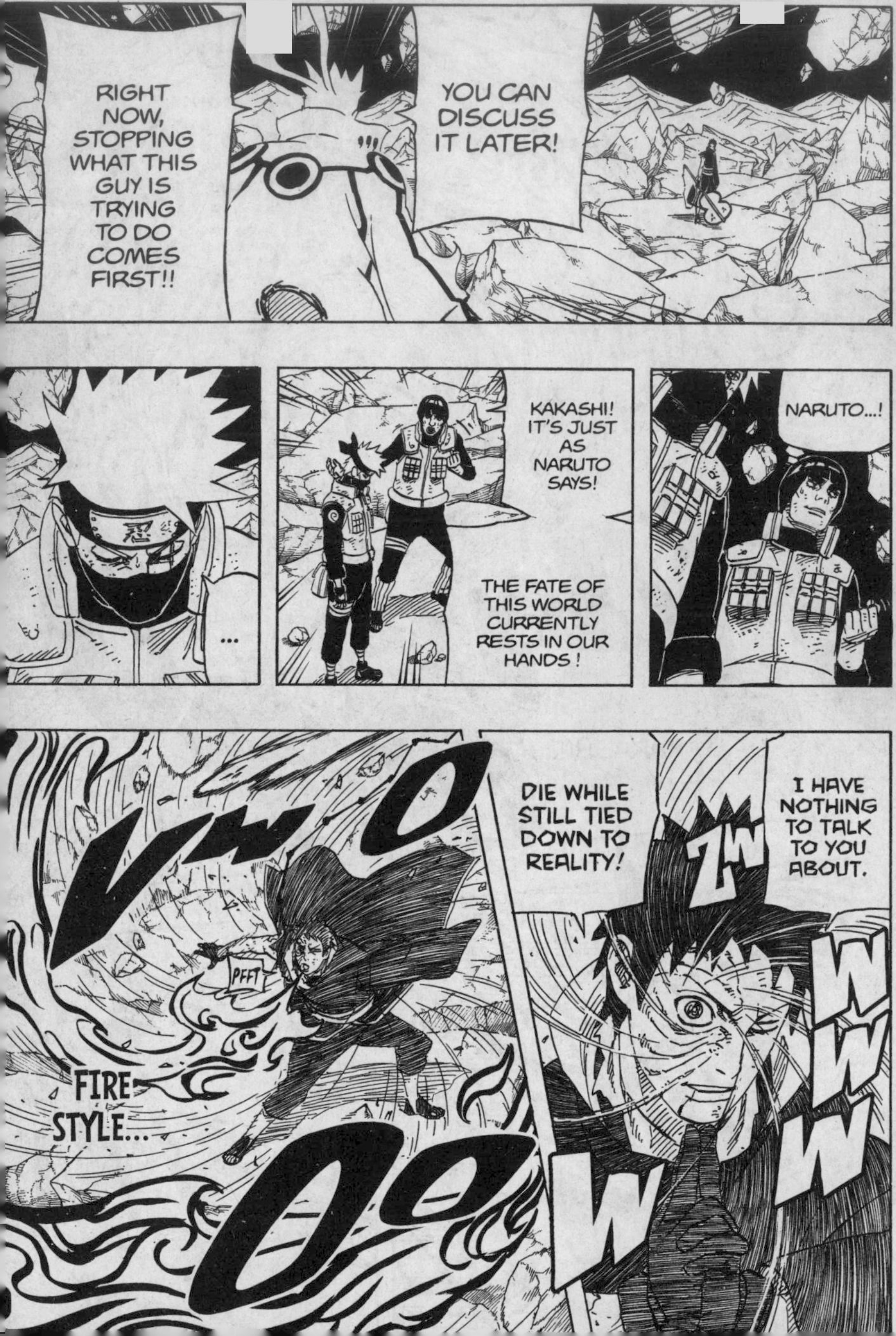
YOU CAN DISCUSS IT LATER!
RIGHT NOW, STOPPING WHAT THIS GUY IS TRYING TO DO COMES FIRST!!
NARUTO...!
KAKASHI! IT'S JUST AS NARUTO SAYS!
THE FATE OF THIS WORLD CURRENTLY RESTS IN OUR HANDS!
...
I HAVE NOTHING TO TALK TO YOU ABOUT.
DIE WHILE STILL TIED DOWN TO REALITY!
ZWWWWWW
PFFT
FIRE STYLE...
VWOOO

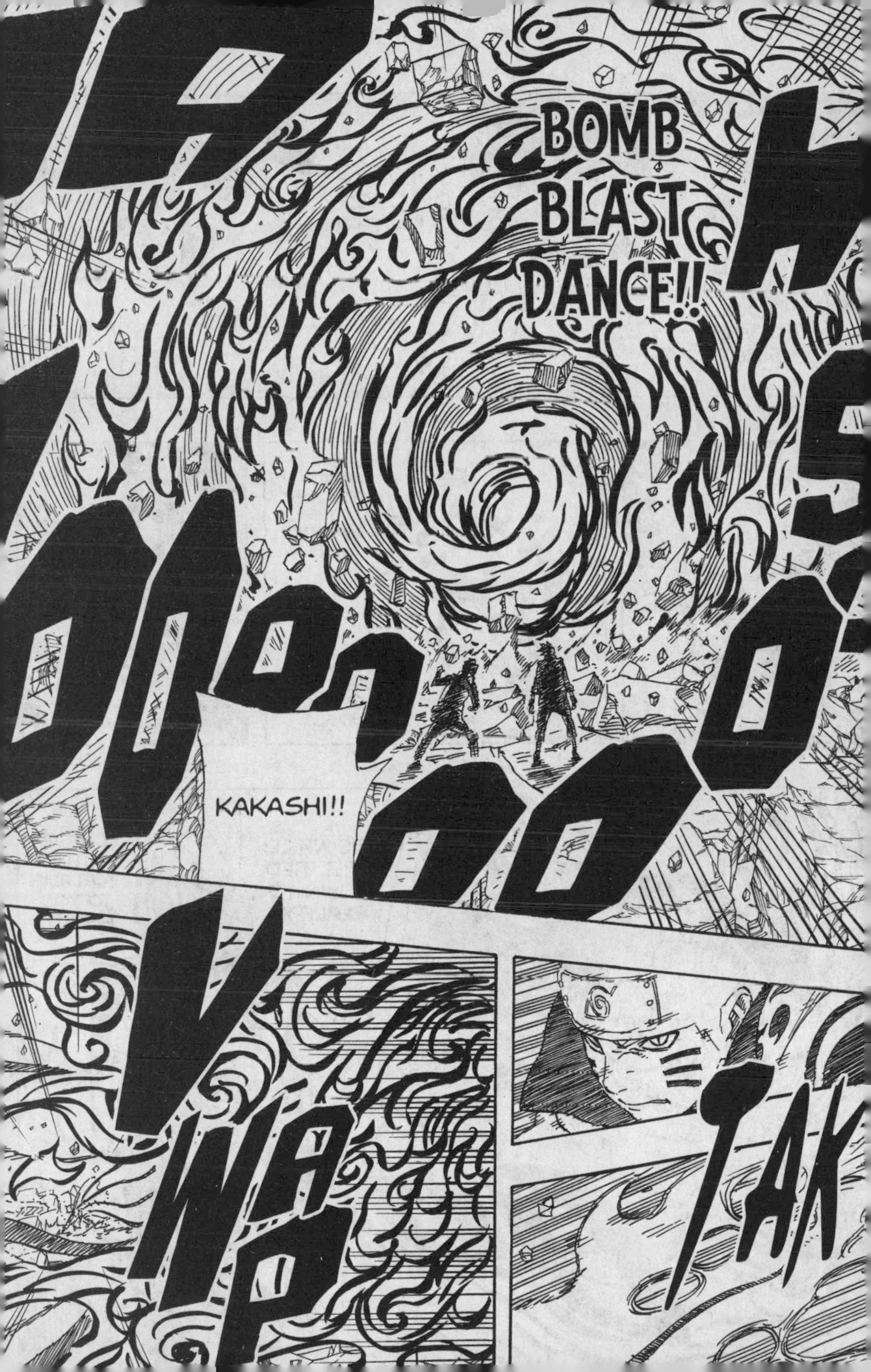
BOMB BLAST DANCE!!
KAKASHI!!
TAK

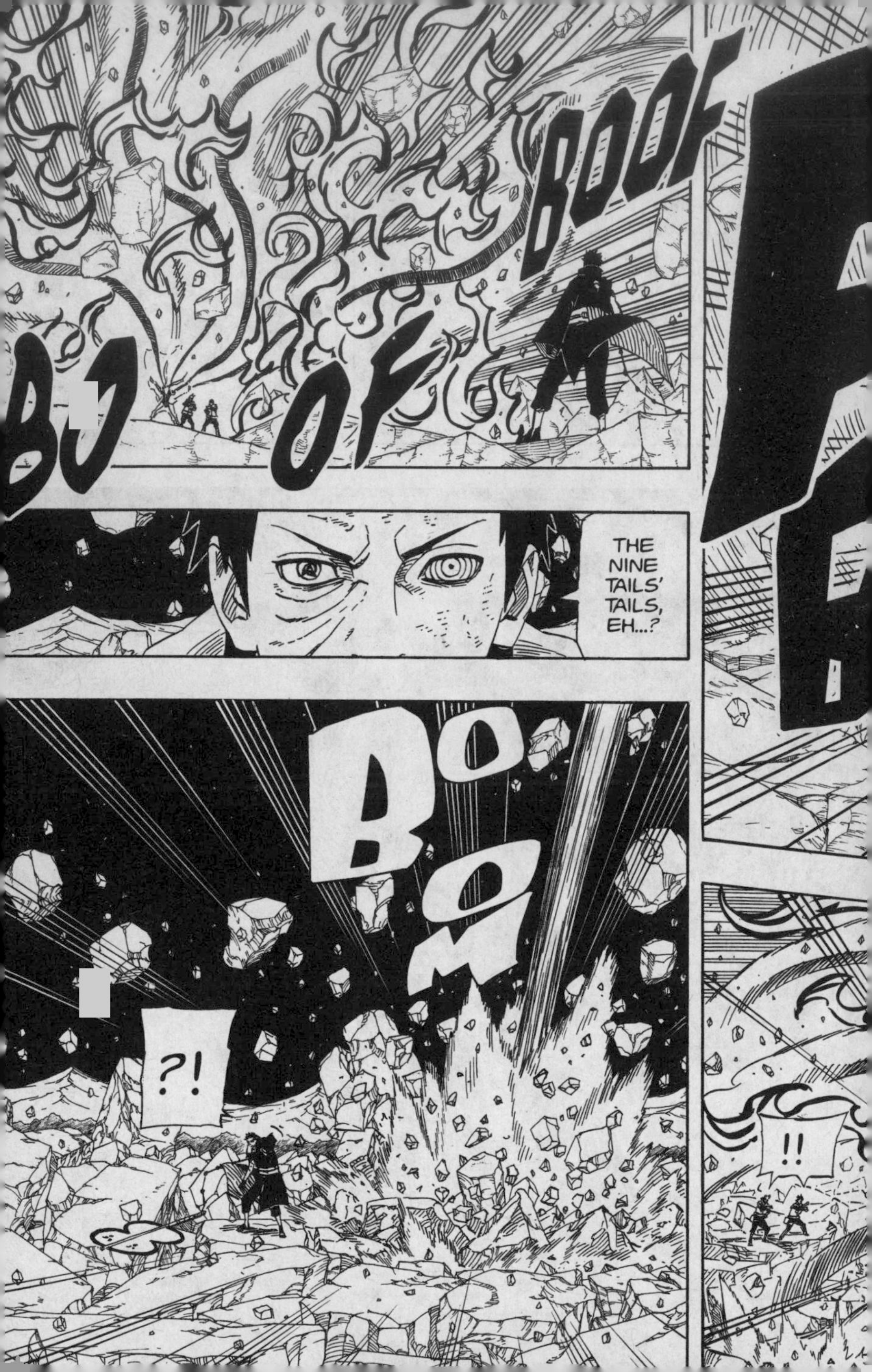
BOOF
BOOF
THE NINE TAILS' TAILS, EH...?
BOOM
?!
!!

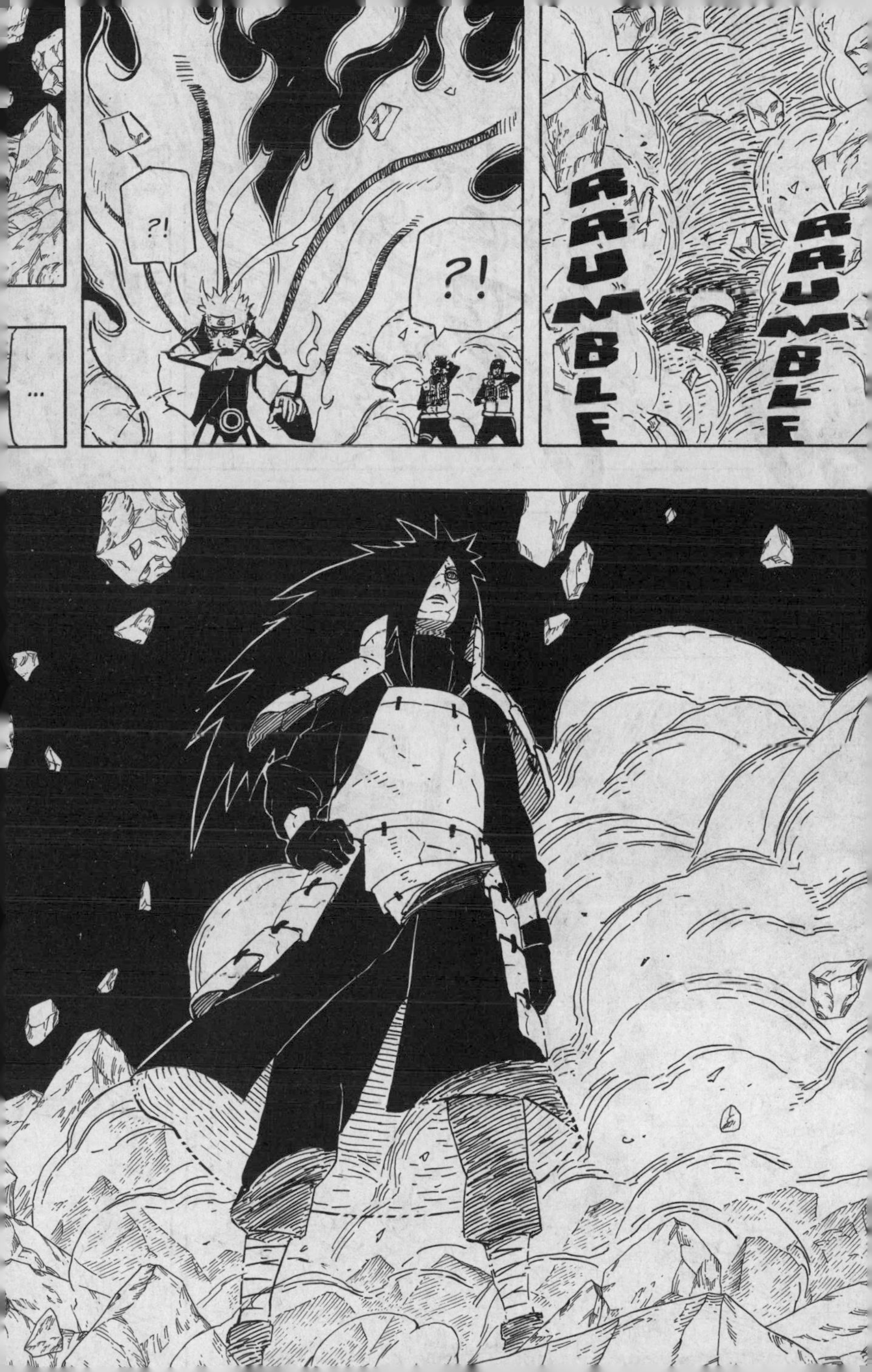
RUMBLE
RUMBLE
?!
?!
...

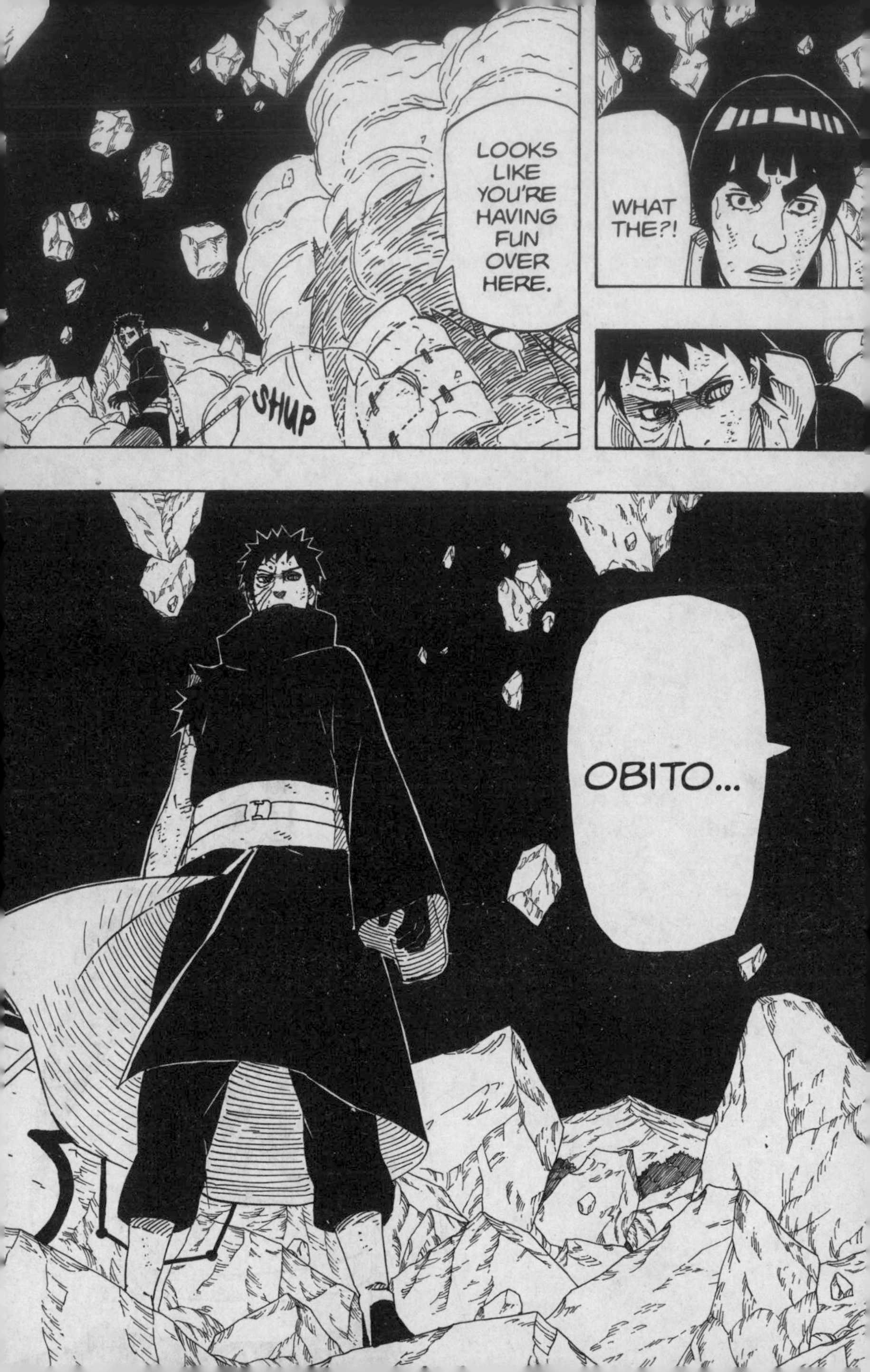
WHAT THE?!
LOOKS LIKE YOU'RE HAVING FUN OVER HERE.
SHUP
OBITO...

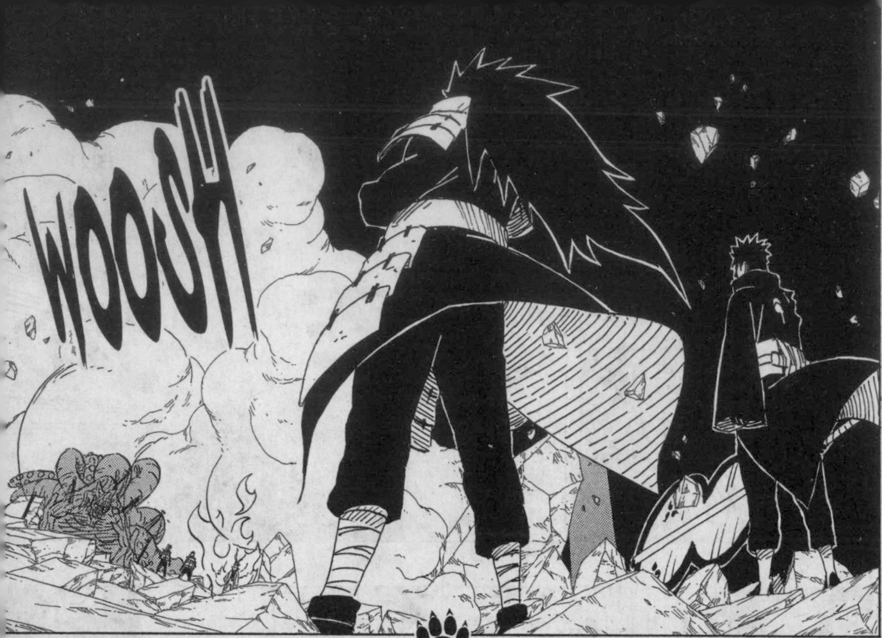
WOOSH

Number 601: Obito and Madara

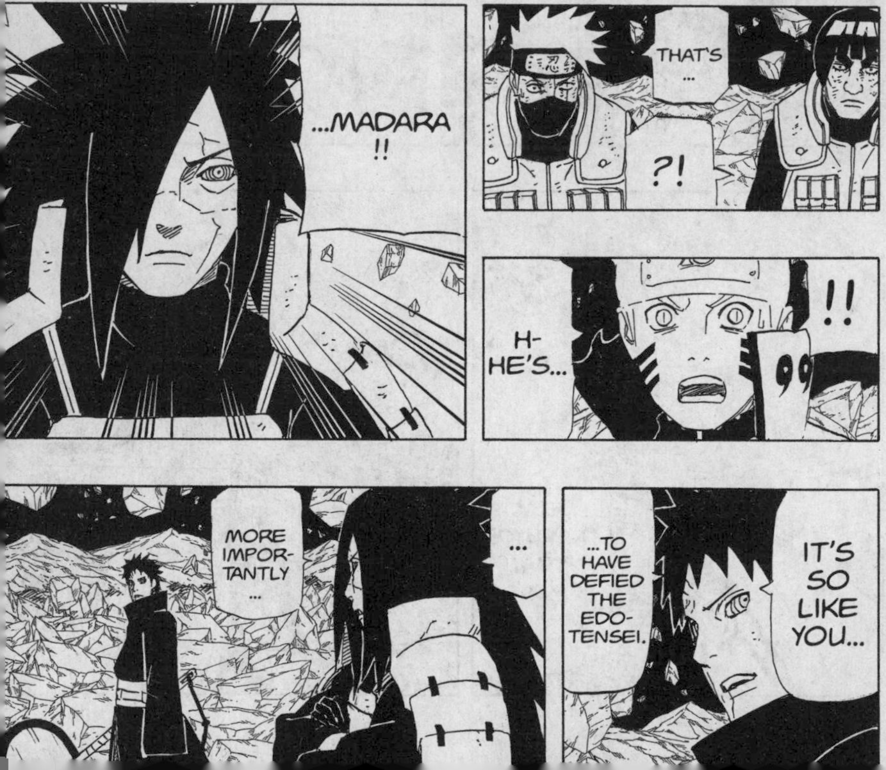
THAT'S ...
?!
!!
H- HE'S...
...MADARA !!
IT'S SO LIKE YOU...
...TO HAVE DEFIED THE EDO-TENSEI.
...
MORE IMPOR-TANTLY ...

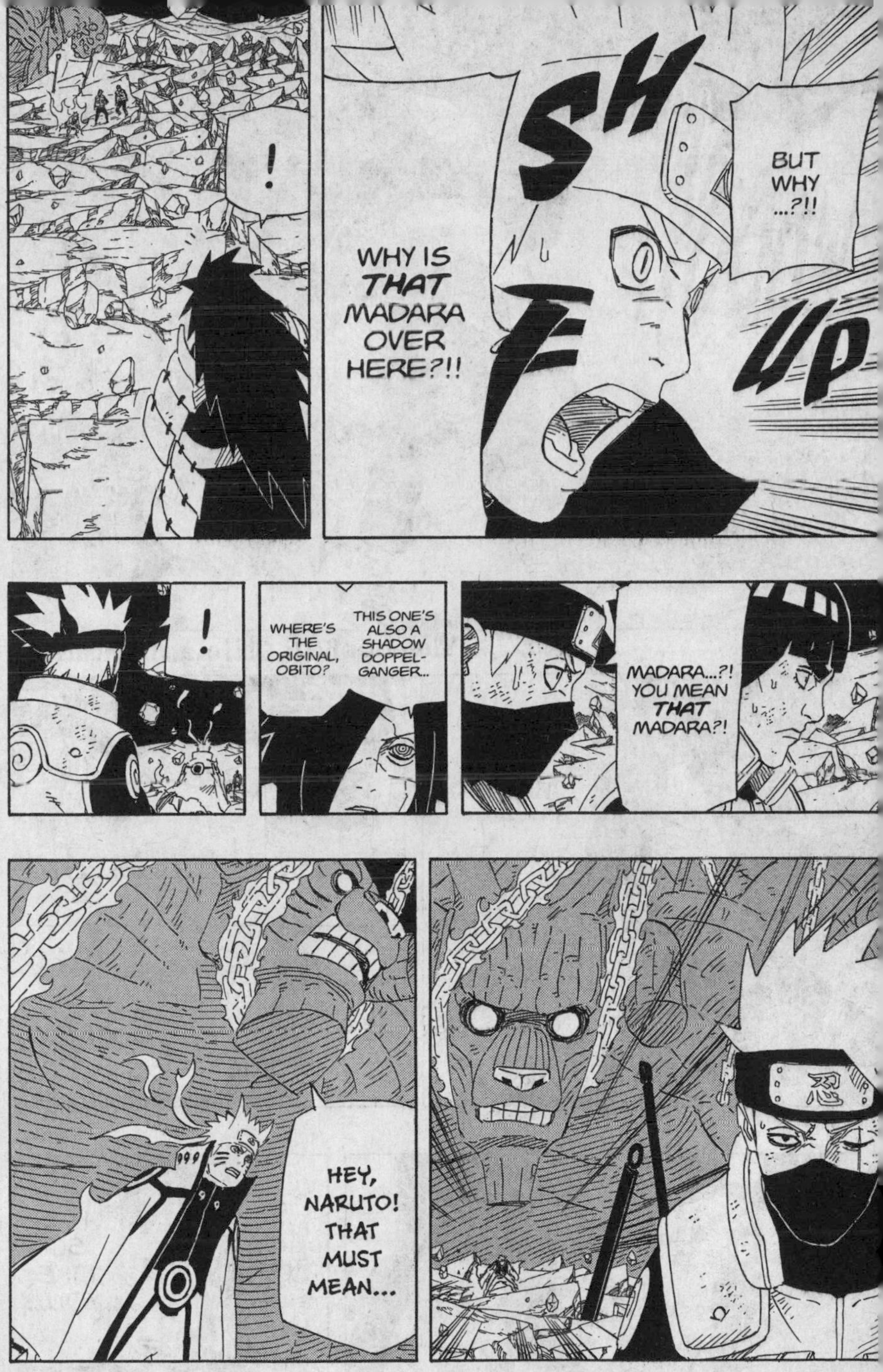
SH
UP
BUT WHY ...?!!
WHY IS *THAT* MADARA OVER HERE?!!
!
MADARA...?! YOU MEAN *THAT* MADARA?!
THIS ONE'S ALSO A SHADOW DOPPEL-GANGER...
WHERE'S THE ORIGINAL, OBITO?
!
HEY, NARUTO! THAT MUST MEAN...

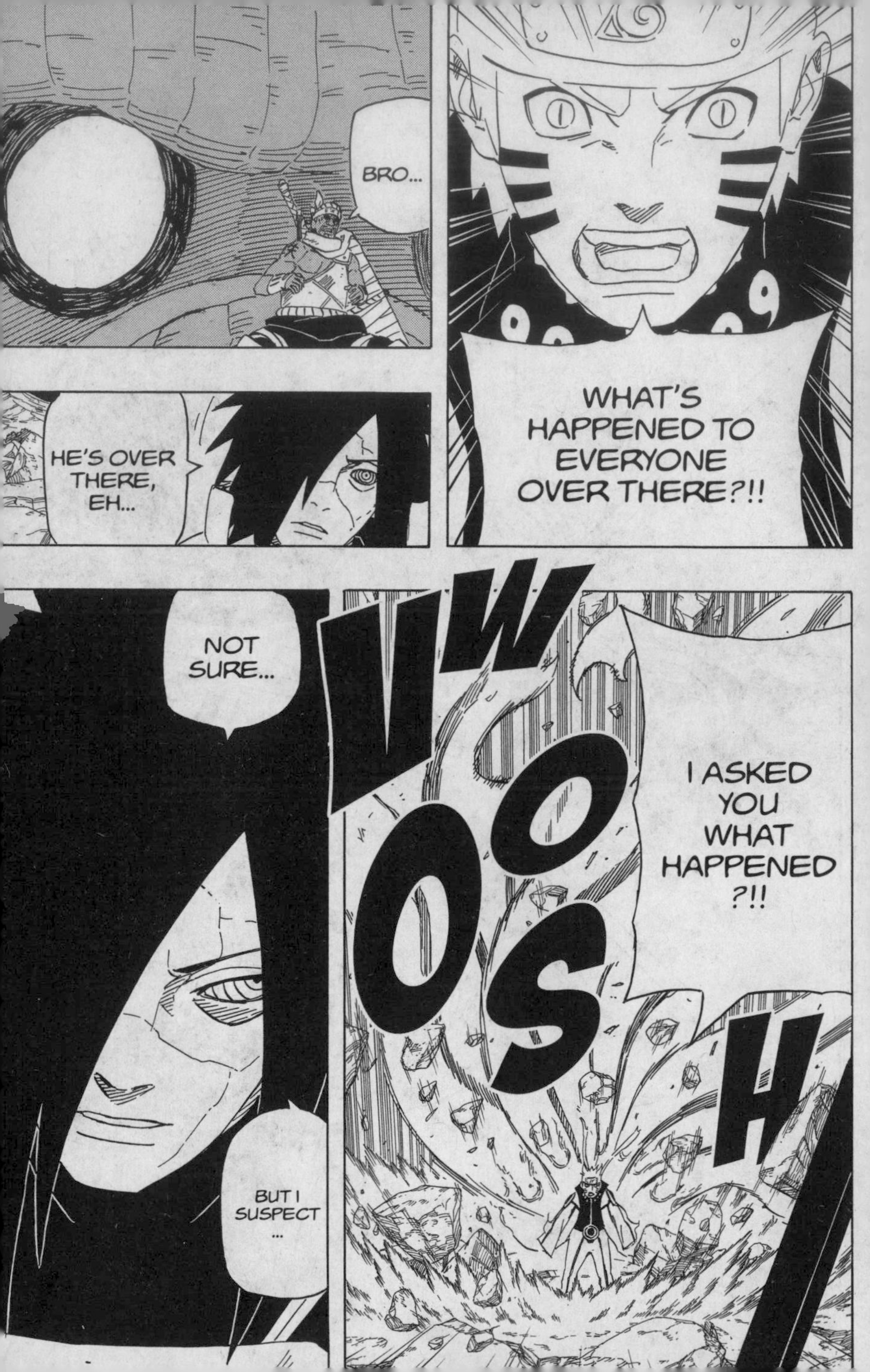
WHAT'S HAPPENED TO EVERYONE OVER THERE?!!
BRO...
HE'S OVER THERE, EH...
WHOOSH
I ASKED YOU WHAT HAPPENED ?!!
NOT SURE...
BUT I SUSPECT ...

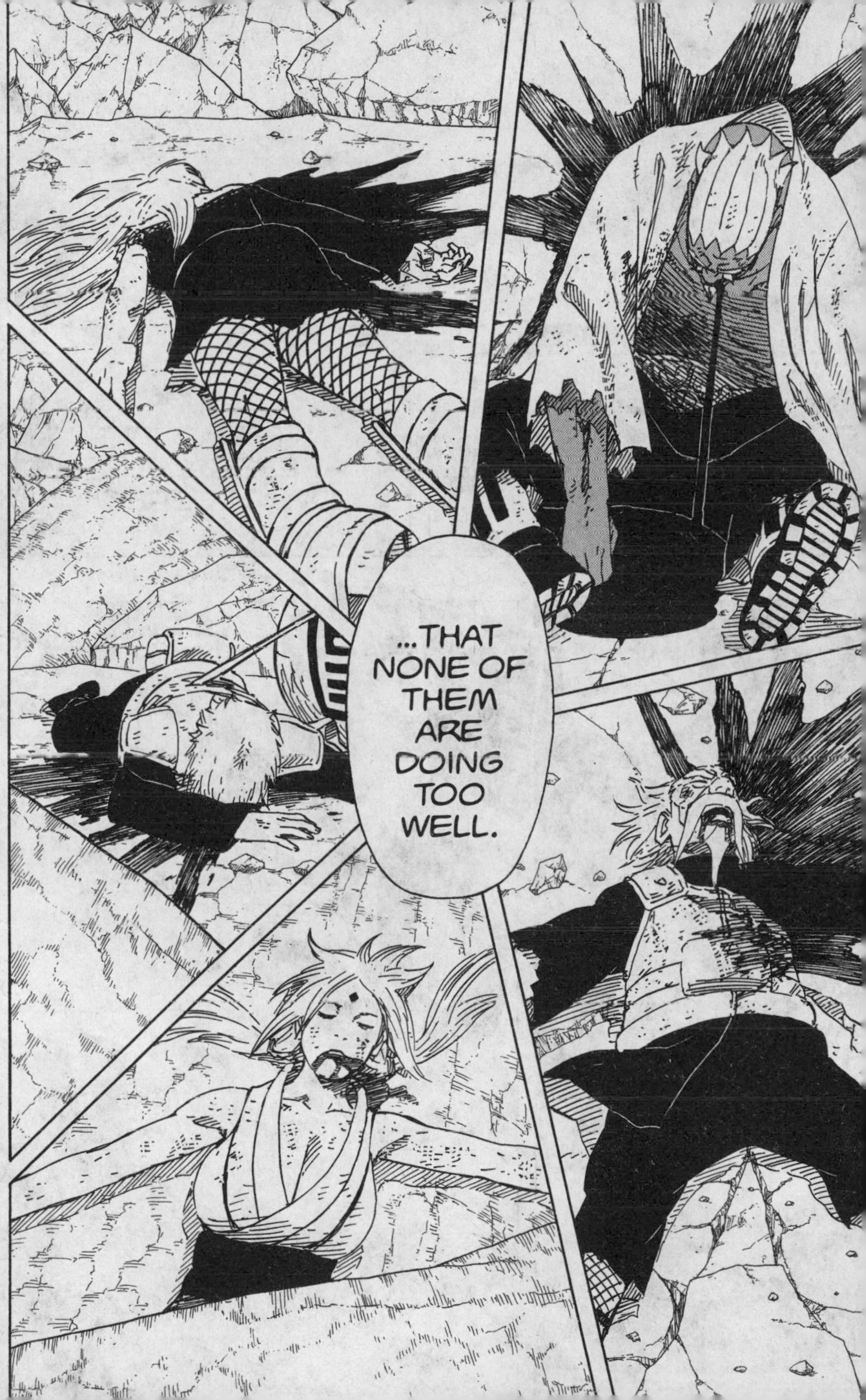
...THAT NONE OF THEM ARE DOING TOO WELL.

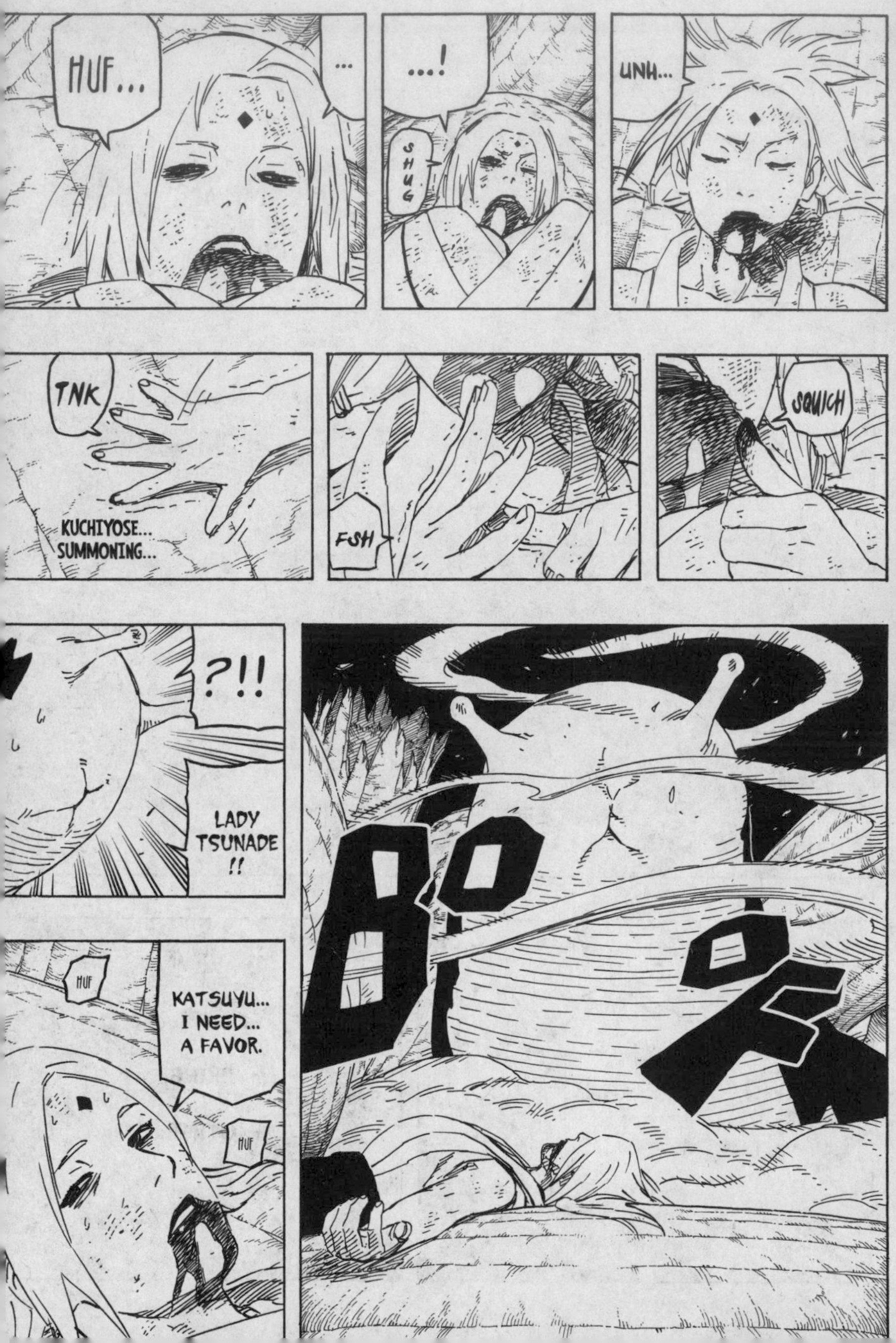
UNH...
...!
SHUG
...
HUF...
SQUICH
FSH
TNK
KUCHIYOSE... SUMMONING...
BOOF
?!!
LADY TSUNADE !!
HUF
KATSUYU... I NEED... A FAVOR.
HUF

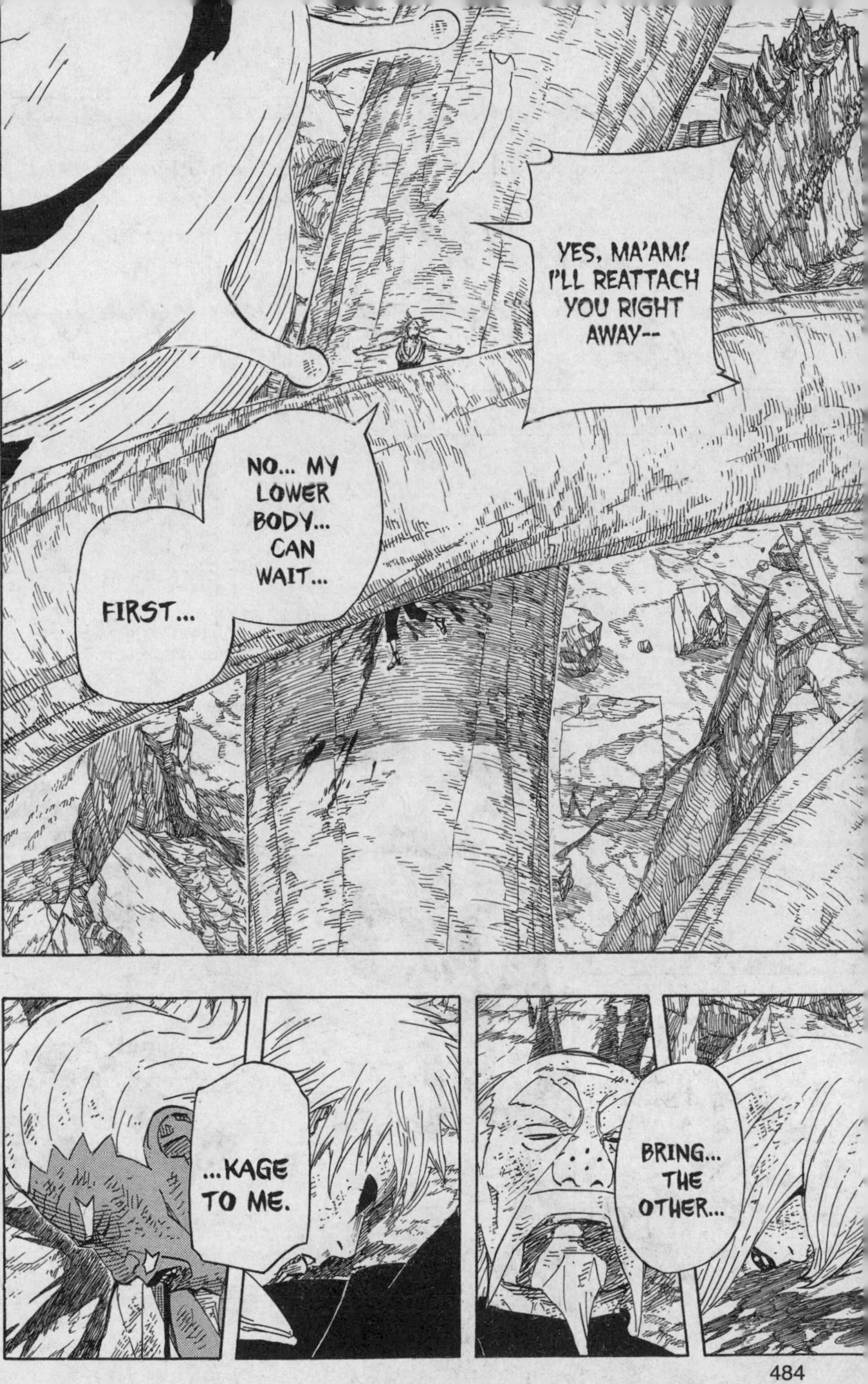
YES, MA'AM! I'LL REATTACH YOU RIGHT AWAY--
NO... MY LOWER BODY... CAN WAIT...
FIRST...
BRING... THE OTHER...
...KAGE TO ME.

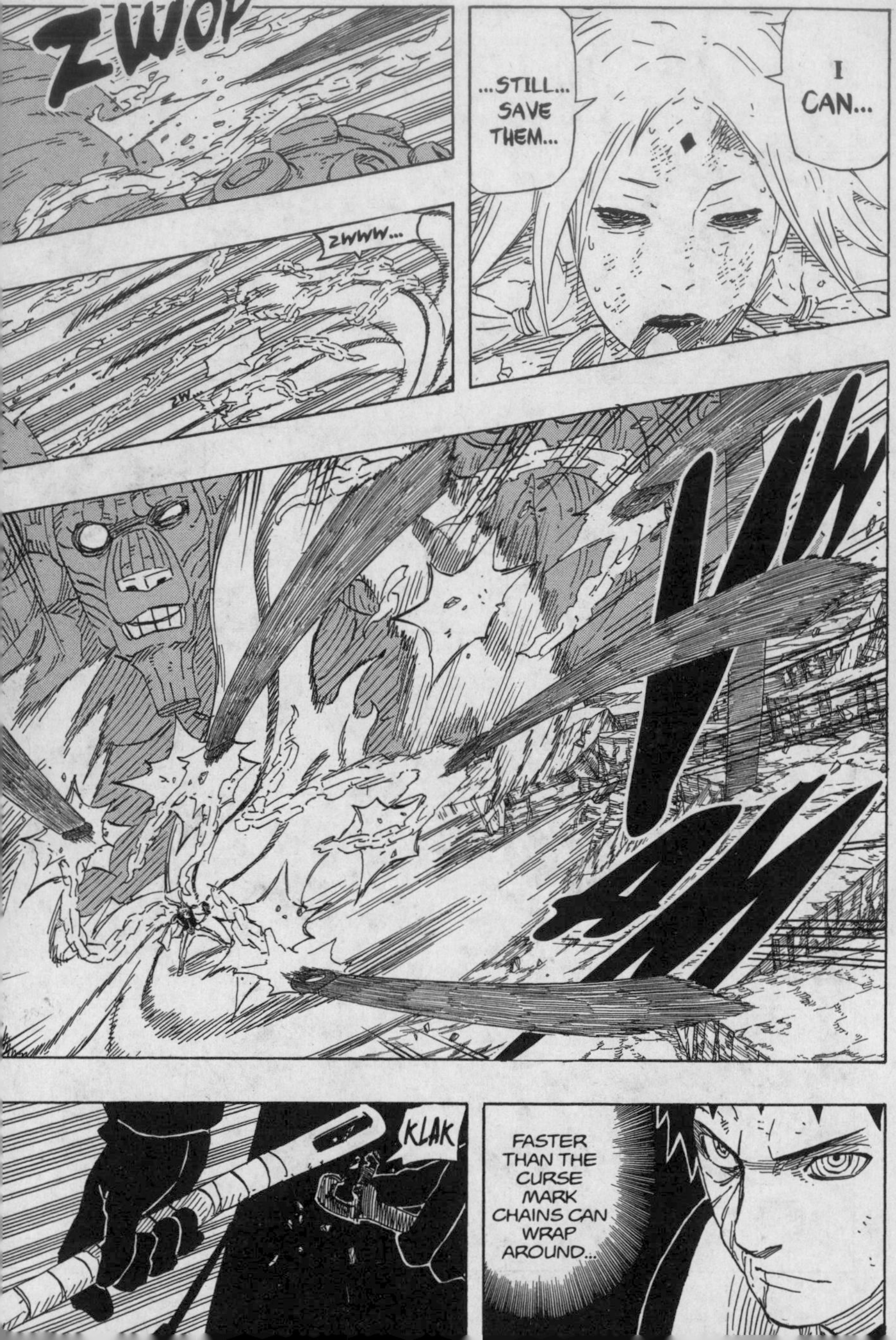
I CAN...
...STILL... SAVE THEM...
ZWOP
ZWWW...
ZW...
FASTER THAN THE CURSE MARK CHAINS CAN WRAP AROUND...
KLAK

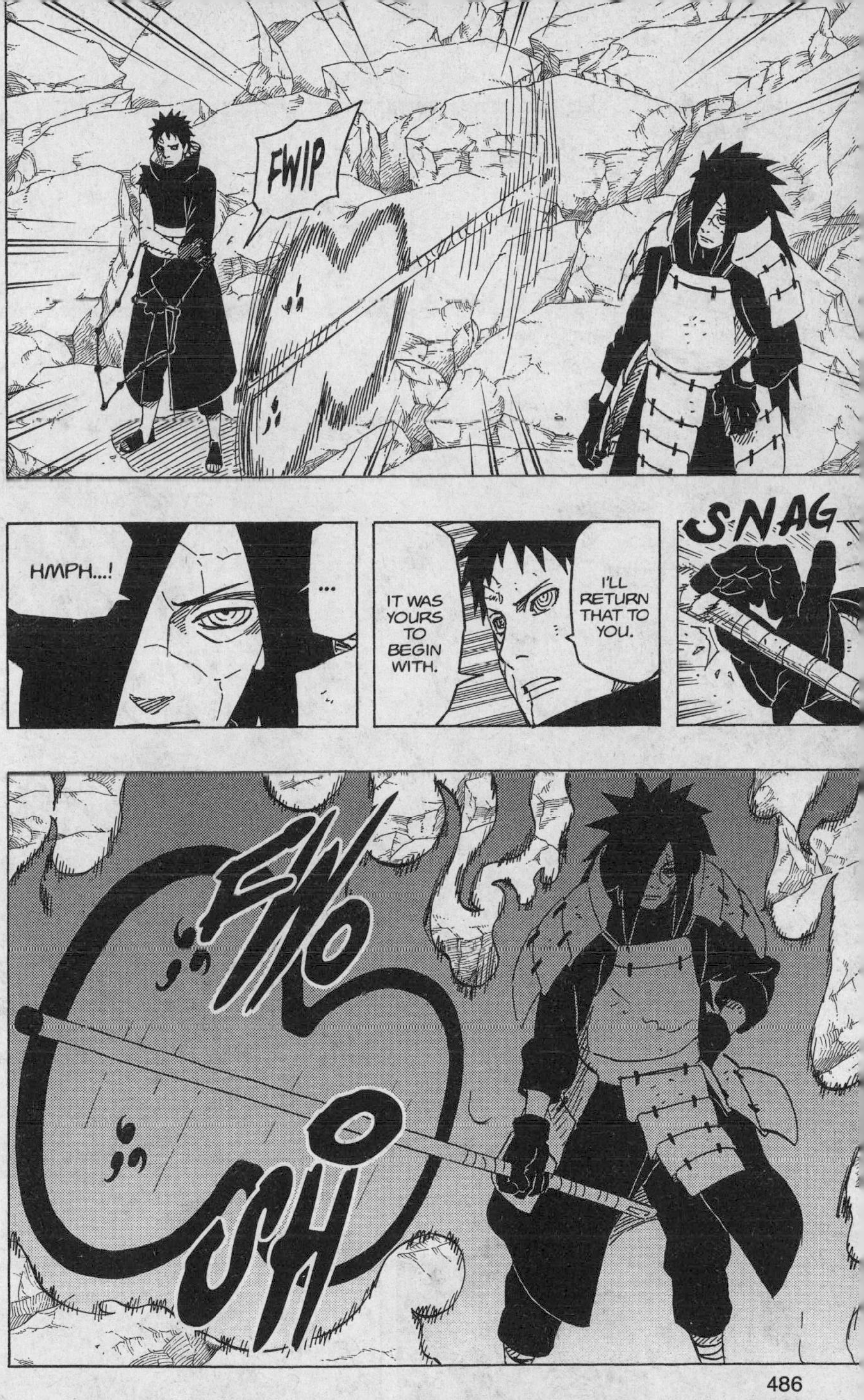
FWIP
SNAG
I'LL RETURN THAT TO YOU.
IT WAS YOURS TO BEGIN WITH.
...
HMPH...!

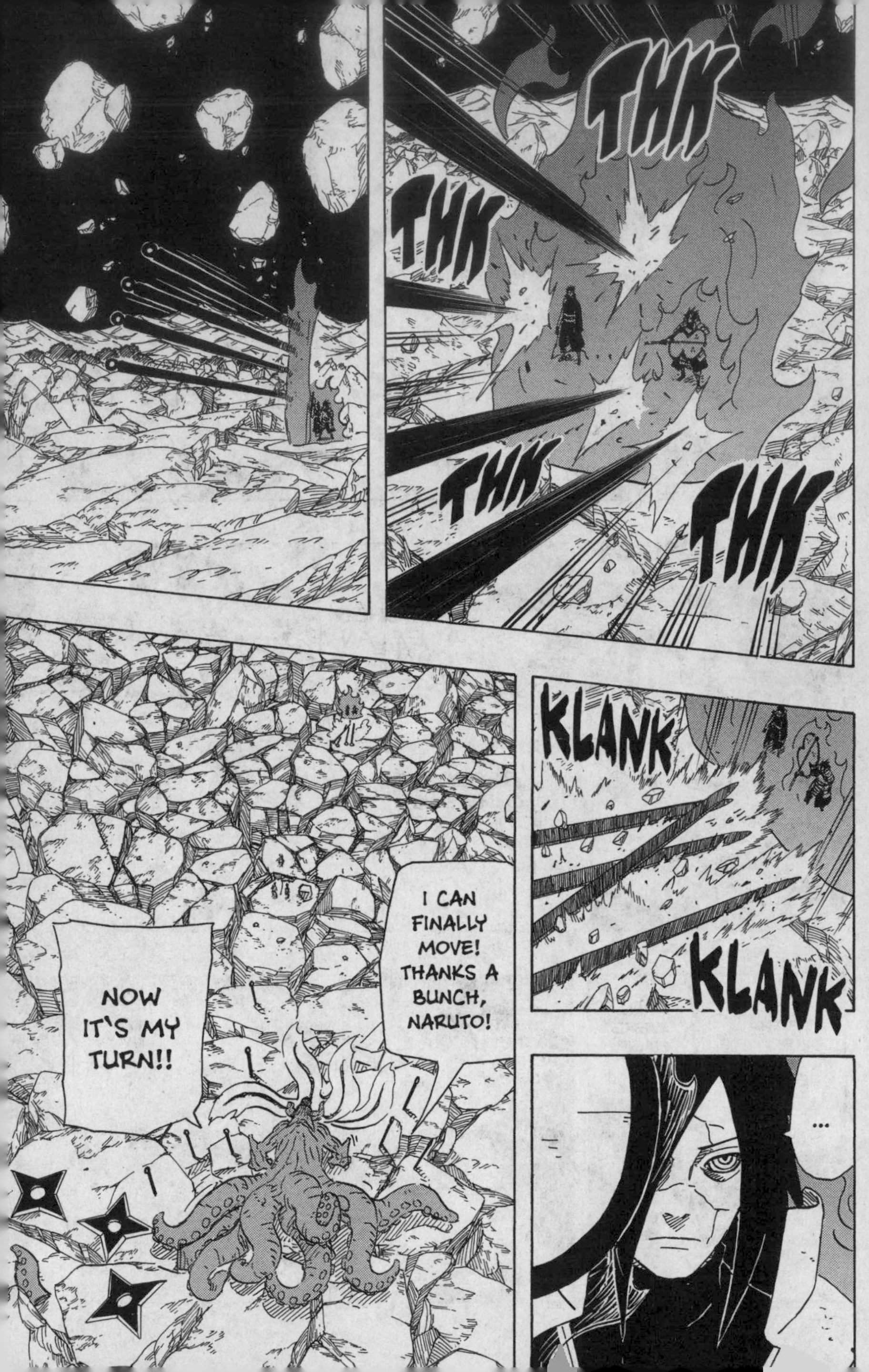
THK
THK
THK
THK
KLANK
KLANK
...
I CAN FINALLY MOVE! THANKS A BUNCH, NARUTO!
NOW IT'S MY TURN!!

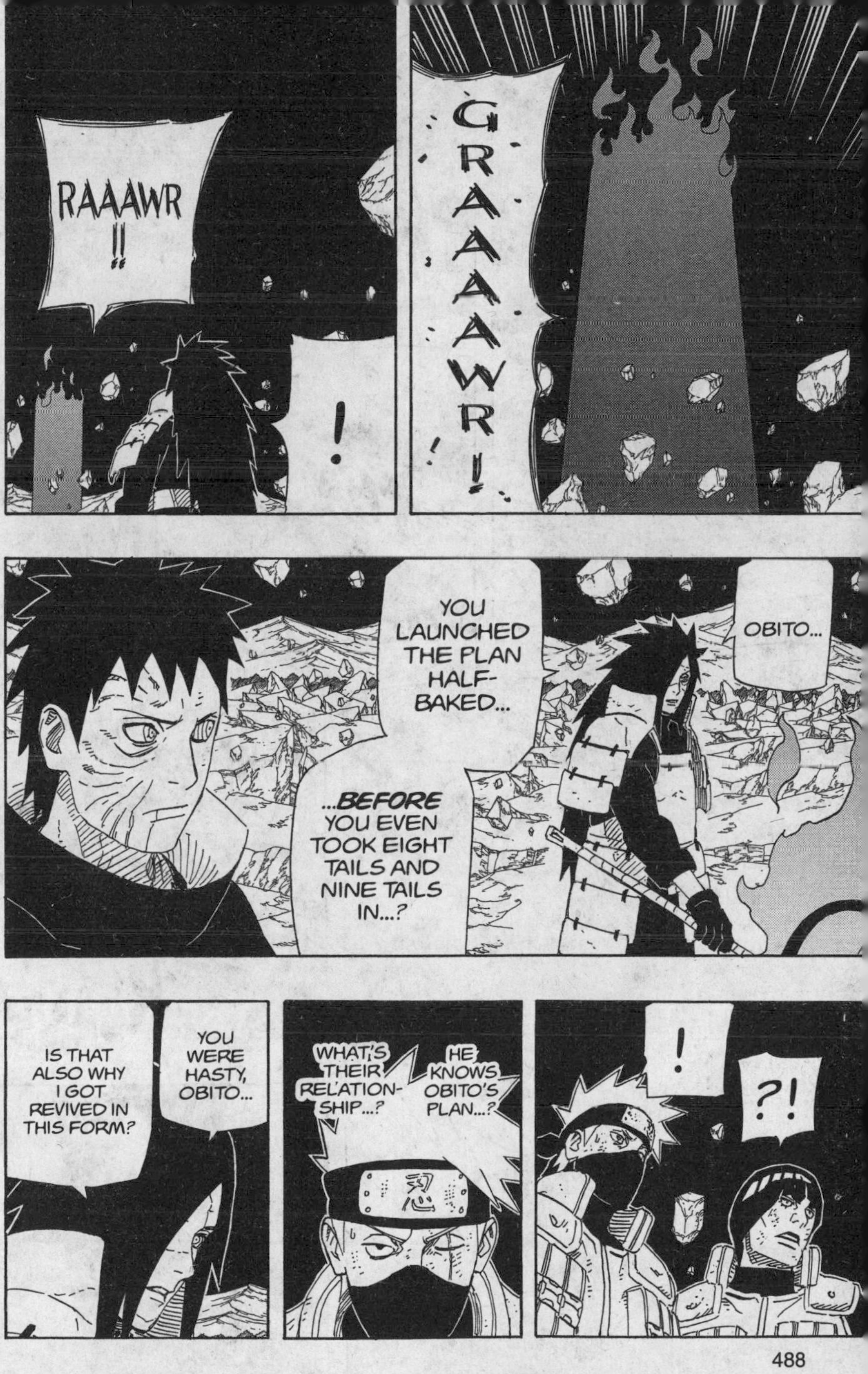
GRAAAAWR!!
RAAAWR!!
!
OBITO...
YOU LAUNCHED THE PLAN HALF-BAKED...
...**BEFORE** YOU EVEN TOOK EIGHT TAILS AND NINE TAILS IN...?
!
?!
HE KNOWS OBITO'S PLAN...?
WHAT'S THEIR RELATIONSHIP...?
YOU WERE HASTY, OBITO...
IS THAT ALSO WHY I GOT REVIVED IN THIS FORM?

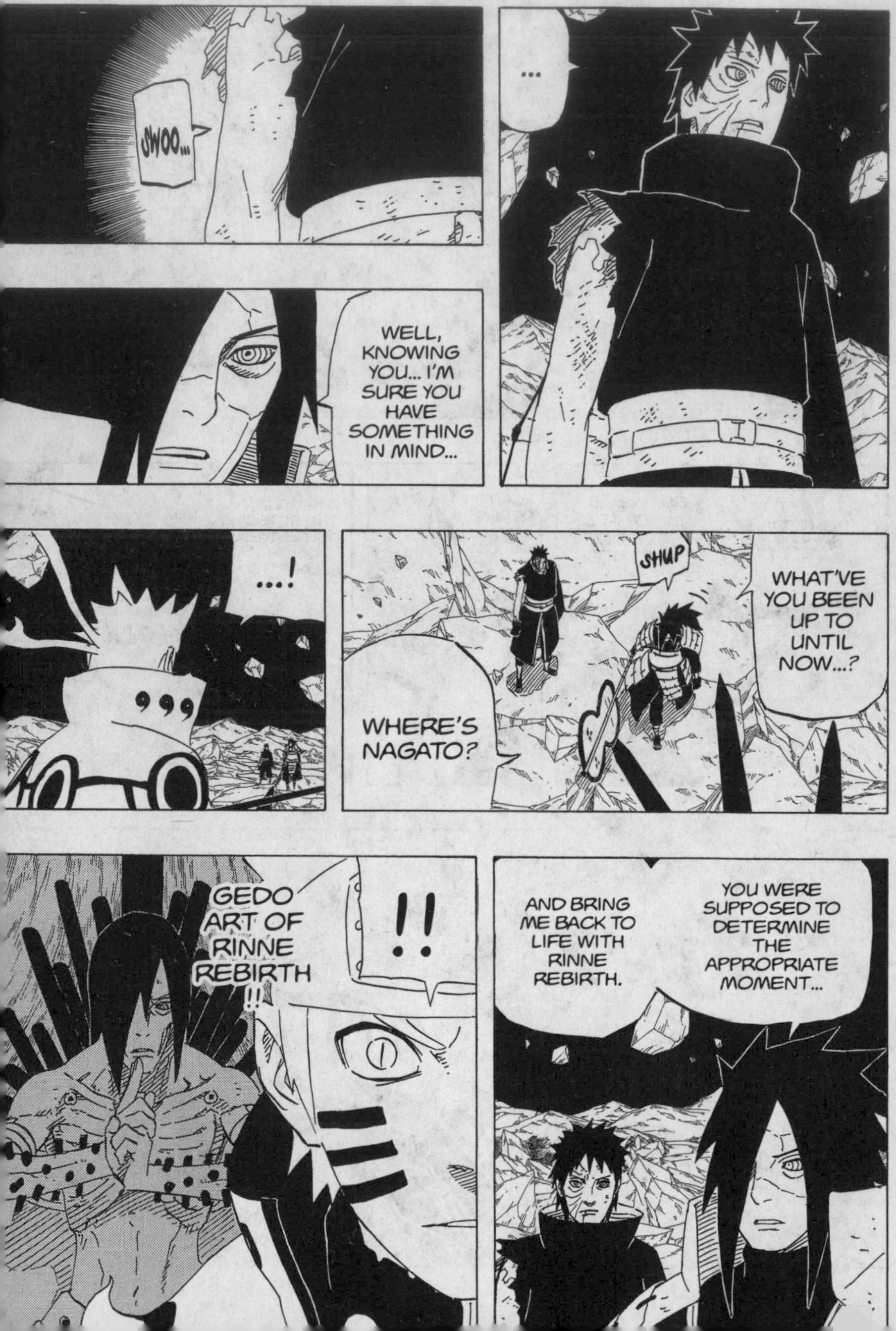
...
SWOO...
WELL, KNOWING YOU... I'M SURE YOU HAVE SOMETHING IN MIND...
SHUP
WHAT'VE YOU BEEN UP TO UNTIL NOW...?
WHERE'S NAGATO?
...!
YOU WERE SUPPOSED TO DETERMINE THE APPROPRIATE MOMENT...
AND BRING ME BACK TO LIFE WITH RINNE REBIRTH.
!!
GEDO ART OF RINNE REBIRTH!!

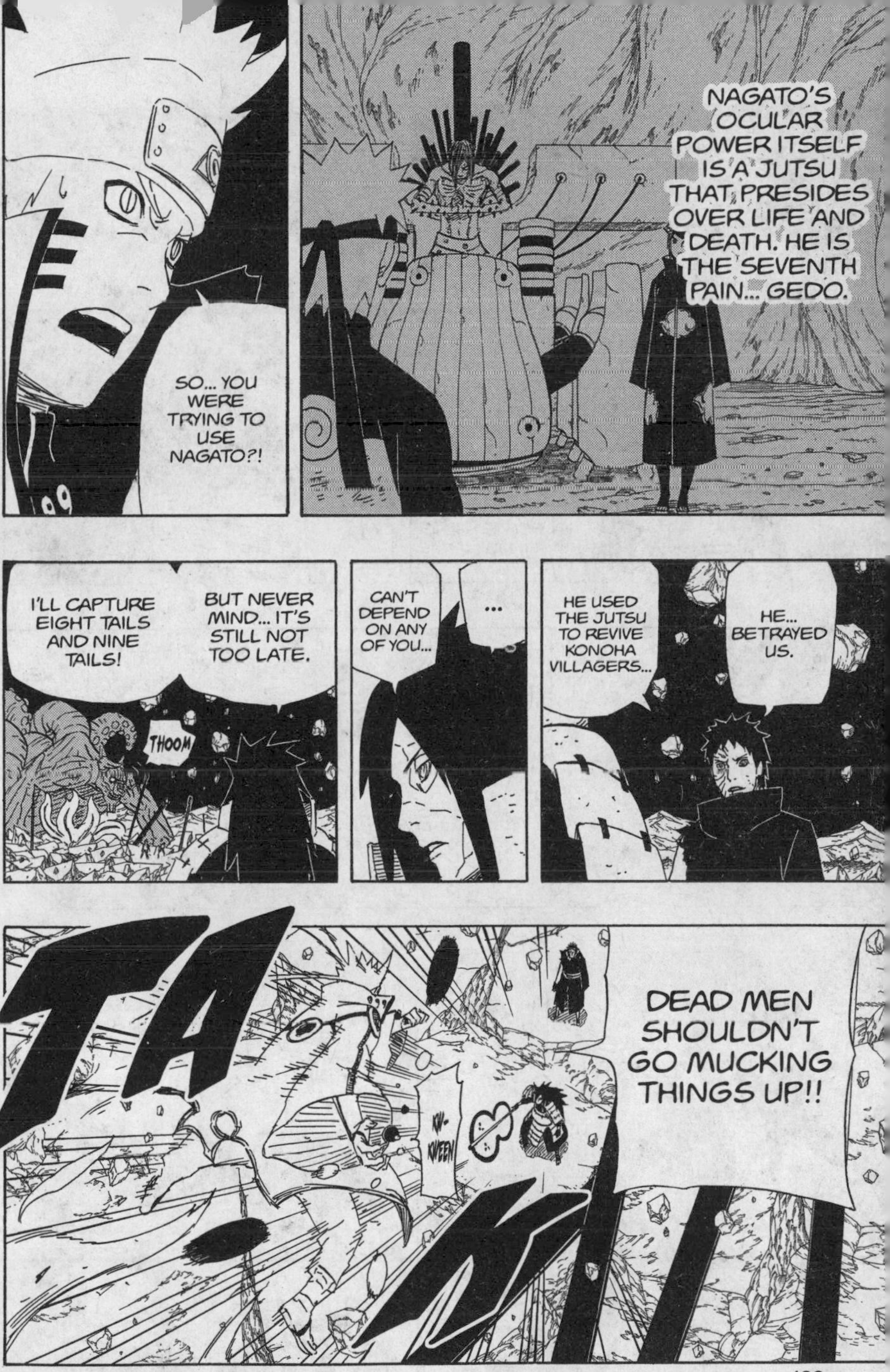
NAGATO'S OCULAR POWER ITSELF IS A JUTSU THAT PRESIDES OVER LIFE AND DEATH. HE IS THE SEVENTH PAIN... GEDO.
SO... YOU WERE TRYING TO USE NAGATO?!
HE... BETRAYED US.
HE USED THE JUTSU TO REVIVE KONOHA VILLAGERS...
...
CAN'T DEPEND ON ANY OF YOU...
BUT NEVER MIND... IT'S STILL NOT TOO LATE.
I'LL CAPTURE EIGHT TAILS AND NINE TAILS!
THOOM
DEAD MEN SHOULDN'T GO MUCKING THINGS UP!!
KW-KWEEN
TA

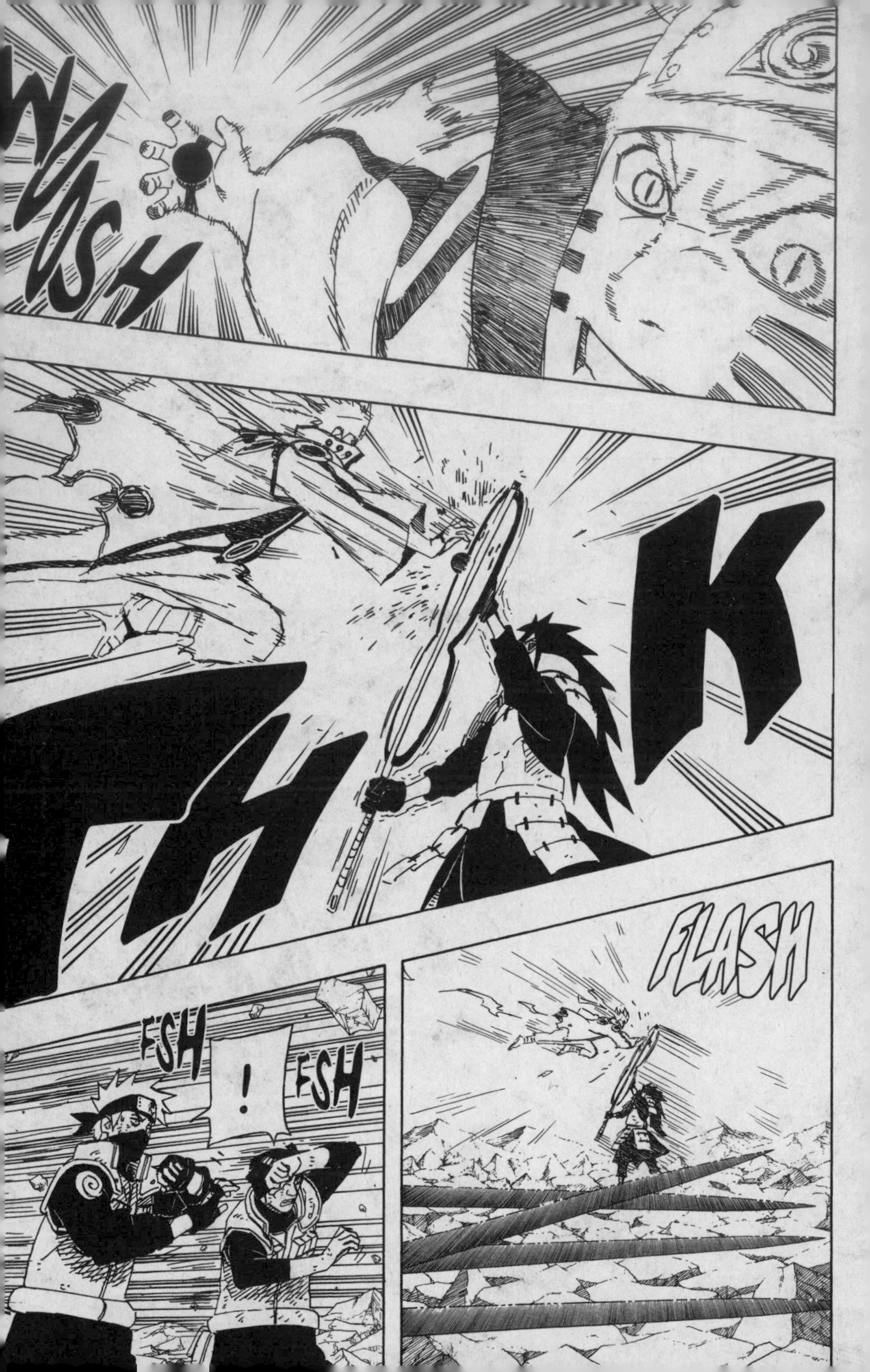
FLASH
FSH
!
FSH

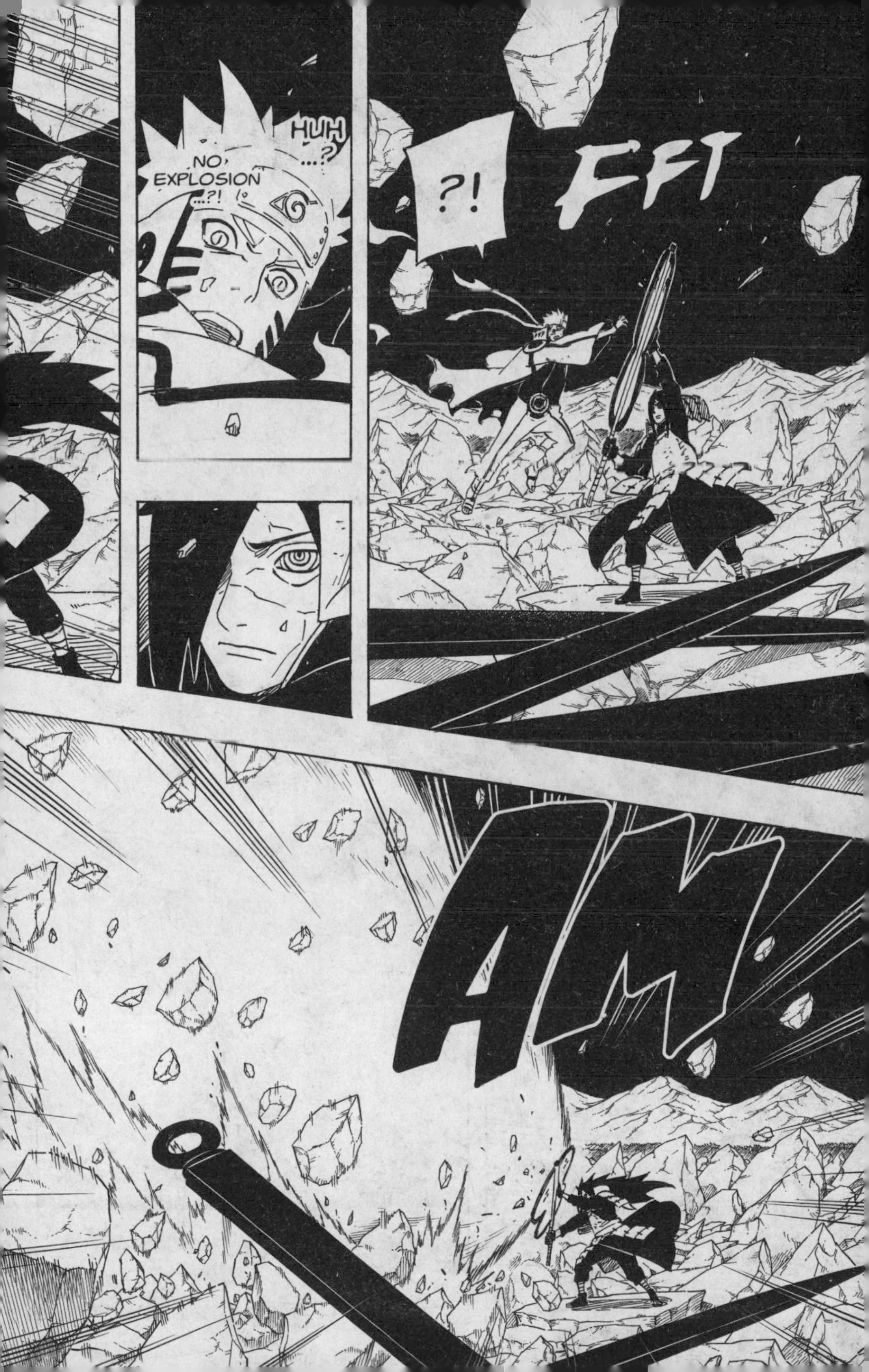
FFT
?!
HUH...?
NO, EXPLOSION...?!
AM!

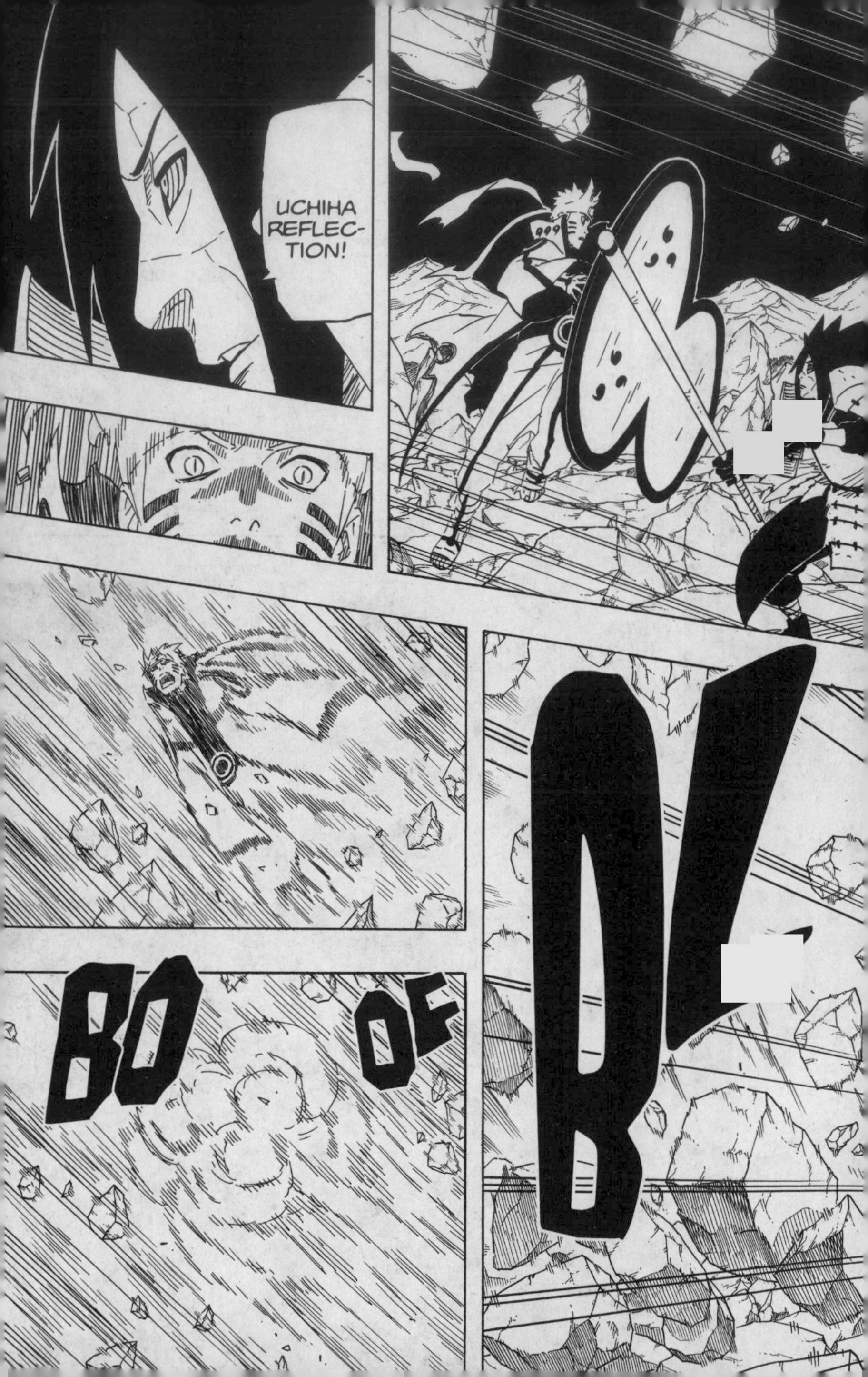
UCHIHA REFLECTION!
BOOF

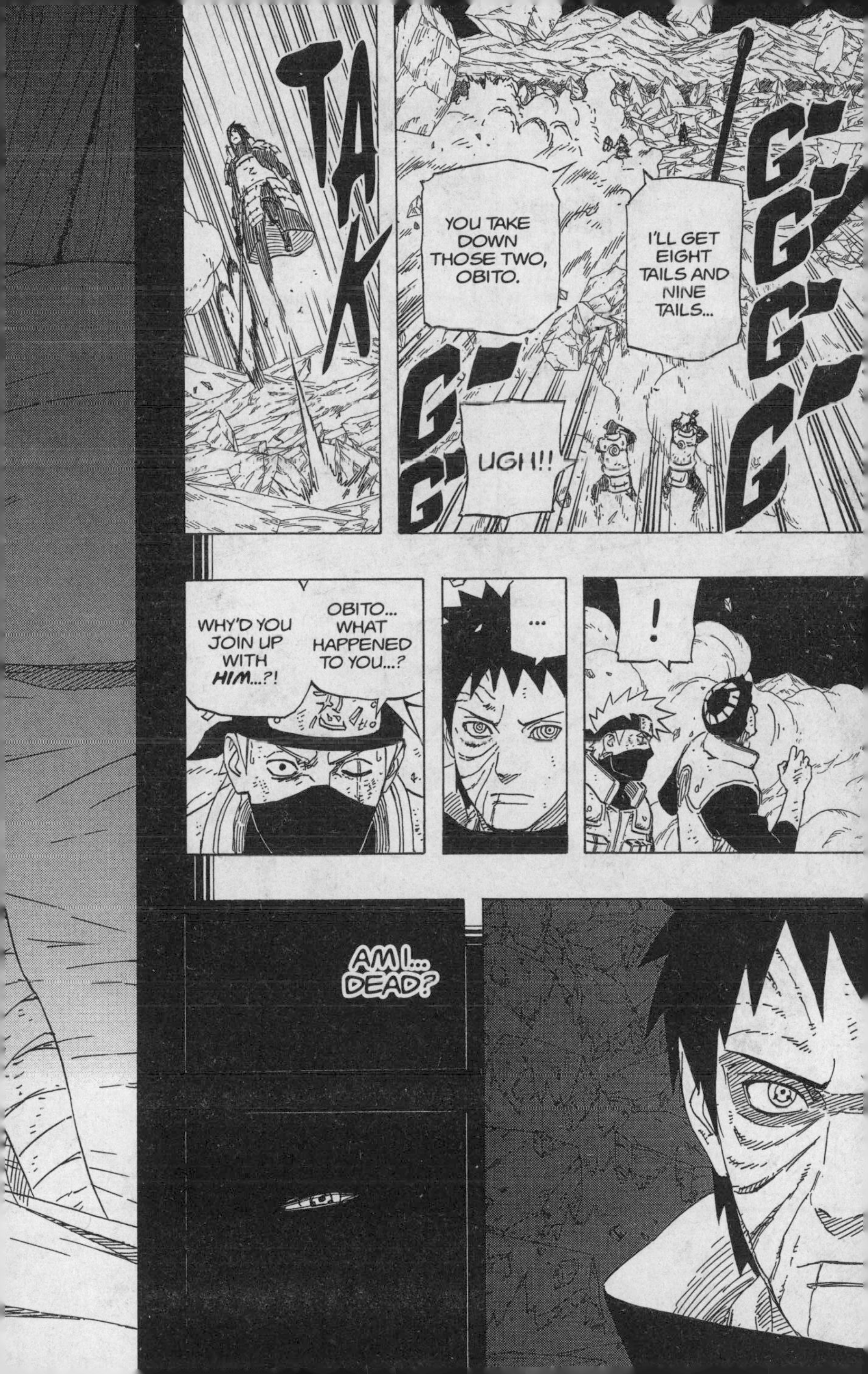
G' G' G' G'
I'LL GET EIGHT TAILS AND NINE TAILS...
YOU TAKE DOWN THOSE TWO, OBITO.
UGH!!
G' G'
TAK
!
...
OBITO... WHAT HAPPENED TO YOU...?
WHY'D YOU JOIN UP WITH *HIM*...?!
AM I... DEAD?

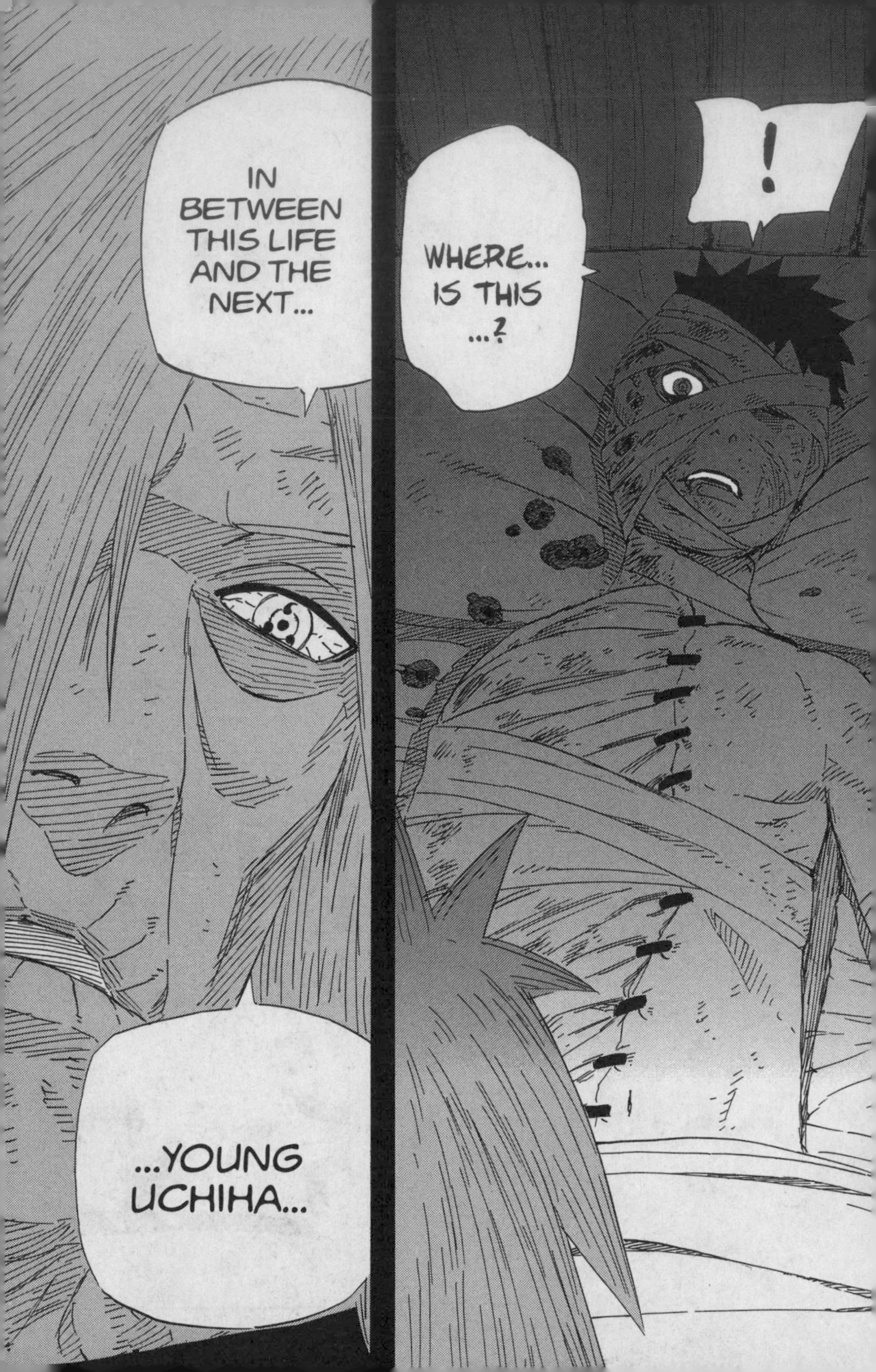
!
WHERE... IS THIS ...?
IN BETWEEN THIS LIFE AND THE NEXT...
...YOUNG UCHIHA...

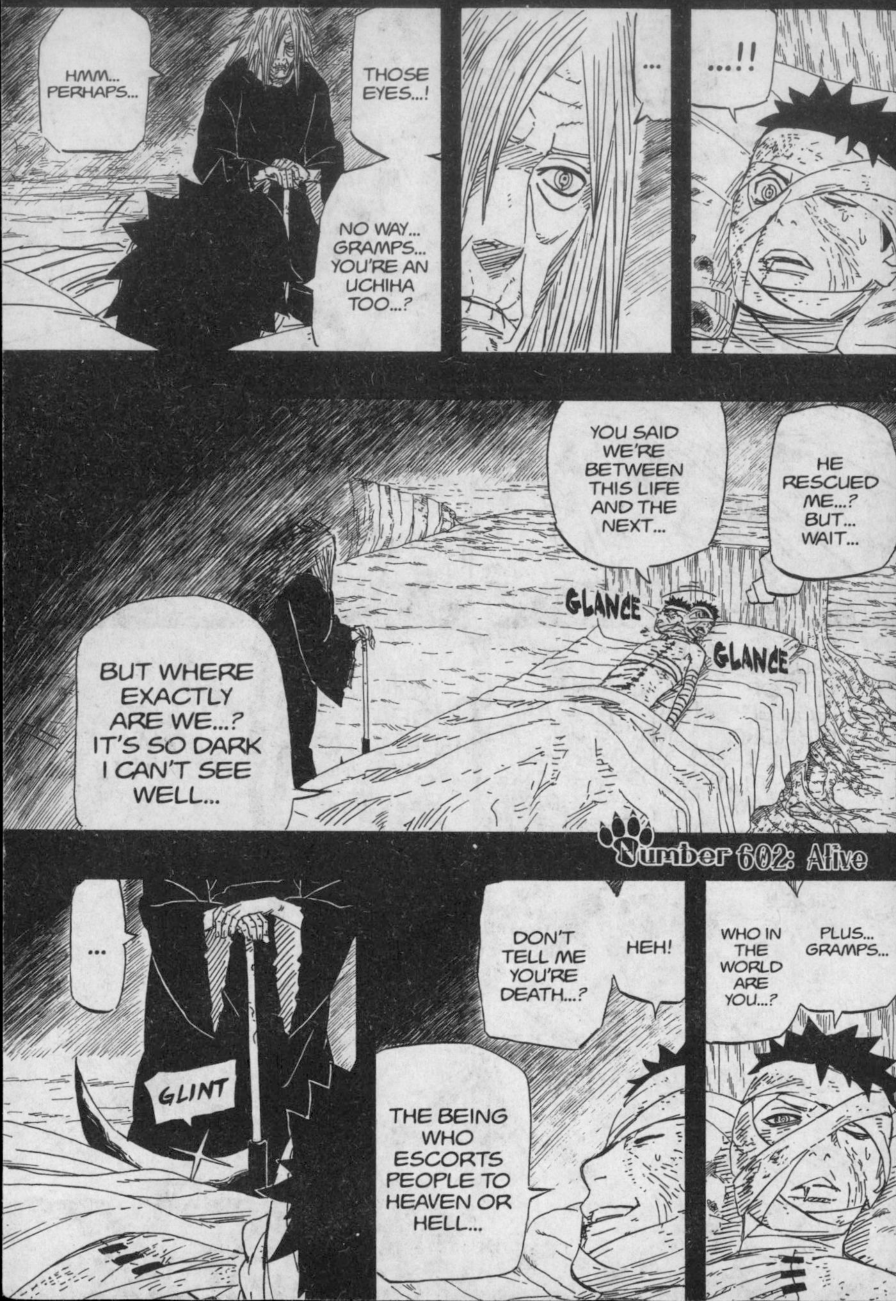
...!!
...
THOSE EYES...!
HMM... PERHAPS...
NO WAY... GRAMPS... YOU'RE AN UCHIHA TOO...?
HE RESCUED ME...? BUT... WAIT...
YOU SAID WE'RE BETWEEN THIS LIFE AND THE NEXT...
GLANCE
GLANCE
BUT WHERE EXACTLY ARE WE...? IT'S SO DARK I CAN'T SEE WELL...
Number 602: Alive
PLUS... GRAMPS...
WHO IN THE WORLD ARE YOU...?
HEH!
DON'T TELL ME YOU'RE DEATH...?
THE BEING WHO ESCORTS PEOPLE TO HEAVEN OR HELL...
...
GLINT

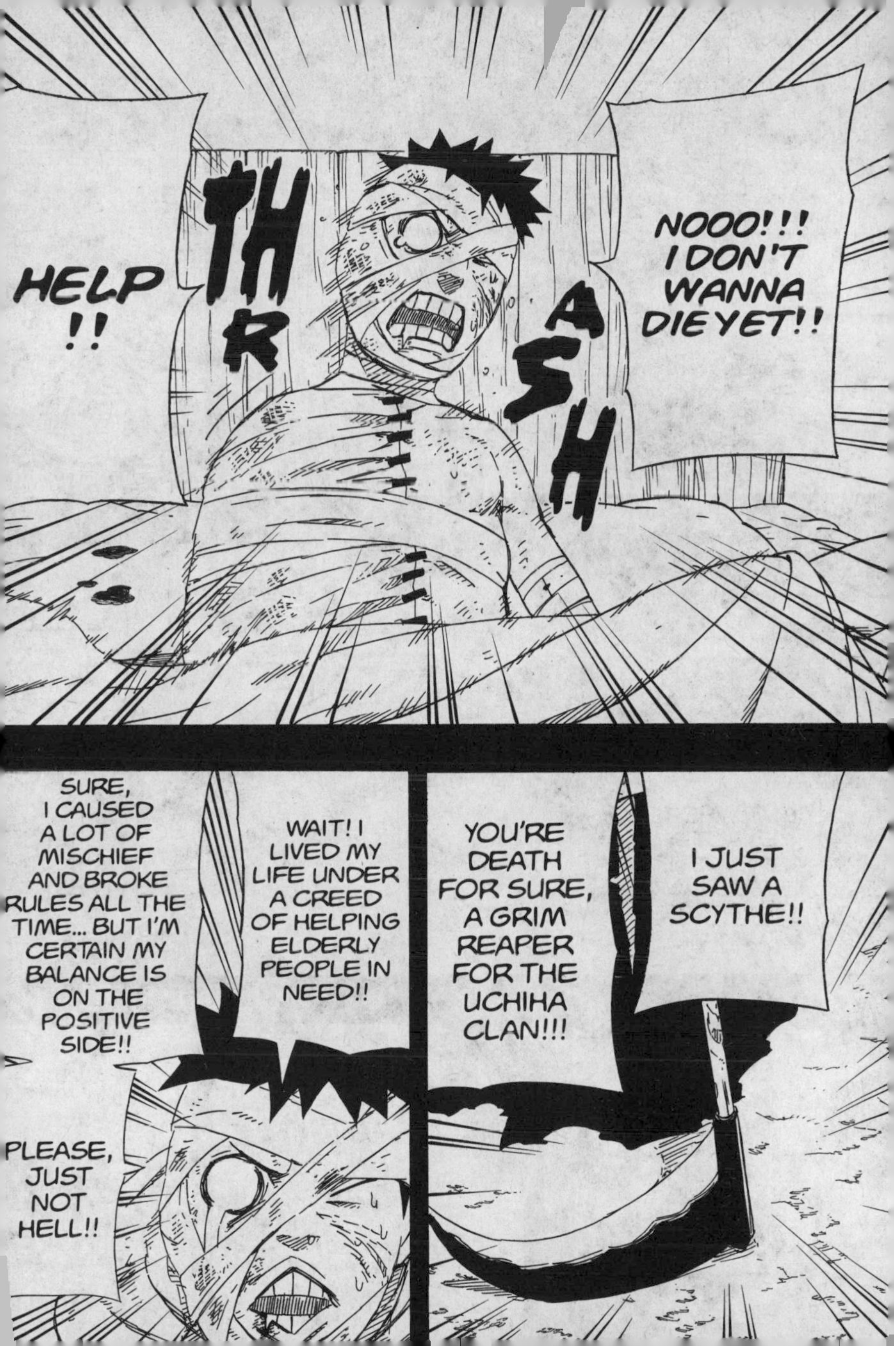
NOOO!!! I DON'T WANNA DIE YET!!
THRASH
HELP!!
I JUST SAW A SCYTHE!!
YOU'RE DEATH FOR SURE, A GRIM REAPER FOR THE UCHIHA CLAN!!!
WAIT! I LIVED MY LIFE UNDER A CREED OF HELPING ELDERLY PEOPLE IN NEED!!
SURE, I CAUSED A LOT OF MISCHIEF AND BROKE RULES ALL THE TIME... BUT I'M CERTAIN MY BALANCE IS ON THE POSITIVE SIDE!!
PLEASE, JUST NOT HELL!!

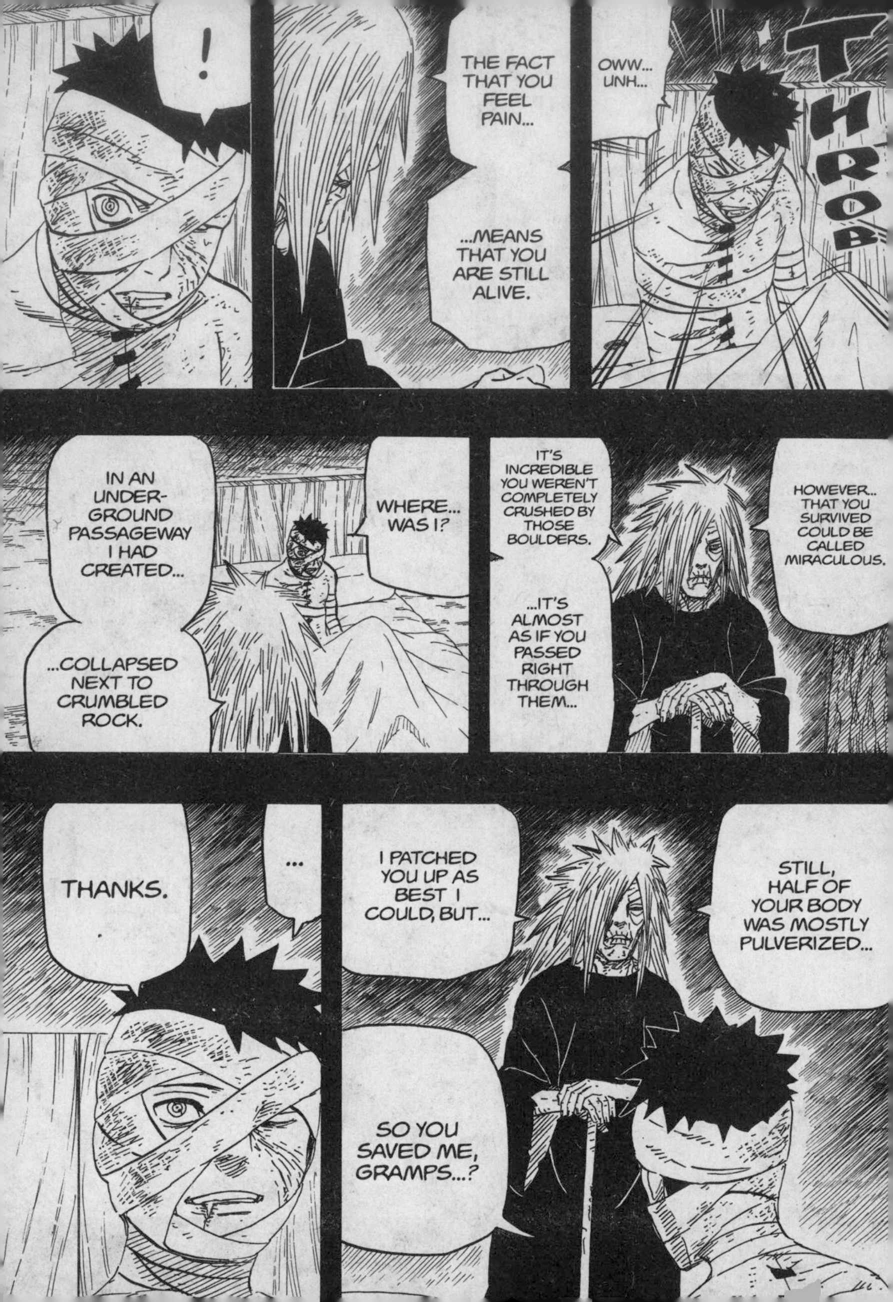
OWW... UNH...
THROB
THE FACT THAT YOU FEEL PAIN...
...MEANS THAT YOU ARE STILL ALIVE.
!
IT'S INCREDIBLE YOU WEREN'T COMPLETELY CRUSHED BY THOSE BOULDERS.
...IT'S ALMOST AS IF YOU PASSED RIGHT THROUGH THEM...
HOWEVER... THAT YOU SURVIVED COULD BE CALLED MIRACULOUS.
WHERE... WAS I?
IN AN UNDER-GROUND PASSAGEWAY I HAD CREATED...
...COLLAPSED NEXT TO CRUMBLED ROCK.
SO YOU SAVED ME, GRAMPS...?
I PATCHED YOU UP AS BEST I COULD, BUT...
STILL, HALF OF YOUR BODY WAS MOSTLY PULVERIZED...
...
THANKS.

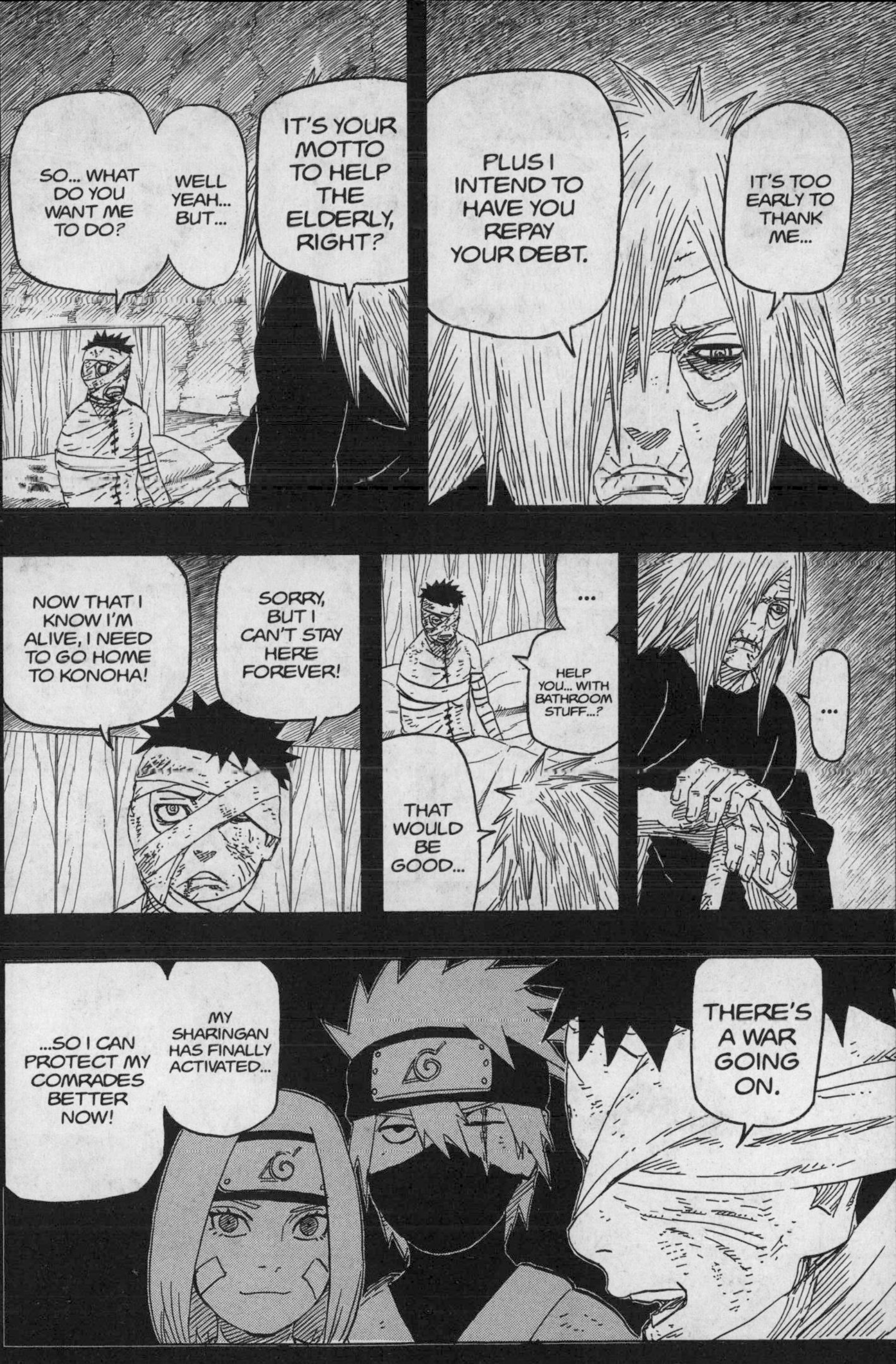
IT'S TOO EARLY TO THANK ME...
PLUS I INTEND TO HAVE YOU REPAY YOUR DEBT.
IT'S YOUR MOTTO TO HELP THE ELDERLY, RIGHT?
WELL YEAH... BUT...
SO... WHAT DO YOU WANT ME TO DO?
...
...
HELP YOU... WITH BATHROOM STUFF...?
THAT WOULD BE GOOD...
SORRY, BUT I CAN'T STAY HERE FOREVER!
NOW THAT I KNOW I'M ALIVE, I NEED TO GO HOME TO KONOHA!
THERE'S A WAR GOING ON.
MY SHARINGAN HAS FINALLY ACTIVATED...
...SO I CAN PROTECT MY COMRADES BETTER NOW!

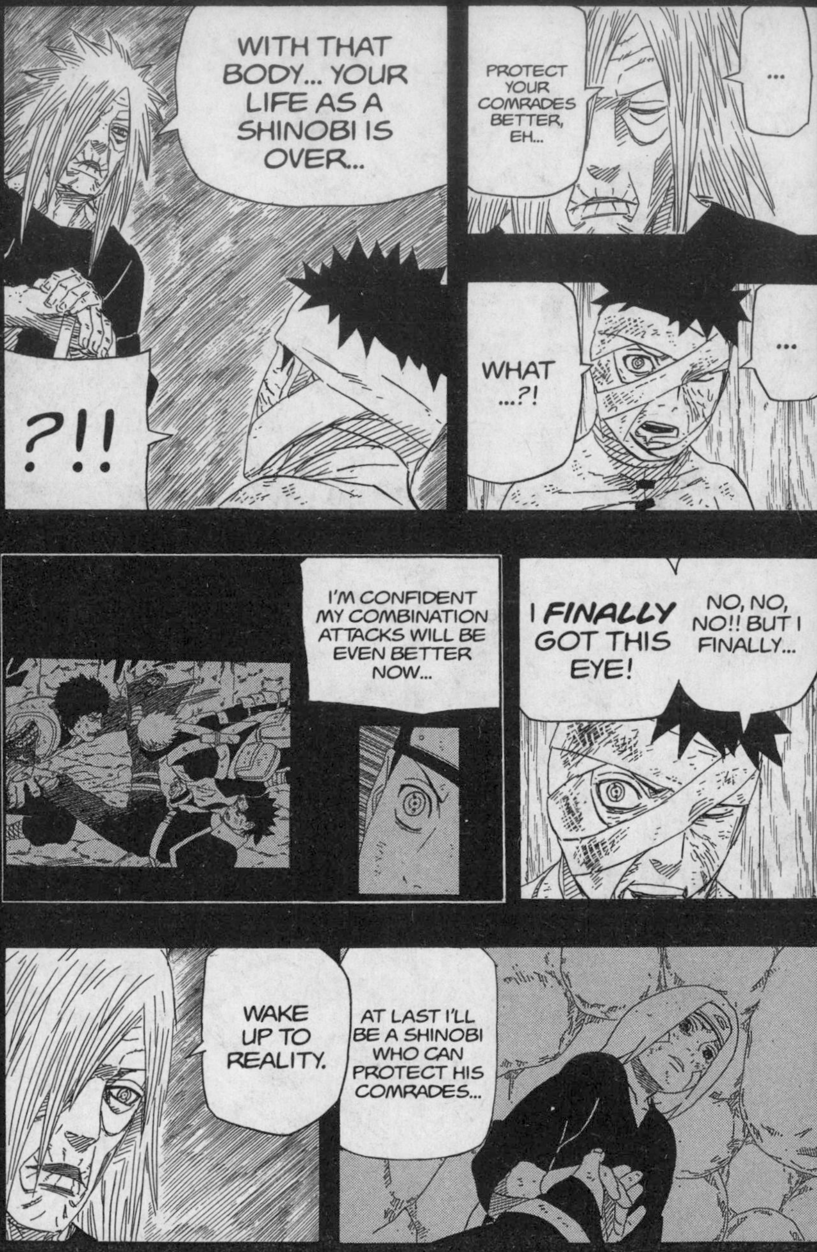
...
PROTECT YOUR COMRADES BETTER, EH...
...
WHAT ...?!
WITH THAT BODY... YOUR LIFE AS A SHINOBI IS OVER...
?!!
NO, NO, NO!! BUT I FINALLY...
I FINALLY GOT THIS EYE!
I'M CONFIDENT MY COMBINATION ATTACKS WILL BE EVEN BETTER NOW...
AT LAST I'LL BE A SHINOBI WHO CAN PROTECT HIS COMRADES...
WAKE UP TO REALITY.

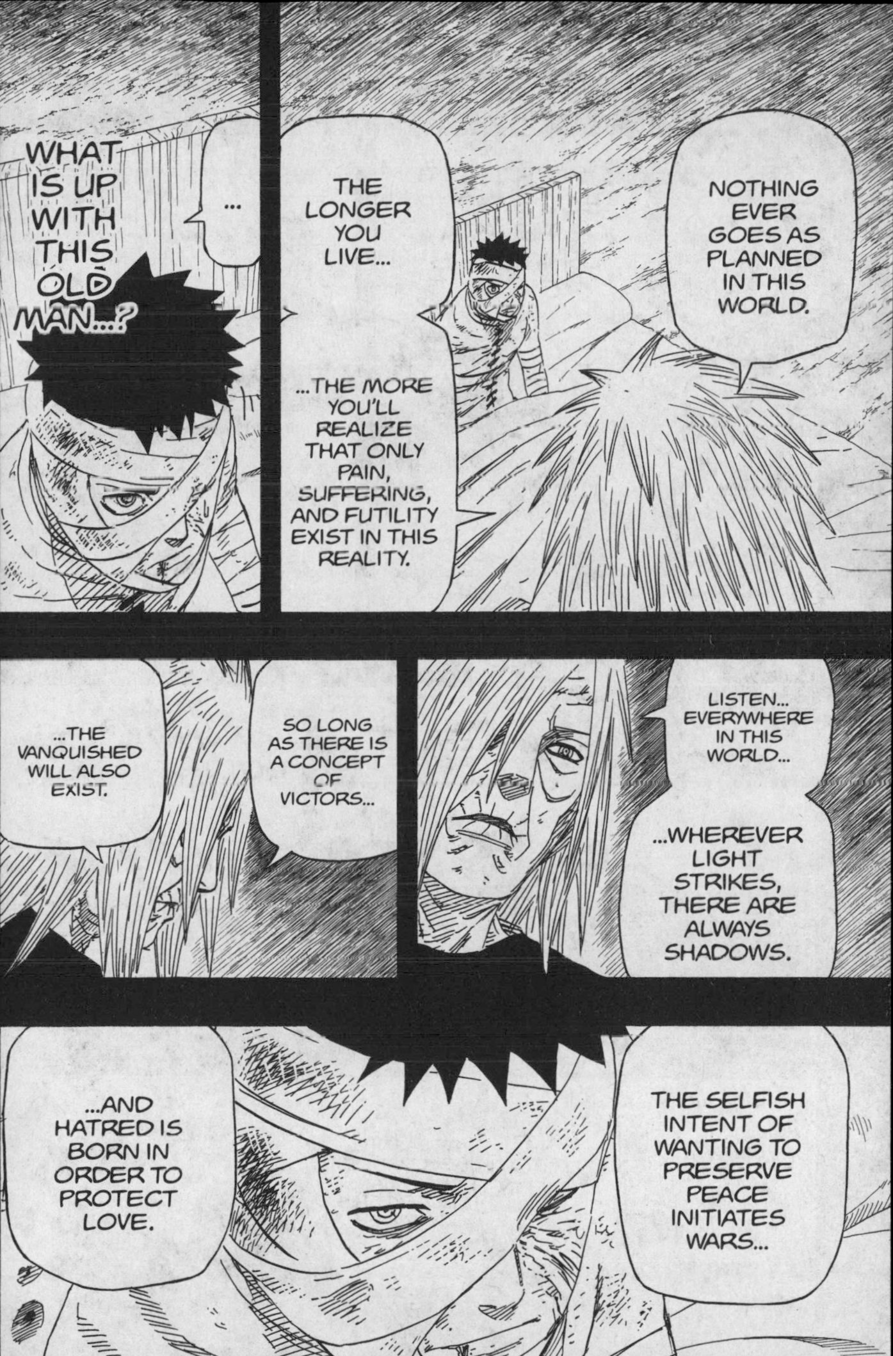

NOTHING EVER GOES AS PLANNED IN THIS WORLD.
THE LONGER YOU LIVE...
...THE MORE YOU'LL REALIZE THAT ONLY PAIN, SUFFERING, AND FUTILITY EXIST IN THIS REALITY.
...
WHAT IS UP WITH THIS OLD MAN...?
LISTEN... EVERYWHERE IN THIS WORLD...
...WHEREVER LIGHT STRIKES, THERE ARE ALWAYS SHADOWS.
SO LONG AS THERE IS A CONCEPT OF VICTORS...
...THE VANQUISHED WILL ALSO EXIST.
THE SELFISH INTENT OF WANTING TO PRESERVE PEACE INITIATES WARS...
...AND HATRED IS BORN IN ORDER TO PROTECT LOVE.

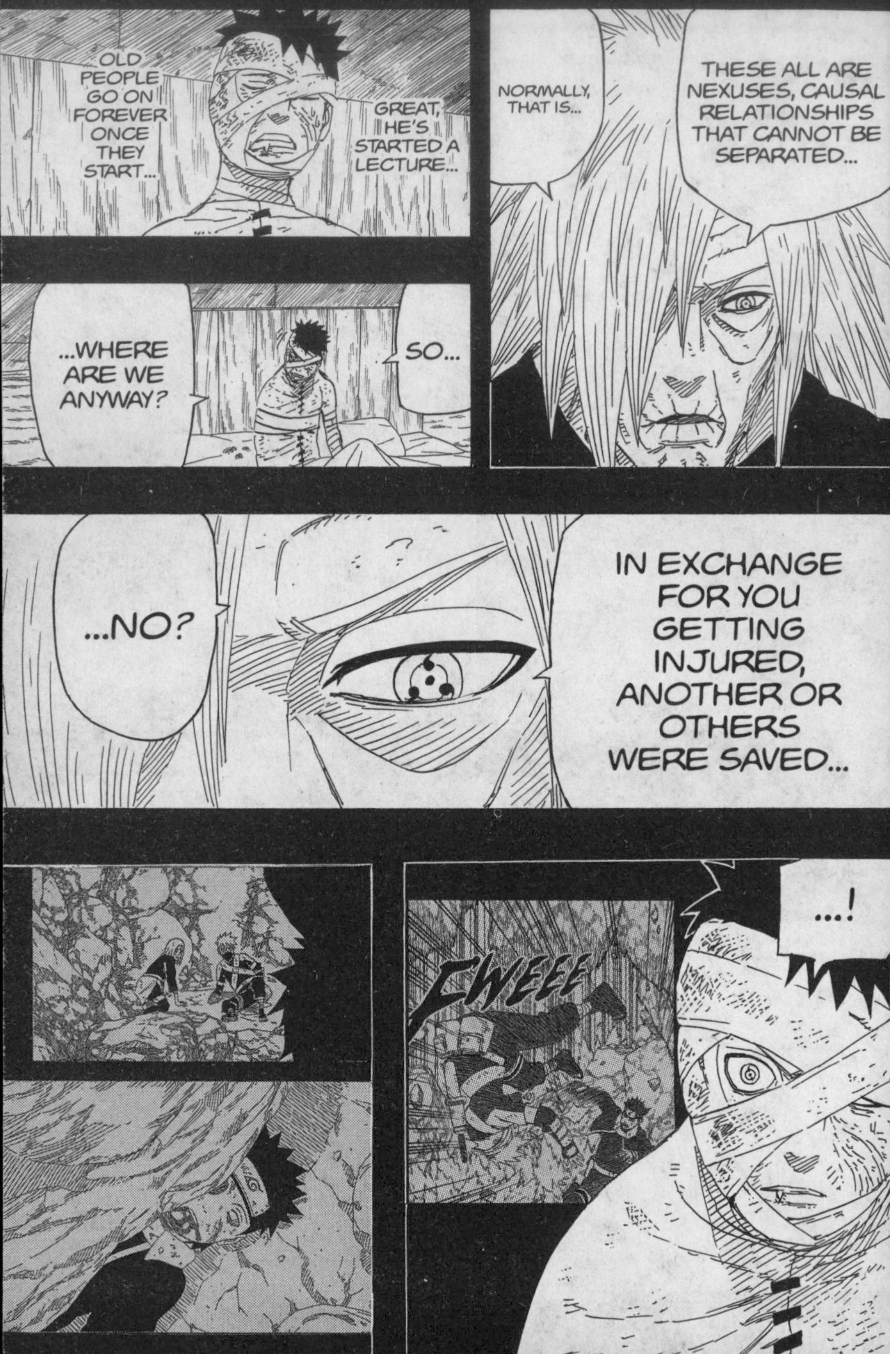
THESE ALL ARE NEXUSES, CAUSAL RELATIONSHIPS THAT CANNOT BE SEPARATED...
NORMALLY, THAT IS...
GREAT, HE'S STARTED A LECTURE...
OLD PEOPLE GO ON FOREVER ONCE THEY START...
SO...
...WHERE ARE WE ANYWAY?
IN EXCHANGE FOR YOU GETTING INJURED, ANOTHER OR OTHERS WERE SAVED...
...NO?
...!
CWEEE

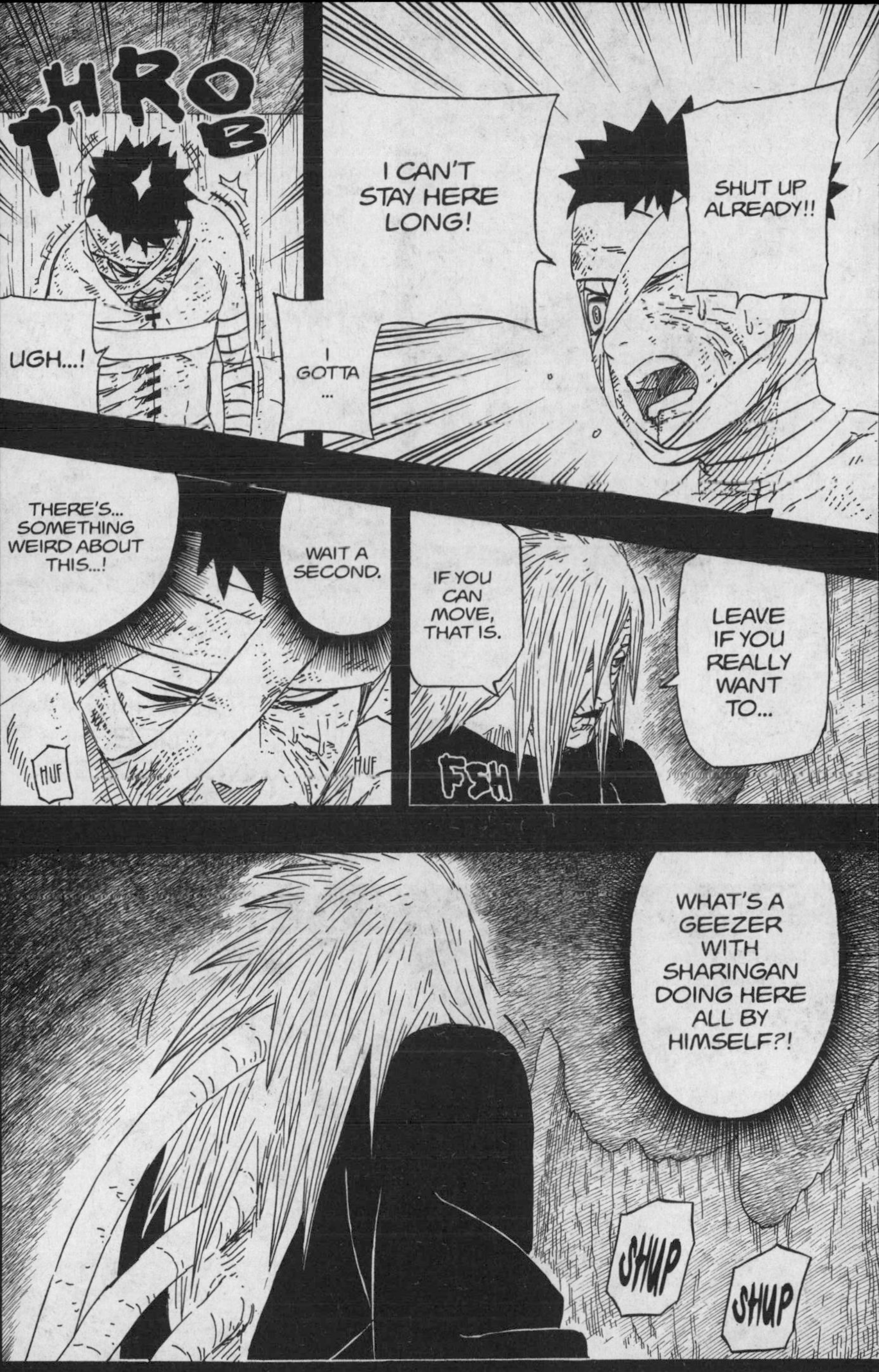
SHUT UP ALREADY!!
I CAN'T STAY HERE LONG!
I GOTTA ...
THROB
UGH...!
LEAVE IF YOU REALLY WANT TO...
IF YOU CAN MOVE, THAT IS.
FSH
WAIT A SECOND.
THERE'S... SOMETHING WEIRD ABOUT THIS...!
HUF
HUF
WHAT'S A GEEZER WITH SHARINGAN DOING HERE ALL BY HIMSELF?!
SHUP
SHUP

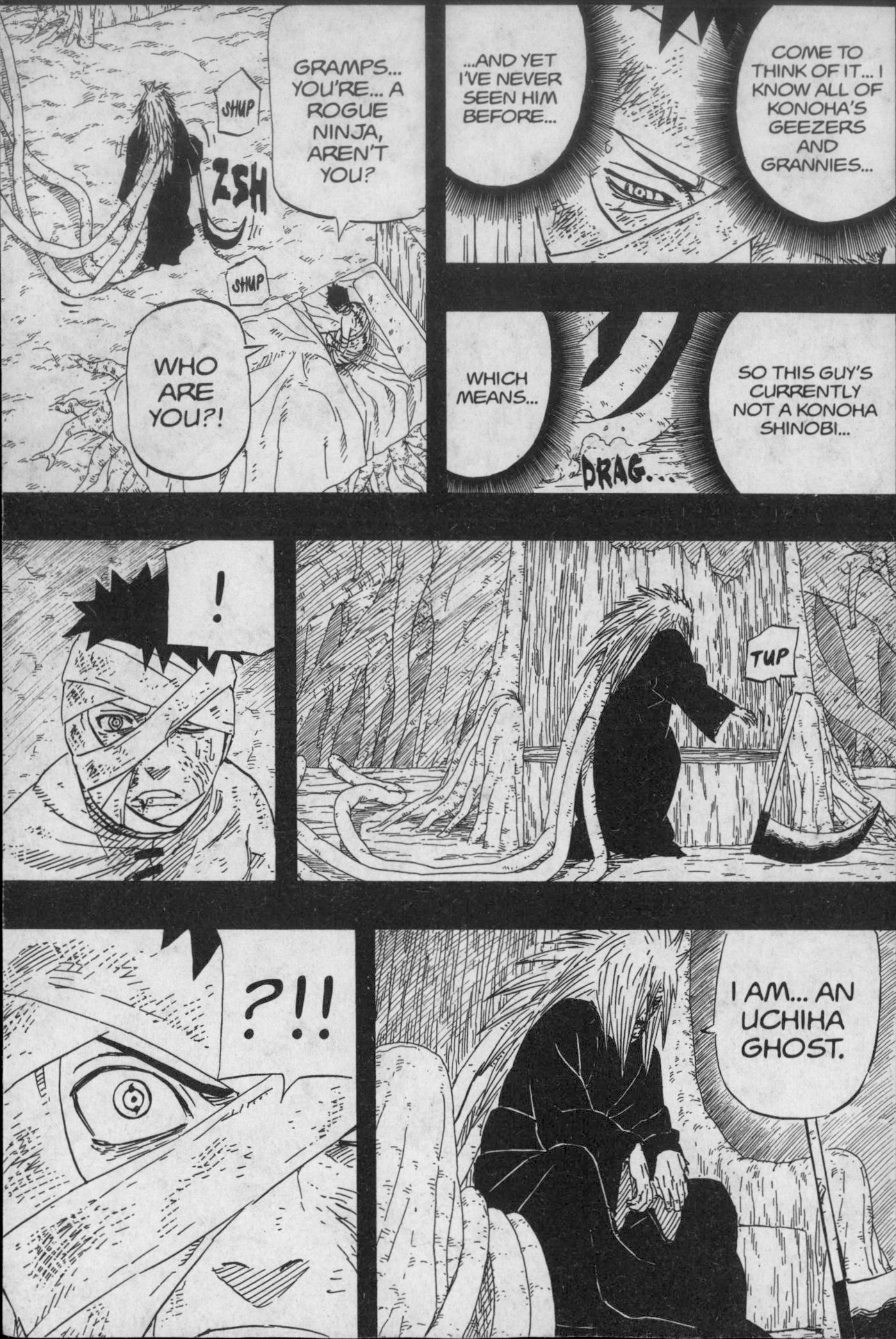
COME TO THINK OF IT... I KNOW ALL OF KONOHA'S GEEZERS AND GRANNIES...
...AND YET I'VE NEVER SEEN HIM BEFORE...
SO THIS GUY'S CURRENTLY NOT A KONOHA SHINOBI...
WHICH MEANS...
DRAG...
GRAMPS... YOU'RE... A ROGUE NINJA, AREN'T YOU?
SHUP
ZSH
SHUP
WHO ARE YOU?!
TUP
!
I AM... AN UCHIHA GHOST.
?!!

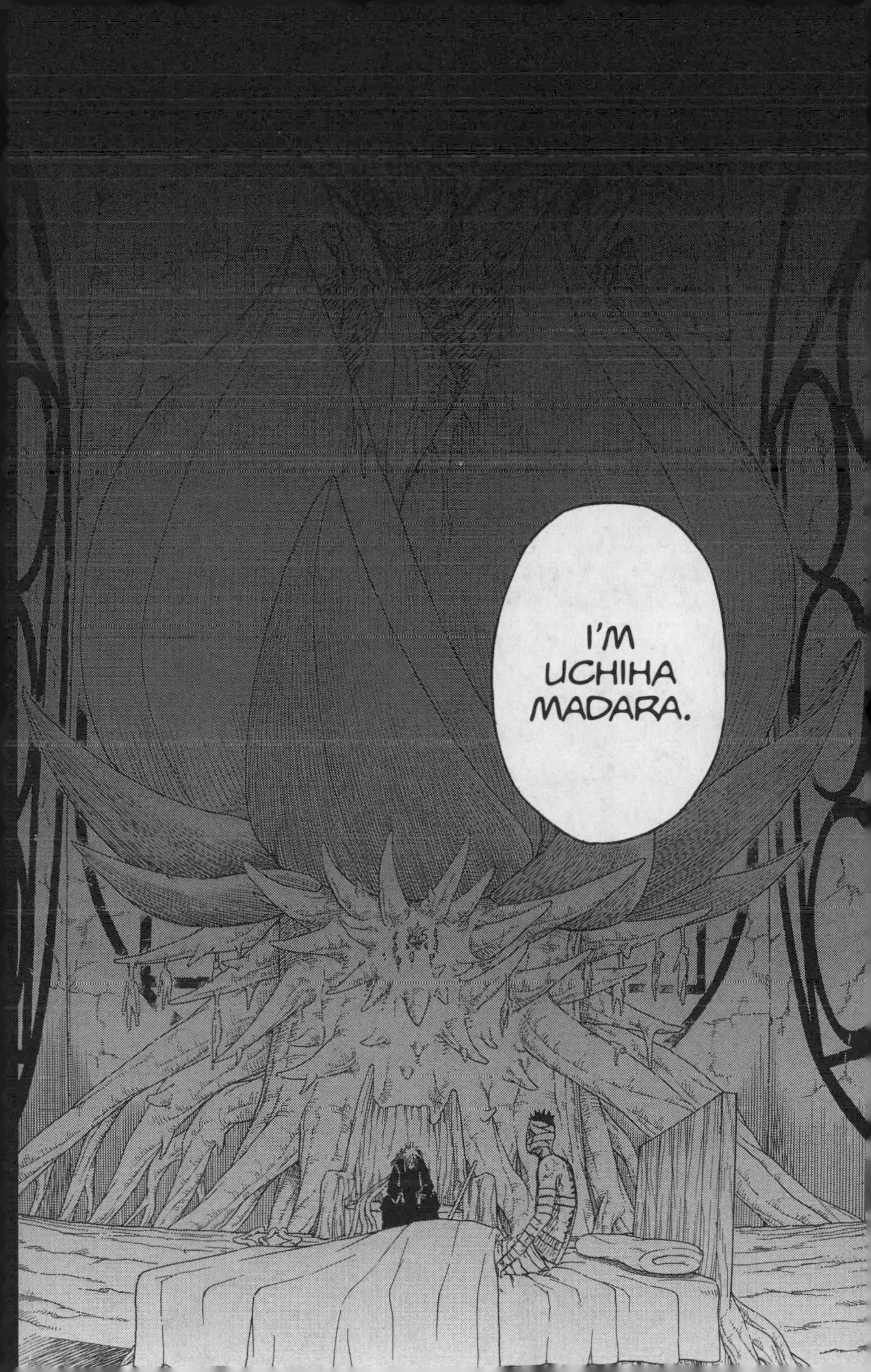
I'M UCHIHA MADARA.

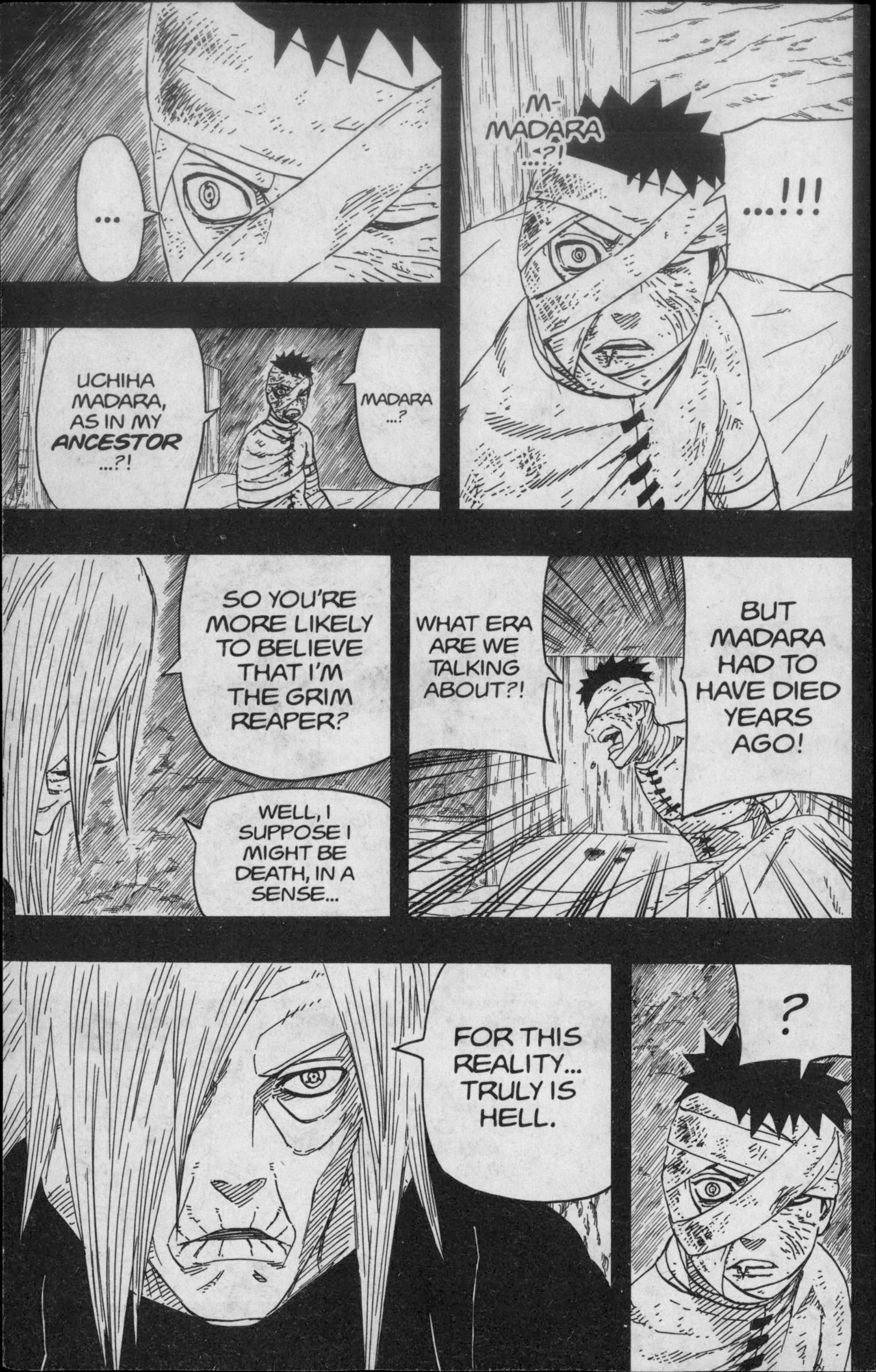
M-MADARA ...?!
...!!!
...
MADARA ...?
UCHIHA MADARA, AS IN MY ANCESTOR ...?!
BUT MADARA HAD TO HAVE DIED YEARS AGO!
WHAT ERA ARE WE TALKING ABOUT?!
SO YOU'RE MORE LIKELY TO BELIEVE THAT I'M THE GRIM REAPER?
WELL, I SUPPOSE I MIGHT BE DEATH, IN A SENSE...
?
FOR THIS REALITY... TRULY IS HELL.

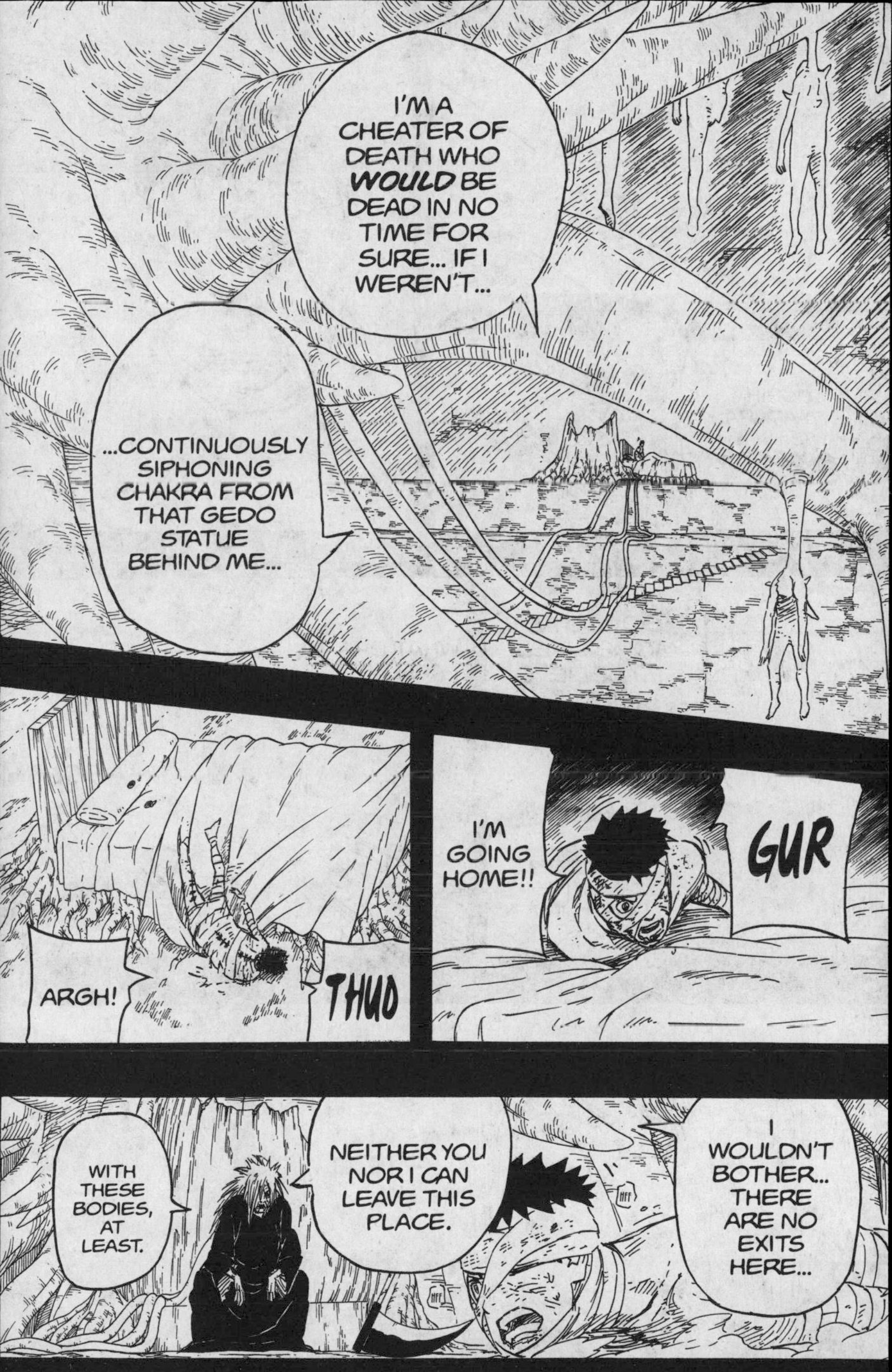
I'M A CHEATER OF DEATH WHO **WOULD** BE DEAD IN NO TIME FOR SURE... IF I WEREN'T...
...CONTINUOUSLY SIPHONING CHAKRA FROM THAT GEDO STATUE BEHIND ME...
I'M GOING HOME!!
GUR
THUD
ARGH!
I WOULDN'T BOTHER... THERE ARE NO EXITS HERE...
NEITHER YOU NOR I CAN LEAVE THIS PLACE.
WITH THESE BODIES, AT LEAST.

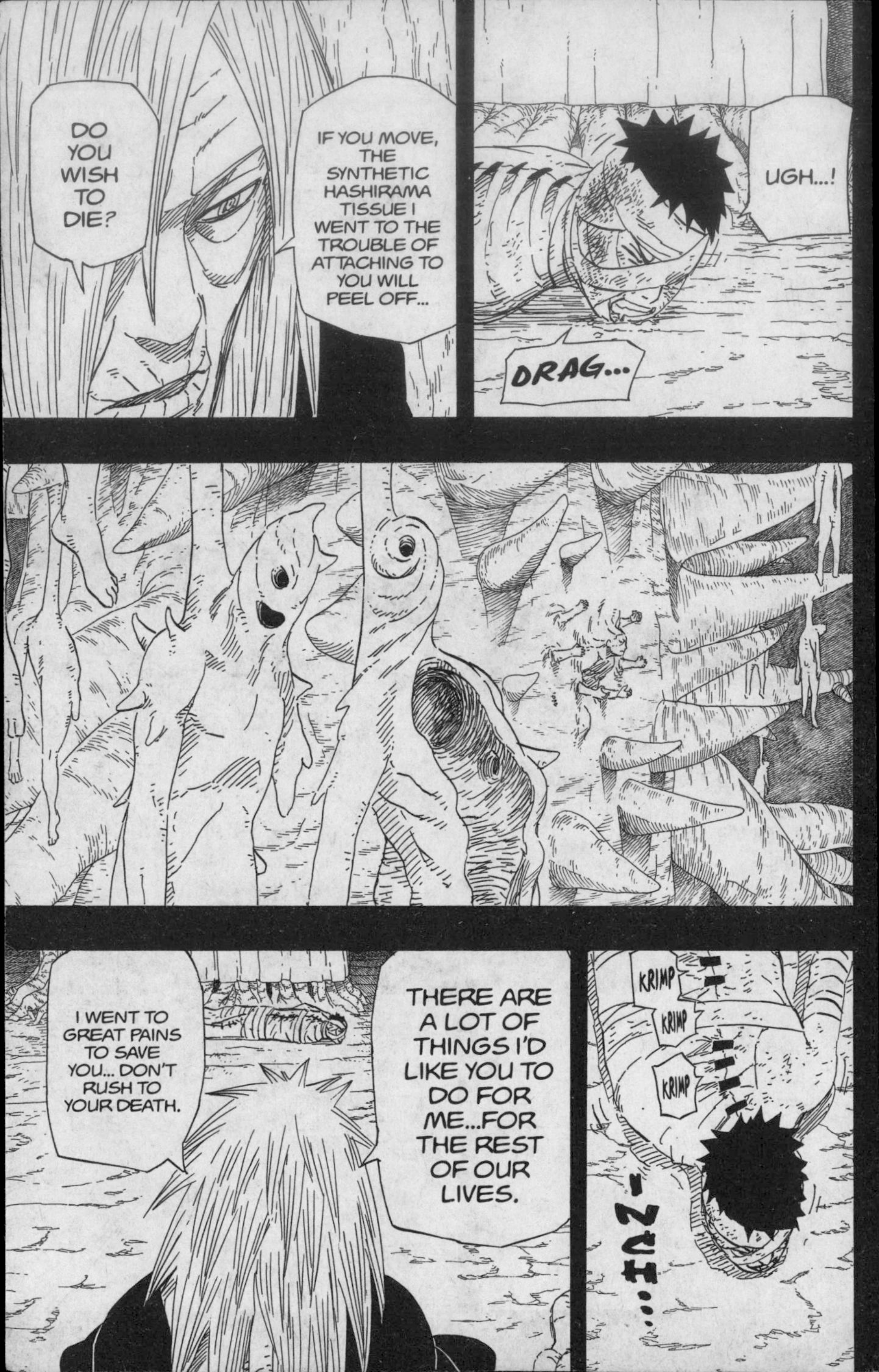
UGH...!
DRAG...
IF YOU MOVE, THE SYNTHETIC HASHIRAMA TISSUE I WENT TO THE TROUBLE OF ATTACHING TO YOU WILL PEEL OFF...
DO YOU WISH TO DIE?
KRIMP
KRIMP
KRIMP
NGH...
THERE ARE A LOT OF THINGS I'D LIKE YOU TO DO FOR ME...FOR THE REST OF OUR LIVES.
I WENT TO GREAT PAINS TO SAVE YOU... DON'T RUSH TO YOUR DEATH.

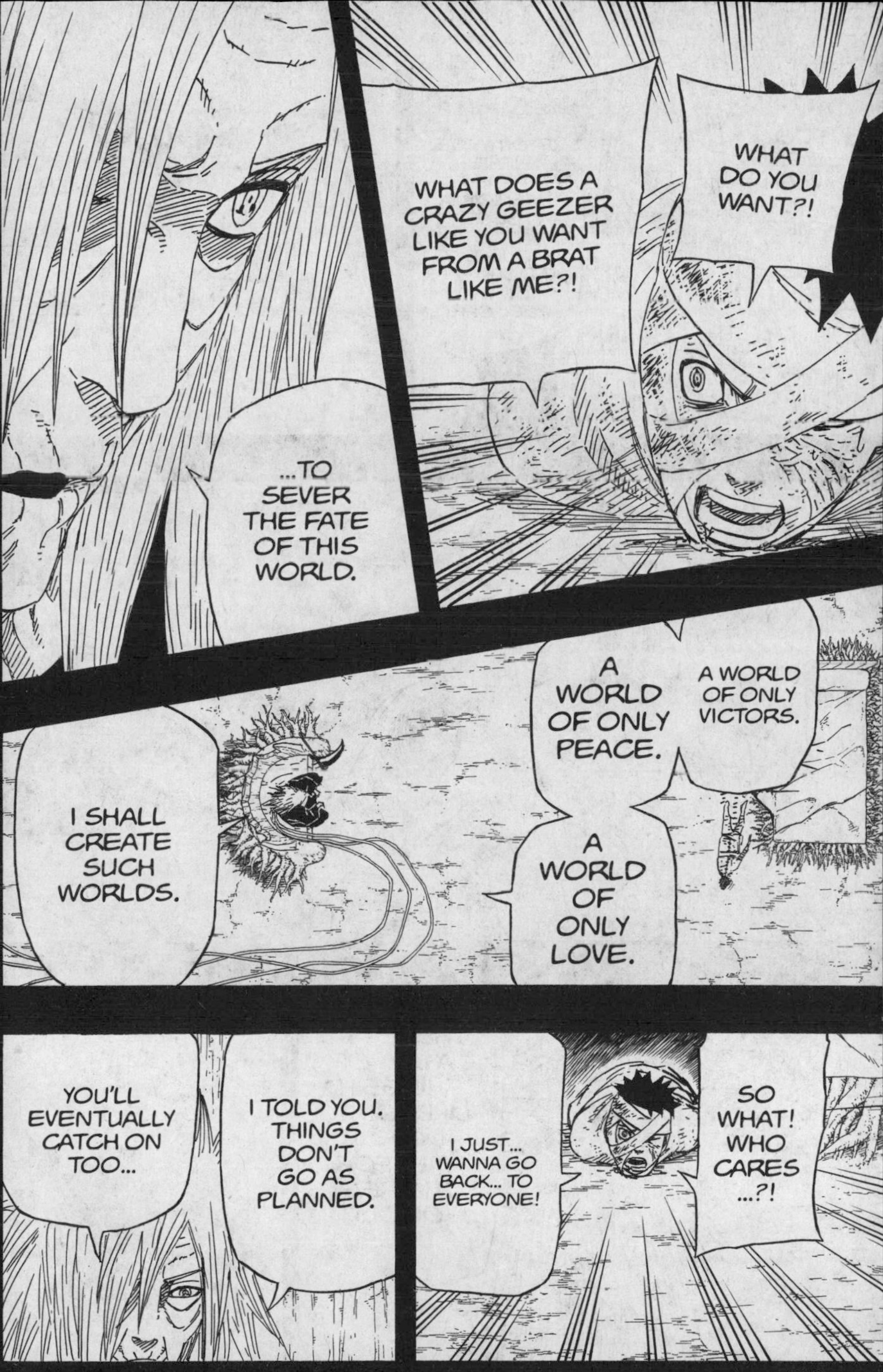
WHAT DO YOU WANT?!
WHAT DOES A CRAZY GEEZER LIKE YOU WANT FROM A BRAT LIKE ME?!
...TO SEVER THE FATE OF THIS WORLD.
A WORLD OF ONLY VICTORS.
A WORLD OF ONLY PEACE.
A WORLD OF ONLY LOVE.
I SHALL CREATE SUCH WORLDS.
SO WHAT! WHO CARES ...?!
I JUST... WANNA GO BACK... TO EVERYONE!
I TOLD YOU. THINGS DON'T GO AS PLANNED.
YOU'LL EVENTUALLY CATCH ON TOO...

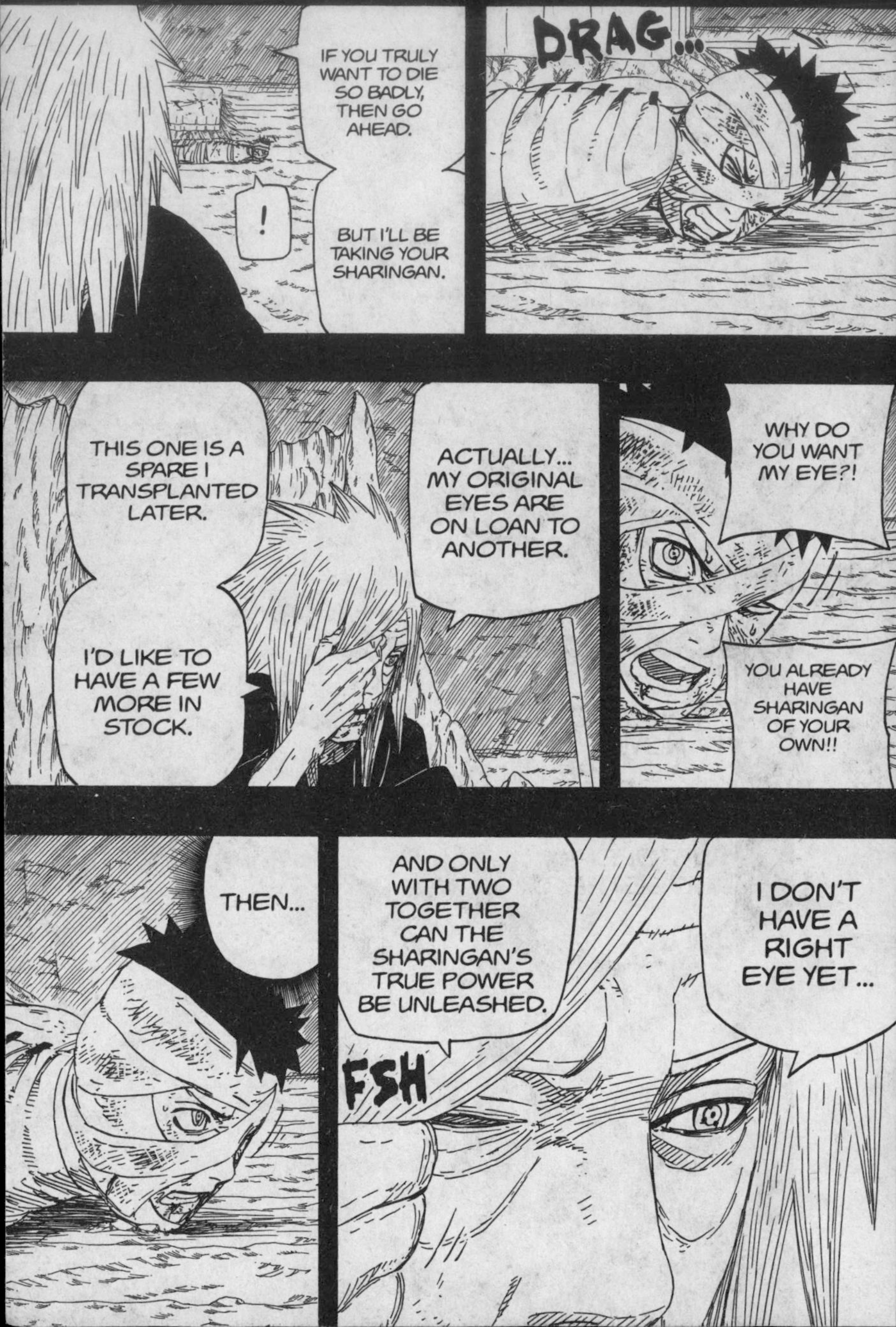
DRAG...
IF YOU TRULY WANT TO DIE SO BADLY, THEN GO AHEAD.
!
BUT I'LL BE TAKING YOUR SHARINGAN.
WHY DO YOU WANT MY EYE?!
YOU ALREADY HAVE SHARINGAN OF YOUR OWN!!
ACTUALLY... MY ORIGINAL EYES ARE ON LOAN TO ANOTHER.
THIS ONE IS A SPARE I TRANSPLANTED LATER.
I'D LIKE TO HAVE A FEW MORE IN STOCK.
I DON'T HAVE A RIGHT EYE YET...
AND ONLY WITH TWO TOGETHER CAN THE SHARINGAN'S TRUE POWER BE UNLEASHED.
FSH
THEN...

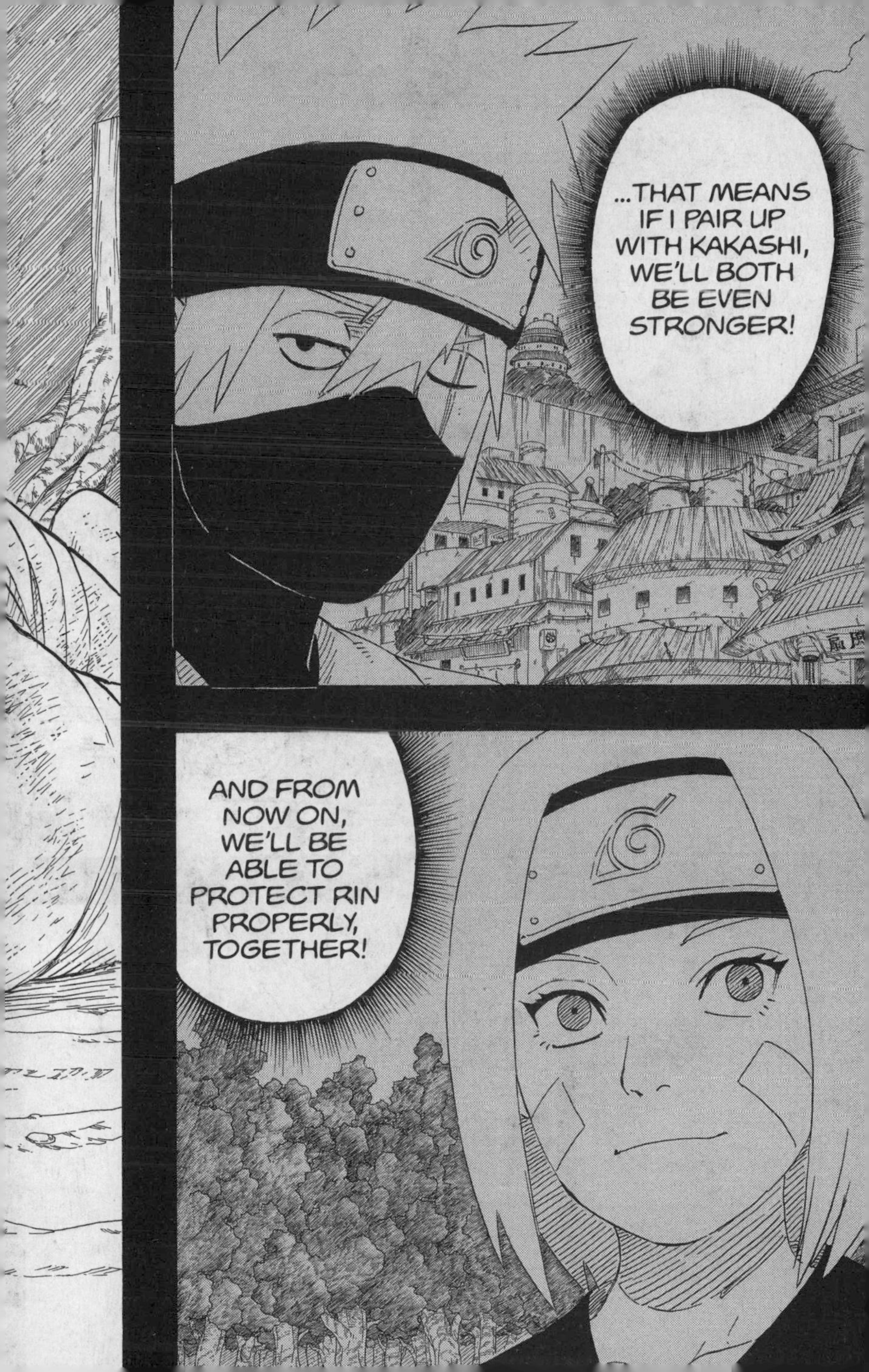
...THAT MEANS IF I PAIR UP WITH KAKASHI, WE'LL BOTH BE EVEN STRONGER!
AND FROM NOW ON, WE'LL BE ABLE TO PROTECT RIN PROPERLY, TOGETHER!

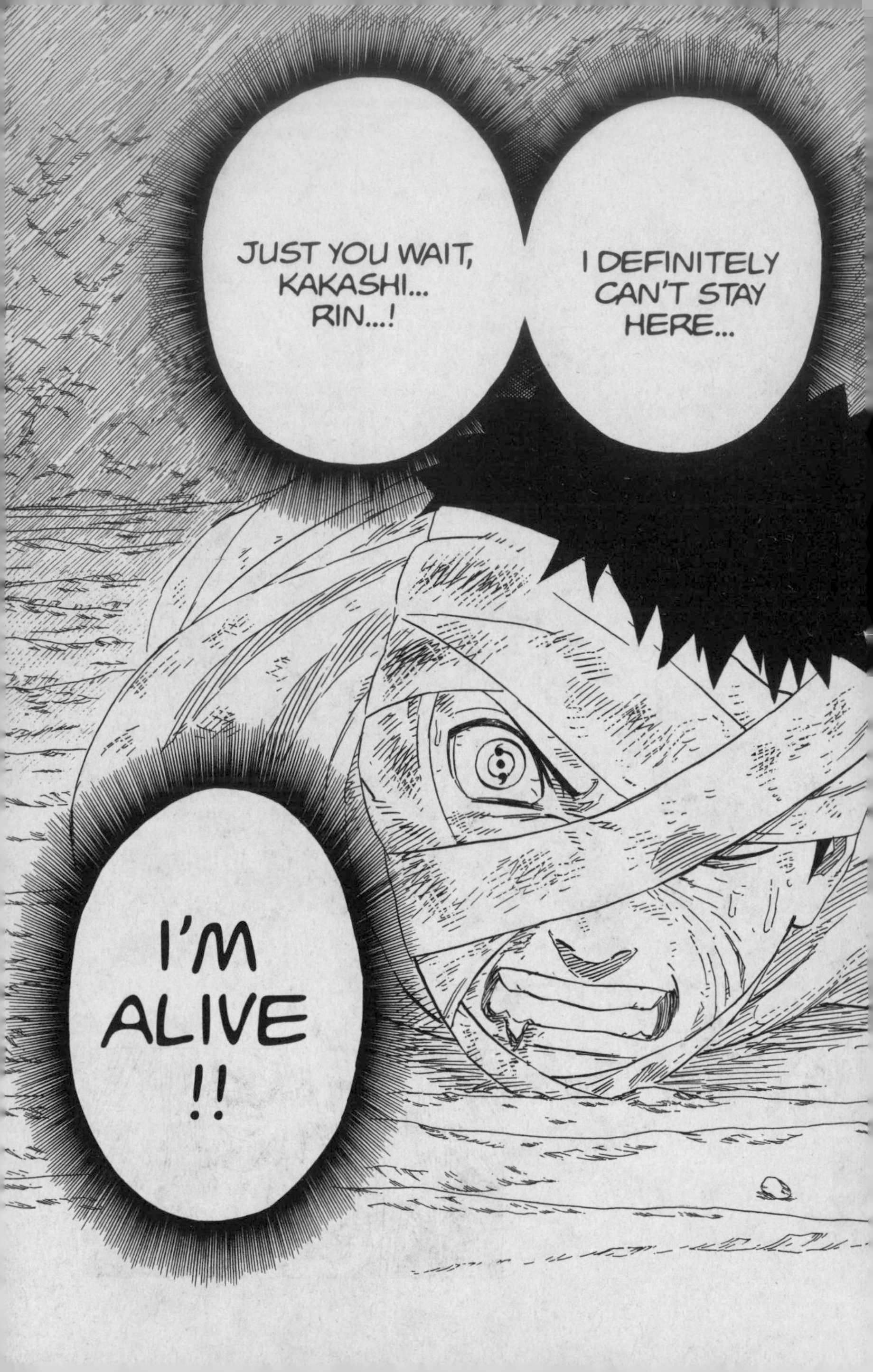
I DEFINITELY CAN'T STAY HERE...
JUST YOU WAIT, KAKASHI... RIN...!
I'M ALIVE !!

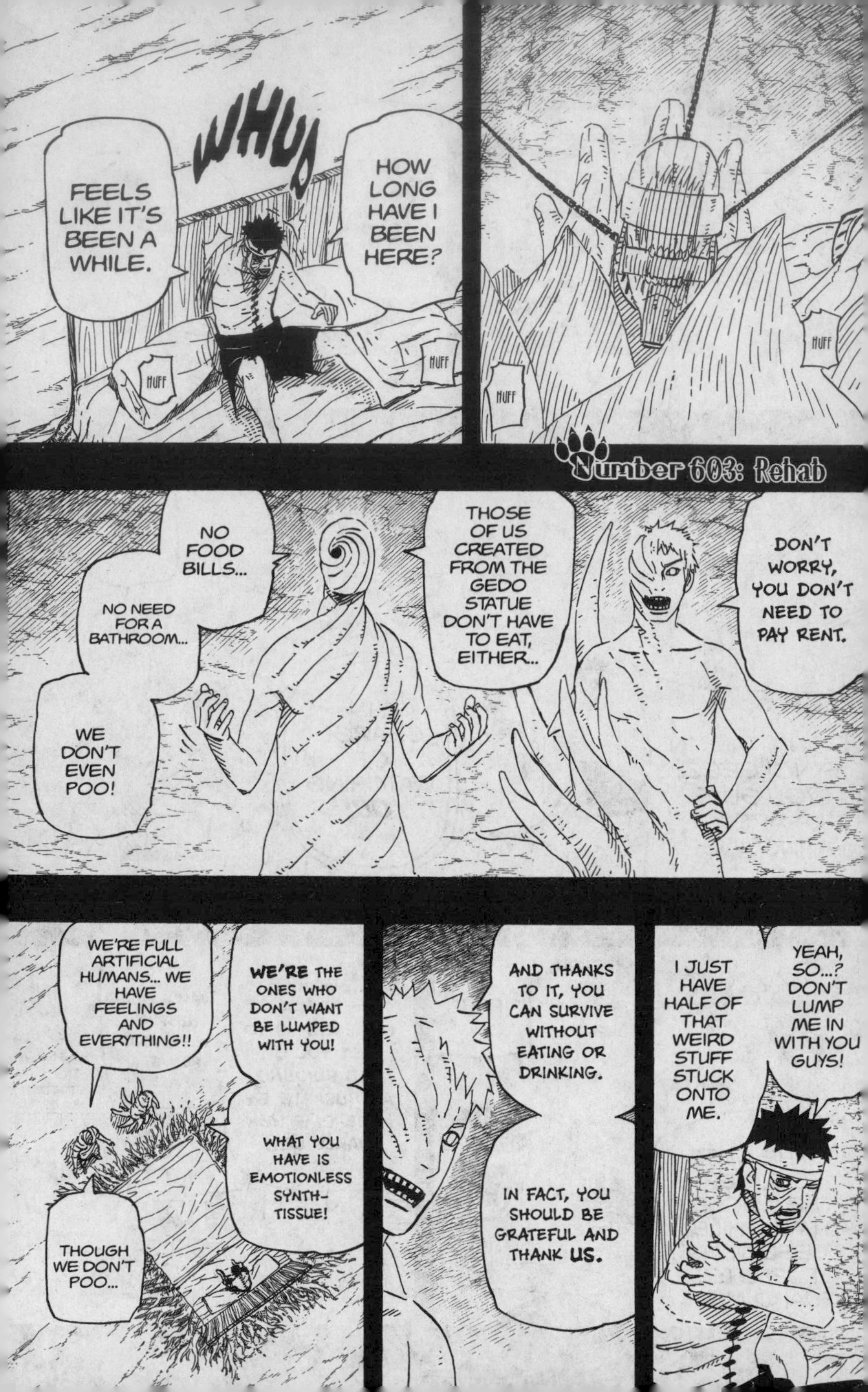
HUFF
HUFF
WHUD
HOW LONG HAVE I BEEN HERE?
FEELS LIKE IT'S BEEN A WHILE.
HUFF
HUFF
Number 603: Rehab
DON'T WORRY, YOU DON'T NEED TO PAY RENT.
THOSE OF US CREATED FROM THE GEDO STATUE DON'T HAVE TO EAT, EITHER...
NO FOOD BILLS...
NO NEED FOR A BATHROOM...
WE DON'T EVEN POO!
YEAH, SO...? DON'T LUMP ME IN WITH YOU GUYS!
I JUST HAVE HALF OF THAT WEIRD STUFF STUCK ONTO ME.
AND THANKS TO IT, YOU CAN SURVIVE WITHOUT EATING OR DRINKING.
IN FACT, YOU SHOULD BE GRATEFUL AND THANK US.
WE'RE THE ONES WHO DON'T WANT BE LUMPED WITH YOU!
WHAT YOU HAVE IS EMOTIONLESS SYNTH-TISSUE!
WE'RE FULL ARTIFICIAL HUMANS... WE HAVE FEELINGS AND EVERYTHING!!
THOUGH WE DON'T POO...

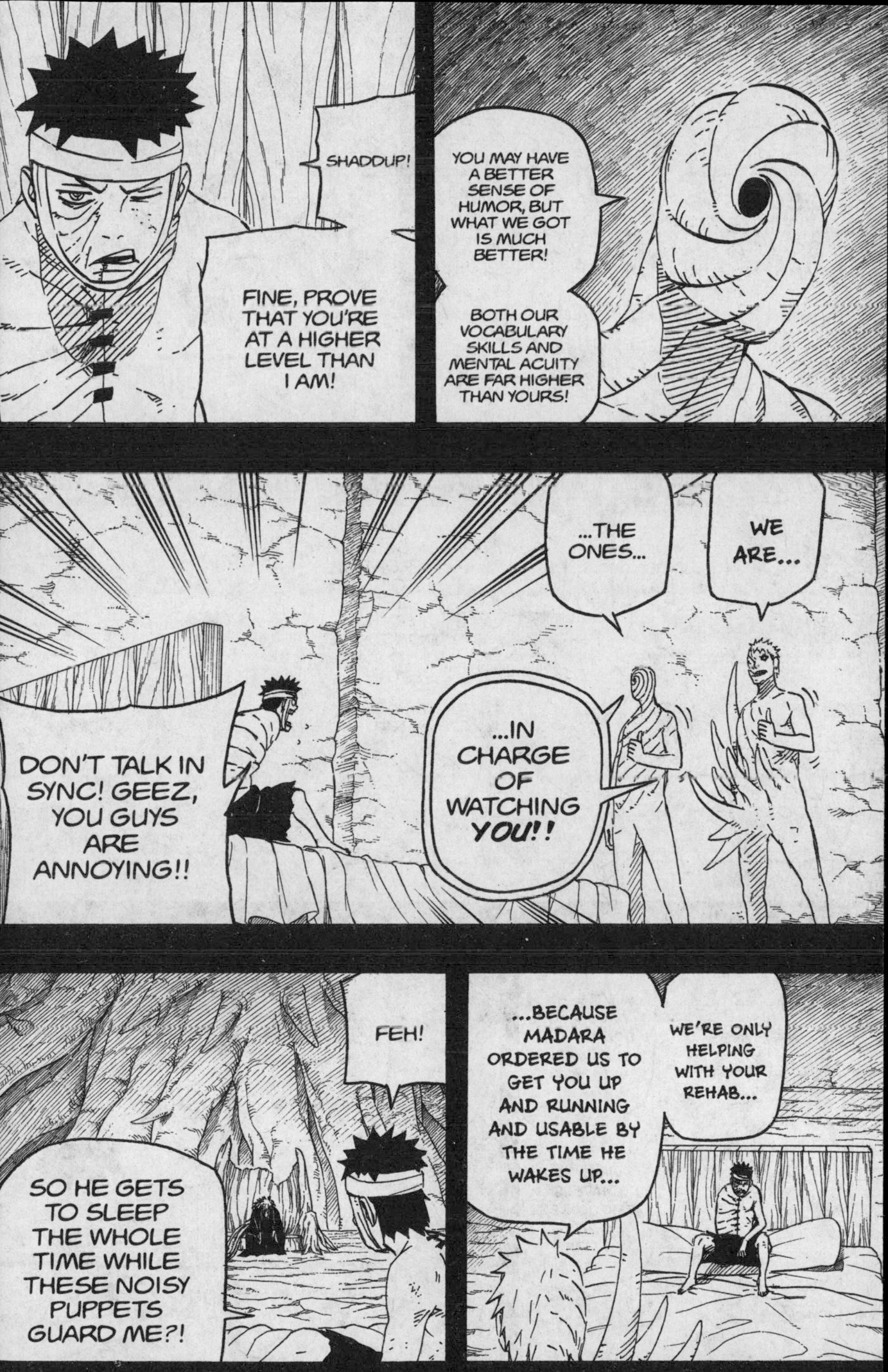
YOU MAY HAVE A BETTER SENSE OF HUMOR, BUT WHAT WE GOT IS MUCH BETTER!
BOTH OUR VOCABULARY SKILLS AND MENTAL ACUITY ARE FAR HIGHER THAN YOURS!
SHADDUP!
FINE, PROVE THAT YOU'RE AT A HIGHER LEVEL THAN I AM!
WE ARE...
...THE ONES...
...IN CHARGE OF WATCHING YOU!!
DON'T TALK IN SYNC! GEEZ, YOU GUYS ARE ANNOYING!!
WE'RE ONLY HELPING WITH YOUR REHAB...
...BECAUSE MADARA ORDERED US TO GET YOU UP AND RUNNING AND USABLE BY THE TIME HE WAKES UP...
FEH!
SO HE GETS TO SLEEP THE WHOLE TIME WHILE THESE NOISY PUPPETS GUARD ME?!

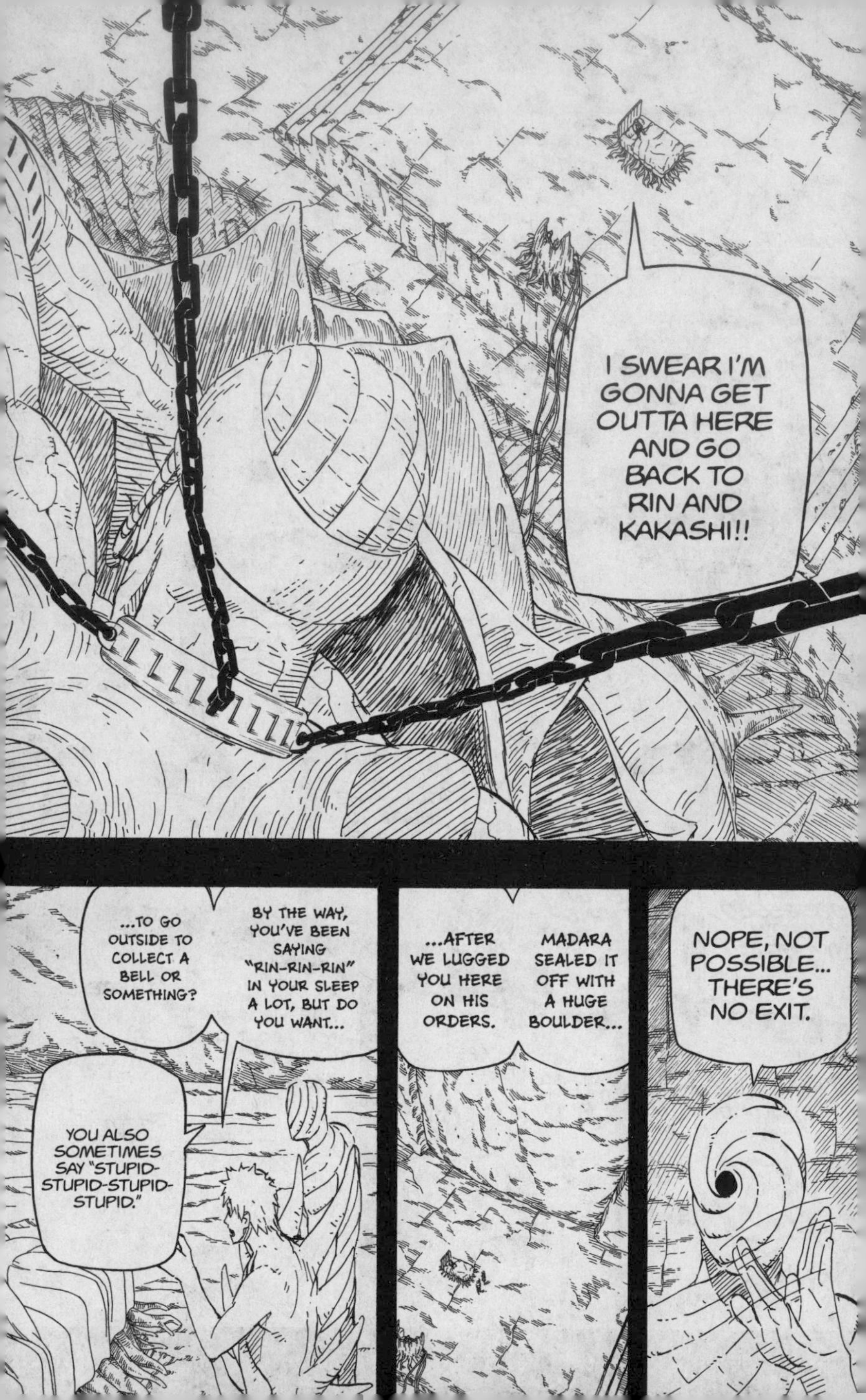
I SWEAR I'M GONNA GET OUTTA HERE AND GO BACK TO RIN AND KAKASHI!!
NOPE, NOT POSSIBLE... THERE'S NO EXIT.
MADARA SEALED IT OFF WITH A HUGE BOULDER...
...AFTER WE LUGGED YOU HERE ON HIS ORDERS.
BY THE WAY, YOU'VE BEEN SAYING "RIN-RIN-RIN" IN YOUR SLEEP A LOT, BUT DO YOU WANT...
...TO GO OUTSIDE TO COLLECT A BELL OR SOMETHING?
YOU ALSO SOMETIMES SAY "STUPID-STUPID-STUPID-STUPID."

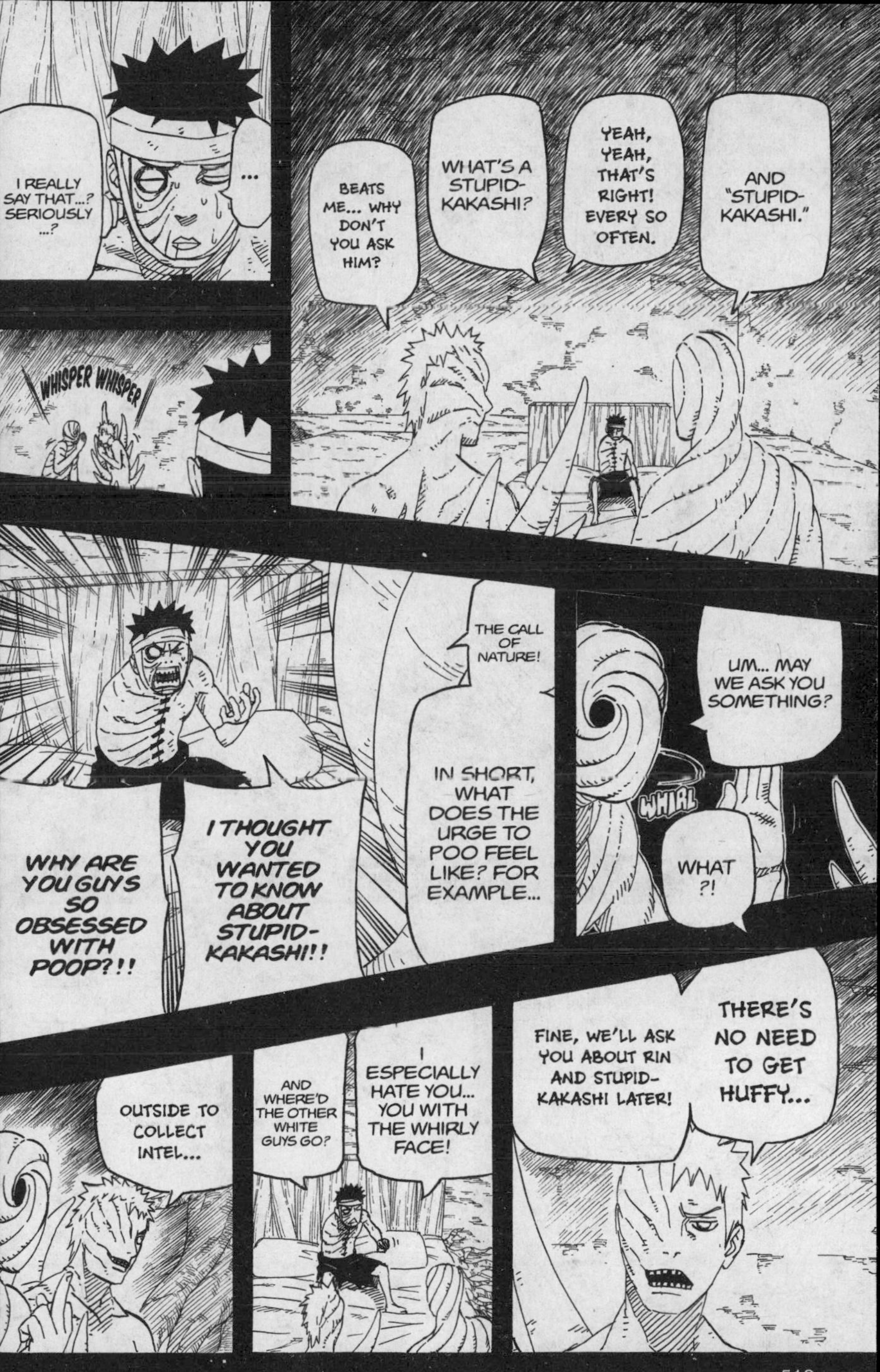
AND "STUPID-KAKASHI."
YEAH, YEAH, THAT'S RIGHT! EVERY SO OFTEN.
WHAT'S A STUPID-KAKASHI?
BEATS ME... WHY DON'T YOU ASK HIM?
...
I REALLY SAY THAT...? SERIOUSLY ...?
WHISPER WHISPER
UM... MAY WE ASK YOU SOMETHING?
WHIRL
WHAT ?!
THE CALL OF NATURE!
IN SHORT, WHAT DOES THE URGE TO POO FEEL LIKE? FOR EXAMPLE...
I THOUGHT YOU WANTED TO KNOW ABOUT STUPID-KAKASHI!!
WHY ARE YOU GUYS SO OBSESSED WITH POOP?!!
THERE'S NO NEED TO GET HUFFY...
FINE, WE'LL ASK YOU ABOUT RIN AND STUPID-KAKASHI LATER!
I ESPECIALLY HATE YOU... YOU WITH THE WHIRLY FACE!
AND WHERE'D THE OTHER WHITE GUYS GO?
OUTSIDE TO COLLECT INTEL...

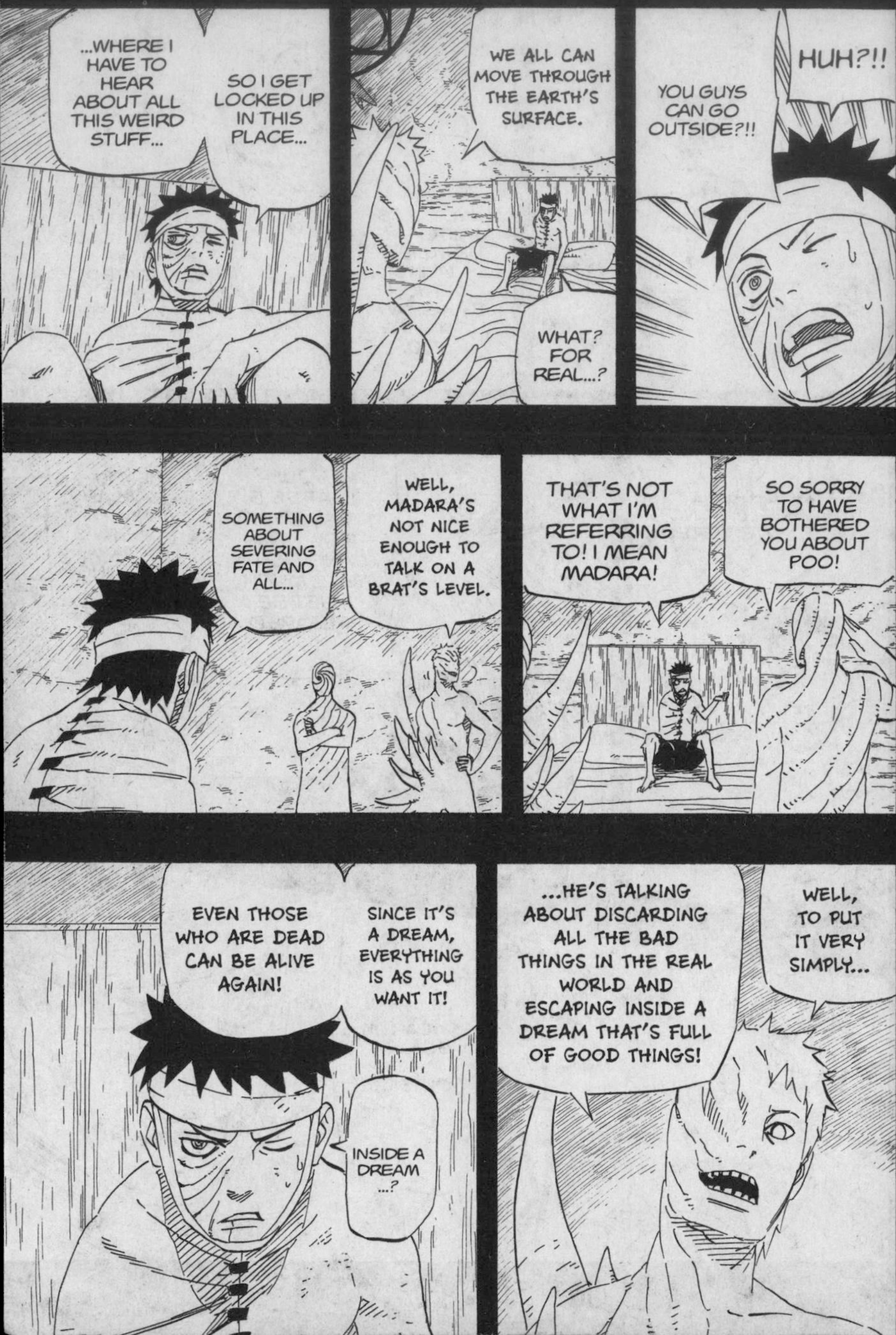
HUH?!!
YOU GUYS CAN GO OUTSIDE?!!
WE ALL CAN MOVE THROUGH THE EARTH'S SURFACE.
WHAT? FOR REAL...?
SO I GET LOCKED UP IN THIS PLACE...
...WHERE I HAVE TO HEAR ABOUT ALL THIS WEIRD STUFF...
SO SORRY TO HAVE BOTHERED YOU ABOUT POO!
THAT'S NOT WHAT I'M REFERRING TO! I MEAN MADARA!
WELL, MADARA'S NOT NICE ENOUGH TO TALK ON A BRAT'S LEVEL.
SOMETHING ABOUT SEVERING FATE AND ALL...
WELL, TO PUT IT VERY SIMPLY...
...HE'S TALKING ABOUT DISCARDING ALL THE BAD THINGS IN THE REAL WORLD AND ESCAPING INSIDE A DREAM THAT'S FULL OF GOOD THINGS!
SINCE IT'S A DREAM, EVERYTHING IS AS YOU WANT IT!
EVEN THOSE WHO ARE DEAD CAN BE ALIVE AGAIN!
INSIDE A DREAM...?

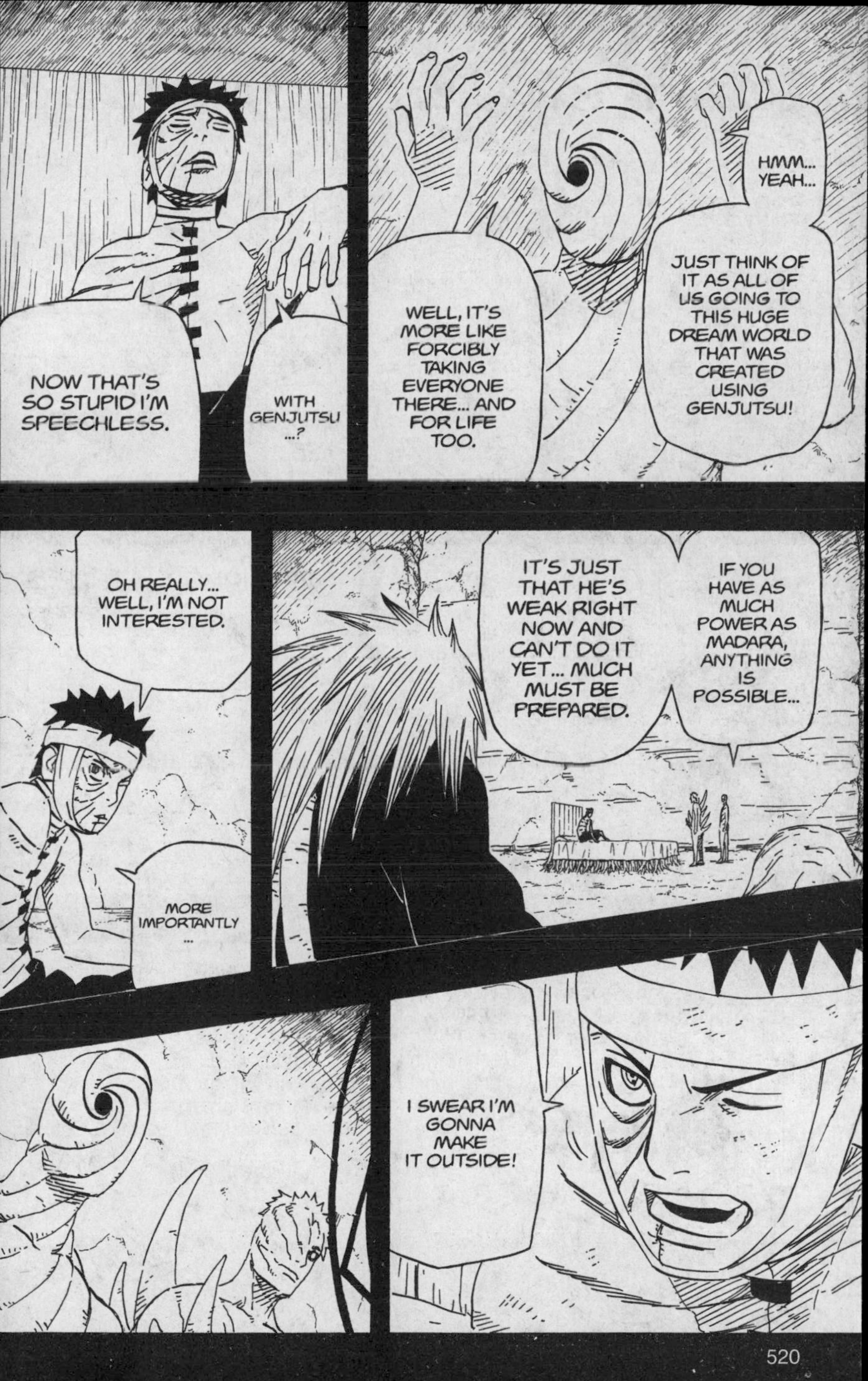
HMM... YEAH...
JUST THINK OF IT AS ALL OF US GOING TO THIS HUGE DREAM WORLD THAT WAS CREATED USING GENJUTSU!
WELL, IT'S MORE LIKE FORCIBLY TAKING EVERYONE THERE... AND FOR LIFE TOO.
WITH GENJUTSU ...?
NOW THAT'S SO STUPID I'M SPEECHLESS.
IF YOU HAVE AS MUCH POWER AS MADARA, ANYTHING IS POSSIBLE...
IT'S JUST THAT HE'S WEAK RIGHT NOW AND CAN'T DO IT YET... MUCH MUST BE PREPARED.
OH REALLY... WELL, I'M NOT INTERESTED.
MORE IMPORTANTLY ...
I SWEAR I'M GONNA MAKE IT OUTSIDE!

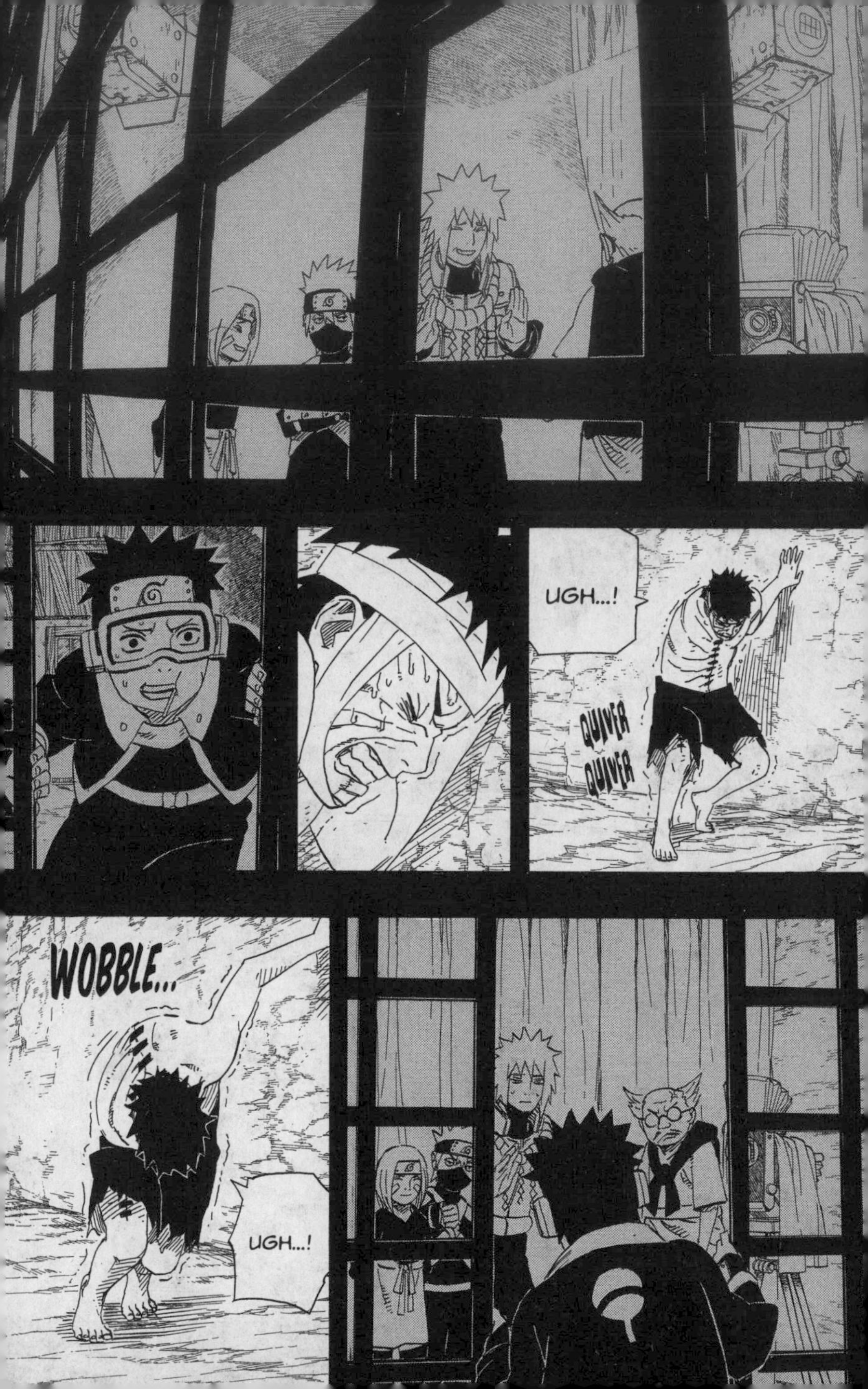
UGH...!
QUIVER
QUIVER
WOBBLE...
UGH...!

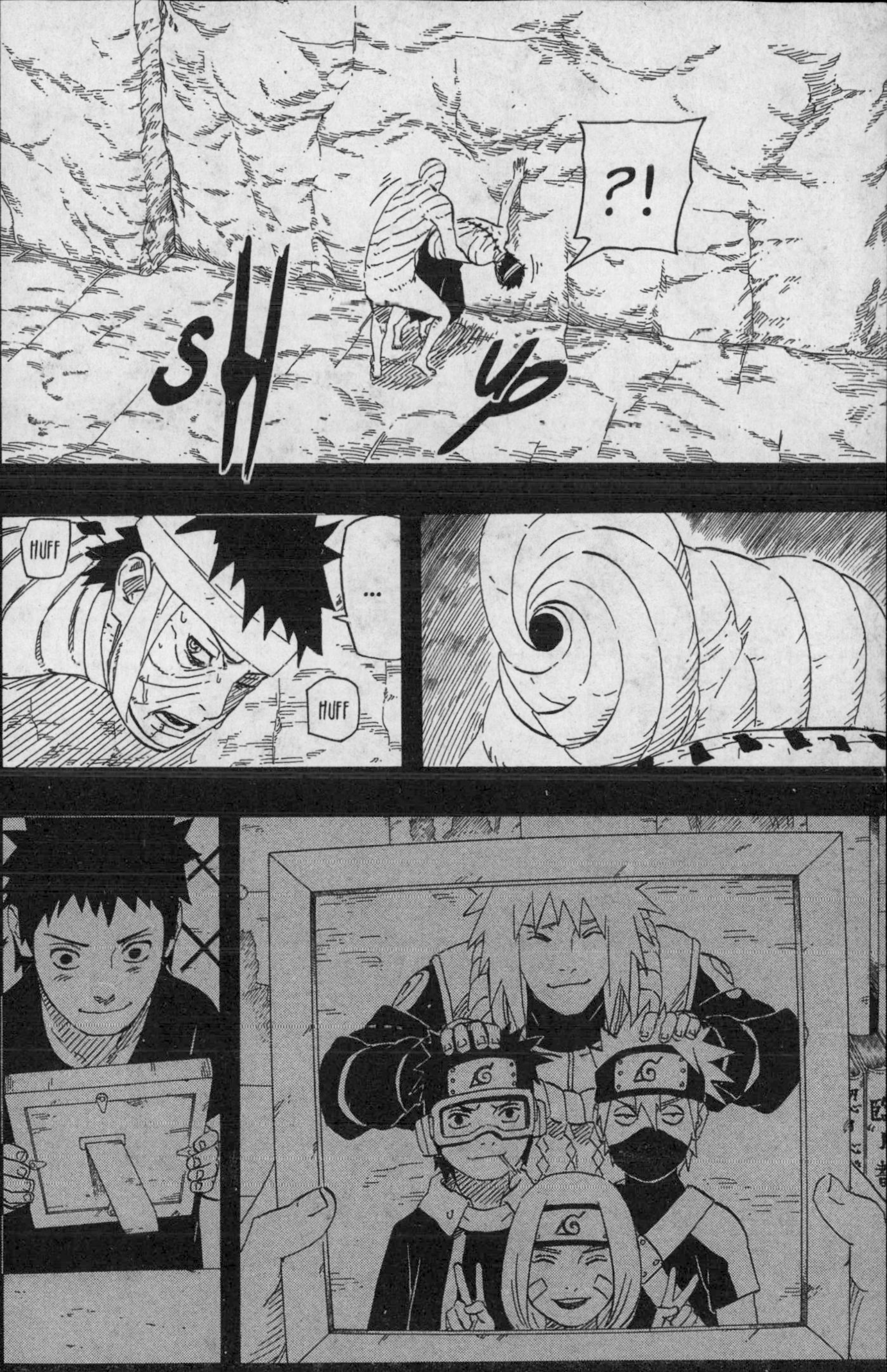
?!
SHUP
HUFF
...
HUFF

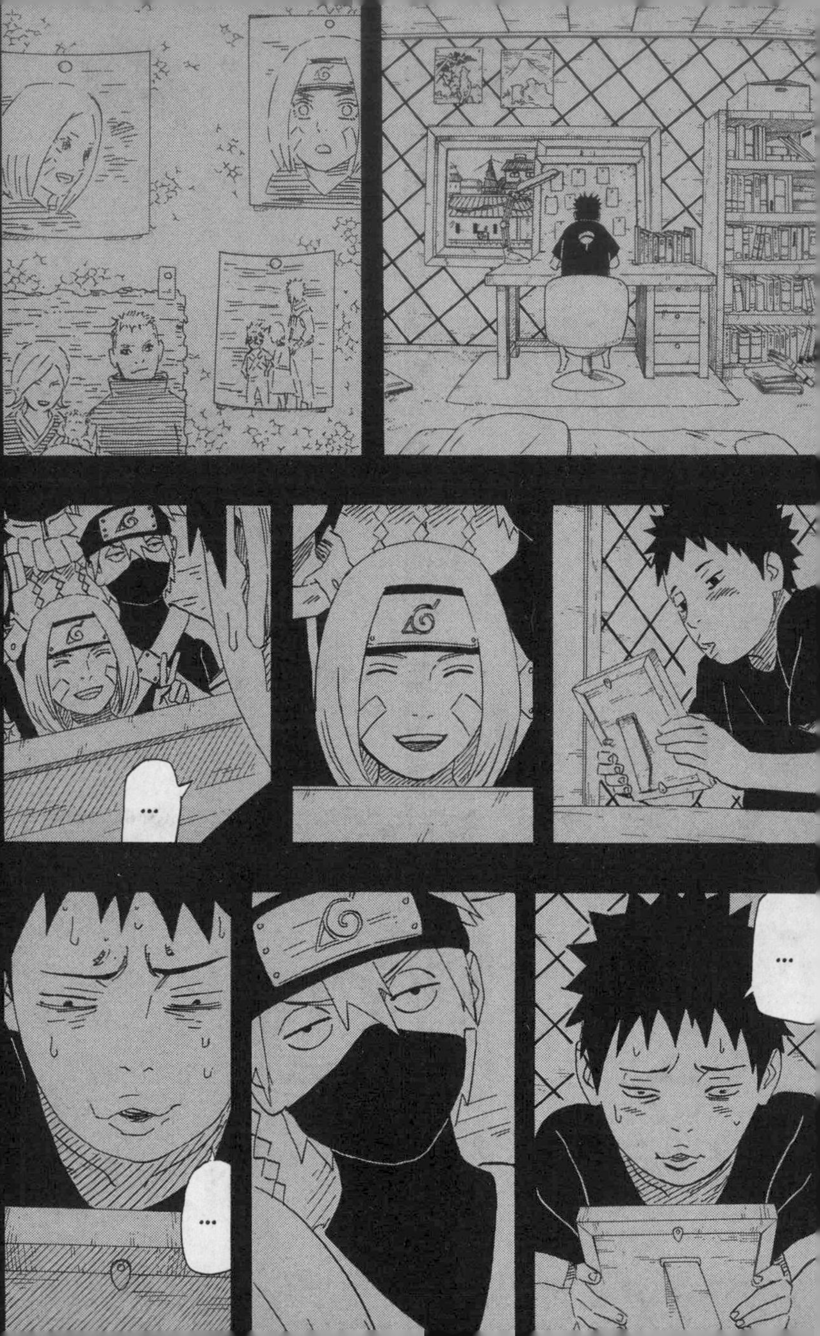
...
...
...

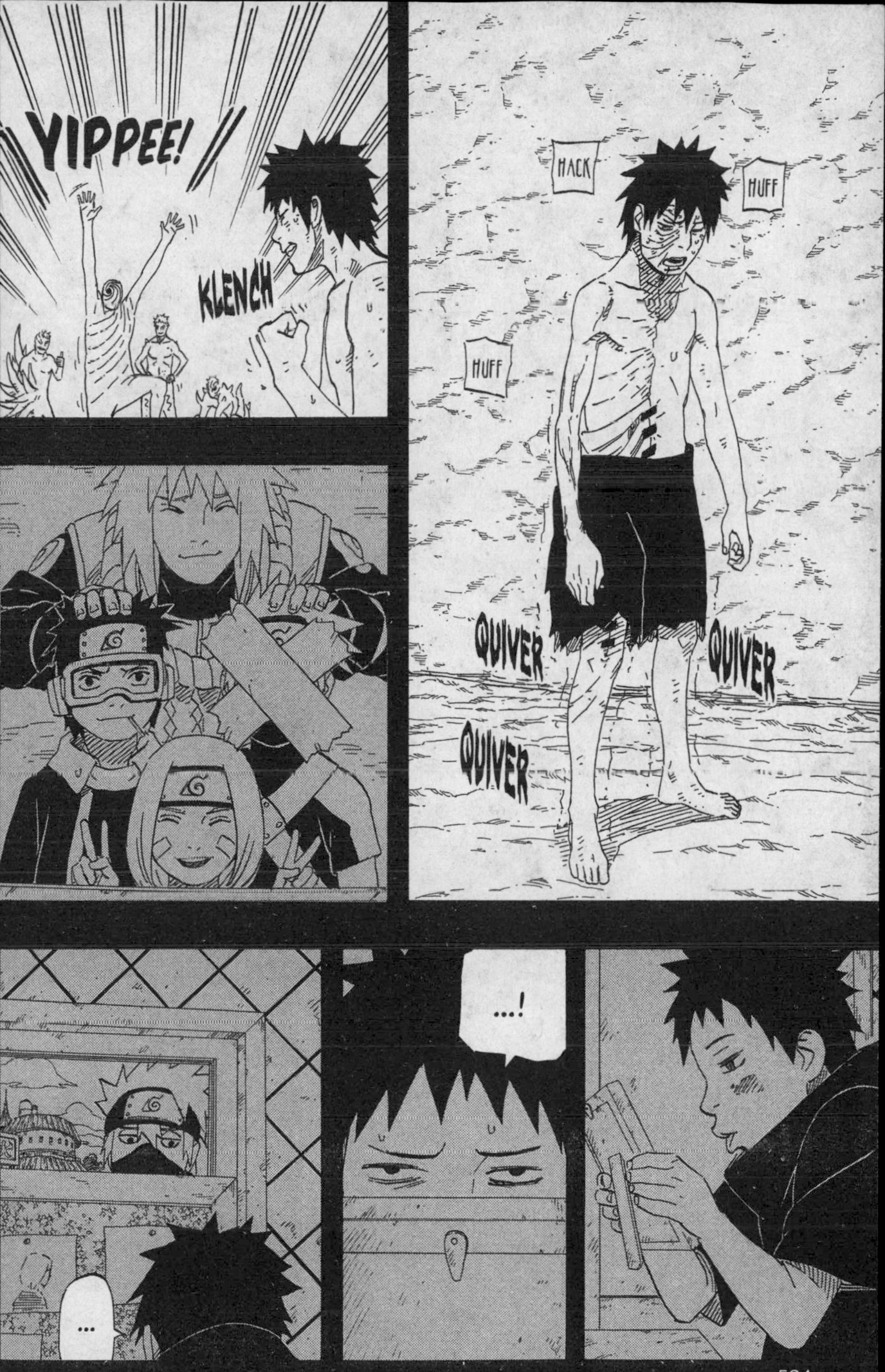
HUFF
HACK
HUFF
QUIVER
QUIVER
QUIVER
YIPPEE!
KLENCH
...!
...

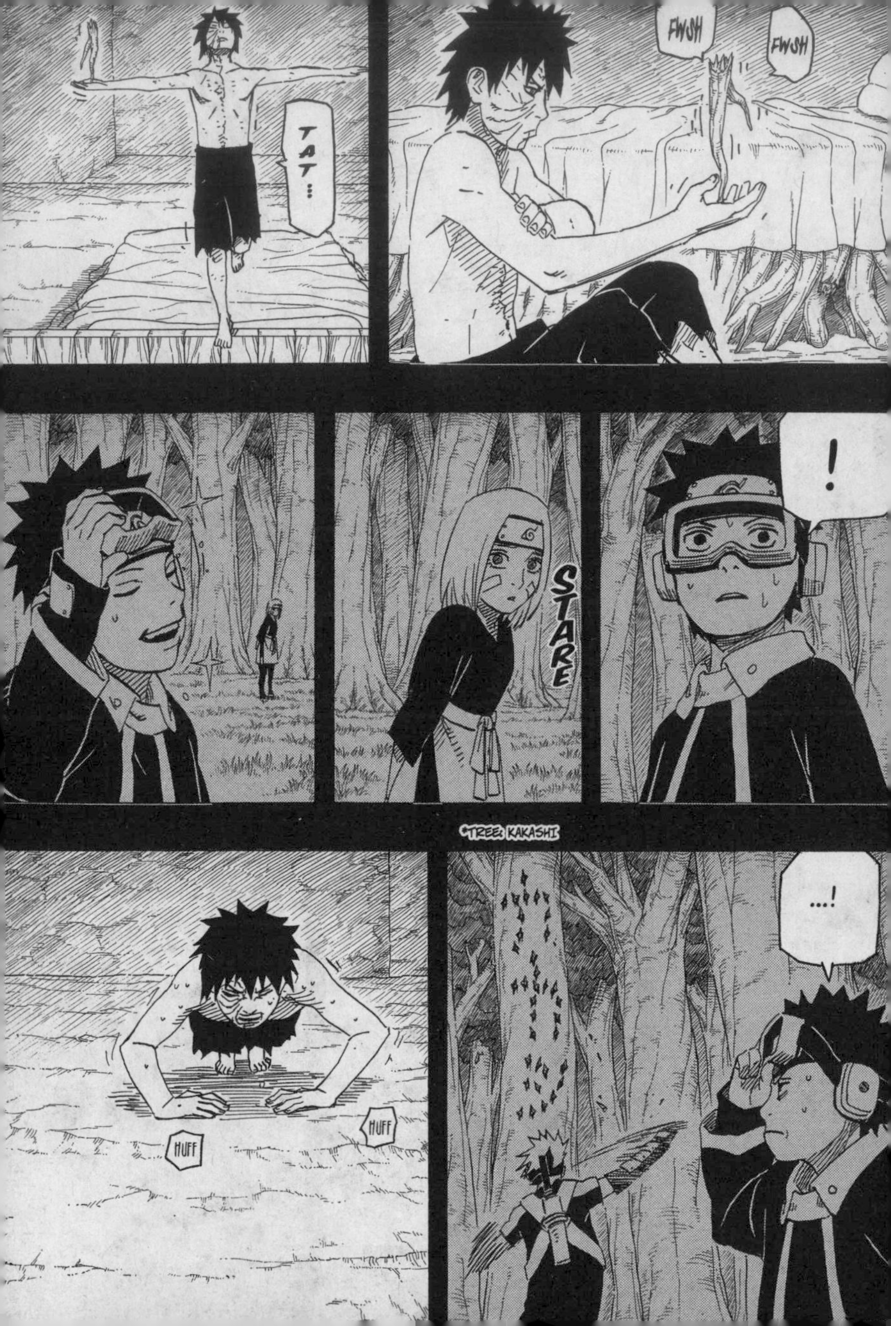
FWSH
FWSH
TAT...
!
STARE
*TREE: KAKASHI
...!
HUFF
HUFF

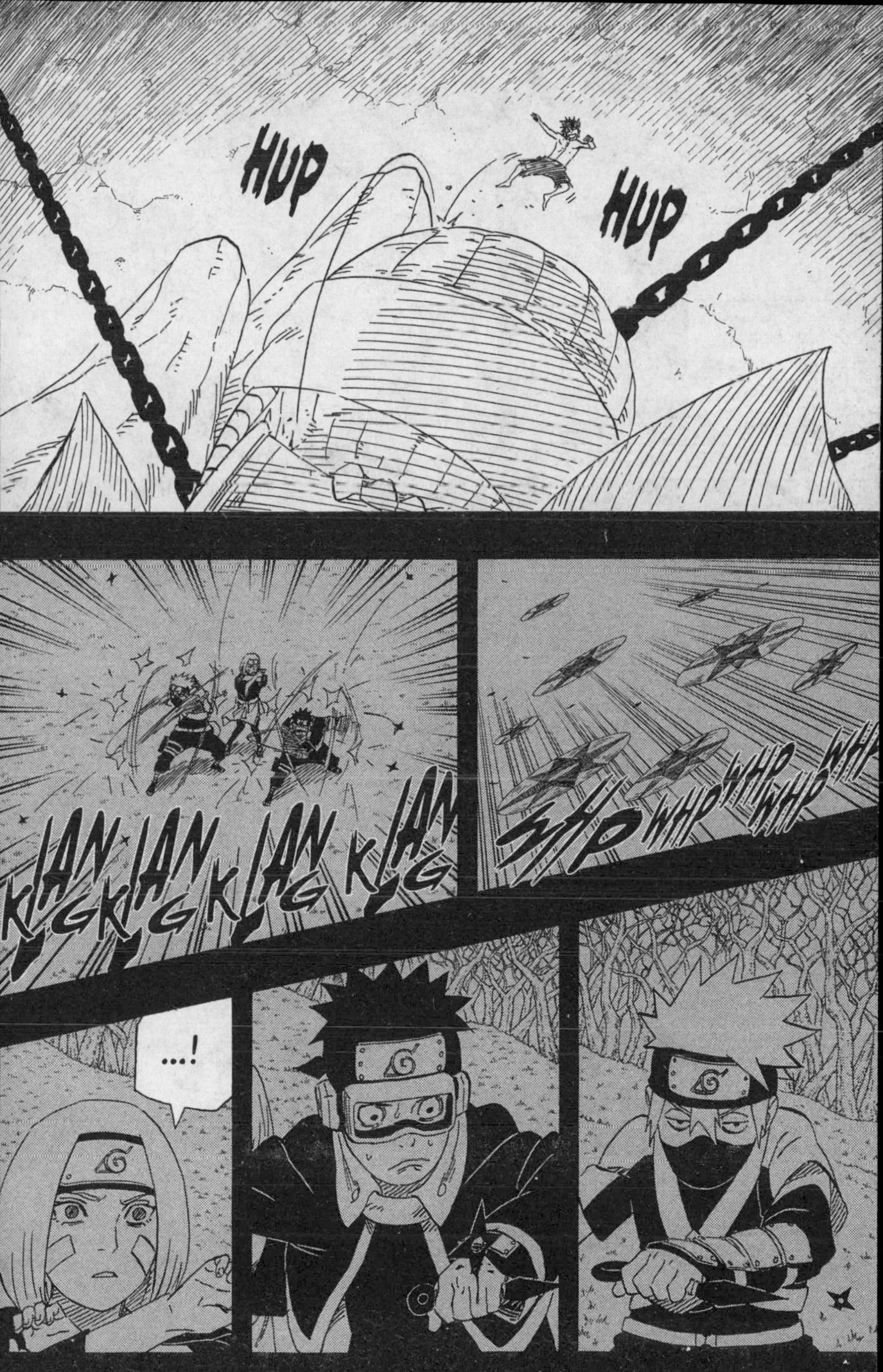
HUP
HUP
WHP
WHP
WHP
WHP
KLANG
KLANG
KLANG
KLANG
...!

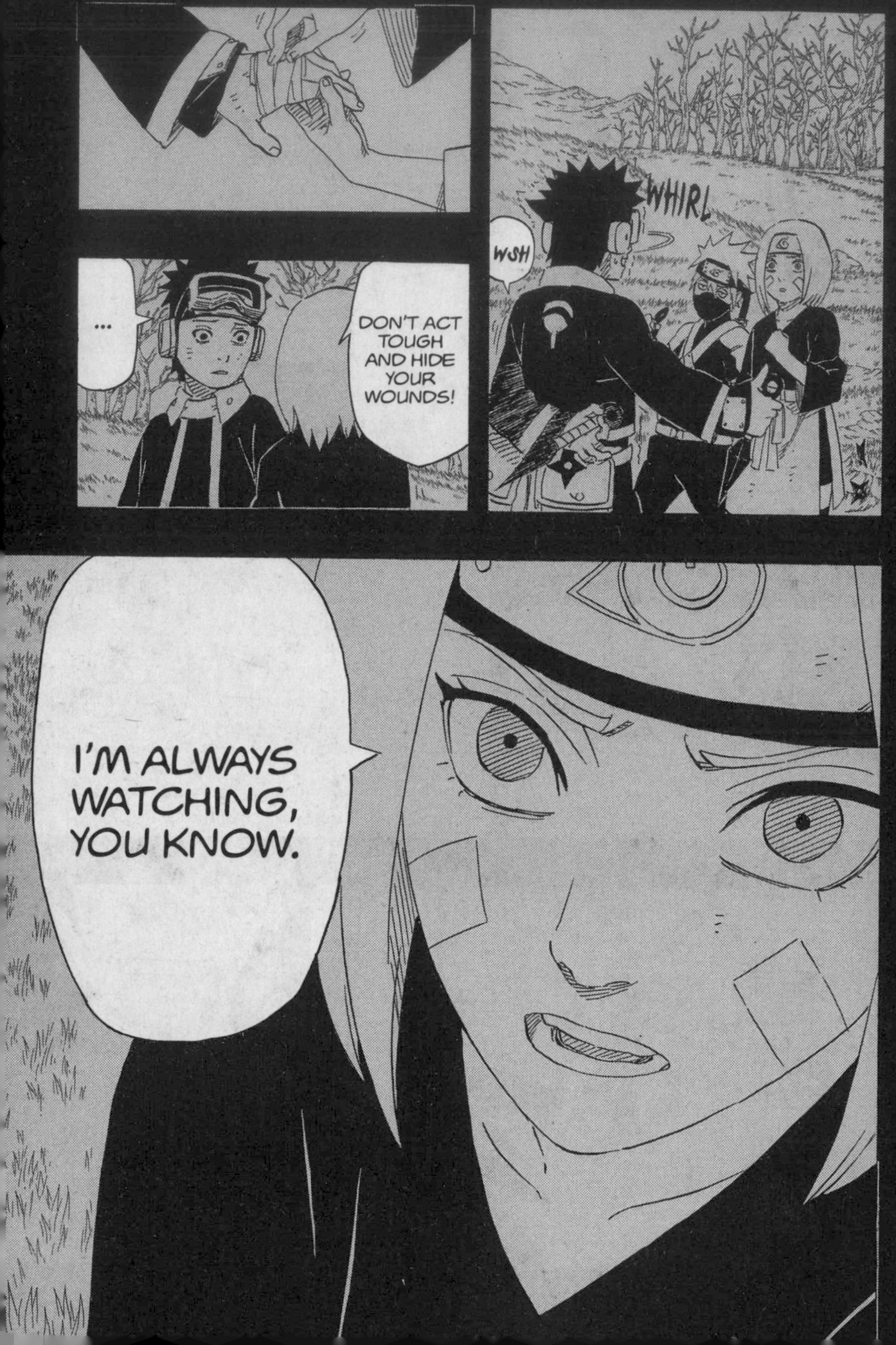
WHIRL
WSH
DON'T ACT TOUGH AND HIDE YOUR WOUNDS!
...
I'M ALWAYS WATCHING, YOU KNOW.

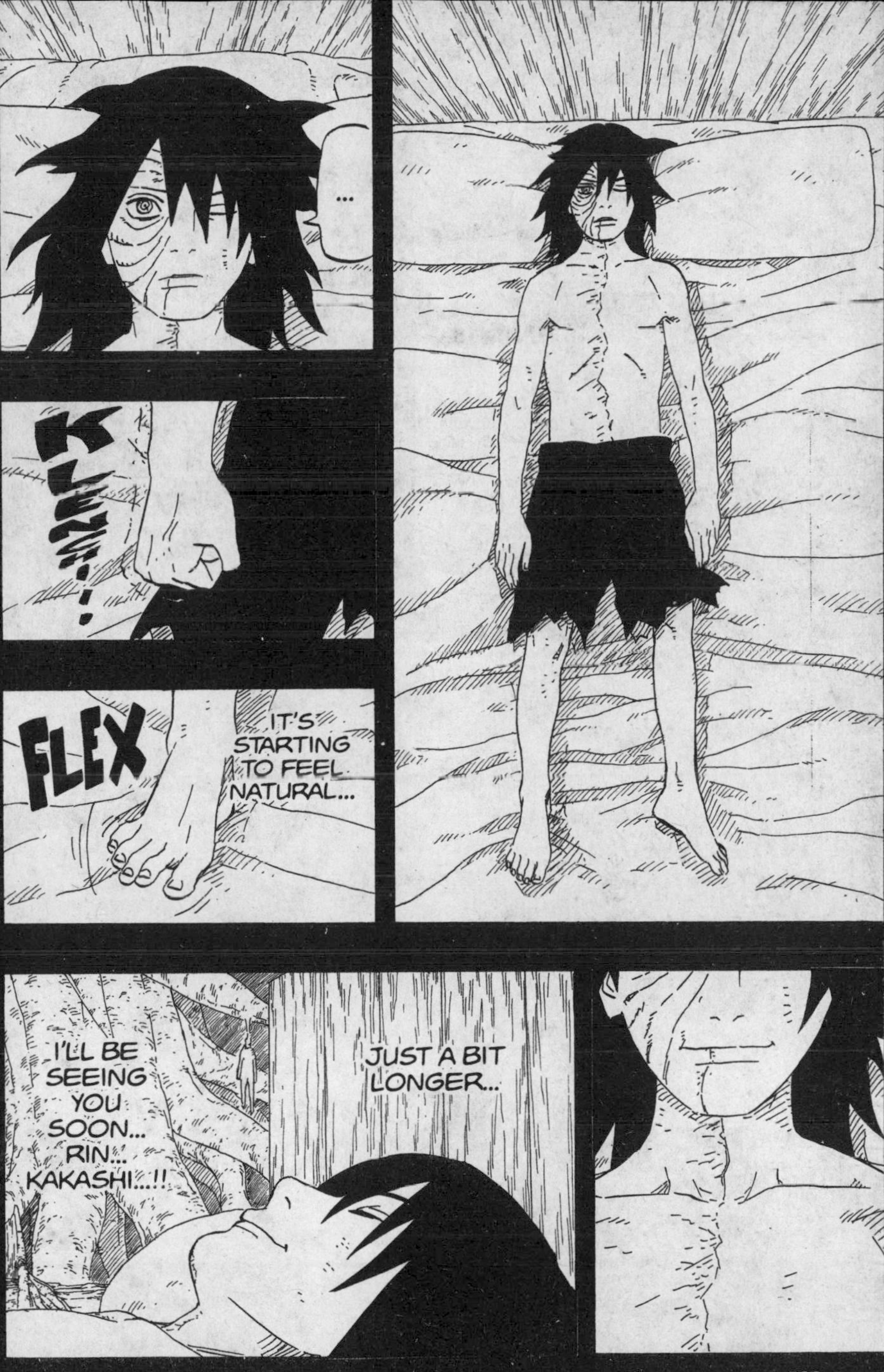
...
KLENCH...
FLEX
IT'S STARTING TO FEEL NATURAL...
JUST A BIT LONGER...
I'LL BE SEEING YOU SOON... RIN... KAKASHI...!!

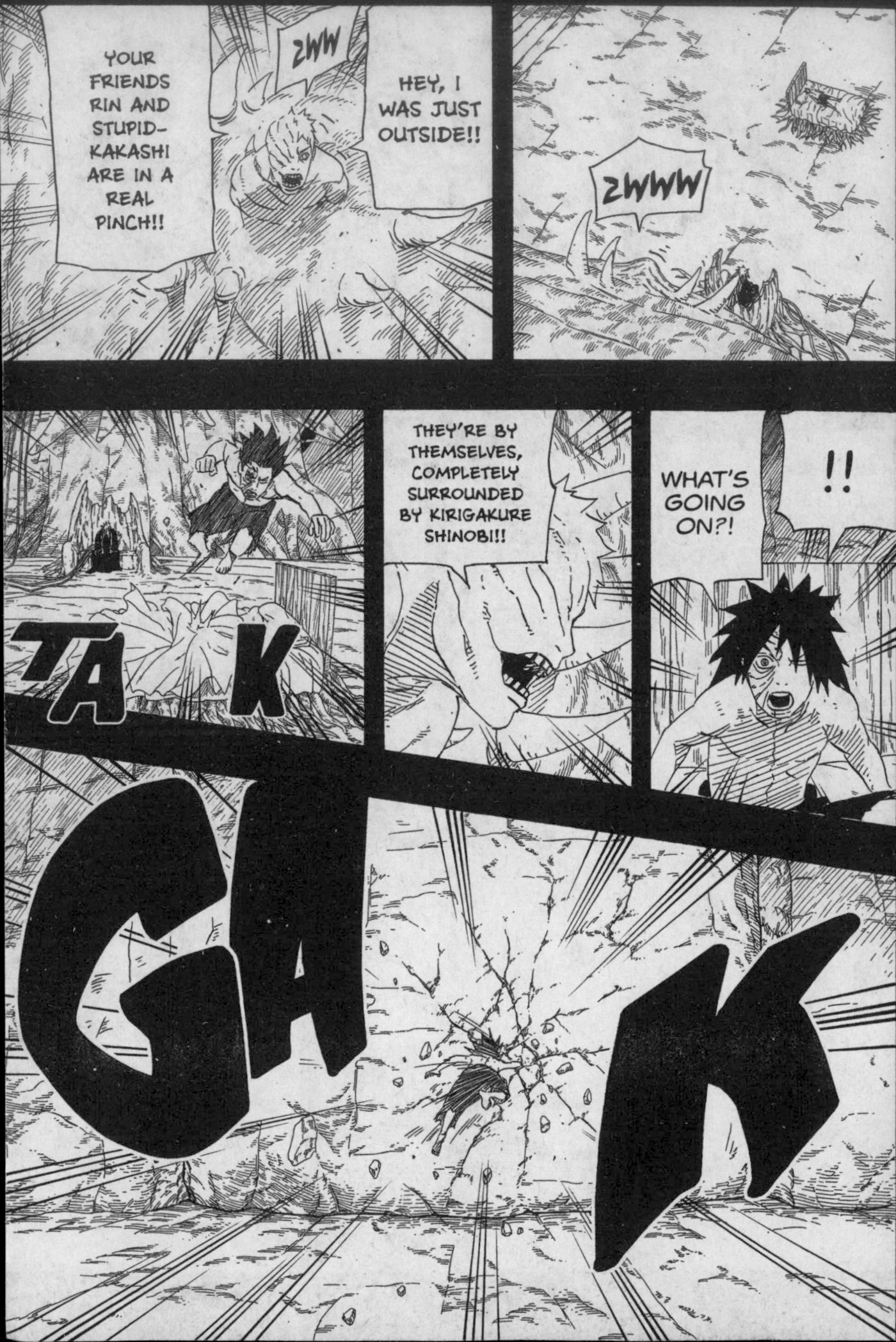

ZWWW
ZWW
HEY, I WAS JUST OUTSIDE!!
YOUR FRIENDS RIN AND STUPID-KAKASHI ARE IN A REAL PINCH!!
!!
WHAT'S GOING ON?!
THEY'RE BY THEMSELVES, COMPLETELY SURROUNDED BY KIRIGAKURE SHINOBI!!!
TAK
GAK

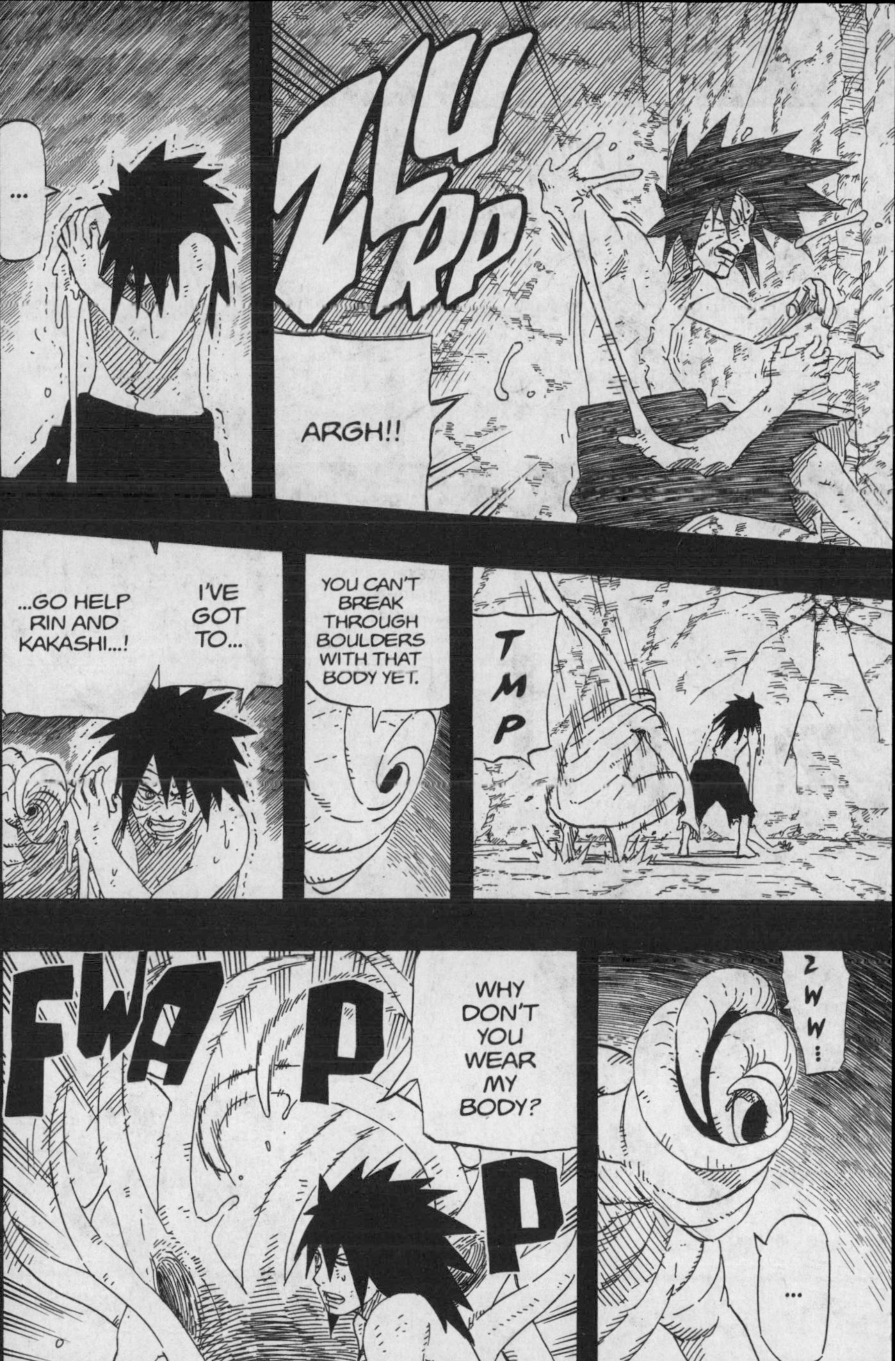
ZLURRP
ARGH!!
...
TMP
YOU CAN'T BREAK THROUGH BOULDERS WITH THAT BODY YET.
I'VE GOT TO...
...GO HELP RIN AND KAKASHI...!
ZWW...
...
WHY DON'T YOU WEAR MY BODY?
FWAP
P

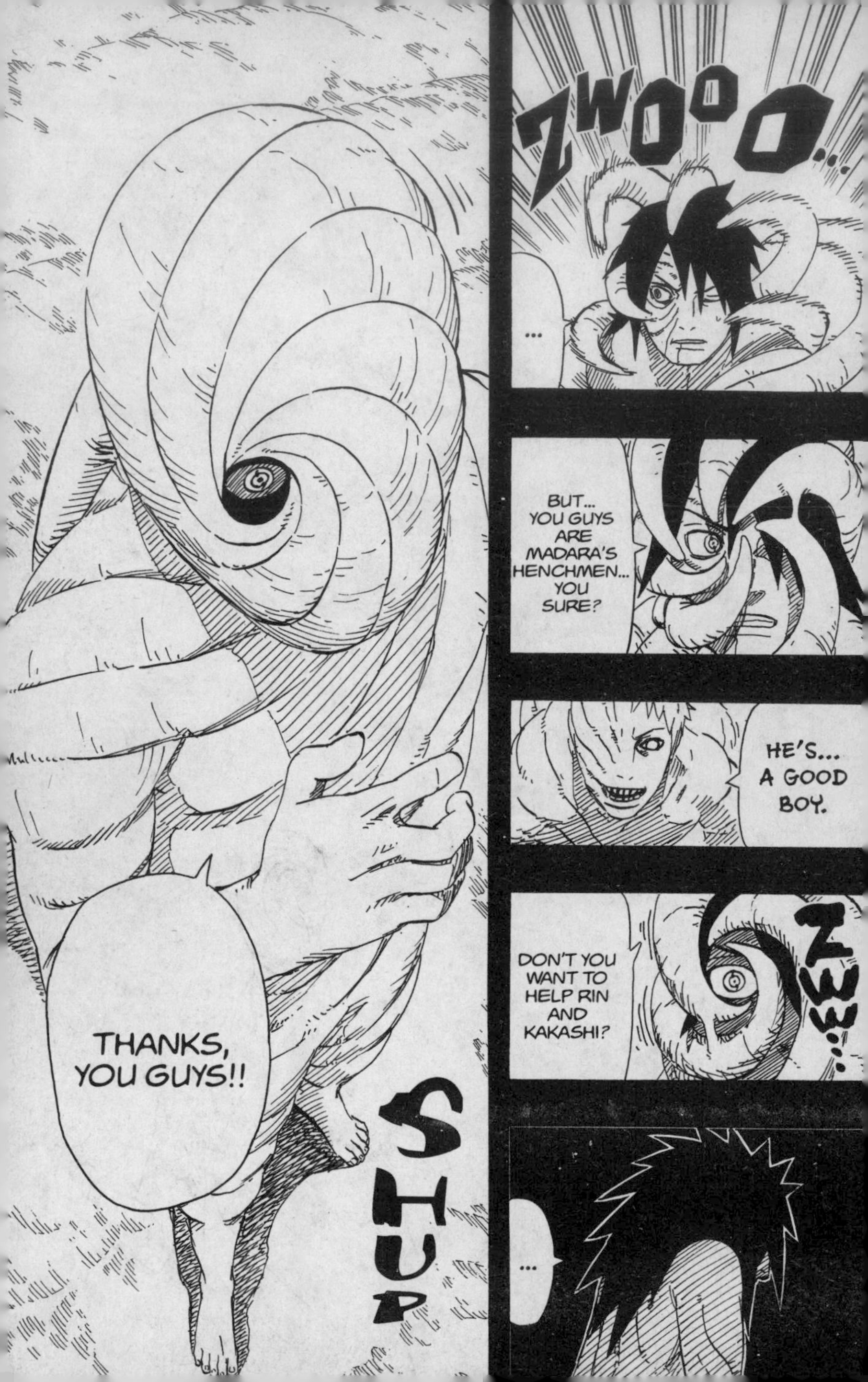
ZWOOO...
...
BUT... YOU GUYS ARE MADARA'S HENCHMEN... YOU SURE?
HE'S... A GOOD BOY.
DON'T YOU WANT TO HELP RIN AND KAKASHI?
NWW...
...
THANKS, YOU GUYS!!
SHUP

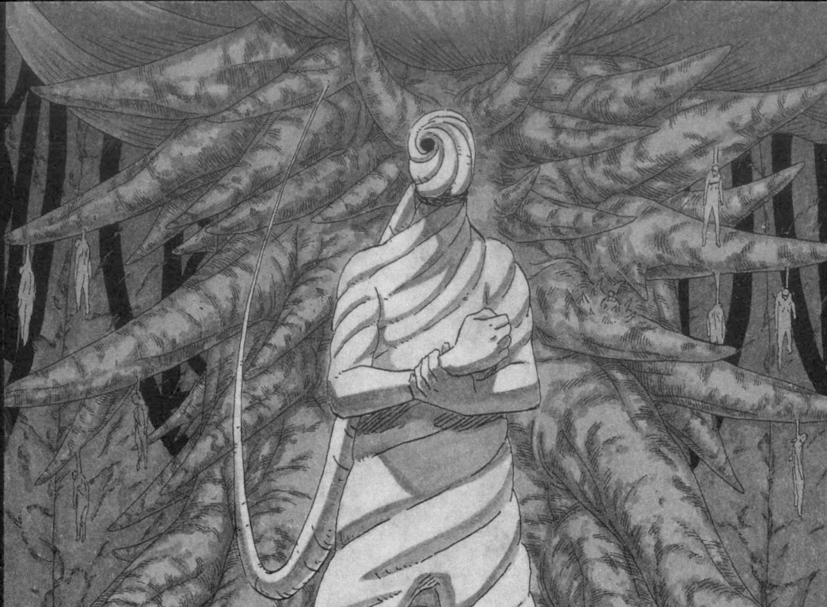

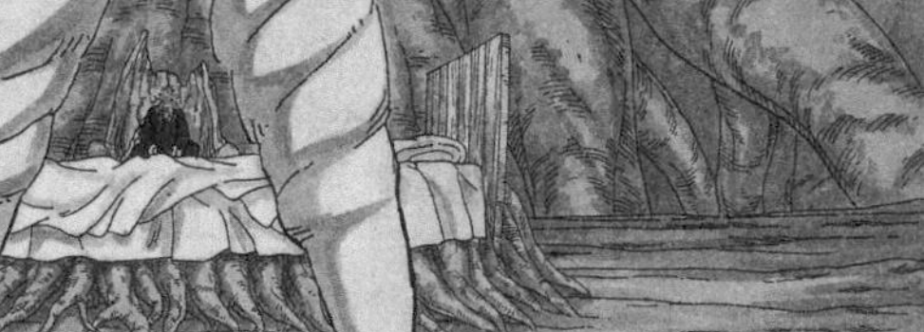

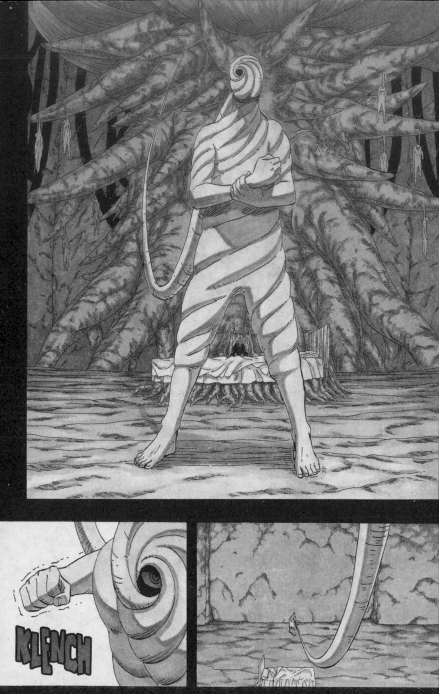

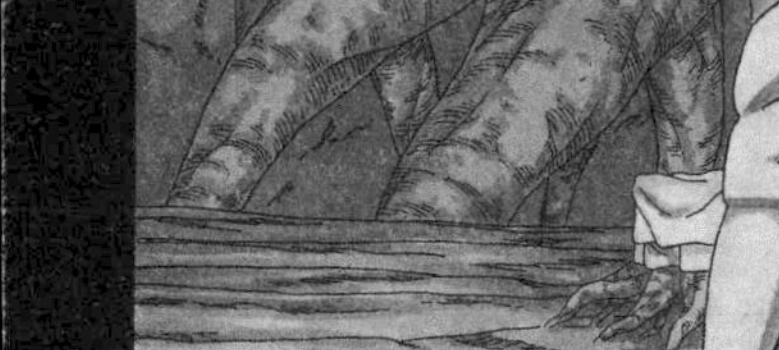
KLENCH

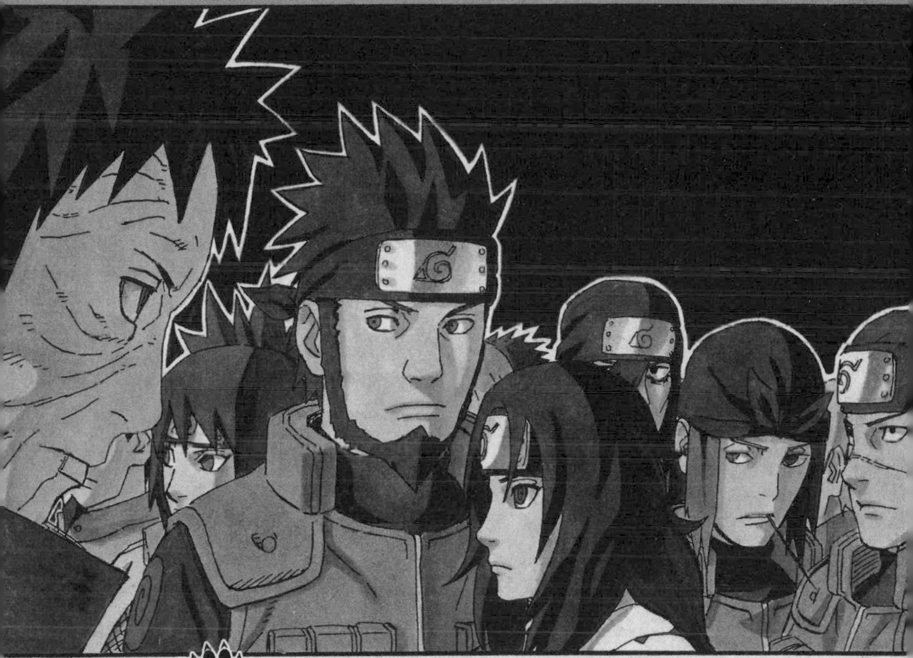

Number 604: Reunion, and Then...

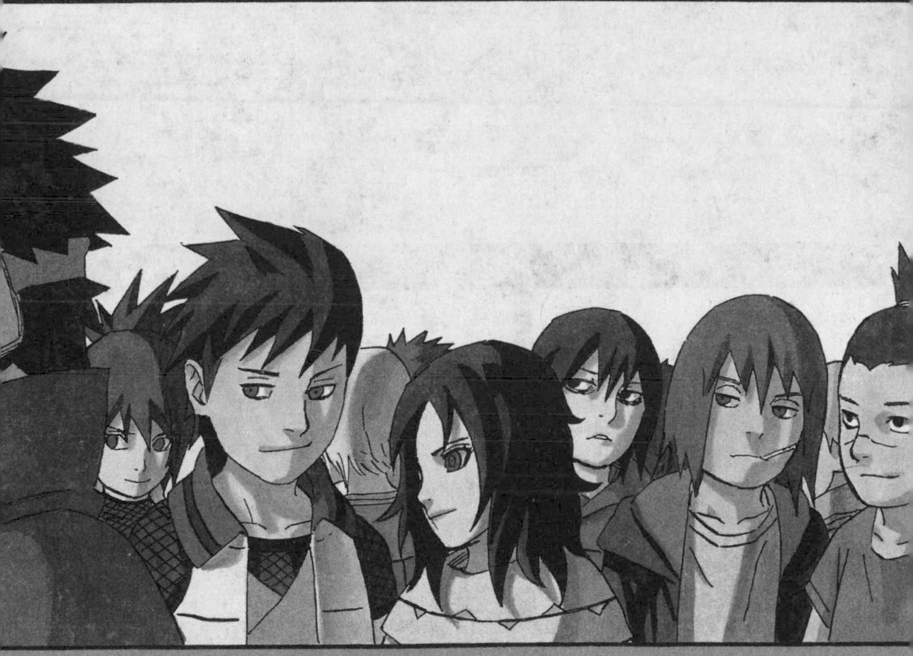

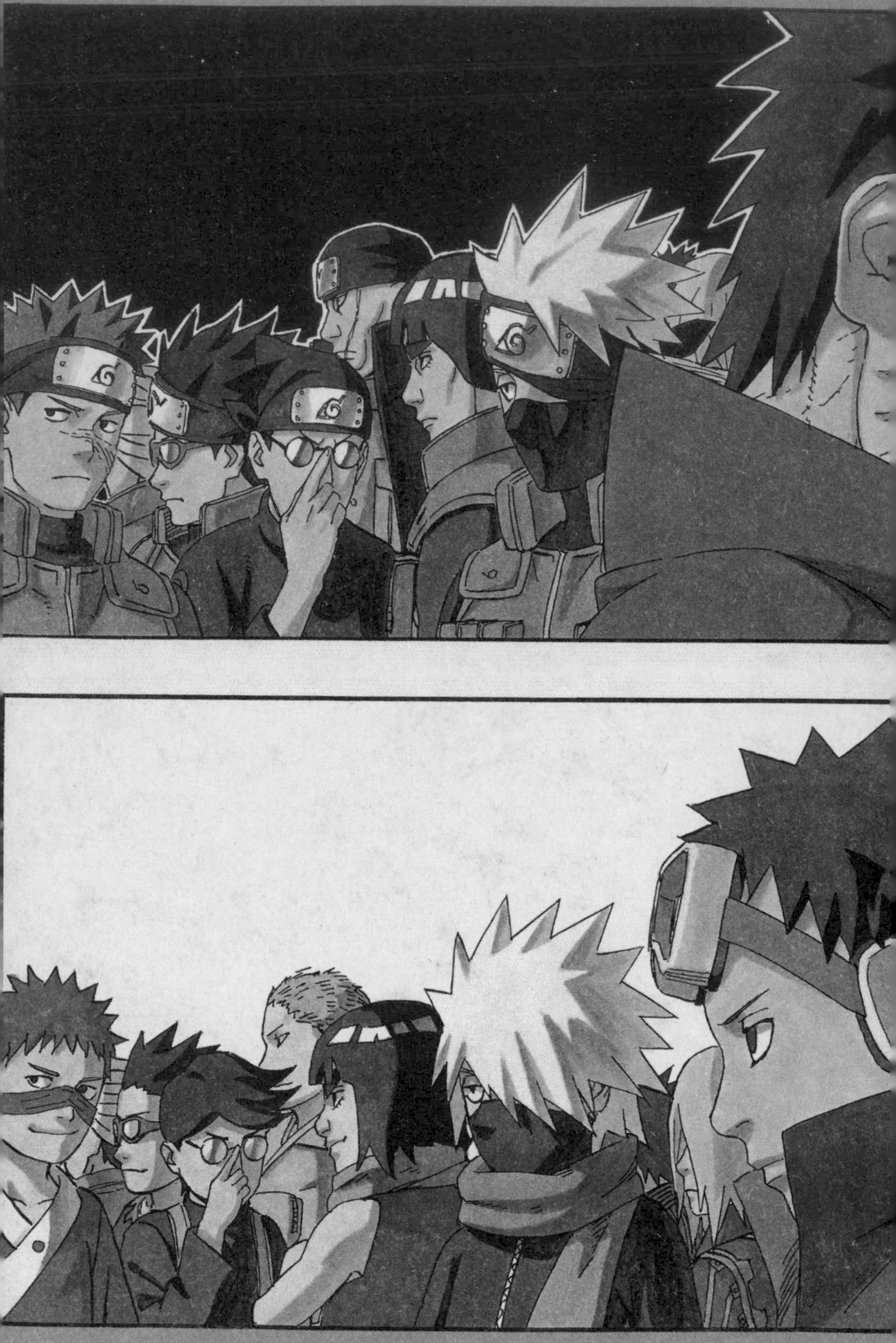

NARUTO

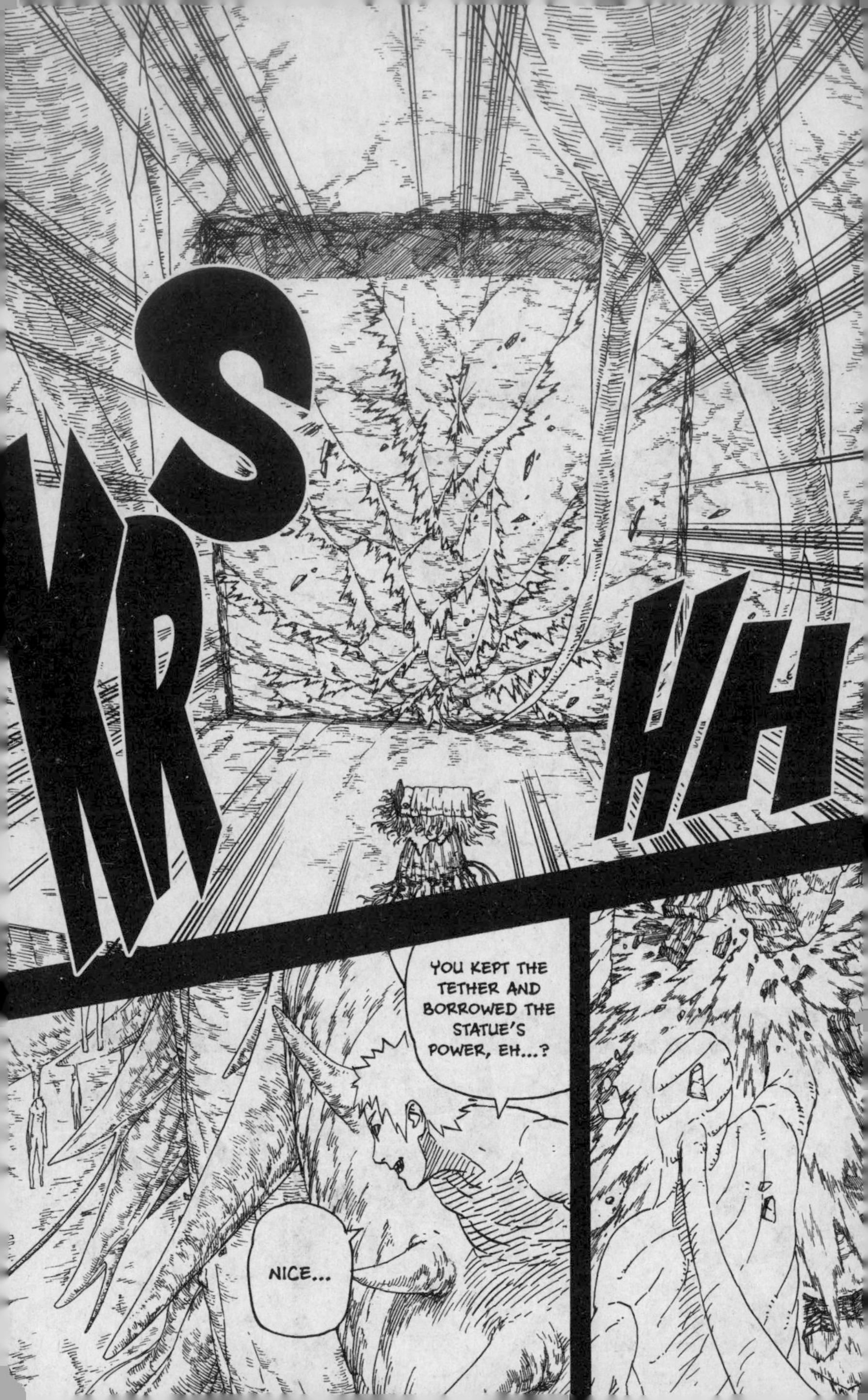
KRSHH
YOU KEPT THE TETHER AND BORROWED THE STATUE'S POWER, EH...?
NICE...

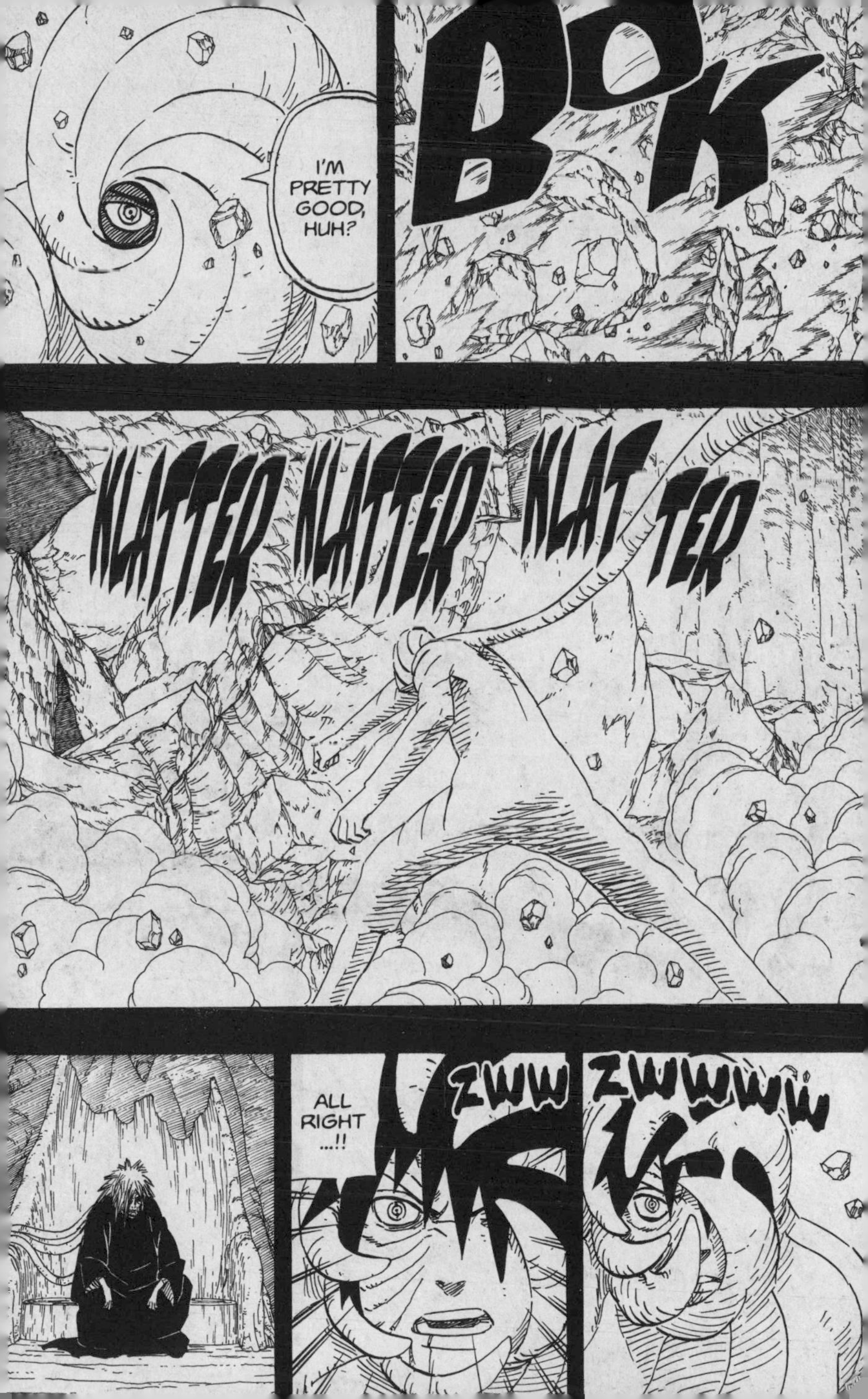
DOK
I'M PRETTY GOOD, HUH?
KLATTER KLATTER KLAT TER
ZWWWWW
ZWW
ALL RIGHT ...!!

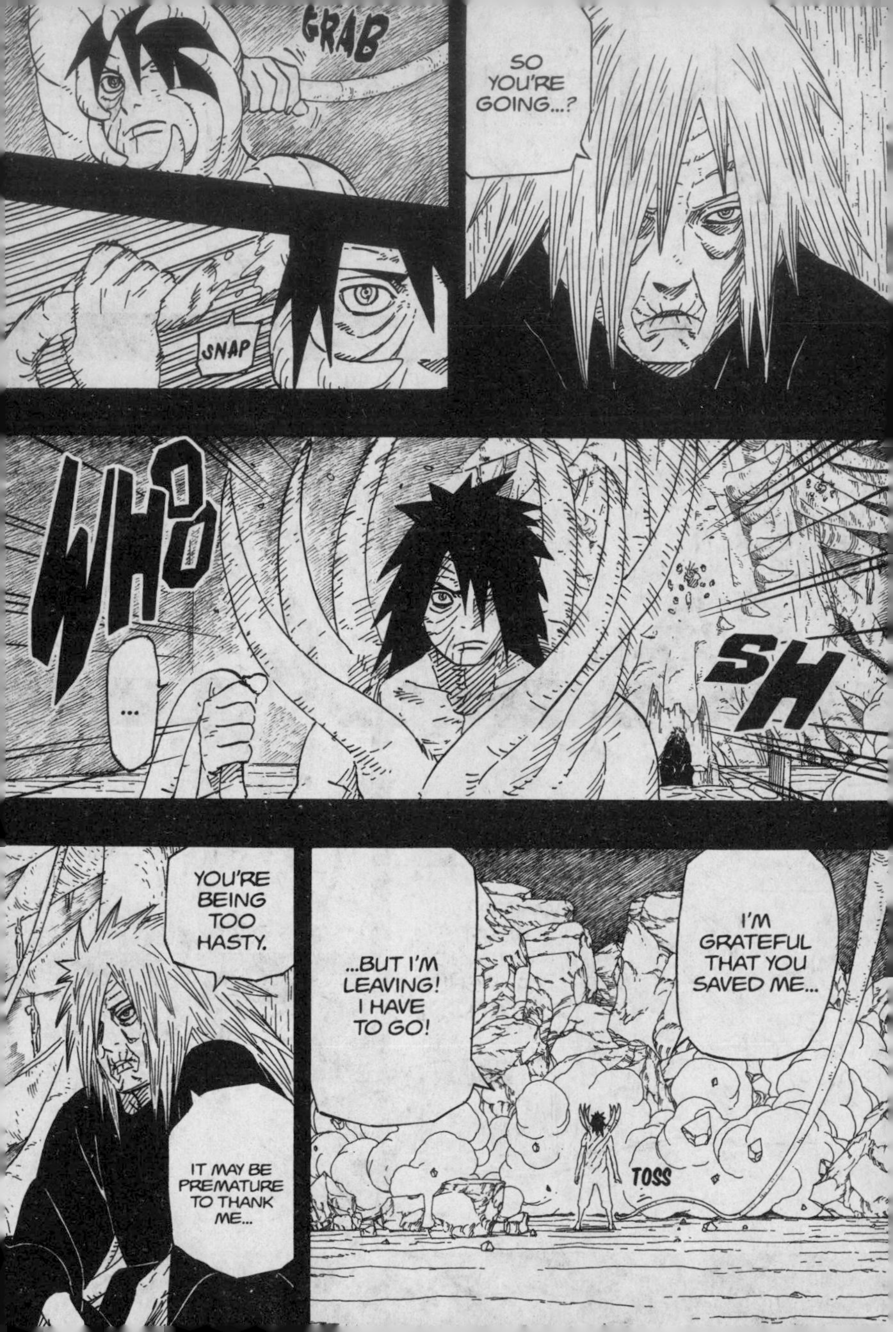
SO YOU'RE GOING...?
GRAB
SNAP
SH
WHOO
...
I'M GRATEFUL THAT YOU SAVED ME...
...BUT I'M LEAVING! I HAVE TO GO!
TOSS
YOU'RE BEING TOO HASTY.
IT MAY BE PREMATURE TO THANK ME...

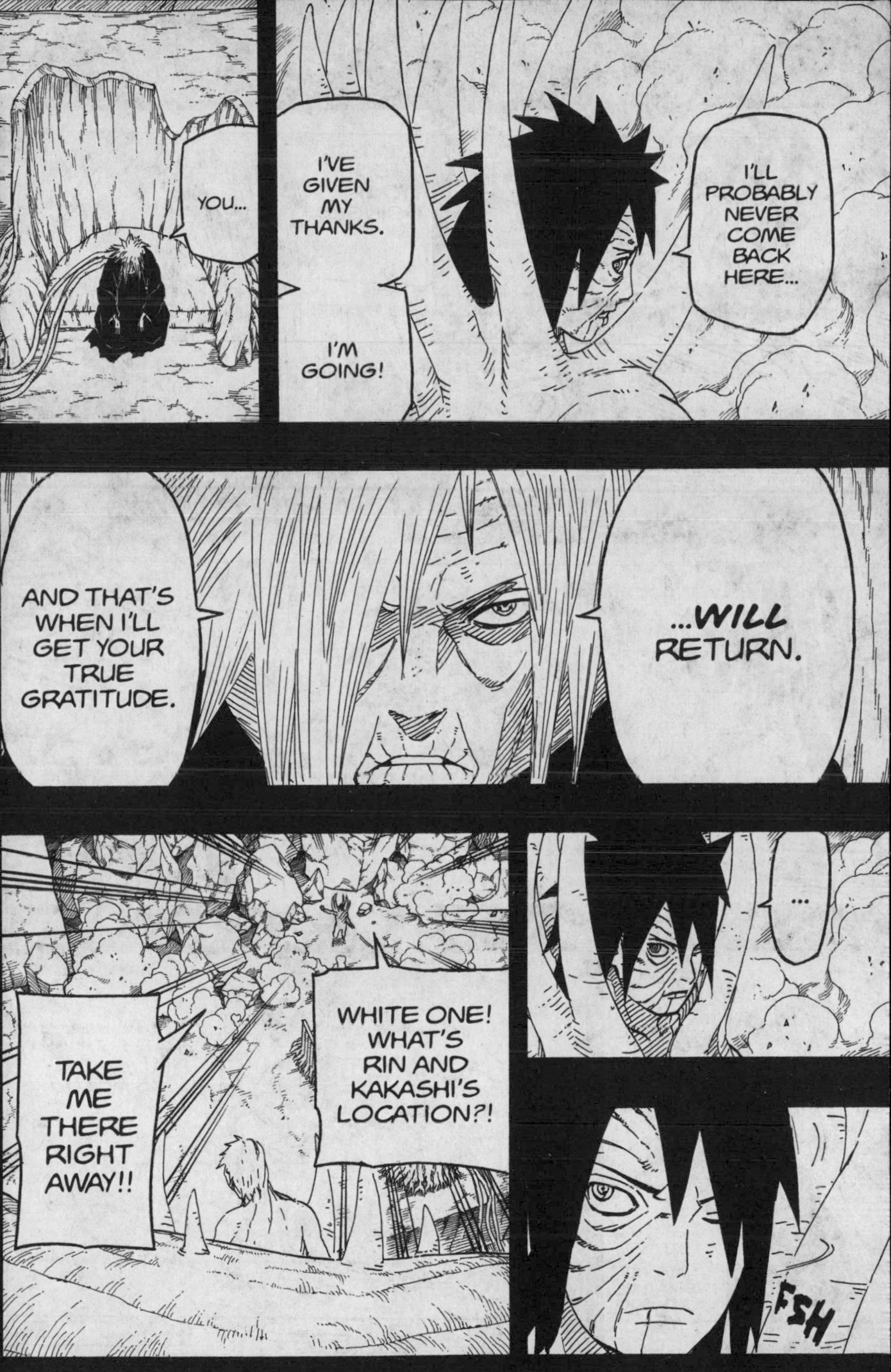
I'LL PROBABLY NEVER COME BACK HERE...
I'VE GIVEN MY THANKS.
I'M GOING!
YOU...
...WILL RETURN.
AND THAT'S WHEN I'LL GET YOUR TRUE GRATITUDE.
...
FSH
WHITE ONE! WHAT'S RIN AND KAKASHI'S LOCATION?!
TAKE ME THERE RIGHT AWAY!!

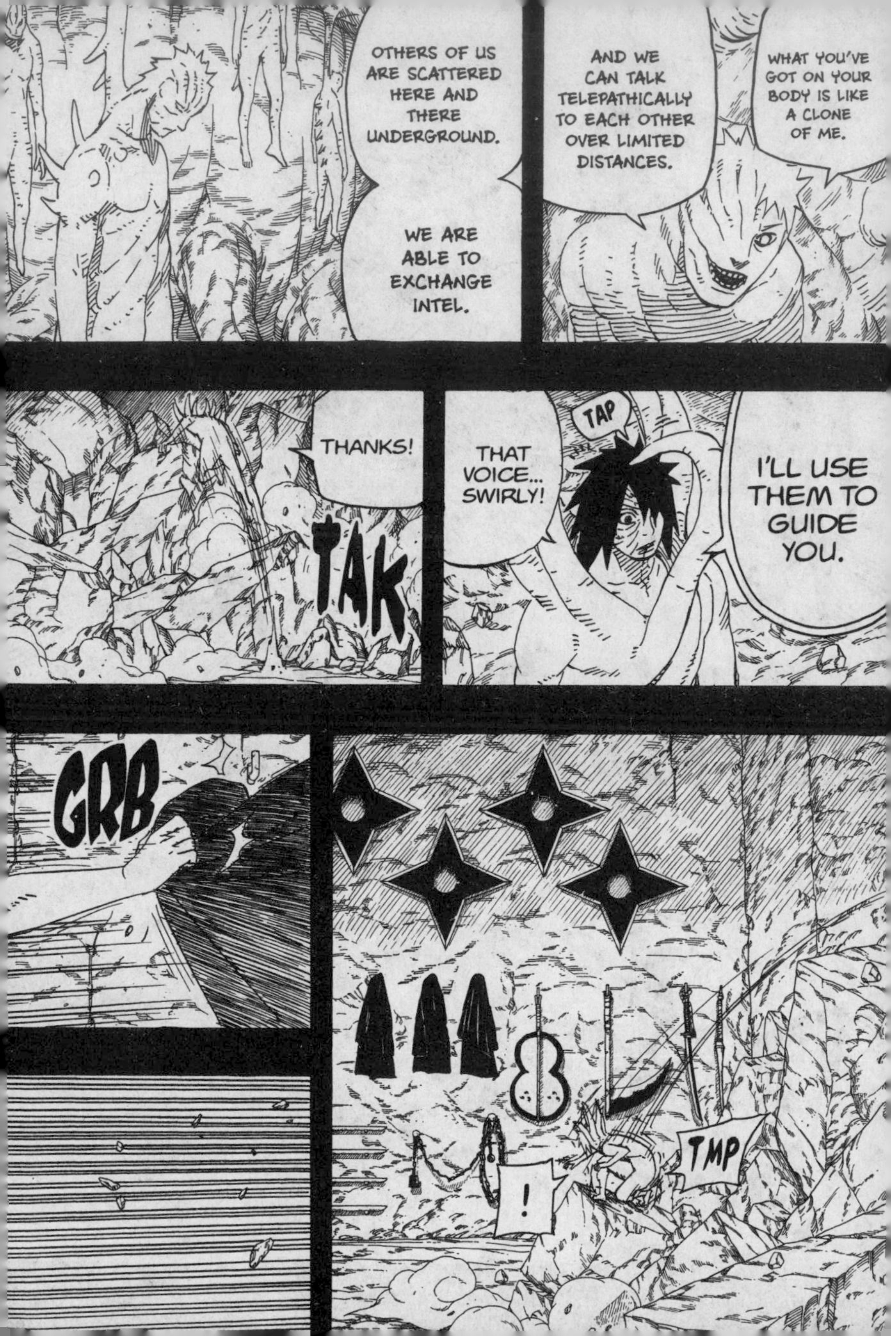
WHAT YOU'VE GOT ON YOUR BODY IS LIKE A CLONE OF ME.
AND WE CAN TALK TELEPATHICALLY TO EACH OTHER OVER LIMITED DISTANCES.
OTHERS OF US ARE SCATTERED HERE AND THERE UNDERGROUND.
WE ARE ABLE TO EXCHANGE INTEL.
I'LL USE THEM TO GUIDE YOU.
TAP
THAT VOICE... SWIRLY!
THANKS!
TAK
TMP
!
GRB

...

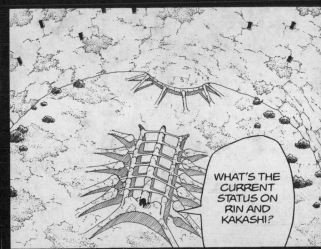

WHAT'S THE CURRENT STATUS ON RIN AND KAKASHI?

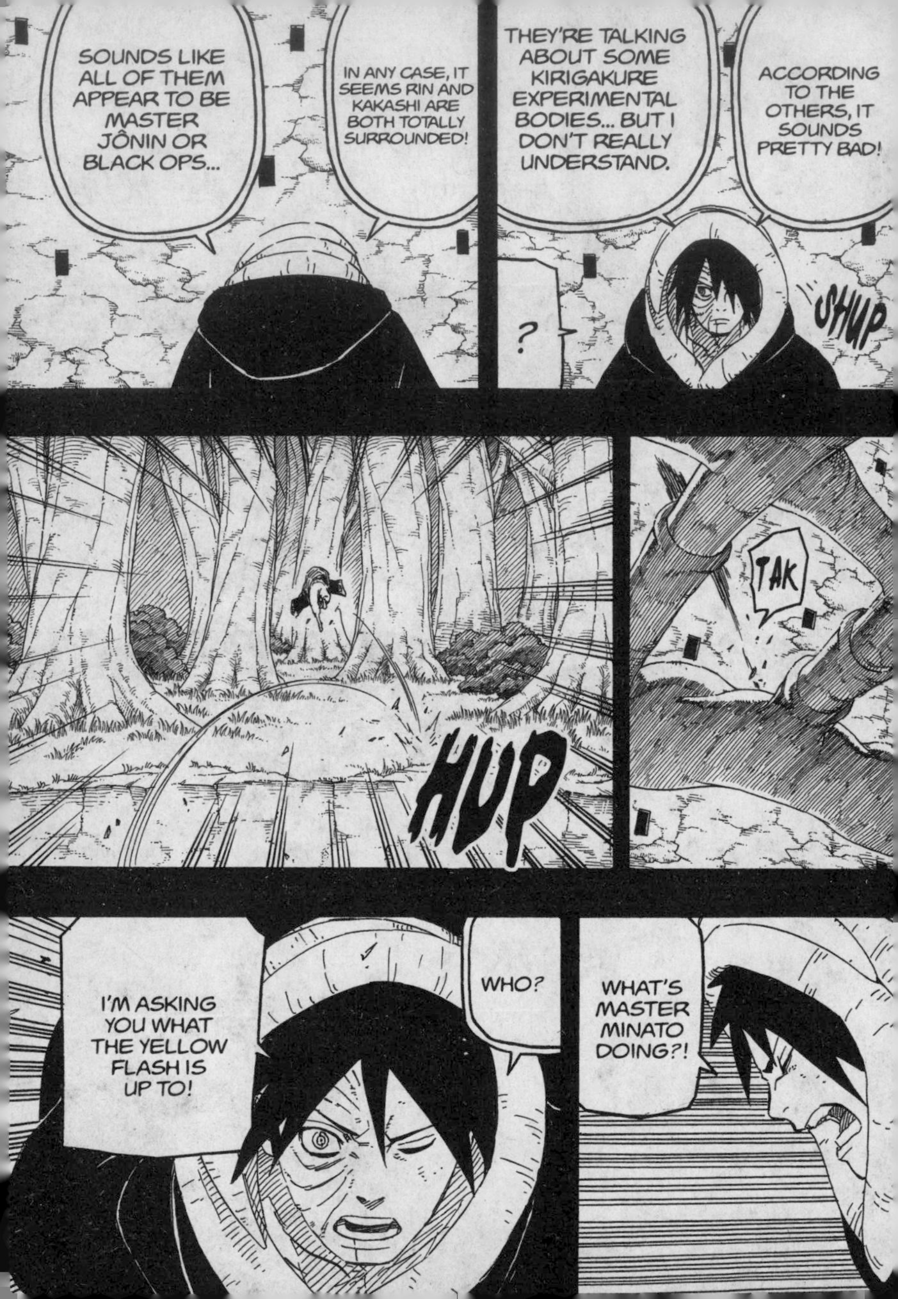
ACCORDING TO THE OTHERS, IT SOUNDS PRETTY BAD!
THEY'RE TALKING ABOUT SOME KIRIGAKURE EXPERIMENTAL BODIES... BUT I DON'T REALLY UNDERSTAND.
SHUP
?
IN ANY CASE, IT SEEMS RIN AND KAKASHI ARE BOTH TOTALLY SURROUNDED!
SOUNDS LIKE ALL OF THEM APPEAR TO BE MASTER JÔNIN OR BLACK OPS...
TAK
HUP
WHAT'S MASTER MINATO DOING?!
WHO?
I'M ASKING YOU WHAT THE YELLOW FLASH IS UP TO!

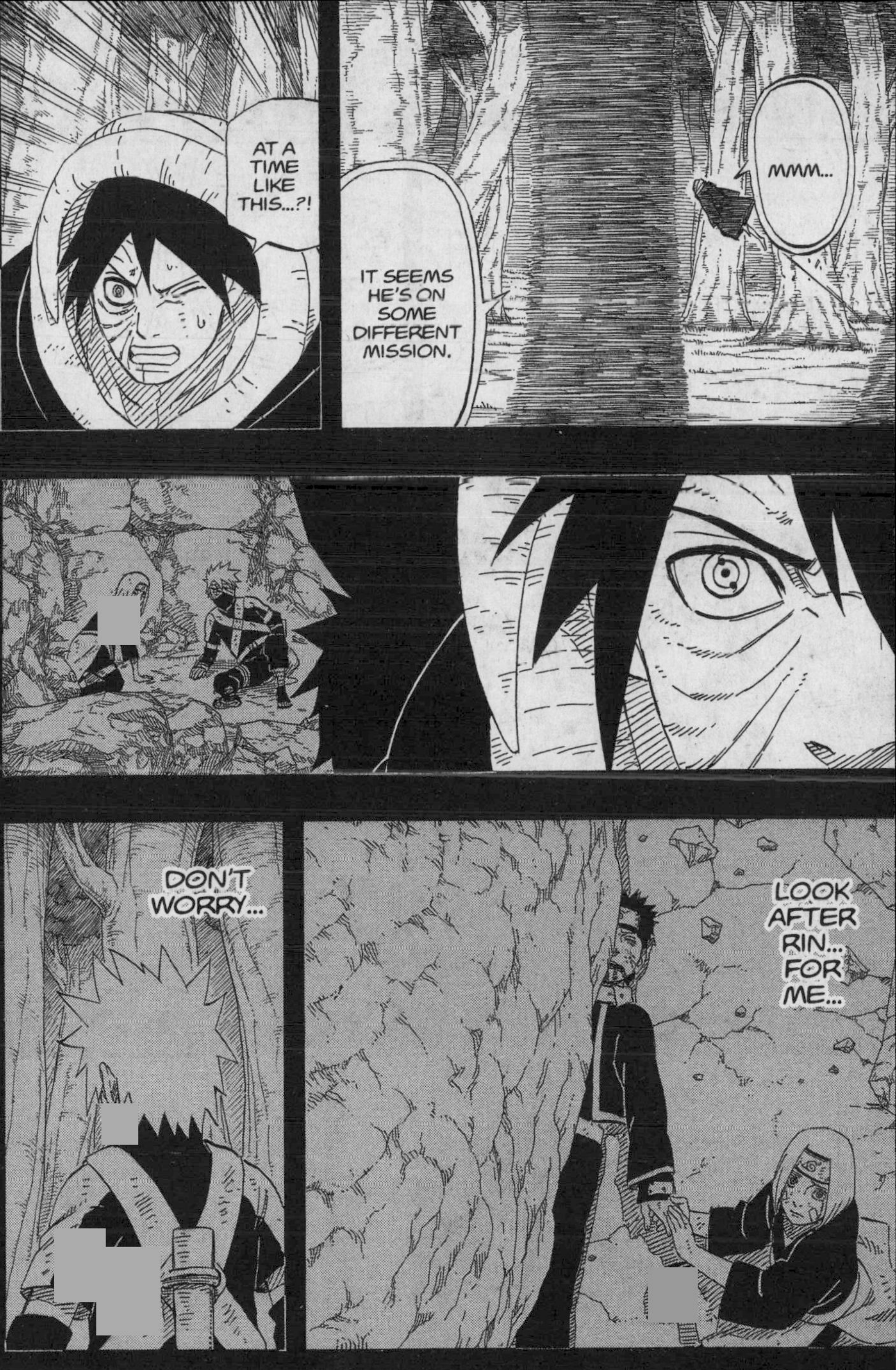
MMM...
IT SEEMS HE'S ON SOME DIFFERENT MISSION.
AT A TIME LIKE THIS...?!
LOOK AFTER RIN... FOR ME...
DON'T WORRY...

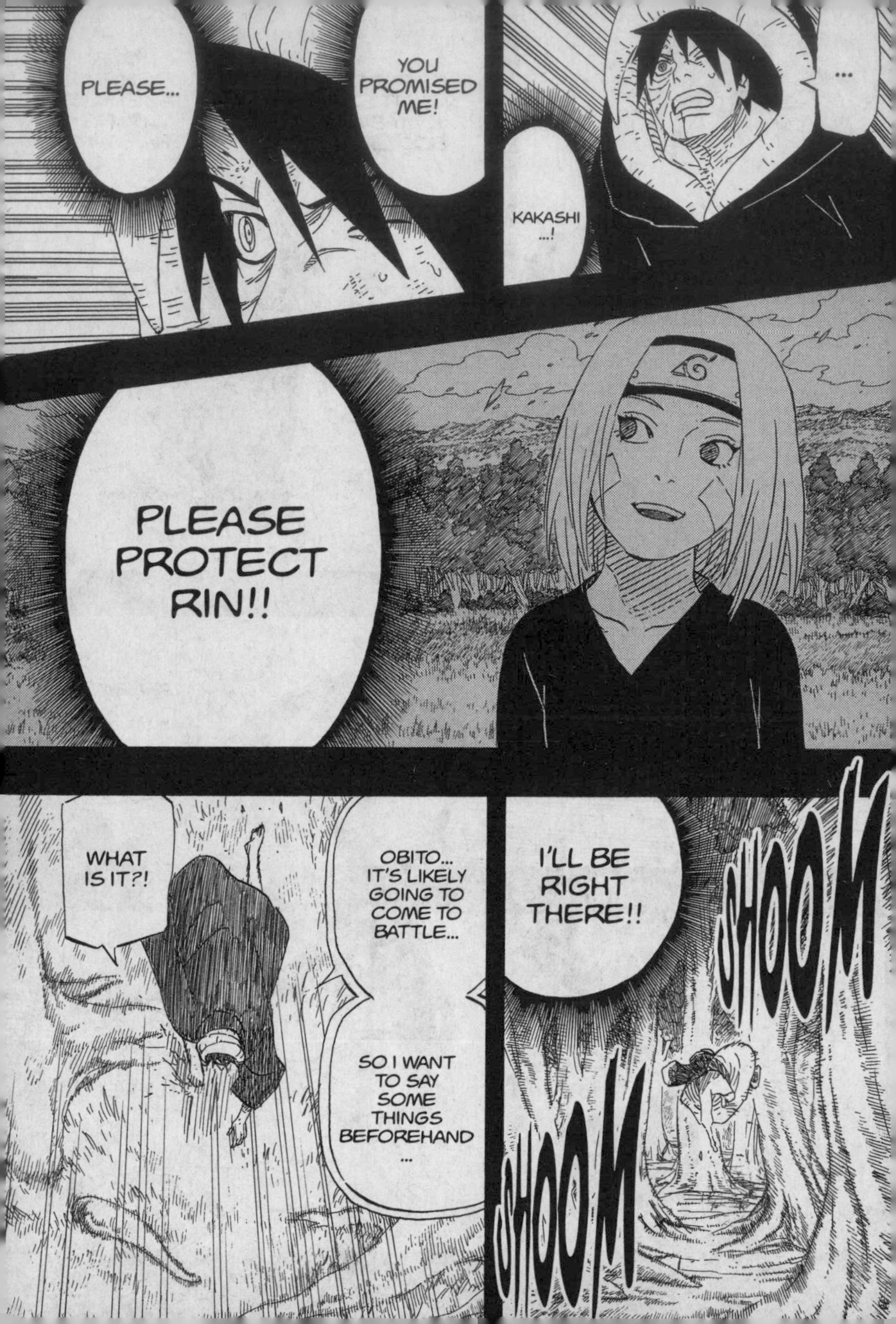
...
KAKASHI ...!
YOU PROMISED ME!
PLEASE...
PLEASE PROTECT RIN!!
I'LL BE RIGHT THERE!!
SHOOM
SHOOM
OBITO... IT'S LIKELY GOING TO COME TO BATTLE...
SO I WANT TO SAY SOME THINGS BEFOREHAND ...
WHAT IS IT?!

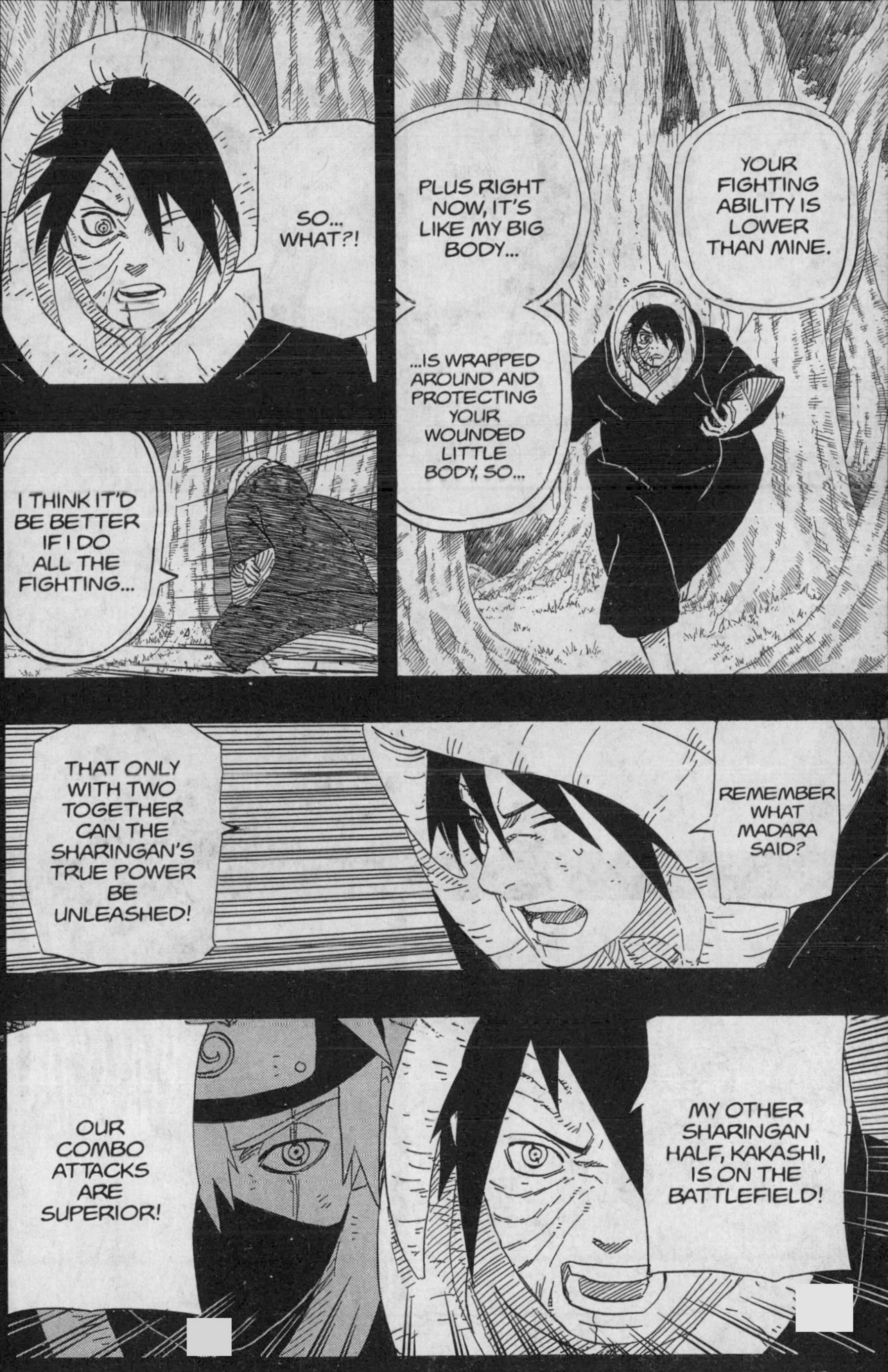
YOUR FIGHTING ABILITY IS LOWER THAN MINE.
PLUS RIGHT NOW, IT'S LIKE MY BIG BODY...
...IS WRAPPED AROUND AND PROTECTING YOUR WOUNDED LITTLE BODY, SO...
SO... WHAT?!
I THINK IT'D BE BETTER IF I DO ALL THE FIGHTING...
REMEMBER WHAT MADARA SAID?
THAT ONLY WITH TWO TOGETHER CAN THE SHARINGAN'S TRUE POWER BE UNLEASHED!
MY OTHER SHARINGAN HALF, KAKASHI, IS ON THE BATTLEFIELD!
OUR COMBO ATTACKS ARE SUPERIOR!

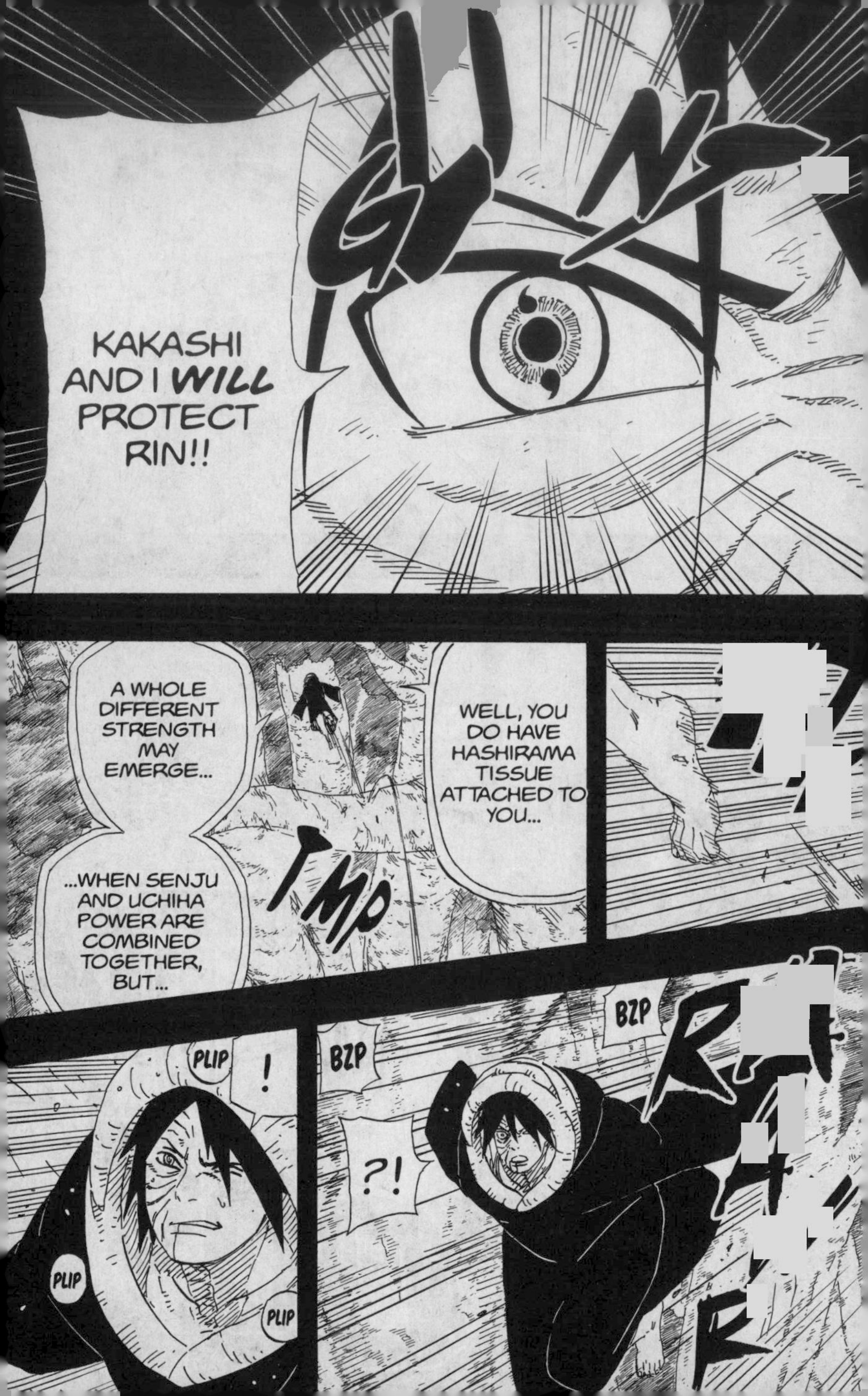
KAKASHI AND I WILL PROTECT RIN!!
WELL, YOU DO HAVE HASHIRAMA TISSUE ATTACHED TO YOU...
A WHOLE DIFFERENT STRENGTH MAY EMERGE...
...WHEN SENJU AND UCHIHA POWER ARE COMBINED TOGETHER, BUT...
TMP
BZP
BZP
?!
PLIP
!
PLIP
PLIP

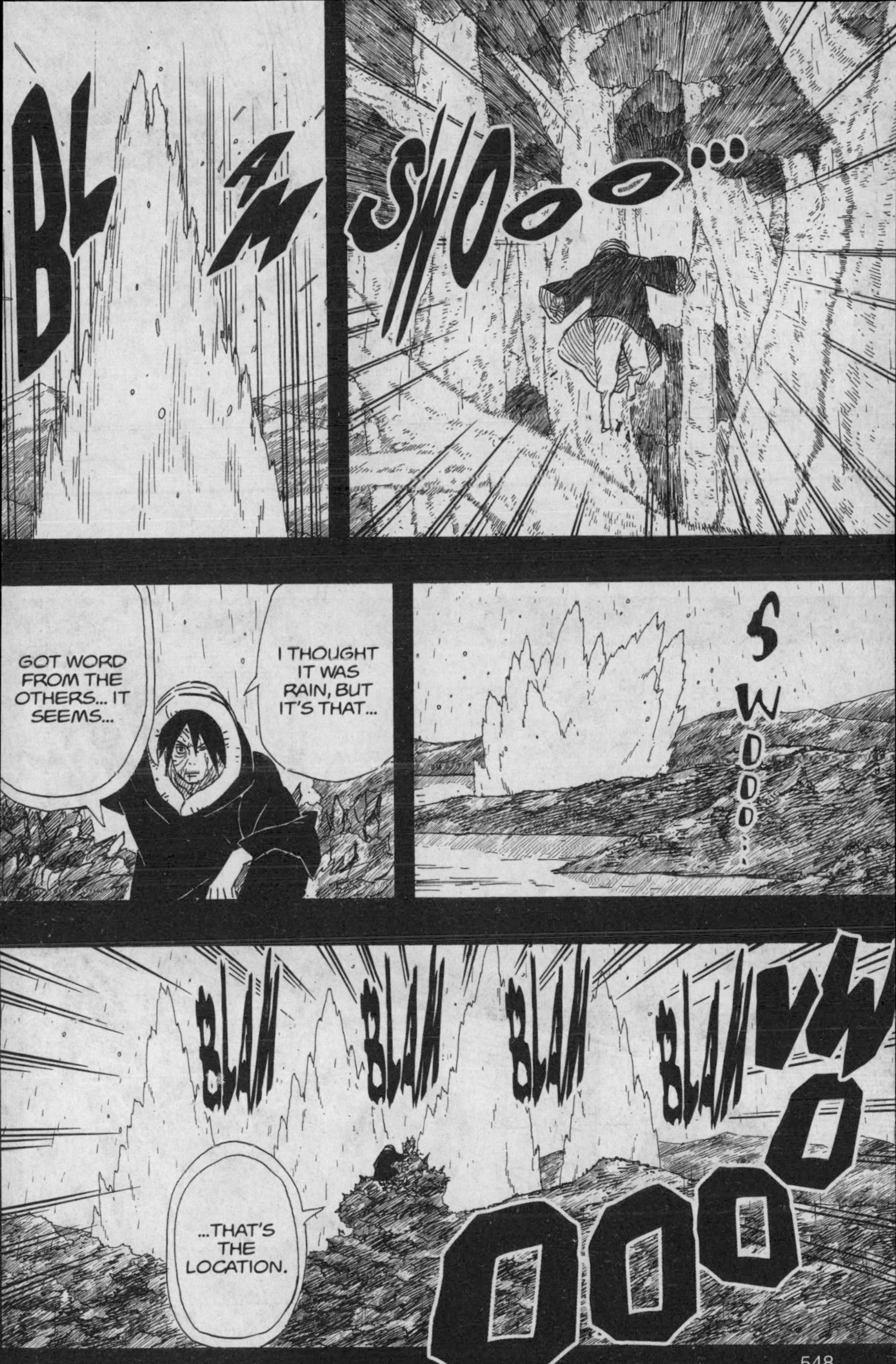
SWOOOO...
BLAM
SWOOOO...
I THOUGHT IT WAS RAIN, BUT IT'S THAT...
GOT WORD FROM THE OTHERS... IT SEEMS...
VWOOOOOO
BLAM
BLAM
BLAM
BLAM
...THAT'S THE LOCATION.

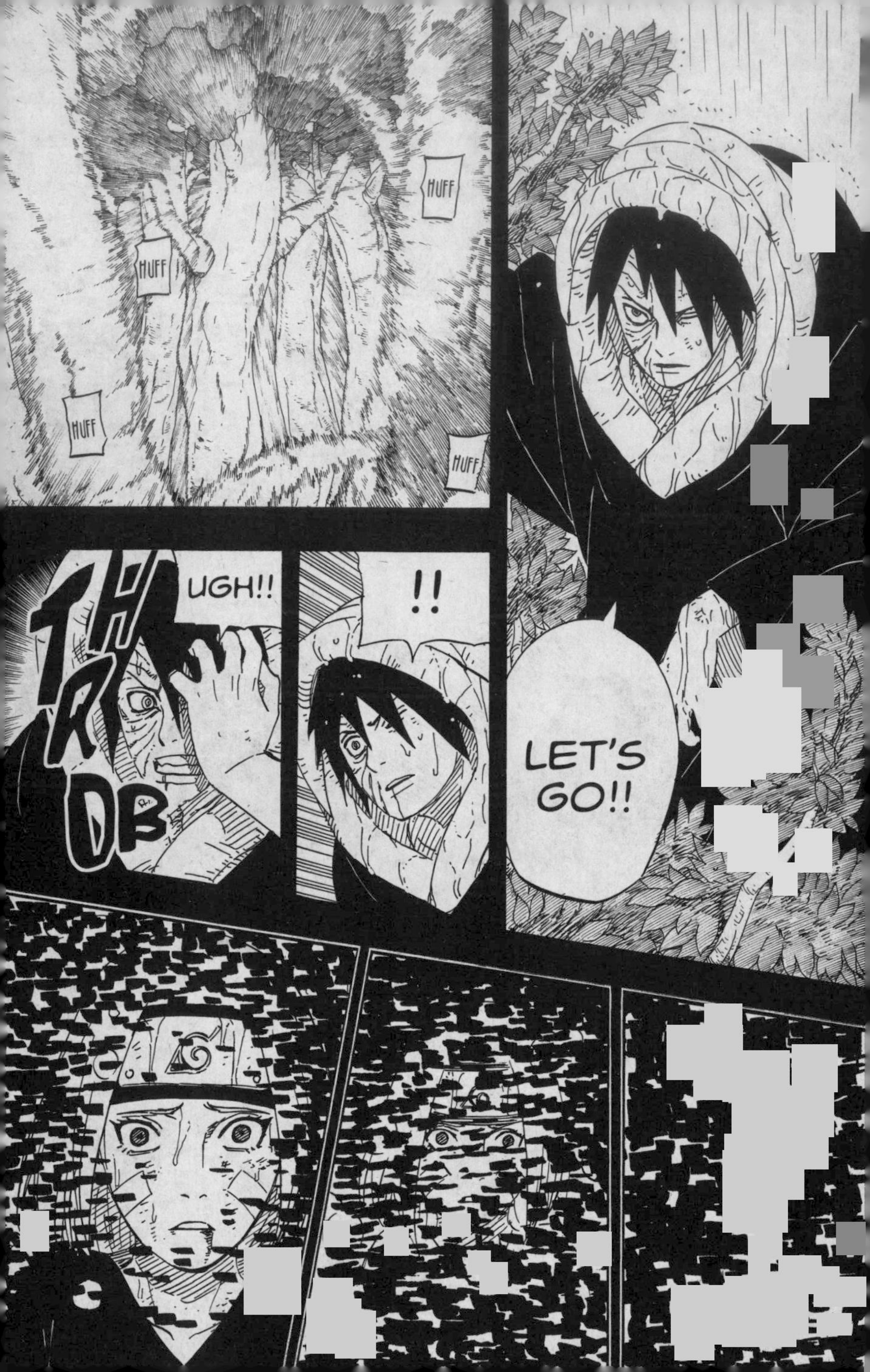
LET'S GO!!
HUFF
HUFF
HUFF
HUFF
!!
UGH!!

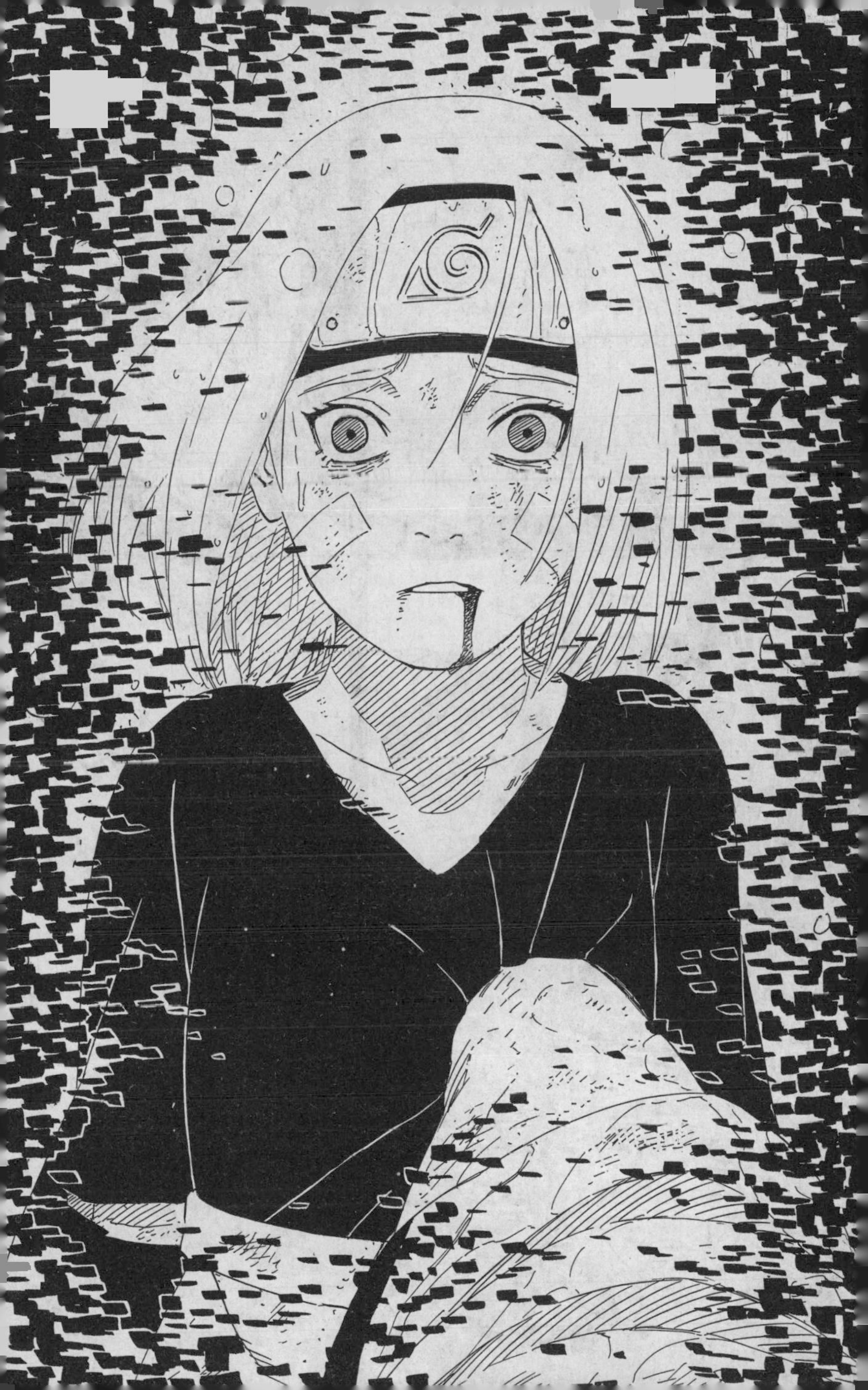

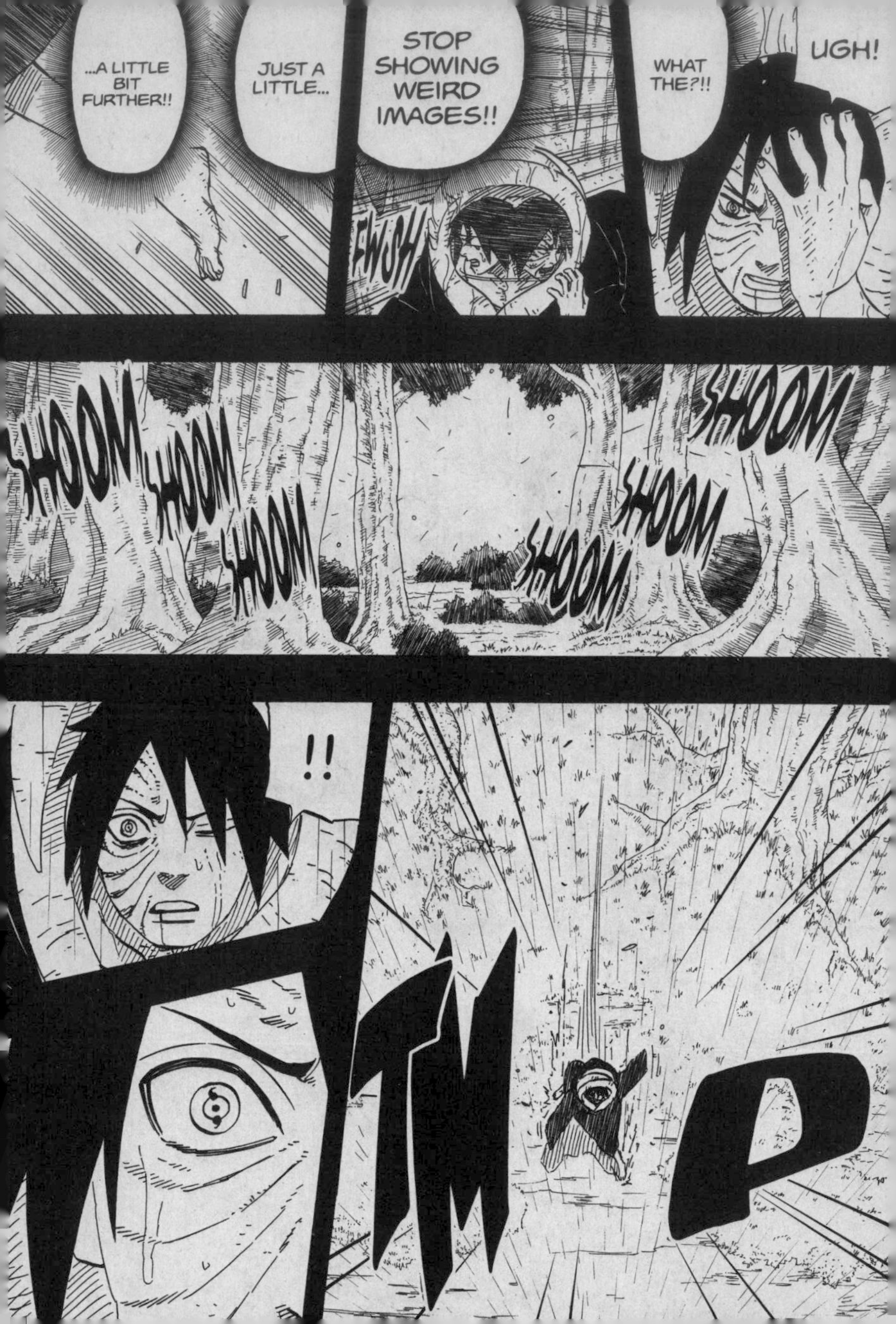
UGH!
WHAT THE?!!
STOP SHOWING WEIRD IMAGES!!
FWSH
JUST A LITTLE...
...A LITTLE BIT FURTHER!!
SHOOM
SHOOM
SHOOM
SHOOM
SHOOM
SHOOM
TMP
!!

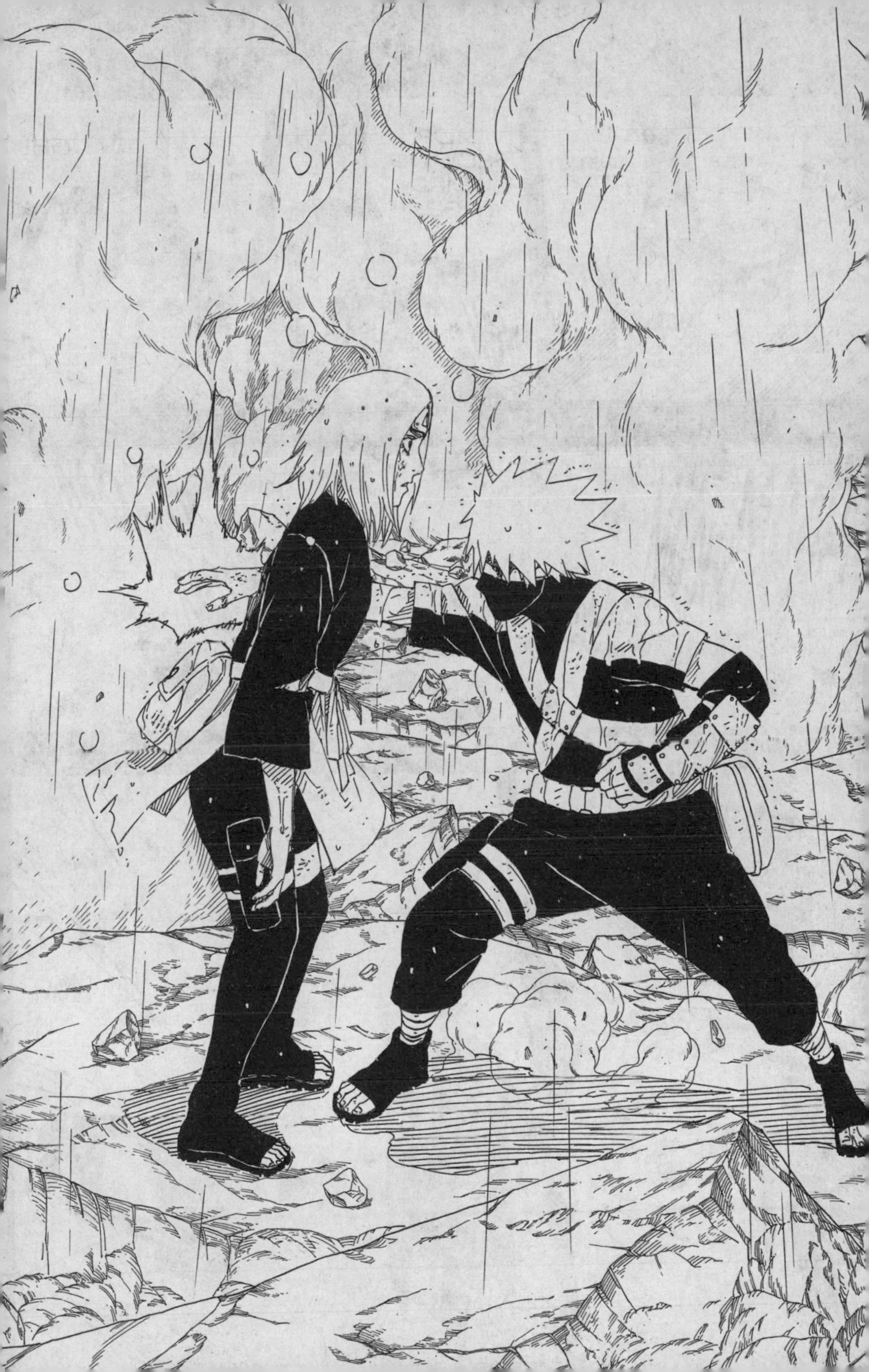

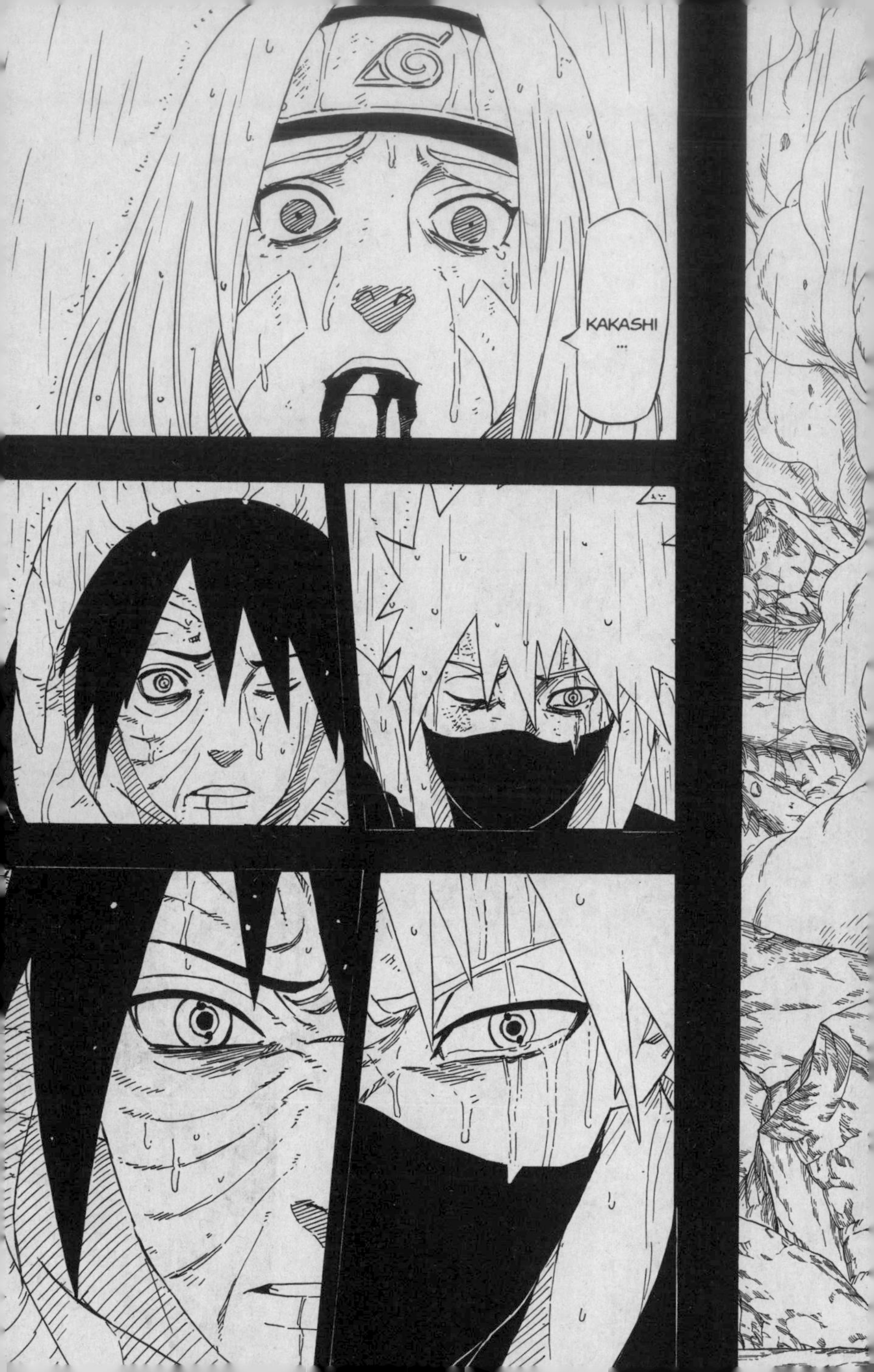
KAKASHI...

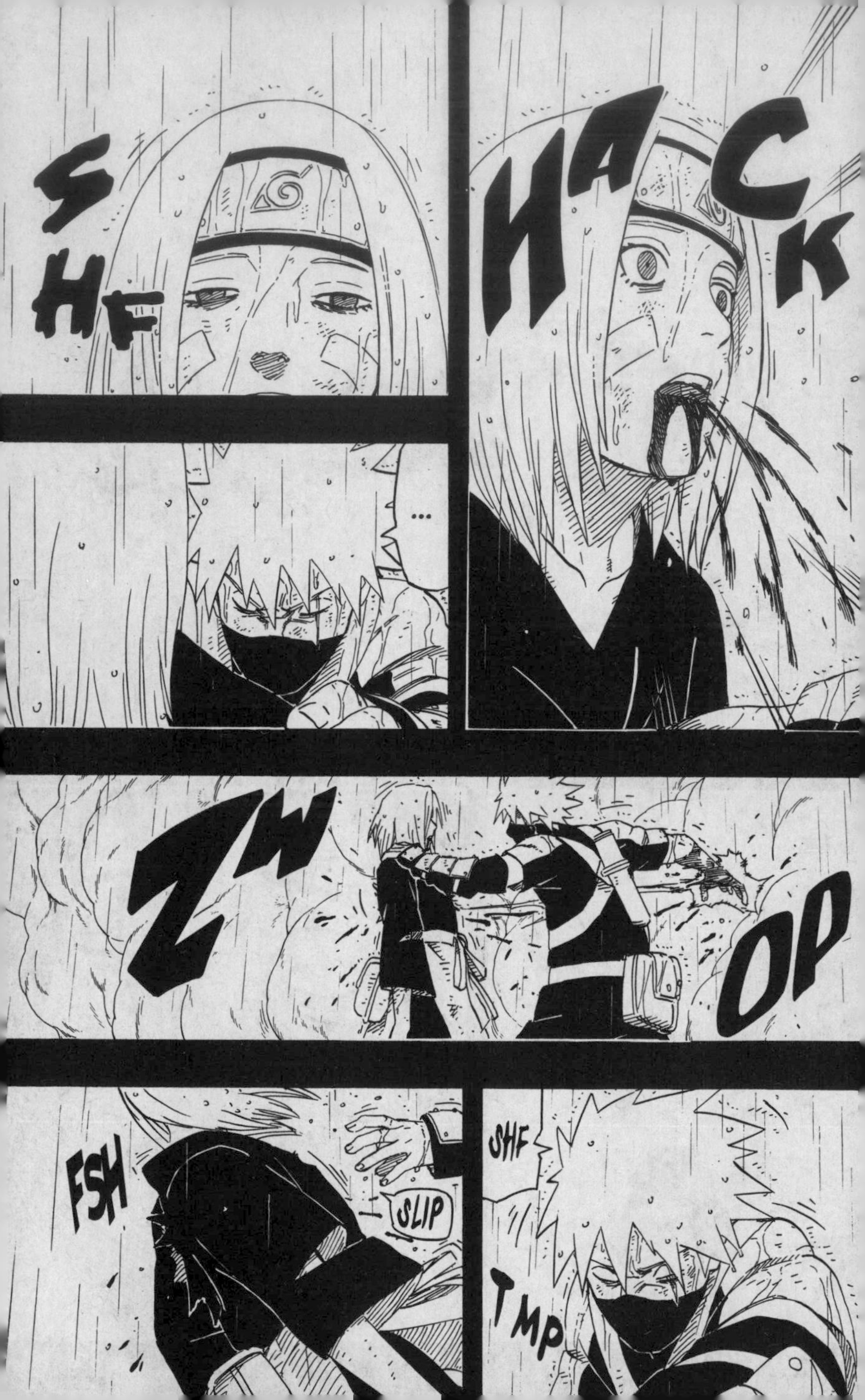
HACK
SHF
...
ZWOP
SHF
TMP
FSH
SLIP

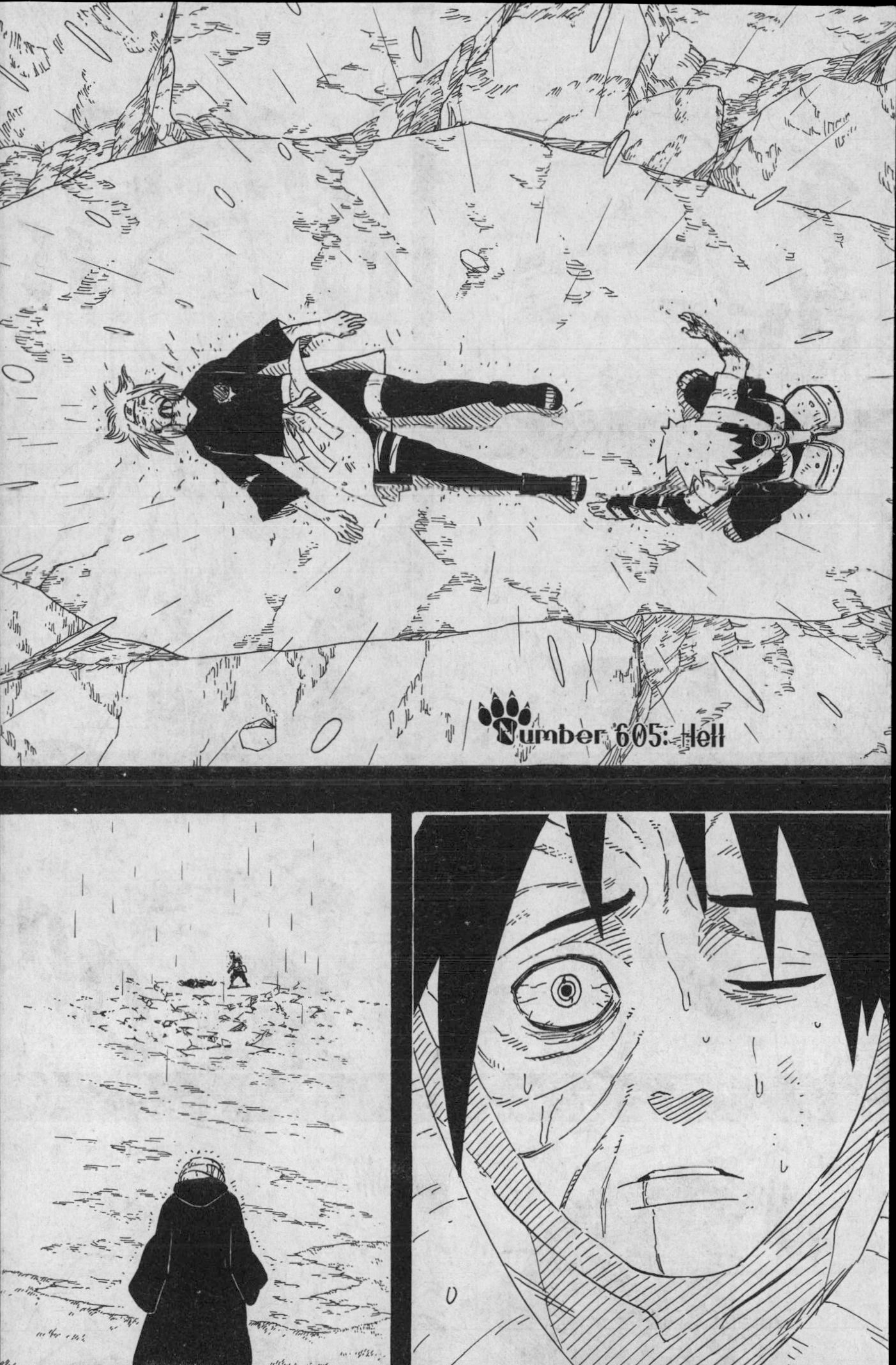
Number 605: Hell

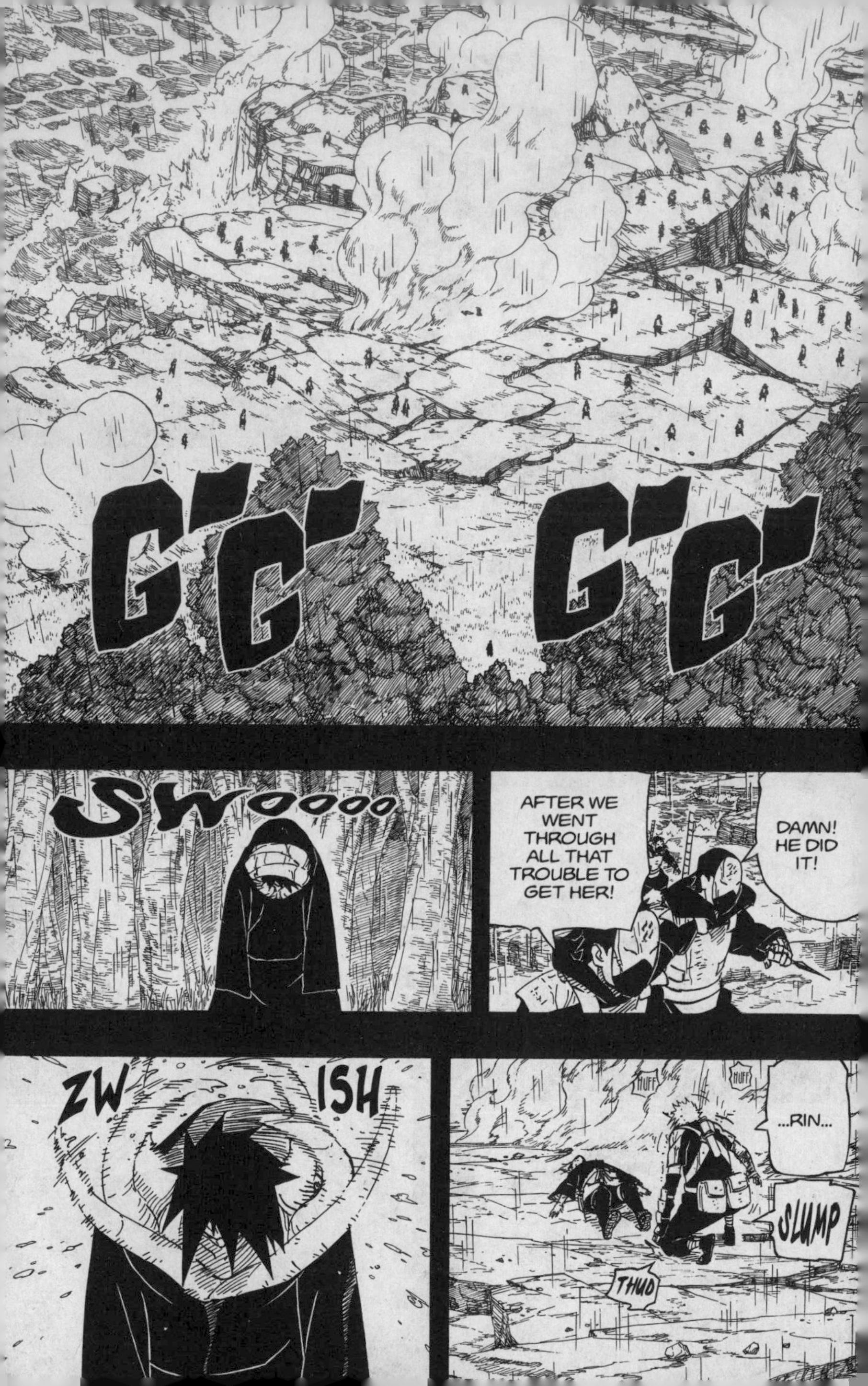
G'G' G'G'
DAMN! HE DID IT!
AFTER WE WENT THROUGH ALL THAT TROUBLE TO GET HER!
SWOOOO
HUFF
HUFF
...RIN...
SLUMP
THUD
ZWISH

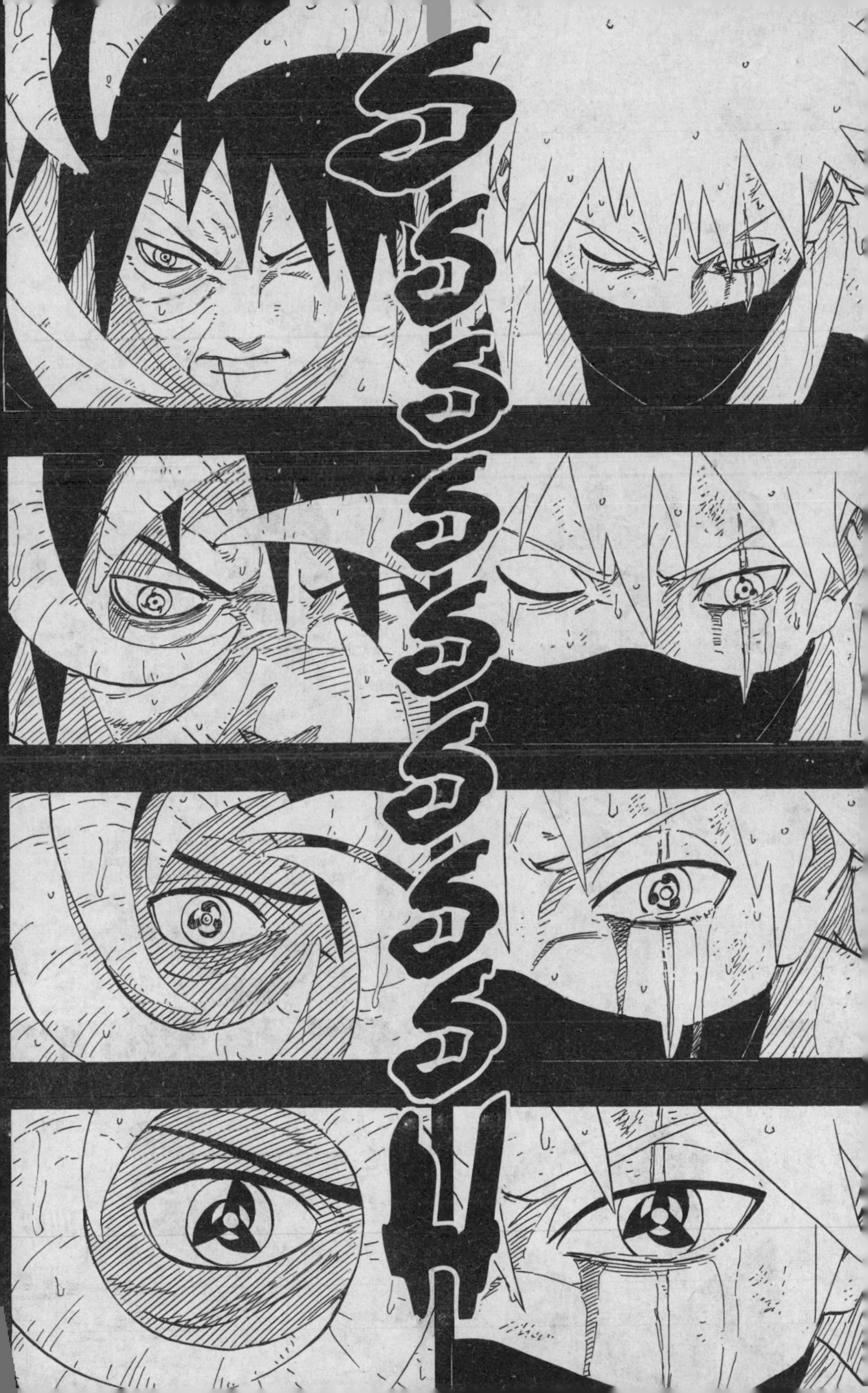
ゴゴゴゴゴゴゴゴ!!

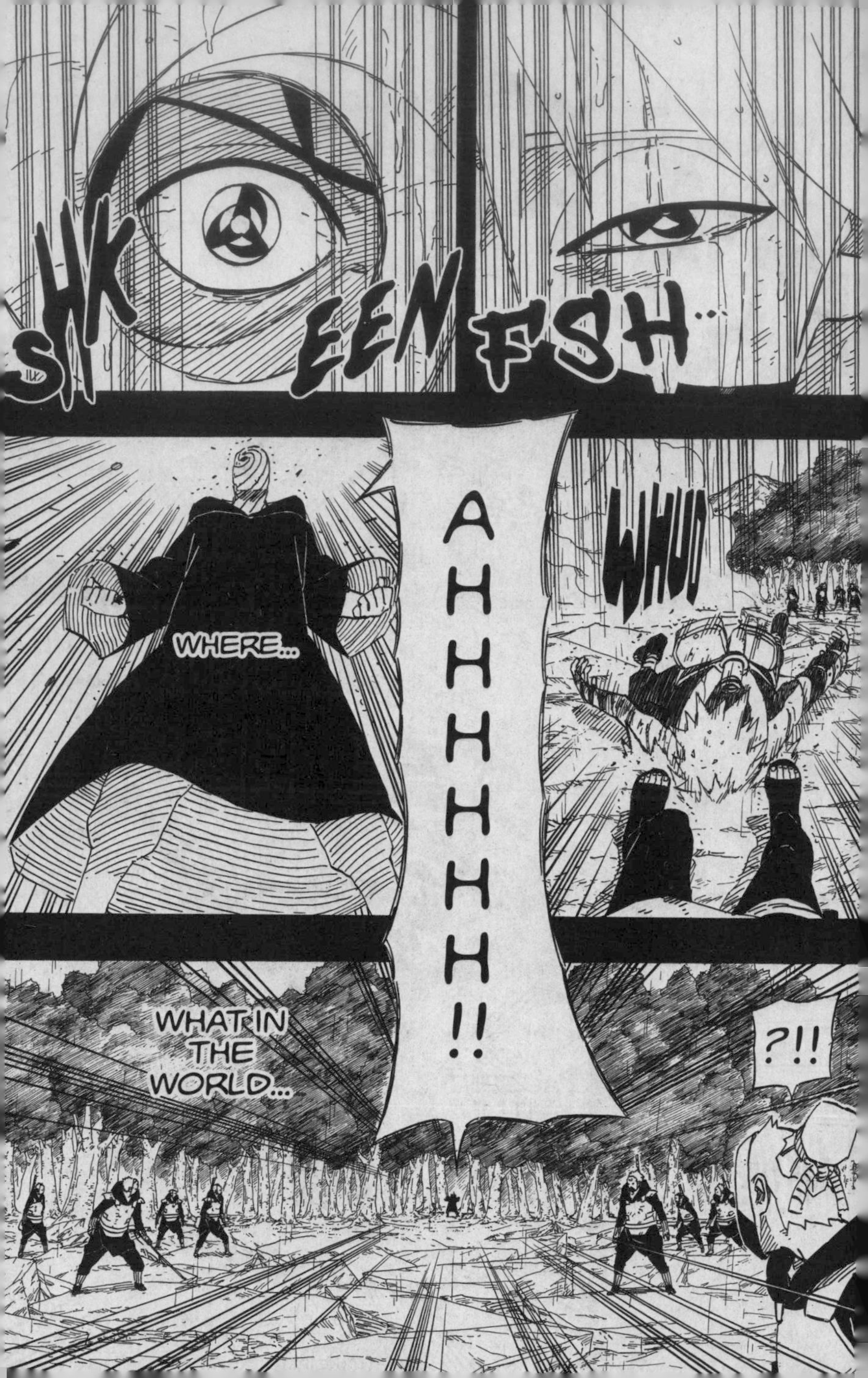
FSH...
SHK
EEN
WHUD
AHHHHHH!!
WHERE...
?!!
WHAT IN THE WORLD...

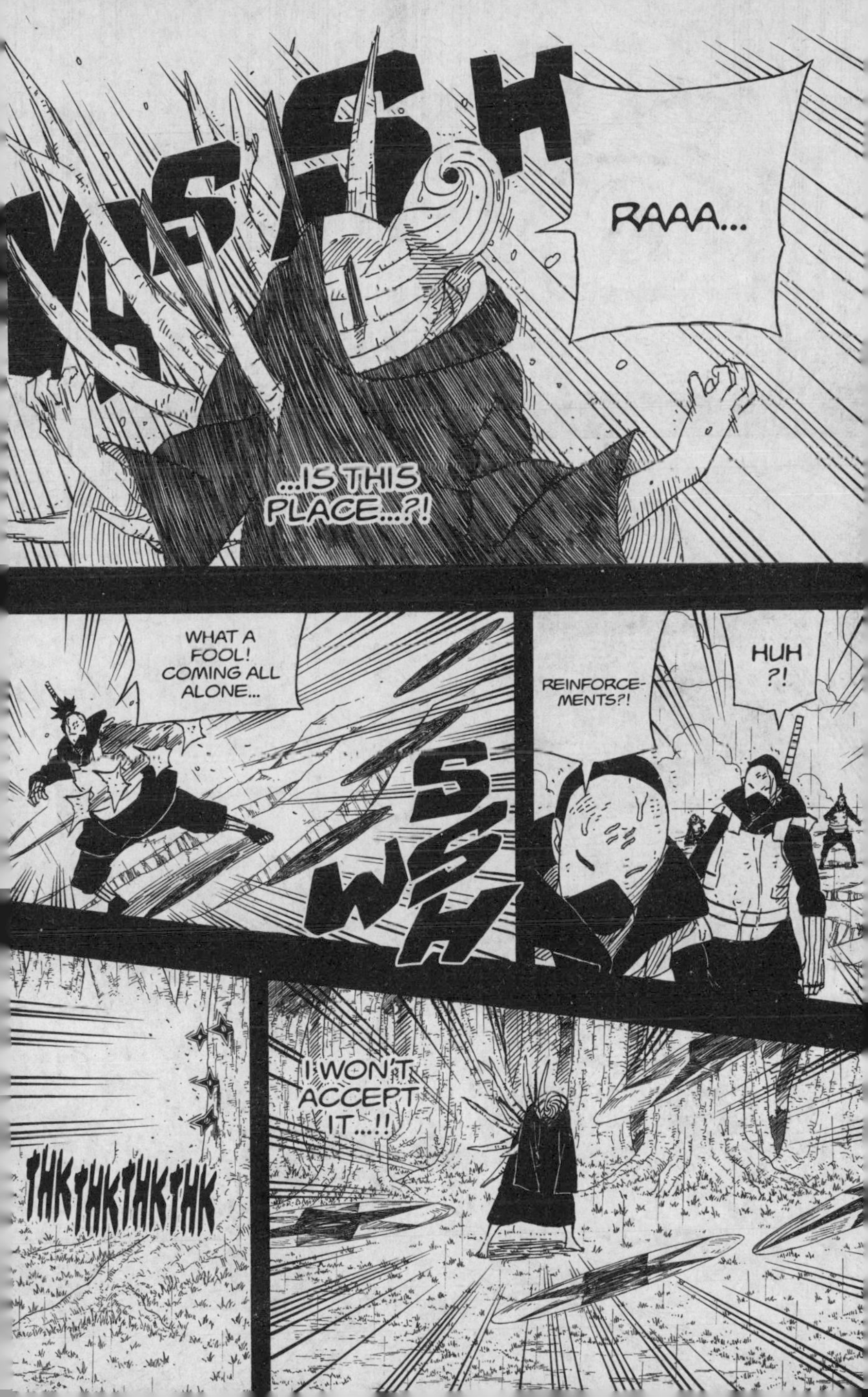
RAAA...
WSSH
...IS THIS PLACE...?!
HUH ?!
REINFORCE-MENTS?!
WHAT A FOOL! COMING ALL ALONE...
SWSH
I WON'T ACCEPT IT...!!
THKTHKTHKTHK

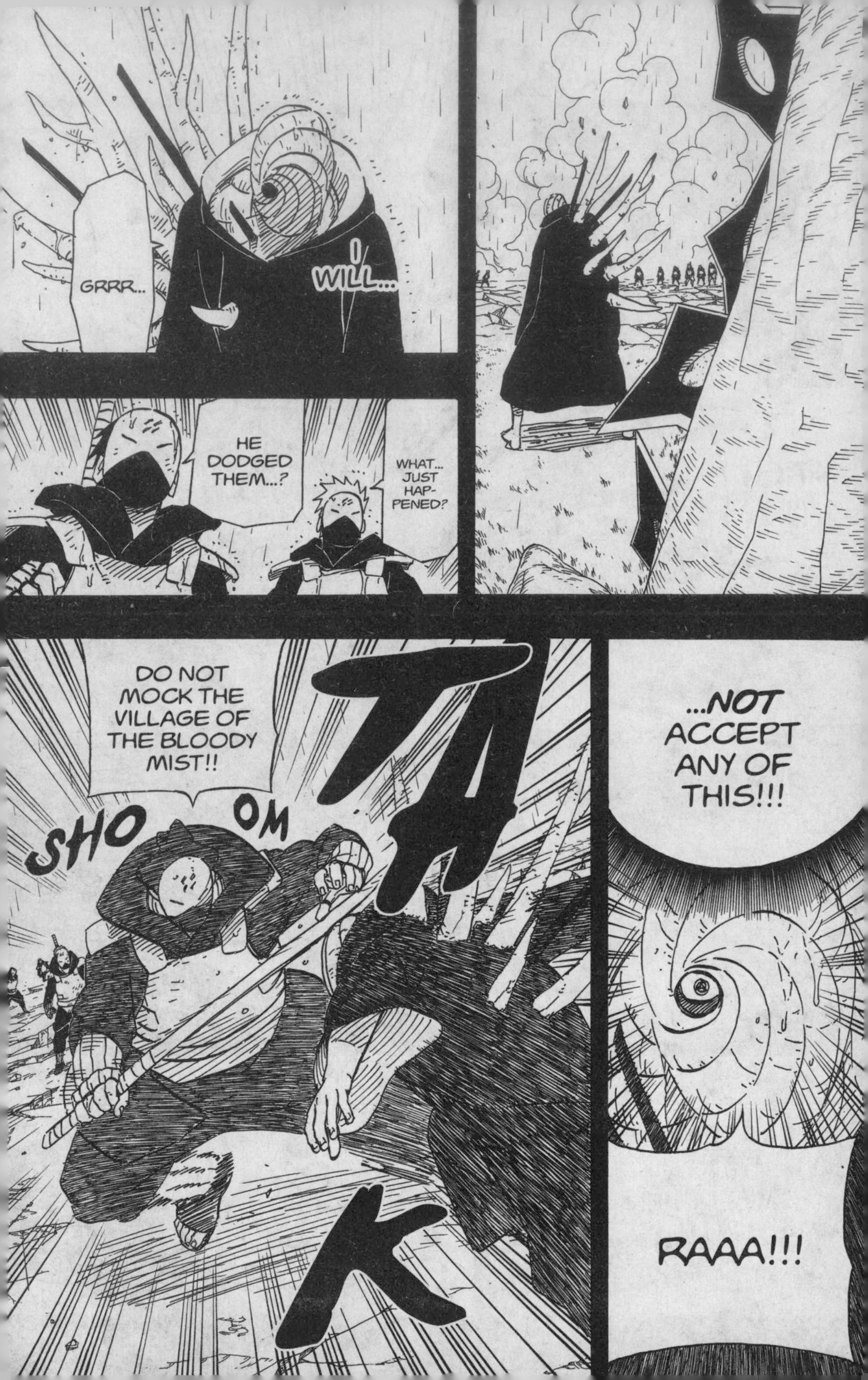
I WILL...
GRRR...
WHAT... JUST HAP-PENED?
HE DODGED THEM...?
...NOT ACCEPT ANY OF THIS!!!
RAAA!!!
DO NOT MOCK THE VILLAGE OF THE BLOODY MIST!!
SHOOM
TAK

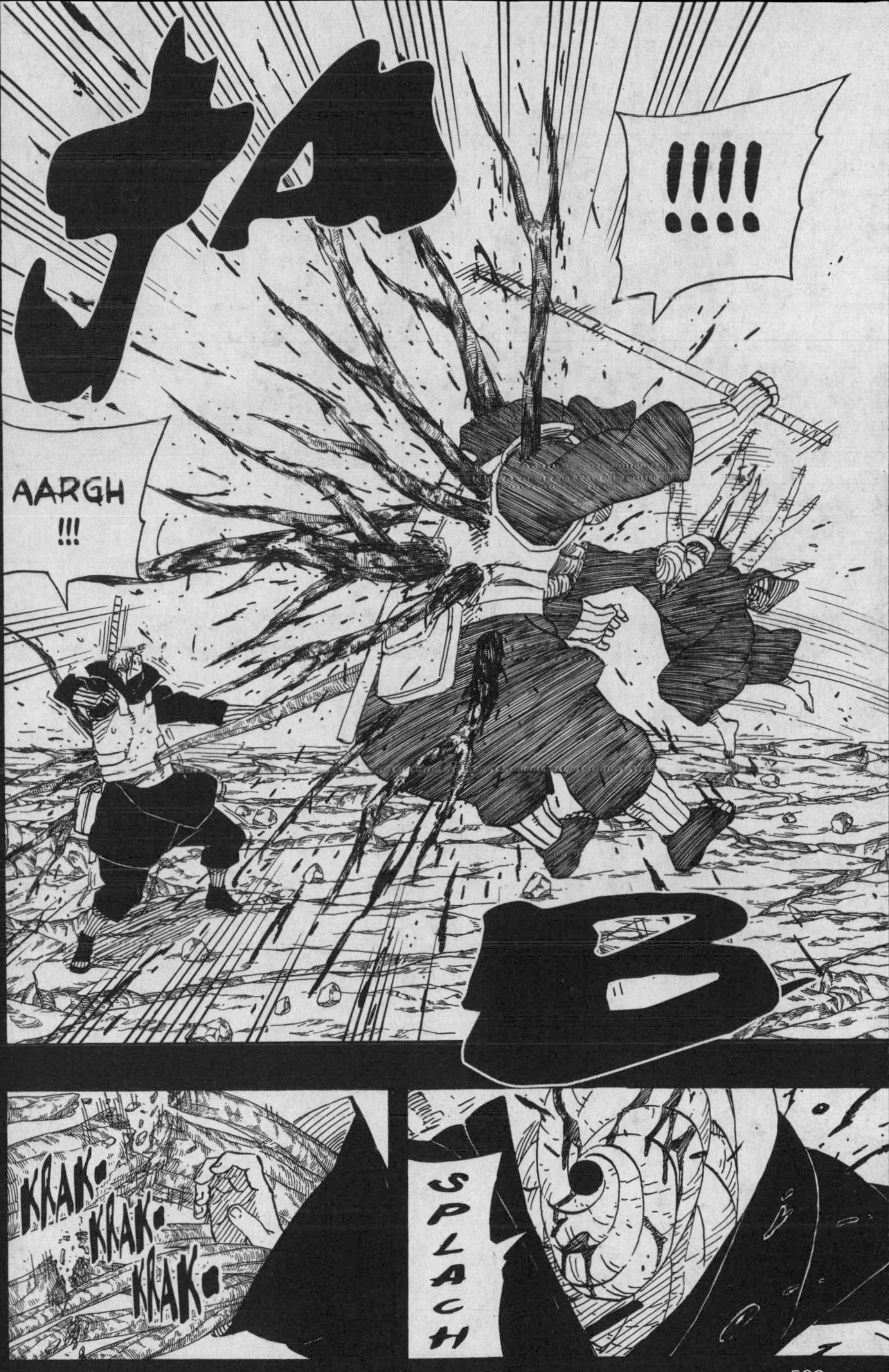
!!!!
JA
AARGH !!!
B
SPLACH
KRAK-
KRAK-
KRAK-

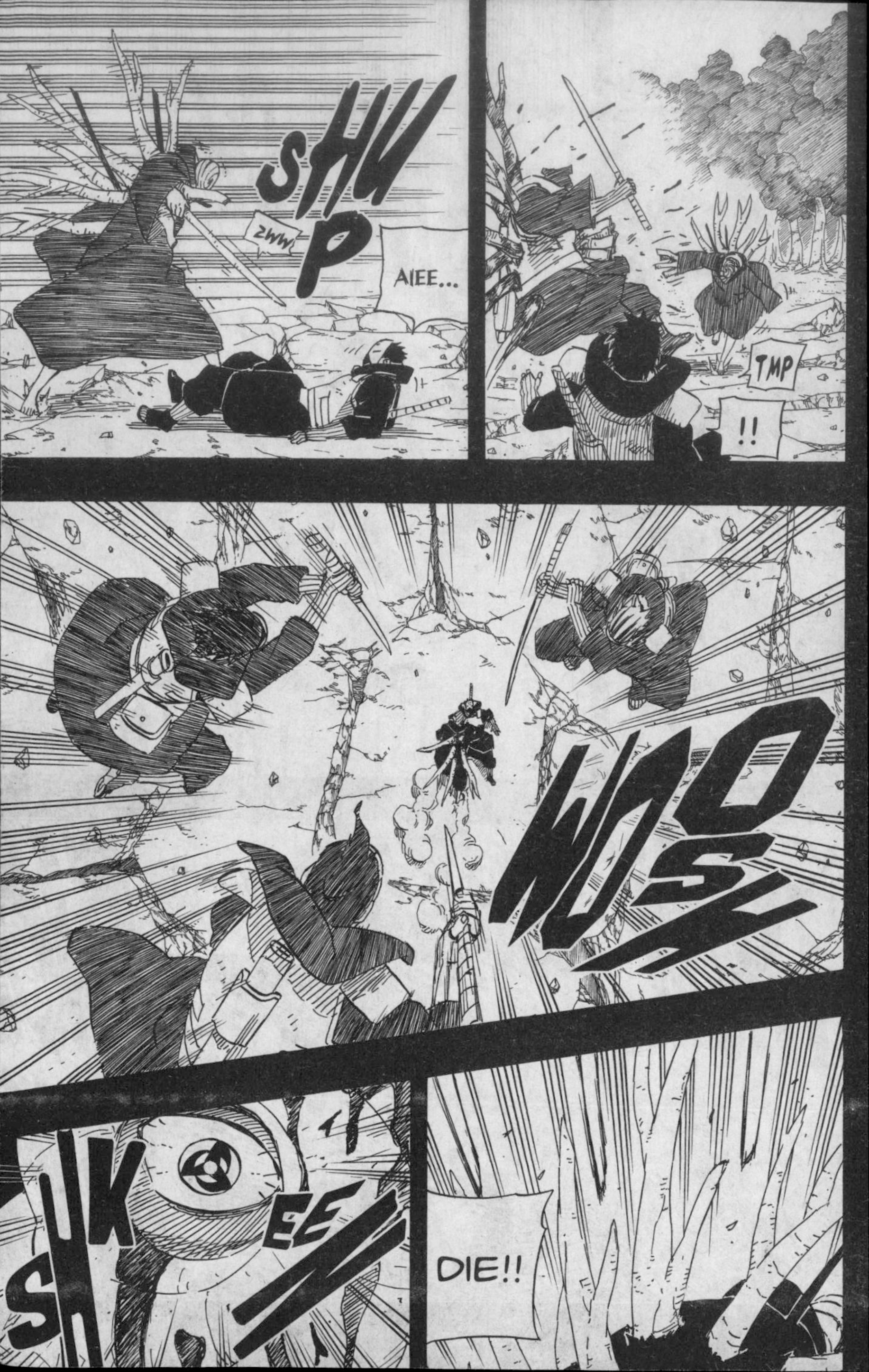
TMP
!!
SHUP
ZWW
AIEE...
WHOOSH
DIE!!
SHKEEN
SH

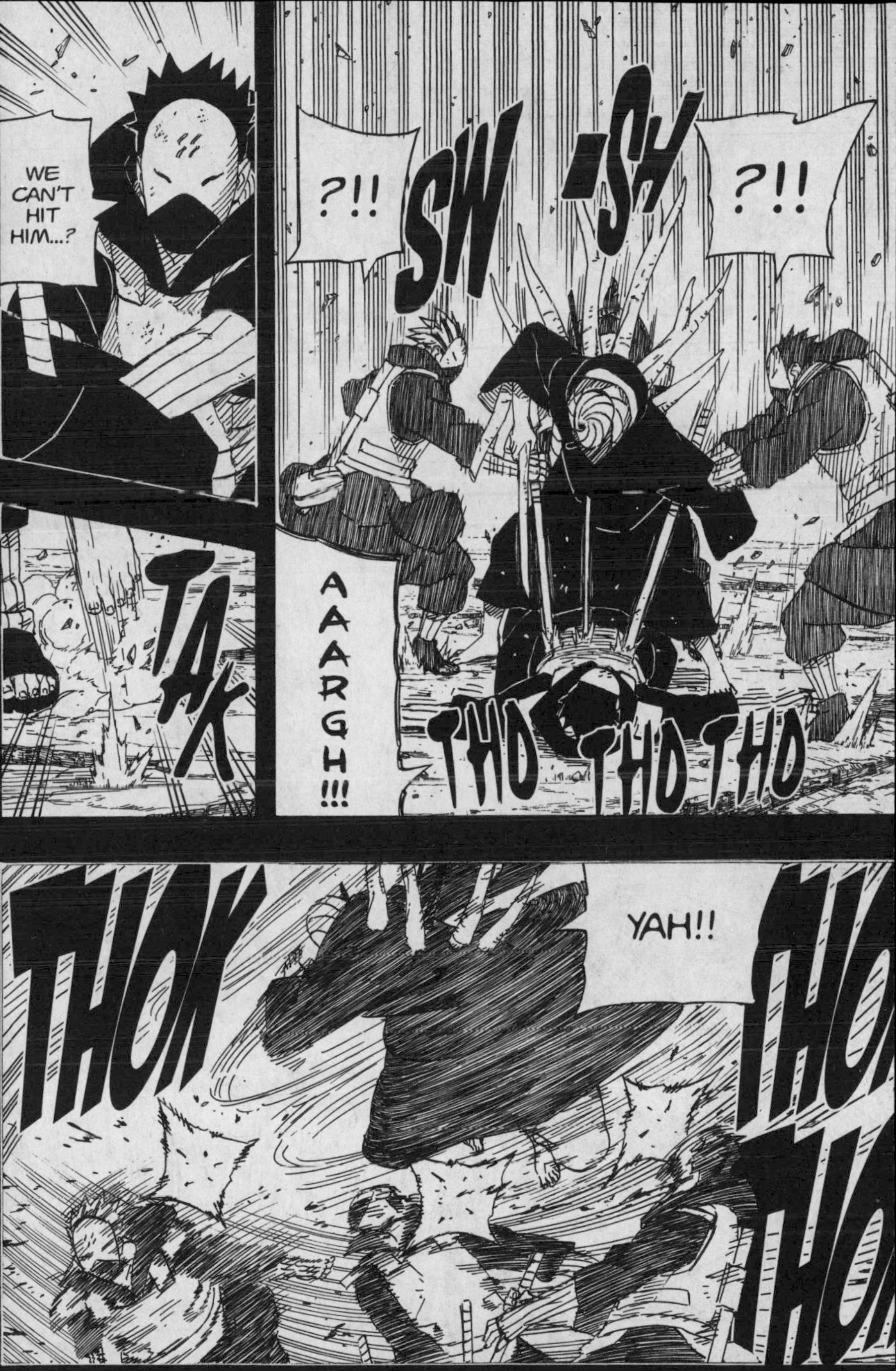

?!!
SW -SH
?!!
AAARGH!!!
THO THO THO
WE CAN'T HIT HIM...?
TAK
YAH!!
THOK

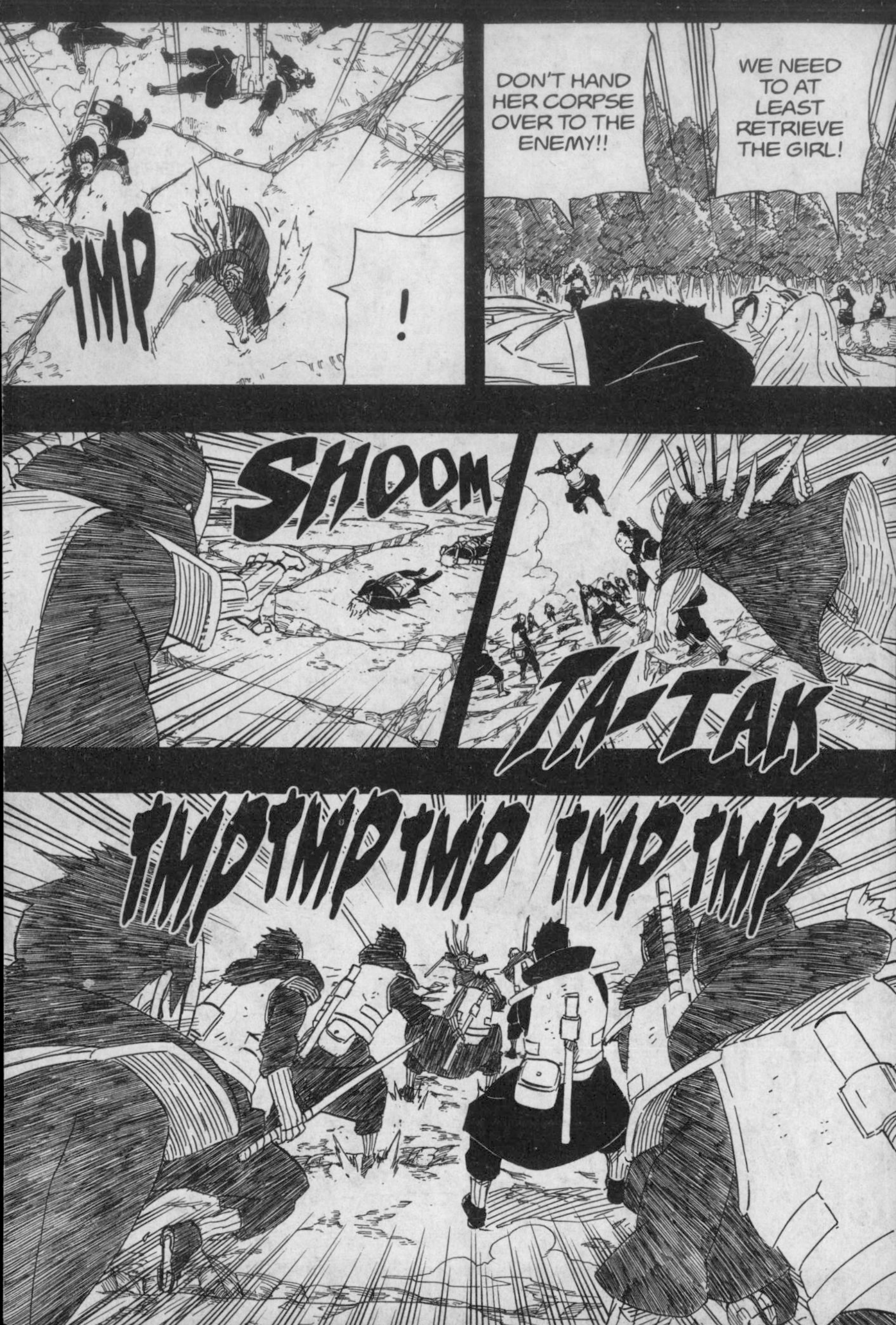
WE NEED TO AT LEAST RETRIEVE THE GIRL!
DON'T HAND HER CORPSE OVER TO THE ENEMY!!
!
TMP
TA-TAK
SHOOM
TMP TMP TMP TMP TMP

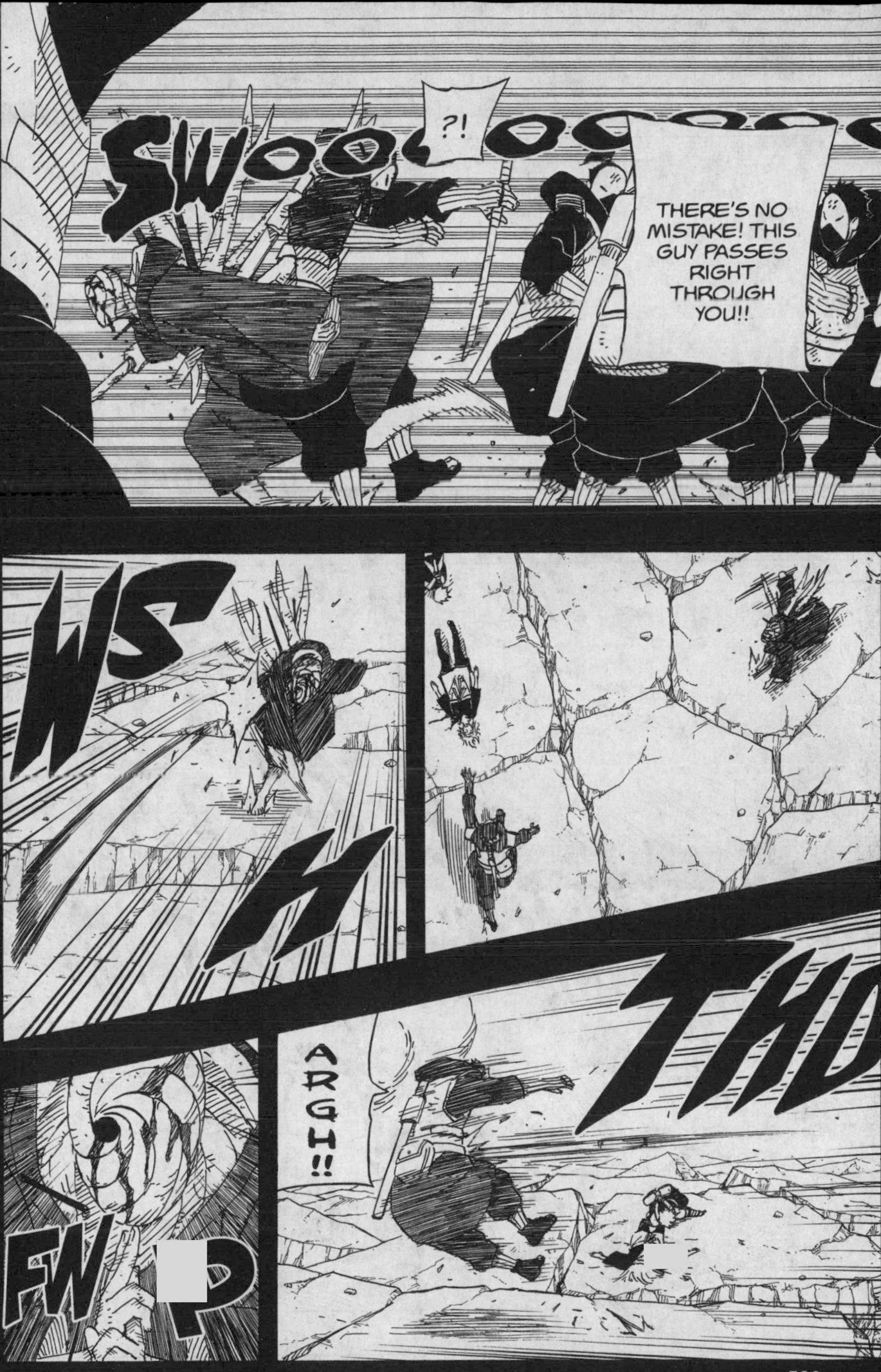
THERE'S NO MISTAKE! THIS GUY PASSES RIGHT THROUGH YOU!!
?!
SWOOOOOOOO
WSH
THD
ARGH!!
FW
P

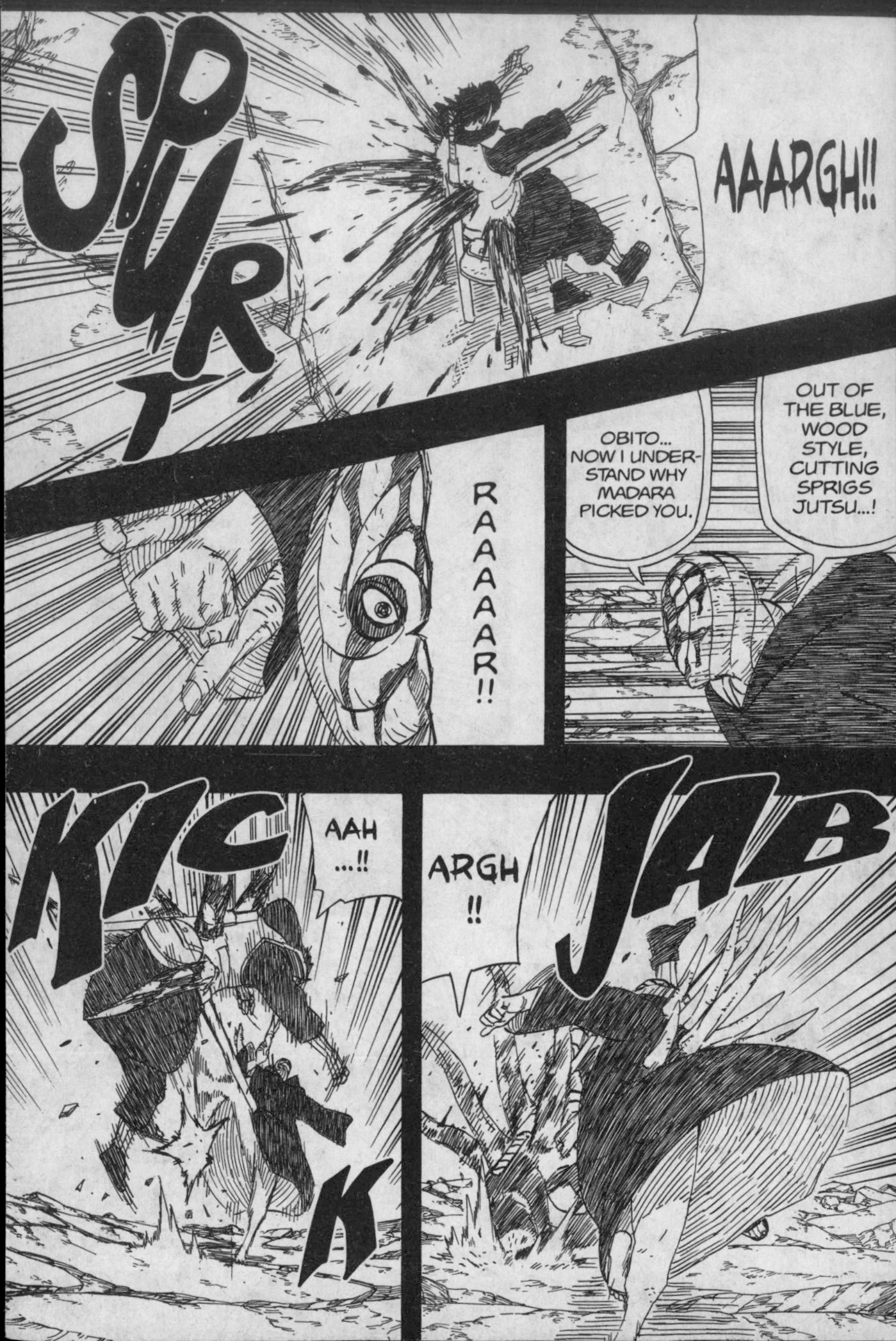
AAARGH!!
SPURT
OUT OF THE BLUE, WOOD STYLE, CUTTING SPRIGS JUTSU...!
OBITO... NOW I UNDER-STAND WHY MADARA PICKED YOU.
RAAAAAAR!!
JAB
ARGH!!
AAH...!!
KICK

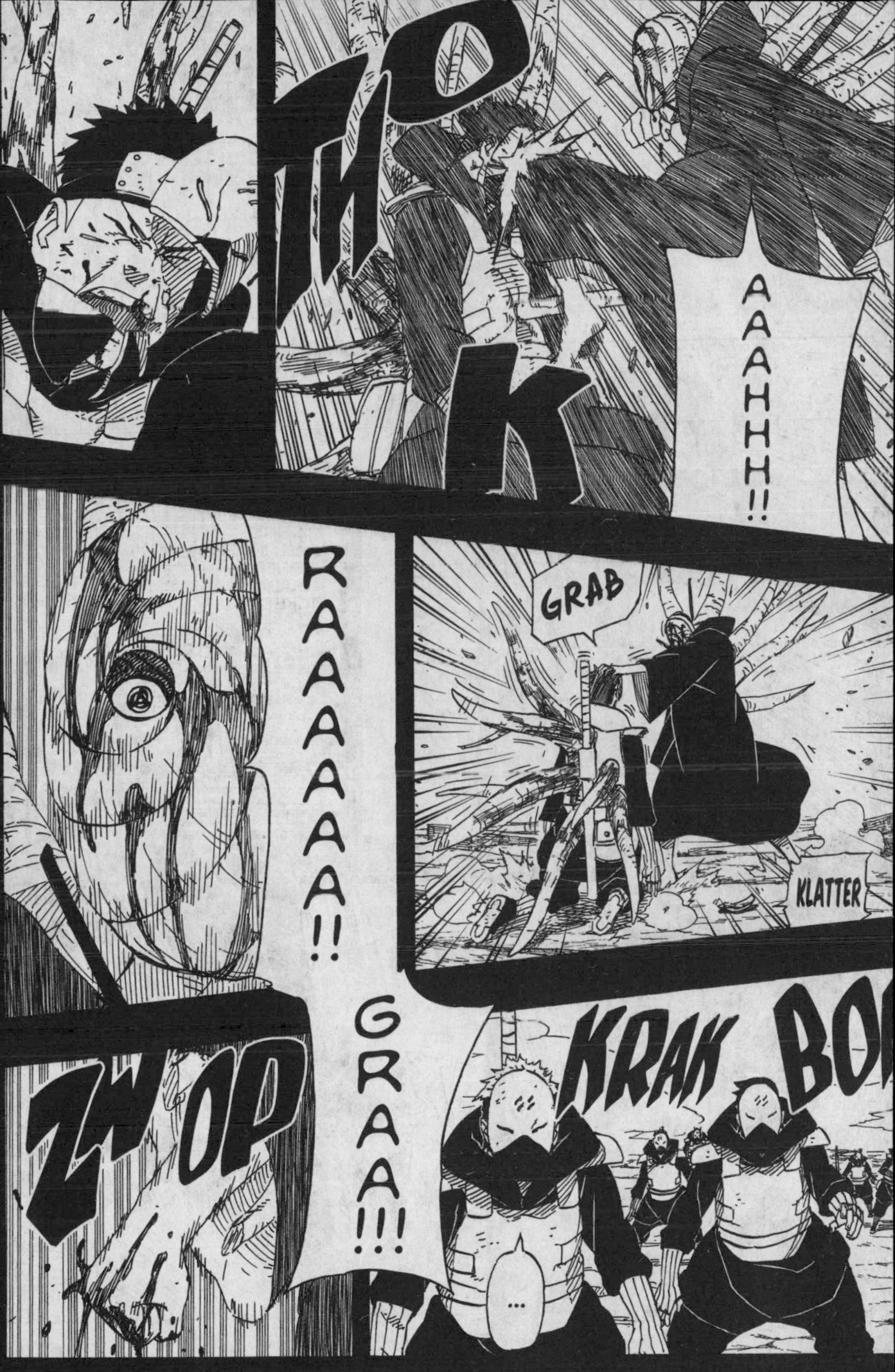
AAAAHHH!!
THK
GRAB
KLATTER
RAAAAAAA!!
KRAK
...
GRAA!!!
ZWOP

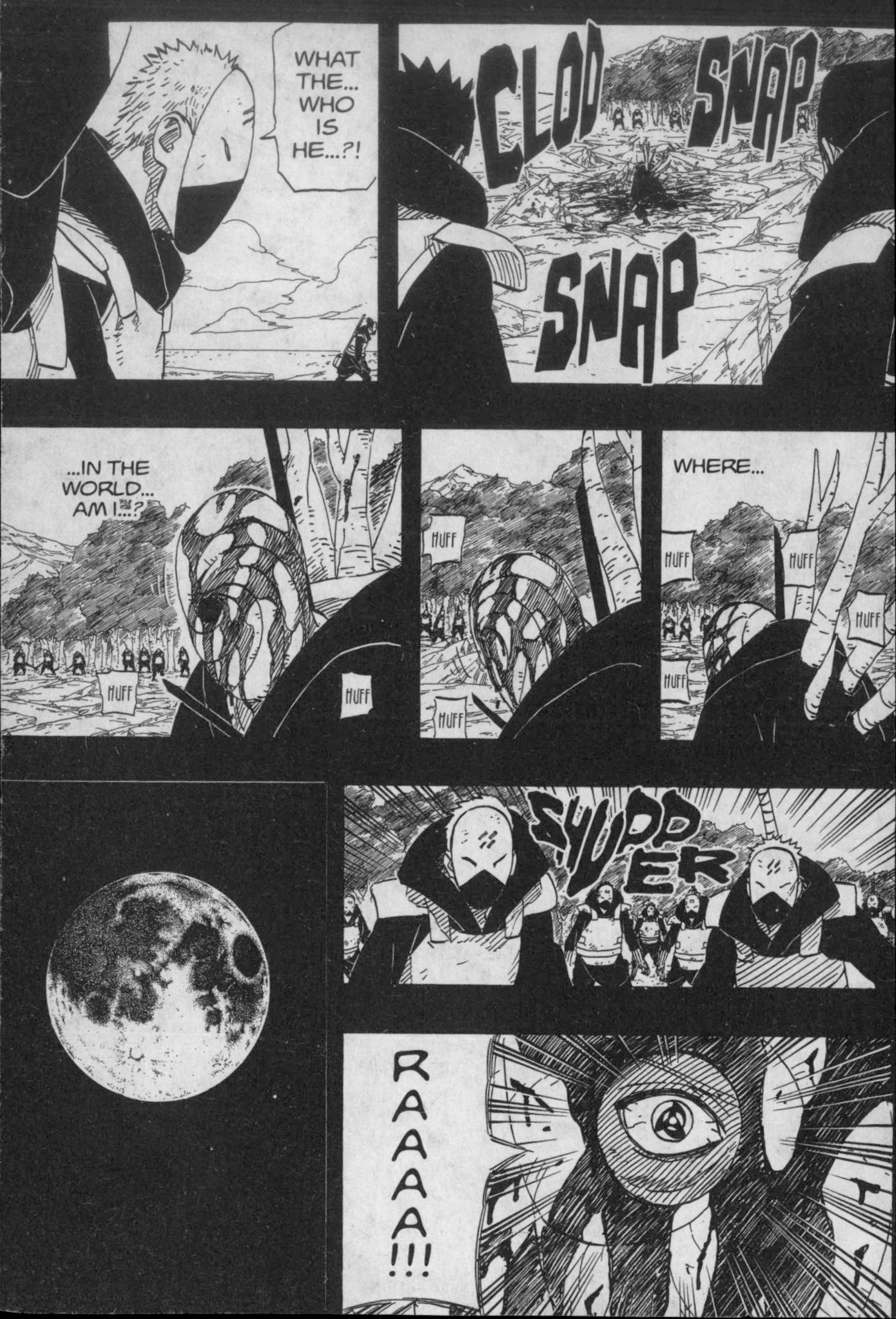
CLOD
SNAP
SNAP
WHAT THE... WHO IS HE...?!
WHERE...
HUFF
HUFF
HUFF
HUFF
HUFF
HUFF
...IN THE WORLD... AM I...?
HUFF
HUFF
SHUDDER
RAAAA!!!

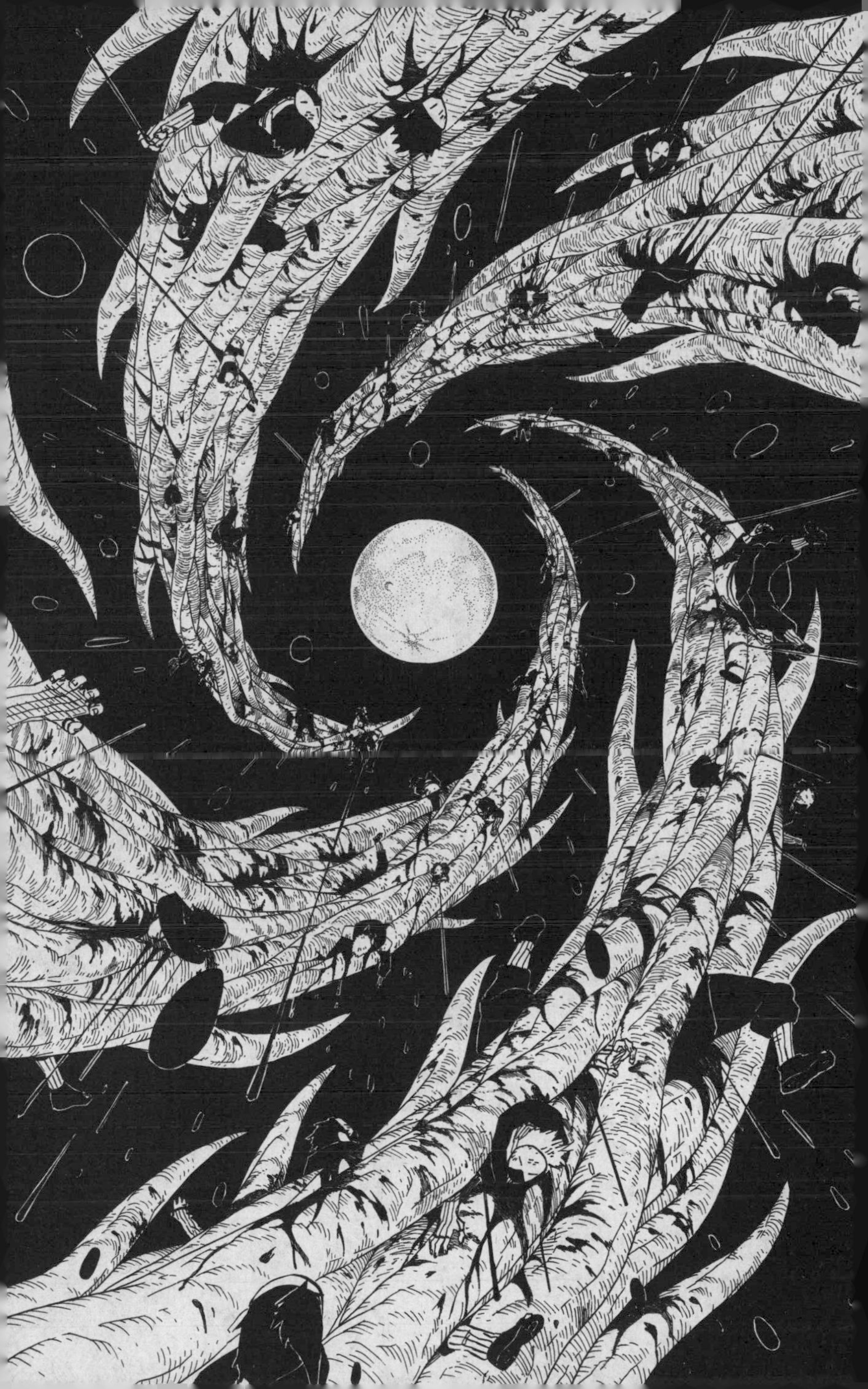

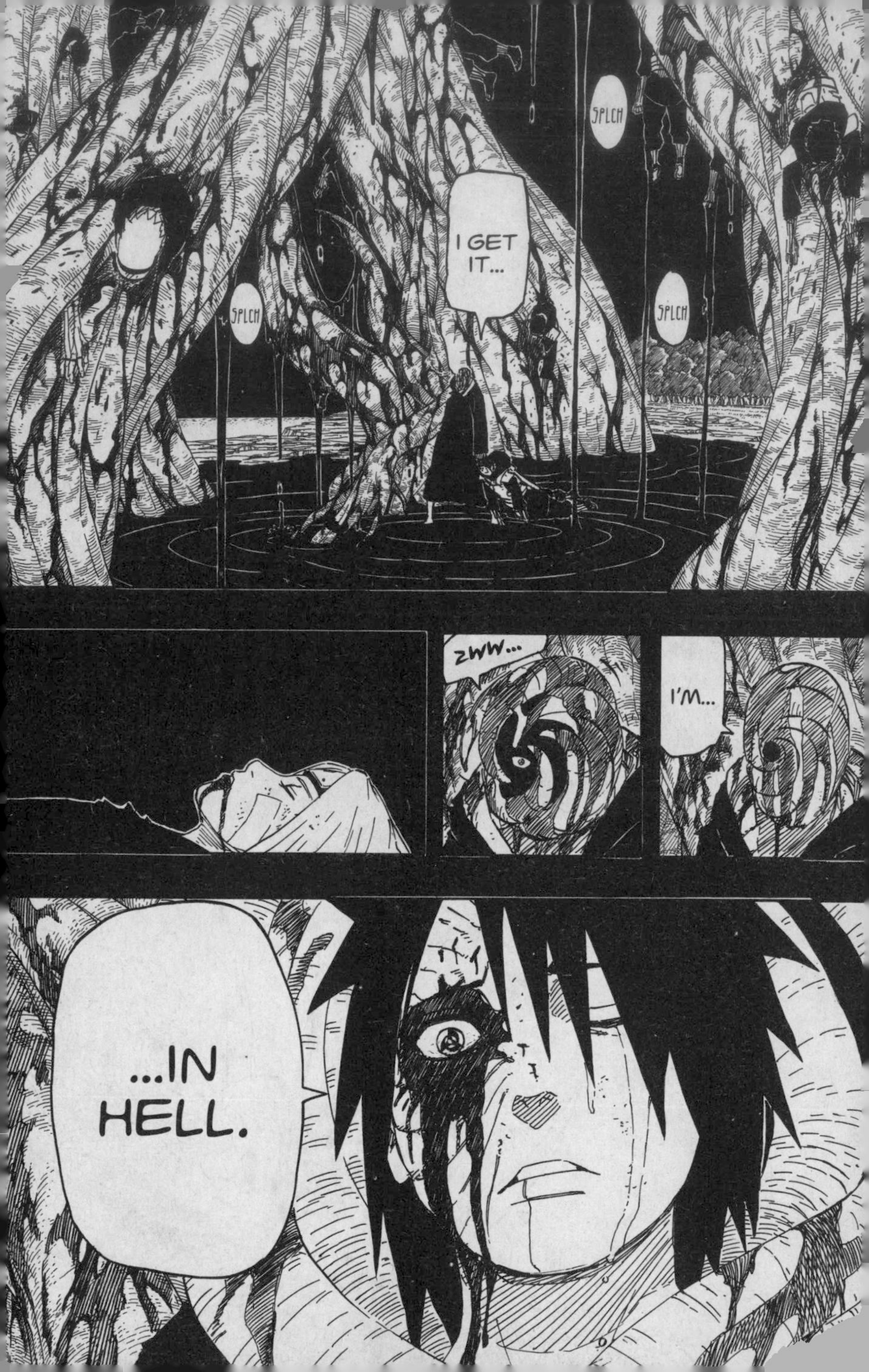
SPLCH
SPLCH
I GET IT...
SPLCH
I'M...
ZWW...
...IN HELL.

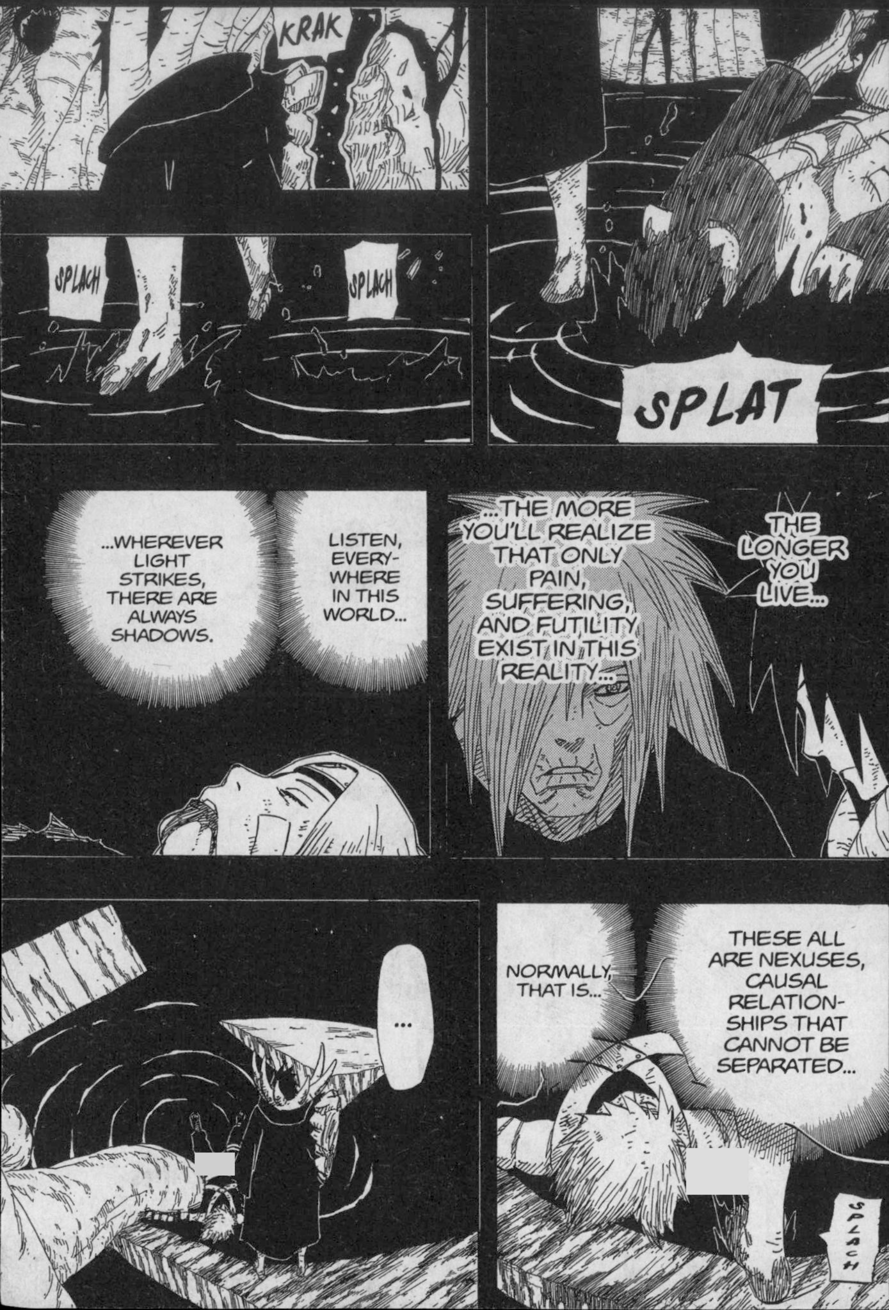
SPLAT
KRAK
SPLACH
SPLACH
THE LONGER YOU LIVE...
...THE MORE YOU'LL REALIZE THAT ONLY PAIN, SUFFERING, AND FUTILITY EXIST IN THIS REALITY...
LISTEN, EVERYWHERE IN THIS WORLD...
...WHEREVER LIGHT STRIKES, THERE ARE ALWAYS SHADOWS.
THESE ALL ARE NEXUSES, CAUSAL RELATIONSHIPS THAT CANNOT BE SEPARATED...
NORMALLY, THAT IS...
SPLACH
...

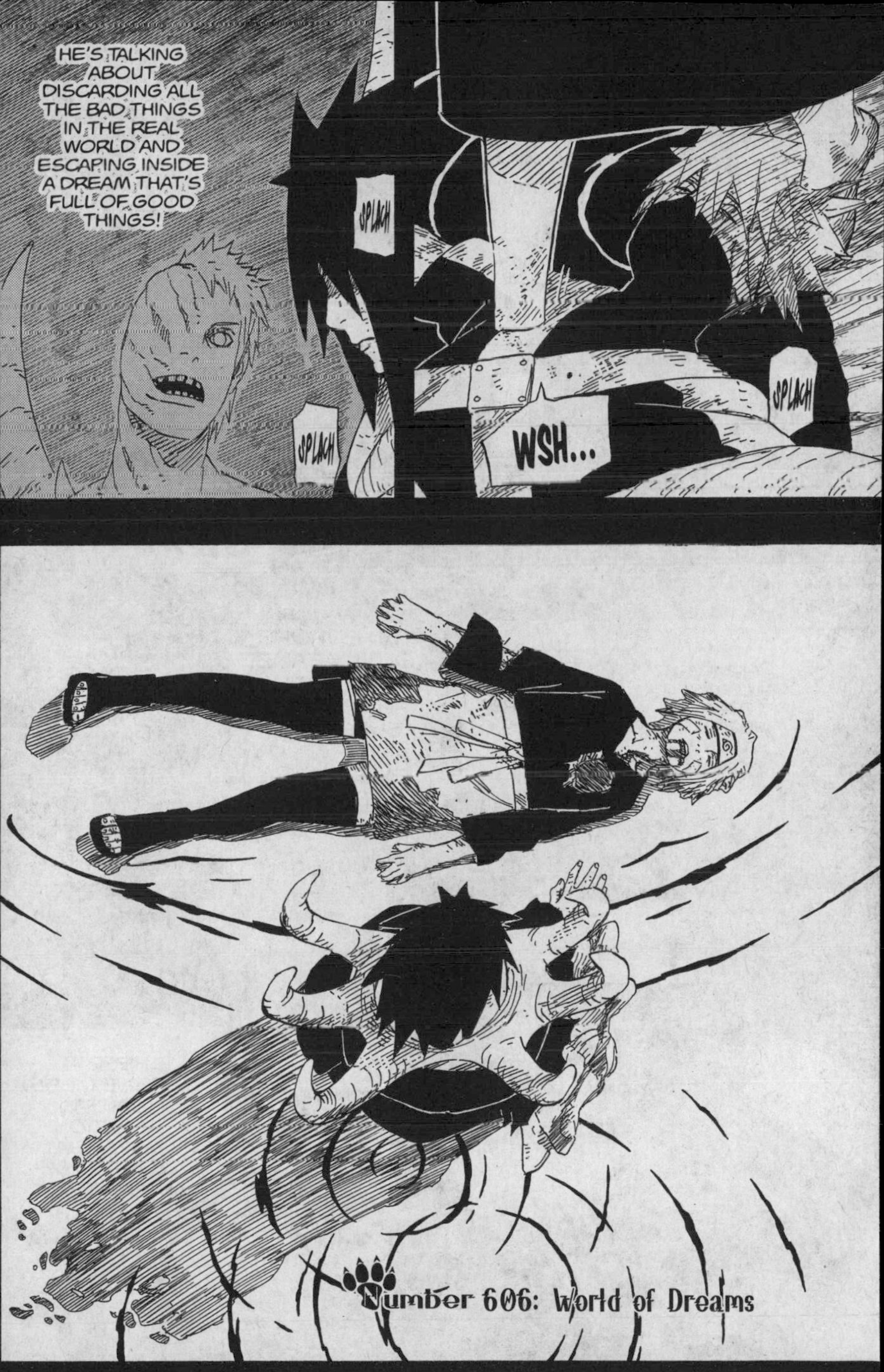
SPLACH
SPLACH
WSH...
HE'S TALKING ABOUT DISCARDING ALL THE BAD THINGS IN THE REAL WORLD AND ESCAPING INSIDE A DREAM THAT'S FULL OF GOOD THINGS!
SPLACH
Number 606: World of Dreams

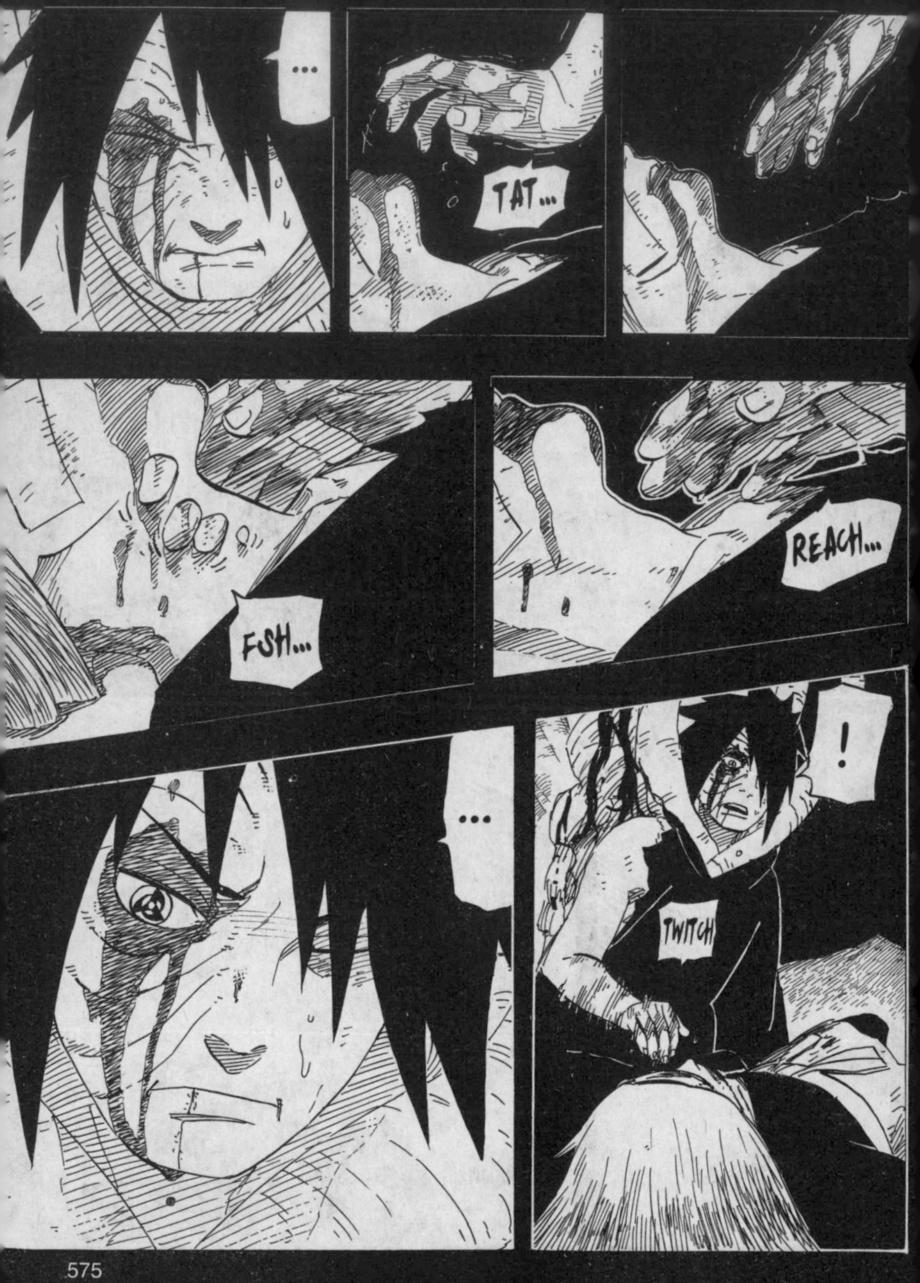
TAT...
...
REACH...
FSH...
!
TWITCH
...

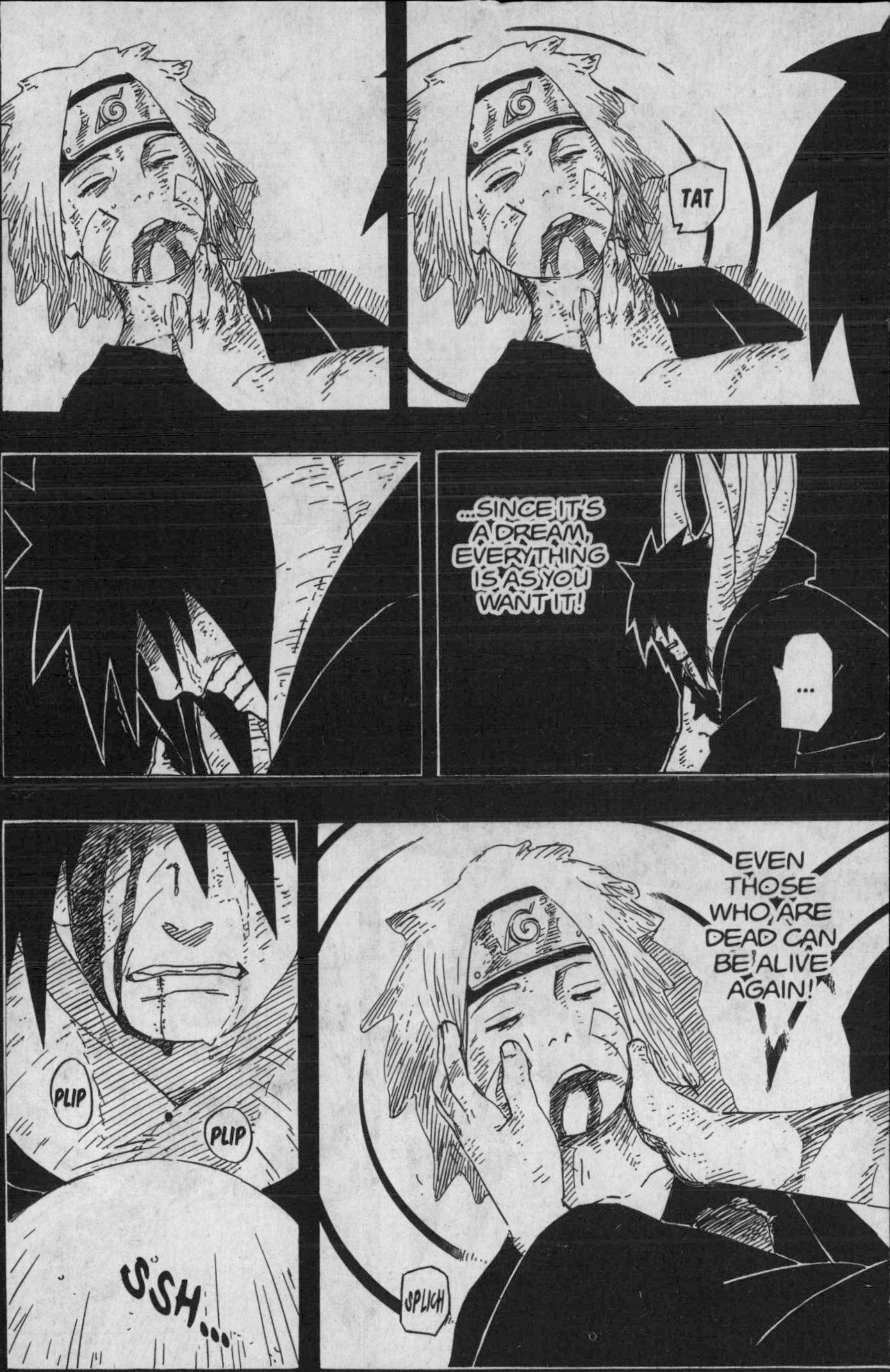
TAT
...SINCE IT'S A DREAM, EVERYTHING IS AS YOU WANT IT!
...
EVEN THOSE WHO ARE DEAD CAN BE ALIVE AGAIN!
SPLICH
PLIP
PLIP
S'SH...

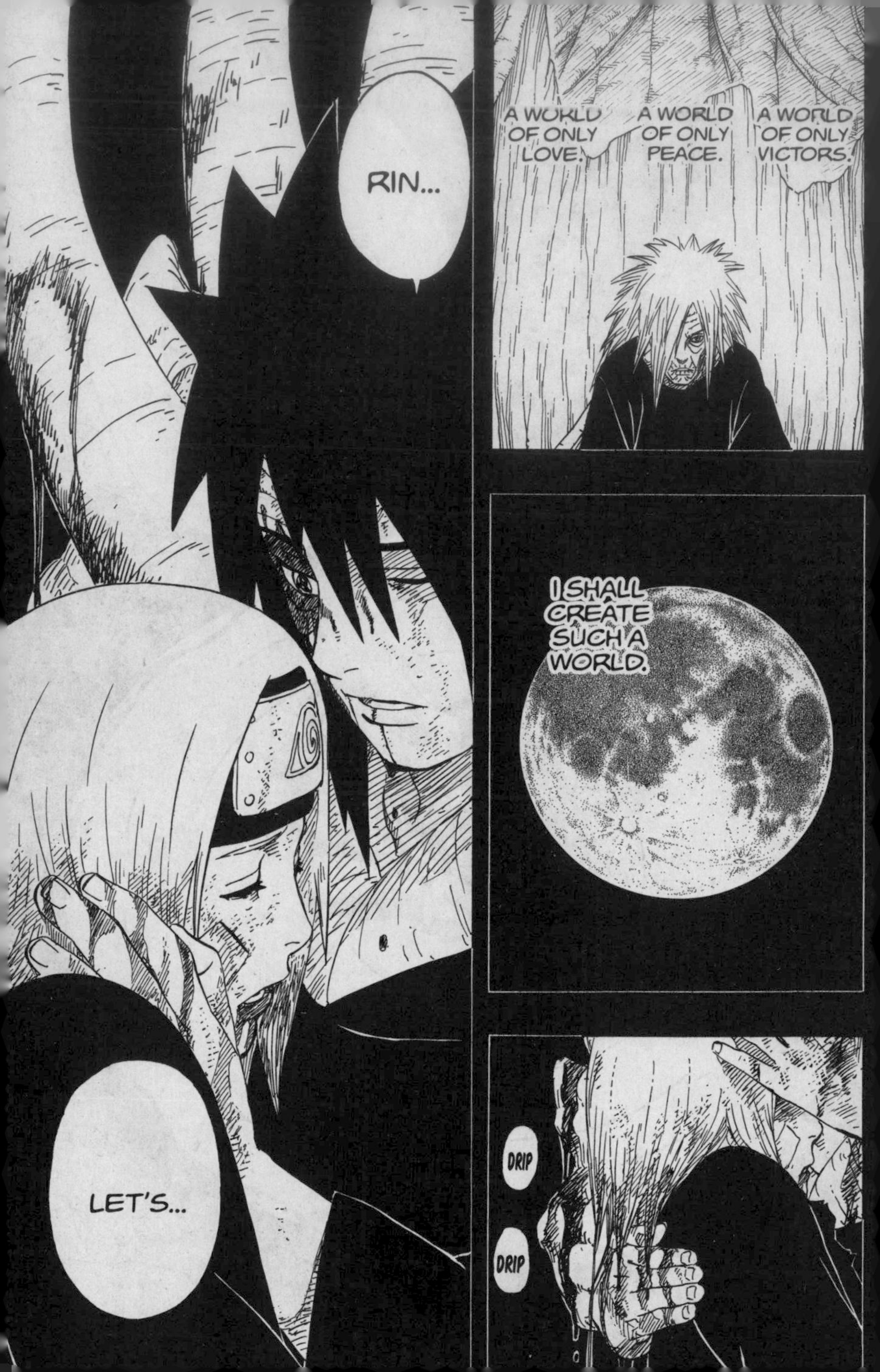
A WORLD OF ONLY VICTORS.
A WORLD OF ONLY PEACE.
A WORLD OF ONLY LOVE.
I SHALL CREATE SUCH A WORLD.
DRIP
DRIP
RIN...
LET'S...

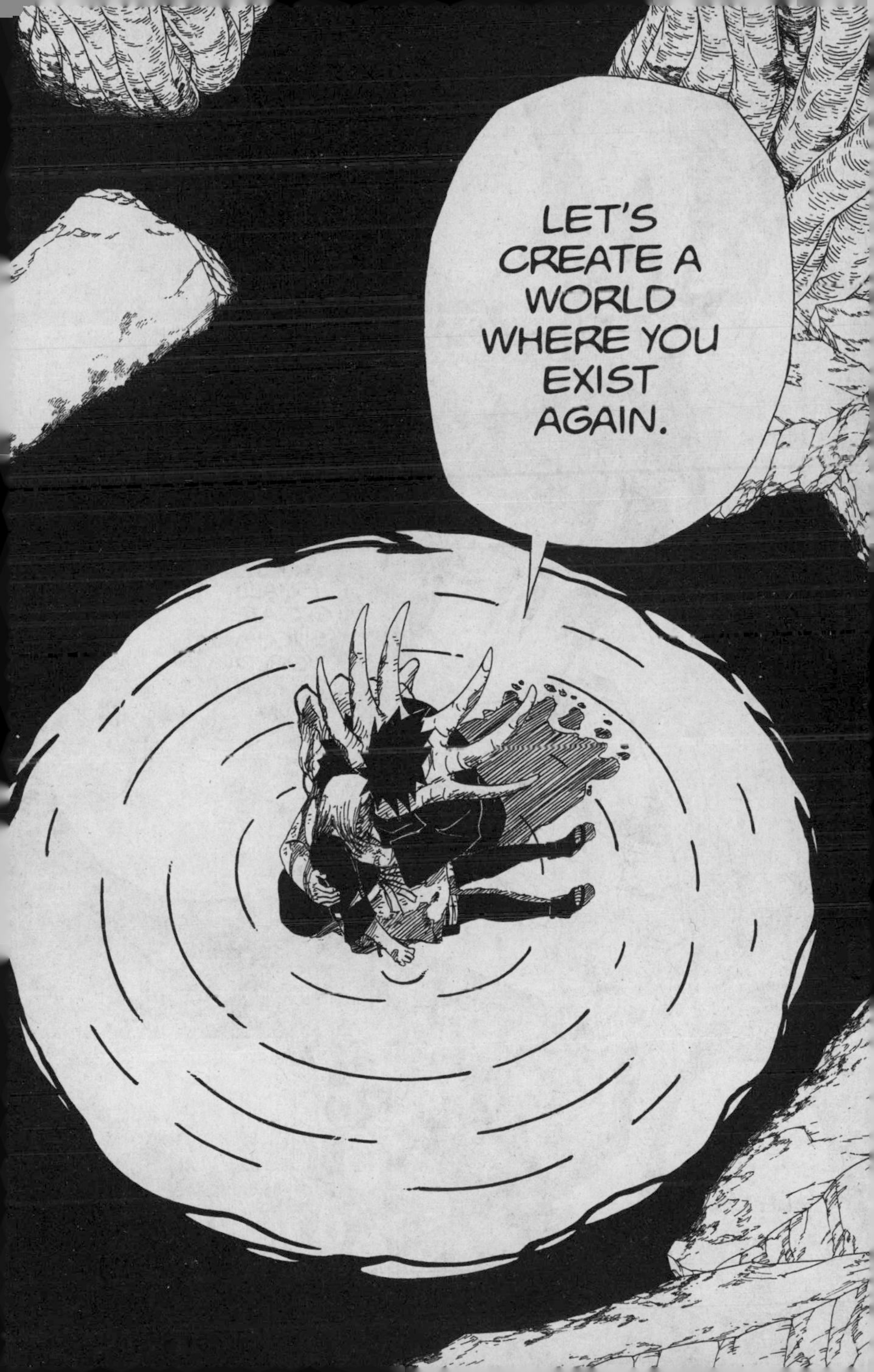
LET'S CREATE A WORLD WHERE YOU EXIST AGAIN.

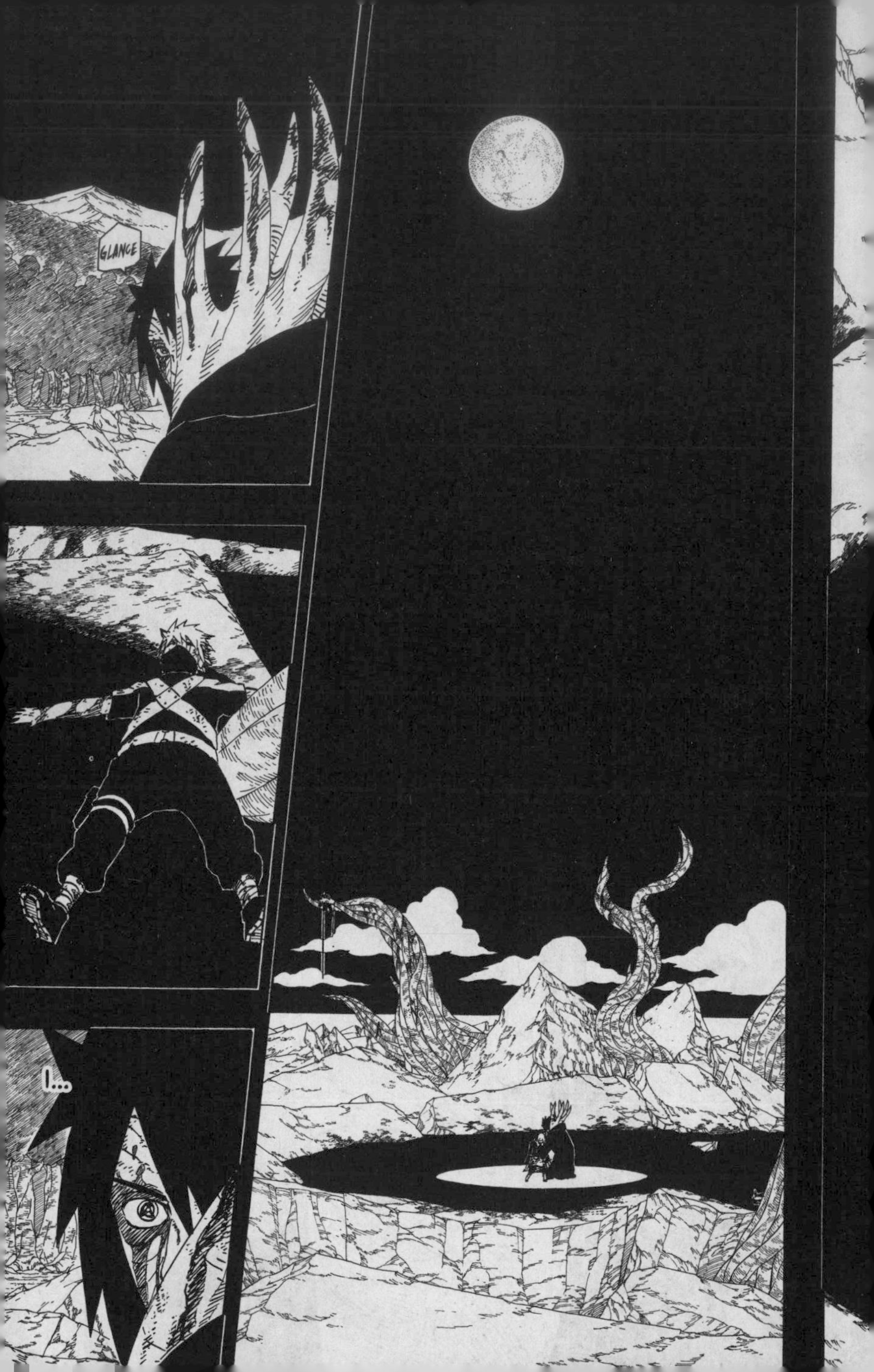
GLANCE
I...

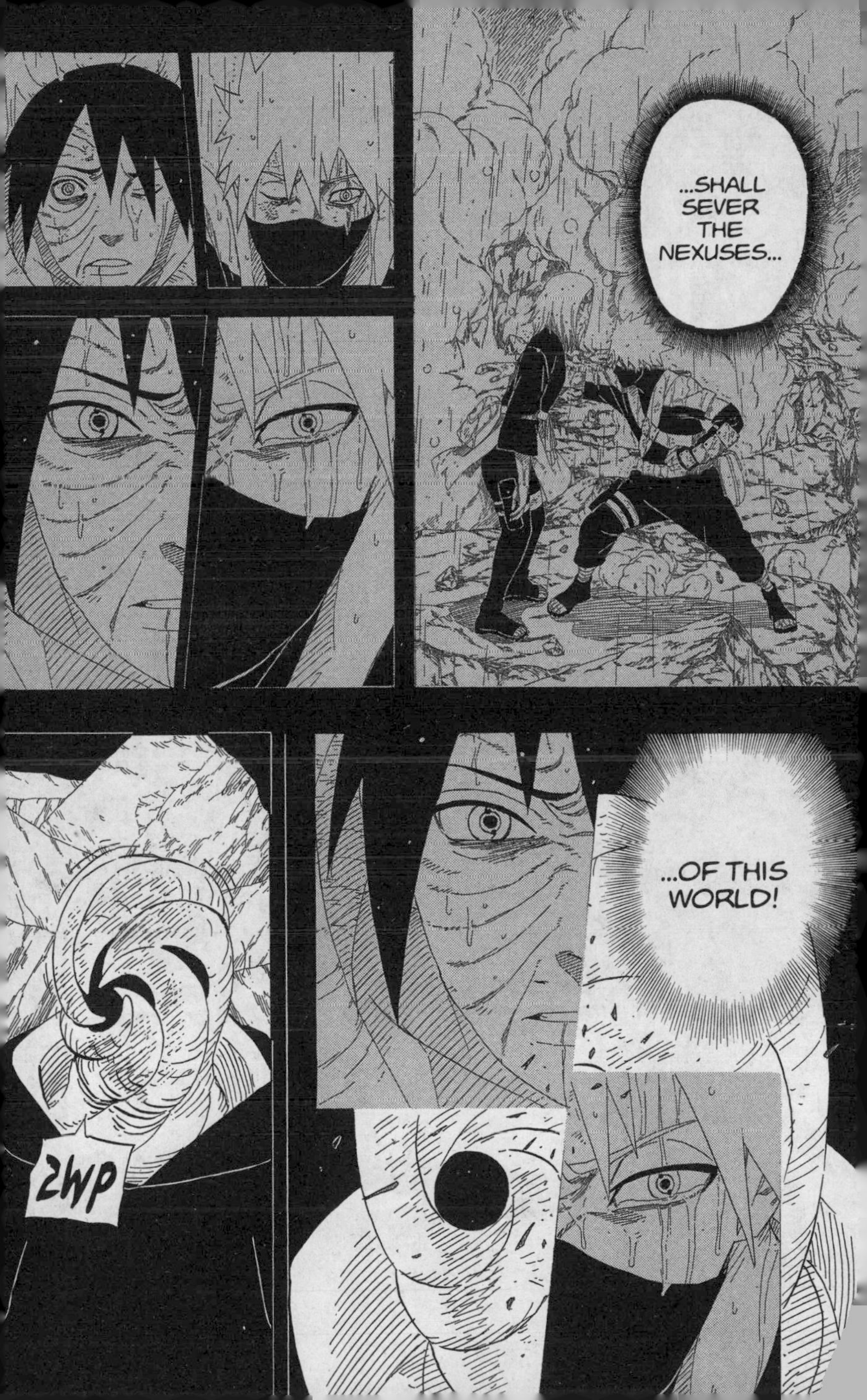
...SHALL SEVER THE NEXUSES...
...OF THIS WORLD!
ZWP

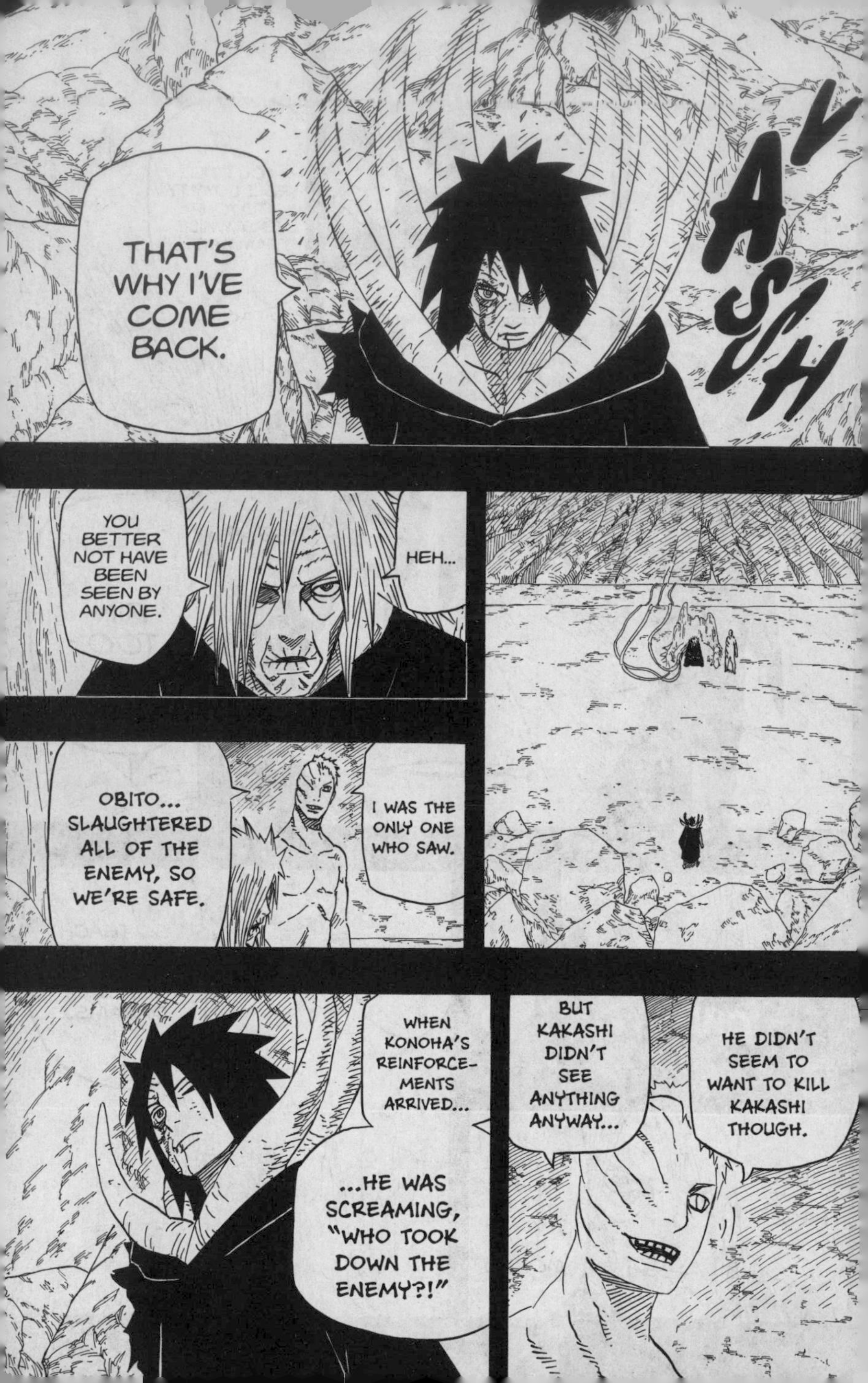
VASH
THAT'S WHY I'VE COME BACK.
HEH...
YOU BETTER NOT HAVE BEEN SEEN BY ANYONE.
I WAS THE ONLY ONE WHO SAW.
OBITO... SLAUGHTERED ALL OF THE ENEMY, SO WE'RE SAFE.
HE DIDN'T SEEM TO WANT TO KILL KAKASHI THOUGH.
BUT KAKASHI DIDN'T SEE ANYTHING ANYWAY...
WHEN KONOHA'S REINFORCE-MENTS ARRIVED...
...HE WAS SCREAMING, "WHO TOOK DOWN THE ENEMY?!"

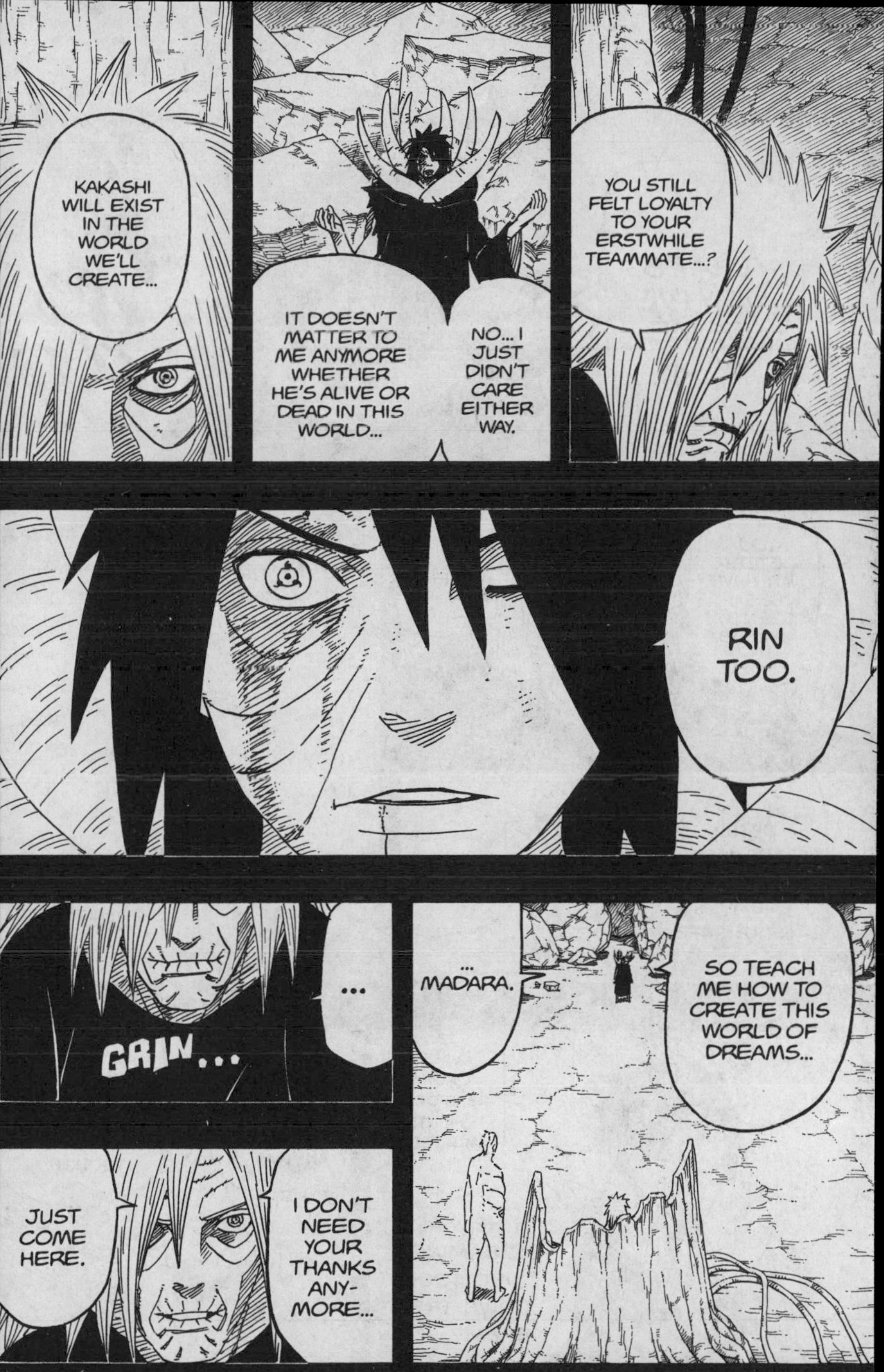
YOU STILL FELT LOYALTY TO YOUR ERSTWHILE TEAMMATE...?
NO... I JUST DIDN'T CARE EITHER WAY.
IT DOESN'T MATTER TO ME ANYMORE WHETHER HE'S ALIVE OR DEAD IN THIS WORLD...
KAKASHI WILL EXIST IN THE WORLD WE'LL CREATE...
RIN TOO.
SO TEACH ME HOW TO CREATE THIS WORLD OF DREAMS...
... MADARA.
...
GRIN...
I DON'T NEED YOUR THANKS ANY-MORE...
JUST COME HERE.

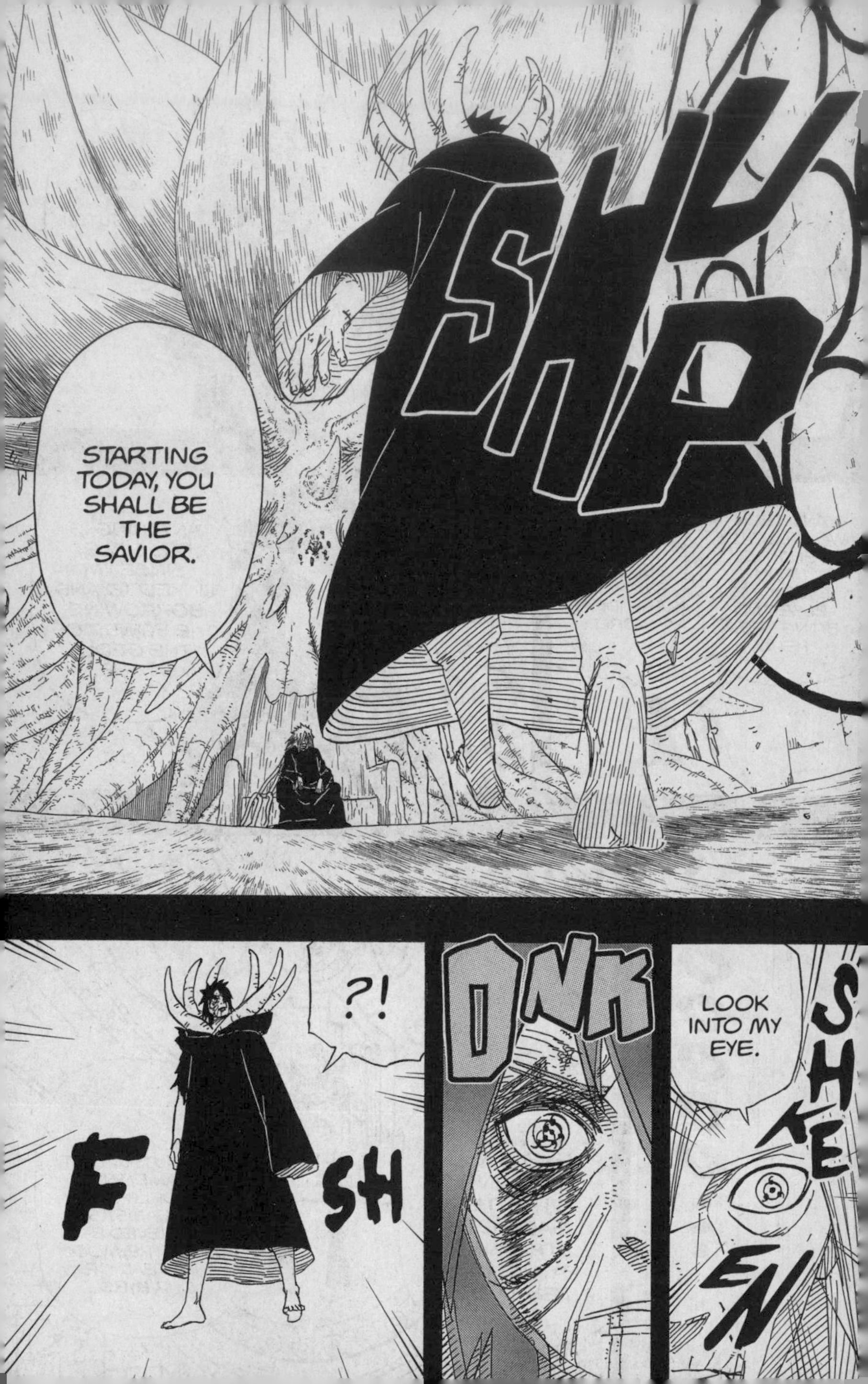
SHUP
STARTING TODAY, YOU SHALL BE THE SAVIOR.
LOOK INTO MY EYE.
SHKEEN
DNK
?!
FSH

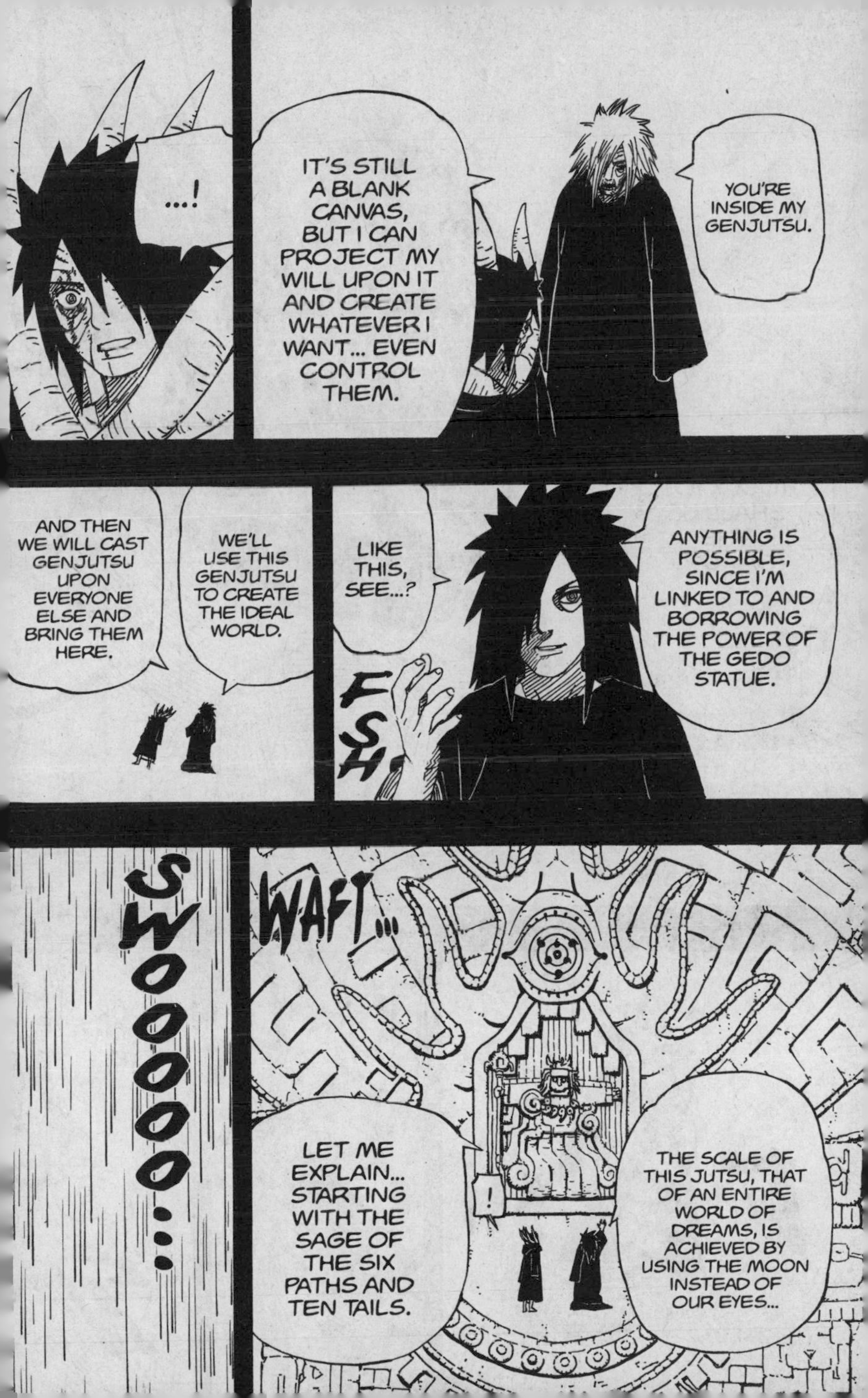
YOU'RE INSIDE MY GENJUTSU.
IT'S STILL A BLANK CANVAS, BUT I CAN PROJECT MY WILL UPON IT AND CREATE WHATEVER I WANT... EVEN CONTROL THEM.
...!
ANYTHING IS POSSIBLE, SINCE I'M LINKED TO AND BORROWING THE POWER OF THE GEDO STATUE.
LIKE THIS, SEE...?
FSH
WE'LL USE THIS GENJUTSU TO CREATE THE IDEAL WORLD.
AND THEN WE WILL CAST GENJUTSU UPON EVERYONE ELSE AND BRING THEM HERE.
WAFT...
THE SCALE OF THIS JUTSU, THAT OF AN ENTIRE WORLD OF DREAMS, IS ACHIEVED BY USING THE MOON INSTEAD OF OUR EYES...
!
LET ME EXPLAIN... STARTING WITH THE SAGE OF THE SIX PATHS AND TEN TAILS.
SWOOOOO...

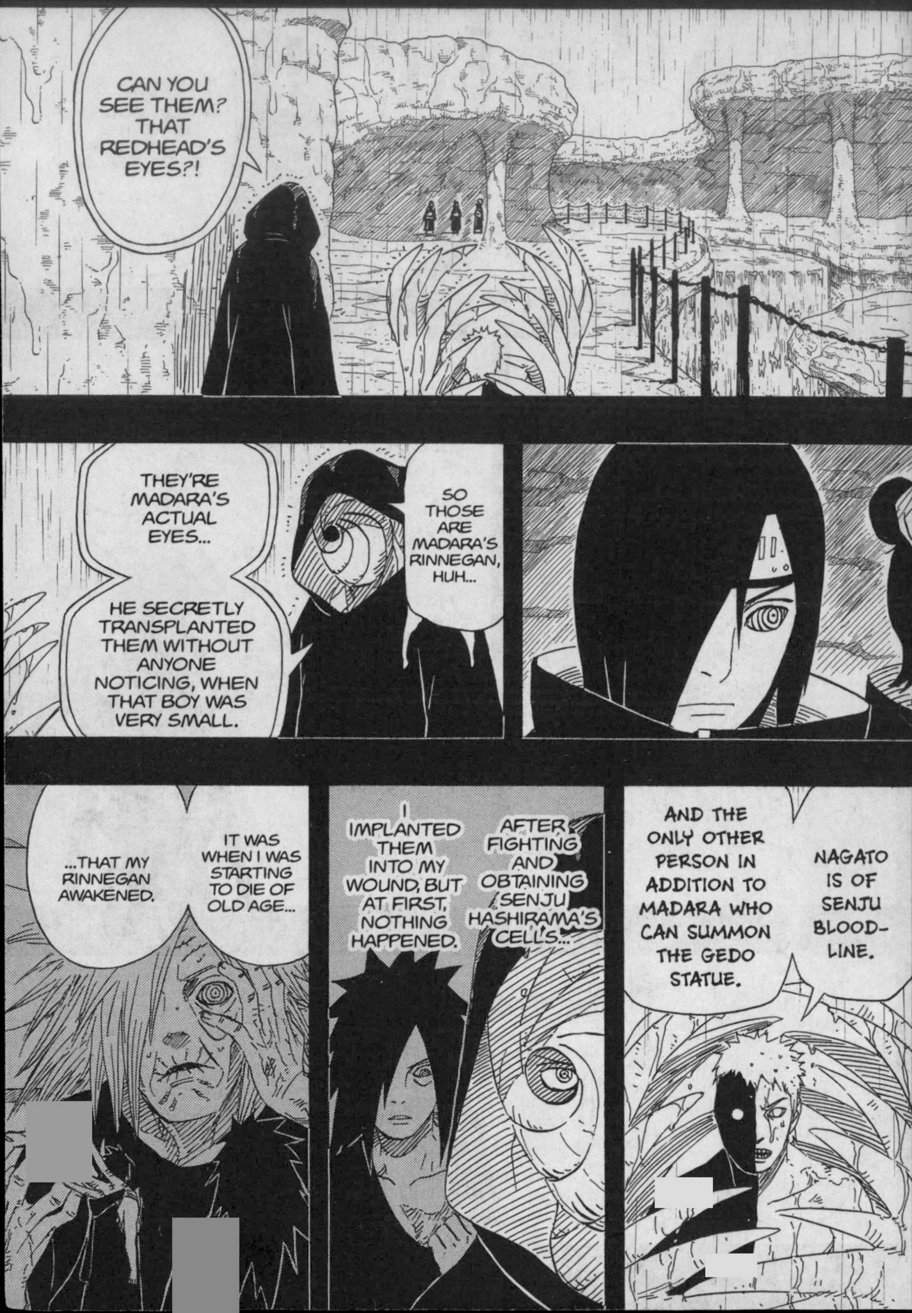
CAN YOU SEE THEM? THAT REDHEAD'S EYES?!
SO THOSE ARE MADARA'S RINNEGAN, HUH...
THEY'RE MADARA'S ACTUAL EYES...
HE SECRETLY TRANSPLANTED THEM WITHOUT ANYONE NOTICING, WHEN THAT BOY WAS VERY SMALL.
NAGATO IS OF SENJU BLOOD-LINE.
AND THE ONLY OTHER PERSON IN ADDITION TO MADARA WHO CAN SUMMON THE GEDO STATUE.
AFTER FIGHTING AND OBTAINING SENJU HASHIRAMA'S CELLS...
I IMPLANTED THEM INTO MY WOUND, BUT AT FIRST, NOTHING HAPPENED.
IT WAS WHEN I WAS STARTING TO DIE OF OLD AGE...
...THAT MY RINNEGAN AWAKENED.

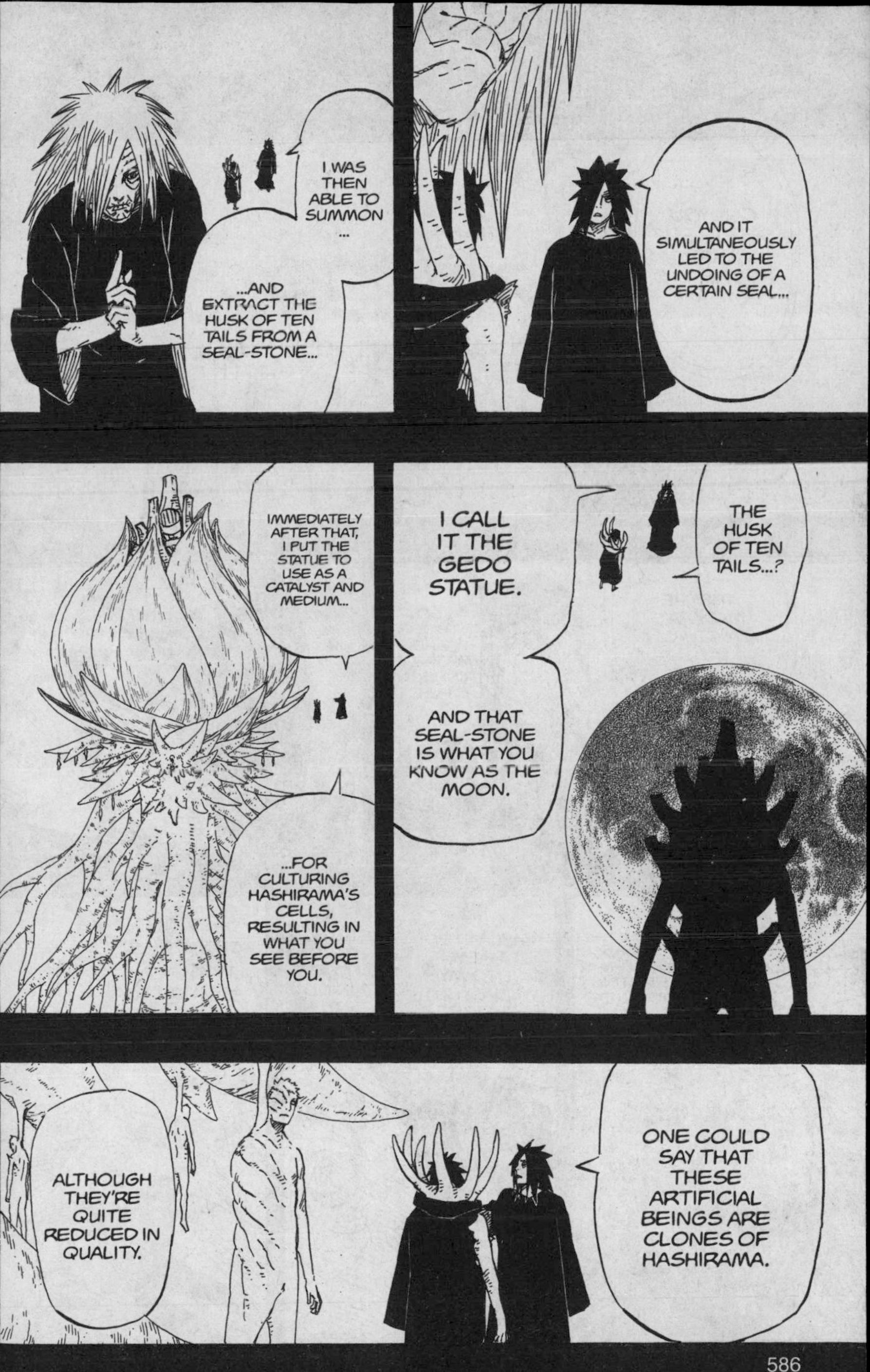
AND IT SIMULTANEOUSLY LED TO THE UNDOING OF A CERTAIN SEAL...
I WAS THEN ABLE TO SUMMON ...
...AND EXTRACT THE HUSK OF TEN TAILS FROM A SEAL-STONE...
THE HUSK OF TEN TAILS...?
I CALL IT THE GEDO STATUE.
AND THAT SEAL-STONE IS WHAT YOU KNOW AS THE MOON.
IMMEDIATELY AFTER THAT, I PUT THE STATUE TO USE AS A CATALYST AND MEDIUM...
...FOR CULTURING HASHIRAMA'S CELLS, RESULTING IN WHAT YOU SEE BEFORE YOU.
ONE COULD SAY THAT THESE ARTIFICIAL BEINGS ARE CLONES OF HASHIRAMA.
ALTHOUGH THEY'RE QUITE REDUCED IN QUALITY.

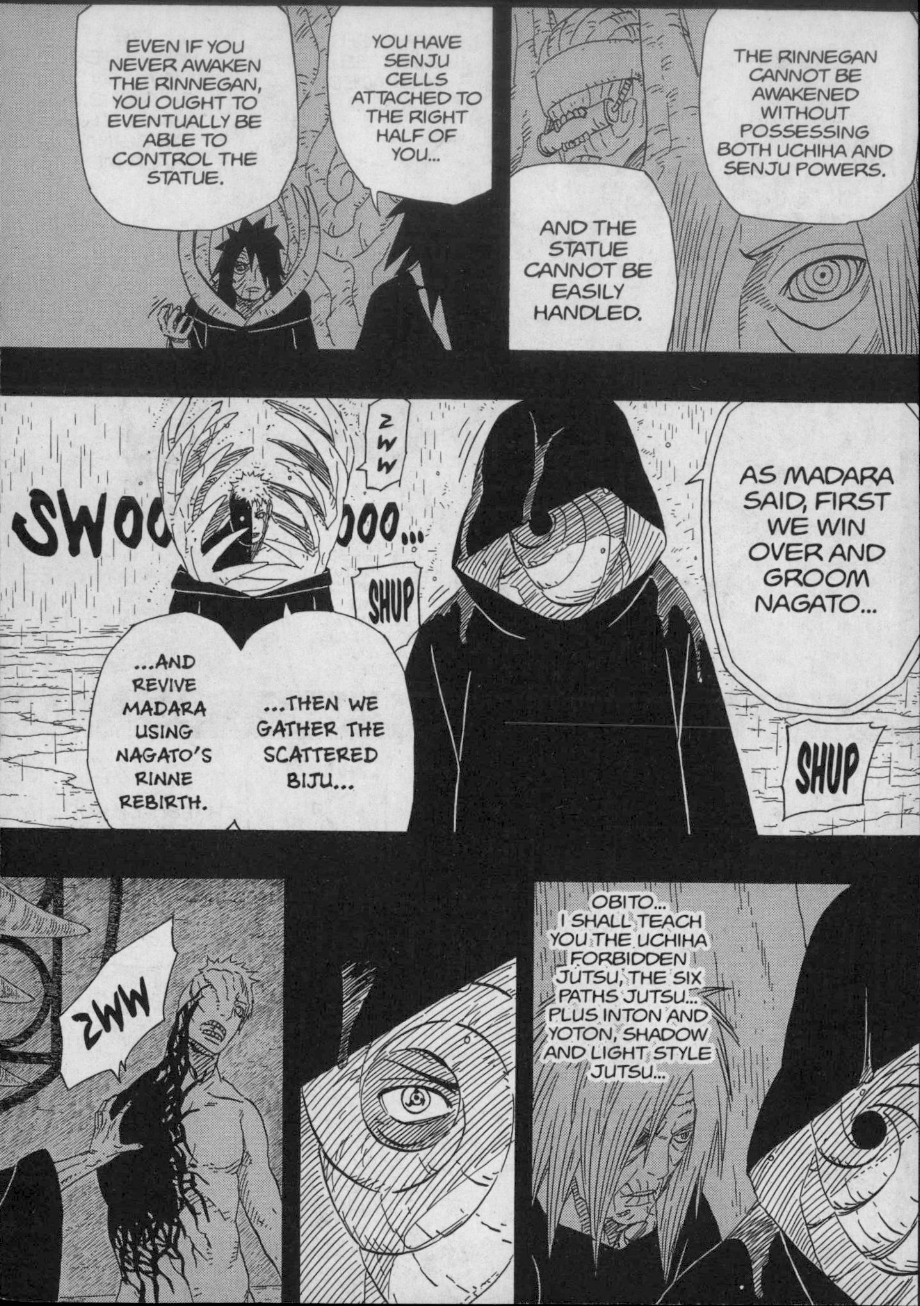
THE RINNEGAN CANNOT BE AWAKENED WITHOUT POSSESSING BOTH UCHIHA AND SENJU POWERS.
AND THE STATUE CANNOT BE EASILY HANDLED.
YOU HAVE SENJU CELLS ATTACHED TO THE RIGHT HALF OF YOU...
EVEN IF YOU NEVER AWAKEN THE RINNEGAN, YOU OUGHT TO EVENTUALLY BE ABLE TO CONTROL THE STATUE.
AS MADARA SAID, FIRST WE WIN OVER AND GROOM NAGATO...
SHUP
SHUP
ZWW
SWOO OOO...
...THEN WE GATHER THE SCATTERED BIJU...
...AND REVIVE MADARA USING NAGATO'S RINNE REBIRTH.
OBITO... I SHALL TEACH YOU THE UCHIHA FORBIDDEN JUTSU, THE SIX PATHS JUTSU... PLUS INTON AND YOTON, SHADOW AND LIGHT STYLE JUTSU...
ZWW

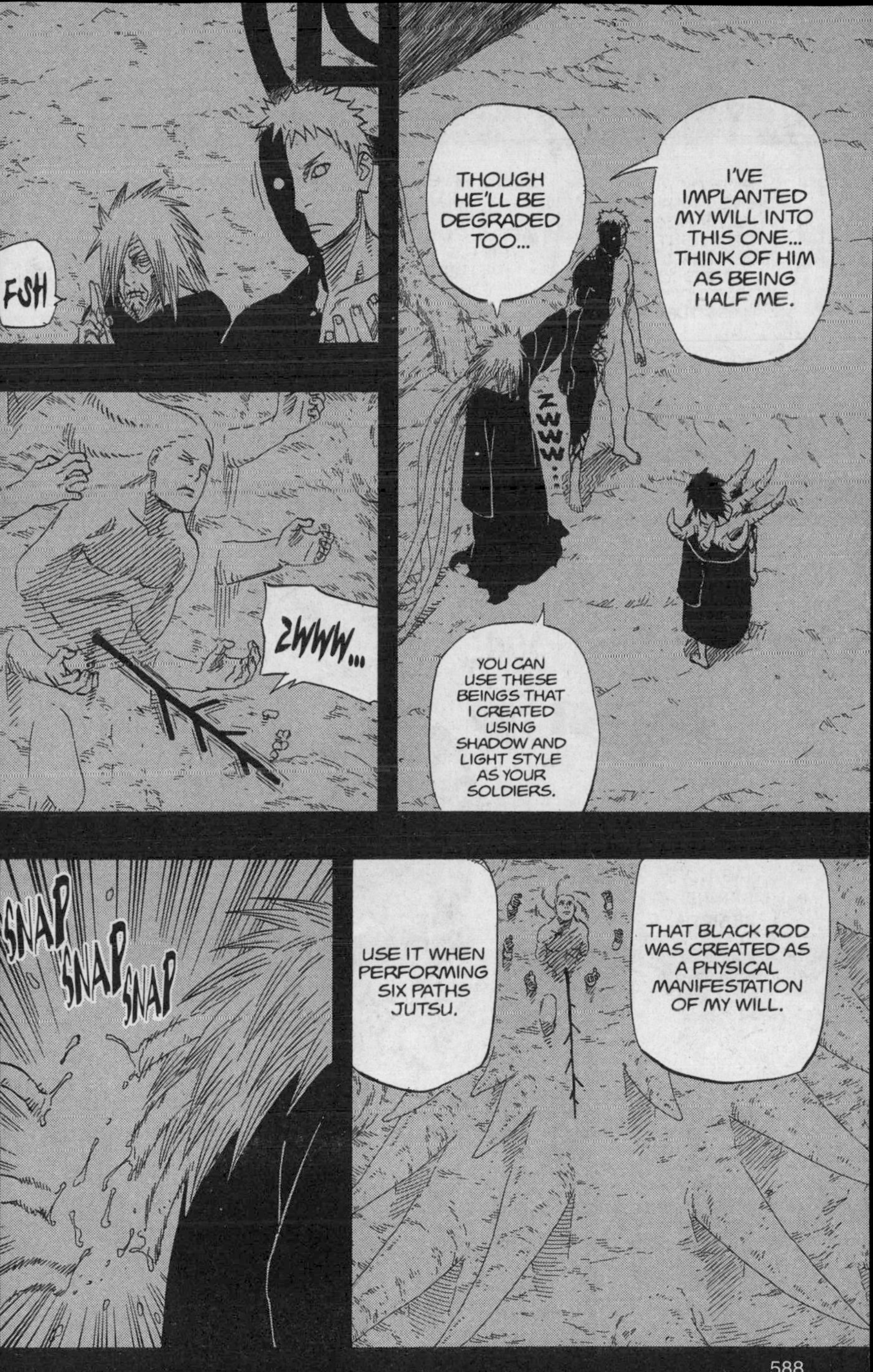
I'VE IMPLANTED MY WILL INTO THIS ONE... THINK OF HIM AS BEING HALF ME.
THOUGH HE'LL BE DEGRADED TOO...
ZWWW...
YOU CAN USE THESE BEINGS THAT I CREATED USING SHADOW AND LIGHT STYLE AS YOUR SOLDIERS.
FSH
ZWWW...
THAT BLACK ROD WAS CREATED AS A PHYSICAL MANIFESTATION OF MY WILL.
USE IT WHEN PERFORMING SIX PATHS JUTSU.
SNAP SNAP SNAP

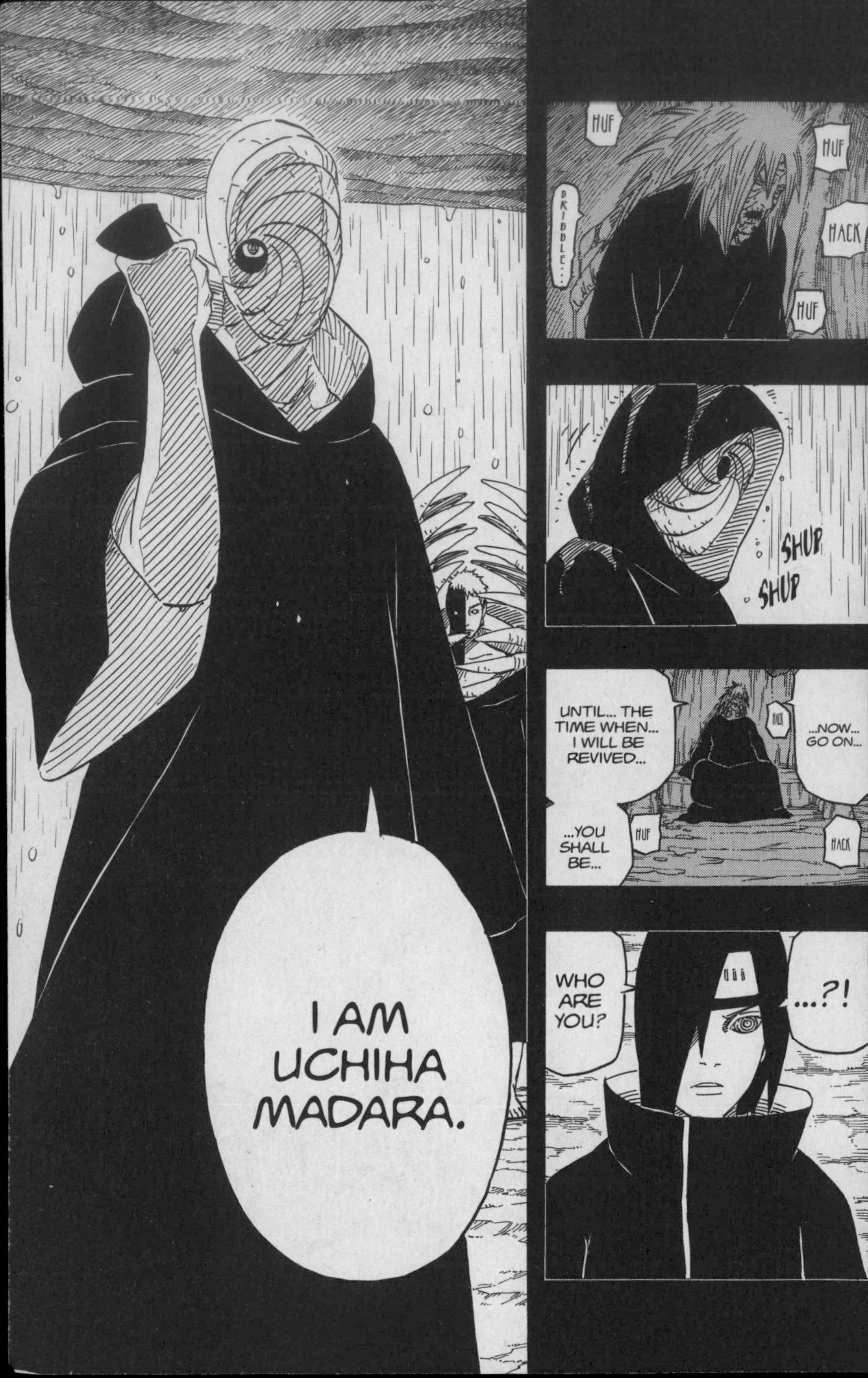
HUF
HACK
HUF
HUF
DRIBBLE...
SHUP
SHUP
...NOW... GO ON...
HACK
UNTIL... THE TIME WHEN... I WILL BE REVIVED...
HACK
HUF
...YOU SHALL BE...
...?!
WHO ARE YOU?
I AM UCHIHA MADARA.

NARUTO

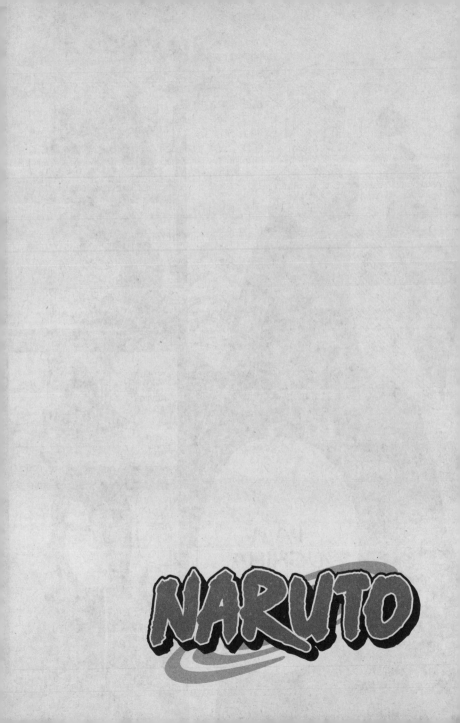

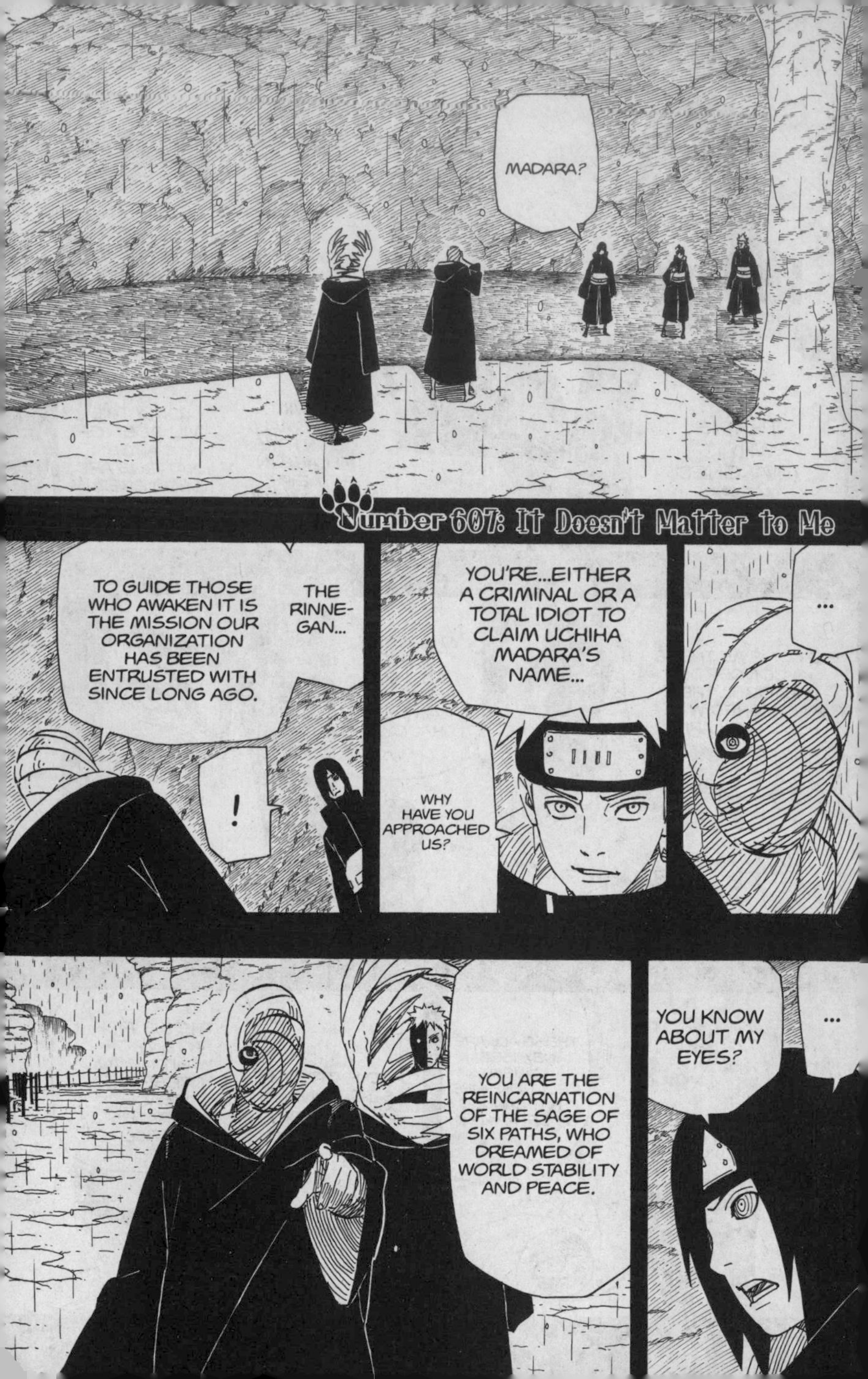
MADARA?
Number 607: It Doesn't Matter to Me
...
YOU'RE...EITHER A CRIMINAL OR A TOTAL IDIOT TO CLAIM UCHIHA MADARA'S NAME...
WHY HAVE YOU APPROACHED US?
THE RINNE-GAN...
TO GUIDE THOSE WHO AWAKEN IT IS THE MISSION OUR ORGANIZATION HAS BEEN ENTRUSTED WITH SINCE LONG AGO.
!
...
YOU KNOW ABOUT MY EYES?
YOU ARE THE REINCARNATION OF THE SAGE OF SIX PATHS, WHO DREAMED OF WORLD STABILITY AND PEACE.

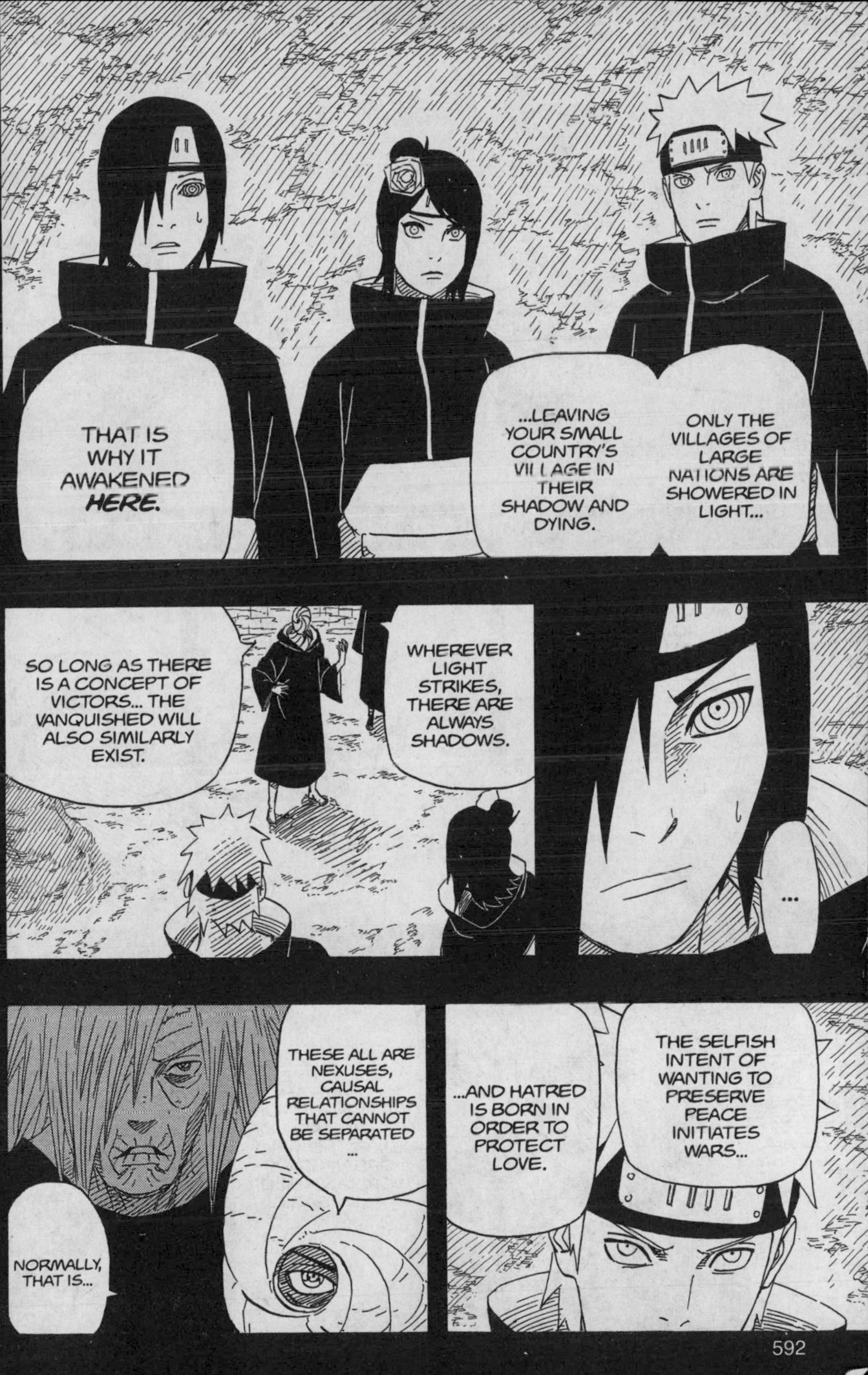
ONLY THE VILLAGES OF LARGE NATIONS ARE SHOWERED IN LIGHT...
...LEAVING YOUR SMALL COUNTRY'S VILLAGE IN THEIR SHADOW AND DYING.
THAT IS WHY IT AWAKENED *HERE.*
...
WHEREVER LIGHT STRIKES, THERE ARE ALWAYS SHADOWS.
SO LONG AS THERE IS A CONCEPT OF VICTORS... THE VANQUISHED WILL ALSO SIMILARLY EXIST.
THE SELFISH INTENT OF WANTING TO PRESERVE PEACE INITIATES WARS...
...AND HATRED IS BORN IN ORDER TO PROTECT LOVE.
THESE ALL ARE NEXUSES, CAUSAL RELATIONSHIPS THAT CANNOT BE SEPARATED ...
NORMALLY, THAT IS...

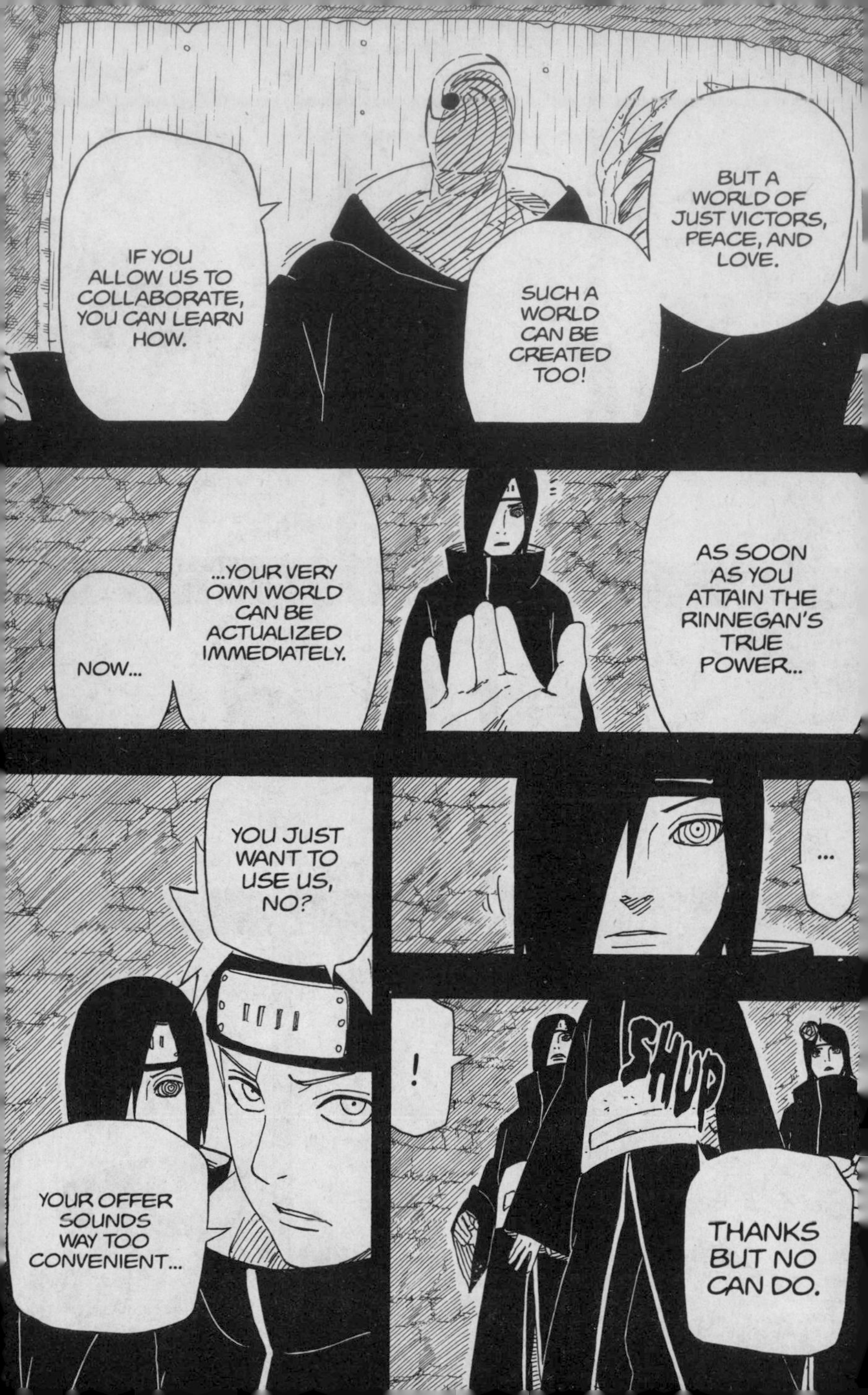
BUT A WORLD OF JUST VICTORS, PEACE, AND LOVE.
SUCH A WORLD CAN BE CREATED TOO!
IF YOU ALLOW US TO COLLABORATE, YOU CAN LEARN HOW.
AS SOON AS YOU ATTAIN THE RINNEGAN'S TRUE POWER...
...YOUR VERY OWN WORLD CAN BE ACTUALIZED IMMEDIATELY.
NOW...
...
!
SHUP
THANKS BUT NO CAN DO.
YOU JUST WANT TO USE US, NO?
YOUR OFFER SOUNDS WAY TOO CONVENIENT...

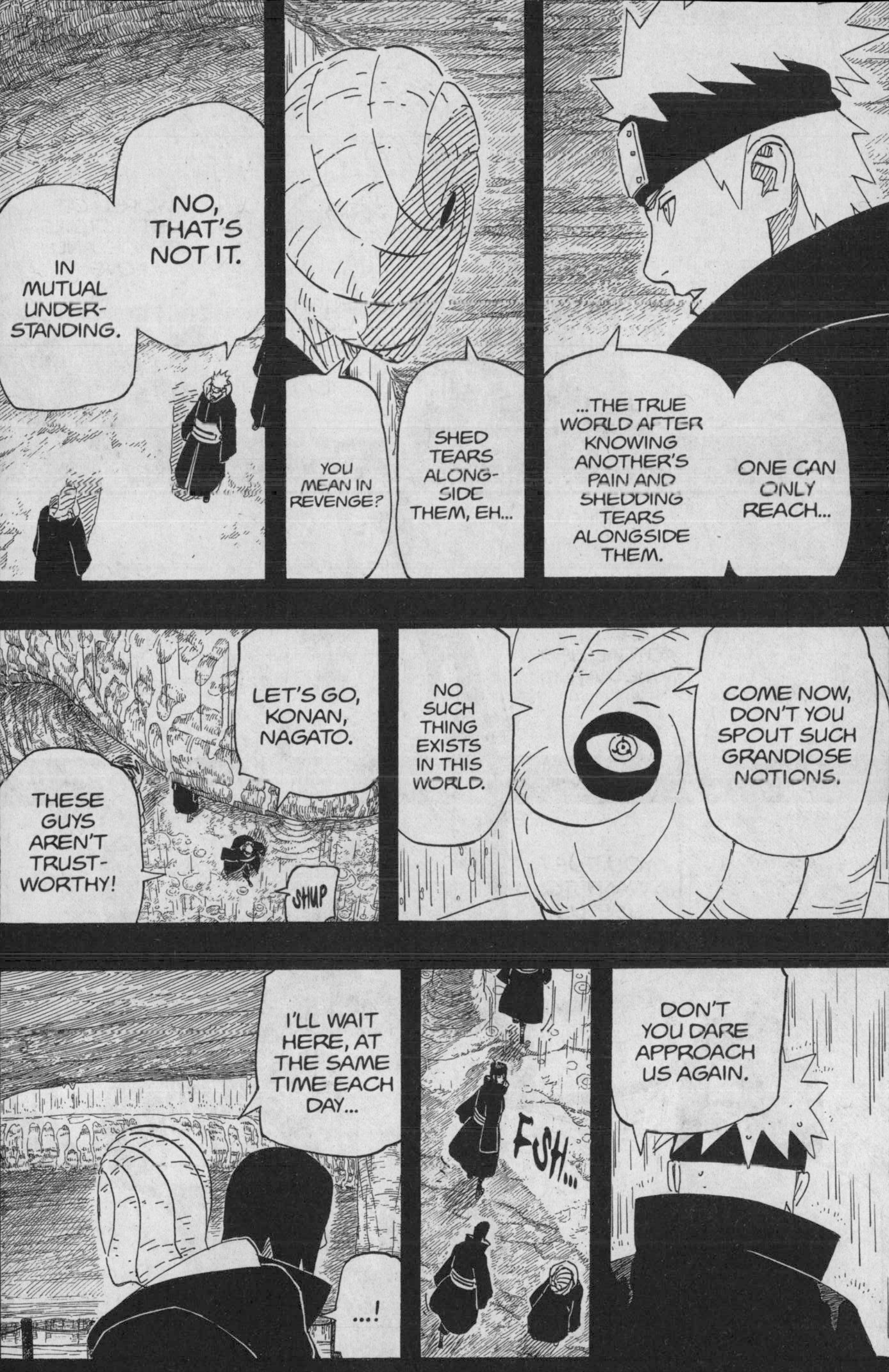
ONE CAN ONLY REACH...
...THE TRUE WORLD AFTER KNOWING ANOTHER'S PAIN AND SHEDDING TEARS ALONGSIDE THEM.
SHED TEARS ALONG-SIDE THEM, EH...
YOU MEAN IN REVENGE?
NO, THAT'S NOT IT.
IN MUTUAL UNDER-STANDING.
COME NOW, DON'T YOU SPOUT SUCH GRANDIOSE NOTIONS.
NO SUCH THING EXISTS IN THIS WORLD.
LET'S GO, KONAN, NAGATO.
THESE GUYS AREN'T TRUST-WORTHY!
SHUP
DON'T YOU DARE APPROACH US AGAIN.
FSH...
I'LL WAIT HERE, AT THE SAME TIME EACH DAY...
...!

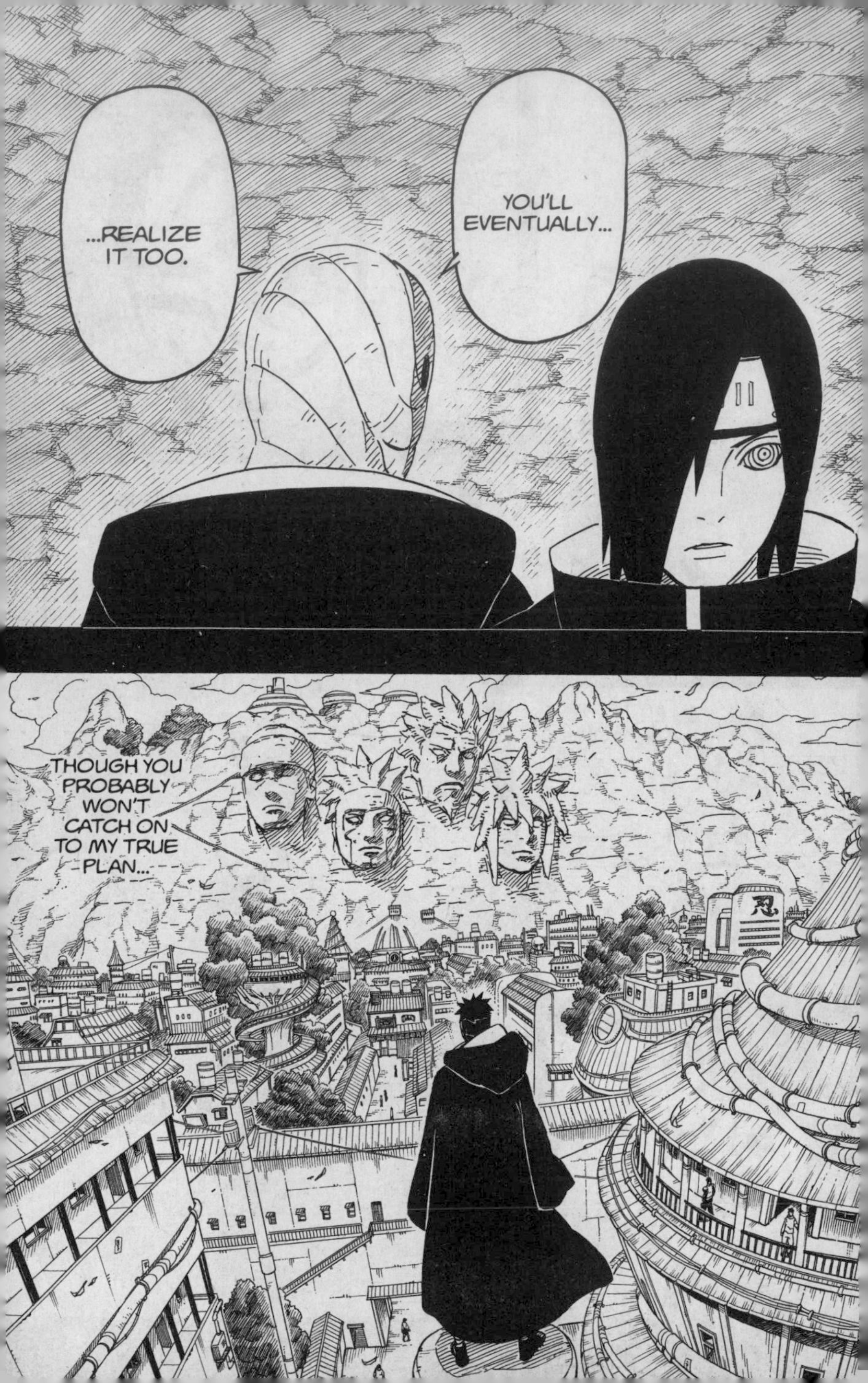
YOU'LL EVENTUALLY...
...REALIZE IT TOO.
THOUGH YOU PROBABLY WON'T CATCH ON TO MY TRUE PLAN...

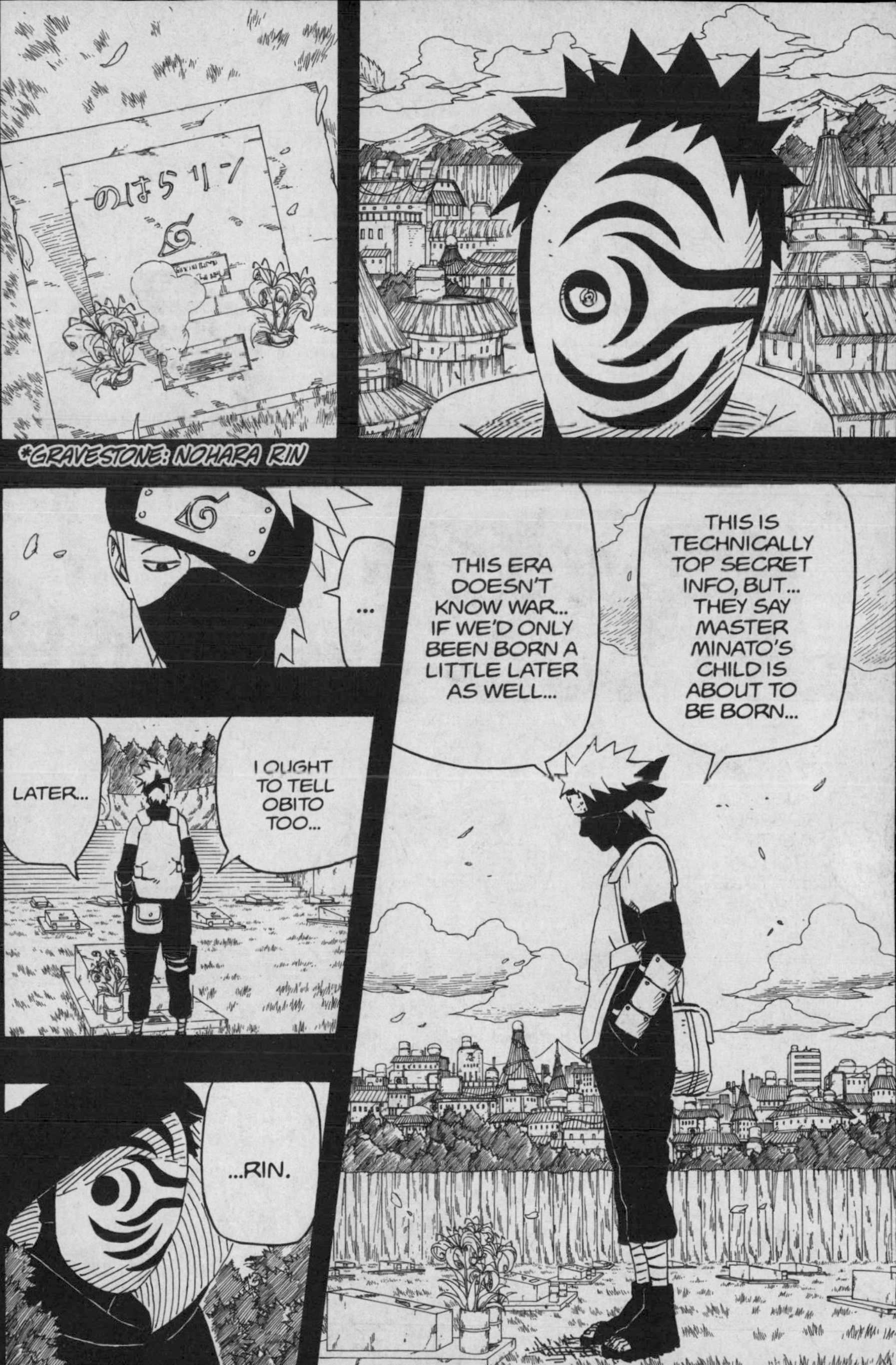
のはらリン
*GRAVESTONE: NOHARA RIN
THIS IS TECHNICALLY TOP SECRET INFO, BUT... THEY SAY MASTER MINATO'S CHILD IS ABOUT TO BE BORN...
THIS ERA DOESN'T KNOW WAR... IF WE'D ONLY BEEN BORN A LITTLE LATER AS WELL...
...
I OUGHT TO TELL OBITO TOO...
LATER...
...RIN.

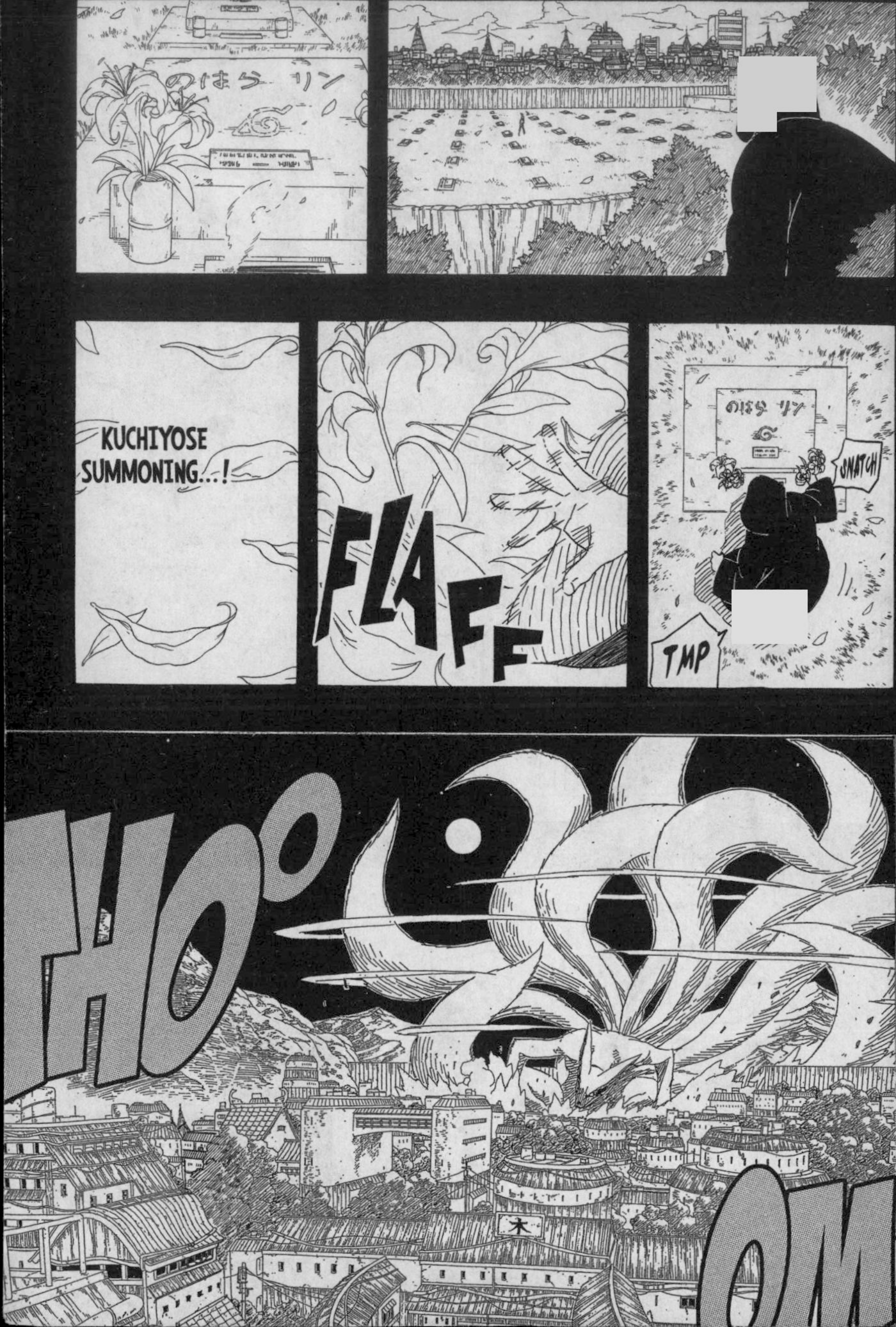
のはら リン
のはら リン
SNATCH
TMP
FLAFF
KUCHIYOSE SUMMONING...!
THOO
OM

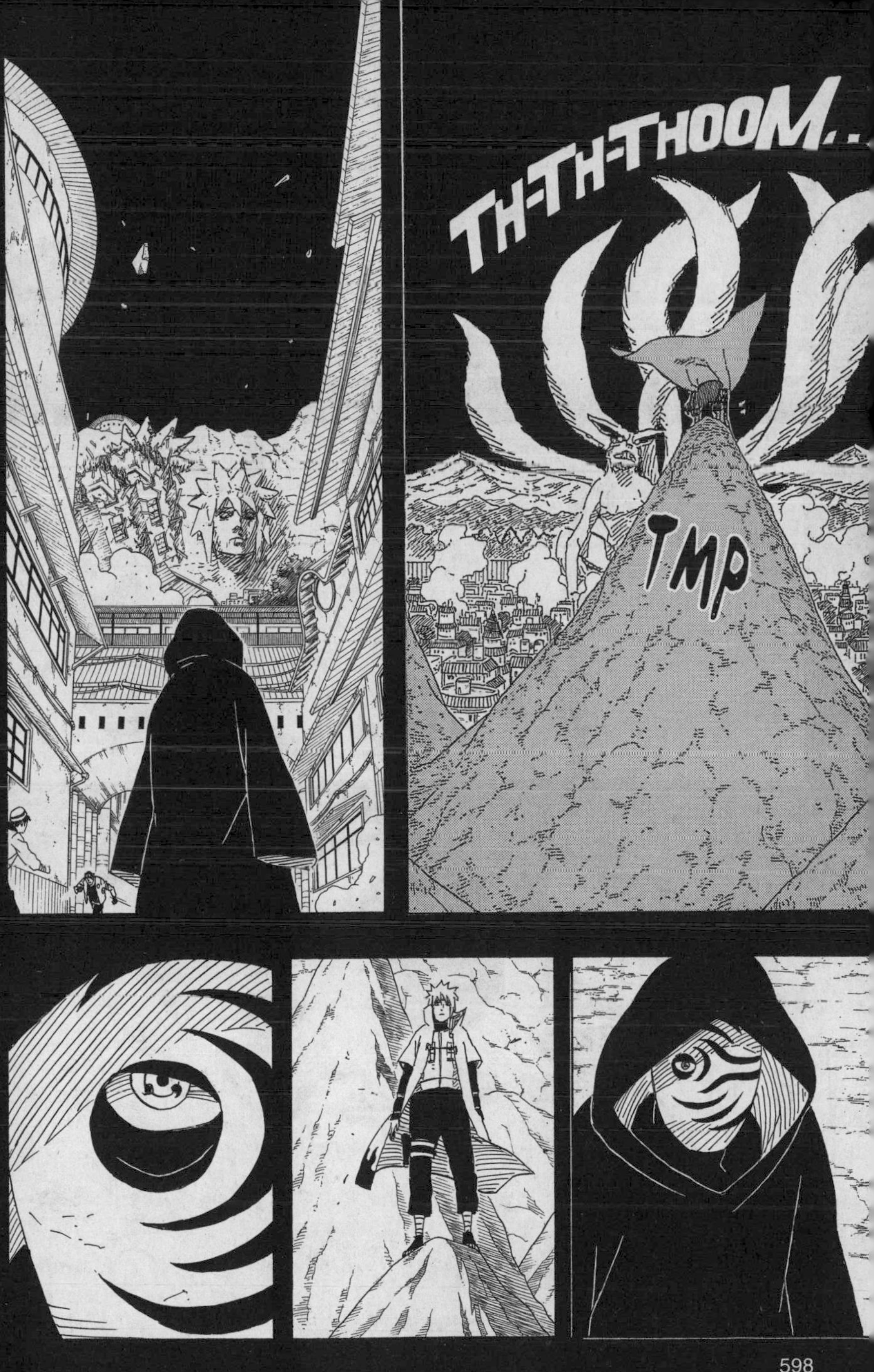
TH-TH-THOOM...
TMP

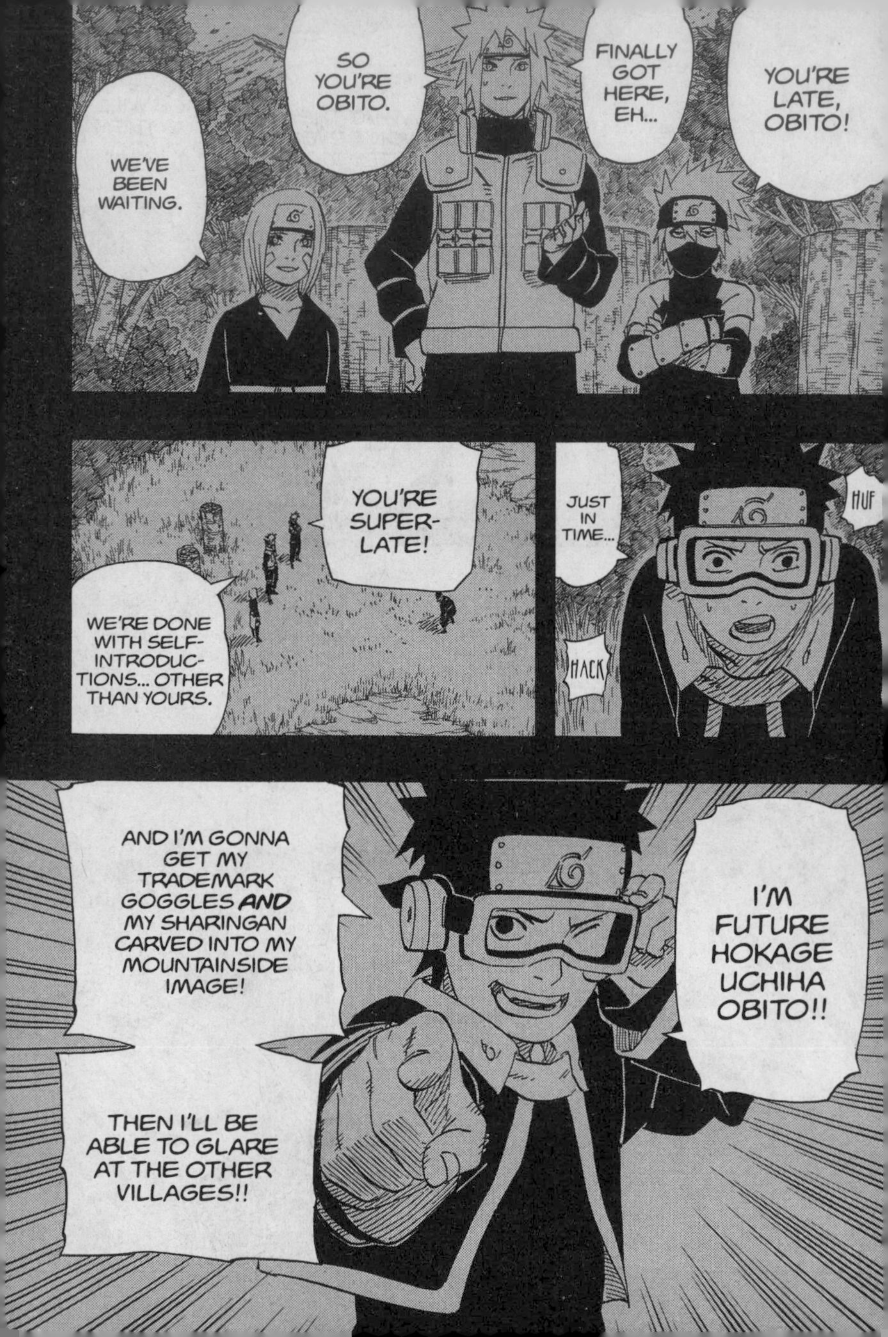
YOU'RE LATE, OBITO!
FINALLY GOT HERE, EH...
SO YOU'RE OBITO.
WE'VE BEEN WAITING.
HUF
JUST IN TIME...
HACK
YOU'RE SUPER-LATE!
WE'RE DONE WITH SELF-INTRODUCTIONS... OTHER THAN YOURS.
I'M FUTURE HOKAGE UCHIHA OBITO!!
AND I'M GONNA GET MY TRADEMARK GOGGLES **AND** MY SHARINGAN CARVED INTO MY MOUNTAINSIDE IMAGE!
THEN I'LL BE ABLE TO GLARE AT THE OTHER VILLAGES!!

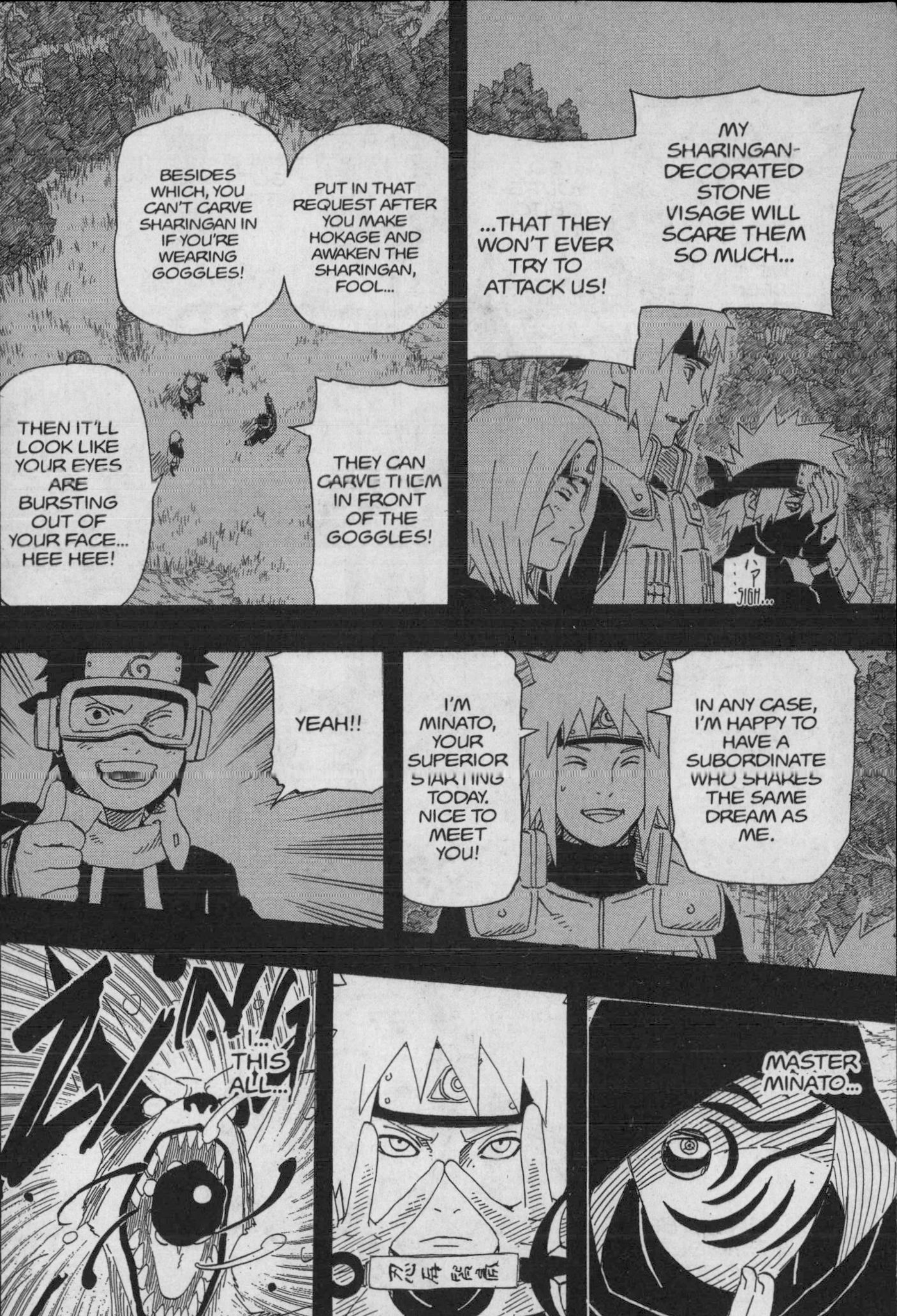
MY SHARINGAN-DECORATED STONE VISAGE WILL SCARE THEM SO MUCH...
...THAT THEY WON'T EVER TRY TO ATTACK US!
ハア... SIGH...
PUT IN THAT REQUEST AFTER YOU MAKE HOKAGE AND AWAKEN THE SHARINGAN, FOOL...
BESIDES WHICH, YOU CAN'T CARVE SHARINGAN IN IF YOU'RE WEARING GOGGLES!
THEY CAN CARVE THEM IN FRONT OF THE GOGGLES!
THEN IT'LL LOOK LIKE YOUR EYES ARE BURSTING OUT OF YOUR FACE... HEE HEE!
IN ANY CASE, I'M HAPPY TO HAVE A SUBORDINATE WHO SHARES THE SAME DREAM AS ME.
I'M MINATO, YOUR SUPERIOR STARTING TODAY. NICE TO MEET YOU!
YEAH!!
MASTER MINATO...
I... THIS ALL...
ZING

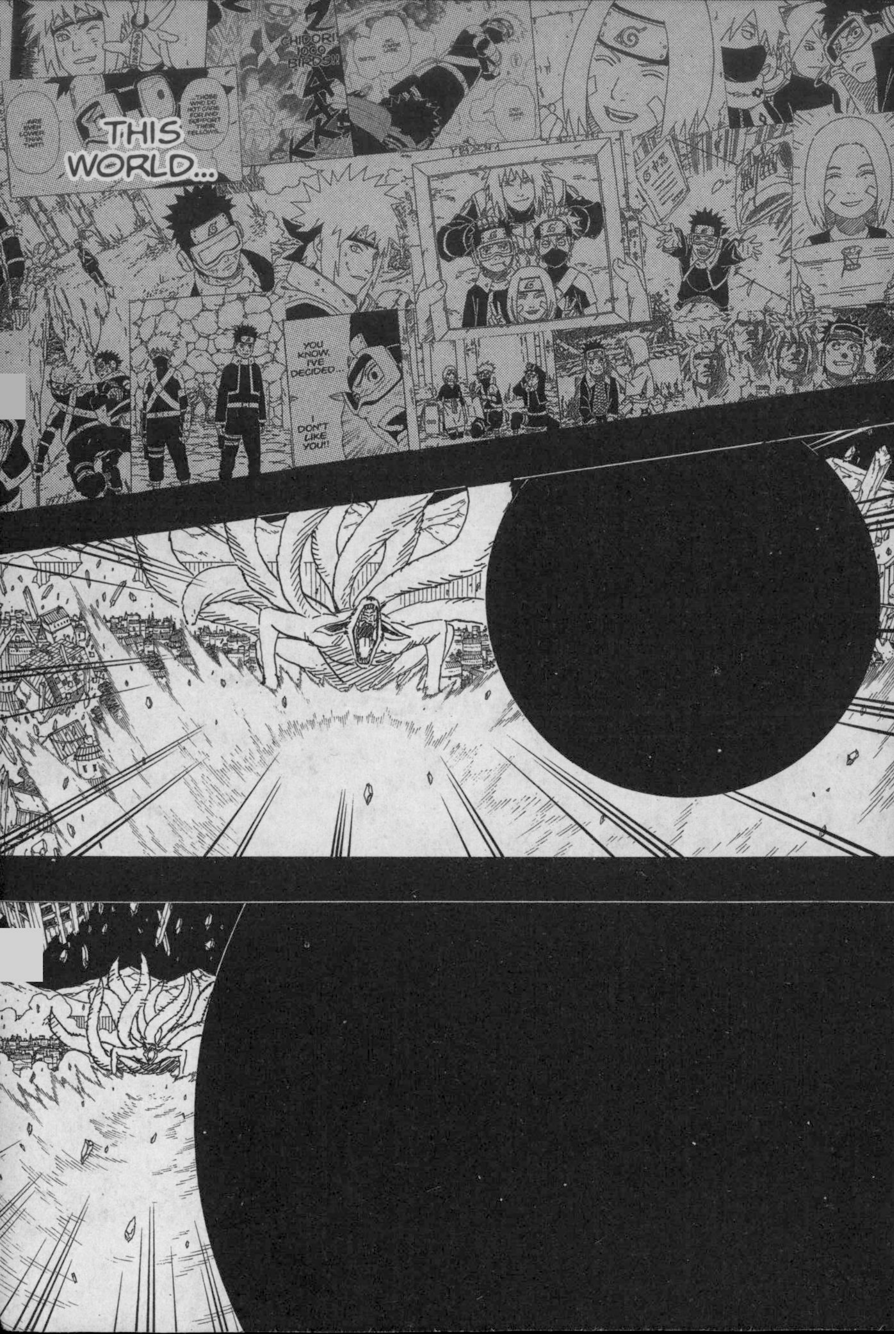
CHIDORI 1000 BIRDS!!
THIS WORLD...
YOU KNOW I'VE DECIDED...
I DON'T LIKE YOU!!

...DOESN'T MATTER TO ME.

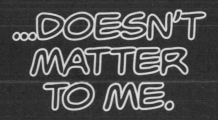

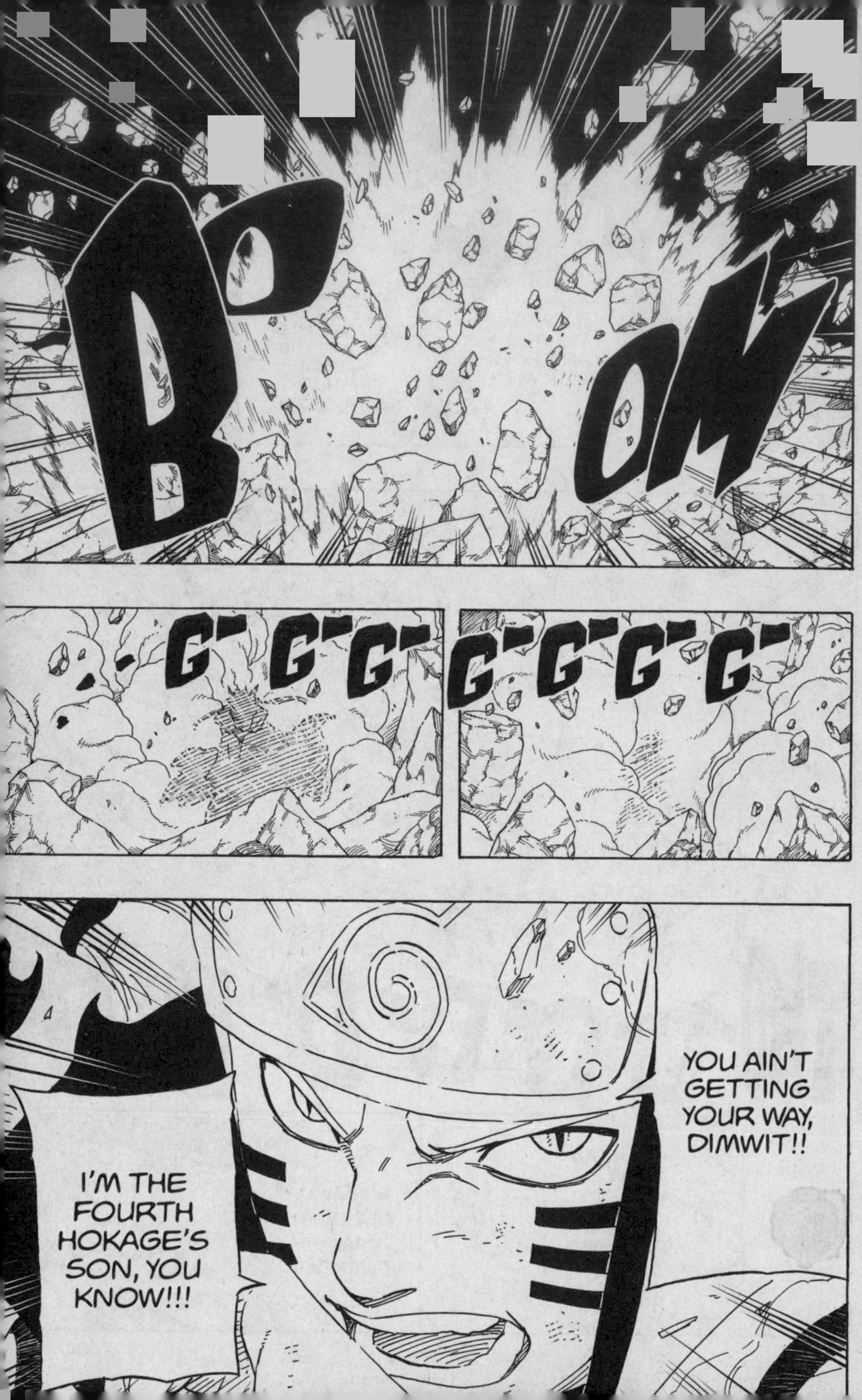
BOOM
G-G-G-G-
G-G-G-
YOU AIN'T GETTING YOUR WAY, DIMWIT!!
I'M THE FOURTH HOKAGE'S SON, YOU KNOW!!!

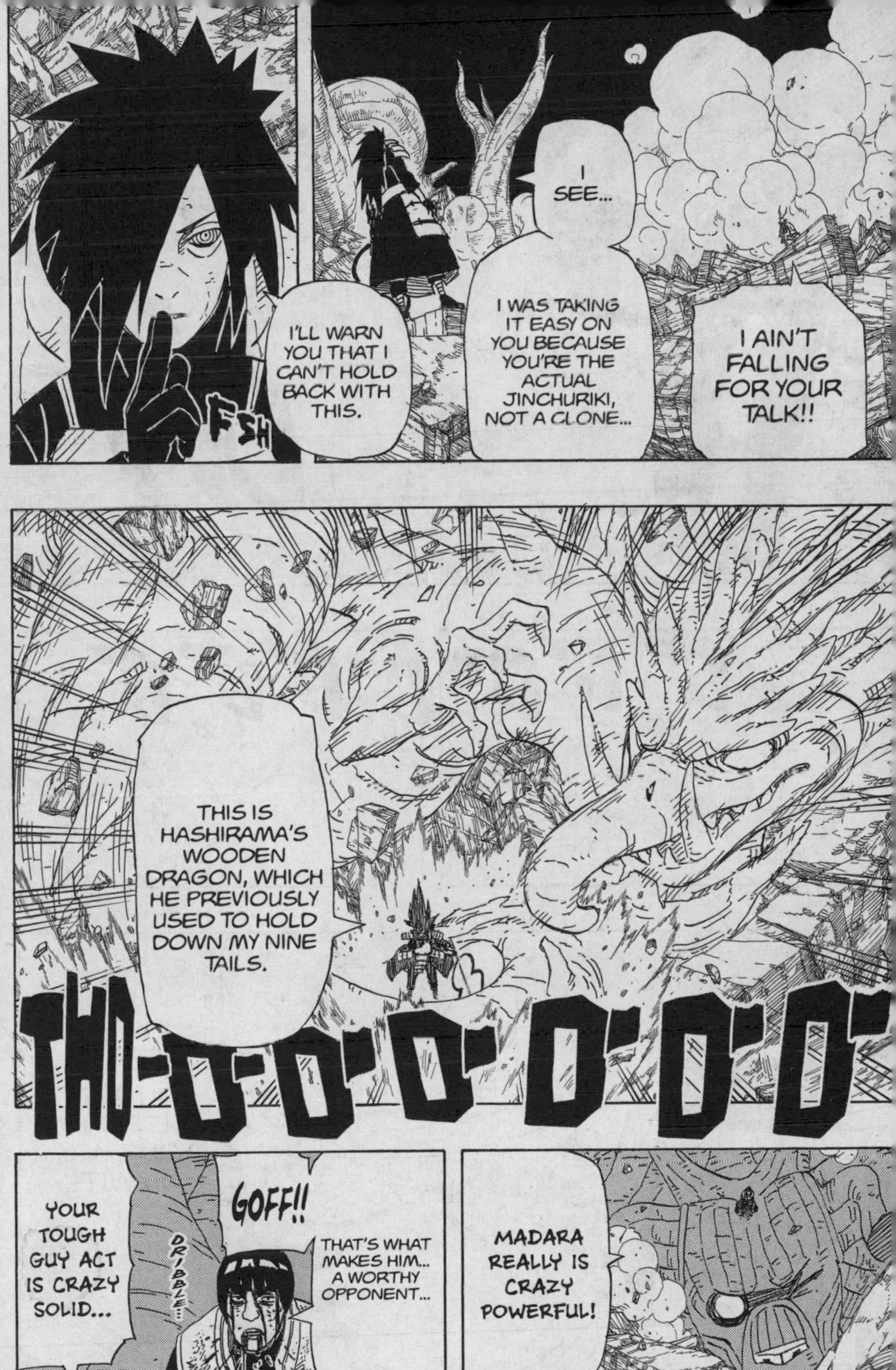
I AIN'T FALLING FOR YOUR TALK!!
I SEE...
I WAS TAKING IT EASY ON YOU BECAUSE YOU'RE THE ACTUAL JINCHURIKI, NOT A CLONE...
I'LL WARN YOU THAT I CAN'T HOLD BACK WITH THIS.
FSH
THIS IS HASHIRAMA'S WOODEN DRAGON, WHICH HE PREVIOUSLY USED TO HOLD DOWN MY NINE TAILS.
THO-O-O-O-O-O-O
MADARA REALLY IS CRAZY POWERFUL!
THAT'S WHAT MAKES HIM... A WORTHY OPPONENT...
GOFF!!
DRIBBLE...
YOUR TOUGH GUY ACT IS CRAZY SOLID...

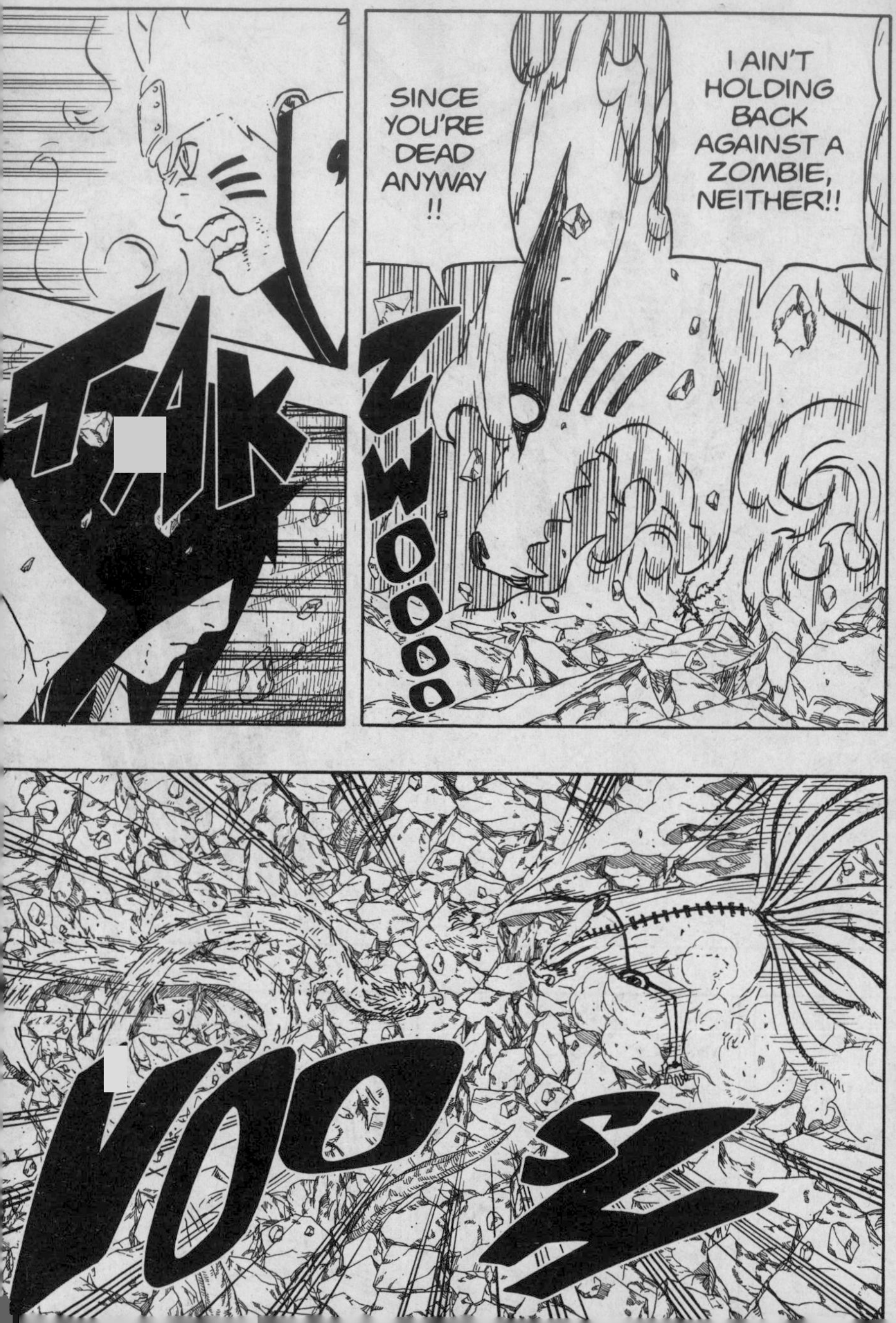
I AIN'T HOLDING BACK AGAINST A ZOMBIE, NEITHER!!
SINCE YOU'RE DEAD ANYWAY!!
ZWOOOOO
TAK
VOOSH

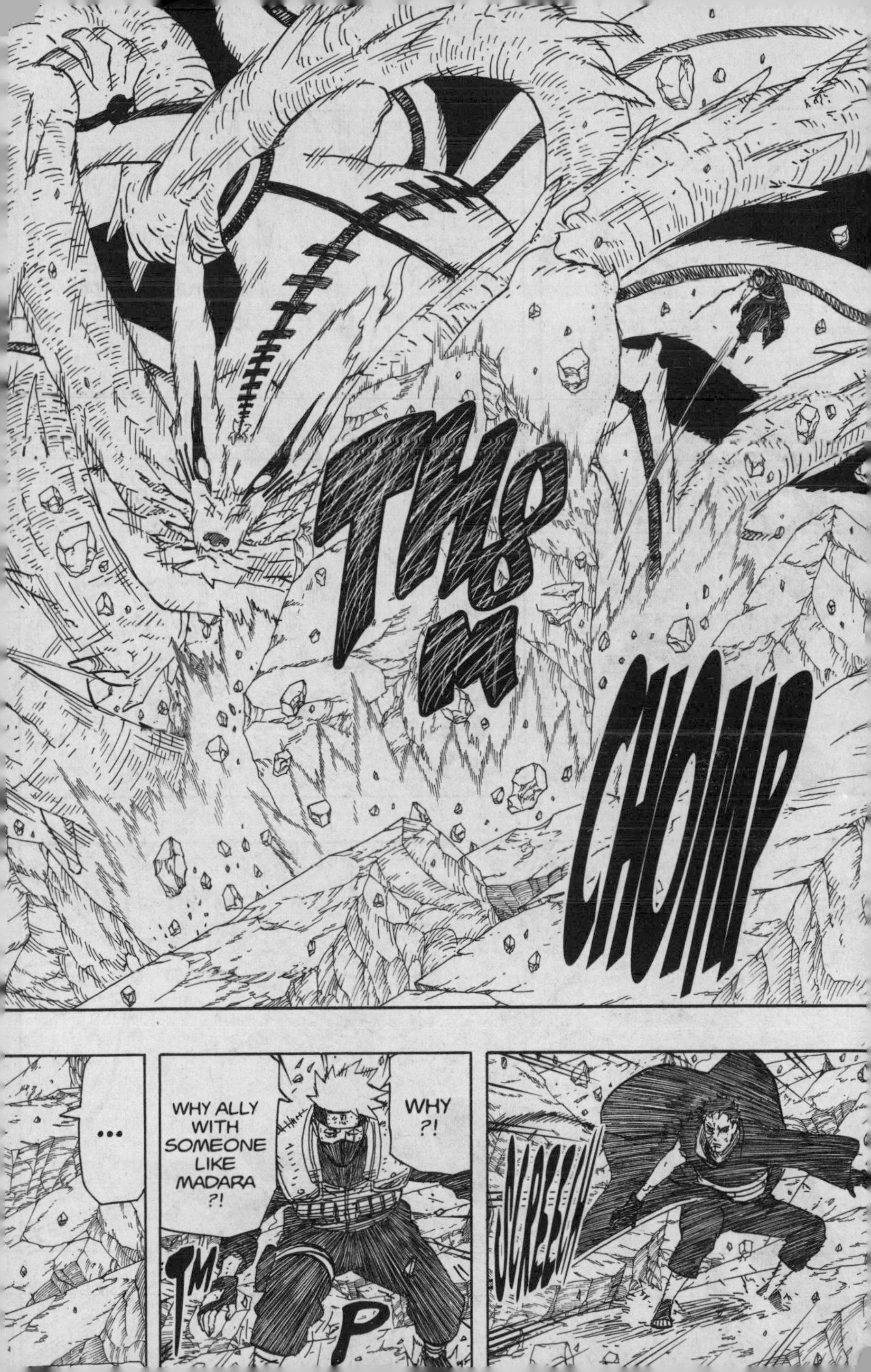
THOOM
CHOMP
SKREESH
WHY ?!
WHY ALLY WITH SOMEONE LIKE MADARA ?!
TMP
...

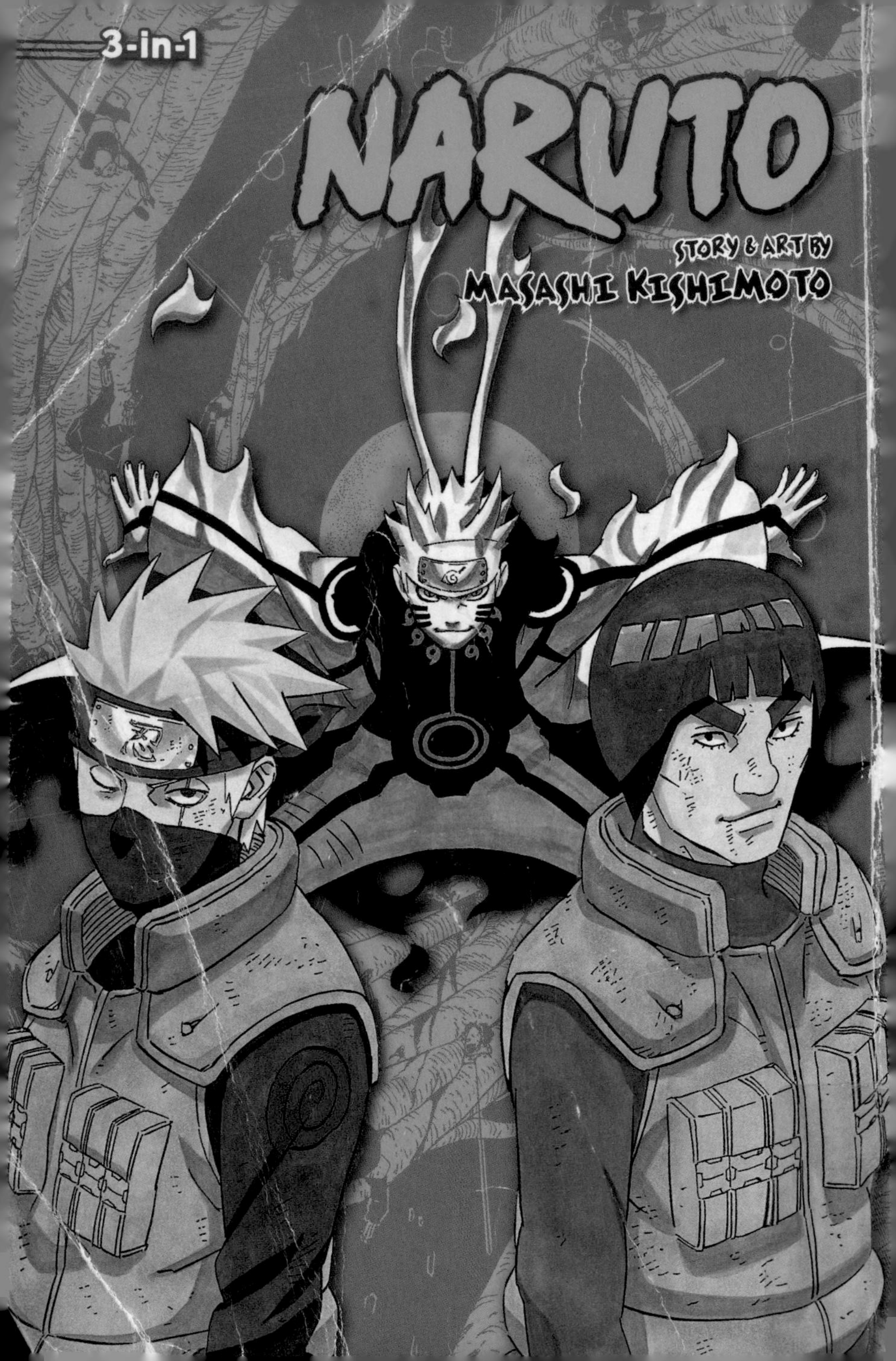
3-in-1
NARUTO
STORY & ART BY
MASASHI KISHIMOTO